THE RECHCIGL
GENEALOGY

Also Authored or Edited by Miloslav Rechcigl, Jr.

Scholarly Publications:
'Canceled Czechs' and Other Uncovered Americans with Czechoslovak Roots
Notable Czech and Slovak Americans. From Explorers and Pioneer Colonists through Activists
Notable Americans of Czechoslovak Ancestry in Arts and Letters and in Education
American Men and Women in Medicine, Applied Sciences and Engineering
American Learned Men and Women with Czechoslovak Roots
Celebrities and Less Famed Americans Married to Women of Bohemian and Czech Ancestry and their Progeny
Notable American Women with Czechoslovak Roots
Notable Americans with Slovak Roots
American Jews with Czechoslovak Roots
Czechs Won't Get Lost in the World, Let Alone in America
Beyond the Sea of Beer. History of Immigration of Bohemians and Czechs to the New World
Encyclopedia of Bohemian and Czech-American Biography 3 vols.
Czech It Out. Czech American Biography Sourcebook
Czech American Timetable. Chronology of Milestones in the History of Czechs in America.
Czech American Bibliography. A Comprehensive Listing
Czechmate. From Bohemian Paradise to American Haven. A Personal Memoir
On Behalf of their Homeland: Fifty Years of SVU
Czechs and Slovaks in America
Czech and Slovak American Archival Materials and their Preservation
Czechoslovak American Archivalia 2 vols.

Czech-American Historic Sites, Monuments, and Memorials
US Legislators with Czechoslovak Roots
Educators with Czechoslovak Roots
Deceased Members of the Czechoslovak Society of Arts and Sciences
Czechoslovak Society of Arts and Sciences Directory: 8 editions
Studies in Czechoslovak History 2 vols.
Czechoslovakia Past and Present 2 vols.
The Czechoslovak Contribution to World Culture

Scientific Monographs:
Nutrition and the World Food Problem
Comparative Animal Nutrition. Vol. 1. Carbohydrates, Lipids, and Accessory Growth Factors
Comparative Animal Nutrition. Vol. 2 Nutrient Elements and Toxicants
Comparative Animal Nutrition. Vol. 3. Nitrogen, Electrolytes, Water and Energy Metabolism
Comparative Animal Nutrition. Vol. 4. Physiology of Growth and Nutrition
Man, Food and Nutrition. Strategies and Technol. Measures for Alleviating the World Food Problem
World Food Problem: A Selective Bibliography of Reviews
Food, Nutrition and Health. A Multidisciplinary Treatise
Enzyme Synthesis and Degradation in Mammalian Systems
Microbodies and Related Particles

Handbook Series in Nutrition and Food: 18 vols.

Czech Publications:
Češi se ve světě neztratí, natož v Americe
Tam za tím mořem piva aneb Naše Amerika, jak ji málokdo zná
Pro Vlast. Padesát let Společnosti pro vědy a umění
Postavy naší Ameriky

THE RECHCIGL GENEALOGY

THE ANCESTRY AND DESCENDANTS OF
MILA RECHCIGL AND EVA EDWARDS
WITH INFORMATION ON ALLIED FAMILIES

Miloslav Rechcigl, Jr.

Scholar-in-Residence and Past President of the Czechoslovak
Society of Arts and Sciences (SVU)

Author's Tranquility Press
ATLANTA, GEORGIA

Copyright © 2023 by MILOSLAV RECHCIGL, JR.

All rights reserved. No part of this publication may be reproduced, distributed or transmitted in any form or by any means, including photocopying, recording, or other electronic or mechanical methods, without the prior written permission of the publisher, except in the case of brief quotations embodied in critical reviews and certain other noncommercial uses permitted by copyright law. For permission requests, write to the publisher, addressed "Attention: Permissions Coordinator," at the address below.

MILOSLAV RECHCIGL, JR./Author's Tranquility Press
3800 Camp Creek Pkwy SW Bldg. 1400-116 #1255
Atlanta, GA 30331, USA
www.authorstranquilitypress.com

Ordering Information:
Quantity sales. Special discounts are available on quantity purchases by corporations, associations, and others. For details, contact the "Special Sales Department" at the address above.

THE RECHCIGL GENEALOGY: THE ANCESTRY AND DESCENDANTS OF MILA RECHCIGL AND EVA EDWARDS WITH INFORMATION ON ALLIED FAMILIES/ MILOSLAV RECHCIGL, JR.
Paperback: 978-1-961908-16-1
eBook: 978-1-961908-17-8

In affection to my amiable and devoted wife Eva,
loving and accomplished children Jack and Karen,
adorable and brilliant grandchildren Kristin, Paul, Lindsey, Kevin
and Greg,
our cutest great-grandson James,
and great granddaughter Evelyn,
dear daughter-in-law Nancy
and
in memory of our beloved parents.

Contents

FOREWORD xiii
PREFACE xiv

I. THE LAND of OUR ANCESTORS
A. The Geographical Setting 2
B. Historical Overview 3
C. The People 8
D. The Economy 8
E. Cultural Life 10
F. The Czech the Musician 14

II. GENEALOGICAL OVERVIEW of OUR FAMILY
A. Ancestors of Mila Rechcigl 20
B. Ancestors of Eva Edwards 63
C. Descendants of Mila Rechcigl and Eva Edwards 73

III. HISTORIES of KEY FAMILIES
A. The Rechcigl Family 76
B. The Rajtr Family 80
C. The Danda Family 81
D. The Eisner Family 82
E. The Taussig Family 84
F. The Steiner Family 86
G. The Steinbach Family 88
H. The Wiener Family 91

IV. GENEALOGIES of ALLIED FAMILIES

A. Mila Rechcigl's Father Side 94
   Rechcigl (Rechziegel) Family 94
   Bergl Family 134
   Mařan Family 143
   Landa Family 148
   Šichta Family 157
   Brož Family 166
   Vela Family 182
   Veselý Family 185
   Pellant Family 189
   Neumann Family of Vlastiborice 191
   Ferkl Family of Chocnejovice 233
   Šifta Family 251
   Janecek Family 254
   Franců Family 262
   Jira Family of Klamorna 263
   Jira Family of Dehtary 265
   Jira Family of Třtí 269
   Zajicek Family 275
   Třešňák Family 279
   Studničný Family 281
   Křikava Family 288
   Roubíček Family 291
   Buriánek Family 294
   Hlavatý Family 297

B. Mila Rechcigl's Mother Side 321
   Rajtr Family 321
   Danda Family 334

- Cimr Family 377
- Ferkl Family of Rostkov 389
- Šverma Family 401
- Balak Family 411
- Huňát Family 415
- Koštejn Family 417
- Barton Family 435
- Novák Family 455
- Brzohohatý Family 478
- Najman Family of Kopernik 485
- Sip Family 502
- Bukvicka Family 505

C. Eva Edwards' Father Side 510
- Edwards (Eisner) Family 510
- Kraus Family 520
- Auer Family 529
- Wiener Family 538

D. Eva Edwards' Mother Side 547
- Taussig Family 547
- Meisl Family 560
- Munk Family 581
- Steindler Family 590
- Svab Family 613
- Weiner Family 620
- Kašpárek Family 633
- Schönfeld Family 635
- Rábl Family 650
- Sedlák Family 667
- Sebek Family 674
- Vodicka Family 681

    Ascher Family 682
    Stránský Family 698
    Syllaba Family 702
    Winternitz Family 705
    Sommer Family 707

E. Jack Rechcigl's Wife Side 711
    Palko Family 711
    Kopcho Family 715
    Vanchissen Family 721
    Rishko Family 727
    Goidich Family 734

F. Karen Rechcigl's Husband Side 742
    Kollecas (Kolecas) Family 742
    Malatras Family 750
    Llaguri Family 756
    Malamosis Family 759
    Hartopoulos Family 765

G. Mila Rechcigl's Sister Side 771
    Žďárský Family 771
    Foltýn Family 779
    Heralecký Family 783

H. Mila Rechcigl's Mother's Sister Side 819
    Koubik Family 819

I. Eva Edwards's Sister Side 821
    Steiner Family 821
    Steinbach Family 824
    Salomon Family 832

J. Eva Edwards' Mother's Sister Side 835
    Winn (Wiener) Family 835
    Růžička Family... 839
    Krajbich Family.. 852
    Ginsburg (Günsburg) Family 854

V. ANCESTOR CHARTS of KEY FAMILIES

Ancestors of Miloslav Rechcigl, Sr..863
B. Ancestors of Marie Rajtrova..864
C. Ancestors of Paul Edwards (Eisner)..865
D. Ancestors of Jirina Taussigova..866

VI. SELECTED BIOGRAPHIES

A. The Rechcigl Family 868
B. Edwards (Eisner) Family 886

VII. Selected Gazetteer 896

BIBLIOGRAPHY...903

GALLERY 909

FOREWORD

Albeit Mila Rechcigl has reached a milestone age up into his 90s, he is not slowing down. The latest of his books is fully devoted to a slightly controversial Czech habit. Czechs tend to hide their identity in plain sight, adopting English sounding names and completely assimilating so that their Czech roots are almost unnoticeable after just a few generations of living in America.

In Jaroslav Hašek's famous satirical novel Good Soldier Švejk, published between 1921–1923, First Lieutenant Lukáš, states: "Let's be Czech and no one has to know." This engrained national habit is what Mila Rechcigl wants to dispel with his newest text. Going over centuries of Czech presence in the United States, Rechcigl traces any possible connections with Czech lands, language, and culture.

I would like to congratulate Mila Rechcigl on his latest book, which proves that a man can have more than one identity and nationality. One cannot hide from his or her roots. Above all, Rechcigl demonstrates once again that he is the man to discover the truth through painstaking research.

Hynek Kmoníček,
Czech Republic Ambassador to the USA

PREFACE

There are several Rechcigl families in today's Czech Republic, some related, others not. They all seem to be located in the northeastern Bohemia. The name is quite ancient, having been spelled in a variety of ways, most commonly as Rechcigl, Rechziegel or Reckziegel.

A name resembling our name appeared in Bohemia already in the midst of 17th century. In the recently published survey of inhabitants of the Mladá Boleslav Region[1] in 1651, there is a reference to one Matěj Rekcigel, a farmer by profession, age 28, and his wife Sybila, age 34, from the village magistrate Kokonín ("Rychta Kukonská"), in the Jablonec n/Nisou District. The same publication lists under the village magistrate Sněhov ("Rychta Sněhovská"), in the village Malá Skála, also in the Jablonec n/Nisou District, Jiřík Rekcigel and his wife Mariana, Krystof Rekcigel and his wife Sybila, Wolf Rekcigel and his wife Anna, and Krystof Rekcigel and his wife Lidmila. Whether these Rekcigels are ancestors of our family could not be determined.

Our most immediate family comes from the Mohelka Valley in the north- northeastern part of Bohemia, neighboring on the most beautiful region of Bohemia, appropriately called "Český Ráj," meaning "Czech Paradise." Our earliest known ancestor František Rechziegel lived in Slavíkov from which the family spread southward along the Mohelka River and settled in the following villages: Třtí, Žďárek, Trávníček, Radostín, Hodkovice, Letařovice, and Chocnějovice. Some family

---

[1] *Soupis poddaných podle víry z roku 1651. Boleslavsko* II (Survey of Subjects according to Faith from 1651).

members moved even further inland, i.e., Malá Bělá and Šárovcova Lhota.

All the Rechcígls in the Mohelka Valley, by tradition, were flour millers. Actually, if you would drive along the Mohelka River, just about every mill you would find belonged to some branch of the Rechcígl family. The mill was usually inherited by the oldest son. However, among Rechcígls, it was traditional for a father to purchase mills for his other sons as well.

This comprehensive genealogy has been long in making and it took a lot of effort, not just because one had to double-check and or update the individual data with the concerned individuals, but the way the genealogy was done. This is not a typical genealogy with the focus on one family. This is a composite genealogy consisting of a plethora of genealogies comprising the related key families.

The opus starts with a brief narrative to provide an overview of the country from which the Rechcigls came. As the readers will note, it is a beautiful country in the heart of Europe about whose strategic position Chancellor Bismarck proclaimed that to rule Europe one needs to rule Bohemia first. Of course, at that time the Kingdom of Bohemia was still in existence, which was in 1918 transformed into a democratic Czechoslovak Republic.

The overview of the section The Land our Ancestors is followed by a Genealogical Overview of our Family. The Histories of Key Families come next, including the Rechcigl Family, the Rajtr Family, the Danda Family, The Eisner Family, the Taussig Family, the Steiner Family, and the Steinbach Family.

A major part of the compendium is in the section entitled Genealogies of Allied Families composed of genealogies of individual families relating to key persons on both their father and mother sides.[2]

The Ancestor and the Descendent Charts comprise the next two sections.

The Appendices include Biographies of selected individuals, Gazeteer of main locations and Selected addresses.

The book ends with a bibliography and a gallery of illustrations.

The present *vade mecum* is unique which should be of interest to professional and amateur genealogists in general. Apart from providing data on multitude of families, it allows researchers to make comparisons between different families in terms of their talent, longevity, or health aspects, in general.

---

[2] Regretfully, we were unable to incorporate diacritical marks in all the genealogies because it would take an enormous effort and the Family Tree Maker which we used, was not suitable.

I.

THE LAND of OUR ANCESTORS

A. The Geographical Setting

1. Physical Features

The Czech Republic is a part is a land-locked state located in the central Europe, covering an area of 78,864 sq km (30,450 sq miles). It comprises the lands of Bohemia and Moravia (the latter also includes part of the historic region known as Silesia, most of which is in Poland). The country is bordered by Poland to the north, Slovakia to the east, Germany to the west and Austria to the south.

Bohemia, the westernmost of the Czech Lands, covers the region drained by the upper Labe (Elbe) and its tributary the Vltava (Moldau), on which the capital, Praha (Prague) stands. The region is a plateau (average height 500 m), bordered to the north-west and south-west by low ranges of mountains, the Krušné hory (Erzgebirge), and the Český les (Böhmerwald), respectively, which form a natural frontier with Germany. The Krkonoše (Riesengebirge) range, the highest of the mountains, marks the border with Poland, rising to 1603 m (5,259 ft) at Mt. Sněžka. Several important rivers, including the Vltava and the Ohře, rise in the south-western hill country and flow north into the Labe, and hence into the North Sea. Moravia, in the east of the country, is a mainly lowland region, which has traditionally been a crossing point between Poland and south-central Europe. It is drained by the Dyje and Morava rivers, the latter forms part of the border with Slovakia and flows south to join the Danube (Dunaj) on the borders of Slovakia and Austria. Eastern Moravia is more rugged and mountainous, with the Little and White Carpathian (Karpaty) mountains, forming the rest of the border with Slovakia.

2. Climate

The climate is typically continental, with cold dry winters and hot, humid summers. The average July temperature in Prague is 19 degrees C (66 degrees F) and the average January temperature is -1 degree C (30 degrees F). Prague receives an average annual rainfall of 485 mm, which often falls as snow in winter months. There is little climatic variation throughout the country.

3. Natural Resources

Although large areas of original forest have been cleared for cultivation and for timber, woodlands remain a characteristic feature of the Czech landscape. Oak, beech, and spruce dominate the forest zones in ascending order of altitude. The timberline runs about 4,500 feet (1,400 m) above the sea level. The country's various wildlife is represented in the Krkonose National Park, which shelters deer and wild sheep but is also extensively developed as a ski resort.

Despite centuries of exploitation, the Czech Republic still has minable metal reserves, including antimony, iron ore, copper, lead, zinc, mercury, gold, and tin. It also has reserve of uranium and low-quality coal.

B. Historical Overview

Most of our ancestors came from Bohemia, a small country in the center of Europe, which because of its strategic position has been frequently called the heart of Europe. Otto Bismarck (1815-1898), the chancellor of German Empire, once declared that to rule Europe one needs to rule Bohemia first.

Bohemia was a part of the historic Czech Lands of the Kingdom of Bohemia, originally consisting of Bohemia, Moravia, Silesia and Lusatia. In the medieval times the Kingdom of Bohemia was an independent country whose ruler held the prestigious position as one of the "Kurfursten" who selected the Holy Roman Emperor.

The historical origin of the name Bohemia goes back to Roman days, when the Romans called the land "Boiohaemum" because it was inhabited by a Celtic tribe the "Boii" The Slav tribes which settled the area around the fifth century A.D. called themselves Czechs, after a legendary chieftain "Čech"who was supposed to have brought them there.

During medieval period the Czechs, together with the Moravians, formed part of the seventh-century state of Samo which came under the sway of Charlemagne. In the ninth century the Great Moravian Empire emerged, of which the Czechs constituted the western part.

The principality of Bohemia which emerged out of the ruins of the Great Moravian state was strongly influenced by Western and Eastern culture, but Western influence clearly predominated. The center of the Kingdom was Prague, seat of the Royal House of the Přemyslids. In the person of Saint Václav (Wenceslas), the prince who died a martyr's death in 929, the Czechs acquired their first national saint.

In 1158 Bohemia became an independent Kingdom when Vladislav II acquired the Royal crown with hereditary rights. Under Přemysl Otakar II (1253-1278) Bohemia reached a position of great strength. Přemysl conquered Austria, Styria, and Carinthia, and extended his possessions southward the Adriatic. He might have maintained his realm had he succeeded in becoming the roman Emperor. But fear of his growing power made the electors choose Rudolph of the Habsburg.

The Přemyslids were followed by the Luxemburg dynasty (1310-1437) during which Bohemia expanded, acquiring Silesia and Lusatia. The Kingdom of Bohemia comprised of four provinces, i.e. Bohemia, Moravia, Silesia, and Lusatia. The Golden Age of the Kingdom falls into a reign of Charles IV (134-1378). The Czech King who also became Holy Roman Emperor, treated Bohemia as the heart of the Europe and Prague became its capital. According to the Golden Bull of 1356 which regulated the manner of imperial elections, the King of Bohemia became the most important of the seven Electors. Prague in 1348 acquired a university (Charles University), the first in central Europe. The Bishopric of Prague was elevated to an Archbishopric, ending dependence on Mainz.

For the church in Bohemia the reign of Charles IV meant increased wealth, power, and prestige, although the abuses began soon to creep in. In the following reign the religious question and, together with the increasing penetration of Czech life by the German element, created grave problems. In connection with the general decline of the Church and of the papacy, a powerful reform movement developed in Bohemia directed against clerical abuses accompanied by strong national sentiment. Finding its leader in Jan Hus, a theologian, preacher and teacher, reform spread through Bohemia. Condemnation of Hus, as a heretic by the Council of Constance and his execution in 1415 precipitated the Hussite wars, which lasted until 1434. Led by such men as Jan Žižka, the Hussites successfully defied the forces of the Empire which undertook crusades against them. The Hussite wars showed the independence and dynamism of the Czech spirit, but they exhausted the nation.

In 1526 the Czech diet elected Ferdinand of Austria King. The Habsburg rulers controlled the Empire, Austria, Bohemia, and part of Hungary, They believed in absolutism and were militantly Catholic. A growing religious conflict accompanied the political disagreement between the Bohemian Diet and the Habsburgs, since Protestantism had spread rapidly in Bohemia, absorbing most of the Hussite element. In 1618 two representatives of the Habsburgs were thrown out of a window in the castle in Prague by angry Czechs. The incident, known as the "Defenestration of Prague," started the Thirty Year War. Unfortunately, The Habsburgs won and the Battle of the White Mountain in 1620 proved a turning point in Czech history.

The Habsburgs inaugurated a series of repressive measures against the Czechs, culminating in the Renewed Land Ordinance of 1627. Because of their rebellion, the Czechs were forced to forfeit their ancient privileges and liberties. Three quarters of the land in Bohemia were confiscated. Protestants were given the choice of either becoming Catholic or emigrating, and about 30,000 families left the country, the rest of the nation became Catholic. Habsburg ruthlessness deprived Czechs of their political and intellectual leaders and reduced the bulk of the people to a condition of a peasantry. The German language was emphasized and eventually made the official language of the country. Czech sank to the level of a peasant dialect.

The enlightened despotic rule of Joseph II brought some advantages to Bohemia, such as religious tolerance and the limitation of serfdom. On the other hand, his strict centralizing policies, which almost integrated Bohemia into Austria, made the matters worse.

These conditions, coupled with the French revolutionary ideas, reinforced by the romantic movement, led to a Czech cultural revival.

The 1848 Revolution, which shook the Habsburg monarchy, opened great possibilities for the Czechs. While advocating a transformation of Austria along federalism lines, the revolutionaries also fought for the Czech right to become a free member of a Habsburg association of nations. Czech hopes for political autonomy were frustrated by the suppression of the revolution in 1849. Their hopes were again revived when, after being defeated by Prussia in 1866, the Habsburgs were ready to make concessions. But the Habsburgs chose to satisfy the Hungarians by transforming the empire into a dual Austro-Hungarian monarchy, whereas the Czech plans for autonomy were rejected and Bohemia was once more relegated to the position of a subordinate province.

At the outbreak of World War I in 1914, the Czech leaders, notably Karel Kramář and Tomáš G. Masaryk, a leading Czech intellectual hoped for concessions from the Habsburg government, but they did not originally aim at complete national independence. Only the progressive disintegration of the Austro-Hungarian Empire under the pressure of war and the reluctance of its government to recognize the right of its component nationalities to self-determination, led the Czech statesmen to seek complete separation. Skillful diplomatic action by Masaryk and the dissolution of the empire as a result of popular movements for independence led in 1918 to the creation of a new nation, Czechoslovakia, including Bohemia, Moravia, Silesia, and Slovakia.

The outbreak of World War I in 1914 gave the Czechs the opportunity of winning complete independence and uniting with the Slovaks, Bohemia, the old traditional Kingdom, lay in the past. Czechoslovakia, a modern republic, became the aim of the Czech leaders. The year 1918 saw the realization of this aim. On October 28, 1918, Czech independence was proclaimed, two days later the Slovaks declared for union with Czechs and the Czechoslovak Republic came into being.

During the era of the first Czechoslovak Republic under President Thomas G. Masaryk Czechs enjoyed unprecedented progress.

The presence in Western Bohemia of many German-speaking citizens gave a pretext for Nazi Germany to occupy Czechoslovakia in the wake of the Munich agreement (1938) and the Czech Lands became a German Protectorate until the Czechoslovak state was restored by the victorious Allies in 1945, at the end of World War II.

After the World WAR II Czechoslovakia came under the domination of the Soviet Union and from 1948 it was ruled by a Communist government. After Communist rule collapsed in 1989, separatist sentiments emerged among the Slovaks, and in 1992 the Czechs and Slovak agreed to break up their federated state. On January 1, 1993, the Czechoslovak Republic was dissolved and replaced by two new countries, the Czech Republic and Slovakia., with the region of Moravia remaining in the former.

C. The People

The western region of the country has traditionally been the westernmost settlement of the Slav people in central Europe. Czechs make up more than nine-tenths of the population, although the Moravians consider themselves a distinct group within the majority. Slovaks constitute the largest minority. Other groups include Poles in the northeastern Moravia, Germans in northwestern Bohemia, and the relatively mobile Rom, or Gypsies.

The official language, Czech, belongs to the group of Slavic languages that uses the Roman rather than the Cyrillic alphabet. Roman Catholics are estimated to make up about 40 percent of the population. There are also various Protestant denominations, including the Bohemian Brethren and Orthodox congregations. As a legacy of the communist period of official atheism, a significant number of people profess no religious affiliation.

About one-fifth of the population is under 15 years of age, whereas one-sixth of the population is 60 years old or older. The birth and death rates produce a relatively low natural rate of growth. Internal migration toward the cities has increased; more than three-fourths of the population is urban.

D. The Economy

Following the collapse of communism in eastern Europe in 1989, the government inaugurated a program of privatization and by 1993 the Czech economy was largely market-oriented. Mining and manufacturing trade, and construction tended to dominate in the

GNP but new service-oriented industries and merchandising were increasingly important.

Czech agriculture is among the most advanced in the central and eastern Europe. The principal crops include sugar beets, wheat, barley, potatoes, corn, and various fruits and vegetables. Bohemia is noted for its hops, used in brewing beer, and there are extensive vineyards along the Vltava river around Mělník and in the Poluží area of southeastern Moravia. Pigs, cattle (both dairy and beef), sheep and poultry are the dominant livestock. Forestry is important mainly in the southern mountains, the hills southwest of Prague, and the northeastern districts.

The country is poor in energy resources; some black coal is mined but the use of lignite (brown coal) predominates in thermal power stations, in home heating, and in the chemical industry. Natural gas and petroleum are produced in limited quantities. Important mineral products include iron ore, magnesite, copper, manganese, lead, zinc, uranium, and various clays and building stone.

Czech manufacturing is highly diversified and is based on domestic and imported raw materials. Major products include iron, steel, and aluminum; refined petroleum products; fertilizers; cement; cotton; wool, and synthetic fibers and clothing; audio and electronic equipment; and road vehicles and railway locomotives. The Czech Republic is noted for precious instruments and for its engineering industry, specializing in factory, power-plant, and transportation-system design and construction. Traditional crafts include glass, porcelain, lace, and wood carving, important for tourism and export.

Tourist activities in the Czech Republic include winter and summer sports, fishing, hunting, and touring in the scenic mountains, numerous historical sites, and traditional regions. Visitors' expenditures are an important source of foreign exchange.

E. Cultural Life

The territory of today's Czech Republic has abounded with culture from the times of the Kingdom of Bohemia and before. German, Czech, and Jewish influences have combined over many centuries to produce a rich and diverse culture in this region. Prague's best-known Jewish authors, Franz Kafka and Franz Werfel, were among the finest German-language novelists of their generation. Important modern Czech literary figures include Jaroslav Hašek, whose *Good Soldier Schweik* is an archetypal Czech hero; émigré authors Josef Škvorecký and Milan Kundera; the Nobel Prize-winning poet, Jaroslav Seifert; and the famous playwright Václav Havel, who was elected president in 1993. Sculpture and painting reached a high point in the late Gothic period and the early 20th century, when Prague was a major center of avant-garde art. The 19th century produced a great trio of Czech classical composers, Dvořák, Smetana, and Janáček, while Prague enjoys fame for its earlier links with the Austrian-born Wolfgang Amadeus Mozart. Nowadays there is a lively jazz scene and heavy rock is another favorite with local people.

An era of continuous artistic development began here with the coming of the Slavs. With the rise of the Great Moravian Empire and the establishment of Christianity, the monumental architecture of stone churches developed. The first written language was Old Church Slavonic, developed in religious hymns and Gregorian chants. From the second half of the 9th century, the art of Great Moravia entered Bohemia, especially the architectural style of the rotunda (St. Kliment in Levý Hradec near Prague).

In the 11th century, under South German influence, architecture and book illustrations (Vyšehrad Codex) developed in particular. The Latin language was dominant in literature until the 14th century, while Romanesque art reached the Central European level, mainly in the form of monastic basilicas (Strahov, Doksany) and noble churches. Princely residences and palaces (Znojmo, Prague), Romanesque castles (Primda) and city homes in the tower style were built.

The 13th century was a period of the ascent of Gothicism, which manifested itself in the construction of castles and in ecclesiastic architecture of the Cistercian monasteries. Noteworthy Gothic structures still erect today are the cathedral in Sedlec near Kutná Hora, and the monasteries of Vyšší Brod and Zlata in South Bohemia. Czech began to be used as a written language.

Gothic art reached its peak during the reign of Charles IV and Vaclav IV, when the Czech lands became one of the focal points of European culture. The artistic center was the workshop of the Saint Vitus Cathedral, led by Matyáš from Arras, and later by P. Parlér (reconstruction of the Prague Castle, construction of the St. Vitus Cathedral, the Přemysl tombs, decoration of the bridge towers). Paintings by court artists Theodorik, Oswald, Wurmser and others were used to decorate Karlštejn, the cloister of the monastery in Emauzy and the chapel of St. Wenceslas in St. Vitus. Religious hymns attained a high standard and in the 14th century independent artistic lay compositions were written. The names of the first composers (Záviš) have been preserved to this day. Renaissance architecture was mediated by Italian builders (Stella, the summer house of Queen Anne), and in particular new types of secular buildings were developed - summer residences, imperial and aristocratic chateaux (Český Krumlov, Jindřichův Hradec, Budějovice), decorated with graffiti, wall paintings and stucco (Hvězda, Kratochvíle).

From the intermingling of domestic and Italian forms arose the shapes of Czech Renaissance, applied significantly in city architecture (city halls, patrician homes, of which Telč is a good example). Music groups of the manor were formed from among the serfs at aristocratic courts. Renaissance vocal polyphonics developed (J. Rychnovský, J.

Trojan, K. Harant from Polžice and Bezdružice). The activities of the Bohemian Brethren and their translation of the Bible (*Kralická Bible*) also contributed to the development of Czech culture.

At the end of the 16th century, an international center of Mannerism arose at the court of Rudolf II (Vries, Spranger, von Aachen, Arcimboldo, and others) and a developed musical culture was cultivated. The post-White Mountain re-Catholicization brought new Baroque artistic elements which asserted themselves in architecture (the Valdštejn buildings in Prague and Jicin), and the design of the buildings of the Jesuit Order (Klementinum), and later even in representative buildings (Černinský Palace in Prague, the Troja chateau). Early Baroque music is represented in particular by Michna from Otradovice, B.M. Černohorský and J.D. Zelenka. Czech Baroque poetry reached its height in the work of B. Bridel.

The influence of Italian Baroque entered Bohemia in the 18th century and was the impulse behind characteristic Czech art of high Baroque. Architecture of this style includes the structure of K. I. Dienzenhofer and the work of G. Santini, creators of a specific phenomenon - Czech Baroque Gothic. In sculpture, the pieces of M. B. Braun and F.M. Brokoff are exemplary. Painting attained its peak in the Brandl painting synthesis of Baroque elements, applied mainly in portraits and altar pieces. Also of significance are the portraits by Kupecký, the wall paintings by Reiner and graphics by Hollar. At that time a number of composers who contributed to the development of world music came from Bohemia, among others these were F. Benda, J. Benda, A. Rejcha, and J. Mysliveček.

At the beginning of the 19th century, Classicism reached its peak in Napoleonic style, applied in sculpture to tombs and monuments. The stagnation in painting was rejuvenated by the activities of F. Machek, A. Mánes and J. Navrátil, who combined Classicism with Romanticism instilled with Revivalist ideals. In Romantic poetic composition, *Máj* by

Karel Hynek Mácha revived Czech literature to again reach a European standard.

During the first half of the 19th century, painting reached the Classic phase through the works of J. Mánes and A. Purkyně and Kosárek's monumental synthesis of the Czech landscape. Czech pseudo historical architecture found its own expression in Neo-Renaissance (J. Zítek, J. Schultz, A. Wiechl), the generation of the National Theater (M. Aleš, F. Ženíšek, V. Hynais, V. Brožík) contributed to the decoration of contemporary, monumental architecture, while at the same time the socially harmonious genre (J. Schikaneder) and realistic landscape painting (A. Chitussi) developed. Efforts to create Czech national music were realized in the works of Bedřich Smetana, Antonín Dvořák, and Zdeněk Fibich. The Czech Philharmonic, an orchestra which has become internationally renowned, was established in 1894. Czech literature was incorporated into the European context by J. Vrchlický J.V. Sládek, and J. Zeyer.

At the beginning of the 20th century, European influences from the generation of the 1890s merged with Czech tradition. Symbolism reached its peak (J. Preisler) and A. Slavíček modified landscape Impressionism. A. Mucha contributed to the development of European Art Nouveau. The Group of Eight (B. Kubišta, O. Kubin), the Tvrdošijní Group and the Group of Graphic Arts associated themselves with Expressionism and Cubism. R. Kremlička combined modern trends into an original synthesis. The painter of circus scenes, F. Tichý, refashioned Seurat impulses. Czech Modernism (J. Gocar, K. Honzík, P. Janák) appeared in architecture, which developed into Functionalism after World War I. Poetism (K. Teige) arose after World War I. The 1930s were also significant for the ascension of Surrealism (J. Styrský, Toyen) and expressive tendencies. Masterpieces of Czech literature were created by Karel Čapek, V. Vančura, J. Durych, J. Čep, Vítězslav Nezval, V. Holan, J. Zahradníček and Jaroslav Seifert. Leading composers of Czech music between 1890 and 1930 were L. Janáček, J.B. Foerster, V. Novák, and J. Suk.

More recently, Czech culture has made sizable contribution to world literature and music. The plays of Karel Čapek, František Langer, Pavel Kohout, and Václav Havel are well known in the west, as are the novels of Jaroslav Hašek, Bohumil Hrabal, and Milan Kundera. The Czech poet Jaroslav Seifert was awarded the Nobel Prize for Literature in 1984. Besides Antonín Dvořák, notable Czech composers have included Bedřich Smetana, Leoš Janáček, and Bohuslav Martinů. Among scientists, Jaroslav Heyrovský was awarded the Nobel Prize for chemistry in 1959.

F. The Czech the Musician

The noted music historian Charles Burney (1726-1814), who traveled through Central Europe in 1772, while collecting material for his History of Music, wrote "I had frequently been told, that the Bohemians were the most musical people, perhaps of all Europe. An eminent German composer, now in London, had declared to me that if they enjoyed the same advantages as the Italians, they would excel them. I crossed the whole Kingdom of Bohemia from south to north; and being very assiduous in my inquiries, how the common people learned music. I found out at length, that, not only in every large town, but in all villages, where there is a reading and writing school, children of both sexes are taught music." In the 18th century, all Europe was flooded with Czech musicians, so that Bohemia became known as the "Music Conservatory of Europe."[3] As Bedřich Smetana[4] proclaimed

---

[3] Charles Burney, *The Present State of Music in German, the Netherlands and United Provinces* (London, 1775). Newly edited by Percy A. Scholes as *An 18th Century Musical Tour in Central Europe and Netherlands* (London: Oxford University Press, 1959), pp. 131-132.
[4] One of the foremost Czech composers.

some 150 years later on the occasion of the groundbreaking ceremony for the National Theatre in Prague, "Music is the life of Czechs."[5]

Bohemia and the Czech Republic can boast a musical tradition that is longer than a millennium. The earliest surviving musical work with a Czech text is the litany "Lord, have mercy upon us" from the tenth century AD. Some two hundred years later, the famous hymn "Saint Wenceslas," invoking St. Wenceslas, Patron Saint of the country, was written, containing the memorable words "Let not ourselves nor or descendants perish." The Hussite movement of the 15th century generated a striking array of hymns and devotional songs that became an important part of the Czech heritage. The Hussite hymns are basically folk songs, simple, but full of melodious strength. The most famous of the hymns, "Ktož jsu boží bojovníci" (All Ye Warriors of Lord) allegedly turned the crusaders sent against the Hussites into panic flight even before the battle.

According to Czech musicologist Karel B. Jirák, one aspect of the proverbial Czech musicality that has received universal recognition is the multitude of extraordinarily beautiful folk songs, recorded and still partly living in all regions of the country. Each has its distinctive characteristics, from the western type musical formulation in Bohemia to the more eastern type in Eastern Moravia.[6]

In the 18th century, Bohemia produced several generations of brilliant composers, most of whom made their reputation abroad. Thus Johann Stamic and Franz Xaver Richter were leaders of the Mannheim School which influenced the transition from the baroque to the classical style of music. Jiří Antonín Benda worked in Thuringia and his brothers František and Josef in Berlin. Josef Mysliveček, Jan Ladislav Dussek, Antonin Rejcha and Jan Václav Voříšek achieved

---

[5] Zdenka E. Fischmann, *Essays on Czech Music* (Boulder: East European Monographs, 2002), p. 7.
[6] Karel B. Jirák, "Music in Czechoslovakia," in: The *Czechoslovak Contribution to World Culture*. Edited by Miloslav Rechcígl, Jr. The Hague/London/Paris: Mouton & Co., 1964, 119-133.

fame in Italy, England, Germany, Russia, France, Vienna and other parts of Europe. Only a few music composers stayed home, among them, the most influential was Francis Xaver Brixi (1732-1771), the music director of the St. Vitus Cathedral in Prague, a prolific composer of more than 400 works for the church. Another composer of note was Vaclav Jan Tomášek (1774-1850), for many years known at the "Music Pope of Prague."

Interestingly, the first music from the Czechlands that crossed the ocean was brought by Moravians who settled in America during the 18th century, chiefly in Pennsylvania and North Carolina[7]. They belonged to a Moravian religious group that was formed in the area of Herrnhut, Saxony, who followed the religious and music tradition of the Bohemian Brethren, the followers of teachings of John Hus and John Amos Comenius.

The central figure of musical revival in the Czechlands in the 19th century was Bedřich Smetana (1824-1884), who almost single-handedly created a national Czech musical style. His comedic opera "The Bartered Bride" remains successful in major opera houses, as does his symphonic tone poem cycle "My Country." Antonín Dvořák (1841-1904) remains today the best-known Czech composer worldwide. His "Slavonic Dances", the symphony "From the New World", Cello Concerto, "American Quartet" and the opera "Rusalka" are played from year to year around the world. During his lifetime, he was highly acclaimed in the United States where he served for several years as the director of a music conservatory in New York City. He is better known abroad than Smetana because his style is more international, based on classicism. The third major composer who was active during Smetana's and Dvorak's lifetime was Zdeněk Fibich (1850-1900), known for his melodramas.

---

[7] Jan Vičar, Echoes of Czech Music in America, in: *Imprints. Essays on Czech Music and Aestehetics* (Olomouc: Palacký University and Togga: Prague, 2005), pp. 19-25.

Among the later composers, one of the most prominent one was Leoš Janáček (1854-1928) who remained unrecognized for a very long time. Only, when his opera "Jenufa" was successfully performed in Prague in 1916, his fame began spreading throughout the world. Apart from this and other operas, Janacek became widely known for his "Glagolitic Mass."

During the undiscovered Janáček years, several Dvořák's pupils dominated Czech music, including Vitězslav Novák (1870-1949) and Josef Suk (1874-1935), Dvořák's own son-in-law.

Their contemporary was Bohemian born Gustav Mahler (1860-1911) who spent his entire career between Vienna and the United States. He wrote nine memorable symphonies and song-cycles. During his life time he was, however, primarily known as one of the world's greatest conductors, in 1907 becoming the new director of the Metropolitan Opera and the following year conductor of the New York Philharmonic.

Bohuslav Martinů (1890-1959), after a checkered start, became the greatest Czech composer of his generation, as well as international figure. In 1941 he came to America where he mastered symphonic writing. He was a prolific composer, writing almost 400 pieces, including 16 operas, concerti and chamber music.

On the music lighter side, a mention should be made of Rudolf Friml (1879-1972), Prague born American composer of operettas. The best known of his thirty-three light operas are "Firefly" (1912), "Rose Marie" (1924) and "The Vagabond King" (1925). Erich Wolfgang Korngold (1897-1957), a native of Brno, made Hollywood music famous with his exquisite scores for such movies as "The Adventures of Robin Hood", "The Sea Hawk" and "The Kings Row."

Among the Czech musicians who have lived abroad in a self-imposed exile, after the Communist takeover of Czechoslovakia in 1948, the most successful were conductors and composers Rafael

Kubelík and Karel B. Jirák, the brilliant pianist Rudolf Firkušný and two younger composers Oskar Morawetz and Karel Husa. We should also add to the list the world famous opera singer Jarmila Novotná who entertained American audiences at the Metropolitan Opera from 1940 to 1956.

II.

GENEALOGICAL OVERVIEW of OUR FAMILY

A. Ancestors of Mila Rechcigl

Generation 1

1. **Mila (Miloslav) Rechcigl Jr.** son of Miloslav Rechcigl and Marie Rajtrová was born on 30 Jul 1930 in Mladá Boleslav, CSR. He was baptized on 17 Aug 1930 in By Alois Novák, parish priest in Loukovec. Employment: Bet. 1958–1968 in Biochemist, National Institutes of Health, Bethesda, MD. Sex: Male. He was educated B.S.,Cornell U. 1954, M.N.S., Cornell U. 1955, Ph.D., Cornell U. 1958. He was also known as "Mila" or "Mike". He was known by the title of Dr.. His address was 1703 Mark Lane / Rockville, MD 20852 / US. His e-mail address was rechcigl@aol.com. His phone number was (301) 881-7222. His religious affiliation was Roman Catholic. Age (wedding): 23 years old. Godmother: Marie Rechcíglová. Godfather: Alois Rechcigl. Midwife: Josefa Silna from Mladá Boleslav.

    Eva Edwards (Eisnerová) daughter of Paul J. Edwards (Pavel Eisner) and Jiřina Taussigová was born on 21 Jan 1932 in Prague, CSR. She was educated B.A., Hofstra College in 1953. Sex: Female. Age (wedding): 21 and 1/2 years old.

    Mila (Miloslav) Rechcigl Jr. and Eva Edwards (Eisnerová) were married on 29 Aug 1953 in New York, NY. They had 2 children.

Generation 2

2. **Miloslav Rechcigl** son of Adolf Rechcigl and Marie Berglová was born on 13 May 1904 in Kocňovice (renamed Chocnějovice) No. 22. He was baptized on 16 May 1904 in By František Hladik, parish priest. Fact 1: May 1948 in Escaped from communist CSR. Fact 2: Feb 1950 in Emigrated to the US. He died on 27 May 1973 in Washington, DC. He was buried on 30 May 1973 in Gates of Heaven, Rockville, MD. Sex: Male. He was educated Commercial Academy, Prague. He was elected Deputy, Czechoslovak Parliament. His address was / Chocnějovice 22, Bohemia / Czechoslovakia. His cause of death was Colon cancer. He was employed as a Miller in Chocnějovice No. 22. His religious affiliation was Roman Catholic. Age (wedding): 22 years old. Godmother: Anna Rechcíglová from Letařovice No. 4. Godfather: František Bergl, cottager

from Kocnejovice No. 28. Midwife: Stefa Janova from Sovenice. Fact 3: Became Editor with Radio Free Europe. Witnesses (wedding): Čeněk Rajtr, farmer from Dolanky No. 7 and Josef Bednar, parish clerk. Married By: Father Josef Gargela, chaplain, U sv. Aloise, Kralovske Vinohrady. Age (death): 69 years old. Death Cause: Colon cancer.

3. **Marie Rajtrová** daughter of Čeněk Rajtr and Marie Dandová was born on 05 Jul 1905 in Dolanky No. 7, Mnichovo Hradiště Co.. She was baptized on 12 Jul 1905 in By Father Josef Pukarek, chaplain. She died on 13 Apr 1982 in Mladá Boleslav. Sex: Female. Her address was / Dolanky 7, /. Her religious affiliation was Roman Catholic. Age (wedding): 21 years old. Godmother: Marie Stránská, midwife from Bakov. Godfather: Václav Cumpelik, cabinet maker from Bakov n. Jiz.. Midwife: Marie Stránská from Bakov. She was buried in Chocnějovice Cemetery.

Miloslav Rechcigl and Marie Rajtrová were married on 26 Jul 1926 in Praha - Kralovske Vinohrady. They had the following children:

+1. i. **Mila (Miloslav) Rechcigl Jr.** was born on 30 Jul 1930 in Mladá Boleslav, CSR. He was baptized on 17 Aug 1930 in By Alois Novák, parish priest in Loukovec. He married Eva Edwards (Eisnerová) on 29 Aug 1953 in New York, NY. Employment: Bet. 1958-1968 in Biochemist, National Institutes of Health, Bethesda, MD. Sex: Male. He was educated B.S.,Cornell U. 1954, M.N.S., Cornell U. 1955, Ph.D., Cornell U. 1958. He was also known as "Mila" or "Mike". He was known by the title of Dr.. His address was 1703 Mark Lane / Rockville, MD 20852 / US. His e-mail address was rechcigl@aol.com. His phone number was (301) 881-7222. His religious affiliation was Roman Catholic. Age (wedding): 23 years old. Godmother: Marie Rechcíglová. Godfather: Alois Rechcigl. Midwife: Josefa Silna from Mladá Boleslav.

ii. **Marta Rechcíglová** was born on 23 May 1933 in Mladá Boleslav. She married František Žďárský on 03 Oct 1953 in Mladá Boleslav. She died on 13 Sep 2018 in Mladá Boleslav. Sex: Female. She was baptized in June 5, 1933. Her address was Chocnějovice 39 / 294

13 Mohelnice nad Jjizerou, / Czech Republic. Her phone number was (420-329) 787020. Godmother: Marta Rajtrová, Marie Rechcíglová. Midwife: Josefa Silna from Mladá Boleslav.

Generation 3

4. **Adolf Rechcigl** son of Petr Rechziegel and Anna Najmanová was born on 21 Aug 1876 in Letařovice No. 4, Český Dub Co.. He was baptized on 22 Aug 1876 in Český Dub parish: By Jan Jesina, dean ("dekan"). He died on 30 Mar 1946 in Šárovcova Lhota No. 16. He was buried on 02 Apr 1946 in Chocnějovice Cemetery. Sex: Male. His address was / Chocnějovice 22, /. He was employed as a A miller. His religious affiliation was Roman Catholic. Godmother: Marie Kovářová, wife of Jan Kovar, cottager from Letarovive No. 3. Godfather: Josef Maruska, cottager from Letařovice No. 2. Midwife: Marie Cubrova. Age (death): 70 years old. Fact 1: A miller in Šárovcova Lhota. Fact 2: A miller in Chocnějovice No. 22. Public Office: Mayor, Chocnějovice. Position: miller in Chocnejovice, then in Sarovcova Lhota, having ledt the mill in Chocnejvice to his son Miloslav Rechcigl..

5. **Marie Berglová** daughter of František Bergl and Marie Mařanová was born on 27 Mar 1880 in Drahotice No. 20, Mnichovo Hradiště Co.. She died on 25 Mar 1917 in Chocnějovice No. 22, Mnichovo Hradiště Co.. She was buried on 28 Mar 1917 in In the Rechcigl family vault at the Chocnějovice Cemetery. Sex: Female. Her cause of death was Heart paralysis ("ochrnuti srdce'). Age (death): 37 years old.

Adolf Rechcigl and Marie Berglová were married about 1900. They had the following children:

    i. **Marie Rechcíglová** was born on 29 Sep 1901 in Kocňovice (renamed Chocnějovice). She died on 03 Oct 1902 in Chocnějovice. Sex: Female. Her cause of death was pneumonia (zanet prudusek). Age (death): 1 year old.

+2. ii. **Miloslav Rechcigl** was born on 13 May 1904 in Kocňovice (renamed Chocnějovice) No. 22. He was baptized on 16 May 1904 in By František Hladik, parish priest. He married Marie Rajtrová on 26 Jul 1926 in Praha - Kralovske Vinohrady. Fact 1: May 1948 in Escaped from communist CSR. Fact 2: Feb 1950 in Emigrated to the US. He died on 27 May 1973 in Washington, DC. He was buried on 30 May 1973 in Gates of Heaven, Rockville, MD. Sex: Male. He was educated Commercial Academy, Prague. He was elected Deputy, Czechoslovak Parliament. His address was / Chocnějovice 22, Bohemia / Czechoslovakia. His cause of death was Colon cancer. He was employed as a Miller in Chocnějovice No. 22. His religious affiliation was Roman Catholic. Age (wedding): 22 years old. Godmother: Anna Rechcíglová from Letařovice No. 4. Godfather: František Bergl, cottager from Kocnejovice No. 28. Midwife: Stefa Janova from Sovenice. Fact 3: Became Editor with Radio Free Europe. Witnesses (wedding): Čeněk Rajtr, farmer from Dolanky No. 7 and Josef Bednar, parish clerk. Married By: Father Josef Gargela, chaplain, U sv. Aloise, Kralovske Vinohrady. Age (death): 69 years old. Death Cause: Colon cancer.

   iii. **Anna Rechcíglová** was born on 10 Feb 1906 in Kocňovice (renamed Chocnějovice) No. 22. She died on 26 Feb 1927 in Chocnějovice. Sex: Female. Her cause of death was pneumonia.

Marie Anna Ferklová daughter of František Ferkl and Anna Saralova was born on 10 Dec 1897 in Chocnějovice No. 2. She died on 31 Dec 1970 in Šárovcova Lhota. She was buried on 07 Jan 1971. Sex: Female. Age (death): 73 years.

Adolf Rechcigl and Marie Anna Ferklová were married on 25 Apr 1917 in St. Alois Church, Praha. They had the following children:

   i. **Stanislav Josef Rechcigl** was born on 10 Oct 1918 in Chocnějovice. He was baptized on Oct 1918. He married Libuše Sedláčková on 17 Jan 1948 in Novy Bydzov. He died on May 1973 in Šárovcova Lhota No. 16. He was buried on 15 May 1973. Sex: Male. He was employed as a A miller in Šárovcova Lhota. Age (death): 54 years old.

   ii. **Adolf Rechcigl** was born on 09 Apr 1920 in Chocnějovice No. 22. He was baptized on 11 Apr 1920. He died on 27 Dec 1944 in Ples. He was buried on 06 Jan 1945. Sex: Male.

6. **Čeněk Rajtr** son of Jan Václav Rajtr and Anna Najmanová[1] was born on 01 Jul 1874 in nky No. 7, Mnichovo Hradiště Dist... He was baptized on 02 Jul 1874 in By Father Antonín Cihlar, parish priest. He died on 27 Oct 1956 in Dolánky No. 7, Mnichovo Hradiště Dist... Sex: Male. He was employed as a A Farmer and ownerof a tree nursery, Dolanky. His religious affiliation was Roman Catholic; since 19212 a membr of Czech-Moravian Church. Godmother: Barbora Brzobohatá, countrywoman from Dolanky. Godfather: Josef Parik, cottager from Cihadky No. 4. Midwife: Josefa Havlickova from Bakov n.J.

7. **Marie Dandová** daughter of František Antonín Danda and Josefa Cimrová[2] was born on 31 Jan 1882 in Hoškovice, No. 14, Mnichovo Hradiště Dist, Bohemia. She was baptized on 31 Jan 1882 in By Father Jan Bernat, chaplain. She died on 05 Jul 1967 in Dolanky No. 7, Mnichovo Hradiště Co.. Sex: Female. Her religious affiliation was Roman Catholic. Godmother: Marie Dandová from Hoškovice. Midwife: Anna Benešová from Mnichovo Hradiště.

Čeněk Rajtr and Marie Dandová were married on 02 Jul 1904 in Mnichovo Hradiště. They had the following children:

+3. i. **Marie Rajtrová** was born on 05 Jul 1905 in Dolanky No. 7, Mnichovo Hradiště Co.. She was baptized on 12 Jul 1905 in By Father Josef Pukarek, chaplain. She married Miloslav Rechcigl on 26 Jul 1926 in Praha - Kralovske Vinohrady. She died on 13 Apr 1982 in Mladá Boleslav. Sex: Female. Her address was / Dolanky 7, /. Her religious affiliation was Roman Catholic. Age (wedding): 21 years old. Godmother: Marie Stránská, midwife from Bakov. Godfather: Václav Cumpelik, cabinet maker from Bakov n. Jiz.. Midwife: Marie Stránská from Bakov. She was buried in Chocnějovice Cemetery.

ii. **Oldrřch Rajtr** was born on 14 Nov 1907 in Dolanky No. 7. He died on 02 Nov 1937. Sex: Male.

iii. **Marta Rajtrová** was born on 10 Jan 1909 in Dolanky u Bakova. She married Josef Knotek in 1934. She died on 29 Nov 1982 in

Mladá Boleslav. She was buried on 03 Dec 1982 in Mladá Boleslav New Cemetery. Sex: Female. Age (death): ca 74 years old.

Generation 4

8. **Petr Rechziegel** son of Petr Rechziegel and Františka Hlavatá was born on 01 Jun 1844 in Hodkovice No. 39. He was baptized on 01 Jun 1844 in Hodkovice parish: By Rev. Josef Hofrichtr in the parish church in Hodkovice. Fact 1: 1872 in Received the Letařovice mill from his father. Fact 2: Abt. 1907 in Gave the mill to his son Zdeněk. He died on 18 Sep 1917 in Letařovice No. 4, Turnov Co.. He was buried on 21 Sep 1917 in Letařovice Cemetery. Sex: Male. His address was / Letařovice No. 32, /. He was employed as a A miller. His religious affiliation was Roman Catholic. Age (wedding): 24 years of age. Godmother: Františka Kaiser, countrywoman ("selka") from Hodkovice No. 100. Godfather: Otokar Presler, businessman from Hodkovice No. 150. Age (death): 74 years old. Position: miller in Letarovice, No. 4. Called Himself: "Josef".

ii. **Anna Najmanová** daughter of Antonín Neumann and Anna Brožová was born on 31 Jul 1849 in Radimovice No. 7, Turnov Co.. She was baptized on 31 Jul 1849 in Vlastibořice parish: By Jan Solc, manor chaplain. She owned in 1904 in Sold the homestead (including mill, inn and farm lands, at Třtí No. 32 to Josef Jira of Dehtary. She died on 05 Jun 1908 in Letařovice. Sex: Female. Her religious affiliation was Roman Catholic. Age (wedding): 19 years old. Godmother: Anna, wife of Vavlav Najman from Radimovice No. 6. Godfather: Václav, son of Josef Skonka from Radimovice No. 2. Witnesses (wedding): Jakub Myrnas, cottager from Třtí and Karel Kvintus, cottager from RybnikI.

Petr Rechziegel and Anna Najmanová were married on 26 Jan 1869 in Radimovice No. 7, Vlastibořice parish., Jan Krt. Hruska officiationg. They had the following children:

> **Josef Rechcigl** was born on 22 Jul 1869 in Radimovice No. 7. He was baptized on 23 Jul 1869 in Vlastibořice parish: By Josef Nemecek, manor chaplain,. He died on 24 Feb 1920 in Letařovice (prob.). He was buried on 28 Feb 1920 in In the Letařovice Cemetery. Sex: Male. His religious affiliation was Roman Catholic. Godmother: Anna,

wife of Josef Šulc, innkeeper from Radimovice. Godfather: August Ulnic, innkeeper from Jilove. Midwife: Anna Vinsova, Žďárek No. 11. Age (death): 51 years old. Cause Of Death (Facts Pag: Serious prolonged illness.

Emilie Rechcíglová was born on 02 Apr 1871 in Letařovice No. 4, Český Dub Co.. She was baptized on 02 Apr 1871 in Český Dub parish: By Rev. Jesina. She died on 18 Feb 1928. She was buried on 22 Feb 1928 in Hodkovice Cemetery. Sex: Female. Her religious affiliation was Roman Catholic. Godmother: Marie Rechziegelová, wife of Petr Rechziegel, miller from Tri No. 8. Godfather: Josef Maruska, cottager from Letařovice No. 2. Midwife: Marie Cubrova. Age (death): 57 years old.

Václav Rechcigl was born on 13 Mar 1873 in Letařovice No. 4, Český Dub Co.. He was baptized on 13 Mar 1873 in By priest Jan Jesina, dean. Sex: Male. He was employed as a A miller near Plzen, western Bohemia. His religious affiliation was Roman Catholic. Godmother: Marie Najmanová, daughter of Antonín Najman, farmer from Radimovice No. 7. Godfather: Wacslav Samal, son of Jan Samal, farmer, Hradcany No. 11. Midwife: Marie Cubrova.

4. iv. **Adolf Rechcigl** was born on 21 Aug 1876 in Letařovice No. 4, Český Dub Co.. He was baptized on 22 Aug 1876 in Český Dub parish: By Jan Jesina, dean ("dekan"). He married Marie Berglová about 1900. He died on 30 Mar 1946 in Šárovcova Lhota No. 16. He was buried on 02 Apr 1946 in Chocnějovice Cemetery. Sex: Male. His address was / Chocnějovice 22, /. He was employed as a A miller. His religious affiliation was Roman Catholic. Godmother: Marie Kovářová, wife of Jan Kovar, cottager from Letarovive No. 3. Godfather: Josef Maruska, cottager from Letařovice No. 2. Midwife: Marie Cubrova. Age (death): 70 years old. Fact 1: A miller in Šárovcova Lhota. Fact 2: A miller in Chocnějovice No. 22. Public Office: Mayor, Chocnějovice. Position: miller in Chocnejovice, then in Sarovcova Lhota, having ledt the mill in Chocnejvice to his son Miloslav Rechcigl..

v. **Arnošt Rechziegel** was born on 07 Sep 1882 in Letařovice No. 4, Český Dub Co.. He died on 12 Oct 1882 in Letařovice No. 4, Český Dub Co.. He was buried on 14 Oct 1882 in Letařovice; Father Sorejs officiating. Sex: Male. His religious affiliation was Roman Catholic. Age (death): 5 weeks. Cause Of Death (Facts Pag: Debilitation ("vysileni").

vi. **Zdeněk Petr Rechcigl** was born on 31 Jul 1884 in Letařovice No. 4, Turnov Dist.. He married Anna Šimůnková on 08 Oct 1906 in Kralovske Vinohrady. Fact 1: 1908 in Received the Letařovice mill from his father. Fact 2: 1925 in Sold the mill to Karel and Anna Bartos. Fact 3: Aft. 1925 in Removed to the Plzen area where he had a mill or had a mill in Komarov. He died on 08 Feb 1962 in Karlovy Vary - Rybare. Sex: Male. His cause of death was Brochopneumonia, hardening of arteries, atherothrombosis of arteries. He was employed as a A miller in Komarov. His religious affiliation was Roman Catholic. Witnesses (wedding): Antonín Fiala, paish clerk and Antonín Planner, parish clerk, Král. Vinohrady. Married By: František Skarda. Age (death): 77 years.

vii. **Bohumil Rechcigl** was born on 09 Apr 1888. He died on 03 Jan 1963 in Český Dub. He was buried on 09 Jan 1963. Sex: Male. He was employed as a A miller, "Na Blejchu", Český Dub. His religious affiliation was Roman Catholic. Age (death): 75 years old.

viii. **Jan Rechziegel** was born on 08 May 1895. Sex: Male. He was employed as a A pharmacist.

10. **František Bergl** son of Josef Bergl and Anna Šichtová was born on 08 Sep 1850 in Podhora No. 16. He died on 22 Nov 1921 in Chocnějovice No. 22/39. Sex: Male. His address was / Drahotice No, 20, /. He was employed as a A shoemaker & cottager in Drahotice No. 20. Age (death): 71 years. Public Service: Mayor of Drahotice. He was buried in Chocnějovice Cemetary.

11. **Marie Mařanová** daughter of Jan Mařan and Kateřina Landová was born on 02 Feb 1860 in Drahotice No. 20. She died on 24 Jun 1924 in

Chocnějovice No. 22/39. Sex: Female. Her cause of death was fell from the stairs and bled to death. Age (death): 64 years. She was buried in Chocnějovice Cemetary.

František Bergl and Marie Mařanová married. They had the following children:

+5. i. **Marie Berglová** was born on 27 Mar 1880 in Drahotice No. 20, Mnichovo Hradiště Co.. She married Adolf Rechcigl about 1900. She died on 25 Mar 1917 in Chocnějovice No. 22, Mnichovo Hradiště Co.. She was buried on 28 Mar 1917 in In the Rechcigl family vault at the Chocnějovice Cemetery. Sex: Female. Her cause of death was Heart paralysis ("ochrnuti srdce'). Age (death): 37 years old.

12. **Jan Václav Rajtr** son of Václav Rajtr and Barbora Koštejn was born on 12 May 1847 in Zvířetice No. 11, Mnichovo Hradiště Co.. He was baptized on 12 May 1847 in By Father Josef Baudis, chaplain. He died on 19 Sep 1903 in Dolanky No. 7. He was buried on 21 Sep 1903 in Bakov nad Jizerou Cemetery. Sex: Male. He was employed as a A cottager, Dolanky No. 7. His religious affiliation was Roman Catholic. Age (wedding): 20 years old. Godmother: Terezie, wife of František Pacelt from Bakov n. Jiz.. Godfather: František Pacelt, laborer from Bakov. Midwife: Jizerou; Terezie Paceltova from Bakov n. Witnesses (wedding): Josef Parik, cottager from Cihadky and Jan Maděra, cottager from Cihadky. Married By: Father František Bubak, parish priest. Age (death): 56 years old. Cause Of Death (Facts Pag: Stroke ("mrtvice mozkova").

13. **Anna Najmanová** daughter of Josef Najman and Alžběta Bartonova was born on 26 Dec 1841 in Dolanky No. 7, Mnichovo Hradiště Co.. She was baptized on 26 Dec 1841. She died on 05 Aug 1900 in Dolanky, Mnichovo Hradiště Co.. She was buried on 08 Aug 1900 in Bakov nad Jizerou Cemetery. Sex: Female. Her cause of death was Stomach and intestinal disorders. Her religious affiliation was Roman Catholic. Age (wedding): 26 years old. Godmother: Barbora Svobodová, wife of a cottager from Chlumin. Godfather: Josef Brzobohatý, farmer from Dolanky. Midwife:

Anna Kyselova from Podhradi. Age (death): 58 years old. Cause Of Death (Facts Pag: Gastrointestinal problems.

Jan Václav Rajtr and Anna Najmanová were married on 09 Jun 1868. They had the following children:

    i. **Vincenc Rajtr** was born on 08 Apr 1871 in Dolanky No. 7. He died on 03 Oct 1871. Sex: Male.

    ii. **Václav Rajtr** was born on 22 Dec 1872 in Dolanky No. 7. He died on 11 Feb 1873 in Dolanky No. 7. Sex: Male.

+ 6. iii. **Čeněk Rajtr**[1] was born on 01 Jul 1874 in nky No. 7, Mnichovo Hradiště Dist... He was baptized on 02 Jul 1874 in By Father Antonín Cihlar, parish priest. He married Marie Dandová on 02 Jul 1904 in Mnichovo Hradiště. He died on 27 Oct 1956 in Dolánky No. 7, Mnichovo Hradiště Dist... Sex: Male. He was employed as a A Farmer and ownerof a tree nursery, Dolanky. His religious affiliation was Roman Catholic; since 19212 a membr of Czech-Moravian Church. Godmother: Barbora Brzobohatá, countrywoman from Dolanky. Godfather: Josef Parik, cottager from Cihadky No. 4. Midwife: Josefa Havlickova from Bakov n.J.

    iv. **Anna Rajtrová** was born on 10 May 1876 in Dolanky No. 7. She died in Jan 1946 in Muzsky No. 19, Mnichovo Hradiště, Co.. Sex: Female.

    v. **Rudolf Rajtr** was born on 15 Nov 1881 in Dolanky No. 7. He died in Mar 1953 in Muzsky No. 6. Sex: Male.

    vi. **Josef Rajtr** was born about 1882 in Dolanky No. 7, Mnichovo Hradiště Cco.. Sex: Male.

14. **František Antonín Danda** son of František Danda and Kateřina Nováková was born on 10 Jun 1857 in Hoškovice, No. 2, Mnichovo Hradiště Dist, Bohemia. He was baptized on 10 Jun 1857. He died on 07 Jun 1900 in Hoškovice, No. 14, Mnichovo Hradiště Dist, Bohemia. He was buried on 09 Jun 1900 in Mnichovo Hradiště Cemetery. Sex: Male. His cause of death was pneumonia. He was employed as a Cottager, Hoškovice No. 14. His religious affiliation was Roman Catholic. Age

(wedding): 23 and 8/12 years old. Godmother: Anna Benešová from Hradiste. Godfather: Josef Buriánek from Hoškovice. Midwife: Anna Benešová from Hradiste. Witnesses (wedding): Josef Bajer from Hoškovice and Václav Danda from Hoškovice. Married By: Father Jan Bernat. Cause Of Death (Facts Pag: Pneumonia. Ownership: His father bought hoim a farm and a pub, Hoškovice No. 14.

15. **Josefa Cimrová** daughter of František Cimr and Anna Ferklová was born on 01 Jan 1859 in Manikovice No. 11, Mnichovo Hradiště Dist.. She was baptized on 02 Jan 1859 in By Father Antonín Cihlar, chaplain. She died on 27 Aug 1923 in Hoškovice No. 14, Mnichovo Hradiště Dist.. She was buried on 29 Aug 1923 in Mnichovo Hradiště Cemetery. Sex: Female. Her cause of death was Heart disease. Her religious affiliation was Roman Catholic. Age (wedding): 22 and 1/12 years old. Cause Of Death (Facts Pag: Heart disease.

František Antonín Danda and Josefa Cimrová were married on 04 Feb 1881 in Manikovice No. 21. They had the following children:

+ 7. i. **Marie Dandová**[2] was born on 31 Jan 1882 in Hoškovice, No. 14, Mnichovo Hradiště Dist, Bohemia. She was baptized on 31 Jan 1882 in By Father Jan Bernat, chaplain. She married Čeněk Rajtr on 02 Jul 1904 in Mnichovo Hradiště. She died on 05 Jul 1967 in Dolanky No. 7, Mnichovo Hradiště Co.. Sex: Female. Her religious affiliation was Roman Catholic. Godmother: Marie Dandová from Hoškovice. Midwife: Anna Benešová from Mnichovo Hradiště.

ii. **Josef Danda** was born on 30 Jan 1884 in Hoškovice, No. 14, Mnichovo Hradiště Dist, Bohemia. He died on 18 Apr 1936 in Dobrá Voda. Sex: Male. He was employed as a Small farmer and tavern keeper in Dobrá Voda. House: Sold the family house in Hoškovice and moved to DobraVvoda.

iii. **Josefa Kateřina Dandová** was born on 04 Oct 1885 in Hoškovice No. 14, Mnichovo Hradiště Dist.. She married Václav Balák after 1925. Sex: Female.

iv. **Anna Dandová** was born on 12 Nov 1886 in Hoškovice, No. 14, Mnichovo Hradiště Dist, Bohemia. She died on 13 May 1972. She was buried on 16 May 1972 in Bakov n. J.. Sex: Female. Age (death): 86 years old.
v. **František Danda** was born on 23 Apr 1888 in Hoškovice, No. 14, Mnichovo Hradiště Dist, Bohemia. He died on 27 Jun 1888 in Hoškovice, No. 14, Mnichovo Hradiště Dist, Bohemia. Sex: Male.
vi. **František Danda** was born on 13 Nov 1889 in Hoškovice No. 14, Mnichovo Hradiště Dist.. He died on 22 Dec 1891 in Hoškovice no. 14, Mnichovo Hradiště Dist, Bohemia. Sex: Male.
vii. **Václav Danda** was born on 05 Sep 1891 in Hoškovice No. 14, Mnichovo Hradiště Dist, Bohemia. He died on 10 Mar 1892 in Hoškovice No. 14, Mnichovo Hradiště Dist, Bohemia. Sex: Male.
viii. **Emilie Dandová** was born on 22 Oct 1893 in Hoškovice No. 14, Mnichovo Hradiště Dist, Bohemia. She married Václav Balák on 18 Sep 1920 in Hoškovice, Mnichovo Hradiště Dist, Bohemia. She died on 06 Apr 1924 in Hoškovice, Mnichovo Hradiště Dist, Bohemia. Sex: Female.

Generation 5

16. **Petr Rechziegel** son of Ing. František Rechziegel and Lidmila Neumanová was born on 10 Jan 1819 in Slavíkov No. 4. Fact 3: Aft. 1850 in Bought the mill in Letařovice No. 4 - from Václav Keller. Fact 2: Bef. 1858 in Leased the mill in Třtí No. 8 - from Janeček. Fact 1: Bef. 1858 in An inn-keeper, Slavíkov No. 3. Fact 4: 1872 in Bought Novy mlyn in Žďárek No. 26, Turnov Co.. Fact 5: 1872 in Gave the Letařovice mill to his son Petr. He died on 17 Oct 1890 in Novy Mlyn, Žďárek. Sex: Male. He was baptized in Vlastibořice parish: By Lustinatz, adm.. He was employed as a A miller. His religious affiliation was Roman Catholic. Age (wedding): 1st wedding - 31 years old. Godfather: Jan Adamu and Matěj Adam, farmers from Vlastibořice. Midwife: Lidmilla H., Radimovice.

17. **Františka Hlavatá** daughter of Unknown and Terezie Hlavatá was born on 27 Feb 1820 in Bzi No. 6. She died on 10 Dec 1857 in Slavíkov No. 4, in Mohelka Creek -. She was buried on 13 Dec 1857 in Český Dub parish: Jan

Jesina, chaplain. Sex: Female. Her religious affiliation was Roman Catholic. Age (wedding): 30 years old. Age (death): 36 years. Cause Of Death (Facts Pag: By drowning- out of distress over the death of her child. Petr Rechziegel and Františka Hlavatá were married on 30 Nov 1850 in Slavíkov No. 3, Vlastibořice parish, Josef Sedláček, officiating. They had the following children:

    i. **Marie Rechziegel** was born on 24 Jan 1841 in Hodkovice No. 39. She was baptized on 24 Jan 1841 in Hodkovice parish. Sex: Female. Her religious affiliation was Roman Catholic. Godmother: Františka, wife of Josef Beisinek from Hodkovice. Godfather: Florián Ganek, small farmer from Bohdankov.

+ 8. ii. **Petr Rechziegel** was born on 01 Jun 1844 in Hodkovice No. 39. He was baptized on 01 Jun 1844 in Hodkovice parish: By Rev. Josef Hofrichtr in the parish church in Hodkovice. He married Anna Najmanová on 26 Jan 1869 in Radimovice No. 7, Vlastibořice parish., Jan Krt. Hruska officiatiatiiong. Fact 1: 1872 in Received the Letařovice mill from his father. Fact 2: Abt. 1907 in Gave the mill to his son Zdeněk. He died on 18 Sep 1917 in Letařovice No. 4, Turnov Co.. He was buried on 21 Sep 1917 in Letařovice Cemetery. Sex: Male. His address was / Letařovice No. 32, /. He was employed as a A miller. His religious affiliation was Roman Catholic. Age (wedding): 24 years of age. Godmother: Františka Kaiser, countrywoman ("selka") from Hodkovice No. 100. Godfather: Otokar Presler, businessman from Hodkovice No. 150. Age (death): 74 years old. Position: miller in Letarovice, No. 4. Called Himself: "Josef".

    iii. **Františka Rechziegel** was born on 05 Jul 1846 in Hodkovice No. 39. She was baptized on 6 Jul 1846 in Hodkovice parish: By Johann Hammerschmied in Hodkovice. She died on 28 Feb 1914 in Ruzodol No. 169. Sex: Female. Her religious affiliation was Roman Catholic. Godmother: Františka Kaiser, countrywoman from Hodkovice No. 100. Godfather: Christoff Wagner, parish clerk from Hodkovice. Age (death): 68 years old. She was buried in Liberec Cemetery.

1   **Václav Rechziegel** was born on 25 Aug 1851 in Slavíkov No. 3. He was baptized on 25 Aug 1851 in His birth certificate lists him as Vacslav Rechziegl. He married Anna Janečková in 1879. He died on 21 Mar 1909 in Radostín No. 13. Sex: Male. His address was / Radostín, /. He was employed as a A cottager ("domkar"), later a miller in Radostín. His religious affiliation was Roman Catholic. Godmother: Anna, wife of František Pluhař, butcher from Dechtary No. 12. Godfather: Stanislav Jiru, bartender from Vlastibořice No. 1 Midwife: Anna Pluhař. Age (death): 58 years old.

2   **Josefa Rechziegelová** was born on 08 Nov 1852 in Slavíkov No. 3. She was baptized on 8 Nov 1852 in Vlastibořice parish: by Jan Krt. Hruska L.. She died on 11 Nov 1852 in Slavíkov No. 3. She was buried on 13 Nov 1852 in Vlastibořice parish: By Jan Krt. Hruska L.. Sex: Female. Her religious affiliation was Roman Catholic. Godmother: Anna, wife of František Pluhař, butcher from Dechtary No.12. Godfather: Václav Hartlich, cottager from Vlastibořice. Midwife: Anna Pluhařová, Slavíkov No. 12. Age (death): 3 days old. Cause Of Death (Facts Pag: Infantile convulsions ("bozec").

vi. **Karel Bor. Rechziegel** was born on 03 Jul 1855 in Slavíkov No. 3. He was baptized on 03 Jul 1855 in Vlastibořice parish: by Jan Krt. Hruska. He died on 24 Oct 1855 in Slavíkov No. 3. He was buried on 27 Oct 1855 in Vlastibořice parish: by Jan Krt. Hruska. Sex: Male. His religious affiliation was Roman Catholic. Godmother: Anna, wife of Jan Vecernik, laborer from Slavíkov No. 16. Godfather: Jan Adam, baker from Vlastibořice No. 13. Midwife: Anna Pluhařová, Slavíkov No. 12. Age (death): 4 months. Cause Of Death (Facts Pag: Infantile convulsions ("psotnik").

Kateřina Koskova daughter of Josef Košek and Marie Jirova was born in 1831 in Třtí No. 6, Turnov Co.. She died on 20 Nov 1902 in Mala Bela, near Bakov. Sex: Female. Her religious affiliation was Roman Catholic. Age (wedding): 26 years old. Witnesses (wedding): Josef Meznar, farmer from Letařovice No. 12 and Staslav Rovac, cottager from Letařovice No. 3. She was buried in Bakov Cemetery.

Petr Rechziegel and Kateřina Koskova were married on 25 May 1858 in Třtí No. 6, Turnov Co., Franz Staznik officiating. They had the following children:

 i. **Josef Rechziegel** was born on 31 Aug 1865 in Třtí No. 8, Turnov Co.. He was baptized on 01 Sep 1865. Fact 1: 19 Jun 1890 in Received from father Novy mlyn, Žďárek No. 26, Turnov Co.. He married Marie Cinkova on 23 Aug 1890 in Parish Church, Mukarov. Fact 3: 1900 in Sold Novy mlyn to Vinc of Žďárek. Fact 4: Abt. 1900 in A miller, Mala Bela, and mayor of the village. He died in 1917. Sex: Male. His religious affiliation was Roman Catholic. Witnesses (wedding): Karel Kvintus, cottager from Rybnik No. 4 and Jan Najman, cottager from Loukov No. 30. Married By: Father Josef Srb, parish priest from Hlavice. Fact 2: Bought a bakery from Zelezny in Hodkovice.

18. **Antonín Neumann** son of Jan Neumann and Kateřina Sivatkova was born in 1828 in Radimovice No. 7, Český Dub Dist.. Sex: Male. He was employed as a Small farmer at Radimovice No. 4. He was employed as a pulsedlak and rolnik, Radimovice No. 7.

19. **Anna Brožová** daughter of Václav Brož and Alžběta Laurinova was born in 1829 in Radimovice No. 10 or Sychrov. Sex: Female. Her religious affiliation was Roman Catholic.

Antonín Neumann and Anna Brožová were married on 08 Feb 1848 in Vlastibořice. They had the following children:

9. i. **Anna Najmanová** was born on 31 Jul 1849 in Radimovice No. 7, Turnov Co.. She was baptized on 31 Jul 1849 in Vlastibořice parish: By Jan Solc, manor chaplain. She married Petr Rechziegel on 26 Jan 1869 in Radimovice No. 7, Vlastibořice parish., Jan Krt. Hruska officiationg. She owned in 1904 in Sold the homestead (including mill, inn and farm lands, at Třtí No. 32 to Josef Jira of

Dehtary. She died on 05 Jun 1908 in Letařovice. Sex: Female. Her religious affiliation was Roman Catholic. Age (wedding): 19 years old. Godmother: Anna, wife of Vavlav Najman from Radimovice No. 6. Godfather: Václav, son of Josef Skonka from Radimovice No. 2. Witnesses (wedding): Jakub Myrnas, cottager from Třtí and Karel Kvintus, cottager from RybnikI.

20. **Josef Bergl** son of Jan Bergl and Kateřina Stránská was born on 28 Dec 1820 in Podhora No. 16. He died on 20 Oct 1861. Sex: Male. His address was / Kocnejovice No. 16, /. He was employed as a cottager ("domkar"), Kocnejovice No. 16l. Position: cottager, tailor.

21. **Anna Šichtová** daughter of Jan Šichta was born on 12 Sep 1824 in Sovinky No. 31. Sex: Female. Josef Bergl and Anna Šichtová married. They had the following children:

    i. **Josef Bergl** was born on 20 Mar 1848 in Kocňovice No. 16. He died on 18 Apr 1856. Sex: Male.

    + 10.ii. **František Bergl** was born on 08 Sep 1850 in Podhora No. 16. He died on 22 Nov 1921 in Chocnějovice No. 22/39. Sex: Male. His address was / Drahotice No, 20, /. He was employed as a A shoemaker & cottager in Drahotice No. 20. Age (death): 71 years. Public Service: Mayor of Drahotice. He was buried in Chocnějovice Cemetary.

    iii. **Jan Bergl** was born on 03 Sep 1854 in Podhora No. 16. Sex: Male.

    iv. **2nd Josef Bergl** was born about 1860 in Podhora No. 16. Sex: Male. Removed: To Neveklovice.

    v. **daughter Berglová** was born about 1850 in Podhora No. 16. Sex: Female.

22. **Jan Mařan** son of Jan Mařan and Anna Konopkova was born in Drahotice No. 20. Sex: Male. His address was / Drahotice No. 20, /. He was employed as a Cottager ("chalupnik") in Drahotice No. 20.
Notes for Jan Mařan:
General Notes:
cottager, Drahotice

23. **Kateřina Landová** daughter of Jan Landa and Anna Polívková was born about 1840 in Drahotice No. 9. Sex: Female.

Jan Mařan and Kateřina Landová married. They had the following children:

    i. **Anna Marie Mařanová** was born on 24 Oct 1855 in Drahotice No. 20. Sex: Female.

28. 11.ii. **Marie Mařanová** was born on 02 Feb 1860 in Drahotice No. 20. She died on 24 Jun 1924 in Chocnějovice No. 22/39. Sex: Female. Her cause of death was fell from the stairs and bled to death. Age (death): 64 years. She was buried in Chocnějovice Cemetary.

14. **Václav Rajtr** son of Václav Rajtr and Dorota Strojsová was born on 15 Sep 1783 in Zvířetice No. 11. He died on 16 Jan 1823 in Zvířetice No. 11, Mnichovo Hradiště Dist., Bohemia. Sex: Male.

15. **Barbora Koštejn** daughter of Jan Koštejn and Terezie Pazderníková was born on 25 Dec 1815 in Zviretica. She died on 28 May 1887 in Chudoplesy No. 9. Sex: Female.

Václav Rajtr and Barbora Koštejn married. They had the following children:

1 12.i. **Jan Václav Rajtr** was born on 12 May 1847 in Zvířetice No. 11, Mnichovo Hradiště Co.. He was baptized on 12 May 1847 in By Father Josef Baudis, chaplain. He married Anna Najmanová on 09 Jun 1868. He died on 19 Sep 1903 in Dolanky No. 7. He was buried on 21 Sep 1903 in Bakov nad Jizerou Cemetery. Sex: Male. He was employed as a A cottager, Dolanky No. 7. His religious affiliation was Roman Catholic. Age (wedding): 20 years old. Godmother: Terezie, wife of František Pacelt from Bakov n. Jiz.. Godfather: František Pacelt, laborer from Bakov. Midwife: Jizerou; Terezie Paceltova from Bakov n. Witnesses (wedding): Josef Parik, cottager from Cihadky and Jan Maděra, cottager from Cihadky. Married By: Father František Bubak, parish priest. Age (death): 56 years old. Cause Of Death (Facts Pag: Stroke ("mrtvice mozkova").

    i. **Marie Rajtrová** was born on 16 Jun 1849. Sex: Female.

ii. **Václav Rajtr** was born on 13 Nov 1857. He died on 16 Nov 1857. He was buried on 18 Nov 1857. Sex: Male.

iii. **Josef Rajtr** was born on 11 Jun 1858. He died on 12 Jun 1858. Sex: Male.

16. **Josef Najman** son of Vojtěch Najman and Anna Gintrova was born in Dolanky No. 7, Mnichovo Hradiště Co.. Sex: Male. He was employed as a A cottager ("chalupnik"), Ddolanky No. 4. His religious affiliation was Roman Catholic.

17. **Alžběta Bartonova** daughter of Václav Barton and Anna Nohýnková was born in Dneboh No. 9, Mnichovo Hradiště Co.. Sex: Female.

Josef Najman and Alžběta Bartonova married. They had the following children:

1 13.i. **Anna Najmanová** was born on 26 Dec 1841 in Dolanky No. 7, Mnichovo Hradiště Co.. She was baptized on 26 Dec 1841. She married Jan Václav Rajtr on 09 Jun 1868. She died on 05 Aug 1900 in Dolanky, Mnichovo Hradiště Co.. She was buried on 08 Aug 1900 in Bakov nad Jizerou Cemetery. Sex: Female. Her cause of death was Stomach and intestinal disorders. Her religious affiliation was Roman Catholic. Age (wedding): 26 years old. Godmother: Barbora Svobodová, wife of a cottager from Chlumin. Godfather: Josef Brzobohatý, farmer from Dolanky. Midwife: Anna Kyselova from Podhradi. Age (death): 58 years old. Cause Of Death (Facts Pag: Gastrointestinal problems.

1 **František Danda** son of Josef Danda and Barbora Buriánková was born on 01 Aug 1817 in Hoškovice, Mnichovo Hradiště Dist, Bohemia. He died on 04 Mar 1904 in Podolí No. 8. Sex: Male.

2 **Kateřina Nováková** daughter of Jan Novák and Dorota Reslerová was born on 03 Jun 1826 in Dalešice no. 5. She died on 29 May 1912 in Podolí No. 8. Sex: Female.

František Danda and Kateřina Nováková married. They had the following children:

i. **Barbora Dandová** was born on 28 Jan 1844 in Hoškovice No. 2, Mnichovo Hradiště Dist, Bohemia. She married Josef Šverma on 27 May 1867 in Hoškovice No. 2, Mnichovo Hradiště Dist, Bohemia. Sex: Female.

ii. **Josef of Kopeček Danda** was born on 16 Jun 1846 in Hoškovice, Mnichovo Hradiště Dist, Bohemia (moved to Hoškovice No. 13 - Kopeček). He died on 21 Sep 1847 in Hoškovice, No. 2, Mnichovo Hradiště Dist, Bohemia. Sex: Male. He was also known as "sycak".

iii. **Václav Danada** was born on 13 May 1848 in Hoškovice, No. 2, Mnichovo Hradiště Dist, Bohemia. He died on 11 Dec 1917 in Hoškovice, Mnichovo Hradiště Dist, Bohemia. Sex: Male.

iv. **Marie Dandová** was born on 16 Sep 1850 in Hoškovice, No. 2, Mnichovo Hradiště Dist, Bohemia. Sex: Female.

v. **Josef Danda** was born on 23 Aug 1854 in Hoškovice, No. 2, Mnichovo Hradiště Dist, Bohemia. Sex: Male.

2 14.vi. **František Antonín Danda** was born on 10 Jun 1857 in Hoškovice, No. 2, Mnichovo Hradiště Dist, Bohemia. He was baptized on 10 Jun 1857. He married Josefa Cimrová on Feb 1881 in Manikovice No. 21. He died on 07 Jun 1900 in Hoškovice, No. 14, Mnichovo Hradiště Dist, Bohemia. He was buried on 09 Jun 1900 in Mnichovo Hradiště Cemetery. Sex: Male. His cause of death was pneumonia. He was employed as a Cottager, Hoškovice No. 14. His religious affiliation was Roman Catholic. Age (wedding): 23 and 8/12 years old. Godmother: Anna Benešová from Hradiste. Godfather: Josef Buriánek from Hoškovice. Midwife: Anna Benešová from Hradiste. Witnesses (wedding): Josef Bajer from Hoškovice and Václav Danda from Hoškovice. Married By: Father Jan Bernat. Cause Of Death (Facts Pag: Pneumonia. Ownership: His father bought hoim a farm and a pub, Hoškovice No. 14.

vii. **Jan Danda** was born on 10 Apr 1860 in Hoškovice, No. 2, Mnichovo Hradiště Dist, Bohemia. He died on 10 Apr 1860 in Hoškovice No. 2,, Mnichovo Hradiště Dist, Bohemia. Sex: Male.

viii. **Kateřina Marie Dandová** was born on 12 Aug 1865 in Hoškovice No. 2,, Mnichovo Hradiště Dist, Bohemia. Sex: Female.

ix. **Antonín Danda** was born on 27 Feb 1868 in Hoškovice, No. 2, Mnichovo Hradiště Dist, Bohemia. He died on 22 Mar 1868. Sex: Male.

30. **František Cimr** son of Josef Cimr and Kodrova ? Anna Kochova was born on 31 Mar 1823 in Manikovice No. 11, Mnichovo Hradiště Co.. He died on 22 Mar 1884. Sex: Male. He was employed as a A farmer ("Sedlák"), Manikovice No. 11. His religious affiliation was Roman Catholic.

31. **Anna Ferklová** daughter of Josef Ferkl and Alžběta Filipová was born in Rostkov No. 3, Mnichovo Hradiště Co.. Sex: Female. Her religious affiliation was Roman Catholic.

František Cimr and Anna Ferklová married. They had the following children:

    i. **Josef Cimr** was born on 06 Jan 1850. Sex: Male.

    ii. **Václav Cimr** was born on 25 Mar 1851. Sex: Male.

    iii. **František Cimr** was born on 26 Jan 1853. Sex: Male.

    iv. **Antonín Cimr** was born on 19 Dec 1855. He died on 17 Mar 1856. Sex: Male.

+ 15.v. **Josefa Cimrová** was born on 01 Jan 1859 in Manikovice No. 11, Mnichovo Hradiště Dist.. She was baptized on 02 Jan 1859 in By Father Antonín Cihlar, chaplain. She married František Antonín Danda on 04 Feb 1881 in Manikovice No. 21. She died on 27 Aug 1923 in Hoškovice No. 14, Mnichovo Hradiště Dist.. She was buried on 29 Aug 1923 in Mnichovo Hradiště Cemetery. Sex: Female. Her cause of death was Heart disease. Her religious affiliation was Roman Catholic. Age (wedding): 22 and 1/12 years old. Cause Of Death (Facts Pag: Heart disease.

    vi. **Štěpán Cimr** was born on 26 May 1860. Sex: Male.

    vii. **Jan Cimr** was born on 21 Apr 1862. Sex: Male.

    viii. **Anna Cimrová** was born on 05 Aug 1864. Sex: Female.

    ix. **Vincenc Cimr** was born on 16 Apr 1870. Sex: Male.

Generation 6

20. **Ing. František Rechziegel** son of František Rechziegel and Alžběta Boelmanova was born on 26 Dec 1789 in Slavíkov No. 4, Český Dub Co.. Godmother: 26 Dec 1789 in Barbora Jirakova, wife of František Jirak, innkeeper from Slavíkov. Godfather: 26 Dec 1789 in Benedykt Richter, miller at Dlouhy Most. He died on 02 Aug 1849 in Slavíkov No. 4. He was buried on 06 Aug 1849 in Parish Vlastibořice: By Josef Sedláček L.. Sex: Male. His address was / Slavíkov No.4, /. He was employed as a A miller in Slavíkov No. 4. His religious affiliation was Roman Catholic. Age (wedding): 21 years old. Witnesses (wedding): Franz Brodky, Vlastibořice. Married By: Gregorius Alexius L.. Age (death): 34 years old. Cause Of Death (Facts Pag: Gastric ulcers ("zaludecni vredy"). Position: miller, Slavikov, No. 4.

21. **Lidmila Neumanová** daughter of Václav Neumann and Lidmila Adamova was born on 28 Jun 1792 in Radimovice No. 6, Český Dub Co.. She died on 09 May 1845 in Slavíkov No. 4. She was buried on 13 May 1845 in Parish Vladstiborice: Bt Josef Sedláček L.. Sex: Female. Her religious affiliation was Roman Catholic. Age (wedding): 18 years old. Age (death): 52 and 3/4 yers old. Cause Of Death (Facts Pag: Internal bleeding ("chrleni krve").

    Ing. František Rechziegel and Lidmila Neumanová were married on 03 Aug 1811 in Slavíkov No. 4, Vlastibořice parish. They had the following children:

    i. **Franz Rechziegel** was born on 03 Aug 1811 in Skavikov No. 4. Sex: Male.

    ii. **František Rechziegel** was born on 26 May 1812 in Slavíkov No. 4. He was buried in Jul 1814 in Vlastibořice parish: By Gregorius Alexius L.. He died on 12 Jul 1814 in Slavíkov No. 4. Sex: Male. He was baptized in Vlastiborive parish: By Gregorius Alexius L.. His religious affiliation was Roman Catholic. Godmother: Terezie, wife of Jiří Jirku, farmer. Godfather: Florián Ledler, baker from Sloup. Midwife: Maria Roubinek, Radostín. Age (death): 2 years old. Cause Of Death (Facts Pag: Infantile convulsions ("bozec").

iii. **Josef Rechziegel** was born on 22 Feb 1814 in Slavíkov No. 4. He died on 06 Jun 1893 in Teplice. He was buried on 09 Jun 1893 in Teplice Catholic Cemetery. Sex: Male. He was baptized in Vlastibořice parish: By Gregorius Alexius L.. He retired in In Teplice, after 56 years of pristhood. His address was / Teplice, /. He was employed as a Roman Catholic priest. His religious affiliation was Roman Catholic. Employment: Parish priest, dean, Jablonec, Mimon Co.. Midwife: Maria Roubinek, Radostín. Age (death): 80 years old. Position: R.C.priest and Dean.

iv. **Marie Rechziegel** was born on 14 Mar 1816 in Slavíkov No. 4. She died on 08 Apr 1846 in Slavíkov No. 4. She was buried on 11 Apr 1846 in Vlastibořice parish: By Josef Sedláček, Sumperk. Sex: Female. She was baptized in Vlastibořice parish: By Gregorius Alexius L.. Her religious affiliation was Roman Catholic. Godmother: Anna, wife of Václav Adam, cottager from Vlastibořice. Godfather: Jan Adam, farmer from Vlastibořice. Midwife: Catharina Jiru, Dechtar. Age (death): 30 years old. Cause Of Death (Facts Pag: Dropsy ("vodnatelnost"). Status: Unmarried.

v. **Františka Rechziegel** was born on 27 Jan 1818 in Slavíkov No. 4. She was buried in Feb 1818 in Vlastibořice parish: By Gregorius Alexius L.. She died on 25 Feb 1818 in Slavíkov, No. 4. Sex: Female. She was baptized in Vlastibořice Parish: Gregorius Alexius L.. Her religious affiliation was Roman Catholic. Godmother: Anna, wife of Václav Adam, cottager of Vlastibořice. Godfather: Jan Adam, farmer of Vlastibořice. Midwife: Catharina Jiru, Dechtar. Cause Of Death (Facts Pag: Birth difficulties.

+ 16.vi. **Petr Rechziegel** was born on 10 Jan 1819 in Slavíkov No. 4. Fact 3: Aft. 1850 in Bought the mill in Letařovice No. 4 - from Václav Keller. He married Františka Hlavatá on 30 Nov 1850 in Slavíkov No. 3, Vlastibořice parish, Josef Sedláček, officiating.

Fact 2: Bef. 1858 in Leased the mill in Třtí No. 8 - from Janeček. Fact 1: Bef. 1858 in An inn-keeper, Slavíkov No. 3. Fact 4: 1872 in Bought Novy mlyn in Žďárek No. 26, Turnov Co.. Fact 5: 1872 in Gave the Letařovice mill to his son Petr. He died on 17 Oct 1890 in Novy Mlyn, Žďárek. Sex: Male. He was baptized in Vlastibořice parish: By Lustinatz, adm.. He was employed as a A miller. His religious affiliation was Roman Catholic. Age (wedding): 1st wedding - 31 years old. Godfather: Jan Adamu and Matěj Adam, farmers from Vlastibořice. Midwife: Lidmilla H., Radimovice.

1   **Františka Johanna Rechziegel** was born on 11 May 1821 in Slavíkov No. 4. She died on 10 Mar 1823 in Slavíkov No. 4. Sex: Female. She was baptized in Vlastibořice parish: By Josef Leynil L.. Her religious affiliation was Roman Catholic. Godmother: Johana Bravowa, parish housekeeper, Vlastibořice No. 23. Godfather: Josef Dolensky, teacher, Vlastibořice No. 9. Midwife: Kateřina, wife of Jan jira, farmer from Dektar. Age (death): 2 years old. Cause Of Death (Facts Pag: Accidental drowning. She was buried in Vlastibořice parish: By Josef Siholy L..

viii. **Antonín Rechziegel** was born on 22 May 1823 in Slavíkov No. 4, Český Dub Co.. He married Anna Šiftová on 11 Feb 1851 in Jivina No. 6. He died on 25 Sep 1888 in Slavíkov No. 4, Cesyu Dub Co.. He was buried on 28 Sep 1888 in Vlastibořice parish: By Josef Kovar, priest. Sex: Male. He was baptized in Vlastibořice parish: By Josephus Soholy L.. He was employed as a A miller. His religious affiliation was Roman Catholic. Age (wedding): 27 and 1/2 years old. Godmother: Anna, wife of Josef Dolensky, teacher from Vlastibořice. Godfather: Matěj Adam, retited farmer from Vlastibořice. Witnesses (wedding): Florián Roubíček. Married By: Josephus Rechziegel. Age (death): 65 years old. Fact 1: A miller in Slavíkov No. 4. Fact 2: An inn-keeper and a lessee of a mill in Třtí. Cause Of Death (Facts Pag: Lung paralysis ("ochrnuti plic"); Asthma ("zaducha"). Position: innkeeper, mill tenant in Trti; miller in Slavikov, No. 4.

ix. **Theresia Rechziegel** was born on 14 Apr 1825 in Slavíkov No. 4. She married Václav Beran on 05 Mar 1845 in Slavíkov No. 4, Vlastibořice parish. Sex: Female. She was baptized in Vlastibořice parish: Jof. Soholy L.. Her religious affiliation was Roman Catholic. Age (wedding): 20 years of age. Godmother: Anna, wife of Josef Dolensky, teacher from Vlastibořice. Godfather: Jan Adam, small farmer("pulsedlak") from Vlastibořice. Witnesses (wedding): Franc Kovar, small farmer from Racany No. 10 and Jan Šulc, farmer from Vlastibořice No. 19. Married By: By Jof. Sedláček.

x. **Anna Rechziegel** was born in Apr 1826 in Slavíkov No. 4. She died on 13 Jul 1826 in Slavíkov No. 4. She was buried on 15 Jul 1826. Sex: Female. Her religious affiliation was Roman Catholic. Age (death): 1/4 year. Cause Of Death (Facts Pag: Infirmity (Slabost").

xi. **Josefa Rechziegelová** was born on 09 May 1827 in Slavíkov No. 4. She married Josef Zajíček on 04 Jun 1851 in Slavíkov No. 4, Vlastibořice parish. She died on 24 Feb 1872 in Jivina No. 16. She was buried on 27 Feb 1872 in Vlastibořice parish: Josef Rechziegel, parish priest in Jablonec, officiated. Sex: Female. She was baptized in Vlastibořice parish: By Josef Soholy L.. Her religious affiliation was Roman Catholic. Age (wedding): 24 yeals old. Godmother: Marie, wife of Jiří Jiru, farmer. Godfather: Josef Dolensky, teacher from Vlastibořice. Witnesses (wedding): Jan Hula, cottager of Vlastibořice No. 10 and Franz Zajíček from Jivina No. 5. Married By: Josephus Rechziegel. Age (death): 45 years old. Cause Of Death (Facts Pag: Internal bleeding.

xii. **Kateřina Rechziegel** was born on 23 Apr 1829 in Slavíkov No. 4. Sex: Female. She was baptized in Vlastibořice parish. Her religious affiliation was Roman Catholic. Godmother: Kateřina, daughter of Jan Jina, lessee ("pachtyr"). Godfather: Josef

Smeidl, cottager from Český Dub. Midwife: Alžběta, widow from Vlastibořice.

xiii. **Karel Rechziegel** was born on 22 Jul 1830 in Slavíkov No. 4. He was baptized on 22 Jul 1830 in Vlastibořice parish. Sex: Male. His religious affiliation was Roman Catholic. Godfather: Matěj Adam, small farmer ("pulsed;lak") fromVvlastiborice.

xiv. **Anna Rechziegel** was born on 09 Feb 1833 in Slavíkov No. 4. She was baptized on 09 Feb 1833 in Vlastibořice parish: By Ignác Hujer, chaplain. She married Johan Fanta on 22 Feb 1859 in Třtí No, 23. Hodkovice parish. Sex: Female. Her religious affiliation was Roman Catholic. Age (wedding): 25 years old. Godmother: Anna Drterova, houskeeper. Midwife: Terezie, wife of František Jiru, Vlastibořice.

xv. **Františka Rechziegel** was born on 04 Oct 1837 in Slavíkov No. 4. She was baptized on 4 Oct 1837 in Vlastibořice parish: By Josef Sedláček L.. She died on 29 Oct 1837 in Slavíkov No. 4. She was buried on 31 Oct 1837 in Parish Vlastibořice: By Josef Sedláček L.. Sex: Female. Her religious affiliation was Roman Catholic. Godmother: Tereza Jirosova, wife of Franta Jiros, innkeeper from Vlastibořice No. 21. Midwife: Terezie from Vlastibořice No. 21. Age (death): 25 days old. Cause Of Death (Facts Pag: Infantile convulsions ("bozec").

34. **Unknown** was born in Bzi No. 6. Sex: Male. He died in Josef Dědek of Hodkovice - pestitel.

35. **Terezie Hlavatá** daughter of František Hlavatý and Anna Glaserova was born on 04 Nov 1800 in Bohumilec 1, Český Dub Co.. Sex: Female. Her religious affiliation was Roman Catholic. Unknown and Terezie Hlavatá met. They had the following children:

+ 17.i. **Františka Hlavatá** was born on 27 Feb 1820 in Bzi No. 6. She married Petr Rechziegel on 30 Nov 1850 in Slavíkov No. 3, Vlastibořice parish, Josef Sedláček, officiating. She died on Dec 1857 in Slavíkov No. 4, in Mohelka Creek -. She was buried on 13 Dec 1857 in Český Dub parish: Jan Jesina, chaplain. Sex: Female.

Her religious affiliation was Roman Catholic. Age (wedding): 30 years old. Age (death): 36 years. Cause Of Death (Facts Pag: By drowning- out of distress over the death of her child.

1 **Jan Neumann** son of Václav Neumann and Lidmila Adamova was born about 1790 in Radimovice No. 7, Český Dub Co.. Sex: Male.

2 **Kateřina Sivatkova** daughter of Václav Sivatko was born in Libic no. 1. Sex: Female.

Jan Neumann and Kateřina Sivatkova married. They had the following children:

    i. **Františka Neumanová** was born on 11 Jan 1810. Sex: Female.

    ii. **Kateřina Neumanová** was born on 22 Feb 1812. Sex: Female.

    iii. **Jan Neumann** was born on 27 Jun 1813 in Radimovice No. 6, Dub Co.. Sex: Male.

    iv. **Anna Neumanová** was born on 10 Nov 1813. Sex: Female.

    v. **František Neumann** was born on 16 Oct 1815. Sex: Male.

    vi. **Václav Neuman** was born on 06 Jan 1817. Sex: Male.

2 18.vii. **Antonín Neumann** was born in 1828 in Radimovice No. 7, Český Dub Dist.. He married Anna Brožová on 08 Feb 1848 in Vlastibořice. Sex: Male. He was employed as a Small farmer at Radimovice No. 4. He was employed as a pulsedlak and rolnik, Radimovice No.

3 **Václav Brož** was born before 1800 in Radimovice No. 10 or Sychrov. Sex: Male. He was employed as a Cottager, Radimovice No. 10.

4 **Alžběta Laurinova** daughter of Václav Laurin and Unknown was born about 1810 in Vselibice No. 19. Sex: Female.

Václav Brož and Alžběta Laurinova married. They had the following children:

+ 19.i. **Anna Brožová** was born in 1829 in Radimovice No. 10 or Sychrov. She married Antonín Neumann on 08 Feb 1848 in Vlastibořice. Sex: Female. Her religious affiliation was Roman Catholic.

41. **Jan Bergl** son of Josef Bergl and Unknown was born in 1789 in Podhora No. 6. He died on 13 Mar 1825. Sex: Male.

42. **Kateřina Stránská** daughter of Jan Stránský and Anna Honcová was born on 06 Sep 1798 in Manikovice No. 6. Sex: Female.
    Jan Bergl and Kateřina Stránská were married on 05 Apr 1818 in Manikovice[3]. They had the following children:
    + 20.i. **Josef Bergl** was born on 28 Dec 1820 in Podhora No. 16. He died on 20 Oct 1861. Sex: Male. His address was / Kocnejovice No. 16, /. He was employed as a cottager ("domkar"), Kocnejovice No. 16l. Position: cottager, tailor.
43. **Jan Šichta** was born in Sovinky No. 31. Sex: Male.
    Jan Šichta and unknown spouse married. They had the following children:
    + 21.i. **Anna Šichtová** was born on 12 Sep 1824 in Sovinky No. 31. Sex: Female.
44. **Jan Mařan** was born in Loukov No. 17. Sex: Male.
45. **Anna Konopkova** daughter of Matěj Konopka and Unknown. Sex: Female.
    Jan Mařan and Anna Konopkova married. They had the following children:
    + 22.i. **Jan Mařan** was born in Drahotice No. 20. Sex: Male. His address was / Drahotice No. 20, He was employed as a Cottager ("chalupnik") in Drahotice No. 20.
46. **Jan Landa** son of František Landa and Kateřina Hozaková was born about 1820 in Drahotice No. 9. Sex: Male. His address was / Drahotice No. 9, /. He was employed as a Cottegere ("chalupnik") in Drahotice No. 9.
47. **Anna Polívková** daughter of Miroslav Polivka and Unknown. Sex: Female. Jan Landa and Anna Polívková married. They had the following children:
    23.i. **Kateřina Landová** was born about 1840 in Drahotice No. 9. Sex: Female.
    Alžběta Nesvadbová daughter of Václav Nesvadba and Barbora Krejčová was born in Sovenice No. 13. Sex: Female.
    Jan Landa and Alžběta Nesvadbová married. They had the following children:

      i.   **Anna Landová** was born on 14 Apr 1849. Sex: Female.

      ii. **František Landa** was born on 06 Aug 1851. Sex: Male.

48. **Václav Rajtr** son of Jan Jri Rajtr and Anna Machackova was born on 15 Sep 1783 in Zvířetice No. 11. He died on 16 Jan 1823 in Zviretic No. 11. Sex: Male.

49. **Dorota Strojsová** daughter of Václav Strojsa and Dorota Wondrakova was born on 24 Jan 1780 in Bitouchov No. 5. Sex: Female.

    Václav Rajtr and Dorota Strojsová were married on 28 Jan 1806 in Bytouchov. They had the following children:

    40 24.i. **Václav Rajtr** was born on 15 Sep 1783 in Zvířetice No. 11. He died on 16 Jan 1823 in Zvířetice No. 11, Mnichovo Hradiště Dist., Bohemia. Sex: Male.

        1   **Václav Rajt** was born on 21 Jun 1807 in Zvířetice. He died on 30 Oct 1871 in Zvířetice. Sex: Male.

1. **Jan Koštejn**. Sex: Male.

2. **Terezie Pazderníková** daughter of Václav Pazderník and Alžběta Jizbova was born in Bitouchov No. 8. Mnichovo Hradiště Co.. Sex: Female.

   Jan Koštejn and Terezie Pazderníková married. They had the following children:

   41. 25.i. **Barbora Koštejn** was born on 25 Dec 1815 in Zviretica. She died on 28 May 1887 in Chudoplesy No. 9. Sex: Female.

3. **Vojtěch Najman** was born in Kopernik No. 2, Mnichovo Hhradiste Co.. Sex: Male. He was employed as a A cottager, Kopernik No. 2.

4. **Anna Gintrova** was born in Kopernik No. 4, Mnichovo Hradiště Co.. Sex: Female. Vojtěch Najman and Anna Gintrova married. They had the following children:

   41. 26.i. **Josef Najman** was born in Dolanky No. 7, Mnichovo Hradiště Co.. Sex: Male. He was employed as a A cottager ("chalupnik"), Ddolanky No. 4. His religious affiliation was Roman Catholic.

5. **Václav Barton** was born in Dneboh No. 9, Mnichovo Hradiště Co.. Sex: Male. He was employed as a A cottager, Kopernik No. 9.

6   **Anna Nohýnková** was born in Sychrov No. 2, Mnichovo Hradiště Co.. Sex: Female. Václav Barton and Anna Nohýnková married. They had the following children:

    41. 27.i. **Alžběta Bartonova** was born in Dneboh No. 9, Mnichovo Hradiště Co.. Sex: Female.

Terezie Cejnarová was born in Benesovice No. 3. Sex: Female.

Václav Barton and Terezie Cejnarová married. They had the following children:

    1   **Josef Bartos** was born on 12 Nov in Sedlisko No. 6. Sex: Male.

    2   **Terezie Bartošová** was born on 02 Aug 1839 in Sedlisko No. 6. Sex: Female.

56. **Josef Danda** son of Josef Danda and Kateřina Tondrová was born on 11 Jun 1783 in Hoškovice No. 2, Mnichovo Hradiště Dist, Bohemia. He died on 07 Oct 1847 in Hoškovice No. 2, Mnichovo Hradiště Dist, Bohemia. Sex: Male. He was employed by in Farmer. His religious affiliation was Roiman Catholic.

57. **Barbora Buriánková** daughter of Václav Buriánek and Kateřina Pryllová was born on 24 Mar 1776 in Hoškovice, Mnichovo Hradiště Co.. Sex: Female. Her religious affiliation was Roman Catholic.

Josef Danda and Barbora Buriánková were married on 30 Jun 1805 in Hoškovice no. 14, Mnichovo Hradiště Dist, Bohemia. They had the following children:

    i.   **Kateřina Dandová** was born on 07 Aug 1806. She married Václav Beran on 11 Feb 1833 in Hoškovice No. 2,, Mnichovo Hradiště Dist, Bohemia. Sex: Female.

    ii. **Barbora Dandová** was born on 15 Jun 1809 in Hoškovice, No. 2, Mnichovo Hradiště Dist, Bohemia. She died on 04 May 1810 in Hoškovice, No. 2, Mnichovo Hradiště Dist, Bohemia. Sex: Female.

    iii. **Barbora Dandová** was born on 23 Mar 1811 in Hoškovice No. 2, Mnichovo Hradiště Dist, Bohemia. She married Josef Bajer on 03 Feb 1835 in Hoškovice No. 2,, Mnichovo Hradiště Dist, Bohemia. Sex: Female.

iv. **Josef Danda** was born on 26 Apr 1813 in Hoškovice No. 2, Mnichovo Hradiště Dist.. He married Marie Wolmanova on 25 Aug 1845 in Mnichovo Hradiště. He died on 02 Apr 1893 in Mnichovoa Hradiště. Sex: Male.

v. **Václav Danda** was born on 15 Jul 1815. Sex: Male.

+ 28.vi. **František Danda** was born on 01 Aug 1817 in Hoškovice, Mnichovo Hradiště Dist, Bohemia. He died on 04 Mar 1904 in Podolí No. 8. Sex: Male.

František Danda was born about 1820 in Hoškovice No. 2, Mnichovo Hradiště Co.. Sex: Male. He was employed as a A farmer ("Sedlák"), Hoškovice No. 14. His religious affiliation was Roman Catholic.

Jan Danda. Sex: Male.

58. **Jan Novák**. Sex: Male.
59. **Dorota Reslerová**. Sex: Female.

Jan Novák and Dorota Reslerová were married on 14 Feb 1843 in Dalešice. They had the following children:

+ 29.i. **Kateřina Nováková** was born on 03 Jun 1826 in Dalešice no. 5. She died on 29 May 1912 in Podolí No. 8. Sex: Female.

60. **Josef Cimr** was born in Manikovice No. 11. Sex: Male. He was employed as a A farmer ("Sedlák"), Manikovice No. 11.
61. **Kodrova ? Anna Kochova** was born in Bitouchov. Sex: Female.

Josef Cimr and Kodrova ? Anna Kochova married. They had the following children:

46. 30.i. **František Cimr** was born on 31 Mar 1823 in Manikovice No. 11, Mnichovo Hradiště Co.. He died on 22 Mar 1884. Sex: Male. He was employed as a A farmer ("Sedlák"), Manikovice No. 11. His religious affiliation was Roman Catholic.

28. **Josef Ferkl** was born in Rostkov No. 3. Sex: Male. He was employed as a A cottager ("chalupnik"), Rostkov.
29. **Alžběta Filipová** was born about 1800 in Sovenice. She died on 11 Aug 1870. Sex: Female.

Josef Ferkl and Alžběta Filipová married. They had the following children:

46. 31.i. **Anna Ferklová** was born in Rostkov No. 3, Mnichovo Hradiště Co.. Sex: Female. Her religious affiliation was Roman Catholic.

Jan Ferkl was born on 22 Mar 1836. He died on 22 Mar 1836 in Rostkov No. 3. Sex: Male.

František Ferkl was born about 1838. He died on 18 Jun 1864 in Rostkov No. 3. Sex: Male.

Generation 7

64. **František Rechziegel** son of Ludvik Rechziegel was born about 1741 in Straz pod Ralskem (Wartenberg), Česká Lipa District, Bohemia (from 1750l resided in Hodkovice, Bohemia). He owned after 1781 in Purchased mill in Slavíkov from Antonín Jagr. He died on 19 Apr 1835 in Slavíkov No. 4 at the age of 94.. He was buried on 22 Apr 1835 in Parish Vlastibořice: By Josef Sedláček L.. Sex: Male. His address was / Slavíkov No. 4, /. He was employed as a A miller in Slavíkov No. 4. His religious affiliation was Roman Catholic. Age (death): 94 years. Cause Of Death (Facts Pg): Respiratory problems ("dusnost").

65. **Alžběta Boelmanova** was born in 1746 in Vlastibořice. She was buried in Aug 1822 in Parish Vlastibořice: By Josef Soholy L.. She died on 21 Aug 1822 in Slavíkov No. 4. Sex: Female. Her religious affiliation was Roman Catholic. Age (death): 76 years old. Cause Of Death (Facts Pag: Dropsy ("vodnatelnost").

František Rechziegel and Alžběta Boelmanova married. They had the following children:

+ 32.i. **Ing. František Rechziegel** was born on 26 Dec 1789 in Slavíkov No. 4, Český Dub Co.. Godmother: 26 Dec 1789 in Barbora Jirakova, wife of František Jirak, innkeeper from Slavíkov. Godfather: 26 Dec 1789 in Benedykt Richter, miller at Dlouhy Most. He married Lidmila Neumanová on 03 Aug 1811 in Slavíkov No. 4, Vlastibořice parish. He died on 02 Aug 1849 in Slavíkov No. 4. He was buried on 06 Aug 1849 in Parish Vlastibořice: By Josef Sedláček L.. Sex: Male. His address was /

Slavíkov No.4, /. He was employed as a A miller in Slavíkov No. 4. His religious affiliation was Roman Catholic. Age (wedding): 21 years old. Witnesses (wedding): Franz Brodky, Vlastibořice. Married By: Gregorius Alexius L.. Age (death): 60 years old. Cause Of Death (Facts Pag: Gastric ulcers ("zaludecni vredy"). Position: miller, Slavikov, No. 4.

66. **Václav Neumann** son of Jan Neumann and Lidmila was born about 1770 in Radimovice No. 6, Dub Co.. Sex: Male. He was employed as a A farmer.
67. **Lidmila Adamova** daughter of Jan Adam and Lidmila was born about 1770 in Vlastibořice No. 10. Sex: Female.

Václav Neumann and Lidmila Adamova married. They had the following children:

+ 36.i. **Jan Neumann** was born about 1790 in Radimovice No. 7, Český Dub Co.. Sex: Male.
  ii. **Kateřina Neumannová** was born about 1790. Sex: Female.
  iii. **Václav Neumann** was born before 1790 in Radimovice No. 8, Český Dub Co.. Sex: Male. Position: Radimovice No. 8; "half farmer".
+ 33.iv. **Lidmila Neumanová** was born on 28 Jun 1792 in Radimovice No. 6, Český Dub Co.. She married Ing. František Rechziegel on 03 Aug 1811 in Slavíkov No. 4, Vlastibořice parish. She died on 09 May 1845 in Slavíkov No. 4. She was buried on 13 May 1845 in Parish Vladstiborice: Bt Josef Sedláček L.. Sex: Female. Her religious affiliation was Roman Catholic. Age (wedding): 18 years old. Age (death): 52 and 3/4 yers old. Cause Of Death (Facts Pag: Internal bleeding ("chrleni krve").
  v. **Jiří Neumann** was born on 26 Oct 1794 in Radimovice, Český Dub Co.. Sex: Male.

70. **František Hlavatý** was born in 1770 in Bzi No. 6. Sex: Male. He was employed as a Farmer ("Sedlák"), Bzove No. 6.
71. **Anna Glaserova** daughter of Josef Glaser and Katharina Skoda was born in 1780 in Bohumilec 1, Český Dub Co.. Sex: Female.

František Hlavatý and Anna Glaserova married. They had the following children:
- + 35.i. **Terezie Hlavatá** was born on 04 Nov 1800 in Bohumilec 1, Český Dub Co.. Sex: Female. Her religious affiliation was Roman Catholic.

74. **Václav Sivatko** was born in Libic no. 1. Sex: Male. He was employed as a Farmer. Václav Sivatko and unknown spouse married. They had the following children:

    55. 37.i. **Kateřina Sivatkova** was born in Libic no. 1. Sex: Female.
35. **Václav Laurin** was born before 1780 in Vselibice No. 19. Sex: Male.
36. **Unknown**. Sex: Female.

    Václav Laurin and Unknown married. They had the following children:
    55. 39.i. **Alžběta Laurinova** was born about 1810 in Vselibice No. 19. Sex: Female.
37. **Josef Bergl** was born after 1760 in Podhora No. 6. Sex: Male.
38. **Unknown**. Sex: Female.

    Josef Bergl and Unknown married. They had the following children:
    55. 40.i. **Jan Bergl** was born in 1789 in Podhora No. 6. He married Kateřina Stránská on 05 Apr 1818 in Manikovice[3]. He died on 13 Mar 1825. Sex: Male.
1 **Jan Stránský** was born bought house in Manikovice No. 6 in 1770. He died after 1770. Sex: Male. Position: farmer.
2 **Anna Honcová** was born in Podkovan. Sex: Female.

    Jan Stránský and Anna Honcová married. They had the following children:
    57. **Jiří Stránský** was born in 1791 in Manikovice No. 6. He died on 10 Oct 1831 in Manikovice No. 6 - murdered by Babinsky. Sex: Male. He was adopted in Farmer.
    60. 41.ii. **Kateřina Stránská** was born on 06 Sep 1798 in Manikovice No. 6. She married Jan Bergl on 05 Apr 1818 in Manikovice[3]. Sex: Female.
36. **Matěj Konopka**. Sex: Male.
37. **Unknown**. Sex: Female.

Matěj Konopka and Unknown married. They had the following children:

    60. 45.i. **Anna Konopkova**. Sex: Female.

38. **František Landa** was born before 1800 in Drahotice No. 14. Sex: Male.
39. **Kateřina Hozaková** was born in Drahotice No. 14. Sex: Female.

František Landa and Kateřina Hozaková married. They had the following children:

    60. 46.i. **Jan Landa** was born about 1820 in Drahotice No. 9. Sex: Male. His address was / Drahotice No. 9, /. He was employed as a Cottegere ("chalupnik") in Drahotice No. 9.

40. **Miroslav Polivka**. Sex: Male.
41. **Unknown**. Sex: Female.

Miroslav Polivka and Unknown married. They had the following children:

    60. 47.i. **Anna Polívková**. Sex: Female.

42. **Jan Jri Rajtr** son of Jiří Rajtr and Kateřina Bylkova was born on 02 Jan 1758 in Zvířetice. He died on 10 Jan 1799 in Zvířetice No. 11, Mnichovo Hradiště Dist., Bohemia. Sex: Male.
43. **Anna Machackova** daughter of Václav Machacek and Alžběta was born in 1758. She died in 1830. Sex: Female.

Jan Jri Rajtr and Anna Machackova married. They had the following children:

    60. 48.i. **Václav Rajtr** was born on 15 Sep 1783 in Zvířetice No. 11. He married Dorota Strojsová on 28 Jan 1806 in Bytouchov. He died on 16 Jan 1823 in Zviretic No. 11. Sex: Male.

44. **Václav Strojsa** was born on 09 Jan 1758 in Bitouchov. Sex: Male.
37. **Dorota Wondrakova** daughter of Jiří Wondrak and Alžběta was born on 06 Feb 1759 in Bitouchov. Sex: Female.

Václav Strojsa and Dorota Wondrakova married. They had the following children:

    + 49.i. **Dorota Strojsová** was born on 24 Jan 1780 in Bitouchov No. 5. She married Václav Rajtr on 28 Jan 1806 in Bytouchov. Sex: Female.

103. **Václav Pazderník** son of Václav Pazderník and Alžběta was born in 1784. He died in 1856. Sex: Male.

104. **Alžběta Jizbova** daughter of Tomáš Jzba and Magdalena was born in Hrdlorezy No. 9. She died in 1870. Sex: Female.
Václav Pazderník and Alžběta Jizbova married. They had the following children:
   51.i. **Terezie Pazderníková** was born in Bitouchov No. 8. Mnichovo Hradiště Co.. Sex: Female.

112. **Josef Danda** son of Josef Danda and Anna Čermáková was born on 08 Feb 1755 in Hoškovice No. 2, Mnichovo Hradiště Dist, Bohemia. He died on 04 Feb 1838 in Hoškovice No. 2, Mnichovo Hradiště Dist, Bohemia. Sex: Male.

113. **Kateřina Tondrová** daughter of Pavel Tondr and Marie Dneboská was born on 01 Apr 1755 in Podolí. She died on 18 Jan 1808 in Hoškovice No. 25,, Mnichovo Hradiště Dist, Bohemia. Sex: Female.
Josef Danda and Kateřina Tondrová were married on 14 Feb 1779 in Podolí No. 4. They had the following children:
   i. **Anna Dandová** was born on 06 Mar 1781 in Hoškovice No. 2, Mnichovo Hradiště Dist, Bohemia. She married Josef Buriánek on 30 Jun 1805 in Hoškovice, No. 2, Mnichovo Hradiště Dist, Bohemia. She died on 16 Jan 1862 in Hoškovice No. 24, Mnichovo Hradiště Dist, Bohemia. Sex: Female.
+ 56.ii. **Josef Danda** was born on 11 Jun 1783 in Hoškovice No. 2, Mnichovo Hradiště Dist, Bohemia. He married Barbora Buriánková on 30 Jun 1805 in Hoškovice no. 14, Mnichovo Hradiště Dist, Bohemia. He died on 07 Oct 1847 in Hoškovice No. 2, Mnichovo Hradiště Dist, Bohemia. Sex: Male. He was employed by in Farmer. His religious affiliation was Roiman Catholic.
   iii. **František Danda** was born on 26 Aug 1785 in Hoškovice, No. 2, Mnichovo Hradiště Dist, Bohemia. He married Kateřina Tondrová on 08 Oct 1805 in Hoškovice, No. 5, Mnichovo Hradiště Dist, Bohemia. He died on 02 Aug 1871 in Hoškovice, No. 2, Mnichovo Hradiště Dist, Bohemia. Sex: Male.
   iv. **Kateřina Dandová** was born on 29 May 1788 in Hoškovice, No. 2, Mnichovo Hradiště Dist, Bohemia. She married Jan Buriánek

on 08 Oct 1895 in Hoškovice, No. 2, Mnichovo Hradiště Dist, Bohemia. Sex: Female.

v. **Marie Dandová** was born on 02 Feb 1791 in Hoškovice No. 2, Mnichovo Hradiště Dist, Bohemia. She married Petr Zámecký on 15 May 1810 in buriankovaHoškovice No. 2, Mnichovo Hradiště Dist, Bohemia. Sex: Female.

114. **Václav Buriánek**. Sex: Male.
115. **Kateřina Pryllová**. Sex: Female.

Václav Buriánek and Kateřina Pryllová married. They had the following children:

57.i. **Barbora Buriánková** was born on 24 Mar 1776 in Hoškovice, Mnichovo Hradiště Co.. She married Josef Danda on 30 Jun 1805 in Hoškovice no. 14, Mnichovo Hradiště Dist, Bohemia. Sex: Female. Her religious affiliation was Roman Catholic.

Generation 8

1 **Ludvik Rechziegel** was born in Straz pod Ralskem (Wartenberg), Česká Lipa District, Bohemia ((in1750 moved to Hodkovice, Bohemia)). Sex: Male.

Ludvik Rechziegel and unknown spouse married. They had the following children:

70. 64.i. **František Rechziegel** was born about 1741 in Straz pod Ralskem (Wartenberg), Česká Lipa District, Bohemia (from 1750l resided in Hodkovice, Bohemia). He owned after 1781 in Purchased mill in Slavíkov from Antonín Jagr. He died on 19 Apr 1835 in Slavíkov No. 4 at the age of 94.. He was buried on 22 Apr 1835 in Parish Vlastibořice: By Josef Sedláček L.. Sex: Male. His address was / Slavíkov No. 4, /. He was employed as a A miller in Slavíkov No. 4. His religious affiliation was Roman Catholic. Age (death): 94 years. Cause Of Death (Facts Pg): Respiratory problems ("dusnost").

132. **Jan Neumann** was born about 1750 in Vlastibořice No. 10. Sex: Male.
133. **Lidmila** was born in 1754. She died in 1824. Sex: Female.

Jan Neumann and Lidmila married. They had the following children:

+ 66.i. **Václav Neumann** was born about 1770 in Radimovice No. 6, Dub Co.. Sex: Male. He was employed as a A farmer.

134. **Jan Adam** was born in No. 10. Sex: Male. He was employed as a farmer and "rychtar" (village magistrate). Position: Vlastibořice; farmer.

135. **Lidmila**. Sex: Female.

Jan Adam and Lidmila married. They had the following children:

+ 67.i. **Lidmila Adamova** was born about 1770 in Vlastibořice No. 10. Sex: Female.

142. **Josef Glaser** was born in 1750 in Bohumilec No. 1. Sex: Male.

143. **Katharina Skoda** was born in 1760 in Třtí No.12. Sex: Female.

Josef Glaser and Katharina Skoda married. They had the following children:

+ 71.i. **Anna Glaserova** was born in 1780 in Bohumilec 1, Český Dub Co.. Sex: Female.

192. **Jiří Rajtr** son of Jakub Rajtr and Marie was born on 16 Apr 1736 in Zvířetice. He died on 30 Jan 1797 in Zvířetice No. 6. Sex: Male. He was employed as a Cottager.

193. **Kateřina Bylkova** daughter of Martin Bylek and Anna was born in 1729. She died on 22 Apr 1797 in Zvířetice No. 6. Sex: Female.

Jiří Rajtr and Kateřina Bylkova were married on 28 Jan 1806 in Bytouchov No. 9. They had the following children:

+ 96.i. **Jan Jri Rajtr** was born on 02 Jan 1758 in Zvířetice. He died on 10 Jan 1799 in Zvířetice No. 11, Mnichovo Hradiště Dist., Bohemia. Sex: Male.

Jiří Rajtr and unknown spouse married. They had the following children:

+ 96.i. **Jan Jiří Rajtr** was born on 02 Jan 1758 in Zvířetice. He died on 10 Jan 1799 in Zvířetice No. 11, Mnichovo Hradiště Dist., Bohemia. Sex: Male.

195. **Václav Machacek**. Sex: Male.

196. **Alžběta**. Sex: Female.

Václav Machacek and Alžběta married. They had the following children:

+ 97.i. **Anna Machackova** was born in 1758. She died in 1830. Sex: Female.
198. **Jiří Wondrak.** Sex: Male.
199. **Alžběta.** Sex: Female.
Jiří Wondrak and Alžběta married. They had the following children:
1 99.i. **Dorota Wondrakova** was born on 06 Feb 1759 in Bitouchov. Sex: Female.
2 **Václav Pazderník** was born in 1744 in Bitouchov. He died in 1820. Sex: Male.
3 **Alžběta** was born in 1755. She died in 1840. Sex: Female.
Václav Pazderník and Alžběta married. They had the following children:
1 102i. **Václav Pazderník** was born in 1784. He died in 1856. Sex: Male.
4 **Tomáš Jzba** was born in Hrdlorezy. Sex: Male.
5 **Magdalena.** Sex: Female.
Tomáš Jzba and Magdalena married. They had the following children:
1 103i. **Alžběta Jizbova** was born in Hrdlorezy No. 9. She died in 1870. Sex: Female.
224. **Josef Danda** son of Jan Danda and Kateřina Berglová was born on 16 Jun 1722 in Kněžmost, Central Bohemia, Czech Republic. He died on 17 Jan 1776 in Hoškovice No. 2,, Central Bohemia, Czech Republic. Sex: Male.
225. **Anna Čermáková** daughter of Václav Čermák and Kateřina Koberová was born on 22 Dec 1726 in Kněžmost, Central Bohemia, Czech Republic. She died on 20 Jan 1746 in Hoškovice, Central Bohemia, Czech Republic. Sex: Female.
Josef Danda and Anna Čermáková were married on 04 Jan 1748 in Kněžmost, Central Bohemia, Czech Republic. They had the following children:
  i. **Anna Dandová** was born on 18 Jun 1749 in Hoškovice No. 2, Mnichovo Hradiště Dist, Bohemia. Sex: Female.
  ii. **Jan Danda** was born on 06 May 1751 in Hoškovice No. 2, Mnichovo Hradiště Dist, Bohemia. He died on 22 Jan 1754 in Hoškovice No. 2, Mnichovo Hradiště Dist, Bohemia. Sex: Male.

iii. **Alžběta Dandová** was born on 25 Feb 1753 in Hoškovice No. 2, Mnichovo Hradiště Dist, Bohemia. She married Josef Presiler on 06 Jan 1780 in Hoškovice No. 2, Mnichovo Hradiště Dist, Bohemia. Sex: Female.

+ 112iv. **Josef Danda** was born on 08 Feb 1755 in Hoškovice No. 2, Mnichovo Hradiště Dist, Bohemia. He married Kateřina Tondrová on 14 Feb 1779 in Podolí No. 4. He died on 04 Feb 1838 in Hoškovice No. 2, Mnichovo Hradiště Dist, Bohemia. Sex: Male.

v. **Kateřina Dandová** was born on 14 May 1757 in Hoškovice, No. 2, Mnichovo Hradiště Dist, Bohemia. She married Jiří Studničný on 04 Nov 1793 in Hoškovice, No. 2, Mnichovo Hradiště Dist, Bohemia. Sex: Female.

vi. **František Danda** was born on 03 Aug 1759 in Hoškovice No. 2, Mnichovo Hradiště Dist, Bohemia. Sex: Male.

vii. **Jan Danda** was born on 07 Sep 1767 in Hoškovice, No. 2, Mnichovo Hradiště Dist, Bohemia. Sex: Male.

50. **Pavel Tondr.** Sex: Male.
51. **Marie Dneboská.** Sex: Female.

Pavel Tondr and Marie Dneboská married. They had the following children:

83. 113i. **Kateřina Tondrová** was born on 01 Apr 1755 in Podolí. She married Josef Danda on 14 Feb 1779 in Podolí No. 4. She died on 18 Jan 1808 in Hoškovice No. 25,, Mnichovo Hradiště Dist, Bohemia. Sex: Female.

Generation 9

384. **Jakub Rajtr** son of Václav Rajtr and Alyna was born in 1701 in Dalešice. He died on 21 Oct 1750 in Zvířetice. Sex: Male.

Marie Rajtrová daughter of Anna. Sex: Female.

Jakub Rajtr and Marie Rajtrová married. They had the following children:

86. 192i. **Jiří Rajtr** was born on 16 Apr 1736 in Zvířetice. He died on 30 Jan 1797 in Zvířetice No. 6. He married Kateřina Bylkova on 28

Jan 1806 in Bytouchov No. 9. Sex: Male. He was employed as a Cottager.

53. **Marie.** Sex: Female.

Jakub Rajtr and Marie married. They had the following children:

86. 192i. **Jiří Rajtr** was born on 16 Apr 1736 in Zvířetice. He died on 30 Jan 1797 in Zvířetice No. 6. He married Kateřina Bylkova on 28 Jan 1806 in Bytouchov No. 9. Sex: Male. He was employed as a Cottager.

54. **Martin Bylek.** Sex: Male.
55. **Anna.** Sex: Female.

Martin Bylek and Anna married. They had the following children:

86. 193i. **Kateřina Bylkova** was born in 1729. She died on 22 Apr 1797 in Zvířetice No. 6. She married Jiří Rajtr on 28 Jan 1806 in Bytouchov No. 9. Sex: Female.

Marie Rajtrová. Sex: Female.

448. **Jan Danda** son of Jan Danda and Salomena was born in 1677 in Boseň, Mladá Boleslav District, Central Bohemian Region. He died on 03 Mar 1732 in Hoškovice, Central Bohemia, Czech Republic. Sex: Male.

449. **Kateřina Berglová** daughter of Jakub Bergl and Mandelina was born on 13 Jul 1696 in Chocnějovice, Mladá Boleslav Dist., Central Bohemia. She died on 20 Jan 1746 in Hoškovice, Central Bohemia. Sex: Female.

Jan Danda and Kateřina Berglová were married on 02 Jun 1721 in Hoškovice, Central Bohemia. They had the following children:

+ 224i. **Josef Danda** was born on 16 Jun 1722 in Kněžmost, Central Bohemia, Czech Republic. He married Anna Čermáková on 04 Jan 1748 in Kněžmost, Central Bohemia, Czech Republic. He died on 17 Jan 1776 in Hoškovice No. 2,, Central Bohemia, Czech Republic. Sex: Male.

ii. **Adam Danda** was born on 01 Jun 1724 in Kněžmost, Central Bohemia, Czech Republic. He died on 19 Jul 1724 in Kněžmost, Central Bohemia, Czech Republic. Sex: Male.

iii. **Eva Dandová** was born on 11 Dec 1725 in Hoškovice, Mnichovo Hradiště Dist., Bohemia. She died on 09 Apr 1726 in Hoškovice, Mnichovo Hradiště Dist., Bohemia. Sex: Female.

iv. **Lidmila Dandová** was born on 11 Dec 1725 in Hoškovice, Mnichovo Hradiště Dist, Bohemia. She died on 14 Apr 1726 in Hoškovice, Mnichovo Hradiště Dist, Bohemia. Sex: Female.

v. **Anna Dandová** was born in 1728. She died on 03 Apr 1729 in Hoškovice, Mnichovo Hradiště Dist., Bohemia. Sex: Female.

vi. **Marie Dandová** was born on 07 Jun 1731 in Hoškovice, Mnichovo Hradiště Dist, Bohemia. Sex: Female.

Dorothea. She died on 29 Jan 1721 in Kněžmost, Central Bohemia, Czech Republic. Sex: Female.

Jan Danda and Dorothea married. They had the following children:

Marie Dandová was born on 04 Jan 1707 in Kněžmost, Mnichovo Hradiště Co., Bohemia. She died on 23 Feb 1707 in Kněžmost, Mnichovo Hradiště Co., Bohemia. Sex: Female.

Kateřina Dandová was born on 19 Apr 1708 in Kněžmost, Mnichovo Hradiště Dist., Bohemia. Sex: Female.

Dorothea Dandová was born on 09 Feb 1712 in Kněžmost, Mnichovo Hradiště Co., Bohemia. She married Václav Mráz on 18 Nov 1736 in Hoškovice, Mnichovo Hradiště Dist, Bohemia. Sex: Female.

Jiří Danda was born on 15 Dec 1714 in Kněžmost, Mnichovo Hradiště Dist., Bohemia. Sex: Male.

Jan Danda was born on 24 Apr 1718 in Kněžmost, Mnichovo Hradiště Dist., Bohemia. Sex: Male.

1 **Václav Čermák.** Sex: Male.
2 **Kateřina Koberová.** Sex: Female.

Václav Čermák and Kateřina Koberová married. They had the following children:

92. 225i. **Anna Čermáková** was born on 22 Dec 1726 in Kněžmost, Central Bohemia, Czech Republic. She died on 20 Jan 1746 in Hoškovice, Central Bohemia, Czech Republic. She married Josef

Danda on 04 Jan 1748 in Kněžmost, Central Bohemia, Czech Republic. Sex: Female.

Generation 10

768. **Václav Rajtr** son of Jakub Rajtr and Magdalena was born in 1659. He died on 03 Sep 1739 in Dalešice. Sex: Male.
769. **Alyna** was born in 1670. She died on 18 Jan 1733 in Dalešice. Sex: Female.

Václav Rajtr and Alyna married. They had the following children:

94. 384i. **Jakub Rajtr** was born in 1701 in Dalešice. He died on 21 Oct 1750 in Zvířetice. Sex: Male.

59. **Jan Danda** was born before 1653 in Boseň, Mladá Boleslav District, Central Bohemian Region. Sex: Male.
60. **Salomena**. Sex: Female.

Jan Danda and Salomena married. They had the following children:

+ 448i. **Jan Danda** was born in 1677 in Boseň, Mladá Boleslav District, Central Bohemian Region. He married Kateřina Berglová on 02 Jun 1721 in Hoškovice, Central Bohemia. He died on 03 Mar 1732 in Hoškovice, Central Bohemia, Czech Republic. Sex: Male.

899. **Jakub Bergl** was born in Chocnějovice, Mladá Boleslav Dist., Central Bohemia. Sex: Male.
900. **Mandelina**. Sex: Female.

Jakub Bergl and Mandelina married. They had the following children:

+ 449i. **Kateřina Berglová** was born on 13 Jul 1696 in Chocnějovice, Mladá Boleslav Dist., Central Bohemia. She married Jan Danda on 02 Jun 1721 in Hoškovice, Central Bohemia. She died on 20 Jan 1746 in Hoškovice, Central Bohemia. Sex: Female.

Generation 11

1536. **Jakub Rajtr.** He died in 1688 (Zvířetice). Sex: Male.
1537. **Magdalena**. Sex: Female.

Jakub Rajtr and Magdalena married. They had the following children:

+ 768i. **Václav Rajtr** was born in 1659. He died on 03 Sep 1739 in Dalešice. Sex: Male.

Sources

1. Matrika krestni, Kniha Z, List 65, Krestni a rodny list.
2. Matrika krestni: Hoškovice, Kniha 104, List 172, Krestni a rodny list.
3. He was 29 and she was 20.

B. Ancestors of Eva Edwards

Generation 1

1   **Eva Edwards (Eisnerová)** daughter of Paul J. Edwards (Pavel Eisner) and Jiřina Taussigová was born on 21 Jan 1932 in Prague, CSR. She was educated B.A., Hofstra College in 1953. Sex: Female. Age (wedding): 21 and 1/2 years old.

Mila (Miloslav) Rechcigl Jr. son of Miloslav Rechcigl and Marie Rajtrová was born on 30 Jul 1930 in Mladá Boleslav, CSR. He was baptized on 17 Aug 1930 in By Alois Novák, parish priest in Loukovec. Employment: Bet. 1958–1968 in Biochemist, National Institutes of Health, Bethesda, MD. Sex: Male. He was educated B.S.,Cornell U. 1954, M.N.S., Cornell U. 1955, Ph.D., Cornell U. 1958. He was also known as "Mila" or "Mike". He was known by the title of Dr.. His address was 1703 Mark Lane / Rockville, MD 20852 / US. His e-mail address was rechcigl@aol.com. His phone number was (301) 881-7222. His religious affiliation was Roman Catholic. Age (wedding): 23 years old. Godmother: Marie Rechcíglová. Godfather: Alois Rechcigl. Midwife: Josefa Silna from Mladá Boleslav.

Mila (Miloslav) Rechcigl Jr. and Eva Edwards (Eisnerová) were married on 29 Aug 1953 in New York, NY. They had 2 children.

Generation 2

1   **Paul J. Edwards (Pavel Eisner)** son of (Jindřich) Henry Eisner and Hortense Auer was born on 29 Jun 1892 in Prague, Klimentska 1. He died on 27 Jun 1964 in Schenectady, NY. Sex: Male. He was educated JUDr., University of Prague. He was employed as a A lawyer.

2   **Jiřina Taussigová** daughter of Oskar Taussig and Klára Munková was born on 24 Apr 1906 in Prague - Kralovske Vinohrady, Nerudova l. She died on 06 Nov 1962 in New York, NY. Sex: Female.

Paul J. Edwards (Pavel Eisner) and Jiřina Taussigová were married on 05 Jun 1926 in Prague. They had the following children:

Helen Edwards (Eisnerova) was born on 29 Apr 1927 in Prague, CSR. She married Frank Steiner on 16 Sep 1948 in New York, NY. Sex: Female.

102. 1. ii. **Eva Edwards (Eisnerová)** was born on 21 Jan 1932 in Prague, CSR. She was educated B.A., Hofstra College in 1953. She married Mila (Miloslav) Rechcigl Jr. on 29 Aug 1953 in New York, NY. Sex: Female. Age (wedding): 21 and 1/2 years old.

Generation 3

32. **(Jindřich) Henry Eisner** son of Karl Eisner and Anna Krausová was born on 12 Mar 1853 in Kaliste u Nemeckeho Brodu, Bohemia. He died on 13 Dec 1956 in New York, NY. Sex: Male. His address was Klimentska 1; later renamed to Revolucni trida / Prague, / Bohemia. He was employed as a Garnet jeweler.

33. **Hortense Auer** daughter of Moritz Auer and Julie Wiener was born in 1869 in Prague, Jakubska 1. She died on 13 Oct 1951 in New York, NY. Sex: Female.

(Jindřich) Henry Eisner and Hortense Auer were married in 1888. They had the following children:

2. i. **Paul J. Edwards (Pavel Eisner)** was born on 29 Jun 1892 in Prague, Klimentska 1. He married Jiřina Taussigová on 05 Jun 1926 in Prague. He died on 27 Jun 1964 in Schenectady, NY. Sex: Male. He was educated JUDr., University of Prague. He was employed as a A lawyer.

ii. **(Karel Eisner) Charles E. Edwards** was born on 26 Apr 1894 in Prague, Bohemia. He married Marta Hanakova on 19 May 1927. He died on 27 Oct 1986. Sex: Male. He was employed as a A jeweler.

iii. **Robert Eisner** was born on 11 Jul 1898 in Prague, Bohemia. He married Mitzi Kratzig in 1926 in Praha, CSR. He died on 31 Oct 1984 in New York, NY. Sex: Male. He was employed as a A cloth merchant.

6. **Oskar Taussig** son of Jakub Taussig and Julie Meislova was born on 22 Jun 1876 in Benešov. He died on 08 Nov 1938 in Prague. He was buried on 10 Nov 1938. Sex: Male. He was known by the title of JUDr.. He was employed as a An attorney, in Prague. Age (death): 62 years old.

7. **Klára Munková** daughter of Rafael Munk and Theresia Steindlerová was born on 21 Dec 1887 in Prague, Bohemia. She died on 18 Jan 1934 in Prague, Bohemia. Sex: Female.
   Oskar Taussig and Klára Munková married. They had the following children:
   + 3. i. **Jiřina Taussigová** was born on 24 Apr 1906 in Prague - Kralovske Vinohrady, Nerudova l. She married Paul J. Edwards (Pavel Eisner) on 05 Jun 1926 in Prague. She died on 06 Nov 1962 in New York, NY. Sex: Female.
   ii. **Hana Taussigová** was born on 26 Feb 1910 in Prague. She married Joseph (Wiener) Winn in 1933. She died on 14 Mar 1999 in New York, NY. Sex: Female.

Generation 4

18. **Karl Eisner** son of Michael Eisner and Klára Hofmanova was born in 1821 in Chotěboř. He died in 1893. Sex: Male. He was employed as a A tanner.
19. **Anna Krausová** daughter of Loebl Kraus and Barbora Fischer was born in 1831 in Dolni Kralovice. She died in 1855. Sex: Female.
    Karl Eisner and Anna Krausová were married about 1852. They had the following children:
    4. i. **(Jindřich) Henry Eisner** was born on 12 Mar 1853 in Kaliste u Nemeckeho Brodu, Bohemia. He married Hortense Auer in 1888. He died on 13 Dec 1956 in New York, NY. Sex: Male. His address was Klimentska 1; later renamed to Revolucni trida / Prague, / Bohemia. He was employed as a Garnet jeweler.
    Julie Eisnerová. Sex: Female.
    Unknown. Sex: Female.
    Karl Eisner and Unknown married. They had no children.
10. **Moritz Auer** son of Bernhard Auer and Therese Lieberman was born in 1841 in Prague, Bohemia (or Serava?). He died in 1915. Sex: Male. His address was Jakubska St. / Prague, / Bohemia.
11. **Julie Wiener** daughter of Jacob Wiener and Marie Hoffmannová was born in 1841 in Prague (probably). She died in 1915. Sex: Female.

Moritz Auer and Julie Wiener married. They had the following children:

32. 5. i. **Hortense Auer** was born in 1869 in Prague, Jakubska 1. She married (Jindřich) Henry Eisner in 1888. She died on 13 Oct 1951 in New York, NY. Sex: Female.

    i **Eugenia Auer**. Sex: Female.

    ii **Thecla Auer** was born about 1876. She died about Aug 1894 in Drowned. Sex: Female.

    iii **Alice Auer** was born about 1878. She died about 1894 in Drowned. Sex: Female.

12. **Jakub Taussig** son of Markus Stoekler and Julia Taussigová was born in 1827 in Bechovice u Prahy. He died on 25 Feb 1896 in Benešov. He was buried on 27 Feb 1896 in Benešov. Sex: Male. He was known by the title of JUDR.. He was employed as a An attorney, Benešov No. 162. Age (death): 68 years old.

13. **Julie Meislova** daughter of Jakub Meisl and Judita Dubova was born in 1838 in Žehušice, Kutná Hora District, Bohemia. She died on 30 May 1913 in Benešov, Bohemia. Sex: Female.

Jakub Taussig and Julie Meislova married. They had the following children:

    i. **Olga Taussigová** was born on 02 Jul 1862. She died on 04 Mar 1905 in Benešov. She was buried on 06 Mar 1905. Sex: Female. Age (death): 38 years old.

    ii. **Julius Taussig** was born on 01 Oct 1862. He died in 1941 in Benešov (probably). Sex: Male. He was known by the title of JUDr.. He was employed as a An attorney, Benešov.

    iii. **Gabriela Taussigová** was born on 23 Sep 1863. She died on 12 Nov 1927. She was buried on 16 Nov 1927. Sex: Female. Age (death): 64 years old.

    iv. **Pavel Taussig** was born in 1864. Sex: Male.

    v. **Jindřich Taussig** was born in 1867. Sex: Male.

    vi. **Artur Taussig** was born on 14 Dec 1869. Sex: Male.

    vii. **Hermina Taussigová** was born on 23 Jun 1871. She died in 1927. Sex: Female.

viii. **Kamila Taussigová** was born on 27 Feb 1873. She died in 1912. Sex: Female.

ix. **Pavla Taussigová** was born on 18 Jan 1875. She died in 1943. Sex: Female.

+ 6. x. **Oskar Taussig** was born on 22 Jun 1876 in Benešov. He died on 08 Nov 1938 in Prague. He was buried on 10 Nov 1938. Sex: Male. He was known by the title of JUDr.. He was employed as a An attorney, in Prague. Age (death): 62 years old.

xi. **Marie Markéta Marta Taussigová** was born on 07 Mar 1879 in Benešov No. 162. She was baptized on 08 Oct 1902. She married Adolf Šváb on 15 Oct 1902 in U Matky Bozi pred Tynem, Prague. She died on 22 Jun 1958 in Plzen. Sex: Female. Her religious affiliation was Roman Catholic. Age (wedding): 23 years old. Witnesses (wedding): JuDr. Viktor Vodička, attorney and Docent Dr. Ladislav Syllaba. Married By: Dr. Eduard Knobloch, parish priest.

xii. **Jindřich Taussig**. Sex: Male.

Julie Meisl daughter of Jakub Meisl and Judita Dubova was born on 13 May 1838 in Žehušice, Kutná Hora District, Bohemia. She died on 30 May 1913 in Benešov, Bohemia. Sex: Female.

Jakub Taussig and Julie Meisl married. They had no children.

14. **Rafael Munk** son of Jakub Munk and Barbora Arnstein was born about 1823 in Chotesov, Plzen Region, Bohemia. He died on 22 Oct 1905 in Benešov. Sex: Male.

15. **Theresia Steindlerová** daughter of Jakub Steindler and Ludmila Bret was born on 07 Nov 1849. Sex: Female.

Rafael Munk and Theresia Steindlerová married. They had the following children:

+ 7. i. **Klára Munková** was born on 21 Dec 1887 in Prague, Bohemia. She died on 18 Jan 1934 in Prague, Bohemia. Sex: Female.

Generation 5

16. **Michael Eisner** son of Elias (Eliezer Zwi Ben Ezechiel) Eisner and Unknown was born in 1771 in Humpolec. He died in 1864. Sex: Male.

17. **Klára Hofmanova** was born in L (Kolin n). Sex: Female.

Michael Eisner and Klára Hofmanova married. They had the following children:
- \+ 8. i. **Karl Eisner** was born in 1821 in Chotěboř. He married Anna Krausová about 1852. He died in 1893. Sex: Male. He was employed as a A tanner.
- ii. **Leopold Eisner**. Sex: Male.

Rachel Reinhalt. Sex: Female.

Michael Eisner and Rachel Reinhalt married. They had no children.

18. **Loebl Kraus**. Sex: Male.
19. **Barbora Fischer** daughter of Fischer and Unknown. Sex: Female.

Loebl Kraus and Barbora Fischer married. They had the following children:
- \+ 9. i. **Anna Krausová** was born in 1831 in Dolni Kralovice. She married Karl Eisner about 1852. She died in 1855. Sex: Female.

20. **Bernhard Auer** was born in Serava, Bohemia. Sex: Male.
21. **Therese Lieberman** daughter of Lieberman and Unknown was born in Bohemia. Sex: Female. Bernhard Auer and Therese Lieberman married. They had the following children:
- \+ 10.i. **Moritz Auer** was born in 1841 in Prague, Bohemia (or Serava?). He died in 1915. Sex: Male. His address was Jakubska St. / Prague, / Bohemia.
- ii. **son Auer** was born before 1841 in Bohemia. He emigrated from US in 1859. Sex: Male. He died in emigrated to US in 1859.

22. **Jacob Wiener** was born in 1811. Sex: Male.
23. **Marie Hoffmannová** daughter of Hoffman and Unknown was born in 1814. Sex: Female. Jacob Wiener and Marie Hoffmannová married. They had the following children:
- \+ 11.i. **Julie Wiener** was born in 1841 in Prague (probably). She died in 1915. Sex: Female.
- ii. **Leopold Wiener** was born in Prague (probably). Sex: Male. He was employed as a A banker and financier, Ferdinand Street, Prague.

24. **Markus Stoekler** was born in 1804 in Zabehlice. Sex: Male.
25. **Julia Taussigová**. Sex: Female.

Markus Stoekler and Julia Taussigová married. They had the following children:

+ 12.i. **Jakub Taussig** was born in 1827 in Bechovice u Prahy. He died on 25 Feb 1896 in Benešov. He was buried on 27 Feb 1896 in Benešov. Sex: Male. He was known by the title of JUDR.. He was employed as a An attorney, Benešov No. 162. Age (death): 68 years old.

26. **Jakub Meisl** was born on 27 Mar 1795 in Žehušice, Kutná Hora District, Bohemia. He died on 08 Jan 1867 in Žehušice, Kutná Hora District, Bohemia. Sex: Male.

27. **Judita Dubova** daughter of Dub and Unknown was born in 1804 in Benešov. Sex: Female. Jakub Meisl and Judita Dubova married. They had the following children:

+ 13.i. **Julie Meislova** was born in 1838 in Žehušice, Kutná Hora District, Bohemia. She died on 30 May 1913 in Benešov, Bohemia. Sex: Female.
  ii. **Anna Meislova** was born on 15 Jul 1830 in Žehušice, Kutná Hora District, Bohemia. She died on 24 Jan 1872 in Turnov, Semily District, Bohemia. Sex: Female.
  iii. **Gabriela Marie Meisl** was born on 28 Sep 1848 in Žehušice, Kutná Hora District, Bohemia. She died on 08 May 1932 in Prague, Czech.. Sex: Female.
  iv. **Leopold Meisl**. Sex: Male.
  v. **Alexander Meisl** was born on 01 Jun 1825 in Žehušice, Kutná Hora District, Bohemia. Sex: Male.
  vi. **Josef Meisl** was born on 13 Sep 1836 in Žehušice, Kutná Hora District, Bohemia. Sex: Male.
  vii. **Julie Meisl** was born on 13 May 1838 in Žehušice, Kutná Hora District, Bohemia. She died on 30 May 1913 in Benešov, Bohemia. Sex: Female.

28. **Jakub Munk**. Sex: Male.
29. **Barbora Arnstein** was born in Chotěšov, Bohemia. Sex: Female.

Jakub Munk and Barbora Arnstein married. They had the following children:

+ 14.i. **Rafael Munk** was born about 1823 in Chotesov, Plzen Region, Bohemia. He died on 22 Oct 1905 in Benešov. Sex: Male.
  ii. **Daniel Munk**. Sex: Male.
  iii. **Isachiel Munk**. Sex: Male.
  iv. **Ariel Munk**. Sex: Male.
  v. **Gabriel Munk** was born on 05 Apr 1831 in Chotysany. He died on 14 Dec 1896 in Struhařov, Benešov District, Bohemia. Sex: Male.
  vi. **Abraham Munk** was born in 1822 in Chotesov, Bohemia. He died on 26 Apr 1891 in Dobromerice, Bohemia. Sex: Male.
30. **Jakub Steindler** son of Moritz Steindler and Unknown was born in 1820 in Benešov, Bohemia. He died on 17 Apr 1873 in Benešov, Bohemia. Sex: Male.
31. **Ludmila Bret** daughter of Elias Bret and Eva Goldberger was born on 24 Dec 1813 in Golcuv Jenikov, Havlickuv Brod District, Moravia. She died on 13 Dec 1849 in Benešov, Bohemia. Sex: Female.

Jakub Steindler and Ludmila Bret married. They had the following children:

1 **Maria Steindlerová** was born in 1838. She died on 29 Apr 1872. Sex: Female.
2 **Francisca Steindlerová** was born on 15 Aug 1840. Sex: Female.
3 **Anna Steindlerová** was born on 17 Sep 1842. Sex: Female.
4 **Helena Steindlerová** was born on 26 Apr 1845. Sex: Female.
2 15.v. **Theresia Steindlerová** was born on 07 Nov 1849. Sex: Female.

Antonie Bret. Sex: Female.

Jakub Steindler and Antonie Bret married. They had the following children:

i. **Moritz Steindler** was born on 15 Dec 1853 in Benešov. He died on 01 Aug 1917 in weinerBenesov, Bohemia. Sex: Male.

Generation 6

34. **Elias (Eliezer Zwi Ben Ezechiel) Eisner** son of Ezechiel and Unknown was born in Dec 1748 in Jenikov. Sex: Male.
33. **Unknown**. Sex: Female.

Elias (Eliezer Zwi Ben Ezechiel) Eisner and Unknown married. They had the following children:

+ 16.i. **Michael Eisner** was born in 1771 in Humpolec. He died in 1864. Sex: Male.

38. **Fischer**. Sex: Male.
39. **Unknown**. Sex: Female.

Fischer and Unknown married. They had the following children:

i. 19.i. **Barbora Fischer**. Sex: Female.

49. **Lieberman**. Sex: Male.
50. **Unknown**. Sex: Female.

Lieberman and Unknown married. They had the following children:

i. 21.i. **Therese Lieberman** was born in Bohemia. Sex: Female.

1 **Hoffman**. Sex: Male.
2 **Unknown**. Sex: Female.

Hoffman and Unknown married. They had the following children:

+ 23.i. **Marie Hoffmannová** was born in 1814. Sex: Female.

54. **Dub**. Sex: Male.
55. **Unknown**. Sex: Female.

Dub and Unknown married. They had the following children:

+ 27.i. **Judita Dubova** was born in 1804 in Benešov. Sex: Female.

60. **Moritz Steindler** was born before 1800. Sex: Male.
61. **Unknown** was born before 1800. Sex: Female.

Moritz Steindler and Unknown married. They had the following children:

+ 30.i. **Jakub Steindler** was born in 1820 in Benešov, Bohemia. He died on 17 Apr 1873 in Benešov, Bohemia. Sex: Male.

62. **Elias Bret**. Sex: Male.
63. **Eva Goldberger**. Sex: Female.

Elias Bret and Eva Goldberger married. They had the following children:

i. **Antonia Bret**. Sex: Female.

+ 31.ii. **Ludmila Bret** was born on 24 Dec 1813 in Golcuv Jenikov, Havlickuv Brod District, Moravia. She died on 13 Dec 1849 in Benešov, Bohemia. Sex: Female.

Generation 7

64. **Ezechiel.** Sex: Male.
65. **Unknown** daughter of Reb Jehuda ben Salomon and Unknown. Sex: Female. Ezechiel and Unknown married. They had the following children:

  + 32.i. **Elias (Eliezer Zwi Ben Ezechiel) Eisner** was born in Dec 1748 in Jenikov. Sex: Male.

Generation 8

130. **Reb Jehuda ben Salomon.** Sex: Male.
131. **Unknown.** Sex: Female.

Reb Jehuda ben Salomon and Unknown married. They had the following children:

  + 65.i. **Unknown.** Sex: Female.

C. Descendants of Mila Rechcigl and Eva Edwards

Generation 1

1. **Mila (Miloslav) Rechcigl Jr.**-1 was born on 30 Jul 1930 in Mladá Boleslav, CSR.
   Eva Edwards (Eisnerová) daughter of Paul J. Edwards (Pavel Eisner) and Jiřina Taussigová was born on 21 Jan 1932 in Prague, CSR.
   Mila (Miloslav) Rechcigl Jr. and Eva Edwards (Eisnerová) were married on 29 Aug 1953 in New York, NY. They had the following children:
   2. i. **John Edward Rechcigl** was born on 27 Feb 1960 in Washington, D.C.. He married Nancy Ann Palko on 30 Jul 1983 in Dover, NJ.
   3. ii. **Karen Rechcigl** was born on 16 Apr 1962 in Washington, DC. She married Ulysses Kollecas on 25 Aug 1990 in Bethesda, MD.

Generation 2

2. **John Edward Rechcigl**-2 (Mila (Miloslav)-1) was born on 27 Feb 1960 in Washington, D.C..
   Nancy Ann Palko daughter of Joseph Palko and Mary Rishko was born on 26 Sep 1961 in Morristown, NJ.
   John Edward Rechcigl and Nancy Ann Palko were married on 30 Jul 1983 in Dover, NJ. They had the following children:
   i. **Gregory John Rechcigl** was born on 19 Dec 1988 in Bradenton, FL.
   5. ii. **Kevin Thomas Rechcigl** was born on 09 Oct 1991 in Bradenton, FL. He married Jordan Robbins on 12 May 2018 in Jacksonville, FL.
   iii. **Lindsey Nicole Rechcigl** was born on 03 Nov 1994 in Bradenton, FL.
3. **Karen Rechcigl**-2 (Mila (Miloslav)-1) was born on 16 Apr 1962 in Washington, DC.
   Ulysses Kollecas son of Christopher Thomas (Kolecas) Collier and Amelia Malatras was born on 20 Mar 1958 in Washington, DC.

Ulysses Kollecas and Karen Rechcigl were married on 25 Aug 1990 in Bethesda, MD. They had the following children:

    i.   **Kristin Kollecas** was born on 04 May 1993 in Albuquerque, NM.

    ii. **Paul Kollecas** was born on 02 Jun 1995 in Albuquerque, NM.

Generation 3

4.   **Kevin Thomas Rechcigl**-3 (John Edward-2, Mila (Miloslav)-1) was born on 09 Oct 1991 in Bradenton, FL.

Jordan Robbins daughter of Douglass Philip Robbins and Ivonne Lavernia was born on 10 Jan 1992 in Camarillo, CA.

Kevin Thomas Rechcigl and Jordan Robbins were married on 12 May 2018 in Jacksonville, FL. They had the following children:

    i. **James Douglas Rechcigl** was born on 05 Jan 2021 in Jacksonville, FL.

    ii. **Evelyn Marie Rechcigl** was born 23 May 2023 in Jacksonville, FL.

III.

HISTORIES of KEY FAMILIES

A. The Rechcigl Family

The Name

As far as I was able to ascertain in the Czech archives, our family name has been spelled in various ways, depending on who actually entered the name in the church registrars. In the 19th century it was usually spelled "Rechziegel," later on the name assumed a more Czech appearance, i.e., "Rechcigl." In addition, I found other spellings, such as Rechcygl, Rechtziegel, Rekcigel, or Reckziegel but cannot say with certainty whether or not any of these families are related to ours. Because of the unusual nature of the name, my guess is that we may be related if we would go far enough into back generations.

The origin of the family name Rechcigl name is not known. It may be based on German words "Recht", meaning "law, right " or "Reck", meaning a "crossbar", and "Siegel", meaning a "seal" or "Ziegel", meaning a "brick." If one were to look for some meaning, the only combination that would make some sense is "Rechtsiegel" which could stand for some legal seal or a person with an authority. Phonetically, the Czech pronunciation of the word "Rechtsiegel" would be actually indistinguishable from the word "Rechcigl." This could be transliterated in English as "Rekhtseegl." For easier pronunciation, most Americans pronounce our name as "Rex Eagle."

In spite of our German sounding family name, all our ancestors were genuine Czechs and all the entries in the church registrars I have been able to examine were written in the Czech language. I have not found any German connection yet and among my contemporaries I am not aware of a single member of our family who could actually boast of his or her knowledge of the German language.

Geography

Our most immediate family comes from the Mohelka Valley in the north- northeastern part of Bohemia, neighboring on the most beautiful region of Bohemia, appropriately called "Český ráj," meaning "Czech Paradise." Our earliest known ancestor František Rechziegel[8] lived in Slavíkov from which the family spread southward along the Mohelka River and settled in the following villages: Třtí, Žďárek, Hodkovice, Letařovice, and Chocnějovice. Some family members moved even further inland, i.e., Malá Bělá and Šárovcova Lhota.

Small villages are scattered throughout the valley, usually about 2-4 kilometers apart. The closest towns are Mnichovo Hradiště, Jablonec and Turnov which the local population visited only when they needed to purchase items that were not available locally, only a few times a year. A typical village had only some thirty houses, usually with a small church and cemetery, a grocery store and a local saloon. Larger villages could also have an elementary school, a smithy or and even a flour mill.

It is a picturesque area, comprised of valleys, through which flows the winding creek "Mohelka," surrounded by green meadows and wooded hills. As I recollect from my childhood, the woods were full of berries, i.e., wild strawberries, whortleberries, blackberries, and raspberries, as well as wild cherries. The women and children would pick them and then preserve them for later use. The woods also abounded with mushrooms which we all learned to recognize and pick from earliest childhood. Those exciting mushroom hunts will forever remain in my memory.

---

[8] I have recently discovered that František Rechziegel may have been son of Ludvik Rechziegel from Stráž pod Ralskem (Wartenberg), Česká Lípa District, Bohemia who presumably moved to Hodkovive, in 1750,where they then resided. However, this needs to be confirmed.

The area had a typical temperate climate with four distinct seasons: Spring, Summer, Autumn, and Winter, each roughly of 3 months duration. Spring and fall were quite mild, with frequent rains. The summers were hot but without humidity. The most beautiful landscape was in winter time when everything was covered with pure white snow.

Occupation

All the Rechcigls in the Mohelka Valley were, by tradition, flour millers. Actually, if you would walk or drive along the Mohelka River, just about every mill you would find belonged to some branch of the Rechcigl family. The mill was usually inherited by the oldest son. However, among Rechcigls, it was traditional for a father to purchase mills for his other sons as well. Miller's trade in those earlier days belonged to among the best professions and it is no wonder that the Rechcigls stayed with it. A miller, who was normally called by everyone "Pan otec" (Mr. Father), was usually considered the most important person in the entire community, partly because of his economic status and partly because of his knowledge and wisdom. To become a miller, you had to not only be a good agriculturist, but you also had to master the rather complex milling technology, in addition to being a good businessman.

History

The oldest ancestor I have been able to find so far is František Rechziegel[9] who was born in Slavíkov, in house No. 4., in the year 1741 and died on April 19, 1835. Apart from the fact that he was a miller by profession, we don't know anything about him. With his wife Alžběta,

---

[9] As mentioned in the previous footnote, I have recently discovered that František Rechziegel may have been son of Ludvik Rechziegel from Stráž pod Ralskem (Wartenberg), Česká Lípa District, Bohemia who presumably moved to Hodkovive, in 1750, where they then resided. However, this needs to be confirmed.

née Boehmanová, he had a son Frantšek, born in the same place on December 26, 1789 and died on August 2, 1849. The latter married Ludmila Neumannová, a daughter of Václav Neumann and Ludmila Najmanová. All known Rechcigls have descended from this couple. We have not been able to ascertain so far, whether František Rechziegel Sr. had other offspring.

A name resembling our name appeared in Bohemia much earlier, however. In the recently published book, *Soupis poddanych podle viry z roku 1651. Boleslavsko II*

(Survey of Subjects according to Faith from 1651), there is a reference to Matěj Rekcigel, a farmer by profession, age 28, and his wife Sybila, age 34, from the village magistrate Kokonín ("Rychta Kukonská"), in the Jablonec n/Nisou County. They also list their children: Anna, age 19, Kryštof, age 17, Jiřík, age 12, Jan, age 9, and Justyna, age 7. The same publication lists under the village magistrate Sněhov ("Rychta Sněhovská"), in the village Malá Skála, also in the Jablonec n/Nisou County), Jiřík Rekcigel and his wife Mariana, Kryštof Rekcigel and his wife Sybila, Wolf Rekcigel and his wife Anna, and Krištof Rekcigel and his wife Lidmila. Whether these Rekcigels are ancestors of our family could not be determined.

Other Rechcigls

There are two other families in Bohemia with similarly sounding names to ours, namely the Rechziegel family of Turnov and the Rechcigl family of Mlčechvosty. No genealogical linkages with these two families were found, so far. Before the World War II there also lived in Jablonec n/Nisou a family Reckziegels. The latter spelling apparently occurs also in Germany. Several members of this family immigrated to Brazil.

B. The Rajtr Family

The Name

The family name "Rajtr" is most likely of German origin. It is probably related to the Czech word "rajtovat" which stands for "horseback riding" or to the word "rajter" which refers to a "cavalryman."

Geography

The Rajtr family came originally from Zvířetice, near Bakov, in Mnichovo Hradiště District. Mila's great-grandfather Jan Václav Rajtr took for his wife Anna Najmanová from a neighboring village Dolánky where the young couple then lived. Both my grandfather and my mother were already born in Dolánky.

Occupations

The entire Rajtr family was of peasant or farmer stock. Grandfather Čeněk Rajtr was an industrious and prosperous man who had the reputation, not only as an excellent farmer but also as an expert tree breeder. His tree nursery belonged to the best in the District. In addition, he was also an avid beekeeper.

History

The oldest known ancestor in the Rajtr line was Václav Rajtr of Zvířietice No. 11, who married Dorota Strojcová. Their son Václav had, with his wife Barbora Koštejnová, four children, of whom two died soon after they were born. The remaining son Jan Václav Rajtr took for his wife Anna Najmannová of Dolánky where he then moved. They had five children. The third-born Vincenc, who later changed his name to Čeněk, was my grandfather. The latter married Marie, nèe Dandová of Hoškovice, who bore him three children, one son Oldřich and daughters Marie, my mother, and another daughter Marta, my aunt.

C. The Danda Family

The Name

Danda is quite a common name, both in the Czech Republic, as well as aboard. It even exists in Nigeria. It is apparently derived from the name Daniel. The basis is a Biblical name of Hebraic origin, Daniel, consisting of words ;'to judge, to adjudicate" and 'God.' The name can just be interpreted as "The Lord is our judge, the Lord is our lawgiver, the Lord is our king; he will save us." as the Bible tell us.

Geography

The earliest known ancestor of this family was Jan Danda born before 1653 in Boseň, in Mladá Boleslav District. His namesake son, who was also born there, married Kateřina Berglová of Hoškovice, located only 5 kilometers from Boseň. From then on, the family resided in Hoškovice, although a few family members moved to Kněžmost, which is also only a few kilometers away.

Occupation

Having lived in rural area, their livelihood was in farming. They were all well to do farmers or cottagers.

History

In the eighth generation from Jan Danda, Marie Dandová (1882-1967), daughter of František Antonín Danda (1857-1900) and Josefa Cimrová (1859-1923), born in Hoškovice, was Mila Rechcigl's grandmother. She married his grandfather, Čeněk Rajtr of Dolanky. They then lived in Dolánky, No. 7, near Bakov n/Jizerou, which is about 11 kilometers distant from Hoškovice.

D. The Eisner Family

The Name

The earliest ancestor we have been able to trace in this family was Reb Jehuda ben Salomon. His son Elias was born in December 1748. At his circumcision on January 8, 1749 he was given the name Eliezer Zwi ben Ezechiel. On May 17, 1785 he took the name Eisner because he worked with iron, probably as a blacksmith. The German word for iron is Eisen - thus the name.

Geography

The Eisner family comes from Bohemia, at one time part of the Austro-Hungarian Empire. After World War II it became Czechoslovakia, and as of this writing (2022), the Czech Republic. Elias Eisner was born in the town of Jeníkov and worked in Prague. His son Michael was born in Humpolec. His son Karel Eisner was born in Chotěboř. The latter's son, Eva's grandfather, Jindřich Eisner, was born in Kaliště, near Německý Brod. Eva's father Pavel Eisner, renamed Edwards, was born in Prague II, Klimenstská Street 1.

Eva and her sister Helen were born in Prague, which was the capital of Czechoslovakia, at that time the most beautiful city in the world. They lived on a street Na Zátorce 10, in the suburb Bubeneč, Prague XIX, an elegant section of the city. Eduard Beneš, who became the second President of Czechoslovakia, lived on the same street. The street was the site of many foreign consulates. During Eva's childhood, the Turkish Embassy was across the street from where they lived. Their home, a three-story yellow stucco house that their family rented, is now the Iraqi Consulate. The Iranian Consulate was just down the hill. The Petschek family, the wealthiest people in the city, during Eva's childhood had their villas in Bubeneč; their houses are now the Russian and American Embassies. A beautiful park with many chestnut trees, called Stromovka, added beauty to the area. Eva's father used to go horseback riding there.

Occupations

The family oldest ancestor, was the chief of the fire and safety division in the Jewish section of the 'Old Town' of Prague. He fought in the war against Swedes in the early 17th century and was seriously wounded at the battle defending the Prague Bridge. His son Michel was in the iron business.

Michael's son, Karel Eisner, owned a tannery and was engaged in the leather business. Eva's grandfather Jindřich Eisner, next in line, was a jeweler, as was his middle son, Karel. He produced Czech garnet jewelry and other items in his workshop in Prague and sold jewelry in that city as well as in the spa, Mariánskè Lázně (Marienbad). Another son of Jindřich, Robert Eisner, was a merchant. The third son, Eva's father Pavel, was a lawyer in Prague and after emigrating to the US, and passing the Bar, he became a lawyer in New York City.

History

In March 1939, Eva's father and his family, and the family of her mother's sister Hanka, came to the US and settled in Brooklyn, NY. They changed their name to Edwards to become more Americanized. Eventually her grandparents arrived via Cuba. Her uncle Robert Eisner and his family already lived in 1939 in London, and he emigrated to the US, as did the third son Charles with his family. Thus the whole family emigrated to the US.

E. The Taussig Family

The Name

Taussig, which was quite a common name in Bohemia, comes from the word "Taus," German translation of the town "Domažlice," located in the western Bohemia. The name was sometimes also spelled "Tausig".

Geography

Our Taussig line comes from Benešov, south of Prague. Our oldest ancestor bearing that name was born in Běchovice near Prague. Oskar Taussig moved from Benešov to Prague where his daughters Jiřina and Hanka were born.

Occupation

Most Taussigs on our side of the family were lawyers. Interestingly enough, the female members of the family, some of whom also opted for the legal profession, had the tendency to select lawyers for their husbands. This was the case of Eva's parents.

History

The oldest known ancestor bearing the name Taussig was Julia Taussigová about whom we know very little. According to some documents, she was the wife of Markus Stoekler of Záběhlice. They had a son Jakub who retained his mother's maiden name Taussig. Why he did not assume his father's name Stoekler is a mystery. Jakub Taussig married Julia Meislová of Žehušice and had with him eleven children: six daughters and five sons. The youngest son Oskar Taussig was the father of Jiřina and Hanka.

Oskar Taussig (1876-1938) was a well-known Prague lawyer and a cousin of the Czech writer Richard Weiner. He was married to Klára Taussig (died 1934). Their children were Hanna (nicknamed Hanka, later Joan Winn) and Jiřina (Georgine) who in 1926 married Pavel Eisner, later known as Paul Edwards).

Julius Taussig (1862-1941) was Oskar's older brother, and their sisters were Hermina Kašpárek (1871-1927), Pavla (1873-1943) and Kamila (1871-1927). Their mother was Julie (née Meislová) (1838-1913). Jiří Kašpárek (George Kasparek) was Oskar's nephew, who worked for Taussig as a lawyer in his firm.

Richard Weiner was born in Pisek, today Písek, Czech Republic, on Nov. 6, 1884 and died Jan. 3, 1937. He graduated as a chemical engineer in 1906 from the University of Prague. After additional studies in Zurich and military service in Bohemia from 1907 to 1908, he decided on a career change and left for Paris to become a correspondent for the Prague newspaper *Samostatnost*. He became a poet and writer and was called the "Czech Franz Kafka." Richard's brother was Kamil Weiner (1886-1960), who was married to Gustav Weiner (1902-1983). In the 1960s, Joan Winn tried to have the works of Richard Weiner published in the US. Today, Richard Weiner's poems are not well known by the general public, but highly recognized by the literary critiques.

Other Taussigs

There were a number of other families in Czechoslovakia bearing the name Taussig or Tausig, with whom we have not been able to find any genealogical linkages. The name also occurred in Vienna, Austria, as well as in Poland and Rumania. Moreover, several Taussig families from Bohemia emigrated around the revolutionary year 1848 to the US. Several of their descendants distinguished themselves as physicians, lawyers, educators and public servants.

F. The Steiner Family

Name

Steiner is a very common name, both in Bohemia and German-speaking countries. "Stein in German means "stone." It is quite possible that people with this name were involved in masonry.

Geography

The Steiner family, as far back as Adolf, grandfather of Frank Steiner, came from Moravia. Adolf Steiner was horn in Prostějov and moved at some time in his life to Židlochovice, also called Selowitz during the Austrian-Hungarian Empire. Židlochovice is a village about 20 km east of Brno. It had an elementary school but for secondary schools~ students had to go to Bmo.

Occupation

Adolf Steiner (1849-1904) and Rosa (Neumannová) Steiner (1851-1935) had a general store in Židlochovice. After Adolf died in 1904, his oldest son Alfred Steiner (1849-1904) took it over and increased the value of the store so that he was considered fairly well-to-do. Adolf Steiner's wife, Rosa moved to Vienna, where her son Johann Steiner lived and worked as mechanical engineer in the Austrian Railroad system. Johann Steiner's son, Frank Steiner, was an engineer, as was his grandson David.

History

As mentioned above, the family moved from Židlochovice to Vienna where they resided until the World War II started. Adolf Steiner's daughters, Anna and Olga also lived in Vienna after they married. Frank Steiner remembers visiting his grandmother Rosa during his youth in her apartment. She died in 1930.

Johann's son, Frank C. Steiner (1922-2000), although born in Prague, was also raised in Vienna..

After the annexation of Austria by Nazi Germany in 1938 and after the Germans occupied Czechoslovakia in 1939, all members of the Steiner family dispersed. Johann and Růža were sent to the concentration camp Terezin in 1941 and survived. They came to the US in 1946. Anna and her husband Gustav perished in Auschwitz, but their sons Otto and Carl escaped and came to the US. Frank Steiner, luckily, was able to move to Prague in June 1938 and in 1939 immigrate to the US.

Olga and the entire Mandel family survived. Olga and Emil, their daughter Alice and her husband Lothar came to the US before World War II. Alfred and Olly perished in a concentration camp but their twin sons Julius and Otto eventually settled in Australia where they died.

G. The Steinbach Family

Name

Steinbach is a German word that could be translated as "stony brook." There is no-good explanation why a family would have such a name other than that the ancestors lived along such a body of water. Steinbach is a common name in German and is found in Christian and Jewish families. In front of London's Albert Hall is a large statue of Prince Albert and the foundation has names of famous Europeans and among them is a person by the name of Steinbach.

Geography

The Bohemian Steinbach family apparently originated in Vysoká, a municipality and village in in Příbram District in the Central Bohemian Region of the Czech Republic. That's where the ancestor Simon Steinbach was definitely born and where he resided. His son Lewis (orig. Ludvik) Weisskopf Steinbach, was also born there. Although his brother Adolf's birthplace is not known with certainty, it is reasonable to assume that Adolf was also born in that village.

Adolf Steinbach, however, seemed to later live in Střebsko (later renamed Třebsko and now again Střebsko). The village is about five miles from the larger town of Příbram. Around 1900 it numbered 51 houses and about 200 people lived there.

Occupation

Karel Steinbach (1894-1990) was a noted physician and general practitioner. For many years he was a civilian doctor for the Army at Governors Island and Fort Hamilton in Brooklyn. During the interwar period he was a well-known Prague obstetrician and an expressive personality of social and cultural life, a close friend of Karel Čapek, F.

Peroutka and Jan Masaryk. Beyond that he was a highly entertaining story-teller and reciter.

Lewis W. Steinbach (1851-1913) who preceded him in the US, was also a distinguished physician and professor of surgery of in Philadelphia Polyclinic and College for Graduates in Medicine.

History

The earliest known ancestor of this family was Lazar Steinbach and Karolina Polak. They had a son, Simon Steinbach (1805-1884), born in Vysoká u Příbramě, who married Rosalie Weisskopf (1814-1901). Simon and Rosalie had 2 daughters: Katharina and Maria Teresa, about whom little is known. They also had 2 sons: Lewis (orig. Ludvik) Weisskopf Steinbach (1851-1913) and Adolf Steinbach (1855-1931). The former immigrated to the US. As for the latter, Adolf Steinbach, he was married twice. His first wife (name unknown) died in childbirth when she delivered Paula in 1887. Adolf then married, in 1899, Marie Hartmannová and they had three children: Růža, Ella and Karel. Karel Steinbach mentions in his memoirs that the family of Marie Hartmannová came from Arcachon near Bordeaux, France. They moved to Příbram where they set up a factory which produced glass beads to make wreaths which were shipped to France and supposedly used to decorate graves.

Adolf and Marie had a general store in Střebsko, and the children worked occasionally in the store. They probably sold the store after WW1 and moved to Prague presumably to be closer to Karel who worked there as a doctor.

Karel Steinbach (1894-1990) lived in Prague at Havlíčkovo náměst 22 until April 1939 when he left for the US. His main residence in New York was at 80-09 35th Ave., Jackson Heights, Queens, NY.

Adolf died in 1931 at the age of 76. Marie developed cancer and required a colostomy. She died in 1935. Both are buried in the new Jewish cemetery and their grave is near that of Franz Kafka. After the war, the names of Paula, Ella and her husband Viktor Reiter, who all perished in Auschwitz, were added to the gravestone of Adolf Steinbach.

The Steinbach name in the family disappeared in in 1990 when Karel Steinbach died on December 31. Previously, other Steinbachs in the US had died: Lewis in 1913, his son Simon in 1945 and Simon's daughter Edna (married to Gold) in 1964.

H. The Wiener Family

Name

This surname is associated with Wien, the German name of Vienna the capital city of Austria, where Jews were living since the 12th century. "Wiener," means something or someone from the city of Wien, in the same way that "New Yorker" is someone from New York. The English word "wiener" comes from this source in German - it refers to a sausage that comes from Wien (or Vienna). So a wiener is technically a Vienna sausage.

Our relative, Joseph Wiener (1901-1983), who immigrated with his family to the US, changed his surname to "Winn."

Geography

The name was common on the territory of former Czechoslovakia, most frequently in Prague, Liberec and Brno. The ancestors of our Wiener relatives came from Rožďálovice, Nymburk District, in the Central Bohemian Region of the Czech Republic. Joseph A. Winn (orig. Wiener) who immigrated to the US, was born in Poděbrady, which is only 28 kilometers distant from there.

Occupation

Dr. Joseph A. Winn (orig. Wiener) was a psychiatrist and a writer. His father was a merchant. Joseph A. Winn's two daughters were journalists. Joseph Ivan Krajbich (1947-) is a physician in Portland, OR, specializing in orthopedic surgery. The latter's brother, George P. Krajbich (1921-1988), was also a physician

History

Josef Wiener (1901-1983), born in Poděbrady (Podiebrad), Bohemia, married Hanna (Hanka) Taussigová, a daughter of the well-known Prague lawyer Oskar Taussig. In August 1939, the Wieners immigrated to the United States with their two daughters, Jana (Janet) and Marie. They changed their family name from Wiener to Winn, and Josef Wiener became Joseph A. Winn. The A stands for his literary pseudonym, Alcantara. His spouse, Hanna Wiener (orig. Taussigová) became Joan Winn. Winn continued with his medical practice as well as with his writings. Joseph Winn died 1983 in New York.

Joseph A. Winn, was a psychiatrist and a writer. He wrote short stories, aphorisms and commentaries, mainly in a satirical and comical style under his pseudonym Alcantara. His works were published largely in *Lidové noviny*, *Tribuna* and *Dobrý den* (satirical biweekly magazine edited by Karel Poláček). While still in Czechoslovakia, Josef Wiener was also a friend and the physician of the members of the "Osvobozené Divadlo" (Liberated Theater), a famous Czech avant-garde theatre (1926-1938).

Joseph A. Winn's mother was Alba ("Babička" - Grandma) Wiener, and his sister was Mařka Krajbich (married to Josef (Bobca) Krajbich). Her sons were Jirka and Ivan Krajbich. Winn's extended family included Elsa Reinisch, his cousin, and her mother Malva Oplatka, his aunt. They emigrated to Chicago in the 1920s. Another of Winn's aunts was Liduša Růžičková, who was married to Herman Růžička (died 1944).

IV.

GENEALOGIES of ALLIED FAMILIES

A. Mila Rechcigl's Father Side

Rechcigl (Rechziegel) Family

Generation 1

1. **Ludvik Rechziegel**-1 was born in Stráž pod Ralskem (Wartenberg), Česká Lipa District, Bohemia ((in 1750 moved to Hodkovice, Bohemia)). Ludvik Rechziegel and unknown spouse married. They had the following children:
   1. i. **František Rechziegel** was born about 1741 in Straz pod Ralskem (Wartenberg), Česká Lipa District, Bohemia (from 1750l resided in Hodkovice, Bohemia). He died on 19 Apr 1835 in Slavíkov No. 4 at the age of 94..

Generation 2

2. **František Rechziegel**-2 (Ludvik-1) was born about 1741 in Straz pod Ralskem (Wartenberg), Česká Lipa District, Bohemia (from 1750l resided in Hodkovice, Bohemia). He died on 19 Apr 1835 in Slavíkov No. 4 at the age of 94..

   Alžběta Boelmanova was born in 1746 in Vlastibořice. She died on 21 Aug 1822 in Slavíkov No. 4. František Rechziegel and Alžběta Boelmanova married. They had the following children:
   3. i. **Ing. František Rechziegel** was born on 26 Dec 1789 in Slavíkov No. 4, Český Dub Co.. He married Lidmila Neumanová on 03 Aug 1811 in Slavíkov No. 4, Vlastibořice parish. He died on 02 Aug 1849 in Slavíkov No. 4.

Generation 3

3. **Ing. František Rechziegel**-3 (František-2, Ludvik-1) was born on 26 Dec 1789 in Slavíkov No. 4, Český Dub Co.. He died on 02 Aug 1849 in Slavíkov No. 4.

   Lidmila Neumanová daughter of Václav Neumann and Lidmila Adamova was born on 28 Jun 1792 in Radimovice No. 6, Český Dub Co.. She died on 09 May 1845 in Slavíkov No. 4.

Ing. František Rechziegel and Lidmila Neumanová were married on 03 Aug 1811 in Slavíkov No. 4, Vlastibořice parish. They had the following children:

    i. **Franz Rechziegel** was born on 03 Aug 1811 in Skavikov No. 4.

    ii. **František Rechziegel** was born on 26 May 1812 in Slavíkov No. 4. He died on 12 Jul 1814 in Slavíkov No. 4.

    iii. **Josef Rechziegel** was born on 22 Feb 1814 in Slavíkov No. 4. He died on 06 Jun 1893 in Teplice.

    iv. **Marie Rechziegel** was born on 14 Mar 1816 in Slavíkov No. 4. She died on 08 Apr 1846 in Slavíkov No. 4.

    v. **Františka Rechziegel** was born on 27 Jan 1818 in Slavíkov No. 4. She died on 25 Feb 1818 in Slavíkov, No. 4.

4.   vi. **Petr Rechziegel** was born on 10 Jan 1819 in Slavíkov No. 4. He married Františka Hlavatá on 30 Nov 1850 in Slavíkov No. 3, Vlastibořice parish, Josef Sedláček, officiating. He died on 17 Oct 1890 in Novy Mlyn, Žďárek.

    vii. **Františka Johanna Rechziegel** was born on 11 May 1821 in Slavíkov No. 4. She died on 10 Mar 1823 in Slavíkov No. 4.

5.   viii. **Antonín Rechziegel** was born on 22 May 1823 in Slavíkov No. 4, Český Dub Co.. He married Anna Šiftová on 11 Feb 1851 in Jivina No. 6. He died on 25 Sep 1888 in Slavíkov No. 4, Cesyu Dub Co..

6.   ix. **Theresia Rechziegel** was born on 14 Apr 1825 in Slavíkov No. 4. She married Václav Beran on 05 Mar 1845 in Slavíkov No. 4, Vlastibořice parish.

    x. **Anna Rechziegel** was born in Apr 1826 in Slavíkov No. 4. She died on 13 Jul 1826 in Slavíkov No. 4.

7.   xi. **Josefa Rechziegelová** was born on 09 May 1827 in Slavíkov No. 4. She married Josef Zajíček on 04 Jun 1851 in Slavíkov No. 4, Vlastibořice parish. She died on 24 Feb 1872 in Jivina No. 16.

    i. **Kateřina Rechziegel** was born on 23 Apr 1829 in Slavíkov No. 4.

    ii. **Karel Rechziegel** was born on 22 Jul 1830 in Slavíkov No. 4.

8.   xiv. **Anna Rechziegel** was born on 09 Feb 1833 in Slavíkov No. 4. She married Johan Fanta on 22 Feb 1859 in Třtí No, 23. Hodkovice parish.

xv. **Františka Rechziegel** was born on 04 Oct 1837 in Slavíkov No. 4. She died on 29 Oct 1837 in Slavíkov No. 4.

Generation 4

4. **Petr Rechziegel**-4 (Ing. František-3, František-2, Ludvik-1) was born on 10 Jan 1819 in Slavíkov No. 4. He died on 17 Oct 1890 in Novy Mlyn, Žďárek.

Františka Hlavatá daughter of Unknown and Terezie Hlavatá was born on 27 Feb 1820 in Bzi No. 6. She died on 10 Dec 1857 in Slavíkov No. 4, in Mohelka Creek -.

Petr Rechziegel and Františka Hlavatá were married on 30 Nov 1850 in Slavíkov No. 3, Vlastibořice parish, Josef Sedláček, officiating. They had the following children:

9. i. **Marie Rechziegel** was born on 24 Jan 1841 in Hodkovice No. 39.
10. ii. **Petr Rechziegel** was born on 01 Jun 1844 in Hodkovice No. 39. He married Anna Najmanová on 26 Jan 1869 in Radimovice No. 7, Vlastibořice parish., Jan Krt. Hruska officiationg. He died on 18 Sep 1917 in Letařovice No. 4, Turnov Co..
11. iii. **Františka Rechziegel** was born on 05 Jul 1846 in Hodkovice No. 39. She died on 28 Feb 1914 in Ruzodol No. 169.
12. iv. **Václav Rechziegel** was born on 25 Aug 1851 in Slavíkov No. 3. He married Anna Janečková in 1879. He died on 21 Mar 1909 in Radostín No. 13.
    v. **Josefa Rechziegelová** was born on 08 Nov 1852 in Slavíkov No. 3. She died on 11 Nov 1852 in Slavíkov No. 3.
    vi. **Karel Bor. Rechziegel** was born on 03 Jul 1855 in Slavíkov No. 3. He died on 24 Oct 1855 in Slavíkov No. 3.

Kateřina Koskova daughter of Josef Košek and Marie Jirova was born in 1831 in Třtí No. 6, Turnov Co.. She died on 20 Nov 1902 in Mala Bela, near Bakov.

Petr Rechziegel and Kateřina Koskova were married on 25 May 1858 in Třtí No. 6, Turnov Co., Franz Staznik officiating. They had the following children:

13. i. **Josef Rechziegel** was born on 31 Aug 1865 in Třtí No. 8, Turnov Co.. He married Marie Cinkova on 23 Aug 1890 in Parish Church, Mukarov. He died in 1917.

5. **Antonín Rechziegel**-4 (Ing. František-3, František-2, Ludvik-1) was born on 22 May 1823 in Slavíkov No. 4, Český Dub Co.. He died on 25 Sep 1888 in Slavíkov No. 4, Cesyu Dub Co..

    Anna Šiftová daughter of František Šifta and Alžběta Černá was born on 27 Jun 1834 in Jivina No. 6. She died on 03 Apr 1854 in Slavíkov No. 4. Antonín Rechziegel and Anna Šiftová were married on 11 Feb 1851 in Jivina No. 6. They had the following children:

    14. i. **Anna Rechziegel** was born on 07 Aug 1852 in Slavíkov No. 4. She married Josef Vela on 6 Feb 1872 in Slavíkov No. 4, Vlastibořice parish. She died on 15 Sep 1931 in Sychrov.
    110. **Josef Rechziegel** was born on 29 Mar 1854 in Slavíkov No. 4. He died on 29 Mar 1854 in Slavíkov No. 4.

    Marie Havliková daughter of Jan Havlik and Kateřina Venclova was born on 08 Nov 1834 in Oujezd Co. 3. She died on 24 Oct 1913 in Loukov - at her daughter's Kateřina Skodova.

    Antonín Rechziegel and Marie Havliková were married on 31 Jul 1854 in Loukov. They had the following children:

    15. i. **Josefa Rechziegel** was born on 15 Jun 1855 in Slavíkov No. 4. She married Václav Jira on 07 Jul 1890 in Slavíkov No. 4. She died on 16 Jul 1945.
        ii. **Josef Rechziegel** was born on 29 Mar 1857 in Slavíkov No. 4. He died on 08 Mar 1912 in Praha.
        iii. **Kateřina Rechziegel** was born on 27 Nov 1859 in Slavíkov No. 4. She died on 24 Jan 1935 in Hodkovice.
    16. iv. **Karel Bor. Rechziegel** was born on 02 Dec 1867 in Slavíkov No. 4. He married Anna Bartošová on 17 Aug 1889 in Český Dub. He died on 09 Jan 1904 in Chvalčovice.

117. **Theresia Rechziegel**-4 (Ing. František-3, František-2, Ludvik-1) was born on 14 Apr 1825 in Slavíkov No. 4.

Václav Beran son of Josef Beran and Alžběta Divinkova was born in 1823 in Trávníček No. 20.
Václav Beran and Theresia Rechziegel were married on 05 Mar 1845 in Slavíkov No. 4, Vlastibořice parish. They had the following children:
  i. **Josef Beran** was born on 12 Jun 1845 in Slavíkov No. 4.
  ii. **Marie Beranová** was born on 12 Sep 1847 in Slavíkov No. 4.

7. **Josefa Rechziegelová**-4 (Ing. František-3, František-2, Ludvik-1) was born on 09 May 1827 in Slavíkov No. 4. She died on 24 Feb 1872 in Jivina No. 16.
Josef Zajíček son of Václav Zajíček and Marie Samalova was born on 12 Nov 1830 in Jivina No. 16. He died in Received house in 1854.
Josef Zajíček and Josefa Rechziegelová were married on 04 Jun 1851 in Slavíkov No. 4, Vlastibořice parish. They had the following children:
  i. **Josef Zajíček** was born on 03 Nov 1851 in Jivina No. 16. He died on 02 Jan 1853 in Jivina No. 16.
  ii. **Jan Zajíček** was born on 11 Dec 1854 in Jivina No. 16. He died on 25 Mar 1855 in Jivina No. 16.
  iii. **Anna Zajickova** was born on 20 Sep 1856 in Jivina No. 16. She married František Richter on 15 Jun 1875 in Jivina No. 1 6; Josef Kovar, parish priest officiating.
  iv. **Josefa Zajickova** was born on 11 May 1859 in Jivina No. 16. She died about 1879. She married Josef Pycha on 11 Nov 1879 in Jivina No. 16, Český Dub Co.; Josef Kovar, parish priest officiating.
18. v. **Marie Zajickova** was born on 24 Aug 1862 in Jivina No. 16. She married Václav Šifta on 14 Jul 1885 in Jivina No. 16, Český Dub Co.; Rev. Josef Kovar, parish priest officiating. She died on 23 Mar 1927 in Jivina No. 16.
  vi. **Emilie Zajickova** was born on 11 Feb 1872 in Jivina No. 16. She died on 14 Feb 1872 in Jivina No. 16.

8. **Anna Rechziegel**-4 (Ing. František-3, František-2, Ludvik-1) was born on 09 Feb 1833 in Slavíkov No. 4.

Johan Fanta son of Johan Fanta and Anna Dopsáková was born about 1834 in Třtí No. 23.

Johan Fanta and Anna Rechziegel were married on 22 Feb 1859 in Třtí No, 23. Hodkovice parish. They had the following children:

    i. **Peter Fanta** was born on 20 Jun 1861 in Třtí No. 23. He married Anna Bussek on 24 Jul 1909 in Vsen.

Generation 5

9. **Marie Rechziegel**-5 (Petr-4, Ing. František-3, František-2, Ludvik-1) was born on 24 Jan 1841 in Hodkovice No. 39.

Václav Janeček son of at and Unknown was born in 1834 in Příšovice. He died on 18 Sep 1909 in Příšovice.

Václav Janeček and Marie Rechziegel married. They had the following children:

18. i. **Anna Janečková**.
    ii. **Petr Janeček**.
    iii. **František Janeček**.

Matejak.

Matejak and Marie Rechziegel met. They had the following children:

    i. **Václav Rechziegel** was born on 24 Apr 1860 in Letařovice No. 4.

10. **Petr Rechziegel**-5 (Petr-4, Ing. František-3, František-2, Ludvik-1) was born on 01 Jun 1844 in Hodkovice No. 39. He died on 18 Sep 1917 in Letařovice No. 4, Turnov Co..

Anna Najmanová daughter of Antonín Neumann and Anna Brožová was born on 31 Jul 1849 in Radimovice No. 7, Turnov Co.. She died on 05 Jun 1908 in Letařovice.

Petr Rechziegel and Anna Najmanová were married on 26 Jan 1869 in Radimovice No. 7, Vlastibořice parish., Jan Krt. Hruska officiationg. They had the following children:

    i. **Josef Rechcigl** was born on 22 Jul 1869 in Radimovice No. 7. He died on 24 Feb 1920 in Letařovice (prob.).

20. ii. **Emilie Rechcíglová** was born on 02 Apr 1871 in Letařovice No. 4, Český Dub Co.. She died on 18 Feb 1928.
   iii. **Václav Rechcigl** was born on 13 Mar 1873 in Letařovice No. 4, Český Dub Co..
20. iv. **Adolf Rechcigl** was born on 21 Aug 1876 in Letařovice No. 4, Český Dub Co.. He married Marie Berglová about 1900. He died on 30 Mar 1946 in Šárovcova Lhota No. 16.
   v. **Arnošt Rechziegel** was born on 07 Sep 1882 in Letařovice No. 4, Český Dub Co.. He died on 12 Oct 1882 in Letařovice No. 4, Český Dub Co..
21. vi. **Zdeněk Petr Rechcigl** was born on 31 Jul 1884 in Letařovice No. 4, Turnov Dist.. He married Anna Šimůnková on 08 Oct 1906 in Kralovske Vinohrady. He died on 08 Feb 1962 in Karlovy Vary - Rybare.
22. vii. **Bohumil Rechcigl** was born on 09 Apr 1888. He died on 03 Jan 1963 in Český Dub.
   viii. **Jan Rechziegel** was born on 08 May 1895.

11. **Františka Rechziegel**-5 (Petr-4, Ing. František-3, František-2, Ludvik-1) was born on 05 Jul 1846 in Hodkovice No. 39. She died on 28 Feb 1914 in Ruzodol No. 169.

    Ullrich was born in Jilove.

    Ullrich and Františka Rechziegel married. They had the following children:

23. ii. **Josef Ullrich** was born in Jilove.

12. **Václav Rechziegel**-5 (Petr-4, Ing. František-3, František-2, Ludvik-1) was born on 25 Aug 1851 in Slavíkov No. 3. He died on 21 Mar 1909 in Radostín No. 13.

    Anna Janečková daughter of František Janeček and Anna Koskova was born on 19 Apr 1855 in Třtí No. 6. She died on 17 Dec 1903 in Hodkovice. Václav Rechziegel and Anna Janečková were married in 1879. They had the following children:

    i. **Adolf Rechziegel**.

ii. **Josef Rechziegel** was born in 1886 in Radostín. He died on 05 Oct 1956 in Radostín.
  iii. **Emilie Rechziegelová**.
25. iv. **Marie Rechziegelová** was born in 1882 in Radostín. She died on 30 Jul 1959 in Radostín.
26. v. **Anna Rechziegelová** was born on 26 Sep 1888 in Radostín. She married Josef Franců about 1925. She died on 10 Oct 1964 in Kacanovy.
27. vi. **Anastazie Rechziegelová** was born on 17 Mar 1894 in Radostín. She married Rudolf Roubíček in Jul 1917. She died on 19 Apr 1984 in Srch.

13. **Josef Rechziegel**-5 (Petr-4, Ing. František-3, František-2, Ludvik-1) was born on 31 Aug 1865 in Třtí No. 8, Turnov Co.. He died in 1917.

Marie Cinkova daughter of Václav Cinka and Anna Štěpánková was born on 05 Jan 1870 in Jivina No. 24, Mnichova Hradiste Co..

Josef Rechziegel and Marie Cinkova were married on 23 Aug 1890 in Parish Church, Mukarov. They had the following children:

  27. i. **Marie Rechcíglová** was born on 11 Mar 1892 in Žďárek No. 26, Turnov Co.. She married Augustin Veselý on 25 Oct 1919 in Král. Vinohrady, Prague. She died on 07 Jul 1968 in Havlickuv Brod.
  28. ii. **Josef Rechcigl** was born on 05 Apr 1893 in Žďárek u Turnova. He married Marie Studničná on 28 Nov 1926 in Prague, CSR. He died on 13 Jun 1933 in Praha.
  29. iii. **Anna Rechcíglová** was born on 12 Jan 1902 in Žďárek. She married Karel Matějů in 1919 in Prague, CSR. She died on 15 Apr 1992 in Brno.

14. **Anna Rechziegel**-5 (Antonín-4, Ing. František-3, František-2, Ludvik-1) was born on 07 Aug 1852 in Slavíkov No. 4. She died on 15 Sep 1931 in Sychrov.

Josef Vela son of Josef Vela and Rozalie Šídová was born on 17 Mar 1844 in Cervenice No. 8. He died on 02 Dec 1928 in Sychrov.

Josef Vela and Anna Rechziegel were married on 06 Feb 1872 in Slavíkov No. 4, Vlastibořice parish. They had the following children:

    i. **Josef Vela** was born on 19 Apr 1873 in Slavíkov No. 3. He died on 07 Jan 1908 in Třtí.

    ii. **Kateřina Velova** was born on 21 Sep 1874 in Slavíkov No. 3. She died on 15 Nov 1931 in Sychrov. She married Čeněk Adam in Slavíkov.

    iii. **Anna Velova** was born on 12 Apr 1877 in Slavíkov No. 3. She died on 22 Apr 1911 in Hruba Skála (Doubravice).

30. iv. **Alois Jan Vela** was born on 14 May 1888 in Slavíkov No. 3. He married Marie Vysatova on 12 Sep 1916 in Vlastibořice. He died on 07 Oct 1974 in Turnov.

15. **Josefa Rechziegel**-5 (Antonín-4, Ing. František-3, František-2, Ludvik-1) was born on 15 Jun 1855 in Slavíkov No. 4. She died on 16 Jul 1945.

Václav Jira son of Josef Jira and Alžběta Růtová was born on 15 Sep 1857 in Klamorna No. 3, Český Dub Co.. He died on 24 May 1931.

Václav Jira and Josefa Rechziegel were married on 07 Jul 1890 in Slavíkov No. 4. They had the following children:

    31. i. **Marie Jirova** was born in 1893. She died on 01 Dec 1959.

16. **Karel Bor. Rechziegel**-5 (Antonín-4, Ing. František-3, František-2, Ludvik-1) was born on 02 Dec 1867 in Slavíkov No. 4. He died on 09 Jan 1904 in Chvalčovice.

Anna Bartošová daughter of Unknown and Kateřina Bartošová was born on 27 Feb 1866 in Chvalčovice No. 12. She died on 30 Sep 1936 in Sobeslavice No. 16.

Karel Bor. Rechziegel and Anna Bartošová were married on 17 Aug 1889 in Český Dub. They had the following children:

    i. **Václav Rechzigel** was born in 1894. He died in 1895.

    32. ii. **Ing. František Rechcigel** was born on 18 Nov 1896 in Chvalčovice. He married Marie Holajova on 12 Nov 1924 in Prague, CSR. He died on 28 Aug 1968 in Český Dub.

16. **Marie Zajickova**-5 (Josefa-4, Ing. František-3, František-2, Ludvik-1) was born on 24 Aug 1862 in Jivina No. 16. She died on 23 Mar 1927 in Jivina No. 16.

Václav Šifta son of Václav Šifta and Karolina Odcházelová was born on 21 Aug 1861 in Jivina No. 1. He died in Received house in 1885.

Václav Šifta and Marie Zajickova were married on 14 Jul 1885 in Jivina No. 16, Český Dub Co.; Rev. Josef Kovar, parish priest officiating. They had the following children:

    Emilie Šiftová was born in 1886 in Jivina No. 1.

    Božena Šiftová was born in 1892 in Jivina No. 1.

ii.   iii. **Josef Šifta** was born in 1898 in Jivina No. 1. He died in 1953.

Generation 6

18. **Anna Janečková**-6 (Marie-5, Petr-4, Ing. František-3, František-2, Ludvik-1).

Kinsky.

Kinsky and Anna Janečková married. They had the following children:
    i. **Miloslav Kinsky.**

19. **Emilie Rechcíglová**-6 (Petr-5, Petr-4, Ing. František-3, František-2, Ludvik-1) was born on 02 Apr 1871 in Letařovice No. 4, Český Dub Co.. She died on 18 Feb 1928.

23. **Josef Ullrich** son of Ullrich and Františka Rechziegel was born in Jilove. Josef Ullrich and Emilie Rechcíglová married. They had the following children:

    i. **Miloslav Ulrich** was born before 1900.

    ii. **Ludvika Ulrichova** was born in 1898. She died on 01 Jun 1945.

20. **Adolf Rechcigl**-6 (Petr-5, Petr-4, Ing. František-3, František-2, Ludvik-1) was born on 21 Aug 1876 in Letařovice No. 4, Český Dub Co.. He died on 30 Mar 1946 in Šárovcova Lhota No. 16.

Marie Berglová daughter of František Bergl and Marie Mařanová was born on 27 Mar 1880 in Drahotice No. 20, Mnichovo Hradiště Co.. She died on 25 Mar 1917 in Chocnějovice No. 22, Mnichovo Hradiště Co..

Adolf Rechcigl and Marie Berglová were married about 1900. They had the following children:

    i. **Marie Rechcíglová** was born on 29 Sep 1901 in Kocňovice (renamed Chocnějovice). She died on 03 Oct 1902 in Chocnějovice.

35 ii. **Miloslav Rechcigl** was born on 13 May 1904 in Kocňovice (renamed Chocnějovice) No. 22. He married Marie Rajtrová on 26 Jul 1926 in Praha - Kralovske Vinohrady. He died on 27 May 1973 in Washington, DC.

iii. **Anna Rechcíglová** was born on 10 Feb 1906 in Kocňovice (renamed Chocnějovice) No. 22. She died on 26 Feb 1927 in Chocnějovice.

Marie Anna Ferklová daughter of František Ferkl and Anna Saralova was born on 10 Dec 1897 in Chocnějovice No. 2. She died on 31 Dec 1970 in Šárovcova Lhota.

Adolf Rechcigl and Marie Anna Ferklová were married on 25 Apr 1917 in St. Alois Church, Praha. They had the following children:

35. i. **Stanislav Josef Rechcigl** was born on 10 Oct 1918 in Chocnějovice. He married Libuše Sedláčková on 17 Jan 1948 in Novy Bydzov. He died on 09 May 1973 in Šárovcova Lhota No. 16.

ii. **Adolf Rechcigl** was born on 09 Apr 1920 in Chocnějovice No. 22. He died on 27 Dec 1944 in Ples.

21. **Zdeněk Petr Rechcigl**-6 (Petr-5, Petr-4, Ing. František-3, František-2, Ludvik-1) was born on 31 Jul 1884 in Letařovice No. 4, Turnov Dist.. He died on 08 Feb 1962 in Karlovy Vary - Rybare.

Anna Šimůnková daughter of Josef Šimůnek and Marie Stejskalová was born on 31 Dec 1884 in Sezemice No. 1, Mnichovo Hradiště Co.. She died on 28 Nov 1907 in After prolonged illnessa.

Zdeněk Petr Rechcigl and Anna Šimůnková were married on 08 Oct 1906 in Kralovske Vinohrady. They had the following children:

36. i. **Božena Rechcíglová** was born on 18 Mar 1907 in Letařovice, Turnov Co.. She married František Křikava on 24 Jul 1926 in Horovice. She died on 11 Aug 1979 in Hospital, Horovice.

Marie Paulu daughter of Paulu was born before 1900. She died in Divorced February 17, 1926.

Zdeněk Petr Rechcigl and Marie Paulu were married on 26 Sep 1908 in Český Dub. They had the following children:

i. **child Rechcigl**. He died in Soon after birth.

ii. **Zdeněk Rechcigl** was born on 06 Jul 1909. He died on 12 Oct 1909.

Marie Reslová daughter of Antonín Resl and Marie Kovářová was born on 25 Mar 1900 in Roven Nio. 45. She died on 02 Dec 1982 in Karlovy Vary.

Zdeněk Petr Rechcigl and Marie Reslová were married on 30 Apr 1926 in Roven. They had the following children:

37. i. **Zdena Rechcíglová** was born on 25 Sep 1926 in Komarov u Horovic. She married Jan Mueller in 1949. She died on 02 Sep 1978 in Karlovy Vary.

Marie - uncertain was born on 11 Jan 1909. She died on 02 Nov 1996. Zdeněk Petr Rechcigl and Marie - uncertain met. They had the following children:

i. **Ludmila Rechcíglová** was born after 1900.

1 **Bohumil Rechcigl**-6 (Petr-5, Petr-4, Ing. František-3, František-2, Ludvik-1) was born on 09 Apr 1888. He died on 03 Jan 1963 in Český Dub. **Růžena Slukova** was born in 1892. She died on 14 Mar 1969 in Český Dub. Bohumil Rechcigl and Růžena Slukova married. They had the following children:

15. i. **Zdeněk Rechcigl** was born on 05 Dec 1913. He married Marie Pavlová on 29 Jan 1944. He died on 01 Nov 1985.

vii. **Věra Rechcíglová** was born in 1915. She died in 1972.

Notes for Věra Rechcíglová:

General Notes:

unmarried

39. iii. **Libuše Rechcíglová** was born on 13 Aug 1916. She married Jan Mančík on 03 Jun 1950. She died in Mar 1997 in Varnsdorf.

23. **Josef Ullrich**-6 (Františka-5, Petr-4, Ing. František-3, František-2, Ludvik-1) was born in Jilove.

19. **Emilie Rechcíglová** daughter of Petr Rechziegel and Anna Najmanová was born on 02 Apr 1871 in Letařovice No. 4, Český Dub Co.. She died on 18 Feb 1928.

Josef Ullrich and Emilie Rechcíglová married. They had the following children:
- i. **Miloslav Ulrich** was born before 1900.
- ii. **Ludvika Ulrichova** was born in 1898. She died on 01 Jun 1945.

24. **Marie Rechziegelová**-6 (Václav-5, Petr-4, Ing. František-3, František-2, Ludvik-1) was born in 1882 in Radostín. She died on 30 Jul 1959 in Radostín.

    Josef Pelech was born in 1885. He died on 09 Feb 1961.

    Josef Pelech and Marie Rechziegelová married. They had the following children:
    - 40. i. **Marie Pelechová**. She died on 09 Aug 1961.

25. **Anna Rechziegelová**-6 (Václav-5, Petr-4, Ing. František-3, František-2, Ludvik-1) was born on 26 Sep 1888 in Radostín. She died on 10 Oct 1964 in Kacanovy.

    Josef Franců was born on 09 Apr 1894 in Kacanovy. He died on 22 Nov 1971 in Turnov.

    Josef Franců and Anna Rechziegelová were married about 1925. They had the following children:
    - 41. i. **Jaromír Franců** was born on 26 Feb 1926 in Kacanovy. He married Marta Lamačová on 4 Nov 1950 in Turnov. He died on 04 Jul 1980 in Jičín.

    Josef Studnička was born in Kacanovy. He died before 1925.

    Notes for Josef Studnička:
    General Notes:
    He went to the Russian Front during the World War I but never returned.

    Josef Studnička and Anna Rechziegelová married. They had the following children:
    - 42. i. **Oldrřch Studnička** was born on 07 Jun 1912 in Kacanovy. He died on 20 Aug 1942 in Kacanovy.

26. **Anastazie Rechziegelová**-6 (Václav-5, Petr-4, Ing. František-3, František-2, Ludvik-1) was born on 17 Mar 1894 in Radostín. She died on 19 Apr 1984 in Srch.

Rudolf Roubíček son of František Roubíček and Marie Roubíčková was born about 1894 in Radostín. He died about Mar 1918.

Rudolf Roubíček and Anastazie Rechziegelová were married in Jul 1917. They had the following children:

43. i. **Jana Roubíčková** was born on 26 Jan 1918 in Radostín. She married Franisek Kvapil on 11 Sep 1943 in Kunetice. She died on 13 Oct 1981 in Lazne Bohdanec.

František Pátek was born in 1894 in Chlum u Hlinska. He died on 05 Feb 1958 in Srchrechziegel.

František Pátek and Anastazie Rechziegelová met. They had the following children:

44. i. **Dalibor Rechziegel** was born on 20 Oct 1924 in Radostín, near Turnov. He married Sona Pražáková on 26 Apr 1948 in Kladno. He died on 12 Aug 1997 in Litomerice.

45. ii. **Drahomir Rechziegel** was born on 19 Nov 1926. He died on 23 Oct 1983.

27. **Marie Rechcíglová**-6 (Josef-5, Petr-4, Ing. František-3, František-2, Ludvik-1) was born on 11 Mar 1892 in Žďárek No. 26, Turnov Co.. She died on 07 Jul 1968 in Havlickuv Brod.

Augustin Veselý son of František Veselý and Anna Helena Pflanzerová was born on 17 Sep 1879 in Blatna. He died on 06 Oct 1947 in Česká Trebova.

Augustin Veselý and Marie Rechcíglová were married on 25 Oct 1919 in Král. Vinohrady, Prague. They had the following children:

46. i. **Věra Veselá** was born on 02 Aug 1920 in Česká Trebova No. 50, Litomysl Co.. She married Arnošt Pellant on 27 Dec 1939 in U sv. Tomase, Brno.

28. **Josef Rechcigl**-6 (Josef-5, Petr-4, Ing. František-3, František-2, Ludvik-1) was born on 05 Apr 1893 in Žďárek u Turnova. He died on 13 Jun 1933 in Praha.

Marie Studničná daughter of Josef Studničný and Otilie Menzelova was born on 09 Feb 1907 in Nova Ves u Bakova nad Jizerou. She died on 20 Dec 1985 in Mala Bela.

Josef Rechcigl and Marie Studničná were married on 28 Nov 1926 in Prague, CSR. They had the following children:

 47. i. **Josef Rechcigl** was born on 19 Feb 1931 in Praha. He married Jitka Prskavcová on 24 Mar 1956 in Praha II.

29. **Anna Rechcíglová**-6 (Josef-5, Petr-4, Ing. František-3, František-2, Ludvik-1) was born on 12 Jan 1902 in Žďárek. She died on 15 Apr 1992 in Brno.

Karel Matějů was born on 01 May 1901 in Prague. He died in May 1945. Karel Matějů and Anna Rechcíglová were married in 1919 in Prague, CSR. They had the following children:

 48. i. **2nd Karel Matějů** was born on 06 Dec 1924 in Brno. He married Anna Třísková on 09 Jun 1951 in Brno. He died on 09 Dec 1992 in Brno.

Miloš Valnicek son of Miloš Valnicek and Emilie Lehka was born in 1902. He died on 14 Oct 1968. Miloš Valnicek and Anna Rechcíglová were married in 1951 in Petrov, Brno. They had no children.

30. **Alois Jan Vela**-6 (Anna-5, Antonín-4, Ing. František-3, František-2, Ludvik-1) was born on 14 May 1888 in Slavíkov No. 3. He died on 07 Oct 1974 in Turnov.

Marie Vysatova was born on 14 May 1895 in Praha. She died on 27 Jan 1971 in Turnov.

Alois Jan Vela and Marie Vysatova were married on 12 Sep 1916 in Vlastibořice. They had the following children:

  i. **Bohumir Vela** was born on 06 Jul 1917 in Sychrov. He married Vlasta Pechanová on 08 May 1956.

 50. ii. **Vladimír Vela** was born on 13 Jul 1922 in Sychrov. He married Alena Vlahova on 22 Jan 1949.

31. **Marie Jirova**-6 (Josefa-5, Antonín-4, Ing. František-3, František-2, Ludvik-1) was born in 1893. She died on 01 Dec 1959.

Josef Jisl was born in 1887 in Trávníček. He died on 12 Feb 1951. Josef Jisl and Marie Jirova married. They had the following children:

 50. i. **Josef Jisl** was born on 02 Dec 1916. He died on 01 May 1991.

32. **Ing. František Rechcigel**-6 (Karel Bor.-5, Antonín-4, Ing. František-3, František-2, Ludvik-1) was born on 18 Nov 1896 in Chvalčovice. He died on 28 Aug 1968 in Český Dub.

    Marie Holajova daughter of Josef Holaj and Marie Hauzrova was born on 18 May 1904 in Český Dub. She died on 27 Nov 1968 in III (Český Dub, No. 31).

    Ing. František Rechcigel and Marie Holajova were married on 12 Nov 1924 in Prague, CSR. They had the following children:

    51. i. **Milan Rechcigel** was born on 12 Sep 1926 in Český Dub. He married Božena Bernardová on 24 Jan 1953. He died on 24 Sep 1980 in Český Dub.
    52. ii. **Ing. Vladko Rechcigel** was born on 29 Aug 1929 in Český Dub. He married Lidmila Lukaskova on 19 Oct 1957.
    53. iii. **Milena Rechcigelova** was born on 10 Mar 1936 in Turnov. She died on 03 May 1983 in Praha.

33. **Josef Šifta**-6 (Marie-5, Josefa-4, Ing. František-3, František-2, Ludvik-1) was born in 1898 in Jivina No. 1. He died in 1953.

    Marie Řepková was born in 1897 in Pacerice. She died in 1985.

    Josef Šifta and Marie Řepková married. They had the following children:

    54. i. **Marie Šiftová** was born on 20 Jun 1923 in Jivina No. 1. She died on 10 Jun 2004.

Generation 7

34. **Miloslav Rechcigl**-7 (Adolf-6, Petr-5, Petr-4, Ing. František-3, František-2, Ludvik-1) was born on 13 May 1904 in Kocňovice (renamed Chocnějovice) No. 22. He died on 27 May 1973 in Washington, DC.

    Marie Rajtrová daughter of Čeněk Rajtr and Marie Dandová was born on 05 Jul 1905 in Dolanky No. 7, Mnichovo Hradiště Co.. She died on 13 Apr 1982 in Mladá Boleslav.

    Miloslav Rechcigl and Marie Rajtrová were married on 26 Jul 1926 in Praha - Kralovske Vinohrady. They had the following children:

    55. i. **Mila (Miloslav) Rechcigl Jr.** was born on 30 Jul 1930 in Mladá Boleslav, CSR. He married Eva Edwards (Eisnerová) on 29 Aug 1953 in New York, NY.

56. ii. **Marta Rechcíglová** was born on 23 May 1933 in Mladá Boleslav. She married František Žďárský on 03 Oct 1953 in Mladá Boleslav. She died on 13 Sep 2018 in Mladá Boleslav.

35. **Stanislav Josef Rechcigl**-7 (Adolf-6, Petr-5, Petr-4, Ing. František-3, František-2, Ludvik-1) was born on 10 Oct 1918 in Chocnějovice. He died on 09 May 1973 in Šárovcova Lhota No. 16.

    Libuše Sedláčková daughter of Bedřich Sedláček and Ludmila was born on 24 Sep 1924 in Staré Smrkovice, Jičín Dist. She died on 03 Apr 2019 in Jičín, Czech.

    Stanislav Josef Rechcigl and Libuše Sedláčková were married on 17 Jan 1948 in Novy Bydzov. They had the following children:

    57. i. **Hana Rechcíglová** was born on 13 Jul 1948 in Novy Bydzov, Hradec Králové Co.. She married Jaroslav Husak on 28 Dec 1968 in Sobotka, Jičín Co..

    58. ii. **Libuše Rechcíglová** was born on 25 Jan 1950 in Novy Bydzov, Hradec Králové Co.. She married Miroslav Vich on 11 Apr 1970 in Ostromer, Jičín Co..

    59. iii. **Stanislav Rechcigl** was born on 24 Mar 1952 in Hořice, Jičín Co.. He married Zdena Pařízková on 24 Mar 1972 in Jičín.

5. **Božena Rechcíglová**-7 (Zdeněk Petr-6, Petr-5, Petr-4, Ing. František-3, František-2, Ludvik-1) was born on 18 Mar 1907 in Letařovice, Turnov Co.. She died on 11 Aug 1979 in Hospital, Horovice.

    František Křikava son of Josef Křikava and Marie Stichová was born on 23 Dec 1890 in Chaloupky, Beroun Co.. He died on 25 Mar 1965 in Komarov u Horovic No. 40.

    František Křikava and Božena Rechcíglová were married on 24 Jul 1926 in Horovice. They had the following children:

    iv. i. **Luděk Křikava** was born on 02 Feb 1927 in Komarov u Horovic No. 40. He died on 23 Sep 1996.

    v. ii. **Sasa Křikava** was born on 02 Dec 1930 in Komarov u Horovic No. 40.

6. **Zdena Rechcíglová**-7 (Zdeněk Petr-6, Petr-5, Petr-4, Ing. František-3, František-2, Ludvik-1) was born on 25 Sep 1926 in Komarov u Horovic. She died on 02 Sep 1978 in Karlovy Vary.

    Jan Mueller son of Jan Karel Mueller and Anna Šašková was born on 05 Feb 1925 in Prague. He died on 01 May 1989 in Karlovy Vary.

    Jan Mueller and Zdena Rechcíglová were married in 1949. They had the following children:

    62. i. **Jana Muellerová** was born on 08 Nov 1952 in Karlovy Vary. She married Jiří Stuchl on 26 Aug 1979 in Manetin, Plzen Sever Co..
    63. ii. **Zdena Muellerová** was born on 01 May 1960 in Karlovy Vary. She married František Petr in 1981 in Karlovy Vary.

38. **Zdeněk Rechcigl**-7 (Bohumil-6, Petr-5, Petr-4, Ing. František-3, František-2, Ludvik-1) was born on 5 Dec 1913. He died on 01 Nov 1985.

    Marie Pavlová was born in Jan 1921 in Vlcetin. She died in Dec 2003.

    Zdeněk Rechcigl and Marie Pavlová were married on 29 Jan 1944. They had the following children:

    64. i. **Radmila Rechcíglová** was born on 29 May 1944. She married Pavel Herák on 14 Sep 1963 in Český Dub.
    65. ii. **Zdeněk Rechcigl** was born on 07 Aug 1946 in Český Dub. He married Věra Vizkova on 30 Dec 1967 in Český Dub.

    Libuše was born on 05 Dec 1917.

    Zdeněk Rechcigl and Libuše were married in 1964. They had no children.

39. **Libuše Rechcíglová**-7 (Bohumil-6, Petr-5, Petr-4, Ing. František-3, František-2, Ludvik-1) was born on 13 Aug 1916. She died in Mar 1997 in Varnsdorf.

    Jan Mančík.

    Jan Mančík and Libuše Rechcíglová were married on 03 Jun 1950. They had the following children:

    66. i. **Jana Mančíková** was born in 1951.
    67. ii. **Irena Mančíková** was born in 1954.

40. **Marie Pelechová**-7 (Marie-6, Václav-5, Petr-4, Ing. František-3, František-2, Ludvik-1). She died on 9 Aug 1961.

    Alois Florián was born resided in Letovice by Brno.

Alois Florián and Marie Pelechová married. They had the following children:
- 68. i. **Marie Floriánová**.
- ii. **Karel Florián**.

41. **Jaromír Franců**-7 (Anna-6, Václav-5, Petr-4, Ing. František-3, František-2, Ludvik-1) was born on 26 Feb 1926 in Kacanovy. He died on 04 Jul 1980 in Jičín.

    Marta Lamačová was born on 06 Jun 1927 in Kacanovy. She died on 04 Nov 1950 in Turnov.

    Jaromír Franců and Marta Lamačová were married on 04 Nov 1950 in Turnov. They had the following children:
    - 69. i. **Jaromír Franců** was born on 21 Aug 1951 in Kacanovy, Turnov. He married Věra Zimova on 29 Dec 1989 in Jičín.

1   **Oldrřch Studnička**-7 (Anna-6, Václav-5, Petr-4, Ing. František-3, František-2, Ludvik-1) was born on 1 Jun 1912 in Kacanovy. He died on 20 Aug 1942 in Kacanovy.

    Notes for Oldrřch Studnička:
    General Notes:
    He was shot by the Nazi during the persecutine of the underground leader Dr. Vladimír. Krajina.

    Bohumila Karaskova was born on 09 May 1913 in Kacanovy. She died on 25 Sep 2000 in Turnov.

    Oldrřch Studnička and Bohumila Karaskova married. They had the following children:
    - 70. i. **Oldrřch Studnička** was born on 31 May 1942 in Kacanovy.

43. **Jana Roubíčková**-7 (Anastazie-6, Václav-5, Petr-4, Ing. František-3, František-2, Ludvik-1) was born on 26 Jan 1918 in Radostín. She died on 13 Oct 1981 in Lazne Bohdanec.

    Franisek Kvapil was born on 24 Nov 1912. He died on 15 Oct 1982.

    Franisek Kvapil and Jana Roubíčková were married on 11 Sep 1943 in Kunetice. They had the following children:
    - 71. i. **Jan Kvapil** was born on 27 May 1944 in Pardubice. He married Eva Nováková on 09 Jun 1962 in Pardubice.

72. ii. **Nada Kvapilová** was born on 11 Feb 1946 in Pardubice. She married Josef Virt on 13 Mar 1971 in Rohovladova Bela.

44. **Dalibor Rechziegel**-7 (Anastazie-6, Václav-5, Petr-4, Ing. František-3, František-2, Ludvik-1) was born on 20 Oct 1924 in Radostín, near Turnov. He died on 12 Aug 1997 in Litomerice.

    Sona Pražáková was born on 23 Sep 1929 in Brandysek, Kladno Co.. Dalibor Rechziegel and Sona Pražáková were married on 26 Apr 1948 in Kladno. They had the following children:
    - i. **Jan Rechziegel** was born on 12 Oct 1951 in Litomerice.
    - ii. **Luboš Rechziegel** was born on 08 Jan 1957 in Litomerice. He married Radka Chládková on 06 Jul 1985 in Litomerice.

45. **Drahomir Rechziegel**-7 (Anastazie-6, Václav-5, Petr-4, Ing. František-3, František-2, Ludvik-1) was born on 19 Nov 1926. He died on 23 Oct 1983.

    Marie Kamenicka was born on 01 Jan 1929 in Kunetice. She died on 18 Apr 1979. Drahomir Rechziegel and Marie Kamenicka married. They had the following children:

    73. i. **Jitka Rechziegelová** was born on 27 Aug 1951.
    74. ii. **Aleš Rechziegel** was born on 15 Jan 1954.
    75. iii. **Drahomir Rechziegel** was born on 10 Feb 1957 in Pardubice.

46. **Věra Veselá**-7 (Marie-6, Josef-5, Petr-4, Ing. František-3, František-2, Ludvik-1) was born on 02 Aug 1920 in Česká Trebova No. 50, Litomysl Co..

    Arnošt Pellant son of Ota Pellant and Antonie Kudlatschkova was born on 11 May 1912 in Okrisky, P.O. Jihlava. He died on 06 Feb 2005 in Hradec Králové.

    Arnošt Pellant and Věra Veselá were married on 27 Dec 1939 in U sv. Tomase, Brno. They had the following children:

    76. i. **Arnošt Pellant** was born on 12 Jun 1943 in Praha. He married Zinaida Poliscukova on 07 Mar 1970 in Praha.
    77. ii. **Karel Pellant** was born on 14 Mar 1946 in Caslav. He married Jitka Kralickova on 01 Aug 1970 in Jevisovice.

47. **Josef Rechcigl**-7 (Josef-6, Josef-5, Petr-4, Ing. František-3, František-2, Ludvik-1) was born on 19 Feb 1931 in Praha.
    Jitka Prskavcová daughter of Josef Prskavec and Anastazie Studničná was born on 02 Feb 1932 in Ptyrov.
    Josef Rechcigl and Jitka Prskavcová were married on 24 Mar 1956 in Praha II. They had the following children:
    78. i. **Jitka Rechcíglová** was born on 09 Oct 1957 in Mladá Boleslav. She married Vladimír Skramusky on 11 Aug 1979 in Bakov nad Jizerou.
    79. ii. **Josef Rechcigl** was born on 03 Mar 1960 in Turnov. He married Věra Laskova on 17 Apr 1987 in Bakov nad Jizerou.
48. **2nd Karel Matějů**-7 (Anna-6, Josef-5, Petr-4, Ing. František-3, František-2, Ludvik-1) was born on 06 Dec 1924 in Brno. He died on 09 Dec 1992 in Brno.
    Anna Třísková daughter of Jindřich Tříska and Anna was born on 26 Jul 1925 in Blansko.
    2nd Karel Matějů and Anna Třísková were married on 09 Jun 1951 in Brno. They had the following children:
    80. i. **3rd Karel Matějů** was born on 15 Nov 1954 in Brno. He married Alena Šrámková on 07 Jul 1979 in Brno.
49. **Vladimír Vela**-7 (Alois Jan-6, Anna-5, Antonín-4, Ing. František-3, František-2, Ludvik-1) was born on 13 Jul 1922 in Sychrov.
    Alena Vlahova was born on 03 Apr 1928. She died on 26 May 1982.
    Vladimír Vela and Alena Vlahova were married on 22 Jan 1949. They had the following children:
    81. i. **Alena Velova** was born on 05 Jan 1951 in Turnov. She married Ladislav Vodhanel on 12 Jul 1972.
    82. ii. **Vladimír Vela** was born on 17 Dec 1954. He married Raduse Dvořáková on 07 Dec 1979.
50. **Josef Jisl**-7 (Marie-6, Josefa-5, Antonín-4, Ing. František-3, František-2, Ludvik-1) was born on 02 Dec 1916. He died on 01 May 1991.
    Marie Pelantová was born on 21 Apr 1916.
    Josef Jisl and Marie Pelantová married. They had the following children:
    83. i. **Marie Jislova** was born on 28 Jul 1947.

51. **Milan Rechcigel**-7 (Ing. František-6, Karel Bor.-5, Antonín-4, Ing. František-3, František-2, Ludvik-1) was born on 12 Sep 1926 in Český Dub. He died on 24 Sep 1980 in Český Dub.
Božena Bernardová daughter of Ladislav Bernard and Bozena Kupcova was born on 04 Jun 1930 in Podrby - Mala Libic.
Milan Rechcigel and Božena Bernardová were married on 24 Jan 1953. They had the following children:
    84. i. **Hana Rechcigelova** was born on 01 Nov 1953 in Český Dub. She died on 27 Jul 2021.
    85. ii. **Ing. Pavel Rechcigel** was born on 19 Jul 1963 in Český Dub.
52. **Ing. Vladko Rechcigel**-7 (Ing. František-6, Karel Bor.-5, Antonín-4, Ing. František-3, František-2, Ludvik-1) was born on 29 Aug 1929 in Český Dub.
Lidmila Lukaskova was born on 28 Mar 1932 in Vresna, nr. Veseli nad Luznici.
Ing. Vladko Rechcigel and Lidmila Lukaskova were married on 19 Oct 1957. They had the following children:
    86. i. **Vladko Rechcigel** was born on 04 Aug 1959 in Prague, CSR.
    87. ii. **Ing. Jan Rechcigel** was born on 02 Feb 1966 in Prague, CSR.
53. **Milena Rechcigelova**-7 (Ing. František-6, Karel Bor.-5, Antonín-4, Ing. František-3, František-2, Ludvik-1) was born on 10 Mar 1936 in Turnov. She died on 03 May 1983 in Praha.
Jiří Nožička was born in 1926.
Jiří Nožička and Milena Rechcigelova married. They had the following children:
    i. **Jiří Nožička** was born on 05 May 1961.
54. **Marie Šiftová**-7 (Josef-6, Marie-5, Josefa-4, Ing. František-3, František-2, Ludvik-1) was born on 20 Jun 1923 in Jivina No. 1. She died on 10 Jun 2004.
Miroslav Třešňák was born on 06 Mar 1921 in Jenisovice -. He died on 11 Jul 1986 in Lived in Jivina No. 1.
Miroslav Třešňák and Marie Šiftová married. They had the following children:

88. i. **Miroslav Třešňák** was born on 25 May 1943 in Jivina No. 1. He married Miluška Hanzlova on 23 Oct 1965. He died on 19 Nov 2005 in moved to Jivina No. 24.
89. ii. **Jiří Třešňák** was born on 22 Jul 1952 in Jivina No. 1. He married Marie Zoubková on 19 Jun 1976. He died in moved to Odolena Voda, Praha vychod.

Generation 8

55. **Mila (Miloslav) Rechcigl Jr.**-8 (Miloslav-7, Adolf-6, Petr-5, Petr-4, Ing. František-3, František-2, Ludvik-1) was born on 30 Jul 1930 in Mladá Boleslav, CSR.
    Eva Edwards (Eisnerová) daughter of Paul J. Edwards (Pavel Eisner) and Jiřina Taussigová was born on 21 Jan 1932 in Prague, CSR.
    Mila (Miloslav) Rechcigl Jr. and Eva Edwards (Eisnerová) were married on 29 Aug 1953 in New York, NY. They had the following children:
    90. i. **John Edward Rechcigl** was born on 27 Feb 1960 in Washington, D.C.. He married Nancy Ann Palko on 30 Jul 1983 in Dover, NJ.
    91. ii. **Karen Rechcigl** was born on 16 Apr 1962 in Washington, DC. She married Ulysses Kollecas on 25 Aug 1990 in Bethesda, MD.
56. **Marta Rechcíglová**-8 (Miloslav-7, Adolf-6, Petr-5, Petr-4, Ing. František-3, František-2, Ludvik-1) was born on 23 May 1933 in Mladá Boleslav. She died on 13 Sep 2018 in Mladá Boleslav.
    František Žďárský son of František Václav Žďárský and Eliška Foltýnová was born on 21 May 1932 in Turnov.
    František Žďárský and Marta Rechcíglová were married on 03 Oct 1953 in Mladá Boleslav. They had the following children:
    92. i. **Marcela Žďárská** was born on 09 May 1954 in Liberec. She married Miroslav Heralecký on 15 Mar 1975 in Sychrov.
    93. ii. **Iveta Žďárská** was born on 29 Aug 1963 in Liberec, Bohemia. She married Vlastimil Berkman on 29 Oct 1983.
57. **Hana Rechcíglová**-8 (Stanislav Josef-7, Adolf-6, Petr-5, Petr-4, Ing. František-3, František-2, Ludvik-1) was born on 13 Jul 1948 in Novy Bydzov, Hradec Králové Co..
    Jaroslav Husak was born on 24 Mar 1946 in Jičín.

Jaroslav Husak and Hana Rechcíglová were married on 28 Dec 1968 in Sobotka, Jičín Co.. They had the following children:
    i. **Martin Husak** was born on 20 Feb 1971 in Hradec Králové. He married Petra Endrychová on 24 Jul 1999 in Hradec Králové.
    ii. **Petra Husakova** was born on 30 Mar 1974 in Hradec Králové.

Tomáš Petříček was born on 18 Dec 1948 in Hradec Králové.
Tomáš Petříček and Hana Rechcíglová were married on 20 Sep 1991 in Hradec Králové. They had no children.

58. **Libuše Rechcíglová**-8 (Stanislav Josef-7, Adolf-6, Petr-5, Petr-4, Ing. František-3, František-2, Ludvik-1) was born on 25 Jan 1950 in Novy Bydzov, Hradec Králové Co..

Miroslav Vich was born on 13 Nov 1950 in Nova Paka, Jičín Co..
Miroslav Vich and Libuše Rechcíglová were married on 11 Apr 1970 in Ostromer, Jičín Co.. They had the following children:

94. i. **Iveta Vichova** was born on 15 Jan 1972 in Jičín. She married Miloš Haltuf on 07 Sep 1991 in Lazne Belohrad, Jičín Co..
    ii. **Miroslav Vich** was born on 10 Mar 1973 in Jičín.
    iii. **Sarka Vichova** was born on 11 Mar 1989 in Hradec Králové.

59. **Stanislav Rechcigl**-8 (Stanislav Josef-7, Adolf-6, Petr-5, Petr-4, Ing. František-3, František-2, Ludvik-1) was born on 24 Mar 1952 in Hořice, Jičín Co..

Zdena Pařízková daughter of Mila Parik and Zdenka was born on 26 Jan 1954 in Hořice, Jičín Dist., Bohemia.
Stanislav Rechcigl and Zdena Pařízková were married on 24 Mar 1972 in Jičín. They had the following children:

95. i. **Stanislava Rechcíglová** was born on 22 Sep 1972 in Hořice, Jičín Dist., Bohemia.
96. ii. **Jana Rechcíglová** was born on 22 Sep 1973 in Hořice, Jičín Co.. She married Karel Spidlen on 29 Apr 1995 in Jičín, Bohemia.
97. iii. **Stanislav Rechcigl** was born on 08 Aug 1975 in Hořice, Jičín Dist., Bohemia. He married Natasha Blackbourn on 19 Jul 2008 in Spalding, Lincolnshire, UK..

Helena Denisova was born on 29 Jun 1944.

Stanislav Rechcigl and Helena Denisova met. They had no children.
60. **Luděk Křikava**-8 (Božena-7, Zdeněk Petr-6, Petr-5, Petr-4, Ing. František-3, František-2, Ludvik-1) was born on 02 Feb 1927 in Komarov u Horovic No. 40. He died on 23 Sep 1996.

Zdenka Krizova was born on 24 Sep 1941 in Komarov u Horovic No. 72. Luděk Křikava and Zdenka Krizova married. They had the following children:

    98. i. **Věra Křikavová** was born on 28 Apr 1966 in Komarov u Horovic No. 40.

    99. ii. **Hanna Křikavová** was born on 07 May 1957 in Komarov u Horovic No. 40. She died on 30 Dec 1997.

    100. iii. **Jan Křikava** was born on 19 Aug 1960 in Komarov u Horovic No. 40.

61. **Sasa Křikava**-8 (Božena-7, Zdeněk Petr-6, Petr-5, Petr-4, Ing. František-3, František-2, Ludvik-1) was born on 02 Dec 1930 in Komarov u Horovic No. 40.

Milada Toclova was born on 24 Jul 1927.

Sasa Křikava and Milada Toclova married. They had the following children:

    i. **Alexander Křikava** was born in 1951 in Komarov u Horovic.

    101. ii. **Hana Křikavová** was born in 1958 in Komarov u Horovic.

62. **Jana Muellerová**-8 (Zdena-7, Zdeněk Petr-6, Petr-5, Petr-4, Ing. František-3, František-2, Ludvik-1) was born on 08 Nov 1952 in Karlovy Vary.

Jiří Stuchl son of Josef Stuchl and Jarmila Šimáňová was born on 14 Nov 1950 in Plzen. He died on 26 Mar 2001 in Praha 10.

Jiří Stuchl and Jana Muellerová were married on 26 Aug 1979 in Manetin, Plzen Sever Co.. They had the following children:

    i. **Lenka Stuchlová** was born on 12 May 1979 in Karlovy Vary. She married Josef Bic on 07 Jul 2007 in Liberec.

    ii. **Jan Stuchl** was born on 24 Feb 1981 in Karlovy Vary.

63. **Zdena Muellerová**-8 (Zdena-7, Zdeněk Petr-6, Petr-5, Petr-4, Ing. František-3, František-2, Ludvik-1) was born on 01 May 1960 in Karlovy Vary.
    František Petr was born on 05 Sep 1958 in Sokolov.
    František Petr and Zdena Muellerová were married in 1981 in Karlovy Vary. They had the following children:
        i. **Miroslav Petr** was born on 30 Oct 1981 in Karlovy Vary.
    103. ii. **Jana Petrová** was born on 29 Jun 1984 in Karlovy Vary.
64. **Radmila Rechcíglová**-8 (Zdeněk-7, Bohumil-6, Petr-5, Petr-4, Ing. František-3, František-2, Ludvik-1) was born on 29 May 1944.
    Pavel Herák was born on 03 Jun 1938 in Brestovany, Slovakia.
    Pavel Herák and Radmila Rechcíglová were married on 14 Sep 1963 in Český Dub. They had the following children:
    103. i. **Petr Herák** was born on 03 Jun 1965. He married Tereza Kovářová on 24 Mar 1990 in Český Dub.
    104. ii. **Pavlina Heráková** was born on 29 Jan 1964. She married Milan Podlipský on 11 Feb 1984 in Milevsko.
    105. iii. **Helena Heráková** was born on 12 Jul 1966. She married Pavel Hudec on 15 Sep 1984 in Český Dub.
65. **Zdeněk Rechcigl**-8 (Zdeněk-7, Bohumil-6, Petr-5, Petr-4, Ing. František-3, František-2, Ludvik-1) was born on 07 Aug 1946 in Český Dub.
    Věra Vizkova was born on 31 Dec 1947 in Hodkovice.
    Zdeněk Rechcigl and Věra Vizkova were married on 30 Dec 1967 in Český Dub. They had the following children:
    106. i. **Martin Rechcigl** was born on 16 Dec 1968. He married Petra Smolakova on 17 Sep 1994 in Český Dub.
66. **Jana Mančíková**-8 (Libuše-7, Bohumil-6, Petr-5, Petr-4, Ing. František-3, František-2, Ludvik-1) was born in 1951.
    Jan Cicka.
    Jan Cicka and Jana Mančíková married. They had the following children:
        i. **Drahomira Cicková** was born in 1971.
    Vladimír Ulver.

Vladimír Ulver and Jana Mančíková married. They had the following children:
    i.   **Jitka Ulverova** was born in 1980.

67. **Irena Mančíková**-8 (Libuše-7, Bohumil-6, Petr-5, Petr-4, Ing. František-3, František-2, Ludvik-1) was born in 1954.
Petr Synek.
Petr Synek and Irena Mančíková married. They had the following children:
    i.   **Veronika Synková** was born on 07 Mar 1979.
    ii. **Jan Synek** was born on 24 May 1980.

68. **Marie Floriánová**-8 (Marie-7, Marie-6, Václav-5, Petr-4, Ing. František-3, František-2, Ludvik-1).
Josef Tomeš was born in Stranov.
Josef Tomeš and Marie Floriánová married. They had the following children:
    i.   **Tomsová-daughter.**
    ii. **son Tomeš.**

69. **Jaromír Franců**-8 (Jaromír-7, Anna-6, Václav-5, Petr-4, Ing. František-3, František-2, Ludvik-1) was born on 21 Aug 1951 in Kacanovy, Turnov.
Věra Zimova was born on 21 Jan 1956 in Turnov.
Jaromír Franců and Věra Zimova were married on 29 Dec 1989 in Jičín. They had the following children:
    i.   **Adam Franců** was born on 12 Jul 1990.
    ii. **Jan Franců** was born on 26 Jul 1993.

70. **Oldrřch Studnička**-8 (Oldrřch-7, Anna-6, Václav-5, Petr-4, Ing. František-3, František-2, Ludvik-1) was born on 31 May 1942 in Kacanovy.
Marie Nováková was born on 06 May 1952 in Vsen, Turnov.
Oldrřch Studnička and Marie Nováková married. They had the following children:
    i.   **Lucie Studničková** was born on 15 Aug 1975 in Praha.

71. **Jan Kvapil**-8 (Jana-7, Anastazie-6, Václav-5, Petr-4, Ing. František-3, František-2, Ludvik-1) was born on 27 May 1944 in Pardubice.
Eva Nováková daughter of Marta Lamacova was born on 21 Dec 1943.

Jan Kvapil and Eva Nováková were married on 09 Jun 1962 in Pardubice. They had the following children:

107. i. **Jan Kvapil** was born on 30 Dec 1963 in Pardubice. He married Iveta Kulichova on 31 Jan 1987 in Lazne Bohdanec.

108. ii. **Jaroslav Kvapil** was born on 26 Feb 1969 in Pardubice. He married Eva Kadlecova on 30 Nov 1991 in Lazne Bohdanec.

109. iii. **Eva Kvapilová** was born on 18 Oct 1973 in Pardubice. He married Tomasz Prcz on 18 May 1996 in Lazne Bohdanec.

110. iv. **Jiri Kvapil** was born on 18 Jan 1980 in Pardubice. He married Zuzana Tomanová on 13 Aug 2005 in Lazne Bohdanec.

72. **Nada Kvapilová**-8 (Jana-7, Anastazie-6, Václav-5, Petr-4, Ing. František-3, František-2, Ludvik-1) was born on 11 Feb 1946 in Pardubice.

    Josef Virt was born on 20 Sep 1933 in Pardubice. He died on 19 Jan 1991. Josef Virt and Nada Kvapilová were married on 13 Mar 1971 in Rohovladova Bela. They had the following children:

    111. i. **Petra Virtova** was born on 17 Aug 1976 in Pardubice. She married Tomáš Tupy on 25 Aug 2000.

73. **Jitka Rechziegelová**-8 (Drahomir-7, Anastazie-6, Václav-5, Petr-4, Ing. František-3, František-2, Ludvik-1) was born on 27 Aug 1951.

    Petr Marek son of Petr Marek and Josefa was born on 16 Jun 1947 in Libec. Petr Marek and Jitka Rechziegelová married. They had the following children:

    i. **Denisa Markova** was born on 28 Aug 1972.

    ii. **Petr Marek** was born on 21 Feb 1975.

74. **Aleš Rechziegel**-8 (Drahomir-7, Anastazie-6, Václav-5, Petr-4, Ing. František-3, František-2, Ludvik-1) was born on 15 Jan 1954.

    Lenka Horčičková daughter of Vladimír Horčička and Unknown was born on 03 Feb 1956. Aleš Rechziegel and Lenka Horčičková married. They had the following children:

    i. **Andrea Rechziegel** was born on 08 Apr 1975.

    ii. **Tomáš Rechziegel** was born on 28 Mar 1979.

75. **Drahomir Rechziegel**-8 (Drahomir-7, Anastazie-6, Václav-5, Petr-4, Ing. František-3, František-2, Ludvik-1) was born on 10 Feb 1957 in Pardubice.
    Alena Rykrova daughter of Jaroslav Rykr and Marie was born in 1965.
    Drahomir Rechziegel and Alena Rykrova married. They had the following children:
    i. **Lukáš Rechziegel** was born on 19 Jan 1985.
76. **Arnošt Pellant**-8 (Věra-7, Marie-6, Josef-5, Petr-4, Ing. František-3, František-2, Ludvik-1) was born on 12 Jun 1943 in Praha.
    Zinaida Poliscukova daughter of Ondřej Poliscuk and Věra Sirova was born on 03 Oct 1943 in Mizoc, Poland; since WWII USSR.
    Arnošt Pellant and Zinaida Poliscukova were married on 07 Mar 1970 in Praha. They had the following children:
    112. i. **Věra Pellantová** was born on 25 Feb 1971 in Hradec Králové. She married Jan Brožík on 24 Aug 2002 in Valdstejn.
    113. ii. **Eva Pellantová** was born on 05 Jul 1974 in Hradec Králové. She married Jan Mejzlik on 9 Jun 2001.
77. **Karel Pellant**-8 (Věra-7, Marie-6, Josef-5, Petr-4, Ing. František-3, František-2, Ludvik-1) was born on 14 Mar 1946 in Caslav.
    Jitka Kralickova was born on 08 Jul 1947 in Ostrava.
    Karel Pellant and Jitka Kralickova were married on 01 Aug 1970 in Jevisovice. They had the following children:
    114. i. **Martina Pellantová** was born on 27 Oct 1971 in Hradec Králové. She married Alan Gernert on 04 Oct 1997 in Jablonec nad Jizetou.
    ii. **Iva Pellantová** was born on 04 Dec 1973 in Brno.
78. **Jitka Rechcíglová**-8 (Josef-7, Josef-6, Josef-5, Petr-4, Ing. František-3, František-2, Ludvik-1) was born on 09 Oct 1957 in Mladá Boleslav.
    Vladimír Skramusky son of Vladimír Skramusky and Miloslava Koutska was born on 15 Jan 1953 in Cista.
    Vladimír Skramusky and Jitka Rechcíglová were married on 11 Aug 1979 in Bakov nad Jizerou. They had the following children:
    i. **Vladimír Skramusky** was born on 17 Jun 1982 in Turnov.

79. **Josef Rechcigl**-8 (Josef-7, Josef-6, Josef-5, Petr-4, Ing. František-3, František-2, Ludvik-1) was born on 03 Mar 1960 in Turnov.
    Věra Laskova daughter of František Laska and Helena Kolocova was born on 05 Oct 1967.
    Josef Rechcigl and Věra Laskova were married on 17 Apr 1987 in Bakov nad Jizerou. They had the following children:
    i. **Zuzana Rechcíglová** was born on 15 Jan 1988 in Mladá Boleslav.
    ii. **Nikola Rechcíglová** was born on 04 Oct 1990 in Mladá Boleslav.
    iii. **Jiří Rechcigl** was born on 06 Oct 1995 in Mladá Boleslav.
80. **3rd Karel Matějů**-8 (2nd Karel-7, Anna-6, Josef-5, Petr-4, Ing. František-3, František-2, Ludvik-1) was born on 15 Nov 1954 in Brno.
    Alena Šrámková daughter of Vit Šrámek and Božena Šrámková was born on 25 Apr 1958 in Brno.
    3rd Karel Matějů and Alena Šrámková were married on 07 Jul 1979 in Brno. They had the following children:
    i. **Lukáš Matějů** was born on 15 Jun 1980 in Brno.
    ii. **Karel Matějů** was born on 06 Oct 1982 in Brno.
    iii. **Martin Matějů** was born on 14 Oct 1992 in Brno.
81. **Alena Velova**-8 (Vladimír-7, Alois Jan-6, Anna-5, Antonín-4, Ing. František-3, František-2, Ludvik-1) was born on 05 Jan 1951 in Turnov.
    Ladislav Vodhanel was born on 29 Dec 1945.
    Ladislav Vodhanel and Alena Velova were married on 12 Jul 1972. They had the following children:
    i. **Miroslava Vodhanelova** was born on 22 Dec 1973 in Turnov.
    Jindřich Novotný.
    Jindřich Novotný and Alena Velova were married on 12 Apr 1976. They had the following children:
    i. **Sarka Novotná** was born on 10 Jun 1977 in Turnov.
82. **Vladimír Vela**-8 (Vladimír-7, Alois Jan-6, Anna-5, Antonín-4, Ing. František-3, František-2, Ludvik-1) was born on 17 Dec 1954.
    Raduse Dvořáková was born on 11 Dec 1959 in Turnov.

Vladimír Vela and Raduse Dvořáková were married on 07 Dec 1979. They had the following children:
   i. **Vladimír Vela** was born on 27 Jul 1980.
   ii. **Jan Vela** was born on 24 Jun 1984.
83. **Marie Jislova**-8 (Josef-7, Marie-6, Josefa-5, Antonín-4, Ing. František-3, František-2, Ludvik-1) was born on 28 Jul 1947.
   Zdeněk Roubíček was born on 23 Jun 1946.
   Zdeněk Roubíček and Marie Jislova married. They had the following children:
   i. **Lada Roubíčková** was born on 30 Dec 1973.
   ii. **Zdeněk Roubíček** was born on 12 Jan 1975.
84. **Hana Rechcigelova**-8 (Milan-7, Ing. František-6, Karel Bor.-5, Antonín-4, Ing. František-3, František-2, Ludvik-1) was born on 01 Nov 1953 in Český Dub. She died on 27 Jul 2021.
   Jiří Maier was born on 21 Mar 1946 in Turnov.
   Jiří Maier and Hana Rechcigelova married. They had the following children:
   i. **Hana Maierova** was born on 03 Mar 1980.
   ii. **Lenka Maierova** was born on 15 Mar 1983.
85. **Ing. Pavel Rechcigel**-8 (Milan-7, Ing. František-6, Karel Bor.-5, Antonín-4, Ing. František-3, František-2, Ludvik-1) was born on 19 Jul 1963 in Český Dub.
   Jana Cadova daughter of Josef Cada and Eva Unknown was born on 18 Apr 1965. Ing. Pavel Rechcigel and Jana Cadova married. They had the following children:
   i. **Jakub Rechcigel** was born on 24 Jul 1990.
86. **Vladko Rechcigel**-8 (Ing. Vladko-7, Ing. František-6, Karel Bor.-5, Antonín-4, Ing. František-3, František-2, Ludvik-1) was born on 04 Aug 1959 in Prague, CSR.
   Eva Vitova was born on 17 May 1958 in Červený Kostelec.
   Vladko Rechcigel and Eva Vitova married. They had the following children:
   i. **Jan Rechcigel** was born on 04 Mar 1988 in Prague, CSR.

ii. **Lukáš Rechcigel** was born on 06 Jun 1990 in Prague, CSR.

87. **Ing. Jan Rechcigel**-8 (Ing. Vladko-7, Ing. František-6, Karel Bor.-5, Antonín-4, Ing. František-3, František-2, Ludvik-1) was born on 02 Feb 1966 in Prague, CSR.

Xenie Wilckova was born on 17 Jan 1968 in Havirov.

Ing. Jan Rechcigel and Xenie Wilckova married. They had the following children:

i. **Tereza Rechciglova** was born on 07 Mar 1994 in Prague, CSR.

ii. **Kristyna Rechciglova** was born on 09 Mar 1998 in Prague, CSR.

88. **Miroslav Třešňák**-8 (Marie-7, Josef-6, Marie-5, Josefa-4, Ing. František-3, František-2, Ludvik-1) was born on 25 May 1943 in Jivina No. 1. He died on 19 Nov 2005 in moved to Jivina No. 24.

Miluška Hanzlova was born on 29 Dec 1944 in Svijany.

Miroslav Třešňák and Miluška Hanzlova were married on 23 Oct 1965. They had the following children:

115. i. **Pavel Třešňák** was born on 25 Feb 1967 in Turnov - moved to Český Dub. He married Radka Černá on 18 Apr 1992.

116. ii. **Luboš Třešňák** was born on 30 Apr 1974 in Turnov - moved to Vrkoslavice. He married Jitka Necaskova on 21 Sep 1996.

89. **Jiří Třešňák**-8 (Marie-7, Josef-6, Marie-5, Josefa-4, Ing. František-3, František-2, Ludvik-1) was born on 22 Jul 1952 in Jivina No. 1. He died in moved to Odolena Voda, Praha vychod.

Marie Zoubková was born on 22 Jun 1956 in Zasada.

Jiří Třešňák and Marie Zoubková were married on 19 Jun 1976. They had the following children:

i. **Lenka Třešňáková** was born on 21 Jan 1978 in Turnov.

ii. **Radka Třešňáková** was born on 30 May 1985 in Brandys nad Labem.

Generation 9

90. **John Edward Rechcigl**-9 (Mila (Miloslav)-8, Miloslav-7, Adolf-6, Petr-5, Petr-4, Ing. František-3, František-2, Ludvik-1) was born on 27 Feb 1960 in Washington, D.C..

Nancy Ann Palko daughter of Joseph Palko and Mary Rishko was born on 26 Sep 1961 in Morristown, NJ.

John Edward Rechcigl and Nancy Ann Palko were married on 30 Jul 1983 in Dover, NJ. They had the following children:
- i. **Gregory John Rechcigl** was born on 19 Dec 1988 in Bradenton, FL.
- 118. ii. **Kevin Thomas Rechcigl** was born on 09 Oct 1991 in Bradenton, FL. He married Jordan Robbins on 12 May 2018 in Jacksonville, FL.
- iii. **Lindsey Nicole Rechcigl** was born on 03 Nov 1994 in Bradenton, FL.

1. **Karen Rechcigl**-9 (Mila (Miloslav)-8, Miloslav-7, Adolf-6, Petr-5, Petr-4, Ing. František-3, František-2, Ludvik-1) was born on 16 Apr 1962 in Washington, DC.

    Ulysses Kollecas son of Christopher Thomas (Kolecas) Collier and Amelia Malatras was born on 20 Mar 1958 in Washington, DC.

    Ulysses Kollecas and Karen Rechcigl were married on 25 Aug 1990 in Bethesda, MD. They had the following children:
    - iii. **Kristin Kollecas** was born on 04 May 1993 in Albuquerque, NM.
    - iv. **Paul Kollecas** was born on 02 Jun 1995 in Albuquerque, NM.

2. **Marcela Žďárská**-9 (Marta-8, Miloslav-7, Adolf-6, Petr-5, Petr-4, Ing. František-3, František-2, Ludvik-1) was born on 09 May 1954 in Liberec.

    Miroslav Heralecký son of Miroslav Heralecký and Marie Bartošová was born on 18 May 1949 in salomonJablonec nad Nisou, Czech.. He died on 20 Feb 2017 in Proseč, Jablonec nad Nisou, Czech..

    Miroslav Heralecký and Marcela Žďárská were married on 15 Mar 1975 in Sychrov. They had the following children:
    - iii. **Vit Heralecký** was born on 16 Jan 1977 in Jablonec nad Nisou. He married Olga Zrubcová on 13 Jul 1996.
3. - ii. **Zuzana Heralecká** was born on 30 Dec 1978 in Jablonec nad Nisou. She married Jaroslav Egrt on 13 Sep 2002 in Jablonec nad Nisou.

3. **Iveta Žďárská**-9 (Marta-8, Miloslav-7, Adolf-6, Petr-5, Petr-4, Ing. František-3, František-2, Ludvik-1) was born on 29 Aug 1963 in Liberec, Bohemia.
   Vlastimil Berkman was born in 1957.
   Vlastimil Berkman and Iveta Žďárská were married on 29 Oct 1983. They had the following children:
   - iii. **Tereza Hriníková** was born on 05 Jun 1984 in Jablonec nad Nisou.

   Jaroslav Hrinik son of Jaroslav Hrinik and Milena Preisslerová was born on 17 Apr 1960.
   Jaroslav Hrinik and Iveta Žďárská were married on 16 Aug 1991 in Zamek Červená Lhota. They had the following children:
   - 1 **Eliška Hriníková** was born on 23 Jun 1992 in Jablonec nad Nisou. She married Jan Ottis on 06 Oct 2018 in Jablonec nad Jizerou, East Bohemia, Czech Republic.

94. **Iveta Vichova**-9 (Libuše-8, Stanislav Josef-7, Adolf-6, Petr-5, Petr-4, Ing. František-3, František-2, Ludvik-1) was born on 15 Jan 1972 in Jičín.
    Miloš Haltuf was born on 03 May 1968 in Chlumec.
    Miloš Haltuf and Iveta Vichova were married on 07 Sep 1991 in Lazne Belohrad, Jičín Co.. They had the following children:
    - i. **Jan Haltuf** was born on 10 Mar 1992 in Hořice, Jičín Co..

95. **Stanislava Rechcíglová**-9 (Stanislav-8, Stanislav Josef-7, Adolf-6, Petr-5, Petr-4, Ing. František-3, František-2, Ludvik-1) was born on 22 Sep 1972 in Hořice, Jičín Dist., Bohemia.
    Josef Bekera was born on 22 Jun 1965.
    Josef Bekera and Stanislava Rechcíglová met. They had the following children:
    - i. **Nikolas Bekera** was born on 23 Sep 2001.
    - ii. **Sebestian Bekera**.
    - iii. **Anastasia Jowefa Bekerová**.

96. **Jana Rechcíglová**-9 (Stanislav-8, Stanislav Josef-7, Adolf-6, Petr-5, Petr-4, Ing. František-3, František-2, Ludvik-1) was born on 22 Sep 1973 in Hořice, Jičín Co..

Karel Spidlen was born on 06 Feb 1972 in Hradec Králové.
Karel Spidlen and Jana Rechcíglová were married on 29 Apr 1995 in Jičín, Bohemia. They had the following children:
    i.   **Karel Spidlen** was born on 15 Oct 1995 in Hořice, Jičín Co..

97. **Stanislav Rechcigl**-9 (Stanislav-8, Stanislav Josef-7, Adolf-6, Petr-5, Petr-4, Ing. František-3, František-2, Ludvik-1) was born on 08 Aug 1975 in Hořice, Jičín Dist., Bohemia.

Natasha Blackbourn.

Stanislav Rechcigl and Natasha Blackbourn were married on 19 Jul 2008 in Spalding, Lincolnshire, UK.. They had the following children:
    i.   **Lily-Grace Rechcíglová** was born on 03 Jul 2011 in Watford, UK.
    ii. **Poppy Sophia Rechcíglová** was born on 13 Oct 2013.

98. **Věra Křikavová**-9 (Luděk-8, Božena-7, Zdeněk Petr-6, Petr-5, Petr-4, Ing. František-3, František-2, Ludvik-1) was born on 28 Apr 1966 in Komarov u Horovic No. 40.

Radek Nešpor was born on 24 Mar 1963 in Horovice.

Radek Nešpor and Věra Křikavová married. They had the following children:
    i.   **David Nešpor** was born on 19 Oct 1987 in Komarov u Horovic No. 40.

99. **Hanna Křikavová**-9 (Luděk-8, Božena-7, Zdeněk Petr-6, Petr-5, Petr-4, Ing. František-3, František-2, Ludvik-1) was born on 07 May 1957 in Komarov u Horovic No. 40. She died on 30 Dec 1997.

Bedřich Mach was born on 13 Feb 1955 in Komarov u Horovic No. 40.

Bedřich Mach and Hanna Křikavová married. They had the following children:
   119. i. **Andrea Machová** was born on 10 Mar 1978 in Komarov u Horovic No. 40.

100. **Jan Křikava**-9 (Luděk-8, Božena-7, Zdeněk Petr-6, Petr-5, Petr-4, Ing. František-3, František-2, Ludvik-1) was born on 19 Aug 1960 in Komarov u Horovic No. 40.

Hana Fedorcaková was born on 05 May 1962 in Kvan near Komarov.

Jan Křikava and Hana Fedorcaková married. They had the following children:
  i. **Jan Křikava** was born on 22 Sep 1983 in Komarov u Horovic No. 40.

Jana Linhartova was born on 14 Feb 1973 in Komarov u Horovic.
Jan Křikava and Jana Linhartova met. They had the following children:
  i. **Johana Křikavová** was born on 27 Nov 2007 in Komarov u Horovic.

101. **Hana Křikavová**-9 (Sasa-8, Božena-7, Zdeněk Petr-6, Petr-5, Petr-4, Ing. František-3, František-2, Ludvik-1) was born in 1958 in Komarov u Horovic.

    Milan Němec was born in 1954 in Komarov u Horovic.
    Milan Němec and Hana Křikavová married. They had the following children:
      i. **Milan Němec** was born in 1978 in Komarov u Horovic.
      ii. **Lubor Němec** was born in 1971 in Komarov u Horovic.

102. **Jana Petrová**-9 (Zdena-8, Zdena-7, Zdeněk Petr-6, Petr-5, Petr-4, Ing. František-3, František-2, Ludvik-1) was born on 29 Jun 1984 in Karlovy Vary.

    Petr Kottnauer.
    Petr Kottnauer and Jana Petrová met. They had the following children:
      i. **Daniel Kottnauer** was born in Karlovy Vary.

103. **Petr Herák**-9 (Radmila-8, Zdeněk-7, Bohumil-6, Petr-5, Petr-4, Ing. František-3, František-2, Ludvik-1) was born on 03 Jun 1965.

    Tereza Kovářová was born on 22 Jul 1973 in Jablonec.
    Petr Herák and Tereza Kovářová were married on 24 Mar 1990 in Český Dub. They had the following children:
      i. **Jan Herák** was born on 11 Sep 1990.
      ii. **Krystyna Heráková** was born on 18 Feb 1997.

104. **Pavlina Heráková**-9 (Radmila-8, Zdeněk-7, Bohumil-6, Petr-5, Petr-4, Ing. František-3, František-2, Ludvik-1) was born on 29 Jan 1964.

    Milan Podlipský was born on 11 Mar 1961.

Milan Podlipský and Pavlina Heráková were married on 11 Feb 1984 in Milevsko. They had the following children:
  i. **Milan Podlipský** was born on 22 Jun 1984.
  ii. **Jakub Podlipský** was born on 19 Mar 1986.

105. **Helena Heráková**-9 (Radmila-8, Zdeněk-7, Bohumil-6, Petr-5, Petr-4, Ing. František-3, František-2, Ludvik-1) was born on 12 Jul 1966.
   Pavel Hudec was born on 01 Jan 1962 in Český Dub.
   Pavel Hudec and Helena Heráková were married on 15 Sep 1984 in Český Dub. They had the following children:
     i. **Kateřina Hudcova** was born on 17 Feb 1985.
     ii. **Martina Hudcova** was born on 12 May 1991.

106. **Martin Rechcigl**-9 (Zdeněk-8, Zdeněk-7, Bohumil-6, Petr-5, Petr-4, Ing. František-3, František-2, Ludvik-1) was born on 16 Dec 1968.
   Petra Smolakova was born on 25 Jan 1973 in Moravia.
   Martin Rechcigl and Petra Smolakova were married on 17 Sep 1994 in Český Dub. They had the following children:
     i. **Lucie Rechcíglová** was born on 05 Apr 1995.
     ii. **David Rechcigl** was born on 08 Aug 2000.

107. **Jan Kvapil**-9 (Jan-8, Jana-7, Anastazie-6, Václav-5, Petr-4, Ing. František-3, František-2, Ludvik-1) was born on 30 Dec 1963 in Pardubice.
   Iveta Kulichova was born on 18 Jan 1969.
   Jan Kvapil and Iveta Kulichova were married on 31 Jan 1987 in Lazne Bohdanec. They had the following children:
     i. **Lucie Kvapilová** was born on 09 Jul 1987 in Pardubice.
     ii. **Pavlina Kvapilová** was born on 05 Sep 1991 in Pardubice.
     iii. **Iveta Kvapilová** was born on 15 Jul 1993 in Pardubice.

108. **Jaroslav Kvapil**-9 (Jan-8, Jana-7, Anastazie-6, Václav-5, Petr-4, Ing. František-3, František-2, Ludvik-1) was born on 26 Feb 1969 in Pardubice.
   Eva Kadlecova was born on 05 Sep 1969.
   Jaroslav Kvapil and Eva Kadlecova were married on 30 Nov 1991 in Lazne Bohdanec. They had the following children:
     i. **Katerina Kvapilová** was born on 21 May 1992 in Pardubice.
     ii. **Monika Kvapilová** was born on 19 Oct 1998 in Pardubice.

iii. **Jakub Kvapil** was born on 05 May 2005 in Pardubice.
109. **Eva Kvapilová**-9 (Jan-8, Jana-7, Anastazie-6, Václav-5, Petr-4, Ing. František-3, František-2, Ludvik-1) was born on 18 Oct 1973 in Pardubice.
Tomasz Prcz was born on 23 May 1970.
Tomasz Prcz and Eva Kvapilová were married on 18 May 1996 in Lazne Bohdanec. They had the following children:
    i. **Martin Prcz** was born on 19 May 1991 in Pardubice.
    ii. **Tomasz Prcz** was born on 05 Oct 1997 in Pardubice.
110. **Jiri Kvapil**-9 (Jan-8, Jana-7, Anastazie-6, Václav-5, Petr-4, Ing. František-3, František-2, Ludvik-1) was born on 18 Jan 1980 in Pardubice.
Zuzana Tomanová was born on 20 Aug 1980.
Jiri Kvapil and Zuzana Tomanová were married on 13 Aug 2005 in Lazne Bohdanec. They had the following children:
    i. **Tereza Kvapilová** was born on 25 Dec 2006 in Pardubice.
    ii. **Jiri Kvapil** was born on 07 Sep 2009 in Pardubice.
111. **Petra Virtova**-9 (Nada-8, Jana-7, Anastazie-6, Václav-5, Petr-4, Ing. František-3, František-2, Ludvik-1) was born on 17 Aug 1976 in Pardubice.
Tomáš Tupy was born on 24 Aug 1975 in Pardubice.
Tomáš Tupy and Petra Virtova were married on 25 Aug 2000. They had the following children:
    i. **Krystyna Tupa** was born on 27 Feb 2001.
    ii. **Aneta Tupa** was born on 21 Apr 2006.
112. **Věra Pellantová**-9 (Arnošt-8, Věra-7, Marie-6, Josef-5, Petr-4, Ing. František-3, František-2, Ludvik-1) was born on 25 Feb 1971 in Hradec Králové.
Jan Brožík son of Jan Brožík and Jarmila Dočkálová was born on 06 Sep 1974 in Kromeriz.
Jan Brožík and Věra Pellantová were married on 24 Aug 2002 in Valdstejn. They had the following children:
    i. **Barbora Brožíková** was born on 05 Dec 2003 in Hradec Králové.

113. **Eva Pellantová**-9 (Arnošt-8, Věra-7, Marie-6, Josef-5, Petr-4, Ing. František-3, František-2, Ludvik-1) was born on 05 Jul 1974 in Hradec Králové.
    Jan Mejzlik son of Josef Mejzlik and Blanka Spustova was born on 13 Mar 1974 in Preckov, Trebic Co..
    Jan Mejzlik and Eva Pellantová were married on 09 Jun 2001. They had the following children:
    i. **Vojtěch Mejzlik** was born on 29 Jan 2003 in Hradec Králové.
    ii. **Antonín Mejzlik** was born on 29 Nov 2006 in Hradec Králové.
114. **Martina Pellantová**-9 (Karel-8, Věra-7, Marie-6, Josef-5, Petr-4, Ing. František-3, František-2, Ludvik-1) was born on 27 Oct 1971 in Hradec Králové.
    Alan Gernert son of Vilém Gernert and Vlasta was born on 26 Mar 1970 in Jilemnice.
    Alan Gernert and Martina Pellantová were married on 04 Oct 1997 in Jablonec nad Jizetou. They had the following children:
    i. **Marek Gernert** was born on 04 Apr 1998.
115. **Pavel Třešňák**-9 (Miroslav-8, Marie-7, Josef-6, Marie-5, Josefa-4, Ing. František-3, František-2, Ludvik-1) was born on 25 Feb 1967 in Turnov - moved to Český Dub.
    Radka Černá was born on 07 Sep 1971 in Česká Lipa.
    Pavel Třešňák and Radka Černá were married on 18 Apr 1992. They had the following children:
    i. **Pavlina Třešňáková** was born on 17 Jun 1999 in Turnov.
116. **Luboš Třešňák**-9 (Miroslav-8, Marie-7, Josef-6, Marie-5, Josefa-4, Ing. František-3, František-2, Ludvik-1) was born on 30 Apr 1974 in Turnov - moved to Vrkoslavice.
    Jitka Necaskova was born on 21 Nov 1969 in Jablonnec nad Nisou.
    Luboš Třešňák and Jitka Necaskova were married on 21 Sep 1996. They had the following children:
    i. **Michaela Třešňáková** was born on 02 Sep 1997 in Jablonec nad Nisou.
    ii. **Matěj Třešňák** was born on 18 May 2001 in Jablonec nad Nisou.

Generation 10

117. **Kevin Thomas Rechcigl**-10 (John Edward-9, Mila (Miloslav)-8, Miloslav-7, Adolf-6, Petr-5, Petr-4, Ing. František-3, František-2, Ludvik-1) was born on 09 Oct 1991 in Bradenton, FL.

    Jordan Robbins daughter of Douglass Robbins and Ivonne was born on 10 Jan 1992 in Camarillo, CA.

    Kevin Thomas Rechcigl and Jordan Robbins were married on 12 May 2018 in Jacksonville, FL. They had the following children:

    i. **James Douglas Rechcigl** was born on 05 Jan 2021 in Jacksonville, FL.

    ii. **Evelyn Marie Rechcigl** was born on 29 May 2023 in Jacksonville, FL.

118. **Zuzana Heralecká**-10 (Marcela-9, Marta-8, Miloslav-7, Adolf-6, Petr-5, Petr-4, Ing. František-3, František-2, Ludvik-1) was born on 30 Dec 1978 in Jablonec nad Nisou.

    Jaroslav Egrt was born on 25 Apr 1974 in Duchcov.

    Jaroslav Egrt and Zuzana Heralecká were married on 13 Sep 2002 in Jablonec nad Nisou. They had the following children:

    i. **Kristina Egrtova** was born on 04 Jan 2008 in Liberec.

    ii. **Jaroslav Egrt** was born on 04 Jan 2008 in Liberec.

119. **Andrea Machová**-10 (Hanna-9, Luděk-8, Božena-7, Zdeněk Petr-6, Petr-5, Petr-4, Ing. František-3, František-2, Ludvik-1) was born on 10 Mar 1978 in Komarov u Horovic No. 40.

    Soeren Christiansen was born in 1975 in Denmark.

    Soeren Christiansen and Andrea Machová met. They had the following children:

    i. **Olivia Machová** was born on 10 May 2007 in Kobenhaven, Denmark.

Bergl Family

Generation 1

1. **Josef Bergl**-1 was born after 1760 in Podhora No. 6.
   Unknown.
   Josef Bergl and Unknown married. They had the following children:
   2. i. **Jan Bergl** was born in 1789 in Podhora No. 6. He married Kateřina Stránská on 05 Apr 1818 in Manikovice[1]. He died on 13 Mar 1825.

Generation 2

2. **Jan Bergl**-2 (Josef-1) was born in 1789 in Podhora No. 6. He died on 13 Mar 1825.
   Kateřina Stránská daughter of Jan Stránský and Anna Honcová was born on 06 Sep 1798 in Manikovice No. 6.
   Jan Bergl and Kateřina Stránská were married on 05 Apr 1818 in Manikovice[1]. They had the following children:
   3. i. **Josef Bergl** was born on 28 Dec 1820 in Podhora No. 16. He died on 20 Oct 1861.

Generation 3

3. **Josef Bergl**-3 (Jan-2, Josef-1) was born on 28 Dec 1820 in Podhora No. 16. He died on 20 Oct 1861.
   Anna Šichtová daughter of Jan Šichta was born on 12 Sep 1824 in Sovinky No. 31.
   Josef Bergl and Anna Šichtová married. They had the following children:

   i. **Josef Bergl** was born on 20 Mar 1848 in Kocňovice No. 16. He died on 18 Apr 1856.

   5. ii. **František Bergl** was born on 08 Sep 1850 in Podhora No. 16. He died on 22 Nov 1921 in Chocnějovice No. 22/39.

   iii. **Jan Bergl** was born on 03 Sep 1854 in Podhora No. 16.

   5. iv. **2nd Josef Bergl** was born about 1860 in Podhora No. 16.

   6. v. **daughter Berglová** was born about 1850 in Podhora No. 16.

Generation 4

4. **František Bergl**-4 (Josef-3, Jan-2, Josef-1) was born on 08 Sep 1850 in Podhora No. 16. He died on 22 Nov 1921 in Chocnějovice No. 22/39.

    Marie Mařanová daughter of Jan Mařan and Kateřina Landová was born on 02 Feb 1860 in Drahotice No. 20. She died on 24 Jun 1924 in Chocnějovice No. 22/39.

    František Bergl and Marie Mařanová married. They had the following children:

    7. i. **Marie Berglová** was born on 27 Mar 1880 in Drahotice No. 20, Mnichovo Hradiště Co.. She married Adolf Rechcigl about 1900. She died on 25 Mar 1917 in Chocnějovice No. 22, Mnichovo Hradiště Co..

5. **2nd Josef Bergl**-4 (Josef-3, Jan-2, Josef-1) was born about 1860 in Podhora No. 16.

    Unknown.

    2nd Josef Bergl and Unknown married. They had the following children:

    i. **3rd Josef Bergl** was born after 1870 in Neveklovice No. 18. He died in killed in war.

    8. ii. **Marie Berglová** was born on 10 Apr 1888 in Neveklovice No. 18.

6. **daughter Berglová**-4 (Josef-3, Jan-2, Josef-1) was born about 1850 in Podhora No. 16.

    Lamač.

    Lamač and daughter Berglová married. They had the following children:

    9. i. **Václav Lamač** was born after 1870.

Generation 5

7. **Marie Berglová**-5 (František-4, Josef-3, Jan-2, Josef-1) was born on 27 Mar 1880 in Drahotice No. 20, Mnichovo Hradiště Co.. She died on 25 Mar 1917 in Chocnějovice No. 22, Mnichovo Hradiště Co..

    Adolf Rechcigl son of Petr Rechziegel and Anna Najmanová was born on 21 Aug 1876 in Letařovice No. 4, Český Dub Co.. He died on 30 Mar 1946 in Šárovcova Lhota No. 16.

    Adolf Rechcigl and Marie Berglová were married about 1900. They had the following children:

BERGL FAMILY

    i. **Marie Rechcíglová** was born on 29 Sep 1901 in Kocňovice (renamed Chocnějovice). She died on 03 Oct 1902 in Chocnějovice.

27 ii. **Miloslav Rechcigl** was born on 13 May 1904 in Kocňovice (renamed Chocnějovice) No. He married Marie Rajtrová on 26 Jul 1926 in Praha - Kralovske Vinohrady. He died on 27 May 1973 in Washington, DC.

    iii. **Anna Rechcíglová** was born on 10 Feb 1906 in Kocňovice (renamed Chocnějovice) No. 22. She died on 26 Feb 1927 in Chocnějovice.

8. **Marie Berglová**-5 (2nd Josef-4, Josef-3, Jan-2, Josef-1) was born on 10 Apr 1888 in Neveklovice No. 18.

Josef Kešner son of Kešner and Unknown was born on 25 Apr 1880 in Neveklovice. He died on 29 Jul 1974 in Neveklovice No. 18.

Josef Kešner and Marie Berglová married. They had the following children:

11. i. **Václav Kešner** was born in 1912 in Neveklovice.

12. ii. **Veroslav Kešner** was born on 21 Apr 1920 in Neveklovice.

9. **Václav Lamač**-5 (daughter-4, Josef-3, Jan-2, Josef-1) was born after 1870.

Václav Lamač and unknown spouse married. They had the following children:

13. i. **Marie Lamačová** was born after 1890 in Podhora.

Generation 6

10. **Miloslav Rechcigl**-6 (Marie-5, František-4, Josef-3, Jan-2, Josef-1) was born on 13 May 1904 in Kocňovice (renamed Chocnějovice) No. 22. He died on 27 May 1973 in Washington, DC.

Marie Rajtrová daughter of Čeněk Rajtr and Marie Dandová was born on 05 Jul 1905 in Dolanky No. 7, Mnichovo Hradiště Co.. She died on 13 Apr 1982 in Mladá Boleslav.

Miloslav Rechcigl and Marie Rajtrová were married on 26 Jul 1926 in Praha - Kralovske Vinohrady. They had the following children:

14. i. **Mila (Miloslav) Rechcigl Jr.** was born on 30 Jul 1930 in Mladá Boleslav, CSR. He married Eva Edwards (Eisnerová) on 29 Aug 1953 in New York, NY.
15. ii. **Marta Rechcíglová** was born on 23 May 1933 in Mladá Boleslav. She married František Žďárský on 03 Oct 1953 in Mladá Boleslav. She died on 13 Sep 2018 in Mladá Boleslav.

11. **Václav Kešner**-6 (Marie-5, 2nd Josef-4, Josef-3, Jan-2, Josef-1) was born in 1912 in Neveklovice.
    Anežka Loudova was born in 1920 in Sezemice.
    Václav Kešner and Anežka Loudova married. They had the following children:
    16. i. **Jiří Kešner**.
    17. ii. **Hana Kešnerová**.

12. **Veroslav Kešner**-6 (Marie-5, 2nd Josef-4, Josef-3, Jan-2, Josef-1) was born on 21 Apr 1920 in Neveklovice.
    Libuše Prylova daughter of Stanislav Pryl was born on 21 Aug 1930 in Solecek No. 1. Veroslav Kešner and Libuše Prylova married. They had the following children:
    18. i. **Stanislav Kešner** was born on 01 Nov 1953 in Turnov.
    19. ii. **Libuše Kešnerová** was born on 20 Dec 1954 in Turnov.

13. **Marie Lamačová**-6 (Václav-5, daughter-4, Josef-3, Jan-2, Josef-1) was born after 1890 in Podhora.
    Jan Šverma son of Jan Šverma and Kateřina Paříková.
    Jan Šverma and Marie Lamačová married. They had the following children:
    20. i. **Jaroslav Šverma** was born on 03 Nov 1917 in Manikovice.
    21. ii. **Ludmila Švermová** was born in 1926. She died about 1996.

Generation 7

14. **Mila (Miloslav) Rechcigl Jr.**-7 (Miloslav-6, Marie-5, František-4, Josef-3, Jan-2, Josef-1) was born on 30 Jul 1930 in Mladá Boleslav, CSR.
    Eva Edwards (Eisnerová) daughter of Paul J. Edwards (Pavel Eisner) and Jiřina Taussigová was born on 21 Jan 1932 in Prague, CSR.

Mila (Miloslav) Rechcigl Jr. and Eva Edwards (Eisnerová) were married on 29 Aug 1953 in New York, NY. They had the following children:

22. i. **John Edward Rechcigl** was born on 27 Feb 1960 in Washington, D.C.. He married Nancy Ann Palko on 30 Jul 1983 in Dover, NJ.

23. ii. **Karen Rechcigl** was born on 16 Apr 1962 in Washington, DC. She married Ulysses Kollecas on 25 Aug 1990 in Bethesda, MD.

15. **Marta Rechcíglová**-7 (Miloslav-6, Marie-5, František-4, Josef-3, Jan-2, Josef-1) was born on 23 May 1933 in Mladá Boleslav. She died on 13 Sep 2018 in Mladá Boleslav.

František Žďárský son of František Václav Žďárský and Eliška Foltýnová was born on 21 May 1932 in Turnov.

František Žďárský and Marta Rechcíglová were married on 03 Oct 1953 in Mladá Boleslav. They had the following children:

24. i. **Marcela Žďárská** was born on 09 May 1954 in Liberec. She married Miroslav Heralecký on 15 Mar 1975 in Sychrov.

25. ii. **Iveta Žďárská** was born on 29 Aug 1963 in Liberec, Bohemia. She married Vlastimil Berkman on 29 Oct 1983.

16. **Jiří Kešner**-7 (Václav-6, Marie-5, 2nd Josef-4, Josef-3, Jan-2, Josef-1). **Věra.**

Jiří Kešner and Věra married. They had the following children:

i. **Monika Kešnerová (adopted).**

17. **Hana Kešnerová**-7 (Václav-6, Marie-5, 2nd Josef-4, Josef-3, Jan-2, Josef-1). **Václav Červa.**

Václav Červa and Hana Kešnerová married. They had the following children:

26. i. **Hana Červová.**

Miloš Makrlik.

Miloš Makrlik and Hana Kešnerová married. They had the following children:

i. **Lenka Makrlikova Makrlik.**

18. **Stanislav Kešner**-7 (Veroslav-6, Marie-5, 2nd Josef-4, Josef-3, Jan-2, Josef-1) was born on 01 Nov 1953 in Turnov.

Miloslava Liblinska was born on 22 Sep 1952 in Liberec.

Stanislav Kešner and Miloslava Liblinska married. They had the following children:
- i. **Vit Kešner** was born on 20 Sep 1981 in Liberec.
- ii. **Tereza Kešnerová** was born on 13 Oct 1982 in Liberec.

19. **Libuše Kešnerová**-7 (Veroslav-6, Marie-5, 2nd Josef-4, Josef-3, Jan-2, Josef-1) was born on 20 Dec 1954 in Turnov.

    Zdeněk Maděra was born on 04 Jul 1954 in Liberec.

    Zdeněk Maděra and Libuše Kešnerová married. They had the following children:
    - i. **Lucie Maděrová** was born on 13 Apr 1979 in Liberec.
    - ii. **Lukáš Maděra** was born on 16 Feb 1983 in Liberec.

20. **Jaroslav Šverma**-7 (Marie-6, Václav-5, daughter-4, Josef-3, Jan-2, Josef-1) was born on 03 Nov 1917 in Manikovice.

    Blažena Novotná was born in Honsov.

    Jaroslav Šverma and Blažena Novotná married. They had the following children:
    - 27. i. **Jaroslav Šverma** was born about 1950.
    - 28. ii. **Jan Šverma** was born about 1948.

21. **Ludmila Švermová**-7 (Marie-6, Václav-5, daughter-4, Josef-3, Jan-2, Josef-1) was born in 1926. She died about 1996.

    Jaromír Štěpánek was born in Bakov nnad Jizerou.

    Jaromír Štěpánek and Ludmila Švermová married. They had the following children:
    - 29. i. **Jaromír Štěpánek**.
    - 30. ii. **Pavel Štěpánek**.

Generation 8

22. **John Edward Rechcigl**-8 (Mila (Miloslav)-7, Miloslav-6, Marie-5, František-4, Josef-3, Jan-2, Josef-1) was born on 27 Feb 1960 in Washington, D.C..

    Nancy Ann Palko daughter of Joseph Palko and Mary Rishko was born on 26 Sep 1961 in Morristown, NJ.

    John Edward Rechcigl and Nancy Ann Palko were married on 30 Jul 1983 in Dover, NJ. They had the following children:

      i. **Gregory John Rechcigl** was born on 19 Dec 1988 in Bradenton, FL.

32. ii. **Kevin Thomas Rechcigl** was born on 09 Oct 1991 in Bradenton, FL. He married Jordan Robbins on 12 May 2018 in Jacksonville, FL.

      iii. **Lindsey Nicole Rechcigl** was born on 03 Nov 1994 in Bradenton, FL.

23. **Karen Rechcigl**-8 (Mila (Miloslav)-7, Miloslav-6, Marie-5, František-4, Josef-3, Jan-2, Josef-1) was born on 16 Apr 1962 in Washington, DC.

Ulysses Kollecas son of Christopher Thomas (Kolecas) Collier and Amelia Malatras was born on 20 Mar 1958 in Washington, DC.

Ulysses Kollecas and Karen Rechcigl were married on 25 Aug 1990 in Bethesda, MD. They had the following children:

      i. **Kristin Kollecas** was born on 04 May 1993 in Albuquerque, NM.

      ii. **Paul Kollecas** was born on 02 Jun 1995 in Albuquerque, NM.

24. **Marcela Žďárská**-8 (Marta-7, Miloslav-6, Marie-5, František-4, Josef-3, Jan-2, Josef-1) was born on 9 May 1954 in Liberec.

Miroslav Heralecký son of Miroslav Heralecký and Marie Bartošová was born on 18 May 1949 in salomonJablonec nad Nisou, Czech.. He died on 20 Feb 2017 in Proseč, Jablonec nad Nisou, Czech..

Miroslav Heralecký and Marcela Žďárská were married on 15 Mar 1975 in Sychrov. They had the following children:

      i. **Vit Heralecký** was born on 16 Jan 1977 in Jablonec nad Nisou. He married Olga Zrubcová on 13 Jul 1996.

33. ii. **Zuzana Heralecká** was born on 30 Dec 1978 in Jablonec nad Nisou. She married Jaroslav Egrt on 13 Sep 2002 in Jablonec nad Nisou.

25. **Iveta Žďárská**-8 (Marta-7, Miloslav-6, Marie-5, František-4, Josef-3, Jan-2, Josef-1) was born on 29 Aug 1963 in Liberec, Bohemia.

Vlastimil Berkman was born in 1957.

Vlastimil Berkman and Iveta Žďárská were married on 29 Oct 1983. They had the following children:

      i. **Tereza Hriníková** was born on 05 Jun 1984 in Jablonec nad Nisou.

Jaroslav Hrinik son of Jaroslav Hrinik and Milena Preisslerová was born on 17 Apr 1960.

Jaroslav Hrinik and Iveta Žďárská were married on 16 Aug 1991 in Zamek Červená Lhota. They had the following children:

    i. **Eliška Hriníková** was born on 23 Jun 1992 in Jablonec nad Nisou. She married Jan Ottis on 06 Oct 2018 in Jablonec nad Jizerou, East Bohemia, Czech Republic.

26. **Hana Červová**-8 (Hana-7, Václav-6, Marie-5, 2nd Josef-4, Josef-3, Jan-2, Josef-1).

Unknown.

Unknown and Hana Červová married. They had the following children:

    i. **Ondřej.**

Unkinown.

Unkinown and Hana Červová married. They had no children.

27. **Jaroslav Šverma**-8 (Jaroslav-7, Marie-6, Václav-5, daughter-4, Josef-3, Jan-2, Josef-1) was born about 1950.

Unknown.

Jaroslav Šverma and Unknown married. They had the following children:

    i. **Robert Šverma** was born about 1977.

    ii. **Jan Šverma** was born about 1980.

    iii. **Otta Šverma** was born about 1990.

28. **Jan Šverma**-8 (Jaroslav-7, Marie-6, Václav-5, daughter-4, Josef-3, Jan-2, Josef-1) was born about 1948.

Unknown.

Jan Šverma and Unknown married. They had the following children:

    i. **son Šverma.**

    ii. **son Šverma.**

29. **Jaromír Štěpánek**-8 (Ludmila-7, Marie-6, Václav-5, daughter-4, Josef-3, Jan-2, Josef-1).

Alenka Vavrova was born in Bakov nad Jizerou.

Jaromír Štěpánek and Alenka Vavrova married. They had the following children:

    i. **Hanička Štěpánková** was born in 1977.

ii.   **Jaromír Štěpánek** was born in 1980.
30. **Pavel Štěpánek**-8 (Ludmila-7, Marie-6, Václav-5, daughter-4, Josef-3, Jan-2, Josef-1).
    Jaruska.
    Pavel Štěpánek and Jaruska married. They had the following children:
    33.   i. **Pavel Štěpánek** was born in 1977.

Generation 9

31. **Kevin Thomas Rechcigl**-9 (John Edward-8, Mila (Miloslav)-7, Miloslav-6, Marie-5, František-4, Josef-3, Jan-2, Josef-1) was born on 09 Oct 1991 in Bradenton, FL.
    Jordan Robbins daughter of Douglass Robbins and Ivonne was born on 10 Jan 1992 in Camarillo, CA.
    Kevin Thomas Rechcigl and Jordan Robbins were married on 12 May 2018 in Jacksonville, FL. They had the following children:
    i.   **James Douglas Rechcigl** was born on 05 Jan 2021 in Jacksonville, FL.
    ii. **Evelyn Marie Rechcigl** was born 29 May 2023 in Jacksonville, FL.
32. **Zuzana Heralecká**-9 (Marcela-8, Marta-7, Miloslav-6, Marie-5, František-4, Josef-3, Jan-2, Josef-1) was born on 30 Dec 1978 in Jablonec nad Nisou.
    Jaroslav Egrt was born on 25 Apr 1974 in Duchcov.
    Jaroslav Egrt and Zuzana Heralecká were married on 13 Sep 2002 in Jablonec nad Nisou. They had the following children:
    i.   **Kristina Egrtova** was born on 04 Jan 2008 in Liberec.
    ii. **Jaroslav Egrt** was born on 04 Jan 2008 in Liberec.
33. **Pavel Štěpánek**-9 (Pavel-8, Ludmila-7, Marie-6, Václav-5, daughter-4, Josef-3, Jan-2, Josef-1) was born in 1977.
    Alžběta was born in 1975.
    Pavel Štěpánek and Alžběta married. They had the following children:
    i.   **Jakub Štěpánek** was born in 2006.

Sources

1 He was 29 and she was 20.

Mařan Family

Generation 1

1. **Jan Mařan**-1 was born in Loukov No. 17.
   Anna Konopkova daughter of Matěj Konopka and Unknown.
   Jan Mařan and Anna Konopkova married. They had the following children:
   2. i. **Jan Mařan** was born in Drahotice No. 20.

Generation 2

2. **Jan Mařan**-2 (Jan-1) was born in Drahotice No. 20.
   Notes for Jan Mařan:
   General Notes:
   cottager, Drahotice
   Kateřina Landová daughter of Jan Landa and Anna Polívková was born about 1840 in Drahotice No. 9.
   Jan Mařan and Kateřina Landová married. They had the following children:
   3. i. **Anna Marie Mařanová** was born on 24 Oct 1855 in Drahotice No. 20.
   4. ii. **Marie Mařanová** was born on 02 Feb 1860 in Drahotice No. 20. She died on 24 Jun 1924 in Chocnějovice No. 22/39.

Generation 3

3. **Anna Marie Mařanová**-3 (Jan-2, Jan-1) was born on 24 Oct 1855 in Drahotice No. 20.
   Václav Jihlavec was born on 20 Jun 1851 in Mukarov.
   Václav Jihlavec and Anna Marie Mařanová married. They had the following children:
   5. i. **Marie Jihlavcová** was born on 20 Jun 1876 in Horni Mohelnice. She died in 1928.
   6. ii. **Anna Jihlavcová** was born on 15 Sep 1882 in Horni Mohelnice.
   iii. **son Jihlavec** was born in Horni Mohelnice. He died in Died.
4. **Marie Mařanová**-3 (Jan-2, Jan-1) was born on 02 Feb 1860 in Drahotice No. 20. She died on 24 Jun 1924 in Chocnějovice No. 22/39.

František Bergl son of Josef Bergl and Anna Šichtová was born on 08 Sep 1850 in Podhora No. 16. He died on 22 Nov 1921 in Chocnějovice No. 22/39.
František Bergl and Marie Mařanová married. They had the following children:
69. i. **Marie Berglová** was born on 27 Mar 1880 in Drahotice No. 20, Mnichovo Hradiště Co.. She married Adolf Rechcigl about 1900. She died on 25 Mar 1917 in Chocnějovice No. 22, Mnichovo Hradiště Co..

Generation 4

5. **Marie Jihlavcová**-4 (Anna Marie-3, Jan-2, Jan-1) was born on 20 Jun 1876 in Horni Mohelnice. She died in 1928.
František Buriánek son of Josef Buriánek and Terezie Bartošová was born on 27 Jul 1869 in Sezemice No. 25. He died in 1944.
František Buriánek and Marie Jihlavcová married. They had the following children:
   i. **Marie Buriánková** was born on 17 Sep 1898 in Sezemice No. 29. She died in 1950.
9. ii. **Josef Buriánek** was born on 05 Feb 1900 in Sezemice No. 29. He died in 1966.
   iii. **František Buriánek** was born on 23 Jan 1902 in Sezemice No. 29. He died in 1936.
9. iv. **Ivo Buriánek**.
6. **Anna Jihlavcová**-4 (Anna Marie-3, Jan-2, Jan-1) was born on 15 Sep 1882 in Horni Mohelnice.
František Dvořák son of Václav Dvořák and Anna Landová was born in 1878 in Malé Podolí. František Dvořák and Anna Jihlavcová married. They had the following children:
   i. **Václav Dvořák** was born in 1905. He died in 1925.
11. ii. **Anna Dvořáková** was born in 1906. She married Jaroslav Sedláček in 1928. She died in 1958.
12. iii. **Marie Dvořáková** was born in 1909. She died in 1985.
13. iv. **Miluše Dvořáková** was born in 1924. She died in 2004.

7. **Marie Berglová**-4 (Marie-3, Jan-2, Jan-1) was born on 27 Mar 1880 in Drahotice No. 20, Mnichovo Hradiště Co.. She died on 25 Mar 1917 in Chocnějovice No. 22, Mnichovo Hradiště Co..
Adolf Rechcigl son of Petr Rechziegel and Anna Najmanová was born on 21 Aug 1876 in Letařovice No. 4, Český Dub Co.. He died on 30 Mar 1946 in Šárovcova Lhota No. 16.
Adolf Rechcigl and Marie Berglová were married about 1900. They had the following children:
    i. **Marie Rechcíglová** was born on 29 Sep 1901 in Kocňovice (renamed Chocnějovice). She died on 03 Oct 1902 in Chocnějovice.

27 ii. **Miloslav Rechcigl** was born on 13 May 1904 in Kocňovice (renamed Chocnějovice) No. 22. He married Marie Rajtrová on 26 Jul 1926 in Praha - Kralovske Vinohrady. He died on May 1973 in Washington, DC.

    iii. **Anna Rechcíglová** was born on 10 Feb 1906 in Kocňovice (renamed Chocnějovice) No. 22. She died on 26 Feb 1927 in Chocnějovice.

Generation 5

8. **Josef Buriánek**-5 (Marie-4, Anna Marie-3, Jan-2, Jan-1) was born on 05 Feb 1900 in Sezemice No. 29. He died in 1966.
Blažena Maruskova was born on 26 Mar 1908 in Sedlistky No. 4. She died in 1989.
Josef Buriánek and Blažena Maruskova married. They had the following children:
    i. **Jaromír Buriánek** was born on 09 Feb 1929 in Koryta No. 29.
    ii. **Vratislav Buriánek** was born on 28 Oct 1935 in Koryta No. 29. He died in 1992.
    iii. **Jana Buriánková** was born on 25 Mar 1944 in Koryta No. 29.

9. **Ivo Buriánek**-5 (Marie-4, Anna Marie-3, Jan-2, Jan-1).
Unknown.
Ivo Buriánek and Unknown married. They had the following children:
    i. **Ivo Buriánek** was born in 1932 in koryta. He died in 1999.

10. **Anna Dvořáková**-5 (Anna-4, Anna Marie-3, Jan-2, Jan-1) was born in 1906. She died in 1958.
    Jaroslav Sedláček was born in 1900 in Loukovec. He died in 1955.
    Jaroslav Sedláček and Anna Dvořáková were married in 1928. They had the following children:
    i. **Břetislav Sedláček** was born in 1935. He died in 1952.
    ii. **Jaroslava Sedláčková** was born in 1930. She died in 2003.
11. **Marie Dvořáková**-5 (Anna-4, Anna Marie-3, Jan-2, Jan-1) was born in 1909. She died in 1985.
    J. Flanderka was born in 1912 in Mohelnica. He died in 1967.
    J. Flanderka and Marie Dvořáková married. They had the following children:
    i. **Miroslav Flanderka**.
    ii. **Blanka Flanderková**.
12. **Miluše Dvořáková**-5 (Anna-4, Anna Marie-3, Jan-2, Jan-1) was born in 1924. She died in 2004.
    Josef Templ was born in Kruhy. He died in 1998.
    Josef Templ and Miluše Dvořáková married. They had the following children:
    i. **Jiřina Templová**.
    ii. **MilušeTemplová**.
    iii. **Bóža Templová**.
13. **Miloslav Rechcigl**-5 (Marie-4, Marie-3, Jan-2, Jan-1) was born on 13 May 1904 in Kocňovice (renamed Chocnějovice) No. 22. He died on 27 May 1973 in Washington, DC.
    Marie Rajtrová daughter of Čeněk Rajtr and Marie Dandová was born on 05 Jul 1905 in Dolanky No. 7, Mnichovo Hradiště Co.. She died on 13 Apr 1982 in Mladá Boleslav.
    Miloslav Rechcigl and Marie Rajtrová were married on 26 Jul 1926 in Praha - Kralovske Vinohrady. They had the following children:
    i. **Mila (Miloslav) Rechcigl Jr.** was born on 30 Jul 1930 in Mladá Boleslav, CSR. He married Eva Edwards (Eisnerová) on 29 Aug 1953 in New York, NY.

ii. **Marta Rechcíglová** was born on 23 May 1933 in Mladá Boleslav. She married František Žďárský on 03 Oct 1953 in Mladá Boleslav. She died on 13 Sep 2018 in Mladá Boleslav.

Landa Family

Generation 1

1. **František Landa**-1 was born before 1800 in Drahotice No. 14.
   Kateřina Hozaková was born in Drahotice No. 14.
   František Landa and Kateřina Hozaková married. They had the following children:
   2. i. **Jan Landa** was born about 1820 in Drahotice No. 9.

Generation 2

3. **Jan Landa**-2 (František-1) was born about 1820 in Drahotice No. 9.
   Anna Polívková daughter of Miroslav Polivka and Unknown.
   Jan Landa and Anna Polívková married. They had the following children:
   3. i. **Kateřina Landová** was born about 1840 in Drahotice No. 9.
   Alžběta Nesvadbová daughter of Václav Nesvadba and Barbora Krejčová was born in Sovenice No. 13.
   Jan Landa and Alžběta Nesvadbová married. They had the following children:
   - i. **Anna Landová** was born on 14 Apr 1849.
   - ii. **František Landa** was born on 06 Aug 1851.

Generation 3

4. **Kateřina Landová**-3 (Jan-2, František-1) was born about 1840 in Drahotice No. 9.
   Jan Mařan son of Jan Mařan and Anna Konopkova was born in Drahotice No. 20.
   Notes for Jan Mařan:
   General Notes:
   cottager, Drahotice
   Jan Mařan and Kateřina Landová married. They had the following children:
   4. i. **Anna Marie Mařanová** was born on 24 Oct 1855 in Drahotice No. 20.

5. ii. **Marie Mařanová** was born on 02 Feb 1860 in Drahotice No. 20. She died on 24 Jun 1924 in Chocnějovice No. 22/39.

Generation 4

4. **Anna Marie Mařanová**-4 (Kateřina-3, Jan-2, František-1) was born on 24 Oct 1855 in Drahotice No. 20.

   Václav Jihlavec was born on 20 un 1851 in Mukar

   Václav Jihlavec and Anna Marie Mařanová married. They had the following children:

   6. i. **Marie Jihlavcová** was born on 20 Jun 1876 in Horni Mohelnice. She died in 1928.
   7. ii. **Anna Jihlavcová** was born on 15 Sep 1882 in Horni Mohelnice.
      iii. **son Jihlavec** was born in Horni Mohelnice. He died in Died.

5. **Marie Mařanová**-4 (Kateřina-3, Jan-2, František-1) was born on 02 Feb 1860 in Drahotice No. 20. She died on 24 Jun 1924 in Chocnějovice No. 22/39.

   František Bergl son of Josef Bergl and Anna Šichtová was born on 08 Sep 1850 in Podhora No. 16. He died on 22 Nov 1921 in Chocnějovice No. 22/39.

   František Bergl and Marie Mařanová married. They had the following children:

   8. i. **Marie Berglová** was born on 27 Mar 1880 in Drahotice No. 20, Mnichovo Hradiště Co.. She married Adolf Rechcigl about 1900. She died on 25 Mar 1917 in Chocnějovice No. 22, Mnichovo Hradiště Co..

Generation 5

6. **Marie Jihlavcová**-5 (Anna Marie-4, Kateřina-3, Jan-2, František-1) was born on 20 Jun 1876 in Horni Mohelnice. She died in 1928.

   František Buriánek son of Josef Buriánek and Terezie Bartošová was born on 27 Jul 1869 in Sezemice No. 25. He died in 1944.

   František Buriánek and Marie Jihlavcová married. They had the following children:

   i. **Marie Buriánková** was born on 17 Sep 1898 in Sezemice No. 29. She died in 1950.

10. ii. **Josef Buriánek** was born on 05 Feb 1900 in Sezemice No. 29. He died in 1966.

   iii. **František Buriánek** was born on 23 Jan 1902 in Sezemice No. 29. He died in 1936.

10. iv. **Ivo Buriánek**.

7. **Anna Jihlavcová**-5 (Anna Marie-4, Kateřina-3, Jan-2, František-1) was born on 15 Sep 1882 in Horni Mohelnice.

   František Dvořák son of Václav Dvořák and Anna Landová was born in 1878 in Malé Podolí. František Dvořák and Anna Jihlavcová married. They had the following children:

   i. **Václav Dvořák** was born in 1905. He died in 1925.

12. ii. **Anna Dvořáková** was born in 1906. She married Jaroslav Sedláček in 1928. She died in 1958.

13. iii. **Marie Dvořáková** was born in 1909. She died in 1985.

13. iv. **Miluše Dvořáková** was born in 1924. She died in 2004.

1 **Marie Berglová**-5 (Marie-4, Kateřina-3, Jan-2, František-1) was born on 27 Mar 1880 in Drahotice No. 20, Mnichovo Hradiště Co.. She died on 25 Mar 1917 in Chocnějovice No. 22, Mnichovo Hradiště Co..

Adolf Rechcigl son of Petr Rechziegel and Anna Najmanová was born on 21 Aug 1876 in Letařovice No. 4, Český Dub Co.. He died on 30 Mar 1946 in Šárovcova Lhota No. 16.

Adolf Rechcigl and Marie Berglová were married about 1900. They had the following children:

   71. **Marie Rechcíglová** was born on 29 Sep 1901 in Kocňovice (renamed Chocnějovice). She died on 03 Oct 1902 in Chocnějovice.

B ii. **Miloslav Rechcigl** was born on 13 May 1904 in Kocňovice (renamed Chocnějovice) No. He married Marie Rajtrová on 26 Jul 1926 in Praha - Kralovske Vinohrady. He died on 27 May 1973 in Washington, DC.

   iii. **Anna Rechcíglová** was born on 10 Feb 1906 in Kocňovice (renamed Chocnějovice) No. 22. She died on 26 Feb 1927 in Chocnějovice.

Generation 6

9. **Josef Buriánek**-6 (Marie-5, Anna Marie-4, Kateřina-3, Jan-2, František-1) was born on 05 Feb 1900 in Sezemice No. 29. He died in 1966.
   Blažena Maruskova was born on 26 Mar 1908 in Sedlistky No. 4. She died in 1989. Josef Buriánek and Blažena Maruskova married. They had the following children:
   - i. **Jaromír Buriánek** was born on 09 Feb 1929 in Koryta No. 29.
   - 16. ii. **Vratislav Buriánek** was born on 28 Oct 1935 in Koryta No. 29. He died in 1992.
   - 17. iii. **Jana Buriánková** was born on 25 Mar 1944 in Koryta No. 29.

10. **Ivo Buriánek**-6 (Marie-5, Anna Marie-4, Kateřina-3, Jan-2, František-1). **Unknown.**
    Ivo Buriánek and Unknown married. They had the following children:
    - 17. i. **Ivo Buriánek** was born in 1932 in koryta. He died in 1999.

11. **Anna Dvořáková**-6 (Anna-5, Anna Marie-4, Kateřina-3, Jan-2, František-1) was born in 1906. She died in 1958.
    Jaroslav Sedláček was born in 1900 in Loukovec. He died in 1955.
    Jaroslav Sedláček and Anna Dvořáková were married in 1928. They had the following children:
    - i. **Břetislav Sedláček** was born in 1935. He died in 1952.
    - ii. **Jaroslava Sedláčková** was born in 1930. She died in 2003.

12. **Marie Dvořáková**-6 (Anna-5, Anna Marie-4, Kateřina-3, Jan-2, František-1) was born in 1909. She died in 1985.
    J. Flanderka was born in 1912 in Mohelnica. He died in 1967.
    J. Flanderka and Marie Dvořáková married. They had the following children:
    - i. **Miroslav Flanderka.**
    - ii. **Blanka Flanderková.**

13. **Miluše Dvořáková**-6 (Anna-5, Anna Marie-4, Kateřina-3, Jan-2, František-1) was born in 1924. She died in 2004.
    Josef Templ was born in Kruhy. He died in 1998.
    Josef Templ and Miluše Dvořáková married. They had the following children:

     i. Jiřina Templová.
    ii. MilušeTemplová.
    iii. Bóža Templová.
14. **Miloslav Rechcigl**-6 (Marie-5, Marie-4, Kateřina-3, Jan-2, František-1) was born on 13 May 1904 in Kocňovice (renamed Chocnějovice) No. 22. He died on 27 May 1973 in Washington, DC.
    Marie Rajtrová daughter of Čeněk Rajtr and Marie Dandová was born on 05 Jul 1905 in Dolanky No. 7, Mnichovo Hradiště Co.. She died on 13 Apr 1982 in Mladá Boleslav.
    Miloslav Rechcigl and Marie Rajtrová were married on 26 Jul 1926 in Praha - Kralovske Vinohrady. They had the following children:
    18. i. **Mila (Miloslav) Rechcigl Jr.** was born on 30 Jul 1930 in Mladá Boleslav, CSR. He married Eva Edwards (Eisnerová) on 29 Aug 1953 in New York, NY.
    19. ii. **Marta Rechcíglová** was born on 23 May 1933 in Mladá Boleslav. She married František Žďárský on 03 Oct 1953 in Mladá Boleslav. She died on 13 Sep 2018 in Mladá Boleslav.

Generation 7

15. **Vratislav Buriánek**-7 (Josef-6, Marie-5, Anna Marie-4, Kateřina-3, Jan-2, František-1) was born on 28 Oct 1935 in Koryta No. 29. He died in 1992.
    Jiřina Schlesingerová was born in Litvinov.
    Vratislav Buriánek and Jiřina Schlesingerová married. They had the following children:
    20. i. **Alena Buriánková** was born on 15 Nov 1960.
16. **Jana Buriánková**-7 (Josef-6, Marie-5, Anna Marie-4, Kateřina-3, Jan-2, František-1) was born on 25 Mar 1944 in Koryta No. 29.
    Bohumil Michalek was born on 30 Nov 1942 in Sedlov No. 1, Kolin.
    Bohumil Michalek and Jana Buriánková married. They had the following children:
    21. i. **Aleš Michalek** was born on 09 Jun 1970.
    22. ii. **Jana Michalkova** was born on 07 Oct 1972 in Loukovec.
17. **Ivo Buriánek**-7 (Ivo-6, Marie-5, Anna Marie-4, Kateřina-3, Jan-2, František-1) was born in 1932 in koryta. He died in 1999.

J. Slajsova.
Ivo Buriánek and J. Slajsova married. They had the following children:
23. i. **Petr Buriánek**. He married Alena Pecharova in 1999.
18. **Mila (Miloslav) Rechcigl Jr.**-7 (Miloslav-6, Marie-5, Marie-4, Kateřina-3, Jan-2, František-1) was born on 30 Jul 1930 in Mladá Boleslav, CSR.
Eva Edwards (Eisnerová) daughter of Paul J. Edwards (Pavel Eisner) and Jiřina Taussigová was born on 21 Jan 1932 in Prague, CSR.
Mila (Miloslav) Rechcigl Jr. and Eva Edwards (Eisnerová) were married on 29 Aug 1953 in New York, NY. They had the following children:
24. i. **John Edward Rechcigl** was born on 27 Feb 1960 in Washington, D.C.. He married Nancy Ann Palko on 30 Jul 1983 in Dover, NJ.
25. ii. **Karen Rechcigl** was born on 16 Apr 1962 in Washington, DC. She married Ulysses Kollecas on 25 Aug 1990 in Bethesda, MD.
19. **Marta Rechcíglová**-7 (Miloslav-6, Marie-5, Marie-4, Kateřina-3, Jan-2, František-1) was born on 23 May 1933 in Mladá Boleslav. She died on 13 Sep 2018 in Mladá Boleslav.
František Žďárský son of František Václav Žďárský and Eliška Foltýnová was born on 21 May 1932 in Turnov.
František Žďárský and Marta Rechcíglová were married on 03 Oct 1953 in Mladá Boleslav. They had the following children:
26. i. **Marcela Žďárská** was born on 09 May 1954 in Liberec. She married Miroslav Heralecký on 15 Mar 1975 in Sychrov.
27. ii. **Iveta Žďárská** was born on 29 Aug 1963 in Liberec, Bohemia. She married Vlastimil Berkman on 29 Oct 1983.

Generation 8

20. **Alena Buriánková**-8 (Vratislav-7, Josef-6, Marie-5, Anna Marie-4, Kateřina-3, Jan-2, František-1) was born on 15 Nov 1960.
Mirek Matlas was born on 20 Sep 1955 in Litvinov.
Mirek Matlas and Alena Buriánková married. They had the following children:
   i. **Alena Matlasová** was born in 1981.
   ii. **daughter Matlasová** was born in 1986.

21. **Aleš Michalek**-8 (Jana-7, Josef-6, Marie-5, Anna Marie-4, Kateřina-3, Jan-2, František-1) was born on 09 Jun 1970.
    Klára Rozenska was born on 08 Sep 1971 in Teplice.
    Aleš Michalek and Klára Rozenska married. They had the following children:
    i. **Terezka Michalkova** was born on 06 Apr 2001.
    ii. **Barbora Michalkova** was born on 03 Apr 2006.
22. **Jana Michalkova**-8 (Jana-7, Josef-6, Marie-5, Anna Marie-4, Kateřina-3, Jan-2, František-1) was born on 07 Oct 1972 in Loukovec.
    Jaromír Terner was born on 27 Jun 1961.
    Jaromír Terner and Jana Michalkova married. They had the following children:
    i. **Anna Ternerova** was born in February 9, 2002.
    ii. **Linda Ternerova** was born in April 7, 2004.
23. **Petr Buriánek**-8 (Ivo-7, Ivo-6, Marie-5, Anna Marie-4, Kateřina-3, Jan-2, František-1).
    Alena Pecharova.
    Petr Buriánek and Alena Pecharova were married in 1999. They had the following children:
    i. **Štěpán Buriánek.**
24. **John Edward Rechcigl**-8 (Mila (Miloslav)-7, Miloslav-6, Marie-5, Marie-4, Kateřina-3, Jan-2, František-1) was born on 27 Feb 1960 in Washington, D.C..
    Nancy Ann Palko daughter of Joseph Palko and Mary Rishko was born on 26 Sep 1961 in Morristown, NJ.
    John Edward Rechcigl and Nancy Ann Palko were married on 30 Jul 1983 in Dover, NJ. They had the following children:
    i. **Gregory John Rechcigl** was born on 19 Dec 1988 in Bradenton, FL.
28. ii. **Kevin Thomas Rechcigl** was born on 09 Oct 1991 in Bradenton, FL. He married Jordan Robbins on 12 May 2018 in Jacksonville, FL.
    iii. **Lindsey Nicole Rechcigl** was born on 03 Nov 1994 in Bradenton, FL.

25. **Karen Rechcigl**-8 (Mila (Miloslav)-7, Miloslav-6, Marie-5, Marie-4, Kateřina-3, Jan-2, František-1) was born on 16 Apr 1962 in Washington, DC.

    Ulysses Kollecas son of Christopher Thomas (Kolecas) Collier and Amelia Malatras was born on 20 Mar 1958 in Washington, DC.

    Ulysses Kollecas and Karen Rechcigl were married on 25 Aug 1990 in Bethesda, MD. They had the following children:
    - i. **Kristin Kollecas** was born on 04 May 1993 in Albuquerque, NM.
    - ii. **Paul Kollecas** was born on 02 Jun 1995 in Albuquerque, NM.

26. **Marcela Žďárská**-8 (Marta-7, Miloslav-6, Marie-5, Marie-4, Kateřina-3, Jan-2, František-1) was born on 09 May 1954 in Liberec.

    Miroslav Heralecký son of Miroslav Heralecký and Marie Bartošová was born on 18 May 1949 in salomonJablonec nad Nisou, Czech.. He died on 20 Feb 2017 in Proseč, Jablonec nad Nisou, Czech..

    Miroslav Heralecký and Marcela Žďárská were married on 15 Mar 1975 in Sychrov. They had the following children:
    - i. **Vit Heralecký** was born on 16 Jan 1977 in Jablonec nad Nisou. He married Olga Zrubcová on 13 Jul 1996.
    - 30. ii. **Zuzana Heralecká** was born on 30 Dec 1978 in Jablonec nad Nisou. She married Jaroslav Egrt on 13 Sep 2002 in Jablonec nad Nisou.

27. **Iveta Žďárská**-8 (Marta-7, Miloslav-6, Marie-5, Marie-4, Kateřina-3, Jan-2, František-1) was born on 29 Aug 1963 in Liberec, Bohemia.

    Vlastimil Berkman was born in 1957.

    Vlastimil Berkman and Iveta Žďárská were married on 29 Oct 1983. They had the following children:
    - i. **Tereza Hriníková** was born on 05 Jun 1984 in Jablonec nad Nisou.

    Jaroslav Hrinik son of Jaroslav Hrinik and Milena Preisslerová was born on 17 Apr 1960.

    Jaroslav Hrinik and Iveta Žďárská were married on 16 Aug 1991 in Zamek Červená Lhota. They had the following children:

i. **Eliška Hriníková** was born on 23 Jun 1992 in Jablonec nad Nisou. She married Jan Ottis on 06 Oct 2018 in Jablonec nad Jizerou, East Bohemia, Czech Republic.

Generation 9

28. **Kevin Thomas Rechcigl**-9 (John Edward-8, Mila (Miloslav)-7, Miloslav-6, Marie-5, Marie-4, Kateřina-3, Jan-2, František-1) was born on 09 Oct 1991 in Bradenton, FL.

Jordan Robbins daughter of Douglass Robbins and Ivonne was born on 10 Jan 1992 in Camarillo, CA.

Kevin Thomas Rechcigl and Jordan Robbins were married on 12 May 2018 in Jacksonville, FL. They had the following children:

   i. **James Douglas Rechcigl** was born on 05 Jan 2021 in Jacksonville, FL.
   ii. **Evelyn Marie Rechcigl** was born 29 May 2023 in Jacksonville, FL.

29. **Zuzana Heralecká**-9 (Marcela-8, Marta-7, Miloslav-6, Marie-5, Marie-4, Kateřina-3, Jan-2, František-1) was born on 30 Dec 1978 in Jablonec nad Nisou.

Jaroslav Egrt was born on 25 Apr 1974 in Duchcov.

Jaroslav Egrt and Zuzana Heralecká were married on 13 Sep 2002 in Jablonec nad Nisou. They had the following children:

   i. **Kristina Egrtova** was born on 04 Jan 2008 in Liberec.
   ii. **Jaroslav Egrt** was born on 04 Jan 2008 in Liberec.

Šichta Family

Generation 1

1. **Jan Šichta**-1 was born in Sovinky No. 31.
   Jan Šichta and unknown spouse married. They had the following children:
   2. i. **Anna Šichtová** was born on 12 Sep 1824 in Sovinky No. 31.

Generation 2

2. **Anna Šichtová**-2 (Jan-1) was born on 12 Sep 1824 in Sovinky No. 31.
   Josef Bergl son of Jan Bergl and Kateřina Stránská was born on 28 Dec 1820 in Podhora No. 16. He died on 20 Oct 1861.
   Josef Bergl and Anna Šichtová married. They had the following children:

   i. **Josef Bergl** was born on 20 Mar 1848 in Kocňovice No. 16. He died on 18 Apr 1856.

   4. ii. **František Bergl** was born on 08 Sep 1850 in Podhora No. 16. He died on 22 Nov 1921 in Chocnějovice No. 22/39.

   iii. **Jan Bergl** was born on 03 Sep 1854 in Podhora No. 16.

   4. iv. **2nd Josef Bergl** was born about 1860 in Podhora No. 16.

   5. v. **daughter Berglová** was born about 1850 in Podhora No. 16.

   Lamač was born about 1821 in Kocňovice.
   Lamač and Anna Šichtová married. They had no children.

Generation 3

3. **František Bergl**-3 (Anna-2, Jan-1) was born on 08 Sep 1850 in Podhora No. 16. He died on 22 Nov 1921 in Chocnějovice No. 22/39.
   Marie Mařanová daughter of Jan Mařan and Kateřina Landová was born on 02 Feb 1860 in Drahotice No. 20. She died on 24 Jun 1924 in Chocnějovice No. 22/39.
   František Bergl and Marie Mařanová married. They had the following children:

   6. i. **Marie Berglová** was born on 27 Mar 1880 in Drahotice No. 20, Mnichovo Hradiště Co.. She married Adolf Rechcigl about 1900. She died on 25 Mar 1917 in Chocnějovice No. 22, Mnichovo Hradiště Co..

4. **2nd Josef Bergl**-3 (Anna-2, Jan-1) was born about 1860 in Podhora No. 16.

Unknown.

2nd Josef Bergl and Unknown married. They had the following children:
- i. **3rd Josef Bergl** was born after 1870 in Neveklovice No. 18. He died in killed in war.
- 7. ii. **Marie Berglová** was born on 10 Apr 1888 in Neveklovice No. 18.

13. **daughter Berglová**-3 (Anna-2, Jan-1) was born about 1850 in Podhora No. 16.

Lamač.

Lamač and daughter Berglová married. They had the following children:
- i. i. **Václav Lamač** was born after 1870.

Generation 4

6. **Marie Berglová**-4 (František-3, Anna-2, Jan-1) was born on 27 Mar 1880 in Drahotice No. 20, Mnichovo Hradiště Co.. She died on 25 Mar 1917 in Chocnějovice No. 22, Mnichovo Hradiště Co..

Adolf Rechcigl son of Petr Rechziegel and Anna Najmanová was born on 21 Aug 1876 in Letařovice No. 4, Český Dub Co.. He died on 30 Mar 1946 in Šárovcova Lhota No. 16.

Adolf Rechcigl and Marie Berglová were married about 1900. They had the following children:
- i. **Marie Rechcíglová** was born on 29 Sep 1901 in Kocňovice (renamed Chocnějovice). She died on 03 Oct 1902 in Chocnějovice.
- 10. ii. **Miloslav Rechcigl** was born on 13 May 1904 in Kocňovice (renamed Chocnějovice) No. 22. He married Marie Rajtrová on 26 Jul 1926 in Praha - Kralovske Vinohrady. He died on 27 May 1973 in Washington, DC.
- iii. **Anna Rechcíglová** was born on 10 Feb 1906 in Kocňovice (renamed Chocnějovice) No. 22. She died on 26 Feb 1927 in Chocnějovice.

7. **Marie Berglová**-4 (2nd Josef-3, Anna-2, Jan-1) was born on 10 Apr 1888 in Neveklovice No. 18.

   Josef Kešner son of Kešner and Unknown was born on 25 Apr 1880 in Neveklovice. He died on 29 Jul 1974 in Neveklovice No. 18.

   Josef Kešner and Marie Berglová married. They had the following children:

   10. i. **Václav Kešner** was born in 1912 in Neveklovice.
   11. ii. **Veroslav Kešner** was born on 21 Apr 1920 in Neveklovice.

8. **Václav Lamač**-4 (daughter-3, Anna-2, Jan-1) was born after 1870.

   Václav Lamač and unknown spouse married. They had the following children:

   12. i. **Marie Lamačová** was born after 1890 in Podhora.

Generation 5

9. **Miloslav Rechcigl**-5 (Marie-4, František-3, Anna-2, Jan-1) was born on 13 May 1904 in Kocňovice (renamed Chocnějovice) No. 22. He died on 27 May 1973 in Washington, DC.

   Marie Rajtrová daughter of Čeněk Rajtr and Marie Dandová was born on 05 Jul 1905 in Dolanky No. 7, Mnichovo Hradiště Co.. She died on 13 Apr 1982 in Mladá Boleslav.

   Miloslav Rechcigl and Marie Rajtrová were married on 26 Jul 1926 in Praha - Kralovske Vinohrady. They had the following children:

   13. i. **Mila (Miloslav) Rechcigl Jr.** was born on 30 Jul 1930 in Mladá Boleslav, CSR. He married Eva Edwards (Eisnerová) on 29 Aug 1953 in New York, NY.
   14. ii. **Marta Rechcíglová** was born on 23 May 1933 in Mladá Boleslav. She married František Žďárský on 03 Oct 1953 in Mladá Boleslav. She died on 13 Sep 2018 in Mladá Boleslav.

10. **Václav Kešner**-5 (Marie-4, 2nd Josef-3, Anna-2, Jan-1) was born in 1912 in Neveklovice.

    Anežka Loudova was born in 1920 in Sezemice.

    Václav Kešner and Anežka Loudova married. They had the following children:

    15. i. **Jiří Kešner**.

16. ii. **Hana Kešnerová.**
11. **Veroslav Kešner**-5 (Marie-4, 2nd Josef-3, Anna-2, Jan-1) was born on 21 Apr 1920 in Neveklovice.

    Libuše Prylova daughter of Stanislav Pryl was born on 21 Aug 1930 in Solecek No. 1.

    Veroslav Kešner and Libuše Prylova married. They had the following children:

    17. i. **Stanislav Kešner** was born on 01 Nov 1953 in Turnov.
    18. ii. **Libuše Kešnerová** was born on 20 Dec 1954 in Turnov.

12. **Marie Lamačová**-5 (Václav-4, daughter-3, Anna-2, Jan-1) was born after 1890 in Podhora.

    Jan Šverma son of Jan Šverma and Kateřina Paříková.

    Jan Šverma and Marie Lamačová married. They had the following children:

    19. i. **Jaroslav Šverma** was born on 03 Nov 1917 in Manikovice.
    20. ii. **Ludmila Švermová** was born in 1926. She died about 1996.

Generation 6

1 **Mila (Miloslav) Rechcigl Jr.**-6 (Miloslav-5, Marie-4, František-3, Anna-2, Jan-1) was born on 30 Jul 1930 in Mladá Boleslav, CSR.

Eva Edwards (Eisnerová) daughter of Paul J. Edwards (Pavel Eisner) and Jiřina Taussigová was born on 21 Jan 1932 in Prague, CSR.

Mila (Miloslav) Rechcigl Jr. and Eva Edwards (Eisnerová) were married on 29 Aug 1953 in New York, NY. They had the following children:

21. i. **John Edward Rechcigl** was born on 27 Feb 1960 in Washington, D.C.. He married Nancy Ann Palko on 30 Jul 1983 in Dover, NJ.
22. ii. **Karen Rechcigl** was born on 16 Apr 1962 in Washington, DC. She married Ulysses Kollecas on 25 Aug 1990 in Bethesda, MD.

14. **Marta Rechcíglová**-6 (Miloslav-5, Marie-4, František-3, Anna-2, Jan-1) was born on 23 May 1933 in Mladá Boleslav. She died on 13 Sep 2018 in Mladá Boleslav.

    František Žďárský son of František Václav Žďárský and Eliška Foltýnová was born on 21 May 1932 in Turnov.

František Žďárský and Marta Rechcíglová were married on 03 Oct 1953 in Mladá Boleslav. They had the following children:

23. i. **Marcela Žďárská** was born on 09 May 1954 in Liberec. She married Miroslav Heralecký on 15 Mar 1975 in Sychrov.

24. ii. **Iveta Žďárská** was born on 29 Aug 1963 in Liberec, Bohemia. She married Vlastimil Berkman on 29 Oct 1983.

15. **Jiří Kešner**-6 (Václav-5, Marie-4, 2nd Josef-3, Anna-2, Jan-1).
Věra.
Jiří Kešner and Věra married. They had the following children:
    i. **Monika Kešnerová (adopted).**

16. **Hana Kešnerová**-6 (Václav-5, Marie-4, 2nd Josef-3, Anna-2, Jan-1).
Václav Červa.
Václav Červa and Hana Kešnerová married. They had the following children:
25. i. **Hana Červová.**
Miloš Makrlik.
Miloš Makrlik and Hana Kešnerová married. They had the following children:
    i. **Lenka Makrlikova Makrlik.**

17. **Stanislav Kešner**-6 (Veroslav-5, Marie-4, 2nd Josef-3, Anna-2, Jan-1) was born on 01 Nov 1953 in Turnov.
Miloslava Liblinska was born on 22 Sep 1952 in Liberec.
Stanislav Kešner and Miloslava Liblinska married. They had the following children:
    i. **Vit Kešner** was born on 20 Sep 1981 in Liberec.
    ii. **Tereza Kešnerová** was born on 13 Oct 1982 in Liberec.

18. **Libuše Kešnerová**-6 (Veroslav-5, Marie-4, 2nd Josef-3, Anna-2, Jan-1) was born on 20 Dec 1954 in Turnov.
Zdeněk Maděra was born on 04 Jul 1954 in Liberec.
Zdeněk Maděra and Libuše Kešnerová married. They had the following children:
    i. **Lucie Maděrová** was born on 13 Apr 1979 in Liberec.
    ii. **Lukáš Maděra** was born on 16 Feb 1983 in Liberec.

19. **Jaroslav Šverma**-6 (Marie-5, Václav-4, daughter-3, Anna-2, Jan-1) was born on 03 Nov 1917 in Manikovice.
    Blažena Novotná was born in Honsov.
    Jaroslav Šverma and Blažena Novotná married. They had the following children:
    26. i. **Jaroslav Šverma** was born about 1950.
    27. ii. **Jan Šverma** was born about 1948.
20. **Ludmila Švermová**-6 (Marie-5, Václav-4, daughter-3, Anna-2, Jan-1) was born in 1926. She died about 1996.
    Jaromír Štěpánek was born in Bakov nnad Jizerou.
    Jaromír Štěpánek and Ludmila Švermová married. They had the following children:
    28. i. **Jaromír Štěpánek**.
    29. ii. **Pavel Štěpánek**.

Generation 7

1   **John Edward Rechcigl**-7 (Mila (Miloslav)-6, Miloslav-5, Marie-4, František-3, Anna-2, Jan-1) was born on 27 Feb 1960 in Washington, D.C..
Nancy Ann Palko daughter of Joseph Palko and Mary Rishko was born on 26 Sep 1961 in Morristown, NJ.
John Edward Rechcigl and Nancy Ann Palko were married on 30 Jul 1983 in Dover, NJ. They had the following children:
  ii. **Gregory John Rechcigl** was born on 19 Dec 1988 in Bradenton, FL.
  2 ii. **Kevin Thomas Rechcigl** was born on 09 Oct 1991 in Bradenton, FL. He married Jordan Robbins on 12 May 2018 in Jacksonville, FL.
  iii. **Lindsey Nicole Rechcigl** was born on 03 Nov 1994 in Bradenton, FL.

22. **Karen Rechcigl**-7 (Mila (Miloslav)-6, Miloslav-5, Marie-4, František-3, Anna-2, Jan-1) was born on 16 Apr 1962 in Washington, DC.
Ulysses Kollecas son of Christopher Thomas (Kolecas) Collier and Amelia Malatras was born on 20 Mar 1958 in Washington, DC.
Ulysses Kollecas and Karen Rechcigl were married on 25 Aug 1990 in Bethesda, MD. They had the following children:

    i. **Kristin Kollecas** was born on 04 May 1993 in Albuquerque, NM.
    ii. **Paul Kollecas** was born on 02 Jun 1995 in Albuquerque, NM.
23. **Marcela Žďárská**-7 (Marta-6, Miloslav-5, Marie-4, František-3, Anna-2, Jan-1) was born on 09 May 1954 in Liberec.
Miroslav Heralecký son of Miroslav Heralecký and Marie Bartošová was born on 18 May 1949 in salomonJablonec nad Nisou, Czech.. He died on 20 Feb 2017 in Proseč, Jablonec nad Nisou, Czech..
Miroslav Heralecký and Marcela Žďárská were married on 15 Mar 1975 in Sychrov. They had the following children:
    i. **Vit Heralecký** was born on 16 Jan 1977 in Jablonec nad Nisou. He married Olga Zrubcová on 13 Jul 1996.
32. ii. **Zuzana Heralecká** was born on 30 Dec 1978 in Jablonec nad Nisou. She married Jaroslav Egrt on 13 Sep 2002 in Jablonec nad Nisou.
24. **Iveta Žďárská**-7 (Marta-6, Miloslav-5, Marie-4, František-3, Anna-2, Jan-1) was born on 29 Aug 1963 in Liberec, Bohemia.
Vlastimil Berkman was born in 1957.
Vlastimil Berkman and Iveta Žďárská were married on 29 Oct 1983. They had the following children:
    i. **Tereza Hriníková** was born on 05 Jun 1984 in Jablonec nad Nisou.
Jaroslav Hrinik son of Jaroslav Hrinik and Milena Preisslerová was born on 17 Apr 1960.
Jaroslav Hrinik and Iveta Žďárská were married on 16 Aug 1991 in Zamek Červená Lhota. They had the following children:
    + **Eliška Hriníková** was born on 23 Jun 1992 in Jablonec nad Nisou. She married Jan Ottis on 06 Oct 2018 in Jablonec nad Jizerou, East Bohemia, Czech Republic.
25. **Hana Červová**-7 (Hana-6, Václav-5, Marie-4, 2nd Josef-3, Anna-2, Jan-1). **Unknown.**
Unknown and Hana Červová married. They had the following children:
    i. **Ondřej.**
Unkinown.

Unkinown and Hana Červová married. They had no children.

26. **Jaroslav Šverma**-7 (Jaroslav-6, Marie-5, Václav-4, daughter-3, Anna-2, Jan-1) was born about 1950.
    Unknown.
    Jaroslav Šverma and Unknown married. They had the following children:
    i. **Robert Šverma** was born about 1977.
    ii. **Jan Šverma** was born about 1980.
    iii. **Otta Šverma** was born about 1990.

27. **Jan Šverma**-7 (Jaroslav-6, Marie-5, Václav-4, daughter-3, Anna-2, Jan-1) was born about 1948.
    Unknown.
    Jan Šverma and Unknown married. They had the following children:
    i. **son Šverma.**
    ii. **son Šverma.**

28. **Jaromír Štěpánek**-7 (Ludmila-6, Marie-5, Václav-4, daughter-3, Anna-2, Jan-1).
    Alenka Vavrova was born in Bakov nad Jizerou.
    Jaromír Štěpánek and Alenka Vavrova married. They had the following children:
    i. **Hanička Štěpánková** was born in 1977.
    ii. **Jaromír Štěpánek** was born in 1980.

29. **Pavel Štěpánek**-7 (Ludmila-6, Marie-5, Václav-4, daughter-3, Anna-2, Jan-1).
    Jaruska.
    Pavel Štěpánek and Jaruska married. They had the following children:
    32. i. **Pavel Štěpánek** was born in 1977.

Generation 8

30. **Kevin Thomas Rechcigl**-8 (John Edward-7, Mila (Miloslav)-6, Miloslav-5, Marie-4, František-3, Anna-2, Jan-1) was born on 09 Oct 1991 in Bradenton, FL.
    Jordan Robbins daughter of Douglass Robbins and Ivonne was born on 10 Jan 1992 in Camarillo, CA.

Kevin Thomas Rechcigl and Jordan Robbins were married on 12 May 2018 in Jacksonville, FL. They had the following children:
  i. **James Douglas Rechcigl** was born on 05 Jan 2021 in Jacksonville, FL.
  ii. **Evelyn Marie Rechcigl** was born 29 May 2023 in Jacksonville, FL.

31. **Zuzana Heralecká**-8 (Marcela-7, Marta-6, Miloslav-5, Marie-4, František-3, Anna-2, Jan-1) was born on 30 Dec 1978 in Jablonec nad Nisou.

    Jaroslav Egrt was born on 25 Apr 1974 in Duchcov.

    Jaroslav Egrt and Zuzana Heralecká were married on 13 Sep 2002 in Jablonec nad Nisou. They had the following children:
      i. **Kristina Egrtova** was born on 04 Jan 2008 in Liberec.
      ii. **Jaroslav Egrt** was born on 04 Jan 2008 in Liberec.

32. **Pavel Štěpánek**-8 (Pavel-7, Ludmila-6, Marie-5, Václav-4, daughter-3, Anna-2, Jan-1) was born in 1977.

    Alžběta was born in 1975.

    Pavel Štěpánek and Alžběta married. They had the following children:
      i. **Jakub Štěpánek** was born in 2006.

Brož Family

Generation 1

1. **Václav Brož**-1 was born before 1800 in Radimovice 10.
   Alžběta Majlenova daughter of Majlenov was born in Chvalčovice No. 19. Václav Brož and Alžběta Majlenova married. They had the following children:
   2. i. **Anna Brožová** was born in 1829 in Radimovice No. 10 or Sychrov. She married Antonín Neumann on 08 Feb 1848 in Vlastibořice.

Generation 2

2. **Anna Brožová**-2 (Václav-1) was born in 1829 in Radimovice No. 10 or Sychrov.
   Antonín Neumann son of Jan Neumann and Kateřina Sivatkova was born in 1828 in Radimovice No. 7, Český Dub Dist..
   Antonín Neumann and Anna Brožová were married on 08 Feb 1848 in Vlastibořice. They had the following children:
   3. i. **Anna Najmanová** was born on 31 Jul 1849 in Radimovice No. 7, Turnov Co.. She married Petr Rechziegel on 26 Jan 1869 in Radimovice No. 7, Vlastibořice parish., Jan Krt. Hruska officiationg. She died on 05 Jun 1908 in Letařovice.

   Antonín Neumann son of Antonín Neumann and Kateřina Hlavacova was born after 1820 in Radimovice No. 7, Dub Co..
   Antonín Neumann and Anna Brožová married. They had the following children:
   3. i. **Anna Najmanová** was born on 31 Jul 1849 in Radimovice No. 7, Turnov Co.. She married Petr Rechziegel on 26 Jan 1869 in Radimovice No. 7, Vlastibořice parish., Jan Krt. Hruska officiationg. She died on 05 Jun 1908 in Letařovice.

Generation 3

3. **Anna Najmanová**-3 (Anna-2, Václav-1) was born on 31 Jul 1849 in Radimovice No. 7, Turnov Co.. She died on 05 Jun 1908 in Letařovice.

Petr Rechziegel son of Petr Rechziegel and Františka Hlavatá was born on 01 Jun 1844 in Hodkovice No. 39. He died on 18 Sep 1917 in Letařovice No. 4, Turnov Co..

Petr Rechziegel and Anna Najmanová were married on 26 Jan 1869 in Radimovice No. 7, Vlastibořice parish., Jan Krt. Hruska officiationg. They had the following children:

    i. **Josef Rechcigl** was born on 22 Jul 1869 in Radimovice No. 7. He died on 24 Feb 1920 in Letařovice (prob.).

5.   ii. **Emilie Rechcíglová** was born on 02 Apr 1871 in Letařovice No. 4, Český Dub Co.. She died on 18 Feb 1928.

    iii. **Václav Rechcigl** was born on 13 Mar 1873 in Letařovice No. 4, Český Dub Co..

5.   iv. **Adolf Rechcigl** was born on 21 Aug 1876 in Letařovice No. 4, Český Dub Co.. He married Marie Berglová about 1900. He died on 30 Mar 1946 in Šárovcova Lhota No. 16.

    v. **Arnošt Rechziegel** was born on 07 Sep 1882 in Letařovice No. 4, Český Dub Co.. He died on 12 Oct 1882 in Letařovice No. 4, Český Dub Co..

6.   vi. **Zdeněk Petr Rechcigl** was born on 31 Jul 1884 in Letařovice No. 4, Turnov Dist.. He married Anna Šimůnková on 08 Oct 1906 in Kralovske Vinohrady. He died on 08 Feb 1962 in Karlovy Vary - Rybare.

7.   vii. **Bohumil Rechcigl** was born on 09 Apr 1888. He died on 03 Jan 1963 in Český Dub.

    viii. **Jan Rechziegel** was born on 08 May 1895.

Generation 4

4. **Emilie Rechcíglová**-4 (Anna-3, Anna-2, Václav-1) was born on 02 Apr 1871 in Letařovice No. 4, Český Dub Co.. She died on 18 Feb 1928.

Josef Ullrich son of Ullrich and Františka Rechziegel was born in Jilove. Josef Ullrich and Emilie Rechcíglová married. They had the following children:

    i. **Miloslav Ulrich** was born before 1900.

    ii. **Ludvika Ulrichova** was born in 1898. She died on 01 Jun 1945.

5. **Adolf Rechcigl**-4 (Anna-3, Anna-2, Václav-1) was born on 21 Aug 1876 in Letařovice No. 4, Český Dub Co.. He died on 30 Mar 1946 in Šárovcova Lhota No. 16.

Marie Berglová daughter of František Bergl and Marie Mařanová was born on 27 Mar 1880 in Drahotice No. 20, Mnichovo Hradiště Co.. She died on 25 Mar 1917 in Chocnějovice No. 22, Mnichovo Hradiště Co..

Adolf Rechcigl and Marie Berglová were married about 1900. They had the following children:

    i. **Marie Rechcíglová** was born on 29 Sep 1901 in Kocňovice (renamed Chocnějovice). She died on 03 Oct 1902 in Chocnějovice.

    ii. **Miloslav Rechcigl** was born on 13 May 1904 in Kocňovice (renamed Chocnějovice) No. 22. He married Marie Rajtrová on 26 Jul 1926 in Praha - Kralovske Vinohrady. He died on 27 May 1973 in Washington, DC.

    iii. **Anna Rechcíglová** was born on 10 Feb 1906 in Kocňovice (renamed Chocnějovice) No. 22. She died on 26 Feb 1927 in Chocnějovice.

Marie Anna Ferklová daughter of František Ferkl and Anna Saralova was born on 10 Dec 1897 in Chocnějovice No. 2. She died on 31 Dec 1970 in Šárovcova Lhota.

Adolf Rechcigl and Marie Anna Ferklová were married on 25 Apr 1917 in St. Alois Church, Praha. They had the following children:

9. i. **Stanislav Josef Rechcigl** was born on 10 Oct 1918 in Chocnějovice. He married Libuše Sedláčková on 17 Jan 1948 in Novy Bydzov. He died on 09 May 1973 in Šárovcova Lhota No. 16.

    ii. **Adolf Rechcigl** was born on 09 Apr 1920 in Chocnějovice No. 22. He died on 27 Dec 1944 in Ples.

1 **Zdeněk Petr Rechcigl**-4 (Anna-3, Anna-2, Václav-1) was born on 31 Jul 1884 in Letařovice No. 4, Turnov Dist.. He died on 08 Feb 1962 in Karlovy Vary - Rybare.

Anna Šimůnková daughter of Josef Šimůnek and Marie Stejskalová was born on 31 Dec 1884 in Sezemice No. 1, Mnichovo Hradiště Co.. She died on 28 Nov 1907 in After prolonged illnessa.
Zdeněk Petr Rechcigl and Anna Šimůnková were married on 08 Oct 1906 in Kralovske Vinohrady. They had the following children:
    62. i. **Božena Rechcíglová** was born on 18 Mar 1907 in Letařovice, Turnov Co.. She married František Křikava on 24 Jul 1926 in Horovice. She died on 11 Aug 1979 in Hospital, Horovice.

Marie Paulu daughter of Paulu was born before 1900. She died in Divorced February 17, 1926.
Zdeněk Petr Rechcigl and Marie Paulu were married on 26 Sep 1908 in Český Dub. They had the following children:
    i. **child Rechcigl**. He died in Soon after birth.
    ii. **Zdeněk Rechcigl** was born on 06 Jul 1909. He died on 12 Oct 1909.

Marie Reslová daughter of Antonín Resl and Marie Kovářová was born on 25 Mar 1900 in Roven Nio. 45. She died on 02 Dec 1982 in Karlovy Vary.
Zdeněk Petr Rechcigl and Marie Reslová were married on 30 Apr 1926 in Roven. They had the following children:
    11. i. **Zdena Rechcíglová** was born on 25 Sep 1926 in Komarov u Horovic. She married Jan Mueller in 1949. She died on 02 Sep 1978 in Karlovy Vary.

Marie - uncertain was born on 11 Jan 1909. She died on 02 Nov 1996.
Zdeněk Petr Rechcigl and Marie - uncertain met. They had the following children:
    i. **Ludmila Rechcíglová** was born after 1900.

7. **Bohumil Rechcigl**-4 (Anna-3, Anna-2, Václav-1) was born on 09 Apr 1888. He died on 03 Jan 1963 in Český Dub.
Růžena Slukova was born in 1892. She died on 14 Mar 1969 in Český Dub. Bohumil Rechcigl and Růžena Slukova married. They had the following children:
    12. i. **Zdeněk Rechcigl** was born on 05 Dec 1913. He married Marie Pavlová on 29 Jan 1944. He died on 01 Nov 1985.

ii. **Věra Rechcíglová** was born in 1915. She died in 1972.
Notes for Věra Rechcíglová:
General Notes:
unmarried

13. iii. **Libuše Rechcíglová** was born on 13 Aug 1916. She married Jan Mančík on 03 Jun 1950. She died in Mar 1997 in Varnsdorf.

Generation 5

8. **Miloslav Rechcigl**-5 (Adolf-4, Anna-3, Anna-2, Václav-1) was born on 13 May 1904 in Kocňovice (renamed Chocnějovice) No. 22. He died on 27 May 1973 in Washington, DC.

   Marie Rajtrová daughter of Čeněk Rajtr and Marie Dandová was born on 05 Jul 1905 in Dolanky No. 7, Mnichovo Hradiště Co.. She died on 13 Apr 1982 in Mladá Boleslav.

   Miloslav Rechcigl and Marie Rajtrová were married on 26 Jul 1926 in Praha - Kralovske Vinohrady. They had the following children:

   14. i. **Mila (Miloslav) Rechcigl Jr.** was born on 30 Jul 1930 in Mladá Boleslav, CSR. He married Eva Edwards (Eisnerová) on 29 Aug 1953 in New York, NY.

   15. ii. **Marta Rechcíglová** was born on 23 May 1933 in Mladá Boleslav. She married František Žďárský on 03 Oct 1953 in Mladá Boleslav. She died on 13 Sep 2018 in Mladá Boleslav.

9. **Stanislav Josef Rechcigl**-5 (Adolf-4, Anna-3, Anna-2, Václav-1) was born on 10 Oct 1918 in Chocnějovice. He died on 09 May 1973 in Šárovcova Lhota No. 16.

   Libuše Sedláčková daughter of Bedřich Sedláček and Ludmila was born on 24 Sep 1924 in Staré Smrkovice, Jičín Dist. She died on 03 Apr 2019 in Jičín, Czech.

   Stanislav Josef Rechcigl and Libuše Sedláčková were married on 17 Jan 1948 in Novy Bydzov. They had the following children:

   16. i. **Hana Rechcíglová** was born on 13 Jul 1948 in Novy Bydzov, Hradec Králové Co.. She married Jaroslav Husak on 28 Dec 1968 in Sobotka, Jičín Co..

17. ii. **Libuše Rechcíglová** was born on 25 Jan 1950 in Novy Bydzov, Hradec Králové Co.. She married Miroslav Vich on 11 Apr 1970 in Ostromer, Jičín Co..
18. iii. **Stanislav Rechcigl** was born on 24 Mar 1952 in Hořice, Jičín Co.. He married Zdena Pařízková on 24 Mar 1972 in Jičín.

10. **Božena Rechcíglová**-5 (Zdeněk Petr-4, Anna-3, Anna-2, Václav-1) was born on 18 Mar 1907 in Letařovice, Turnov Co.. She died on 11 Aug 1979 in Hospital, Horovice.

    František Křikava son of Josef Křikava and Marie Stichová was born on 23 Dec 1890 in Chaloupky, Beroun Co.. He died on 25 Mar 1965 in Komarov u Horovic No. 40.

    František Křikava and Božena Rechcíglová were married on 24 Jul 1926 in Horovice. They had the following children:

    19. i. **Luděk Křikava** was born on 02 Feb 1927 in Komarov u Horovic No. 40. He died on 23 Sep 1996.
    20. ii. **Sasa Křikava** was born on 02 Dec 1930 in Komarov u Horovic No. 40.

11. **Zdena Rechcíglová**-5 (Zdeněk Petr-4, Anna-3, Anna-2, Václav-1) was born on 25 Sep 1926 in Komarov u Horovic. She died on 02 Sep 1978 in Karlovy Vary.

    Jan Mueller son of Jan Karel Mueller and Anna Šašková was born on 05 Feb 1925 in Prague. He died on 01 May 1989 in Karlovy Vary.

    Jan Mueller and Zdena Rechcíglová were married in 1949. They had the following children:

    21. i. **Jana Muellerová** was born on 08 Nov 1952 in Karlovy Vary. She married Jiří Stuchl on 26 Aug 1979 in Manetin, Plzen Sever Co..
    22. ii. **Zdena Muellerová** was born on 01 May 1960 in Karlovy Vary. She married František Petr in 1981 in Karlovy Vary.

12. **Zdeněk Rechcigl**-5 (Bohumil-4, Anna-3, Anna-2, Václav-1) was born on 05 Dec 1913. He died on 01 Nov 1985.

    Marie Pavlová was born in Jan 1921 in Vlcetin. She died in Dec 2003. Zdeněk Rechcigl and Marie Pavlová were married on 29 Jan 1944. They had the following children:

23. i. **Radmila Rechcíglová** was born on 29 May 1944. She married Pavel Herák on 14 Sep 1963 in Český Dub.
24. ii. **Zdeněk Rechcigl** was born on 07 Aug 1946 in Český Dub. He married Věra Vizkova on 30 Dec 1967 in Český Dub.

Libuše was born on 05 Dec 1917.

Zdeněk Rechcigl and Libuše were married in 1964. They had no children.

13. **Libuše Rechcíglová**-5 (Bohumil-4, Anna-3, Anna-2, Václav-1) was born on 13 Aug 1916. She died in Mar 1997 in Varnsdorf.

Jan Mančík.

Jan Mančík and Libuše Rechcíglová were married on 03 Jun 1950. They had the following children:

25. i. **Jana Mančíková** was born in 1951.
26. ii. **Irena Mančíková** was born in 1954.

Generation 6

14. **Mila (Miloslav) Rechcigl Jr.**-6 (Miloslav-5, Adolf-4, Anna-3, Anna-2, Václav-1) was born on 30 Jul 1930 in Mladá Boleslav, CSR.

Eva Edwards (Eisnerová) daughter of Paul J. Edwards (Pavel Eisner) and Jiřina Taussigová was born on 21 Jan 1932 in Prague, CSR.

Mila (Miloslav) Rechcigl Jr. and Eva Edwards (Eisnerová) were married on 29 Aug 1953 in New York, NY. They had the following children:

27. i. **John Edward Rechcigl** was born on 27 Feb 1960 in Washington, D.C.. He married Nancy Ann Palko on 30 Jul 1983 in Dover, NJ.
28. ii. **Karen Rechcigl** was born on 16 Apr 1962 in Washington, DC. She married Ulysses Kollecas on 25 Aug 1990 in Bethesda, MD.

15. **Marta Rechcíglová**-6 (Miloslav-5, Adolf-4, Anna-3, Anna-2, Václav-1) was born on 23 May 1933 in Mladá Boleslav. She died on 13 Sep 2018 in Mladá Boleslav.

František Žďárský son of František Václav Žďárský and Eliška Foltýnová was born on 21 May 1932 in Turnov.

František Žďárský and Marta Rechcíglová were married on 03 Oct 1953 in Mladá Boleslav. They had the following children:

29. i. **Marcela Žďárská** was born on 09 May 1954 in Liberec. She married Miroslav Heralecký on 15 Mar 1975 in Sychrov.

30. ii. **Iveta Žďárská** was born on 29 Aug 1963 in Liberec, Bohemia. She married Vlastimil Berkman on 29 Oct 1983.

16. **Hana Rechcíglová**-6 (Stanislav Josef-5, Adolf-4, Anna-3, Anna-2, Václav-1) was born on 13 Jul 1948 in Novy Bydzov, Hradec Králové Co..
Jaroslav Husak was born on 24 Mar 1946 in Jičín.
Jaroslav Husak and Hana Rechcíglová were married on 28 Dec 1968 in Sobotka, Jičín Co.. They had the following children:
    i. **Martin Husak** was born on 20 Feb 1971 in Hradec Králové. He married Petra Endrychová on 24 Jul 1999 in Hradec Králové.
    ii. **Petra Husakova** was born on 30 Mar 1974 in Hradec Králové.
Tomáš Petříček was born on 18 Dec 1948 in Hradec Králové.
Tomáš Petříček and Hana Rechcíglová were married on 20 Sep 1991 in Hradec Králové. They had no children.

17. **Libuše Rechcíglová**-6 (Stanislav Josef-5, Adolf-4, Anna-3, Anna-2, Václav-1) was born on 25 Jan 1950 in Novy Bydzov, Hradec Králové Co..
Miroslav Vich was born on 13 Nov 1950 in Nova Paka, Jičín Co..
Miroslav Vich and Libuše Rechcíglová were married on 11 Apr 1970 in Ostromer, Jičín Co.. They had the following children:
31. i. **Iveta Vichova** was born on 15 Jan 1972 in Jičín. She married Miloš Haltuf on 07 Sep 1991 in Lazne Belohrad, Jičín Co..
    ii. **Miroslav Vich** was born on 10 Mar 1973 in Jičín.
    iii. **Sarka Vichova** was born on 11 Mar 1989 in Hradec Králové.

18. **Stanislav Rechcigl**-6 (Stanislav Josef-5, Adolf-4, Anna-3, Anna-2, Václav-1) was born on 24 Mar 1952 in Hořice, Jičín Co..
Zdena Pařízková daughter of Mila Parik and Zdenka was born on 26 Jan 1954 in Hořice, Jičín Dist., Bohemia.
Stanislav Rechcigl and Zdena Pařízková were married on 24 Mar 1972 in Jičín. They had the following children:
32. i. **Stanislava Rechcíglová** was born on 22 Sep 1972 in Hořice, Jičín Dist., Bohemia.
33. ii. **Jana Rechcíglová** was born on 22 Sep 1973 in Hořice, Jičín Co.. She married Karel Spidlen on 29 Apr 1995 in Jičín, Bohemia.

34. iii. **Stanislav Rechcigl** was born on 08 Aug 1975 in Hořice, Jičín Dist., Bohemia. He married Natasha Blackbourn on 19 Jul 2008 in Spalding, Lincolnshire, UK..
Helena Denisova was born on 29 Jun 1944.
Stanislav Rechcigl and Helena Denisova met. They had no children.

19. **Luděk Křikava**-6 (Božena-5, Zdeněk Petr-4, Anna-3, Anna-2, Václav-1) was born on 02 Feb 1927 in Komarov u Horovic No. 40. He died on 23 Sep 1996.
Zdenka Krizova was born on 24 Sep 1941 in Komarov u Horovic No. 72.
Luděk Křikava and Zdenka Krizova married. They had the following children:
    35. i. **Věra Křikavová** was born on 28 Apr 1966 in Komarov u Horovic No. 40.
    36. ii. **Hanna Křikavová** was born on 07 May 1957 in Komarov u Horovic No. 40. She died on 30 Dec 1997.
    37. iii. **Jan Křikava** was born on 19 Aug 1960 in Komarov u Horovic No. 40.

20. **Sasa Křikava**-6 (Božena-5, Zdeněk Petr-4, Anna-3, Anna-2, Václav-1) was born on 02 Dec 1930 in Komarov u Horovic No. 40.
Milada Toclova was born on 24 Jul 1927.
Sasa Křikava and Milada Toclova married. They had the following children:
    i. **Alexander Křikava** was born in 1951 in Komarov u Horovic.
    38. ii. **Hana Křikavová** was born in 1958 in Komarov u Horovic.

21. **Jana Muellerová**-6 (Zdena-5, Zdeněk Petr-4, Anna-3, Anna-2, Václav-1) was born on 08 Nov 1952 in Karlovy Vary.
Jiří Stuchl son of Josef Stuchl and Jarmila Šimáňová was born on 14 Nov 1950 in Plzen. He died on 26 Mar 2001 in Praha 10.
Jiří Stuchl and Jana Muellerová were married on 26 Aug 1979 in Manetin, Plzen Sever Co.. They had the following children:
    i. **Lenka Stuchlová** was born on 12 May 1979 in Karlovy Vary. She married Josef Bic on 07 Jul 2007 in Liberec.
    ii. **Jan Stuchl** was born on 24 Feb 1981 in Karlovy Vary.

22. **Zdena Muellerová**-6 (Zdena-5, Zdeněk Petr-4, Anna-3, Anna-2, Václav-1) was born on 01 May 1960 in Karlovy Vary.
    František Petr was born on 05 Sep 1958 in Sokolov.
    František Petr and Zdena Muellerová were married in 1981 in Karlovy Vary. They had the following children:
    - i. **Miroslav Petr** was born on 30 Oct 1981 in Karlovy Vary.
    - 40. ii. **Jana Petrová** was born on 29 Jun 1984 in Karlovy Vary.
23. **Radmila Rechcíglová**-6 (Zdeněk-5, Bohumil-4, Anna-3, Anna-2, Václav-1) was born on 29 May 1944.
    Pavel Herák was born on 03 Jun 1938 in Brestovany, Slovakia.
    Pavel Herák and Radmila Rechcíglová were married on 14 Sep 1963 in Český Dub. They had the following children:
    - 40. i. **Petr Herák** was born on 03 Jun 1965. He married Tereza Kovářová on 24 Mar 1990 in Český Dub.
    - 41. ii. **Pavlina Heráková** was born on 29 Jan 1964. She married Milan Podlipský on 11 Feb 1984 in Milevsko.
    - 42. iii. **Helena Heráková** was born on 12 Jul 1966. She married Pavel Hudec on 15 Sep 1984 in Český Dub.
24. **Zdeněk Rechcigl**-6 (Zdeněk-5, Bohumil-4, Anna-3, Anna-2, Václav-1) was born on 07 Aug 1946 in Český Dub.
    Věra Vizkova was born on 31 Dec 1947 in Hodkovice.
    Zdeněk Rechcigl and Věra Vizkova were married on 30 Dec 1967 in Český Dub. They had the following children:
    - 43. i. **Martin Rechcigl** was born on 16 Dec 1968. He married Petra Smolakova on 17 Sep 1994 in Český Dub.
25. **Jana Mančíková**-6 (Libuše-5, Bohumil-4, Anna-3, Anna-2, Václav-1) was born in 1951.
    Jan Cicka.
    Jan Cicka and Jana Mančíková married. They had the following children:
    - i. **Drahomira Cicková** was born in 1971.

    Vladimír Ulver.
    Vladimír Ulver and Jana Mančíková married. They had the following children:

i. **Jitka Ulverova** was born in 1980.
26. **Irena Mančíková**-6 (Libuše-5, Bohumil-4, Anna-3, Anna-2, Václav-1) was born in 1954.

    Petr Synek.

    Petr Synek and Irena Mančíková married. They had the following children:

    i. **Veronika Synková** was born on 07 Mar 1979.

    ii. **Jan Synek** was born on 24 May 1980.

Generation 7

27. **John Edward Rechcigl**-7 (Mila (Miloslav)-6, Miloslav-5, Adolf-4, Anna-3, Anna-2, Václav-1) was born on 27 Feb 1960 in Washington, D.C..

    Nancy Ann Palko daughter of Joseph Palko and Mary Rishko was born on 26 Sep 1961 in Morristown, NJ.

    John Edward Rechcigl and Nancy Ann Palko were married on 30 Jul 1983 in Dover, NJ. They had the following children:

    i. **Gregory John Rechcigl** was born on 19 Dec 1988 in Bradenton, FL.

    45. ii. **Kevin Thomas Rechcigl** was born on 09 Oct 1991 in Bradenton, FL. He married Jordan Robbins on 12 May 2018 in Jacksonville, FL.

    iii. **Lindsey Nicole Rechcigl** was born on 03 Nov 1994 in Bradenton, FL.

28. **Karen Rechcigl**-7 (Mila (Miloslav)-6, Miloslav-5, Adolf-4, Anna-3, Anna-2, Václav-1) was born on 16 Apr 1962 in Washington, DC.

    Ulysses Kollecas son of Christopher Thomas (Kolecas) Collier and Amelia Malatras was born on 20 Mar 1958 in Washington, DC.

    Ulysses Kollecas and Karen Rechcigl were married on 25 Aug 1990 in Bethesda, MD. They had the following children:

    i. **Kristin Kollecas** was born on 04 May 1993 in Albuquerque, NM.

    ii. **Paul Kollecas** was born on 02 Jun 1995 in Albuquerque, NM.

29. **Marcela Žďárská**-7 (Marta-6, Miloslav-5, Adolf-4, Anna-3, Anna-2, Václav-1) was born on 09 May 1954 in Liberec.

Miroslav Heralecký son of Miroslav Heralecký and Marie Bartošová was born on 18 May 1949 in salomonJablonec nad Nisou, Czech.. He died on 20 Feb 2017 in Proseč, Jablonec nad Nisou, Czech..
Miroslav Heralecký and Marcela Žďárská were married on 15 Mar 1975 in Sychrov. They had the following children:
- i. **Vit Heralecký** was born on 16 Jan 1977 in Jablonec nad Nisou. He married Olga Zrubcová on 13 Jul 1996.
- 46. ii. **Zuzana Heralecká** was born on 30 Dec 1978 in Jablonec nad Nisou. She married Jaroslav Egrt on 13 Sep 2002 in Jablonec nad Nisou.

30. **Iveta Žďárská**-7 (Marta-6, Miloslav-5, Adolf-4, Anna-3, Anna-2, Václav-1) was born on 29 Aug 1963 in Liberec, Bohemia.
Vlastimil Berkman was born in 1957.
Vlastimil Berkman and Iveta Žďárská were married on 29 Oct 1983. They had the following children:
- i. **Tereza Hriníková** was born on 05 Jun 1984 in Jablonec nad Nisou.

Jaroslav Hrinik son of Jaroslav Hrinik and Milena Preisslerová was born on 17 Apr 1960.
Jaroslav Hrinik and Iveta Žďárská were married on 16 Aug 1991 in Zamek Červená Lhota. They had the following children:
- i. **Eliška Hriníková** was born on 23 Jun 1992 in Jablonec nad Nisou. She married Jan Ottis on 06 Oct 2018 in Jablonec nad Jizerou, East Bohemia, Czech Republic.

1 **Iveta Vichova**-7 (Libuše-6, Stanislav Josef-5, Adolf-4, Anna-3, Anna-2, Václav-1) was born on 15 Jan 1972 in Jičín.
Miloš Haltuf was born on 03 May 1968 in Chlumec.
Miloš Haltuf and Iveta Vichova were married on 07 Sep 1991 in Lazne Belohrad, Jičín Co.. They had the following children:
- 34. **Jan Haltuf** was born on 10 Mar 1992 in Hořice, Jičín Co..

2 **Stanislava Rechcíglová**-7 (Stanislav-6, Stanislav Josef-5, Adolf-4, Anna-3, Anna-2, Václav-1) was born on 22 Sep 1972 in Hořice, Jičín Dist., Bohemia.
Josef Bekera was born on 22 Jun 1965.

Josef Bekera and Stanislava Rechcíglová met. They had the following children:

    34. **Nikolas Bekera** was born on 23 Sep 2001.

    ii. **Sebestian Bekera**.

    iii. **Anastasia Jowefa Bekerová**.

33. **Jana Rechcíglová**-7 (Stanislav-6, Stanislav Josef-5, Adolf-4, Anna-3, Anna-2, Václav-1) was born on 22 Sep 1973 in Hořice, Jičín Co..

Karel Spidlen was born on 06 Feb 1972 in Hradec Králové.

Karel Spidlen and Jana Rechcíglová were married on 29 Apr 1995 in Jičín, Bohemia. They had the following children:

    i. **Karel Spidlen** was born on 15 Oct 1995 in Hořice, Jičín Co..

34. **Stanislav Rechcigl**-7 (Stanislav-6, Stanislav Josef-5, Adolf-4, Anna-3, Anna-2, Václav-1) was born on 08 Aug 1975 in Hořice, Jičín Dist., Bohemia.

Natasha Blackbourn.

Stanislav Rechcigl and Natasha Blackbourn were married on 19 Jul 2008 in Spalding, Lincolnshire, UK.. They had the following children:

    i. **Lily-Grace Rechcíglová** was born on 03 Jul 2011 in Watford, UK.

    ii. **Poppy Sophia Rechcíglová** was born on 13 Oct 2013.

35. **Věra Křikavová**-7 (Luděk-6, Božena-5, Zdeněk Petr-4, Anna-3, Anna-2, Václav-1) was born on 28 Apr 1966 in Komarov u Horovic No. 40.

Radek Nešpor was born on 24 Mar 1963 in Horovice.

Radek Nešpor and Věra Křikavová married. They had the following children:

    i. **David Nešpor** was born on 19 Oct 1987 in Komarov u Horovic No. 40.

36. **Hanna Křikavová**-7 (Luděk-6, Božena-5, Zdeněk Petr-4, Anna-3, Anna-2, Václav-1) was born on 07 May 1957 in Komarov u Horovic No. 40. She died on 30 Dec 1997.

Bedřich Mach was born on 13 Feb 1955 in Komarov u Horovic No. 40. Bedřich Mach and Hanna Křikavová married. They had the following children:

    46. i. **Andrea Machová** was born on 10 Mar 1978 in Komarov u Horovic No. 40.

37. **Jan Křikava**-7 (Luděk-6, Božena-5, Zdeněk Petr-4, Anna-3, Anna-2, Václav-1) was born on 19 Aug 1960 in Komarov u Horovic No. 40.
    Hana Fedorcaková was born on 05 May 1962 in Kvan near Komarov.
    Jan Křikava and Hana Fedorcaková married. They had the following children:
    i. **Jan Křikava** was born on 22 Sep 1983 in Komarov u Horovic No. 40.
    ii. **Jana Linhartova** was born on 14 Feb 1973 in Komarov u Horovic.
    Jan Křikava and Jana Linhartova met. They had the following children:
    i. **Johana Křikavová** was born on 27 Nov 2007 in Komarov u Horovic.
38. **Hana Křikavová**-7 (Sasa-6, Božena-5, Zdeněk Petr-4, Anna-3, Anna-2, Václav-1) was born in 1958 in Komarov u Horovic.
    Milan Němec was born in 1954 in Komarov u Horovic.
    Milan Němec and Hana Křikavová married. They had the following children:
    i. **Milan Němec** was born in 1978 in Komarov u Horovic.
    ii. **Lubor Němec** was born in 1971 in Komarov u Horovic.
39. **Jana Petrová**-7 (Zdena-6, Zdena-5, Zdeněk Petr-4, Anna-3, Anna-2, Václav-1) was born on 29 Jun 1984 in Karlovy Vary.
    Petr Kottnauer.
    Petr Kottnauer and Jana Petrová met. They had the following children:
    i. **Daniel Kottnauer** was born in Karlovy Vary.
40. **Petr Herák**-7 (Radmila-6, Zdeněk-5, Bohumil-4, Anna-3, Anna-2, Václav-1) was born on 03 Jun 1965.
    Tereza Kovářová was born on 22 Jul 1973 in Jablonec.
    Petr Herák and Tereza Kovářová were married on 24 Mar 1990 in Český Dub. They had the following children:
    i. **Jan Herák** was born on 11 Sep 1990.
    ii. **Krystyna Heráková** was born on 18 Feb 1997.
41. **Pavlina Heráková**-7 (Radmila-6, Zdeněk-5, Bohumil-4, Anna-3, Anna-2, Václav-1) was born on 29 Jan 1964.

Milan Podlipský was born on 11 Mar 1961.

Milan Podlipský and Pavlina Heráková were married on 11 Feb 1984 in Milevsko. They had the following children:
    i. **Milan Podlipský** was born on 22 Jun 1984.
    ii. **Jakub Podlipský** was born on 19 Mar 1986.

42. **Helena Heráková**-7 (Radmila-6, Zdeněk-5, Bohumil-4, Anna-3, Anna-2, Václav-1) was born on 12 Jul 1966.

Pavel Hudec was born on 01 Jan 1962 in Český Dub.

Pavel Hudec and Helena Heráková were married on 15 Sep 1984 in Český Dub. They had the following children:
    i. **Kateřina Hudcova** was born on 17 Feb 1985.
    ii. **Martina Hudcova** was born on 12 May 1991.

43. **Martin Rechcigl**-7 (Zdeněk-6, Zdeněk-5, Bohumil-4, Anna-3, Anna-2, Václav-1) was born on 16 Dec 1968.

Petra Smolakova was born on 25 Jan 1973 in Moravia.

Martin Rechcigl and Petra Smolakova were married on 17 Sep 1994 in Český Dub. They had the following children:
    i. **Lucie Rechcíglová** was born on 05 Apr 1995.
    ii. **David Rechcigl** was born on 08 Aug 2000.

Generation 8

44. **Kevin Thomas Rechcigl**-8 (John Edward-7, Mila (Miloslav)-6, Miloslav-5, Adolf-4, Anna-3, Anna-2, Václav-1) was born on 09 Oct 1991 in Bradenton, FL.

Jordan Robbins daughter of Douglass Robbins and Ivonne was born on 10 Jan 1992 in Camarillo, CA.

Kevin Thomas Rechcigl and Jordan Robbins were married on 12 May 2018 in Jacksonville, FL. They had the following children:
    i. **James Douglas Rechcigl** was born on 05 Jan 2021 in Jacksonville, FL.
    ii. **Evelyn Marie Rechcigl** was born 29 May 2023 in Jacksonville, FL.

45. **Zuzana Heralecká**-8 (Marcela-7, Marta-6, Miloslav-5, Adolf-4, Anna-3, Anna-2, Václav-1) was born on 30 Dec 1978 in Jablonec nad Nisou.

Jaroslav Egrt was born on 25 Apr 1974 in Duchcov.

Jaroslav Egrt and Zuzana Heralecká were married on 13 Sep 2002 in Jablonec nad Nisou. They had the following children:
- i. **Kristina Egrtova** was born on 04 Jan 2008 in Liberec.
- ii. **Jaroslav Egrt** was born on 04 Jan 2008 in Liberec.

46. **Andrea Machová**-8 (Hanna-7, Luděk-6, Božena-5, Zdeněk Petr-4, Anna-3, Anna-2, Václav-1) was born on 10 Mar 1978 in Komarov u Horovic No. 40.

Soeren Christiansen was born in 1975 in Denmark.

Soeren Christiansen and Andrea Machová met. They had the following children:
- i. **Olivia Machová** was born on 10 May 2007 in Kobenhaven, Denmark.

Vela Family

Generation 1

1. **Josef Vela**-1 was born on 18 Nov 1818 in Cervenice No. 8. He died on 19 Mar 1899 in Cervenice No. 8.

   Rozalie Šídová daughter of Josef Šída and Unknown was born on 20 Nov 1821 in Cervenice No. 2. She died on 06 May 1891.

   Josef Vela and Rozalie Šídová were married in 1843. They had the following children:

   2. i. **Josef Vela** was born on 17 Mar 1844 in Cervenice No. 8. He married Anna Rechziegel on 06 Feb 1872 in Slavíkov No. 4, Vlastibořice parish. He died on 02 Dec 1928 in Sychrov.
   ii. **Zofie Velova** was born on 14 Oct 1846. She died on 30 Jun 1910.
   iii. **Františka Velova** was born on 04 Aug 1848. She died in 1896.
   iv. **Maria Velova** was born in 1851. She died on 21 Jul 1851.
   v. **Rozalia Velova** was born on 21 Jul 1852. She died on 03 Nov 1852.
   vi. **Jan Vela** was born on 18 Oct 1853. He died on 15 Apr 1861.

Generation 2

2. **Josef Vela**-2 (Josef-1) was born on 17 Mar 1844 in Cervenice No. 8. He died on 02 Dec 1928 in Sychrov.

   Anna Rechziegel daughter of Antonín Rechziegel and Anna Šiftová was born on 07 Aug 1852 in Slavíkov No. 4. She died on 15 Sep 1931 in Sychrov. Josef Vela and Anna Rechziegel were married on 06 Feb 1872 in Slavíkov No. 4, Vlastibořice parish. They had the following children:

   i. **Josef Vela** was born on 19 Apr 1873 in Slavíkov No. 3. He died on 07 Jan 1908 in Třtí.
   ii. **Kateřina Velova** was born on 21 Sep 1874 in Slavíkov No. 3. She died on 15 Nov 1931 in Sychrov. She married Čeněk Adam in Slavíkov.
   iii. **Anna Velova** was born on 12 Apr 1877 in Slavíkov No. 3. She died on 22 Apr 1911 in Hruba Skála (Doubravice).

4. iv. **Alois Jan Vela** was born on 14 May 1888 in Slavíkov No. 3. He married Marie Vysatova on 12 Sep 1916 in Vlastibořice. He died on 07 Oct 1974 in Turnov.

Generation 3

3. **Alois Jan Vela**-3 (Josef-2, Josef-1) was born on 14 May 1888 in Slavíkov No. 3. He died on 07 Oct 1974 in Turnov.
Marie Vysatova was born on 14 May 1895 in Praha. She died on 27 Jan 1971 in Turnov.
Alois Jan Vela and Marie Vysatova were married on 12 Sep 1916 in Vlastibořice. They had the following children:
   i. **Bohumir Vela** was born on 06 Jul 1917 in Sychrov. He married Vlasta Pechanová on 08 May 1956.
4. ii. **Vladimír Vela** was born on 13 Jul 1922 in Sychrov. He married Alena Vlahova on 22 Jan 1949.

Generation 4

4. **Vladimír Vela**-4 (Alois Jan-3, Josef-2, Josef-1) was born on 13 Jul 1922 in Sychrov.
Alena Vlahova was born on 03 Apr 1928. She died on 26 May 1982.
Vladimír Vela and Alena Vlahova were married on 22 Jan 1949. They had the following children:
5. i. **Alena Velova** was born on 05 Jan 1951 in Turnov. She married Ladislav Vodhanel on 12 Jul 1972.
6. ii. **Vladimír Vela** was born on 17 Dec 1954. He married Raduse Dvořáková on 07 Dec 1979.

Generation 5

5. **Alena Velova**-5 (Vladimír-4, Alois Jan-3, Josef-2, Josef-1) was born on 05 Jan 1951 in Turnov.
Ladislav Vodhanel was born on 29 Dec 1945.
Ladislav Vodhanel and Alena Velova were married on 12 Jul 1972. They had the following children:
   i. **Miroslava Vodhanelova** was born on 22 Dec 1973 in Turnov.
Jindřich Novotný.

Jindřich Novotný and Alena Velova were married on 12 Apr 1976. They had the following children:

    i.   **Sarka Novotná** was born on 10 Jun 1977 in Turnov.

6. **Vladimír Vela**-5 (Vladimír-4, Alois Jan-3, Josef-2, Josef-1) was born on 17 Dec 1954.

Raduse Dvořáková was born on 11 Dec 1959 in Turnov.

Vladimír Vela and Raduse Dvořáková were married on 07 Dec 1979. They had the following children:

    i.   **Vladimír Vela** was born on 27 Jul 1980.

    ii.   **Jan Vela** was born on 24 Jun 1984.

Veselý Family

Generation 1

1. **František Veselý**-1 was born in Blatna.
   Anna Pflanzerová was born in Kolin.
   František Veselý and Anna Pflanzerová married. They had the following children:
   2. i. **Augustin Veselý** was born in Blatna No. 1.

Generation 2

2. **Augustin Veselý**-2 (František-1) was born in Blatna No. 1.
   Anna Bodkynová daughter of Josef Bodkyn.
   Augustin Veselý and Anna Bodkynová married. They had the following children:
   3. i. **František Veselý** was born on 29 Mar 1835 in Komarice, Southren bohemia. He married Anna Helena Pflanzerová on 06 Aug 1878 in Kolin. He died on 21 Jun 1895 in Blatna.

Generation 3

3. **František Veselý**-3 (Augustin-2, František-1) was born on 29 Mar 1835 in Komarice, Southren bohemia. He died on 21 Jun 1895 in Blatna.
   Anna Helena Pflanzerová daughter of Gustav Pflanzer and Sofie Langova was born on 12 May 1857 in Horazdovice. She died on 26 Dec 1902 in Praha - Smichov.
   František Veselý and Anna Helena Pflanzerová were married on 06 Aug 1878 in Kolin. They had the following children:
   4. i. **Augustin Veselý** was born on 17 Sep 1879 in Blatna. He married Marie Rechcíglová on 25 Oct 1919 in Král. Vinohrady, Prague. He died on 06 Oct 1947 in Česká Trebova.
      ii. **Kamila Veselá** was born on 19 May 1882 in Blatna. She died on 19 Feb 1889 in Blatna.
      iii. **František Veselý** was born on 11 Jun 1886 in Blatna. He died on 20 Jun 1889.
      iv. **Otto Veselý** was born on 22 Jun 1888 in Blatna. He died on 13 Mar 1952 in České budejovice.

5. v. **Anna Veselá** was born on 16 Sep 1890 in Blatna. She married Alfred Pflanzer on 18 Jul 1910. She died on 04 Dec 1913 in Praha XI.

Generation 4

4. **Augustin Veselý**-4 (František-3, Augustin-2, František-1) was born on 17 Sep 1879 in Blatna. He died on 06 Oct 1947 in Česká Trebova.

   Marie Rechcíglová daughter of Josef Rechziegel and Marie Cinkova was born on 11 Mar 1892 in Žďárek No. 26, Turnov Co.. She died on 07 Jul 1968 in Havlickuv Brod.

   Augustin Veselý and Marie Rechcíglová were married on 25 Oct 1919 in Král. Vinohrady, Prague. They had the following children:

   6. i. **Věra Veselá** was born on 02 Aug 1920 in Česká Trebova No. 50, Litomysl Co.. She married Arnošt Pellant on 27 Dec 1939 in U sv. Tomase, Brno.

2. **Anna Veselá**-4 (František-3, Augustin-2, František-1) was born on 16 Sep 1890 in Blatna. She died on 04 Dec 1913 in Praha XI.

   Alfred Pflanzer son of Jan Pflanzer and Olga Fesalova was born on 09 May 1882 in Praha - Smichov. He died on 15 Mar 1953 in Praha - Smichov.

   Alfred Pflanzer and Anna Veselá were married on 18 Jul 1910. They had the following children:

   + i. **Věra Pflanzerová** was born on 18 Apr 1911 in Praha. She married František Přerovský in 1930.

Generation 5

6. **Věra Veselá**-5 (Augustin-4, František-3, Augustin-2, František-1) was born on 02 Aug 1920 in Česká Trebova No. 50, Litomysl Co..

   Arnošt Pellant son of Ota Pellant and Antonie Kudlatschkova was born on 11 May 1912 in Okrisky, P.O. Jihlava. He died on 06 Feb 2005 in Hradec Králové.

   Arnošt Pellant and Věra Veselá were married on 27 Dec 1939 in U sv. Tomase, Brno. They had the following children:

   8. i. **Arnošt Pellant** was born on 12 Jun 1943 in Praha. He married Zinaida Poliscukova on 07 Mar 1970 in Praha.
   9. ii. **Karel Pellant** was born on 14 Mar 1946 in Caslav. He married Jitka Kralickova on 01 Aug 1970 in Jevisovice.

7. **Věra Pflanzerová**-5 (Anna-4, František-3, Augustin-2, František-1) was born on 18 Apr 1911 in Praha.
   František Přerovský was born on 17 Nov 1900 in Moravska Ostrava. František Přerovský and Věra Pflanzerová were married in 1930. They had the following children:
   - 10. i. **František Jan Přerovský** was born on 16 Aug 1931 in Praha.

Generation 6

8. **Arnošt Pellant**-6 (Věra-5, Augustin-4, František-3, Augustin-2, František-1) was born on 12 Jun 1943 in Praha.
   Zinaida Poliscukova daughter of Ondřej Poliscuk and Věra Sirova was born on 03 Oct 1943 in Mizoc, Poland; since WWII USSR.
   Arnošt Pellant and Zinaida Poliscukova were married on 07 Mar 1970 in Praha. They had the following children:
   - 24 i. **Věra Pellantová** was born on 25 Feb 1971 in Hradec Králové. She married Jan Brožík on 24 Aug 2002 in Valdstejn.
   - 12. ii. **Eva Pellantová** was born on 05 Jul 1974 in Hradec Králové. She married Jan Mejzlik on 9 Jun 2001.

9. **Karel Pellant**-6 (Věra-5, Augustin-4, František-3, Augustin-2, František-1) was born on 14 Mar 1946 in Caslav.
   Jitka Kralickova was born on 08 Jul 1947 in Ostrava.
   Karel Pellant and Jitka Kralickova were married on 01 Aug 1970 in Jevisovice. They had the following children:
   - 13. i. **Martina Pellantová** was born on 27 Oct 1971 in Hradec Králové. She married Alan Gernert on 04 Oct 1997 in Jablonec nad Jizetou.
   - ii. **Iva Pellantová** was born on 04 Dec 1973 in Brno.

10. **František Jan Přerovský**-6 (Věra-5, Anna-4, František-3, Augustin-2, František-1) was born on 16 Aug 1931 in Praha.
    Danuse Zadakova was born on 19 May 1933 in Hlubos.
    František Jan Přerovský and Danuse Zadakova married. They had the following children:
    - i. **Ivan Přerovský** was born on 16 Jul 1958 in Pribram.
    - ii. **Eva Přerovská** was born on 10 Jun 1960 in Pribram.

Generation 7

11. **Věra Pellantová**-7 (Arnošt-6, Věra-5, Augustin-4, František-3, Augustin-2, František-1) was born on 25 Feb 1971 in Hradec Králové.

    Jan Brožík son of Jan Brožík and Jarmila Dočkálová was born on 06 Sep 1974 in Kromeriz.

    Jan Brožík and Věra Pellantová were married on 24 Aug 2002 in Valdstejn. They had the following children:

    i. **Barbora Brožíková** was born on 05 Dec 2003 in Hradec Králové.

    i. **Eva Pellantová**-7 (Arnošt-6, Věra-5, Augustin-4, František-3, Augustin-2, František-1) was born on 05 Jul 1974 in Hradec Králové.

    Jan Mejzlik son of Josef Mejzlik and Blanka Spustova was born on 13 Mar 1974 in Preckov, Trebic Co..

    Jan Mejzlik and Eva Pellantová were married on 09 Jun 2001. They had the following children:

    i. **Vojtěch Mejzlik** was born on 29 Jan 2003 in Hradec Králové.

    ii. **Antonín Mejzlik** was born on 29 Nov 2006 in Hradec Králové.

13. **Martina Pellantová**-7 (Karel-6, Věra-5, Augustin-4, František-3, Augustin-2, František-1) was born on 27 Oct 1971 in Hradec Králové.

    Alan Gernert son of Vilém Gernert and Vlasta was born on 26 Mar 1970 in Jilemnice.

    Alan Gernert and Martina Pellantová were married on 04 Oct 1997 in Jablonec nad Jizetou. They had the following children:

    i. **Marek Gernert** was born on 04 Apr 1998.

Pellant Family

Generation 1

1. **Ota Pellant**-1 was born in Okrizky.
   Antonie Kudlatschkova daughter of František Kudlatschek.
   Ota Pellant and Antonie Kudlatschkova married. They had the following children:
   - i. **Otilie Pellant** was born in 1909. She died in 1994.
   - ii. **Hilda Pellantová** was born in 1910.
   - iii. **Jana Pellant** was born in 1918. She died in 2000.
   - 3. iv. **Arnošt Pellant** was born on 11 May 1912 in Okrisky, P.O. Jihlava. He married Věra Veselá on 27 Dec 1939 in U sv. Tomase, Brno. He died on 06 Feb 2005 in Hradec Králové.
   - v. **Ota Pellant**.

Generation 2

2. **Arnošt Pellant**-2 (Ota-1) was born on 11 May 1912 in Okrisky, P.O. Jihlava. He died on 06 Feb 2005 in Hradec Králové.
   Věra Veselá daughter of Augustin Veselý and Marie Rechcíglová was born on 02 Aug 1920 in Česká Trebova No. 50, Litomysl Co..
   Arnošt Pellant and Věra Veselá were married on 27 Dec 1939 in U sv. Tomase, Brno. They had the following children:
   - 3. i. **Arnošt Pellant** was born on 12 Jun 1943 in Praha. He married Zinaida Poliscukova on 07 Mar 1970 in Praha.
   - 4. ii. **Karel Pellant** was born on 14 Mar 1946 in Caslav. He married Jitka Kralickova on 01 Aug 1970 in Jevisovice.

Generation 3

3. **Arnošt Pellant**-3 (Arnošt-2, Ota-1) was born on 12 Jun 1943 in Praha.
   Zinaida Poliscukova daughter of Ondřej Poliscuk and Věra Sirova was born on 03 Oct 1943 in Mizoc, Poland; since WWII USSR.
   Arnošt Pellant and Zinaida Poliscukova were married on 07 Mar 1970 in Praha. They had the following children:
   - 5. i. **Věra Pellantová** was born on 25 Feb 1971 in Hradec Králové. She married Jan Brožík on 24 Aug 2002 in Valdstejn.

6. ii. **Eva Pellantová** was born on 05 Jul 1974 in Hradec Králové. She married Jan Mejzlik on 9 Jun 2001.
4. **Karel Pellant**-3 (Arnošt-2, Ota-1) was born on 14 Mar 1946 in Caslav.
Jitka Kralickova was born on 08 Jul 1947 in Ostrava.
Karel Pellant and Jitka Kralickova were married on 01 Aug 1970 in Jevisovice. They had the following children:
7. i. **Martina Pellantová** was born on 27 Oct 1971 in Hradec Králové. She married Alan Gernert on 04 Oct 1997 in Jablonec nad Jizetou.
   ii. **Iva Pellantová** was born on 04 Dec 1973 in Brno.

Generation 4

5. **Věra Pellantová**-4 (Arnošt-3, Arnošt-2, Ota-1) was born on 25 Feb 1971 in Hradec Králové.
Jan Brožík son of Jan Brožík and Jarmila Dočkálová was born on 06 Sep 1974 in Kromeriz.
Jan Brožík and Věra Pellantová were married on 24 Aug 2002 in Valdstejn. They had the following children:
   i. **Barbora Brožíková** was born on 05 Dec 2003 in Hradec Králové.
6. **Eva Pellantová**-4 (Arnošt-3, Arnošt-2, Ota-1) was born on 05 Jul 1974 in Hradec Králové.
Jan Mejzlik son of Josef Mejzlik and Blanka Spustova was born on 13 Mar 1974 in Preckov, Trebic Co..
Jan Mejzlik and Eva Pellantová were married on 09 Jun 2001. They had the following children:
   i. **Vojtěch Mejzlik** was born on 29 Jan 2003 in Hradec Králové.
   ii. **Antonín Mejzlik** was born on 29 Nov 2006 in Hradec Králové.
7. **Martina Pellantová**-4 (Karel-3, Arnošt-2, Ota-1) was born on 27 Oct 1971 in Hradec Králové.
Alan Gernert son of Vilém Gernert and Vlasta was born on 26 Mar 1970 in Jilemnice.
Alan Gernert and Martina Pellantová were married on 04 Oct 1997 in Jablonec nad Jizetou. They had the following children:
   i. **Marek Gernert** was born on 04 Apr 1998.

Neumann Family of Vlastiborice

Generation 1

1. **Jan Neumann**-1 was born about 1750 in Vlastibořice No. 10.
   Lidmila was born in 1754. She died in 1824.
   Jan Neumann and Lidmila married. They had the following children:
   - 2. i. **Václav Neumann** was born about 1770 in Radimovice No. 6, Dub Co..

Generation 2

2. **Václav Neumann**-2 (Jan-1) was born about 1770 in Radimovice No. 6, Dub Co..
   Lidmila Adamova daughter of Jan Adam and Lidmila was born about 1770 in Vlastibořice No. 10. Václav Neumann and Lidmila Adamova married. They had the following children:
   - 3. i. **Jan Neumann** was born about 1790 in Radimovice No. 7, Český Dub Co..
   - 4. ii. **Kateřina Neumannová** was born about 1790.
   - 5. iii. **Václav Neumann** was born before 1790 in Radimovice No. 8, Český Dub Co..
   - 6. iv. **Lidmila Neumanová** was born on 28 Jun 1792 in Radimovice No. 6, Český Dub Co.. She married Ing. František Rechziegel on 03 Aug 1811 in Slavíkov No. 4, Vlastibořice parish. She died on 09 May 1845 in Slavíkov No. 4.
   - v. **Jiří Neumann** was born on 26 Oct 1794 in Radimovice, Český Dub Co..

Generation 3

3. **Jan Neumann**-3 (Václav-2, Jan-1) was born about 1790 in Radimovice No. 7, Český Dub Co..
   Kateřina Sivatkova daughter of Václav Sivatko was born in Libic no. 1. Jan Neumann and Kateřina Sivatkova married. They had the following children:
   - i. **Františka Neumanová** was born on 11 Jan 1810.
   - ii. **Kateřina Neumanová** was born on 22 Feb 1812.

    iii. **Jan Neumann** was born on 27 Jun 1813 in Radimovice No. 6, Dub Co..
    iv. **Anna Neumanová** was born on 10 Nov 1813.
    v. **František Neumann** was born on 16 Oct 1815.
    vi. **Václav Neuman** was born on 06 Jan 1817.
8. vii. **Antonín Neumann** was born in 1828 in Radimovice No. 7, Český Dub Dist.. He married Anna Brožová on 08 Feb 1848 in Vlastibořice.

4. **Kateřina Neumannová**-3 (Václav-2, Jan-1) was born about 1790.
Franc Beran.
Franc Beran and Kateřina Neumannová married. They had the following children:
    i. **Josef Beran** was born on 19 Oct 1812.

5. **Václav Neumann**-3 (Václav-2, Jan-1) was born before 1790 in Radimovice No. 8, Český Dub Co..
Terezie Kitova daughter of Karel Kita and Kateřina Matoušová was born in Trávníček.
Václav Neumann and Terezie Kitova married. They had the following children:
    i. **Jan Neumann** was born on 01 Jan 1807 in Radimovice No. 6, Dub Co..
    ii. **Kateřina Neumanová** was born on 13 Sep 1808 in Radimovice No. 6, Dub Co..
    iii. **Eleonora Neumannová** was born on 31 Jan 1813 in Radimovice No. 6, Dub Co..
    iv. **Barbora Neumanová** was born on 28 May 1815 in Radimovice No. 6, Dub Co..
    v. **Anna Neumannová** was born on 27 Jan 1817 in Radimovice No. 6, Dub Co..
    vi. **Václav Neumann** was born on 29 Dec 1820 in Radimovice No. 6, Dub Co..

Therezie Jiru daughter of Karel Jiru and Kateřina Matoušová.
Václav Neumann and Therezie Jiru married. They had the following children:

    i. **Therezie Neumannová** was born on 23 Dec 1810 in Radimovice No. 6, Český Dub Co..
    ii. **Eleonora Neumannová** was born on 31 Jan 1813 in Radimovice No. 6, Český Dub Co..
6. **Lidmila Neumanová**-3 (Václav-2, Jan-1) was born on 28 Jun 1792 in Radimovice No. 6, Český Dub Co.. She died on 09 May 1845 in Slavíkov No. 4.

    Ing. František Rechziegel son of František Rechziegel and Alžběta Boelmanova was born on 26 Dec 1789 in Slavíkov No. 4, Český Dub Co.. He died on 02 Aug 1849 in Slavíkov No. 4.

    Ing. František Rechziegel and Lidmila Neumanová were married on 03 Aug 1811 in Slavíkov No. 4, Vlastibořice parish. They had the following children:
    i. **Franz Rechziegel** was born on 03 Aug 1811 in Skavikov No. 4.
    ii. **František Rechziegel** was born on 26 May 1812 in Slavíkov No. 4. He died on 12 Jul 1814 in Slavíkov No. 4.
    iii. **Josef Rechziegel** was born on 22 Feb 1814 in Slavíkov No. 4. He died on 06 Jun 1893 in Teplice.
    iv. **Marie Rechziegel** was born on 14 Mar 1816 in Slavíkov No. 4. She died on 08 Apr 1846 in Slavíkov No. 4.
    v. **Františka Rechziegel** was born on 27 Jan 1818 in Slavíkov No. 4. She died on 25 Feb 1818 in Slavíkov, No. 4.
8. vi. **Petr Rechziegel** was born on 10 Jan 1819 in Slavíkov No. 4. He married Františka Hlavatá on 30 Nov 1850 in Slavíkov No. 3, Vlastibořice parish, Josef Sedláček, officiating. He died on 17 Oct 1890 in Novy Mlyn, Žďárek.
    vii. **Františka Johanna Rechziegel** was born on 11 May 1821 in Slavíkov No. 4. She died on 10 Mar 1823 in Slavíkov No. 4.
9. viii. **Antonín Rechziegel** was born on 22 May 1823 in Slavíkov No. 4, Český Dub Co.. He married Anna Šiftová on 11 Feb 1851 in Jivina No. 6. He died on 25 Sep 1888 in Slavíkov No. 4, Cesyu Dub Co..

10. ix. **Theresia Rechziegel** was born on 14 Apr 1825 in Slavíkov No. 4. She married Václav Beran on 05 Mar 1845 in Slavíkov No. 4, Vlastibořice parish.

    x. **Anna Rechziegel** was born in Apr 1826 in Slavíkov No. 4. She died on 13 Jul 1826 in Slavíkov No. 4.

11. xi. **Josefa Rechziegelová** was born on 09 May 1827 in Slavíkov No. 4. She married Josef Zajíček on 04 Jun 1851 in Slavíkov No. 4, Vlastibořice parish. She died on 24 Feb 1872 in Jivina No. 16.

    xii. **Kateřina Rechziegel** was born on 23 Apr 1829 in Slavíkov No. 4.

    xiii. **Karel Rechziegel** was born on 22 Jul 1830 in Slavíkov No. 4.

12. xiv. **Anna Rechziegel** was born on 09 Feb 1833 in Slavíkov No. 4. She married Johan Fanta on 22 Feb 1859 in Třtí No, 23. Hodkovice parish.

    xv. **Františka Rechziegel** was born on 04 Oct 1837 in Slavíkov No. 4. She died on 29 Oct 1837 in Slavíkov No. 4.

Generation 4

7. **Antonín Neumann**-4 (Jan-3, Václav-2, Jan-1) was born in 1828 in Radimovice No. 7, Český Dub Dist..

Anna Brožová daughter of Václav Brož and Alžběta Laurinova was born in 1829 in Radimovice No. 10 or Sychrov.

Antonín Neumann and Anna Brožová were married on 08 Feb 1848 in Vlastibořice. They had the following children:

13. i. **Anna Najmanová** was born on 31 Jul 1849 in Radimovice No. 7, Turnov Co.. She married Petr Rechziegel on 26 Jan 1869 in Radimovice No. 7, Vlastibořice parish., Jan Krt. Hruska officationg. She died on 05 Jun 1908 in Letařovice.

8. **Petr Rechziegel**-4 (Lidmila-3, Václav-2, Jan-1) was born on 10 Jan 1819 in Slavíkov No. 4. He died on 17 Oct 1890 in Novy Mlyn, Žďárek.

Františka Hlavatá daughter of Unknown and Terezie Hlavatá was born on 27 Feb 1820 in Bzi No. 6. She died on 10 Dec 1857 in Slavíkov No. 4, in Mohelka Creek -.

Petr Rechziegel and Františka Hlavatá were married on 30 Nov 1850 in Slavíkov No. 3, Vlastibořice parish, Josef Sedláček, officiating. They had the following children:

14. i. **Marie Rechziegel** was born on 24 Jan 1841 in Hodkovice No. 39.
15. ii. **Petr Rechziegel** was born on 01 Jun 1844 in Hodkovice No. 39. He married Anna Najmanová on 26 Jan 1869 in Radimovice No. 7, Vlastibořice parish., Jan Krt. Hruska officiationg. He died on 18 Sep 1917 in Letařovice No. 4, Turnov Co..
16. iii. **Františka Rechziegel** was born on 05 Jul 1846 in Hodkovice No. 39. She died on 28 Feb 1914 in Ruzodol No. 169.
17. iv. **Václav Rechziegel** was born on 25 Aug 1851 in Slavíkov No. 3. He married Anna Janečková in 1879. He died on 21 Mar 1909 in Radostín No. 13.
    v. **Josefa Rechziegelová** was born on 08 Nov 1852 in Slavíkov No. 3. She died on 11 Nov 1852 in Slavíkov No. 3.
    vi. **Karel Bor. Rechziegel** was born on 03 Jul 1855 in Slavíkov No. 3. He died on 24 Oct 1855 in Slavíkov No. 3.

Kateřina Koskova daughter of Josef Košek and Marie Jirova was born in 1831 in Třtí No. 6, Turnov Co.. She died on 20 Nov 1902 in Mala Bela, near Bakov.

Petr Rechziegel and Kateřina Koskova were married on 25 May 1858 in Třtí No. 6, Turnov Co., Franz Staznik officiating. They had the following children:

18. i. **Josef Rechziegel** was born on 31 Aug 1865 in Třtí No. 8, Turnov Co.. He married Marie Cinkova on 23 Aug 1890 in Parish Church, Mukarov. He died in 1917.

9. **Antonín Rechziegel**-4 (Lidmila-3, Václav-2, Jan-1) was born on 22 May 1823 in Slavíkov No. 4, Český Dub Co.. He died on 25 Sep 1888 in Slavíkov No. 4, Cesyu Dub Co..

Anna Šiftová daughter of František Šifta and Alžběta Černá was born on 27 Jun 1834 in Jivina No. 6. She died on 03 Apr 1854 in Slavíkov No. 4. Antonín Rechziegel and Anna Šiftová were married on 11 Feb 1851 in Jivina No. 6. They had the following children:

19. i. **Anna Rechziegel** was born on 07 Aug 1852 in Slavíkov No. 4. She married Josef Vela on 6 Feb 1872 in Slavíkov No. 4, Vlastibořice parish. She died on 15 Sep 1931 in Sychrov.

    ii. **Josef Rechziegel** was born on 29 Mar 1854 in Slavíkov No. 4. He died on 29 Mar 1854 in Slavíkov No. 4.

Marie Havlikova daughter of Jan Havlik and Kateřina Venclova was born on 08 Nov 1834 in Oujezd Co. 3. She died on 24 Oct 1913 in Loukov - at her daughter's Kateřina Skodova.

Antonín Rechziegel and Marie Havliková were married on 31 Jul 1854 in Loukov. They had the following children:

20. i. **Josefa Rechziegel** was born on 15 Jun 1855 in Slavíkov No. 4. She married Václav Jira on 07 Jul 1890 in Slavíkov No. 4. She died on 16 Jul 1945.

    ii. **Josef Rechziegel** was born on 29 Mar 1857 in Slavíkov No. 4. He died on 08 Mar 1912 in Praha.

    iii. **Kateřina Rechziegel** was born on 27 Nov 1859 in Slavíkov No. 4. She died on 24 Jan 1935 in Hodkovice.

21. iv. **Karel Bor. Rechziegel** was born on 02 Dec 1867 in Slavíkov No. 4. He married Anna Bartošová on 17 Aug 1889 in Český Dub. He died on 09 Jan 1904 in Chvalčovice.

10. **Theresia Rechziegel**-4 (Lidmila-3, Václav-2, Jan-1) was born on 14 Apr 1825 in Slavíkov No. 4.

Václav Beran son of Josef Beran and Alžběta Divinkova was born in 1823 in Trávníček No. 20.

Václav Beran and Theresia Rechziegel were married on 05 Mar 1845 in Slavíkov No. 4, Vlastibořice parish. They had the following children:

    i. **Josef Beran** was born on 12 Jun 1845 in Slavíkov No. 4.

    ii. **Marie Beranová** was born on 12 Sep 1847 in Slavíkov No. 4.

11. **Josefa Rechziegelová**-4 (Lidmila-3, Václav-2, Jan-1) was born on 09 May 1827 in Slavíkov No. 4. She died on 24 Feb 1872 in Jivina No. 16.

Josef Zajíček son of Václav Zajíček and Marie Samalova was born on 12 Nov 1830 in Jivina No. 16. He died in Received house in 1854.

Josef Zajíček and Josefa Rechziegelová were married on 04 Jun 1851 in Slavíkov No. 4, Vlastibořice parish. They had the following children:
   i. **Josef Zajíček** was born on 03 Nov 1851 in Jivina No. 16. He died on 02 Jan 1853 in Jivina No. 16.
   ii. **Jan Zajíček** was born on 11 Dec 1854 in Jivina No. 16. He died on 25 Mar 1855 in Jivina No. 16.
   iii. **Anna Zajickova** was born on 20 Sep 1856 in Jivina No. 16. She married František Richter on 15 Jun 1875 in Jivina No. 1 6; Josef Kovar, parish priest officiating.
   iv. **Josefa Zajickova** was born on 11 May 1859 in Jivina No. 16. She died about 1879. She married Josef Pycha on 11 Nov 1879 in Jivina No. 16, Český Dub Co.; Josef Kovar, parish priest officiating.
23. v. **Marie Zajickova** was born on 24 Aug 1862 in Jivina No. 16. She married Václav Šifta on 14 Jul 1885 in Jivina No. 16, Český Dub Co.; Rev. Josef Kovar, parish priest officiating. She died on 23 Mar 1927 in Jivina No. 16.
   vi. **Emilie Zajickova** was born on 11 Feb 1872 in Jivina No. 16. She died on 14 Feb 1872 in Jivina No. 16.

12. **Anna Rechziegel**-4 (Lidmila-3, Václav-2, Jan-1) was born on 09 Feb 1833 in Slavíkov No. 4.

Johan Fanta son of Johan Fanta and Anna Dopsáková was born about 1834 in Třtí No. 23.

Johan Fanta and Anna Rechziegel were married on 22 Feb 1859 in Třtí No, 23. Hodkovice parish. They had the following children:
   i. **Peter Fanta** was born on 20 Jun 1861 in Třtí No. 23. He married Anna Bussek on 24 Jul 1909 in Vsen.

Generation 5

13. **Anna Najmanová**-5 (Antonín-4, Jan-3, Václav-2, Jan-1) was born on 31 Jul 1849 in Radimovice No. 7, Turnov Co.. She died on 05 Jun 1908 in Letařovice.

Petr Rechziegel son of Petr Rechziegel and Františka Hlavatá was born on 01 Jun 1844 in Hodkovice No. 39. He died on 18 Sep 1917 in Letařovice No. 4, Turnov Co..

Petr Rechziegel and Anna Najmanová were married on 26 Jan 1869 in Radimovice No. 7, Vlastibořice parish., Jan Krt. Hruska officiationg. They had the following children:

    i. **Josef Rechcigl** was born on 22 Jul 1869 in Radimovice No. 7. He died on 24 Feb 1920 in Letařovice (prob.).

24. ii. **Emilie Rechcíglová** was born on 02 Apr 1871 in Letařovice No. 4, Český Dub Co.. She died on 18 Feb 1928.

    iii. **Václav Rechcigl** was born on 13 Mar 1873 in Letařovice No. 4, Český Dub Co..

24. iv. **Adolf Rechcigl** was born on 21 Aug 1876 in Letařovice No. 4, Český Dub Co.. He married Marie Berglová about 1900. He died on 30 Mar 1946 in Šárovcova Lhota No. 16.

    v. **Arnošt Rechziegel** was born on 07 Sep 1882 in Letařovice No. 4, Český Dub Co.. He died on 12 Oct 1882 in Letařovice No. 4, Český Dub Co..

25. vi. **Zdeněk Petr Rechcigl** was born on 31 Jul 1884 in Letařovice No. 4, Turnov Dist.. He married Anna Šimůnková on 08 Oct 1906 in Kralovske Vinohrady. He died on 08 Feb 1962 in Karlovy Vary - Rybare.

26. vii. **Bohumil Rechcigl** was born on 09 Apr 1888. He died on 03 Jan 1963 in Český Dub.

    viii. **Jan Rechziegel** was born on 08 May 1895.

14. **Marie Rechziegel**-5 (Petr-4, Lidmila-3, Václav-2, Jan-1) was born on 24 Jan 1841 in Hodkovice No. 39.

Václav Janeček son of at and Unknown was born in 1834 in Příšovice. He died on 18 Sep 1909 in Příšovice.

Václav Janeček and Marie Rechziegel married. They had the following children:

27. i. **Anna Janečková**.

    ii. **Petr Janeček**.

    iii. **František Janeček**.

Matejak.

Matejak and Marie Rechziegel met. They had the following children:

i. **Václav Rechziegel** was born on 24 Apr 1860 in Letařovice No. 4.

15. **Petr Rechziegel**-5 (Petr-4, Lidmila-3, Václav-2, Jan-1) was born on 01 Jun 1844 in Hodkovice No. 39. He died on 18 Sep 1917 in Letařovice No. 4, Turnov Co..

Anna Najmanová daughter of Antonín Neumann and Anna Brožová was born on 31 Jul 1849 in Radimovice No. 7, Turnov Co.. She died on 05 Jun 1908 in Letařovice.

Petr Rechziegel and Anna Najmanová were married on 26 Jan 1869 in Radimovice No. 7, Vlastibořice parish., Jan Krt. Hruska officiationg. They had the following children:

    i. **Josef Rechcigl** was born on 22 Jul 1869 in Radimovice No. 7. He died on 24 Feb 1920 in Letařovice (prob.).

24. ii. **Emilie Rechcíglová** was born on 02 Apr 1871 in Letařovice No. 4, Český Dub Co.. She died on 18 Feb 1928.

    iii. **Václav Rechcigl** was born on 13 Mar 1873 in Letařovice No. 4, Český Dub Co..

24. iv. **Adolf Rechcigl** was born on 21 Aug 1876 in Letařovice No. 4, Český Dub Co.. He married Marie Berglová about 1900. He died on 30 Mar 1946 in Šárovcova Lhota No. 16.

    v. **Arnošt Rechziegel** was born on 07 Sep 1882 in Letařovice No. 4, Český Dub Co.. He died on 12 Oct 1882 in Letařovice No. 4, Český Dub Co..

25. vi. **Zdeněk Petr Rechcigl** was born on 31 Jul 1884 in Letařovice No. 4, Turnov Dist.. He married Anna Šimůnková on 08 Oct 1906 in Kralovske Vinohrady. He died on 08 Feb 1962 in Karlovy Vary - Rybare.

26. vii. **Bohumil Rechcigl** was born on 09 Apr 1888. He died on 03 Jan 1963 in Český Dub.

    viii. **Jan Rechziegel** was born on 08 May 1895.

16. **Františka Rechziegel**-5 (Petr-4, Lidmila-3, Václav-2, Jan-1) was born on 05 Jul 1846 in Hodkovice No. 39. She died on 28 Feb 1914 in Ruzodol No. 169.

Ullrich was born in Jilove.

Ullrich and Františka Rechziegel married. They had the following children:
- i. **Adolf Ullrich** was born in Jilove.
- 28. ii. **Josef Ullrich** was born in Jilove.

17. **Václav Rechziegel**-5 (Petr-4, Lidmila-3, Václav-2, Jan-1) was born on 25 Aug 1851 in Slavíkov No. 3. He died on 21 Mar 1909 in Radostín No. 13.

    Anna Janečková daughter of František Janeček and Anna Koskova was born on 19 Apr 1855 in Třtí No. 6. She died on 17 Dec 1903 in Hodkovice. Václav Rechziegel and Anna Janečková were married in 1879. They had the following children:
    - i. **Adolf Rechziegel**.
    - ii. **Josef Rechziegel** was born in 1886 in Radostín. He died on 05 Oct 1956 in Radostín.
    - iii. **Emilie Rechziegelová**.
    - 30. iv. **Marie Rechziegelová** was born in 1882 in Radostín. She died on 30 Jul 1959 in Radostín.
    - 31. v. **Anna Rechziegelová** was born on 26 Sep 1888 in Radostín. She married Josef Franců about 1925. She died on 10 Oct 1964 in Kacanovy.
    - 32. vi. **Anastazie Rechziegelová** was born on 17 Mar 1894 in Radostín. She married Rudolf Roubíček in Jul 1917. She died on 19 Apr 1984 in Srch.

18. **Josef Rechziegel**-5 (Petr-4, Lidmila-3, Václav-2, Jan-1) was born on 31 Aug 1865 in Třtí No. 8, Turnov Co.. He died in 1917.

    Marie Cinkova daughter of Václav Cinka and Anna Štěpánková was born on 05 Jan 1870 in Jivina No. 24, Mnichova Hradiste Co..

    Josef Rechziegel and Marie Cinkova were married on 23 Aug 1890 in Parish Church, Mukarov. They had the following children:
    - 32. i. **Marie Rechcíglová** was born on 11 Mar 1892 in Žďárek No. 26, Turnov Co.. She married Augustin Veselý on 25 Oct 1919 in Král. Vinohrady, Prague. She died on 07 Jul 1968 in Havlickuv Brod.

33. ii. **Josef Rechcigl** was born on 05 Apr 1893 in Žďárek u Turnova. He married Marie Studničná on 28 Nov 1926 in Prague, CSR. He died on 13 Jun 1933 in Praha.

34. iii. **Anna Rechcíglová** was born on 12 Jan 1902 in Žďárek. She married Karel Matějů in 1919 in Prague, CSR. She died on 15 Apr 1992 in Brno.

19. **Anna Rechziegel**-5 (Antonín-4, Lidmila-3, Václav-2, Jan-1) was born on 07 Aug 1852 in Slavíkov No. 4. She died on 15 Sep 1931 in Sychrov.

    Josef Vela son of Josef Vela and Rozalie Šídová was born on 17 Mar 1844 in Cervenice No. 8. He died on 02 Dec 1928 in Sychrov.

    Josef Vela and Anna Rechziegel were married on 06 Feb 1872 in Slavíkov No. 4, Vlastibořice parish. They had the following children:

    i. **Josef Vela** was born on 19 Apr 1873 in Slavíkov No. 3. He died on 07 Jan 1908 in Třtí.

    ii. **Kateřina Velova** was born on 21 Sep 1874 in Slavíkov No. 3. She died on 15 Nov 1931 in Sychrov. She married Čeněk Adam in Slavíkov.

    iii. **Anna Velova** was born on 12 Apr 1877 in Slavíkov No. 3. She died on 22 Apr 1911 in Hruba Skála (Doubravice).

35. iv. **Alois Jan Vela** was born on 14 May 1888 in Slavíkov No. 3. He married Marie Vysatova on 12 Sep 1916 in Vlastibořice. He died on 07 Oct 1974 in Turnov.

20. **Josefa Rechziegel**-5 (Antonín-4, Lidmila-3, Václav-2, Jan-1) was born on 15 Jun 1855 in Slavíkov No. 4. She died on 16 Jul 1945.

    Václav Jira son of Josef Jira and Alžběta Růtová was born on 15 Sep 1857 in Klamorna No. 3, Český Dub Co.. He died on 24 May 1931.

    Václav Jira and Josefa Rechziegel were married on 07 Jul 1890 in Slavíkov No. 4. They had the following children:

36. i. **Marie Jirova** was born in 1893. She died on 01 Dec 1959.

21. **Karel Bor. Rechziegel**-5 (Antonín-4, Lidmila-3, Václav-2, Jan-1) was born on 02 Dec 1867 in Slavíkov No. 4. He died on 09 Jan 1904 in Chvalčovice.

Anna Bartošová daughter of Unknown and Kateřina Bartošová was born on 27 Feb 1866 in Chvalčovice No. 12. She died on 30 Sep 1936 in Sobeslavice No. 16.

Karel Bor. Rechziegel and Anna Bartošová were married on 17 Aug 1889 in Český Dub. They had the following children:
- i. **Václav Rechziegel** was born in 1894. He died in 1895.
- 37. ii. **Ing. František Rechcigel** was born on 18 Nov 1896 in Chvalčovice. He married Marie Holajova on 12 Nov 1924 in Prague, CSR. He died on 28 Aug 1968 in Český Dub.

22. **Marie Zajickova**-5 (Josefa-4, Lidmila-3, Václav-2, Jan-1) was born on 24 Aug 1862 in Jivina No. 16. She died on 23 Mar 1927 in Jivina No. 16.

Václav Šifta son of Václav Šifta and Karolina Odcházelová was born on 21 Aug 1861 in Jivina No. 1. He died in Received house in 1885.

Václav Šifta and Marie Zajickova were married on 14 Jul 1885 in Jivina No. 16, Český Dub Co.; Rev. Josef Kovar, parish priest officiating. They had the following children:
- i. **Emilie Šiftová** was born in 1886 in Jivina No. 1.
- ii. **Božena Šiftová** was born in 1892 in Jivina No. 1.
- 39. iii. **Josef Šifta** was born in 1898 in Jivina No. 1. He died in 1953.

Generation 6

23. **Emilie Rechcíglová**-6 (Anna-5, Antonín-4, Jan-3, Václav-2, Jan-1) was born on 02 Apr 1871 in Letařovice No. 4, Český Dub Co.. She died on 18 Feb 1928.

28. **Josef Ullrich** son of Ullrich and Františka Rechziegel was born in Jilove. Josef Ullrich and Emilie Rechcíglová married. They had the following children:
    - i. **Miloslav Ulrich** was born before 1900.
    - ii. **Ludvika Ulrichova** was born in 1898. She died on 01 Jun 1945.

24. **Adolf Rechcigl**-6 (Anna-5, Antonín-4, Jan-3, Václav-2, Jan-1) was born on 21 Aug 1876 in Letařovice No. 4, Český Dub Co.. He died on 30 Mar 1946 in Šárovcova Lhota No. 16.

Marie Berglová daughter of František Bergl and Marie Mařanová was born on 27 Mar 1880 in Drahotice No. 20, Mnichovo Hradiště Co.. She died on 25 Mar 1917 in Chocnějovice No. 22, Mnichovo Hradiště Co..
Adolf Rechcigl and Marie Berglová were married about 1900. They had the following children:
  i. **Marie Rechcíglová** was born on 29 Sep 1901 in Kocňovice (renamed Chocnějovice). She died on 03 Oct 1902 in Chocnějovice.
40. ii. **Miloslav Rechcigl** was born on 13 May 1904 in Kocňovice (renamed Chocnějovice) No. 27. He married Marie Rajtrová on 26 Jul 1926 in Praha - Kralovske Vinohrady. He died on 27 May 1973 in Washington, DC.
  Anna Rechcíglová was born on 10 Feb 1906 in Kocňovice (renamed Chocnějovice) No. She died on 26 Feb 1927 in Chocnějovice.

Marie Anna Ferklová daughter of František Ferkl and Anna Saralova was born on 10 Dec 1897 in Chocnějovice No. 2. She died on 31 Dec 1970 in Šárovcova Lhota.
Adolf Rechcigl and Marie Anna Ferklová were married on 25 Apr 1917 in St. Alois Church, Praha. They had the following children:
40. i. **Stanislav Josef Rechcigl** was born on 10 Oct 1918 in Chocnějovice. He married Libuše Sedláčková on 17 Jan 1948 in Novy Bydzov. He died on 09 May 1973 in Šárovcova Lhota No. 16.
  ii. **Adolf Rechcigl** was born on 09 Apr 1920 in Chocnějovice No. 22. He died on 27 Dec 1944 in Ples.

25. **Zdeněk Petr Rechcigl**-6 (Anna-5, Antonín-4, Jan-3, Václav-2, Jan-1) was born on 31 Jul 1884 in Letařovice No. 4, Turnov Dist.. He died on 08 Feb 1962 in Karlovy Vary - Rybare.
Anna Šimůnková daughter of Josef Šimůnek and Marie Stejskalová was born on 31 Dec 1884 in Sezemice No. 1, Mnichovo Hradiště Co.. She died on 28 Nov 1907 in After prolonged illnessa.
Zdeněk Petr Rechcigl and Anna Šimůnková were married on 08 Oct 1906 in Kralovske Vinohrady. They had the following children:

41. i. **Božena Rechcíglová** was born on 18 Mar 1907 in Letařovice, Turnov Co.. She married František Křikava on 24 Jul 1926 in Horovice. She died on 11 Aug 1979 in Hospital, Horovice.

Marie Paulu daughter of Paulu was born before 1900. She died in Divorced February 17, 1926.

Zdeněk Petr Rechcigl and Marie Paulu were married on 26 Sep 1908 in Český Dub. They had the following children:
  i. **child Rechcigl**. He died in Soon after birth.
  ii. **Zdeněk Rechcigl** was born on 06 Jul 1909. He died on 12 Oct 1909.

Marie Reslová daughter of Antonín Resl and Marie Kovářová was born on 25 Mar 1900 in Roven Nio. 45. She died on 02 Dec 1982 in Karlovy Vary. Zdeněk Petr Rechcigl and Marie Reslová were married on 30 Apr 1926 in Roven. They had the following children:

42. i. **Zdena Rechcíglová** was born on 25 Sep 1926 in Komarov u Horovic. She married Jan Mueller in 1949. She died on 02 Sep 1978 in Karlovy Vary.

Marie - uncertain was born on 11 Jan 1909. She died on 02 Nov 1996. Zdeněk Petr Rechcigl and Marie - uncertain met. They had the following children:
  i. **Ludmila Rechcíglová** was born after 1900.

26. **Bohumil Rechcigl**-6 (Anna-5, Antonín-4, Jan-3, Václav-2, Jan-1) was born on 09 Apr 1888. He died on 03 Jan 1963 in Český Dub.

Růžena Slukova was born in 1892. She died on 14 Mar 1969 in Český Dub. Bohumil Rechcigl and Růžena Slukova married. They had the following children:

43. i. **Zdeněk Rechcigl** was born on 05 Dec 1913. He married Marie Pavlová on 29 Jan 1944. He died on 01 Nov 1985.
  ii. **Věra Rechcíglová** was born in 1915. She died in 1972.
      Notes for Věra Rechcíglová:
      General Notes:
      unmarried

44. iii. **Libuše Rechcíglová** was born on 13 Aug 1916. She married Jan Mančík on 03 Jun 1950. She died in Mar 1997 in Varnsdorf.

27. **Anna Janečková**-6 (Marie-5, Petr-4, Lidmila-3, Václav-2, Jan-1).
Kinsky.
Kinsky and Anna Janečková married. They had the following children:
   i. **Miloslav Kinsky**.

28. **Josef Ullrich**-6 (Františka-5, Petr-4, Lidmila-3, Václav-2, Jan-1) was born in Jilove.

23. **Emilie Rechcíglová** daughter of Petr Rechziegel and Anna Najmanová was born on 02 Apr 1871 in Letařovice No. 4, Český Dub Co.. She died on 18 Feb 1928.
Josef Ullrich and Emilie Rechcíglová married. They had the following children:
   i. **Miloslav Ulrich** was born before 1900.
   ii. **Ludvika Ulrichova** was born in 1898. She died on 01 Jun 1945.

29. **Marie Rechziegelová**-6 (Václav-5, Petr-4, Lidmila-3, Václav-2, Jan-1) was born in 1882 in Radostín. She died on 30 Jul 1959 in Radostín.
Josef Pelech was born in 1885. He died on 09 Feb 1961.
Josef Pelech and Marie Rechziegelová married. They had the following children:
45. i. **Marie Pelechová**. She died on 09 Aug 1961.

30. **Anna Rechziegelová**-6 (Václav-5, Petr-4, Lidmila-3, Václav-2, Jan-1) was born on 26 Sep 1888 in Radostín. She died on 10 Oct 1964 in Kacanovy.
Josef Franců was born on 09 Apr 1894 in Kacanovy. He died on 22 Nov 1971 in Turnov.
Josef Franců and Anna Rechziegelová were married about 1925. They had the following children:
4   i. **Jaromír Franců** was born on 26 Feb 1926 in Kacanovy. He married Marta Lamačová on 4 Nov 1950 in Turnov. He died on 04 Jul 1980 in Jičín.

Josef Studnička was born in Kacanovy. He died before 1925.
Notes for Josef Studnička:
General Notes:

He went to the Russian Front during the World War I but never returned. Josef Studnička and Anna Rechziegelová married. They had the following children:

    47. i. **Oldrřch Studnička** was born on 07 Jun 1912 in Kacanovy. He died on 20 Aug 1942 in Kacanovy.

31. **Anastazie Rechziegelová**-6 (Václav-5, Petr-4, Lidmila-3, Václav-2, Jan-1) was born on 17 Mar 1894 in Radostín. She died on 19 Apr 1984 in Srch.

Rudolf Roubíček son of František Roubíček and Marie Roubíčková was born about 1894 in Radostín. He died about Mar 1918.

Rudolf Roubíček and Anastazie Rechziegelová were married in Jul 1917. They had the following children:

    11 i. **Jana Roubíčková** was born on 26 Jan 1918 in Radostín. She married Franisek Kvapil on 11 Sep 1943 in Kunetice. She died on 13 Oct 1981 in Lazne Bohdanec.

František Pátek was born in 1894 in Chlum u Hlinska. He died on 05 Feb 1958 in Srchrechziegel.

František Pátek and Anastazie Rechziegelová met. They had the following children:

    49. i. **Dalibor Rechziegel** was born on 20 Oct 1924 in Radostín, near Turnov. He married Sona Pražáková on 26 Apr 1948 in Kladno. He died on 12 Aug 1997 in Litomerice.

    50. ii. **Drahomir Rechziegel** was born on 19 Nov 1926. He died on 23 Oct 1983.

32. **Marie Rechcíglová**-6 (Josef-5, Petr-4, Lidmila-3, Václav-2, Jan-1) was born on 11 Mar 1892 in Žďárek No. 26, Turnov Co.. She died on 07 Jul 1968 in Havlickuv Brod.

Augustin Veselý son of František Veselý and Anna Helena Pflanzerová was born on 17 Sep 1879 in Blatna. He died on 06 Oct 1947 in Česká Trebova.

Augustin Veselý and Marie Rechcíglová were married on 25 Oct 1919 in Král. Vinohrady, Prague. They had the following children:

51. i. **Věra Veselá** was born on 02 Aug 1920 in Česká Trebova No. 50, Litomysl Co.. She married Arnošt Pellant on 27 Dec 1939 in U sv. Tomase, Brno.

33. **Josef Rechcigl**-6 (Josef-5, Petr-4, Lidmila-3, Václav-2, Jan-1) was born on 05 Apr 1893 in Žďárek u Turnova. He died on 13 Jun 1933 in Praha.

    Marie Studničná daughter of Josef Studničný and Otilie Menzelova was born on 09 Feb 1907 in Nova Ves u Bakova nad Jizerou. She died on 20 Dec 1985 in Mala Bela.

    Josef Rechcigl and Marie Studničná were married on 28 Nov 1926 in Prague, CSR. They had the following children:

    15. i. **Josef Rechcigl** was born on 19 Feb 1931 in Praha. He married Jitka Prskavcová on 24 Mar 1956 in Praha II.

1   **Anna Rechcíglová**-6 (Josef-5, Petr-4, Lidmila-3, Václav-2, Jan-1) was born on 12 Jan 1902 in Žďárek. She died on 15 Apr 1992 in Brno.

    Karel Matějů was born on 01 May 1901 in Prague. He died in May 1945. Karel Matějů and Anna Rechcíglová were married in 1919 in Prague, CSR. They had the following children:

    53. i. **2nd Karel Matějů** was born on 06 Dec 1924 in Brno. He married Anna Třísková on 09 Jun 1951 in Brno. He died on 09 Dec 1992 in Brno.

    Miloš Valnicek son of Miloš Valnicek and Emilie Lehka was born in 1902. He died on 14 Oct 1968. Miloš Valnicek and Anna Rechcíglová were married in 1951 in Petrov, Brno. They had no children.

35. **Alois Jan Vela**-6 (Anna-5, Antonín-4, Lidmila-3, Václav-2, Jan-1) was born on 14 May 1888 in Slavíkov No. 3. He died on 07 Oct 1974 in Turnov.

    Marie Vysatova was born on 14 May 1895 in Praha. She died on 27 Jan 1971 in Turnov.

    Alois Jan Vela and Marie Vysatova were married on 12 Sep 1916 in Vlastibořice. They had the following children:

    i. **Bohumir Vela** was born on 06 Jul 1917 in Sychrov. He married Vlasta Pechanová on 08 May 1956.

    55. ii. **Vladimír Vela** was born on 13 Jul 1922 in Sychrov. He married Alena Vlahova on 22 Jan 1949.

36. **Marie Jirova**-6 (Josefa-5, Antonín-4, Lidmila-3, Václav-2, Jan-1) was born in 1893. She died on 01 Dec 1959.

    Josef Jisl was born in 1887 in Trávníček. He died on 12 Feb 1951. Josef Jisl and Marie Jirova married. They had the following children:

    55. i. **Josef Jisl** was born on 02 Dec 1916. He died on 01 May 1991.

37. **Ing. František Rechcigel**-6 (Karel Bor.-5, Antonín-4, Lidmila-3, Václav-2, Jan-1) was born on 18 Nov 1896 in Chvalčovice. He died on 28 Aug 1968 in Český Dub.

    Marie Holajova daughter of Josef Holaj and Marie Hauzrova was born on 18 May 1904 in Český Dub. She died on 27 Nov 1968 in III (Český Dub, No. 31).

    Ing. František Rechcigel and Marie Holajova were married on 12 Nov 1924 in Prague, CSR. They had the following children:

    56. i. **Milan Rechcigel** was born on 12 Sep 1926 in Český Dub. He married Božena Bernardová on 24 Jan 1953. He died on 24 Sep 1980 in Český Dub.
    57. ii. **Ing. Vladko Rechcigel** was born on 29 Aug 1929 in Český Dub. He married Lidmila Lukaskova on 19 Oct 1957.
    58. iii. **Milena Rechcigelova** was born on 10 Mar 1936 in Turnov. She died on 03 May 1983 in Praha.

38. **Josef Šifta**-6 (Marie-5, Josefa-4, Lidmila-3, Václav-2, Jan-1) was born in 1898 in Jivina No. 1. He died in 1953.

    Marie Řepková was born in 1897 in Pacerice. She died in 1985.

    Josef Šifta and Marie Řepková married. They had the following children:

    59. i. **Marie Šiftová** was born on 20 Jun 1923 in Jivina No. 1. She died on 10 Jun 2004.

Generation 7

39. **Miloslav Rechcigl**-7 (Adolf-6, Anna-5, Antonín-4, Jan-3, Václav-2, Jan-1) was born on 13 May 1904 in Kocňovice (renamed Chocnějovice) No. 22. He died on 27 May 1973 in Washington, DC.

    Marie Rajtrová daughter of Čeněk Rajtr and Marie Dandová was born on 05 Jul 1905 in Dolanky No. 7, Mnichovo Hradiště Co.. She died on 13 Apr 1982 in Mladá Boleslav.

Miloslav Rechcigl and Marie Rajtrová were married on 26 Jul 1926 in Praha - Kralovske Vinohrady. They had the following children:

    60. i. **Mila (Miloslav) Rechcigl Jr.** was born on 30 Jul 1930 in Mladá Boleslav, CSR. He married Eva Edwards (Eisnerová) on 29 Aug 1953 in New York, NY.

    61. ii. **Marta Rechcíglová** was born on 23 May 1933 in Mladá Boleslav. She married František Žďárský on 03 Oct 1953 in Mladá Boleslav. She died on 13 Sep 2018 in Mladá Boleslav.

40. **Stanislav Josef Rechcigl**-7 (Adolf-6, Anna-5, Antonín-4, Jan-3, Václav-2, Jan-1) was born on 10 Oct 1918 in Chocnějovice. He died on 09 May 1973 in Šárovcova Lhota No. 16.

Libuše Sedláčková daughter of Bedřich Sedláček and Ludmila was born on 24 Sep 1924 in Staré Smrkovice, Jičín Dist. She died on 03 Apr 2019 in Jičín, Czech.

Stanislav Josef Rechcigl and Libuše Sedláčková were married on 17 Jan 1948 in Novy Bydzov. They had the following children:

    62. i. **Hana Rechcíglová** was born on 13 Jul 1948 in Novy Bydzov, Hradec Králové Co.. She married Jaroslav Husak on 28 Dec 1968 in Sobotka, Jičín Co..

    63. ii. **Libuše Rechcíglová** was born on 25 Jan 1950 in Novy Bydzov, Hradec Králové Co.. She married Miroslav Vich on 11 Apr 1970 in Ostromer, Jičín Co..

    64. iii. **Stanislav Rechcigl** was born on 24 Mar 1952 in Hořice, Jičín Co.. He married Zdena Pařízková on 24 Mar 1972 in Jičín.

41. **Božena Rechcíglová**-7 (Zdeněk Petr-6, Anna-5, Antonín-4, Jan-3, Václav-2, Jan-1) was born on 18 Mar 1907 in Letařovice, Turnov Co.. She died on 11 Aug 1979 in Hospital, Horovice.

František Křikava son of Josef Křikava and Marie Stichová was born on 23 Dec 1890 in Chaloupky, Beroun Co.. He died on 25 Mar 1965 in Komarov u Horovic No. 40.

František Křikava and Božena Rechcíglová were married on 24 Jul 1926 in Horovice. They had the following children:

65. i. **Luděk Křikava** was born on 02 Feb 1927 in Komarov u Horovic No. 40. He died on 23 Sep 1996.
66. ii. **Sasa Křikava** was born on 02 Dec 1930 in Komarov u Horovic No. 40.

42. **Zdena Rechcíglová**-7 (Zdeněk Petr-6, Anna-5, Antonín-4, Jan-3, Václav-2, Jan-1) was born on 25 Sep 1926 in Komarov u Horovic. She died on 02 Sep 1978 in Karlovy Vary.

Jan Mueller son of Jan Karel Mueller and Anna Šašková was born on 05 Feb 1925 in Prague. He died on 01 May 1989 in Karlovy Vary.

Jan Mueller and Zdena Rechcíglová were married in 1949. They had the following children:

i. **Jana Muellerová** was born on 08 Nov 1952 in Karlovy Vary. She married Jiří Stuchl on 26 Aug 1979 in Manetin, Plzen Sever Co..

ii. **Zdena Muellerová** was born on 01 May 1960 in Karlovy Vary. She married František Petr in 1981 in Karlovy Vary.

43. **Zdeněk Rechcigl**-7 (Bohumil-6, Anna-5, Antonín-4, Jan-3, Václav-2, Jan-1) was born on 05 Dec 1913. He died on 01 Nov 1985.

Marie Pavlová was born in Jan 1921 in Vlcetin. She died in Dec 2003.

Zdeněk Rechcigl and Marie Pavlová were married on 29 Jan 1944. They had the following children:

69. i. **Radmila Rechcíglová** was born on 29 May 1944. She married Pavel Herák on 14 Sep 1963 in Český Dub.
70. ii. **Zdeněk Rechcigl** was born on 07 Aug 1946 in Český Dub. He married Věra Vizkova on 30 Dec 1967 in Český Dub.

Libuše was born on 05 Dec 1917.

Zdeněk Rechcigl and Libuše were married in 1964. They had no children.

44. **Libuše Rechcíglová**-7 (Bohumil-6, Anna-5, Antonín-4, Jan-3, Václav-2, Jan-1) was born on 13 Aug 1916. She died in Mar 1997 in Varnsdorf.

Jan Mančík.

Jan Mančík and Libuše Rechcíglová were married on 03 Jun 1950. They had the following children:

71. i. **Jana Mančíková** was born in 1951.

72. ii. **Irena Mančíková** was born in 1954.
45. **Marie Pelechová**-7 (Marie-6, Václav-5, Petr-4, Lidmila-3, Václav-2, Jan-1). She died on 09 Aug 1961.

    Alois Florián was born resided in Letovice by Brno.

    Alois Florián and Marie Pelechová married. They had the following children:

    73. i. **Marie Floriánová**.

    ii. **Karel Florián**.

46. **Jaromír Franců**-7 (Anna-6, Václav-5, Petr-4, Lidmila-3, Václav-2, Jan-1) was born on 26 Feb 1926 in Kacanovy. He died on 04 Jul 1980 in Jičín.

    Marta Lamačová was born on 06 Jun 1927 in Kacanovy. She died on 04 Nov 1950 in Turnov.

    Jaromír Franců and Marta Lamačová were married on 04 Nov 1950 in Turnov. They had the following children:

    74. i. **Jaromír Franců** was born on 21 Aug 1951 in Kacanovy, Turnov. He married Věra Zimova on 29 Dec 1989 in Jičín.

47. **Oldrřch Studnička**-7 (Anna-6, Václav-5, Petr-4, Lidmila-3, Václav-2, Jan-1) was born on 07 Jun 1912 in Kacanovy. He died on 20 Aug 1942 in Kacanovy.

    Notes for Oldrřch Studnička:

    General Notes:

    He was shot by the Nazi during the persecutine of the underground leader Dr. Vladimír. Krajina.

    Bohumila Karaskova was born on 09 May 1913 in Kacanovy. She died on 25 Sep 2000 in Turnov. Oldrřch Studnička and Bohumila Karaskova married. They had the following children:

    75. i. **Oldrřch Studnička** was born on 31 May 1942 in Kacanovy.

48. **Jana Roubíčková**-7 (Anastazie-6, Václav-5, Petr-4, Lidmila-3, Václav-2, Jan-1) was born on 26 Jan 1918 in Radostín. She died on 13 Oct 1981 in Lazne Bohdanec.

    Franisek Kvapil was born on 24 Nov 1912. He died on 15 Oct 1982.

    Franisek Kvapil and Jana Roubíčková were married on 11 Sep 1943 in Kunetice. They had the following children:

76. i. **Jan Kvapil** was born on 27 May 1944 in Pardubice. He married Eva Nováková on 09 Jun 1962 in Pardubice.
77. ii. **Nada Kvapilová** was born on 11 Feb 1946 in Pardubice. She married Josef Virt on 13 Mar 1971 in Rohovladova Bela.

49. **Dalibor Rechziegel**-7 (Anastazie-6, Václav-5, Petr-4, Lidmila-3, Václav-2, Jan-1) was born on 20 Oct 1924 in Radostín, near Turnov. He died on 12 Aug 1997 in Litomerice.
    Sona Pražáková was born on 23 Sep 1929 in Brandysek, Kladno Co.. Dalibor Rechziegel and Sona Pražáková were married on 26 Apr 1948 in Kladno. They had the following children:
    i. **Jan Rechziegel** was born on 12 Oct 1951 in Litomerice.
    ii. **Luboš Rechziegel** was born on 08 Jan 1957 in Litomerice. He married Radka Chládková on 06 Jul 1985 in Litomerice.

50. **Drahomir Rechziegel**-7 (Anastazie-6, Václav-5, Petr-4, Lidmila-3, Václav-2, Jan-1) was born on 19 Nov 1926. He died on 23 Oct 1983.
    Marie Kamenicka was born on 01 Jan 1929 in Kunetice. She died on 18 Apr 1979. Drahomir Rechziegel and Marie Kamenicka married. They had the following children:
78. i. **Jitka Rechziegelová** was born on 27 Aug 1951.
79. ii. **Aleš Rechziegel** was born on 15 Jan 1954.
80. iii. **Drahomir Rechziegel** was born on 10 Feb 1957 in Pardubice.

51. **Věra Veselá**-7 (Marie-6, Josef-5, Petr-4, Lidmila-3, Václav-2, Jan-1) was born on 02 Aug 1920 in Česká Trebova No. 50, Litomysl Co..
    Arnošt Pellant son of Ota Pellant and Antonie Kudlatschkova was born on 11 May 1912 in Okrisky, P.O. Jihlava. He died on 06 Feb 2005 in Hradec Králové.
    Arnošt Pellant and Věra Veselá were married on 27 Dec 1939 in U sv. Tomase, Brno. They had the following children:
81. i. **Arnošt Pellant** was born on 12 Jun 1943 in Praha. He married Zinaida Poliscukova on 07 Mar 1970 in Praha.
82. ii. **Karel Pellant** was born on 14 Mar 1946 in Caslav. He married Jitka Kralickova on 01 Aug 1970 in Jevisovice.

52. **Josef Rechcigl**-7 (Josef-6, Josef-5, Petr-4, Lidmila-3, Václav-2, Jan-1) was born on 19 Feb 1931 in Praha.
    Jitka Prskavcová daughter of Josef Prskavec and Anastazie Studničná was born on 02 Feb 1932 in Ptyrov.
    Josef Rechcigl and Jitka Prskavcová were married on 24 Mar 1956 in Praha II. They had the following children:
    - 83. i. **Jitka Rechcíglová** was born on 09 Oct 1957 in Mladá Boleslav. She married Vladimír Skramusky on 11 Aug 1979 in Bakov nad Jizerou.
    - 84. ii. **Josef Rechcigl** was born on 03 Mar 1960 in Turnov. He married Věra Laskova on 17 Apr 1987 in Bakov nad Jizerou.

53. **2nd Karel Matějů**-7 (Anna-6, Josef-5, Petr-4, Lidmila-3, Václav-2, Jan-1) was born on 06 Dec 1924 in Brno. He died on 09 Dec 1992 in Brno.
    Anna Třísková daughter of Jindřich Tříska and Anna was born on 26 Jul 1925 in Blansko.
    2nd Karel Matějů and Anna Třísková were married on 09 Jun 1951 in Brno. They had the following children:
    - 85. i. **3rd Karel Matějů** was born on 15 Nov 1954 in Brno. He married Alena Šrámková on 07 Jul 1979 in Brno.

54. **Vladimír Vela**-7 (Alois Jan-6, Anna-5, Antonín-4, Lidmila-3, Václav-2, Jan-1) was born on 13 Jul 1922 in Sychrov.
    Alena Vlahova was born on 03 Apr 1928. She died on 26 May 1982.
    Vladimír Vela and Alena Vlahova were married on 22 Jan 1949. They had the following children:
    - 86. i. **Alena Velova** was born on 05 Jan 1951 in Turnov. She married Ladislav Vodhanel on 12 Jul 1972.
    - 87. ii. **Vladimír Vela** was born on 17 Dec 1954. He married Raduse Dvořáková on 07 Dec 1979.

55. **Josef Jisl**-7 (Marie-6, Josefa-5, Antonín-4, Lidmila-3, Václav-2, Jan-1) was born on 02 Dec 1916. He died on 01 May 1991.
    Marie Pelantová was born on 21 Apr 1916.
    Josef Jisl and Marie Pelantová married. They had the following children:
    - 88. i. **Marie Jislova** was born on 28 Jul 1947.

56. **Milan Rechcigel**-7 (Ing. František-6, Karel Bor.-5, Antonín-4, Lidmila-3, Václav-2, Jan-1) was born on 12 Sep 1926 in Český Dub. He died on 24 Sep 1980 in Český Dub.

    Božena Bernardová daughter of Ladislav Bernard and Bozena Kupcova was born on 04 Jun 1930 in Podrby - Mala Libic.

    Milan Rechcigel and Božena Bernardová were married on 24 Jan 1953. They had the following children:

    89. i. **Hana Rechcigelova** was born on 01 Nov 1953 in Český Dub. She died on 27 Jul 2021.
    90. ii. **Ing. Pavel Rechcigel** was born on 19 Jul 1963 in Český Dub.

57. **Ing. Vladko Rechcigel**-7 (Ing. František-6, Karel Bor.-5, Antonín-4, Lidmila-3, Václav-2, Jan-1) was born on 29 Aug 1929 in Český Dub.

    Lidmila Lukaskova was born on 28 Mar 1932 in Vresna, nr. Veseli nad Luznici.

    Ing. Vladko Rechcigel and Lidmila Lukaskova were married on 19 Oct 1957. They had the following children:

    91. i. **Vladko Rechcigel** was born on 04 Aug 1959 in Prague, CSR.
    92. ii. **Ing. Jan Rechcigel** was born on 02 Feb 1966 in Prague, CSR.

58. **Milena Rechcigelova**-7 (Ing. František-6, Karel Bor.-5, Antonín-4, Lidmila-3, Václav-2, Jan-1) was born on 10 Mar 1936 in Turnov. She died on 03 May 1983 in Praha.

    Jiří Nožička was born in 1926.

    Jiří Nožička and Milena Rechcigelova married. They had the following children:

    i. **Jiří Nožička** was born on 05 May 1961.

59. **Marie Šiftová**-7 (Josef-6, Marie-5, Josefa-4, Lidmila-3, Václav-2, Jan-1) was born on 20 Jun 1923 in Jivina No. 1. She died on 10 Jun 2004.

    Miroslav Třešňák was born on 06 Mar 1921 in Jenisovice -. He died on 11 Jul 1986 in Lived in Jivina No. 1.

    Miroslav Třešňák and Marie Šiftová married. They had the following children:

93. i. **Miroslav Třešňák** was born on 25 May 1943 in Jivina No. 1. He married Miluška Hanzlova on 23 Oct 1965. He died on 19 Nov 2005 in moved to Jivina No. 24.
94. ii. **Jiří Třešňák** was born on 22 Jul 1952 in Jivina No. 1. He married Marie Zoubková on 19 Jun 1976. He died in moved to Odolena Voda, Praha vychod.

Generation 8

60. **Mila (Miloslav) Rechcigl Jr.**-8 (Miloslav-7, Adolf-6, Anna-5, Antonín-4, Jan-3, Václav-2, Jan-1) was born on 30 Jul 1930 in Mladá Boleslav, CSR.
Eva Edwards (Eisnerová) daughter of Paul J. Edwards (Pavel Eisner) and Jiřina Taussigová was born on 21 Jan 1932 in Prague, CSR.
Mila (Miloslav) Rechcigl Jr. and Eva Edwards (Eisnerová) were married on 29 Aug 1953 in New York, NY. They had the following children:

95. i. **John Edward Rechcigl** was born on 27 Feb 1960 in Washington, D.C.. He married Nancy Ann Palko on 30 Jul 1983 in Dover, NJ.
96. ii. **Karen Rechcigl** was born on 16 Apr 1962 in Washington, DC. She married Ulysses Kollecas on 25 Aug 1990 in Bethesda, MD.

24 **Marta Rechcíglová**-8 (Miloslav-7, Adolf-6, Anna-5, Antonín-4, Jan-3, Václav-2, Jan-1) was born on 23 May 1933 in Mladá Boleslav. She died on 13 Sep 2018 in Mladá Boleslav.
František Žďárský son of František Václav Žďárský and Eliška Foltýnová was born on 21 May 1932 in Turnov.
František Žďárský and Marta Rechcíglová were married on 03 Oct 1953 in Mladá Boleslav. They had the following children:

97. i. **Marcela Žďárská** was born on 09 May 1954 in Liberec. She married Miroslav Heralecký on 15 Mar 1975 in Sychrov.
98. ii. **Iveta Žďárská** was born on 29 Aug 1963 in Liberec, Bohemia. She married Vlastimil Berkman on 29 Oct 1983.

62. **Hana Rechcíglová**-8 (Stanislav Josef-7, Adolf-6, Anna-5, Antonín-4, Jan-3, Václav-2, Jan-1) was born on 13 Jul 1948 in Novy Bydzov, Hradec Králové Co..
Jaroslav Husak was born on 24 Mar 1946 in Jičín.

Jaroslav Husak and Hana Rechcíglová were married on 28 Dec 1968 in Sobotka, Jičín Co.. They had the following children:
    i. **Martin Husak** was born on 20 Feb 1971 in Hradec Králové. He married Petra Endrychová on 24 Jul 1999 in Hradec Králové.
    ii. **Petra Husakova** was born on 30 Mar 1974 in Hradec Králové.

Tomáš Petříček was born on 18 Dec 1948 in Hradec Králové.
Tomáš Petříček and Hana Rechcíglová were married on 20 Sep 1991 in Hradec Králové. They had no children.

63. **Libuše Rechcíglová**-8 (Stanislav Josef-7, Adolf-6, Anna-5, Antonín-4, Jan-3, Václav-2, Jan-1) was born on 25 Jan 1950 in Novy Bydzov, Hradec Králové Co..

Miroslav Vich was born on 13 Nov 1950 in Nova Paka, Jičín Co..
Miroslav Vich and Libuše Rechcíglová were married on 11 Apr 1970 in Ostromer, Jičín Co.. They had the following children:
99. i. **Iveta Vichova** was born on 15 Jan 1972 in Jičín. She married Miloš Haltuf on 07 Sep 1991 in Lazne Belohrad, Jičín Co..
    ii. **Miroslav Vich** was born on 10 Mar 1973 in Jičín.
    iii. **Sarka Vichova** was born on 11 Mar 1989 in Hradec Králové.

64. **Stanislav Rechcigl**-8 (Stanislav Josef-7, Adolf-6, Anna-5, Antonín-4, Jan-3, Václav-2, Jan-1) was born on 24 Mar 1952 in Hořice, Jičín Co..

Zdena Pařízková daughter of Mila Parik and Zdenka was born on 26 Jan 1954 in Hořice, Jičín Dist., Bohemia.
Stanislav Rechcigl and Zdena Pařízková were married on 24 Mar 1972 in Jičín. They had the following children:
100. i. **Stanislava Rechcíglová** was born on 22 Sep 1972 in Hořice, Jičín Dist., Bohemia.
101. ii. **Jana Rechcíglová** was born on 22 Sep 1973 in Hořice, Jičín Co.. She married Karel Spidlen on 29 Apr 1995 in Jičín, Bohemia.
102. iii. **Stanislav Rechcigl** was born on 08 Aug 1975 in Hořice, Jičín Dist., Bohemia. He married Natasha Blackbourn on 19 Jul 2008 in Spalding, Lincolnshire, UK..

Helena Denisova was born on 29 Jun 1944.
Stanislav Rechcigl and Helena Denisova met. They had no children.

65. **Luděk Křikava**-8 (Božena-7, Zdeněk Petr-6, Anna-5, Antonín-4, Jan-3, Václav-2, Jan-1) was born on 02 Feb 1927 in Komarov u Horovic No. 40. He died on 23 Sep 1996.
    Zdenka Krizova was born on 24 Sep 1941 in Komarov u Horovic No. 72.
    Luděk Křikava and Zdenka Krizova married. They had the following children:
    103. i. **Věra Křikavová** was born on 28 Apr 1966 in Komarov u Horovic No. 40.
    104. ii. **Hanna Křikavová** was born on 07 May 1957 in Komarov u Horovic No. 40. She died on 30 Dec 1997.
    105. iii. **Jan Křikava** was born on 19 Aug 1960 in Komarov u Horovic No. 40.
66. **Sasa Křikava**-8 (Božena-7, Zdeněk Petr-6, Anna-5, Antonín-4, Jan-3, Václav-2, Jan-1) was born on 2 Dec 1930 in Komarov u Horovic No. 40.
    Milada Toclova was born on 24 Jul 1927.
    Sasa Křikava and Milada Toclova married. They had the following children:
    i. **Alexander Křikava** was born in 1951 in Komarov u Horovic.
    106. ii. **Hana Křikavová** was born in 1958 in Komarov u Horovic.
67. **Jana Muellerová**-8 (Zdena-7, Zdeněk Petr-6, Anna-5, Antonín-4, Jan-3, Václav-2, Jan-1) was born on 08 Nov 1952 in Karlovy Vary.
    Jiří Stuchl son of Josef Stuchl and Jarmila Šimáňová was born on 14 Nov 1950 in Plzen. He died on 26 Mar 2001 in Praha 10.
    Jiří Stuchl and Jana Muellerová were married on 26 Aug 1979 in Manetin, Plzen Sever Co.. They had the following children:
    i. **Lenka Stuchlová** was born on 12 May 1979 in Karlovy Vary. She married Josef Bic on 07 Jul 2007 in Liberec.
    ii. **Jan Stuchl** was born on 24 Feb 1981 in Karlovy Vary.
68. **Zdena Muellerová**-8 (Zdena-7, Zdeněk Petr-6, Anna-5, Antonín-4, Jan-3, Václav-2, Jan-1) was born on 01 May 1960 in Karlovy Vary.
    František Petr was born on 05 Sep 1958 in Sokolov.
    František Petr and Zdena Muellerová were married in 1981 in Karlovy Vary. They had the following children:

i. **Miroslav Petr** was born on 30 Oct 1981 in Karlovy Vary.

108. ii. **Jana Petrová** was born on 29 Jun 1984 in Karlovy Vary.

69. **Radmila Rechcíglová**-8 (Zdeněk-7, Bohumil-6, Anna-5, Antonín-4, Jan-3, Václav-2, Jan-1) was born on 29 May 1944.

    Pavel Herák was born on 03 Jun 1938 in Brestovany, Slovakia.

    Pavel Herák and Radmila Rechcíglová were married on 14 Sep 1963 in Český Dub. They had the following children:

    108. i. **Petr Herák** was born on 03 Jun 1965. He married Tereza Kovářová on 24 Mar 1990 in Český Dub.
    109. ii. **Pavlina Heráková** was born on 29 Jan 1964. She married Milan Podlipský on 11 Feb 1984 in Milevsko.
    110. iii. **Helena Heráková** was born on 12 Jul 1966. She married Pavel Hudec on 15 Sep 1984 in Český Dub.

70. **Zdeněk Rechcigl**-8 (Zdeněk-7, Bohumil-6, Anna-5, Antonín-4, Jan-3, Václav-2, Jan-1) was born on 7 Aug 1946 in Český Dub.

    Věra Vizkova was born on 31 Dec 1947 in Hodkovice.

    Zdeněk Rechcigl and Věra Vizkova were married on 30 Dec 1967 in Český Dub. They had the following children:

    111. i. **Martin Rechcigl** was born on 16 Dec 1968. He married Petra Smolakova on 17 Sep 1994 in Český Dub.

71. **Jana Mančíková**-8 (Libuše-7, Bohumil-6, Anna-5, Antonín-4, Jan-3, Václav-2, Jan-1) was born in 1951.

    Jan Cicka.

    Jan Cicka and Jana Mančíková married. They had the following children:

    i. **Drahomira Cicková** was born in 1971.

    Vladimír Ulver.

    Vladimír Ulver and Jana Mančíková married. They had the following children:

    i. **Jitka Ulverova** was born in 1980.

72. **Irena Mančíková**-8 (Libuše-7, Bohumil-6, Anna-5, Antonín-4, Jan-3, Václav-2, Jan-1) was born in 1954.

    Petr Synek.

Petr Synek and Irena Mančíková married. They had the following children:
- i. **Veronika Synková** was born on 07 Mar 1979.
- ii. **Jan Synek** was born on 24 May 1980.

73. **Marie Floriánová**-8 (Marie-7, Marie-6, Václav-5, Petr-4, Lidmila-3, Václav-2, Jan-1).

    Josef Tomeš was born in Stranov.

    Josef Tomeš and Marie Floriánová married. They had the following children:
    - i. **Tomsová-daughter.**
    - ii. **son Tomeš.**

74. **Jaromír Franců**-8 (Jaromír-7, Anna-6, Václav-5, Petr-4, Lidmila-3, Václav-2, Jan-1) was born on 21 Aug 1951 in Kacanovy, Turnov.

    Věra Zimova was born on 21 Jan 1956 in Turnov.

    Jaromír Franců and Věra Zimova were married on 29 Dec 1989 in Jičín. They had the following children:
    - i. **Adam Franců** was born on 12 Jul 1990.
    - ii. **Jan Franců** was born on 26 Jul 1993.

32. **Oldrřch Studnička**-8 (Oldrřch-7, Anna-6, Václav-5, Petr-4, Lidmila-3, Václav-2, Jan-1) was born on 31 May 1942 in Kacanovy.

    Marie Nováková was born on 06 May 1952 in Vsen, Turnov.

    Oldrřch Studnička and Marie Nováková married. They had the following children:
    - i. **Lucie Studničková** was born on 15 Aug 1975 in Praha.

76. **Jan Kvapil**-8 (Jana-7, Anastazie-6, Václav-5, Petr-4, Lidmila-3, Václav-2, Jan-1) was born on 27 May 1944 in Pardubice.

    Eva Nováková daughter of Marta Lamacova was born on 21 Dec 1943.

    Jan Kvapil and Eva Nováková were married on 09 Jun 1962 in Pardubice. They had the following children:
    - 112. i. **Jan Kvapil** was born on 30 Dec 1963 in Pardubice. He married Iveta Kulichova on 31 Jan 1987 in Lazne Bohdanec.
    - 113. ii. **Jaroslav Kvapil** was born on 26 Feb 1969 in Pardubice. He married Eva Kadlecova on 30 Nov 1991 in Lazne Bohdanec.

114. iii. **Eva Kvapilová** was born on 18 Oct 1973 in Pardubice. He married Tomasz Prcz on 18 May 1996 in Lazne Bohdanec.

115. iv. **Jiri Kvapil** was born on 18 Jan 1980 in Pardubice. He married Zuzana Tomanová on 13 Aug 2005 in Lazne Bohdanec.

77. **Nada Kvapilová**-8 (Jana-7, Anastazie-6, Václav-5, Petr-4, Lidmila-3, Václav-2, Jan-1) was born on 11 Feb 1946 in Pardubice.

    Josef Virt was born on 20 Sep 1933 in Pardubice. He died on 19 Jan 1991. Josef Virt and Nada Kvapilová were married on 13 Mar 1971 in Rohovladova Bela. They had the following children:

    116. i. **Petra Virtova** was born on 17 Aug 1976 in Pardubice. She married Tomáš Tupy on 25 Aug 2000.

78. **Jitka Rechziegelová**-8 (Drahomir-7, Anastazie-6, Václav-5, Petr-4, Lidmila-3, Václav-2, Jan-1) was born on 27 Aug 1951.

    Petr Marek son of Petr Marek and Josefa was born on 16 Jun 1947 in Libec. Petr Marek and Jitka Rechziegelová married. They had the following children:

    i. **Denisa Markova** was born on 28 Aug 1972.

    ii. **Petr Marek** was born on 21 Feb 1975.

79. **Aleš Rechziegel**-8 (Drahomir-7, Anastazie-6, Václav-5, Petr-4, Lidmila-3, Václav-2, Jan-1) was born on 15 Jan 1954.

    Lenka Horčičková daughter of Vladimír Horčička and Unknown was born on 03 Feb 1956. Aleš Rechziegel and Lenka Horčičková married. They had the following children:

    i. **Andrea Rechziegel** was born on 08 Apr 1975.

    ii. **Tomáš Rechziegel** was born on 28 Mar 1979.

80. **Drahomir Rechziegel**-8 (Drahomir-7, Anastazie-6, Václav-5, Petr-4, Lidmila-3, Václav-2, Jan-1) was born on 10 Feb 1957 in Pardubice.

    Alena Rykrova daughter of Jaroslav Rykr and Marie was born in 1965. Drahomir Rechziegel and Alena Rykrova married. They had the following children:

    i. **Lukáš Rechziegel** was born on 19 Jan 1985.

81. **Arnošt Pellant**-8 (Věra-7, Marie-6, Josef-5, Petr-4, Lidmila-3, Václav-2, Jan-1) was born on 12 Jun 1943 in Praha.

Zinaida Poliscukova daughter of Ondřej Poliscuk and Věra Sirova was born on 03 Oct 1943 in Mizoc, Poland; since WWII USSR.
Arnošt Pellant and Zinaida Poliscukova were married on 07 Mar 1970 in Praha. They had the following children:

   117. i. **Věra Pellantová** was born on 25 Feb 1971 in Hradec Králové. She married Jan Brožík on 24 Aug 2002 in Valdstejn.

   118. ii. **Eva Pellantová** was born on 05 Jul 1974 in Hradec Králové. She married Jan Mejzlik on 9 Jun 2001.

82. **Karel Pellant**-8 (Věra-7, Marie-6, Josef-5, Petr-4, Lidmila-3, Václav-2, Jan-1) was born on 14 Mar 1946 in Caslav.

Jitka Kralickova was born on 08 Jul 1947 in Ostrava.

Karel Pellant and Jitka Kralickova were married on 01 Aug 1970 in Jevisovice. They had the following children:

   119. i. **Martina Pellantová** was born on 27 Oct 1971 in Hradec Králové. She married Alan Gernert on 04 Oct 1997 in Jablonec nad Jizetou.

        ii. **Iva Pellantová** was born on 04 Dec 1973 in Brno.

83. **Jitka Rechcíglová**-8 (Josef-7, Josef-6, Josef-5, Petr-4, Lidmila-3, Václav-2, Jan-1) was born on 09 Oct 1957 in Mladá Boleslav.

Vladimír Skramusky son of Vladimír Skramusky and Miloslava Koutska was born on 15 Jan 1953 in Cista.

Vladimír Skramusky and Jitka Rechcíglová were married on 11 Aug 1979 in Bakov nad Jizerou. They had the following children:

        i. **Vladimír Skramusky** was born on 17 Jun 1982 in Turnov.

84. **Josef Rechcigl**-8 (Josef-7, Josef-6, Josef-5, Petr-4, Lidmila-3, Václav-2, Jan-1) was born on 03 Mar 1960 in Turnov.

Věra Laskova daughter of František Laska and Helena Kolocova was born on 05 Oct 1967.

Josef Rechcigl and Věra Laskova were married on 17 Apr 1987 in Bakov nad Jizerou. They had the following children:

        i. **Zuzana Rechcíglová** was born on 15 Jan 1988 in Mladá Boleslav.

        ii. **Nikola Rechcíglová** was born on 04 Oct 1990 in Mladá Boleslav.

        iii. **Jiří Rechcigl** was born on 06 Oct 1995 in Mladá Boleslav.

85. **3rd Karel Matějů**-8 (2nd Karel-7, Anna-6, Josef-5, Petr-4, Lidmila-3, Václav-2, Jan-1) was born on 15 Nov 1954 in Brno.
    Alena Šrámková daughter of Vit Šrámek and Božena Šrámková was born on 25 Apr 1958 in Brno.
    3rd Karel Matějů and Alena Šrámková were married on 07 Jul 1979 in Brno. They had the following children:
    i. **Lukáš Matějů** was born on 15 Jun 1980 in Brno.
    ii. **Karel Matějů** was born on 06 Oct 1982 in Brno.
    iii. **Martin Matějů** was born on 14 Oct 1992 in Brno.
86. **Alena Velova**-8 (Vladimír-7, Alois Jan-6, Anna-5, Antonín-4, Lidmila-3, Václav-2, Jan-1) was born on 5 Jan 1951 in Turnov.
    Ladislav Vodhanel was born on 29 Dec 1945.
    Ladislav Vodhanel and Alena Velova were married on 12 Jul 1972. They had the following children:
    i. **Miroslava Vodhanelova** was born on 22 Dec 1973 in Turnov.
    Jindřich Novotný.
    Jindřich Novotný and Alena Velova were married on 12 Apr 1976. They had the following children:
    i. **Sarka Novotná** was born on 10 Jun 1977 in Turnov.
87. **Vladimír Vela**-8 (Vladimír-7, Alois Jan-6, Anna-5, Antonín-4, Lidmila-3, Václav-2, Jan-1) was born on 17 Dec 1954.
    Raduse Dvořáková was born on 11 Dec 1959 in Turnov.
    Vladimír Vela and Raduse Dvořáková were married on 07 Dec 1979. They had the following children:
    i. **Vladimír Vela** was born on 27 Jul 1980.
    ii. **Jan Vela** was born on 24 Jun 1984.
88. **Marie Jislova**-8 (Josef-7, Marie-6, Josefa-5, Antonín-4, Lidmila-3, Václav-2, Jan-1) was born on 28 Jul 1947.
    Zdeněk Roubíček was born on 23 Jun 1946.
    Zdeněk Roubíček and Marie Jislova married. They had the following children:
    i. **Lada Roubíčková** was born on 30 Dec 1973.
    ii. **Zdeněk Roubíček** was born on 12 Jan 1975.

89. **Hana Rechcigelova**-8 (Milan-7, Ing. František-6, Karel Bor.-5, Antonín-4, Lidmila-3, Václav-2, Jan-1) was born on 01 Nov 1953 in Český Dub. She died on 27 Jul 2021.

    Jiří Maier was born on 21 Mar 1946 in Turnov.

    Jiří Maier and Hana Rechcigelova married. They had the following children:
    i. **Hana Maierova** was born on 03 Mar 1980.
    ii. **Lenka Maierova** was born on 15 Mar 1983.

90. **Ing. Pavel Rechcigel**-8 (Milan-7, Ing. František-6, Karel Bor.-5, Antonín-4, Lidmila-3, Václav-2, Jan-1) was born on 19 Jul 1963 in Český Dub.

    Jana Cadova daughter of Josef Cada and Eva Unknown was born on 18 Apr 1965. Ing. Pavel Rechcigel and Jana Cadova married. They had the following children:
    i. **Jakub Rechcigel** was born on 24 Jul 1990.

91. **Vladko Rechcigel**-8 (Ing. Vladko-7, Ing. František-6, Karel Bor.-5, Antonín-4, Lidmila-3, Václav-2, Jan-1) was born on 04 Aug 1959 in Prague, CSR.

    Eva Vitova was born on 17 May 1958 in Červený Kostelec.

    Vladko Rechcigel and Eva Vitova married. They had the following children:
    i. **Jan Rechcigel** was born on 04 Mar 1988 in Prague, CSR.
    ii. **Lukáš Rechcigel** was born on 06 Jun 1990 in Prague, CSR.

92. **Ing. Jan Rechcigel**-8 (Ing. Vladko-7, Ing. František-6, Karel Bor.-5, Antonín-4, Lidmila-3, Václav-2, Jan-1) was born on 02 Feb 1966 in Prague, CSR.

    Xenie Wilckova was born on 17 Jan 1968 in Havirov.

    Ing. Jan Rechcigel and Xenie Wilckova married. They had the following children:
    i. **Tereza Rechciglova** was born on 07 Mar 1994 in Prague, CSR.
    ii. **Kristyna Rechciglova** was born on 09 Mar 1998 in Prague, CSR.

93. **Miroslav Třešňák**-8 (Marie-7, Josef-6, Marie-5, Josefa-4, Lidmila-3, Václav-2, Jan-1) was born on 25 May 1943 in Jivina No. 1. He died on 19 Nov 2005 in moved to Jivina No. 24.

Miluška Hanzlova was born on 29 Dec 1944 in Svijany.
Miroslav Třešňák and Miluška Hanzlova were married on 23 Oct 1965. They had the following children:
- 120. i. **Pavel Třešňák** was born on 25 Feb 1967 in Turnov - moved to Český Dub. He married Radka Černá on 18 Apr 1992.
- 121. ii. **Luboš Třešňák** was born on 30 Apr 1974 in Turnov - moved to Vrkoslavice. He married Jitka Necaskova on 21 Sep 1996.

94. **Jiří Třešňák**-8 (Marie-7, Josef-6, Marie-5, Josefa-4, Lidmila-3, Václav-2, Jan-1) was born on 22 Jul 1952 in Jivina No. 1. He died in moved to Odolena Voda, Praha vychod.
Marie Zoubková was born on 22 Jun 1956 in Zasada.
Jiří Třešňák and Marie Zoubková were married on 19 Jun 1976. They had the following children:
- i. **Lenka Třešňáková** was born on 21 Jan 1978 in Turnov.
- ii. **Radka Třešňáková** was born on 30 May 1985 in Brandys nad Labem.

Generation 9

95. **John Edward Rechcigl**-9 (Mila (Miloslav)-8, Miloslav-7, Adolf-6, Anna-5, Antonín-4, Jan-3, Václav-2, Jan-1) was born on 27 Feb 1960 in Washington, D.C..
Nancy Ann Palko daughter of Joseph Palko and Mary Rishko was born on 26 Sep 1961 in Morristown, NJ.
John Edward Rechcigl and Nancy Ann Palko were married on 30 Jul 1983 in Dover, NJ. They had the following children:
- i. **Gregory John Rechcigl** was born on 19 Dec 1988 in Bradenton, FL.
- 123. ii. **Kevin Thomas Rechcigl** was born on 09 Oct 1991 in Bradenton, FL. He married Jordan Robbins on 12 May 2018 in Jacksonville, FL.
- iii. **Lindsey Nicole Rechcigl** was born on 03 Nov 1994 in Bradenton, FL.

96. **Karen Rechcigl**-9 (Mila (Miloslav)-8, Miloslav-7, Adolf-6, Anna-5, Antonín-4, Jan-3, Václav-2, Jan-1) was born on 16 Apr 1962 in Washington, DC.

Ulysses Kollecas son of Christopher Thomas (Kolecas) Collier and Amelia Malatras was born on 20 Mar 1958 in Washington, DC.
Ulysses Kollecas and Karen Rechcigl were married on 25 Aug 1990 in Bethesda, MD. They had the following children:
- i. **Kristin Kollecas** was born on 04 May 1993 in Albuquerque, NM.
- ii. **Paul Kollecas** was born on 02 Jun 1995 in Albuquerque, NM.

97. **Marcela Žďárská**-9 (Marta-8, Miloslav-7, Adolf-6, Anna-5, Antonín-4, Jan-3, Václav-2, Jan-1) was born on 09 May 1954 in Liberec.
Miroslav Heralecký son of Miroslav Heralecký and Marie Bartošová was born on 18 May 1949 in salomonJablonec nad Nisou, Czech.. He died on 20 Feb 2017 in Proseč, Jablonec nad Nisou, Czech..
Miroslav Heralecký and Marcela Žďárská were married on 15 Mar 1975 in Sychrov. They had the following children:
- i. **Vit Heralecký** was born on 16 Jan 1977 in Jablonec nad Nisou. He married Olga Zrubcová on 13 Jul 1996.
- 124. ii. **Zuzana Heralecká** was born on 30 Dec 1978 in Jablonec nad Nisou. She married Jaroslav Egrt on 13 Sep 2002 in Jablonec nad Nisou.

98. **Iveta Žďárská**-9 (Marta-8, Miloslav-7, Adolf-6, Anna-5, Antonín-4, Jan-3, Václav-2, Jan-1) was born on 29 Aug 1963 in Liberec, Bohemia.
Vlastimil Berkman was born in 1957.
Vlastimil Berkman and Iveta Žďárská were married on 29 Oct 1983. They had the following children:
- i. **Tereza Hriníková** was born on 05 Jun 1984 in Jablonec nad Nisou.

Jaroslav Hrinik son of Jaroslav Hrinik and Milena Preisslerová was born on 17 Apr 1960.
Jaroslav Hrinik and Iveta Žďárská were married on 16 Aug 1991 in Zamek Červená Lhota. They had the following children:
- i. **Eliška Hriníková** was born on 23 Jun 1992 in Jablonec nad Nisou. She married Jan Ottis on 06 Oct 2018 in Jablonec nad Jizerou, East Bohemia, Czech Republic.

99. **Iveta Vichova**-9 (Libuše-8, Stanislav Josef-7, Adolf-6, Anna-5, Antonín-4, Jan-3, Václav-2, Jan-1) was born on 15 Jan 1972 in Jičín.
    Miloš Haltuf was born on 03 May 1968 in Chlumec.
    Miloš Haltuf and Iveta Vichova were married on 07 Sep 1991 in Lazne Belohrad, Jičín Co.. They had the following children:
    i. **Jan Haltuf** was born on 10 Mar 1992 in Hořice, Jičín Co..
100. **Stanislava Rechcíglová**-9 (Stanislav-8, Stanislav Josef-7, Adolf-6, Anna-5, Antonín-4, Jan-3, Václav-2, Jan-1) was born on 22 Sep 1972 in Hořice, Jičín Dist., Bohemia.
    Josef Bekera was born on 22 Jun 1965.
    Josef Bekera and Stanislava Rechcíglová met. They had the following children:
    i. **Nikolas Bekera** was born on 23 Sep 2001.
    ii. **Sebestian Bekera**.
    iii. **Anastasia Jowefa Bekerová**.
101. **Jana Rechcíglová**-9 (Stanislav-8, Stanislav Josef-7, Adolf-6, Anna-5, Antonín-4, Jan-3, Václav-2, Jan-1) was born on 22 Sep 1973 in Hořice, Jičín Co..
    Karel Spidlen was born on 06 Feb 1972 in Hradec Králové.
    Karel Spidlen and Jana Rechcíglová were married on 29 Apr 1995 in Jičín, Bohemia. They had the following children:
    i. **Karel Spidlen** was born on 15 Oct 1995 in Hořice, Jičín Co..
102. **Stanislav Rechcigl**-9 (Stanislav-8, Stanislav Josef-7, Adolf-6, Anna-5, Antonín-4, Jan-3, Václav-2, Jan-1) was born on 08 Aug 1975 in Hořice, Jičín Dist., Bohemia.
    Natasha Blackbourn.
    Stanislav Rechcigl and Natasha Blackbourn were married on 19 Jul 2008 in Spalding, Lincolnshire, UK.. They had the following children:
    i. **Lily-Grace Rechcíglová** was born on 03 Jul 2011 in Watford, UK.
    ii. **Poppy Sophia Rechcíglová** was born on 13 Oct 2013.

103. **Věra Křikavová**-9 (Luděk-8, Božena-7, Zdeněk Petr-6, Anna-5, Antonín-4, Jan-3, Václav-2, Jan-1) was born on 28 Apr 1966 in Komarov u Horovic No. 40.
Radek Nešpor was born on 24 Mar 1963 in Horovice.
Radek Nešpor and Věra Křikavová married. They had the following children:
    i. **David Nešpor** was born on 19 Oct 1987 in Komarov u Horovic No. 40.

104. **Hanna Křikavová**-9 (Luděk-8, Božena-7, Zdeněk Petr-6, Anna-5, Antonín-4, Jan-3, Václav-2, Jan-1) was born on 07 May 1957 in Komarov u Horovic No. 40. She died on 30 Dec 1997.
Bedřich Mach was born on 13 Feb 1955 in Komarov u Horovic No. 40.
Bedřich Mach and Hanna Křikavová married. They had the following children:
    124. i. **Andrea Machová** was born on 10 Mar 1978 in Komarov u Horovic No. 40.

105. **Jan Křikava**-9 (Luděk-8, Božena-7, Zdeněk Petr-6, Anna-5, Antonín-4, Jan-3, Václav-2, Jan-1) was born on 19 Aug 1960 in Komarov u Horovic No. 40.
Hana Fedorcaková was born on 05 May 1962 in Kvan near Komarov.
Jan Křikava and Hana Fedorcaková married. They had the following children:
    i. **Jan Křikava** was born on 22 Sep 1983 in Komarov u Horovic No. 40.
Jana Linhartova was born on 14 Feb 1973 in Komarov u Horovic.
Jan Křikava and Jana Linhartova met. They had the following children:
    i. **Johana Křikavová** was born on 27 Nov 2007 in Komarov u Horovic.

106. **Hana Křikavová**-9 (Sasa-8, Božena-7, Zdeněk Petr-6, Anna-5, Antonín-4, Jan-3, Václav-2, Jan-1) was born in 1958 in Komarov u Horovic.
Milan Němec was born in 1954 in Komarov u Horovic.
Milan Němec and Hana Křikavová married. They had the following children:

      i.   **Milan Němec** was born in 1978 in Komarov u Horovic.

     ii.   **Lubor Němec** was born in 1971 in Komarov u Horovic.

107. **Jana Petrová**-9 (Zdena-8, Zdena-7, Zdeněk Petr-6, Anna-5, Antonín-4, Jan-3, Václav-2, Jan-1) was born on 29 Jun 1984 in Karlovy Vary.
Petr Kottnauer.
Petr Kottnauer and Jana Petrová met. They had the following children:

      i.   **Daniel Kottnauer** was born in Karlovy Vary.

108. **Petr Herák**-9 (Radmila-8, Zdeněk-7, Bohumil-6, Anna-5, Antonín-4, Jan-3, Václav-2, Jan-1) was born on 03 Jun 1965.
Tereza Kovářová was born on 22 Jul 1973 in Jablonec.
Petr Herák and Tereza Kovářová were married on 24 Mar 1990 in Český Dub. They had the following children:

      i.   **Jan Herák** was born on 11 Sep 1990.

     ii.   **Krystyna Heráková** was born on 18 Feb 1997.

109. **Pavlina Heráková**-9 (Radmila-8, Zdeněk-7, Bohumil-6, Anna-5, Antonín-4, Jan-3, Václav-2, Jan-1) was born on 29 Jan 1964.
Milan Podlipský was born on 11 Mar 1961.
Milan Podlipský and Pavlina Heráková were married on 11 Feb 1984 in Milevsko. They had the following children:

     iii.   **Milan Podlipský** was born on 22 Jun 1984.

     iv.   **Jakub Podlipský** was born on 19 Mar 1986.

110. **Helena Heráková**-9 (Radmila-8, Zdeněk-7, Bohumil-6, Anna-5, Antonín-4, Jan-3, Václav-2, Jan-1) was born on 12 Jul 1966.
Pavel Hudec was born on 01 Jan 1962 in Český Dub.
Pavel Hudec and Helena Heráková were married on 15 Sep 1984 in Český Dub. They had the following children:

     v.   **Kateřina Hudcova** was born on 17 Feb 1985.

     vi.   **Martina Hudcova** was born on 12 May 1991.

111. **Martin Rechcigl**-9 (Zdeněk-8, Zdeněk-7, Bohumil-6, Anna-5, Antonín-4, Jan-3, Václav-2, Jan-1) was born on 16 Dec 1968.
Petra Smolakova was born on 25 Jan 1973 in Moravia.
Martin Rechcigl and Petra Smolakova were married on 17 Sep 1994 in Český Dub. They had the following children:

vii. **Lucie Rechcíglová** was born on 05 Apr 1995.

viii. **David Rechcigl** was born on 08 Aug 2000.

112. **Jan Kvapil**-9 (Jan-8, Jana-7, Anastazie-6, Václav-5, Petr-4, Lidmila-3, Václav-2, Jan-1) was born on 30 Dec 1963 in Pardubice.

    Iveta Kulichova was born on 18 Jan 1969.

    Jan Kvapil and Iveta Kulichova were married on 31 Jan 1987 in Lazne Bohdanec. They had the following children:

    i. **Lucie Kvapilová** was born on 09 Jul 1987 in Pardubice.

    ii. **Pavlina Kvapilová** was born on 05 Sep 1991 in Pardubice.

    iii. **Iveta Kvapilová** was born on 15 Jul 1993 in Pardubice.

113. **Jaroslav Kvapil**-9 (Jan-8, Jana-7, Anastazie-6, Václav-5, Petr-4, Lidmila-3, Václav-2, Jan-1) was born on 26 Feb 1969 in Pardubice.

    Eva Kadlecova was born on 05 Sep 1969.

    Jaroslav Kvapil and Eva Kadlecova were married on 30 Nov 1991 in Lazne Bohdanec. They had the following children:

    i. **Katerina Kvapilová** was born on 21 May 1992 in Pardubice.

    ii. **Monika Kvapilová** was born on 19 Oct 1998 in Pardubice.

    iii. **Jakub Kvapil** was born on 05 May 2005 in Pardubice.

114. **Eva Kvapilová**-9 (Jan-8, Jana-7, Anastazie-6, Václav-5, Petr-4, Lidmila-3, Václav-2, Jan-1) was born on 18 Oct 1973 in Pardubice.

    Tomasz Prcz was born on 23 May 1970.

    Tomasz Prcz and Eva Kvapilová were married on 18 May 1996 in Lazne Bohdanec. They had the following children:

    iv. **Martin Prcz** was born on 19 May 1991 in Pardubice.

    v. **Tomasz Prcz** was born on 05 Oct 1997 in Pardubice.

115. **Jiri Kvapil**-9 (Jan-8, Jana-7, Anastazie-6, Václav-5, Petr-4, Lidmila-3, Václav-2, Jan-1) was born on 18 Jan 1980 in Pardubice.

    Zuzana Tomanová was born on 20 Aug 1980.

    Jiri Kvapil and Zuzana Tomanová were married on 13 Aug 2005 in Lazne Bohdanec. They had the following children:

    i. **Tereza Kvapilová** was born on 25 Dec 2006 in Pardubice.

    ii. **Jiri Kvapil** was born on 07 Sep 2009 in Pardubice.

116. **Petra Virtova**-9 (Nada-8, Jana-7, Anastazie-6, Václav-5, Petr-4, Lidmila-3, Václav-2, Jan-1) was born on 17 Aug 1976 in Pardubice.
Tomáš Tupy was born on 24 Aug 1975 in Pardubice.
Tomáš Tupy and Petra Virtova were married on 25 Aug 2000. They had the following children:
    i. **Krystyna Tupa** was born on 27 Feb 2001.
    ii. **Aneta Tupa** was born on 21 Apr 2006.
117. **Věra Pellantová**-9 (Arnošt-8, Věra-7, Marie-6, Josef-5, Petr-4, Lidmila-3, Václav-2, Jan-1) was born on 25 Feb 1971 in Hradec Králové.
Jan Brožík son of Jan Brožík and Jarmila Dočkálová was born on 06 Sep 1974 in Kromeriz.
Jan Brožík and Věra Pellantová were married on 24 Aug 2002 in Valdstejn. They had the following children:
    iii. **Barbora Brožíková** was born on 05 Dec 2003 in Hradec Králové.
118. **Eva Pellantová**-9 (Arnošt-8, Věra-7, Marie-6, Josef-5, Petr-4, Lidmila-3, Václav-2, Jan-1) was born on 05 Jul 1974 in Hradec Králové.
Jan Mejzlik son of Josef Mejzlik and Blanka Spustova was born on 13 Mar 1974 in Preckov, Trebic Co..
Jan Mejzlik and Eva Pellantová were married on 09 Jun 2001. They had the following children:
    iv. **Vojtěch Mejzlik** was born on 29 Jan 2003 in Hradec Králové.
    v. **Antonín Mejzlik** was born on 29 Nov 2006 in Hradec Králové.
119. **Martina Pellantová**-9 (Karel-8, Věra-7, Marie-6, Josef-5, Petr-4, Lidmila-3, Václav-2, Jan-1) was born on 27 Oct 1971 in Hradec Králové.
Alan Gernert son of Vilém Gernert and Vlasta was born on 26 Mar 1970 in Jilemnice.
Alan Gernert and Martina Pellantová were married on 04 Oct 1997 in Jablonec nad Jizetou. They had the following children:
    vi. **Marek Gernert** was born on 04 Apr 1998.
120. **Pavel Třešňák**-9 (Miroslav-8, Marie-7, Josef-6, Marie-5, Josefa-4, Lidmila-3, Václav-2, Jan-1) was born on 25 Feb 1967 in Turnov - moved to Český Dub.
Radka Černá was born on 07 Sep 1971 in Česká Lipa.

Pavel Třešňák and Radka Černá were married on 18 Apr 1992. They had the following children:

    vii. **Pavlina Třešňáková** was born on 17 Jun 1999 in Turnov.

121. **Luboš Třešňák**-9 (Miroslav-8, Marie-7, Josef-6, Marie-5, Josefa-4, Lidmila-3, Václav-2, Jan-1) was born on 30 Apr 1974 in Turnov - moved to Vrkoslavice.

Jitka Necaskova was born on 21 Nov 1969 in Jablonnec nad Nisou.

Luboš Třešňák and Jitka Necaskova were married on 21 Sep 1996. They had the following children:

    i. **Michaela Třešňáková** was born on 02 Sep 1997 in Jablonec nad Nisou.

    ii. **Matěj Třešňák** was born on 18 May 2001 in Jablonec nad Nisou.

Generation 10

122. **Kevin Thomas Rechcigl**-10 (John Edward-9, Mila (Miloslav)-8, Miloslav-7, Adolf-6, Anna-5, Antonín-4, Jan-3, Václav-2, Jan-1) was born on 09 Oct 1991 in Bradenton, FL.

Jordan Robbins daughter of Douglass Robbins and Ivonne was born on 10 Jan 1992 in Camarillo, CA.

Kevin Thomas Rechcigl and Jordan Robbins were married on 12 May 2018 in Jacksonville, FL. They had the following children:

    i. **James Douglas Rechcigl** was born on 05 Jan 2021 in Jacksonville, FL.

    ii. **Evelyn Marie Rechcigl** was born 29 May 2023 in Jacksonville, FL.

123. **Zuzana Heralecká**-10 (Marcela-9, Marta-8, Miloslav-7, Adolf-6, Anna-5, Antonín-4, Jan-3, Václav-2, Jan-1) was born on 30 Dec 1978 in Jablonec nad Nisou.

Jaroslav Egrt was born on 25 Apr 1974 in Duchcov.

Jaroslav Egrt and Zuzana Heralecká were married on 13 Sep 2002 in Jablonec nad Nisou. They had the following children:

    iii. **Kristina Egrtova** was born on 04 Jan 2008 in Liberec.

    iv. **Jaroslav Egrt** was born on 04 Jan 2008 in Liberec.

124. **Andrea Machová**-10 (Hanna-9, Luděk-8, Božena-7, Zdeněk Petr-6, Anna-5, Antonín-4, Jan-3, Václav-2, Jan-1) was born on 10 Mar 1978 in Komarov u Horovic No. 40.

Soeren Christiansen was born in 1975 in Denmark.

Soeren Christiansen and Andrea Machová met. They had the following children:

    Olivia Machová was born on 10 May 2007 in Kobenhaven, Denmark.

Ferkl Family of Chocnejovice

Generation 1

Jiří Ferkl-1 was born in 1682 in Kocňovice. He died in 1748.

Marie Magdalena Horáková daughter of Jan Horák was born in 1685 in Neveklovice. She died in 1758.

Jiří Ferkl and Marie Magdalena Horáková were married in 1707. They had the following children:

- i. **Josef Ferkl** was born in 1707 in Kocňovice No. 2. He married Anna Šimáně in 1754. He died on 11 Aug 1774.
- ii. **Václav Ferkl** was born in 1710 in Kocnevice No. 2. He married Marie Šnajdrová in 1735.
- iii. **Jiří Ferkl** was born in 1713 in Kocňovice No. 2. He married Anna Holasova in 1743. He died on 11 Aug 1783 in lived in Kocňovice No. 11.

Generation 2

Josef Ferkl-2 (Jiří-1) was born in 1707 in Kocňovice No. 2. He died on 11 Aug 1774.

Anna Šimáně daughter of Jiří Šimáně was born in 1736 in Kocňovice. She died on 11 Jul 1808. Josef Ferkl and Anna Šimáně were married in 1754. They had the following children:

- i. **Jan Vojtěch Ferkl** was born on 19 Jan 1756 in Kocňovice No. 2. He married Kateřina Kolotzova in 1789.
- ii. **Josef Ferkl** was born on 15 Sep 1758 in Kocňovice No. 2. He married Dorota Paříková on 18 Jun 1782.

  Anna Ferklová was born on 15 Sep 1758.

  Václav Ferkl was born in 1760.

  Kateřina Ferkl was born on 10 Apr 1763.

  Václav Ferkl was born on 28 Feb 1764.

  Dorota Ferkl was born on 30 May 1767.
- viii. **František Ferkl** was born on 24 Nov 1769 in Kocňovice. He married Kateřina Nohýnková in 1795. He died on 16 Apr 1840 in Sychrov No, 16.

Pavel Ferkl was born on 06 Jul 1772. He died in 1774.

Matěj Ferkl was born on 28 Jun 1774. He died in 1774.

Václav Ferkl-2 (Jiří-1) was born in 1710 in Kocnevice No. 2.

Marie Šnajdrová daughter of Adam Šnajdr was born in 1713 in Kocňovice. She died on 08 Jun 1772. Václav Ferkl and Marie Šnajdrová were married in 1735. They had the following children:

> Mary Ferkl was born in 1735.
>
> ii. Josef Ferkl was born on 28 Jan 1737. He married Kateřina Studničná in 1768. He died in Lived in Honsob No. 5.
>
> iii. Anna Marie Ferkl was born in 1740.
>
> iv. Jan Ferkl was born on 09 Jun 1743. He married Anna Kostkova in 1772. He died in Lived in Jivina No. 6.
>
> v. Václav Ferkl was born in 1749. He died on 16 Feb 1805 in Bukovina No. 6.
>
> vi. Jiří Ferkl was born on 07 May 1750 in lived in Kocňovice No. 11.

Jiří Ferkl-2 (Jiří-1) was born in 1713 in Kocňovice No. 2. He died on 11 Aug 1783 in lived in Kocňovice No. 11.

Anna Holasova daughter of Jan Holas was born in 1723 in Kocňovice. She died in 1792. Jiří Ferkl and Anna Holasova were married in 1743. They had the following children:

> Anna Ferklová was born in 1744 in Kocňovice.
>
> Jiří Ferkl was born in 1746 in Kocňovice.
>
> iii. Josef Ferkl was born on 18 Feb 1751 in Kocňovice No. 11. He married Anna Nohýnková in 1777.
>
> iv. Vojtěch Ferkl was born on 02 Sep 1753 in Kocňovice. He married Kateřina Douděrová in 1782. He died on 02 Oct 1843.
>
> Kateřina Ferklová was born in 1756 in Kocňovice.
>
> Václav Ferkl was born in 1759 in Kocňovice.

Generation 3

Jan Vojtěch Ferkl-3 (Josef-2, Jiří-1) was born on 19 Jan 1756 in Kocňovice No. 2.

Kateřina Kolotzova was born in 1766 in Mukarov No. 17.

Jan Vojtěch Ferkl and Kateřina Kolotzova were married in 1789. They had the following children:
- i. **František Ferkl** was born on 06 Nov 1794 in Kocňovice No. 2, Mnichovo Hradiště Co.. He died on 13 Apr 1868.

Josef Ferkl-3 (Josef-2, Jiří-1) was born on 15 Sep 1758 in Kocňovice No. 2.

Dorota Paříková daughter of Vojtěch Parik was born in 1758 in Jivina No. 19.

Josef Ferkl and Dorota Paříková were married on 18 Jun 1782. They had the following children:

> **Anna Ferklová** was born on 15 Sep 1782 in Kocňovice No. 2.
>
> **Matěj Josef Ferkl** was born on 22 Feb 1785 in Kocňovice No. 2. He died in 1785.
>
> **Josef Ferkl** was born on 11 Feb 1786 in Kocňovice No. 2.
>
> **František Ferkl** was born on 14 Jul 1788 in Kocňovice No. 2. He died in 1788.
>
> **Dorota Ferklová** was born on 02 Oct 1789 in Kocňovice No. 2. She died in 1789.
>
> **Marie Magdalena Ferklová** was born on 19 Feb 1791 in Kocňovice No. 2.

- vii. **Jan Ferkl** was born in 1794 in Kocňovice No. 2. He married Anna Šnajdrová in 1830. He died in Lived in Kocňovice No. 25.
- viii. **Václav Ferkl** was born on 30 Jun 1795 in Kocňovice No. 11. He married Kateřina Nohýnková on 11 Nov 1815.

František Ferkl-3 (Josef-2, Jiří-1) was born on 24 Nov 1769 in Kocňovice. He died on 16 Apr 1840 in Sychrov No, 16.

Kateřina Nohýnková daughter of Josef Nohynek and Unknown was born on 16 Apr 1771 in Sychrov. She died on 30 Jan 1806.

František Ferkl and Kateřina Nohýnková were married in 1795. They had the following children:

> **Kateřina Ferklová** was born on 09 Jun 1795 in Sychrov No. 16. She died in 1795.
>
> **Kateřina Ferklová** was born on 16 Jul 1797 in Sychrov No. 16. She died in 1828.

iii. **Josef Ferkl** was born on 07 Nov 1799 in Sychrov No. 16. He married Kateřina Zamecka in 1830. He died on 08 Sep 1863.

iv. **Jan Ferkl** was born on 19 Jan 1802 in Sychrov No. 16. He died before 1875.

v. **František Ferkl** was born on 30 Jan 1806 in Sychrov No. 16. He married Dorota Rejzkova in 1829.

Kateřina Nohýnková daughter of Jan Nohynek was born in 1774 in Podolí. She died on 26 Aug 1830.

František Ferkl and Kateřina Nohýnková were married in 1806. They had no children.

Josef Ferkl-3 (Václav-2, Jiří-1) was born on 28 Jan 1737. He died in Lived in Honsob No. 5.

Kateřina Studničná daughter of Jan Studničný was born in 1750.

Josef Ferkl and Kateřina Studničná were married in 1768. They had the following children:

Václav Ferkl was born in 1774 in Honsob No. 5.

Josef Ferkl was born in 1779 in Honsob No.5.

Anna Marie Ferkl-3 (Václav-2, Jiří-1) was born in 1740.

Unknown.

Unknown and Anna Marie Ferkl married. They had the following children:

Josef Ferkl was born in 1779 in Honsob No.5.

Jan Ferkl-3 (Václav-2, Jiří-1) was born on 09 Jun 1743. He died in Lived in Jivina No. 6.

Anna Kostkova daughter of Krystof Kostka was born on 03 Oct 1752.

Jan Ferkl and Anna Kostkova were married in 1772. They had the following children:

Jan Ferkl was born in 1774 in Jivina No. 6. He died in 1776.

ii. **Josef Ferkl** was born on 30 Jan 1776 in Jivina No. 6. He married Cecile Kinterova in 1793.

Jan Krtitel Ferkl was born in 1780 in Jivina No. 6. He died in 1780.

> Jan Ferkl was born on 23 Jan 1783 in Jivina No. 6. He married Anna Machová in 1803.
>
> František Ferkl was born in 1786 in Jivina No. 6. He died in 1786.

Václav Ferkl-3 (Václav-2, Jiří-1) was born in 1749. He died on 16 Feb 1805 in Bukovina No. 6.

Dorota Scheiblova daughter of Pavel Scheibel was born in 1748. She died on 20 Jan 1824.

Václav Ferkl and Dorota Scheiblova married. They had the following children:

> i. Josef Ferkl was born on 26 Jan 1782. He died on 30 Dec 1846 in Lived in Dolni Bukovina No. 11.
>
> Jiří Ferkl was born in 1784.
>
> iii. Marie Ferklová was born in 1800.

Jiří Ferkl-3 (Václav-2, Jiří-1) was born on 07 May 1750 in lived in Kocňovice No. 11.

Anna Nohýnková was born in 1750 in Rostkov.

Jiří Ferkl and Anna Nohýnková married. They had the following children:

> Anna Ferklová was born in 1776.
>
> Jan Ferkl was born in 1778.
>
> Josef Ferkl was born in 1780.
>
> Kateřina Ferklová was born in 1784.
>
> Václav Ferkl was born in 1787.
>
> Dorota Ferklová was born in 1794.

Josef Ferkl-3 (Jiří-2, Jiří-1) was born on 18 Feb 1751 in Kocňovice No. 11.

Anna Nohýnková daughter of Tomáš Nohynek was born in 1755 in Sychrov.

Josef Ferkl and Anna Nohýnková were married in 1777. They had the following children:

> Anna Ferklová was born in 1778 in Kocňovice No. 11. She died in 1778.
>
> ii. Josef Ferkl was born in 1790 in Kocňovice No. 11. He married Dorota Jirešová in 1810.

Vojtěch Ferkl-3 (Jiří-2, Jiří-1) was born on 02 Sep 1753 in Kocňovice. He died on 02 Oct 1843.

Kateřina Douděrová daughter of Pavel Douděra was born in 1755.

Vojtěch Ferkl and Kateřina Douděrová were married in 1782. They had the following children:

> **Jan Ferkl** was born in Kocňovice No. 6.
> **Josef Ferkl** was born in Kocňovice No. 15.
> **Dorota Ferklová** was born in Kocňovice No. 6.
> **Anna Ferklová** was born in 1785 in Kocňovice No. 6. She died in 1821.
> **Kateria Terezie Ferklová** was born in 1785 in Kocňovice No. 6. She died in 1821.

Generation 4

František Ferkl-4 (Jan Vojtěch-3, Josef-2, Jiří-1) was born on 06 Nov 1794 in Kocňovice No. 2, Mnichovo Hradiště Co.. He died on 13 Apr 1868.

Dorota Vondrakova daughter of Josef Vondrak and Anna Strejcova was born in 1802 in Bitouchov No. 14. She died on 14 Aug 1863.

František Ferkl and Dorota Vondrakova married. They had the following children:

> **Josef Ferkl** was born on 20 Apr 1827.
> **Josef Ferkl** was born on 23 Jun 1830.
> iii. **František Ferkl** was born on 19 Mar 1838 in Kocňovice No. 2, Mnichovo Hradiště Co.. He married Alžběta Horáčková on 05 Feb 1862. He died on 06 Feb 1906.

Jan Ferkl-4 (Josef-3, Josef-2, Jiří-1) was born in 1794 in Kocňovice No. 2. He died in Lived in Kocňovice No. 25.

Anna Šnajdrová daughter of František Šnajdr and Marie Kolomaznikova was born in 1795 in Podhora.

Jan Ferkl and Anna Šnajdrová were married in 1830. They had the following children:

> **Marie Ferklová** was born on 15 Jun 1827.
> ii. **Josef Ferkl** was born on 21 Oct 1831. He married Barbora Nevyhoštěná before 1886.

Václav Ferkl was born on 23 Aug 1834.
Václav Ferkl was born on 02 Sep 1835. He died on 16 Jul 1898.
František Ferkl was born on 16 Oct 1838. He married Barbora Koci in 1859.
Antonín Ferkl was born in 1843. He died in 1845.
Jan Ferkl was born on 03 Jul 1845. He died in 1847.

Václav Ferkl-4 (Josef-3, Josef-2, Jiří-1) was born on 30 Jun 1795 in Kocňovice No. 11.

Kateřina Nohýnková daughter of Václav Nohynek and Kateřina Formánková was born in 1791 in Hoškovice No. 3.

Václav Ferkl and Kateřina Nohýnková were married on 11 Nov 1815. They had the following children:

Josef Ferkl was born on 20 Jun 1817 in Hoškovice No. 11.
Anna Ferklová was born on 26 Jul 1819 in Hoškovice No. 3.
Kateřina Ferklová was born on 26 Dec 1820 in Kocňovice No. 11.

Josef Ferkl-4 (František-3, Josef-2, Jiří-1) was born on 07 Nov 1799 in Sychrov No. 16. He died on Sep 1863.

Kateřina Zamecka daughter of Václav Zamecky and Anna Čermáková was born in 1812 in Sychrov No. 11. She died on 01 Oct 1866.

Josef Ferkl and Kateřina Zamecka were married in 1830. They had the following children:

i. **Václav Ferkl** was born on 09 Jan 1833 in Sychrov No. 53.
Anna Ferkl was born on 23 Aug 1835 in Sychrov No. 53. She died in 1836 in Sychrov No. 50.
Anna Ferkl was born on 08 Nov 1837 in Sychrov No. 11.
Josef Ferkl was born on 04 Apr 1840 in Klaster No. 84. He died in 1841.

Jan Ferkl-4 (František-3, Josef-2, Jiří-1) was born on 19 Jan 1802 in Sychrov No. 16. He died before 1875.

Veronika Peterková daughter of Václav Peterka and Anna Lochmanová was born in 1803 in Mala Bela. She died on 27 May 1845.

Jan Ferkl and Veronika Peterková married. They had the following children:
> **Marie Ferklová** was born on 08 Aug 1829 in Klaster No. 26.
>
> **Jan Nepomucký Ferkl** was born on 16 May 1834 in Klaster No. 53. He died in 1835.
>
> **Barbora Ferklová** was born in 1834 in Klaster No. 1. She died in 1875.
>
> **Antonie Ferklová** was born on 13 Sep 1839 in Klaster No. 74. She died in 1841 in Klaster No. 70.
>
> v. **Josefa Ferklová** was born in 1845 in Klaster.

František Ferkl-4 (František-3, Josef-2, Jiří-1) was born on 30 Jan 1806 in Sychrov No. 16.

Dorota Rejzkova was born in 1807.

František Ferkl and Dorota Rejzkova were married in 1829. They had the following children:
> **Anna Ferklová** was born in 1830. She died in 1830.
>
> **Kateřina Ferklová** was born on 14 Mar 1830.
>
> **Josef Ferkl** was born on 07 Feb 1835. He died in 1835.

Kateřina Nohýnková daughter of Jan Nohynek was born in 1774 in Podolí. She died on 26 Aug 1830.

František Ferkl and Kateřina Nohýnková married. They had no children.

Josef Ferkl-4 (Jan-3, Václav-2, Jiří-1) was born on 30 Jan 1776 in Jivina No. 6.
> **Cecile Kinterova** daughter of Václav Kintera and Kateřina was born in 1773 in Hoškovice N o. 15. Josef Ferkl and Cecile Kinterova were married in 1793. They had the following children:
>
> **Antonín Ferkl** was born in 1798.
>
> **Josefa Ferkl** was born in 1800.
>
> **Kateřina Ferkl** was born in 1800. She died in 1800.
>
> iv. **Josef Ferkl** was born on 19 May 1802 in Jivina No. 6.

Josef Ferkl-4 (Václav-3, Václav-2, Jiří-1) was born on 26 Jan 1782. He died on 30 Dec 1846 in Lived in Dolni Bukovina No. 11.

Marie Augustinova daughter of Jan Augustin was born in 1770. She died on 22 Oct 1840. Josef Ferkl and Marie Augustinova married. They had the following children:

    Jan Nepomucký Ferkl was born in 1805. He died in 1807.
    Kateřina Ferkl was born in 1808.
    Anna Ferkl was born in 1810.
    Barabora Ferkl was born in 1812. She died in 1815.
  v. **Josef Ferkl** was born on 19 Oct 1815 in Dolni Bukovina No. 11. He died in Bukovina No. 11.
    Marie Ferkl was born in 1818.
    Jan Krtitel Ferkl was born in 1820. He died in 1825.
    Jan Ferkl was born in 1823 in Dolni Bukovina No. 11.
    Jan Nepomucký Ferkl was born in 1823.

Marie Ferklová-4 (Václav-3, Václav-2, Jiří-1) was born in 1800.
Marie Ferklová and unknown spouse married. They had the following children:

    Václav Ferkl was born in 1830. He died in 1830.

Josef Ferkl-4 (Josef-3, Jiří-2, Jiří-1) was born in 1790 in Kocňovice No. 11.
Dorota Jirešová daughter of Jan Jireš and Anna Zamecka was born in 1790 in Sychrov No. 3. Josef Ferkl and Dorota Jirešová were married in 1810. They had the following children:

    Josef Ferkl was born in 1810 in Sychrov No. 3. He died in 1811.
    Josef Ferkl was born in 1812 in Sychrov No. 3.
    Václav Ferkl was born in 1814 in Sychrov No. 3.
  iv. **Anna Ferklová** was born in 1817 in Sychrov No. 3.

Generation 5

František Ferkl-5 (František-4, Jan Vojtěch-3, Josef-2, Jiří-1) was born on 19 Mar 1838 in Kocňovice No. 2, Mnichovo Hradiště Co.. He died on 06 Feb 1906.

Alžběta Horáčková daughter of Josef Horáček and Kateřina Němcová was born on 14 Apr 1842 in Hrdlorezy No. 24. She died on 23 Oct 1906 in Kocnevice Cemetary.

František Ferkl and Alžběta Horáčková were married on 05 Feb 1862. They had the following children:
> son Ferkl.
> son Ferkl.
> son Ferkl.
> son Ferkl.
> son Ferkl.
> **Josef Ferkl** was born on 20 Jan 1863 in Kocňovice No. 2.
> vii. **František Ferkl** was born on 21 Jan 1865 in Kocňovice No. 2. He died on 26 Jul 1943 in Kocnevuce Cemetery.

Josef Ferkl-5 (Jan-4, Josef-3, Josef-2, Jiří-1) was born on 21 Oct 1831.

Barbora Nevyhoštěná daughter of Jan Nevyhoštěný and Terezie Hykova was born in 1850 in Mohelnice No. 31.

Josef Ferkl and Barbora Nevyhoštěná were married before 1886. They had the following children:
> **Josef Ferkl** was born on 09 Oct 1886. He died in 1886.
> **Anna Ferklová** was born on 19 Jan 1889. She died in 1890.
> **Josef Ferkl** was born on 29 Dec 1892.

Barbora Koci daughter of Václav Koci and Barbora Hejdukova was born in 1834 in Tatobyty No. 19. She died before 1885.

Josef Ferkl and Barbora Koci were married on 07 Nov 1859. They had the following children:
> **Anna Ferklová** was born on 04 May 1860 in Mohelnice.
> ii. **Marie Ferklová** was born on 13 Aug 1862 in Hnevosice No. 4.
> **Josef Karel Ferkl** was born on 28 Jan 1865. He died in 1868 in Mohelnice No. 33.
> **Kateřina Ferklová** was born on 04 Feb 1867 in Mohelnice No. 42. She died on 29 Jan 1895 in Mohelnice No. 32.
> **Václav Ferkl** was born before 28 Sep 1869 in Mohelnice No. 27.
> **Paulina Ferklová** was born before 22 Mar 1872 in Mohelnice No. 42.
> **Marie Ferklová** was born before 19 Jun 1874 in Mohelnice No. 42.

Václav Ferkl-5 (Josef-4, František-3, Josef-2, Jiří-1) was born on 09 Jan 1833 in Sychrov No. 53.

Terezie Venclakova daughter of Josef Venclak and Dorota Marouskova was born in 1840 in Borovice No. 25.

Václav Ferkl and Terezie Venclakova married. They had the following children:

    i. **Josef Ferkl** was born on 11 Feb 1865 in Borovice. He married Marie Lambergova in 1897. He died in Lived in Klaster No. 84.

    Marie Ferkl was born in 1869 in Klaster No. 84. She died in 1869.

    Josefa Ferkl was born in 1872 in Klaster No. 84.

    Františka Ferkl was born in 1875 in Klaster No. 84.

    Antonia Ferkl was born in 1877 in Klaster No. 84. She died in 1877.

    Václav Ferkl was born in 1878 in Klaster No. 84. He died in 1878.

    Václav Ferkl was born in 1879 in Klaster No. 84. He died in 1951.

    František Ferkl was born in 1882 in Klaster No. 84. He died in 1883.

    František Ferkl was born in 1884 in Klaster No. 84. He died in 1884.

Josefa Ferklová-5 (Jan-4, František-3, Josef-2, Jiří-1) was born in 1845 in Klaster.

Unknown.

Unknown and Josefa Ferklová married. They had the following children:

    Antonín Ferkl was born on 18 Oct 1880 in Klaster No. 45. He died in 1880.

Josef Ferkl-5 (Josef-4, Jan-3, Václav-2, Jiří-1) was born on 19 May 1802 in Jivina No. 6.

Marie Tomková was born in 1802 in Mohelnice No. 10.

Josef Ferkl and Marie Tomková married. They had the following children:

    Marie Ferklová Ferkl was born in 1825 in Mohelnice No. 10.

    Jiří Ferkl was born in 1832 in Jivina No. 6. He married Anna Nedvědová in 1851 in Dobrá Voda.

Josef Ferkl-5 (Josef-4, Václav-3, Václav-2, Jiří-1) was born on 19 Oct 1815 in Dolni Bukovina No. 11. He died in Bukovina No. 11.

Marie Čupíková son of Josef Čupík and Anna Nedomova was born in 1820. He died in 1884.

Josef Ferkl and Marie Čupíková married. They had the following children:

    Anna Ferklová was born in 1839.

    Barbora Ferklová was born in 1840.

    iii. **Josef Ferkl** was born on 13 Jul 1842 in Dolni Bukovina No. 11. He married Barbora Fidlerova in 1869.

    iv. **Anna Ferklová** was born in 1844 in Dolni Bukovina No. 11.

    Jan Ferkl was born in 1847 in Dolni Bukovina No. 11.

    Kateřina Ferklová was born in 1850 in Dolni Bukovina No. 11.

    vii. **Václav Ferkl** was born on 01 Jun 1851 in Dolni Bukovina No. 11. He died in Bukovina.

    Antonín Ferkl was born on 07 Apr 1853 in Dolni Bukovina No. 11. He died on 15 Dec 1924 in Bukovina No. 11.

    František Ferkl was born in 1857 in Dolni Bukovina No. 11. He died in 1891.

    Jiří Ferkl was born in 1859 in Dolni Bukovina No. 11.

Anna Ferklová-5 (Josef-4, Josef-3, Jiří-2, Jiří-1) was born in 1817 in Sychrov No. 3.

Unknown.

Unknown and Anna Ferklová married. They had the following children:

    Josef was born in 1839 in Kocňovice No. 30.

Generation 6

František Ferkl-6 (František-5, František-4, Jan Vojtěch-3, Josef-2, Jiří-1) was born on 21 Jan 1865 in Kocňovice No. 2. He died on 26 Jul 1943 in Kocnevuce Cemetary.

Anna Saralova daughter of Václav Saral and Josefa Pluhařová was born on 03 Oct 1878 in Cervenice No. 7, near Radimovice. She died on 25 Jan 1938.

František Ferkl and Anna Saralova married. They had the following children:

i. **Marie Anna Ferklová** was born on 10 Dec 1897 in Chocnějovice No. 2. She married Adolf Rechcigl on 25 Apr 1917 in St. Alois Church, Praha. She died on 31 Dec 1970 in Šárovcova Lhota.

ii. **Josef Ferkl** was born on 07 Jul 1899 in Chocnějovice No. 2. He married Blažena Koskova on 02 Aug 1926.

Marie Ferklová-6 (Josef-5, Jan-4, Josef-3, Josef-2, Jiří-1) was born on 13 Aug 1862 in Hnevosice No. 4.

Unknown.

Unknown and Marie Ferklová married. They had the following children:

Božena Ferklová was born on 03 Jul 1899. She died in 1899.

Josef Ferkl-6 (Václav-5, Josef-4, František-3, Josef-2, Jiří-1) was born on 11 Feb 1865 in Borovice. He died in Lived in Klaster No. 84.

Marie Lambergova daughter of Václav Lamberg and Terezie Hyblova was born on 23 Jul 1863 in Voderady 7.

Josef Ferkl and Marie Lambergova were married in 1897. They had the following children:

František Ferkl was born in 1891 in Klaster No. 84.

Josef Ferkl was born in 1893. He married Anna Maskova in 1917.

Ladislav Ferkl.

Zdeněk Ferkl was born in 1904.

Josef Ferkl-6 (Josef-5, Josef-4, Václav-3, Václav-2, Jiří-1) was born on 13 Jul 1842 in Dolni Bukovina No. 11.

Barbora Fidlerova was born on 07 Sep 1842. She died in 1899.

Josef Ferkl and Barbora Fidlerova were married in 1869. They had the following children:

Anna Ferklová was born in 1866 in Bila Hlina No. 22.

Josef Ferkl was born in 1866 in Bila Hlina No. 27.

František Ferkl was born in 1870 in Dolni Bukopvina No. 16.

Václav Ferkl was born in 1875 in Dolni Bukovina No. 17.

v. **Barbora Kateřina Ferklová** was born in 1880 in Dolni Bukovina No. 17.

Anna Ferklová-6 (Josef-5, Josef-4, Václav-3, Václav-2, Jiří-1) was born in 1844 in Dolni Bukovina No. 11.

Unknown.

Unknown and Anna Ferklová married. They had the following children:

Marie Ferklová was born in 1866.

Václav Ferkl-6 (Josef-5, Josef-4, Václav-3, Václav-2, Jiří-1) was born on 01 Jun 1851 in Dolní Bukovina No. 11. He died in Bukovina.

Marie Horáková was born on 16 Aug 1848.

Václav Ferkl and Marie Horáková married. They had the following children:

Anna Ferklová was born in 1881.

Barbora Ferklová was born in 1883. She died in 1890.

Marie Ferklová was born in 1888.

Barbora Ferklová was born in 1893.

Generation 7

Marie Anna Ferklová-7 (František-6, František-5, František-4, Jan Vojtěch-3, Josef-2, Jiří-1) was born on 10 Dec 1897 in Chocnějovice No. 2. She died on 31 Dec 1970 in Šárovcova Lhota.

Adolf Rechcigl son of Petr Rechziegel and Anna Najmanová was born on 21 Aug 1876 in Letařovice No. 4, Český Dub Co.. He died on 30 Mar 1946 in Šárovcova Lhota No. 16.

Adolf Rechcigl and Marie Anna Ferklová were married on 25 Apr 1917 in St. Alois Church, Praha. They had the following children:

i. **Stanislav Josef Rechcigl** was born on 10 Oct 1918 in Chocnějovice. He married Libuše Sedláčková on 17 Jan 1948 in Novy Bydzov. He died on 09 May 1973 in Šárovcova Lhota No. 16.

Adolf Rechcigl was born on 09 Apr 1920 in Chocnějovice No. 22. He died on 27 Dec 1944 in Ples.

Josef Ferkl-7 (František-6, František-5, František-4, Jan Vojtěch-3, Josef-2, Jiří-1) was born on 07 Jul 1899 in Chocnějovice No. 2.

Blažena Koskova daughter of Florián Košek and Antonie Sedláčková was born on 05 May 1900 in Burinsko No. 1.

Josef Ferkl and Blažena Koskova were married on 02 Aug 1926. They had the following children:

> i. **Hana Ferklová** was born on 03 Jan 1927 in Chocnějovice No. 2. She married Ladislav Šulc on 09 Sep 1950 in Loukov. She died about 2005.

Barbora Kateřina Ferklová-7 (Josef-6, Josef-5, Josef-4, Václav-3, Václav-2, Jiří-1) was born in 1880 in Dolni Bukovina No. 17.

Barbora Kateřina Ferklová and unknown spouse married. They had the following children:

> **Marie Ferklová**. She died in 1900.

Generation 8

Stanislav Josef Rechcigl-8 (Marie Anna-7, František-6, František-5, František-4, Jan Vojtěch-3, Josef-2, Jiří-1) was born on 10 Oct 1918 in Chocnějovice. He died on 09 May 1973 in Šárovcova Lhota No. 16.

Libuše Sedláčková daughter of Bedřich Sedláček and Ludmila was born on 24 Sep 1924 in Staré Smrkovice, Jičín Dist. She died on 03 Apr 2019 in Jičín, Czech.

Stanislav Josef Rechcigl and Libuše Sedláčková were married on 17 Jan 1948 in Novy Bydzov. They had the following children:

> i. **Hana Rechcíglová** was born on 13 Jul 1948 in Novy Bydzov, Hradec Králové Co.. She married Jaroslav Husak on 28 Dec 1968 in Sobotka, Jičín Co..
>
> ii. **Libuše Rechcíglová** was born on 25 Jan 1950 in Novy Bydzov, Hradec Králové Co.. She married Miroslav Vich on 11 Apr 1970 in Ostromer, Jičín Co..
>
> iii. **Stanislav Rechcigl** was born on 24 Mar 1952 in Hořice, Jičín Co.. He married Zdena Pařízková on 24 Mar 1972 in Jičín.

Hana Ferklová-8 (Josef-7, František-6, František-5, František-4, Jan Vojtěch-3, Josef-2, Jiří-1) was born on 03 Jan 1927 in Chocnějovice No. 2. She died about 2005.

Ladislav Šulc son of Václav Šulc and Kristina Stránská was born on 11 Jan 1926 in Klaster No. 115.

Ladislav Šulc and Hana Ferklová were married on 09 Sep 1950 in Loukov. They had the following children:

> **Jaromira Šulc** was born on 08 Oct 1953.

Hana Šulcová was born on 15 Apr 1955.

Generation 9

Hana Rechcíglová-9 (Stanislav Josef-8, Marie Anna-7, František-6, František-5, František-4, Jan Vojtěch-3, Josef-2, Jiří-1) was born on 13 Jul 1948 in Novy Bydzov, Hradec Králové Co..

Jaroslav Husak was born on 24 Mar 1946 in Jičín.

Jaroslav Husak and Hana Rechcíglová were married on 28 Dec 1968 in Sobotka, Jičín Co.. They had the following children:

>**Martin Husak** was born on 20 Feb 1971 in Hradec Králové. He married Petra Endrychová on 24 Jul 1999 in Hradec Králové.
>
>**Petra Husakova** was born on 30 Mar 1974 in Hradec Králové.

Tomáš Petříček was born on 18 Dec 1948 in Hradec Králové.

Tomáš Petříček and Hana Rechcíglová were married on 20 Sep 1991 in Hradec Králové. They had no children.

Libuše Rechcíglová-9 (Stanislav Josef-8, Marie Anna-7, František-6, František-5, František-4, Jan Vojtěch-3, Josef-2, Jiří-1) was born on 25 Jan 1950 in Novy Bydzov, Hradec Králové Co..

Miroslav Vich was born on 13 Nov 1950 in Nova Paka, Jičín Co..

Miroslav Vich and Libuše Rechcíglová were married on 11 Apr 1970 in Ostromer, Jičín Co.. They had the following children:

>i. **Iveta Vichova** was born on 15 Jan 1972 in Jičín. She married Miloš Haltuf on 07 Sep 1991 in Lazne Belohrad, Jičín Co..
>
>**Miroslav Vich** was born on 10 Mar 1973 in Jičín.
>
>**Sarka Vichova** was born on 11 Mar 1989 in Hradec Králové.

Stanislav Rechcigl-9 (Stanislav Josef-8, Marie Anna-7, František-6, František-5, František-4, Jan Vojtěch-3, Josef-2, Jiří-1) was born on 24 Mar 1952 in Hořice, Jičín Co..

Zdena Pařízková daughter of Mila Parik and Zdenka was born on 26 Jan 1954 in Hořice, Jičín Dist., Bohemia.

Stanislav Rechcigl and Zdena Pařízková were married on 24 Mar 1972 in Jičín. They had the following children:

>i. **Stanislava Rechcíglová** was born on 22 Sep 1972 in Hořice, Jičín Dist., Bohemia.

ii. **Jana Rechcíglová** was born on 22 Sep 1973 in Hořice, Jičín Co.. She married Karel Spidlen on 29 Apr 1995 in Jičín, Bohemia.

iii. **Stanislav Rechcigl** was born on 08 Aug 1975 in Hořice, Jičín Dist., Bohemia. He married Natasha Blackbourn on 19 Jul 2008 in Spalding, Lincolnshire, UK..

Helena Denisova was born on 29 Jun 1944.

Stanislav Rechcigl and Helena Denisova met. They had no children.

Generation 10

Iveta Vichova-10 (Libuše-9, Stanislav Josef-8, Marie Anna-7, František-6, František-5, František-4, Jan Vojtěch-3, Josef-2, Jiří-1) was born on 15 Jan 1972 in Jičín.

Miloš Haltuf was born on 03 May 1968 in Chlumec.

Miloš Haltuf and Iveta Vichova were married on 07 Sep 1991 in Lazne Belohrad, Jičín Co.. They had the following children:

    Jan Haltuf was born on 10 Mar 1992 in Hořice, Jičín Co..

Stanislava Rechcíglová-10 (Stanislav-9, Stanislav Josef-8, Marie Anna-7, František-6, František-5, František-4, Jan Vojtěch-3, Josef-2, Jiří-1) was born on 22 Sep 1972 in Hořice, Jičín Dist., Bohemia.

Josef Bekera was born on 22 Jun 1965.

Josef Bekera and Stanislava Rechcíglová met. They had the following children:

    Nikolas Bekera was born on 23 Sep 2001.
    Sebestian Bekera.
    Anastasia Jowefa Bekerová.

Jana Rechcíglová-10 (Stanislav-9, Stanislav Josef-8, Marie Anna-7, František-6, František-5, František-4, Jan Vojtěch-3, Josef-2, Jiří-1) was born on 22 Sep 1973 in Hořice, Jičín Co..

Karel Spidlen was born on 06 Feb 1972 in Hradec Králové.

Karel Spidlen and Jana Rechcíglová were married on 29 Apr 1995 in Jičín, Bohemia. They had the following children:

    Karel Spidlen was born on 15 Oct 1995 in Hořice, Jičín Co..

Stanislav Rechcigl-10 (Stanislav-9, Stanislav Josef-8, Marie Anna-7, František-6, František-5, František-4, Jan Vojtěch-3, Josef-2, Jiří-1) was born on 08 Aug 1975 in Hořice, Jičín Dist., Bohemia.
Natasha Blackbourn.
Stanislav Rechcigl and Natasha Blackbourn were married on 19 Jul 2008 in Spalding, Lincolnshire, UK.. They had the following children:

    Lily-Grace Rechcíglová was born on 03 Jul 2011 in Watford, UK.

    Poppy Sophia Rechcíglová was born on 13 Oct 2013.

Šifta Family

Generation 1

Václav Šifta-1 was born before 1840 in Jivina No. 1.

Karolina Odcházelová daughter of František Odchazel and Unknown was born in Jivina No. 1, Český Dub Co..

Václav Šifta and Karolina Odcházelová married. They had the following children:

> i. **Václav Šifta** was born on 21 Aug 1861 in Jivina No. 1. He married Marie Zajickova on 14 Jul 1885 in Jivina No. 16, Český Dub Co.; Rev. Josef Kovar, parish priest officiating. He died in Received house in 1885.

Generation 2

Václav Šifta-2 (Václav-1) was born on 21 Aug 1861 in Jivina No. 1. He died in Received house in 1885.

Marie Zajickova daughter of Josef Zajíček and Josefa Rechziegelová was born on 24 Aug 1862 in Jivina No. 16. She died on 23 Mar 1927 in Jivina No. 16.

Václav Šifta and Marie Zajickova were married on 14 Jul 1885 in Jivina No. 16, Český Dub Co.; Rev. Josef Kovar, parish priest officiating. They had the following children:

> **Emilie Šiftová** was born in 1886 in Jivina No. 1.
>
> **Božena Šiftová** was born in 1892 in Jivina No. 1.
>
> iii. **Josef Šifta** was born in 1898 in Jivina No. 1. He died in 1953.

Generation 3

Josef Šifta-3 (Václav-2, Václav-1) was born in 1898 in Jivina No. 1. He died in 1953.

Marie Řepková was born in 1897 in Pacerice. She died in 1985.

Josef Šifta and Marie Řepková married. They had the following children:

> i. **Marie Šiftová** was born on 20 Jun 1923 in Jivina No. 1. She died on 10 Jun 2004.

Generation 4

Marie Šiftová-4 (Josef-3, Václav-2, Václav-1) was born on 20 Jun 1923 in Jivina No. 1. She died on 10 Jun 2004.

Miroslav Třešňák was born on 06 Mar 1921 in Jenisovice -. He died on 11 Jul 1986 in Lived in Jivina No. 1.

Miroslav Třešňák and Marie Šiftová married. They had the following children:

> i. **Miroslav Třešňák** was born on 25 May 1943 in Jivina No. 1. He married Miluška Hanzlova on 23 Oct 1965. He died on 19 Nov 2005 in moved to Jivina No. 24.
>
> ii. **Jiří Třešňák** was born on 22 Jul 1952 in Jivina No. 1. He married Marie Zoubková on 19 Jun 1976. He died in moved to Odolena Voda, Praha vychod.

Generation 5

Miroslav Třešňák-5 (Marie-4, Josef-3, Václav-2, Václav-1) was born on 25 May 1943 in Jivina No. 1. He died on 19 Nov 2005 in moved to Jivina No. 24.

Miluška Hanzlova was born on 29 Dec 1944 in Svijany.

Miroslav Třešňák and Miluška Hanzlova were married on 23 Oct 1965. They had the following children:

> i. **Pavel Třešňák** was born on 25 Feb 1967 in Turnov - moved to Český Dub. He married Radka Černá on 18 Apr 1992.
>
> ii. **Luboš Třešňák** was born on 30 Apr 1974 in Turnov - moved to Vrkoslavice. He married Jitka Necaskova on 21 Sep 1996.

Jiří Třešňák-5 (Marie-4, Josef-3, Václav-2, Václav-1) was born on 22 Jul 1952 in Jivina No. 1. He died in moved to Odolena Voda, Praha vychod.

Marie Zoubková was born on 22 Jun 1956 in Zasada.

Jiří Třešňák and Marie Zoubková were married on 19 Jun 1976. They had the following children:

> **Lenka Třešňáková** was born on 21 Jan 1978 in Turnov.
>
> **Radka Třešňáková** was born on 30 May 1985 in Brandys nad Labem.

Generation 6

Pavel Třešňák-6 (Miroslav-5, Marie-4, Josef-3, Václav-2, Václav-1) was born on 25 Feb 1967 in Turnov - moved to Český Dub.

Radka Černá was born on 07 Sep 1971 in Česká Lipa.

Pavel Třešňák and Radka Černá were married on 18 Apr 1992. They had the following children:

    Pavlina Třešňáková was born on 17 Jun 1999 in Turnov.

Luboš Třešňák-6 (Miroslav-5, Marie-4, Josef-3, Václav-2, Václav-1) was born on 30 Apr 1974 in Turnov - moved to Vrkoslavice.

Jitka Necaskova was born on 21 Nov 1969 in Jablonnec nad Nisou.

Luboš Třešňák and Jitka Necaskova were married on 21 Sep 1996. They had the following children:

    Michaela Třešňáková was born on 02 Sep 1997 in Jablonec nad Nisou.

    Matěj Třešňák was born on 18 May 2001 in Jablonec nad Nisou.

Janecek Family

Generation 1

František Janeček-1 was born in Třtí, No. 6.

Anna Koskova was born in Třtí.

František Janeček and Anna Koskova married. They had the following children:

>**František Janeček.**
>**Františka Janečková.**
>**Kateřina Janečková.**
>**Marie Janečková.**
>v. **Václav Janeček** was born in 1834 in Příšovice. He died on 18 Sep 1909 in Příšovice.
>vi. **Anna Janečková** was born on 19 Apr 1855 in Třtí No. 6. She married Václav Rechziegel in 1879. She died on 17 Dec 1903 in Hodkovice.

Generation 2

Václav Janeček-2 (František-1) was born in 1834 in Příšovice. He died on 18 Sep 1909 in Příšovice.

Marie Rechziegel daughter of Petr Rechziegel and Františka Hlavatá was born on 24 Jan 1841 in Hodkovice No. 39.

Václav Janeček and Marie Rechziegel married. They had the following children:

>i. **Anna Janečková.**
>**Petr Janeček.**
>**František Janeček.**

Anna Janečková-2 (František-1) was born on 19 Apr 1855 in Třtí No. 6. She died on 17 Dec 1903 in Hodkovice.

Václav Rechziegel son of Petr Rechziegel and Františka Hlavatá was born on 25 Aug 1851 in Slavíkov No. 3. He died on 21 Mar 1909 in Radostín No. 13.

Václav Rechziegel and Anna Janečková were married in 1879. They had the following children:

Adolf Rechziegel.

Josef Rechziegel was born in 1886 in Radostín. He died on 05 Oct 1956 in Radostín.

Emilie Rechziegelová.

iv. **Marie Rechziegelová** was born in 1882 in Radostín. She died on 30 Jul 1959 in Radostín.

v. **Anna Rechziegelová** was born on 26 Sep 1888 in Radostín. She married Josef Franců about 1925. She died on 10 Oct 1964 in Kacanovy.

vi. **Anastazie Rechziegelová** was born on 17 Mar 1894 in Radostín. She married Rudolf Roubíček in Jul 1917. She died on 19 Apr 1984 in Srch.

Generation 3

Anna Janečková-3 (Václav-2, František-1).

Kinsky.

Kinsky and Anna Janečková married. They had the following children:

i. **Miloslav Kinsky.**

Marie Rechziegelová-3 (Anna-2, František-1) was born in 1882 in Radostín. She died on 30 Jul 1959 in Radostín.

Josef Pelech was born in 1885. He died on 09 Feb 1961.

Josef Pelech and Marie Rechziegelová married. They had the following children:

i. **Marie Pelechová.** She died on 09 Aug 1961.

Anna Rechziegelová-3 (Anna-2, František-1) was born on 26 Sep 1888 in Radostín. She died on 10 Oct 1964 in Kacanovy.

Josef Franců was born on 09 Apr 1894 in Kacanovy. He died on 22 Nov 1971 in Turnov.

Josef Franců and Anna Rechziegelová were married about 1925. They had the following children:

i. **Jaromír Franců** was born on 26 Feb 1926 in Kacanovy. He married Marta Lamačová on 04 Nov 1950 in Turnov. He died on 04 Jul 1980 in Jičín.

Josef Studnička was born in Kacanovy. He died before 1925.

Notes for Josef Studnička:
General Notes:
He went to the Russian Front during the World War I but never returned.
Josef Studnička and Anna Rechziegelová married. They had the following children:
- i. **Oldrřch Studnička** was born on 07 Jun 1912 in Kacanovy. He died on 20 Aug 1942 in Kacanovy.

Anastazie Rechziegelová-3 (Anna-2, František-1) was born on 17 Mar 1894 in Radostín. She died on 19 Apr 1984 in Srch.

Rudolf Roubíček son of František Roubíček and Marie Roubíčková was born about 1894 in Radostín. He died about Mar 1918.

Rudolf Roubíček and Anastazie Rechziegelová were married in Jul 1917. They had the following children:
- i. **Jana Roubíčková** was born on 26 Jan 1918 in Radostín. She married Franisek Kvapil on Sep 1943 in Kunetice. She died on 13 Oct 1981 in Lazne Bohdanec.

František Pátek was born in 1894 in Chlum u Hlinska. He died on 05 Feb 1958 in Srchrechziegel.

František Pátek and Anastazie Rechziegelová met. They had the following children:
- i. **Dalibor Rechziegel** was born on 20 Oct 1924 in Radostín, near Turnov. He married Sona Pražáková on 26 Apr 1948 in Kladno. He died on 12 Aug 1997 in Litomerice.
- ii. **Drahomir Rechziegel** was born on 19 Nov 1926. He died on 23 Oct 1983.

Generation 4

Marie Pelechová-4 (Marie-3, Anna-2, František-1). She died on 09 Aug 1961.

Alois Florián was born resided in Letovice by Brno.

Alois Florián and Marie Pelechová married. They had the following children:
- i. **Marie Floriánová**.
- ii. **Karel Florián**.

Jaromír Franců-4 (Anna-3, Anna-2, František-1) was born on 26 Feb 1926 in Kacanovy. He died on Jul 1980 in Jičín.

Marta Lamačová was born on 06 Jun 1927 in Kacanovy. She died on 04 Nov 1950 in Turnov.

Jaromír Franců and Marta Lamačová were married on 04 Nov 1950 in Turnov. They had the following children:

    i. **Jaromír Franců** was born on 21 Aug 1951 in Kacanovy, Turnov. He married Věra Zimova on 29 Dec 1989 in Jičín.

Oldrřch Studnička-4 (Anna-3, Anna-2, František-1) was born on 07 Jun 1912 in Kacanovy. He died on 20 Aug 1942 in Kacanovy.

Notes for Oldrřch Studnička:

General Notes:

He was shot by the Nazi during the persecutine of the underground leader Dr. Vladimír. Krajina.

Bohumila Karaskova was born on 09 May 1913 in Kacanovy. She died on 25 Sep 2000 in Turnov. Oldrřch Studnička and Bohumila Karaskova married. They had the following children:

    i. **Oldrřch Studnička** was born on 31 May 1942 in Kacanovy.

Jana Roubíčková-4 (Anastazie-3, Anna-2, František-1) was born on 26 Jan 1918 in Radostín. She died on 13 Oct 1981 in Lazne Bohdanec.

Franisek Kvapil was born on 24 Nov 1912. He died on 15 Oct 1982.

Franisek Kvapil and Jana Roubíčková were married on 11 Sep 1943 in Kunetice. They had the following children:

    i. **Jan Kvapil** was born on 27 May 1944 in Pardubice. He married Eva Nováková on 09 Jun 1962 in Pardubice.

    ii. **Nada Kvapilová** was born on 11 Feb 1946 in Pardubice. She married Josef Virt on 13 Mar 1971 in Rohovladova Bela.

Dalibor Rechziegel-4 (Anastazie-3, Anna-2, František-1) was born on 20 Oct 1924 in Radostín, near Turnov. He died on 12 Aug 1997 in Litomerice.

Sona Pražáková was born on 23 Sep 1929 in Brandysek, Kladno Co..

Dalibor Rechziegel and Sona Pražáková were married on 26 Apr 1948 in Kladno. They had the following children:

    Jan Rechziegel was born on 12 Oct 1951 in Litomerice.

Luboš Rechziegel was born on 08 Jan 1957 in Litomerice. He married Radka Chládková on 06 Jul 1985 in Litomerice.

Drahomir Rechziegel-4 (Anastazie-3, Anna-2, František-1) was born on 19 Nov 1926. He died on 23 Oct 1983.

Marie Kamenicka was born on 01 Jan 1929 in Kunetice. She died on 18 Apr 1979.

Drahomir Rechziegel and Marie Kamenicka married. They had the following children:

    i. **Jitka Rechziegelová** was born on 27 Aug 1951.

    ii. **Aleš Rechziegel** was born on 15 Jan 1954.

    iii. **Drahomir Rechziegel** was born on 10 Feb 1957 in Pardubice.

Generation 5

Marie Floriánová-5 (Marie-4, Marie-3, Anna-2, František-1).

Josef Tomeš was born in Stranov.

Josef Tomeš and Marie Floriánová married. They had the following children:

    Tomsová-daughter.

    son Tomeš.

Jaromír Franců-5 (Jaromír-4, Anna-3, Anna-2, František-1) was born on 21 Aug 1951 in Kacanovy, Turnov.

Věra Zimova was born on 21 Jan 1956 in Turnov.

Jaromír Franců and Věra Zimova were married on 29 Dec 1989 in Jičín. They had the following children:

    Adam Franců was born on 12 Jul 1990.

    Jan Franců was born on 26 Jul 1993.

Oldrřch Studnička-5 (Oldrřch-4, Anna-3, Anna-2, František-1) was born on 31 May 1942 in Kacanovy.

Marie Nováková was born on 06 May 1952 in Vsen, Turnov.

Oldrřch Studnička and Marie Nováková married. They had the following children:

    Lucie Studničková was born on 15 Aug 1975 in Praha.

Jan Kvapil-5 (Jana-4, Anastazie-3, Anna-2, František-1) was born on 27 May 1944 in Pardubice.

Eva Nováková daughter of Marta Lamacova was born on 21 Dec 1943. Jan Kvapil and Eva Nováková were married on 09 Jun 1962 in Pardubice. They had the following children:

    i. **Jan Kvapil** was born on 30 Dec 1963 in Pardubice. He married Iveta Kulichova on 31 Jan 1987 in Lazne Bohdanec.

    ii. **Jaroslav Kvapil** was born on 26 Feb 1969 in Pardubice. He married Eva Kadlecova on 30 Nov 1991 in Lazne Bohdanec.

    iii. **Eva Kvapilová** was born on 18 Oct 1973 in Pardubice. He married Tomasz Prcz on 18 May 1996 in Lazne Bohdanec.

    iv. **Jiri Kvapil** was born on 18 Jan 1980 in Pardubice. He married Zuzana Tomanová on 13 Aug 2005 in Lazne Bohdanec.

Nada Kvapilová-5 (Jana-4, Anastazie-3, Anna-2, František-1) was born on 11 Feb 1946 in Pardubice.

Josef Virt was born on 20 Sep 1933 in Pardubice. He died on 19 Jan 1991. Josef Virt and Nada Kvapilová were married on 13 Mar 1971 in Rohovladova Bela. They had the following children:

    i. **Petra Virtova** was born on 17 Aug 1976 in Pardubice. She married Tomáš Tupy on 25 Aug 2000.

Jitka Rechziegelová-5 (Drahomir-4, Anastazie-3, Anna-2, František-1) was born on 27 Aug 1951.

Petr Marek son of Petr Marek and Josefa was born on 16 Jun 1947 in Libec.

Petr Marek and Jitka Rechziegelová married. They had the following children:

    Denisa Markova was born on 28 Aug 1972.

    Petr Marek was born on 21 Feb 1975.

Aleš Rechziegel-5 (Drahomir-4, Anastazie-3, Anna-2, František-1) was born on 15 Jan 1954.

Lenka Horčičková daughter of Vladimír Horčička and Unknown was born on 03 Feb 1956. Aleš Rechziegel and Lenka Horčičková married. They had the following children:

    Andrea Rechziegel was born on 08 Apr 1975.

    Tomáš Rechziegel was born on 28 Mar 1979.

Drahomir Rechziegel-5 (Drahomir-4, Anastazie-3, Anna-2, František-1) was born on 10 Feb 1957 in Pardubice.

Alena Rykrova daughter of Jaroslav Rykr and Marie was born in 1965. Drahomir Rechziegel and Alena Rykrova married. They had the following children:

    Lukáš Rechziegel was born on 19 Jan 1985.

Generation 6

Jan Kvapil-6 (Jan-5, Jana-4, Anastazie-3, Anna-2, František-1) was born on 30 Dec 1963 in Pardubice.

Iveta Kulichova was born on 18 Jan 1969.

Jan Kvapil and Iveta Kulichova were married on 31 Jan 1987 in Lazne Bohdanec. They had the following children:

    Lucie Kvapilová was born on 09 Jul 1987 in Pardubice.

    Pavlina Kvapilová was born on 05 Sep 1991 in Pardubice.

    Iveta Kvapilová was born on 15 Jul 1993 in Pardubice.

Jaroslav Kvapil-6 (Jan-5, Jana-4, Anastazie-3, Anna-2, František-1) was born on 26 Feb 1969 in Pardubice.

Eva Kadlecova was born on 05 Sep 1969.

Jaroslav Kvapil and Eva Kadlecova were married on 30 Nov 1991 in Lazne Bohdanec. They had the following children:

    Katerina Kvapilová was born on 21 May 1992 in Pardubice.

    Monika Kvapilová was born on 19 Oct 1998 in Pardubice.

    Jakub Kvapil was born on 05 May 2005 in Pardubice.

Eva Kvapilová-6 (Jan-5, Jana-4, Anastazie-3, Anna-2, František-1) was born on 18 Oct 1973 in Pardubice.

Tomasz Prcz was born on 23 May 1970.

Tomasz Prcz and Eva Kvapilová were married on 18 May 1996 in Lazne Bohdanec. They had the following children:

    Martin Prcz was born on 19 May 1991 in Pardubice.

    Tomasz Prcz was born on 05 Oct 1997 in Pardubice.

Jiri Kvapil-6 (Jan-5, Jana-4, Anastazie-3, Anna-2, František-1) was born on 18 Jan 1980 in Pardubice.

Zuzana Tomanová was born on 20 Aug 1980.

Jiri Kvapil and Zuzana Tomanová were married on 13 Aug 2005 in Lazne Bohdanec. They had the following children:

> **Tereza Kvapilová** was born on 25 Dec 2006 in Pardubice.
>
> **Jiri Kvapil** was born on 07 Sep 2009 in Pardubice.

Petra Virtova-6 (Nada-5, Jana-4, Anastazie-3, Anna-2, František-1) was born on 17 Aug 1976 in Pardubice.

Tomáš Tupy was born on 24 Aug 1975 in Pardubice.

Tomáš Tupy and Petra Virtova were married on 25 Aug 2000. They had the following children:

> **Krystyna Tupa** was born on 27 Feb 2001.
>
> **Aneta Tupa** was born on 21 Apr 2006.

Franců Family

Generation 1

Josef Franců-1 was born on 09 Apr 1894 in Kacanovy. He died on 22 Nov 1971 in Turnov.

Anna Rechziegelová daughter of Václav Rechziegel and Anna Janečková was born on 26 Sep 1888 in Radostín. She died on 10 Oct 1964 in Kacanovy. Josef Franců and Anna Rechziegelová were married about 1925. They had the following children:

    i. **Jaromír Franců** was born on 26 Feb 1926 in Kacanovy. He married Marta Lamačová on Nov 1950 in Turnov. He died on 04 Jul 1980 in Jičín.

Generation 2

Jaromír Franců-2 (Josef-1) was born on 26 Feb 1926 in Kacanovy. He died on 04 Jul 1980 in Jičín.

Marta Lamačová was born on 06 Jun 1927 in Kacanovy. She died on 04 Nov 1950 in Turnov.

Jaromír Franců and Marta Lamačová were married on 04 Nov 1950 in Turnov. They had the following children:

    i. **Jaromír Franců** was born on 21 Aug 1951 in Kacanovy, Turnov. He married Věra Zimova on 29 Dec 1989 in Jičín.

Generation 3

Jaromír Franců-3 (Jaromír-2, Josef-1) was born on 21 Aug 1951 in Kacanovy, Turnov.

Věra Zimova was born on 21 Jan 1956 in Turnov.

Jaromír Franců and Věra Zimova were married on 29 Dec 1989 in Jičín. They had the following children:

    Adam Franců was born on 12 Jul 1990.

    Jan Franců was born on 26 Jul 1993.

Jira Family of Klamorna

Generation 1

Václav Jira-1.

    Dorota Roubinková was born in Selovice No. `3.

    Václav Jira and Dorota Roubinková married. They had the following children:

        i. **Josef Jira** was born in Klamorna No. 3, Český Dub Co..

Generation 2

Josef Jira-2 (Václav-1) was born in Klamorna No. 3, Český Dub Co..

    Alžběta Růtová daughter of Josef Růta and Unknown was born in Doubi No. 8, Český Dub Co.. Josef Jira and Alžběta Růtová married. They had the following children:

        i. **Václav Jira** was born on 15 Sep 1857 in Klamorna No. 3, Český Dub Co.. He married Josefa Rechziegel on 07 Jul 1890 in Slavíkov No. 4. He died on 24 May 1931.

    Marie Pelantová daughter of František Pelant and Alžběta Šimková.

    Josef Jira and Marie Pelantová married. They had the following children:

        i. **Jan Jira** was born in 1867.

Generation 3

Václav Jira-3 (Josef-2, Václav-1) was born on 15 Sep 1857 in Klamorna No. 3, Český Dub Co.. He died on 24 May 1931.

    Josefa Rechziegel daughter of Antonín Rechziegel and Marie Havliková was born on 15 Jun 1855 in Slavíkov No. 4. She died on 16 Jul 1945.

    Václav Jira and Josefa Rechziegel were married on 07 Jul 1890 in Slavíkov No. 4. They had the following children:

        i. **Marie Jirova** was born in 1893. She died on 01 Dec 1959.

Generation 4

Marie Jirova-4 (Václav-3, Josef-2, Václav-1) was born in 1893. She died on 01 Dec 1959.

    Josef Jisl was born in 1887 in Trávníček. He died on 12 Feb 1951.

    Josef Jisl and Marie Jirova married. They had the following children:

i. **Josef Jisl** was born on 02 Dec 1916. He died on 01 May 1991.

Generation 5

Josef Jisl-5 (Marie-4, Václav-3, Josef-2, Václav-1) was born on 02 Dec 1916. He died on 01 May 1991.

Marie Pelantová was born on 21 Apr 1916.

Josef Jisl and Marie Pelantová married. They had the following children:

6. i. **Marie Jislova** was born on 28 Jul 1947.

Generation 6

Marie Jislova-6 (Josef-5, Marie-4, Václav-3, Josef-2, Václav-1) was born on 28 Jul 1947.

Zdeněk Roubíček was born on 23 Jun 1946.

Zdeněk Roubíček and Marie Jislova married. They had the following children:

> **Lada Roubíčková** was born on 30 Dec 1973.
>
> **Zdeněk Roubíček** was born on 12 Jan 1975.

Jira Family of Dehtary

Generation 1

Jan Jira-1 was born in Dehtary No. 10.

Kateřina Lautska was born in Vlastibořice.

Jan Jira and Kateřina Lautska married. They had the following children:

    i. **Kateřina Jirova** was born in 1807 in Dehtary No. 10.

Generation 2

Kateřina Jirova-2 (Jan-1) was born in 1807 in Dehtary No. 10.

Josef Bartos son of Josef Bartos and Anna Hudcova was born in 1791 in Chvalčovice No. 12. He died in 1865.

Josef Bartos and Kateřina Jirova married. They had the following children:

    i. **Kateřina Bartošová** was born in Chvalčovice No. 12.

Generation 3

Kateřina Bartošová-3 (Kateřina-2, Jan-1) was born in Chvalčovice No. 12.

Unknown.

Unknown and Kateřina Bartošová met. They had the following children:

    i. **Anna Bartošová** was born on 27 Feb 1866 in Chvalčovice No. 12. She married Karel Bor. Rechziegel on 17 Aug 1889 in Český Dub. She died on 30 Sep 1936 in Sobeslavice No. 16.

Josef Beran.

Josef Beran and Kateřina Bartošová were married after 1866. They had no children.

Generation 4

Anna Bartošová-4 (Kateřina-3, Kateřina-2, Jan-1) was born on 27 Feb 1866 in Chvalčovice No. 12. She died on 30 Sep 1936 in Sobeslavice No. 16.

Karel Bor. Rechziegel son of Antonín Rechziegel and Marie Havliková was born on 02 Dec 1867 in Slavíkov No. 4. He died on 09 Jan 1904 in Chvalčovice.

Karel Bor. Rechziegel and Anna Bartošová were married on 17 Aug 1889 in Český Dub. They had the following children:

    Václav Rechziegel was born in 1894. He died in 1895.

ii. **Ing. František Rechcigel** was born on 18 Nov 1896 in Chvalčovice. He married Marie Holajova on 12 Nov 1924 in Prague, CSR. He died on 28 Aug 1968 in Český Dub.

František Tvrzník was born in 1861 in Sobeslavice No. 16. He died in 1938.

František Tvrzník and Anna Bartošová were married after 1904. They had no children.

Generation 5

Ing. František Rechcigel-5 (Anna-4, Kateřina-3, Kateřina-2, Jan-1) was born on 18 Nov 1896 in Chvalčovice. He died on 28 Aug 1968 in Český Dub.

Marie Holajova daughter of Josef Holaj and Marie Hauzrova was born on 18 May 1904 in Český Dub. She died on 27 Nov 1968 in III (Český Dub, No. 31).

Ing. František Rechcigel and Marie Holajova were married on 12 Nov 1924 in Prague, CSR. They had the following children:

    i. **Milan Rechcigel** was born on 12 Sep 1926 in Český Dub. He married Božena Bernardová on 24 Jan 1953. He died on 24 Sep 1980 in Český Dub.

    ii. **Ing. Vladko Rechcigel** was born on 29 Aug 1929 in Český Dub. He married Lidmila Lukaskova on 19 Oct 1957.

    iii. **Milena Rechcigelova** was born on 10 Mar 1936 in Turnov. She died on 03 May 1983 in Praha.

Generation 6

Milan Rechcigel-6 (Ing. František-5, Anna-4, Kateřina-3, Kateřina-2, Jan-1) was born on 12 Sep 1926 in Český Dub. He died on 24 Sep 1980 in Český Dub.

Božena Bernardová daughter of Ladislav Bernard and Bozena Kupcova was born on 04 Jun 1930 in Podrby - Mala Libic.

Milan Rechcigel and Božena Bernardová were married on 24 Jan 1953. They had the following children:

    i. **Hana Rechcigelova** was born on 01 Nov 1953 in Český Dub. She died on 27 Jul 2021.

    ii. **Ing. Pavel Rechcigel** was born on 19 Jul 1963 in Český Dub.

Ing. Vladko Rechcigel-6 (Ing. František-5, Anna-4, Kateřina-3, Kateřina-2, Jan-1) was born on 29 Aug 1929 in Český Dub.

Lidmila Lukaskova was born on 28 Mar 1932 in Vresna, nr. Veseli nad Luznici.

Ing. Vladko Rechcigel and Lidmila Lukaskova were married on 19 Oct 1957. They had the following children:

    i. **Vladko Rechcigel** was born on 04 Aug 1959 in Prague, CSR.

    ii. **Ing. Jan Rechcigel** was born on 02 Feb 1966 in Prague, CSR.

Milena Rechcigelova-6 (Ing. František-5, Anna-4, Kateřina-3, Kateřina-2, Jan-1) was born on 10 Mar 1936 in Turnov. She died on 03 May 1983 in Praha.

Jiří Nožička was born in 1926.

Jiří Nožička and Milena Rechcigelova married. They had the following children:

    i. **Jiří Nožička** was born on 05 May 1961.

Generation 7

Hana Rechcigelova-7 (Milan-6, Ing. František-5, Anna-4, Kateřina-3, Kateřina-2, Jan-1) was born on 01 Nov 1953 in Český Dub. She died on 27 Jul 2021.

Jiří Maier was born on 21 Mar 1946 in Turnov.

Jiří Maier and Hana Rechcigelova married. They had the following children:

    Hana Maierova was born on 03 Mar 1980.

    Lenka Maierova was born on 15 Mar 1983.

Ing. Pavel Rechcigel-7 (Milan-6, Ing. František-5, Anna-4, Kateřina-3, Kateřina-2, Jan-1) was born on 19 Jul 1963 in Český Dub.

Jana Cadova daughter of Josef Cada and Eva Unknown was born on 18 Apr 1965.

Ing. Pavel Rechcigel and Jana Cadova married. They had the following children:

    Jakub Rechcigel was born on 24 Jul 1990.

Vladko Rechcigel-7 (Ing. Vladko-6, Ing. František-5, Anna-4, Kateřina-3, Kateřina-2, Jan-1) was born on 04 Aug 1959 in Prague, CSR.

Eva Vitova was born on 17 May 1958 in Červený Kostelec.

Vladko Rechcigel and Eva Vitova married. They had the following children:

> **Jan Rechcigel** was born on 04 Mar 1988 in Prague, CSR.
>
> **Lukáš Rechcigel** was born on 06 Jun 1990 in Prague, CSR.

Ing. Jan Rechcigel-7 (Ing. Vladko-6, Ing. František-5, Anna-4, Kateřina-3, Kateřina-2, Jan-1) was born on 02 Feb 1966 in Prague, CSR.

Xenie Wilckova was born on 17 Jan 1968 in Havirov.

Ing. Jan Rechcigel and Xenie Wilckova married. They had the following children:

> **Tereza Rechciglova** was born on 07 Mar 1994 in Prague, CSR.
>
> **Kristyna Rechciglova** was born on 09 Mar 1998 in Prague, CSR.

Jira Family of Třtí

Generation 1

Josef Jira-1 was born in Třtí No. 7.

Unknown.

Josef Jira and Unknown married. They had the following children:

    i. **Marie Jirova** was born in Třtí No. 7.

Generation 2

Marie Jirova-2 (Josef-1) was born in Třtí No. 7.

    Josef Košek was born in Třtí No. 6, Turnov Co..

    Josef Košek and Marie Jirova married. They had the following children:

        i. **Kateřina Koskova** was born in 1831 in Třtí No. 6, Turnov Co.. She married Petr Rechziegel on 25 May 1858 in Třtí No. 6, Turnov Co., Franz Staznik officiating. She died on 20 Nov 1902 in Mala Bela, near Bakov.

Generation 3

Kateřina Koskova-3 (Marie-2, Josef-1) was born in 1831 in Třtí No. 6, Turnov Co.. She died on 20 Nov 1902 in Mala Bela, near Bakov.

Petr Rechziegel son of Ing. František Rechziegel and Lidmila Neumanová was born on 10 Jan 1819 in Slavíkov No. 4. He died on 17 Oct 1890 in Novy Mlyn, Žďárek.

Petr Rechziegel and Kateřina Koskova were married on 25 May 1858 in Třtí No. 6, Turnov Co., Franz Staznik officiating. They had the following children:

    i. **Josef Rechziegel** was born on 31 Aug 1865 in Třtí No. 8, Turnov Co.. He married Marie Cinkova on 23 Aug 1890 in Parish Church, Mukarov. He died in 1917.

Generation 4

Josef Rechziegel-4 (Kateřina-3, Marie-2, Josef-1) was born on 31 Aug 1865 in Třtí No. 8, Turnov Co.. He died in 1917.

    Marie Cinkova daughter of Václav Cinka and Anna Štěpánková was born on 05 Jan 1870 in Jivina No. 24, Mnichova Hradiste Co..

Josef Rechziegel and Marie Cinkova were married on 23 Aug 1890 in Parish Church, Mukarov. They had the following children:
>   i. **Marie Rechcíglová** was born on 11 Mar 1892 in Žďárek No. 26, Turnov Co.. She married Augustin Veselý on 25 Oct 1919 in Král. Vinohrady, Prague. She died on 07 Jul 1968 in Havlickuv Brod.
>   ii. **Josef Rechcigl** was born on 05 Apr 1893 in Žďárek u Turnova. He married Marie Studničná on 28 Nov 1926 in Prague, CSR. He died on 13 Jun 1933 in Praha.
>   iii. **Anna Rechcíglová** was born on 12 Jan 1902 in Žďárek. She married Karel Matějů in 1919 in Prague, CSR. She died on 15 Apr 1992 in Brno.

Generation 5

Marie Rechcíglová-5 (Josef-4, Kateřina-3, Marie-2, Josef-1) was born on 11 Mar 1892 in Žďárek No. 26, Turnov Co.. She died on 07 Jul 1968 in Havlickuv Brod.

Augustin Veselý son of František Veselý and Anna Helena Pflanzerová was born on 17 Sep 1879 in Blatna. He died on 06 Oct 1947 in Česká Trebova.

Augustin Veselý and Marie Rechcíglová were married on 25 Oct 1919 in Král. Vinohrady, Prague. They had the following children:
>   i. **Věra Veselá** was born on 02 Aug 1920 in Česká Trebova No. 50, Litomysl Co.. She married Arnošt Pellant on 27 Dec 1939 in U sv. Tomase, Brno.

Josef Rechcigl-5 (Josef-4, Kateřina-3, Marie-2, Josef-1) was born on 05 Apr 1893 in Žďárek u Turnova. He died on 13 Jun 1933 in Praha.

Marie Studničná daughter of Josef Studničný and Otilie Menzelova was born on 09 Feb 1907 in Nova Ves u Bakova nad Jizerou. She died on 20 Dec 1985 in Mala Bela.

Josef Rechcigl and Marie Studničná were married on 28 Nov 1926 in Prague, CSR. They had the following children:
>   i. **Josef Rechcigl** was born on 19 Feb 1931 in Praha. He married Jitka Prskavcová on 24 Mar 1956 in Praha II.

Anna Rechcíglová-5 (Josef-4, Kateřina-3, Marie-2, Josef-1) was born on 12 Jan 1902 in Žďárek. She died on 15 Apr 1992 in Brno.
Karel Matějů was born on 01 May 1901 in Prague. He died in May 1945. Karel Matějů and Anna Rechcíglová were married in 1919 in Prague, CSR. They had the following children:
    i. **2nd Karel Matějů** was born on 06 Dec 1924 in Brno. He married Anna Třísková on 09 Jun 1951 in Brno. He died on 09 Dec 1992 in Brno.

Miloš Valnicek son of Miloš Valnicek and Emilie Lehka was born in 1902. He died on 14 Oct 1968.
Miloš Valnicek and Anna Rechcíglová were married in 1951 in Petrov, Brno. They had no children.

Generation 6

Věra Veselá-6 (Marie-5, Josef-4, Kateřina-3, Marie-2, Josef-1) was born on 02 Aug 1920 in Česká Trebova No. 50, Litomysl Co..
Arnošt Pellant son of Ota Pellant and Antonie Kudlatschkova was born on 11 May 1912 in Okrisky, P.O. Jihlava. He died on 06 Feb 2005 in Hradec Králové.
Arnošt Pellant and Věra Veselá were married on 27 Dec 1939 in U sv. Tomase, Brno. They had the following children:
    i. **Arnošt Pellant** was born on 12 Jun 1943 in Praha. He married Zinaida Poliscukova on 07 Mar 1970 in Praha.
    ii. **Karel Pellant** was born on 14 Mar 1946 in Caslav. He married Jitka Kralickova on 01 Aug 1970 in Jevisovice.

Josef Rechcigl-6 (Josef-5, Josef-4, Kateřina-3, Marie-2, Josef-1) was born on 19 Feb 1931 in Praha.
Jitka Prskavcová daughter of Josef Prskavec and Anastazie Studničná was born on 02 Feb 1932 in Ptyrov.
Josef Rechcigl and Jitka Prskavcová were married on 24 Mar 1956 in Praha II. They had the following children:
    i. **Jitka Rechcíglová** was born on 09 Oct 1957 in Mladá Boleslav. She married Vladimír Skramusky on 11 Aug 1979 in Bakov nad Jizerou.

ii. **Josef Rechcigl** was born on 03 Mar 1960 in Turnov. He married Věra Laskova on 17 Apr 1987 in Bakov nad Jizerou.

2nd Karel Matějů-6 (Anna-5, Josef-4, Kateřina-3, Marie-2, Josef-1) was born on 06 Dec 1924 in Brno. He died on 09 Dec 1992 in Brno.

Anna Třísková daughter of Jindřich Tříska and Anna was born on 26 Jul 1925 in Blansko.

2nd Karel Matějů and Anna Třísková were married on 09 Jun 1951 in Brno. They had the following children:

i. **3rd Karel Matějů** was born on 15 Nov 1954 in Brno. He married Alena Šrámková on 07 Jul 1979 in Brno.

Generation 7

Arnošt Pellant-7 (Věra-6, Marie-5, Josef-4, Kateřina-3, Marie-2, Josef-1) was born on 12 Jun 1943 in Praha.

Zinaida Poliscukova daughter of Ondřej Poliscuk and Věra Sirova was born on 03 Oct 1943 in Mizoc, Poland; since WWII USSR.

Arnošt Pellant and Zinaida Poliscukova were married on 07 Mar 1970 in Praha. They had the following children:

i. **Věra Pellantová** was born on 25 Feb 1971 in Hradec Králové. She married Jan Brožík on Aug 2002 in Valdstejn.

ii. **Eva Pellantová** was born on 05 Jul 1974 in Hradec Králové. She married Jan Mejzlik on Jun 2001.

Karel Pellant-7 (Věra-6, Marie-5, Josef-4, Kateřina-3, Marie-2, Josef-1) was born on 14 Mar 1946 in Caslav.

Jitka Kralickova was born on 08 Jul 1947 in Ostrava.

Karel Pellant and Jitka Kralickova were married on 01 Aug 1970 in Jevisovice. They had the following children:

i. **Martina Pellantová** was born on 27 Oct 1971 in Hradec Králové. She married Alan Gernert on 04 Oct 1997 in Jablonec nad Jizetou.

Iva Pellantová was born on 04 Dec 1973 in Brno.

Jitka Rechcíglová-7 (Josef-6, Josef-5, Josef-4, Kateřina-3, Marie-2, Josef-1) was born on 09 Oct 1957 in Mladá Boleslav.

Vladimír Skramusky son of Vladimír Skramusky and Miloslava Koutska was born on 15 Jan 1953 in Cista.

Vladimír Skramusky and Jitka Rechcíglová were married on 11 Aug 1979 in Bakov nad Jizerou. They had the following children:

>**Vladimír Skramusky** was born on 17 Jun 1982 in Turnov.

Josef Rechcigl-7 (Josef-6, Josef-5, Josef-4, Kateřina-3, Marie-2, Josef-1) was born on 03 Mar 1960 in Turnov.

Věra Laskova daughter of František Laska and Helena Kolocova was born on 05 Oct 1967.

Josef Rechcigl and Věra Laskova were married on 17 Apr 1987 in Bakov nad Jizerou. They had the following children:

>**Zuzana Rechcíglová** was born on 15 Jan 1988 in Mladá Boleslav.
>**Nikola Rechcíglová** was born on 04 Oct 1990 in Mladá Boleslav.
>**Jiří Rechcigl** was born on 06 Oct 1995 in Mladá Boleslav.

3rd **Karel Matějů**-7 (2nd Karel-6, Anna-5, Josef-4, Kateřina-3, Marie-2, Josef-1) was born on 15 Nov 1954 in Brno.

Alena Šrámková daughter of Vit Šrámek and Božena Šrámková was born on 25 Apr 1958 in Brno.

3rd Karel Matějů and Alena Šrámková were married on 07 Jul 1979 in Brno. They had the following children:

>**Lukáš Matějů** was born on 15 Jun 1980 in Brno.
>**Karel Matějů** was born on 06 Oct 1982 in Brno.
>**Martin Matějů** was born on 14 Oct 1992 in Brno.

Generation 8

Věra Pellantová-8 (Arnošt-7, Věra-6, Marie-5, Josef-4, Kateřina-3, Marie-2, Josef-1) was born on 25 Feb 1971 in Hradec Králové.

Jan Brožík son of Jan Brožík and Jarmila Dočkálová was born on 06 Sep 1974 in Kromeriz.

Jan Brožík and Věra Pellantová were married on 24 Aug 2002 in Valdstejn. They had the following children:

>**Barbora Brožíková** was born on 05 Dec 2003 in Hradec Králové.

Eva Pellantová-8 (Arnošt-7, Věra-6, Marie-5, Josef-4, Kateřina-3, Marie-2, Josef-1) was born on 05 Jul 1974 in Hradec Králové.

Jan Mejzlik son of Josef Mejzlik and Blanka Spustova was born on 13 Mar 1974 in Preckov, Trebic Co..

Jan Mejzlik and Eva Pellantová were married on 09 Jun 2001. They had the following children:

    Vojtěch Mejzlik was born on 29 Jan 2003 in Hradec Králové.

    Antonín Mejzlik was born on 29 Nov 2006 in Hradec Králové.

Martina Pellantová-8 (Karel-7, Věra-6, Marie-5, Josef-4, Kateřina-3, Marie-2, Josef-1) was born on Oct 1971 in Hradec Králové.

Alan Gernert son of Vilém Gernert and Vlasta was born on 26 Mar 1970 in Jilemnice.

Alan Gernert and Martina Pellantová were married on 04 Oct 1997 in Jablonec nad Jizetou. They had the following children:

    i. **Marek Gernert** was born on 04 Apr 1998.

Zajicek Family

Generation 1

Jan Zajíček-1 was born before 1750 in lived in Jivina No. 16. He died after 1787 in Sold house to son Jiří in 1787.

Unknown.

Jan Zajíček and Unknown married. They had the following children:

    i. **Jiří Zajíček** was born after 1760 in Jivina No. 16. He died about 1830.

Generation 2

Jiří Zajíček-2 (Jan-1) was born after 1760 in Jivina No. 16. He died about 1830.

Unknown.

Jiří Zajíček and Unknown married. They had the following children:

    i. **Václav Zajíček** was born after 1800. He died after 1854 in bought house No. 16 in Jivina in 1831.

Generation 3

Václav Zajíček-3 (Jiří-2, Jan-1) was born after 1800. He died after 1854 in bought house No. 16 in Jivina in 1831.

Marie Samalova daughter of Václav Samal and Unknown was born in Racany No. 11. Václav Zajíček and Marie Samalova married. They had the following children:

    i. **Josef Zajíček** was born on 12 Nov 1830 in Jivina No. 16. He married Josefa Rechziegelová on 04 Jun 1851 in Slavíkov No. 4, Vlastibořice parish. He died in Received house in 1854.

    Jiří Zajíček was born in Jivina No. 16.

Generation 4

Josef Zajíček-4 (Václav-3, Jiří-2, Jan-1) was born on 12 Nov 1830 in Jivina No. 16. He died in Received house in 1854.

Josefa Rechziegelová daughter of Ing. František Rechziegel and Lidmila Neumanová was born on 09 May 1827 in Slavíkov No. 4. She died on 24 Feb 1872 in Jivina No. 16.

Josef Zajíček and Josefa Rechziegelová were married on 04 Jun 1851 in Slavíkov No. 4, Vlastibořice parish. They had the following children:

> **Josef Zajíček** was born on 03 Nov 1851 in Jivina No. 16. He died on 02 Jan 1853 in Jivina No. 16.
>
> **Jan Zajíček** was born on 11 Dec 1854 in Jivina No. 16. He died on 25 Mar 1855 in Jivina No. 16.
>
> **Anna Zajickova** was born on 20 Sep 1856 in Jivina No. 16. She married František Richter on 15 Jun 1875 in Jivina No. 1 6; Josef Kovar, parish priest officiating.
>
> **Josefa Zajickova** was born on 11 May 1859 in Jivina No. 16. She died about 1879. She married Josef Pycha on 11 Nov 1879 in Jivina No. 16, Český Dub Co.; Josef Kovar, parish priest officiating.
>
> v. **Marie Zajickova** was born on 24 Aug 1862 in Jivina No. 16. She married Václav Šifta on 14 Jul 1885 in Jivina No. 16, Český Dub Co.; Rev. Josef Kovar, parish priest officiating. She died on 23 Mar 1927 in Jivina No. 16.
>
> **Emilie Zajickova** was born on 11 Feb 1872 in Jivina No. 16. She died on 14 Feb 1872 in Jivina No. 16.

Kateřina Retrová was born in Kameni.

Josef Zajíček and Kateřina Retrová were married about 1872. They had the following children:

> **Josef Zajíček** was born in 1873 in Jivina No. 16.
>
> **František Zajíček** was born in 1875 in Jivina No. 16. He died in 1902 in Jivna No. 16.
>
> **Emilie Zajickova** was born in 1878 in Jivina No. 16.
>
> **Kateřina Zajickova** was born in 1884 in Jivina No. 16.

Generation 5

Marie Zajickova-5 (Josef-4, Václav-3, Jiří-2, Jan-1) was born on 24 Aug 1862 in Jivina No. 16. She died on 23 Mar 1927 in Jivina No. 16.

Václav Šifta son of Václav Šifta and Karolina Odcházelová was born on 21 Aug 1861 in Jivina No. 1. He died in Received house in 1885.

Václav Šifta and Marie Zajickova were married on 14 Jul 1885 in Jivina No. 16, Český Dub Co.; Rev. Josef Kovar, parish priest officiating. They had the following children:
> **Emilie Šiftová** was born in 1886 in Jivina No. 1.
> **Božena Šiftová** was born in 1892 in Jivina No. 1.
> iii. **Josef Šifta** was born in 1898 in Jivina No. 1. He died in 1953.

Generation 6
Josef Šifta-6 (Marie-5, Josef-4, Václav-3, Jiří-2, Jan-1) was born in 1898 in Jivina No. 1. He died in 1953.
Marie Řepková was born in 1897 in Pacerice. She died in 1985.
Josef Šifta and Marie Řepková married. They had the following children:
> 7. i. **Marie Šiftová** was born on 20 Jun 1923 in Jivina No. 1. She died on 10 Jun 2004.

Generation 7
Marie Šiftová-7 (Josef-6, Marie-5, Josef-4, Václav-3, Jiří-2, Jan-1) was born on 20 Jun 1923 in Jivina No. 1. She died on 10 Jun 2004.
Miroslav Třešňák was born on 06 Mar 1921 in Jenisovice -. He died on 11 Jul 1986 in Lived in Jivina No. 1.
Miroslav Třešňák and Marie Šiftová married. They had the following children:
> i. **Miroslav Třešňák** was born on 25 May 1943 in Jivina No. 1. He married Miluška Hanzlova on 23 Oct 1965. He died on 19 Nov 2005 in moved to Jivina No. 24.
> ii. **Jiří Třešňák** was born on 22 Jul 1952 in Jivina No. 1. He married Marie Zoubková on 19 Jun 1976. He died in moved to Odolena Voda, Praha vychod.

Generation 8
Miroslav Třešňák-8 (Marie-7, Josef-6, Marie-5, Josef-4, Václav-3, Jiří-2, Jan-1) was born on 25 May 1943 in Jivina No. 1. He died on 19 Nov 2005 in moved to Jivina No. 24.
Miluška Hanzlova was born on 29 Dec 1944 in Svijany.

Miroslav Třešňák and Miluška Hanzlova were married on 23 Oct 1965. They had the following children:
    i. **Pavel Třešňák** was born on 25 Feb 1967 in Turnov - moved to Český Dub. He married Radka Černá on 18 Apr 1992.
    ii. **Luboš Třešňák** was born on 30 Apr 1974 in Turnov - moved to Vrkoslavice. He married Jitka Necaskova on 21 Sep 1996.

Jiří Třešňák-8 (Marie-7, Josef-6, Marie-5, Josef-4, Václav-3, Jiří-2, Jan-1) was born on 22 Jul 1952 in Jivina No. 1. He died in moved to Odolena Voda, Praha vychod.

Marie Zoubková was born on 22 Jun 1956 in Zasada.

Jiří Třešňák and Marie Zoubková were married on 19 Jun 1976. They had the following children:
    Lenka Třešňáková was born on 21 Jan 1978 in Turnov.
    Radka Třešňáková was born on 30 May 1985 in Brandys nad Labem.

Generation 9

Pavel Třešňák-9 (Miroslav-8, Marie-7, Josef-6, Marie-5, Josef-4, Václav-3, Jiří-2, Jan-1) was born on 25 Feb 1967 in Turnov - moved to Český Dub.

Radka Černá was born on 07 Sep 1971 in Česká Lipa.

Pavel Třešňák and Radka Černá were married on 18 Apr 1992. They had the following children:
    Pavlina Třešňáková was born on 17 Jun 1999 in Turnov.

Luboš Třešňák-9 (Miroslav-8, Marie-7, Josef-6, Marie-5, Josef-4, Václav-3, Jiří-2, Jan-1) was born on 30 Apr 1974 in Turnov - moved to Vrkoslavice.

Jitka Necaskova was born on 21 Nov 1969 in Jablonnec nad Nisou.

Luboš Třešňák and Jitka Necaskova were married on 21 Sep 1996. They had the following children:
    Michaela Třešňáková was born on 02 Sep 1997 in Jablonec nad Nisou.
    Matěj Třešňák was born on 18 May 2001 in Jablonec nad Nisou.

Třešňák Family

Generation 1

Miroslav Třešňák-1 was born on 06 Mar 1921 in Jenisovice -. He died on 11 Jul 1986 in Lived in Jivina No. 1.

Marie Šiftová daughter of Josef Šifta and Marie Řepková was born on 20 Jun 1923 in Jivina No. 1. She died on 10 Jun 2004.

Miroslav Třešňák and Marie Šiftová married. They had the following children:

    i. **Miroslav Třešňák** was born on 25 May 1943 in Jivina No. 1. He married Miluška Hanzlova on 23 Oct 1965. He died on 19 Nov 2005 in moved to Jivina No. 24.

    ii. **Jiří Třešňák** was born on 22 Jul 1952 in Jivina No. 1. He married Marie Zoubková on 19 Jun 1976. He died in moved to Odolena Voda, Praha vychod.

Generation 2

Miroslav Třešňák-2 (Miroslav-1) was born on 25 May 1943 in Jivina No. 1. He died on 19 Nov 2005 in moved to Jivina No. 24.

Miluška Hanzlova was born on 29 Dec 1944 in Svijany.

Miroslav Třešňák and Miluška Hanzlova were married on 23 Oct 1965. They had the following children:

    i. **Pavel Třešňák** was born on 25 Feb 1967 in Turnov - moved to Český Dub. He married Radka Černá on 18 Apr 1992.

    ii. **Luboš Třešňák** was born on 30 Apr 1974 in Turnov - moved to Vrkoslavice. He married Jitka Necaskova on 21 Sep 1996.

Jiří Třešňák-2 (Miroslav-1) was born on 22 Jul 1952 in Jivina No. 1. He died in moved to Odolena Voda, Praha vychod.

Marie Zoubková was born on 22 Jun 1956 in Zasada.

Jiří Třešňák and Marie Zoubková were married on 19 Jun 1976. They had the following children:

    Lenka Třešňáková was born on 21 Jan 1978 in Turnov.

    Radka Třešňáková was born on 30 May 1985 in Brandys nad Labem.

Generation 3

Pavel Třešňák-3 (Miroslav-2, Miroslav-1) was born on 25 Feb 1967 in Turnov - moved to Český Dub.

Radka Černá was born on 07 Sep 1971 in Česká Lipa.

Pavel Třešňák and Radka Černá were married on 18 Apr 1992. They had the following children:

    Pavlina Třešňáková was born on 17 Jun 1999 in Turnov.

Luboš Třešňák-3 (Miroslav-2, Miroslav-1) was born on 30 Apr 1974 in Turnov - moved to Vrkoslavice.

Jitka Necaskova was born on 21 Nov 1969 in Jablonnec nad Nisou.

Luboš Třešňák and Jitka Necaskova were married on 21 Sep 1996. They had the following children:

    Michaela Třešňáková was born on 02 Sep 1997 in Jablonec nad Nisou.

    Matěj Třešňák was born on 18 May 2001 in Jablonec nad Nisou.

Studničný Family

Generation 1

Josef Studnicny-1 was born before 1790 in Honcov No. 8.
Barbora Mansfeldova was born in Manikovice No. 7.
Josef Studnicny and Barbora Mansfeldova married. They had the following children:
- i. **Josef Studničný** was born before 1820 in Honcob.
- ii. **Václav Studničný** was born after 1820 in Buda 18.

Generation 2

Josef Studničný-2 (Josef-1) was born before 1820 in Honcob.
Marie Baierova was born in Bela No. 12.
Josef Studničný and Marie Baierova married. They had the following children:
- i. **Jan Studničný** was born on 20 Feb 1839 in Honcob No. 8.

Václav Studničný-2 (Josef-1) was born after 1820 in Buda 18.
Barbora Štěpánková daughter of Václav Štěpánek and Barbora Ticha was born in Buda No. 22. Václav Studničný and Barbora Štěpánková married. They had the following children:
- i. **Antonín Studničný** was born on 07 Oct 1850 in Buda. He married Marie Pecinová in Resided Veselá No. 6 and 17. He died in Lived in Veselá No. 46.
- ii. **Josef Studničný** was born about 1850.

Generation 3

Jan Studničný-3 (Josef-2, Josef-1) was born on 20 Feb 1839 in Honcob No. 8.
Alžběta Stránská daughter of Josef Stránský and Kateřina Tůmová was born on 05 Jun 1843 in Zolldorf.
Jan Studničný and Alžběta Stránská married. They had the following children:
- i. **Josef Studničný** was born on 05 Jul 1870 in Manikovice.

Antonín Studničný-3 (Václav-2, Josef-1) was born on 07 Oct 1850 in Buda. He died in Lived in Veselá No. 46.

Marie Pecinová daughter of Josef Pecina and Kateřina Stránská was born on 13 Jan 1854 in Veselá No. 46.

Antonín Studničný and Marie Pecinová were married in Resided Veselá No. 6 and 17. They had the following children:

    i. **Marie Studničná** was born after 1870 in Veselá. She died on 12 Apr 1942. She married Antonín Stránský in Resided Veselá No. 21.

    Antonín Studničný was born after 1870 in Veselá. He died in on Serbian front during World War I.

    iii. **Josef Studničný** was born after 1870 in Veselá No. 17. He died in 1944 in Lived in Veselá No. 17. He married Marie Fidlerova in Resided in Veselá No. 17.

    iv. **František Studničný** was born on 28 Apr 1878 in Veselá No. 46. He died on 27 Feb 1958 in Lived in Veselá.

Josef Studničný-3 (Václav-2, Josef-1) was born about 1850.

Unknown.

Josef Studničný and Unknown married. They had the following children:

    Josef Studničný was born in 1881. He died in 1939 in Lived in Veselá.

    František Studničný was born in 1882. He died in 1917 in World War I.

Generation 4

Josef Studničný-4 (Jan-3, Josef-2, Josef-1) was born on 05 Jul 1870 in Manikovice.

Otilie Menzelova daughter of Karel Menzel and Marie Kubrtova was born on 23 Jan 1877 in Kralovske Vinohrady.

Josef Studničný and Otilie Menzelova married. They had the following children:

    Otilie Studničná.

    ii. **Josef Studničný.**

    iii. **Marie Studničná** was born on 09 Feb 1907 in Nova Ves u Bakova nad Jizerou. She married Josef Rechcigl on 28 Nov 1926 in Prague, CSR. She died on 20 Dec 1985 in Mala Bela.

Marie Studničná-4 (Antonín-3, Václav-2, Josef-1) was born after 1870 in Veselá. She died on 12 Apr 1942.
Antonín Stránský. He died in Lived in Veselá No. 21.
Antonín Stránský and Marie Studničná were married in Resided Veselá No. 21. They had the following children:
> **František Stránský** was born on 06 Oct 1910 in Veselá No. 21`. He married Anna Brožová on 28 Apr 1937 in Resided Veselá No. 21. He died on 09 Jan 1993 in Lived in Veselá No. 21.
>
> **Václav Stránský** was born in 1908 in Veselá No. 21. He died on 23 Jul 1995 in Lived in Mnichovo Hradiště No. 603. He married Marue Duerichová in Resided Mnichovo Hradiště No. 603.

Josef Studničný-4 (Antonín-3, Václav-2, Josef-1) was born after 1870 in Veselá No. 17. He died in 1944 in Lived in Veselá No. 17.
Marie Fidlerova was born in Lhotice. She died in 1946.
Josef Studničný and Marie Fidlerova were married in Resided in Veselá No. 17. They had the following children:
> **Anna Studničná** was born on 27 Jan 1915 in Veselá No. 17. She died on 18 Sep 1995. She married Jan Martinek in Resided in Mnichovo Hradiště.
>
> **Marie Studničná** was born on 30 Aug 1917 in Veselá No. 17. She died on 24 Dec 1999.

František Studničný-4 (Antonín-3, Václav-2, Josef-1) was born on 28 Apr 1878 in Veselá No. 46. He died on 27 Feb 1958 in Lived in Veselá.
Marie Pavlistova was born on 12 Aug 1885 in Veselá No. 28. She died on 27 Jan 1961. František Studničný and Marie Pavlistova married. They had the following children:
> i. **Ludmila Studničná** was born on 03 Dec 1908 in Veselá No. 157. She died on 12 Oct 1997. She married Václav Šverma in Resided in Veselá No. 157.
>
> ii. **Miroslav Studničný** was born on 04 May 1923 in Veselá No. 15. He died on 26 Feb 2003 in Lived in Diolni Pocernice.
>
> **Miloslav Studničný** was born in Veselá.

Zdeněk Studničný was born in Veselá.

Generation 5

Josef Studničný-5 (Josef-4, Jan-3, Josef-2, Josef-1).
Ludmila was born in 1901 in Stare Smrkovice.
Josef Studničný and Ludmila married. They had the following children:
Josef Studničný.

Marie Studničná-5 (Josef-4, Jan-3, Josef-2, Josef-1) was born on 09 Feb 1907 in Nova Ves u Bakova nad Jizerou. She died on 20 Dec 1985 in Mala Bela.
Josef Rechcigl son of Josef Rechziegel and Marie Cinkova was born on 05 Apr 1893 in Žďárek u Turnova. He died on 13 Jun 1933 in Praha.
Josef Rechcigl and Marie Studničná were married on 28 Nov 1926 in Prague, CSR. They had the following children:
  i. **Josef Rechcigl** was born on 19 Feb 1931 in Praha. He married Jitka Prskavcová on 24 Mar 1956 in Praha II.

Karel Halmann was born on 19 May 1905. He died in 1943.
Karel Halmann and Marie Studničná were married on 09 Dec 1942. They had no children.

Ludmila Studničná-5 (František-4, Antonín-3, Václav-2, Josef-1) was born on 03 Dec 1908 in Veselá No. 157. She died on 12 Oct 1997.
Václav Šverma son of Václav Šverma and Růžena Stránská was born on 13 Nov 1904 in Maly Ptyrov No. 2. He died on 28 Sep 1960.
Václav Šverma and Ludmila Studničná were married in Resided in Veselá No. 157. They had the following children:
  i. **Vratislav Šverma** was born on 29 Jan 1936 in Veselá No. 157. He married Zdenka Simonova in Resided at Veselá No. 98.
  ii. **Lubomir Šverma** was born on 18 Nov 1937 in Veselá No. 157.
    Alena Švermová was born on 02 Jul 1943 in Veselá No. 157. She married Harwey Salmon in Resude in England.

Miroslav Studničný-5 (František-4, Antonín-3, Václav-2, Josef-1) was born on 04 May 1923 in Veselá No. 15. He died on 26 Feb 2003 in Lived in Diolni Pocernice.
Věra Seraková was born on 16 Nov 1927 in Studanka.

Miroslav Studničný and Věra Seraková married. They had the following children:
> i. **Miroslav Studničný** was born on 20 Jul 1949 in Veselá 15.
>
> ii. **Veroslav Studničný** was born on 04 Aug 1950 in Veselá 15.

Generation 6

Josef Rechcigl-6 (Marie-5, Josef-4, Jan-3, Josef-2, Josef-1) was born on 19 Feb 1931 in Praha.

Jitka Prskavcová daughter of Josef Prskavec and Anastazie Studničná was born on 02 Feb 1932 in Ptyrov.

Josef Rechcigl and Jitka Prskavcová were married on 24 Mar 1956 in Praha II. They had the following children:
> i. **Jitka Rechcíglová** was born on 09 Oct 1957 in Mladá Boleslav. She married Vladimír Skramusky on 11 Aug 1979 in Bakov nad Jizerou.
>
> ii. **Josef Rechcigl** was born on 03 Mar 1960 in Turnov. He married Věra Laskova on 17 Apr 1987 in Bakov nad Jizerou.

Vratislav Šverma-6 (Ludmila-5, František-4, Antonín-3, Václav-2, Josef-1) was born on 29 Jan 1936 in Veselá No. 157.

Zdenka Simonova was born on 21 May 1936 in Veselá No. 96. She died on 20 Jan 1990.

Vratislav Šverma and Zdenka Simonova were married in Resided at Veselá No. 98. They had the following children:
> i. **Martin Šverma** was born on 15 Dec 1966 in Veselá No. 98.
>
> **Ondřej Šverma** was born on 03 May 1972 in Veselá No. 98. He married Michaela Knizkova on 25 Sep 2004 in Resided at Veselá No. 216.

Lubomir Šverma-6 (Ludmila-5, František-4, Antonín-3, Václav-2, Josef-1) was born on 18 Nov 1937 in Veselá No. 157.

Jiřina Matejova was born on 11 Feb 1940 in Bakov No. 248.

Lubomir Šverma and Jiřina Matejova married. They had the following children:
> i. **Lubomir Šverma** was born on 12 Jun 1971 in Veselá No. 157.
>
> ii. **Radmila Švermová** was born on 23 Mar 1968 in Veselá No. 157.

Veroslav Studničný-6 (Miroslav-5, František-4, Antonín-3, Václav-2, Josef-1) was born on 04 Aug 1950 in Veselá 15.

Alena Unknown was born in Praha - Prosek.

Veroslav Studničný and Alena Unknown married. They had the following children:

> **Radek Studničný** was born on 19 Apr 1977 in Praha - Prosek.

Generation 7

Jitka Rechcíglová-7 (Josef-6, Marie-5, Josef-4, Jan-3, Josef-2, Josef-1) was born on 09 Oct 1957 in Mladá Boleslav.

Vladimír Skramusky son of Vladimír Skramusky and Miloslava Koutska was born on 15 Jan 1953 in Cista.

Vladimír Skramusky and Jitka Rechcíglová were married on 11 Aug 1979 in Bakov nad Jizerou. They had the following children:

> **Vladimír Skramusky** was born on 17 Jun 1982 in Turnov.

Josef Rechcigl-7 (Josef-6, Marie-5, Josef-4, Jan-3, Josef-2, Josef-1) was born on 03 Mar 1960 in Turnov.

Věra Laskova daughter of František Laska and Helena Kolocova was born on 05 Oct 1967.

Josef Rechcigl and Věra Laskova were married on 17 Apr 1987 in Bakov nad Jizerou. They had the following children:

> **Zuzana Rechcíglová** was born on 15 Jan 1988 in Mladá Boleslav.
>
> **Nikola Rechcíglová** was born on 04 Oct 1990 in Mladá Boleslav.
>
> **Jiří Rechcigl** was born on 06 Oct 1995 in Mladá Boleslav.

Martin Šverma-7 (Vratislav-6, Ludmila-5, František-4, Antonín-3, Václav-2, Josef-1) was born on 15 Dec 1966 in Veselá No. 98.

Jaroslava Wernerova was born on 03 Sep 1969 in Sedlec No. 27.

Martin Šverma and Jaroslava Wernerova married. They had the following children:

> **Martin Šverma** was born on 04 Mar 1991 in Veselá No. 98.
>
> **Veronika Švermová** was born on 06 Jan 1995 in Veselá No. 98.

Lubomir Šverma-7 (Lubomir-6, Ludmila-5, František-4, Antonín-3, Václav-2, Josef-1) was born on 12 Jun 1971 in Veselá No. 157.

Eva Matejovska was born on 20 Jun 1971 in Mnichovo Hradiště. Lubomir Šverma and Eva Matejovska married. They had the following children:

> **Jakub Šverma** was born on 10 Feb 1991.

Radmila Švermová-7 (Lubomir-6, Ludmila-5, František-4, Antonín-3, Václav-2, Josef-1) was born on Mar 1968 in Veselá No. 157.

Karel Maděra was born on 12 Oct 1967 in Mnichovo Hradiště, Sadova. Karel Maděra and Radmila Švermová married. They had the following children:

> **Karel Maděra** was born on 30 Jan 1996 in Mnichovo Hradiště, Na kamenci No. 137.
>
> **Jan Maděra** was born on 21 Jul 1997 in Mnichovo Hradiště, Na kamenci No. 137.

Křikava Family

Generation 1

Antonín Křikava-1 was born in Bechcin No. 2.

Anna Táborská was born in Bechcin No. 11.

Antonín Křikava and Anna Táborská married. They had the following children:

    i. **Josef Křikava** was born in Chaloupky No. 36.

Generation 2

Josef Křikava-2 (Antonín-1) was born in Chaloupky No. 36.

Marie Stichová daughter of Josef Sticha and Terezie Bělohlávková was born in Chaloupky. Josef Křikava and Marie Stichová married. They had the following children:

    i. **František Křikava** was born on 23 Dec 1890 in Chaloupky, Beroun Co.. He died on 25 Mar 1965 in Komarov u Horovic No. 40.

Generation 3

František Křikava-3 (Josef-2, Antonín-1) was born on 23 Dec 1890 in Chaloupky, Beroun Co.. He died on 25 Mar 1965 in Komarov u Horovic No. 40.

Anna Wimrova was born in 1890. She died in 1921.

František Křikava and Anna Wimrova married. They had the following children:

    Jaromír Křikava was born in 1921. He died in 2001.

Božena Rechcíglová daughter of Zdeněk Petr Rechcigl and Anna Šimůnková was born on 18 Mar 1907 in Letařovice, Turnov Co.. She died on 11 Aug 1979 in Hospital, Horovice.

František Křikava and Božena Rechcíglová were married on 24 Jul 1926 in Horovice. They had the following children:

    i. **Luděk Křikava** was born on 02 Feb 1927 in Komarov u Horovic No. 40. He died on 23 Sep 1996.

    ii. **Sasa Křikava** was born on 02 Dec 1930 in Komarov u Horovic No. 40.

Generation 4

Luděk Křikava-4 (František-3, Josef-2, Antonín-1) was born on 02 Feb 1927 in Komarov u Horovic No. 40. He died on 23 Sep 1996.

Zdenka Krizova was born on 24 Sep 1941 in Komarov u Horovic No. 72.

Luděk Křikava and Zdenka Krizova married. They had the following children:

    i. **Věra Křikavová** was born on 28 Apr 1966 in Komarov u Horovic No. 40.

    ii. **Hanna Křikavová** was born on 07 May 1957 in Komarov u Horovic No. 40. She died on 30 Dec 1997.

    iii. **Jan Křikava** was born on 19 Aug 1960 in Komarov u Horovic No. 40.

Sasa Křikava-4 (František-3, Josef-2, Antonín-1) was born on 02 Dec 1930 in Komarov u Horovic No. 40.

Milada Toclova was born on 24 Jul 1927.

Sasa Křikava and Milada Toclova married. They had the following children:

    i. **Alexander Křikava** was born in 1951 in Komarov u Horovic.

    ii. **Hana Křikavová** was born in 1958 in Komarov u Horovic.

Generation 5

Věra Křikavová-5 (Luděk-4, František-3, Josef-2, Antonín-1) was born on 28 Apr 1966 in Komarov u Horovic No. 40.

Radek Nešpor was born on 24 Mar 1963 in Horovice.

Radek Nešpor and Věra Křikavová married. They had the following children:

    David Nešpor was born on 19 Oct 1987 in Komarov u Horovic No. 40.

Hanna Křikavová-5 (Luděk-4, František-3, Josef-2, Antonín-1) was born on 07 May 1957 in Komarov u Horovic No. 40. She died on 30 Dec 1997.

Bedřich Mach was born on 13 Feb 1955 in Komarov u Horovic No. 40. Bedřich Mach and Hanna Křikavová married. They had the following children:

> i. **Andrea Machová** was born on 10 Mar 1978 in Komarov u Horovic No. 40.

Jan Křikava-5 (Luděk-4, František-3, Josef-2, Antonín-1) was born on 19 Aug 1960 in Komarov u Horovic No. 40.

Hana Fedorcaková was born on 05 May 1962 in Kvan near Komarov.

Jan Křikava and Hana Fedorcaková married. They had the following children:

> **Jan Křikava** was born on 22 Sep 1983 in Komarov u Horovic No. 40.

Jana Linhartova was born on 14 Feb 1973 in Komarov u Horovic.

Jan Křikava and Jana Linhartova met. They had the following children:

> **Johana Křikavová** was born on 27 Nov 2007 in Komarov u Horovic.

Hana Křikavová-5 (Sasa-4, František-3, Josef-2, Antonín-1) was born in 1958 in Komarov u Horovic.

Milan Němec was born in 1954 in Komarov u Horovic.

Milan Němec and Hana Křikavová married. They had the following children:

> **Milan Němec** was born in 1978 in Komarov u Horovic.
>
> **Lubor Němec** was born in 1971 in Komarov u Horovic.

Generation 6

Andrea Machová-6 (Hanna-5, Luděk-4, František-3, Josef-2, Antonín-1) was born on 10 Mar 1978 in Komarov u Horovic No. 40.

Soeren Christiansen was born in 1975 in Denmark.

Soeren Christiansen and Andrea Machová met. They had the following children:

> **Olivia Machová** was born on 10 May 2007 in Kobenhaven, Denmark.

Roubíček Family

Generation 1

1. **František Roubíček**-1 was born in Radostín No. 12.

Marie Roubíčková daughter of František Roubíček was born in Radostín No. 9. František Roubíček and Marie Roubíčková married. They had the following children:

    i. **Rudolf Roubíček** was born about 1894 in Radostín. He married Anastazie Rechziegelová in Jul 1917. He died about Mar 1918.

František Roubíček and unknown spouse married. They had the following children:

3. i. **Marie Roubíčková** was born in Radostín No. 9.

Generation 2

Rudolf Roubíček-2 (František-1) was born about 1894 in Radostín. He died about Mar 1918.

Anastazie Rechziegelová daughter of Václav Rechziegel and Anna Janečková was born on 17 Mar 1894 in Radostín. She died on 19 Apr 1984 in Srch.

Rudolf Roubíček and Anastazie Rechziegelová were married in Jul 1917. They had the following children:

    i. **Jana Roubíčková** was born on 26 Jan 1918 in Radostín. She married Franisek Kvapil on Sep 1943 in Kunetice. She died on 13 Oct 1981 in Lazne Bohdanec.

Marie Roubíčková-2 (František-1) was born in Radostín No. 9.

František Roubíček was born in Radostín No. 12.

František Roubíček and Marie Roubíčková married. They had the following children:

    i. **Rudolf Roubíček** was born about 1894 in Radostín. He married Anastazie Rechziegelová in Jul 1917. He died about Mar 1918.

Generation 3

Jana Roubíčková-3 (Rudolf-2, František-1) was born on 26 Jan 1918 in Radostín. She died on 13 Oct 1981 in Lazne Bohdanec.

Franisek Kvapil was born on 24 Nov 1912. He died on 15 Oct 1982.

Franisek Kvapil and Jana Roubíčková were married on 11 Sep 1943 in Kunetice. They had the following children:
- i. **Jan Kvapil** was born on 27 May 1944 in Pardubice. He married Eva Nováková on 09 Jun 1962 in Pardubice.
- ii. **Nada Kvapilová** was born on 11 Feb 1946 in Pardubice. She married Josef Virt on 13 Mar 1971 in Rohovladova Bela.

Generation 4

Jan Kvapil-4 (Jana-3, Rudolf-2, František-1) was born on 27 May 1944 in Pardubice.

Eva Nováková daughter of Marta Lamacova was born on 21 Dec 1943.

Jan Kvapil and Eva Nováková were married on 09 Jun 1962 in Pardubice. They had the following children:
- i. **Jan Kvapil** was born on 30 Dec 1963 in Pardubice. He married Iveta Kulichova on 31 Jan 1987 in Lazne Bohdanec.
- ii. **Jaroslav Kvapil** was born on 26 Feb 1969 in Pardubice. He married Eva Kadlecova on 30 Nov 1991 in Lazne Bohdanec.
- iii. **Eva Kvapilová** was born on 18 Oct 1973 in Pardubice. He married Tomasz Prcz on 18 May 1996 in Lazne Bohdanec.
- iv. **Jiri Kvapil** was born on 18 Jan 1980 in Pardubice. He married Zuzana Tomanová on 13 Aug 2005 in Lazne Bohdanec.

Nada Kvapilová-4 (Jana-3, Rudolf-2, František-1) was born on 11 Feb 1946 in Pardubice.

Josef Virt was born on 20 Sep 1933 in Pardubice. He died on 19 Jan 1991. Josef Virt and Nada Kvapilová were married on 13 Mar 1971 in Rohovladova Bela. They had the following children:
- i. **Petra Virtova** was born on 17 Aug 1976 in Pardubice. She married Tomáš Tupy on 25 Aug 2000.

Generation 5

Jan Kvapil-5 (Jan-4, Jana-3, Rudolf-2, František-1) was born on 30 Dec 1963 in Pardubice.

Iveta Kulichova was born on 18 Jan 1969.

Jan Kvapil and Iveta Kulichova were married on 31 Jan 1987 in Lazne Bohdanec. They had the following children:

>**Lucie Kvapilová** was born on 09 Jul 1987 in Pardubice.
>
>**Pavlina Kvapilová** was born on 05 Sep 1991 in Pardubice.
>
>**Iveta Kvapilová** was born on 15 Jul 1993 in Pardubice.

Jaroslav Kvapil-5 (Jan-4, Jana-3, Rudolf-2, František-1) was born on 26 Feb 1969 in Pardubice.

Eva Kadlecova was born on 05 Sep 1969.

Jaroslav Kvapil and Eva Kadlecova were married on 30 Nov 1991 in Lazne Bohdanec. They had the following children:

>**Katerina Kvapilová** was born on 21 May 1992 in Pardubice.
>
>**Monika Kvapilová** was born on 19 Oct 1998 in Pardubice.
>
>**Jakub Kvapil** was born on 05 May 2005 in Pardubice.

Eva Kvapilová-5 (Jan-4, Jana-3, Rudolf-2, František-1) was born on 18 Oct 1973 in Pardubice.

Tomasz Prcz was born on 23 May 1970.

Tomasz Prcz and Eva Kvapilová were married on 18 May 1996 in Lazne Bohdanec. They had the following children:

>**Martin Prcz** was born on 19 May 1991 in Pardubice.
>
>**Tomasz Prcz** was born on 05 Oct 1997 in Pardubice.

Jiri Kvapil-5 (Jan-4, Jana-3, Rudolf-2, František-1) was born on 18 Jan 1980 in Pardubice.

Zuzana Tomanová was born on 20 Aug 1980.

Jiri Kvapil and Zuzana Tomanová were married on 13 Aug 2005 in Lazne Bohdanec. They had the following children:

>**Tereza Kvapilová** was born on 25 Dec 2006 in Pardubice.
>
>**Jiri Kvapil** was born on 07 Sep 2009 in Pardubice.

Petra Virtova-5 (Nada-4, Jana-3, Rudolf-2, František-1) was born on 17 Aug 1976 in Pardubice.

Tomáš Tupy was born on 24 Aug 1975 in Pardubice.

Tomáš Tupy and Petra Virtova were married on 25 Aug 2000. They had the following children:

>**Krystyna Tupa** was born on 27 Feb 2001.
>
>**Aneta Tupa** was born on 21 Apr 2006.

Buriánek Family

Generation 1

Václav Buriánek-1 was born in Sezemice No. 39.

Anna Havlova was born in Sezemice No. 5.

Václav Buriánek and Anna Havlova married. They had the following children:

    i. **Josef Buriánek** was born on 07 Dec 1830 in Sezemice No. 39.

Generation 2

Josef Buriánek-2 (Václav-1) was born on 07 Dec 1830 in Sezemice No. 39.

Terezie Bartošová daughter of Václav Barton and Terezie Cejnarová was born on 02 Aug 1839 in Sedlisko No. 6.

Josef Buriánek and Terezie Bartošová married. They had the following children:

    Josef Buriánek was born on 27 Oct 1861 in Sezemice No. 25.

    Václav Buriánek was born on 04 Aug 1865 in Sezemice No. 25.

    iii. **František Buriánek** was born on 27 Jul 1869 in Sezemice No. 25. He died in 1944.

    Emil Buriánek was born on 17 Oct 1886 in Sezemice No. 25.

Generation 3

František Buriánek-3 (Josef-2, Václav-1) was born on 27 Jul 1869 in Sezemice No. 25. He died in 1944.

Marie Jihlavcová daughter of Václav Jihlavec and Anna Marie Mařanová was born on 20 Jun 1876 in Horni Mohelnice. She died in 1928.

František Buriánek and Marie Jihlavcová married. They had the following children:

    Marie Buriánková was born on 17 Sep 1898 in Sezemice No. 29. She died in 1950.

    ii. **Josef Buriánek** was born on 05 Feb 1900 in Sezemice No. 29. He died in 1966.

    František Buriánek was born on 23 Jan 1902 in Sezemice No. 29. He died in 1936.

    iv. **Ivo Buriánek**.

Generation 4

Josef Buriánek-4 (František-3, Josef-2, Václav-1) was born on 05 Feb 1900 in Sezemice No. 29. He died in 1966.

Blažena Maruskova was born on 26 Mar 1908 in Sedlistky No. 4. She died in 1989. Josef Buriánek and Blažena Maruskova married. They had the following children:

    i. **Jaromír Buriánek** was born on 09 Feb 1929 in Koryta No. 29.

    ii. **Vratislav Buriánek** was born on 28 Oct 1935 in Koryta No. 29. He died in 1992.

    iii. **Jana Buriánková** was born on 25 Mar 1944 in Koryta No. 29.

Ivo Buriánek-4 (František-3, Josef-2, Václav-1).

Unknown.

Ivo Buriánek and Unknown married. They had the following children:

    i. **Ivo Buriánek** was born in 1932 in koryta. He died in 1999.

Generation 5

Vratislav Buriánek-5 (Josef-4, František-3, Josef-2, Václav-1) was born on 28 Oct 1935 in Koryta No. 29. He died in 1992.

Jiřina Schlesingerová was born in Litvinov.

Vratislav Buriánek and Jiřina Schlesingerová married. They had the following children:

    i. **Alena Buriánková** was born on 15 Nov 1960.

Jana Buriánková-5 (Josef-4, František-3, Josef-2, Václav-1) was born on 25 Mar 1944 in Koryta No. 29.

Bohumil Michalek was born on 30 Nov 1942 in Sedlov No. 1, Kolin.

Bohumil Michalek and Jana Buriánková married. They had the following children:

    i. **Aleš Michalek** was born on 09 Jun 1970.

    ii. **Jana Michalkova** was born on 07 Oct 1972 in Loukovec.

Ivo Buriánek-5 (Ivo-4, František-3, Josef-2, Václav-1) was born in 1932 in koryta. He died in 1999.

J. Slajsova.

Ivo Buriánek and J. Slajsova married. They had the following children:

    12. i. **Petr Buriánek.** He married Alena Pecharova in 1999.

Generation 6

Alena Buriánková-6 (Vratislav-5, Josef-4, František-3, Josef-2, Václav-1) was born on 15 Nov 1960.

Mirek Matlas was born on 20 Sep 1955 in Litvinov.

Mirek Matlas and Alena Buriánková married. They had the following children:

> **Alena Matlasová** was born in 1981.
>
> **daughter Matlasová** was born in 1986.

Aleš Michalek-6 (Jana-5, Josef-4, František-3, Josef-2, Václav-1) was born on 09 Jun 1970.

Klára Rozenska was born on 08 Sep 1971 in Teplice.

Aleš Michalek and Klára Rozenska married. They had the following children:

> **Terezka Michalkova** was born on 06 Apr 2001.
>
> **Barbora Michalkova** was born on 03 Apr 2006.

Jana Michalkova-6 (Jana-5, Josef-4, František-3, Josef-2, Václav-1) was born on 07 Oct 1972 in Loukovec.

Jaromír Terner was born on 27 Jun 1961.

Jaromír Terner and Jana Michalkova married. They had the following children:

> **Anna Ternerova** was born in February 9, 2002.
>
> **Linda Ternerova** was born in April 7, 2004.

Petr Buriánek-6 (Ivo-5, Ivo-4, František-3, Josef-2, Václav-1).

Alena Pecharova.

Petr Buriánek and Alena Pecharova were married in 1999. They had the following children:

> **Štěpán Buriánek**.

Hlavatý Family

Generation 1

František Hlavatý-1 was born in 1770 in Bzi No. 6.

Anna Glaserova daughter of Josef Glaser and Katharina Skoda was born in 1780 in Bohumilec 1, Český Dub Co..

František Hlavatý and Anna Glaserova married. They had the following children:

    i. **Terezie Hlavatá** was born on 04 Nov 1800 in Bohumilec 1, Český Dub Co..

Generation 2

Terezie Hlavatá-2 (František-1) was born on 04 Nov 1800 in Bohumilec 1, Český Dub Co..

Unknown was born in Bzi No. 6. He died in Josef Dědek of Hodkovice - pestitel.

Unknown and Terezie Hlavatá met. They had the following children:

    i. **Františka Hlavatá** was born on 27 Feb 1820 in Bzi No. 6. She married Petr Rechziegel on Nov 1850 in Slavíkov No. 3, Vlastibořice parish, Josef Sedláček, officiating. She died on Dec 1857 in Slavíkov No. 4, in Mohelka Creek -.

Generation 3

Františka Hlavatá-3 (Terezie-2, František-1) was born on 27 Feb 1820 in Bzi No. 6. She died on 10 Dec 1857 in Slavíkov No. 4, in Mohelka Creek.

Petr Rechziegel son of Ing. František Rechziegel and Lidmila Neumanová was born on 10 Jan 1819 in Slavíkov No. 4. He died on 17 Oct 1890 in Novy Mlyn, Žďárek.

Petr Rechziegel and Františka Hlavatá were married on 30 Nov 1850 in Slavíkov No. 3, Vlastibořice parish, Josef Sedláček, officiating. They had the following children:

    i. **Marie Rechziegel** was born on 24 Jan 1841 in Hodkovice No. 39.

    ii. **Petr Rechziegel** was born on 01 Jun 1844 in Hodkovice No. 39. He married Anna Najmanová on 26 Jan 1869 in Radimovice No. 7,

Vlastibořice parish., Jan Krt. Hruska officiationg. He died on 18 Sep 1917 in Letařovice No. 4, Turnov Co..

iii. **Františka Rechziegel** was born on 05 Jul 1846 in Hodkovice No. 39. She died on 28 Feb 1914 in Ruzodol No. 169.

iv. **Václav Rechziegel** was born on 25 Aug 1851 in Slavíkov No. 3. He married Anna Janečková in 1879. He died on 21 Mar 1909 in Radostín No. 13.

Josefa Rechziegelová was born on 08 Nov 1852 in Slavíkov No. 3. She died on 11 Nov 1852 in Slavíkov No. 3.

Karel Bor. Rechziegel was born on 03 Jul 1855 in Slavíkov No. 3. He died on 24 Oct 1855 in Slavíkov No. 3.

Generation 4

Marie Rechziegel-4 (Františka-3, Terezie-2, František-1) was born on 24 Jan 1841 in Hodkovice No. 39.

Václav Janeček son of at and Unknown was born in 1834 in Příšovice. He died on 18 Sep 1909 in Příšovice.

Václav Janeček and Marie Rechziegel married. They had the following children:

i. **Anna Janečková.**

Petr Janeček.

František Janeček.

Matejak.

Matejak and Marie Rechziegel met. They had the following children:

Václav Rechziegel was born on 24 Apr 1860 in Letařovice No. 4.

Petr Rechziegel-4 (Františka-3, Terezie-2, František-1) was born on 01 Jun 1844 in Hodkovice No. He died on 18 Sep 1917 in Letařovice No. 4, Turnov Co..

Anna Najmanová daughter of Antonín Neumann and Anna Brožová was born on 31 Jul 1849 in Radimovice No. 7, Turnov Co.. She died on 05 Jun 1908 in Letařovice.

Petr Rechziegel and Anna Najmanová were married on 26 Jan 1869 in Radimovice No. 7, Vlastibořice parish., Jan Krt. Hruska officiationg. They had the following children:

Josef Rechcigl was born on 22 Jul 1869 in Radimovice No. 7. He died on 24 Feb 1920 in Letařovice (prob.).

ii. **Emilie Rechcíglová** was born on 02 Apr 1871 in Letařovice No. 4, Český Dub Co.. She died on 18 Feb 1928.

Václav Rechcigl was born on 13 Mar 1873 in Letařovice No. 4, Český Dub Co..

iv. **Adolf Rechcigl** was born on 21 Aug 1876 in Letařovice No. 4, Český Dub Co.. He married Marie Berglová about 1900. He died on 30 Mar 1946 in Šárovcova Lhota No. 16.

Arnošt Rechziegel was born on 07 Sep 1882 in Letařovice No. 4, Český Dub Co.. He died on 12 Oct 1882 in Letařovice No. 4, Český Dub Co..

vi. **Zdeněk Petr Rechcigl** was born on 31 Jul 1884 in Letařovice No. 4, Turnov Dist.. He married Anna Šimůnková on 08 Oct 1906 in Kralovske Vinohrady. He died on 08 Feb 1962 in Karlovy Vary - Rybare.

vii. **Bohumil Rechcigl** was born on 09 Apr 1888. He died on 03 Jan 1963 in Český Dub.

Jan Rechziegel was born on 08 May 1895.

Františka Rechziegel-4 (Františka-3, Terezie-2, František-1) was born on 05 Jul 1846 in Hodkovice No. 39. She died on 28 Feb 1914 in Ruzodol No. 169.

Ullrich was born in Jilove.

Ullrich and Františka Rechziegel married. They had the following children:

i. **Adolf Ullrich** was born in Jilove.

ii. **Josef Ullrich** was born in Jilove.

Václav Rechziegel-4 (Františka-3, Terezie-2, František-1) was born on 25 Aug 1851 in Slavíkov No. He died on 21 Mar 1909 in Radostín No. 13.

Anna Janečková daughter of František Janeček and Anna Koskova was born on 19 Apr 1855 in Trtí No. 6. She died on 17 Dec 1903 in Hodkovice. Václav Rechziegel and Anna Janečková were married in 1879. They had the following children:

Adolf Rechziegel.

Josef Rechziegel was born in 1886 in Radostín. He died on 05 Oct 1956 in Radostín.

Emilie Rechziegelová.

iv. **Marie Rechziegelová** was born in 1882 in Radostín. She died on 30 Jul 1959 in Radostín.

v. **Anna Rechziegelová** was born on 26 Sep 1888 in Radostín. She married Josef Franců about 1925. She died on 10 Oct 1964 in Kacanovy.

vi. **Anastazie Rechziegelová** was born on 17 Mar 1894 in Radostín. She married Rudolf Roubíček in Jul 1917. She died on 19 Apr 1984 in Srch.

Generation 5

Anna Janečková-5 (Marie-4, Františka-3, Terezie-2, František-1).

Kinsky.

Kinsky and Anna Janečková married. They had the following children:

Miloslav Kinsky.

Emilie Rechcíglová-5 (Petr-4, Františka-3, Terezie-2, František-1) was born on 02 Apr 1871 in Letařovice No. 4, Český Dub Co.. She died on 18 Feb 1928.

Josef Ullrich son of Ullrich and Františka Rechziegel was born in Jilove. Josef Ullrich and Emilie Rechcíglová married. They had the following children:

Miloslav Ulrich was born before 1900.

Ludvika Ulrichova was born in 1898. She died on 01 Jun 1945.

Adolf Rechcigl-5 (Petr-4, Františka-3, Terezie-2, František-1) was born on 21 Aug 1876 in Letařovice No. 4, Český Dub Co.. He died on 30 Mar 1946 in Šárovcova Lhota No. 16.

Marie Berglová daughter of František Bergl and Marie Mařanová was born on 27 Mar 1880 in Drahotice No. 20, Mnichovo Hradiště Co.. She died on 25 Mar 1917 in Chocnějovice No. 22, Mnichovo Hradiště Co..

Adolf Rechcigl and Marie Berglová were married about 1900. They had the following children:

Marie Rechcíglová was born on 29 Sep 1901 in Kocňovice (renamed Chocnějovice). She died on 03 Oct 1902 in Chocnějovice.

ii. **Miloslav Rechcigl** was born on 13 May 1904 in Kocňovice (renamed Chocnějovice) No. He married Marie Rajtrová on 26 Jul 1926 in Praha - Kralovske Vinohrady. He died on May 1973 in Washington, DC.

Anna Rechcíglová was born on 10 Feb 1906 in Kocňovice (renamed Chocnějovice) No. She died on 26 Feb 1927 in Chocnějovice.

Marie Anna Ferklová daughter of František Ferkl and Anna Saralova was born on 10 Dec 1897 in Chocnějovice No. 2. She died on 31 Dec 1970 in Šárovcova Lhota.

Adolf Rechcigl and Marie Anna Ferklová were married on 25 Apr 1917 in St. Alois Church, Praha. They had the following children:

i. **Stanislav Josef Rechcigl** was born on 10 Oct 1918 in Chocnějovice. He married Libuše Sedláčková on 17 Jan 1948 in Novy Bydzov. He died on 09 May 1973 in Šárovcova Lhota No. 16.

Adolf Rechcigl was born on 09 Apr 1920 in Chocnějovice No. 22. He died on 27 Dec 1944 in Ples.

Zdeněk Petr Rechcigl-5 (Petr-4, Františka-3, Terezie-2, František-1) was born on 31 Jul 1884 in Letařovice No. 4, Turnov Dist.. He died on 08 Feb 1962 in Karlovy Vary - Rybare.

Anna Šimůnková daughter of Josef Šimůnek and Marie Stejskalová was born on 31 Dec 1884 in Sezemice No. 1, Mnichovo Hradiště Co.. She died on 28 Nov 1907 in After prolonged illnessa.

Zdeněk Petr Rechcigl and Anna Šimůnková were married on 08 Oct 1906 in Kralovske Vinohrady. They had the following children:

i. **Božena Rechcíglová** was born on 18 Mar 1907 in Letařovice, Turnov Co.. She married František Křikava on 24 Jul 1926 in Horovice. She died on 11 Aug 1979 in Hospital, Horovice.

Marie Paulu daughter of Paulu was born before 1900. She died in Divorced February 17, 1926.

Zdeněk Petr Rechcigl and Marie Paulu were married on 26 Sep 1908 in Český Dub. They had the following children:
    i. **child Rechcigl**. He died in Soon after birth.
    ii. **Zdeněk Rechcigl** was born on 06 Jul 1909. He died on 12 Oct 1909.
Marie Reslová daughter of Antonín Resl and Marie Kovářová was born on 25 Mar 1900 in Roven Nio. 45. She died on 02 Dec 1982 in Karlovy Vary. Zdeněk Petr Rechcigl and Marie Reslová were married on 30 Apr 1926 in Roven. They had the following children:
    i. **Zdena Rechcíglová** was born on 25 Sep 1926 in Komarov u Horovic. She married Jan Mueller in 1949. She died on 02 Sep 1978 in Karlovy Vary.
Marie - uncertain was born on 11 Jan 1909. She died on 02 Nov 1996. Zdeněk Petr Rechcigl and Marie - uncertain met. They had the following children:
    Ludmila Rechcíglová was born after 1900.
Bohumil Rechcigl-5 (Petr-4, Františka-3, Terezie-2, František-1) was born on 09 Apr 1888. He died on 03 Jan 1963 in Český Dub.
Růžena Slukova was born in 1892. She died on 14 Mar 1969 in Český Dub. Bohumil Rechcigl and Růžena Slukova married. They had the following children:
    i. **Zdeněk Rechcigl** was born on 05 Dec 1913. He married Marie Pavlová on 29 Jan 1944. He died on 01 Nov 1985.
    Věra Rechcíglová was born in 1915. She died in 1972.
    Notes for Věra Rechcíglová:
    General Notes:
    unmarried
    iii. **Libuše Rechcíglová** was born on 13 Aug 1916. She married Jan Mančík on 03 Jun 1950. She died in Mar 1997 in Varnsdorf.
Josef Ullrich-5 (Františka-4, Františka-3, Terezie-2, František-1) was born in Jilove.
Emilie Rechcíglová daughter of Petr Rechziegel and Anna Najmanová was born on 02 Apr 1871 in Letařovice No. 4, Český Dub Co.. She died on 18 Feb 1928.

Josef Ullrich and Emilie Rechcíglová married. They had the following children:

> **Miloslav Ulrich** was born before 1900.
>
> **Ludvika Ulrichova** was born in 1898. She died on 01 Jun 1945.

Marie Rechziegelová-5 (Václav-4, Františka-3, Terezie-2, František-1) was born in 1882 in Radostín. She died on 30 Jul 1959 in Radostín.

Josef Pelech was born in 1885. He died on 09 Feb 1961.

Josef Pelech and Marie Rechziegelová married. They had the following children:

> i. **Marie Pelechová.** She died on 09 Aug 1961.

Anna Rechziegelová-5 (Václav-4, Františka-3, Terezie-2, František-1) was born on 26 Sep 1888 in Radostín. She died on 10 Oct 1964 in Kacanovy.

Josef Franců was born on 09 Apr 1894 in Kacanovy. He died on 22 Nov 1971 in Turnov.

Josef Franců and Anna Rechziegelová were married about 1925. They had the following children:

> i. **Jaromír Franců** was born on 26 Feb 1926 in Kacanovy. He married Marta Lamačová on Nov 1950 in Turnov. He died on 04 Jul 1980 in Jičín.

Josef Studnička was born in Kacanovy. He died before 1925.

Notes for Josef Studnička:

General Notes:

He went to the Russian Front during the World War I but never returned.

Josef Studnička and Anna Rechziegelová married. They had the following children:

> i. **Oldrřch Studnička** was born on 07 Jun 1912 in Kacanovy. He died on 20 Aug 1942 in Kacanovy.

Anastazie Rechziegelová-5 (Václav-4, Františka-3, Terezie-2, František-1) was born on 17 Mar 1894 in Radostín. She died on 19 Apr 1984 in Srch.

Rudolf Roubíček son of František Roubíček and Marie Roubíčková was born about 1894 in Radostín. He died about Mar 1918.

Rudolf Roubíček and Anastazie Rechziegelová were married in Jul 1917. They had the following children:

i. **Jana Roubíčková** was born on 26 Jan 1918 in Radostín. She married Franisek Kvapil on Sep 1943 in Kunetice. She died on 13 Oct 1981 in Lazne Bohdanec.

František Pátek was born in 1894 in Chlum u Hlinska. He died on 05 Feb 1958 in Srchrechziegel.

František Pátek and Anastazie Rechziegelová met. They had the following children:

    i. **Dalibor Rechziegel** was born on 20 Oct 1924 in Radostín, near Turnov. He married Sona Pražáková on 26 Apr 1948 in Kladno. He died on 12 Aug 1997 in Litomerice.

    ii. **Drahomir Rechziegel** was born on 19 Nov 1926. He died on 23 Oct 1983.

Generation 6

Miloslav Rechcigl-6 (Adolf-5, Petr-4, Františka-3, Terezie-2, František-1) was born on 13 May 1904 in Kocňovice (renamed Chocnějovice) No. 22. He died on 27 May 1973 in Washington, DC.

Marie Rajtrová daughter of Čeněk Rajtr and Marie Dandová was born on 05 Jul 1905 in Dolanky No. 7, Mnichovo Hradiště Co.. She died on 13 Apr 1982 in Mladá Boleslav.

Miloslav Rechcigl and Marie Rajtrová were married on 26 Jul 1926 in Praha - Kralovske Vinohrady. They had the following children:

    i. **Mila (Miloslav) Rechcigl Jr.** was born on 30 Jul 1930 in Mladá Boleslav, CSR. He married Eva Edwards (Eisnerová) on 29 Aug 1953 in New York, NY.

    ii. **Marta Rechcíglová** was born on 23 May 1933 in Mladá Boleslav. She married František Žďárský on 03 Oct 1953 in Mladá Boleslav. She died on 13 Sep 2018 in Mladá Boleslav.

Stanislav Josef Rechcigl-6 (Adolf-5, Petr-4, Františka-3, Terezie-2, František-1) was born on 10 Oct 1918 in Chocnějovice. He died on 09 May 1973 in Šárovcova Lhota No. 16.

Libuše Sedláčková daughter of Bedřich Sedláček and Ludmila was born on 24 Sep 1924 in Staré Smrkovice, Jičín Dist. She died on 03 Apr 2019 in Jičín, Czech.

Stanislav Josef Rechcigl and Libuše Sedláčková were married on 17 Jan 1948 in Novy Bydzov. They had the following children:
- i. **Hana Rechcíglová** was born on 13 Jul 1948 in Novy Bydzov, Hradec Králové Co.. She married Jaroslav Husak on 28 Dec 1968 in Sobotka, Jičín Co..
- ii. **Libuše Rechcíglová** was born on 25 Jan 1950 in Novy Bydzov, Hradec Králové Co.. She married Miroslav Vich on 11 Apr 1970 in Ostromer, Jičín Co..
- iii. **Stanislav Rechcigl** was born on 24 Mar 1952 in Hořice, Jičín Co.. He married Zdena Pařízková on 24 Mar 1972 in Jičín.

Božena Rechcíglová-6 (Zdeněk Petr-5, Petr-4, Františka-3, Terezie-2, František-1) was born on 18 Mar 1907 in Letařovice, Turnov Co.. She died on 11 Aug 1979 in Hospital, Horovice.

František Křikava son of Josef Křikava and Marie Stichová was born on 23 Dec 1890 in Chaloupky, Beroun Co.. He died on 25 Mar 1965 in Komarov u Horovic No. 40.

František Křikava and Božena Rechcíglová were married on 24 Jul 1926 in Horovice. They had the following children:
- i. **Luděk Křikava** was born on 02 Feb 1927 in Komarov u Horovic No. 40. He died on 23 Sep 1996.
- ii. **Sasa Křikava** was born on 02 Dec 1930 in Komarov u Horovic No. 40.

Zdena Rechcíglová-6 (Zdeněk Petr-5, Petr-4, Františka-3, Terezie-2, František-1) was born on 25 Sep 1926 in Komarov u Horovic. She died on 02 Sep 1978 in Karlovy Vary.

Jan Mueller son of Jan Karel Mueller and Anna Šašková was born on 05 Feb 1925 in Prague. He died on 01 May 1989 in Karlovy Vary.

Jan Mueller and Zdena Rechcíglová were married in 1949. They had the following children:
- i. **Jana Muellerová** was born on 08 Nov 1952 in Karlovy Vary. She married Jiří Stuchl on 26 Aug 1979 in Manetin, Plzen Sever Co..
- ii. **Zdena Muellerová** was born on 01 May 1960 in Karlovy Vary. She married František Petr in 1981 in Karlovy Vary.

Zdeněk Rechcigl-6 (Bohumil-5, Petr-4, Františka-3, Terezie-2, František-1) was born on 05 Dec 1913. He died on 01 Nov 1985.

Marie Pavlová was born in Jan 1921 in Vlcetin. She died in Dec 2003.

Zdeněk Rechcigl and Marie Pavlová were married on 29 Jan 1944. They had the following children:

    i. **Radmila Rechcíglová** was born on 29 May 1944. She married Pavel Herák on 14 Sep 1963 in Český Dub.

    ii. **Zdeněk Rechcigl** was born on 07 Aug 1946 in Český Dub. He married Věra Vizkova on 30 Dec 1967 in Český Dub.

Libuše was born on 05 Dec 1917.

Zdeněk Rechcigl and Libuše were married in 1964. They had no children.

Libuše Rechcíglová-6 (Bohumil-5, Petr-4, Františka-3, Terezie-2, František-1) was born on 13 Aug 1916. She died in Mar 1997 in Varnsdorf.

Jan Mančík.

Jan Mančík and Libuše Rechcíglová were married on 03 Jun 1950. They had the following children:

    i. **Jana Mančíková** was born in 1951.

    ii. **Irena Mančíková** was born in 1954.

Marie Pelechová-6 (Marie-5, Václav-4, Františka-3, Terezie-2, František-1). She died on 09 Aug 1961.

Alois Florián was born resided in Letovice by Brno.

Alois Florián and Marie Pelechová married. They had the following children:

    i. **Marie Floriánová**.

    ii. **Karel Florián**.

Jaromír Franců-6 (Anna-5, Václav-4, Františka-3, Terezie-2, František-1) was born on 26 Feb 1926 in Kacanovy. He died on 04 Jul 1980 in Jičín.

Marta Lamačová was born on 06 Jun 1927 in Kacanovy. She died on 04 Nov 1950 in Turnov.

Jaromír Franců and Marta Lamačová were married on 04 Nov 1950 in Turnov. They had the following children:

    i. **Jaromír Franců** was born on 21 Aug 1951 in Kacanovy, Turnov. He married Věra Zimova on 29 Dec 1989 in Jičín.

Oldrřch Studnička-6 (Anna-5, Václav-4, Františka-3, Terezie-2, František-1) was born on 07 Jun 1912 in Kacanovy. He died on 20 Aug 1942 in Kacanovy. Notes for Oldrřch Studnička:
General Notes:
He was shot by the Nazi during the persecutine of the underground leader Dr. Vladimír Krajina.

Bohumila Karaskova was born on 09 May 1913 in Kacanovy. She died on 25 Sep 2000 in Turnov. Oldrřch Studnička and Bohumila Karaskova married. They had the following children:

    i. **Oldrřch Studnička** was born on 31 May 1942 in Kacanovy.

Jana Roubíčková-6 (Anastazie-5, Václav-4, Františka-3, Terezie-2, František-1) was born on 26 Jan 1918 in Radostín. She died on 13 Oct 1981 in Lazne Bohdanec.

Franisek Kvapil was born on 24 Nov 1912. He died on 15 Oct 1982. Franisek Kvapil and Jana Roubíčková were married on 11 Sep 1943 in Kunetice. They had the following children:

    i. **Jan Kvapil** was born on 27 May 1944 in Pardubice. He married Eva Nováková on 09 Jun 1962 in Pardubice.

    ii. **Nada Kvapilová** was born on 11 Feb 1946 in Pardubice. She married Josef Virt on 13 Mar 1971 in Rohovladova Bela.

Dalibor Rechziegel-6 (Anastazie-5, Václav-4, Františka-3, Terezie-2, František-1) was born on 20 Oct 1924 in Radostín, near Turnov. He died on 12 Aug 1997 in Litomerice.

Sona Pražáková was born on 23 Sep 1929 in Brandysek, Kladno Co.. Dalibor Rechziegel and Sona Pražáková were married on 26 Apr 1948 in Kladno. They had the following children:

    Jan Rechziegel was born on 12 Oct 1951 in Litomerice.

    Luboš Rechziegel was born on 08 Jan 1957 in Litomerice. He married Radka Chládková on 06 Jul 1985 in Litomerice.

Drahomir Rechziegel-6 (Anastazie-5, Václav-4, Františka-3, Terezie-2, František-1) was born on 19 Nov 1926. He died on 23 Oct 1983.

Marie Kamenicka was born on 01 Jan 1929 in Kunetice. She died on 18 Apr 1979.

Drahomir Rechziegel and Marie Kamenicka married. They had the following children:

    i. **Jitka Rechziegelová** was born on 27 Aug 1951.

    ii. **Aleš Rechziegel** was born on 15 Jan 1954.

    iii. **Drahomir Rechziegel** was born on 10 Feb 1957 in Pardubice.

Generation 7

Mila (Miloslav) Rechcigl Jr.-7 (Miloslav-6, Adolf-5, Petr-4, Františka-3, Terezie-2, František-1) was born on 30 Jul 1930 in Mladá Boleslav, CSR.

Eva Edwards (Eisnerová) daughter of Paul J. Edwards (Pavel Eisner) and Jiřina Taussigová was born on 21 Jan 1932 in Prague, CSR.

Mila (Miloslav) Rechcigl Jr. and Eva Edwards (Eisnerová) were married on 29 Aug 1953 in New York, NY. They had the following children:

    i. **John Edward Rechcigl** was born on 27 Feb 1960 in Washington, D.C.. He married Nancy Ann Palko on 30 Jul 1983 in Dover, NJ.

    ii. **Karen Rechcigl** was born on 16 Apr 1962 in Washington, DC. She married Ulysses Kollecas on 25 Aug 1990 in Bethesda, MD.

Marta Rechcíglová-7 (Miloslav-6, Adolf-5, Petr-4, Františka-3, Terezie-2, František-1) was born on May 1933 in Mladá Boleslav. She died on 13 Sep 2018 in Mladá Boleslav.

František Žďárský son of František Václav Žďárský and Eliška Foltýnová was born on 21 May 1932 in Turnov.

František Žďárský and Marta Rechcíglová were married on 03 Oct 1953 in Mladá Boleslav. They had the following children:

    i. **Marcela Žďárská** was born on 09 May 1954 in Liberec. She married Miroslav Heralecký on 15 Mar 1975 in Sychrov.

    ii. **Iveta Žďárská** was born on 29 Aug 1963 in Liberec, Bohemia. She married Vlastimil Berkman on 29 Oct 1983.

Hana Rechcíglová-7 (Stanislav Josef-6, Adolf-5, Petr-4, Františka-3, Terezie-2, František-1) was born on 13 Jul 1948 in Novy Bydzov, Hradec Králové Co..

Jaroslav Husak was born on 24 Mar 1946 in Jičín.

Jaroslav Husak and Hana Rechcíglová were married on 28 Dec 1968 in Sobotka, Jičín Co.. They had the following children:

Martin Husak was born on 20 Feb 1971 in Hradec Králové. He married Petra Endrychová on 24 Jul 1999 in Hradec Králové.

Petra Husakova was born on 30 Mar 1974 in Hradec Králové.

Tomáš Petříček was born on 18 Dec 1948 in Hradec Králové.

Tomáš Petříček and Hana Rechcíglová were married on 20 Sep 1991 in Hradec Králové. They had no children.

Libuše Rechcíglová-7 (Stanislav Josef-6, Adolf-5, Petr-4, Františka-3, Terezie-2, František-1) was born on 25 Jan 1950 in Novy Bydzov, Hradec Králové Co..

Miroslav Vich was born on 13 Nov 1950 in Nova Paka, Jičín Co..

Miroslav Vich and Libuše Rechcíglová were married on 11 Apr 1970 in Ostromer, Jičín Co.. They had the following children:

- i. **Iveta Vichova** was born on 15 Jan 1972 in Jičín. She married Miloš Haltuf on 07 Sep 1991 in Lazne Belohrad, Jičín Co..
- **Miroslav Vich** was born on 10 Mar 1973 in Jičín.
- **Sarka Vichova** was born on 11 Mar 1989 in Hradec Králové.

Stanislav Rechcigl-7 (Stanislav Josef-6, Adolf-5, Petr-4, Františka-3, Terezie-2, František-1) was born on 24 Mar 1952 in Hořice, Jičín Co..

Zdena Pařízková daughter of Mila Parik and Zdenka was born on 26 Jan 1954 in Hořice, Jičín Dist., Bohemia.

Stanislav Rechcigl and Zdena Pařízková were married on 24 Mar 1972 in Jičín. They had the following children:

- i. **Stanislava Rechcíglová** was born on 22 Sep 1972 in Hořice, Jičín Dist., Bohemia.
- ii. **Jana Rechcíglová** was born on 22 Sep 1973 in Hořice, Jičín Co.. She married Karel Spidlen on 29 Apr 1995 in Jičín, Bohemia.
- iii. **Stanislav Rechcigl** was born on 08 Aug 1975 in Hořice, Jičín Dist., Bohemia. He married Natasha Blackbourn on 19 Jul 2008 in Spalding, Lincolnshire, UK..

Helena Denisova was born on 29 Jun 1944.

Stanislav Rechcigl and Helena Denisova met. They had no children.

Luděk Křikava-7 (Božena-6, Zdeněk Petr-5, Petr-4, Františka-3, Terezie-2, František-1) was born on 02 Feb 1927 in Komarov u Horovic No. 40. He died on 23 Sep 1996.

Zdenka Krizova was born on 24 Sep 1941 in Komarov u Horovic No. 72. Luděk Křikava and Zdenka Krizova married. They had the following children:

    i. **Věra Křikavová** was born on 28 Apr 1966 in Komarov u Horovic No. 40.

    ii. **Hanna Křikavová** was born on 07 May 1957 in Komarov u Horovic No. 40. She died on 30 Dec 1997.

    iii. **Jan Křikava** was born on 19 Aug 1960 in Komarov u Horovic No. 40.

Sasa Křikava-7 (Božena-6, Zdeněk Petr-5, Petr-4, Františka-3, Terezie-2, František-1) was born on Dec 1930 in Komarov u Horovic No. 40.

Milada Toclova was born on 24 Jul 1927.

Sasa Křikava and Milada Toclova married. They had the following children:

    i. **Alexander Křikava** was born in 1951 in Komarov u Horovic.

    ii. **Hana Křikavová** was born in 1958 in Komarov u Horovic.

Jana Muellerová-7 (Zdena-6, Zdeněk Petr-5, Petr-4, Františka-3, Terezie-2, František-1) was born on 08 Nov 1952 in Karlovy Vary.

Jiří Stuchl son of Josef Stuchl and Jarmila Šimáňová was born on 14 Nov 1950 in Plzen. He died on Mar 2001 in Praha 10.

Jiří Stuchl and Jana Muellerová were married on 26 Aug 1979 in Manetin, Plzen Sever Co.. They had the following children:

    Lenka Stuchlová was born on 12 May 1979 in Karlovy Vary. She married Josef Bic on 07 Jul 2007 in Liberec.

    Jan Stuchl was born on 24 Feb 1981 in Karlovy Vary.

Zdena Muellerová-7 (Zdena-6, Zdeněk Petr-5, Petr-4, Františka-3, Terezie-2, František-1) was born on 01 May 1960 in Karlovy Vary.

František Petr was born on 05 Sep 1958 in Sokolov.

František Petr and Zdena Muellerová were married in 1981 in Karlovy Vary. They had the following children:

Miroslav Petr was born on 30 Oct 1981 in Karlovy Vary.

  ii. Jana Petrová was born on 29 Jun 1984 in Karlovy Vary.

Radmila Rechcíglová-7 (Zdeněk-6, Bohumil-5, Petr-4, Františka-3, Terezie-2, František-1) was born on 29 May 1944.

Pavel Herák was born on 03 Jun 1938 in Brestovany, Slovakia.

Pavel Herák and Radmila Rechcíglová were married on 14 Sep 1963 in Český Dub. They had the following children:

  i. **Petr Herák** was born on 03 Jun 1965. He married Tereza Kovářová on 24 Mar 1990 in Český Dub.

  ii. **Pavlina Heráková** was born on 29 Jan 1964. She married Milan Podlipský on 11 Feb 1984 in Milevsko.

  iii. **Helena Heráková** was born on 12 Jul 1966. She married Pavel Hudec on 15 Sep 1984 in Český Dub.

Zdeněk Rechcigl-7 (Zdeněk-6, Bohumil-5, Petr-4, Františka-3, Terezie-2, František-1) was born on 07 Aug 1946 in Český Dub.

Věra Vizkova was born on 31 Dec 1947 in Hodkovice.

Zdeněk Rechcigl and Věra Vizkova were married on 30 Dec 1967 in Český Dub. They had the following children:

  i. **Martin Rechcigl** was born on 16 Dec 1968. He married Petra Smolakova on 17 Sep 1994 in Český Dub.

Jana Mančíková-7 (Libuše-6, Bohumil-5, Petr-4, Františka-3, Terezie-2, František-1) was born in 1951.

Jan Cicka.

Jan Cicka and Jana Mančíková married. They had the following children:

  Drahomira Cicková was born in 1971.

Vladimír Ulver.

Vladimír Ulver and Jana Mančíková married. They had the following children:

  Jitka Ulverova was born in 1980.

Irena Mančíková-7 (Libuše-6, Bohumil-5, Petr-4, Františka-3, Terezie-2, František-1) was born in 1954.

Petr Synek.

Petr Synek and Irena Mančíková married. They had the following children:

    Veronika Synková was born on 07 Mar 1979.

    Jan Synek was born on 24 May 1980.

Marie Floriánová-7 (Marie-6, Marie-5, Václav-4, Františka-3, Terezie-2, František-1).

Josef Tomeš was born in Stranov.

Josef Tomeš and Marie Floriánová married. They had the following children:

    Tomsová-daughter.

    son Tomeš.

Jaromír Franců-7 (Jaromír-6, Anna-5, Václav-4, Františka-3, Terezie-2, František-1) was born on 21 Aug 1951 in Kacanovy, Turnov.

Věra Zimova was born on 21 Jan 1956 in Turnov.

Jaromír Franců and Věra Zimova were married on 29 Dec 1989 in Jičín. They had the following children:

    i. **Adam Franců** was born on 12 Jul 1990.

    Jan Franců was born on 26 Jul 1993.

Oldrřch Studnička-7 (Oldrřch-6, Anna-5, Václav-4, Františka-3, Terezie-2, František-1) was born on May 1942 in Kacanovy.

Marie Nováková was born on 06 May 1952 in Vsen, Turnov.

Oldrřch Studnička and Marie Nováková married. They had the following children:

    Lucie Studničková was born on 15 Aug 1975 in Praha.

Jan Kvapil-7 (Jana-6, Anastazie-5, Václav-4, Františka-3, Terezie-2, František-1) was born on 27 May 1944 in Pardubice.

Eva Nováková daughter of Marta Lamacova was born on 21 Dec 1943.

Jan Kvapil and Eva Nováková were married on 09 Jun 1962 in Pardubice. They had the following children:

    i. **Jan Kvapil** was born on 30 Dec 1963 in Pardubice. He married Iveta Kulichova on 31 Jan 1987 in Lazne Bohdanec.

    ii. **Jaroslav Kvapil** was born on 26 Feb 1969 in Pardubice. He married Eva Kadlecova on 30 Nov 1991 in Lazne Bohdanec.

      iii. **Eva Kvapilová** was born on 18 Oct 1973 in Pardubice. He married Tomasz Prcz on 18 May 1996 in Lazne Bohdanec.

      iv. **Jiri Kvapil** was born on 18 Jan 1980 in Pardubice. He married Zuzana Tomanová on 13 Aug 2005 in Lazne Bohdanec.

Nada Kvapilová-7 (Jana-6, Anastazie-5, Václav-4, Františka-3, Terezie-2, František-1) was born on Feb 1946 in Pardubice.

Josef Virt was born on 20 Sep 1933 in Pardubice. He died on 19 Jan 1991. Josef Virt and Nada Kvapilová were married on 13 Mar 1971 in Rohovladova Bela. They had the following children:

      i. **Petra Virtova** was born on 17 Aug 1976 in Pardubice. She married Tomáš Tupy on 25 Aug 2000.

Jitka Rechziegelová-7 (Drahomir-6, Anastazie-5, Václav-4, Františka-3, Terezie-2, František-1) was born on 27 Aug 1951.

Petr Marek son of Petr Marek and Josefa was born on 16 Jun 1947 in Libec. Petr Marek and Jitka Rechziegelová married. They had the following children:

    Denisa Markova was born on 28 Aug 1972.

    Petr Marek was born on 21 Feb 1975.

Aleš Rechziegel-7 (Drahomir-6, Anastazie-5, Václav-4, Františka-3, Terezie-2, František-1) was born on 15 Jan 1954.

Lenka Horčičková daughter of Vladimír Horčička and Unknown was born on 03 Feb 1956. Aleš Rechziegel and Lenka Horčičková married. They had the following children:

    Andrea Rechziegel was born on 08 Apr 1975.

    Tomáš Rechziegel was born on 28 Mar 1979.

Drahomir Rechziegel-7 (Drahomir-6, Anastazie-5, Václav-4, Františka-3, Terezie-2, František-1) was born on 10 Feb 1957 in Pardubice.

Alena Rykrova daughter of Jaroslav Rykr and Marie was born in 1965. Drahomir Rechziegel and Alena Rykrova married. They had the following children:

    Lukáš Rechziegel was born on 19 Jan 1985.

Generation 8

John Edward Rechcigl-8 (Mila (Miloslav)-7, Miloslav-6, Adolf-5, Petr-4, Františka-3, Terezie-2, František-1) was born on 27 Feb 1960 in Washington, D.C..

Nancy Ann Palko daughter of Joseph Palko and Mary Rishko was born on 26 Sep 1961 in Morristown, NJ.

John Edward Rechcigl and Nancy Ann Palko were married on 30 Jul 1983 in Dover, NJ. They had the following children:

> **Gregory John Rechcigl** was born on 19 Dec 1988 in Bradenton, FL.
>
> ii. **Kevin Thomas Rechcigl** was born on 09 Oct 1991 in Bradenton, FL. He married Jordan Robbins on 12 May 2018 in Jacksonville, FL.
>
> **Lindsey Nicole Rechcigl** was born on 03 Nov 1994 in Bradenton, FL.

Karen Rechcigl-8 (Mila (Miloslav)-7, Miloslav-6, Adolf-5, Petr-4, Františka-3, Terezie-2, František-1) was born on 16 Apr 1962 in Washington, DC.

Ulysses Kollecas son of Christopher Thomas (Kolecas) Collier and Amelia Malatras was born on 20 Mar 1958 in Washington, DC.

Ulysses Kollecas and Karen Rechcigl were married on 25 Aug 1990 in Bethesda, MD. They had the following children:

> **Kristin Kollecas** was born on 04 May 1993 in Albuquerque, NM.
>
> **Paul Kollecas** was born on 02 Jun 1995 in Albuquerque, NM.

Marcela Žďárská-8 (Marta-7, Miloslav-6, Adolf-5, Petr-4, Františka-3, Terezie-2, František-1) was born on 09 May 1954 in Liberec.

Miroslav Heralecký son of Miroslav Heralecký and Marie Bartošová was born on 18 May 1949 in salomonJablonec nad Nisou, Czech.. He died on 20 Feb 2017 in Proseč, Jablonec nad Nisou, Czech..

Miroslav Heralecký and Marcela Žďárská were married on 15 Mar 1975 in Sychrov. They had the following children:

> **Vit Heralecký** was born on 16 Jan 1977 in Jablonec nad Nisou. He married Olga Zrubcová on 13 Jul 1996.

ii. **Zuzana Heralecká** was born on 30 Dec 1978 in Jablonec nad Nisou. She married Jaroslav Egrt on 13 Sep 2002 in Jablonec nad Nisou.

Iveta Žďárská-8 (Marta-7, Miloslav-6, Adolf-5, Petr-4, Františka-3, Terezie-2, František-1) was born on 29 Aug 1963 in Liberec, Bohemia.

Vlastimil Berkman was born in 1957.

Vlastimil Berkman and Iveta Žďárská were married on 29 Oct 1983. They had the following children:

    Tereza Hriníková was born on 05 Jun 1984 in Jablonec nad Nisou.

Jaroslav Hrinik son of Jaroslav Hrinik and Milena Preisslerová was born on 17 Apr 1960.

Jaroslav Hrinik and Iveta Žďárská were married on 16 Aug 1991 in Zamek Červená Lhota. They had the following children:

    Eliška Hriníková was born on 23 Jun 1992 in Jablonec nad Nisou. She married Jan Ottis on 06 Oct 2018 in Jablonec nad Jizerou, East Bohemia, Czech Republic.

Iveta Vichova-8 (Libuše-7, Stanislav Josef-6, Adolf-5, Petr-4, Františka-3, Terezie-2, František-1) was born on 15 Jan 1972 in Jičín.

Miloš Haltuf was born on 03 May 1968 in Chlumec.

Miloš Haltuf and Iveta Vichova were married on 07 Sep 1991 in Lazne Belohrad, Jičín Co.. They had the following children:

    Jan Haltuf was born on 10 Mar 1992 in Hořice, Jičín Co..

Stanislava Rechcíglová-8 (Stanislav-7, Stanislav Josef-6, Adolf-5, Petr-4, Františka-3, Terezie-2, František-1) was born on 22 Sep 1972 in Hořice, Jičín Dist., Bohemia.

Josef Bekera was born on 22 Jun 1965.

Josef Bekera and Stanislava Rechcíglová met. They had the following children:

    Nikolas Bekera was born on 23 Sep 2001.
    Sebestian Bekera.
    Anastasia Jowefa Bekerová.

Jana Rechcíglová-8 (Stanislav-7, Stanislav Josef-6, Adolf-5, Petr-4, Františka-3, Terezie-2, František-1) was born on 22 Sep 1973 in Hořice, Jičín Co..
Karel Spidlen was born on 06 Feb 1972 in Hradec Králové.
Karel Spidlen and Jana Rechcíglová were married on 29 Apr 1995 in Jičín, Bohemia. They had the following children:
> **Karel Spidlen** was born on 15 Oct 1995 in Hořice, Jičín Co..

Stanislav Rechcigl-8 (Stanislav-7, Stanislav Josef-6, Adolf-5, Petr-4, Františka-3, Terezie-2, František-1) was born on 08 Aug 1975 in Hořice, Jičín Dist., Bohemia.
Natasha Blackbourn.
Stanislav Rechcigl and Natasha Blackbourn were married on 19 Jul 2008 in Spalding, Lincolnshire, UK.. They had the following children:
> **Lily-Grace Rechcíglová** was born on 03 Jul 2011 in Watford, UK.
>
> **Poppy Sophia Rechcíglová** was born on 13 Oct 2013.

Věra Křikavová-8 (Luděk-7, Božena-6, Zdeněk Petr-5, Petr-4, Františka-3, Terezie-2, František-1) was born on 28 Apr 1966 in Komarov u Horovic No. 40.
Radek Nešpor was born on 24 Mar 1963 in Horovice.
Radek Nešpor and Věra Křikavová married. They had the following children:
> **David Nešpor** was born on 19 Oct 1987 in Komarov u Horovic No. 40.

Hanna Křikavová-8 (Luděk-7, Božena-6, Zdeněk Petr-5, Petr-4, Františka-3, Terezie-2, František-1) was born on 07 May 1957 in Komarov u Horovic No. 40. She died on 30 Dec 1997.
Bedřich Mach was born on 13 Feb 1955 in Komarov u Horovic No. 40. Bedřich Mach and Hanna Křikavová married. They had the following children:
> i. **Andrea Machová** was born on 10 Mar 1978 in Komarov u Horovic No. 40.

Jan Křikava-8 (Luděk-7, Božena-6, Zdeněk Petr-5, Petr-4, Františka-3, Terezie-2, František-1) was born on 19 Aug 1960 in Komarov u Horovic No. 40.

Hana Fedorcaková was born on 05 May 1962 in Kvan near Komarov.

Jan Křikava and Hana Fedorcaková married. They had the following children:

    i.   **Jan Křikava** was born on 22 Sep 1983 in Komarov u Horovic No. 40.

Jana Linhartova was born on 14 Feb 1973 in Komarov u Horovic.

Jan Křikava and Jana Linhartova met. They had the following children:

    Johana Křikavová was born on 27 Nov 2007 in Komarov u Horovic.

Hana Křikavová-8 (Sasa-7, Božena-6, Zdeněk Petr-5, Petr-4, Františka-3, Terezie-2, František-1) was born in 1958 in Komarov u Horovic.

Milan Němec was born in 1954 in Komarov u Horovic.

Milan Němec and Hana Křikavová married. They had the following children:

    Milan Němec was born in 1978 in Komarov u Horovic.

    Lubor Němec was born in 1971 in Komarov u Horovic.

Jana Petrová-8 (Zdena-7, Zdena-6, Zdeněk Petr-5, Petr-4, Františka-3, Terezie-2, František-1) was born on 29 Jun 1984 in Karlovy Vary.

Petr Kottnauer.

Petr Kottnauer and Jana Petrová met. They had the following children:

    Daniel Kottnauer was born in Karlovy Vary.

Petr Herák-8 (Radmila-7, Zdeněk-6, Bohumil-5, Petr-4, Františka-3, Terezie-2, František-1) was born on 03 Jun 1965.

Tereza Kovářová was born on 22 Jul 1973 in Jablonec.

Petr Herák and Tereza Kovářová were married on 24 Mar 1990 in Český Dub. They had the following children:

    Jan Herák was born on 11 Sep 1990.

    Krystyna Heráková was born on 18 Feb 1997.

Pavlina Heráková-8 (Radmila-7, Zdeněk-6, Bohumil-5, Petr-4, Františka-3, Terezie-2, František-1) was born on 29 Jan 1964.

Milan Podlipský was born on 11 Mar 1961.

Milan Podlipský and Pavlina Heráková were married on 11 Feb 1984 in Milevsko. They had the following children:

Milan Podlipský was born on 22 Jun 1984.

Jakub Podlipský was born on 19 Mar 1986.

Helena Heráková-8 (Radmila-7, Zdeněk-6, Bohumil-5, Petr-4, Františka-3, Terezie-2, František-1) was born on 12 Jul 1966.

Pavel Hudec was born on 01 Jan 1962 in Český Dub.

Pavel Hudec and Helena Heráková were married on 15 Sep 1984 in Český Dub. They had the following children:

>Kateřina Hudcova was born on 17 Feb 1985.
>
>Martina Hudcova was born on 12 May 1991.

Martin Rechcigl-8 (Zdeněk-7, Zdeněk-6, Bohumil-5, Petr-4, Františka-3, Terezie-2, František-1) was born on 16 Dec 1968.

Petra Smolakova was born on 25 Jan 1973 in Moravia.

Martin Rechcigl and Petra Smolakova were married on 17 Sep 1994 in Český Dub. They had the following children:

>Lucie Rechcíglová was born on 05 Apr 1995.
>
>David Rechcigl was born on 08 Aug 2000.

Jan Kvapil-8 (Jan-7, Jana-6, Anastazie-5, Václav-4, Františka-3, Terezie-2, František-1) was born on Dec 1963 in Pardubice.

Iveta Kulichova was born on 18 Jan 1969.

Jan Kvapil and Iveta Kulichova were married on 31 Jan 1987 in Lazne Bohdanec. They had the following children:

>Lucie Kvapilová was born on 09 Jul 1987 in Pardubice.
>
>Pavlina Kvapilová was born on 05 Sep 1991 in Pardubice.
>
>Iveta Kvapilová was born on 15 Jul 1993 in Pardubice.

Jaroslav Kvapil-8 (Jan-7, Jana-6, Anastazie-5, Václav-4, Františka-3, Terezie-2, František-1) was born on 26 Feb 1969 in Pardubice.

Eva Kadlecova was born on 05 Sep 1969.

Jaroslav Kvapil and Eva Kadlecova were married on 30 Nov 1991 in Lazne Bohdanec. They had the following children:

>Katerina Kvapilová was born on 21 May 1992 in Pardubice.
>
>Monika Kvapilová was born on 19 Oct 1998 in Pardubice.
>
>Jakub Kvapil was born on 05 May 2005 in Pardubice.

Eva Kvapilová-8 (Jan-7, Jana-6, Anastazie-5, Václav-4, Františka-3, Terezie-2, František-1) was born on 18 Oct 1973 in Pardubice.

Tomasz Prcz was born on 23 May 1970.

Tomasz Prcz and Eva Kvapilová were married on 18 May 1996 in Lazne Bohdanec. They had the following children:

>**Martin Prcz** was born on 19 May 1991 in Pardubice.
>
>**Tomasz Prcz** was born on 05 Oct 1997 in Pardubice.

Jiri Kvapil-8 (Jan-7, Jana-6, Anastazie-5, Václav-4, Františka-3, Terezie-2, František-1) was born on Jan 1980 in Pardubice.

Zuzana Tomanová was born on 20 Aug 1980.

Jiri Kvapil and Zuzana Tomanová were married on 13 Aug 2005 in Lazne Bohdanec. They had the following children:

>**Tereza Kvapilová** was born on 25 Dec 2006 in Pardubice.
>
>**Jiri Kvapil** was born on 07 Sep 2009 in Pardubice.

Petra Virtova-8 (Nada-7, Jana-6, Anastazie-5, Václav-4, Františka-3, Terezie-2, František-1) was born on 17 Aug 1976 in Pardubice.

Tomáš Tupy was born on 24 Aug 1975 in Pardubice.

Tomáš Tupy and Petra Virtova were married on 25 Aug 2000. They had the following children:

>**Krystyna Tupa** was born on 27 Feb 2001.
>
>**Aneta Tupa** was born on 21 Apr 2006.

Generation 9

Kevin Thomas Rechcigl-9 (John Edward-8, Mila (Miloslav)-7, Miloslav-6, Adolf-5, Petr-4, Františka-3, Terezie-2, František-1) was born on 09 Oct 1991 in Bradenton, FL.

Jordan Robbins daughter of Douglass Robbins and Ivonne was born on 10 Jan 1992 in Camarillo, CA.

Kevin Thomas Rechcigl and Jordan Robbins were married on 12 May 2018 in Jacksonville, FL. They had the following children:

>**James Douglas Rechcigl** was born on 05 Jan 2021 in Jacksonville, FL.
>
>**Evelyn Marie Rechcigl** was born 29 May 2023 in Jacksonville, FL.

Zuzana Heralecká-9 (Marcela-8, Marta-7, Miloslav-6, Adolf-5, Petr-4, Františka-3, Terezie-2, František-1) was born on 30 Dec 1978 in Jablonec nad Nisou.

Jaroslav Egrt was born on 25 Apr 1974 in Duchcov.

Jaroslav Egrt and Zuzana Heralecká were married on 13 Sep 2002 in Jablonec nad Nisou. They had the following children:

>**Kristina Egrtova** was born on 04 Jan 2008 in Liberec.
>
>**Jaroslav Egrt** was born on 04 Jan 2008 in Liberec.

Andrea Machová-9 (Hanna-8, Luděk-7, Božena-6, Zdeněk Petr-5, Petr-4, Františka-3, Terezie-2, František-1) was born on 10 Mar 1978 in Komarov u Horovic No. 40.

Soeren Christiansen was born in 1975 in Denmark.

Soeren Christiansen and Andrea Machová met. They had the following children:

>**Olivia Machová** was born on 10 May 2007 in Kobenhaven, Denmark.

B. Mila Rechcigl's Mother Side

Rajtr Family

Generation 1

1. **Jakub Rajtr**-1. He died in 1688 (Zvířetice).
   Magdalena.
   Jakub Rajtr and Magdalena married. They had the following children:
   2. i. **Václav Rajtr** was born in 1659. He died on 03 Sep 1739 in Dalešice.

Generation 2

2. **Václav Rajtr**-2 (Jakub-1) was born in 1659. He died on 03 Sep 1739 in Dalešice.
   Alyna was born in 1670. She died on 18 Jan 1733 in Dalešice.
   Václav Rajtr and Alyna married. They had the following children:
   3. i. **Jakub Rajtr** was born in 1701 in Dalešice. He died on 21 Oct 1750 in Zvířetice.

Generation 3

3. **Jakub Rajtr**-3 (Václav-2, Jakub-1) was born in 1701 in Dalešice. He died on 21 Oct 1750 in Zvířetice.
   Marie Rajtrová daughter of Anna.
   Jakub Rajtr and Marie Rajtrová married. They had the following children:
   4. i. **Jiří Rajtr** was born on 16 Apr 1736 in Zvířetice. He died on 30 Jan 1797 in Zvířetice No. 6. He married Kateřina Bylkova on 28 Jan 1806 in Bytouchov No. 9.

   Marie.
   Jakub Rajtr and Marie married. They had the following children:
   25. i. **Jiří Rajtr** was born on 16 Apr 1736 in Zvířetice. He died on 30 Jan 1797 in Zvířetice No. 6. He married Kateřina Bylkova on 28 Jan 1806 in Bytouchov No. 9.

Generation 4

4. **Jiří Rajtr**-4 (Jakub-3, Václav-2, Jakub-1) was born on 16 Apr 1736 in Zvířetice. He died on 30 Jan 1797 in Zvířetice No. 6.
   Kateřina Bylkova daughter of Martin Bylek and Anna was born in 1729. She died on 22 Apr 1797 in Zvířetice No. 6.
   Jiří Rajtr and Kateřina Bylkova were married on 28 Jan 1806 in Bytouchov No. 9. They had the following children:
   - 5. i. **Jan Jri Rajtr** was born on 02 Jan 1758 in Zvířetice. He died on 10 Jan 1799 in Zvířetice No. 11, Mnichovo Hradiště Dist., Bohemia.

   Jiří Rajtr and unknown spouse married. They had the following children:
   - 5. i. **Jan Jri Rajtr** was born on 02 Jan 1758 in Zvířetice. He died on 10 Jan 1799 in Zvířetice No. 11, Mnichovo Hradiště Dist., Bohemia.

Generation 5

5. **Jan Jri Rajtr**-5 (Jiří-4, Jakub-3, Václav-2, Jakub-1) was born on 02 Jan 1758 in Zvířetice. He died on 10 Jan 1799 in Zvířetice No. 11, Mnichovo Hradiště Dist., Bohemia.
   Anna Machackova daughter of Václav Machacek and Alžběta was born in 1758. She died in 1830.
   Jan Jri Rajtr and Anna Machackova married. They had the following children:
   - 6. i. **Václav Rajtr** was born on 15 Sep 1783 in Zvířetice No. 11. He married Dorota Strojsová on 28 Jan 1806 in Bytouchov. He died on 16 Jan 1823 in Zviretic No. 11.

Generation 6

6. **Václav Rajtr**-6 (Jan Jri-5, Jiří-4, Jakub-3, Václav-2, Jakub-1) was born on 15 Sep 1783 in Zvířetice No. 11. He died on 16 Jan 1823 in Zviretic No. 11.
   Dorota Strojsová daughter of Václav Strojsa and Dorota Wondrakova was born on 24 Jan 1780 in Bitouchov No. 5.
   Václav Rajtr and Dorota Strojsová were married on 28 Jan 1806 in Bytouchov. They had the following children:
   - 7. i. **Václav Rajtr** was born on 15 Sep 1783 in Zvířetice No. 11. He died on 16 Jan 1823 in Zvířetice No. 11, Mnichovo Hradiště Dist., Bohemia.
   - ii. **Václav Rajt** was born on 21 Jun 1807 in Zvířetice. He died on 30

Oct 1871 in Zvířetice.

Generation 7

7. **Václav Rajtr**-7 (Václav-6, Jan Jri-5, Jiří-4, Jakub-3, Václav-2, Jakub-1) was born on 15 Sep 1783 in Zvířetice No. 11. He died on 16 Jan 1823 in Zvířetice No. 11, Mnichovo Hradiště Dist., Bohemia.

    Barbora Koštejn daughter of Jan Koštejn and Terezie Pazderníková was born on 25 Dec 1815 in Zviretica. She died on 28 May 1887 in Chudoplesy No. 9.

    Václav Rajtr and Barbora Koštejn married. They had the following children:

    8. i. **Jan Václav Rajtr** was born on 12 May 1847 in Zvířetice No. 11, Mnichovo Hradiště Co.. He married Anna Najmanová on 09 Jun 1868. He died on 19 Sep 1903 in Dolanky No. 7.

    ii. **Marie Rajtrová** was born on 16 Jun 1849.

    iii. **Václav Rajtr** was born on 13 Nov 1857. He died on 16 Nov 1857.

    iv. **Josef Rajtr** was born on 11 Jun 1858. He died on 12 Jun 1858.

Generation 8

8. **Jan Václav Rajtr**-8 (Václav-7, Václav-6, Jan Jri-5, Jiří-4, Jakub-3, Václav-2, Jakub-1) was born on 12 May 1847 in Zvířetice No. 11, Mnichovo Hradiště Co.. He died on 19 Sep 1903 in Dolanky No. 7.

    Anna Najmanová daughter of Josef Najman and Alžběta Bartonova was born on 26 Dec 1841 in Dolanky No. 7, Mnichovo Hradiště Co.. She died on 05 Aug 1900 in Dolanky, Mnichovo Hradiště Co.. Jan Václav Rajtr and Anna Najmanová were married on 09 Jun 1868. They had the following children:

    i. **Vincenc Rajtr** was born on 08 Apr 1871 in Dolanky No. 7. He died on 03 Oct 1871.

    ii. **Václav Rajtr** was born on 22 Dec 1872 in Dolanky No. 7. He died on 11 Feb 1873 in Dolanky No. 7.

    10. iii. **Čeněk Rajtr**[1] was born on 01 Jul 1874 in nky No. 7, Mnichovo Hradiště Dist... He married Marie Dandová on 02 Jul 1904 in Mnichovo Hradiště. He died on 27 Oct 1956 in Dolánky No. 7, Mnichovo Hradiště Dist...

11. iv. **Anna Rajtrová** was born on 10 May 1876 in Dolanky No. 7. She died in Jan 1946 in Muzsky No. 19, Mnichovo Hradiště, Co..
12. v. **Rudolf Rajtr** was born on 15 Nov 1881 in Dolanky No. 7. He died in Mar 1953 in Muzsky No. 6.
13. vi. **Josef Rajtr** was born about 1882 in Dolanky No. 7, Mnichovo Hradiště Cco..

Generation 9

9. **Čeněk Rajtr**-9 (Jan Václav-8, Václav-7, Václav-6, Jan Jri-5, Jiří-4, Jakub-3, Václav-2, Jakub-1)[1] was born on 01 Jul 1874 in nky No. 7, Mnichovo Hradiště Dist... He died on 27 Oct 1956 in Dolánky No. 7, Mnichovo Hradiště Dist...

    Marie Dandová daughter of František Antonín Danda and Josefa Cimrová[2] was born on 31 Jan 1882 in Hoškovice, No. 14, Mnichovo Hradiště Dist, Bohemia. She died on 05 Jul 1967 in Dolanky No. 7, Mnichovo Hradiště Co..

    Čeněk Rajtr and Marie Dandová were married on 02 Jul 1904 in Mnichovo Hradiště. They had the following children:

    13. i. **Marie Rajtrová** was born on 05 Jul 1905 in Dolanky No. 7, Mnichovo Hradiště Co.. She married Miloslav Rechcigl on 26 Jul 1926 in Praha - Kralovske Vinohrady. She died on 13 Apr 1982 in Mladá Boleslav.
    ii. **Oldrřch Rajtr** was born on 14 Nov 1907 in Dolanky No. 7. He died on 02 Nov 1937.
    14. iii. **Marta Rajtrová** was born on 10 Jan 1909 in Dolanky u Bakova. She married Josef Knotek in 1934. She died on 29 Nov 1982 in Mladá Boleslav.

10. **Anna Rajtrová**-9 (Jan Václav-8, Václav-7, Václav-6, Jan Jri-5, Jiří-4, Jakub-3, Václav-2, Jakub-1) was born on 10 May 1876 in Dolanky No. 7. She died in Jan 1946 in Muzsky No. 19, Mnichovo Hradiště, Co..

    Václav Brzohohaty was born about 1870 in Muzsky No. 8, Mnichovo Hradiště Co.. He died in 1918 in Muzsky No. 8, Mnichovo Hradiště Co..

    Václav Brzohohaty and Anna Rajtrová married. They had the following children:

15. i. **Marie Brzobohatá** was born on 18 Dec 1900 in Muzsky No. 8, Mnichovo Hradiště Co.. She died on 21 Sep 1969 in Liberec.
16. ii. **Václav Brzobohatý** was born on 25 Aug 1902 in Muzsky No. 8, Mnichovo Hradiště Co.. He married Julie Kolomaznikova on 17 Nov 1928 in Mnichovo Hradiště. He died on 28 Jul 1974 in Mladá Boleslav.
    iii. **Bohumil Brzobohatý** was born about 1904 in Muzsky No. 8, Mnichovo Hradiště Co.. He died in 1930 in Muzsky No. 8, Mnichovo Hradiště Co..
17. iv. **Božena Brzobohatá** was born on 22 Jul 1906 in Muzsky No. 8, Mnichovo Hradiště Co.. She died on 02 Apr 1989.

11. **Rudolf Rajtr**-9 (Jan Václav-8, Václav-7, Václav-6, Jan Jri-5, Jiří-4, Jakub-3, Václav-2, Jakub-1) was born on 15 Nov 1881 in Dolanky No. 7. He died in Mar 1953 in Muzsky No. 6.

    Božena Maděrová was born in Muzsky. She died on 04 Dec 1964 in Muzsky. Rudolf Rajtr and Božena Maděrová married. They had the following children:

    18. i. **Josef Rajtr** was born on 27 Apr 1911 in Muzsky No. 6, Mnichovo Hradiště Co.. He died on 22 Mar 1978 in Liberec. He married Marie Janoušková on 27 Oct.
    19. ii. **Václav Rajtr** was born on 13 Jun 1912 in Muzsky No. 6, Mnichovo Hradiště Co.. He married Jarmila Maděrová on 10 Nov 1940 in Farni urad Bosen. He died on 12 Mar 1989 in Muzsky.
        iii. **Božena Rajtrová** was born after 1912 in Muzsky No. 6, Mnichovo Hradiště Co.. She died in Drowned aet. 8 years old.

12. **Josef Rajtr**-9 (Jan Václav-8, Václav-7, Václav-6, Jan Jri-5, Jiří-4, Jakub-3, Václav-2, Jakub-1) was born about 1882 in Dolanky No. 7, Mnichovo Hradiště Cco..

    Františka Kobosilova was born after 1880 in Prepere No. 15, Turnov Co.. Josef Rajtr and Františka Kobosilova married. They had the following children:

    20. i. **Josef Rajtr** was born on 30 Jun 1902 in Prepere No. 15, Turnov Co.. He married Zdenka Karlasova on 02 Nov 1924 in Turnov. He died on

09 Jul 1978 in Prepere No. 15, Turnov Co..

13. ii. **Marie Rajtrová** was born on 05 Jul 1905 in Dolanky No. 7, Mnichovo Hradiště Co.. She married Miloslav Rechcigl on 26 Jul 1926 in Praha - Kralovske Vinohrady. She died on 13 Apr 1982 in Mladá Boleslav.

Generation 10

13. **Marie Rajtrová**-10 (Čeněk-9, Jan Václav-8, Václav-7, Václav-6, Jan Jri-5, Jiří-4, Jakub-3, Václav-2, Jakub-1) was born on 05 Jul 1905 in Dolanky No. 7, Mnichovo Hradiště Co.. She died on 13 Apr 1982 in Mladá Boleslav.

    Miloslav Rechcigl son of Adolf Rechcigl and Marie Berglová was born on 13 May 1904 in Kocňovice (renamed Chocnějovice) No. 22. He died on 27 May 1973 in Washington, DC.

    Miloslav Rechcigl and Marie Rajtrová were married on 26 Jul 1926 in Praha - Kralovske Vinohrady. They had the following children:

    21. i. **Mila (Miloslav) Rechcigl Jr.** was born on 30 Jul 1930 in Mladá Boleslav, CSR. He married Eva Edwards (Eisnerová) on 29 Aug 1953 in New York, NY.

    22. ii. **Marta Rechcíglová** was born on 23 May 1933 in Mladá Boleslav. She married František Žďárský on 03 Oct 1953 in Mladá Boleslav. She died on 13 Sep 2018 in Mladá Boleslav.

14. **Marta Rajtrová**-10 (Čeněk-9, Jan Václav-8, Václav-7, Václav-6, Jan Jri-5, Jiří-4, Jakub-3, Václav-2, Jakub-1) was born on 10 Jan 1909 in Dolanky u Bakova. She died on 29 Nov 1982 in Mladá Boleslav.

    Josef Knotek was born between 1905-1907 in Mala Bela, p. Bakov nad Jizerou. He died in 1934.

    Josef Knotek and Marta Rajtrová were married in 1934. They had no children.

    Miroslav Koubik son of Koubik was born in 1908 in Terezin. He died in 1968 in Havlickuv Brod.

    Miroslav Koubik and Marta Rajtrová were married on 26 Jul 1938 in Praha. They had the following children:

    23. i. **Jiří Koubik** was born on 29 Jan 1940 in Prague. He married Jiřina Muellerová on 31 Jan 1962 in Praha. He died on 26 Jun 1998 in

Brandys nad Labem.

Emil Pazderník was born after 1900.

Emil Pazderník and Marta Rajtrová were married after 1945. They had no children.

Karel Horáček.

Karel Horáček and Marta Rajtrová met. They had no children.

15. **Marie Brzobohatá**-10 (Anna-9, Jan Václav-8, Václav-7, Václav-6, Jan Jri-5, Jiří-4, Jakub-3, Václav-2, Jakub-1) was born on 18 Dec 1900 in Muzsky No. 8, Mnichovo Hradiště Co.. She died on 21 Sep 1969 in Liberec.

    Václav Krausner was born on 19 Feb 1900 in Pribyslavice No. 4, Turnov Co.. He died on 08 Mar 1979 in Liberec.

    Václav Krausner and Marie Brzobohatá married. They had the following children:

    24. i. **Olga Krausnerova** was born on 24 Apr 1933 in Pribyslavice No. 4, Turnov Co.. She married Miloslav Rajtr on 16 Jan 1954 in Selibice.

    25. ii. **Milena Krausnerova** was born on 15 Dec 1931 in Pribyslavice No. 4, Turnov Co.. She married Jaroslav Pabišta on 06 Dec 1952 in Vselibice.

16. **Václav Brzobohatý**-10 (Anna-9, Jan Václav-8, Václav-7, Václav-6, Jan Jri-5, Jiří-4, Jakub-3, Václav-2, Jakub-1) was born on 25 Aug 1902 in Muzsky No. 8, Mnichovo Hradiště Co.. He died on 28 Jul 1974 in Mladá Boleslav.

    Julie Kolomaznikova was born on 17 Feb 1906 in Rostkov, Mnichovo Hradiště Co.. She died on 04 Apr 1975 in Kosmonosy.

    Václav Brzobohatý and Julie Kolomaznikova were married on 17 Nov 1928 in Mnichovo Hradiště. They had the following children:

    26. i. **Jaroslava Brzobohatá** was born on 06 Feb 1929 in Muzsky No. 8, Mnichovo Hradiště Co.. She married Václav Huňát on 03 Feb 1951 in MnV Knezmost, Mladá Boleslav Co..

    27. ii. **Hana Brzobohatá** was born on 28 Feb 1930 in Muzsky No. 8. Mnichovo Hradiště Co.. She married Stanislav Pic on 29 Jan 1949 in Farni urad Bosen.

        iii. **Václav Brzobohatý** was born on 10 Dec 1944 in Muzsky No. 8, Mnichovo Hradiště Co.. He died in Mar 1946 in Turnov.

17. **Božena Brzobohatá**-10 (Anna-9, Jan Václav-8, Václav-7, Václav-6, Jan Jri-5, Jiří-4, Jakub-3, Václav-2, Jakub-1) was born on 22 Jul 1906 in Muzsky No. 8, Mnichovo Hradiště Co.. She died on 02 Apr 1989.
    František Příhoda was born in Příšovice.
    František Příhoda and Božena Brzobohatá married. They had the following children:
    28. i. **Luboš Příhoda** was born in 1928.
    František Košek was born on 01 Nov 1904 in Borovice, Mnichovo Hradiště Co.. He died on 25 Jan 1968 in Licenice, Litomerice Co..
    František Košek and Božena Brzobohatá were married in 1936 in Listopec. They had the following children:
    29. i. **Danuse Koskova** was born on 19 Dec 1937 in Horka u Bakova. She married Victor Svoboda on 01 Mar 1958 in Ustek, Litomerice Co..
18. **Josef Rajtr**-10 (Rudolf-9, Jan Václav-8, Václav-7, Václav-6, Jan Jri-5, Jiří-4, Jakub-3, Václav-2, Jakub-1) was born on 27 Apr 1911 in Muzsky No. 6, Mnichovo Hradiště Co.. He died on 22 Mar 1978 in Liberec.
    Marie Janoušková was born on 22 Feb 1915 in Dolni Bukovina, Mnichovo Hradiště Co.. She died on Dec 1973 in Liberec.
    Josef Rajtr and Marie Janoušková were married on 27 Oct. They had the following children:
    30. i. **Marie Rajtrová** was born on 19 Sep 1941 in Knezmost, Mnichovo Hradiště Co.. She married Zdeněk Kilian on 05 Jul 1969 in Praha.
    31. ii. **Josef Rajtr** was born on 30 May 1947 in Nova Ves u Branzeze, Mladá Boleslav Co.. He married Helena Klimesova on 06 Apr 1974 in Sychrov.
19. **Václav Rajtr**-10 (Rudolf-9, Jan Václav-8, Václav-7, Václav-6, Jan Jri-5, Jiří-4, Jakub-3, Václav-2, Jakub-1) was born on 13 Jun 1912 in Muzsky No. 6, Mnichovo Hradiště Co.. He died on 12 Mar 1989 in Muzsky.
    Jarmila Maděrová was born on 18 Jun 1920 in Muzsky. She died on 09 Feb 2002 in Kosmonosy.
    Václav Rajtr and Jarmila Maděrová were married on 10 Nov 1940 in Farni urad Bosen. They had the following children:
    32. i. **Václav Rajtr** was born on 02 Feb 1942 in Muzsky No. 6, Mnichovo

Hradiště Co.. He married Jana Karaskova on 17 Apr 1965 in Rakovnik.
33. ii. **Věra Rajtrová** was born on 19 Feb 1947 in Muzsky No. 6, Mnichovo Hradiště Co.. She married Jaroslav Verner on 08 Jan 1966 in Mnichovo Hradiště.

20. **Josef Rajtr**-10 (Josef-9, Jan Václav-8, Václav-7, Václav-6, Jan Jri-5, Jiří-4, Jakub-3, Václav-2, Jakub-1) was born on 30 Jun 1902 in Prepere No. 15, Turnov Co.. He died on 09 Jul 1978 in Prepere No. 15, Turnov Co..

    Zdenka Karlasova was born on 23 Oct 1901 in Sekyrkovy Loucky. She died on 09 Jan 1978 in Prepere No. 15.

    Josef Rajtr and Zdenka Karlasova were married on 02 Nov 1924 in Turnov. They had the following children:
    i. **Josef Rajtr** was born after 1920 in Prepere No. 15. He died after 1920 in Prepere No. 15.
    ii. **František Rajtr** was born after 1920 in Prepere No. 15. He died after 1920.

Generation 11

21. **Mila (Miloslav) Rechcigl Jr.**-11 (Marie-10, Čeněk-9, Jan Václav-8, Václav-7, Václav-6, Jan Jri-5, Jiří-4, Jakub-3, Václav-2, Jakub-1) was born on 30 Jul 1930 in Mladá Boleslav, CSR.

    Eva Edwards (Eisnerová) daughter of Paul J. Edwards (Pavel Eisner) and Jiřina Taussigová was born on 21 Jan 1932 in Prague, CSR.

    Mila (Miloslav) Rechcigl Jr. and Eva Edwards (Eisnerová) were married on 29 Aug 1953 in New York, NY. They had the following children:
    i. **John Edward Rechcigl** was born on 27 Feb 1960 in Washington, D.C.. He married Nancy Ann Palko on 30 Jul 1983 in Dover, NJ.
    ii. **Karen Rechcigl** was born on 16 Apr 1962 in Washington, DC. She married Ulysses Kollecas on 25 Aug 1990 in Bethesda, MD.

22. **Marta Rechcíglová**-11 (Marie-10, Čeněk-9, Jan Václav-8, Václav-7, Václav-6, Jan Jri-5, Jiří-4, Jakub-3, Václav-2, Jakub-1) was born on 23 May 1933 in Mladá Boleslav. She died on 13 Sep 2018 in Mladá Boleslav.

    František Žďárský son of František Václav Žďárský and Eliška Foltýnová was born on 21 May 1932 in Turnov.

    František Žďárský and Marta Rechcíglová were married on 03 Oct 1953

in Mladá Boleslav. They had the following children:
   i. **Marcela Žďárská** was born on 09 May 1954 in Liberec. She married Miroslav Heralecký on 15 Mar 1975 in Sychrov.
   ii. **Iveta Žďárská** was born on 29 Aug 1963 in Liberec, Bohemia. She married Vlastimil Berkman on 29 Oct 1983.
23. **Jiří Koubik**-11 (Marta-10, Čeněk-9, Jan Václav-8, Václav-7, Václav-6, Jan Jri-5, Jiří-4, Jakub-3, Václav-2, Jakub-1) was born on 29 Jan 1940 in Prague. He died on 26 Jun 1998 in Brandys nad Labem.
    Jiřina Muellerová was born on 27 Feb 1943 in Buda.
    Jiří Koubik and Jiřina Muellerová were married on 31 Jan 1962 in Praha. They had the following children:
    i. **Marta Koubikova** was born on 04 Jul 1962 in Mladá Boleslav. She married Vladimír Stibor on 17 Apr 1981.
    ii. **2nd Jiří Koubik** was born on 13 May 1965 in Praha. He married Andrea Dunebierová on 04 Apr 1987 in Brandys nad Labem.
24. **Olga Krausnerova**-11 (Marie-10, Anna-9, Jan Václav-8, Václav-7, Václav-6, Jan Jri-5, Jiří-4, Jakub-3, Václav-2, Jakub-1) was born on 24 Apr 1933 in Pribyslavice No. 4, Turnov Co..
    Miloslav Rajtr was born on 21 Apr 1930 in Straziste No. 18, Mnichovo Hradiště Co..
    Miloslav Rajtr and Olga Krausnerova were married on 16 Jan 1954 in Selibice. They had the following children:
    i. **Hana Rajtrová** was born on 02 Aug 1955 in Turnov. She married Milan Ludvik on 26 Mar 1977 in Sychrov.
    ii. **Miroslav Rajtr** was born on 29 Oct 1960 in Mladá Boleslav. He married Zdena Bartošová on 22 Mar 1980 in Český Dub.
25. **Milena Krausnerova**-11 (Marie-10, Anna-9, Jan Václav-8, Václav-7, Václav-6, Jan Jri-5, Jiří-4, Jakub-3, Václav-2, Jakub-1) was born on 15 Dec 1931 in Pribyslavice No. 4, Turnov Co..
    Jaroslav Pabišta was born on 29 Dec 1929 in Budikov.
    Jaroslav Pabišta and Milena Krausnerova were married on 06 Dec 1952 in Vselibice. They had the following children:
    i. **Milena Pabištová** was born on 03 Aug 1955 in Liberec. She

married Jiří Bobek on 24 Aug 1974 in Sychrov.

26. **Jaroslava Brzbohatá**-11 (Václav-10, Anna-9, Jan Václav-8, Václav-7, Václav-6, Jan Jri-5, Jiří-4, Jakub-3, Václav-2, Jakub-1) was born on 06 Feb 1929 in Muzsky No. 8, Mnichovo Hradiště Co..

    Václav Huňát son of Václav Huňát and Božena Červinková was born on 29 Jun 1922 in Ptyrov No. 14, Mnichovo Hradiště Co.. He died on 20 Jul 1982 in Ptyrov No. 14, Mnichovo Hradiště Co..

    Václav Huňát and Jaroslava Brzbohatá were married on 03 Feb 1951 in MnV Knezmost, Mladá Boleslav Co.. They had the following children:

    i. **Hana Huňátová** was born on 01 Feb 1955 in Turnov. She married Milan Lauryn on 12 Jul 1974 in Mnichovo Hradiště.

    ii. **Václav Huňát** was born on 16 Apr 1953 in Turnov. He married Jiřina Durianciková on 26 Nov 1982 in Bakov nad Jizerou.

27. **Hana Brzbohatá**-11 (Václav-10, Anna-9, Jan Václav-8, Václav-7, Václav-6, Jan Jri-5, Jiří-4, Jakub-3, Václav-2, Jakub-1) was born on 28 Feb 1930 in Muzsky No. 8. Mnichovo Hradiště Co..

    Stanislav Pic was born on 07 Jun 1928 in Bycina No. 2 u Knezmosta, Mnichovo Hradiště Co.. He died on 12 Oct 2005 in Praha.

    Stanislav Pic and Hana Brzbohatá were married on 29 Jan 1949 in Farni urad Bosen. They had the following children:

    i. **Stanislav (Pic) Brzbohatý** was born on 26 Dec 1949 in Turnov. He married Jaroslava Hatašová on 17 Dec 1971 in Sychrov.

    ii. **Jiří Pic** was born on 14 Feb 1954 in Turnov. He married Lida Havelková on 22 Apr 1976 in Bakov mad Jizerou.

28. **Luboš Příhoda**-11 (Božena-10, Anna-9, Jan Václav-8, Václav-7, Václav-6, Jan Jri-5, Jiří-4, Jakub-3, Václav-2, Jakub-1) was born in 1928.
    Unknown.
    Luboš Příhoda and Unknown married. They had the following children:

    i. **son Příhoda** was born about 1950.

29. **Danuse Koskova**-11 (Božena-10, Anna-9, Jan Václav-8, Václav-7, Václav-6, Jan Jri-5, Jiří-4, Jakub-3, Václav-2, Jakub-1) was born on 19 Dec 1937 in Horka u Bakova.

    Victor Svoboda was born on 05 Oct 1937 in Brnany, Litomerice Co.. He died on 14 Aug 1985.

Victor Svoboda and Danuse Koskova were married on 01 Mar 1958 in Ustek, Litomerice Co.. They had the following children:

    i. **Danuse Svobodová** was born on 24 Sep 1958 in Litomerice. She married Otakar Gabriel on 15 Jul 1978 in MNV Terezin.

    ii. **Václav Svoboda** was born on 25 Sep 1959 in Litomerice. He married Miroslava Safrová on 21 Jun 1980 in MNV Terezin.

    iii. **Hana Svobodová** was born on 02 Mar 1972 in Litomerice. She married Martin Gaper on 13 Jun 1992 in MNV Terezin.

30. **Marie Rajtrová**-11 (Josef-10, Rudolf-9, Jan Václav-8, Václav-7, Václav-6, Jan Jri-5, Jiří-4, Jakub-3, Václav-2, Jakub-1) was born on 19 Sep 1941 in Knezmost, Mnichovo Hradiště Co..

    Zdeněk Kilian was born on 16 Jan 1929. He died on 30 Aug 1999.

    Zdeněk Kilian and Marie Rajtrová were married on 05 Jul 1969 in Praha. They had the following children:

        i. **Ester Kilianova** was born on 14 Apr 1973 in Jablonec nad Nisou. She married Ivo Srb on 09 Sep 1995 in Liberec.

        ii. **Pavlina Kilianova** was born on 17 Feb 1976.

31. **Josef Rajtr**-11 (Josef-10, Rudolf-9, Jan Václav-8, Václav-7, Václav-6, Jan Jri-5, Jiří-4, Jakub-3, Václav-2, Jakub-1) was born on 30 May 1947 in Nova Ves u Branzeze, Mladá Boleslav Co..

    Helena Klimesova was born on 18 Aug 1951 in Liberec.

    Josef Rajtr and Helena Klimesova were married on 06 Apr 1974 in Sychrov. They had the following children:

        i. **Helena Rajtrová** was born on 02 Feb 1976 in Jablonec nad Nisou.

        ii. **Tomáš Rajtr** was born on 04 Apr 1977 in Liberec.

32. **Václav Rajtr**-11 (Václav-10, Rudolf-9, Jan Václav-8, Václav-7, Václav-6, Jan Jri-5, Jiří-4, Jakub-3, Václav-2, Jakub-1) was born on 02 Feb 1942 in Muzsky No. 6, Mnichovo Hradiště Co..

    Jana Karaskova was born on 11 Feb 1945 in Rakovnik.

    Václav Rajtr and Jana Karaskova were married on 17 Apr 1965 in Rakovnik. They had the following children:

i. **Jana Rajtrová** was born on 14 Apr 1966 in Rakovnik. She married Jaromír Kamenik on 08 Mar 1986 in Rakovnik.

33. **Věra Rajtrová**-11 (Václav-10, Rudolf-9, Jan Václav-8, Václav-7, Václav-6, Jan Jri-5, Jiří-4, Jakub-3, Václav-2, Jakub-1) was born on 19 Feb 1947 in Muzsky No. 6, Mnichovo Hradiště Co..

    Jaroslav Verner was born on 27 Mar 1941 in Knezmost.

    Jaroslav Verner and Věra Rajtrová were married on 08 Jan 1966 in Mnichovo Hradiště. They had the following children:

    i. **Jolana Vernerova** was born on 19 Oct 1967 in Mladá Boleslav. She married Jaroslav Zdobinsky on 15 Sep 1989.
    ii. **Věra Vernerova** was born on 26 Nov 1968 in Knezmost. She married Petr Holas on 24 Apr 1990.

Sources

1   Matrika krestni, Kniha Z, List 65, Krestni a rodny list.
2   Matrika krestni: Hoškovice, Kniha 104, List 172, Krestni a rodny list.

Danda Family

Generation 1

1. **Jan Danda**-1 was born before 1653 in Boseň, Mladá Boleslav District, Central Bohemian Region.
   Salomena.
   Jan Danda and Salomena married. They had the following children:
   2. i. **Jan Danda** was born in 1677 in Boseň, Mladá Boleslav District, Central Bohemian Region. He married Kateřina Berglová on 02 Jun 1721 in Hoškovice, Central Bohemia. He died on 03 Mar 1732 in Hoškovice, Central Bohemia, Czech Republic.

Generation 2

2. **Jan Danda**-2 (Jan-1) was born in 1677 in Boseň, Mladá Boleslav District, Central Bohemian Region. He died on 03 Mar 1732 in Hoškovice, Central Bohemia, Czech Republic.
   Kateřina Berglová daughter of Jakub Bergl and Mandelina was born on 13 Jul 1696 in Chocnějovice, Mladá Boleslav Dist., Central Bohemia. She died on 20 Jan 1746 in Hoškovice, Central Bohemia.
   Jan Danda and Kateřina Berglová were married on 02 Jun 1721 in Hoškovice, Central Bohemia. They had the following children:
   3. i. **Josef Danda** was born on 16 Jun 1722 in Kněžmost, Central Bohemia, Czech Republic. He married Anna Čermáková on 04 Jan 1748 in Kněžmost, Central Bohemia, Czech Republic. He died on 17 Jan 1776 in Hoškovice No. 2,, Central Bohemia, Czech Republic.
   ii. **Adam Danda** was born on 01 Jun 1724 in Kněžmost, Central Bohemia, Czech Republic. He died on 19 Jul 1724 in Kněžmost, Central Bohemia, Czech Republic.
   iii. **Eva Dandová** was born on 11 Dec 1725 in Hoškovice, Mnichovo Hradiště Dist., Bohemia. She died on 09 Apr 1726 in Hoškovice, Mnichovo Hradiště Dist., Bohemia.
   iv. **Lidmila Dandová** was born on 11 Dec 1725 in Hoškovice, Mnichovo Hradiště Dist, Bohemia. She died on 14 Apr 1726 in Hoškovice, Mnichovo Hradiště Dist, Bohemia.

v. **Anna Dandová** was born in 1728. She died on 03 Apr 1729 in Hoškovice, Mnichovo Hradiště Dist., Bohemia.

vi. **Marie Dandová** was born on 07 Jun 1731 in Hoškovice, Mnichovo Hradiště Dist, Bohemia.

Dorothea. She died on 29 Jan 1721 in Kněžmost, Central Bohemia, Czech Republic.

Jan Danda and Dorothea married. They had the following children:

i. **Marie Dandová** was born on 04 Jan 1707 in Kněžmost, Mnichovo Hradiště Co., Bohemia. She died on 23 Feb 1707 in Kněžmost, Mnichovo Hradiště Co., Bohemia.

ii. **Kateřina Dandová** was born on 19 Apr 1708 in Kněžmost, Mnichovo Hradiště Dist., Bohemia.

iii. **Dorothea Dandová** was born on 09 Feb 1712 in Kněžmost, Mnichovo Hradiště Co., Bohemia. She married Václav Mráz on 18 Nov 1736 in Hoškovice, Mnichovo Hradiště Dist, Bohemia.

iv. **Jiří Danda** was born on 15 Dec 1714 in Kněžmost, Mnichovo Hradiště Dist., Bohemia.

v. **Jan Danda** was born on 24 Apr 1718 in Kněžmost, Mnichovo Hradiště Dist., Bohemia.

Generation 3

3. **Josef Danda**-3 (Jan-2, Jan-1) was born on 16 Jun 1722 in Kněžmost, Central Bohemia, Czech Republic. He died on 17 Jan 1776 in Hoškovice No. 2,, Central Bohemia, Czech Republic.

Anna Čermáková daughter of Václav Čermák and Kateřina Koberová was born on 22 Dec 1726 in Kněžmost, Central Bohemia, Czech Republic. She died on 20 Jan 1746 in Hoškovice, Central Bohemia, Czech Republic. Josef Danda and Anna Čermáková were married on 04 Jan 1748 in Kněžmost, Central Bohemia, Czech Republic. They had the following children:

i. **Anna Dandová** was born on 18 Jun 1749 in Hoškovice No. 2, Mnichovo Hradiště Dist, Bohemia.

ii. **Jan Danda** was born on 06 May 1751 in Hoškovice No. 2, Mnichovo Hradiště Dist, Bohemia. He died on 22 Jan 1754 in

Hoškovice No. 2, Mnichovo Hradiště Dist, Bohemia.

    iii. **Alžběta Dandová** was born on 25 Feb 1753 in Hoškovice No. 2, Mnichovo Hradiště Dist, Bohemia. She married Josef Presiler on 06 Jan 1780 in Hoškovice No. 2, Mnichovo Hradiště Dist, Bohemia.

5. iv. **Josef Danda** was born on 08 Feb 1755 in Hoškovice No. 2, Mnichovo Hradiště Dist, Bohemia. He married Kateřina Tondrová on 14 Feb 1779 in Podolí No. 4. He died on 04 Feb 1838 in Hoškovice No. 2, Mnichovo Hradiště Dist, Bohemia.

    v. **Kateřina Dandová** was born on 14 May 1757 in Hoškovice, No. 2, Mnichovo Hradiště Dist, Bohemia. She married Jiří Studničný on 04 Nov 1793 in Hoškovice, No. 2, Mnichovo Hradiště Dist, Bohemia.

    vi. **František Danda** was born on 03 Aug 1759 in Hoškovice No. 2, Mnichovo Hradiště Dist, Bohemia.

    vii. **Jan Danda** was born on 07 Sep 1767 in Hoškovice, No. 2, Mnichovo Hradiště Dist, Bohemia.

Generation 4

4. **Josef Danda**-4 (Josef-3, Jan-2, Jan-1) was born on 08 Feb 1755 in Hoškovice No. 2, Mnichovo Hradiště Dist, Bohemia. He died on 04 Feb 1838 in Hoškovice No. 2, Mnichovo Hradiště Dist, Bohemia.

Kateřina Tondrová daughter of Pavel Tondr and Marie Dneboská was born on 01 Apr 1755 in Podolí. She died on 18 Jan 1808 in Hoškovice No. 25,, Mnichovo Hradiště Dist, Bohemia.

Josef Danda and Kateřina Tondrová were married on 14 Feb 1779 in Podolí No. 4. They had the following children:

    i. **Anna Dandová** was born on 06 Mar 1781 in Hoškovice No. 2, Mnichovo Hradiště Dist, Bohemia. She married Josef Buriánek on 30 Jun 1805 in Hoškovice, No. 2, Mnichovo Hradiště Dist, Bohemia. She died on 16 Jan 1862 in Hoškovice No. 24, Mnichovo Hradiště Dist, Bohemia.

7. ii. **Josef Danda** was born on 11 Jun 1783 in Hoškovice No. 2, Mnichovo Hradiště Dist, Bohemia. He married Barbora Buriánková on 30 Jun

1805 in Hoškovice no. 14, Mnichovo Hradiště Dist, Bohemia. He died on 07 Oct 1847 in Hoškovice No. 2, Mnichovo Hradiště Dist, Bohemia.

8. iii. **František Danda** was born on 26 Aug 1785 in Hoškovice, No. 2, Mnichovo Hradiště Dist, Bohemia. He married Kateřina Tondrová on 08 Oct 1805 in Hoškovice, No. 5, Mnichovo Hradiště Dist, Bohemia. He died on 02 Aug 1871 in Hoškovice, No. 2, Mnichovo Hradiště Dist, Bohemia.

iv. **Kateřina Dandová** was born on 29 May 1788 in Hoškovice, No. 2, Mnichovo Hradiště Dist, Bohemia. She married Jan Buriánek on 08 Oct 1895 in Hoškovice, No. 2, Mnichovo Hradiště Dist, Bohemia.

v. **Marie Dandová** was born on 02 Feb 1791 in Hoškovice No. 2, Mnichovo Hradiště Dist, Bohemia. She married Petr Zámecký on 15 May 1810 in buriankovaHoškovice No. 2, Mnichovo Hradiště Dist, Bohemia.

Generation 5

5. **Josef Danda**-5 (Josef-4, Josef-3, Jan-2, Jan-1) was born on 11 Jun 1783 in Hoškovice No. 2, Mnichovo Hradiště Dist, Bohemia. He died on 07 Oct 1847 in Hoškovice No. 2, Mnichovo Hradiště Dist, Bohemia.

Barbora Buriánková daughter of Václav Buriánek and Kateřina Pryllová was born on 24 Mar 1776 in Hoškovice, Mnichovo Hradiště Co.. Josef Danda and Barbora Buriánková were married on 30 Jun 1805 in Hoškovice no. 14, Mnichovo Hradiště Dist, Bohemia. They had the following children:

i. **Kateřina Dandová** was born on 07 Aug 1806. She married Václav Beran on 11 Feb 1833 in Hoškovice No. 2,, Mnichovo Hradiště Dist, Bohemia.

ii. **Barbora Dandová** was born on 15 Jun 1809 in Hoškovice, No. 2, Mnichovo Hradiště Dist, Bohemia. She died on 04 May 1810 in Hoškovice, No. 2, Mnichovo Hradiště Dist, Bohemia.

iii. **Barbora Dandová** was born on 23 Mar 1811 in Hoškovice No. 2, Mnichovo Hradiště Dist, Bohemia. She married Josef Bajer on 03 Feb 1835 in Hoškovice No. 2,, Mnichovo Hradiště Dist, Bohemia.

8. iv. **Josef Danda** was born on 26 Apr 1813 in Hoškovice No. 2, Mnichovo Hradiště Dist.. He married Marie Wolmanova on 25 Aug 1845 in Mnichovo Hradiště. He died on 02 Apr 1893 in Mnichovoa Hradiště.
   v. **Václav Danda** was born on 15 Jul 1815.
9. vi. **František Danda** was born on 01 Aug 1817 in Hoškovice, Mnichovo Hradiště Dist, Bohemia. He died on 04 Mar 1904 in Podolí No. 8.
10. vii. **František Danda** was born about 1820 in Hoškovice No. 2, Mnichovo Hradiště Co..
11. viii. **Jan Danda.**

6. **František Danda**-5 (Josef-4, Josef-3, Jan-2, Jan-1) was born on 26 Aug 1785 in Hoškovice, No. 2, Mnichovo Hradiště Dist, Bohemia. He died on 02 Aug 1871 in Hoškovice, No. 2, Mnichovo Hradiště Dist, Bohemia. **Kateřina Tondrová** daughter of Jan Tondr and Anna Chlebnová was born on 26 Mar 1788 in Hoškovice, No. 5, Mnichovo Hradiště Dist, Bohemia. She died on 04 Jun 1878 in Hoškovice, No. 5, Mnichovo Hradiště Dist, Bohemia. František Danda and Kateřina Tondrová were married on 08 Oct 1805 in Hoškovice, No. 5, Mnichovo Hradiště Dist, Bohemia. They had the following children:
   i. **Anna Dandová** was born on 08 Sep 1809 in Hoškovice, No. 5, Mnichovo Hradiště Dist, Bohemia. She married Josef Kovář on 12 Jan 1836 in Hoškovice No. 5, Mnichovo Hradiště Dist, Bohemia. She died on 05 Mar 1867 in Jivina No. 6.
12. ii. **Marie Dandová** was born on 01 Feb 1812 in Hoškovice, No. 5, Mnichovo Hradiště Dist, Bohemia. She married Josef Maděra on 22 Feb 1830 in Hoškovice, No. 5, Mnichovo Hradiště Dist, Bohemia.
   iii. **Josef Danda** was born on 04 Feb 1815 in Hoškovice, No. 5, Mnichovo Hradiště Dist, Bohemia. He died on 11 Jan 1818 in Hoškovice, No. 5, Mnichovo Hradiště Dist, Bohemia.
12. iv. **Kateřina Dandová** was born on 18 May 1817 in Hoškovice, No. 5, Mnichovo Hradiště Dist, Bohemia. She married František Dědek in 1837 in Hoškovice, No. 5, Mnichovo Hradiště Dist, Bohemia.
   v. **Václav Danda** was born on 03 Nov 1819 in Hoškovice, No. 5, Mnichovo Hradiště Dist, Bohemia. He died on 04 May 1824 in

Hoškovice, No. 5, Mnichovo Hradiště Dist, Bohemia.

13. vi. **František Danda** was born on 19 Jan 1824 in Hoškovice, No. 5, Mnichovo Hradiště Dist, Bohemia. He married Barbora Holasova on 31 May 1842 in Neveklovice No. 19. He died on 26 Nov 1883 in Hoškovice, No. 5, Mnichovo Hradiště Dist, Bohemia.

vii. **Jan Danda** was born on 10 Jul 1827 in Hoškovice, Mnichovo Hradiště Dist, Bohemia.

Generation 6

7. **Josef Danda**-6 (Josef-5, Josef-4, Josef-3, Jan-2, Jan-1) was born on 26 Apr 1813 in Hoškovice No. 2, Mnichovo Hradiště Dist.. He died on 02 Apr 1893 in Mnichovoa Hradiště.

    Marie Wolmanova daughter of Ferdinand Wolman and Kateřina Václavová was born in Mnichovo Hradiště No. 6.

    Josef Danda and Marie Wolmanova were married on 25 Aug 1845 in Mnichovo Hradiště. They had the following children:

    i. **Josef Ambroz Danda** was born on 07 Dec 1854 in Mnichovo Hradiště No. 341.

    ii. **Václav Josef Danda** was born in 1846 in Mnichovo Hradiště No. 341.

8. **František Danda**-6 (Josef-5, Josef-4, Josef-3, Jan-2, Jan-1) was born on 01 Aug 1817 in Hoškovice, Mnichovo Hradiště Dist, Bohemia. He died on 04 Mar 1904 in Podolí No. 8.

    Kateřina Nováková daughter of Jan Novák and Dorota Reslerová was born on 03 Jun 1826 in Dalešice no. 5. She died on 29 May 1912 in Podolí No. 8.

    František Danda and Kateřina Nováková married. They had the following children:

    i. **Barbora Dandová** was born on 28 Jan 1844 in Hoškovice No. 2, Mnichovo Hradiště Dist, Bohemia. She married Josef Šverma on 27 May 1867 in Hoškovice No. 2, Mnichovo Hradiště Dist, Bohemia.

15. ii. **Josef of Kopeček Danda** was born on 16 Jun 1846 in Hoškovice, Mnichovo Hradiště Dist, Bohemia (moved to Hoškovice No. 13 -

Kopeček). He died on 21 Sep 1847 in Hoškovice, No. 2, Mnichovo Hradiště Dist, Bohemia.

    iii. **Václav Danada** was born on 13 May 1848 in Hoškovice, No. 2, Mnichovo Hradiště Dist, Bohemia. He died on 11 Dec 1917 in Hoškovice, Mnichovo Hradiště Dist, Bohemia.

    iv. **Marie Dandová** was born on 16 Sep 1850 in Hoškovice, No. 2, Mnichovo Hradiště Dist, Bohemia.

    v. **Josef Danda** was born on 23 Aug 1854 in Hoškovice, No. 2, Mnichovo Hradiště Dist, Bohemia.

16. vi. **František Antonín Danda** was born on 10 Jun 1857 in Hoškovice, No. 2, Mnichovo Hradiště Dist, Bohemia. He married Josefa Cimrová on 04 Feb 1881 in Manikovice No. 21. He died on 07 Jun 1900 in Hoškovice, No. 14, Mnichovo Hradiště Dist, Bohemia.

    vii. **Jan Danda** was born on 10 Apr 1860 in Hoškovice, No. 2, Mnichovo Hradiště Dist, Bohemia. He died on 10 Apr 1860 in Hoškovice No. 2,, Mnichovo Hradiště Dist, Bohemia.

    viii. **Kateřina Marie Dandová** was born on 12 Aug 1865 in Hoškovice No. 2,, Mnichovo Hradiště Dist, Bohemia.

    ix. **Antonín Danda** was born on 27 Feb 1868 in Hoškovice, No. 2, Mnichovo Hradiště Dist, Bohemia. He died on 22 Mar 1868.

9. **František Danda**-6 (Josef-5, Josef-4, Josef-3, Jan-2, Jan-1) was born about 1820 in Hoškovice No. 2, Mnichovo Hradiště Co..

Kateřina Nováková daughter of Jan Novák and Dorota Reslová was born in Dalešice No. 5. František Danda and Kateřina Nováková married. They had the following children:

16. i. **Václav Danda** was born on 13 May 1848 in Hoškovice No. 2, Mnichovo Hradiště Dist, Bohemia. He married Marie Štěpánková on 07 Feb 1871 in Dobrá Voda, Bohemia. He died on 11 Dec 1917 in February 7, Hoškovice, Mnichovo Hradiště Dist, Bohemia.

17. ii. **son Danda** was born in Hoškovice 2, Mnichovo Hradiště Co..

18. iii. **Anna Dandová** was born in Hoškovice No. 2,.

19. iv. **Barbora Dandová** was born in Hoškovice No. 2, Mnichovo Hradiště Co..

15. v. **František Antonín Danda** was born on 10 Jun 1857 in Hoškovice, No. 2, Mnichovo Hradiště Dist, Bohemia. He married Josefa Cimrová on 04 Feb 1881 in Manikovice No. 21. He died on 07 Jun 1900 in Hoškovice, No. 14, Mnichovo Hradiště Dist, Bohemia.

10. **Jan Danda**-6 (Josef-5, Josef-4, Josef-3, Jan-2, Jan-1).
    Anna Frydrychova daughter of Jiří Frydrychova and Padlerova.
    Jan Danda and Anna Frydrychova married. They had the following children:
    i. **Kristina Dandová** was born on 19 Apr 1850 in Mnichovo Hradiště No. 208.

11. **Marie Dandová**-6 (František-5, Josef-4, Josef-3, Jan-2, Jan-1) was born on 01 Feb 1812 in Hoškovice, No. 5, Mnichovo Hradiště Dist, Bohemia.
    Josef Maděra was born in Kněžmost No. 58.
    Josef Maděra and Marie Dandová were married on 22 Feb 1830 in Hoškovice, No. 5, Mnichovo Hradiště Dist, Bohemia. They had the following children:
    i. **František Maděra** was born on 02 Mar 1832 in Kněžmost 58, Mnichovo Hradiště Co., Bohemia.
    ii. **Amnna Maria Maděová** was born on 09 Mar 1834 in Kněžmost 58, Mnichovo Hradiště Co., Bohemia.
    iii. **Josef Maděra** was born on 19 Apr 1837 in Kněžmost, Mnichovo Hradiště Dist., Bohemia.
    iv. **Marie Maděrová** was born on 05 Nov 1839 in Kněžmost 58, Mnichovo Hradiště Co., Bohemia.

12. **Kateřina Dandová**-6 (František-5, Josef-4, Josef-3, Jan-2, Jan-1) was born on 18 May 1817 in Hoškovice, No. 5, Mnichovo Hradiště Dist, Bohemia.
    František Dědek was born in 1813 in Veselá.
    František Dědek and Kateřina Dandová were married in 1837 in Hoškovice, No. 5, Mnichovo Hradiště Dist, Bohemia. They had the following children:
    i. **Marie Dědková**.

13. **František Danda**-6 (František-5, Josef-4, Josef-3, Jan-2, Jan-1) was born on 19 Jan 1824 in Hoškovice, No. 5, Mnichovo Hradiště Dist, Bohemia. He

died on 26 Nov 1883 in Hoškovice, No. 5, Mnichovo Hradiště Dist, Bohemia.

Barbora Holasova daughter of Václav Holas and Barbora Černá was born on 27 Apr 1818 in Neveklovice, Mukařov. She died on 29 Jun 1865 in Hoškovice, No. 5, Mnichovo Hradiště Dist, Bohemia.

František Danda and Barbora Holasova were married on 31 May 1842 in Neveklovice No. 19. They had the following children:

20. i. **Anna Dandová** was born on 29 May 1843 in Hoškovice No. 5, Mnichovo Hradiště Dist, Bohemia. She married Jan Šverma on 30 Jan 1866 in Hoškovice, Mnichovo Hradiště Dist, Bohemia. She died on 22 Jul 1897.

    ii. **Kateřina Dandová** was born on 29 Aug 1844 in Hoškovice, Mnichovo Hradiště Dist, Bohemia. She died on 24 Dec 1844 in Hoškovice, Mnichovo Hradiště Dist, Bohemia.

    iii. **Barbora Dandová** was born on 26 Oct 1849 in Hoškovice No. 5, Mnichovo Hradiště Dist, Bohemia. She died on 16 Apr 1850 in Hoškovice No. 5, Mnichovo Hradiště Dist, Bohemia.

21. iv. **František Danda** was born on 02 Nov 1851 in Hoškovice No. 5, Mnichovo Hradiště Dist, Bohemia. He married Marie Šámalová on 24 Oct 1876 in Hoškovice No. 25, Mnichovo Hradiště Dist, Bohemia. He died on 12 May 1929 in Hoškovice No. 25, Mnichovo Hradiště Dist, Bohemia.

14. v. **Josef of Kopeček Danda** was born on 16 Jun 1846 in Hoškovice, Mnichovo Hradiště Dist, Bohemia (moved to Hoškovice No. 13 - Kopeček). He died on 21 Sep 1847 in Hoškovice, No. 2, Mnichovo Hradiště Dist, Bohemia.

Kateřina Horáková was born on 08 Oct 1831 in Dneboh No. 4. She died on 28 Nov 1888 in Dneboh No. 2.

František Danda and Kateřina Horáková were married on 23 Nov 1883 in Hoškovice No. 23,, Mnichovo Hradiště Dist, Bohemia. They had the following children:

   i. **Václav Danda** was born on 01 Jul 1873 in Dneboh No. 2.

Generation 7

14. **Josef of Kopeček Danda**-7 (František-6, Josef-5, Josef-4, Josef-3, Jan-2, Jan-1) was born on 16 Jun 1846 in Hoškovice, Mnichovo Hradiště Dist, Bohemia (moved to Hoškovice No. 13 - Kopeček). He died on 21 Sep 1847 in Hoškovice, No. 2, Mnichovo Hradiště Dist, Bohemia.
    Anna Horáková was born on 01 Jun 1849 in Dneboh No. 2. She died on 27 Apr 1872 in Hoškovice No. 13, Mnichovo Hradiště Dist, Bohemia.
    Josef of Kopeček Danda and Anna Horáková married. They had the following children:
    i. **Barbora Dandová** was born on 21 Jun 1870 in Hoškovice No. 5, Mnichovo Hradiště Dist, Bohemia. She died on 17 Jun 1889 in Hoškovice No. 34, Mnichovo Hradiště Dist, Bohemia.
    ii. **son Danda** was born on 27 Apr 1872 in Hoškovice No. 13, Mnichovo Hradiště Dist, Bohemia. He died on 27 Apr 1872 in Hoškovice No. 13, Mnichovo Hradiště Dist, Bohemia.
    iii. **Barbora Dandová** was born on 21 Jun 1889 in Hoškovice No. 34.

    Josefa Picková was born on 12 Jun 1862 in Mohelnice No. 16. She died after 1900.
    Josef of Kopeček Danda and Josefa Picková were married on 12 Nov 1862 in Mohelnice No. 16. They had the following children:
    i. **František Danda** was born on 25 Sep 1884 in Hoškovice No. 13, Mnichovo Hradiště Dist, Bohemia. He died in Hoškovice, Mnichovo Hradiště Dist, Bohemia.
    ii. **Růžena Josefa Dandová** was born on 17 Mar 1886 in Hoškovice No. 13, Mnichovo Hradiště Dist, Bohemia. She married Gunzel in Zittau, Saxony, Germany.
    iii. **Zdenka Marie Dandová** was born on 14 Sep 1887 in Hoškovice No. 13, Mnichovo Hradiště Dist, Bohemia.
    iv. **Emilie Barbora Dandová** was born on 12 Nov 1889 in Hoškovice No. 13, Mnichovo Hradiště Dist, Bohemia. She died on 04 Dec 1889 in Hoškovice No. 13, Mnichovo Hradiště Dist, Bohemia.
    v. **Bohumil Janda** was born on 08 Feb 1892 in Hoškovice No. 13, Mnichovo Hradiště Dist, Bohemia. He died on 05 Mar 1915 in

Rusko.

22. vi. **Jaroslav Danda** was born on 25 Mar 1895 in Hoškovice No. 13, Mnichovo Hradiště Dist, Bohemia. He married Marie Svobodová on 26 Feb 1929 in Semily. He died in 1956 in Mnichovo Hradište, Central Bohemia, Czech Republic.

   vii. **Miloslav Danda** was born on 27 Jan 1898 in Hoškovice No. 13, Mnichovo Hradiště Dist, Bohemia. He died on 19 Feb 1898 in Hoškovice No. 13, Mnichovo Hradiště Dist, Bohemia.

23. viii. **Miloslav Danda** was born on 20 May 1900 in Hoškovice No. 13, Mnichovo Hradiště Dist, Bohemia. He died on 13 Sep 1952 in Hoškovice No. 13, Mnichovo Hradiště Dist, Bohemia.

   ix. **Božena Dandová**.

Kateřina Horáková was born on 25 Jan 1852 in Dneboh No. 2. She died on 13 Jul 1877 in Hoškovice No. 13, Mnichovo Hradiště Dist, Bohemia. Josef of Kopeček Danda and Kateřina Horáková were married on 26 Nov 1872 in Dneboh No. 2. They had the following children:

   i. **Josef Danda** was born on 29 Dec 1872 in Hoškovice No.13, Mnichovo Hradiště Dist, Bohemia. He died on 02 Jun 1901 in Hoškovice No. 34m Mnichovo Hradiště Dist, Bohemia.

24. ii. **Václav Danda** was born on 10 Sep 1874 in Hoškovice No. 13. He died on 27 Jun 1912 in Dneboh No. 17.

   iii. **Marie Dandová** was born on 13 Oct 1876 in Hoškovice No.13, Mnichovo Hradiště Dist, Bohemia. She died on 19 Jul 1877 in Hoškovice No.13, Mnichovo Hradiště Dist, Bohemia.

Anna Nezdarová daughter of Petr Nezdara and Teresie was born on 20 Oct 1855 in Sovenice No. 1. She died on 02 Jan 1882 in Hoškovice No. 13. Josef of Kopeček Danda and Anna Nezdarová were married on 28 May 1879. They had the following children:

   František Danda was born on 09 Oct 1880 in Hoškovice No. 13, Mnichovo Hradiště Dist, Bohemia. He died on 14 Oct 1880 in Hoškovice No. 13, Mnichovo Hradiště Dist, Bohemia.

   nna Dandová was born on 02 Jan 1882 in Hoškovice No.13, Mnichovo Hradiště Dist, Bohemia. She died on 19 Dec 1882 in Hoškovice No.13, Mnichovo Hradiště Dist, Bohemia.

15. **František Antonín Danda**-7 (František-6, Josef-5, Josef-4, Josef-3, Jan-2, Jan-1) was born on 10 Jun 1857 in Hoškovice, No. 2, Mnichovo Hradiště Dist, Bohemia. He died on 07 Jun 1900 in Hoškovice, No. 14, Mnichovo Hradiště Dist, Bohemia.

Josefa Cimrová daughter of František Cimr and Anna Ferklová was born on 01 Jan 1859 in Manikovice No. 11, Mnichovo Hradiště Dist.. She died on 27 Aug 1923 in Hoškovice No. 14, Mnichovo Hradiště Dist..

František Antonín Danda and Josefa Cimrová were married on 04 Feb 1881 in Manikovice No. 21. They had the following children:

25. i. **Marie Dandová**[1] was born on 31 Jan 1882 in Hoškovice, No. 14, Mnichovo Hradiště Dist, Bohemia. She married Čeněk Rajtr on 02 Jul 1904 in Mnichovo Hradiště. She died on 05 Jul 1967 in Dolanky No. 7, Mnichovo Hradiště Co..

26. ii. **Josef Danda** was born on 30 Jan 1884 in Hoškovice, No. 14, Mnichovo Hradiště Dist, Bohemia. He died on 18 Apr 1936 in Dobrá Voda.

iii. **Josefa Kateřina Dandová** was born on 04 Oct 1885 in Hoškovice No. 14, Mnichovo Hradiště Dist.. She married Václav Balák after 1925.

iv. **Anna Dandová** was born on 12 Nov 1886 in Hoškovice, No. 14, Mnichovo Hradiště Dist, Bohemia. She died on 13 May 1972.

v. **František Danda** was born on 23 Apr 1888 in Hoškovice, No. 14, Mnichovo Hradiště Dist, Bohemia. He died on 27 Jun 1888 in Hoškovice, No. 14, Mnichovo Hradiště Dist, Bohemia.

vi. **František Danda** was born on 13 Nov 1889 in Hoškovice No. 14, Mnichovo Hradiště Dist.. He died on 22 Dec 1891 in Hoškovice no. 14, Mnichovo Hradiště Dist, Bohemia.

vii. **Václav Danda** was born on 05 Sep 1891 in Hoškovice No. 14, Mnichovo Hradiště Dist, Bohemia. He died on 10 Mar 1892 in Hoškovice No. 14, Mnichovo Hradiště Dist, Bohemia.

27. viii. **Emilie Dandová** was born on 22 Oct 1893 in Hoškovice No. 14, Mnichovo Hradiště Dist, Bohemia. She married Václav Balák on 18

Sep 1920 in Hoškovice, Mnichovo Hradiště Dist, Bohemia. She died on 06 Apr 1924 in Hoškovice, Mnichovo Hradiště Dist, Bohemia.

16. **Václav Danda**-7 (František-6, Josef-5, Josef-4, Josef-3, Jan-2, Jan-1) was born on 13 May 1848 in Hoškovice No. 2, Mnichovo Hradiště Dist, Bohemia. He died on 11 Dec 1917 in February 7, Hoškovice, Mnichovo Hradiště Dist, Bohemia.

Marie Štěpánková daughter of Antonín Štěpánek and Anna Koťátková was born on 28 Jun 1847 in Dobrá Voda No.. 10. She died on 16 Apr 1914 in Hoškovice No. 2, Mnichovo Hradiště Dist, Bohemia.

Václav Danda and Marie Štěpánková were married on 07 Feb 1871 in Dobrá Voda, Bohemia. They had the following children:

    28. i. **Anna Dandová** was born on 07 Feb 1872 in Hoškovice No. 2,, Mnichovo Hradiště Dist, Bohemia. She married Václav Šverma on 23 Nov 1897 in Hoškovice No. 10, Mnichovo Hradiště Dist, Bohemia. She died on 31 May 1927.

    ii. **Josef Danda** was born on 17 Mar 1873 in Hoškovice No. 2, Mnichovo Hradiště Dist, Bohemia. He died on 07 Oct 1900 in Hoškovice No. 2, Mnichovo Hradiště Dist, Bohemia.

    29. iii. **Emilie Kateřina Dandová** was born on 17 Feb 1874 in Hoškovice, No. 2, Mnichovo Hradiště Dist, Bohemia. She married František Stejskal on 22 Nov 1904. She died on 28 Apr 1954.

17. **son Danda**-7 (František-6, Josef-5, Josef-4, Josef-3, Jan-2, Jan-1) was born in Hoškovice 2, Mnichovo Hradiště Co..

Unknown.

son Danda and Unknown married. They had the following children:

    i. **daughter Dandová**.

    31. ii. **daughter Dandová**.

18. **Anna Dandová**-7 (František-6, Josef-5, Josef-4, Josef-3, Jan-2, Jan-1) was born in Hoškovice No. 2,.

Červinka was born in Nasldelnice.

Červinka and Anna Dandová married. They had the following children:

    i. **Emilie Červinková**.

19. **Barbora Dandová**-7 (František-6, Josef-5, Josef-4, Josef-3, Jan-2, Jan-1)

was born in Hoškovice No. 2, Mnichovo Hradiště Co..

Barbora Dandová and unknown spouse married. They had the following children:

31. i. **Marie Švermová** was born about 1880.
32. ii. **Antonín Šverma** was born before 1890 in Podolí, Mnichovo Hradiště Co..
33. iii. **František Šverma** was born before 1890.
34. iv. **Václav Šverma** was born before 1890.

20. **Anna Dandová**-7 (František-6, František-5, Josef-4, Josef-3, Jan-2, Jan-1) was born on 29 May 1843 in Hoškovice No. 5, Mnichovo Hradiště Dist, Bohemia. She died on 22 Jul 1897.

    Jan Šverma son of Josef Šverma and Marie Tondrová was born on 17 Jan 1844 in Hoškovice No. 10, Mnichovo Hradiště Dist, Bohemia. He died on 22 Sep 1922 in Hoškovice, Mnichovo Hradiště Dist, Bohemia.

    Jan Šverma and Anna Dandová were married on 30 Jan 1866 in Hoškovice, Mnichovo Hradiště Dist, Bohemia. They had the following children:

    i. **Václav Šverma** was born on 28 Apr 1866 in Hoškovice no. 14, Mnichovo Hradiště Dist, Bohemia.

    ii. **Anna Švermová** was born on 09 Sep 1867 in Hoškovice, Mnichovo Hradiště Dist, Bohemia. She died on 07 Oct 1869.

    iii. **Barbora Švermová** was born on 18 Jan 1869 in Hoškovice, Mnichovo Hradiště Dist, Bohemia. She died on 08 Oct 1869 in Hoškovice, Mnichovo Hradiště Dist, Bohemia.

35. iv. **Václav Šverma** was born on 12 Aug 1870 in Podolí. He married Anna Dandová on 23 Nov 1897 in Hoškovice No. 10, Mnichovo Hradiště Dist, Bohemia. He died on 08 Apr 1943 in Hoškovice No. 10, Mnichovo Hradiště Dist, Bohemia.

    v. **Josef Šverma** was born on 01 Dec 1871 in Hoškovice, Mnichovo Hradiště Dist, Bohemia.

36. vi. **Marie Švermová** was born on 07 Jul 1873 in Hoškovice, Mnichovo Hradiště Dist, Bohemia. She married Pazderník on 01 Feb 1896.

    vii. **Emiilie Švermová** was born on 07 Mar 1875 in Hoškovice,

Mnichovo Hradiště Dist, Bohemia. She married Jan Frydrych on 20 Nov 1897 in Hoškovice, Mnichovo Hradiště Dist, Bohemia.

21. **František Danda**-7 (František-6, František-5, Josef-4, Josef-3, Jan-2, Jan-1) was born on 02 Nov 1851 in Hoškovice No. 5, Mnichovo Hradiště Dist, Bohemia. He died on 12 May 1929 in Hoškovice No. 25, Mnichovo Hradiště Dist, Bohemia.

    Marie Šámalová daughter of Jiří Šámal and Dorota Fidlerová was born on 20 Oct 1854 in Hoškovice No. 25, Mnichovo Hradiště Dist, Bohemia. She died on 03 Mar 1927 in Hoškovice No. 25, Mnichovo Hradiště Dist, Bohemia.

    František Danda and Marie Šámalová were married on 24 Oct 1876 in Hoškovice No. 25, Mnichovo Hradiště Dist, Bohemia. They had the following children:

    37. i. **Bohuslav Jiří Danda** was born on 17 Mar 1875 in Hoškovice No. 25, Mnichovo Hradiště Dist, Bohemia. He died on 13 Aug 1953.

    ii. **Adolf František Danda** was born on 31 May 1878 in Hoškovice No.25, Mnichovo Hradiště Dist, Bohemia. He died on 30 Aug 1878 in Hoškovice No.25, Mnichovo Hradiště Dist, Bohemia.

    iii. **Jaroslav Danda** was born on 13 Mar 1892 in Hoškovice No. 25, Mnichovo Hradiště Dist, Bohemia. He died on 06 Nov 1979 in Mnichovo Hradište, Central Bohemia, Czech Republic.

Generation 8

1 **Jaroslav Danda**-8 (Josef of Kopeček-7, František-6, Josef-5, Josef-4, Josef-3, Jan-2, Jan-1) was born on 25 Mar 1895 in Hoškovice No. 13, Mnichovo Hradiště Dist, Bohemia. He died in 1956 in Mnichovo Hradište, Central Bohemia, Czech Republic.

    Marie Svobodová was born in 1904 in Hoškovice. She died in 1968 in Mnichovo Hradiště.

    Jaroslav Danda and Marie Svobodová were married on 26 Feb 1929 in Semily. They had the following children:

    39. i. **Jaroslava Dandová** was born in 1930.

    ii. **Zdeněk Danda** was born in 1932.

23. **Miloslav Danda**-8 (Josef of Kopeček-7, František-6, Josef-5, Josef-4,

Josef-3, Jan-2, Jan-1) was born on 20 May 1900 in Hoškovice No. 13, Mnichovo Hradiště Dist, Bohemia. He died on 13 Sep 1952 in Hoškovice No. 13, Mnichovo Hradiště Dist, Bohemia.

Anna Švermová daughter of Václav Šverma and Unknown was born on 16 Aug 1901 in Podolí. She died on 05 Mar 1972 in Hoškovice No. 13.

Miloslav Danda and Anna Švermová married. They had the following children:

    40. i. **Miloslav Danda** was born on 03 Sep 1931 in Hoškovice No. 13. He died on 05 Jun 2002 in Hoškovice No. 13.

    ii. **Miloslav Danda**.

24. **Václav Danda**-8 (Josef of Kopeček-7, František-6, Josef-5, Josef-4, Josef-3, Jan-2, Jan-1) was born on 10 Sep 1874 in Hoškovice No. 13. He died on 27 Jun 1912 in Dneboh No. 17.

Božena Novotná was born on 26 Jun 1879 in Dneboh No. 17.

Václav Danda and Božena Novotná married. They had the following children:

    41. i. **Josef Danda** was born on 05 Apr 1904 in Dneboh No. 17. He married Emilie Rajtrová on 24 Jan 1931 in Brezina.

    42. ii. **Václav Danda** was born on 16 Jul 1909 in Dneboh No. 17. He married Marie Krejčí on 22 Sep 1934 in Bosen. He died on 08 Dec 1972 in Dneboh No. 34.

25. **Marie Dandová**-8 (František Antonín-7, František-6, Josef-5, Josef-4, Josef-3, Jan-2, Jan-1)[1] was born on 31 Jan 1882 in Hoškovice, No. 14, Mnichovo Hradiště Dist, Bohemia. She died on 05 Jul 1967 in Dolanky No. 7, Mnichovo Hradiště Co..

Čeněk Rajtr son of Jan Václav Rajtr and Anna Najmanová[2] was born on 01 Jul 1874 in nky No. 7, Mnichovo Hradiště Dist... He died on 27 Oct 1956 in Dolánky No. 7, Mnichovo Hradiště Dist...

Čeněk Rajtr and Marie Dandová were married on 02 Jul 1904 in Mnichovo Hradiště. They had the following children:

    43. i. **Marie Rajtrová** was born on 05 Jul 1905 in Dolanky No. 7, Mnichovo Hradiště Co.. She married Miloslav Rechcigl on 26 Jul 1926 in Praha - Kralovske Vinohrady. She died on 13 Apr 1982 in

Mladá Boleslav.

    ii. **Oldrřch Rajtr** was born on 14 Nov 1907 in Dolanky No. 7. He died on 02 Nov 1937.

44. iii. **Marta Rajtrová** was born on 10 Jan 1909 in Dolanky u Bakova. She married Josef Knotek in 1934. She died on 29 Nov 1982 in Mladá Boleslav.

26. **Josef Danda**-8 (František Antonín-7, František-6, Josef-5, Josef-4, Josef-3, Jan-2, Jan-1) was born on 30 Jan 1884 in Hoškovice, No. 14, Mnichovo Hradiště Dist, Bohemia. He died on 18 Apr 1936 in Dobrá Voda.

Božena Slavíková daughter of Josef Slavik and Anna Jirova was born on 05 Sep 1889 in Lesnovky, Turnov Dist... She died on 06 Oct 1965 in Dobrá Voda.

Josef Danda and Božena Slavíková married. They had the following children:

  45. i. **Oldřich Danda** was born on 29 Jan 1922 in Hoškovice No. 10, Mnichovo Hradiště Dist, Bohemia. He died on 30 Jan 1983 in Dobrá Voda, Mnichovo Hradiště Co..

27. **Emilie Dandová**-8 (František Antonín-7, František-6, Josef-5, Josef-4, Josef-3, Jan-2, Jan-1) was born on 22 Oct 1893 in Hoškovice No. 14, Mnichovo Hradiště Dist, Bohemia. She died on 06 Apr 1924 in Hoškovice, Mnichovo Hradiště Dist, Bohemia.

Václav Balák son of Václav Balak and Kateřina Janoušková was born about 1890 in Nová Ves No. 13, Mnichovo Hradiště District.

Václav Balák and Emilie Dandová were married on 18 Sep 1920 in Hoškovice, Mnichovo Hradiště Dist, Bohemia. They had the following children:

  46. i. **Marie Balakova** was born on 16 Feb 1921 in Hoškovice No. 14, Mnichovo Hradiště Dist.. She married Otakar Lochman on 04 Nov 1942 in Mnichovo Hradiště.

  47. ii. **Václav Balak** was born on 06 Jun 1922 in Hoškovice. He died on 24 Jan 2001. He married Zdenka Štolbová on 31 Dec.

  48. iii. **Vlasta Balakova** was born on 02 Sep 1923 in Hoškovice, Mnichovo Hradiště Co.. She married Milous Bičík in 1948.

28. **Anna Dandová**-8 (Václav-7, František-6, Josef-5, Josef-4, Josef-3, Jan-2, Jan-1) was born on 07 Feb 1872 in Hoškovice No. 2,, Mnichovo Hradiště Dist, Bohemia. She died on 31 May 1927.

    Václav Šverma son of Jan Šverma and Anna Dandová was born on 12 Aug 1870 in Podolí. He died on 08 Apr 1943 in Hoškovice No. 10, Mnichovo Hradiště Dist, Bohemia.

    Václav Šverma and Anna Dandová were married on 23 Nov 1897 in Hoškovice No. 10, Mnichovo Hradiště Dist, Bohemia. They had the following children:

    49. i. **Marie Švermová** was born on 20 Aug 1898 in Hoškovice No. 10, Mnichovo Hradiště Dist, Bohemia. She married Ladislav Šíp on 02 Oct 1920 in Hoškovice, Mnichovo Hradiště Dist, Bohemia. She died on 12 Apr 1986.

29. **Emilie Kateřina Dandová**-8 (Václav-7, František-6, Josef-5, Josef-4, Josef-3, Jan-2, Jan-1) was born on 17 Feb 1874 in Hoškovice, No. 2, Mnichovo Hradiště Dist, Bohemia. She died on 28 Apr 1954.

    František Stejskal son of Jan Stejskal and Barbora Sritrova was born on 12 Sep 1876 in Proseč. He died on 19 Mar 1931.

    František Stejskal and Emilie Kateřina Dandová were married on 22 Nov 1904. They had the following children:

    50. i. **Josef Stejskal** was born on 02 Aug 1905 in Hoškovice No. 2, Mnichovo Hradiště Co.. He died on 14 Aug 1987.
    51. ii. **Marie Stejskalová** was born in 1910. She died in 1945.

30. **daughter Dandová**-8 (son-7, František-6, Josef-5, Josef-4, Josef-3, Jan-2, Jan-1).

    Unknown.

    Unknown and daughter Dandová married. They had the following children:

    52. i. **Marie Floriánová**.

31. **Marie Švermová**-8 (Barbora-7, František-6, Josef-5, Josef-4, Josef-3, Jan-2, Jan-1) was born about 1880.

    Josef Bukvička was born before 1880 in Hoškovice No. 5.

    Josef Bukvička and Marie Švermová married. They had the following

children:
- 54. i. **Antonín Bukvička** was born in Hoškovice.
- 55. ii. **Josef Bukvička** was born on 27 Jan 1898. He died on 14 Feb 1970.
- 56. iii. **Marie Bukvičková** was born about 1899 in Hoškovice No. 5.
- 57. iv. **Bohuslav Bukvička**.

32. **Antonín Šverma**-8 (Barbora-7, František-6, Josef-5, Josef-4, Josef-3, Jan-2, Jan-1) was born before 1890 in Podolí, Mnichovo Hradiště Co..

    Růžena Švermová was born before 1890 in Manikovice, Mnichovo Hradiště Co.. Antonín Šverma and Růžena Švermová married. They had the following children:
    - 57. i. **Růžena Švermová** was born in 1907 in Podolí, Mnichovo Hradiště Co..

33. **František Šverma**-8 (Barbora-7, František-6, Josef-5, Josef-4, Josef-3, Jan-2, Jan-1) was born before 1890.

    Anna was born in Bycin.

    František Šverma and Anna married. They had the following children:
    - i. **František Šverma**.
    - ii. **Anna Švermová**.

34. **Václav Šverma**-8 (Barbora-7, František-6, Josef-5, Josef-4, Josef-3, Jan-2, Jan-1) was born before 1890.

    Unknown.

    Václav Šverma and Unknown married. They had the following children:
    - i. **Václav Šverma**.
    - 58. ii. **Anna Švermová** was born on 16 Aug 1901 in Podolí. She died on 05 Mar 1972 in Hoškovice No. 13.
    - iii. **Ladislav Šverma**.
    - iv. **Josef Šverma**.

35. **Václav Šverma**-8 (Anna-7, František-6, František-5, Josef-4, Josef-3, Jan-2, Jan-1) was born on 12 Aug 1870 in Podolí. He died on 08 Apr 1943 in Hoškovice No. 10, Mnichovo Hradiště Dist, Bohemia.

    Anna Dandová daughter of Václav Danda and Marie Štěpánková was born on 07 Feb 1872 in Hoškovice No. 2,, Mnichovo Hradiště Dist, Bohemia. She died on 31 May 1927.

Václav Šverma and Anna Dandová were married on 23 Nov 1897 in Hoškovice No. 10, Mnichovo Hradiště Dist, Bohemia. They had the following children:

49. i. **Marie Švermová** was born on 20 Aug 1898 in Hoškovice No. 10, Mnichovo Hradiště Dist, Bohemia. She married Ladislav Šíp on 02 Oct 1920 in Hoškovice, Mnichovo Hradiště Dist, Bohemia. She died on 12 Apr 1986.

36. **Marie Švermová**-8 (Anna-7, František-6, František-5, Josef-4, Josef-3, Jan-2, Jan-1) was born on 07 Jul 1873 in Hoškovice, Mnichovo Hradiště Dist, Bohemia.

    Pazderník was born on 13 Jul 1866.

    Pazderník and Marie Švermová were married on 01 Feb 1896. They had no children.

    Friedrich.

    Friedrich and Marie Švermová married. They had the following children:

    i. **daughter Friedrichova.**

    ii. **daughetr Friedrichova.**

37. **Bohuslav Jiří Danda**-8 (František-7, František-6, František-5, Josef-4, Josef-3, Jan-2, Jan-1) was born on 17 Mar 1875 in Hoškovice No. 25, Mnichovo Hradiště Dist, Bohemia. He died on 13 Aug 1953.

    Milada Brechlerová was born on 22 May 1881 in Chocnějovice,, Mnichovo Hradiště Dist.. She died on 21 May 1960 in Mnichovo Hradište, Central Bohemia, Czech Republic.

    Bohuslav Jiří Danda and Milada Brechlerová married. They had the following children:

    i. **Dana Dandová.**

    ii. **Marie Dandová.**

    59. iii. **Bohuslav Danda** was born on 24 Apr 1902 in Mohelnice nad Jizerou, Central Bohemia, Czech Republic. He died on 14 Oct 1967 in Javornice.

38. **Jaroslav Danda**-8 (František-7, František-6, František-5, Josef-4, Josef-3, Jan-2, Jan-1) was born on 13 Mar 1892 in Hoškovice No. 25, Mnichovo

Hradiště Dist, Bohemia. He died on 06 Nov 1979 in Mnichovo Hradište, Central Bohemia, Czech Republic.

Marie Tondrová daughter of Tondr was born about 1895 in Hoškovice No. 35.

Jaroslav Danda and Marie Tondrová married. They had the following children:

60. i. **Jiří Danda** was born on 16 Mar 1921 in Hoškovice No. 25, Mnichovo Hradiště Co.. He married Věra Prskavcová on 15 Apr 1950. He died on 13 Nov 1990 in Mladá Boleslav.

Generation 9

39. **Jaroslava Dandová**-9 (Jaroslav-8, Josef of Kopeček-7, František-6, Josef-5, Josef-4, Josef-3, Jan-2, Jan-1) was born in 1930.

Jaroslav Fanta was born in Mnichovo Hradiště.

Jaroslav Fanta and Jaroslava Dandová married. They had the following children:

    i. **Michaela 'Misa' Fantova.**

40. **Miloslav Danda**-9 (Miloslav-8, Josef of Kopeček-7, František-6, Josef-5, Josef-4, Josef-3, Jan-2, Jan-1) was born on 03 Sep 1931 in Hoškovice No. 13. He died on 05 Jun 2002 in Hoškovice No. 13.

Jiřina Hykova was born in Dneboh. She died in 1968 in Dneboh.

Miloslav Danda and Jiřina Hykova married. They had the following children:

61. i. **Jiří Danda** was born on 29 Mar 1962.

41. **Josef Danda**-9 (Václav-8, Josef of Kopeček-7, František-6, Josef-5, Josef-4, Josef-3, Jan-2, Jan-1) was born on 05 Apr 1904 in Dneboh No. 17.

Emilie Rajtrová daughter of Jan Rajtr and Kateřina Volfova was born on 14 May 1909 in Olsina.

Josef Danda and Emilie Rajtrová were married on 24 Jan 1931 in Brezina. They had the following children:

62. i. **Josef Danda** was born on 11 Nov 1931 in Dneboh No. 17. He died on 27 Aug 2013 in Dbeboh No. 17.

42. **Václav Danda**-9 (Václav-8, Josef of Kopeček-7, František-6, Josef-5, Josef-4, Josef-3, Jan-2, Jan-1) was born on 16 Jul 1909 in Dneboh No. 17.

He died on 08 Dec 1972 in Dneboh No. 34.

Marie Krejčí daughter of Josef Krejčí and Anna Havlasová was born on 11 Aug 1913 in Olsina. She died on 26 May 1998 in Dneboh.

Václav Danda and Marie Krejčí were married on 22 Sep 1934 in Bosen. They had the following children:

    63. i. **Vratislav Danda** was born on 29 Mar 1935 in Dneboh No. 34. He married Zdenka Smidova on 15 Feb 1958 in Solec - Solecek.

43. **Marie Rajtrová**-9 (Marie-8, František Antonín-7, František-6, Josef-5, Josef-4, Josef-3, Jan-2, Jan-1) was born on 05 Jul 1905 in Dolanky No. 7, Mnichovo Hradiště Co.. She died on 13 Apr 1982 in Mladá Boleslav.

Miloslav Rechcigl son of Adolf Rechcigl and Marie Berglová was born on 13 May 1904 in Kocňovice (renamed Chocnějovice) No. 22. He died on 27 May 1973 in Washington, DC.

Miloslav Rechcigl and Marie Rajtrová were married on 26 Jul 1926 in Praha - Kralovske Vinohrady. They had the following children:

    64. i. **Mila (Miloslav) Rechcigl Jr.** was born on 30 Jul 1930 in Mladá Boleslav, CSR. He married Eva Edwards (Eisnerová) on 29 Aug 1953 in New York, NY.

    65. ii. **Marta Rechcíglová** was born on 23 May 1933 in Mladá Boleslav. She married František Žďárský on 03 Oct 1953 in Mladá Boleslav. She died on 13 Sep 2018 in Mladá Boleslav.

44. **Marta Rajtrová**-9 (Marie-8, František Antonín-7, František-6, Josef-5, Josef-4, Josef-3, Jan-2, Jan-1) was born on 10 Jan 1909 in Dolanky u Bakova. She died on 29 Nov 1982 in Mladá Boleslav.

Josef Knotek was born between 1905-1907 in Mala Bela, p. Bakov nad Jizerou. He died in 1934. Josef Knotek and Marta Rajtrová were married in 1934. They had no children.

Miroslav Koubik son of Koubik was born in 1908 in Terezin. He died in 1968 in Havlickuv Brod.

Miroslav Koubik and Marta Rajtrová were married on 26 Jul 1938 in Praha. They had the following children:

    66. i. **Jiří Koubik** was born on 29 Jan 1940 in Prague. He married Jiřina Muellerová on 31 Jan 1962 in Praha. He died on 26 Jun 1998 in

Brandys nad Labem.

Emil Pazderník was born after 1900.

Emil Pazderník and Marta Rajtrová were married after 1945. They had no children.

Karel Horáček.

Karel Horáček and Marta Rajtrová met. They had no children.

45. **Oldřich Danda**-9 (Josef-8, František Antonín-7, František-6, Josef-5, Josef-4, Josef-3, Jan-2, Jan-1) was born on 29 Jan 1922 in Hoškovice No. 10, Mnichovo Hradiště Dist, Bohemia. He died on 30 Jan 1983 in Dobrá Voda, Mnichovo Hradiště Co..

    Marie Augustinova was born on 01 Jun 1923 in Dobrá Voda, Mnichovo Hradiště Co.. She died on 03 Jan 2003 in Dobrá Voda, Mnichovo Hradiště Co..

    Oldřich Danda and Marie Augustinova married. They had the following children:

        i. **Oldrřch Danda** was born on 06 Sep 1958 in Turnov.

        ii. **Marie Dandová** was born on 12 Jun 1946 in Mnichovo Hradiště.

46. **Marie Balakova**-9 (Emilie-8, František Antonín-7, František-6, Josef-5, Josef-4, Josef-3, Jan-2, Jan-1) was born on 16 Feb 1921 in Hoškovice No. 14, Mnichovo Hradiště Dist..

    Otakar Lochman was born on 13 Jan 1917 in Hradec, Mnichovo Hrtadiste Dist.. He died on 22 Sep 1980.

    Otakar Lochman and Marie Balakova were married on 04 Nov 1942 in Mnichovo Hradiště. They had the following children:

    68. i. **Otakar Lochman** was born on 24 Dec 1944 in Mnichovo Hradiště. He married Václava Bártová on 12 Nov 1966 in Turnov.

47. **Václav Balak**-9 (Emilie-8, František Antonín-7, František-6, Josef-5, Josef-4, Josef-3, Jan-2, Jan-1) was born on 06 Jun 1922 in Hoškovice. He died on 24 Jan 2001.

    Zdenka Štolbová was born on 22 Dec 1930. She died on 01 Jan 1985.

    Václav Balak and Zdenka Štolbová were married on 31 Dec. They had the following children:

        i. **Sarka Balakova** was born about 1950.

69. ii. **Zdenka Balakova** was born on 16 Nov 1952. She married Bohumil Konicek on 08 Jun 1974.

48. **Vlasta Balakova**-9 (Emilie-8, František Antonín-7, František-6, Josef-5, Josef-4, Josef-3, Jan-2, Jan-1) was born on 02 Sep 1923 in Hoškovice, Mnichovo Hradiště Co..

    Milous Bičík was born on 28 Jun 1920. He died on 24 Mar 1988.

    Milous Bičík and Vlasta Balakova were married in 1948. They had the following children:

    70. i. **Emilie Bičíková** was born on 08 Mar 1949 in Turnov. She married Oldrřch Šnajdr on 08 Oct 1970.

49. **Marie Švermová**-9 (Anna-8, Václav-7, František-6, Josef-5, Josef-4, Josef-3, Jan-2, Jan-1) was born on 20 Aug 1898 in Hoškovice No. 10, Mnichovo Hradiště Dist, Bohemia. She died on 12 Apr 1986.

    Ladislav Šíp son of Václav Šíp and Julie Chvalinová was born on 30 Sep 1888 in Vesec u Turnova, Turnov Co.. He died on 01 Apr 1967 in Prague, Czechoslovakia.

    Ladislav Šíp and Marie Švermová were married on 02 Oct 1920 in Hoškovice, Mnichovo Hradiště Dist, Bohemia. They had the following children:

    71. i. **Ladislav Šíp** was born on 08 Oct 1922 in Prague, Czechoslavakia. He married Mirka Langova about 13 Apr 1950. He died on 10 Jun 1993 in Prague, Czechoslavakia.

    72. ii. **Eva Šípová** was born in 1927.

50. **Josef Stejskal**-9 (Emilie Kateřina-8, Václav-7, František-6, Josef-5, Josef-4, Josef-3, Jan-2, Jan-1) was born on 02 Aug 1905 in Hoškovice No. 2, Mnichovo Hradiště Co.. He died on 14 Aug 1987.

    Marie Maděrová daughter of František Maděra and Marie Dubská was born on 08 Apr 1910 in Bosen No. 38. She died on 10 Oct 1945.

    Josef Stejskal and Marie Maděrová married. They had the following children:

    73. i. **Josef Stejskal** was born in 1932. He died in 2003.

        ii. **Jaromír Stejskal** was born on 18 Jul 1937. He died on 13 Aug 1995.

51. **Marie Stejskalová**-9 (Emilie Kateřina-8, Václav-7, František-6, Josef-5, Josef-4, Josef-3, Jan-2, Jan-1) was born in 1910. She died in 1945.
    Oldrřch Bergman was born in Mnichovo Hradiště.
    Oldrřch Bergman and Marie Stejskalová married. They had the following children:
    i. **Jana Bergmannová** was born in Mnichovo Hradiště.
    ii. **Pavel Bergmann**.
52. **Marie Floriánová**-9 (daughter-8, son-7, František-6, Josef-5, Josef-4, Josef-3, Jan-2, Jan-1).
    Josef Tomeš was born in Stranov.
    Josef Tomeš and Marie Floriánová married. They had the following children:
    i. **Tomsová-daughter**.
    ii. **son Tomeš**.
53. **Antonín Bukvička**-9 (Marie-8, Barbora-7, František-6, Josef-5, Josef-4, Josef-3, Jan-2, Jan-1) was born in Hoškovice.
    Ludmila Baierova daughter of Václav Baier and Marie Buriánková.
    Antonín Bukvička and Ludmila Baierova married. They had the following children:
    74. i. **Jaroslav Bukvička** was born in 1928.
    75. ii. **Jiří Bukvička** was born in 1935 in Hoškovice. He died on 11 May 1998.
54. **Josef Bukvička**-9 (Marie-8, Barbora-7, František-6, Josef-5, Josef-4, Josef-3, Jan-2, Jan-1) was born on 27 Jan 1898. He died on 14 Feb 1970.
    Ludmila Tondrová daughter of Tondr was born on 10 Oct 1899 in Hoškovice No.. 35. She died on 23 Feb 1992.
    Josef Bukvička and Ludmila Tondrová married. They had the following children:
    76. i. **Josef Bukvička** was born on 16 Mar 1926 in Hoškovice No. 34.
    77. ii. **Jiřina Bukvičková** was born on 07 Sep 1922 in Hoškovice No. 6.
55. **Marie Bukvičková**-9 (Marie-8, Barbora-7, František-6, Josef-5, Josef-4, Josef-3, Jan-2, Jan-1) was born about 1899 in Hoškovice No. 5.
    Miroslav Hyka was born in Mnichovo Hradiště.

Miroslav Hyka and Marie Bukvičková married. They had the following children:
- 78. i. **Miroslav Hyka** was born about 1925.
- 79. ii. **Milena Hykova**.

56. **Bohuslav Bukvička**-9 (Marie-8, Barbora-7, František-6, Josef-5, Josef-4, Josef-3, Jan-2, Jan-1).
Zofie Tomášová was born in Stranov.
Bohuslav Bukvička and Zofie Tomášová married. They had the following children:
- 80. i. **Bohuslav Bukvička** was born on 20 Oct 1929. He died on 11 Nov 1988.
- 81. ii. **Drahoslava Bukvičková** was born on 07 Nov 1933.

57. **Růžena Švermová**-9 (Antonín-8, Barbora-7, František-6, Josef-5, Josef-4, Josef-3, Jan-2, Jan-1) was born in 1907 in Podolí, Mnichovo Hradiště Co..
Josef Vochvesta was born in 1908 in Sezemice.
Josef Vochvesta and Růžena Švermová married. They had the following children:
- 82. i. **Květa Vochvestova** was born on 02 Nov 1932 in Podolí, Mnichovo Hradiště Co..

58. **Anna Švermová**-9 (Václav-8, Barbora-7, František-6, Josef-5, Josef-4, Josef-3, Jan-2, Jan-1) was born on 16 Aug 1901 in Podolí. She died on 05 Mar 1972 in Hoškovice No. 13.
Miloslav Danda son of Josef of Kopeček Danda and Josefa Picková was born on 20 May 1900 in Hoškovice No. 13, Mnichovo Hradiště Dist, Bohemia. He died on 13 Sep 1952 in Hoškovice No. 13, Mnichovo Hradiště Dist, Bohemia.
Miloslav Danda and Anna Švermová married. They had the following children:
- 40. i. **Miloslav Danda** was born on 03 Sep 1931 in Hoškovice No. 13. He died on 05 Jun 2002 in Hoškovice No. 13.
- ii. **Miloslav Danda.**

60. **Bohuslav Danda**-9 (Bohuslav Jiří-8, František-7, František-6, František-5, Josef-4, Josef-3, Jan-2, Jan-1) was born on 24 Apr 1902 in Mohelnice

nad Jizerou, Central Bohemia, Czech Republic. He died on 14 Oct 1967 in Javornice.

Anna Hykova was born in Olsina.

Bohuslav Danda and Anna Hykova married. They had the following children:

    83. i. **Bohuslav Zdeněk Danda** was born on 30 Jun 1932 in Primda. He married Libuše Vinklarova in Dec 1950 in Kneznice. He died on 25 May 1989 in Kneznice.

60. **Jiří Danda**-9 (Jaroslav-8, František-7, František-6, František-5, Josef-4, Josef-3, Jan-2, Jan-1) was born on 16 Mar 1921 in Hoškovice No. 25, Mnichovo Hradiště Co.. He died on 13 Nov 1990 in Mladá Boleslav.

Věra Prskavcová daughter of Josef Prskavec and Anastazie Studničná was born on 12 Dec 1929 in Ptyrov.

Jiří Danda and Věra Prskavcová were married on 15 Apr 1950. They had the following children:

    84. i. **Eva Dandová** was born on 11 Feb 1951 in Mladá Boleslav. She married Milan Dědič on 28 Jan 1977 in Mnichovo Hradiště No. 208.

    85. ii. **Jiřina Dandová** was born on 15 Feb 1955 in Turnov. She died on 02 Oct 2015 in Rozstani (cancer).

Generation 10

61. **Jiří Danda**-10 (Miloslav-9, Miloslav-8, Josef of Kopeček-7, František-6, Josef-5, Josef-4, Josef-3, Jan-2, Jan-1) was born on 29 Mar 1962.

Iveta Mucskova.

Jiří Danda and Iveta Mucskova married. They had the following children:

    i. **Yveta Dandová.**

    ii. **Lucie Dandová** was born on 07 Sep 1988.

62. **Josef Danda**-10 (Josef-9, Václav-8, Josef of Kopeček-7, František-6, Josef-5, Josef-4, Josef-3, Jan-2, Jan-1) was born on 11 Nov 1931 in Dneboh No. 17. He died on 27 Aug 2013 in Dbeboh No. 17.

Alena Patočková was born on 02 Jul 1935 in Semily. She died on 01 Dec 2005 in Dneboh No. 17. Josef Danda and Alena Patočková married. They had the following children:

86. i. **Josef Danda** was born on 26 Jul 1958 in Turnov. He married Marcela Zemánková in Dneboh No. 9.

87. ii. **Pavel Danda** was born on 12 Aug 1963 in Mladá Boleslav. He married Jana Hozaková in Dneboh No.66.

63. **Vratislav Danda**-10 (Václav-9, Václav-8, Josef of Kopeček-7, František-6, Josef-5, Josef-4, Josef-3, Jan-2, Jan-1) was born on 29 Mar 1935 in Dneboh No. 34.

Zdenka Smidova was born on 01 Apr 1936 in Knezmost. She died on 14 Aug 2012 in Dneboh No. 34.

Vratislav Danda and Zdenka Smidova were married on 15 Feb 1958 in Solec - Solecek. They had the following children:

    i. **Alena Dandová** was born on 14 Dec 1959.

    ii. **Roman Danda** was born on 01 Dec 1962.

64. **Mila (Miloslav) Rechcigl Jr.**-10 (Marie-9, Marie-8, František Antonín-7, František-6, Josef-5, Josef-4, Josef-3, Jan-2, Jan-1) was born on 30 Jul 1930 in Mladá Boleslav, CSR.

Eva Edwards (Eisnerová) daughter of Paul J. Edwards (Pavel Eisner) and Jiřina Taussigová was born on 21 Jan 1932 in Prague, CSR.

Mila (Miloslav) Rechcigl Jr. and Eva Edwards (Eisnerová) were married on 29 Aug 1953 in New York, NY. They had the following children:

88. i. **John Edward Rechcigl** was born on 27 Feb 1960 in Washington, D.C.. He married Nancy Ann Palko on 30 Jul 1983 in Dover, NJ.

89. ii. **Karen Rechcigl** was born on 16 Apr 1962 in Washington, DC. She married Ulysses Kollecas on 25 Aug 1990 in Bethesda, MD.

65. **Marta Rechcíglová**-10 (Marie-9, Marie-8, František Antonín-7, František-6, Josef-5, Josef-4, Josef-3, Jan-2, Jan-1) was born on 23 May 1933 in Mladá Boleslav. She died on 13 Sep 2018 in Mladá Boleslav.

František Žďárský son of František Václav Žďárský and Eliška Foltýnová was born on 21 May 1932 in Turnov.

František Žďárský and Marta Rechcíglová were married on 03 Oct 1953 in Mladá Boleslav. They had the following children:

90. i. **Marcela Žďárská** was born on 09 May 1954 in Liberec. She married Miroslav Heralecký on 15 Mar 1975 in Sychrov.

91. ii. **Iveta Žďárská** was born on 29 Aug 1963 in Liberec, Bohemia. She married Vlastimil Berkman on 29 Oct 1983.

66. **Jiří Koubik**-10 (Marta-9, Marie-8, František Antonín-7, František-6, Josef-5, Josef-4, Josef-3, Jan-2, Jan-1) was born on 29 Jan 1940 in Prague. He died on 26 Jun 1998 in Brandys nad Labem.

    Jiřina Muellerová was born on 27 Feb 1943 in Buda.

    Jiří Koubik and Jiřina Muellerová were married on 31 Jan 1962 in Praha. They had the following children:

    92. i. **Marta Koubikova** was born on 04 Jul 1962 in Mladá Boleslav. She married Vladimír Stibor on 17 Apr 1981.
    93. ii. **2nd Jiří Koubik** was born on 13 May 1965 in Praha. He married Andrea Dunebierová on 04 Apr 1987 in Brandys nad Labem.

67. **Marie Dandová**-10 (Oldřich-9, Josef-8, František Antonín-7, František-6, Josef-5, Josef-4, Josef-3, Jan-2, Jan-1) was born on 12 Jun 1946 in Mnichovo Hradiště.

    Květoslav Červený was born on 07 Mar 1945 in Bosen, Mladá Boleslav Co.. Květoslav Červený and Marie Dandová married. They had the following children:

    94. i. **Luděk Červený** was born on 17 Aug 1968 in Mladá Boleslav. He married Lenka Kovacova on 11 Mar 1989.
    95. ii. **Radek Červený** was born on 23 May 1972 in Mladá Boleslav. He married Renata Bejrová on 05 Nov 1994.

68. **Otakar Lochman**-10 (Marie-9, Emilie-8, František Antonín-7, František-6, Josef-5, Josef-4, Josef-3, Jan-2, Jan-1) was born on 24 Dec 1944 in Mnichovo Hradiště.

    Václava Bártová was born on 26 Sep 1948 in Mladá Boleslav.

    Otakar Lochman and Václava Bártová were married on 12 Nov 1966 in Turnov. They had the following children:

    96. i. **Otakar Lochman** was born on 01 Apr 1968 in Mladá Boleslav. He married Štěpánka Jandová on 27 Aug 1988 in Mnichovo Hradiště.
    97. ii. **Václava Lochmanová** was born on 21 May 1972 in Mladá Boleslav. She married Vladimír Pecina on 09 Sep 1995 in Mnichovo Hradiště.
    98. iii. **Iva Lochmanová** was born on 28 Apr 1976 in Mladá Boleslav.

She married Libor Janoušek on 21 Mar 1997 in Bakov nad Jizerou.
69. **Zdenka Balakova**-10 (Václav-9, Emilie-8, František Antonín-7, František-6, Josef-5, Josef-4, Josef-3, Jan-2, Jan-1) was born on 16 Nov 1952.
Bohumil Konicek was born on 19 Jun 1953.
Bohumil Konicek and Zdenka Balakova were married on 08 Jun 1974. They had the following children:
99. i. **Sarka Konickova** was born on 17 Dec 1974.
ii. **Lukáš Konicek** was born on 14 May 1985.
70. **Emilie Bičíková**-10 (Vlasta-9, Emilie-8, František Antonín-7, František-6, Josef-5, Josef-4, Josef-3, Jan-2, Jan-1) was born on 08 Mar 1949 in Turnov.
Oldrřch Šnajdr was born on 07 May 1949 in Brehy.
Oldrřch Šnajdr and Emilie Bičíková were married on 08 Oct 1970. They had the following children:
100. i. **Oldrřch Šnajdr** was born on 04 Apr 1971 in Turnov. He married Daniela Synková on 16 Mar 1991.
ii. **Jiří Šnajdr** was born on 10 Nov 1977 in Turnov.
71. **Ladislav Šíp**-10 (Marie-9, Anna-8, Václav-7, František-6, Josef-5, Josef-4, Josef-3, Jan-2, Jan-1) was born on 08 Oct 1922 in Prague, Czechoslavakia. He died on 10 Jun 1993 in Prague, Czechoslavakia.
Mirka Langova was born on 19 Feb 1925. She died in 2005.
Ladislav Šíp and Mirka Langova were married about 13 Apr 1950. They had the following children:
101. i. **Marie Šípová** was born on 08 Jun 1956 in Praha.
102. ii. **Ladislav Šíp** was born on 11 Sep 1958 in Praha.
72. **Eva Šípová**-10 (Marie-9, Anna-8, Václav-7, František-6, Josef-5, Josef-4, Josef-3, Jan-2, Jan-1) was born in 1927.
Jan Klos was born on 20 May 1912. He died on 05 Jan 1984. Jan Klos and Eva Šípová married. They had the following children:
i. **Eva Klosova.**
73. **Josef Stejskal**-10 (Josef-9, Emilie Kateřina-8, Václav-7, František-6, Josef-5, Josef-4, Josef-3, Jan-2, Jan-1) was born in 1932. He died in 2003.
Růžena Patočková was born in 1935 in Mnichovo Hradiště.
Josef Stejskal and Růžena Patočková married. They had the following

children:
- 103. i. **Milan Stejskal** was born in 1960.
- ii. **Vit Stejskal** was born in 1963.

74. **Jaroslav Bukvička**-10 (Antonín-9, Marie-8, Barbora-7, František-6, Josef-5, Josef-4, Josef-3, Jan-2, Jan-1) was born in 1928.
Ludmila Machatova was born in 1935.
Jaroslav Bukvička and Ludmila Machatova married. They had the following children:
- i. **Dana Bukvičková**.
- ii. **Ivana Bukvičková**.

75. **Jiří Bukvička**-10 (Antonín-9, Marie-8, Barbora-7, František-6, Josef-5, Josef-4, Josef-3, Jan-2, Jan-1) was born in 1935 in Hoškovice. He died on 11 May 1998.
Milena Tomsová was born on 13 Apr 1935 in Loukov No. 17.
Jiří Bukvička and Milena Tomsová married. They had the following children:
- i. **Milena Bukvičková** was born on 14 Apr 1959 in Mladá Boleslav.
- 104. ii. **Sona Bukvičková** was born on 26 Jan 1965 in Mladá Boleslav.

76. **Josef Bukvička**-10 (Josef-9, Marie-8, Barbora-7, František-6, Josef-5, Josef-4, Josef-3, Jan-2, Jan-1) was born on 16 Mar 1926 in Hoškovice No. 34.
Vlasta Benešová was born on 23 Mar 1930 in Hoškovice.
Josef Bukvička and Vlasta Benešová married. They had the following children:
- 105. i. **Ludmila Bukvičková** was born on 31 Aug 1959 in Mladá Boleslav. She married Frantiosek Šafránek on 09 Sep 1984.
- ii. **Josef Bukvička** was born on 06 Nov 1963 in Mladá Boleslav.

77. **Jiřina Bukvičková**-10 (Josef-9, Marie-8, Barbora-7, František-6, Josef-5, Josef-4, Josef-3, Jan-2, Jan-1) was born on 07 Sep 1922 in Hoškovice No. 6.
Antonín Wagenknecht was born on 05 Sep 1913.
Antonín Wagenknecht and Jiřina Bukvičková married. They had the following children:
- 106. i. **Jiří Wagenknecht** was born on 10 Jan 1946.
- 107. ii. **Jan Wagenknecht** was born on 30 Nov 1949.

78. **Miroslav Hyka**-10 (Marie-9, Marie-8, Barbora-7, František-6, Josef-5, Josef-4, Josef-3, Jan-2, Jan-1) was born about 1925.
Emilie.
Miroslav Hyka and Emilie married. They had the following children:
   108. i. **Mirek Hyka.**
   109. ii. **Jan Hyka.**
79. **Milena Hykova**-10 (Marie-9, Marie-8, Barbora-7, František-6, Josef-5, Josef-4, Josef-3, Jan-2, Jan-1).
Ladislav Sedláček was born in Mladá Boleslav.
Ladislav Sedláček and Milena Hykova married. They had the following children:
   110. i. **Ladislav Sedláček.**
   111. ii. **Milena Sedláčková.**
80. **Bohuslav Bukvička**-10 (Bohuslav-9, Marie-8, Barbora-7, František-6, Josef-5, Josef-4, Josef-3, Jan-2, Jan-1) was born on 20 Oct 1929. He died on 11 Nov 1988.
Marie was born on 09 Sep 1932.
Bohuslav Bukvička and Marie married. They had the following children:
   i. **Pavel Bukvička** was born on 08 Aug 1953. He died on 01 Dec 1977.
   ii. **Hana Bukvičková** was born on 13 Jan 1960.
81. **Drahoslava Bukvičková**-10 (Bohuslav-9, Marie-8, Barbora-7, František-6, Josef-5, Josef-4, Josef-3, Jan-2, Jan-1) was born on 07 Nov 1933.
Jaroslav Vochvesta. He died on Unknown.
Jaroslav Vochvesta and Drahoslava Bukvičková married. They had the following children:
   i. **Jaroslav Vochvesta.**
   ii. **Zuzana Vochvestova.**
82. **Květa Vochvestova**-10 (Růžena-9, Antonín-8, Barbora-7, František-6, Josef-5, Josef-4, Josef-3, Jan-2, Jan-1) was born on 02 Nov 1932 in Podolí, Mnichovo Hradiště Co..
Zdeněk Hrůša was born on 18 Nov 1928 in Dneboh.
Zdeněk Hrůša and Květa Vochvestova married. They had the following

children:
- 112. i. **Jitka Hrušová** was born on 11 Nov 1956 in Turnov.
- 113. ii. **Zdeněk Hrůša** was born in Nov 1957 in Turnov.
- 114. iii. **Josef Hrůša** was born on 13 Aug 1959 in Turnov.

83. **Bohuslav Zdeněk Danda**-10 (Bohuslav-9, Bohuslav Jiří-8, František-7, František-6, František-5, Josef-4, Josef-3, Jan-2, Jan-1) was born on 30 Jun 1932 in Primda. He died on 25 May 1989 in Kneznice.

    Libuše Vinklarova was born on 30 Dec 1933 in Kneznice.

    Bohuslav Zdeněk Danda and Libuše Vinklarova were married in Dec 1950 in Kneznice. They had the following children:
    - 115. i. **Iva Dandová** was born on 04 Apr 1951 in Kneznice.
    - 116. ii. **Zdeněk Danda** was born on 30 Jun 1952 in Kneznice.
    - 117. iii. **Radomil Danda** was born on 10 Apr 1956 in Kneznice.

84. **Eva Dandová**-10 (Jiří-9, Jaroslav-8, František-7, František-6, František-5, Josef-4, Josef-3, Jan-2, Jan-1) was born on 11 Feb 1951 in Mladá Boleslav.

    Milan Dědič son of Josef Dědič and Marie Svobodová was born on 06 Oct 1953 in Bysice.

    Milan Dědič and Eva Dandová were married on 28 Jan 1977 in Mnichovo Hradiště No. 208. They had the following children:
    - 118. i. **Milan Dědič** was born on 03 Oct 1977 in Prague, Czechoslovakia.
    - 119. ii. **Jaroslav Dědič** was born on 08 Jan 1980 in Prague, Czechoslovakia.
    - 120. iii. **Petr Dědič** was born on 27 Apr 1985 in Prague, Czechoslovakia.

85. **Jiřina Dandová**-10 (Jiří-9, Jaroslav-8, František-7, František-6, František-5, Josef-4, Josef-3, Jan-2, Jan-1) was born on 15 Feb 1955 in Turnov. She died on 02 Oct 2015 in Rozstani (cancer).

    Vladimír Vystejn was born on 01 Feb 1950.

    Vladimír Vystejn and Jiřina Dandová married. They had the following children:
    - i. **Jiří Vystejn** was born on 22 Dec 1981.
    - ii. **Jan Vystejn** was born on 08 Feb 1985.

Generation 11

86. **Josef Danda**-11 (Josef-10, Josef-9, Václav-8, Josef of Kopeček-7, František-6, Josef-5, Josef-4, Josef-3, Jan-2, Jan-1) was born on 26 Jul 1958 in Turnov.
    Marcela Zemánková was born on 18 Oct 1963 in Mladá Boleslav.
    Josef Danda and Marcela Zemánková were married in Dneboh No. 9. They had the following children:
    - i. **Petr Danda** was born on 21 Jul 1984 in Mladá Boleslav.
    - ii. **Pavel Danda** was born on 17 May 1985 in Mladá Boleslav, Central Bohemia, Czech Republic.

87. **Pavel Danda**-11 (Josef-10, Josef-9, Václav-8, Josef of Kopeček-7, František-6, Josef-5, Josef-4, Josef-3, Jan-2, Jan-1) was born on 12 Aug 1963 in Mladá Boleslav.
    Jana Hozaková was born on 05 Mar 1966 in Liberec.
    Pavel Danda and Jana Hozaková were married in Dneboh No.66. They had the following children:
    - i. **Michal Danda** was born on 28 Oct 1997 in Mladá Boleslav.
    - ii. **Jan Danda** was born on 10 Jan 2011 in Mladá Boleslav.

88. **John Edward Rechcigl**-11 (Mila (Miloslav)-10, Marie-9, Marie-8, František Antonín-7, František-6, Josef-5, Josef-4, Josef-3, Jan-2, Jan-1) was born on 27 Feb 1960 in Washington, D.C..
    Nancy Ann Palko daughter of Joseph Palko and Mary Rishko was born on 26 Sep 1961 in Morristown, NJ.
    John Edward Rechcigl and Nancy Ann Palko were married on 30 Jul 1983 in Dover, NJ. They had the following children:
    - i. **Gregory John Rechcigl** was born on 19 Dec 1988 in Bradenton, FL.
    - 121. ii. **Kevin Thomas Rechcigl** was born on 09 Oct 1991 in Bradenton, FL. He married Jordan Robbins on 12 May 2018 in Jacksonville, FL.
    - iii. **Lindsey Nicole Rechcigl** was born on 03 Nov 1994 in Bradenton, FL.

89. **Karen Rechcigl**-11 (Mila (Miloslav)-10, Marie-9, Marie-8, František Antonín-7, František-6, Josef-5, Josef-4, Josef-3, Jan-2, Jan-1) was born on 16 Apr 1962 in Washington, DC.

Ulysses Kollecas son of Christopher Thomas (Kolecas) Collier and Amelia Malatras was born on 20 Mar 1958 in Washington, DC.
Ulysses Kollecas and Karen Rechcigl were married on 25 Aug 1990 in Bethesda, MD. They had the following children:
    i. **Kristin Kollecas** was born on 04 May 1993 in Albuquerque, NM.
    ii. **Paul Kollecas** was born on 02 Jun 1995 in Albuquerque, NM.

90. **Marcela Žďárská**-11 (Marta-10, Marie-9, Marie-8, František Antonín-7, František-6, Josef-5, Josef-4, Josef-3, Jan-2, Jan-1) was born on 09 May 1954 in Liberec.

Miroslav Heralecký son of Miroslav Heralecký and Marie Bartošová was born on 18 May 1949 in salomonJablonec nad Nisou, Czech.. He died on 20 Feb 2017 in Proseč, Jablonec nad Nisou, Czech..
Miroslav Heralecký and Marcela Žďárská were married on 15 Mar 1975 in Sychrov. They had the following children:
    i. **Vit Heralecký** was born on 16 Jan 1977 in Jablonec nad Nisou. He married Olga Zrubcová on 13 Jul 1996.
  123. ii. **Zuzana Heralecká** was born on 30 Dec 1978 in Jablonec nad Nisou. She married Jaroslav Egrt on 13 Sep 2002 in Jablonec nad Nisou.

91. **Iveta Žďárská**-11 (Marta-10, Marie-9, Marie-8, František Antonín-7, František-6, Josef-5, Josef-4, Josef-3, Jan-2, Jan-1) was born on 29 Aug 1963 in Liberec, Bohemia.

Vlastimil Berkman was born in 1957.
Vlastimil Berkman and Iveta Žďárská were married on 29 Oct 1983. They had the following children:
    i. **Tereza Hriníková** was born on 05 Jun 1984 in Jablonec nad Nisou.

Jaroslav Hrinik son of Jaroslav Hrinik and Milena Preisslerová was born on 17 Apr 1960.
Jaroslav Hrinik and Iveta Žďárská were married on 16 Aug 1991 in Zamek Červená Lhota. They had the following children:
    i. **Eliška Hriníková** was born on 23 Jun 1992 in Jablonec nad Nisou. She married Jan Ottis on 06 Oct 2018 in Jablonec nad

Jizerou, East Bohemia, Czech Republic.

92. **Marta Koubikova**-11 (Jiří-10, Marta-9, Marie-8, František Antonín-7, František-6, Josef-5, Josef-4, Josef-3, Jan-2, Jan-1) was born on 04 Jul 1962 in Mladá Boleslav.

    Vladimír Stibor was born on 04 Jun 1959 in Praha.

    Vladimír Stibor and Marta Koubikova were married on 17 Apr 1981. They had the following children:

    123. i. **Lucie Stiborová** was born on 29 Aug 1982 in Mladá Boleslav.

         ii. **Tadeáš Stibor** was born on 25 Jul 1988 in Mladá Boleslav.

93. **2nd Jiří Koubik**-11 (Jiří-10, Marta-9, Marie-8, František Antonín-7, František-6, Josef-5, Josef-4, Josef-3, Jan-2, Jan-1) was born on 13 May 1965 in Praha.

    Andrea Dunebierová was born on 25 Nov 1964 in Praha.

    2nd Jiří Koubik and Andrea Dunebierová were married on 04 Apr 1987 in Brandys nad Labem. They had the following children:

    124. i. **Roman Koubik** was born on 07 Aug 1987 in Brandys nad Labem.

         ii. **Vojtěch Koubik** was born on 24 Mar 1989 in Brandys nad Labem.

94. **Luděk Červený**-11 (Marie-10, Oldřich-9, Josef-8, František Antonín-7, František-6, Josef-5, Josef-4, Josef-3, Jan-2, Jan-1) was born on 17 Aug 1968 in Mladá Boleslav.

    Lenka Kovacova was born in Bratislava, Slovakia.

    Luděk Červený and Lenka Kovacova were married on 11 Mar 1989. They had the following children:

         i. **Lukáš Červený** was born on 05 Sep 1989.

         ii. **Roman Červený** was born on 06 Oct 1992.

95. **Radek Červený**-11 (Marie-10, Oldřich-9, Josef-8, František Antonín-7, František-6, Josef-5, Josef-4, Josef-3, Jan-2, Jan-1) was born on 23 May 1972 in Mladá Boleslav.

    Renata Bejrová was born in Koprnik, Mladá Boleslav Co..

    Radek Červený and Renata Bejrová were married on 05 Nov 1994. They had the following children:

         i. **Veronika Červená** was born on 20 May 1995.

         ii. **Štěpán Červený** was born on 11 Aug 2001.

96. **Otakar Lochman**-11 (Otakar-10, Marie-9, Emilie-8, František Antonín-7, František-6, Josef-5, Josef-4, Josef-3, Jan-2, Jan-1) was born on 01 Apr 1968 in Mladá Boleslav.
Štěpánka Jandová was born on 25 Oct 1970.
Otakar Lochman and Štěpánka Jandová were married on 27 Aug 1988 in Mnichovo Hradiště. They had the following children:
 i. **Otakar Lochman** was born on 17 Jan 1989 in Mladá Boleslav.
Ladislava (Viznerová) Černá was born on 15 Feb 1970 in Kladno.
Otakar Lochman and Ladislava (Viznerová) Černá were married on 25 Apr 1992 in Mnhichovo Hradiste. They had the following children:
 i. **Lucie Lochmanová** was born on 29 Jan 1992 in Mladá Boleslav.
 ii. **Luboš Lochman** was born on 19 Jan 2002 in Mlada Bolesalav.
98. **Václava Lochmanová**-11 (Otakar-10, Marie-9, Emilie-8, František Antonín-7, František-6, Josef-5, Josef-4, Josef-3, Jan-2, Jan-1) was born on 21 May 1972 in Mladá Boleslav.
Vladimír Pecina was born on 23 Oct 1961 in Mladá Boleslav.
Vladimír Pecina and Václava Lochmanová were married on 09 Sep 1995 in Mnichovo Hradiště. They had the following children:
 i. **Jana Pecinová** was born on 29 Jan 1996 in Mladá Boleslav.
 ii. **Václava Pecinová** was born on 07 Jan 1998 in Mladá Boleslav.
 iii. **Jitka Pecinová** was born on 01 May 2000 in Mladá Boleslav.
99. **Iva Lochmanová**-11 (Otakar-10, Marie-9, Emilie-8, František Antonín-7, František-6, Josef-5, Josef-4, Josef-3, Jan-2, Jan-1) was born on 28 Apr 1976 in Mladá Boleslav.
Libor Janoušek was born on 04 Aug 1976 in Mladá Boleslav.
Libor Janoušek and Iva Lochmanová were married on 21 Mar 1997 in Bakov nad Jizerou. They had the following children:
 i. **Pavla Janoušková** was born on 27 Jan 1999 in Mladá Boleslav.
100. **Sarka Konickova**-11 (Zdenka-10, Václav-9, Emilie-8, František Antonín-7, František-6, Josef-5, Josef-4, Josef-3, Jan-2, Jan-1) was born on 17 Dec 1974.
Miroslav Kaliban was born on 25 Nov 1973.
Miroslav Kaliban and Sarka Konickova married. They had the following

children:
   i.   **Tereza Kalibanova** was born on 14 May 2000.
100. **Oldrřch Šnajdr**-11 (Emilie-10, Vlasta-9, Emilie-8, František Antonín-7, František-6, Josef-5, Josef-4, Josef-3, Jan-2, Jan-1) was born on 04 Apr 1971 in Turnov.
   Daniela Synková was born in Mladá Boleslav.
   Oldrřch Šnajdr and Daniela Synková were married on 16 Mar 1991. They had the following children:
   i.   **Iveta Šnajdrová** was born on 11 Sep 1991 in Turnov.
   ii. **Filip Šnajdr** was born on 05 Apr 1995 in Turnov.
101. **Marie Šípová**-11 (Ladislav-10, Marie-9, Anna-8, Václav-7, František-6, Josef-5, Josef-4, Josef-3, Jan-2, Jan-1) was born on 08 Jun 1956 in Praha.
   Petr Retek son of Retek was born on 21 Jan 1944.
   Petr Retek and Marie Šípová married. They had the following children:
   i.   **Magdalena Retková** was born on 31 Dec 1982 in Praha.
102. **Ladislav Šíp**-11 (Ladislav-10, Marie-9, Anna-8, Václav-7, František-6, Josef-5, Josef-4, Josef-3, Jan-2, Jan-1) was born on 11 Sep 1958 in Praha.
   Hanička Kratochvílová was born on 24 Jun 1960 in Praha.
   Ladislav Šíp and Hanička Kratochvílová married. They had the following children:
   i.   **Ladislav Šíp** was born on 22 Nov 1984 in Praha.
   ii. **Martin Šíp** was born on 11 Nov 1985 in Praha.
103. **Milan Stejskal**-11 (Josef-10, Josef-9, Emilie Kateřina-8, Václav-7, František-6, Josef-5, Josef-4, Josef-3, Jan-2, Jan-1) was born in 1960.
   Lenka Soupkova was born in 1963.
   Milan Stejskal and Lenka Soupkova married. They had the following children:
   i.   **Martin Stejskal** was born in 1989.
   ii. **Jiří Stejskal** was born in 1990.
104. **Sona Bukvičková**-11 (Jiří-10, Antonín-9, Marie-8, Barbora-7, František-6, Josef-5, Josef-4, Josef-3, Jan-2, Jan-1) was born on 26 Jan 1965 in Mladá Boleslav.
   Imrich Rigo.

Imrich Rigo and Sona Bukvičková married. They had the following children:
- i. **Zuzanka Rigová** was born on 13 Apr 1987 in Mladá Boleslav.
- ii. **Janicka Rigová** was born on 05 Feb 1990 in Mladá Boleslav.

105. **Ludmila Bukvičková**-11 (Josef-10, Josef-9, Marie-8, Barbora-7, František-6, Josef-5, Josef-4, Josef-3, Jan-2, Jan-1) was born on 31 Aug 1959 in Mladá Boleslav.

    Frantiosek Šafránek was born on 09 Apr 1959 in Dymokury.

    Frantiosek Šafránek and Ludmila Bukvičková were married on 09 Sep 1984. They had the following children:
    - i. **František Šafránek** was born on 15 Jun 1984.
    - ii. **Petr Šafránek** was born on 12 Aug 1986.
    - iii. **Jan Šafránek** was born on 05 Dec 1988.

106. **Jiří Wagenknecht**-11 (Jiřina-10, Josef-9, Marie-8, Barbora-7, František-6, Josef-5, Josef-4, Josef-3, Jan-2, Jan-1) was born on 10 Jan 1946.

    Vendulka Zahorska was born on 06 Jun 1949.

    Jiří Wagenknecht and Vendulka Zahorska married. They had the following children:
    - i. **Jan Wagenknecht** was born on 16 Feb 1974.
    - ii. **Lenka Wagenknechtova** was born on 14 Jan 1980.

107. **Jan Wagenknecht**-11 (Jiřina-10, Josef-9, Marie-8, Barbora-7, František-6, Josef-5, Josef-4, Josef-3, Jan-2, Jan-1) was born on 30 Nov 1949.

    Jana Nováková was born on 08 Apr 1955.

    Jan Wagenknecht and Jana Nováková married. They had the following children:
    - i. **Jana Wagenknechtova** was born on 09 Sep 1978.
    - ii. **Pavlina Wagenknechtova** was born on 15 Jun 1984.

108. **Mirek Hyka**-11 (Miroslav-10, Marie-9, Marie-8, Barbora-7, František-6, Josef-5, Josef-4, Josef-3, Jan-2, Jan-1).

    Unknown.

    Mirek Hyka and Unknown married. They had the following children:
    - i. **Mirek Hyka**.
    - ii. **daughter Hyka**.

109. **Jan Hyka**-11 (Miroslav-10, Marie-9, Marie-8, Barbora-7, František-6, Josef-5, Josef-4, Josef-3, Jan-2, Jan-1).
Olga.
Jan Hyka and Olga married. They had the following children:
   i. **Jan Hyka.**
110. **Ladislav Sedláček**-11 (Milena-10, Marie-9, Marie-8, Barbora-7, František-6, Josef-5, Josef-4, Josef-3, Jan-2, Jan-1).
Unknown.
Ladislav Sedláček and Unknown married. They had the following children:
   i. **son Sedláček.**
111. **Milena Sedláčková**-11 (Milena-10, Marie-9, Marie-8, Barbora-7, František-6, Josef-5, Josef-4, Josef-3, Jan-2, Jan-1).
Michetslaeger was born in Turnov.
Michetslaeger and Milena Sedláčková married. They had the following children:
   i. **daughter Michetslaegerova.**
   ii. **son Michetslaeger.**
112. **Jitka Hrušová**-11 (Květa-10, Růžena-9, Antonín-8, Barbora-7, František-6, Josef-5, Josef-4, Josef-3, Jan-2, Jan-1) was born on 11 Nov 1956 in Turnov.
Josef Brzobohatý was born on 02 Jul 1955 in Knezmost.
Josef Brzobohatý and Jitka Hrušová married. They had the following children:
   i. **Petra Brzobohatá** was born on 05 Feb 1980.
   ii. **Josef Brzobohatý** was born on 21 Jun 1984.
113. **Zdeněk Hrůša**-11 (Květa-10, Růžena-9, Antonín-8, Barbora-7, František-6, Josef-5, Josef-4, Josef-3, Jan-2, Jan-1) was born in Nov 1957 in Turnov.
Libuše Machackova.
Zdeněk Hrůša and Libuše Machackova married. They had the following children:
   i. **Ondřej Hrůša** was born on 05 Oct 1987 in Turnov.
114. **Josef Hrůša**-11 (Květa-10, Růžena-9, Antonín-8, Barbora-7, František-6,

Josef-5, Josef-4, Josef-3, Jan-2, Jan-1) was born on 13 Aug 1959 in Turnov.
Jana Kindlova.
Josef Hrůša and Jana Kindlova married. They had the following children:
  i. **Zuzana Hrušová** was born on 28 Mar 1984.
115. **Iva Dandová**-11 (Bohuslav Zdeněk-10, Bohuslav-9, Bohuslav Jiří-8, František-7, František-6, František-5, Josef-4, Josef-3, Jan-2, Jan-1) was born on 04 Apr 1951 in Kneznice.
Kožený.
Kožený and Iva Dandová married. They had the following children:
  i. **Olina Kožená.**
  ii. **Aleš Kožený.**
116. **Zdeněk Danda**-11 (Bohuslav Zdeněk-10, Bohuslav-9, Bohuslav Jiří-8, František-7, František-6, František-5, Josef-4, Josef-3, Jan-2, Jan-1) was born on 30 Jun 1952 in Kneznice.
Radka Kopecka was born in Ktova.
Zdeněk Danda and Radka Kopecka married. They had the following children:
  i. **Petra Dandová.**
  ii. **Zdeněk Danda.**
117. **Radomil Danda**-11 (Bohuslav Zdeněk-10, Bohuslav-9, Bohuslav Jiří-8, František-7, František-6, František-5, Josef-4, Josef-3, Jan-2, Jan-1) was born on 10 Apr 1956 in Kneznice.
Ludmila Spisová was born in Rulcova.
Radomil Danda and Ludmila Spisová married. They had the following children:
  125. i. **Radek Danda.**
  ii. **Tomáš Danda.**
118. **Milan Dědič**-11 (Eva-10, Jiří-9, Jaroslav-8, František-7, František-6, František-5, Josef-4, Josef-3, Jan-2, Jan-1) was born on 03 Oct 1977 in Prague, Czechoslovakia.
Eva Stanislavska daughter of Jaroslav Stanislavsky and Dana was born on 16 Jun 1978 in Polepy u Melnika.
Milan Dědič and Eva Stanislavska married. They had the following

children:
   i. **Ema Dědičová** was born on 07 Oct 2007 in Melnik.
   ii. **Berta Dědičová** was born on 12 Jan 2011 in Melnik.
119. **Jaroslav Dědič**-11 (Eva-10, Jiří-9, Jaroslav-8, František-7, František-6, František-5, Josef-4, Josef-3, Jan-2, Jan-1) was born on 08 Jan 1980 in Prague, Czechoslovakia.
   Jaroslav Dědič and unknown spouse married. They had the following children:
   i. **Matylda Dědičová**.
120. **Petr Dědič**-11 (Eva-10, Jiří-9, Jaroslav-8, František-7, František-6, František-5, Josef-4, Josef-3, Jan-2, Jan-1) was born on 27 Apr 1985 in Prague, Czechoslovakia.
   Veroniika Šulcová was born in 1985 in Mladá Boleslav.
   Petr Dědič and Veroniika Šulcová married. They had the following children:
   i. **Sarlota Dědičová** was born on 30 Dec 2015 in Mladá Boleslav.
   ii. **Simon Dědič** was born on 26 Aug 2018.

Generation 12

121. **Kevin Thomas Rechcigl**-12 (John Edward-11, Mila (Miloslav)-10, Marie-9, Marie-8, František Antonín-7, František-6, Josef-5, Josef-4, Josef-3, Jan-2, Jan-1) was born on 09 Oct 1991 in Bradenton, FL.
   Jordan Robbins daughter of Douglass Robbins and Ivonne was born on 10 Jan 1992 in Camarillo, CA.
   Kevin Thomas Rechcigl and Jordan Robbins were married on 12 May 2018 in Jacksonville, FL. They had the following children:
   i. **James Douglas Rechcigl** was born on 05 Jan 2021 in Jacksonville, FL.
   ii. **Evelyn Marie Rechcigl** was born 29 May 2023 in Jacksonville, FL.
122. **Zuzana Heralecká**-12 (Marcela-11, Marta-10, Marie-9, Marie-8, František Antonín-7, František-6, Josef-5, Josef-4, Josef-3, Jan-2, Jan-1) was born on 30 Dec 1978 in Jablonec nad Nisou.
   Jaroslav Egrt was born on 25 Apr 1974 in Duchcov.
   Jaroslav Egrt and Zuzana Heralecká were married on 13 Sep 2002 in

Jablonec nad Nisou. They had the following children:
- iii. **Kristina Egrtova** was born on 04 Jan 2008 in Liberec.
- iv. **Jaroslav Egrt** was born on 04 Jan 2008 in Liberec.

123. **Lucie Stiborová**-12 (Marta-11, Jiří-10, Marta-9, Marie-8, František Antonín-7, František-6, Josef-5, Josef-4, Josef-3, Jan-2, Jan-1) was born on 29 Aug 1982 in Mladá Boleslav.
Novotný.
Novotný and Lucie Stiborová married. They had the following children:
- v. **Tobias Novotný.**

124. **Roman Koubik**-12 (2nd Jiří-11, Jiří-10, Marta-9, Marie-8, František Antonín-7, František-6, Josef-5, Josef-4, Josef-3, Jan-2, Jan-1) was born on 07 Aug 1987 in Brandys nad Labem.
Martina.
Roman Koubik and Martina married. They had the following children:
- i. **Roman Koubik.**

125. **Radek Danda**-12 (Radomil-11, Bohuslav Zdeněk-10, Bohuslav-9, Bohuslav Jiří-8, František-7, František-6, František-5, Josef-4, Josef-3, Jan-2, Jan-1).
Radek Danda and unknown spouse married. They had the following children:
- i. **daughter Dandová.**
- ii. **daughter Dandová.**

Sources

1 Matrika krestni: Hoškovice, Kniha 104, List 172, Krestni a rodny list.
2 Matrika krestni, Kniha Z, List 65, Krestni a rodny list.

Cimr Family

Generation 1

1. **Josef Cimr**-1 was born in Manikovice No. 11.
   Kodrova ? Anna Kochova was born in Bitouchov.
   Josef Cimr and Kodrova ? Anna Kochova married. They had the following children:
   2. i. **František Cimr** was born on 31 Mar 1823 in Manikovice No. 11, Mnichovo Hradiště Co.. He died on 22 Mar 1884.

Generation 2

2. **František Cimr**-2 (Josef-1) was born on 31 Mar 1823 in Manikovice No. 11, Mnichovo Hradiště Co.. He died on 22 Mar 1884.
   Anna Ferklová daughter of Josef Ferkl and Alžběta Filipová was born in Rostkov No. 3, Mnichovo Hradiště Co..
   František Cimr and Anna Ferklová married. They had the following children:
   i. **Josef Cimr** was born on 06 Jan 1850.
   ii. **Václav Cimr** was born on 25 Mar 1851.
   iii. **František Cimr** was born on 26 Jan 1853.
   iv. **Antonín Cimr** was born on 19 Dec 1855. He died on 17 Mar 1856.
   4. v. **Josefa Cimrová** was born on 01 Jan 1859 in Manikovice No. 11, Mnichovo Hradiště Dist.. She married František Antonín Danda on 04 Feb 1881 in Manikovice No. 21. She died on 27 Aug 1923 in Hoškovice No. 14, Mnichovo Hradiště Dist..
   vi. **Štěpán Cimr** was born on 26 May 1860.
   vii. **Jan Cimr** was born on 21 Apr 1862.
   viii. **Anna Cimrová** was born on 05 Aug 1864.
   ix. **Vincenc Cimr** was born on 16 Apr 1870.

Generation 3

3. **Josefa Cimrová**-3 (František-2, Josef-1) was born on 01 Jan 1859 in Manikovice No. 11, Mnichovo Hradiště Dist.. She died on 27 Aug 1923 in Hoškovice No. 14, Mnichovo Hradiště Dist..
   František Antonín Danda son of František Danda and Kateřina

Nováková was born on 10 Jun 1857 in Hoškovice, No. 2, Mnichovo Hradiště Dist, Bohemia. He died on 07 Jun 1900 in Hoškovice, No. 14, Mnichovo Hradiště Dist, Bohemia.

František Antonín Danda and Josefa Cimrová were married on 04 Feb 1881 in Manikovice No. 21. They had the following children:

4. i. **Marie Dandová**[1] was born on 31 Jan 1882 in Hoškovice, No. 14, Mnichovo Hradiště Dist, Bohemia. She married Čeněk Rajtr on 02 Jul 1904 in Mnichovo Hradiště. She died on 05 Jul 1967 in Dolanky No. 7, Mnichovo Hradiště Co..
5. ii. **Josef Danda** was born on 30 Jan 1884 in Hoškovice, No. 14, Mnichovo Hradiště Dist, Bohemia. He died on 18 Apr 1936 in Dobrá Voda.
    iii. **Josefa Kateřina Dandová** was born on 04 Oct 1885 in Hoškovice No. 14, Mnichovo Hradiště Dist.. She married Václav Balák after 1925.
    iv. **Anna Dandová** was born on 12 Nov 1886 in Hoškovice, No. 14, Mnichovo Hradiště Dist, Bohemia. She died on 13 May 1972.
    v. **František Danda** was born on 23 Apr 1888 in Hoškovice, No. 14, Mnichovo Hradiště Dist, Bohemia. He died on 27 Jun 1888 in Hoškovice, No. 14, Mnichovo Hradiště Dist, Bohemia.
    vi. **František Danda** was born on 13 Nov 1889 in Hoškovice No. 14, Mnichovo Hradiště Dist.. He died on 22 Dec 1891 in Hoškovice no. 14, Mnichovo Hradiště Dist, Bohemia.
    vii. **Václav Danda** was born on 05 Sep 1891 in Hoškovice No. 14, Mnichovo Hradiště Dist, Bohemia. He died on 10 Mar 1892 in Hoškovice No. 14, Mnichovo Hradiště Dist, Bohemia.
6. viii. **Emilie Dandová** was born on 22 Oct 1893 in Hoškovice No. 14, Mnichovo Hradiště Dist, Bohemia. She married Václav Balák on 18 Sep 1920 in Hoškovice, Mnichovo Hradiště Dist, Bohemia. She died on 06 Apr 1924 in Hoškovice, Mnichovo Hradiště Dist, Bohemia.

Generation 4

4. **Marie Dandová**-4 (Josefa-3, František-2, Josef-1)[1] was born on 31 Jan 1882 in Hoškovice, No. 14, Mnichovo Hradiště Dist, Bohemia. She died on 05 Jul 1967 in Dolanky No. 7, Mnichovo Hradiště Co..

   Čeněk Rajtr son of Jan Václav Rajtr and Anna Najmanová[2] was born on 01 Jul 1874 in nky No. 7, Mnichovo Hradiště Dist... He died on 27 Oct 1956 in Dolánky No. 7, Mnichovo Hradiště Dist...

   Čeněk Rajtr and Marie Dandová were married on 02 Jul 1904 in Mnichovo Hradiště. They had the following children:

   7. i. **Marie Rajtrová** was born on 05 Jul 1905 in Dolanky No. 7, Mnichovo Hradiště Co.. She married Miloslav Rechcigl on 26 Jul 1926 in Praha - Kralovske Vinohrady. She died on 13 Apr 1982 in Mladá Boleslav.

      ii. **Oldrřch Rajtr** was born on 14 Nov 1907 in Dolanky No. 7. He died on 02 Nov 1937.

   8. iii. **Marta Rajtrová** was born on 10 Jan 1909 in Dolanky u Bakova. She married Josef Knotek in 1934. She died on 29 Nov 1982 in Mladá Boleslav.

5. **Josef Danda**-4 (Josefa-3, František-2, Josef-1) was born on 30 Jan 1884 in Hoškovice, No. 14, Mnichovo Hradiště Dist, Bohemia. He died on 18 Apr 1936 in Dobrá Voda.

   Božena Slavíková daughter of Josef Slavik and Anna Jirova was born on 05 Sep 1889 in Lesnovky, Turnov Dist... She died on 06 Oct 1965 in Dobrá Voda.

   Josef Danda and Božena Slavíková married. They had the following children:

   9. i. **Oldřich Danda** was born on 29 Jan 1922 in Hoškovice No. 10, Mnichovo Hradiště Dist, Bohemia. He died on 30 Jan 1983 in Dobrá Voda, Mnichovo Hradiště Co..

6. **Emilie Dandová**-4 (Josefa-3, František-2, Josef-1) was born on 22 Oct 1893 in Hoškovice No. 14, Mnichovo Hradiště Dist, Bohemia. She died on 06 Apr 1924 in Hoškovice, Mnichovo Hradiště Dist, Bohemia.

   Václav Balák son of Václav Balak and Kateřina Janoušková was born about 1890 in Nová Ves No. 13, Mnichovo Hradiště District.

Václav Balák and Emilie Dandová were married on 18 Sep 1920 in Hoškovice, Mnichovo Hradiště Dist, Bohemia. They had the following children:

10. i. **Marie Balakova** was born on 16 Feb 1921 in Hoškovice No. 14, Mnichovo Hradiště Dist.. She married Otakar Lochman on 04 Nov 1942 in Mnichovo Hradiště.

11. ii. **Václav Balak** was born on 06 Jun 1922 in Hoškovice. He died on 24 Jan 2001. He married Zdenka Štolbová on 31 Dec.

12. iii. **Vlasta Balakova** was born on 02 Sep 1923 in Hoškovice, Mnichovo Hradiště Co.. She married Milous Bičík in 1948.

Generation 5

7. **Marie Rajtrová**-5 (Marie-4, Josefa-3, František-2, Josef-1) was born on 05 Jul 1905 in Dolanky No. 7, Mnichovo Hradiště Co.. She died on 13 Apr 1982 in Mladá Boleslav.

Miloslav Rechcigl son of Adolf Rechcigl and Marie Berglová was born on 13 May 1904 in Kocňovice (renamed Chocnějovice) No. 22. He died on 27 May 1973 in Washington, DC.

Miloslav Rechcigl and Marie Rajtrová were married on 26 Jul 1926 in Praha - Kralovske Vinohrady. They had the following children:

13. i. **Mila (Miloslav) Rechcigl Jr.** was born on 30 Jul 1930 in Mladá Boleslav, CSR. He married Eva Edwards (Eisnerová) on 29 Aug 1953 in New York, NY.

14. ii. **Marta Rechcíglová** was born on 23 May 1933 in Mladá Boleslav. She married František Žďárský on 03 Oct 1953 in Mladá Boleslav. She died on 13 Sep 2018 in Mladá Boleslav.

8. **Marta Rajtrová**-5 (Marie-4, Josefa-3, František-2, Josef-1) was born on 10 Jan 1909 in Dolanky u Bakova. She died on 29 Nov 1982 in Mladá Boleslav.

Josef Knotek was born between 1905-1907 in Mala Bela, p. Bakov nad Jizerou. He died in 1934. Josef Knotek and Marta Rajtrová were married in 1934. They had no children.

Miroslav Koubik son of Koubik was born in 1908 in Terezin. He died in

1968 in Havlickuv Brod.

Miroslav Koubik and Marta Rajtrová were married on 26 Jul 1938 in Praha. They had the following children:

15. i. **Jiří Koubik** was born on 29 Jan 1940 in Prague. He married Jiřina Muellerová on 31 Jan 1962 in Praha. He died on 26 Jun 1998 in Brandys nad Labem.

Emil Pazderník was born after 1900.

Emil Pazderník and Marta Rajtrová were married after 1945. They had no children.

Karel Horáček.

Karel Horáček and Marta Rajtrová met. They had no children.

9. **Oldřich Danda**-5 (Josef-4, Josefa-3, František-2, Josef-1) was born on 29 Jan 1922 in Hoškovice No. 10, Mnichovo Hradiště Dist, Bohemia. He died on 30 Jan 1983 in Dobrá Voda, Mnichovo Hradiště Co..

Marie Augustinova was born on 01 Jun 1923 in Dobrá Voda, Mnichovo Hradiště Co.. She died on 03 Jan 2003 in Dobrá Voda, Mnichovo Hradiště Co..

Oldřich Danda and Marie Augustinova married. They had the following children:

   i. **Oldrřch Danda** was born on 06 Sep 1958 in Turnov.

17. ii. **Marie Dandová** was born on 12 Jun 1946 in Mnichovo Hradiště.

10. **Marie Balakova**-5 (Emilie-4, Josefa-3, František-2, Josef-1) was born on 16 Feb 1921 in Hoškovice No. 14, Mnichovo Hradiště Dist..

Otakar Lochman was born on 13 Jan 1917 in Hradec, Mnichovo Hrtadiste Dist.. He died on 22 Sep 1980.

Otakar Lochman and Marie Balakova were married on 04 Nov 1942 in Mnichovo Hradiště. They had the following children:

17. i. **Otakar Lochman** was born on 24 Dec 1944 in Mnichovo Hradiště. He married Václava Bártová on 12 Nov 1966 in Turnov.

11. **Václav Balak**-5 (Emilie-4, Josefa-3, František-2, Josef-1) was born on 06 Jun 1922 in Hoškovice. He died on 24 Jan 2001.

Zdenka Štolbová was born on 22 Dec 1930. She died on 01 Jan 1985.

Václav Balak and Zdenka Štolbová were married on 31 Dec. They had

the following children:
- i. **Sarka Balakova** was born about 1950.
- 19. ii. **Zdenka Balakova** was born on 16 Nov 1952. She married Bohumil Konicek on 08 Jun 1974.

12. **Vlasta Balakova**-5 (Emilie-4, Josefa-3, František-2, Josef-1) was born on 02 Sep 1923 in Hoškovice, Mnichovo Hradiště Co..
Milous Bičík was born on 28 Jun 1920. He died on 24 Mar 1988.
Milous Bičík and Vlasta Balakova were married in 1948. They had the following children:
- 19. i. **Emilie Bičíková** was born on 08 Mar 1949 in Turnov. She married Oldrřch Šnajdr on 08 Oct 1970.

Generation 6

13. **Mila (Miloslav) Rechcigl Jr.**-6 (Marie-5, Marie-4, Josefa-3, František-2, Josef-1) was born on 30 Jul 1930 in Mladá Boleslav, CSR.
Eva Edwards (Eisnerová) daughter of Paul J. Edwards (Pavel Eisner) and Jiřina Taussigová was born on 21 Jan 1932 in Prague, CSR.
Mila (Miloslav) Rechcigl Jr. and Eva Edwards (Eisnerová) were married on 29 Aug 1953 in New York, NY. They had the following children:
- 20. i. **John Edward Rechcigl** was born on 27 Feb 1960 in Washington, D.C.. He married Nancy Ann Palko on 30 Jul 1983 in Dover, NJ.
- 21. ii. **Karen Rechcigl** was born on 16 Apr 1962 in Washington, DC. She married Ulysses Kollecas on 25 Aug 1990 in Bethesda, MD.

14. **Marta Rechcíglová**-6 (Marie-5, Marie-4, Josefa-3, František-2, Josef-1) was born on 23 May 1933 in Mladá Boleslav. She died on 13 Sep 2018 in Mladá Boleslav.
František Žďárský son of František Václav Žďárský and Eliška Foltýnová was born on 21 May 1932 in Turnov.
František Žďárský and Marta Rechcíglová were married on 03 Oct 1953 in Mladá Boleslav. They had the following children:
- 22. i. **Marcela Žďárská** was born on 09 May 1954 in Liberec. She married Miroslav Heralecký on 15 Mar 1975 in Sychrov.
- 23. ii. **Iveta Žďárská** was born on 29 Aug 1963 in Liberec, Bohemia. She married Vlastimil Berkman on 29 Oct 1983.

15. **Jiří Koubik**-6 (Marta-5, Marie-4, Josefa-3, František-2, Josef-1) was born on 29 Jan 1940 in Prague. He died on 26 Jun 1998 in Brandys nad Labem.
    Jiřina Muellerová was born on 27 Feb 1943 in Buda.
    Jiří Koubik and Jiřina Muellerová were married on 31 Jan 1962 in Praha. They had the following children:
    24. i. **Marta Koubikova** was born on 04 Jul 1962 in Mladá Boleslav. She married Vladimír Stibor on 17 Apr 1981.
    25. ii. **2nd Jiří Koubik** was born on 13 May 1965 in Praha. He married Andrea Dunebierová on 4 Apr 1987 in Brandys nad Labem.
16. **Marie Dandová**-6 (Oldřich-5, Josef-4, Josefa-3, František-2, Josef-1) was born on 12 Jun 1946 in Mnichovo Hradiště.
    Květoslav Červený was born on 07 Mar 1945 in Bosen, Mladá Boleslav Co..
    Květoslav Červený and Marie Dandová married. They had the following children:
    26. i. **Luděk Červený** was born on 17 Aug 1968 in Mladá Boleslav. He married Lenka Kovacova on 11 Mar 1989.
    27. ii. **Radek Červený** was born on 23 May 1972 in Mladá Boleslav. He married Renata Bejrová on 05 Nov 1994.
17. **Otakar Lochman**-6 (Marie-5, Emilie-4, Josefa-3, František-2, Josef-1) was born on 24 Dec 1944 in Mnichovo Hradiště.
    Václava Bártová was born on 26 Sep 1948 in Mladá Boleslav.
    Otakar Lochman and Václava Bártová were married on 12 Nov 1966 in Turnov. They had the following children:
    28. i. **Otakar Lochman** was born on 01 Apr 1968 in Mladá Boleslav. He married Štěpánka Jandová on 27 Aug 1988 in Mnichovo Hradiště.
    29. ii. **Václava Lochmanová** was born on 21 May 1972 in Mladá Boleslav. She married Vladimír Pecina on 09 Sep 1995 in Mnichovo Hradiště.
    30. iii. **Iva Lochmanová** was born on 28 Apr 1976 in Mladá Boleslav. She married Libor Janoušek on 21 Mar 1997 in Bakov nad Jizerou.
18. **Zdenka Balakova**-6 (Václav-5, Emilie-4, Josefa-3, František-2, Josef-1) was born on 16 Nov 1952.
    Bohumil Konicek was born on 19 Jun 1953.

Bohumil Konicek and Zdenka Balakova were married on 08 Jun 1974. They had the following children:
- 31. i. **Sarka Konickova** was born on 17 Dec 1974.
-      ii. **Lukáš Konicek** was born on 14 May 1985.

19. **Emilie Bičíková**-6 (Vlasta-5, Emilie-4, Josefa-3, František-2, Josef-1) was born on 08 Mar 1949 in Turnov.
    Oldrřch Šnajdr was born on 07 May 1949 in Brehy.
    Oldrřch Šnajdr and Emilie Bičíková were married on 08 Oct 1970. They had the following children:
    - 32. i. **Oldrřch Šnajdr** was born on 04 Apr 1971 in Turnov. He married Daniela Synková on 16 Mar 1991.
    -      ii. **Jiří Šnajdr** was born on 10 Nov 1977 in Turnov.

Generation 7

20. **John Edward Rechcigl**-7 (Mila (Miloslav)-6, Marie-5, Marie-4, Josefa-3, František-2, Josef-1) was born on 27 Feb 1960 in Washington, D.C..
    Nancy Ann Palko daughter of Joseph Palko and Mary Rishko was born on 26 Sep 1961 in Morristown, NJ.
    John Edward Rechcigl and Nancy Ann Palko were married on 30 Jul 1983 in Dover, NJ. They had the following children:
    -      i. **Gregory John Rechcigl** was born on 19 Dec 1988 in Bradenton, FL.
    - 33. ii. **Kevin Thomas Rechcigl** was born on 09 Oct 1991 in Bradenton, FL. He married Jordan Robbins on 12 May 2018 in Jacksonville, FL.
    -      iii. **Lindsey Nicole Rechcigl** was born on 03 Nov 1994 in Bradenton, FL.

21. **Karen Rechcigl**-7 (Mila (Miloslav)-6, Marie-5, Marie-4, Josefa-3, František-2, Josef-1) was born on 16 Apr 1962 in Washington, DC.
    Ulysses Kollecas son of Christopher Thomas (Kolecas) Collier and Amelia Malatras was born on 20 Mar 1958 in Washington, DC.
    Ulysses Kollecas and Karen Rechcigl were married on 25 Aug 1990 in Bethesda, MD. They had the following children:
    -      i. **Kristin Kollecas** was born on 04 May 1993 in Albuquerque, NM.
    -      ii. **Paul Kollecas** was born on 02 Jun 1995 in Albuquerque, NM.

22. **Marcela Žďárská**-7 (Marta-6, Marie-5, Marie-4, Josefa-3, František-2, Josef-1) was born on 09 May 1954 in Liberec.

    Miroslav Heralecký son of Miroslav Heralecký and Marie Bartošová was born on 18 May 1949 in salomonJablonec nad Nisou, Czech.. He died on 20 Feb 2017 in Proseč, Jablonec nad Nisou, Czech..

    Miroslav Heralecký and Marcela Žďárská were married on 15 Mar 1975 in Sychrov. They had the following children:

    - i. **Vit Heralecký** was born on 16 Jan 1977 in Jablonec nad Nisou. He married Olga Zrubcová on 13 Jul 1996.
    - 35. ii. **Zuzana Heralecká** was born on 30 Dec 1978 in Jablonec nad Nisou. She married Jaroslav Egrt on 13 Sep 2002 in Jablonec nad Nisou.

23. **Iveta Žďárská**-7 (Marta-6, Marie-5, Marie-4, Josefa-3, František-2, Josef-1) was born on 29 Aug 1963 in Liberec, Bohemia.

    Vlastimil Berkman was born in 1957.

    Vlastimil Berkman and Iveta Žďárská were married on 29 Oct 1983. They had the following children:

    - i. **Tereza Hriníková** was born on 05 Jun 1984 in Jablonec nad Nisou.

    Jaroslav Hrinik son of Jaroslav Hrinik and Milena Preisslerová was born on 17 Apr 1960.

    Jaroslav Hrinik and Iveta Žďárská were married on 16 Aug 1991 in Zamek Červená Lhota. They had the following children:

    - i. **Eliška Hriníková** was born on 23 Jun 1992 in Jablonec nad Nisou. She married Jan Ottis on 06 Oct 2018 in Jablonec nad Jizerou, East Bohemia, Czech Republic.

24. **Marta Koubikova**-7 (Jiří-6, Marta-5, Marie-4, Josefa-3, František-2, Josef-1) was born on 04 Jul 1962 in Mladá Boleslav.

    Vladimír Stibor was born on 04 Jun 1959 in Praha.

    Vladimír Stibor and Marta Koubikova were married on 17 Apr 1981. They had the following children:

    - 35. i. **Lucie Stiborová** was born on 29 Aug 1982 in Mladá Boleslav.
    - ii. **Tadeáš Stibor** was born on 25 Jul 1988 in Mladá Boleslav.

25. **2nd Jiří Koubik**-7 (Jiří-6, Marta-5, Marie-4, Josefa-3, František-2, Josef-1) was born on 13 May 1965 in Praha.
    Andrea Dunebierová was born on 25 Nov 1964 in Praha.
    2nd Jiří Koubik and Andrea Dunebierová were married on 04 Apr 1987 in Brandys nad Labem. They had the following children:
    36. i. **Roman Koubik** was born on 07 Aug 1987 in Brandys nad Labem.
        ii. **Vojtěch Koubik** was born on 24 Mar 1989 in Brandys nad Labem.
26. **Luděk Červený**-7 (Marie-6, Oldřich-5, Josef-4, Josefa-3, František-2, Josef-1) was born on 17 Aug 1968 in Mladá Boleslav.
    Lenka Kovacova was born in Bratislava, Slovakia.
    Luděk Červený and Lenka Kovacova were married on 11 Mar 1989. They had the following children:
    i. **Lukáš Červený** was born on 05 Sep 1989.
    ii. **Roman Červený** was born on 06 Oct 1992.
27. **Radek Červený**-7 (Marie-6, Oldřich-5, Josef-4, Josefa-3, František-2, Josef-1) was born on 23 May 1972 in Mladá Boleslav.
    Renata Bejrová was born in Koprnik, Mladá Boleslav Co..
    Radek Červený and Renata Bejrová were married on 05 Nov 1994. They had the following children:
    i. **Veronika Červená** was born on 20 May 1995.
    ii. **Štěpán Červený** was born on 11 Aug 2001.
28. **Otakar Lochman**-7 (Otakar-6, Marie-5, Emilie-4, Josefa-3, František-2, Josef-1) was born on 01 Apr 1968 in Mladá Boleslav.
    Štěpánka Jandová was born on 25 Oct 1970.
    Otakar Lochman and Štěpánka Jandová were married on 27 Aug 1988 in Mnichovo Hradiště. They had the following children:
    i. **Otakar Lochman** was born on 17 Jan 1989 in Mladá Boleslav.
    Ladislava (Viznerová) Černá was born on 15 Feb 1970 in Kladno.
    Otakar Lochman and Ladislava (Viznerová) Černá were married on 25 Apr 1992 in Mnhichovo Hradiste. They had the following children:
    i. **Lucie Lochmanová** was born on 29 Jan 1992 in Mladá Boleslav.
    ii. **Luboš Lochman** was born on 19 Jan 2002 in Mlada Bolesalav.
29. **Václava Lochmanová**-7 (Otakar-6, Marie-5, Emilie-4, Josefa-3,

František-2, Josef-1) was born on 21 May 1972 in Mladá Boleslav.
Vladimír Pecina was born on 23 Oct 1961 in Mladá Boleslav.
Vladimír Pecina and Václava Lochmanová were married on 09 Sep 1995 in Mnichovo Hradiště. They had the following children:
   i. **Jana Pecinová** was born on 29 Jan 1996 in Mladá Boleslav.
   ii. **Václava Pecinová** was born on 07 Jan 1998 in Mladá Boleslav.
   iii. **Jitka Pecinová** was born on 01 May 2000 in Mladá Boleslav.
30. **Iva Lochmanová**-7 (Otakar-6, Marie-5, Emilie-4, Josefa-3, František-2, Josef-1) was born on 28 Apr 1976 in Mladá Boleslav.
Libor Janoušek was born on 04 Aug 1976 in Mladá Boleslav.
Libor Janoušek and Iva Lochmanová were married on 21 Mar 1997 in Bakov nad Jizerou. They had the following children:
   i. **Pavla Janoušková** was born on 27 Jan 1999 in Mladá Boleslav.
31. **Sarka Konickova**-7 (Zdenka-6, Václav-5, Emilie-4, Josefa-3, František-2, Josef-1) was born on 17 Dec 1974.
Miroslav Kaliban was born on 25 Nov 1973.
Miroslav Kaliban and Sarka Konickova married. They had the following children:
   i. **Tereza Kalibanova** was born on 14 May 2000.
32. **Oldrřch Šnajdr**-7 (Emilie-6, Vlasta-5, Emilie-4, Josefa-3, František-2, Josef-1) was born on 04 Apr 1971 in Turnov.
Daniela Synková was born in Mladá Boleslav.
Oldrřch Šnajdr and Daniela Synková were married on 16 Mar 1991. They had the following children:
   i. **Iveta Šnajdrová** was born on 11 Sep 1991 in Turnov.
   ii. **Filip Šnajdr** was born on 05 Apr 1995 in Turnov.

Generation 8

33. **Kevin Thomas Rechcigl**-8 (John Edward-7, Mila (Miloslav)-6, Marie-5, Marie-4, Josefa-3, František-2, Josef-1) was born on 09 Oct 1991 in Bradenton, FL.
Jordan Robbins daughter of Douglass Robbins and Ivonne was born on 10 Jan 1992 in Camarillo, CA.
Kevin Thomas Rechcigl and Jordan Robbins were married on 12 May

2018 in Jacksonville, FL. They had the following children:
  i. **James Douglas Rechcigl** was born on 05 Jan 2021 in Jacksonville, FL.
  ii. **Evelyn Marie Rechcigl** was born 29 May 2023 in Jacksonville, FL.
34. **Zuzana Heralecká**-8 (Marcela-7, Marta-6, Marie-5, Marie-4, Josefa-3, František-2, Josef-1) was born on 30 Dec 1978 in Jablonec nad Nisou.
Jaroslav Egrt was born on 25 Apr 1974 in Duchcov.
Jaroslav Egrt and Zuzana Heralecká were married on 13 Sep 2002 in Jablonec nad Nisou. They had the following children:
  i. **Kristina Egrtova** was born on 04 Jan 2008 in Liberec.
  ii. **Jaroslav Egrt** was born on 04 Jan 2008 in Liberec.
35. **Lucie Stiborová**-8 (Marta-7, Jiří-6, Marta-5, Marie-4, Josefa-3, František-2, Josef-1) was born on 29 Aug 1982 in Mladá Boleslav.
Novotný.
Novotný and Lucie Stiborová married. They had the following children:
  i. **Tobias Novotný.**
36. **Roman Koubik**-8 (2nd Jiří-7, Jiří-6, Marta-5, Marie-4, Josefa-3, František-2, Josef-1) was born on 07 Aug 1987 in Brandys nad Labem.
Martina.
Roman Koubik and Martina married. They had the following children:
  i. **Roman Koubik.**

Sources

1. Matrika krestni: Hoškovice, Kniha 104, List 172, Krestni a rodny list.
2. Matrika krestni, Kniha Z, List 65, Krestni a rodny list.

Ferkl Family of Rostkov

Generation 1

1. **Josef Ferkl**-1 was born in Rostkov No. 3.
    Alžběta Filipová was born about 1800 in Sovenice. She died on 11 Aug 1870. Josef Ferkl and Alžběta Filipová married. They had the following children:
    2. i. **Anna Ferklová** was born in Rostkov No. 3, Mnichovo Hradiště Co..
        ii. **Jan Ferkl** was born on 22 Mar 1836. He died on 22 Mar 1836 in Rostkov No. 3.
        iii. **František Ferkl** was born about 1838. He died on 18 Jun 1864 in Rostkov No. 3.

Generation 2

2. **Anna Ferklová**-2 (Josef-1) was born in Rostkov No. 3, Mnichovo Hradiště Co..
    František Cimr son of Josef Cimr and Kodrova ? Anna Kochova was born on 31 Mar 1823 in Manikovice No. 11, Mnichovo Hradiště Co.. He died on 22 Mar 1884.
    František Cimr and Anna Ferklová married. They had the following children:
    i. **Josef Cimr** was born on 06 Jan 1850.
    ii. **Václav Cimr** was born on 25 Mar 1851.
    iii. **František Cimr** was born on 26 Jan 1853.
    iv. **Antonín Cimr** was born on 19 Dec 1855. He died on 17 Mar 1856.
    4. v. **Josefa Cimrová** was born on 01 Jan 1859 in Manikovice No. 11, Mnichovo Hradiště Dist.. She married František Antonín Danda on 04 Feb 1881 in Manikovice No. 21. She died on 27 Aug 1923 in Hoškovice No. 14, Mnichovo Hradiště Dist..
        vi. **Štěpán Cimr** was born on 26 May 1860.
        vii. **Jan Cimr** was born on 21 Apr 1862.
        viii. **Anna Cimrová** was born on 05 Aug 1864.
        ix. **Vincenc Cimr** was born on 16 Apr 1870.

Generation 3

3. **Josefa Cimrová**-3 (Anna-2, Josef-1) was born on 01 Jan 1859 in Manikovice No. 11, Mnichovo Hradiště Dist.. She died on 27 Aug 1923 in Hoškovice No. 14, Mnichovo Hradiště Dist..

   František Antonín Danda son of František Danda and Kateřina Nováková was born on 10 Jun 1857 in Hoškovice, No. 2, Mnichovo Hradiště Dist, Bohemia. He died on 07 Jun 1900 in Hoškovice, No. 14, Mnichovo Hradiště Dist, Bohemia.

   František Antonín Danda and Josefa Cimrová were married on 04 Feb 1881 in Manikovice No. 21. They had the following children:

   4. i. **Marie Dandová**[1] was born on 31 Jan 1882 in Hoškovice, No. 14, Mnichovo Hradiště Dist, Bohemia. She married Čeněk Rajtr on 02 Jul 1904 in Mnichovo Hradiště. She died on 05 Jul 1967 in Dolanky No. 7, Mnichovo Hradiště Co..
   5. ii. **Josef Danda** was born on 30 Jan 1884 in Hoškovice, No. 14, Mnichovo Hradiště Dist, Bohemia. He died on 18 Apr 1936 in Dobrá Voda.
      iii. **Josefa Kateřina Dandová** was born on 04 Oct 1885 in Hoškovice No. 14, Mnichovo Hradiště Dist.. She married Václav Balák after 1925.
      iv. **Anna Dandová** was born on 12 Nov 1886 in Hoškovice, No. 14, Mnichovo Hradiště Dist, Bohemia. She died on 13 May 1972.
      v. **František Danda** was born on 23 Apr 1888 in Hoškovice, No. 14, Mnichovo Hradiště Dist, Bohemia. He died on 27 Jun 1888 in Hoškovice, No. 14, Mnichovo Hradiště Dist, Bohemia.
      vi. **František Danda** was born on 13 Nov 1889 in Hoškovice No. 14, Mnichovo Hradiště Dist.. He died on 22 Dec 1891 in Hoškovice no. 14, Mnichovo Hradiště Dist, Bohemia.
      vii. **Václav Danda** was born on 05 Sep 1891 in Hoškovice No. 14, Mnichovo Hradiště Dist, Bohemia. He died on 10 Mar 1892 in Hoškovice No. 14, Mnichovo Hradiště Dist, Bohemia.
   6. viii. **Emilie Dandová** was born on 22 Oct 1893 in Hoškovice No. 14, Mnichovo Hradiště Dist, Bohemia. She married Václav Balák on 18

Sep 1920 in Hoškovice, Mnichovo Hradiště Dist, Bohemia. She died on 06 Apr 1924 in Hoškovice, Mnichovo Hradiště Dist, Bohemia.

Generation 4

4. **Marie Dandová**-4 (Josefa-3, Anna-2, Josef-1)[1] was born on 31 Jan 1882 in Hoškovice, No. 14, Mnichovo Hradiště Dist, Bohemia. She died on 05 Jul 1967 in Dolanky No. 7, Mnichovo Hradiště Co..

    Čeněk Rajtr son of Jan Václav Rajtr and Anna Najmanová[2] was born on 01 Jul 1874 in nky No. 7, Mnichovo Hradiště Dist... He died on 27 Oct 1956 in Dolánky No. 7, Mnichovo Hradiště Dist...

    Čeněk Rajtr and Marie Dandová were married on 02 Jul 1904 in Mnichovo Hradiště. They had the following children:

    7. i. **Marie Rajtrová** was born on 05 Jul 1905 in Dolanky No. 7, Mnichovo Hradiště Co.. She married Miloslav Rechcigl on 26 Jul 1926 in Praha - Kralovske Vinohrady. She died on 13 Apr 1982 in Mladá Boleslav.

       ii. **Oldrřch Rajtr** was born on 14 Nov 1907 in Dolanky No. 7. He died on 02 Nov 1937.

    8. iii. **Marta Rajtrová** was born on 10 Jan 1909 in Dolanky u Bakova. She married Josef Knotek in 1934. She died on 29 Nov 1982 in Mladá Boleslav.

5. **Josef Danda**-4 (Josefa-3, Anna-2, Josef-1) was born on 30 Jan 1884 in Hoškovice, No. 14, Mnichovo Hradiště Dist, Bohemia. He died on 18 Apr 1936 in Dobrá Voda.

    Božena Slavíková daughter of Josef Slavik and Anna Jirova was born on 05 Sep 1889 in Lesnovky, Turnov Dist... She died on 06 Oct 1965 in Dobrá Voda.

    Josef Danda and Božena Slavíková married. They had the following children:

    9. i. **Oldřich Danda** was born on 29 Jan 1922 in Hoškovice No. 10, Mnichovo Hradiště Dist, Bohemia. He died on 30 Jan 1983 in Dobrá Voda, Mnichovo Hradiště Co..

6. **Emilie Dandová**-4 (Josefa-3, Anna-2, Josef-1) was born on 22 Oct 1893 in Hoškovice No. 14, Mnichovo Hradiště Dist, Bohemia. She died on 06 Apr

1924 in Hoškovice, Mnichovo Hradiště Dist, Bohemia.

Václav Balák son of Václav Balak and Kateřina Janoušková was born about 1890 in Nová Ves No. 13, Mnichovo Hradiště District.

Václav Balák and Emilie Dandová were married on 18 Sep 1920 in Hoškovice, Mnichovo Hradiště Dist, Bohemia. They had the following children:

10. i. **Marie Balakova** was born on 16 Feb 1921 in Hoškovice No. 14, Mnichovo Hradiště Dist.. She married Otakar Lochman on 04 Nov 1942 in Mnichovo Hradiště.
11. ii. **Václav Balak** was born on 06 Jun 1922 in Hoškovice. He died on 24 Jan 2001. He married Zdenka Štolbová on 31 Dec.
12. iii. **Vlasta Balakova** was born on 02 Sep 1923 in Hoškovice, Mnichovo Hradiště Co.. She married Milous Bičík in 1948.

Generation 5

7. **Marie Rajtrová**-5 (Marie-4, Josefa-3, Anna-2, Josef-1) was born on 05 Jul 1905 in Dolanky No. 7, Mnichovo Hradiště Co.. She died on 13 Apr 1982 in Mladá Boleslav.

Miloslav Rechcigl son of Adolf Rechcigl and Marie Berglová was born on 13 May 1904 in Kocňovice (renamed Chocnějovice) No. 22. He died on 27 May 1973 in Washington, DC.

Miloslav Rechcigl and Marie Rajtrová were married on 26 Jul 1926 in Praha - Kralovske Vinohrady. They had the following children:

13. i. **Mila (Miloslav) Rechcigl Jr.** was born on 30 Jul 1930 in Mladá Boleslav, CSR. He married Eva Edwards (Eisnerová) on 29 Aug 1953 in New York, NY.
14. ii. **Marta Rechcíglová** was born on 23 May 1933 in Mladá Boleslav. She married František Žďárský on 03 Oct 1953 in Mladá Boleslav. She died on 13 Sep 2018 in Mladá Boleslav.

8. **Marta Rajtrová**-5 (Marie-4, Josefa-3, Anna-2, Josef-1) was born on 10 Jan 1909 in Dolanky u Bakova. She died on 29 Nov 1982 in Mladá Boleslav.

Josef Knotek was born between 1905-1907 in Mala Bela, p. Bakov nad Jizerou. He died in 1934. Josef Knotek and Marta Rajtrová were married in 1934. They had no children.

Miroslav Koubik son of Koubik was born in 1908 in Terezin. He died in 1968 in Havlickuv Brod.

Miroslav Koubik and Marta Rajtrová were married on 26 Jul 1938 in Praha. They had the following children:

15. i. **Jiří Koubik** was born on 29 Jan 1940 in Prague. He married Jiřina Muellerová on 31 Jan 1962 in Praha. He died on 26 Jun 1998 in Brandys nad Labem.

Emil Pazderník was born after 1900.

Emil Pazderník and Marta Rajtrová were married after 1945. They had no children.

Karel Horáček.

Karel Horáček and Marta Rajtrová met. They had no children.

9. **Oldřich Danda**-5 (Josef-4, Josefa-3, Anna-2, Josef-1) was born on 29 Jan 1922 in Hoškovice No. 10, Mnichovo Hradiště Dist, Bohemia. He died on 30 Jan 1983 in Dobrá Voda, Mnichovo Hradiště Co..

    Marie Augustinova was born on 01 Jun 1923 in Dobrá Voda, Mnichovo Hradiště Co.. She died on 03 Jan 2003 in Dobrá Voda, Mnichovo Hradiště Co..

    Oldřich Danda and Marie Augustinova married. They had the following children:

    i. **Oldrřch Danda** was born on 06 Sep 1958 in Turnov.

    17. ii. **Marie Dandová** was born on 12 Jun 1946 in Mnichovo Hradiště.

10. **Marie Balakova**-5 (Emilie-4, Josefa-3, Anna-2, Josef-1) was born on 16 Feb 1921 in Hoškovice No. 14, Mnichovo Hradiště Dist..

    Otakar Lochman was born on 13 Jan 1917 in Hradec, Mnichovo Hrtadiste Dist.. He died on 22 Sep 1980.

    Otakar Lochman and Marie Balakova were married on 04 Nov 1942 in Mnichovo Hradiště. They had the following children:

    17. i. **Otakar Lochman** was born on 24 Dec 1944 in Mnichovo Hradiště. He married Václava Bártová on 12 Nov 1966 in Turnov.

11. **Václav Balak**-5 (Emilie-4, Josefa-3, Anna-2, Josef-1) was born on 06 Jun 1922 in Hoškovice. He died on 24 Jan 2001.

    Zdenka Štolbová was born on 22 Dec 1930. She died on 01 Jan 1985.

Václav Balak and Zdenka Štolbová were married on 31 Dec. They had the following children:
- i. **Sarka Balakova** was born about 1950.
- 19. ii. **Zdenka Balakova** was born on 16 Nov 1952. She married Bohumil Konicek on 08 Jun 1974.

12. **Vlasta Balakova**-5 (Emilie-4, Josefa-3, Anna-2, Josef-1) was born on 02 Sep 1923 in Hoškovice, Mnichovo Hradiště Co..
Milous Bičík was born on 28 Jun 1920. He died on 24 Mar 1988.
Milous Bičík and Vlasta Balakova were married in 1948. They had the following children:
- 19. i. **Emilie Bičíková** was born on 08 Mar 1949 in Turnov. She married Oldrřch Šnajdr on 08 Oct 1970.

Generation 6

13. **Mila (Miloslav) Rechcigl Jr.**-6 (Marie-5, Marie-4, Josefa-3, Anna-2, Josef-1) was born on 30 Jul 1930 in Mladá Boleslav, CSR.
Eva Edwards (Eisnerová) daughter of Paul J. Edwards (Pavel Eisner) and Jiřina Taussigová was born on 21 Jan 1932 in Prague, CSR.
Mila (Miloslav) Rechcigl Jr. and Eva Edwards (Eisnerová) were married on 29 Aug 1953 in New York, NY. They had the following children:
- 20. i. **John Edward Rechcigl** was born on 27 Feb 1960 in Washington, D.C.. He married Nancy Ann Palko on 30 Jul 1983 in Dover, NJ.
- 21. ii. **Karen Rechcigl** was born on 16 Apr 1962 in Washington, DC. She married Ulysses Kollecas on 25 Aug 1990 in Bethesda, MD.

14. **Marta Rechcíglová**-6 (Marie-5, Marie-4, Josefa-3, Anna-2, Josef-1) was born on 23 May 1933 in Mladá Boleslav. She died on 13 Sep 2018 in Mladá Boleslav.
František Žďárský son of František Václav Žďárský and Eliška Foltýnová was born on 21 May 1932 in Turnov.
František Žďárský and Marta Rechcíglová were married on 03 Oct 1953 in Mladá Boleslav. They had the following children:
- 22. i. **Marcela Žďárská** was born on 09 May 1954 in Liberec. She married Miroslav Heralecký on 15 Mar 1975 in Sychrov.
- 23. ii. **Iveta Žďárská** was born on 29 Aug 1963 in Liberec, Bohemia. She

married Vlastimil Berkman on 29 Oct 1983.
15. **Jiří Koubik**-6 (Marta-5, Marie-4, Josefa-3, Anna-2, Josef-1) was born on 29 Jan 1940 in Prague. He died on 26 Jun 1998 in Brandys nad Labem.
Jiřina Muellerová was born on 27 Feb 1943 in Buda.
Jiří Koubik and Jiřina Muellerová were married on 31 Jan 1962 in Praha. They had the following children:
   24. i. **Marta Koubikova** was born on 04 Jul 1962 in Mladá Boleslav. She married Vladimír Stibor on 17 Apr 1981.
   25. ii. **2nd Jiří Koubik** was born on 13 May 1965 in Praha. He married Andrea Dunebierová on 4 Apr 1987 in Brandys nad Labem.
16. **Marie Dandová**-6 (Oldřich-5, Josef-4, Josefa-3, Anna-2, Josef-1) was born on 12 Jun 1946 in Mnichovo Hradiště.
Květoslav Červený was born on 07 Mar 1945 in Bosen, Mladá Boleslav Co.. Květoslav Červený and Marie Dandová married. They had the following children:
   26. i. **Luděk Červený** was born on 17 Aug 1968 in Mladá Boleslav. He married Lenka Kovacova on 11 Mar 1989.
   27. ii. **Radek Červený** was born on 23 May 1972 in Mladá Boleslav. He married Renata Bejrová on 05 Nov 1994.
17. **Otakar Lochman**-6 (Marie-5, Emilie-4, Josefa-3, Anna-2, Josef-1) was born on 24 Dec 1944 in Mnichovo Hradiště.
Václava Bártová was born on 26 Sep 1948 in Mladá Boleslav.
Otakar Lochman and Václava Bártová were married on 12 Nov 1966 in Turnov. They had the following children:
   28. i. **Otakar Lochman** was born on 01 Apr 1968 in Mladá Boleslav. He married Štěpánka Jandová on 27 Aug 1988 in Mnichovo Hradiště.
   29. ii. **Václava Lochmanová** was born on 21 May 1972 in Mladá Boleslav. She married Vladimír Pecina on 09 Sep 1995 in Mnichovo Hradiště.
   30. iii. **Iva Lochmanová** was born on 28 Apr 1976 in Mladá Boleslav. She married Libor Janoušek on 21 Mar 1997 in Bakov nad Jizerou.
18. **Zdenka Balakova**-6 (Václav-5, Emilie-4, Josefa-3, Anna-2, Josef-1) was born on 16 Nov 1952.

Bohumil Konicek was born on 19 Jun 1953.
Bohumil Konicek and Zdenka Balakova were married on 08 Jun 1974. They had the following children:
    31. i. **Sarka Konickova** was born on 17 Dec 1974.
        ii. **Lukáš Konicek** was born on 14 May 1985.

19. **Emilie Bičíková**-6 (Vlasta-5, Emilie-4, Josefa-3, Anna-2, Josef-1) was born on 08 Mar 1949 in Turnov.
Oldrřch Šnajdr was born on 07 May 1949 in Brehy.
Oldrřch Šnajdr and Emilie Bičíková were married on 08 Oct 1970. They had the following children:
    32. i. **Oldrřch Šnajdr** was born on 04 Apr 1971 in Turnov. He married Daniela Synková on 16 Mar 1991.
        ii. **Jiří Šnajdr** was born on 10 Nov 1977 in Turnov.

Generation 7

20. **John Edward Rechcigl**-7 (Mila (Miloslav)-6, Marie-5, Marie-4, Josefa-3, Anna-2, Josef-1) was born on 27 Feb 1960 in Washington, D.C..
Nancy Ann Palko daughter of Joseph Palko and Mary Rishko was born on 26 Sep 1961 in Morristown, NJ.
John Edward Rechcigl and Nancy Ann Palko were married on 30 Jul 1983 in Dover, NJ. They had the following children:
        i. **Gregory John Rechcigl** was born on 19 Dec 1988 in Bradenton, FL.
    34. ii. **Kevin Thomas Rechcigl** was born on 09 Oct 1991 in Bradenton, FL. He married Jordan Robbins on 12 May 2018 in Jacksonville, FL.
        iii. **Lindsey Nicole Rechcigl** was born on 03 Nov 1994 in Bradenton, FL.

21. **Karen Rechcigl**-7 (Mila (Miloslav)-6, Marie-5, Marie-4, Josefa-3, Anna-2, Josef-1) was born on 16 Apr 1962 in Washington, DC.
Ulysses Kollecas son of Christopher Thomas (Kolecas) Collier and Amelia Malatras was born on 20 Mar 1958 in Washington, DC.
Ulysses Kollecas and Karen Rechcigl were married on 25 Aug 1990 in Bethesda, MD. They had the following children:
        i. **Kristin Kollecas** was born on 04 May 1993 in Albuquerque, NM.

ii. **Paul Kollecas** was born on 02 Jun 1995 in Albuquerque, NM.
22. **Marcela Žďárská**-7 (Marta-6, Marie-5, Marie-4, Josefa-3, Anna-2, Josef-1) was born on 09 May 1954 in Liberec.
Miroslav Heralecký son of Miroslav Heralecký and Marie Bartošová was born on 18 May 1949 in salomonJablonec nad Nisou, Czech.. He died on 20 Feb 2017 in Proseč, Jablonec nad Nisou, Czech..
Miroslav Heralecký and Marcela Žďárská were married on 15 Mar 1975 in Sychrov. They had the following children:
    i. **Vit Heralecký** was born on 16 Jan 1977 in Jablonec nad Nisou. He married Olga Zrubcová on 13 Jul 1996.
35. ii. **Zuzana Heralecká** was born on 30 Dec 1978 in Jablonec nad Nisou. She married Jaroslav Egrt on 13 Sep 2002 in Jablonec nad Nisou.
23. **Iveta Žďárská**-7 (Marta-6, Marie-5, Marie-4, Josefa-3, Anna-2, Josef-1) was born on 29 Aug 1963 in Liberec, Bohemia.
Vlastimil Berkman was born in 1957.
Vlastimil Berkman and Iveta Žďárská were married on 29 Oct 1983. They had the following children:
    i. **Tereza Hriníková** was born on 05 Jun 1984 in Jablonec nad Nisou.
Jaroslav Hrinik son of Jaroslav Hrinik and Milena Preisslerová was born on 17 Apr 1960.
Jaroslav Hrinik and Iveta Žďárská were married on 16 Aug 1991 in Zamek Červená Lhota. They had the following children:
    i. **Eliška Hriníková** was born on 23 Jun 1992 in Jablonec nad Nisou. She married Jan Ottis on 06 Oct 2018 in Jablonec nad Jizerou, East Bohemia, Czech Republic.
24. **Marta Koubikova**-7 (Jiří-6, Marta-5, Marie-4, Josefa-3, Anna-2, Josef-1) was born on 04 Jul 1962 in Mladá Boleslav.
Vladimír Stibor was born on 04 Jun 1959 in Praha.
Vladimír Stibor and Marta Koubikova were married on 17 Apr 1981. They had the following children:
35. i. **Lucie Stiborová** was born on 29 Aug 1982 in Mladá Boleslav.
    ii. **Tadeáš Stibor** was born on 25 Jul 1988 in Mladá Boleslav.
25. **2nd Jiří Koubik**-7 (Jiří-6, Marta-5, Marie-4, Josefa-3, Anna-2, Josef-1)

was born on 13 May 1965 in Praha.
Andrea Dunebierová was born on 25 Nov 1964 in Praha.
2nd Jiří Koubik and Andrea Dunebierová were married on 04 Apr 1987 in Brandys nad Labem. They had the following children:

    36. i. **Roman Koubik** was born on 07 Aug 1987 in Brandys nad Labem.
         ii. **Vojtěch Koubik** was born on 24 Mar 1989 in Brandys nad Labem.

26. **Luděk Červený**-7 (Marie-6, Oldřich-5, Josef-4, Josefa-3, Anna-2, Josef-1) was born on 17 Aug 1968 in Mladá Boleslav.
Lenka Kovacova was born in Bratislava, Slovakia.
Luděk Červený and Lenka Kovacova were married on 11 Mar 1989. They had the following children:
    i. **Lukáš Červený** was born on 05 Sep 1989.
    ii. **Roman Červený** was born on 06 Oct 1992.

27. **Radek Červený**-7 (Marie-6, Oldřich-5, Josef-4, Josefa-3, Anna-2, Josef-1) was born on 23 May 1972 in Mladá Boleslav.
Renata Bejrová was born in Koprnik, Mladá Boleslav Co..
Radek Červený and Renata Bejrová were married on 05 Nov 1994. They had the following children:
    i. **Veronika Červená** was born on 20 May 1995.
    ii. **Štěpán Červený** was born on 11 Aug 2001.

28. **Otakar Lochman**-7 (Otakar-6, Marie-5, Emilie-4, Josefa-3, Anna-2, Josef-1) was born on 01 Apr 1968 in Mladá Boleslav.
Štěpánka Jandová was born on 25 Oct 1970.
Otakar Lochman and Štěpánka Jandová were married on 27 Aug 1988 in Mnichovo Hradiště. They had the following children:
    i. **Otakar Lochman** was born on 17 Jan 1989 in Mladá Boleslav.
Ladislava (Viznerová) Černá was born on 15 Feb 1970 in Kladno.
Otakar Lochman and Ladislava (Viznerová) Černá were married on 25 Apr 1992 in Mnhichovo Hradiste. They had the following children:
    i. **Lucie Lochmanová** was born on 29 Jan 1992 in Mladá Boleslav.
    ii. **Luboš Lochman** was born on 19 Jan 2002 in Mlada Bolesalv.

29. **Václava Lochmanová**-7 (Otakar-6, Marie-5, Emilie-4, Josefa-3, Anna-2, Josef-1) was born on 21 May 1972 in Mladá Boleslav.

Vladimír Pecina was born on 23 Oct 1961 in Mladá Boleslav.

Vladimír Pecina and Václava Lochmanová were married on 09 Sep 1995 in Mnichovo Hradiště. They had the following children:

    i. **Jana Pecinová** was born on 29 Jan 1996 in Mladá Boleslav.

    ii. **Václava Pecinová** was born on 07 Jan 1998 in Mladá Boleslav.

    iii. **Jitka Pecinová** was born on 01 May 2000 in Mladá Boleslav.

30. **Iva Lochmanová**-7 (Otakar-6, Marie-5, Emilie-4, Josefa-3, Anna-2, Josef-1) was born on 28 Apr 1976 in Mladá Boleslav.

Libor Janoušek was born on 04 Aug 1976 in Mladá Boleslav.

Libor Janoušek and Iva Lochmanová were married on 21 Mar 1997 in Bakov nad Jizerou. They had the following children:

    i. **Pavla Janoušková** was born on 27 Jan 1999 in Mladá Boleslav.

31. **Sarka Konickova**-7 (Zdenka-6, Václav-5, Emilie-4, Josefa-3, Anna-2, Josef-1) was born on 17 Dec 1974.

Miroslav Kaliban was born on 25 Nov 1973.

Miroslav Kaliban and Sarka Konickova married. They had the following children:

    i. **Tereza Kalibanova** was born on 14 May 2000.

32. **Oldrřch Šnajdr**-7 (Emilie-6, Vlasta-5, Emilie-4, Josefa-3, Anna-2, Josef-1) was born on 04 Apr 1971 in Turnov.

Daniela Synková was born in Mladá Boleslav.

Oldrřch Šnajdr and Daniela Synková were married on 16 Mar 1991. They had the following children:

    i. **Iveta Šnajdrová** was born on 11 Sep 1991 in Turnov.

    ii. **Filip Šnajdr** was born on 05 Apr 1995 in Turnov.

Generation 8

33. **Kevin Thomas Rechcigl**-8 (John Edward-7, Mila (Miloslav)-6, Marie-5, Marie-4, Josefa-3, Anna-2, Josef-1) was born on 09 Oct 1991 in Bradenton, FL.

Jordan Robbins daughter of Douglass Robbins and Ivonne was born on 10 Jan 1992 in Camarillo, CA.

Kevin Thomas Rechcigl and Jordan Robbins were married on 12 May 2018 in Jacksonville, FL. They had the following children:

      i. **James Douglas Rechcigl** was born on 05 Jan 2021 in Jacksonville, FL.

      ii. **Evelyn Marie Rechcigl** was born 29 May 2023 in Jacksonville, FL.

31 **Zuzana Heralecká**-8 (Marcela-7, Marta-6, Marie-5, Marie-4, Josefa-3, Anna-2, Josef-1) was born on 30 Dec 1978 in Jablonec nad Nisou.
Jaroslav Egrt was born on 25 Apr 1974 in Duchcov.
Jaroslav Egrt and Zuzana Heralecká were married on 13 Sep 2002 in Jablonec nad Nisou. They had the following children:

      i. **Kristina Egrtova** was born on 04 Jan 2008 in Liberec.

      ii. **Jaroslav Egrt** was born on 04 Jan 2008 in Liberec.

35. **Lucie Stiborová**-8 (Marta-7, Jiří-6, Marta-5, Marie-4, Josefa-3, Anna-2, Josef-1) was born on 29 Aug 1982 in Mladá Boleslav.
Novotný.
Novotný and Lucie Stiborová married. They had the following children:

      i. **Tobias Novotný**.

36. **Roman Koubik**-8 (2nd Jiří-7, Jiří-6, Marta-5, Marie-4, Josefa-3, Anna-2, Josef-1) was born on 07 Aug 1987 in Brandys nad Labem.
Martina.
Roman Koubik and Martina married. They had the following children:

      i. **Roman Koubik**.

Sources

1 Matrika krestni: Hoškovice, Kniha 104, List 172, Krestni a rodny list.
2 Matrika krestni, Kniha Z, List 65, Krestni a rodny list.

Šverma Family

Generation 1

Jiří Šverma-1 was born in Velký Ptýrov No. 13 (married into the family in 1809).

Anna Mansfeldova was born in Velký Ptýrov No. 13.

Jiří Šverma and Anna Mansfeldova were married in 1819 in Resided at Velký Ptýrov No. 13. They had the following children:

    i. **Josef Šverma** was born in Podolí.

    ii. **Jan Šverma** was born in Hoškovice No. 34.

    iii. **Jiří Šverma** was born in Velký Ptýrov No. 13.

Generation 2

Josef Šverma-2 (Jiří-1) was born in Podolí.

Marie Tondrová daughter of Josef Tondr and Kateřina Peldova was born in Podolí.

Josef Šverma and Marie Tondrová married. They had the following children:

    i. **Jan Šverma** was born on 17 Jan 1844 in Hoškovice No. 10, Mnichovo Hradiště Dist, Bohemia. He married Anna Dandová on 30 Jan 1866 in Hoškovice, Mnichovo Hradiště Dist, Bohemia. He died on 22 Sep 1922 in Hoškovice, Mnichovo Hradiště Dist, Bohemia.

Jan Šverma-2 (Jiří-1) was born in Hoškovice No. 34.

Kateřina Lochmanová daughter of Jan Lochman and Anna Kinzrova was born in Hoškovice No. 23. Jan Šverma and Kateřina Lochmanová married. They had the following children:

    i. **Jan Šverma** was born on 17 Sep 1851 in Maly Ptyrove No. 2.

    ii. **son Šverma**.

    iii. **son Šverma**.

Generation 3

Jan Šverma-3 (Josef-2, Jiří-1) was born on 17 Jan 1844 in Hoškovice No. 10, Mnichovo Hradiště Dist, Bohemia. He died on 22 Sep 1922 in Hoškovice, Mnichovo Hradiště Dist, Bohemia.

Anna Dandová daughter of František Danda and Barbora Holasova was born on 29 May 1843 in Hoškovice No. 5, Mnichovo Hradiště Dist, Bohemia. She died on 22 Jul 1897.

Jan Šverma and Anna Dandová were married on 30 Jan 1866 in Hoškovice, Mnichovo Hradiště Dist, Bohemia. They had the following children:

> **Václav Šverma** was born on 28 Apr 1866 in Hoškovice no. 14, Mnichovo Hradiště Dist, Bohemia.
>
> **Anna Švermová** was born on 09 Sep 1867 in Hoškovice, Mnichovo Hradiště Dist, Bohemia. She died on 07 Oct 1869.
>
> **Barbora Švermová** was born on 18 Jan 1869 in Hoškovice, Mnichovo Hradiště Dist, Bohemia. She died on 08 Oct 1869 in Hoškovice, Mnichovo Hradiště Dist, Bohemia.
>
> iv. **Václav Šverma** was born on 12 Aug 1870 in Podolí. He married Anna Dandová on 23 Nov 1897 in Hoškovice No. 10, Mnichovo Hradiště Dist, Bohemia. He died on 08 Apr 1943 in Hoškovice No. 10, Mnichovo Hradiště Dist, Bohemia.
>
> **Josef Šverma** was born on 01 Dec 1871 in Hoškovice, Mnichovo Hradiště Dist, Bohemia.
>
> vi. **Marie Švermová** was born on 07 Jul 1873 in Hoškovice, Mnichovo Hradiště Dist, Bohemia. She married Pazderník on 01 Feb 1896.
>
> **Emiilie Švermová** was born on 07 Mar 1875 in Hoškovice, Mnichovo Hradiště Dist, Bohemia. She married Jan Frydrych on 20 Nov 1897 in Hoškovice, Mnichovo Hradiště Dist, Bohemia.

Jan Šverma-3 (Jan-2, Jiří-1) was born on 17 Sep 1851 in Maly Ptyrove No. 2.

Alžběta Formánková daughter of Josef Formánek and Anna Haslarova was born on 23 Sep 1852 in Maly Ptyrov No. 10.

Jan Šverma and Alžběta Formánková married. They had the following children:

> i. **Václav Šverma** was born on 09 Nov 1875 in Maly Ptyrov No. 2. He died on 01 May 1929.
>
> ii. **Jan Šverma** was born in Maly Ptyrov No. 2.
>
> **son Šverma** was born in Maly Ptyrov No. 2.

son Šverma-3 (Jan-2, Jiří-1).

Unknown.

son Šverma and Unknown married. They had the following children:

    i. **Josef Šverma** was born in Vicmanov No. 9.

son Šverma-3 (Jan-2, Jiří-1).

Unknown.

son Šverma and Unknown married. They had the following children:

    i. **Antonín Šverma** was born in Mnichovo Hradiště.

Generation 4

Václav Šverma-4 (Jan-3, Josef-2, Jiří-1) was born on 12 Aug 1870 in Podolí. He died on 08 Apr 1943 in Hoškovice No. 10, Mnichovo Hradiště Dist, Bohemia.

Anna Dandová daughter of Václav Danda and Marie Štěpánková was born on 07 Feb 1872 in Hoškovice No. 2,, Mnichovo Hradiště Dist, Bohemia. She died on 31 May 1927.

Václav Šverma and Anna Dandová were married on 23 Nov 1897 in Hoškovice No. 10, Mnichovo Hradiště Dist, Bohemia. They had the following children:

    i. **Marie Švermová** was born on 20 Aug 1898 in Hoškovice No. 10, Mnichovo Hradiště Dist, Bohemia. She married Ladislav Šíp on 02 Oct 1920 in Hoškovice, Mnichovo Hradiště Dist, Bohemia. She died on 12 Apr 1986.

Marie Švermová-4 (Jan-3, Josef-2, Jiří-1) was born on 07 Jul 1873 in Hoškovice, Mnichovo Hradiště Dist, Bohemia.

Pazderník was born on 13 Jul 1866.

Pazderník and Marie Švermová were married on 01 Feb 1896. They had no children.

Friedrich.

Friedrich and Marie Švermová married. They had the following children:

    daughter Friedrichova.
    daughetr Friedrichova.

Václav Šverma-4 (Jan-3, Jan-2, Jiří-1) was born on 09 Nov 1875 in Maly Ptyrov No. 2. He died on 01 May 1929.

Růžena Stránská daughter of Josef Stránský and Barbora Paříková was born on 19 Sep 1881 in Manikovice No. 6. She died on 21 Feb 1964.
Václav Šverma and Růžena Stránská married. They had the following children:

    i. **Václav Šverma** was born on 13 Nov 1904 in Maly Ptyrov No. 2. He died on 28 Sep 1960. He married Ludmila Studničná in Resided in Veselá No. 157.

    ii. **Josef Šverma** was born on 19 Apr 1907 in Maly Ptyrov No. 2. He died on 06 Feb 1969. He married Věra Harvánková in Resoided in Ptyrov.

    iii. **Miroslav Šverma** was born on 21 Oct 1909 in Maly Ptyrov No. 2. He died on 05 Nov 1982. He married Anna Kasparove in Moved to Ostrava.

    son Šverma was born in Maly Ptyrov No. 2.

Jan Šverma-4 (Jan-3, Jan-2, Jiří-1) was born in Maly Ptyrov No. 2.
Unknown.
Jan Šverma and Unknown married. They had the following children:

    i. **Jan Šverma** was born in Mnichovo Hradiště.

Vlasta Švermová was born in Mnichovo Hradiště. She married Mates in Moved to South America.

Josef Šverma-4 (son-3, Jan-2, Jiří-1) was born in Vicmanov No. 9.
Unknown.
Josef Šverma and Unknown married. They had the following children:

    i. **Václav Šverma** was born in 1912 in Vicmanov No. 9.

    ii. **Josef Šverma** was born in 1911 in Vicmanov No. 9.

Antonín Šverma-4 (son-3, Jan-2, Jiří-1) was born in Mnichovo Hradiště.
Marie Horoldová.
Antonín Šverma and Marie Horoldová married. They had the following children:

    i. **Jan Šverma** was born in 1901 in Mnichovo Hradiště. He died on 10 Nov 1944 in Chabenec, Slovakia.

Generation 5

Marie Švermová-5 (Václav-4, Jan-3, Josef-2, Jiří-1) was born on 20 Aug 1898 in Hoškovice No. 10, Mnichovo Hradiště Dist, Bohemia. She died on 12 Apr 1986.

Ladislav Šíp son of Václav Šíp and Julie Chvalinová was born on 30 Sep 1888 in Vesec u Turnova, Turnov Co.. He died on 01 Apr 1967 in Prague, Czechoslovakia.

Ladislav Šíp and Marie Švermová were married on 02 Oct 1920 in Hoškovice, Mnichovo Hradiště Dist, Bohemia. They had the following children:

- i. **Ladislav Šíp** was born on 08 Oct 1922 in Prague, Czechoslavakia. He married Mirka Langova about 13 Apr 1950. He died on 10 Jun 1993 in Prague, Czechoslavakia.
- ii. **Eva Šípová** was born in 1927.

Václav Šverma-5 (Václav-4, Jan-3, Jan-2, Jiří-1) was born on 13 Nov 1904 in Maly Ptyrov No. 2. He died on 28 Sep 1960.

Ludmila Studničná daughter of František Studničný and Marie Pavlistova was born on 03 Dec 1908 in Veselá No. 157. She died on 12 Oct 1997.

Václav Šverma and Ludmila Studničná were married in Resided in Veselá No. 157. They had the following children:

- i. **Vratislav Šverma** was born on 29 Jan 1936 in Veselá No. 157. He married Zdenka Simonova in Resided at Veselá No. 98.
- ii. **Lubomir Šverma** was born on 18 Nov 1937 in Veselá No. 157.
    Alena Švermová was born on 02 Jul 1943 in Veselá No. 157. She married Harwey Salmon in Resude in England.

Josef Šverma-5 (Václav-4, Jan-3, Jan-2, Jiří-1) was born on 19 Apr 1907 in Maly Ptyrov No. 2. He died on 06 Feb 1969.

Věra Harvánková was born on 26 Jun 1919 in Mnichovo Hradiště, Boleslavska No. 289.

Josef Šverma and Věra Harvánková were married in Resoided in Ptyrov. They had the following children:

- i. **Josef Šverma** was born on 23 Jul 1943 in Ptyrov No. 2.
- ii. **Věra Švermová** was born on 03 Sep 1949 in Ptyrov No. 2.

Miroslav Šverma-5 (Václav-4, Jan-3, Jan-2, Jiří-1) was born on 21 Oct 1909 in Maly Ptyrov No. 2. He died on 05 Nov 1982.

Anna Kasparove was born on 12 Mar 1914 in Haskov. She died on 27 Oct 1964.

Miroslav Šverma and Anna Kasparove were married in Moved to Ostrava. They had the following children:

    i. **Jana Švermová** was born on 22 Feb 1940 in Ostrava No. 1.

    ii. **Pavel Šverma** was born on 25 Jun 1843 in Ostrava No. 1.

Jan Šverma-5 (Jan-4, Jan-3, Jan-2, Jiří-1) was born in Mnichovo Hradiště.

Marie Svernova daughter of František Šverma and Marie Unknown was born in Haskov. Jan Šverma and Marie Svernova married. They had the following children:

    i. **Jan Šverma** was born in Mnichovo Hradiště.

    daughter Švermová was born in Mnichovo Hradiště.

Václav Šverma-5 (Josef-4, son-3, Jan-2, Jiří-1) was born in 1912 in Vicmanov No. 9.

Unknown.

Václav Šverma and Unknown married. They had the following children:

    Radoslav Šverma was born in 1939.

    Vladislav Šverma was born in 1931.

Josef Šverma-5 (Josef-4, son-3, Jan-2, Jiří-1) was born in 1911 in Vicmanov No. 9.

Unknown.

Josef Šverma and Unknown married. They had the following children:

    Josef Šverma was born in 1950 in Mukarov.

    daughter Švermová was born in 1955 in Mukarov.

Jan Šverma-5 (Antonín-4, son-3, Jan-2, Jiří-1) was born in 1901 in Mnichovo Hradiště. He died on 10 Nov 1944 in Chabenec, Slovakia.

Jan Šverma and unknown spouse married. They had the following children:

    Jiřina Sverova was born in Mnichovo Hradiště.

Generation 6

Ladislav Šíp-6 (Marie-5, Václav-4, Jan-3, Josef-2, Jiří-1) was born on 08 Oct 1922 in Prague, Czechoslavakia. He died on 10 Jun 1993 in Prague,

Czechoslavakia.

Mirka Langova was born on 19 Feb 1925. She died in 2005.

Ladislav Šíp and Mirka Langova were married about 13 Apr 1950. They had the following children:

    i. **Marie Šípová** was born on 08 Jun 1956 in Praha.

    ii. **Ladislav Šíp** was born on 11 Sep 1958 in Praha.

Eva Šípová-6 (Marie-5, Václav-4, Jan-3, Josef-2, Jiří-1) was born in 1927.

Jan Klos was born on 20 May 1912. He died on 05 Jan 1984.

Jan Klos and Eva Šípová married. They had the following children:

    Eva Klosova.

Vratislav Šverma-6 (Václav-5, Václav-4, Jan-3, Jan-2, Jiří-1) was born on 29 Jan 1936 in Veselá No. 157.

Zdenka Simonova was born on 21 May 1936 in Veselá No. 96. She died on 20 Jan 1990.

Vratislav Šverma and Zdenka Simonova were married in Resided at Veselá No. 98. They had the following children:

    i. **Martin Šverma** was born on 15 Dec 1966 in Veselá No. 98.

    Ondřej Šverma was born on 03 May 1972 in Veselá No. 98. He married Michaela Knizkova on 25 Sep 2004 in Resided at Veselá No. 216.

Lubomir Šverma-6 (Václav-5, Václav-4, Jan-3, Jan-2, Jiří-1) was born on 18 Nov 1937 in Veselá No. 157.

Jiřina Matejova was born on 11 Feb 1940 in Bakov No. 248.

Lubomir Šverma and Jiřina Matejova married. They had the following children:

    i. **Lubomir Šverma** was born on 12 Jun 1971 in Veselá No. 157.

    ii. **Radmila Švermová** was born on 23 Mar 1968 in Veselá No. 157.

Josef Šverma-6 (Josef-5, Václav-4, Jan-3, Jan-2, Jiří-1) was born on 23 Jul 1943 in Ptyrov No. 2.

Emilie Langova was born on 25 Feb 1945.

Josef Šverma and Emilie Langova married. They had the following children:

    Josef Šverma was born on 02 Oct 1978 in Ptyrov No. 2.

ii. **Renata Švermová** was born on 07 Aug 1972 in Ptyrov No. 2.

Věra Švermová-6 (Josef-5, Václav-4, Jan-3, Jan-2, Jiří-1) was born on 03 Sep 1949 in Ptyrov No. 2.

Jiří Zizka was born in Mnichovo Hradiště.

Jiří Zizka and Věra Švermová married. They had the following children:

    Radek Zizka was born on 04 Nov 1976.

Ivan Smolik was born on 20 Apr 1954 in Mnichovo Hradiště.

Ivan Smolik and Věra Švermová married. They had the following children:

    i. **Jan Smolik** was born on 17 Jul 1981.

Jana Švermová-6 (Miroslav-5, Václav-4, Jan-3, Jan-2, Jiří-1) was born on 22 Feb 1940 in Ostrava No. 1.

František Zak was born on 05 Jun 1940.

František Zak and Jana Švermová married. They had the following children:

    Petr Zak was born on 03 Nov 1974 in Ostrava No. 1.

Pavel Šverma-6 (Miroslav-5, Václav-4, Jan-3, Jan-2, Jiří-1) was born on 25 Jun 1843 in Ostrava No. 1.

Eva Jebava was born on 20 Jun 1946 in Hradec Králové.

Pavel Šverma and Eva Jebava married. They had the following children:

    Jakub Šverma was born on 09 Apr 1973.

    Lucie Švermová was born on 24 Sep 1976.

Jan Šverma-6 (Jan-5, Jan-4, Jan-3, Jan-2, Jiří-1) was born in Mnichovo Hradiště.

Unknown.

Jan Šverma and Unknown married. They had the following children:

    i. **Miloš Šverma.**

Generation 7

Marie Šípová-7 (Ladislav-6, Marie-5, Václav-4, Jan-3, Josef-2, Jiří-1) was born on 08 Jun 1956 in Praha.

Petr Retek son of Retek was born on 21 Jan 1944.

Petr Retek and Marie Šípová married. They had the following children:

    Magdalena Retková was born on 31 Dec 1982 in Praha.

Ladislav Šíp-7 (Ladislav-6, Marie-5, Václav-4, Jan-3, Josef-2, Jiří-1) was born on 11 Sep 1958 in Praha.
Hanička Kratochvílová was born on 24 Jun 1960 in Praha.
Ladislav Šíp and Hanička Kratochvílová married. They had the following children:
>**Ladislav Šíp** was born on 22 Nov 1984 in Praha.
>**Martin Šíp** was born on 11 Nov 1985 in Praha.

Martin Šverma-7 (Vratislav-6, Václav-5, Václav-4, Jan-3, Jan-2, Jiří-1) was born on 15 Dec 1966 in Veselá No. 98.
Jaroslava Wernerova was born on 03 Sep 1969 in Sedlec No. 27.
Martin Šverma and Jaroslava Wernerova married. They had the following children:
>**Martin Šverma** was born on 04 Mar 1991 in Veselá No. 98.
>**Veronika Švermová** was born on 06 Jan 1995 in Veselá No. 98.

Lubomir Šverma-7 (Lubomir-6, Václav-5, Václav-4, Jan-3, Jan-2, Jiří-1) was born on 12 Jun 1971 in Veselá No. 157.
Eva Matejovska was born on 20 Jun 1971 in Mnichovo Hradiště.
Lubomir Šverma and Eva Matejovska married. They had the following children:
>**Jakub Šverma** was born on 10 Feb 1991.

Radmila Švermová-7 (Lubomir-6, Václav-5, Václav-4, Jan-3, Jan-2, Jiří-1) was born on 23 Mar 1968 in Veselá No. 157.
Karel Maděra was born on 12 Oct 1967 in Mnichovo Hradiště, Sadova.
Karel Maděra and Radmila Švermová married. They had the following children:
>**Karel Maděra** was born on 30 Jan 1996 in Mnichovo Hradiště, Na kamenci No. 137.
>**Jan Maděra** was born on 21 Jul 1997 in Mnichovo Hradiště, Na kamenci No. 137.

Renata Švermová-7 (Josef-6, Josef-5, Václav-4, Jan-3, Jan-2, Jiří-1) was born on 07 Aug 1972 in Ptyrov No. 2.
Petr Palousek was born on 05 Nov 1963.
Petr Palousek and Renata Švermová married. They had the following

children:
>
> **Lanka Palousek** was born on 11 Jun 1993.
>
> **Petr Palousek** was born on 14 Oct 1987.
>
> **Jan Palousek** was born on 14 Jun 2002.

Jan Smolik-7 (Věra-6, Josef-5, Václav-4, Jan-3, Jan-2, Jiří-1) was born on 17 Jul 1981.

Radka Bartošová was born on 03 Sep 1980.

Jan Smolik and Radka Bartošová married. They had the following children:
>
> **Natalie Smolikova** was born on 21 Dec 2005.

Balak Family

Generation 1

Václav Balak-1 was born in Nova Ves No. 13, Mnichovo Hradiště Dist..

Kateřina Janoušková daughter of Josef Janoušek was born in Nova Ves. Václav Balak and Kateřina Janoušková married. They had the following children:

> i. **Václav Balák** was born about 1890 in Nová Ves No. 13, Mnichovo Hradiště District. He married Emilie Dandová on 18 Sep 1920 in Hoškovice, Mnichovo Hradiště Dist, Bohemia.

Generation 2

Václav Balák-2 (Václav-1) was born about 1890 in Nová Ves No. 13, Mnichovo Hradiště District.

Emilie Dandová daughter of František Antonín Danda and Josefa Cimrová was born on 22 Oct 1893 in Hoškovice No. 14, Mnichovo Hradiště Dist, Bohemia. She died on 06 Apr 1924 in Hoškovice, Mnichovo Hradiště Dist, Bohemia.

Václav Balák and Emilie Dandová were married on 18 Sep 1920 in Hoškovice, Mnichovo Hradiště Dist, Bohemia. They had the following children:

> i. **Marie Balakova** was born on 16 Feb 1921 in Hoškovice No. 14, Mnichovo Hradiště Dist.. She married Otakar Lochman on 04 Nov 1942 in Mnichovo Hradiště.
>
> ii. **Václav Balak** was born on 06 Jun 1922 in Hoškovice. He died on 24 Jan 2001. He married Zdenka Štolbová on 31 Dec.
>
> iii. **Vlasta Balakova** was born on 02 Sep 1923 in Hoškovice, Mnichovo Hradiště Co.. She married Milous Bičík in 1948.

Josefa Kateřina Dandová daughter of František Antonín Danda and Josefa Cimrová was born on 04 Oct 1885 in Hoškovice No. 14, Mnichovo Hradiště Dist..

Václav Balák and Josefa Kateřina Dandová were married after 1925. They had no children.

Generation 3

Marie Balakova-3 (Václav-2, Václav-1) was born on 16 Feb 1921 in Hoškovice No. 14, Mnichovo Hradiště Dist..

Otakar Lochman was born on 13 Jan 1917 in Hradec, Mnichovo Hrtadiste Dist.. He died on 22 Sep 1980.

Otakar Lochman and Marie Balakova were married on 04 Nov 1942 in Mnichovo Hradiště. They had the following children:

    i. **Otakar Lochman** was born on 24 Dec 1944 in Mnichovo Hradiště. He married Václava Bártová on 12 Nov 1966 in Turnov.

Václav Balak-3 (Václav-2, Václav-1) was born on 06 Jun 1922 in Hoškovice. He died on 24 Jan 2001.

Zdenka Štolbová was born on 22 Dec 1930. She died on 01 Jan 1985.

Václav Balak and Zdenka Štolbová were married on 31 Dec. They had the following children:

    i. **Sarka Balakova** was born about 1950.

    ii. **Zdenka Balakova** was born on 16 Nov 1952. She married Bohumil Konicek on 08 Jun 1974.

Vlasta Balakova-3 (Václav-2, Václav-1) was born on 02 Sep 1923 in Hoškovice, Mnichovo Hradiště Co..

Milous Bičík was born on 28 Jun 1920. He died on 24 Mar 1988.

Milous Bičík and Vlasta Balakova were married in 1948. They had the following children:

    i. **Emilie Bičíková** was born on 08 Mar 1949 in Turnov. She married Oldrřch Šnajdr on 08 Oct 1970.

Generation 4

Otakar Lochman-4 (Marie-3, Václav-2, Václav-1) was born on 24 Dec 1944 in Mnichovo Hradiště.

Václava Bártová was born on 26 Sep 1948 in Mladá Boleslav.

Otakar Lochman and Václava Bártová were married on 12 Nov 1966 in Turnov. They had the following children:

    i. **Otakar Lochman** was born on 01 Apr 1968 in Mladá Boleslav. He married Štěpánka Jandová on 27 Aug 1988 in Mnichovo Hradiště.

    ii. **Václava Lochmanová** was born on 21 May 1972 in Mladá Boleslav.

She married Vladimír Pecina on 09 Sep 1995 in Mnichovo Hradiště.

    iii. **Iva Lochmanová** was born on 28 Apr 1976 in Mladá Boleslav. She married Libor Janoušek on 21 Mar 1997 in Bakov nad Jizerou.

Zdenka Balakova-4 (Václav-3, Václav-2, Václav-1) was born on 16 Nov 1952.

Bohumil Konicek was born on 19 Jun 1953.

Bohumil Konicek and Zdenka Balakova were married on 08 Jun 1974. They had the following children:

    i. **Sarka Konickova** was born on 17 Dec 1974.

    ii. **Lukáš Konicek** was born on 14 May 1985.

Emilie Bičíková-4 (Vlasta-3, Václav-2, Václav-1) was born on 08 Mar 1949 in Turnov.

Oldrřch Šnajdr was born on 07 May 1949 in Brehy.

Oldrřch Šnajdr and Emilie Bičíková were married on 08 Oct 1970. They had the following children:

    i. **Oldrřch Šnajdr** was born on 04 Apr 1971 in Turnov. He married Daniela Synková on 16 Mar 1991.

    Jiří Šnajdr was born on 10 Nov 1977 in Turnov.

Generation 5

Otakar Lochman-5 (Otakar-4, Marie-3, Václav-2, Václav-1) was born on 01 Apr 1968 in Mladá Boleslav.

Štěpánka Jandová was born on 25 Oct 1970.

Otakar Lochman and Štěpánka Jandová were married on 27 Aug 1988 in Mnichovo Hradiště. They had the following children:

    Otakar Lochman was born on 17 Jan 1989 in Mladá Boleslav.

Ladislava (Viznerová) Černá was born on 15 Feb 1970 in Kladno.

Otakar Lochman and Ladislava (Viznerová) Černá were married on 25 Apr 1992 in Mnhichovo Hradiste. They had the following children:

    Lucie Lochmanová was born on 29 Jan 1992 in Mladá Boleslav.

    Luboš Lochman was born on 19 Jan 2002 in Mlada Bolesalav.

Václava Lochmanová-5 (Otakar-4, Marie-3, Václav-2, Václav-1) was born on 21 May 1972 in Mladá Boleslav.

Vladimír Pecina was born on 23 Oct 1961 in Mladá Boleslav.

Vladimír Pecina and Václava Lochmanová were married on 09 Sep 1995 in Mnichovo Hradiště. They had the following children:
>	**Jana Pecinová** was born on 29 Jan 1996 in Mladá Boleslav.
>	**Václava Pecinová** was born on 07 Jan 1998 in Mladá Boleslav.
>	**Jitka Pecinová** was born on 01 May 2000 in Mladá Boleslav.

Iva Lochmanová-5 (Otakar-4, Marie-3, Václav-2, Václav-1) was born on 28 Apr 1976 in Mladá Boleslav.
Libor Janoušek was born on 04 Aug 1976 in Mladá Boleslav.
Libor Janoušek and Iva Lochmanová were married on 21 Mar 1997 in Bakov nad Jizerou. They had the following children:
>	**Pavla Janoušková** was born on 27 Jan 1999 in Mladá Boleslav.

Sarka Konickova-5 (Zdenka-4, Václav-3, Václav-2, Václav-1) was born on 17 Dec 1974.
Miroslav Kaliban was born on 25 Nov 1973.
Miroslav Kaliban and Sarka Konickova married. They had the following children:
>	**Tereza Kalibanova** was born on 14 May 2000.

Oldrřch Šnajdr-5 (Emilie-4, Vlasta-3, Václav-2, Václav-1) was born on 04 Apr 1971 in Turnov.
Daniela Synková was born in Mladá Boleslav.
Oldrřch Šnajdr and Daniela Synková were married on 16 Mar 1991. They had the following children:
>	**Iveta Šnajdrová** was born on 11 Sep 1991 in Turnov.
>	**Filip Šnajdr** was born on 05 Apr 1995 in Turnov.

Huňát Family

Generation 1

Václav Huňát-1 was born in Trencin.

Božena Červinková daughter of Václav Červinka and Marie Pospíšilová was born on 15 Jan 1900 in Ptyrov - Branka No. 14.

Václav Huňát and Božena Červinková were married on 28 Jan 1922. They had the following children:

    i. **Václav Huňát** was born on 29 Jun 1922 in Ptyrov No. 14, Mnichovo Hradiště Co.. He married Jaroslava Brzobohatá on 03 Feb 1951 in MnV Knezmost, Mladá Boleslav Co.. He died on 20 Jul 1982 in Ptyrov No. 14, Mnichovo Hradiště Co..

    Božena Huňátová was born on 08 Oct 1929. She married Vladimír Malina on 21 Mar 1953.

Generation 2

Václav Huňát-2 (Václav-1) was born on 29 Jun 1922 in Ptyrov No. 14, Mnichovo Hradiště Co.. He died on 20 Jul 1982 in Ptyrov No. 14, Mnichovo Hradiště Co..

Jaroslava Brzobohatá daughter of Václav Brzobohatý and Julie Kolomaznikova was born on 06 Feb 1929 in Muzsky No. 8, Mnichovo Hradiště Co..

Václav Huňát and Jaroslava Brzobohatá were married on 03 Feb 1951 in MnV Knezmost, Mladá Boleslav Co.. They had the following children:

    i. **Hana Huňátová** was born on 01 Feb 1955 in Turnov. She married Milan Lauryn on 12 Jul 1974 in Mnichovo Hradiště.

    ii. **Václav Huňát** was born on 16 Apr 1953 in Turnov. He married Jiřina Durianciková on 26 Nov 1982 in Bakov nad Jizerou.

Generation 3

Hana Huňátová-3 (Václav-2, Václav-1) was born on 01 Feb 1955 in Turnov.

Milan Lauryn was born on 08 Feb 1951 in Ptyrov.

Milan Lauryn and Hana Huňátová were married on 12 Jul 1974 in Mnichovo Hradiště. They had the following children:

    i. **Hana Laurynova** was born on 08 Jan 1975 in Mladá Boleslav. She married Luboš Vodilan on 09 Jun 2001 in Mnichovo Hradiště.

    ii. **Milena Laurynova** was born on 25 Aug 1976 in Mladá Boleslav. She married Jiří Koštejn on 29 Sep 1995 in Mnichovo Hradiště.

Václav Huňát-3 (Václav-2, Václav-1) was born on 16 Apr 1953 in Turnov.

Jiřina Durianciková was born on 06 Jun 1954.

Václav Huňát and Jiřina Durianciková were married on 26 Nov 1982 in Bakov nad Jizerou. They had the following children:

    i. **Václav Huňát** was born on 09 May 1983 in Mladá Boleslav.

Generation 4

Hana Laurynova-4 (Hana-3, Václav-2, Václav-1) was born on 08 Jan 1975 in Mladá Boleslav.

Luboš Vodilan was born on 06 Jul 1974 in Mladá Boleslav.

Luboš Vodilan and Hana Laurynova were married on 09 Jun 2001 in Mnichovo Hradiště. They had the following children:

    Michaela Vodilanova was born on 10 May 2002.

Milena Laurynova-4 (Hana-3, Václav-2, Václav-1) was born on 25 Aug 1976 in Mladá Boleslav.

Jiří Koštejn was born on 01 Jun 1970 in Mladá Boleslav.

Jiří Koštejn and Milena Laurynova were married on 29 Sep 1995 in Mnichovo Hradiště. They had the following children:

    Jiří Koštejn was born on 18 Jul 1997 in Mladá Boleslav.

    Adela Koštejn was born on 01 Jan 2004 in Mladá Boleslav.

Koštejn Family

Generation 1

1. **Jan Koštejn**-1 was born in Zvířetice No. 4, Mnichovo Hradiště Co..

Terezie Pazderníková daughter of Václav Pazderník and Alžběta Jizbova was born in Bitouchov No. 8. Mnichovo Hradiště Co..

Jan Koštejn and Terezie Pazderníková married. They had the following children:

- i. **Václav Koštejn** was born in Zvířetice No. 4. He died on 10 Oct 1856.

  Kateřina Koštejn.

  Alžběta Koštejn.

  František Koštejn.

  Terezie Koštejn.

- vi. **Barbora Koštejn** was born on 25 Dec 1815 in Zviretica. She died on 28 May 1887 in Chudoplesy No. 9.

Generation 2

Václav Koštejn-2 (Jan-1) was born in Zvířetice No. 4. He died on 10 Oct 1856.

Marie.

Václav Koštejn and Marie married. They had the following children:

- **Anna Koštejn** was born on 31 May 1848. She married Vilém Pánek in 1870. She died in 1925.
- **Marie Koštejn** was born on 18 May 1852. She died on 11 Jan 1881.

Barbora Koštejn-2 (Jan-1) was born on 25 Dec 1815 in Zviretica. She died on 28 May 1887 in Chudoplesy No. 9.

Václav Rajt son of Václav Rajtr and Dorota Strojsová was born on 21 Jun 1807 in Zvířetice. He died on 30 Oct 1871 in Zvířetice.

Václav Rajt and Barbora Koštejn married. They had no children.

Václav Rajtr son of Václav Rajtr and Dorota Strojsová was born on 15 Sep 1783 in Zvířetice No. 11. He died on 16 Jan 1823 in Zvířetice No. 11, Mnichovo Hradiště Dist., Bohemia.

Václav Rajtr and Barbora Koštejn married. They had the following

children:

> i. **Jan Václav Rajtr** was born on 12 May 1847 in Zvířetice No. 11, Mnichovo Hradiště Co.. He married Anna Najmanová on 09 Jun 1868. He died on 19 Sep 1903 in Dolanky No. 7.
>
> **Marie Rajtrová** was born on 16 Jun 1849.
>
> **Václav Rajtr** was born on 13 Nov 1857. He died on 16 Nov 1857.
>
> iv. **Josef Rajtr** was born on 11 Jun 1858. He died on 12 Jun 1858.

Generation 3

Jan Václav Rajtr-3 (Barbora-2, Jan-1) was born on 12 May 1847 in Zvířetice No. 11, Mnichovo Hradiště Co.. He died on 19 Sep 1903 in Dolanky No. 7. **Anna Najmanová** daughter of Josef Najman and Alžběta Bartonova was born on 26 Dec 1841 in Dolanky No. 7, Mnichovo Hradiště Co.. She died on 05 Aug 1900 in Dolanky, Mnichovo Hradiště Co.. Jan Václav Rajtr and Anna Najmanová were married on 09 Jun 1868. They had the following children:

> **Vincenc Rajtr** was born on 08 Apr 1871 in Dolanky No. 7. He died on 03 Oct 1871.
>
> **Václav Rajtr** was born on 22 Dec 1872 in Dolanky No. 7. He died on 11 Feb 1873 in Dolanky No. 7.
>
> iii. **Čeněk Rajtr**[1] was born on 01 Jul 1874 in nky No. 7, Mnichovo Hradiště Dist... He married Marie Dandová on 02 Jul 1904 in Mnichovo Hradiště. He died on 27 Oct 1956 in Dolánky No. 7, Mnichovo Hradiště Dist...
>
> iv. **Anna Rajtrová** was born on 10 May 1876 in Dolanky No. 7. She died in Jan 1946 in Muzsky No. 19, Mnichovo Hradiště, Co..
>
> v. **Rudolf Rajtr** was born on 15 Nov 1881 in Dolanky No. 7. He died in Mar 1953 in Muzsky No. 6.
>
> vi. **Josef Rajtr** was born about 1882 in Dolanky No. 7, Mnichovo Hradiště Cco..

Generation 4

Čeněk Rajtr-4 (Jan Václav-3, Barbora-2, Jan-1)[1] was born on 01 Jul 1874 in nky No. 7, Mnichovo Hradiště Dist... He died on 27 Oct 1956 in Dolánky No. 7, Mnichovo Hradiště Dist...

Marie Dandová daughter of František Antonín Danda and Josefa Cimrová[2] was born on 31 Jan 1882 in Hoškovice, No. 14, Mnichovo Hradiště Dist, Bohemia. She died on 05 Jul 1967 in Dolanky No. 7, Mnichovo Hradiště Co..

Čeněk Rajtr and Marie Dandová were married on 02 Jul 1904 in Mnichovo Hradiště. They had the following children:

    i. **Marie Rajtrová** was born on 05 Jul 1905 in Dolanky No. 7, Mnichovo Hradiště Co.. She married Miloslav Rechcigl on 26 Jul 1926 in Praha - Kralovske Vinohrady. She died on 13 Apr 1982 in Mladá Boleslav.

    Oldrřch Rajtr was born on 14 Nov 1907 in Dolanky No. 7. He died on 02 Nov 1937.

    iii. **Marta Rajtrová** was born on 10 Jan 1909 in Dolanky u Bakova. She married Josef Knotek in 1934. She died on 29 Nov 1982 in Mladá Boleslav.

Anna Rajtrová-4 (Jan Václav-3, Barbora-2, Jan-1) was born on 10 May 1876 in Dolanky No. 7. She died in Jan 1946 in Muzsky No. 19, Mnichovo Hradiště, Co..

Václav Brzohohaty was born about 1870 in Muzsky No. 8, Mnichovo Hradiště Co.. He died in 1918 in Muzsky No. 8, Mnichovo Hradiště Co..

Václav Brzohohaty and Anna Rajtrová married. They had the following children:

    i. **Marie Brzobohatá** was born on 18 Dec 1900 in Muzsky No. 8, Mnichovo Hradiště Co.. She died on 21 Sep 1969 in Liberec.

    ii. **Václav Brzobohatý** was born on 25 Aug 1902 in Muzsky No. 8, Mnichovo Hradiště Co.. He married Julie Kolomaznikova on 17 Nov 1928 in Mnichovo Hradiště. He died on 28 Jul 1974 in Mladá Boleslav.

    Bohumil Brzobohatý was born about 1904 in Muzsky No. 8, Mnichovo Hradiště Co.. He died in 1930 in Muzsky No. 8, Mnichovo Hradiště Co..

    iv. **Božena Brzobohatá** was born on 22 Jul 1906 in Muzsky No. 8, Mnichovo Hradiště Co.. She died on 02 Apr 1989.

Rudolf Rajtr-4 (Jan Václav-3, Barbora-2, Jan-1) was born on 15 Nov 1881 in Dolanky No. 7. He died in Mar 1953 in Muzsky No. 6.

Božena Maděrová was born in Muzsky. She died on 04 Dec 1964 in Muzsky. Rudolf Rajtr and Božena Maděrová married. They had the following children:

    i. **Josef Rajtr** was born on 27 Apr 1911 in Muzsky No. 6, Mnichovo Hradiště Co.. He died on 22 Mar 1978 in Liberec. He married Marie Janoušková on 27 Oct.

    ii. **Václav Rajtr** was born on 13 Jun 1912 in Muzsky No. 6, Mnichovo Hradiště Co.. He married Jarmila Maděrová on 10 Nov 1940 in Farni urad Bosen. He died on 12 Mar 1989 in Muzsky.

    Božena Rajtrová was born after 1912 in Muzsky No. 6, Mnichovo Hradiště Co.. She died in Drowned aet. 8 years old.

Josef Rajtr-4 (Jan Václav-3, Barbora-2, Jan-1) was born about 1882 in Dolanky No. 7, Mnichovo Hradiště Cco..

Františka Kobosilova was born after 1880 in Prepere No. 15, Turnov Co.. Josef Rajtr and Františka Kobosilova married. They had the following children:

    i. **Josef Rajtr** was born on 30 Jun 1902 in Prepere No. 15, Turnov Co.. He married Zdenka Karlasova on 02 Nov 1924 in Turnov. He died on 09 Jul 1978 in Prepere No. 15, Turnov Co..

    ii. **Marie Rajtrová** was born on 05 Jul 1905 in Dolanky No. 7, Mnichovo Hradiště Co.. She married Miloslav Rechcigl on 26 Jul 1926 in Praha - Kralovske Vinohrady. She died on 13 Apr 1982 in Mladá Boleslav.

Generation 5

Marie Rajtrová-5 (Čeněk-4, Jan Václav-3, Barbora-2, Jan-1) was born on 05 Jul 1905 in Dolanky No. 7, Mnichovo Hradiště Co.. She died on 13 Apr 1982 in Mladá Boleslav.

Miloslav Rechcigl son of Adolf Rechcigl and Marie Berglová was born on 13 May 1904 in Kocňovice (renamed Chocnějovice) No. 22. He died on 27 May 1973 in Washington, DC.

Miloslav Rechcigl and Marie Rajtrová were married on 26 Jul 1926 in

Praha - Kralovske Vinohrady. They had the following children:
  i. **Mila (Miloslav) Rechcigl Jr.** was born on 30 Jul 1930 in Mladá Boleslav, CSR. He married Eva Edwards (Eisnerová) on 29 Aug 1953 in New York, NY.
  ii. **Marta Rechcíglová** was born on 23 May 1933 in Mladá Boleslav. She married František Žďárský on 03 Oct 1953 in Mladá Boleslav. She died on 13 Sep 2018 in Mladá Boleslav.

Marta Rajtrová-5 (Čeněk-4, Jan Václav-3, Barbora-2, Jan-1) was born on 10 Jan 1909 in Dolanky u Bakova. She died on 29 Nov 1982 in Mladá Boleslav.

Josef Knotek was born between 1905-1907 in Mala Bela, p. Bakov nad Jizerou. He died in 1934. Josef Knotek and Marta Rajtrová were married in 1934. They had no children.

Miroslav Koubik son of Koubik was born in 1908 in Terezin. He died in 1968 in Havlickuv Brod.

Miroslav Koubik and Marta Rajtrová were married on 26 Jul 1938 in Praha. They had the following children:
  i. **Jiří Koubik** was born on 29 Jan 1940 in Prague. He married Jiřina Muellerová on 31 Jan 1962 in Praha. He died on 26 Jun 1998 in Brandys nad Labem.

Emil Pazderník was born after 1900.

Emil Pazderník and Marta Rajtrová were married after 1945. They had no children.

Karel Horáček.

Karel Horáček and Marta Rajtrová met. They had no children.

Marie Brzobohatá-5 (Anna-4, Jan Václav-3, Barbora-2, Jan-1) was born on 18 Dec 1900 in Muzsky No. 8, Mnichovo Hradiště Co.. She died on 21 Sep 1969 in Liberec.

Václav Krausner was born on 19 Feb 1900 in Pribyslavice No. 4, Turnov Co.. He died on 08 Mar 1979 in Liberec.

Václav Krausner and Marie Brzobohatá married. They had the following children:
  i. **Olga Krausnerova** was born on 24 Apr 1933 in Pribyslavice No. 4, Turnov Co.. She married Miloslav Rajtr on 16 Jan 1954 in Selibice.

ii. **Milena Krausnerova** was born on 15 Dec 1931 in Pribyslavice No. 4, Turnov Co.. She married Jaroslav Pabišta on 06 Dec 1952 in Vselibice.

Václav Brzobohatý-5 (Anna-4, Jan Václav-3, Barbora-2, Jan-1) was born on 25 Aug 1902 in Muzsky No. 8, Mnichovo Hradiště Co.. He died on 28 Jul 1974 in Mladá Boleslav.

Julie Kolomaznikova was born on 17 Feb 1906 in Rostkov, Mnichovo Hradiště Co.. She died on 04 Apr 1975 in Kosmonosy.

Václav Brzobohatý and Julie Kolomaznikova were married on 17 Nov 1928 in Mnichovo Hradiště. They had the following children:

i. **Jaroslava Brzobohatá** was born on 06 Feb 1929 in Muzsky No. 8, Mnichovo Hradiště Co.. She married Václav Huňát on 03 Feb 1951 in MnV Knezmost, Mladá Boleslav Co..

ii. **Hana Brzobohatá** was born on 28 Feb 1930 in Muzsky No. 8. Mnichovo Hradiště Co.. She married Stanislav Pic on 29 Jan 1949 in Farni urad Bosen.

Václav Brzobohatý was born on 10 Dec 1944 in Muzsky No. 8, Mnichovo Hradiště Co.. He died in Mar 1946 in Turnov.

Božena Brzobohatá-5 (Anna-4, Jan Václav-3, Barbora-2, Jan-1) was born on 22 Jul 1906 in Muzsky No. 8, Mnichovo Hradiště Co.. She died on 02 Apr 1989.

František Příhoda was born in Příšovice.

František Příhoda and Božena Brzobohatá married. They had the following children:

i. **Luboš Příhoda** was born in 1928.

František Košek was born on 01 Nov 1904 in Borovice, Mnichovo Hradiště Co.. He died on 25 Jan 1968 in Licenice, Litomerice Co..

František Košek and Božena Brzobohatá were married in 1936 in Listopec. They had the following children:

i. **Danuse Koskova** was born on 19 Dec 1937 in Horka u Bakova. She married Victor Svoboda on 01 Mar 1958 in Ustek, Litomerice Co..

Josef Rajtr-5 (Rudolf-4, Jan Václav-3, Barbora-2, Jan-1) was born on 27 Apr 1911 in Muzsky No. 6, Mnichovo Hradiště Co.. He died on 22 Mar 1978 in

Liberec.

Marie Janoušková was born on 22 Feb 1915 in Dolni Bukovina, Mnichovo Hradiště Co.. She died on Dec 1973 in Liberec.

Josef Rajtr and Marie Janoušková were married on 27 Oct. They had the following children:

    i. **Marie Rajtrová** was born on 19 Sep 1941 in Knezmost, Mnichovo Hradiště Co.. She married Zdeněk Kilian on 05 Jul 1969 in Praha.

    ii. **Josef Rajtr** was born on 30 May 1947 in Nova Ves u Branzeze, Mladá Boleslav Co.. He married Helena Klimesova on 06 Apr 1974 in Sychrov.

Václav Rajtr-5 (Rudolf-4, Jan Václav-3, Barbora-2, Jan-1) was born on 13 Jun 1912 in Muzsky No. 6, Mnichovo Hradiště Co.. He died on 12 Mar 1989 in Muzsky.

Jarmila Maděrová was born on 18 Jun 1920 in Muzsky. She died on 09 Feb 2002 in Kosmonosy.

Václav Rajtr and Jarmila Maděrová were married on 10 Nov 1940 in Farni urad Bosen. They had the following children:

    i. **Václav Rajtr** was born on 02 Feb 1942 in Muzsky No. 6, Mnichovo Hradiště Co.. He married Jana Karaskova on 17 Apr 1965 in Rakovnik.

    ii. **Věra Rajtrová** was born on 19 Feb 1947 in Muzsky No. 6, Mnichovo Hradiště Co.. She married Jaroslav Verner on 08 Jan 1966 in Mnichovo Hradiště.

Josef Rajtr-5 (Josef-4, Jan Václav-3, Barbora-2, Jan-1) was born on 30 Jun 1902 in Prepere No. 15, Turnov Co.. He died on 09 Jul 1978 in Prepere No. 15, Turnov Co..

Zdenka Karlasova was born on 23 Oct 1901 in Sekyrkovy Loucky. She died on 09 Jan 1978 in Prepere No. 15.

Josef Rajtr and Zdenka Karlasova were married on 02 Nov 1924 in Turnov. They had the following children:

    Josef Rajtr was born after 1920 in Prepere No. 15. He died after 1920 in Prepere No. 15.

    František Rajtr was born after 1920 in Prepere No. 15. He died after 1920.

Generation 6

Mila (Miloslav) Rechcigl Jr.-6 (Marie-5, Čeněk-4, Jan Václav-3, Barbora-2, Jan-1) was born on 30 Jul 1930 in Mladá Boleslav, CSR.

Eva Edwards (Eisnerová) daughter of Paul J. Edwards (Pavel Eisner) and Jiřina Taussigová was born on 21 Jan 1932 in Prague, CSR.

Mila (Miloslav) Rechcigl Jr. and Eva Edwards (Eisnerová) were married on 29 Aug 1953 in New York, NY. They had the following children:

    i. **John Edward Rechcigl** was born on 27 Feb 1960 in Washington, D.C.. He married Nancy Ann Palko on 30 Jul 1983 in Dover, NJ.

    ii. **Karen Rechcigl** was born on 16 Apr 1962 in Washington, DC. She married Ulysses Kollecas on 25 Aug 1990 in Bethesda, MD.

Marta Rechcíglová-6 (Marie-5, Čeněk-4, Jan Václav-3, Barbora-2, Jan-1) was born on 23 May 1933 in Mladá Boleslav. She died on 13 Sep 2018 in Mladá Boleslav.

František Žďárský son of František Václav Žďárský and Eliška Foltýnová was born on 21 May 1932 in Turnov.

František Žďárský and Marta Rechcíglová were married on 03 Oct 1953 in Mladá Boleslav. They had the following children:

    i. **Marcela Žďárská** was born on 09 May 1954 in Liberec. She married Miroslav Heralecký on 15 Mar 1975 in Sychrov.

    ii. **Iveta Žďárská** was born on 29 Aug 1963 in Liberec, Bohemia. She married Vlastimil Berkman on 29 Oct 1983.

Jiří Koubik-6 (Marta-5, Čeněk-4, Jan Václav-3, Barbora-2, Jan-1) was born on 29 Jan 1940 in Prague. He died on 26 Jun 1998 in Brandys nad Labem.

Jiřina Muellerová was born on 27 Feb 1943 in Buda.

Jiří Koubik and Jiřina Muellerová were married on 31 Jan 1962 in Praha. They had the following children:

    i. **Marta Koubikova** was born on 04 Jul 1962 in Mladá Boleslav. She married Vladimír Stibor on 17 Apr 1981.

    ii. **2nd Jiří Koubik** was born on 13 May 1965 in Praha. He married Andrea Dunebierová on 04 Apr 1987 in Brandys nad Labem.

Olga Krausnerova-6 (Marie-5, Anna-4, Jan Václav-3, Barbora-2, Jan-1) was born on 24 Apr 1933 in Pribyslavice No. 4, Turnov Co..

Miloslav Rajtr was born on 21 Apr 1930 in Straziste No. 18, Mnichovo Hradiště Co..

Miloslav Rajtr and Olga Krausnerova were married on 16 Jan 1954 in Selibice. They had the following children:

    i. **Hana Rajtrová** was born on 02 Aug 1955 in Turnov. She married Milan Ludvik on 26 Mar 1977 in Sychrov.

    ii. **Miroslav Rajtr** was born on 29 Oct 1960 in Mladá Boleslav. He married Zdena Bartošová on 22 Mar 1980 in Český Dub.

Milena Krausnerova-6 (Marie-5, Anna-4, Jan Václav-3, Barbora-2, Jan-1) was born on 15 Dec 1931 in Pribyslavice No. 4, Turnov Co..

Jaroslav Pabišta was born on 29 Dec 1929 in Budikov.

Jaroslav Pabišta and Milena Krausnerova were married on 06 Dec 1952 in Vselibice. They had the following children:

    i. **Milena Pabištová** was born on 03 Aug 1955 in Liberec. She married Jiří Bobek on 24 Aug 1974 in Sychrov.

Jaroslava Brzobohatá-6 (Václav-5, Anna-4, Jan Václav-3, Barbora-2, Jan-1) was born on 06 Feb 1929 in Muzsky No. 8, Mnichovo Hradiště Co..

Václav Huňát son of Václav Huňát and Božena Červinková was born on 29 Jun 1922 in Ptyrov No. 14, Mnichovo Hradiště Co.. He died on 20 Jul 1982 in Ptyrov No. 14, Mnichovo Hradiště Co..

Václav Huňát and Jaroslava Brzobohatá were married on 03 Feb 1951 in MnV Knezmost, Mladá Boleslav Co.. They had the following children:

    i. **Hana Huňátová** was born on 01 Feb 1955 in Turnov. She married Milan Lauryn on 12 Jul 1974 in Mnichovo Hradiště.

    ii. **Václav Huňát** was born on 16 Apr 1953 in Turnov. He married Jiřina Duriancikova on 26 Nov 1982 in Bakov nad Jizerou.

Hana Brzobohatá-6 (Václav-5, Anna-4, Jan Václav-3, Barbora-2, Jan-1) was born on 28 Feb 1930 in Muzsky No. 8. Mnichovo Hradiště Co..

Stanislav Pic was born on 07 Jun 1928 in Bycina No. 2 u Knezmosta, Mnichovo Hradiště Co.. He died on 12 Oct 2005 in Praha.

Stanislav Pic and Hana Brzobohatá were married on 29 Jan 1949 in Farni urad Bosen. They had the following children:

    i. **Stanislav (Pic) Brzobohatý** was born on 26 Dec 1949 in Turnov. He married Jaroslava Hatašová on 17 Dec 1971 in Sychrov.
    ii. **Jiří Pic** was born on 14 Feb 1954 in Turnov. He married Lida Havelková on 22 Apr 1976 in Bakov mad Jizerou.

Luboš Příhoda-6 (Božena-5, Anna-4, Jan Václav-3, Barbora-2, Jan-1) was born in 1928.

Unknown.

Luboš Příhoda and Unknown married. They had the following children:
    i. **son Příhoda** was born about 1950.

Danuse Koskova-6 (Božena-5, Anna-4, Jan Václav-3, Barbora-2, Jan-1) was born on 19 Dec 1937 in Horka u Bakova.

Victor Svoboda was born on 05 Oct 1937 in Brnany, Litomerice Co.. He died on 14 Aug 1985.

Victor Svoboda and Danuse Koskova were married on 01 Mar 1958 in Ustek, Litomerice Co.. They had the following children:
    i. **Danuse Svobodová** was born on 24 Sep 1958 in Litomerice. She married Otakar Gabriel on 15 Jul 1978 in MNV Terezin.
    ii. **Václav Svoboda** was born on 25 Sep 1959 in Litomerice. He married Miroslava Safrová on 21 Jun 1980 in MNV Terezin.
    iii. **Hana Svobodová** was born on 02 Mar 1972 in Litomerice. She married Martin Gaper on Jun 1992 in MNV Terezin.

Marie Rajtrová-6 (Josef-5, Rudolf-4, Jan Václav-3, Barbora-2, Jan-1) was born on 19 Sep 1941 in Knezmost, Mnichovo Hradiště Co..

Zdeněk Kilian was born on 16 Jan 1929. He died on 30 Aug 1999.

Zdeněk Kilian and Marie Rajtrová were married on 05 Jul 1969 in Praha. They had the following children:
    i. **Ester Kilianova** was born on 14 Apr 1973 in Jablonec nad Nisou. She married Ivo Srb on 09 Sep 1995 in Liberec.
       Pavlina Kilianova was born on 17 Feb 1976.

Josef Rajtr-6 (Josef-5, Rudolf-4, Jan Václav-3, Barbora-2, Jan-1) was born on 30 May 1947 in Nova Ves u Branzeze, Mladá Boleslav Co..

Helena Klimesova was born on 18 Aug 1951 in Liberec.

Josef Rajtr and Helena Klimesova were married on 06 Apr 1974 in

Sychrov. They had the following children:

>**Helena Rajtrová** was born on 02 Feb 1976 in Jablonec nad Nisou.
>
>**Tomáš Rajtr** was born on 04 Apr 1977 in Liberec.

Václav Rajtr-6 (Václav-5, Rudolf-4, Jan Václav-3, Barbora-2, Jan-1) was born on 02 Feb 1942 in Muzsky No. 6, Mnichovo Hradiště Co..

Jana Karaskova was born on 11 Feb 1945 in Rakovnik.

Václav Rajtr and Jana Karaskova were married on 17 Apr 1965 in Rakovnik. They had the following children:

>i. **Jana Rajtrová** was born on 14 Apr 1966 in Rakovnik. She married Jaromír Kamenik on 08 Mar 1986 in Rakovnik.

Věra Rajtrová-6 (Václav-5, Rudolf-4, Jan Václav-3, Barbora-2, Jan-1) was born on 19 Feb 1947 in Muzsky No. 6, Mnichovo Hradiště Co..

Jaroslav Verner was born on 27 Mar 1941 in Knezmost.

Jaroslav Verner and Věra Rajtrová were married on 08 Jan 1966 in Mnichovo Hradiště. They had the following children:

>i. **Jolana Vernerova** was born on 19 Oct 1967 in Mladá Boleslav. She married Jaroslav Zdobinsky on 15 Sep 1989.
>
>ii. **Věra Vernerova** was born on 26 Nov 1968 in Knezmost. She married Petr Holas on 24 Apr 1990.

Generation 7

John Edward Rechcigl-7 (Mila (Miloslav)-6, Marie-5, Čeněk-4, Jan Václav-3, Barbora-2, Jan-1) was born on 27 Feb 1960 in Washington, D.C..

Nancy Ann Palko daughter of Joseph Palko and Mary Rishko was born on 26 Sep 1961 in Morristown, NJ.

John Edward Rechcigl and Nancy Ann Palko were married on 30 Jul 1983 in Dover, NJ. They had the following children:

>**Gregory John Rechcigl** was born on 19 Dec 1988 in Bradenton, FL.
>
>ii. **Kevin Thomas Rechcigl** was born on 09 Oct 1991 in Bradenton, FL. He married Jordan Robbins on 12 May 2018 in Jacksonville, FL.
>
>**Lindsey Nicole Rechcigl** was born on 03 Nov 1994 in Bradenton, FL.

Karen Rechcigl-7 (Mila (Miloslav)-6, Marie-5, Čeněk-4, Jan Václav-3, Barbora-2, Jan-1) was born on 16 Apr 1962 in Washington, DC.
Ulysses Kollecas son of Christopher Thomas (Kolecas) Collier and Amelia Malatras was born on 20 Mar 1958 in Washington, DC.
Ulysses Kollecas and Karen Rechcigl were married on 25 Aug 1990 in Bethesda, MD. They had the following children:
>**Kristin Kollecas** was born on 04 May 1993 in Albuquerque, NM.
>**Paul Kollecas** was born on 02 Jun 1995 in Albuquerque, NM.

Marcela Žďárská-7 (Marta-6, Marie-5, Čeněk-4, Jan Václav-3, Barbora-2, Jan-1) was born on 09 May 1954 in Liberec.
Miroslav Heralecký son of Miroslav Heralecký and Marie Bartošová was born on 18 May 1949 in salomonJablonec nad Nisou, Czech.. He died on 20 Feb 2017 in Proseč, Jablonec nad Nisou, Czech..
Miroslav Heralecký and Marcela Žďárská were married on 15 Mar 1975 in Sychrov. They had the following children:
>**Vit Heralecký** was born on 16 Jan 1977 in Jablonec nad Nisou. He married Olga Zrubcová on 13 Jul 1996.
>
>ii. **Zuzana Heralecká** was born on 30 Dec 1978 in Jablonec nad Nisou. She married Jaroslav Egrt on 13 Sep 2002 in Jablonec nad Nisou.

Iveta Žďárská-7 (Marta-6, Marie-5, Čeněk-4, Jan Václav-3, Barbora-2, Jan-1) was born on 29 Aug 1963 in Liberec, Bohemia.
Vlastimil Berkman was born in 1957.
Vlastimil Berkman and Iveta Žďárská were married on 29 Oct 1983. They had the following children:
>**Tereza Hriníková** was born on 05 Jun 1984 in Jablonec nad Nisou.

Jaroslav Hrinik son of Jaroslav Hrinik and Milena Preisslerová was born on 17 Apr 1960.
Jaroslav Hrinik and Iveta Žďárská were married on 16 Aug 1991 in Zamek Červená Lhota. They had the following children:
>**Eliška Hriníková** was born on 23 Jun 1992 in Jablonec nad Nisou. She married Jan Ottis on 06 Oct 2018 in Jablonec nad Jizerou, East Bohemia, Czech Republic.

Marta Koubikova-7 (Jiří-6, Marta-5, Čeněk-4, Jan Václav-3, Barbora-2, Jan-1) was born on 04 Jul 1962 in Mladá Boleslav.
Vladimír Stibor was born on 04 Jun 1959 in Praha.
Vladimír Stibor and Marta Koubikova were married on 17 Apr 1981. They had the following children:
    i. **Lucie Stiborová** was born on 29 Aug 1982 in Mladá Boleslav.
    Tadeáš Stibor was born on 25 Jul 1988 in Mladá Boleslav.
2nd Jiří Koubik-7 (Jiří-6, Marta-5, Čeněk-4, Jan Václav-3, Barbora-2, Jan-1) was born on 13 May 1965 in Praha.
Andrea Dunebierová was born on 25 Nov 1964 in Praha.
2nd Jiří Koubik and Andrea Dunebierová were married on 04 Apr 1987 in Brandys nad Labem. They had the following children:
    i. **Roman Koubik** was born on 07 Aug 1987 in Brandys nad Labem.
    Vojtěch Koubik was born on 24 Mar 1989 in Brandys nad Labem.
Hana Rajtrová-7 (Olga-6, Marie-5, Anna-4, Jan Václav-3, Barbora-2, Jan-1) was born on 02 Aug 1955 in Turnov.
Milan Ludvik was born on 31 Jan 1953 in Turnov.
Milan Ludvik and Hana Rajtrová were married on 26 Mar 1977 in Sychrov. They had the following children:
    Martin Ludvik was born on 29 May 1979 in Jablonec nad Nisou.
Miroslav Rajtr-7 (Olga-6, Marie-5, Anna-4, Jan Václav-3, Barbora-2, Jan-1) was born on 29 Oct 1960 in Mladá Boleslav.
Zdena Bartošová was born on 05 Oct 1961 in Liberec.
Miroslav Rajtr and Zdena Bartošová were married on 22 Mar 1980 in Český Dub. They had the following children:
    Jana Rajtrová was born on 23 Aug 1980 in Liberec.
    Helena Rajtrová was born on 02 Jan 1993 in Liberec.
Milena Pabištová-7 (Milena-6, Marie-5, Anna-4, Jan Václav-3, Barbora-2, Jan-1) was born on 03 Aug 1955 in Liberec.
Jiří Bobek was born on 27 Mar 1948 in Turnov.
Jiří Bobek and Milena Pabištová were married on 24 Aug 1974 in Sychrov. They had the following children:
    i. **Aleš Bobek** was born on 27 Jul 1975 in Liberec. He married Petra

Coufalova on 07 Aug 1999.

Jiří Bobek was born on 20 May 1982 in Liberec.

Hana Huňátová-7 (Jaroslava-6, Václav-5, Anna-4, Jan Václav-3, Barbora-2, Jan-1) was born on 01 Feb 1955 in Turnov.

Milan Lauryn was born on 08 Feb 1951 in Ptyrov.

Milan Lauryn and Hana Huňátová were married on 12 Jul 1974 in Mnichovo Hradiště. They had the following children:

    i. **Hana Laurynova** was born on 08 Jan 1975 in Mladá Boleslav. She married Luboš Vodilan on 09 Jun 2001 in Mnichovo Hradiště.

    ii. **Milena Laurynova** was born on 25 Aug 1976 in Mladá Boleslav. She married Jiří Koštejn on 29 Sep 1995 in Mnichovo Hradiště.

Václav Huňát-7 (Jaroslava-6, Václav-5, Anna-4, Jan Václav-3, Barbora-2, Jan-1) was born on 16 Apr 1953 in Turnov.

Jiřina Durianciková was born on 06 Jun 1954.

Václav Huňát and Jiřina Durianciková were married on 26 Nov 1982 in Bakov nad Jizerou. They had the following children:

    Václav Huňát was born on 09 May 1983 in Mladá Boleslav.

Stanislav (Pic) Brzobohatý-7 (Hana-6, Václav-5, Anna-4, Jan Václav-3, Barbora-2, Jan-1) was born on 26 Dec 1949 in Turnov.

Jaroslava Hatašová was born on 18 Jan 1948 in Mnichovo Hradiště.

Stanislav (Pic) Brzobohatý and Jaroslava Hatašová were married on 17 Dec 1971 in Sychrov. They had the following children:

    i. **Stanislava Brzobohatá** was born on 03 Mar 1973 in Mladá Boleslav. She married Michal Stárek on 07 Dec 1993 in Sychrov.

    Jaroslava Brzobohatá was born on 01 Feb 1977 in Mladá Boleslav.

Jiří Pic-7 (Hana-6, Václav-5, Anna-4, Jan Václav-3, Barbora-2, Jan-1) was born on 14 Feb 1954 in Turnov.

Lida Havelková was born on 24 Aug 1955 in Mladá Boleslav.

Jiří Pic and Lida Havelková were married on 22 Apr 1976 in Bakov mad Jizerou. They had the following children:

    Jiří Pic was born on 25 Apr 1977 in Mladá Boleslav.

    Martin Pic was born on 24 May 1980 in Mladá Boleslav.

son Příhoda-7 (Luboš-6, Božena-5, Anna-4, Jan Václav-3, Barbora-2, Jan-1) was born about 1950.

Unknown.

son Příhoda and Unknown married. They had the following children:

children Příhoda.

Danuse Svobodová-7 (Danuse-6, Božena-5, Anna-4, Jan Václav-3, Barbora-2, Jan-1) was born on Sep 1958 in Litomerice.

Otakar Gabriel was born on 28 Jan 1958.

Otakar Gabriel and Danuse Svobodová were married on 15 Jul 1978 in MNV Terezin. They had the following children:

> **Lenka Gabrielová** was born on 07 Dec 1978 in Litomerice.
>
> **Oto Gabrie** was born on 26 May 1981 in Roudnice nad Labem.

Václav Svoboda-7 (Danuse-6, Božena-5, Anna-4, Jan Václav-3, Barbora-2, Jan-1) was born on 25 Sep 1959 in Litomerice.

Miroslava Safrová was born on 01 Jan 1961.

Václav Svoboda and Miroslava Safrová were married on 21 Jun 1980 in MNV Terezin. They had the following children:

> **Lucie Svobodová** was born on 04 Mar 1981 in Litomerice.
>
> **Vendula Svobodová** was born on 19 Mar 1982 in Litomerice.
>
> **Václav Svoboda** was born on 25 Jul 1985 in Litomerice.

Hana Svobodová-7 (Danuse-6, Božena-5, Anna-4, Jan Václav-3, Barbora-2, Jan-1) was born on 02 Mar 1972 in Litomerice.

Martin Gaper was born in Doksany.

Martin Gaper and Hana Svobodová were married on 13 Jun 1992 in MNV Terezin. They had the following children:

> **Martin Gaper** was born on 19 Sep 1992 in Litomerice.

Ester Kilianova-7 (Marie-6, Josef-5, Rudolf-4, Jan Václav-3, Barbora-2, Jan-1) was born on 14 Apr 1973 in Jablonec nad Nisou.

Ivo Srb.

Ivo Srb and Ester Kilianova were married on 09 Sep 1995 in Liberec. They had the following children:

> **Jakub Srb** was born on 15 Feb 1996.

Jana Rajtrová-7 (Václav-6, Václav-5, Rudolf-4, Jan Václav-3, Barbora-2, Jan-

1) was born on 14 Apr 1966 in Rakovnik.

Jaromír Kamenik was born on 12 Jan 1963 in Kutna Hora.

Jaromír Kamenik and Jana Rajtrová were married on 08 Mar 1986 in Rakovnik. They had the following children:

> **Alena Kamenikova** was born on 02 Aug 1985 in Rakovnik.
>
> **Petr Kamenik** was born on 31 Jan 1993 in Rakovnik.

Jolana Vernerova-7 (Věra-6, Václav-5, Rudolf-4, Jan Václav-3, Barbora-2, Jan-1) was born on 19 Oct 1967 in Mladá Boleslav.

Jaroslav Zdobinsky was born on 16 Dec 1963.

Jaroslav Zdobinsky and Jolana Vernerova were married on 15 Sep 1989. They had the following children:

> **Jaroslav Zobinsky** was born on 26 Mar 1992 in Mladá Boleslav.
>
> **Nela Zdobinska** was born on 29 Feb 2000 in Mladá Boleslav.

Věra Vernerova-7 (Věra-6, Václav-5, Rudolf-4, Jan Václav-3, Barbora-2, Jan-1) was born on 26 Nov 1968 in Knezmost.

Petr Holas was born on 11 Feb 1965 in Mladá Boleslav.

Petr Holas and Věra Vernerova were married on 24 Apr 1990. They had the following children:

> **Vojta Holas** was born on 08 Mar 1993 in Turnov.

Generation 8

Kevin Thomas Rechcigl-8 (John Edward-7, Mila (Miloslav)-6, Marie-5, Čeněk-4, Jan Václav-3, Barbora-2, Jan-1) was born on 09 Oct 1991 in Bradenton, FL.

Jordan Robbins daughter of Douglass Robbins and Ivonne was born on 10 Jan 1992 in Camarillo, CA.

Kevin Thomas Rechcigl and Jordan Robbins were married on 12 May 2018 in Jacksonville, FL. They had the following children:

> **James Douglas Rechcigl** was born on 05 Jan 2021 in Jacksonville, FL.
>
> **Evelyn Marie Rechcigl** was born 29 May 2023 in Jacksonville, FL.

Zuzana Heralecká-8 (Marcela-7, Marta-6, Marie-5, Čeněk-4, Jan Václav-3, Barbora-2, Jan-1) was born on 30 Dec 1978 in Jablonec nad Nisou.

Jaroslav Egrt was born on 25 Apr 1974 in Duchcov.

Jaroslav Egrt and Zuzana Heralecká were married on 13 Sep 2002 in Jablonec nad Nisou. They had the following children:
   i. **Kristina Egrtova** was born on 04 Jan 2008 in Liberec.
   Jaroslav Egrt was born on 04 Jan 2008 in Liberec.

Lucie Stiborová-8 (Marta-7, Jiří-6, Marta-5, Čeněk-4, Jan Václav-3, Barbora-2, Jan-1) was born on Aug 1982 in Mladá Boleslav.
Novotný.
Novotný and Lucie Stiborová married. They had the following children:
   Tobias Novotný.

Roman Koubik-8 (2nd Jiří-7, Jiří-6, Marta-5, Čeněk-4, Jan Václav-3, Barbora-2, Jan-1) was born on Aug 1987 in Brandys nad Labem.
Martina.
Roman Koubik and Martina married. They had the following children:
   Roman Koubik.

Aleš Bobek-8 (Milena-7, Milena-6, Marie-5, Anna-4, Jan Václav-3, Barbora-2, Jan-1) was born on 27 Jul 1975 in Liberec.
Petra Coufalova was born in 1974.
Aleš Bobek and Petra Coufalova were married on 07 Aug 1999. They had the following children:
   Alena Bobková was born on 02 Feb 2002 in Liberec.
   Antonia Bobková was born on 16 Jul 2004 in Liberec.

Hana Laurynova-8 (Hana-7, Jaroslava-6, Václav-5, Anna-4, Jan Václav-3, Barbora-2, Jan-1) was born on 08 Jan 1975 in Mladá Boleslav.
Luboš Vodilan was born on 06 Jul 1974 in Mladá Boleslav.
Luboš Vodilan and Hana Laurynova were married on 09 Jun 2001 in Mnichovo Hradiště. They had the following children:
   Michaela Vodilanova was born on 10 May 2002.

Milena Laurynova-8 (Hana-7, Jaroslava-6, Václav-5, Anna-4, Jan Václav-3, Barbora-2, Jan-1) was born on 25 Aug 1976 in Mladá Boleslav.
Jiří Koštejn was born on 01 Jun 1970 in Mladá Boleslav.
Jiří Koštejn and Milena Laurynova were married on 29 Sep 1995 in Mnichovo Hradiště. They had the following children:
   Jiří Koštejn was born on 18 Jul 1997 in Mladá Boleslav.

KOŠTEJN FAMILY

Adela Koštejn was born on 01 Jan 2004 in Mladá Boleslav.

Stanislava Brzobohatá-8 (Stanislav (Pic)-7, Hana-6, Václav-5, Anna-4, Jan Václav-3, Barbora-2, Jan-1) was born on 03 Mar 1973 in Mladá Boleslav.

Michal Stárek.

Michal Stárek and Stanislava Brzobohatá were married on 07 Dec 1993 in Sychrov. They had the following children:

 Michal Stárek was born on 06 Jun 1994 in Mladá Boleslav.

 David Stárek was born on 26 Jan 2000 in Liberec.

Sources

Matrika krestni, Kniha Z, List 65, Krestni a rodny list.

Matrika krestni: Hoškovice, Kniha 104, List 172, Krestni a rodny list.

Barton Family

Generation 1

Václav Barton-1 was born in Dneboh No. 9, Mnichovo Hradiště Co..

Anna Nohýnková was born in Sychrov No. 2, Mnichovo Hradiště Co..

Václav Barton and Anna Nohýnková married. They had the following children:

    i. **Alžběta Bartonova** was born in Dneboh No. 9, Mnichovo Hradiště Co..

Terezie Cejnarová was born in Benesovice No. 3.

Václav Barton and Terezie Cejnarová married. They had the following children:

    i. **Josef Bartos** was born on 12 Nov in Sedlisko No. 6.

    ii. **Terezie Bartošová** was born on 02 Aug 1839 in Sedlisko No. 6.

Generation 2

Alžběta Bartonova-2 (Václav-1) was born in Dneboh No. 9, Mnichovo Hradiště Co..

Josef Najman son of Vojtěch Najman and Anna Gintrova was born in Dolanky No. 7, Mnichovo Hradiště Co..

Josef Najman and Alžběta Bartonova married. They had the following children:

    i. **Anna Najmanová** was born on 26 Dec 1841 in Dolanky No. 7, Mnichovo Hradiště Co.. She married Jan Václav Rajtr on 09 Jun 1868. She died on 05 Aug 1900 in Dolanky, Mnichovo Hradiště Co..

Terezie Bartošová-2 (Václav-1) was born on 02 Aug 1839 in Sedlisko No. 6.

Josef Buriánek son of Václav Buriánek and Anna Havlova was born on 07 Dec 1830 in Sezemice No. 39.

Josef Buriánek and Terezie Bartošová married. They had the following children:

    Josef Buriánek was born on 27 Oct 1861 in Sezemice No. 25.

    Václav Buriánek was born on 04 Aug 1865 in Sezemice No. 25.

    iii. **František Buriánek** was born on 27 Jul 1869 in Sezemice No. 25.

He died in 1944.

Emil Buriánek was born on 17 Oct 1886 in Sezemice No. 25.

Generation 3

Anna Najmanová-3 (Alžběta-2, Václav-1) was born on 26 Dec 1841 in Dolanky No. 7, Mnichovo Hradiště Co.. She died on 05 Aug 1900 in Dolanky, Mnichovo Hradiště Co..

Jan Václav Rajtr son of Václav Rajtr and Barbora Koštejn was born on 12 May 1847 in Zvířetice No. 11, Mnichovo Hradiště Co.. He died on 19 Sep 1903 in Dolanky No. 7.

Jan Václav Rajtr and Anna Najmanová were married on 09 Jun 1868. They had the following children:

> **Vincenc Rajtr** was born on 08 Apr 1871 in Dolanky No. 7. He died on 03 Oct 1871.
>
> **Václav Rajtr** was born on 22 Dec 1872 in Dolanky No. 7. He died on 11 Feb 1873 in Dolanky No. 7.
>
> iii. **Čeněk Rajtr**[1] was born on 01 Jul 1874 in nky No. 7, Mnichovo Hradiště Dist... He married Marie Dandová on 02 Jul 1904 in Mnichovo Hradiště. He died on 27 Oct 1956 in Dolánky No. 7, Mnichovo Hradiště Dist...
>
> iv. **Anna Rajtrová** was born on 10 May 1876 in Dolanky No. 7. She died in Jan 1946 in Muzsky No. 19, Mnichovo Hradiště, Co..
>
> v. **Rudolf Rajtr** was born on 15 Nov 1881 in Dolanky No. 7. He died in Mar 1953 in Muzsky No. 6.
>
> vi. **Josef Rajtr** was born about 1882 in Dolanky No. 7, Mnichovo Hradiště Cco..

František Buriánek-3 (Terezie-2, Václav-1) was born on 27 Jul 1869 in Sezemice No. 25. He died in 1944.

Marie Jihlavcová daughter of Václav Jihlavec and Anna Marie Mařanová was born on 20 Jun 1876 in Horni Mohelnice. She died in 1928. František Buriánek and Marie Jihlavcová married. They had the following children:

> **Marie Buriánková** was born on 17 Sep 1898 in Sezemice No. 29. She died in 1950.

    ii. **Josef Buriánek** was born on 05 Feb 1900 in Sezemice No. 29. He died in 1966.

    František Buriánek was born on 23 Jan 1902 in Sezemice No. 29. He died in 1936.

    iv. **Ivo Buriánek**.

Generation 4

Čeněk Rajtr-4 (Anna-3, Alžběta-2, Václav-1)[1] was born on 01 Jul 1874 in nky No. 7, Mnichovo Hradiště Dist... He died on 27 Oct 1956 in Dolánky No. 7, Mnichovo Hradiště Dist...

Marie Dandová daughter of František Antonín Danda and Josefa Cimrová[2] was born on 31 Jan 1882 in Hoškovice, No. 14, Mnichovo Hradiště Dist, Bohemia. She died on 05 Jul 1967 in Dolanky No. 7, Mnichovo Hradiště Co..

Čeněk Rajtr and Marie Dandová were married on 02 Jul 1904 in Mnichovo Hradiště. They had the following children:

   i. **Marie Rajtrová** was born on 05 Jul 1905 in Dolanky No. 7, Mnichovo Hradiště Co.. She married Miloslav Rechcigl on 26 Jul 1926 in Praha - Kralovske Vinohrady. She died on 13 Apr 1982 in Mladá Boleslav.

   Oldrřch Rajtr was born on 14 Nov 1907 in Dolanky No. 7. He died on 02 Nov 1937.

   iii. **Marta Rajtrová** was born on 10 Jan 1909 in Dolanky u Bakova. She married Josef Knotek in 1934. She died on 29 Nov 1982 in Mladá Boleslav.

Anna Rajtrová-4 (Anna-3, Alžběta-2, Václav-1) was born on 10 May 1876 in Dolanky No. 7. She died in Jan 1946 in Muzsky No. 19, Mnichovo Hradiště, Co..

Václav Brzohohaty was born about 1870 in Muzsky No. 8, Mnichovo Hradiště Co.. He died in 1918 in Muzsky No. 8, Mnichovo Hradiště Co..

Václav Brzohohaty and Anna Rajtrová married. They had the following children:

   i. **Marie Brzobohatá** was born on 18 Dec 1900 in Muzsky No. 8, Mnichovo Hradiště Co.. She died on 21 Sep 1969 in Liberec.

ii. **Václav Brzobohatý** was born on 25 Aug 1902 in Muzsky No. 8, Mnichovo Hradiště Co.. He married Julie Kolomaznikova on 17 Nov 1928 in Mnichovo Hradiště. He died on 28 Jul 1974 in Mladá Boleslav.

Bohumil Brzobohatý was born about 1904 in Muzsky No. 8, Mnichovo Hradiště Co.. He died in 1930 in Muzsky No. 8, Mnichovo Hradiště Co..

iv. **Božena Brzobohatá** was born on 22 Jul 1906 in Muzsky No. 8, Mnichovo Hradiště Co.. She died on 02 Apr 1989.

Rudolf Rajtr-4 (Anna-3, Alžběta-2, Václav-1) was born on 15 Nov 1881 in Dolanky No. 7. He died in Mar 1953 in Muzsky No. 6.

Božena Maděrová was born in Muzsky. She died on 04 Dec 1964 in Muzsky. Rudolf Rajtr and Božena Maděrová married. They had the following children:

i. **Josef Rajtr** was born on 27 Apr 1911 in Muzsky No. 6, Mnichovo Hradiště Co.. He died on 22 Mar 1978 in Liberec. He married Marie Janoušková on 27 Oct.

ii. **Václav Rajtr** was born on 13 Jun 1912 in Muzsky No. 6, Mnichovo Hradiště Co.. He married Jarmila Maděrová on 10 Nov 1940 in Farni urad Bosen. He died on 12 Mar 1989 in Muzsky.

Božena Rajtrová was born after 1912 in Muzsky No. 6, Mnichovo Hradiště Co.. She died in Drowned aet. 8 years old.

Josef Rajtr-4 (Anna-3, Alžběta-2, Václav-1) was born about 1882 in Dolanky No. 7, Mnichovo Hradiště Cco..

Františka Kobosilova was born after 1880 in Prepere No. 15, Turnov Co.. Josef Rajtr and Františka Kobosilova married. They had the following children:

i. **Josef Rajtr** was born on 30 Jun 1902 in Prepere No. 15, Turnov Co.. He married Zdenka Karlasova on 02 Nov 1924 in Turnov. He died on 09 Jul 1978 in Prepere No. 15, Turnov Co..

ii. **Marie Rajtrová** was born on 05 Jul 1905 in Dolanky No. 7, Mnichovo Hradiště Co.. She married Miloslav Rechcigl on 26 Jul 1926 in Praha - Kralovske Vinohrady. She died on 13 Apr 1982 in Mladá Boleslav.

Josef Buriánek-4 (František-3, Terezie-2, Václav-1) was born on 05 Feb 1900 in Sezemice No. 29. He died in 1966.

Blažena Maruskova was born on 26 Mar 1908 in Sedlistky No. 4. She died in 1989. Josef Buriánek and Blažena Maruskova married. They had the following children:

    i. **Jaromír Buriánek** was born on 09 Feb 1929 in Koryta No. 29.

    ii. **Vratislav Buriánek** was born on 28 Oct 1935 in Koryta No. 29. He died in 1992.

    iii. **Jana Buriánková** was born on 25 Mar 1944 in Koryta No. 29.

Ivo Buriánek-4 (František-3, Terezie-2, Václav-1).

Unknown.

Ivo Buriánek and Unknown married. They had the following children:

    i. **Ivo Buriánek** was born in 1932 in koryta. He died in 1999.

Generation 5

Marie Rajtrová-5 (Čeněk-4, Anna-3, Alžběta-2, Václav-1) was born on 05 Jul 1905 in Dolanky No. 7, Mnichovo Hradiště Co.. She died on 13 Apr 1982 in Mladá Boleslav.

Miloslav Rechcigl son of Adolf Rechcigl and Marie Berglová was born on 13 May 1904 in Kocňovice (renamed Chocnějovice) No. 22. He died on 27 May 1973 in Washington, DC.

Miloslav Rechcigl and Marie Rajtrová were married on 26 Jul 1926 in Praha - Kralovske Vinohrady. They had the following children:

    i. **Mila (Miloslav) Rechcigl Jr.** was born on 30 Jul 1930 in Mladá Boleslav, CSR. He married Eva Edwards (Eisnerová) on 29 Aug 1953 in New York, NY.

    ii. **Marta Rechcíglová** was born on 23 May 1933 in Mladá Boleslav. She married František Žďárský on 03 Oct 1953 in Mladá Boleslav. She died on 13 Sep 2018 in Mladá Boleslav.

Marta Rajtrová-5 (Čeněk-4, Anna-3, Alžběta-2, Václav-1) was born on 10 Jan 1909 in Dolanky u Bakova. She died on 29 Nov 1982 in Mladá Boleslav.

Josef Knotek was born between 1905-1907 in Mala Bela, p. Bakov nad Jizerou. He died in 1934. Josef Knotek and Marta Rajtrová were married in 1934. They had no children.

Miroslav Koubik son of Koubik was born in 1908 in Terezin. He died in 1968 in Havlickuv Brod.

Miroslav Koubik and Marta Rajtrová were married on 26 Jul 1938 in Praha. They had the following children:

    i. **Jiří Koubik** was born on 29 Jan 1940 in Prague. He married Jiřina Muellerová on 31 Jan 1962 in Praha. He died on 26 Jun 1998 in Brandys nad Labem.

Emil Pazderník was born after 1900.

Emil Pazderník and Marta Rajtrová were married after 1945. They had no children.

Karel Horáček.

Karel Horáček and Marta Rajtrová met. They had no children.

Marie Brzobohatá-5 (Anna-4, Anna-3, Alžběta-2, Václav-1) was born on 18 Dec 1900 in Muzsky No. 8, Mnichovo Hradiště Co.. She died on 21 Sep 1969 in Liberec.

Václav Krausner was born on 19 Feb 1900 in Pribyslavice No. 4, Turnov Co.. He died on 08 Mar 1979 in Liberec.

Václav Krausner and Marie Brzobohatá married. They had the following children:

    i. **Olga Krausnerova** was born on 24 Apr 1933 in Pribyslavice No. 4, Turnov Co.. She married Miloslav Rajtr on 16 Jan 1954 in Selibice.

    ii. **Milena Krausnerova** was born on 15 Dec 1931 in Pribyslavice No. 4, Turnov Co.. She married Jaroslav Pabišta on 06 Dec 1952 in Vselibice.

Václav Brzobohatý-5 (Anna-4, Anna-3, Alžběta-2, Václav-1) was born on 25 Aug 1902 in Muzsky No. 8, Mnichovo Hradiště Co.. He died on 28 Jul 1974 in Mladá Boleslav.

Julie Kolomaznikova was born on 17 Feb 1906 in Rostkov, Mnichovo Hradiště Co.. She died on 04 Apr 1975 in Kosmonosy.

Václav Brzobohatý and Julie Kolomaznikova were married on 17 Nov 1928 in Mnichovo Hradiště. They had the following children:

> i. **Jaroslava Brzobohatá** was born on 06 Feb 1929 in Muzsky No. 8, Mnichovo Hradiště Co.. She married Václav Huňát on 03 Feb 1951 in MnV Knezmost, Mladá Boleslav Co..
>
> ii. **Hana Brzobohatá** was born on 28 Feb 1930 in Muzsky No. 8. Mnichovo Hradiště Co.. She married Stanislav Pic on 29 Jan 1949 in Farni urad Bosen.
>
> **Václav Brzobohatý** was born on 10 Dec 1944 in Muzsky No. 8, Mnichovo Hradiště Co.. He died in Mar 1946 in Turnov.

Božena Brzobohatá-5 (Anna-4, Anna-3, Alžběta-2, Václav-1) was born on 22 Jul 1906 in Muzsky No. 8, Mnichovo Hradiště Co.. She died on 02 Apr 1989.
František Příhoda was born in Příšovice.
František Příhoda and Božena Brzobohatá married. They had the following children:

> 30. i. **Luboš Příhoda** was born in 1928.

František Košek was born on 01 Nov 1904 in Borovice, Mnichovo Hradiště Co.. He died on 25 Jan 1968 in Licenice, Litomerice Co..
František Košek and Božena Brzobohatá were married in 1936 in Listopec. They had the following children:

> i. **Danuse Koskova** was born on 19 Dec 1937 in Horka u Bakova. She married Victor Svoboda on 01 Mar 1958 in Ustek, Litomerice Co..

Josef Rajtr-5 (Rudolf-4, Anna-3, Alžběta-2, Václav-1) was born on 27 Apr 1911 in Muzsky No. 6, Mnichovo Hradiště Co.. He died on 22 Mar 1978 in Liberec.
Marie Janoušková was born on 22 Feb 1915 in Dolni Bukovina, Mnichovo Hradiště Co.. She died on Dec 1973 in Liberec.
Josef Rajtr and Marie Janoušková were married on 27 Oct. They had the following children:

> i. **Marie Rajtrová** was born on 19 Sep 1941 in Knezmost, Mnichovo Hradiště Co.. She married Zdeněk Kilian on 05 Jul 1969 in Praha.
>
> ii. **Josef Rajtr** was born on 30 May 1947 in Nova Ves u Branzeze, Mladá Boleslav Co.. He married Helena Klimesova on 06 Apr 1974 in Sychrov.

Václav Rajtr-5 (Rudolf-4, Anna-3, Alžběta-2, Václav-1) was born on 13 Jun

1912 in Muzsky No. 6, Mnichovo Hradiště Co.. He died on 12 Mar 1989 in Muzsky.

Jarmila Maděrová was born on 18 Jun 1920 in Muzsky. She died on 09 Feb 2002 in Kosmonosy.

Václav Rajtr and Jarmila Maděrová were married on 10 Nov 1940 in Farni urad Bosen. They had the following children:

    i. **Václav Rajtr** was born on 02 Feb 1942 in Muzsky No. 6, Mnichovo Hradiště Co.. He married Jana Karaskova on 17 Apr 1965 in Rakovnik.

    ii. **Věra Rajtrová** was born on 19 Feb 1947 in Muzsky No. 6, Mnichovo Hradiště Co.. She married Jaroslav Verner on 08 Jan 1966 in Mnichovo Hradiště.

Josef Rajtr-5 (Josef-4, Anna-3, Alžběta-2, Václav-1) was born on 30 Jun 1902 in Prepere No. 15, Turnov Co.. He died on 09 Jul 1978 in Prepere No. 15, Turnov Co..

Zdenka Karlasova was born on 23 Oct 1901 in Sekyrkovy Loucky. She died on 09 Jan 1978 in Prepere No. 15.

Josef Rajtr and Zdenka Karlasova were married on 02 Nov 1924 in Turnov. They had the following children:

    Josef Rajtr was born after 1920 in Prepere No. 15. He died after 1920 in Prepere No. 15.

    František Rajtr was born after 1920 in Prepere No. 15. He died after 1920.

Vratislav Buriánek-5 (Josef-4, František-3, Terezie-2, Václav-1) was born on 28 Oct 1935 in Koryta No. 29. He died in 1992.

Jiřina Schlesingerová was born in Litvinov.

Vratislav Buriánek and Jiřina Schlesingerová married. They had the following children:

    i. **Alena Buriánková** was born on 15 Nov 1960.

Jana Buriánková-5 (Josef-4, František-3, Terezie-2, Václav-1) was born on 25 Mar 1944 in Koryta No. 29.

Bohumil Michalek was born on 30 Nov 1942 in Sedlov No. 1, Kolin.

Bohumil Michalek and Jana Buriánková married. They had the following

children:
:   i. **Aleš Michalek** was born on 09 Jun 1970.
:   ii. **Jana Michalkova** was born on 07 Oct 1972 in Loukovec.

Ivo Buriánek-5 (Ivo-4, František-3, Terezie-2, Václav-1) was born in 1932 in koryta. He died in 1999.

J. Slajsova.

Ivo Buriánek and J. Slajsova married. They had the following children:

39. i. **Petr Buriánek**. He married Alena Pecharova in 1999.

Generation 6

Mila (Miloslav) Rechcigl Jr.-6 (Marie-5, Čeněk-4, Anna-3, Alžběta-2, Václav-1) was born on 30 Jul 1930 in Mladá Boleslav, CSR.

Eva Edwards (Eisnerová) daughter of Paul J. Edwards (Pavel Eisner) and Jiřina Taussigová was born on 21 Jan 1932 in Prague, CSR.

Mila (Miloslav) Rechcigl Jr. and Eva Edwards (Eisnerová) were married on 29 Aug 1953 in New York, NY. They had the following children:
:   i. **John Edward Rechcigl** was born on 27 Feb 1960 in Washington, D.C.. He married Nancy Ann Palko on 30 Jul 1983 in Dover, NJ.
:   ii. **Karen Rechcigl** was born on 16 Apr 1962 in Washington, DC. She married Ulysses Kollecas on 25 Aug 1990 in Bethesda, MD.

Marta Rechcíglová-6 (Marie-5, Čeněk-4, Anna-3, Alžběta-2, Václav-1) was born on 23 May 1933 in Mladá Boleslav. She died on 13 Sep 2018 in Mladá Boleslav.

František Žďárský son of František Václav Žďárský and Eliška Foltýnová was born on 21 May 1932 in Turnov.

František Žďárský and Marta Rechcíglová were married on 03 Oct 1953 in Mladá Boleslav. They had the following children:
:   i. **Marcela Žďárská** was born on 09 May 1954 in Liberec. She married Miroslav Heralecký on 15 Mar 1975 in Sychrov.
:   ii. **Iveta Žďárská** was born on 29 Aug 1963 in Liberec, Bohemia. She married Vlastimil Berkman on 29 Oct 1983.

Jiří Koubik-6 (Marta-5, Čeněk-4, Anna-3, Alžběta-2, Václav-1) was born on 29 Jan 1940 in Prague. He died on 26 Jun 1998 in Brandys nad Labem.

Jiřina Muellerová was born on 27 Feb 1943 in Buda.

Jiří Koubik and Jiřina Muellerová were married on 31 Jan 1962 in Praha. They had the following children:
> i. **Marta Koubikova** was born on 04 Jul 1962 in Mladá Boleslav. She married Vladimír Stibor on 17 Apr 1981.
>
> ii. **2nd Jiří Koubik** was born on 13 May 1965 in Praha. He married Andrea Dunebierová on 04 Apr 1987 in Brandys nad Labem.

Olga Krausnerova-6 (Marie-5, Anna-4, Anna-3, Alžběta-2, Václav-1) was born on 24 Apr 1933 in Pribyslavice No. 4, Turnov Co..

Miloslav Rajtr was born on 21 Apr 1930 in Straziste No. 18, Mnichovo Hradiště Co..

Miloslav Rajtr and Olga Krausnerova were married on 16 Jan 1954 in Selibice. They had the following children:
> i. **Hana Rajtrová** was born on 02 Aug 1955 in Turnov. She married Milan Ludvik on 26 Mar 1977 in Sychrov.
>
> ii. **Miroslav Rajtr** was born on 29 Oct 1960 in Mladá Boleslav. He married Zdena Bartošová on 22 Mar 1980 in Český Dub.

Milena Krausnerova-6 (Marie-5, Anna-4, Anna-3, Alžběta-2, Václav-1) was born on 15 Dec 1931 in Pribyslavice No. 4, Turnov Co..

Jaroslav Pabišta was born on 29 Dec 1929 in Budikov.

Jaroslav Pabišta and Milena Krausnerova were married on 06 Dec 1952 in Vselibice. They had the following children:
> i. **Milena Pabištová** was born on 03 Aug 1955 in Liberec. She married Jiří Bobek on 24 Aug 1974 in Sychrov.

Jaroslava Brzobohatá-6 (Václav-5, Anna-4, Anna-3, Alžběta-2, Václav-1) was born on 06 Feb 1929 in Muzsky No. 8, Mnichovo Hradiště Co..

Václav Huňát son of Václav Huňát and Božena Červinková was born on 29 Jun 1922 in Ptyrov No. 14, Mnichovo Hradiště Co.. He died on 20 Jul 1982 in Ptyrov No. 14, Mnichovo Hradiště Co..

Václav Huňát and Jaroslava Brzobohatá were married on 03 Feb 1951 in MnV Knezmost, Mladá Boleslav Co.. They had the following children:
> i. **Hana Huňátová** was born on 01 Feb 1955 in Turnov. She married Milan Lauryn on 12 Jul 1974 in Mnichovo Hradiště.
>
> ii. **Václav Huňát** was born on 16 Apr 1953 in Turnov. He married

Jiřina Duriancikova on 26 Nov 1982 in Bakov nad Jizerou.

Hana Brzobohatá-6 (Václav-5, Anna-4, Anna-3, Alžběta-2, Václav-1) was born on 28 Feb 1930 in Muzsky No. 8. Mnichovo Hradiště Co..

Stanislav Pic was born on 07 Jun 1928 in Bycina No. 2 u Knezmosta, Mnichovo Hradiště Co.. He died on 12 Oct 2005 in Praha.

Stanislav Pic and Hana Brzobohatá were married on 29 Jan 1949 in Farni urad Bosen. They had the following children:

    i. **Stanislav (Pic) Brzobohatý** was born on 26 Dec 1949 in Turnov. He married Jaroslava Hatašová on 17 Dec 1971 in Sychrov.

    ii. **Jiří Pic** was born on 14 Feb 1954 in Turnov. He married Lida Havelková on 22 Apr 1976 in Bakov mad Jizerou.

Luboš Příhoda-6 (Božena-5, Anna-4, Anna-3, Alžběta-2, Václav-1) was born in 1928.

Unknown.

Luboš Příhoda and Unknown married. They had the following children:

    i. **son Příhoda** was born about 1950.

Danuse Koskova-6 (Božena-5, Anna-4, Anna-3, Alžběta-2, Václav-1) was born on 19 Dec 1937 in Horka u Bakova.

Victor Svoboda was born on 05 Oct 1937 in Brnany, Litomerice Co.. He died on 14 Aug 1985.

Victor Svoboda and Danuse Koskova were married on 01 Mar 1958 in Ustek, Litomerice Co.. They had the following children:

    i. **Danuse Svobodová** was born on 24 Sep 1958 in Litomerice. She married Otakar Gabriel on 15 Jul 1978 in MNV Terezin.

    ii. **Václav Svoboda** was born on 25 Sep 1959 in Litomerice. He married Miroslava Safrová on 21 Jun 1980 in MNV Terezin.

    iii. **Hana Svobodová** was born on 02 Mar 1972 in Litomerice. She married Martin Gaper on Jun 1992 in MNV Terezin.

Marie Rajtrová-6 (Josef-5, Rudolf-4, Anna-3, Alžběta-2, Václav-1) was born on 19 Sep 1941 in Knezmost, Mnichovo Hradiště Co..

Zdeněk Kilian was born on 16 Jan 1929. He died on 30 Aug 1999.

Zdeněk Kilian and Marie Rajtrová were married on 05 Jul 1969 in Praha. They had the following children:

       i. **Ester Kilianova** was born on 14 Apr 1973 in Jablonec nad Nisou. She married Ivo Srb on 09 Sep 1995 in Liberec.

       Pavlina Kilianova was born on 17 Feb 1976.

Josef Rajtr-6 (Josef-5, Rudolf-4, Anna-3, Alžběta-2, Václav-1) was born on 30 May 1947 in Nova Ves u Branzeze, Mladá Boleslav Co..

Helena Klimesova was born on 18 Aug 1951 in Liberec.

Josef Rajtr and Helena Klimesova were married on 06 Apr 1974 in Sychrov. They had the following children:

       Helena Rajtrová was born on 02 Feb 1976 in Jablonec nad Nisou.

       Tomáš Rajtr was born on 04 Apr 1977 in Liberec.

Václav Rajtr-6 (Václav-5, Rudolf-4, Anna-3, Alžběta-2, Václav-1) was born on 02 Feb 1942 in Muzsky No. 6, Mnichovo Hradiště Co..

Jana Karaskova was born on 11 Feb 1945 in Rakovnik.

Václav Rajtr and Jana Karaskova were married on 17 Apr 1965 in Rakovnik. They had the following children:

       i. **Jana Rajtrová** was born on 14 Apr 1966 in Rakovnik. She married Jaromír Kamenik on 08 Mar 1986 in Rakovnik.

Věra Rajtrová-6 (Václav-5, Rudolf-4, Anna-3, Alžběta-2, Václav-1) was born on 19 Feb 1947 in Muzsky No. 6, Mnichovo Hradiště Co..

Jaroslav Verner was born on 27 Mar 1941 in Knezmost.

Jaroslav Verner and Věra Rajtrová were married on 08 Jan 1966 in Mnichovo Hradiště. They had the following children:

       i. **Jolana Vernerova** was born on 19 Oct 1967 in Mladá Boleslav. She married Jaroslav Zdobinsky on 15 Sep 1989.

       ii. **Věra Vernerova** was born on 26 Nov 1968 in Knezmost. She married Petr Holas on 24 Apr 1990.

Alena Buriánková-6 (Vratislav-5, Josef-4, František-3, Terezie-2, Václav-1) was born on 15 Nov 1960.

Mirek Matlas was born on 20 Sep 1955 in Litvinov.

Mirek Matlas and Alena Buriánková married. They had the following children:

       Alena Matlasová was born in 1981.

       daughter Matlasová was born in 1986.

Aleš Michalek-6 (Jana-5, Josef-4, František-3, Terezie-2, Václav-1) was born on 09 Jun 1970.

Klára Rozenska was born on 08 Sep 1971 in Teplice.

Aleš Michalek and Klára Rozenska married. They had the following children:

>**Terezka Michalkova** was born on 06 Apr 2001.
>
>**Barbora Michalkova** was born on 03 Apr 2006.

Jana Michalkova-6 (Jana-5, Josef-4, František-3, Terezie-2, Václav-1) was born on 07 Oct 1972 in Loukovec.

Jaromír Terner was born on 27 Jun 1961.

Jaromír Terner and Jana Michalkova married. They had the following children:

>**Anna Ternerova** was born in February 9, 2002.
>
>**Linda Ternerova** was born in April 7, 2004.

Petr Buriánek-6 (Ivo-5, Ivo-4, František-3, Terezie-2, Václav-1).

Alena Pecharova.

Petr Buriánek and Alena Pecharova were married in 1999. They had the following children:

>**Štěpán Buriánek.**

Generation 7

John Edward Rechcigl-7 (Mila (Miloslav)-6, Marie-5, Čeněk-4, Anna-3, Alžběta-2, Václav-1) was born on 27 Feb 1960 in Washington, D.C..

Nancy Ann Palko daughter of Joseph Palko and Mary Rishko was born on 26 Sep 1961 in Morristown, NJ.

John Edward Rechcigl and Nancy Ann Palko were married on 30 Jul 1983 in Dover, NJ. They had the following children:

>**Gregory John Rechcigl** was born on 19 Dec 1988 in Bradenton, FL.
>
>ii. **Kevin Thomas Rechcigl** was born on 09 Oct 1991 in Bradenton, FL. He married Jordan Robbins on 12 May 2018 in Jacksonville, FL.
>
>**Lindsey Nicole Rechcigl** was born on 03 Nov 1994 in Bradenton, FL.

Karen Rechcigl-7 (Mila (Miloslav)-6, Marie-5, Čeněk-4, Anna-3, Alžběta-2, Václav-1) was born on 16 Apr 1962 in Washington, DC.

Ulysses Kollecas son of Christopher Thomas (Kolecas) Collier and Amelia Malatras was born on 20 Mar 1958 in Washington, DC.

Ulysses Kollecas and Karen Rechcigl were married on 25 Aug 1990 in Bethesda, MD. They had the following children:

> **Kristin Kollecas** was born on 04 May 1993 in Albuquerque, NM.
>
> **Paul Kollecas** was born on 02 Jun 1995 in Albuquerque, NM.

Marcela Žďárská-7 (Marta-6, Marie-5, Čeněk-4, Anna-3, Alžběta-2, Václav-1) was born on 09 May 1954 in Liberec.

Miroslav Heralecký son of Miroslav Heralecký and Marie Bartošová was born on 18 May 1949 in salomonJablonec nad Nisou, Czech.. He died on 20 Feb 2017 in Proseč, Jablonec nad Nisou, Czech..

Miroslav Heralecký and Marcela Žďárská were married on 15 Mar 1975 in Sychrov. They had the following children:

> **Vit Heralecký** was born on 16 Jan 1977 in Jablonec nad Nisou. He married Olga Zrubcová on 13 Jul 1996.
>
> ii. **Zuzana Heralecká** was born on 30 Dec 1978 in Jablonec nad Nisou. She married Jaroslav Egrt on 13 Sep 2002 in Jablonec nad Nisou.

Iveta Žďárská-7 (Marta-6, Marie-5, Čeněk-4, Anna-3, Alžběta-2, Václav-1) was born on 29 Aug 1963 in Liberec, Bohemia.

Vlastimil Berkman was born in 1957.

Vlastimil Berkman and Iveta Žďárská were married on 29 Oct 1983. They had the following children:

> **Tereza Hriníková** was born on 05 Jun 1984 in Jablonec nad Nisou.

Jaroslav Hrinik son of Jaroslav Hrinik and Milena Preisslerová was born on 17 Apr 1960.

Jaroslav Hrinik and Iveta Žďárská were married on 16 Aug 1991 in Zamek Červená Lhota. They had the following children:

> **Eliška Hriníková** was born on 23 Jun 1992 in Jablonec nad Nisou. She married Jan Ottis on 06 Oct 2018 in Jablonec nad

Jizerou, East Bohemia, Czech Republic.

Marta Koubikova-7 (Jiří-6, Marta-5, Čeněk-4, Anna-3, Alžběta-2, Václav-1) was born on 04 Jul 1962 in Mladá Boleslav.

Vladimír Stibor was born on 04 Jun 1959 in Praha.

Vladimír Stibor and Marta Koubikova were married on 17 Apr 1981. They had the following children:

    i. **Lucie Stiborová** was born on 29 Aug 1982 in Mladá Boleslav.

    Tadeáš Stibor was born on 25 Jul 1988 in Mladá Boleslav.

2nd Jiří Koubik-7 (Jiří-6, Marta-5, Čeněk-4, Anna-3, Alžběta-2, Václav-1) was born on 13 May 1965 in Praha.

Andrea Dunebierová was born on 25 Nov 1964 in Praha.

2nd Jiří Koubik and Andrea Dunebierová were married on 04 Apr 1987 in Brandys nad Labem. They had the following children:

    i. **Roman Koubik** was born on 07 Aug 1987 in Brandys nad Labem.

    Vojtěch Koubik was born on 24 Mar 1989 in Brandys nad Labem.

Hana Rajtrová-7 (Olga-6, Marie-5, Anna-4, Anna-3, Alžběta-2, Václav-1) was born on 02 Aug 1955 in Turnov.

Milan Ludvik was born on 31 Jan 1953 in Turnov.

Milan Ludvik and Hana Rajtrová were married on 26 Mar 1977 in Sychrov. They had the following children:

    Martin Ludvik was born on 29 May 1979 in Jablonec nad Nisou.

Miroslav Rajtr-7 (Olga-6, Marie-5, Anna-4, Anna-3, Alžběta-2, Václav-1) was born on 29 Oct 1960 in Mladá Boleslav.

Zdena Bartošová was born on 05 Oct 1961 in Liberec.

Miroslav Rajtr and Zdena Bartošová were married on 22 Mar 1980 in Český Dub. They had the following children:

    Jana Rajtrová was born on 23 Aug 1980 in Liberec.

    Helena Rajtrová was born on 02 Jan 1993 in Liberec.

Milena Pabištová-7 (Milena-6, Marie-5, Anna-4, Anna-3, Alžběta-2, Václav-1) was born on 03 Aug 1955 in Liberec.

Jiří Bobek was born on 27 Mar 1948 in Turnov.

Jiří Bobek and Milena Pabištová were married on 24 Aug 1974 in Sychrov. They had the following children:

i. **Aleš Bobek** was born on 27 Jul 1975 in Liberec. He married Petra Coufalova on 07 Aug 1999.

Jiří Bobek was born on 20 May 1982 in Liberec.

Hana Huňátová-7 (Jaroslava-6, Václav-5, Anna-4, Anna-3, Alžběta-2, Václav-1) was born on 01 Feb 1955 in Turnov.

Milan Lauryn was born on 08 Feb 1951 in Ptyrov.

Milan Lauryn and Hana Huňátová were married on 12 Jul 1974 in Mnichovo Hradiště. They had the following children:

i. **Hana Laurynova** was born on 08 Jan 1975 in Mladá Boleslav. She married Luboš Vodilan on 09 Jun 2001 in Mnichovo Hradiště.

ii. **Milena Laurynova** was born on 25 Aug 1976 in Mladá Boleslav. She married Jiří Koštejn on 29 Sep 1995 in Mnichovo Hradiště.

Václav Huňát-7 (Jaroslava-6, Václav-5, Anna-4, Anna-3, Alžběta-2, Václav-1) was born on 16 Apr 1953 in Turnov.

Jiřina Durianciková was born on 06 Jun 1954.

Václav Huňát and Jiřina Duriancikov**á were married on 26 Nov 1982 in Bakov nad Jizerou. They had the following children:

Václav Huňát was born on 09 May 1983 in Mladá Boleslav.

Stanislav (Pic) Brzobohatý-7 (Hana-6, Václav-5, Anna-4, Anna-3, Alžběta-2, Václav-1) was born on Dec 1949 in Turnov.

Jaroslava Hatašová was born on 18 Jan 1948 in Mnichovo Hradiště.

Stanislav (Pic) Brzobohatý and Jaroslava Hatašová were married on 17 Dec 1971 in Sychrov. They had the following children:

i. **Stanislava Brzobohatá** was born on 03 Mar 1973 in Mladá Boleslav. She married Michal Stárek on 07 Dec 1993 in Sychrov.

Jaroslava Brzobohatá was born on 01 Feb 1977 in Mladá Boleslav.

Jiří Pic-7 (Hana-6, Václav-5, Anna-4, Anna-3, Alžběta-2, Václav-1) was born on 14 Feb 1954 in Turnov.

Lida Havelková was born on 24 Aug 1955 in Mladá Boleslav.

Jiří Pic and Lida Havelková were married on 22 Apr 1976 in Bakov mad Jizerou. They had the following children:

Jiří Pic was born on 25 Apr 1977 in Mladá Boleslav.

Martin Pic was born on 24 May 1980 in Mladá Boleslav.

son **Příhoda**-7 (Luboš-6, Božena-5, Anna-4, Anna-3, Alžběta-2, Václav-1) was born about 1950.

Unknown.

son Příhoda and Unknown married. They had the following children:

children Příhoda.

Danuse Svobodová-7 (Danuse-6, Božena-5, Anna-4, Anna-3, Alžběta-2, Václav-1) was born on 24 Sep 1958 in Litomerice.

Otakar Gabriel was born on 28 Jan 1958.

Otakar Gabriel and Danuse Svobodová were married on 15 Jul 1978 in MNV Terezin. They had the following children:

>**Lenka Gabrielová** was born on 07 Dec 1978 in Litomerice.
>
>**Oto Gabrie** was born on 26 May 1981 in Roudnice nad Labem.

Václav Svoboda-7 (Danuse-6, Božena-5, Anna-4, Anna-3, Alžběta-2, Václav-1) was born on 25 Sep 1959 in Litomerice.

Miroslava Safrová was born on 01 Jan 1961.

Václav Svoboda and Miroslava Safrová were married on 21 Jun 1980 in MNV Terezin. They had the following children:

>**Lucie Svobodová** was born on 04 Mar 1981 in Litomerice.
>
>**Vendula Svobodová** was born on 19 Mar 1982 in Litomerice.
>
>**Václav Svoboda** was born on 25 Jul 1985 in Litomerice.

Hana Svobodová-7 (Danuse-6, Božena-5, Anna-4, Anna-3, Alžběta-2, Václav-1) was born on 02 Mar 1972 in Litomerice.

Martin Gaper was born in Doksany.

Martin Gaper and Hana Svobodová were married on 13 Jun 1992 in MNV Terezin. They had the following children:

>**Martin Gaper** was born on 19 Sep 1992 in Litomerice.

Ester Kilianova-7 (Marie-6, Josef-5, Rudolf-4, Anna-3, Alžběta-2, Václav-1) was born on 14 Apr 1973 in Jablonec nad Nisou.

Ivo Srb.

Ivo Srb and Ester Kilianova were married on 09 Sep 1995 in Liberec. They had the following children:

>**Jakub Srb** was born on 15 Feb 1996.

Jana Rajtrová-7 (Václav-6, Václav-5, Rudolf-4, Anna-3, Alžběta-2, Václav-1) was born on 14 Apr 1966 in Rakovnik.

Jaromír Kamenik was born on 12 Jan 1963 in Kutna Hora.

Jaromír Kamenik and Jana Rajtrová were married on 08 Mar 1986 in Rakovnik. They had the following children:

> **Alena Kamenikova** was born on 02 Aug 1985 in Rakovnik.
>
> **Petr Kamenik** was born on 31 Jan 1993 in Rakovnik.

Jolana Vernerova-7 (Věra-6, Václav-5, Rudolf-4, Anna-3, Alžběta-2, Václav-1) was born on 19 Oct 1967 in Mladá Boleslav.

Jaroslav Zdobinsky was born on 16 Dec 1963.

Jaroslav Zdobinsky and Jolana Vernerova were married on 15 Sep 1989. They had the following children:

> **Jaroslav Zobinsky** was born on 26 Mar 1992 in Mladá Boleslav.
>
> **Nela Zdobinska** was born on 29 Feb 2000 in Mladá Boleslav.

Věra Vernerova-7 (Věra-6, Václav-5, Rudolf-4, Anna-3, Alžběta-2, Václav-1) was born on 26 Nov 1968 in Knezmost.

Petr Holas was born on 11 Feb 1965 in Mladá Boleslav.

Petr Holas and Věra Vernerova were married on 24 Apr 1990. They had the following children:

> **Vojta Holas** was born on 08 Mar 1993 in Turnov.

Generation 8

Kevin Thomas Rechcigl-8 (John Edward-7, Mila (Miloslav)-6, Marie-5, Čeněk-4, Anna-3, Alžběta-2, Václav-1) was born on 09 Oct 1991 in Bradenton, FL.

Jordan Robbins daughter of Douglass Robbins and Ivonne was born on 10 Jan 1992 in Camarillo, CA.

Kevin Thomas Rechcigl and Jordan Robbins were married on 12 May 2018 in Jacksonville, FL. They had the following children:

> **James Douglas Rechcigl** was born on 05 Jan 2021 in Jacksonville, FL.
>
> **Evelyn Marie Rechcigl** was born 29 May 2023 in Jacksonville, FL.

Zuzana Heralecká-8 (Marcela-7, Marta-6, Marie-5, Čeněk-4, Anna-3, Alžběta-2, Václav-1) was born on 30 Dec 1978 in Jablonec nad Nisou.

Jaroslav Egrt was born on 25 Apr 1974 in Duchcov.

Jaroslav Egrt and Zuzana Heralecká were married on 13 Sep 2002 in Jablonec nad Nisou. They had the following children:
>   **Kristina Egrtova** was born on 04 Jan 2008 in Liberec.
>   **Jaroslav Egrt** was born on 04 Jan 2008 in Liberec.

Lucie Stiborová-8 (Marta-7, Jiří-6, Marta-5, Čeněk-4, Anna-3, Alžběta-2, Václav-1) was born on 29 Aug 1982 in Mladá Boleslav.
Novotný.
Novotný and Lucie Stiborová married. They had the following children:
>   **Tobias Novotný**.

Roman Koubik-8 (2nd Jiří-7, Jiří-6, Marta-5, Čeněk-4, Anna-3, Alžběta-2, Václav-1) was born on 07 Aug 1987 in Brandys nad Labem.
Martina.
Roman Koubik and Martina married. They had the following children:
>   **Roman Koubik**.

Aleš Bobek-8 (Milena-7, Milena-6, Marie-5, Anna-4, Anna-3, Alžběta-2, Václav-1) was born on 27 Jul 1975 in Liberec.
Petra Coufalova was born in 1974.
Aleš Bobek and Petra Coufalova were married on 07 Aug 1999. They had the following children:
>   **Alena Bobková** was born on 02 Feb 2002 in Liberec.
>   **Antonia Bobková** was born on 16 Jul 2004 in Liberec.

Hana Laurynova-8 (Hana-7, Jaroslava-6, Václav-5, Anna-4, Anna-3, Alžběta-2, Václav-1) was born on 08 Jan 1975 in Mladá Boleslav.
Luboš Vodilan was born on 06 Jul 1974 in Mladá Boleslav.
Luboš Vodilan and Hana Laurynova were married on 09 Jun 2001 in Mnichovo Hradiště. They had the following children:
>   **Michaela Vodilanova** was born on 10 May 2002.

Milena Laurynova-8 (Hana-7, Jaroslava-6, Václav-5, Anna-4, Anna-3, Alžběta-2, Václav-1) was born on 25 Aug 1976 in Mladá Boleslav.
Jiří Koštejn was born on 01 Jun 1970 in Mladá Boleslav.
Jiří Koštejn and Milena Laurynova were married on 29 Sep 1995 in Mnichovo Hradiště. They had the following children:
>   **Jiří Koštejn** was born on 18 Jul 1997 in Mladá Boleslav.

Adela Koštejn was born on 01 Jan 2004 in Mladá Boleslav.

Stanislava Brzobohatá-8 (Stanislav (Pic)-7, Hana-6, Václav-5, Anna-4, Anna-3, Alžběta-2, Václav-1) was born on 03 Mar 1973 in Mladá Boleslav. **Michal Stárek**.

Michal Stárek and Stanislava Brzobohatá were married on 07 Dec 1993 in Sychrov. They had the following children:

    Michal Stárek was born on 06 Jun 1994 in Mladá Boleslav.

    David Stárek was born on 26 Jan 2000 in Liberec.

Sources

Matrika krestni, Kniha Z, List 65, Krestni a rodny list.

Matrika krestni: Hoškovice, Kniha 104, List 172, Krestni a rodny list.

Novák Family

Generation 1

Jan Novák-1 was born in Dalešice No. 5.

Dorota Reslová was born in Bitouchov.

Jan Novák and Dorota Reslová married. They had the following children:

    i. **Kateřina Nováková** was born in Dalešice No. 5.

Generation 2

Kateřina Nováková-2 (Jan-1) was born in Dalešice No. 5.

František Danda son of Josef Danda and Barbora Buriánková was born about 1820 in Hoškovice No. 2, Mnichovo Hradiště Co..

František Danda and Kateřina Nováková married. They had the following children:

    i. **Václav Danda** was born on 13 May 1848 in Hoškovice No. 2, Mnichovo Hradiště Dist, Bohemia. He married Marie Štěpánková on 07 Feb 1871 in Dobrá Voda, Bohemia. He died on 11 Dec 1917 in February 7, Hoškovice, Mnichovo Hradiště Dist, Bohemia.

    ii. **son Danda** was born in Hoškovice 2, Mnichovo Hradiště Co..

    iii. **Anna Dandová** was born in Hoškovice No. 2,.

    iv. **Barbora Dandová** was born in Hoškovice No. 2, Mnichovo Hradiště Co..

    v. **František Antonín Danda** was born on 10 Jun 1857 in Hoškovice, No. 2, Mnichovo Hradiště Dist, Bohemia. He married Josefa Cimrová on 04 Feb 1881 in Manikovice No. 21. He died on 07 Jun 1900 in Hoškovice, No. 14, Mnichovo Hradiště Dist, Bohemia.

Generation 3

Václav Danda-3 (Kateřina-2, Jan-1) was born on 13 May 1848 in Hoškovice No. 2, Mnichovo Hradiště Dist, Bohemia. He died on 11 Dec 1917 in February 7, Hoškovice, Mnichovo Hradiště Dist, Bohemia.

Marie Štěpánková daughter of Antonín Štěpánek and Anna Koťátková was born on 28 Jun 1847 in Dobrá Voda No.. 10. She died on 16 Apr 1914 in Hoškovice No. 2, Mnichovo Hradiště Dist, Bohemia.

Václav Danda and Marie Štěpánková were married on 07 Feb 1871 in

Dobrá Voda, Bohemia. They had the following children:
> i. **Anna Dandová** was born on 07 Feb 1872 in Hoškovice No. 2,, Mnichovo Hradiště Dist, Bohemia. She married Václav Šverma on 23 Nov 1897 in Hoškovice No. 10, Mnichovo Hradiště Dist, Bohemia. She died on 31 May 1927.
>> **Josef Danda** was born on 17 Mar 1873 in Hoškovice No. 2, Mnichovo Hradiště Dist, Bohemia. He died on 07 Oct 1900 in Hoškovice No. 2, Mnichovo Hradiště Dist, Bohemia.
>
> iii. **Emilie Kateřina Dandová** was born on 17 Feb 1874 in Hoškovice, No. 2, Mnichovo Hradiště Dist, Bohemia. She married František Stejskal on 22 Nov 1904. She died on 28 Apr 1954.

son Danda-3 (Kateřina-2, Jan-1) was born in Hoškovice 2, Mnichovo Hradiště Co..

Unknown.

son Danda and Unknown married. They had the following children:
> **daughter Dandová.**
>
> ii. **daughter Dandová.**

Anna Dandová-3 (Kateřina-2, Jan-1) was born in Hoškovice No. 2,.

Červinka was born in Nasldelnice.

Červinka and Anna Dandová married. They had the following children:
> **Emilie Červinková.**

Barbora Dandová-3 (Kateřina-2, Jan-1) was born in Hoškovice No. 2, Mnichovo Hradiště Co.. Barbora Dandová and unknown spouse married. They had the following children:
> i. **Marie Švermová** was born about 1880.
>
> ii. **Antonín Šverma** was born before 1890 in Podolí, Mnichovo Hradiště Co..
>
> iii. **František Šverma** was born before 1890.
>
> iv. **Václav Šverma** was born before 1890.

František Antonín Danda-3 (Kateřina-2, Jan-1) was born on 10 Jun 1857 in Hoškovice, No. 2, Mnichovo Hradiště Dist, Bohemia. He died on 07 Jun 1900 in Hoškovice, No. 14, Mnichovo Hradiště Dist, Bohemia.

Josefa Cimrová daughter of František Cimr and Anna Ferklová was born on 01 Jan 1859 in Manikovice No. 11, Mnichovo Hradiště Dist.. She died on 27 Aug 1923 in Hoškovice No. 14, Mnichovo Hradiště Dist.. František Antonín Danda and Josefa Cimrová were married on 04 Feb 1881 in Manikovice No. 21. They had the following children:

    i. **Marie Dandová**[1] was born on 31 Jan 1882 in Hoškovice, No. 14, Mnichovo Hradiště Dist, Bohemia. She married Čeněk Rajtr on 02 Jul 1904 in Mnichovo Hradiště. She died on 05 Jul 1967 in Dolanky No. 7, Mnichovo Hradiště Co..

    ii. **Josef Danda** was born on 30 Jan 1884 in Hoškovice, No. 14, Mnichovo Hradiště Dist, Bohemia. He died on 18 Apr 1936 in Dobrá Voda.

Josefa Kateřina Dandová was born on 04 Oct 1885 in Hoškovice No. 14, Mnichovo Hradiště Dist.. She married Václav Balák after 1925.

Anna Dandová was born on 12 Nov 1886 in Hoškovice, No. 14, Mnichovo Hradiště Dist, Bohemia. She died on 13 May 1972.

František Danda was born on 23 Apr 1888 in Hoškovice, No. 14, Mnichovo Hradiště Dist, Bohemia. He died on 27 Jun 1888 in Hoškovice, No. 14, Mnichovo Hradiště Dist, Bohemia.

František Danda was born on 13 Nov 1889 in Hoškovice No. 14, Mnichovo Hradiště Dist.. He died on 22 Dec 1891 in Hoškovice no. 14, Mnichovo Hradiště Dist, Bohemia.

Václav Danda was born on 05 Sep 1891 in Hoškovice No. 14, Mnichovo Hradiště Dist, Bohemia. He died on 10 Mar 1892 in Hoškovice No. 14, Mnichovo Hradiště Dist, Bohemia.

    viii. **Emilie Dandová** was born on 22 Oct 1893 in Hoškovice No. 14, Mnichovo Hradiště Dist, Bohemia. She married Václav Balák on 18 Sep 1920 in Hoškovice, Mnichovo Hradiště Dist, Bohemia. She died on 06 Apr 1924 in Hoškovice, Mnichovo Hradiště Dist, Bohemia.

Generation 4

Anna Dandová-4 (Václav-3, Kateřina-2, Jan-1) was born on 07 Feb 1872 in Hoškovice No. 2,, Mnichovo Hradiště Dist, Bohemia. She died on 31 May

1927.

Václav Šverma son of Jan Šverma and Anna Dandová was born on 12 Aug 1870 in Podolí. He died on 08 Apr 1943 in Hoškovice No. 10, Mnichovo Hradiště Dist, Bohemia.

Václav Šverma and Anna Dandová were married on 23 Nov 1897 in Hoškovice No. 10, Mnichovo Hradiště Dist, Bohemia. They had the following children:

    i. **Marie Švermová** was born on 20 Aug 1898 in Hoškovice No. 10, Mnichovo Hradiště Dist, Bohemia. She married Ladislav Šíp on 02 Oct 1920 in Hoškovice, Mnichovo Hradiště Dist, Bohemia. She died on 12 Apr 1986.

Emilie Kateřina Dandová-4 (Václav-3, Kateřina-2, Jan-1) was born on 17 Feb 1874 in Hoškovice, No. 2, Mnichovo Hradiště Dist, Bohemia. She died on 28 Apr 1954.

František Stejskal son of Jan Stejskal and Barbora Sritrova was born on 12 Sep 1876 in Proseč. He died on 19 Mar 1931.

František Stejskal and Emilie Kateřina Dandová were married on 22 Nov 1904. They had the following children:

    i. **Josef Stejskal** was born on 02 Aug 1905 in Hoškovice No. 2, Mnichovo Hradiště Co.. He died on 14 Aug 1987.

    ii. **Marie Stejskalová** was born in 1910. She died in 1945.

daughter Dandová-4 (son-3, Kateřina-2, Jan-1).

Unknown.

Unknown and daughter Dandová married. They had the following children:

    i. **Marie Floriánová**.

Marie Švermová-4 (Barbora-3, Kateřina-2, Jan-1) was born about 1880.

Josef Bukvička was born before 1880 in Hoškovice No. 5.

Josef Bukvička and Marie Švermová married. They had the following children:

    i. **Antonín Bukvička** was born in Hoškovice.

    ii. **Josef Bukvička** was born on 27 Jan 1898. He died on 14 Feb 1970.

    iii. **Marie Bukvičková** was born about 1899 in Hoškovice No. 5.

iv. **Bohuslav Bukvička**.

Antonín Šverma-4 (Barbora-3, Kateřina-2, Jan-1) was born before 1890 in Podolí, Mnichovo Hradiště Co..

Růžena Švermová was born before 1890 in Manikovice, Mnichovo Hradiště Co.. Antonín Šverma and Růžena Švermová married. They had the following children:

    i. **Růžena Švermová** was born in 1907 in Podolí, Mnichovo Hradiště Co..

František Šverma-4 (Barbora-3, Kateřina-2, Jan-1) was born before 1890.

Anna was born in Bycin.

František Šverma and Anna married. They had the following children:
    František Šverma.
    Anna Švermová.

Václav Šverma-4 (Barbora-3, Kateřina-2, Jan-1) was born before 1890.

Unknown.

Václav Šverma and Unknown married. They had the following children:
    Václav Šverma.

    ii. **Anna Švermová** was born on 16 Aug 1901 in Podolí. She died on 05 Mar 1972 in Hoškovice No. 13.

    Ladislav Šverma.

    Josef Šverma.

Marie Dandová-4 (František Antonín-3, Kateřina-2, Jan-1)[1] was born on 31 Jan 1882 in Hoškovice, No. 14, Mnichovo Hradiště Dist, Bohemia. She died on 05 Jul 1967 in Dolanky No. 7, Mnichovo Hradiště Co..

Čeněk Rajtr son of Jan Václav Rajtr and Anna Najmanová[2] was born on 01 Jul 1874 in nky No. 7, Mnichovo Hradiště Dist... He died on 27 Oct 1956 in Dolánky No. 7, Mnichovo Hradiště Dist...

Čeněk Rajtr and Marie Dandová were married on 02 Jul 1904 in Mnichovo Hradiště. They had the following children:

    i. **Marie Rajtrová** was born on 05 Jul 1905 in Dolanky No. 7, Mnichovo Hradiště Co.. She married Miloslav Rechcigl on 26 Jul 1926 in Praha - Kralovske Vinohrady. She died on 13 Apr 1982 in Mladá Boleslav.

Oldrřch Rajtr was born on 14 Nov 1907 in Dolanky No. 7. He died on 02 Nov 1937.

iii. **Marta Rajtrová** was born on 10 Jan 1909 in Dolanky u Bakova. She married Josef Knotek in 1934. She died on 29 Nov 1982 in Mladá Boleslav.

Josef Danda-4 (František Antonín-3, Kateřina-2, Jan-1) was born on 30 Jan 1884 in Hoškovice, No. 14, Mnichovo Hradiště Dist, Bohemia. He died on 18 Apr 1936 in Dobrá Voda.

Božena Slavíková daughter of Josef Slavik and Anna Jirova was born on 05 Sep 1889 in Lesnovky, Turnov Dist... She died on 06 Oct 1965 in Dobrá Voda.

Josef Danda and Božena Slavíková married. They had the following children:

i. **Oldřich Danda** was born on 29 Jan 1922 in Hoškovice No. 10, Mnichovo Hradiště Dist, Bohemia. He died on 30 Jan 1983 in Dobrá Voda, Mnichovo Hradiště Co..

Emilie Dandová-4 (František Antonín-3, Kateřina-2, Jan-1) was born on 22 Oct 1893 in Hoškovice No. 14, Mnichovo Hradiště Dist, Bohemia. She died on 06 Apr 1924 in Hoškovice, Mnichovo Hradiště Dist, Bohemia.

Václav Balák son of Václav Balak and Kateřina Janoušková was born about 1890 in Nová Ves No. 13, Mnichovo Hradiště District.

Václav Balák and Emilie Dandová were married on 18 Sep 1920 in Hoškovice, Mnichovo Hradiště Dist, Bohemia. They had the following children:

i. **Marie Balakova** was born on 16 Feb 1921 in Hoškovice No. 14, Mnichovo Hradiště Dist.. She married Otakar Lochman on 04 Nov 1942 in Mnichovo Hradiště.

ii. **Václav Balak** was born on 06 Jun 1922 in Hoškovice. He died on 24 Jan 2001. He married Zdenka Štolbová on 31 Dec.

iii. **Vlasta Balakova** was born on 02 Sep 1923 in Hoškovice, Mnichovo Hradiště Co.. She married Milous Bičík in 1948.

Generation 5

Marie Švermová-5 (Anna-4, Václav-3, Kateřina-2, Jan-1) was born on 20 Aug

1898 in Hoškovice No. 10, Mnichovo Hradiště Dist, Bohemia. She died on 12 Apr 1986.

Ladislav Šíp son of Václav Šíp and Julie Chvalinová was born on 30 Sep 1888 in Vesec u Turnova, Turnov Co.. He died on 01 Apr 1967 in Prague, Czechoslovakia.

Ladislav Šíp and Marie Švermová were married on 02 Oct 1920 in Hoškovice, Mnichovo Hradiště Dist, Bohemia. They had the following children:

> i. **Ladislav Šíp** was born on 08 Oct 1922 in Prague, Czechoslavakia. He married Mirka Langova about 13 Apr 1950. He died on 10 Jun 1993 in Prague, Czechoslavakia.
>
> ii. **Eva Šípová** was born in 1927.

Josef Stejskal-5 (Emilie Kateřina-4, Václav-3, Kateřina-2, Jan-1) was born on 02 Aug 1905 in Hoškovice No. 2, Mnichovo Hradiště Co.. He died on 14 Aug 1987.

Marie Maděrová daughter of František Maděra and Marie Dubská was born on 08 Apr 1910 in Bosen No. 38. She died on 10 Oct 1945.

Josef Stejskal and Marie Maděrová married. They had the following children:

> i. **Josef Stejskal** was born in 1932. He died in 2003.

Jaromír Stejskal was born on 18 Jul 1937. He died on 13 Aug 1995.

Marie Stejskalová-5 (Emilie Kateřina-4, Václav-3, Kateřina-2, Jan-1) was born in 1910. She died in 1945.

Oldrřch Bergman was born in Mnichovo Hradiště.

Oldrřch Bergman and Marie Stejskalová married. They had the following children:

> **Jana Bergmannová** was born in Mnichovo Hradiště.
>
> **Pavel Bergmann.**

Marie Floriánová-5 (daughter-4, son-3, Kateřina-2, Jan-1).

Josef Tomeš was born in Stranov.

Josef Tomeš and Marie Floriánová married. They had the following children:

> **Tomsová-daughter.**

son Tomeš.

Antonín Bukvička-5 (Marie-4, Barbora-3, Kateřina-2, Jan-1) was born in Hoškovice.

Ludmila Baierova daughter of Václav Baier and Marie Buriánková.

Antonín Bukvička and Ludmila Baierova married. They had the following children:

    i. **Jaroslav Bukvička** was born in 1928.

    ii. **Jiří Bukvička** was born in 1935 in Hoškovice. He died on 11 May 1998.

Josef Bukvička-5 (Marie-4, Barbora-3, Kateřina-2, Jan-1) was born on 27 Jan 1898. He died on 14 Feb 1970.

Ludmila Tondrová daughter of Tondr was born on 10 Oct 1899 in Hoškovice No.. 35. She died on 23 Feb 1992.

Josef Bukvička and Ludmila Tondrová married. They had the following children:

    i. **Josef Bukvička** was born on 16 Mar 1926 in Hoškovice No. 34.

    ii. **Jiřina Bukvičková** was born on 07 Sep 1922 in Hoškovice No. 6.

Marie Bukvičková-5 (Marie-4, Barbora-3, Kateřina-2, Jan-1) was born about 1899 in Hoškovice No. 5.

Miroslav Hyka was born in Mnichovo Hradiště.

Miroslav Hyka and Marie Bukvičková married. They had the following children:

    i. **Miroslav Hyka** was born about 1925.

    ii. **Milena Hykova**.

Bohuslav Bukvička-5 (Marie-4, Barbora-3, Kateřina-2, Jan-1).

Zofie Tomášová was born in Stranov.

Bohuslav Bukvička and Zofie Tomášová married. They had the following children:

    i. **Bohuslav Bukvička** was born on 20 Oct 1929. He died on 11 Nov 1988.

    ii. **Drahoslava Bukvičková** was born on 07 Nov 1933.

Růžena Švermová-5 (Antonín-4, Barbora-3, Kateřina-2, Jan-1) was born in 1907 in Podolí, Mnichovo Hradiště Co..

Josef Vochvesta was born in 1908 in Sezemice.
Josef Vochvesta and Růžena Švermová married. They had the following children:

    i. **Květa Vochvestova** was born on 02 Nov 1932 in Podolí, Mnichovo Hradiště Co..

Anna Švermová-5 (Václav-4, Barbora-3, Kateřina-2, Jan-1) was born on 16 Aug 1901 in Podolí. She died on 05 Mar 1972 in Hoškovice No. 13.

Miloslav Danda son of Josef of Kopeček Danda and Josefa Picková was born on 20 May 1900 in Hoškovice No. 13, Mnichovo Hradiště Dist, Bohemia. He died on 13 Sep 1952 in Hoškovice No. 13, Mnichovo Hradiště Dist, Bohemia.

Miloslav Danda and Anna Švermová married. They had the following children:

    i. **Miloslav Danda** was born on 03 Sep 1931 in Hoškovice No. 13. He died on 05 Jun 2002 in Hoškovice No. 13.

    Miloslav Danda.

Marie Rajtrová-5 (Marie-4, František Antonín-3, Kateřina-2, Jan-1) was born on 05 Jul 1905 in Dolanky No. 7, Mnichovo Hradiště Co.. She died on 13 Apr 1982 in Mladá Boleslav.

Miloslav Rechcigl son of Adolf Rechcigl and Marie Berglová was born on 13 May 1904 in Kočnovice (renamed Chocnějovice) No. 22. He died on 27 May 1973 in Washington, DC.

Miloslav Rechcigl and Marie Rajtrová were married on 26 Jul 1926 in Praha - Kralovske Vinohrady. They had the following children:

    i. **Mila (Miloslav) Rechcigl Jr.** was born on 30 Jul 1930 in Mladá Boleslav, CSR. He married Eva Edwards (Eisnerová) on 29 Aug 1953 in New York, NY.

    ii. **Marta Rechcíglová** was born on 23 May 1933 in Mladá Boleslav. She married František Žďárský on 03 Oct 1953 in Mladá Boleslav. She died on 13 Sep 2018 in Mladá Boleslav.

Marta Rajtrová-5 (Marie-4, František Antonín-3, Kateřina-2, Jan-1) was born on 10 Jan 1909 in Dolanky u Bakova. She died on 29 Nov 1982 in Mladá Boleslav.

Josef Knotek was born between 1905-1907 in Mala Bela, p. Bakov nad Jizerou. He died in 1934. Josef Knotek and Marta Rajtrová were married in 1934. They had no children.

Miroslav Koubik son of Koubik was born in 1908 in Terezin. He died in 1968 in Havlickuv Brod.

Miroslav Koubik and Marta Rajtrová were married on 26 Jul 1938 in Praha. They had the following children:

    i. **Jiří Koubik** was born on 29 Jan 1940 in Prague. He married Jiřina Muellerová on 31 Jan 1962 in Praha. He died on 26 Jun 1998 in Brandys nad Labem.

Emil Pazderník was born after 1900.

Emil Pazderník and Marta Rajtrová were married after 1945. They had no children.

Karel Horáček.

Karel Horáček and Marta Rajtrová met. They had no children.

Oldřich Danda-5 (Josef-4, František Antonín-3, Kateřina-2, Jan-1) was born on 29 Jan 1922 in Hoškovice No. 10, Mnichovo Hradiště Dist, Bohemia. He died on 30 Jan 1983 in Dobrá Voda, Mnichovo Hradiště Co..

Marie Augustinova was born on 01 Jun 1923 in Dobrá Voda, Mnichovo Hradiště Co.. She died on 03 Jan 2003 in Dobrá Voda, Mnichovo Hradiště Co..

Oldřich Danda and Marie Augustinova married. They had the following children:

    i. **Oldrřch Danda** was born on 06 Sep 1958 in Turnov.

    ii. **Marie Dandová** was born on 12 Jun 1946 in Mnichovo Hradiště.

Marie Balakova-5 (Emilie-4, František Antonín-3, Kateřina-2, Jan-1) was born on 16 Feb 1921 in Hoškovice No. 14, Mnichovo Hradiště Dist..

Otakar Lochman was born on 13 Jan 1917 in Hradec, Mnichovo Hrtadiste Dist.. He died on 22 Sep 1980.

Otakar Lochman and Marie Balakova were married on 04 Nov 1942 in Mnichovo Hradiště. They had the following children:

    i. **Otakar Lochman** was born on 24 Dec 1944 in Mnichovo Hradiště. He married Václava Bártová on 12 Nov 1966 in Turnov.

Václav Balak-5 (Emilie-4, František Antonín-3, Kateřina-2, Jan-1) was born on 06 Jun 1922 in Hoškovice. He died on 24 Jan 2001.
Zdenka Štolbová was born on 22 Dec 1930. She died on 01 Jan 1985.
Václav Balak and Zdenka Štolbová were married on 31 Dec. They had the following children:
>   **Sarka Balakova** was born about 1950.
>   ii. **Zdenka Balakova** was born on 16 Nov 1952. She married Bohumil Konicek on 08 Jun 1974.

Vlasta Balakova-5 (Emilie-4, František Antonín-3, Kateřina-2, Jan-1) was born on 02 Sep 1923 in Hoškovice, Mnichovo Hradiště Co..
Milous Bičík was born on 28 Jun 1920. He died on 24 Mar 1988.
Milous Bičík and Vlasta Balakova were married in 1948. They had the following children:
>   i. **Emilie Bičíková** was born on 08 Mar 1949 in Turnov. She married Oldrřch Šnajdr on 08 Oct 1970.

Generation 6

Ladislav Šíp-6 (Marie-5, Anna-4, Václav-3, Kateřina-2, Jan-1) was born on 08 Oct 1922 in Prague, Czechoslavakia. He died on 10 Jun 1993 in Prague, Czechoslavakia.
Mirka Langova was born on 19 Feb 1925. She died in 2005.
Ladislav Šíp and Mirka Langova were married about 13 Apr 1950. They had the following children:
>   i. **Marie Šípová** was born on 08 Jun 1956 in Praha.
>   ii. **Ladislav Šíp** was born on 11 Sep 1958 in Praha.

Eva Šípová-6 (Marie-5, Anna-4, Václav-3, Kateřina-2, Jan-1) was born in 1927.
Jan Klos was born on 20 May 1912. He died on 05 Jan 1984.
Jan Klos and Eva Šípová married. They had the following children:
>   **Eva Klosova**.

Josef Stejskal-6 (Josef-5, Emilie Kateřina-4, Václav-3, Kateřina-2, Jan-1) was born in 1932. He died in 2003.
Růžena Patočková was born in 1935 in Mnichovo Hradiště.
Josef Stejskal and Růžena Patočková married. They had the following

children:
> i. **Milan Stejskal** was born in 1960.
>
> **Vit Stejskal** was born in 1963.

Jaroslav Bukvička-6 (Antonín-5, Marie-4, Barbora-3, Kateřina-2, Jan-1) was born in 1928.

Ludmila Machatova was born in 1935.

Jaroslav Bukvička and Ludmila Machatova married. They had the following children:
> **Dana Bukvičková**.
>
> **Ivana Bukvičková**.

Jiří Bukvička-6 (Antonín-5, Marie-4, Barbora-3, Kateřina-2, Jan-1) was born in 1935 in Hoškovice. He died on 11 May 1998.

Milena Tomsová was born on 13 Apr 1935 in Loukov No. 17.

Jiří Bukvička and Milena Tomsová married. They had the following children:
> **Milena Bukvičková** was born on 14 Apr 1959 in Mladá Boleslav.
>
> ii. **Sona Bukvičková** was born on 26 Jan 1965 in Mladá Boleslav.

Josef Bukvička-6 (Josef-5, Marie-4, Barbora-3, Kateřina-2, Jan-1) was born on 16 Mar 1926 in Hoškovice No. 34.

Vlasta Benešová was born on 23 Mar 1930 in Hoškovice.

Josef Bukvička and Vlasta Benešová married. They had the following children:
> i. **Ludmila Bukvičková** was born on 31 Aug 1959 in Mladá Boleslav. She married Frantiosek Šafránek on 09 Sep 1984.
>
> **Josef Bukvička** was born on 06 Nov 1963 in Mladá Boleslav.

Jiřina Bukvičková-6 (Josef-5, Marie-4, Barbora-3, Kateřina-2, Jan-1) was born on 07 Sep 1922 in Hoškovice No. 6.

Antonín Wagenknecht was born on 05 Sep 1913.

Antonín Wagenknecht and Jiřina Bukvičková married. They had the following children:
> i. **Jiří Wagenknecht** was born on 10 Jan 1946.
>
> ii. **Jan Wagenknecht** was born on 30 Nov 1949.

Miroslav Hyka-6 (Marie-5, Marie-4, Barbora-3, Kateřina-2, Jan-1) was born about 1925.

Emilie.

Miroslav Hyka and Emilie married. They had the following children:
  i. **Mirek Hyka.**
  ii. **Jan Hyka.**

Milena Hykova-6 (Marie-5, Marie-4, Barbora-3, Kateřina-2, Jan-1).

Ladislav Sedláček was born in Mladá Boleslav.

Ladislav Sedláček and Milena Hykova married. They had the following children:
  i. **Ladislav Sedláček.**
  ii. **Milena Sedláčková.**

Bohuslav Bukvička-6 (Bohuslav-5, Marie-4, Barbora-3, Kateřina-2, Jan-1) was born on 20 Oct 1929. He died on 11 Nov 1988.

Marie was born on 09 Sep 1932.

Bohuslav Bukvička and Marie married. They had the following children:

  Pavel Bukvička was born on 08 Aug 1953. He died on 01 Dec 1977.

  Hana Bukvičková was born on 13 Jan 1960.

Drahoslava Bukvičková-6 (Bohuslav-5, Marie-4, Barbora-3, Kateřina-2, Jan-1) was born on 07 Nov 1933.

Jaroslav Vochvesta. He died on Unknown.

Jaroslav Vochvesta and Drahoslava Bukvičková married. They had the following children:

  Jaroslav Vochvesta.

  Zuzana Vochvestova.

Květa Vochvestova-6 (Růžena-5, Antonín-4, Barbora-3, Kateřina-2, Jan-1) was born on 02 Nov 1932 in Podolí, Mnichovo Hradiště Co..

Zdeněk Hrůša was born on 18 Nov 1928 in Dneboh.

Zdeněk Hrůša and Květa Vochvestova married. They had the following children:
  i. **Jitka Hrušová** was born on 11 Nov 1956 in Turnov.
  ii. **Zdeněk Hrůša** was born in Nov 1957 in Turnov.
  iii. **Josef Hrůša** was born on 13 Aug 1959 in Turnov.

Miloslav Danda-6 (Anna-5, Václav-4, Barbora-3, Kateřina-2, Jan-1) was born on 03 Sep 1931 in Hoškovice No. 13. He died on 05 Jun 2002 in Hoškovice No. 13.

Jiřina Hykova was born in Dneboh. She died in 1968 in Dneboh.

Miloslav Danda and Jiřina Hykova married. They had the following children:

> i. **Jiří Danda** was born on 29 Mar 1962.

Mila (Miloslav) Rechcigl Jr.-6 (Marie-5, Marie-4, František Antonín-3, Kateřina-2, Jan-1) was born on 30 Jul 1930 in Mladá Boleslav, CSR.

Eva Edwards (Eisnerová) daughter of Paul J. Edwards (Pavel Eisner) and Jiřina Taussigová was born on 21 Jan 1932 in Prague, CSR.

Mila (Miloslav) Rechcigl Jr. and Eva Edwards (Eisnerová) were married on 29 Aug 1953 in New York, NY. They had the following children:

> i. **John Edward Rechcigl** was born on 27 Feb 1960 in Washington, D.C.. He married Nancy Ann Palko on 30 Jul 1983 in Dover, NJ.
>
> ii. **Karen Rechcigl** was born on 16 Apr 1962 in Washington, DC. She married Ulysses Kollecas on 25 Aug 1990 in Bethesda, MD.

Marta Rechcíglová-6 (Marie-5, Marie-4, František Antonín-3, Kateřina-2, Jan-1) was born on 23 May 1933 in Mladá Boleslav. She died on 13 Sep 2018 in Mladá Boleslav.

František Žďárský son of František Václav Žďárský and Eliška Foltýnová was born on 21 May 1932 in Turnov.

František Žďárský and Marta Rechcíglová were married on 03 Oct 1953 in Mladá Boleslav. They had the following children:

> i. **Marcela Žďárská** was born on 09 May 1954 in Liberec. She married Miroslav Heralecký on 15 Mar 1975 in Sychrov.
>
> ii. **Iveta Žďárská** was born on 29 Aug 1963 in Liberec, Bohemia. She married Vlastimil Berkman on 29 Oct 1983.

Jiří Koubik-6 (Marta-5, Marie-4, František Antonín-3, Kateřina-2, Jan-1) was born on 29 Jan 1940 in Prague. He died on 26 Jun 1998 in Brandys nad Labem.

Jiřina Muellerová was born on 27 Feb 1943 in Buda.

Jiří Koubik and Jiřina Muellerová were married on 31 Jan 1962 in Praha.

They had the following children:
- i. **Marta Koubikova** was born on 04 Jul 1962 in Mladá Boleslav. She married Vladimír Stibor on 17 Apr 1981.
- ii. **2nd Jiří Koubik** was born on 13 May 1965 in Praha. He married Andrea Dunebierová on 04 Apr 1987 in Brandys nad Labem.

Marie Dandová-6 (Oldřich-5, Josef-4, František Antonín-3, Kateřina-2, Jan-1) was born on 12 Jun 1946 in Mnichovo Hradiště.

Květoslav Červený was born on 07 Mar 1945 in Bosen, Mladá Boleslav Co.. Květoslav Červený and Marie Dandová married. They had the following children:
- i. **Luděk Červený** was born on 17 Aug 1968 in Mladá Boleslav. He married Lenka Kovacova on 11 Mar 1989.
- ii. **Radek Červený** was born on 23 May 1972 in Mladá Boleslav. He married Renata Bejrová on 05 Nov 1994.

Otakar Lochman-6 (Marie-5, Emilie-4, František Antonín-3, Kateřina-2, Jan-1) was born on 24 Dec 1944 in Mnichovo Hradiště.

Václava Bártová was born on 26 Sep 1948 in Mladá Boleslav.

Otakar Lochman and Václava Bártová were married on 12 Nov 1966 in Turnov. They had the following children:
- i. **Otakar Lochman** was born on 01 Apr 1968 in Mladá Boleslav. He married Štěpánka Jandová on 27 Aug 1988 in Mnichovo Hradiště.
- ii. **Václava Lochmanová** was born on 21 May 1972 in Mladá Boleslav. She married Vladimír Pecina on 09 Sep 1995 in Mnichovo Hradiště.
- iii. **Iva Lochmanová** was born on 28 Apr 1976 in Mladá Boleslav. She married Libor Janoušek on 21 Mar 1997 in Bakov nad Jizerou.

Zdenka Balakova-6 (Václav-5, Emilie-4, František Antonín-3, Kateřina-2, Jan-1) was born on 16 Nov 1952.

Bohumil Konicek was born on 19 Jun 1953.

Bohumil Konicek and Zdenka Balakova were married on 08 Jun 1974. They had the following children:
- i. **Sarka Konickova** was born on 17 Dec 1974.

    Lukáš Konicek was born on 14 May 1985.

Emilie Bičíková-6 (Vlasta-5, Emilie-4, František Antonín-3, Kateřina-2, Jan-1) was born on 08 Mar 1949 in Turnov.

Oldrřch Šnajdr was born on 07 May 1949 in Brehy.

Oldrřch Šnajdr and Emilie Bičíková were married on 08 Oct 1970. They had the following children:

    i. **Oldrřch Šnajdr** was born on 04 Apr 1971 in Turnov. He married Daniela Synková on 16 Mar 1991.

    Jiří Šnajdr was born on 10 Nov 1977 in Turnov.

Generation 7

Marie Šípová-7 (Ladislav-6, Marie-5, Anna-4, Václav-3, Kateřina-2, Jan-1) was born on 08 Jun 1956 in Praha.

Petr Retek son of Retek was born on 21 Jan 1944.

Petr Retek and Marie Šípová married. They had the following children:

    Magdalena Retková was born on 31 Dec 1982 in Praha.

Ladislav Šíp-7 (Ladislav-6, Marie-5, Anna-4, Václav-3, Kateřina-2, Jan-1) was born on 11 Sep 1958 in Praha.

Hanička Kratochvílová was born on 24 Jun 1960 in Praha.

Ladislav Šíp and Hanička Kratochvílová married. They had the following children:

    Ladislav Šíp was born on 22 Nov 1984 in Praha.

    Martin Šíp was born on 11 Nov 1985 in Praha.

Milan Stejskal-7 (Josef-6, Josef-5, Emilie Kateřina-4, Václav-3, Kateřina-2, Jan-1) was born in 1960.

Lenka Soupkova was born in 1963.

Milan Stejskal and Lenka Soupkova married. They had the following children:

    Martin Stejskal was born in 1989.

    Jiří Stejskal was born in 1990.

Sona Bukvičková-7 (Jiří-6, Antonín-5, Marie-4, Barbora-3, Kateřina-2, Jan-1) was born on 26 Jan 1965 in Mladá Boleslav.

Imrich Rigo.

Imrich Rigo and Sona Bukvičková married. They had the following children:

Zuzanka Rigová was born on 13 Apr 1987 in Mladá Boleslav.

Janicka Rigová was born on 05 Feb 1990 in Mladá Boleslav.

Ludmila Bukvičková-7 (Josef-6, Josef-5, Marie-4, Barbora-3, Kateřina-2, Jan-1) was born on 31 Aug 1959 in Mladá Boleslav.

Frantiosek Šafránek was born on 09 Apr 1959 in Dymokury.

Frantiosek Šafránek and Ludmila Bukvičková were married on 09 Sep 1984. They had the following children:

>   **František Šafránek** was born on 15 Jun 1984.
>
>   **Petr Šafránek** was born on 12 Aug 1986.
>
>   **Jan Šafránek** was born on 05 Dec 1988.

Jiří Wagenknecht-7 (Jiřina-6, Josef-5, Marie-4, Barbora-3, Kateřina-2, Jan-1) was born on 10 Jan 1946.

Vendulka Zahorska was born on 06 Jun 1949.

Jiří Wagenknecht and Vendulka Zahorska married. They had the following children:

>   **Jan Wagenknecht** was born on 16 Feb 1974.
>
>   **Lenka Wagenknechtova** was born on 14 Jan 1980.

Jan Wagenknecht-7 (Jiřina-6, Josef-5, Marie-4, Barbora-3, Kateřina-2, Jan-1) was born on 30 Nov 1949.

Jana Nováková was born on 08 Apr 1955.

Jan Wagenknecht and Jana Nováková married. They had the following children:

>   **Jana Wagenknechtova** was born on 09 Sep 1978.
>
>   **Pavlina Wagenknechtova** was born on 15 Jun 1984.

Mirek Hyka-7 (Miroslav-6, Marie-5, Marie-4, Barbora-3, Kateřina-2, Jan-1).

Unknown.

Mirek Hyka and Unknown married. They had the following children:

>   **Mirek Hyka.**
>
>   **daughter Hyka.**

Jan Hyka-7 (Miroslav-6, Marie-5, Marie-4, Barbora-3, Kateřina-2, Jan-1).

Olga.

Jan Hyka and Olga married. They had the following children:

>   **Jan Hyka.**

Ladislav Sedláček-7 (Milena-6, Marie-5, Marie-4, Barbora-3, Kateřina-2, Jan-1).
Unknown.
Ladislav Sedláček and Unknown married. They had the following children:
    son Sedláček.
Milena Sedláčková-7 (Milena-6, Marie-5, Marie-4, Barbora-3, Kateřina-2, Jan-1).
Michetslaeger was born in Turnov.
Michetslaeger and Milena Sedláčková married. They had the following children:
    daughter Michetslaegerova.
    son Michetslaeger.
Jitka Hrušová-7 (Květa-6, Růžena-5, Antonín-4, Barbora-3, Kateřina-2, Jan-1) was born on 11 Nov 1956 in Turnov.
Josef Brzobohatý was born on 02 Jul 1955 in Knezmost.
Josef Brzobohatý and Jitka Hrušová married. They had the following children:
    Petra Brzobohatá was born on 05 Feb 1980.
    Josef Brzobohatý was born on 21 Jun 1984.
Zdeněk Hrůša-7 (Květa-6, Růžena-5, Antonín-4, Barbora-3, Kateřina-2, Jan-1) was born in Nov 1957 in Turnov.
Libuše Machackova.
Zdeněk Hrůša and Libuše Machackova married. They had the following children:
    Ondřej Hrůša was born on 05 Oct 1987 in Turnov.
Josef Hrůša-7 (Květa-6, Růžena-5, Antonín-4, Barbora-3, Kateřina-2, Jan-1) was born on 13 Aug 1959 in Turnov.
Jana Kindlova.
Josef Hrůša and Jana Kindlova married. They had the following children:
    Zuzana Hrušová was born on 28 Mar 1984.
Jiří Danda-7 (Miloslav-6, Anna-5, Václav-4, Barbora-3, Kateřina-2, Jan-1) was born on 29 Mar 1962.

Iveta Mucskova.

Jiří Danda and Iveta Mucskova married. They had the following children:

> Yveta Dandová.
> Lucie Dandová was born on 07 Sep 1988.

John Edward Rechcigl-7 (Mila (Miloslav)-6, Marie-5, Marie-4, František Antonín-3, Kateřina-2, Jan-1) was born on 27 Feb 1960 in Washington, D.C..

Nancy Ann Palko daughter of Joseph Palko and Mary Rishko was born on 26 Sep 1961 in Morristown, NJ.

John Edward Rechcigl and Nancy Ann Palko were married on 30 Jul 1983 in Dover, NJ. They had the following children:

> **Gregory John Rechcigl** was born on 19 Dec 1988 in Bradenton, FL.
>
> ii. **Kevin Thomas Rechcigl** was born on 09 Oct 1991 in Bradenton, FL. He married Jordan Robbins on 12 May 2018 in Jacksonville, FL.
>
> **Lindsey Nicole Rechcigl** was born on 03 Nov 1994 in Bradenton, FL.

Karen Rechcigl-7 (Mila (Miloslav)-6, Marie-5, Marie-4, František Antonín-3, Kateřina-2, Jan-1) was born on 16 Apr 1962 in Washington, DC.

Ulysses Kollecas son of Christopher Thomas (Kolecas) Collier and Amelia Malatras was born on 20 Mar 1958 in Washington, DC.

Ulysses Kollecas and Karen Rechcigl were married on 25 Aug 1990 in Bethesda, MD. They had the following children:

> **Kristin Kollecas** was born on 04 May 1993 in Albuquerque, NM.
> **Paul Kollecas** was born on 02 Jun 1995 in Albuquerque, NM.

Marcela Žďárská-7 (Marta-6, Marie-5, Marie-4, František Antonín-3, Kateřina-2, Jan-1) was born on May 1954 in Liberec.

Miroslav Heralecký son of Miroslav Heralecký and Marie Bartošová was born on 18 May 1949 in salomonJablonec nad Nisou, Czech.. He died on 20 Feb 2017 in Proseč, Jablonec nad Nisou, Czech..

Miroslav Heralecký and Marcela Žďárská were married on 15 Mar 1975 in Sychrov. They had the following children:

>**Vit Heralecký** was born on 16 Jan 1977 in Jablonec nad Nisou. He married Olga Zrubcová on 13 Jul 1996.
>
>ii. **Zuzana Heralecká** was born on 30 Dec 1978 in Jablonec nad Nisou. She married Jaroslav Egrt on 13 Sep 2002 in Jablonec nad Nisou.

Iveta Žďárská-7 (Marta-6, Marie-5, Marie-4, František Antonín-3, Kateřina-2, Jan-1) was born on 29 Aug 1963 in Liberec, Bohemia.

Vlastimil Berkman was born in 1957.

Vlastimil Berkman and Iveta Žďárská were married on 29 Oct 1983. They had the following children:

>**Tereza Hriníková** was born on 05 Jun 1984 in Jablonec nad Nisou.

Jaroslav Hrinik son of Jaroslav Hrinik and Milena Preisslerová was born on 17 Apr 1960.

Jaroslav Hrinik and Iveta Žďárská were married on 16 Aug 1991 in Zamek Červená Lhota. They had the following children:

>**Eliška Hriníková** was born on 23 Jun 1992 in Jablonec nad Nisou. She married Jan Ottis on 06 Oct 2018 in Jablonec nad Jizerou, East Bohemia, Czech Republic.

Marta Koubikova-7 (Jiří-6, Marta-5, Marie-4, František Antonín-3, Kateřina-2, Jan-1) was born on 04 Jul 1962 in Mladá Boleslav.

Vladimír Stibor was born on 04 Jun 1959 in Praha.

Vladimír Stibor and Marta Koubikova were married on 17 Apr 1981. They had the following children:

>i. **Lucie Stiborová** was born on 29 Aug 1982 in Mladá Boleslav.
>
>**Tadeáš Stibor** was born on 25 Jul 1988 in Mladá Boleslav.

2nd Jiří Koubik-7 (Jiří-6, Marta-5, Marie-4, František Antonín-3, Kateřina-2, Jan-1) was born on 13 May 1965 in Praha.

Andrea Dunebierová was born on 25 Nov 1964 in Praha.

2nd Jiří Koubik and Andrea Dunebierová were married on 04 Apr 1987 in Brandys nad Labem. They had the following children:

>i. **Roman Koubik** was born on 07 Aug 1987 in Brandys nad Labem.

Vojtěch Koubik was born on 24 Mar 1989 in Brandys nad Labem.
Luděk Červený-7 (Marie-6, Oldřich-5, Josef-4, František Antonín-3, Kateřina-2, Jan-1) was born on 17 Aug 1968 in Mladá Boleslav.
Lenka Kovacova was born in Bratislava, Slovakia.
Luděk Červený and Lenka Kovacova were married on 11 Mar 1989. They had the following children:

    i. **Lukáš Červený** was born on 05 Sep 1989.

    Roman Červený was born on 06 Oct 1992.

Radek Červený-7 (Marie-6, Oldřich-5, Josef-4, František Antonín-3, Kateřina-2, Jan-1) was born on May 1972 in Mladá Boleslav.
Renata Bejrová was born in Koprnik, Mladá Boleslav Co..
Radek Červený and Renata Bejrová were married on 05 Nov 1994. They had the following children:

    i. **Veronika Červená** was born on 20 May 1995.

    Štěpán Červený was born on 11 Aug 2001.

Otakar Lochman-7 (Otakar-6, Marie-5, Emilie-4, František Antonín-3, Kateřina-2, Jan-1) was born on Apr 1968 in Mladá Boleslav.
Štěpánka Jandová was born on 25 Oct 1970.
Otakar Lochman and Štěpánka Jandová were married on 27 Aug 1988 in Mnichovo Hradiště. They had the following children:

    i.   **Otakar Lochman** was born on 17 Jan 1989 in Mladá Boleslav.

Ladislava (Viznerová) Černá was born on 15 Feb 1970 in Kladno.
Otakar Lochman and Ladislava (Viznerová) Černá were married on 25 Apr 1992 in Mnhichovo Hradiste. They had the following children:

    Lucie Lochmanová was born on 29 Jan 1992 in Mladá Boleslav.

    Luboš Lochman was born on 19 Jan 2002 in Mlada Boleslav.

Václava Lochmanová-7 (Otakar-6, Marie-5, Emilie-4, František Antonín-3, Kateřina-2, Jan-1) was born on 21 May 1972 in Mladá Boleslav.
Vladimír Pecina was born on 23 Oct 1961 in Mladá Boleslav.
Vladimír Pecina and Václava Lochmanová were married on 09 Sep 1995 in Mnichovo Hradiště. They had the following children:

    Jana Pecinová was born on 29 Jan 1996 in Mladá Boleslav.

    ii. **Václava Pecinová** was born on 07 Jan 1998 in Mladá Boleslav.

> Jitka Pecinová was born on 01 May 2000 in Mladá Boleslav.

Iva Lochmanová-7 (Otakar-6, Marie-5, Emilie-4, František Antonín-3, Kateřina-2, Jan-1) was born on Apr 1976 in Mladá Boleslav.

Libor Janoušek was born on 04 Aug 1976 in Mladá Boleslav.

Libor Janoušek and Iva Lochmanová were married on 21 Mar 1997 in Bakov nad Jizerou. They had the following children:

> Pavla Janoušková was born on 27 Jan 1999 in Mladá Boleslav.

Sarka Konickova-7 (Zdenka-6, Václav-5, Emilie-4, František Antonín-3, Kateřina-2, Jan-1) was born on 17 Dec 1974.

Miroslav Kaliban was born on 25 Nov 1973.

Miroslav Kaliban and Sarka Konickova married. They had the following children:

> Tereza Kalibanova was born on 14 May 2000.

Oldrřch Šnajdr-7 (Emilie-6, Vlasta-5, Emilie-4, František Antonín-3, Kateřina-2, Jan-1) was born on Apr 1971 in Turnov.

Daniela Synková was born in Mladá Boleslav.

Oldrřch Šnajdr and Daniela Synková were married on 16 Mar 1991. They had the following children:

> Iveta Šnajdrová was born on 11 Sep 1991 in Turnov.
>
> Filip Šnajdr was born on 05 Apr 1995 in Turnov.

Generation 8

Kevin Thomas Rechcigl-8 (John Edward-7, Mila (Miloslav)-6, Marie-5, Marie-4, František Antonín-3, Kateřina-2, Jan-1) was born on 09 Oct 1991 in Bradenton, FL.

Jordan Robbins daughter of Douglass Robbins and Ivonne was born on 10 Jan 1992 in Camarillo, CA.

Kevin Thomas Rechcigl and Jordan Robbins were married on 12 May 2018 in Jacksonville, FL. They had the following children:

> James Douglas Rechcigl was born on 05 Jan 2021 in Jacksonville, FL.
>
> Evelyn Marie Rechcigl was born 29 May 2023 in Jacksonville, FL.

Zuzana Heralecká-8 (Marcela-7, Marta-6, Marie-5, Marie-4, František Antonín-3, Kateřina-2, Jan-1) was born on 30 Dec 1978 in Jablonec nad

Nisou.

Jaroslav Egrt was born on 25 Apr 1974 in Duchcov.

Jaroslav Egrt and Zuzana Heralecká were married on 13 Sep 2002 in Jablonec nad Nisou. They had the following children:

    Kristina Egrtova was born on 04 Jan 2008 in Liberec.

    Jaroslav Egrt was born on 04 Jan 2008 in Liberec.

Lucie Stiborová-8 (Marta-7, Jiří-6, Marta-5, Marie-4, František Antonín-3, Kateřina-2, Jan-1) was born on 29 Aug 1982 in Mladá Boleslav.

Novotný.

Novotný and Lucie Stiborová married. They had the following children:

    Tobias Novotný.

Roman Koubik-8 (2nd Jiří-7, Jiří-6, Marta-5, Marie-4, František Antonín-3, Kateřina-2, Jan-1) was born on 07 Aug 1987 in Brandys nad Labem.

Martina.

Roman Koubik and Martina married. They had the following children:

    Roman Koubik.

Sources

Matrika krestni: Hoškovice, Kniha 104, List 172, Krestni a rodny list.

Matrika krestni, Kniha Z, List 65, Krestni a rodny list.

Brzohohatý Family

Generation 1

Václav Brzohohaty-1 was born about 1870 in Muzsky No. 8, Mnichovo Hradiště Co.. He died in 1918 in Muzsky No. 8, Mnichovo Hradiště Co..

Anna Rajtrová daughter of Jan Václav Rajtr and Anna Najmanová was born on 10 May 1876 in Dolanky No. 7. She died in Jan 1946 in Muzsky No. 19, Mnichovo Hradiště, Co..

Václav Brzohohaty and Anna Rajtrová married. They had the following children:

    i. **Marie Brzobohatá** was born on 18 Dec 1900 in Muzsky No. 8, Mnichovo Hradiště Co.. She died on 21 Sep 1969 in Liberec.

    ii. **Václav Brzobohatý** was born on 25 Aug 1902 in Muzsky No. 8, Mnichovo Hradiště Co.. He married Julie Kolomaznikova on 17 Nov 1928 in Mnichovo Hradiště. He died on 28 Jul 1974 in Mladá Boleslav.

    Bohumil Brzobohatý was born about 1904 in Muzsky No. 8, Mnichovo Hradiště Co.. He died in 1930 in Muzsky No. 8, Mnichovo Hradiště Co..

    iv. **Božena Brzobohatá** was born on 22 Jul 1906 in Muzsky No. 8, Mnichovo Hradiště Co.. She died on 02 Apr 1989.

Generation 2

Marie Brzobohatá-2 (Václav-1) was born on 18 Dec 1900 in Muzsky No. 8, Mnichovo Hradiště Co.. She died on 21 Sep 1969 in Liberec.

Václav Krausner was born on 19 Feb 1900 in Pribyslavice No. 4, Turnov Co.. He died on 08 Mar 1979 in Liberec.

Václav Krausner and Marie Brzobohatá married. They had the following children:

    i. **Olga Krausnerova** was born on 24 Apr 1933 in Pribyslavice No. 4, Turnov Co.. She married Miloslav Rajtr on 16 Jan 1954 in Selibice.

    ii. **Milena Krausnerova** was born on 15 Dec 1931 in Pribyslavice No. 4, Turnov Co.. She married Jaroslav Pabišta on 06 Dec 1952 in Vselibice.

Václav Brzobohatý-2 (Václav-1) was born on 25 Aug 1902 in Muzsky No. 8, Mnichovo Hradiště Co.. He died on 28 Jul 1974 in Mladá Boleslav.

Julie Kolomaznikova was born on 17 Feb 1906 in Rostkov, Mnichovo Hradiště Co.. She died on 04 Apr 1975 in Kosmonosy.

Václav Brzobohatý and Julie Kolomaznikova were married on 17 Nov 1928 in Mnichovo Hradiště. They had the following children:

    i. **Jaroslava Brzobohatá** was born on 06 Feb 1929 in Muzsky No. 8, Mnichovo Hradiště Co.. She married Václav Huňát on 03 Feb 1951 in MnV Knezmost, Mladá Boleslav Co..

    ii. **Hana Brzobohatá** was born on 28 Feb 1930 in Muzsky No. 8. Mnichovo Hradiště Co.. She married Stanislav Pic on 29 Jan 1949 in Farni urad Bosen.

    Václav Brzobohatý was born on 10 Dec 1944 in Muzsky No. 8, Mnichovo Hradiště Co.. He died in Mar 1946 in Turnov.

Božena Brzobohatá-2 (Václav-1) was born on 22 Jul 1906 in Muzsky No. 8, Mnichovo Hradiště Co.. She died on 02 Apr 1989.

František Příhoda was born in Příšovice.

František Příhoda and Božena Brzobohatá married. They had the following children:

    i. **Luboš Příhoda** was born in 1928.

František Košek was born on 01 Nov 1904 in Borovice, Mnichovo Hradiště Co.. He died on 25 Jan 1968 in Licenice, Litomerice Co..

František Košek and Božena Brzobohatá were married in 1936 in Listopec. They had the following children:

    i. **Danuse Koskova** was born on 19 Dec 1937 in Horka u Bakova. She married Victor Svoboda on 01 Mar 1958 in Ustek, Litomerice Co..

Generation 3

Olga Krausnerova-3 (Marie-2, Václav-1) was born on 24 Apr 1933 in Pribyslavice No. 4, Turnov Co..

Miloslav Rajtr was born on 21 Apr 1930 in Straziste No. 18, Mnichovo Hradiště Co..

Miloslav Rajtr and Olga Krausnerova were married on 16 Jan 1954 in Selibice. They had the following children:

i. **Hana Rajtrová** was born on 02 Aug 1955 in Turnov. She married Milan Ludvik on 26 Mar 1977 in Sychrov.

ii. **Miroslav Rajtr** was born on 29 Oct 1960 in Mladá Boleslav. He married Zdena Bartošová on 22 Mar 1980 in Český Dub.

Milena Krausnerova-3 (Marie-2, Václav-1) was born on 15 Dec 1931 in Pribyslavice No. 4, Turnov Co..

Jaroslav Pabišta was born on 29 Dec 1929 in Budikov.

Jaroslav Pabišta and Milena Krausnerova were married on 06 Dec 1952 in Vselibice. They had the following children:

i. **Milena Pabištová** was born on 03 Aug 1955 in Liberec. She married Jiří Bobek on 24 Aug 1974 in Sychrov.

Jaroslava Brzobohatá-3 (Václav-2, Václav-1) was born on 06 Feb 1929 in Muzsky No. 8, Mnichovo Hradiště Co..

Václav Huňát son of Václav Huňát and Božena Červinková was born on 29 Jun 1922 in Ptyrov No. 14, Mnichovo Hradiště Co.. He died on 20 Jul 1982 in Ptyrov No. 14, Mnichovo Hradiště Co..

Václav Huňát and Jaroslava Brzobohatá were married on 03 Feb 1951 in MnV Knezmost, Mladá Boleslav Co.. They had the following children:

i. **Hana Huňátová** was born on 01 Feb 1955 in Turnov. She married Milan Lauryn on 12 Jul 1974 in Mnichovo Hradiště.

ii. **Václav Huňát** was born on 16 Apr 1953 in Turnov. He married Jiřina Duriancikova on 26 Nov 1982 in Bakov nad Jizerou.

Hana Brzobohatá-3 (Václav-2, Václav-1) was born on 28 Feb 1930 in Muzsky No. 8. Mnichovo Hradiště Co..

Stanislav Pic was born on 07 Jun 1928 in Bycina No. 2 u Knezmosta, Mnichovo Hradiště Co.. He died on 12 Oct 2005 in Praha.

Stanislav Pic and Hana Brzobohatá were married on 29 Jan 1949 in Farni urad Bosen. They had the following children:

i. **Stanislav (Pic) Brzobohatý** was born on 26 Dec 1949 in Turnov. He married Jaroslava Hatašová on 17 Dec 1971 in Sychrov.

ii. **Jiří Pic** was born on 14 Feb 1954 in Turnov. He married Lida Havelková on 22 Apr 1976 in Bakov mad Jizerou.

Luboš Příhoda-3 (Božena-2, Václav-1) was born in 1928.

Unknown.
Luboš Příhoda and Unknown married. They had the following children:
   i. **son Příhoda** was born about 1950.

Danuse Koskova-3 (Božena-2, Václav-1) was born on 19 Dec 1937 in Horka u Bakova.

Victor Svoboda was born on 05 Oct 1937 in Brnany, Litomerice Co.. He died on 14 Aug 1985.

Victor Svoboda and Danuse Koskova were married on 01 Mar 1958 in Ustek, Litomerice Co.. They had the following children:
   i. **Danuse Svobodová** was born on 24 Sep 1958 in Litomerice. She married Otakar Gabriel on 15 Jul 1978 in MNV Terezin.
   ii. **Václav Svoboda** was born on 25 Sep 1959 in Litomerice. He married Miroslava Safrová on 21 Jun 1980 in MNV Terezin.
   iii. **Hana Svobodová** was born on 02 Mar 1972 in Litomerice. She married Martin Gaper on Jun 1992 in MNV Terezin.

Generation 4

Hana Rajtrová-4 (Olga-3, Marie-2, Václav-1) was born on 02 Aug 1955 in Turnov.

Milan Ludvik was born on 31 Jan 1953 in Turnov.

Milan Ludvik and Hana Rajtrová were married on 26 Mar 1977 in Sychrov. They had the following children:
   Martin Ludvik was born on 29 May 1979 in Jablonec nad Nisou.

Miroslav Rajtr-4 (Olga-3, Marie-2, Václav-1) was born on 29 Oct 1960 in Mladá Boleslav.

Zdena Bartošová was born on 05 Oct 1961 in Liberec.

Miroslav Rajtr and Zdena Bartošová were married on 22 Mar 1980 in Český Dub. They had the following children:
   Jana Rajtrová was born on 23 Aug 1980 in Liberec.
   Helena Rajtrová was born on 02 Jan 1993 in Liberec.

Milena Pabištová-4 (Milena-3, Marie-2, Václav-1) was born on 03 Aug 1955 in Liberec.

Jiří Bobek was born on 27 Mar 1948 in Turnov.

Jiří Bobek and Milena Pabištová were married on 24 Aug 1974 in Sychrov. They had the following children:
> i. **Aleš Bobek** was born on 27 Jul 1975 in Liberec. He married Petra Coufalova on 07 Aug 1999.
>
> **Jiří Bobek** was born on 20 May 1982 in Liberec.

Hana Huňátová-4 (Jaroslava-3, Václav-2, Václav-1) was born on 01 Feb 1955 in Turnov.

Milan Lauryn was born on 08 Feb 1951 in Ptyrov.

Milan Lauryn and Hana Huňátová were married on 12 Jul 1974 in Mnichovo Hradiště. They had the following children:
> i. **Hana Laurynova** was born on 08 Jan 1975 in Mladá Boleslav. She married Luboš Vodilan on 09 Jun 2001 in Mnichovo Hradiště.
>
> ii. **Milena Laurynova** was born on 25 Aug 1976 in Mladá Boleslav. She married Jiří Koštejn on 29 Sep 1995 in Mnichovo Hradiště.

Václav Huňát-4 (Jaroslava-3, Václav-2, Václav-1) was born on 16 Apr 1953 in Turnov.

Jiřina Durianciková was born on 06 Jun 1954.

Václav Huňát and Jiřina Durianciková were married on 26 Nov 1982 in Bakov nad Jizerou. They had the following children:
> **Václav Huňát** was born on 09 May 1983 in Mladá Boleslav.

Stanislav (Pic) Brzobohatý-4 (Hana-3, Václav-2, Václav-1) was born on 26 Dec 1949 in Turnov.

Jaroslava Hatašová was born on 18 Jan 1948 in Mnichovo Hradiště.

Stanislav (Pic) Brzobohatý and Jaroslava Hatašová were married on 17 Dec 1971 in Sychrov. They had the following children:
> i. **Stanislava Brzobohatá** was born on 03 Mar 1973 in Mladá Boleslav. She married Michal Stárek on 07 Dec 1993 in Sychrov.
>
> **Jaroslava Brzobohatá** was born on 01 Feb 1977 in Mladá Boleslav.

Jiří Pic-4 (Hana-3, Václav-2, Václav-1) was born on 14 Feb 1954 in Turnov.

Lida Havelková was born on 24 Aug 1955 in Mladá Boleslav.

Jiří Pic and Lida Havelková were married on 22 Apr 1976 in Bakov mad Jizerou. They had the following children:

Jiří Pic was born on 25 Apr 1977 in Mladá Boleslav.

Martin Pic was born on 24 May 1980 in Mladá Boleslav.

son Příhoda-4 (Luboš-3, Božena-2, Václav-1) was born about 1950.

Unknown.

son Příhoda and Unknown married. They had the following children:

children Příhoda.

Danuse Svobodová-4 (Danuse-3, Božena-2, Václav-1) was born on 24 Sep 1958 in Litomerice.

Otakar Gabriel was born on 28 Jan 1958.

Otakar Gabriel and Danuse Svobodová were married on 15 Jul 1978 in MNV Terezin. They had the following children:

    Lenka Gabrielová was born on 07 Dec 1978 in Litomerice.

    Oto Gabrie was born on 26 May 1981 in Roudnice nad Labem.

Václav Svoboda-4 (Danuse-3, Božena-2, Václav-1) was born on 25 Sep 1959 in Litomerice.

Miroslava Safrová was born on 01 Jan 1961.

Václav Svoboda and Miroslava Safrová were married on 21 Jun 1980 in MNV Terezin. They had the following children:

    Lucie Svobodová was born on 04 Mar 1981 in Litomerice.

    Vendula Svobodová was born on 19 Mar 1982 in Litomerice.

    Václav Svoboda was born on 25 Jul 1985 in Litomerice.

Hana Svobodová-4 (Danuse-3, Božena-2, Václav-1) was born on 02 Mar 1972 in Litomerice.

Martin Gaper was born in Doksany.

Martin Gaper and Hana Svobodová were married on 13 Jun 1992 in MNV Terezin. They had the following children:

    Martin Gaper was born on 19 Sep 1992 in Litomerice.

Generation 5

Aleš Bobek-5 (Milena-4, Milena-3, Marie-2, Václav-1) was born on 27 Jul 1975 in Liberec.

Petra Coufalova was born in 1974.

Aleš Bobek and Petra Coufalova were married on 07 Aug 1999. They had the following children:

> Alena Bobková was born on 02 Feb 2002 in Liberec.
>
> Antonia Bobková was born on 16 Jul 2004 in Liberec.

Hana Laurynova-5 (Hana-4, Jaroslava-3, Václav-2, Václav-1) was born on 08 Jan 1975 in Mladá Boleslav.

Luboš Vodilan was born on 06 Jul 1974 in Mladá Boleslav.

Luboš Vodilan and Hana Laurynova were married on 09 Jun 2001 in Mnichovo Hradiště. They had the following children:

> Michaela Vodilanova was born on 10 May 2002.

Milena Laurynova-5 (Hana-4, Jaroslava-3, Václav-2, Václav-1) was born on 25 Aug 1976 in Mladá Boleslav.

Jiří Koštejn was born on 01 Jun 1970 in Mladá Boleslav.

Jiří Koštejn and Milena Laurynova were married on 29 Sep 1995 in Mnichovo Hradiště. They had the following children:

> Jiří Koštejn was born on 18 Jul 1997 in Mladá Boleslav.
>
> Adela Koštejn was born on 01 Jan 2004 in Mladá Boleslav.

Stanislava Brzobohatá-5 (Stanislav (Pic)-4, Hana-3, Václav-2, Václav-1) was born on 03 Mar 1973 in Mladá Boleslav.

Michal Stárek.

Michal Stárek and Stanislava Brzobohatá were married on 07 Dec 1993 in Sychrov. They had the following children:

> Michal Stárek was born on 06 Jun 1994 in Mladá Boleslav.
>
> David Stárek was born on 26 Jan 2000 in Liberec.

Najman Family of Kopernik

Generation 1

Vojtěch Najman-1 was born in Kopernik No. 2, Mnichovo Hhradiste Co..

Anna Gintrova was born in Kopernik No. 4, Mnichovo Hradiště Co..
Vojtěch Najman and Anna Gintrova married. They had the following children:

    i. **Josef Najman** was born in Dolanky No. 7, Mnichovo Hradiště Co..

Generation 2

Josef Najman-2 (Vojtěch-1) was born in Dolanky No. 7, Mnichovo Hradiště Co..

Alžběta Bartonova daughter of Václav Barton and Anna Nohýnková was born in Dneboh No. 9, Mnichovo Hradiště Co..

Josef Najman and Alžběta Bartonova married. They had the following children:

    i. **Anna Najmanová** was born on 26 Dec 1841 in Dolanky No. 7, Mnichovo Hradiště Co.. She married Jan Václav Rajtr on 09 Jun 1868. She died on 05 Aug 1900 in Dolanky, Mnichovo Hradiště Co..

Generation 3

Anna Najmanová-3 (Josef-2, Vojtěch-1) was born on 26 Dec 1841 in Dolanky No. 7, Mnichovo Hradiště Co.. She died on 05 Aug 1900 in Dolanky, Mnichovo Hradiště Co..

Jan Václav Rajtr son of Václav Rajtr and Barbora Koštejn was born on 12 May 1847 in Zvířetice No. 11, Mnichovo Hradiště Co.. He died on 19 Sep 1903 in Dolanky No. 7.

Jan Václav Rajtr and Anna Najmanová were married on 09 Jun 1868. They had the following children:

    Vincenc Rajtr was born on 08 Apr 1871 in Dolanky No. 7. He died on 03 Oct 1871.

    Václav Rajtr was born on 22 Dec 1872 in Dolanky No. 7. He died on 11 Feb 1873 in Dolanky No. 7.

    iii. **Čeněk Rajtr**[1] was born on 01 Jul 1874 in nky No. 7, Mnichovo

Hradiště Dist... He married Marie Dandová on 02 Jul 1904 in Mnichovo Hradiště. He died on 27 Oct 1956 in Dolánky No. 7, Mnichovo Hradiště Dist...

iv. **Anna Rajtrová** was born on 10 May 1876 in Dolanky No. 7. She died in Jan 1946 in Muzsky No. 19, Mnichovo Hradiště, Co..

v. **Rudolf Rajtr** was born on 15 Nov 1881 in Dolanky No. 7. He died in Mar 1953 in Muzsky No. 6.

vi. **Josef Rajtr** was born about 1882 in Dolanky No. 7, Mnichovo Hradiště Cco..

Generation 4

Čeněk Rajtr-4 (Anna-3, Josef-2, Vojtěch-1)[1] was born on 01 Jul 1874 in nky No. 7, Mnichovo Hradiště Dist... He died on 27 Oct 1956 in Dolánky No. 7, Mnichovo Hradiště Dist...

Marie Dandová daughter of František Antonín Danda and Josefa Cimrová[2] was born on 31 Jan 1882 in Hoškovice, No. 14, Mnichovo Hradiště Dist, Bohemia. She died on 05 Jul 1967 in Dolanky No. 7, Mnichovo Hradiště Co..

Čeněk Rajtr and Marie Dandová were married on 02 Jul 1904 in Mnichovo Hradiště. They had the following children:

i. **Marie Rajtrová** was born on 05 Jul 1905 in Dolanky No. 7, Mnichovo Hradiště Co.. She married Miloslav Rechcigl on 26 Jul 1926 in Praha - Kralovske Vinohrady. She died on 13 Apr 1982 in Mladá Boleslav.

Oldrřch Rajtr was born on 14 Nov 1907 in Dolanky No. 7. He died on 02 Nov 1937.

iii. **Marta Rajtrová** was born on 10 Jan 1909 in Dolanky u Bakova. She married Josef Knotek in 1934. She died on 29 Nov 1982 in Mladá Boleslav.

Anna Rajtrová-4 (Anna-3, Josef-2, Vojtěch-1) was born on 10 May 1876 in Dolanky No. 7. She died in Jan 1946 in Muzsky No. 19, Mnichovo Hradiště, Co..

Václav Brzohohaty was born about 1870 in Muzsky No. 8, Mnichovo Hradiště Co.. He died in 1918 in Muzsky No. 8, Mnichovo Hradiště Co..

Václav Brzohohaty and Anna Rajtrová married. They had the following children:

 i. **Marie Brzobohatá** was born on 18 Dec 1900 in Muzsky No. 8, Mnichovo Hradiště Co.. She died on 21 Sep 1969 in Liberec.

 ii. **Václav Brzobohatý** was born on 25 Aug 1902 in Muzsky No. 8, Mnichovo Hradiště Co.. He married Julie Kolomaznikova on 17 Nov 1928 in Mnichovo Hradiště. He died on 28 Jul 1974 in Mladá Boleslav.

  Bohumil Brzobohatý was born about 1904 in Muzsky No. 8, Mnichovo Hradiště Co.. He died in 1930 in Muzsky No. 8, Mnichovo Hradiště Co..

 iv. **Božena Brzobohatá** was born on 22 Jul 1906 in Muzsky No. 8, Mnichovo Hradiště Co.. She died on 02 Apr 1989.

Rudolf Rajtr-4 (Anna-3, Josef-2, Vojtěch-1) was born on 15 Nov 1881 in Dolanky No. 7. He died in Mar 1953 in Muzsky No. 6.

Božena Maděrová was born in Muzsky. She died on 04 Dec 1964 in Muzsky. Rudolf Rajtr and Božena Maděrová married. They had the following children:

 i. **Josef Rajtr** was born on 27 Apr 1911 in Muzsky No. 6, Mnichovo Hradiště Co.. He died on 22 Mar 1978 in Liberec. He married Marie Janoušková on 27 Oct.

 ii. **Václav Rajtr** was born on 13 Jun 1912 in Muzsky No. 6, Mnichovo Hradiště Co.. He married Jarmila Maděrová on 10 Nov 1940 in Farni urad Bosen. He died on 12 Mar 1989 in Muzsky.

  Božena Rajtrová was born after 1912 in Muzsky No. 6, Mnichovo Hradiště Co.. She died in Drowned aet. 8 years old.

Josef Rajtr-4 (Anna-3, Josef-2, Vojtěch-1) was born about 1882 in Dolanky No. 7, Mnichovo Hradiště Cco..

Františka Kobosilova was born after 1880 in Prepere No. 15, Turnov Co.. Josef Rajtr and Františka Kobosilova married. They had the following children:

 i. **Josef Rajtr** was born on 30 Jun 1902 in Prepere No. 15, Turnov Co.. He married Zdenka Karlasova on 02 Nov 1924 in Turnov. He died on 09 Jul 1978 in Prepere No. 15, Turnov Co..

ii. **Marie Rajtrová** was born on 05 Jul 1905 in Dolanky No. 7, Mnichovo Hradiště Co.. She married Miloslav Rechcigl on 26 Jul 1926 in Praha - Kralovske Vinohrady. She died on 13 Apr 1982 in Mladá Boleslav.

Generation 5

Marie Rajtrová-5 (Čeněk-4, Anna-3, Josef-2, Vojtěch-1) was born on 05 Jul 1905 in Dolanky No. 7, Mnichovo Hradiště Co.. She died on 13 Apr 1982 in Mladá Boleslav.

Miloslav Rechcigl son of Adolf Rechcigl and Marie Berglová was born on 13 May 1904 in Kocňovice (renamed Chocnějovice) No. 22. He died on 27 May 1973 in Washington, DC.

Miloslav Rechcigl and Marie Rajtrová were married on 26 Jul 1926 in Praha - Kralovske Vinohrady. They had the following children:

i. **Mila (Miloslav) Rechcigl Jr.** was born on 30 Jul 1930 in Mladá Boleslav, CSR. He married Eva Edwards (Eisnerová) on 29 Aug 1953 in New York, NY.

ii. **Marta Rechcíglová** was born on 23 May 1933 in Mladá Boleslav. She married František Žďárský on 03 Oct 1953 in Mladá Boleslav. She died on 13 Sep 2018 in Mladá Boleslav.

Marta Rajtrová-5 (Čeněk-4, Anna-3, Josef-2, Vojtěch-1) was born on 10 Jan 1909 in Dolanky u Bakova. She died on 29 Nov 1982 in Mladá Boleslav.

Josef Knotek was born between 1905-1907 in Mala Bela, p. Bakov nad Jizerou. He died in 1934. Josef Knotek and Marta Rajtrová were married in 1934. They had no children.

Miroslav Koubik son of Koubik was born in 1908 in Terezin. He died in 1968 in Havlickuv Brod.

Miroslav Koubik and Marta Rajtrová were married on 26 Jul 1938 in Praha. They had the following children:

i. **Jiří Koubik** was born on 29 Jan 1940 in Prague. He married Jiřina Muellerová on 31 Jan 1962 in Praha. He died on 26 Jun 1998 in Brandys nad Labem.

Emil Pazderník was born after 1900.

Emil Pazderník and Marta Rajtrová were married after 1945. They had no children.

Karel Horáček.

Karel Horáček and Marta Rajtrová met. They had no children.

Marie Brzobohatá-5 (Anna-4, Anna-3, Josef-2, Vojtěch-1) was born on 18 Dec 1900 in Muzsky No. 8, Mnichovo Hradiště Co.. She died on 21 Sep 1969 in Liberec.

Václav Krausner was born on 19 Feb 1900 in Pribyslavice No. 4, Turnov Co.. He died on 08 Mar 1979 in Liberec.

Václav Krausner and Marie Brzobohatá married. They had the following children:

    i. **Olga Krausnerova** was born on 24 Apr 1933 in Pribyslavice No. 4, Turnov Co.. She married Miloslav Rajtr on 16 Jan 1954 in Selibice.

    ii. **Milena Krausnerova** was born on 15 Dec 1931 in Pribyslavice No. 4, Turnov Co.. She married Jaroslav Pabišta on 06 Dec 1952 in Vselibice.

Václav Brzobohatý-5 (Anna-4, Anna-3, Josef-2, Vojtěch-1) was born on 25 Aug 1902 in Muzsky No. 8, Mnichovo Hradiště Co.. He died on 28 Jul 1974 in Mladá Boleslav.

Julie Kolomaznikova was born on 17 Feb 1906 in Rostkov, Mnichovo Hradiště Co.. She died on 04 Apr 1975 in Kosmonosy.

Václav Brzobohatý and Julie Kolomaznikova were married on 17 Nov 1928 in Mnichovo Hradiště. They had the following children:

    i. **Jaroslava Brzobohatá** was born on 06 Feb 1929 in Muzsky No. 8, Mnichovo Hradiště Co.. She married Václav Huňát on 03 Feb 1951 in MnV Knezmost, Mladá Boleslav Co..

    ii. **Hana Brzobohatá** was born on 28 Feb 1930 in Muzsky No. 8. Mnichovo Hradiště Co.. She married Stanislav Pic on 29 Jan 1949 in Farni urad Bosen.

    Václav Brzobohatý was born on 10 Dec 1944 in Muzsky No. 8, Mnichovo Hradiště Co.. He died in Mar 1946 in Turnov.

Božena Brzobohatá-5 (Anna-4, Anna-3, Josef-2, Vojtěch-1) was born on 22 Jul 1906 in Muzsky No. 8, Mnichovo Hradiště Co.. She died on 02 Apr 1989.

František Příhoda was born in Příšovice.

František Příhoda and Božena Brzobohatá married. They had the following children:

    i. **Luboš Příhoda** was born in 1928.

František Košek was born on 01 Nov 1904 in Borovice, Mnichovo Hradiště Co.. He died on 25 Jan 1968 in Licenice, Litomerice Co..

František Košek and Božena Brzobohatá were married in 1936 in Listopec. They had the following children:

    i. **Danuse Koskova** was born on 19 Dec 1937 in Horka u Bakova. She married Victor Svoboda on 01 Mar 1958 in Ustek, Litomerice Co..

Josef Rajtr-5 (Rudolf-4, Anna-3, Josef-2, Vojtěch-1) was born on 27 Apr 1911 in Muzsky No. 6, Mnichovo Hradiště Co.. He died on 22 Mar 1978 in Liberec.

Marie Janoušková was born on 22 Feb 1915 in Dolni Bukovina, Mnichovo Hradiště Co.. She died on 18 Dec 1973 in Liberec.

Josef Rajtr and Marie Janoušková were married on 27 Oct. They had the following children:

    i. **Marie Rajtrová** was born on 19 Sep 1941 in Knezmost, Mnichovo Hradiště Co.. She married Zdeněk Kilian on 05 Jul 1969 in Praha.

    ii. **Josef Rajtr** was born on 30 May 1947 in Nova Ves u Branzeze, Mladá Boleslav Co.. He married Helena Klimesova on 06 Apr 1974 in Sychrov.

Václav Rajtr-5 (Rudolf-4, Anna-3, Josef-2, Vojtěch-1) was born on 13 Jun 1912 in Muzsky No. 6, Mnichovo Hradiště Co.. He died on 12 Mar 1989 in Muzsky.

Jarmila Maděrová was born on 18 Jun 1920 in Muzsky. She died on 09 Feb 2002 in Kosmonosy.

Václav Rajtr and Jarmila Maděrová were married on 10 Nov 1940 in Farni urad Bosen. They had the following children:

    i. **Václav Rajtr** was born on 02 Feb 1942 in Muzsky No. 6, Mnichovo Hradiště Co.. He married Jana Karaskova on 17 Apr 1965 in Rakovnik.

    ii. **Věra Rajtrová** was born on 19 Feb 1947 in Muzsky No. 6, Mnichovo Hradiště Co.. She married Jaroslav Verner on 08 Jan

1966 in Mnichovo Hradiště.

Josef Rajtr-5 (Josef-4, Anna-3, Josef-2, Vojtěch-1) was born on 30 Jun 1902 in Prepere No. 15, Turnov Co.. He died on 09 Jul 1978 in Prepere No. 15, Turnov Co..

Zdenka Karlasova was born on 23 Oct 1901 in Sekyrkovy Loucky. She died on 09 Jan 1978 in Prepere No. 15.

Josef Rajtr and Zdenka Karlasova were married on 02 Nov 1924 in Turnov. They had the following children:

> **Josef Rajtr** was born after 1920 in Prepere No. 15. He died after 1920 in Prepere No. 15.
>
> **František Rajtr** was born after 1920 in Prepere No. 15. He died after 1920.

Generation 6

Mila (Miloslav) Rechcigl Jr.-6 (Marie-5, Čeněk-4, Anna-3, Josef-2, Vojtěch-1) was born on 30 Jul 1930 in Mladá Boleslav, CSR.

Eva Edwards (Eisnerová) daughter of Paul J. Edwards (Pavel Eisner) and Jiřina Taussigová was born on 21 Jan 1932 in Prague, CSR.

Mila (Miloslav) Rechcigl Jr. and Eva Edwards (Eisnerová) were married on 29 Aug 1953 in New York, NY. They had the following children:

> i. **John Edward Rechcigl** was born on 27 Feb 1960 in Washington, D.C.. He married Nancy Ann Palko on 30 Jul 1983 in Dover, NJ.
>
> ii. **Karen Rechcigl** was born on 16 Apr 1962 in Washington, DC. She married Ulysses Kollecas on 25 Aug 1990 in Bethesda, MD.

Marta Rechcíglová-6 (Marie-5, Čeněk-4, Anna-3, Josef-2, Vojtěch-1) was born on 23 May 1933 in Mladá Boleslav. She died on 13 Sep 2018 in Mladá Boleslav.

František Žďárský son of František Václav Žďárský and Eliška Foltýnová was born on 21 May 1932 in Turnov.

František Žďárský and Marta Rechcíglová were married on 03 Oct 1953 in Mladá Boleslav. They had the following children:

> i. **Marcela Žďárská** was born on 09 May 1954 in Liberec. She married Miroslav Heralecký on 15 Mar 1975 in Sychrov.
>
> ii. **Iveta Žďárská** was born on 29 Aug 1963 in Liberec, Bohemia. She

married Vlastimil Berkman on 29 Oct 1983.

Jiří Koubik-6 (Marta-5, Čeněk-4, Anna-3, Josef-2, Vojtěch-1) was born on 29 Jan 1940 in Prague. He died on 26 Jun 1998 in Brandys nad Labem.

Jiřina Muellerová was born on 27 Feb 1943 in Buda.

Jiří Koubik and Jiřina Muellerová were married on 31 Jan 1962 in Praha. They had the following children:

    i. **Marta Koubikova** was born on 04 Jul 1962 in Mladá Boleslav. She married Vladimír Stibor on 17 Apr 1981.

    ii. **2nd Jiří Koubik** was born on 13 May 1965 in Praha. He married Andrea Dunebierová on 04 Apr 1987 in Brandys nad Labem.

Olga Krausnerova-6 (Marie-5, Anna-4, Anna-3, Josef-2, Vojtěch-1) was born on 24 Apr 1933 in Pribyslavice No. 4, Turnov Co..

Miloslav Rajtr was born on 21 Apr 1930 in Straziste No. 18, Mnichovo Hradiště Co..

Miloslav Rajtr and Olga Krausnerova were married on 16 Jan 1954 in Selibice. They had the following children:

    i. **Hana Rajtrová** was born on 02 Aug 1955 in Turnov. She married Milan Ludvik on 26 Mar 1977 in Sychrov.

    ii. **Miroslav Rajtr** was born on 29 Oct 1960 in Mladá Boleslav. He married Zdena Bartošová on 22 Mar 1980 in Český Dub.

Milena Krausnerova-6 (Marie-5, Anna-4, Anna-3, Josef-2, Vojtěch-1) was born on 15 Dec 1931 in Pribyslavice No. 4, Turnov Co..

Jaroslav Pabišta was born on 29 Dec 1929 in Budikov.

Jaroslav Pabišta and Milena Krausnerova were married on 06 Dec 1952 in Vselibice. They had the following children:

    i. **Milena Pabištová** was born on 03 Aug 1955 in Liberec. She married Jiří Bobek on 24 Aug 1974 in Sychrov.

Jaroslava Brzobohatá-6 (Václav-5, Anna-4, Anna-3, Josef-2, Vojtěch-1) was born on 06 Feb 1929 in Muzsky No. 8, Mnichovo Hradiště Co..

Václav Huňát son of Václav Huňát and Božena Červinková was born on 29 Jun 1922 in Ptyrov No. 14, Mnichovo Hradiště Co.. He died on 20 Jul 1982 in Ptyrov No. 14, Mnichovo Hradiště Co..

Václav Huňát and Jaroslava Brzobohatá were married on 03 Feb 1951 in

MnV Knezmost, Mladá Boleslav Co.. They had the following children:
  i. **Hana Huňátová** was born on 01 Feb 1955 in Turnov. She married Milan Lauryn on 12 Jul 1974 in Mnichovo Hradiště.
  ii. **Václav Huňát** was born on 16 Apr 1953 in Turnov. He married Jiřina Durianciková on 26 Nov 1982 in Bakov nad Jizerou.

Hana Brzobohatá-6 (Václav-5, Anna-4, Anna-3, Josef-2, Vojtěch-1) was born on 28 Feb 1930 in Muzsky No. 8. Mnichovo Hradiště Co..

Stanislav Pic was born on 07 Jun 1928 in Bycina No. 2 u Knezmosta, Mnichovo Hradiště Co.. He died on 12 Oct 2005 in Praha.

Stanislav Pic and Hana Brzobohatá were married on 29 Jan 1949 in Farni urad Bosen. They had the following children:
  i. **Stanislav (Pic) Brzobohatý** was born on 26 Dec 1949 in Turnov. He married Jaroslava Hatašová on 17 Dec 1971 in Sychrov.
  ii. **Jiří Pic** was born on 14 Feb 1954 in Turnov. He married Lida Havelková on 22 Apr 1976 in Bakov mad Jizerou.

Luboš Příhoda-6 (Božena-5, Anna-4, Anna-3, Josef-2, Vojtěch-1) was born in 1928.

Unknown.

Luboš Příhoda and Unknown married. They had the following children:
  i. **son Příhoda** was born about 1950.

Danuse Koskova-6 (Božena-5, Anna-4, Anna-3, Josef-2, Vojtěch-1) was born on 19 Dec 1937 in Horka u Bakova.

Victor Svoboda was born on 05 Oct 1937 in Brnany, Litomerice Co.. He died on 14 Aug 1985.

Victor Svoboda and Danuse Koskova were married on 01 Mar 1958 in Ustek, Litomerice Co.. They had the following children:
  i. **Danuse Svobodová** was born on 24 Sep 1958 in Litomerice. She married Otakar Gabriel on 15 Jul 1978 in MNV Terezin.
  ii. **Václav Svoboda** was born on 25 Sep 1959 in Litomerice. He married Miroslava Safrová on 21 Jun 1980 in MNV Terezin.
  iii. **Hana Svobodová** was born on 02 Mar 1972 in Litomerice. She married Martin Gaper on Jun 1992 in MNV Terezin.

Marie Rajtrová-6 (Josef-5, Rudolf-4, Anna-3, Josef-2, Vojtěch-1) was born on

19 Sep 1941 in Knezmost, Mnichovo Hradiště Co..

Zdeněk Kilian was born on 16 Jan 1929. He died on 30 Aug 1999. Zdeněk Kilian and Marie Rajtrová were married on 05 Jul 1969 in Praha. They had the following children:

>   i. **Ester Kilianova** was born on 14 Apr 1973 in Jablonec nad Nisou. She married Ivo Srb on Sep 1995 in Liberec.
>
>   **Pavlina Kilianova** was born on 17 Feb 1976.

Josef Rajtr-6 (Josef-5, Rudolf-4, Anna-3, Josef-2, Vojtěch-1) was born on 30 May 1947 in Nova Ves u Branzeze, Mladá Boleslav Co..

Helena Klimesova was born on 18 Aug 1951 in Liberec.

Josef Rajtr and Helena Klimesova were married on 06 Apr 1974 in Sychrov. They had the following children:

>   **Helena Rajtrová** was born on 02 Feb 1976 in Jablonec nad Nisou.
>
>   **Tomáš Rajtr** was born on 04 Apr 1977 in Liberec.

Václav Rajtr-6 (Václav-5, Rudolf-4, Anna-3, Josef-2, Vojtěch-1) was born on 02 Feb 1942 in Muzsky No. 6, Mnichovo Hradiště Co..

Jana Karaskova was born on 11 Feb 1945 in Rakovnik.

Václav Rajtr and Jana Karaskova were married on 17 Apr 1965 in Rakovnik. They had the following children:

>   i. **Jana Rajtrová** was born on 14 Apr 1966 in Rakovnik. She married Jaromír Kamenik on 08 Mar 1986 in Rakovnik.

Věra Rajtrová-6 (Václav-5, Rudolf-4, Anna-3, Josef-2, Vojtěch-1) was born on 19 Feb 1947 in Muzsky No. 6, Mnichovo Hradiště Co..

Jaroslav Verner was born on 27 Mar 1941 in Knezmost.

Jaroslav Verner and Věra Rajtrová were married on 08 Jan 1966 in Mnichovo Hradiště. They had the following children:

>   i. **Jolana Vernerova** was born on 19 Oct 1967 in Mladá Boleslav. She married Jaroslav Zdobinsky on 15 Sep 1989.
>
>   ii. **Věra Vernerova** was born on 26 Nov 1968 in Knezmost. She married Petr Holas on 24 Apr 1990.

Generation 7

John Edward Rechcigl-7 (Mila (Miloslav)-6, Marie-5, Čeněk-4, Anna-3, Josef-2, Vojtěch-1) was born on 27 Feb 1960 in Washington, D.C..

Nancy Ann Palko daughter of Joseph Palko and Mary Rishko was born on 26 Sep 1961 in Morristown, NJ.

John Edward Rechcigl and Nancy Ann Palko were married on 30 Jul 1983 in Dover, NJ. They had the following children:

>**Gregory John Rechcigl** was born on 19 Dec 1988 in Bradenton, FL.
>
>ii. **Kevin Thomas Rechcigl** was born on 09 Oct 1991 in Bradenton, FL. He married Jordan Robbins on 12 May 2018 in Jacksonville, FL.
>
>**Lindsey Nicole Rechcigl** was born on 03 Nov 1994 in Bradenton, FL.

Karen Rechcigl-7 (Mila (Miloslav)-6, Marie-5, Čeněk-4, Anna-3, Josef-2, Vojtěch-1) was born on 16 Apr 1962 in Washington, DC.

Ulysses Kollecas son of Christopher Thomas (Kolecas) Collier and Amelia Malatras was born on 20 Mar 1958 in Washington, DC.

Ulysses Kollecas and Karen Rechcigl were married on 25 Aug 1990 in Bethesda, MD. They had the following children:

>**Kristin Kollecas** was born on 04 May 1993 in Albuquerque, NM.
>
>**Paul Kollecas** was born on 02 Jun 1995 in Albuquerque, NM.

Marcela Žďárská-7 (Marta-6, Marie-5, Čeněk-4, Anna-3, Josef-2, Vojtěch-1) was born on 09 May 1954 in Liberec.

Miroslav Heralecký son of Miroslav Heralecký and Marie Bartošová was born on 18 May 1949 in salomonJablonec nad Nisou, Czech.. He died on 20 Feb 2017 in Proseč, Jablonec nad Nisou, Czech..

Miroslav Heralecký and Marcela Žďárská were married on 15 Mar 1975 in Sychrov. They had the following children:

>**Vit Heralecký** was born on 16 Jan 1977 in Jablonec nad Nisou. He married Olga Zrubcová on 13 Jul 1996.
>
>ii. **Zuzana Heralecká** was born on 30 Dec 1978 in Jablonec nad Nisou. She married Jaroslav Egrt on 13 Sep 2002 in Jablonec nad Nisou.

Iveta Žďárská-7 (Marta-6, Marie-5, Čeněk-4, Anna-3, Josef-2, Vojtěch-1) was born on 29 Aug 1963 in Liberec, Bohemia.

Vlastimil Berkman was born in 1957.

Vlastimil Berkman and Iveta Žďárská were married on 29 Oct 1983. They had the following children:

 Tereza Hriníková was born on 05 Jun 1984 in Jablonec nad Nisou.

Jaroslav Hrinik son of Jaroslav Hrinik and Milena Preisslerová was born on 17 Apr 1960.

Jaroslav Hrinik and Iveta Žďárská were married on 16 Aug 1991 in Zamek Červená Lhota. They had the following children:

 Eliška Hriníková was born on 23 Jun 1992 in Jablonec nad Nisou. She married Jan Ottis on 06 Oct 2018 in Jablonec nad Jizerou, East Bohemia, Czech Republic.

Marta Koubikova-7 (Jiří-6, Marta-5, Čeněk-4, Anna-3, Josef-2, Vojtěch-1) was born on 04 Jul 1962 in Mladá Boleslav.

Vladimír Stibor was born on 04 Jun 1959 in Praha.

Vladimír Stibor and Marta Koubikova were married on 17 Apr 1981. They had the following children:

 i. **Lucie Stiborová** was born on 29 Aug 1982 in Mladá Boleslav.

 Tadeáš Stibor was born on 25 Jul 1988 in Mladá Boleslav.

2nd Jiří Koubik-7 (Jiří-6, Marta-5, Čeněk-4, Anna-3, Josef-2, Vojtěch-1) was born on 13 May 1965 in Praha.

Andrea Dunebierová was born on 25 Nov 1964 in Praha.

2nd Jiří Koubik and Andrea Dunebierová were married on 04 Apr 1987 in Brandys nad Labem. They had the following children:

 i. **Roman Koubik** was born on 07 Aug 1987 in Brandys nad Labem.

 Vojtěch Koubik was born on 24 Mar 1989 in Brandys nad Labem.

Hana Rajtrová-7 (Olga-6, Marie-5, Anna-4, Anna-3, Josef-2, Vojtěch-1) was born on 02 Aug 1955 in Turnov.

Milan Ludvik was born on 31 Jan 1953 in Turnov.

Milan Ludvik and Hana Rajtrová were married on 26 Mar 1977 in Sychrov. They had the following children:

 Martin Ludvik was born on 29 May 1979 in Jablonec nad Nisou.

Miroslav Rajtr-7 (Olga-6, Marie-5, Anna-4, Anna-3, Josef-2, Vojtěch-1) was born on 29 Oct 1960 in Mladá Boleslav.

Zdena Bartošová was born on 05 Oct 1961 in Liberec.

Miroslav Rajtr and Zdena Bartošová were married on 22 Mar 1980 in Český Dub. They had the following children:

    Jana Rajtrová was born on 23 Aug 1980 in Liberec.

    Helena Rajtrová was born on 02 Jan 1993 in Liberec.

Milena Pabištová-7 (Milena-6, Marie-5, Anna-4, Anna-3, Josef-2, Vojtěch-1) was born on 03 Aug 1955 in Liberec.

Jiří Bobek was born on 27 Mar 1948 in Turnov.

Jiří Bobek and Milena Pabištová were married on 24 Aug 1974 in Sychrov. They had the following children:

    i. **Aleš Bobek** was born on 27 Jul 1975 in Liberec. He married Petra Coufalova on 07 Aug 1999.

    Jiří Bobek was born on 20 May 1982 in Liberec.

Hana Huňátová-7 (Jaroslava-6, Václav-5, Anna-4, Anna-3, Josef-2, Vojtěch-1) was born on 01 Feb 1955 in Turnov.

Milan Lauryn was born on 08 Feb 1951 in Ptyrov.

Milan Lauryn and Hana Huňátová were married on 12 Jul 1974 in Mnichovo Hradiště. They had the following children:

    i. **Hana Laurynova** was born on 08 Jan 1975 in Mladá Boleslav. She married Luboš Vodilan on 09 Jun 2001 in Mnichovo Hradiště.

    ii. **Milena Laurynova** was born on 25 Aug 1976 in Mladá Boleslav. She married Jiří Koštejn on 29 Sep 1995 in Mnichovo Hradiště.

Václav Huňát-7 (Jaroslava-6, Václav-5, Anna-4, Anna-3, Josef-2, Vojtěch-1) was born on 16 Apr 1953 in Turnov.

Jiřina Duriancikovά was born on 06 Jun 1954.

Václav Huňát and Jiřina Durianciková were married on 26 Nov 1982 in Bakov nad Jizerou. They had the following children:

    Václav Huňát was born on 09 May 1983 in Mladá Boleslav.

Stanislav (Pic) Brzobohatý-7 (Hana-6, Václav-5, Anna-4, Anna-3, Josef-2, Vojtěch-1) was born on Dec 1949 in Turnov.

Jaroslava Hatašová was born on 18 Jan 1948 in Mnichovo Hradiště.

Stanislav (Pic) Brzobohatý and Jaroslava Hatašová were married on 17

Dec 1971 in Sychrov. They had the following children:
  i. **Stanislava Brzobohatá** was born on 03 Mar 1973 in Mladá Boleslav. She married Michal Stárek on 07 Dec 1993 in Sychrov.
  Jaroslava Brzobohatá was born on 01 Feb 1977 in Mladá Boleslav.

Jiří Pic-7 (Hana-6, Václav-5, Anna-4, Anna-3, Josef-2, Vojtěch-1) was born on 14 Feb 1954 in Turnov.

Lida Havelková was born on 24 Aug 1955 in Mladá Boleslav.

Jiří Pic and Lida Havelková were married on 22 Apr 1976 in Bakov mad Jizerou. They had the following children:
  Jiří Pic was born on 25 Apr 1977 in Mladá Boleslav.
  Martin Pic was born on 24 May 1980 in Mladá Boleslav.

son Příhoda-7 (Luboš-6, Božena-5, Anna-4, Anna-3, Josef-2, Vojtěch-1) was born about 1950.

Unknown.

son Příhoda and Unknown married. They had the following children:
  children Příhoda.

Danuse Svobodová-7 (Danuse-6, Božena-5, Anna-4, Anna-3, Josef-2, Vojtěch-1) was born on 24 Sep 1958 in Litomerice.

Otakar Gabriel was born on 28 Jan 1958.

Otakar Gabriel and Danuse Svobodová were married on 15 Jul 1978 in MNV Terezin. They had the following children:
  Lenka Gabrielová was born on 07 Dec 1978 in Litomerice.
  Oto Gabrie was born on 26 May 1981 in Roudnice nad Labem.

Václav Svoboda-7 (Danuse-6, Božena-5, Anna-4, Anna-3, Josef-2, Vojtěch-1) was born on 25 Sep 1959 in Litomerice.

Miroslava Safrová was born on 01 Jan 1961.

Václav Svoboda and Miroslava Safrová were married on 21 Jun 1980 in MNV Terezin. They had the following children:
  Lucie Svobodová was born on 04 Mar 1981 in Litomerice.
  Vendula Svobodová was born on 19 Mar 1982 in Litomerice.
  Václav Svoboda was born on 25 Jul 1985 in Litomerice.

Hana Svobodová-7 (Danuse-6, Božena-5, Anna-4, Anna-3, Josef-2, Vojtěch-

1) was born on 02 Mar 1972 in Litomerice.

Martin Gaper was born in Doksany.

Martin Gaper and Hana Svobodová were married on 13 Jun 1992 in MNV Terezin. They had the following children:

    Martin Gaper was born on 19 Sep 1992 in Litomerice.

Ester Kilianova-7 (Marie-6, Josef-5, Rudolf-4, Anna-3, Josef-2, Vojtěch-1) was born on 14 Apr 1973 in Jablonec nad Nisou.

Ivo Srb.

Ivo Srb and Ester Kilianova were married on 09 Sep 1995 in Liberec. They had the following children:

    Jakub Srb was born on 15 Feb 1996.

Jana Rajtrová-7 (Václav-6, Václav-5, Rudolf-4, Anna-3, Josef-2, Vojtěch-1) was born on 14 Apr 1966 in Rakovnik.

Jaromír Kamenik was born on 12 Jan 1963 in Kutna Hora.

Jaromír Kamenik and Jana Rajtrová were married on 08 Mar 1986 in Rakovnik. They had the following children:

    Alena Kamenikova was born on 02 Aug 1985 in Rakovnik.

    Petr Kamenik was born on 31 Jan 1993 in Rakovnik.

Jolana Vernerova-7 (Věra-6, Václav-5, Rudolf-4, Anna-3, Josef-2, Vojtěch-1) was born on 19 Oct 1967 in Mladá Boleslav.

Jaroslav Zdobinsky was born on 16 Dec 1963.

Jaroslav Zdobinsky and Jolana Vernerova were married on 15 Sep 1989. They had the following children:

    Jaroslav Zobinsky was born on 26 Mar 1992 in Mladá Boleslav.

    Nela Zdobinska was born on 29 Feb 2000 in Mladá Boleslav.

Věra Vernerova-7 (Věra-6, Václav-5, Rudolf-4, Anna-3, Josef-2, Vojtěch-1) was born on 26 Nov 1968 in Knezmost.

Petr Holas was born on 11 Feb 1965 in Mladá Boleslav.

Petr Holas and Věra Vernerova were married on 24 Apr 1990. They had the following children:

    i. **Vojta Holas** was born on 08 Mar 1993 in Turnov.

Generation 8

Kevin Thomas Rechcigl-8 (John Edward-7, Mila (Miloslav)-6, Marie-5, Čeněk-4, Anna-3, Josef-2, Vojtěch-1) was born on 09 Oct 1991 in Bradenton, FL.

Jordan Robbins daughter of Douglass Robbins and Ivonne was born on 10 Jan 1992 in Camarillo, CA.

Kevin Thomas Rechcigl and Jordan Robbins were married on 12 May 2018 in Jacksonville, FL. They had the following children:

> **James Douglas Rechcigl** was born on 05 Jan 2021 in Jacksonville, FL.
>
> **Evelyn Marie Rechcigl** was born 29 May 2023 in Jacksonville, FL.

Zuzana Heralecká-8 (Marcela-7, Marta-6, Marie-5, Čeněk-4, Anna-3, Josef-2, Vojtěch-1) was born on 30 Dec 1978 in Jablonec nad Nisou.

Jaroslav Egrt was born on 25 Apr 1974 in Duchcov.

Jaroslav Egrt and Zuzana Heralecká were married on 13 Sep 2002 in Jablonec nad Nisou. They had the following children:

> **Kristina Egrtova** was born on 04 Jan 2008 in Liberec.
>
> **Jaroslav Egrt** was born on 04 Jan 2008 in Liberec.

Lucie Stiborová-8 (Marta-7, Jiří-6, Marta-5, Čeněk-4, Anna-3, Josef-2, Vojtěch-1) was born on 29 Aug 1982 in Mladá Boleslav.

Novotný.

Novotný and Lucie Stiborová married. They had the following children:

> **Tobias Novotný**.

Roman Koubik-8 (2nd Jiří-7, Jiří-6, Marta-5, Čeněk-4, Anna-3, Josef-2, Vojtěch-1) was born on 07 Aug 1987 in Brandys nad Labem.

Martina.

Roman Koubik and Martina married. They had the following children:

> **Roman Koubik**.

Aleš Bobek-8 (Milena-7, Milena-6, Marie-5, Anna-4, Anna-3, Josef-2, Vojtěch-1) was born on 27 Jul 1975 in Liberec.

Petra Coufalova was born in 1974.

Aleš Bobek and Petra Coufalova were married on 07 Aug 1999. They had the following children:

> i. **Alena Bobková** was born on 02 Feb 2002 in Liberec.

Antonia Bobková was born on 16 Jul 2004 in Liberec.

Hana Laurynova-8 (Hana-7, Jaroslava-6, Václav-5, Anna-4, Anna-3, Josef-2, Vojtěch-1) was born on Jan 1975 in Mladá Boleslav.

Luboš Vodilan was born on 06 Jul 1974 in Mladá Boleslav.

Luboš Vodilan and Hana Laurynova were married on 09 Jun 2001 in Mnichovo Hradiště. They had the following children:

>Michaela Vodilanova was born on 10 May 2002.

Milena Laurynova-8 (Hana-7, Jaroslava-6, Václav-5, Anna-4, Anna-3, Josef-2, Vojtěch-1) was born on 25 Aug 1976 in Mladá Boleslav.

Jiří Koštejn was born on 01 Jun 1970 in Mladá Boleslav.

Jiří Koštejn and Milena Laurynova were married on 29 Sep 1995 in Mnichovo Hradiště. They had the following children:

>Jiří Koštejn was born on 18 Jul 1997 in Mladá Boleslav.

>Adela Koštejn was born on 01 Jan 2004 in Mladá Boleslav.

Stanislava Brzobohatá-8 (Stanislav (Pic)-7, Hana-6, Václav-5, Anna-4, Anna-3, Josef-2, Vojtěch-1) was born on 03 Mar 1973 in Mladá Boleslav.

Michal Stárek.

Michal Stárek and Stanislava Brzobohatá were married on 07 Dec 1993 in Sychrov. They had the following children:

>Michal Stárek was born on 06 Jun 1994 in Mladá Boleslav.

>David Stárek was born on 26 Jan 2000 in Liberec.

Sources

Matrika krestni, Kniha Z, List 65, Krestni a rodny list.

Matrika krestni: Hoškovice, Kniha 104, List 172, Krestni a rodny list.

Sip Family

Generation 1

Václav Šíp-1.
Eva.
Václav Šíp and Eva married. They had the following children:
   i. **Václav Šíp**. He married Kateřina Halikova in 1725.

Generation 2

Václav Šíp-2 (Václav-1).
Kateřina Halikova.
Václav Šíp and Kateřina Halikova were married in 1725. They had the following children:
   i. **Jan Šíp** was born in 1726. He married Ludmila Houzvicková after 1770. He died in 1806.

Generation 3

3. **Jan Šíp**-3 (Václav-2, Václav-1) was born in 1726. He died in 1806.
Ludmila Houzvicková.
Jan Šíp and Ludmila Houzvicková were married after 1770. They had the following children:
4. i. **Václav Šíp** was born on 09 Sep 1782 in Pecice.
Ludmila was born in 1746. She died on 18 Mar 1770.
Jan Šíp and Ludmila married. They had no children.

Generation 4

Václav Šíp-4 (Jan-3, Václav-2, Václav-1) was born on 09 Sep 1782 in Pecice.
Anna Konickova daughter of Josef Konicek.
Václav Šíp and Anna Konickova married. They had the following children:
   i. **Václav Šíp** was born on 09 Oct 1818 in Pecice.

Generation 5

Václav Šíp-5 (Václav-4, Jan-3, Václav-2, Václav-1) was born on 09 Oct 1818 in Pecice.
Kateřina Polívková daughter of František Polivka and Kateřina Nováková was born on 17 Aug 1817. Václav Šíp and Kateřina Polívková

married. They had the following children:
> i. **Václav Šíp** was born on 05 Nov 1858. He died in 1937.

Generation 6

Václav Šíp-6 (Václav-5, Václav-4, Jan-3, Václav-2, Václav-1) was born on 05 Nov 1858. He died in 1937.

Julie Chvalinová daughter of František Chvalina and Anna Sediva was born on 11 Jan 1864. She died in 1938.

Václav Šíp and Julie Chvalinová married. They had the following children:
> i. **Ladislav Šíp** was born on 30 Sep 1888 in Vesec u Turnova, Turnov Co.. He married Marie Švermová on 02 Oct 1920 in Hoškovice, Mnichovo Hradiště Dist, Bohemia. He died on 01 Apr 1967 in Prague, Czechoslavakia.

Generation 7

Ladislav Šíp-7 (Václav-6, Václav-5, Václav-4, Jan-3, Václav-2, Václav-1) was born on 30 Sep 1888 in Vesec u Turnova, Turnov Co.. He died on 01 Apr 1967 in Prague, Czechoslovakia.

Marie Švermová daughter of Václav Šverma and Anna Dandová was born on 20 Aug 1898 in Hoškovice No. 10, Mnichovo Hradiště Dist, Bohemia. She died on 12 Apr 1986.

Ladislav Šíp and Marie Švermová were married on 02 Oct 1920 in Hoškovice, Mnichovo Hradiště Dist, Bohemia. They had the following children:
> i. **Ladislav Šíp** was born on 08 Oct 1922 in Prague, Czechoslavakia. He married Mirka Langova about 13 Apr 1950. He died on 10 Jun 1993 in Prague, Czechoslavakia.
>
> ii. **Eva Šípová** was born in 1927.

Generation 8

Ladislav Šíp-8 (Ladislav-7, Václav-6, Václav-5, Václav-4, Jan-3, Václav-2, Václav-1) was born on 08 Oct 1922 in Prague, Czechoslavakia. He died on 10 Jun 1993 in Prague, Czechoslavakia.

Mirka Langova was born on 19 Feb 1925. She died in 2005.

Ladislav Šíp and Mirka Langova were married about 13 Apr 1950. They had the following children:

    i. **Marie Šípová** was born on 08 Jun 1956 in Praha.

    ii. **Ladislav Šíp** was born on 11 Sep 1958 in Praha.

Eva Šípová-8 (Ladislav-7, Václav-6, Václav-5, Václav-4, Jan-3, Václav-2, Václav-1) was born in 1927.

Jan Klos was born on 20 May 1912. He died on 05 Jan 1984. Jan Klos and Eva Šípová married. They had the following children:

    i. **Eva Klosova.**

Generation 9

Marie Šípová-9 (Ladislav-8, Ladislav-7, Václav-6, Václav-5, Václav-4, Jan-3, Václav-2, Václav-1) was born on 08 Jun 1956 in Praha.

Petr Retek son of Retek was born on 21 Jan 1944.

Petr Retek and Marie Šípová married. They had the following children:

    Magdalena Retková was born on 31 Dec 1982 in Praha.

Ladislav Šíp-9 (Ladislav-8, Ladislav-7, Václav-6, Václav-5, Václav-4, Jan-3, Václav-2, Václav-1) was born on 11 Sep 1958 in Praha.

Hanička Kratochvílová was born on 24 Jun 1960 in Praha.

Ladislav Šíp and Hanička Kratochvílová married. They had the following children:

    Ladislav Šíp was born on 22 Nov 1984 in Praha.

    Martin Šíp was born on 11 Nov 1985 in Praha.

Bukvicka Family

Generation 1

Josef Bukvička-1 was born before 1880 in Hoškovice No. 5.

Marie Švermová daughter of Barbora Dandová was born about 1880.

Josef Bukvička and Marie Švermová married. They had the following children:

    i. **Antonín Bukvička** was born in Hoškovice.

    ii. **Josef Bukvička** was born on 27 Jan 1898. He died on 14 Feb 1970.

    iii. **Marie Bukvičková** was born about 1899 in Hoškovice No. 5.

    iv. **Bohuslav Bukvička.**

Generation 2

Antonín Bukvička-2 (Josef-1) was born in Hoškovice.

Ludmila Baierova daughter of Václav Baier and Marie Buriánková.

Antonín Bukvička and Ludmila Baierova married. They had the following children:

    i. **Jaroslav Bukvička** was born in 1928.

    ii. **Jiří Bukvička** was born in 1935 in Hoškovice. He died on 11 May 1998.

Josef Bukvička-2 (Josef-1) was born on 27 Jan 1898. He died on 14 Feb 1970.

Ludmila Tondrová daughter of Tondr was born on 10 Oct 1899 in Hoškovice No.. 35. She died on 23 Feb 1992.

Josef Bukvička and Ludmila Tondrová married. They had the following children:

    i. **Josef Bukvička** was born on 16 Mar 1926 in Hoškovice No. 34.

    ii. **Jiřina Bukvičková** was born on 07 Sep 1922 in Hoškovice No. 6.

Marie Bukvičková-2 (Josef-1) was born about 1899 in Hoškovice No. 5.

Miroslav Hyka was born in Mnichovo Hradiště.

Miroslav Hyka and Marie Bukvičková married. They had the following children:

    i. **Miroslav Hyka** was born about 1925.

    ii. **Milena Hykova.**

Bohuslav Bukvička-2 (Josef-1).

Zofie Tomášová was born in Stranov.

Bohuslav Bukvička and Zofie Tomášová married. They had the following children:

    i. **Bohuslav Bukvička** was born on 20 Oct 1929. He died on 11 Nov 1988.

    ii. **Drahoslava Bukvičková** was born on 07 Nov 1933.

Generation 3

Jaroslav Bukvička-3 (Antonín-2, Josef-1) was born in 1928.

Ludmila Machatova was born in 1935.

Jaroslav Bukvička and Ludmila Machatova married. They had the following children:

    Dana Bukvičková.

    Ivana Bukvičková.

Jiří Bukvička-3 (Antonín-2, Josef-1) was born in 1935 in Hoškovice. He died on 11 May 1998.

Milena Tomsová was born on 13 Apr 1935 in Loukov No. 17.

Jiří Bukvička and Milena Tomsová married. They had the following children:

    Milena Bukvičková was born on 14 Apr 1959 in Mladá Boleslav.

    ii. **Sona Bukvičková** was born on 26 Jan 1965 in Mladá Boleslav.

Josef Bukvička-3 (Josef-2, Josef-1) was born on 16 Mar 1926 in Hoškovice No. 34.

Vlasta Benešová was born on 23 Mar 1930 in Hoškovice.

Josef Bukvička and Vlasta Benešová married. They had the following children:

    i. **Ludmila Bukvičková** was born on 31 Aug 1959 in Mladá Boleslav. She married Frantiosek Šafránek on 09 Sep 1984.

    Josef Bukvička was born on 06 Nov 1963 in Mladá Boleslav.

Jiřina Bukvičková-3 (Josef-2, Josef-1) was born on 07 Sep 1922 in Hoškovice No. 6.

Antonín Wagenknecht was born on 05 Sep 1913.

Antonín Wagenknecht and Jiřina Bukvičková married. They had the following children:

i. **Jiří Wagenknecht** was born on 10 Jan 1946.

ii. **Jan Wagenknecht** was born on 30 Nov 1949.

Miroslav Hyka-3 (Marie-2, Josef-1) was born about 1925.

Emilie.

Miroslav Hyka and Emilie married. They had the following children:

i. **Mirek Hyka.**

ii. **Jan Hyka.**

Milena Hykova-3 (Marie-2, Josef-1).

Ladislav Sedláček was born in Mladá Boleslav.

Ladislav Sedláček and Milena Hykova married. They had the following children:

i. **Ladislav Sedláček.**

ii. **Milena Sedláčková.**

Bohuslav Bukvička-3 (Bohuslav-2, Josef-1) was born on 20 Oct 1929. He died on 11 Nov 1988.

Marie was born on 09 Sep 1932.

Bohuslav Bukvička and Marie married. They had the following children:

Pavel Bukvička was born on 08 Aug 1953. He died on 01 Dec 1977.

Hana Bukvičková was born on 13 Jan 1960.

Drahoslava Bukvičková-3 (Bohuslav-2, Josef-1) was born on 07 Nov 1933.

Jaroslav Vochvesta. He died on Unknown.

Jaroslav Vochvesta and Drahoslava Bukvičková married. They had the following children:

Jaroslav Vochvesta.

Zuzana Vochvestova.

Generation 4

Sona Bukvičková-4 (Jiří-3, Antonín-2, Josef-1) was born on 26 Jan 1965 in Mladá Boleslav.

Imrich Rigo.

Imrich Rigo and Sona Bukvičková married. They had the following children:

Zuzanka Rigová was born on 13 Apr 1987 in Mladá Boleslav.

Janicka Rigová was born on 05 Feb 1990 in Mladá Boleslav.

Ludmila Bukvičková-4 (Josef-3, Josef-2, Josef-1) was born on 31 Aug 1959 in Mladá Boleslav.

Frantiosek Šafránek was born on 09 Apr 1959 in Dymokury.

Frantiosek Šafránek and Ludmila Bukvičková were married on 09 Sep 1984. They had the following children:

 František Šafránek was born on 15 Jun 1984.

 Petr Šafránek was born on 12 Aug 1986.

 Jan Šafránek was born on 05 Dec 1988.

Jiří Wagenknecht-4 (Jiřina-3, Josef-2, Josef-1) was born on 10 Jan 1946.

Vendulka Zahorska was born on 06 Jun 1949.

Jiří Wagenknecht and Vendulka Zahorska married. They had the following children:

 Jan Wagenknecht was born on 16 Feb 1974.

 Lenka Wagenknechtova was born on 14 Jan 1980.

Jan Wagenknecht-4 (Jiřina-3, Josef-2, Josef-1) was born on 30 Nov 1949.

Jana Nováková was born on 08 Apr 1955.

Jan Wagenknecht and Jana Nováková married. They had the following children:

 Jana Wagenknechtova was born on 09 Sep 1978.

 Pavlina Wagenknechtova was born on 15 Jun 1984.

Mirek Hyka-4 (Miroslav-3, Marie-2, Josef-1).

Unknown.

Mirek Hyka and Unknown married. They had the following children:

 Mirek Hyka.

 daughter Hyka.

Jan Hyka-4 (Miroslav-3, Marie-2, Josef-1).

Olga.

Jan Hyka and Olga married. They had the following children:

 Jan Hyka.

Ladislav Sedláček-4 (Milena-3, Marie-2, Josef-1).

Unknown.

Ladislav Sedláček and Unknown married. They had the following

children:
>
> **son Sedláček.**

Milena Sedláčková-4 (Milena-3, Marie-2, Josef-1).

Michetslaeger was born in Turnov.

Michetslaeger and Milena Sedláčková married. They had the following children:
>
> **daughter Michetslaegerova.**
>
> **son Michetslaeger.**

C. Eva Edwards' Father Side

Edwards (Eisner) Family

Generation 1

1. **Michael Eisner**-1 was born in 1771 in Humpolec. He died in 1864.
   Klára Hofmanova was born in L (Kolin n).
   Michael Eisner and Klára Hofmanova married. They had the following children:
   - 3. i. **Karl Eisner** was born in 1821 in Chotěboř. He married Anna Krausová about 1852. He died in 1893.
   - 4. ii. **Leopold Eisner**.

   Rachel Reinhalt.
   Michael Eisner and Rachel Reinhalt married. They had no children.

Generation 2

2. **Karl Eisner**-2 (Michael-1) was born in 1821 in Chotěboř. He died in 1893.
   Anna Krausová daughter of Loebl Kraus and Barbora Fischer was born in 1831 in Dolni Kralovice. She died in 1855.
   Karl Eisner and Anna Krausová were married about 1852. They had the following children:
   - 4. i. **(Jindřich) Henry Eisner** was born on 12 Mar 1853 in Kaliste u Nemeckeho Brodu, Bohemia. He married Hortense Auer in 1888. He died on 13 Dec 1956 in New York, NY.
   - 5. ii. **Julie Eisnerová**.

   Unknown.
   Karl Eisner and Unknown married. They had no children.

3. **Leopold Eisner**-2 (Michael-1).
   Leopold Eisner and unknown spouse married. They had the following children:
   - 6. i. **Siegmund Eisner**.

Generation 3

4. **(Jindřich) Henry Eisner**-3 (Karl-2, Michael-1) was born on 12 Mar 1853 in Kaliste u Nemeckeho Brodu, Bohemia. He died on 13 Dec 1956 in New York, NY.

    Hortense Auer daughter of Moritz Auer and Julie Wiener was born in 1869 in Prague, Jakubska 1. She died on 13 Oct 1951 in New York, NY.

    (Jindřich) Henry Eisner and Hortense Auer were married in 1888. They had the following children:

    7. i. **Paul J. Edwards (Pavel Eisner)** was born on 29 Jun 1892 in Prague, Klimentska 1. He married Jiřina Taussigová on 05 Jun 1926 in Prague. He died on 27 Jun 1964 in Schenectady, NY.
    8. ii. **(Karel Eisner) Charles E. Edwards** was born on 26 Apr 1894 in Prague, Bohemia. He married Marta Hanakova on 19 May 1927. He died on 27 Oct 1986.
    9. iii. **Robert Eisner** was born on 11 Jul 1898 in Prague, Bohemia. He married Mitzi Kratzig in 1926 in Praha, CSR. He died on 31 Oct 1984 in New York, NY.

5. **Julie Eisnerová**-3 (Karl-2, Michael-1).

    Unknown.

    Unknown and Julie Eisnerová married. They had the following children:

    i. **Arnošt** was born in Krchleby.
    ii. **Anna** was born in Krchleby.
    iii. **Otto** was born in Krchleby.

6. **Siegmund Eisner**-3 (Leopold-2, Michael-1).

    Unknown.

    Siegmund Eisner and Unknown married. They had the following children:

    i. **Adolf Eisner.**

Generation 4

7. **Paul J. Edwards (Pavel Eisner)**-4 ((Jindřich) Henry-3, Karl-2, Michael-1) was born on 29 Jun 1892 in Prague, Klimentska 1. He died on 27 Jun 1964 in Schenectady, NY.

    Jiřina Taussigová daughter of Oskar Taussig and Klára Munková was born on 24 Apr 1906 in Prague - Kralovske Vinohrady, Nerudova l. She died on 06 Nov 1962 in New York, NY.

Paul J. Edwards (Pavel Eisner) and Jiřina Taussigová were married on 05 Jun 1926 in Prague. They had the following children:

10. i. **Helen Edwards (Eisnerova)** was born on 29 Apr 1927 in Prague, CSR. She married Frank Steiner on 16 Sep 1948 in New York, NY.

11. ii. **Eva Edwards (Eisnerová)** was born on 21 Jan 1932 in Prague, CSR. She married Mila (Miloslav) Rechcigl Jr. on 29 Aug 1953 in New York, NY.

8. **(Karel Eisner) Charles E. Edwards**-4 ((Jindřich) Henry-3, Karl-2, Michael-1) was born on 26 Apr 1894 in Prague, Bohemia. He died on 27 Oct 1986.

Marta Hanakova daughter of Sigmund Hanák and Klára Loewy was born on 01 May 1905 in Zatec. She died on 25 Nov 1985.

(Karel Eisner) Charles E. Edwards and Marta Hanakova were married on 19 May 1927. They had the following children:

12. i. **(Hana Ruth Eisnerová) Joan Ruth Edwards** was born on 14 Jun 1930 in Prague. She married Bernie Hulkower on 20 Nov 1955. She died on 21 Apr 2021.

13. ii. **Doris Věra Edwards** was born on 09 Apr 1932 in Prague, Bohemia. She married John ("Jack") Rodney Gordon on 09 May 1954.

9. **Robert Eisner**-4 ((Jindřich) Henry-3, Karl-2, Michael-1) was born on 11 Jul 1898 in Prague, Bohemia. He died on 31 Oct 1984 in New York, NY.

Mitzi Kratzig was born on 12 Oct 1900 in Liberec, CSR. She died in 1991 in New York, NY.

Robert Eisner and Mitzi Kratzig were married in 1926 in Praha, CSR. They had the following children:

14. i. **Thomas Michael Eisner** was born on 10 Mar 1931 in Prague, CSR. He married Savilla Gamble on 21 Dec 1957 in Vancouver, WA. He died on 13 Feb 1992 in Santa Fe, NM.

15. ii. **Stephen Alexander Eisner** was born on 28 Jul 1932 in Prague, CSR. He married Arlene Zohn on 28 Sep 1972.

Generation 5

10. **Helen Edwards (Eisnerova)**-5 (Paul J. Edwards-4, (Jindřich) Henry-3, Karl-2, Michael-1) was born on 29 Apr 1927 in Prague, CSR.
    Frank Steiner son of Johann (Hans) Steiner and Růžena Steinbachova was born on 23 Apr 1922 in Prague, Bohemia. He died on 14 Sep 2000 in Scotia, NY.
    Frank Steiner and Helen Edwards (Eisnerova) were married on 16 Sep 1948 in New York, NY. They had the following children:
    - 16. i. **Linda Claire Steiner** was born on 01 Mar 1950 in Schenectady, NY. She married Edward Salomon on 05 Jun 1977 in Scotia, NY.
    - 17. ii. **David Henry Steiner** was born on 13 Mar 1952 in Schenectady, NY. He married Carol Ann Mastaliz on 07 Jul 1979 in So. Deerfield, MA.

11. **Eva Edwards (Eisnerová)**-5 (Paul J. Edwards-4, (Jindřich) Henry-3, Karl-2, Michael-1) was born on 21 Jan 1932 in Prague, CSR.
    Mila (Miloslav) Rechcigl Jr. son of Miloslav Rechcigl and Marie Rajtrová was born on 30 Jul 1930 in Mladá Boleslav, CSR.
    Mila (Miloslav) Rechcigl Jr. and Eva Edwards (Eisnerová) were married on 29 Aug 1953 in New York, NY. They had the following children:
    - 18. i. **John Edward Rechcigl** was born on 27 Feb 1960 in Washington, D.C.. He married Nancy Ann Palko on 30 Jul 1983 in Dover, NJ.
    - 19. ii. **Karen Rechcigl** was born on 16 Apr 1962 in Washington, DC. She married Ulysses Kollecas on 25 Aug 1990 in Bethesda, MD.

12. **(Hana Ruth Eisnerová) Joan Ruth Edwards**-5 ((Karel Eisner) Charles E.-4, (Jindřich) Henry-3, Karl-2, Michael-1) was born on 14 Jun 1930 in Prague. She died on 21 Apr 2021.
    Bernie Hulkower was born on 23 Jul 1928 in New York City.
    Bernie Hulkower and (Hana Ruth Eisnerová) Joan Ruth Edwards were married on 20 Nov 1955. They had the following children:
    - 20. i. **Seth Hulkower** was born on 14 Mar 1958 in Queens, NY. He married Lissa Perlman on 16 Jun 1991.
    - 21. ii. **Daniel Hulkower** was born on 22 Dec 1961 in Queens, NY. He married Lynda J. Greenberg on 19 Nov 1989.

13. **Doris Věra Edwards**-5 ((Karel Eisner) Charles E.-4, (Jindřich) Henry-3,

Karl-2, Michael-1) was born on 09 Apr 1932 in Prague, Bohemia.

John ("Jack") Rodney Gordon was born on 13 Mar 1929 in Brooklyn, NY. John ("Jack") Rodney Gordon and Doris Věra Edwards were married on 09 May 1954. They had the following children:

22. i. **Wayne Peter Gordon** was born on 02 May 1957 in Queens, NY. He married Claire Lin Ward on 01 Sep 1991 in NC.
23. ii. **Melissa Rose Gordon** was born on 18 Feb 1960 in Queens, NY. She married Jeffrey Clark on 03 Mar 1984.
24. iii. **Dean Mark Gordon** was born on 18 Jun 1963 in Long Island, NY. He married Angela Müller on 29 Feb 1992.

14. **Thomas Michael Eisner**-5 (Robert-4, (Jindřich) Henry-3, Karl-2, Michael-1) was born on 10 Mar 1931 in Prague, CSR. He died on 13 Feb 1992 in Santa Fe, NM.

Savilla Gamble was born on 26 Oct 1937 in Ft. George Mead, MD.

Thomas Michael Eisner and Savilla Gamble were married on 21 Dec 1957 in Vancouver, WA. They had the following children:

25. i. **Stephen Mark Eisner** was born on 29 Nov 1958 in Chuquicamata, Chile, SA. He married Staci Suzanne Johnson on 14 Jun 1986 in Ft. Worth, TX.
26. ii. **Andrea Savilla Eisner** was born on 23 Nov 1959 in Sewell, Chile, SA. She married Todd Allen Barnett on 27 Jun 1993 in Carmel, CA.
    iii. **Phillip Robert Eisner** was born on 23 Aug 1965 in Ft. Worth, TX.

Kim Davey was born in 1949.

Thomas Michael Eisner and Kim Davey were married on 04 Jan 1990. They had no children.

15. **Stephen Alexander Eisner**-5 (Robert-4, (Jindřich) Henry-3, Karl-2, Michael-1) was born on 28 Jul 1932 in Prague, CSR.

Arlene Zohn was born on 30 Oct 1940 in New York, NY. She died 15 Apr 2013.

Stephen Alexander Eisner and Arlene Zohn were married on 28 Sep 1972. They had the following children:

i. **Andrew Calvin Eisner** was born on 16 Jul 1974 in New York, NY. He was married to Stacy Lynn Hischberg on 10 Sep 2005 in

Mamaroneck, NY. They have 2 children:
Parker Thomas Eisner was born 24 May 2008 in New York, NY.
Zachary Robert Eisner was born 15 May 2010 in New York, NY.
   ii. **Douglas Randall Eisner** was born on 21 Jul 1978 in New York, NY. He was married to Victoria Jordan Tobias. She was born on 24 Dec 1984 in Vancouver, BC, Canada. They have 2 children:
Jack August Eisner was born on 23 Feb 2017 in Las Vegas, NV.
Levi Thomas Eisner was born on 29 Dec 2018 in Las Vegas, NV.

Generation 6

16. **Linda Claire Steiner**-6 (Helen Edwards-5, Paul J. Edwards-4, (Jindřich) Henry-3, Karl-2, Michael-1) was born on 01 Mar 1950 in Schenectady, NY. **Edward Salomon** son of Jerome Salomon and Rachel Finchel was born on 12 Feb 1951 in Jersey city, NJ.
Edward Salomon and Linda Claire Steiner were married on 05 Jun 1977 in Scotia, NY. They had the following children:
   i. **Sarah Beth Salomon** was born on 28 Jan 1980 in Chicago, IL.
   ii. **Paul Nathan Salomon** was born on 02 Jan 1983 in Chicago, IL.

17. **David Henry Steiner**-6 (Helen Edwards-5, Paul J. Edwards-4, (Jindřich) Henry-3, Karl-2, Michael-1) was born on 13 Mar 1952 in Schenectady, NY. **Carol Ann Mastaliz** daughter of Frank Peter Mastaliz and Helen Carline Macko was born on 26 Oct 1952 (Greenfield, MA).
David Henry Steiner and Carol Ann Mastaliz were married on 07 Jul 1979 in So. Deerfield, MA. They had the following children:
27. i. **Erin Marie Steiner** was born on 01 Aug 1981 in Chicago, IL. She married Michael John Malick on 27 Jul 2013 in Poulsbo, WA.
   ii. **Jonathan Robert Steiner** was born on 30 Dec 1984 in Concord, MA.

18. **John Edward Rechcigl**-6 (Eva Edwards-5, Paul J. Edwards-4, (Jindřich) Henry-3, Karl-2, Michael-1) was born on 27 Feb 1960 in Washington, D.C.. **Nancy Ann Palko** daughter of Joseph Palko and Mary Rishko was born on 26 Sep 1961 in Morristown, NJ.
John Edward Rechcigl and Nancy Ann Palko were married on 30 Jul 1983 in Dover, NJ. They had the following children:

  i. **Gregory John Rechcigl** was born on 19 Dec 1988 in Bradenton, FL.

29. ii. **Kevin Thomas Rechcigl** was born on 09 Oct 1991 in Bradenton, FL. He married Jordan Robbins on 12 May 2018 in Jacksonville, FL.

  iii. **Lindsey Nicole Rechcigl** was born on 03 Nov 1994 in Bradenton, FL.

19. **Karen Rechcigl**-6 (Eva Edwards-5, Paul J. Edwards-4, (Jindřich) Henry-3, Karl-2, Michael-1) was born on 16 Apr 1962 in Washington, DC.

Ulysses Kollecas son of Christopher Thomas (Kolecas) Collier and Amelia Malatras was born on 20 Mar 1958 in Washington, DC.

Ulysses Kollecas and Karen Rechcigl were married on 25 Aug 1990 in Bethesda, MD. They had the following children:

  i. **Kristin Kollecas** was born on 04 May 1993 in Albuquerque, NM.

  ii. **Paul Kollecas** was born on 02 Jun 1995 in Albuquerque, NM.

20. **Seth Hulkower**-6 ((Hana Ruth Eisnerová) Joan Ruth-5, (Karel Eisner) Charles E.-4, (Jindřich) Henry-3, Karl-2, Michael-1) was born on 14 Mar 1958 in Queens, NY.

Lissa Perlman was born on 24 Dec 1955 in New Haven, CT.

Seth Hulkower and Lissa Perlman were married on 16 Jun 1991. They had the following children:

  i. **Talia Minna Hulkower** was born on 20 Jun 1994 in New York City.

  ii. **Sasha Regina Hulkower** was born on 16 Aug 1996 in New York City.

21. **Daniel Hulkower**-6 ((Hana Ruth Eisnerová) Joan Ruth-5, (Karel Eisner) Charles E.-4, (Jindřich) Henry-3, Karl-2, Michael-1) was born on 22 Dec 1961 in Queens, NY.

Lynda J. Greenberg was born on 26 Dec 1954 in New York City, NY.

Daniel Hulkower and Lynda J. Greenberg were married on 19 Nov 1989. They had the following children:

  i. **Anna Marta Hulkower** was born on 12 Sep 1990 in York, PA.

  ii. **Isabel Sophia Hulkower** was born on 27 May 1994 in York, PA.

22. **Wayne Peter Gordon**-6 (Doris Věra-5, (Karel Eisner) Charles E.-4,

(Jindřich) Henry-3, Karl-2, Michael-1) was born on 02 May 1957 in Queens, NY.

Claire Lin Ward was born on 07 Oct 1964 in NC.

Wayne Peter Gordon and Claire Lin Ward were married on 01 Sep 1991 in NC. They had the following children:

    i. **Dominick Lin Gordon** was born on 31 May 1993 in Los Angeles, CA.

    ii. **Anthony John Gordon** was born on 08 Feb 1995 in Los Angeles, CA.

Susan Reifer was born on 05 Apr 1962 in CA.

Wayne Peter Gordon and Susan Reifer were married on 10 Oct 2002 in Hawaii. They had the following children:

    i. **Nicholas Gordon** was born about 2006.

23. **Melissa Rose Gordon**-6 (Doris Věra-5, (Karel Eisner) Charles E.-4, (Jindřich) Henry-3, Karl-2, Michael-1) was born on 18 Feb 1960 in Queens, NY.

Jeffrey Clark was born on 23 Feb 1953 in Los Angeles, CA.

Jeffrey Clark and Melissa Rose Gordon were married on 03 Mar 1984. They had the following children:

    i. **Brandon Andrew Clark** was born on 01 Nov 1989 in Los Angeles, CA.

    ii. **Madison Ross Clark** was born on 01 Jun 1994 in Los Angeles, CA.

    iii. **Kaitlin Elizabeth Clark** was born on 27 Jan 1999 in Los Angeles, CA.

24. **Dean Mark Gordon**-6 (Doris Věra-5, (Karel Eisner) Charles E.-4, (Jindřich) Henry-3, Karl-2, Michael-1) was born on 18 Jun 1963 in Long Island, NY.

Angela Müller was born on 09 Nov 1964 in Los Angeles, CA.

Dean Mark Gordon and Angela Müller were married on 29 Feb 1992. They had the following children:

    i. **Sam Walter Gordon** was born on 02 Sep 1994 in New York City.

    ii. **Joseph Charles Gordon** was born on 26 Aug 1996 in Los

Angeles, CA.
    iii. **Greta Kelly Gordon** was born on 15 Oct 1998 in Chicago, IL.

25. **Stephen Mark Eisner**-6 (Thomas Michael-5, Robert-4, (Jindřich) Henry-3, Karl-2, Michael-1) was born on 29 Nov 1958 in Chuquicamata, Chile, SA.

Staci Suzanne Johnson.

Stephen Mark Eisner and Staci Suzanne Johnson were married on 14 Jun 1986 in Ft. Worth, TX. They had the following children:
    i. **Kathryn Bliss Eisner** was born on 19 Oct 1988 in Ft. Worth, TX.
    ii. **Patrick Thomas Eisner** was born on 23 Apr 1994 in Ft. Worth, TX.

26. **Andrea Savilla Eisner**-6 (Thomas Michael-5, Robert-4, (Jindřich) Henry-3, Karl-2, Michael-1) was born on 23 Nov 1959 in Sewell, Chile, SA.

Todd Allen Barnett.

Todd Allen Barnett and Andrea Savilla Eisner were married on 27 Jun 1993 in Carmel, CA. They had the following children:
    i. **Benjamin Michael Barnett** was born on 30 Apr 1997 in Bellevue, WA.
    ii. **Daniel Barnett.**

Generation 7

27. **Erin Marie Steiner**-7 (David Henry-6, Helen Edwards-5, Paul J. Edwards-4, (Jindřich) Henry-3, Karl-2, Michael-1) was born on 01 Aug 1981 in Chicago, IL.

Michael John Malick was born on 01 Aug 1981 in Chicago, IL.

Michael John Malick and Erin Marie Steiner were married on 27 Jul 2013 in Poulsbo, WA. They had the following children:
    i. **Henry Francsz Malick** was born on 18 Feb 2018 in Seattle, WA.

28. **Kevin Thomas Rechcigl**-7 (John Edward-6, Eva Edwards-5, Paul J. Edwards-4, (Jindřich) Henry-3, Karl-2, Michael-1) was born on 09 Oct 1991 in Bradenton, FL.

Jordan Robbins daughter of Douglass Robbins and Ivonne was born on 10 Jan 1992 in Camarillo, CA.

Kevin Thomas Rechcigl and Jordan Robbins were married on 12 May 2018 in Jacksonville, FL. They had the following children:
  i. **James Douglas Rechcigl** was born on 05 Jan 2021 in Jacksonville, FL.
  ii. **Evelyn Marie Rechcigl** was born 29 May 2023 in Jacksonville, FL.

Kraus Family

Generation 1

1. **Loebl Kraus**-1.
Barbora Fischer daughter of Fischer and Unknown.
Loebl Kraus and Barbora Fischer married. They had the following children:
   2. i. **Anna Krausová** was born in 1831 in Dolni Kralovice. She married Karl Eisner about 1852. She died in 1855.

Generation 2

2. **Anna Krausová**-2 (Loebl-1) was born in 1831 in Dolni Kralovice. She died in 1855.
Karl Eisner son of Michael Eisner and Klára Hofmanova was born in 1821 in Chotěboř. He died in 1893.
Karl Eisner and Anna Krausová were married about 1852. They had the following children:
   3. i. **(Jindřich) Henry Eisner** was born on 12 Mar 1853 in Kaliste u Nemeckeho Brodu, Bohemia. He married Hortense Auer in 1888. He died on 13 Dec 1956 in New York, NY.
   4. ii. **Julie Eisnerová**.

Unknown was born in Bohemia.
Unknown and Anna Krausová were married about 1850. They had the following children:
   5. i. **Josef Kraus** was born about 1851 in Bohemia.

Generation 3

3. **(Jindřich) Henry Eisner**-3 (Anna-2, Loebl-1) was born on 12 Mar 1853 in Kaliste u Nemeckeho Brodu, Bohemia. He died on 13 Dec 1956 in New York, NY.
Hortense Auer daughter of Moritz Auer and Julie Wiener was born in 1869 in Prague, Jakubska 1. She died on 13 Oct 1951 in New York, NY.
(Jindřich) Henry Eisner and Hortense Auer were married in 1888. They had the following children:
   6. i. **Paul J. Edwards (Pavel Eisner)** was born on 29 Jun 1892 in

Prague, Klimentska 1. He married Jiřina Taussigová on 05 Jun 1926 in Prague. He died on 27 Jun 1964 in Schenectady, NY.
7. ii. **(Karel Eisner) Charles E. Edwards** was born on 26 Apr 1894 in Prague, Bohemia. He married Marta Hanakova on 19 May 1927. He died on 27 Oct 1986.
8. iii. **Robert Eisner** was born on 11 Jul 1898 in Prague, Bohemia. He married Mitzi Kratzig in 1926 in Praha, CSR. He died on 31 Oct 1984 in New York, NY.

4. **Julie Eisnerová**-3 (Anna-2, Loebl-1).
Unknown.
Unknown and Julie Eisnerová married. They had the following children:
   i. **Arnošt** was born in Krchleby.
   ii. **Anna** was born in Krchleby.
   iii. **Otto** was born in Krchleby.

5. **Josef Kraus**-3 (Anna-2, Loebl-1) was born about 1851 in Bohemia.
Emma.
Josef Kraus and Emma married. They had the following children:
   i. **Max Kraus** was born in Bohemia. He died in Resided in Cleveland, OH.
   ii. **Anna Krausová** was born in Bohemia.
   iii. **daughter Krausová** was born in Bohemia.

Generation 4

6. **Paul J. Edwards (Pavel Eisner)**-4 ((Jindřich) Henry-3, Anna-2, Loebl-1) was born on 29 Jun 1892 in Prague, Klimentska 1. He died on 27 Jun 1964 in Schenectady, NY.
Jiřina Taussigová daughter of Oskar Taussig and Klára Munková was born on 24 Apr 1906 in Prague - Kralovske Vinohrady, Nerudova l. She died on 06 Nov 1962 in New York, NY.
Paul J. Edwards (Pavel Eisner) and Jiřina Taussigová were married on 05 Jun 1926 in Prague. They had the following children:
9. i. **Helen Edwards (Eisnerova)** was born on 29 Apr 1927 in Prague, CSR. She married Frank Steiner on 16 Sep 1948 in New York, NY.
10. ii. **Eva Edwards (Eisnerová)** was born on 21 Jan 1932 in Prague,

CSR. She married Mila (Miloslav) Rechcigl Jr. on 29 Aug 1953 in New York, NY.

7. **(Karel Eisner) Charles E. Edwards**-4 ((Jindřich) Henry-3, Anna-2, Loebl-1) was born on 26 Apr 1894 in Prague, Bohemia. He died on 27 Oct 1986.
   Marta Hanakova daughter of Sigmund Hanák and Klára Loewy was born on 01 May 1905 in Zatec. She died on 25 Nov 1985.
   (Karel Eisner) Charles E. Edwards and Marta Hanakova were married on 19 May 1927. They had the following children:
   11. i. **(Hana Ruth Eisnerová) Joan Ruth Edwards** was born on 14 Jun 1930 in Prague. She married Bernie Hulkower on 20 Nov 1955. She died on 21 Apr 2021.
   12. ii. **Doris Věra Edwards** was born on 09 Apr 1932 in Prague, Bohemia. She married John ("Jack") Rodney Gordon on 09 May 1954.

8. **Robert Eisner**-4 ((Jindřich) Henry-3, Anna-2, Loebl-1) was born on 11 Jul 1898 in Prague, Bohemia. He died on 31 Oct 1984 in New York, NY.
   Mitzi Kratzig was born on 12 Oct 1900 in Liberec, CSR. She died in 1991 in New York, NY.
   Robert Eisner and Mitzi Kratzig were married in 1926 in Praha, CSR. They had the following children:
   13. i. **Thomas Michael Eisner** was born on 10 Mar 1931 in Prague, CSR. He married Savilla Gamble on 21 Dec 1957 in Vancouver, WA. He died on 13 Feb 1992 in Santa Fe, NM.
   14. ii. **Stephen Alexander Eisner** was born on 28 Jul 1932 in Prague, CSR. He married Arlene Zohn on 28 Sep 1972.

Generation 5

9. **Helen Edwards (Eisnerova)**-5 (Paul J. Edwards-4, (Jindřich) Henry-3, Anna-2, Loebl-1) was born on 29 Apr 1927 in Prague, CSR.
   Frank Steiner son of Johann (Hans) Steiner and Růžena Steinbachova was born on 23 Apr 1922 in Prague, Bohemia. He died on 14 Sep 2000 in Scotia, NY.
   Frank Steiner and Helen Edwards (Eisnerova) were married on 16 Sep 1948 in New York, NY. They had the following children:
   15. i. **Linda Claire Steiner** was born on 01 Mar 1950 in Schenectady,

NY. She married Edward Salomon on 05 Jun 1977 in Scotia, NY.

16.   ii. **David Henry Steiner** was born on 13 Mar 1952 in Schenectady, NY. He married Carol Ann Mastaliz on 07 Jul 1979 in So. Deerfield, MA.

10. **Eva Edwards (Eisnerová)**-5 (Paul J. Edwards-4, (Jindřich) Henry-3, Anna-2, Loebl-1) was born on 21 Jan 1932 in Prague, CSR.

    Mila (Miloslav) Rechcigl Jr. son of Miloslav Rechcigl and Marie Rajtrová was born on 30 Jul 1930 in Mladá Boleslav, CSR.

    Mila (Miloslav) Rechcigl Jr. and Eva Edwards (Eisnerová) were married on 29 Aug 1953 in New York, NY. They had the following children:

    17.   i. **John Edward Rechcigl** was born on 27 Feb 1960 in Washington, D.C.. He married Nancy Ann Palko on 30 Jul 1983 in Dover, NJ.

    18.   ii. **Karen Rechcigl** was born on 16 Apr 1962 in Washington, DC. She married Ulysses Kollecas on 25 Aug 1990 in Bethesda, MD.

11. **(Hana Ruth Eisnerová) Joan Ruth Edwards**-5 ((Karel Eisner) Charles E.-4, (Jindřich) Henry-3, Anna-2, Loebl-1) was born on 14 Jun 1930 in Prague. She died on 21 Apr 2021.

    Bernie Hulkower was born on 23 Jul 1928 in New York City.

    Bernie Hulkower and (Hana Ruth Eisnerová) Joan Ruth Edwards were married on 20 Nov 1955. They had the following children:

    19.   i. **Seth Hulkower** was born on 14 Mar 1958 in Queens, NY. He married Lissa Perlman on 16 Jun 1991.

    20.   ii. **Daniel Hulkower** was born on 22 Dec 1961 in Queens, NY. He married Lynda J. Greenberg on 19 Nov 1989.

12. **Doris Věra Edwards**-5 ((Karel Eisner) Charles E.-4, (Jindřich) Henry-3, Anna-2, Loebl-1) was born on 09 Apr 1932 in Prague, Bohemia.

    John ("Jack") Rodney Gordon was born on 13 Mar 1929 in Brooklyn, NY. John ("Jack") Rodney Gordon and Doris Věra Edwards were married on 09 May 1954. They had the following children:

    21.   i. **Wayne Peter Gordon** was born on 02 May 1957 in Queens, NY. He married Claire Lin Ward on 01 Sep 1991 in NC.

    22.   ii. **Melissa Rose Gordon** was born on 18 Feb 1960 in Queens, NY. She married Jeffrey Clark on 03 Mar 1984.

23. iii. **Dean Mark Gordon** was born on 18 Jun 1963 in Long Island, NY. He married Angela Müller on 29 Feb 1992.

13. **Thomas Michael Eisner**-5 (Robert-4, (Jindřich) Henry-3, Anna-2, Loebl-1) was born on 10 Mar 1931 in Prague, CSR. He died on 13 Feb 1992 in Santa Fe, NM.
Savilla Gamble was born on 26 Oct 1937 in Ft. George Mead, MD.
Thomas Michael Eisner and Savilla Gamble were married on 21 Dec 1957 in Vancouver, WA. They had the following children:

24. i. **Stephen Mark Eisner** was born on 29 Nov 1958 in Chuquicamata, Chile, SA. He married Staci Suzanne Johnson on 14 Jun 1986 in Ft. Worth, TX.

25. ii. **Andrea Savilla Eisner** was born on 23 Nov 1959 in Sewell, Chile, SA. She married Todd Allen Barnett on 27 Jun 1993 in Carmel, CA.

   iii. **Phillip Robert Eisner** was born on 23 Aug 1965 in Ft. Worth, TX.
Kim Davey was born in 1949.
Thomas Michael Eisner and Kim Davey were married on 04 Jan 1990. They had no children.

14. **Stephen Alexander Eisner**-5 (Robert-4, (Jindřich) Henry-3, Anna-2, Loebl-1) was born on 28 Jul 1932 in Prague, CSR.
Arlene Zohn was born on 30 Oct 1940 in New York, NY. She died 15 Apr 2013.
Stephen Alexander Eisner and Arlene Zohn were married on 28 Sep 1972. They had the following children:

   i. **Andrew Calvin Eisner** was born on 16 Jul 1974 in New York, NY. He married Stacy Lynn Hischberg on 10 Sep 2005 in Mamaroneck, NY.

   ii. **Douglas Randall Eisner** was born on 21 Jul 1978 in New York, NY.

Generation 6

15. **Linda Claire Steiner**-6 (Helen Edwards-5, Paul J. Edwards-4, (Jindřich) Henry-3, Anna-2, Loebl-1) was born on 01 Mar 1950 in Schenectady, NY.
Edward Salomon son of Jerome Salomon and Rachel Finchel was born on 12 Feb 1951 in Jersey city, NJ.
Edward Salomon and Linda Claire Steiner were married on 05 Jun 1977

in Scotia, NY. They had the following children:
  i. **Sarah Beth Salomon** was born on 28 Jan 1980 in Chicago, IL.
  ii. **Paul Nathan Salomon** was born on 02 Jan 1983 in Chicago, IL.

16. **David Henry Steiner**-6 (Helen Edwards-5, Paul J. Edwards-4, (Jindřich) Henry-3, Anna-2, Loebl-1) was born on 13 Mar 1952 in Schenectady, NY. **Carol Ann Mastaliz** daughter of Frank Peter Mastaliz and Helen Carline Macko was born on 26 Oct 1952 (Greenfield, MA).
David Henry Steiner and Carol Ann Mastaliz were married on 07 Jul 1979 in So. Deerfield, MA. They had the following children:
  26. i. **Erin Marie Steiner** was born on 01 Aug 1981 in Chicago, IL. She married Michael John Malick on 27 Jul 2013 in Poulsbo, WA.
  ii. **Jonathan Robert Steiner** was born on 30 Dec 1984 in Concord, MA.

17. **John Edward Rechcigl**-6 (Eva Edwards-5, Paul J. Edwards-4, (Jindřich) Henry-3, Anna-2, Loebl-1) was born on 27 Feb 1960 in Washington, D.C.. **Nancy Ann Palko** daughter of Joseph Palko and Mary Rishko was born on 26 Sep 1961 in Morristown, NJ.
John Edward Rechcigl and Nancy Ann Palko were married on 30 Jul 1983 in Dover, NJ. They had the following children:
  i. **Gregory John Rechcigl** was born on 19 Dec 1988 in Bradenton, FL.
  28. ii. **Kevin Thomas Rechcigl** was born on 09 Oct 1991 in Bradenton, FL. He married Jordan Robbins on 12 May 2018 in Jacksonville, FL.
  ii. **Lindsey Nicole Rechcigl** was born on 03 Nov 1994 in Bradenton, FL.

18. **Karen Rechcigl**-6 (Eva Edwards-5, Paul J. Edwards-4, (Jindřich) Henry-3, Anna-2, Loebl-1) was born on 16 Apr 1962 in Washington, DC. **Ulysses Kollecas** son of Christopher Thomas (Kolecas) Collier and Amelia Malatras was born on 20 Mar 1958 in Washington, DC.
Ulysses Kollecas and Karen Rechcigl were married on 25 Aug 1990 in Bethesda, MD. They had the following children:
  i. **Kristin Kollecas** was born on 04 May 1993 in Albuquerque, NM.
  ii. **Paul Kollecas** was born on 02 Jun 1995 in Albuquerque, NM.

19. **Seth Hulkower**-6 ((Hana Ruth Eisnerová) Joan Ruth-5, (Karel Eisner) Charles E.-4, (Jindřich) Henry-3, Anna-2, Loebl-1) was born on 14 Mar 1958 in Queens, NY.
    Lissa Perlman was born on 24 Dec 1955 in New Haven, CT.
    Seth Hulkower and Lissa Perlman were married on 16 Jun 1991. They had the following children:
    i. **Talia Minna Hulkower** was born on 20 Jun 1994 in New York City.
    ii. **Sasha Regina Hulkower** was born on 16 Aug 1996 in New York City.
20. **Daniel Hulkower**-6 ((Hana Ruth Eisnerová) Joan Ruth-5, (Karel Eisner) Charles E.-4, (Jindřich) Henry-3, Anna-2, Loebl-1) was born on 22 Dec 1961 in Queens, NY.
    Lynda J. Greenberg was born on 26 Dec 1954 in New York City, NY.
    Daniel Hulkower and Lynda J. Greenberg were married on 19 Nov 1989. They had the following children:
    i. **Anna Marta Hulkower** was born on 12 Sep 1990 in York, PA.
    ii. **Isabel Sophia Hulkower** was born on 27 May 1994 in York, PA.
21. **Wayne Peter Gordon**-6 (Doris Věra-5, (Karel Eisner) Charles E.-4, (Jindřich) Henry-3, Anna-2, Loebl-1) was born on 02 May 1957 in Queens, NY.
    Claire Lin Ward was born on 07 Oct 1964 in NC.
    Wayne Peter Gordon and Claire Lin Ward were married on 01 Sep 1991 in NC. They had the following children:
    i. **Dominick Lin Gordon** was born on 31 May 1993 in Los Angeles, CA.
    ii. **Anthony John Gordon** was born on 08 Feb 1995 in Los Angeles, CA.
    Susan Reifer was born on 05 Apr 1962 in CA.
    Wayne Peter Gordon and Susan Reifer were married on 10 Oct 2002 in Hawaii. They had the following children:
    i. **Nicholas Gordon** was born about 2006.
22. **Melissa Rose Gordon**-6 (Doris Věra-5, (Karel Eisner) Charles E.-4,

(Jindřich) Henry-3, Anna-2, Loebl-1) was born on 18 Feb 1960 in Queens, NY.

Jeffrey Clark was born on 23 Feb 1953 in Los Angeles, CA.

Jeffrey Clark and Melissa Rose Gordon were married on 03 Mar 1984. They had the following children:

    47. **Brandon Andrew Clark** was born on 01 Nov 1989 in Los Angeles, CA.

    48. **Madison Ross Clark** was born on 01 Jun 1994 in Los Angeles, CA.

    49. **Kaitlin Elizabeth Clark** was born on 27 Jan 1999 in Los Angeles, CA.

23. **Dean Mark Gordon**-6 (Doris Věra-5, (Karel Eisner) Charles E.-4, (Jindřich) Henry-3, Anna-2, Loebl-1) was born on 18 Jun 1963 in Long Island, NY.

Angela Müller was born on 09 Nov 1964 in Los Angeles, CA.

Dean Mark Gordon and Angela Müller were married on 29 Feb 1992. They had the following children:

    i. **Sam Walter Gordon** was born on 02 Sep 1994 in New York City.

    ii. **Joseph Charles Gordon** was born on 26 Aug 1996 in Los Angeles, CA.

    iii. **Greta Kelly Gordon** was born on 15 Oct 1998 in Chicago, IL.

24. **Stephen Mark Eisner**-6 (Thomas Michael-5, Robert-4, (Jindřich) Henry-3, Anna-2, Loebl-1) was born on 29 Nov 1958 in Chuquicamata, Chile, SA.

Staci Suzanne Johnson.

Stephen Mark Eisner and Staci Suzanne Johnson were married on 14 Jun 1986 in Ft. Worth, TX. They had the following children:

    i. **Kathryn Bliss Eisner** was born on 19 Oct 1988 in Ft. Worth, TX.

    ii. **Patrick Thomas Eisner** was born on 23 Apr 1994 in Ft. Worth, TX.

25. **Andrea Savilla Eisner**-6 (Thomas Michael-5, Robert-4, (Jindřich) Henry-3, Anna-2, Loebl-1) was born on 23 Nov 1959 in Sewell, Chile, SA.

Todd Allen Barnett.

Todd Allen Barnett and Andrea Savilla Eisner were married on 27 Jun

1993 in Carmel, CA. They had the following children:
   i. **Benjamin Michael Barnett** was born on 30 Apr 1997 in Bellevue, WA.
   ii. **Daniel Barnett**.

Generation 7

26. **Erin Marie Steiner**-7 (David Henry-6, Helen Edwards-5, Paul J. Edwards-4, (Jindřich) Henry-3, Anna-2, Loebl-1) was born on 01 Aug 1981 in Chicago, IL.
    Michael John Malick was born on 01 Aug 1981 in Chicago, IL.
    Michael John Malick and Erin Marie Steiner were married on 27 Jul 2013 in Poulsbo, WA. They had the following children:
    i. **Henry Francsz Malick** was born on 18 Feb 2018 in Seattle, WA.

27. **Kevin Thomas Rechcigl**-7 (John Edward-6, Eva Edwards-5, Paul J. Edwards-4, (Jindřich) Henry-3, Anna-2, Loebl-1) was born on 09 Oct 1991 in Bradenton, FL.
    Jordan Robbins daughter of Douglass Robbins and Ivonne was born on 10 Jan 1992 in Camarillo, CA.
    Kevin Thomas Rechcigl and Jordan Robbins were married on 12 May 2018 in Jacksonville, FL. They had the following children:
    i. **James Douglas Rechcigl** was born on 05 Jan 2021 in Jacksonville, FL.
    ii. **Evelyn Marie Rechcigl** was born 29 May 2023 in Jacksonville, FL.

Auer Family

Generation 1

1. **Bernhard Auer**-1 was born in Serava, Bohemia.

   Therese Lieberman daughter of Lieberman and Unknown was born in Bohemia. Bernhard Auer and Therese Lieberman married. They had the following children:

   2. i. **Moritz Auer** was born in 1841 in Prague, Bohemia (or Serava?). He died in 1915.

   ii. **son Auer** was born before 1841 in Bohemia. He died in emigrated to US in 1859.

Generation 2

2. **Moritz Auer**-2 (Bernhard-1) was born in 1841 in Prague, Bohemia (or Serava?). He died in 1915.

   Julie Wiener daughter of Jacob Wiener and Marie Hoffmannová was born in 1841 in Prague (probably). She died in 1915.

   Moritz Auer and Julie Wiener married. They had the following children:

   3. i. **Hortense Auer** was born in 1869 in Prague, Jakubska 1. She married (Jindřich) Henry Eisner in 1888. She died on 13 Oct 1951 in New York, NY.

   ii. **Eugenia Auer**.

   iii. **Thecla Auer** was born about 1876. She died about Aug 1894 in Drowned.

   iv. **Alice Auer** was born about 1878. She died about 1894 in Drowned.

Generation 3

3. **Hortense Auer**-3 (Moritz-2, Bernhard-1) was born in 1869 in Prague, Jakubska 1. She died on 13 Oct 1951 in New York, NY.

   (Jindřich) Henry Eisner son of Karl Eisner and Anna Krausová was born on 12 Mar 1853 in Kaliste u Nemeckeho Brodu, Bohemia. He died on 13 Dec 1956 in New York, NY.

   (Jindřich) Henry Eisner and Hortense Auer were married in 1888. They had the following children:

4. i. **Paul J. Edwards (Pavel Eisner)** was born on 29 Jun 1892 in Prague, Klimentska 1. He married Jiřina Taussigová on 05 Jun 1926 in Prague. He died on 27 Jun 1964 in Schenectady, NY.
5. ii. **(Karel Eisner) Charles E. Edwards** was born on 26 Apr 1894 in Prague, Bohemia. He married Marta Hanakova on 19 May 1927. He died on 27 Oct 1986.
6. iii. **Robert Eisner** was born on 11 Jul 1898 in Prague, Bohemia. He married Mitzi Kratzig in 1926 in Praha, CSR. He died on 31 Oct 1984 in New York, NY.

Generation 4

4. **Paul J. Edwards (Pavel Eisner)**-4 (Hortense-3, Moritz-2, Bernhard-1) was born on 29 Jun 1892 in Prague, Klimentska 1. He died on 27 Jun 1964 in Schenectady, NY.

Jiřina Taussigová daughter of Oskar Taussig and Klára Munková was born on 24 Apr 1906 in Prague - Kralovske Vinohrady, Nerudova l. She died on 06 Nov 1962 in New York, NY.

Paul J. Edwards (Pavel Eisner) and Jiřina Taussigová were married on 05 Jun 1926 in Prague. They had the following children:

7. i. **Helen Edwards (Eisnerova)** was born on 29 Apr 1927 in Prague, CSR. She married Frank Steiner on 16 Sep 1948 in New York, NY.
8. ii. **Eva Edwards (Eisnerová)** was born on 21 Jan 1932 in Prague, CSR. She married Mila (Miloslav) Rechcigl Jr. on 29 Aug 1953 in New York, NY.

5. **(Karel Eisner) Charles E. Edwards**-4 (Hortense-3, Moritz-2, Bernhard-1) was born on 26 Apr 1894 in Prague, Bohemia. He died on 27 Oct 1986.

Marta Hanakova daughter of Sigmund Hanák and Klára Loewy was born on 01 May 1905 in Zatec. She died on 25 Nov 1985.

(Karel Eisner) Charles E. Edwards and Marta Hanakova were married on 19 May 1927. They had the following children:

9. i. **(Hana Ruth Eisnerová) Joan Ruth Edwards** was born on 14 Jun 1930 in Prague. She married Bernie Hulkower on 20 Nov 1955. She died on 21 Apr 2021.

10. ii. **Doris Věra Edwards** was born on 09 Apr 1932 in Prague, Bohemia. She married John ("Jack") Rodney Gordon on 09 May 1954.
6. **Robert Eisner**-4 (Hortense-3, Moritz-2, Bernhard-1) was born on 11 Jul 1898 in Prague, Bohemia. He died on 31 Oct 1984 in New York, NY.
Mitzi Kratzig was born on 12 Oct 1900 in Liberec, CSR. She died in 1991 in New York, NY.
Robert Eisner and Mitzi Kratzig were married in 1926 in Praha, CSR. They had the following children:
11. i. **Thomas Michael Eisner** was born on 10 Mar 1931 in Prague, CSR. He married Savilla Gamble on 21 Dec 1957 in Vancouver, WA. He died on 13 Feb 1992 in Santa Fe, NM.
12. ii. **Stephen Alexander Eisner** was born on 28 Jul 1932 in Prague, CSR. He married Arlene Zohn on 28 Sep 1972.

Generation 5

7. **Helen Edwards (Eisnerova)**-5 (Paul J. Edwards-4, Hortense-3, Moritz-2, Bernhard-1) was born on 29 Apr 1927 in Prague, CSR.
Frank Steiner son of Johann (Hans) Steiner and Růžena Steinbachova was born on 23 Apr 1922 in Prague, Bohemia. He died on 14 Sep 2000 in Scotia, NY.
Frank Steiner and Helen Edwards (Eisnerova) were married on 16 Sep 1948 in New York, NY. They had the following children:
13. i. **Linda Claire Steiner** was born on 01 Mar 1950 in Schenectady, NY. She married Edward Salomon on 05 Jun 1977 in Scotia, NY.
14. ii. **David Henry Steiner** was born on 13 Mar 1952 in Schenectady, NY. He married Carol Ann Mastaliz on 07 Jul 1979 in So. Deerfield, MA.
58. **Eva Edwards (Eisnerová)**-5 (Paul J. Edwards-4, Hortense-3, Moritz-2, Bernhard-1) was born on 21 Jan 1932 in Prague, CSR.
Mila (Miloslav) Rechcigl Jr. son of Miloslav Rechcigl and Marie Rajtrová was born on 30 Jul 1930 in Mladá Boleslav, CSR.
Mila (Miloslav) Rechcigl Jr. and Eva Edwards (Eisnerová) were married on 29 Aug 1953 in New York, NY. They had the following children:
ii. i. **John Edward Rechcigl** was born on 27 Feb 1960 in Washington, D.C.. He married Nancy Ann Palko on 30 Jul 1983 in Dover, NJ.

iii. ii. **Karen Rechcigl** was born on 16 Apr 1962 in Washington, DC. She married Ulysses Kollecas on 25 Aug 1990 in Bethesda, MD.

59. **(Hana Ruth Eisnerová) Joan Ruth Edwards**-5 ((Karel Eisner) Charles E.-4, Hortense-3, Moritz-2, Bernhard-1) was born on 14 Jun 1930 in Prague. She died on 21 Apr 2021.

    Bernie Hulkower was born on 23 Jul 1928 in New York City.

    Bernie Hulkower and (Hana Ruth Eisnerová) Joan Ruth Edwards were married on 20 Nov 1955. They had the following children:

    17. i. **Seth Hulkower** was born on 14 Mar 1958 in Queens, NY. He married Lissa Perlman on 16 Jun 1991.
    18. ii. **Daniel Hulkower** was born on 22 Dec 1961 in Queens, NY. He married Lynda J. Greenberg on 19 Nov 1989.

9 **Doris Věra Edwards**-5 ((Karel Eisner) Charles E.-4, Hortense-3, Moritz-2, Bernhard-1) was born on 9 Apr 1932 in Prague, Bohemia.

    John ("Jack") Rodney Gordon was born on 13 Mar 1929 in Brooklyn, NY. John ("Jack") Rodney Gordon and Doris Věra Edwards were married on 09 May 1954. They had the following children:

    19. i. **Wayne Peter Gordon** was born on 02 May 1957 in Queens, NY. He married Claire Lin Ward on 01 Sep 1991 in NC.
    20. ii. **Melissa Rose Gordon** was born on 18 Feb 1960 in Queens, NY. She married Jeffrey Clark on 03 Mar 1984.
    21. iii. **Dean Mark Gordon** was born on 18 Jun 1963 in Long Island, NY. He married Angela Müller on 29 Feb 1992.

11. **Thomas Michael Eisner**-5 (Robert-4, Hortense-3, Moritz-2, Bernhard-1) was born on 10 Mar 1931 in Prague, CSR. He died on 13 Feb 1992 in Santa Fe, NM.

    Savilla Gamble was born on 26 Oct 1937 in Ft. George Mead, MD.

    Thomas Michael Eisner and Savilla Gamble were married on 21 Dec 1957 in Vancouver, WA. They had the following children:

    22. i. **Stephen Mark Eisner** was born on 29 Nov 1958 in Chuquicamata, Chile, SA. He married Staci Suzanne Johnson on 14 Jun 1986 in Ft. Worth, TX.
    23. ii. **Andrea Savilla Eisner** was born on 23 Nov 1959 in Sewell, Chile,

SA. She married Todd Allen Barnett on 27 Jun 1993 in Carmel, CA.

iii. **Phillip Robert Eisner** was born on 23 Aug 1965 in Ft. Worth, TX.

Kim Davey was born in 1949.

Thomas Michael Eisner and Kim Davey were married on 04 Jan 1990. They had no children.

12. **Stephen Alexander Eisner**-5 (Robert-4, Hortense-3, Moritz-2, Bernhard-1) was born on 28 Jul 1932 in Prague, CSR.

Arlene Zohn was born on 30 Oct 1940 in New York, NY. She died 15 Apr 2013.

Stephen Alexander Eisner and Arlene Zohn were married on 28 Sep 1972. They had the following children:

   i. **Andrew Calvin Eisner** was born on 16 Jul 1974 in New York, NY. He married Stacy Lynn Hischberg on 10 Sep 2005 in Mamaroneck, NY.

   ii. **Douglas Randall Eisner** was born on 21 Jul 1978 in New York, NY.

Generation 6

1 **Linda Claire Steiner**-6 (Helen Edwards-5, Paul J. Edwards-4, Hortense-3, Moritz-2, Bernhard-1) was born on 01 Mar 1950 in Schenectady, NY.

Edward Salomon son of Jerome Salomon and Rachel Finchel was born on 12 Feb 1951 in Jersey city, NJ.

Edward Salomon and Linda Claire Steiner were married on 05 Jun 1977 in Scotia, NY. They had the following children:

   1 **Sarah Beth Salomon** was born on 28 Jan 1980 in Chicago, IL.

   2 **Paul Nathan Salomon** was born on 02 Jan 1983 in Chicago, IL.

2 **David Henry Steiner**-6 (Helen Edwards-5, Paul J. Edwards-4, Hortense-3, Moritz-2, Bernhard-1) was born on 13 Mar 1952 in Schenectady, NY.

Carol Ann Mastaliz daughter of Frank Peter Mastaliz and Helen Carline Macko was born on 26 Oct 1952 (Greenfield, MA).

David Henry Steiner and Carol Ann Mastaliz were married on 07 Jul 1979 in So. Deerfield, MA. They had the following children:

24. i. **Erin Marie Steiner** was born on 01 Aug 1981 in Chicago, IL. She married Michael John Malick on 27 Jul 2013 in Poulsbo, WA.

ii. **Jonathan Robert Steiner** was born on 30 Dec 1984 in Concord, MA.

15. **John Edward Rechcigl**-6 (Eva Edwards-5, Paul J. Edwards-4, Hortense-3, Moritz-2, Bernhard-1) was born on 27 Feb 1960 in Washington, D.C..
Nancy Ann Palko daughter of Joseph Palko and Mary Rishko was born on 26 Sep 1961 in Morristown, NJ.
John Edward Rechcigl and Nancy Ann Palko were married on 30 Jul 1983 in Dover, NJ. They had the following children:
    i. **Gregory John Rechcigl** was born on 19 Dec 1988 in Bradenton, FL.
26. ii. **Kevin Thomas Rechcigl** was born on 09 Oct 1991 in Bradenton, FL. He married Jordan Robbins on 12 May 2018 in Jacksonville, FL.
    iii. **Lindsey Nicole Rechcigl** was born on 03 Nov 1994 in Bradenton, FL.

16. **Karen Rechcigl**-6 (Eva Edwards-5, Paul J. Edwards-4, Hortense-3, Moritz-2, Bernhard-1) was born on 16 Apr 1962 in Washington, DC.
Ulysses Kollecas son of Christopher Thomas (Kolecas) Collier and Amelia Malatras was born on 20 Mar 1958 in Washington, DC.
Ulysses Kollecas and Karen Rechcigl were married on 25 Aug 1990 in Bethesda, MD. They had the following children:
    i. **Kristin Kollecas** was born on 04 May 1993 in Albuquerque, NM.
    ii. **Paul Kollecas** was born on 02 Jun 1995 in Albuquerque, NM.

17. **Seth Hulkower**-6 ((Hana Ruth Eisnerová) Joan Ruth-5, (Karel Eisner) Charles E.-4, Hortense-3, Moritz-2, Bernhard-1) was born on 14 Mar 1958 in Queens, NY.
Lissa Perlman was born on 24 Dec 1955 in New Haven, CT.
Seth Hulkower and Lissa Perlman were married on 16 Jun 1991. They had the following children:
    i. **Talia Minna Hulkower** was born on 20 Jun 1994 in New York City.
    ii. **Sasha Regina Hulkower** was born on 16 Aug 1996 in New York City.

18. **Daniel Hulkower**-6 ((Hana Ruth Eisnerová) Joan Ruth-5, (Karel Eisner)

Charles E.-4, Hortense-3, Moritz-2, Bernhard-1) was born on 22 Dec 1961 in Queens, NY.

Lynda J. Greenberg was born on 26 Dec 1954 in New York City, NY.

Daniel Hulkower and Lynda J. Greenberg were married on 19 Nov 1989. They had the following children:
  i. **Anna Marta Hulkower** was born on 12 Sep 1990 in York, PA.
  ii. **Isabel Sophia Hulkower** was born on 27 May 1994 in York, PA.

19. **Wayne Peter Gordon**-6 (Doris Věra-5, (Karel Eisner) Charles E.-4, Hortense-3, Moritz-2, Bernhard-1) was born on 02 May 1957 in Queens, NY.

Claire Lin Ward was born on 07 Oct 1964 in NC.

Wayne Peter Gordon and Claire Lin Ward were married on 01 Sep 1991 in NC. They had the following children:
  i. **Dominick Lin Gordon** was born on 31 May 1993 in Los Angeles, CA.
  ii. **Anthony John Gordon** was born on 08 Feb 1995 in Los Angeles, CA.

Susan Reifer was born on 05 Apr 1962 in CA.

Wayne Peter Gordon and Susan Reifer were married on 10 Oct 2002 in Hawaii. They had the following children:
  i. **Nicholas Gordon** was born about 2006.

20. **Melissa Rose Gordon**-6 (Doris Věra-5, (Karel Eisner) Charles E.-4, Hortense-3, Moritz-2, Bernhard-1) was born on 18 Feb 1960 in Queens, NY.

Jeffrey Clark was born on 23 Feb 1953 in Los Angeles, CA.

Jeffrey Clark and Melissa Rose Gordon were married on 03 Mar 1984. They had the following children:
  i. **Brandon Andrew Clark** was born on 01 Nov 1989 in Los Angeles, CA.
  ii. **Madison Ross Clark** was born on 01 Jun 1994 in Los Angeles, CA.
  iii. **Kaitlin Elizabeth Clark** was born on 27 Jan 1999 in Los Angeles, CA.

21. **Dean Mark Gordon**-6 (Doris Věra-5, (Karel Eisner) Charles E.-4, Hortense-3, Moritz-2, Bernhard-1) was born on 18 Jun 1963 in Long

Island, NY.

Angela Müller was born on 09 Nov 1964 in Los Angeles, CA.

Dean Mark Gordon and Angela Müller were married on 29 Feb 1992. They had the following children:

    i. **Sam Walter Gordon** was born on 02 Sep 1994 in New York City.

    ii. **Joseph Charles Gordon** was born on 26 Aug 1996 in Los Angeles, CA.

    iii. **Greta Kelly Gordon** was born on 15 Oct 1998 in Chicago, IL.

22. **Stephen Mark Eisner**-6 (Thomas Michael-5, Robert-4, Hortense-3, Moritz-2, Bernhard-1) was born on 29 Nov 1958 in Chuquicamata, Chile, SA.

Staci Suzanne Johnson.

Stephen Mark Eisner and Staci Suzanne Johnson were married on 14 Jun 1986 in Ft. Worth, TX. They had the following children:

    i. **Kathryn Bliss Eisner** was born on 19 Oct 1988 in Ft. Worth, TX.

    ii. **Patrick Thomas Eisner** was born on 23 Apr 1994 in Ft. Worth, TX.

23. **Andrea Savilla Eisner**-6 (Thomas Michael-5, Robert-4, Hortense-3, Moritz-2, Bernhard-1) was born on 23 Nov 1959 in Sewell, Chile, SA.

Todd Allen Barnett.

Todd Allen Barnett and Andrea Savilla Eisner were married on 27 Jun 1993 in Carmel, CA. They had the following children:

    i. **Benjamin Michael Barnett** was born on 30 Apr 1997 in Bellevue, WA.

    ii. **Daniel Barnett**.

Generation 7

24. **Erin Marie Steiner**-7 (David Henry-6, Helen Edwards-5, Paul J. Edwards-4, Hortense-3, Moritz-2, Bernhard-1) was born on 01 Aug 1981 in Chicago, IL.

Michael John Malick was born on 01 Aug 1981 in Chicago, IL.

Michael John Malick and Erin Marie Steiner were married on 27 Jul 2013 in Poulsbo, WA. They had the following children:

    i. **Henry Francsz Malick** was born on 18 Feb 2018 in Seattle, WA.

25. **Kevin Thomas Rechcigl**-7 (John Edward-6, Eva Edwards-5, Paul J. Edwards-4, Hortense-3, Moritz-2, Bernhard-1) was born on 09 Oct 1991 in Bradenton, FL.

    Jordan Robbins daughter of Douglass Robbins and Ivonne was born on 10 Jan 1992 in Camarillo, CA.

    Kevin Thomas Rechcigl and Jordan Robbins were married on 12 May 2018 in Jacksonville, FL. They had the following children:

    i. **James Douglas Rechcigl** was born on 05 Jan 2021 in Jacksonville, FL.

    ii. **Evelyn Marie Rechcigl** was born 29 May 2023 in Jacksonville, FL.

Wiener Family

Generation 1

1   **Jacob Wiener**-1 was born in 1811.

Marie Hoffmannová daughter of Hoffman and Unknown was born in 1814. Jacob Wiener and Marie Hoffmannová married. They had the following children:

1. i. **Julie Wiener** was born in 1841 in Prague (probably). She died in 1915.
   ii. **Leopold Wiener** was born in Prague (probably).

Generation 2

2   **Julie Wiener**-2 (Jacob-1) was born in 1841 in Prague (probably). She died in 1915.

Moritz Auer son of Bernhard Auer and Therese Lieberman was born in 1841 in Prague, Bohemia (or Serava?). He died in 1915.

Moritz Auer and Julie Wiener married. They had the following children:

3. i. **Hortense Auer** was born in 1869 in Prague, Jakubska 1. She married (Jindřich) Henry Eisner in 1888. She died on 13 Oct 1951 in New York, NY.
   ii. **Eugenia Auer**.
   iii. **Thecla Auer** was born about 1876. She died about Aug 1894 in Drowned.
   iv. **Alice Auer** was born about 1878. She died about 1894 in Drowned.

Generation 3

3. **Hortense Auer**-3 (Julie-2, Jacob-1) was born in 1869 in Prague, Jakubska 1. She died on 13 Oct 1951 in New York, NY.

(Jindřich) Henry Eisner son of Karl Eisner and Anna Krausová was born on 12 Mar 1853 in Kaliste u Nemeckeho Brodu, Bohemia. He died on 13 Dec 1956 in New York, NY.

(Jindřich) Henry Eisner and Hortense Auer were married in 1888. They had the following children:

4. i. **Paul J. Edwards (Pavel Eisner)** was born on 29 Jun 1892 in

Prague, Klimentska 1. He married Jiřina Taussigová on 05 Jun 1926 in Prague. He died on 27 Jun 1964 in Schenectady, NY.
5. ii. **(Karel Eisner) Charles E. Edwards** was born on 26 Apr 1894 in Prague, Bohemia. He married Marta Hanakova on 19 May 1927. He died on 27 Oct 1986.
6. iii. **Robert Eisner** was born on 11 Jul 1898 in Prague, Bohemia. He married Mitzi Kratzig in 1926 in Praha, CSR. He died on 31 Oct 1984 in New York, NY.

Generation 4

Paul J. Edwards (Pavel Eisner)-4 (Hortense-3, Julie-2, Jacob-1) was born on 29 Jun 1892 in Prague, Klimentska 1. He died on 27 Jun 1964 in Schenectady, NY.

Jiřina Taussigová daughter of Oskar Taussig and Klára Munková was born on 24 Apr 1906 in Prague - Kralovske Vinohrady, Nerudova l. She died on 06 Nov 1962 in New York, NY.

Paul J. Edwards (Pavel Eisner) and Jiřina Taussigová were married on 05 Jun 1926 in Prague. They had the following children:

7. i. **Helen Edwards (Eisnerova)** was born on 29 Apr 1927 in Prague, CSR. She married Frank Steiner on 16 Sep 1948 in New York, NY.
8. ii. **Eva Edwards (Eisnerová)** was born on 21 Jan 1932 in Prague, CSR. She married Mila (Miloslav) Rechcigl Jr. on 29 Aug 1953 in New York, NY.

5. **(Karel Eisner) Charles E. Edwards**-4 (Hortense-3, Julie-2, Jacob-1) was born on 26 Apr 1894 in Prague, Bohemia. He died on 27 Oct 1986.

Marta Hanakova daughter of Sigmund Hanák and Klára Loewy was born on 01 May 1905 in Zatec. She died on 25 Nov 1985.

(Karel Eisner) Charles E. Edwards and Marta Hanakova were married on 19 May 1927. They had the following children:

9. i. **(Hana Ruth Eisnerová) Joan Ruth Edwards** was born on 14 Jun 1930 in Prague. She married Bernie Hulkower on 20 Nov 1955. She died on 21 Apr 2021.
10. ii. **Doris Věra Edwards** was born on 09 Apr 1932 in Prague, Bohemia. She married John ("Jack") Rodney Gordon on 09 May 1954.

6. **Robert Eisner**-4 (Hortense-3, Julie-2, Jacob-1) was born on 11 Jul 1898 in Prague, Bohemia. He died on 31 Oct 1984 in New York, NY.

   Mitzi Kratzig was born on 12 Oct 1900 in Liberec, CSR. She died in 1991 in New York, NY.

   Robert Eisner and Mitzi Kratzig were married in 1926 in Praha, CSR. They had the following children:

   11. i. **Thomas Michael Eisner** was born on 10 Mar 1931 in Prague, CSR. He married Savilla Gamble on 21 Dec 1957 in Vancouver, WA. He died on 13 Feb 1992 in Santa Fe, NM.
   12. ii. **Stephen Alexander Eisner** was born on 28 Jul 1932 in Prague, CSR. He married Arlene Zohn on 28 Sep 1972.

Generation 5

7. **Helen Edwards (Eisnerova)**-5 (Paul J. Edwards-4, Hortense-3, Julie-2, Jacob-1) was born on 29 Apr 1927 in Prague, CSR.

   Frank Steiner son of Johann (Hans) Steiner and Růžena Steinbachova was born on 23 Apr 1922 in Prague, Bohemia. He died on 14 Sep 2000 in Scotia, NY.

   Frank Steiner and Helen Edwards (Eisnerova) were married on 16 Sep 1948 in New York, NY. They had the following children:

   13. i. **Linda Claire Steiner** was born on 01 Mar 1950 in Schenectady, NY. She married Edward Salomon on 05 Jun 1977 in Scotia, NY.
   14. ii. **David Henry Steiner** was born on 13 Mar 1952 in Schenectady, NY. He married Carol Ann Mastaliz on 07 Jul 1979 in So. Deerfield, MA.

8. **Eva Edwards (Eisnerová)**-5 (Paul J. Edwards-4, Hortense-3, Julie-2, Jacob-1) was born on 21 Jan 1932 in Prague, CSR.

   Mila (Miloslav) Rechcigl Jr. son of Miloslav Rechcigl and Marie Rajtrová was born on 30 Jul 1930 in Mladá Boleslav, CSR.

   Mila (Miloslav) Rechcigl Jr. and Eva Edwards (Eisnerová) were married on 29 Aug 1953 in New York, NY. They had the following children:

   15. i. **John Edward Rechcigl** was born on 27 Feb 1960 in Washington, D.C.. He married Nancy Ann Palko on 30 Jul 1983 in Dover, NJ.
   16. ii. **Karen Rechcigl** was born on 16 Apr 1962 in Washington, DC. She married Ulysses Kollecas on 25 Aug 1990 in Bethesda, MD.

9. **(Hana Ruth Eisnerová) Joan Ruth Edwards**-5 ((Karel Eisner) Charles E.-4, Hortense-3, Julie-2, Jacob-1) was born on 14 Jun 1930 in Prague. She died on 21 Apr 2021.

    Bernie Hulkower was born on 23 Jul 1928 in New York City.

    Bernie Hulkower and (Hana Ruth Eisnerová) Joan Ruth Edwards were married on 20 Nov 1955. They had the following children:

    17. i. **Seth Hulkower** was born on 14 Mar 1958 in Queens, NY. He married Lissa Perlman on 16 Jun 1991.
    18. ii. **Daniel Hulkower** was born on 22 Dec 1961 in Queens, NY. He married Lynda J. Greenberg on 19 Nov 1989.

10. **Doris Věra Edwards**-5 ((Karel Eisner) Charles E.-4, Hortense-3, Julie-2, Jacob-1) was born on 09 Apr 1932 in Prague, Bohemia.

    John ("Jack") Rodney Gordon was born on 13 Mar 1929 in Brooklyn, NY. John ("Jack") Rodney Gordon and Doris Věra Edwards were married on 09 May 1954. They had the following children:

    19. i. **Wayne Peter Gordon** was born on 02 May 1957 in Queens, NY. He married Claire Lin Ward on 01 Sep 1991 in NC.
    20. ii. **Melissa Rose Gordon** was born on 18 Feb 1960 in Queens, NY. She married Jeffrey Clark on 03 Mar 1984.
    21. iii. **Dean Mark Gordon** was born on 18 Jun 1963 in Long Island, NY. He married Angela Müller on 29 Feb 1992.

11. **Thomas Michael Eisner**-5 (Robert-4, Hortense-3, Julie-2, Jacob-1) was born on 10 Mar 1931 in Prague, CSR. He died on 13 Feb 1992 in Santa Fe, NM.

    Savilla Gamble was born on 26 Oct 1937 in Ft. George Mead, MD.

    Thomas Michael Eisner and Savilla Gamble were married on 21 Dec 1957 in Vancouver, WA. They had the following children:

    22. i. **Stephen Mark Eisner** was born on 29 Nov 1958 in Chuquicamata, Chile, SA. He married Staci Suzanne Johnson on 14 Jun 1986 in Ft. Worth, TX.
    23. ii. **Andrea Savilla Eisner** was born on 23 Nov 1959 in Sewell, Chile, SA. She married Todd Allen Barnett on 27 Jun 1993 in Carmel, CA.
    iii. **Phillip Robert Eisner** was born on 23 Aug 1965 in Ft. Worth,

TX.

Kim Davey was born in 1949.

Thomas Michael Eisner and Kim Davey were married on 04 Jan 1990. They had no children.

12. **Stephen Alexander Eisner**-5 (Robert-4, Hortense-3, Julie-2, Jacob-1) was born on 28 Jul 1932 in Prague, CSR.

    Arlene Zohn was born on 30 Oct 1940 in New York, NY. She died 15 Apr 2013.

    Stephen Alexander Eisner and Arlene Zohn were married on 28 Sep 1972. They had the following children:

    i. **Andrew Calvin Eisner** was born on 16 Jul 1974 in New York, NY. He married Stacy Lynn Hischberg on 10 Sep 2005 in Mamaroneck, NY.

    ii. **Douglas Randall Eisner** was born on 21 Jul 1978 in New York, NY.

Generation 6

13. **Linda Claire Steiner**-6 (Helen Edwards-5, Paul J. Edwards-4, Hortense-3, Julie-2, Jacob-1) was born on 01 Mar 1950 in Schenectady, NY.

    Edward Salomon son of Jerome Salomon and Rachel Finchel was born on 12 Feb 1951 in Jersey city, NJ.

    Edward Salomon and Linda Claire Steiner were married on 05 Jun 1977 in Scotia, NY. They had the following children:

    i. **Sarah Beth Salomon** was born on 28 Jan 1980 in Chicago, IL.

    ii. **Paul Nathan Salomon** was born on 02 Jan 1983 in Chicago, IL.

14. **David Henry Steiner**-6 (Helen Edwards-5, Paul J. Edwards-4, Hortense-3, Julie-2, Jacob-1) was born on 13 Mar 1952 in Schenectady, NY.

    Carol Ann Mastaliz daughter of Frank Peter Mastaliz and Helen Carline Macko was born on 26 Oct 1952 (Greenfield, MA).

    David Henry Steiner and Carol Ann Mastaliz were married on 07 Jul 1979 in So. Deerfield, MA. They had the following children:

    24. i. **Erin Marie Steiner** was born on 01 Aug 1981 in Chicago, IL. She married Michael John Malick on 27 Jul 2013 in Poulsbo, WA.

        ii. **Jonathan Robert Steiner** was born on 30 Dec 1984 in Concord,

MA.

15. **John Edward Rechcigl**-6 (Eva Edwards-5, Paul J. Edwards-4, Hortense-3, Julie-2, Jacob-1) was born on 27 Feb 1960 in Washington, D.C..

    Nancy Ann Palko daughter of Joseph Palko and Mary Rishko was born on 26 Sep 1961 in Morristown, NJ.

    John Edward Rechcigl and Nancy Ann Palko were married on 30 Jul 1983 in Dover, NJ. They had the following children:

    i. **Gregory John Rechcigl** was born on 19 Dec 1988 in Bradenton, FL.

    26. ii. **Kevin Thomas Rechcigl** was born on 09 Oct 1991 in Bradenton, FL. He married Jordan Robbins on 12 May 2018 in Jacksonville, FL.

    iii. **Lindsey Nicole Rechcigl** was born on 03 Nov 1994 in Bradenton, FL.

16. **Karen Rechcigl**-6 (Eva Edwards-5, Paul J. Edwards-4, Hortense-3, Julie-2, Jacob-1) was born on 16 Apr 1962 in Washington, DC.

    Ulysses Kollecas son of Christopher Thomas (Kolecas) Collier and Amelia Malatras was born on 20 Mar 1958 in Washington, DC.

    Ulysses Kollecas and Karen Rechcigl were married on 25 Aug 1990 in Bethesda, MD. They had the following children:

    i. **Kristin Kollecas** was born on 04 May 1993 in Albuquerque, NM.

    ii. **Paul Kollecas** was born on 02 Jun 1995 in Albuquerque, NM.

17. **Seth Hulkower**-6 ((Hana Ruth Eisnerová) Joan Ruth-5, (Karel Eisner) Charles E.-4, Hortense-3, Julie-2, Jacob-1) was born on 14 Mar 1958 in Queens, NY.

    Lissa Perlman was born on 24 Dec 1955 in New Haven, CT.

    Seth Hulkower and Lissa Perlman were married on 16 Jun 1991. They had the following children:

    i. **Talia Minna Hulkower** was born on 20 Jun 1994 in New York City.

    ii. **Sasha Regina Hulkower** was born on 16 Aug 1996 in New York City.

18. **Daniel Hulkower**-6 ((Hana Ruth Eisnerová) Joan Ruth-5, (Karel Eisner) Charles E.-4, Hortense-3, Julie-2, Jacob-1) was born on 22 Dec 1961 in

Queens, NY.

Lynda J. Greenberg was born on 26 Dec 1954 in New York City, NY.

Daniel Hulkower and Lynda J. Greenberg were married on 19 Nov 1989. They had the following children:

    i. **Anna Marta Hulkower** was born on 12 Sep 1990 in York, PA.

    ii. **Isabel Sophia Hulkower** was born on 27 May 1994 in York, PA.

19. **Wayne Peter Gordon**-6 (Doris Věra-5, (Karel Eisner) Charles E.-4, Hortense-3, Julie-2, Jacob-1) was born on 02 May 1957 in Queens, NY.

Claire Lin Ward was born on 07 Oct 1964 in NC.

Wayne Peter Gordon and Claire Lin Ward were married on 01 Sep 1991 in NC. They had the following children:

    i. **Dominick Lin Gordon** was born on 31 May 1993 in Los Angeles, CA.

    ii. **Anthony John Gordon** was born on 08 Feb 1995 in Los Angeles, CA.

Susan Reifer was born on 05 Apr 1962 in CA.

Wayne Peter Gordon and Susan Reifer were married on 10 Oct 2002 in Hawaii. They had the following children:

    i. **Nicholas Gordon** was born about 2006.

20. **Melissa Rose Gordon**-6 (Doris Věra-5, (Karel Eisner) Charles E.-4, Hortense-3, Julie-2, Jacob-1) was born on 18 Feb 1960 in Queens, NY.

Jeffrey Clark was born on 23 Feb 1953 in Los Angeles, CA.

Jeffrey Clark and Melissa Rose Gordon were married on 03 Mar 1984. They had the following children:

    i. **Brandon Andrew Clark** was born on 01 Nov 1989 in Los Angeles, CA.

    ii. **Madison Ross Clark** was born on 01 Jun 1994 in Los Angeles, CA.

    iii. **Kaitlin Elizabeth Clark** was born on 27 Jan 1999 in Los Angeles, CA.

21. **Dean Mark Gordon**-6 (Doris Věra-5, (Karel Eisner) Charles E.-4, Hortense-3, Julie-2, Jacob-1) was born on 18 Jun 1963 in Long Island, NY.

Angela Müller was born on 09 Nov 1964 in Los Angeles, CA.

Dean Mark Gordon and Angela Müller were married on 29 Feb 1992.

They had the following children:
- i. **Sam Walter Gordon** was born on 02 Sep 1994 in New York City.
- ii. **Joseph Charles Gordon** was born on 26 Aug 1996 in Los Angeles, CA.
- iii. **Greta Kelly Gordon** was born on 15 Oct 1998 in Chicago, IL.

22. **Stephen Mark Eisner**-6 (Thomas Michael-5, Robert-4, Hortense-3, Julie-2, Jacob-1) was born on 29 Nov 1958 in Chuquicamata, Chile, SA.
Staci Suzanne Johnson.
Stephen Mark Eisner and Staci Suzanne Johnson were married on 14 Jun 1986 in Ft. Worth, TX. They had the following children:
- i. **Kathryn Bliss Eisner** was born on 19 Oct 1988 in Ft. Worth, TX.
- ii. **Patrick Thomas Eisner** was born on 23 Apr 1994 in Ft. Worth, TX.

23. **Andrea Savilla Eisner**-6 (Thomas Michael-5, Robert-4, Hortense-3, Julie-2, Jacob-1) was born on 23 Nov 1959 in Sewell, Chile, SA.
Todd Allen Barnett.
Todd Allen Barnett and Andrea Savilla Eisner were married on 27 Jun 1993 in Carmel, CA. They had the following children:
- i. **Benjamin Michael Barnett** was born on 30 Apr 1997 in Bellevue, WA.
- ii. **Daniel Barnett**.

Generation 7

24. **Erin Marie Steiner**-7 (David Henry-6, Helen Edwards-5, Paul J. Edwards-4, Hortense-3, Julie-2, Jacob-1) was born on 01 Aug 1981 in Chicago, IL.
Michael John Malick was born on 01 Aug 1981 in Chicago, IL.
Michael John Malick and Erin Marie Steiner were married on 27 Jul 2013 in Poulsbo, WA. They had the following children:
- i. **Henry Francsz Malick** was born on 18 Feb 2018 in Seattle, WA.

25. **Kevin Thomas Rechcigl**-7 (John Edward-6, Eva Edwards-5, Paul J. Edwards-4, Hortense-3, Julie-2, Jacob-1) was born on 09 Oct 1991 in Bradenton, FL.
Jordan Robbins daughter of Douglass Robbins and Ivonne was born on 10 Jan 1992 in Camarillo, CA.

Kevin Thomas Rechcigl and Jordan Robbins were married on 12 May 2018 in Jacksonville, FL. They had the following children:
> i. **James Douglas Rechcigl** was born on 05 Jan 2021 in Jacksonville, FL.
> ii. **Evelyn Marie Rechcigl** was born 29 May 2023 in Jacksonville, FL.

D. Eva Edwards' Mother Side

Taussig Family

Generation 1

1. **Julia Taussigová**-1.
   Markus Stoekler was born in 1804 in Zabehlice.
   Markus Stoekler and Julia Taussigová married. They had the following children:
   - 2. i. **Jakub Taussig** was born in 1827 in Bechovice u Prahy. He died on 25 Feb 1896 in Benešov.

Generation 2

2. **Jakub Taussig**-2 (Julia-1) was born in 1827 in Bechovice u Prahy. He died on 25 Feb 1896 in Benešov.
   Julie Meislova daughter of Jakub Meisl and Judita Dubova was born in 1838 in Žehušice, Kutná Hora District, Bohemia. She died on 30 May 1913 in Benešov, Bohemia.
   Jakub Taussig and Julie Meislova married. They had the following children:
   - i. **Olga Taussigová** was born on 02 Jul 1862. She died on 04 Mar 1905 in Benešov.
   - ii. **Julius Taussig** was born on 01 Oct 1862. He died in 1941 in Benešov (probably).
   - 4. iii. **Gabriela Taussigová** was born on 23 Sep 1863. She died on 12 Nov 1927.
   - iv. **Pavel Taussig** was born in 1864.
   - v. **Jindřich Taussig** was born in 1867.
   - vi. **Artur Taussig** was born on 14 Dec 1869.
   - 4. vii. **Hermina Taussigová** was born on 23 Jun 1871. She died in 1927.
   - 5. viii. **Kamila Taussigová** was born on 27 Feb 1873. She died in 1912.
   - 6. ix. **Pavla Taussigová** was born on 18 Jan 1875. She died in 1943.
   - 7. x. **Oskar Taussig** was born on 22 Jun 1876 in Benešov. He died on

08 Nov 1938 in Prague.
8. xi. **Marie Markéta Marta Taussigová** was born on 07 Mar 1879 in Benešov No. 162. She married Adolf Šváb on 15 Oct 1902 in U Matky Bozi pred Tynem, Prague. She died on 22 Jun 1958 in Plzen.

xii. **Jindřich Taussig**.

Julie Meisl daughter of Jakub Meisl and Judita Dubova was born on 13 May 1838 in Žehušice, Kutná Hora District, Bohemia. She died on 30 May 1913 in Benešov, Bohemia.

Jakub Taussig and Julie Meisl married. They had no children.

Generation 3

3. **Gabriela Taussigová**-3 (Jakub-2, Julia-1) was born on 23 Sep 1863. She died on 12 Nov 1927.

   Gustav Weiner son of Moses Weiner and Rosalia Hindl Stricker was born in 1850 in Pisek, Písek District, Bohemia. He died in 1919 in Prague, Czechoslovakia.

   Gustav Weiner and Gabriela Taussigová married. They had the following children:

   i. **Richard Weiner** was born on 06 Nov 1884 in Pisek, Písek District, Bohemia. He died on 03 Jan 1937 in Prague, Czech..

   ii. **Kamil Weiner** was born in 1886. He died in 1960.

   iii. **Marta Weinerova** was born in 1893. She died in 1918.

10. iv. **Jiří Weiner** was born in 1896.

11. v. **Zdena Weinerova** was born in 1898. She died in 1975.

4. **Hermina Taussigová**-3 (Jakub-2, Julia-1) was born on 23 Jun 1871. She died in 1927.

   František Kašpárek son of Kašpárek and Unknown.

   František Kašpárek and Hermina Taussigová married. They had the following children:

   i. **Jiří Kašpárek** was born in 1909. He married Zdena Kracmerova in 1939. He died in 1983.

11. ii. **Ivan Kašpárek** was born in 1910. He died in 1985.

   iii. **Petr Kašpárek** was born in 1912.

5. **Kamila Taussigová**-3 (Jakub-2, Julia-1) was born on 27 Feb 1873. She

died in 1912.

Viktor Vodička son of Vodička and Unknown.

Viktor Vodička and Kamila Taussigová married. They had the following children:

12. i. **Vladimír Vodička** was born before 1893. He died on 12 Feb 1954.
    ii. **Marenka Vodičková** was born in 1893. She died on 09 Feb 1898 in Pisek.

6. **Pavla Taussigová**-3 (Jakub-2, Julia-1) was born on 18 Jan 1875. She died in 1943.

Emil Bloch.

Emil Bloch and Pavla Taussigová married. They had the following children:
    i. **Karel Bloch.**
13. ii. **Helena Bloch.**

7. **Oskar Taussig**-3 (Jakub-2, Julia-1) was born on 22 Jun 1876 in Benešov. He died on 08 Nov 1938 in Prague.

Klára Munková daughter of Rafael Munk and Theresia Steindlerová was born on 21 Dec 1887 in Prague, Bohemia. She died on 18 Jan 1934 in Prague, Bohemia.

Oskar Taussig and Klára Munková married. They had the following children:

14. i. **Jiřina Taussigová** was born on 24 Apr 1906 in Prague - Kralovske Vinohrady, Nerudova l. She married Paul J. Edwards (Pavel Eisner) on 05 Jun 1926 in Prague. She died on 06 Nov 1962 in New York, NY.
15. ii. **Hana Taussigová** was born on 26 Feb 1910 in Prague. She married Joseph (Wiener) Winn in 1933. She died on 14 Mar 1999 in New York, NY.

8. **Marie Markéta Marta Taussigová**-3 (Jakub-2, Julia-1) was born on 07 Mar 1879 in Benešov No. 162. She died on 22 Jun 1958 in Plzen.

Adolf Šváb son of Jan Krtitel Šváb and Barbora Sedláková was born on 18 Apr 1876 in Bystrice No. 138, Benešov Co.. He died on 26 Apr 1954 in Plzen.

Adolf Šváb and Marie Markéta Marta Taussigová were married on 15 Oct

1902 in U Matky Bozi pred Tynem, Prague. They had the following children:
- 16. i. **Vladislav Šváb** was born on 08 Aug 1903 in Vysoke nad Jizerou. He married Julie Zacharova on 11 Oct 1932 in Prague. He died on 23 Oct 1947 in Tabor, Czechoslovakia.
- 17. ii. **Adolf Šváb** was born on 15 Apr 1905 in Vysoke nad Jizerou No. 267. He married Zdenka Sigmundova on 17 Sep 1932 in Plzen. He died in 1976 in Plzen.
- 18. iii. **Kamil Šváb** was born in 1907 in Vysoke nad Jizerou. He married Augusta (Gusta) Hyblerova in 1936. He died in 1982 in Praha, Bohemia.
- iv. **Věra Švábová** was born in 1910 in Vysoke nad Jizerou. She married Čeněk Simerka in 1936. She died in 1985 in Plzen.

Generation 4

9. **Jiří Weiner**-4 (Gabriela-3, Jakub-2, Julia-1) was born in 1896.
Kateřina.
Jiří Weiner and Kateřina married. They had the following children:
- i. **Jadviga Weiner**.

10. **Zdena Weinerova**-4 (Gabriela-3, Jakub-2, Julia-1) was born in 1898. She died in 1975.
Vladimír Vochoc. He died in 1987.
Vladimír Vochoc and Zdena Weinerova married. They had the following children:
- i. **Nanynka Vochocova**.

Antonín Pavel was born in 1887. He died in 1958.
Antonín Pavel and Zdena Weinerova married. They had no children.

11. **Ivan Kašpárek**-4 (Hermina-3, Jakub-2, Julia-1) was born in 1910. He died in 1985.
Mila Novotná was born in 1916.
Ivan Kašpárek and Mila Novotná married. They had the following children:
- 19. i. **Eva Kašpárková** was born in 1944.

12. **Vladimír Vodička**-4 (Kamila-3, Jakub-2, Julia-1) was born before 1893.

He died on 12 Feb 1954.

Růžena Krausová.

Vladimír Vodička and Růžena Krausová married. They had the following children:

    20. i. **Vladimír Vodička** was born on 05 May 1925 in Benešov.

          ii. **daughter Vodička.**

13. **Helena Bloch**-4 (Pavla-3, Jakub-2, Julia-1).

Salinger.

Salinger and Helena Bloch married. They had the following children:

        i. **Henry Salinger.**

Kahn.

Kahn and Helena Bloch married. They had the following children:

        i. **son Kahn.**

14. **Jiřina Taussigová**-4 (Oskar-3, Jakub-2, Julia-1) was born on 24 Apr 1906 in Prague - Kralovske Vinohrady, Nerudova l. She died on 06 Nov 1962 in New York, NY.

Paul J. Edwards (Pavel Eisner) son of (Jindřich) Henry Eisner and Hortense Auer was born on 29 Jun 1892 in Prague, Klimentska 1. He died on 27 Jun 1964 in Schenectady, NY.

Paul J. Edwards (Pavel Eisner) and Jiřina Taussigová were married on 05 Jun 1926 in Prague. They had the following children:

    21. i. **Helen Edwards (Eisnerova)** was born on 29 Apr 1927 in Prague, CSR. She married Frank Steiner on 16 Sep 1948 in New York, NY.

    22. ii. **Eva Edwards (Eisnerová)** was born on 21 Jan 1932 in Prague, CSR. She married Mila (Miloslav) Rechcigl Jr. on 29 Aug 1953 in New York, NY.

15. **Hana Taussigová**-4 (Oskar-3, Jakub-2, Julia-1) was born on 26 Feb 1910 in Prague. She died on 14 Mar 1999 in New York, NY.

Joseph (Wiener) Winn son of Maurice Wiener and Alba Růžičková was born on 02 Feb 1901 in Prague. He died on 08 Feb 1983 in New York City. Joseph (Wiener) Winn and Hana Taussigová were married in 1933. They had the following children:

    23. i. **Janet (Jana) Winn** was born on 08 Jul 1934 in Prague. She married

Donald Malcolm on Apr 1956 in New York City.

24. ii. **Marie Winn** was born on 21 Oct 1936 in Prague. She married Allan Miller on 28 Apr 1961 in New York City.

16. **Vladislav Šváb**-4 (Marie Markéta Marta-3, Jakub-2, Julia-1) was born on 08 Aug 1903 in Vysoke nad Jizerou. He died on 23 Oct 1947 in Tabor, Czechoslovakia.

    Julie Zacharova daughter of Nikolaj Michajlovic Zacharov and Julie Filipovna Obrevko-Zdanov was born on 03 Mar 1901 in Moscow, Russia. She died on 24 Jan 1999 in Tabor, Bbohemia.

    Vladislav Šváb and Julie Zacharova were married on 11 Oct 1932 in Prague. They had the following children:

    25. i. **Julie ("Jaska") Švábová** was born on 24 Feb 1945 in Tabor. She married Vladimír Sarsa on 26 Jun 1969 in Ostrava.

17. **Adolf Šváb**-4 (Marie Markéta Marta-3, Jakub-2, Julia-1) was born on 15 Apr 1905 in Vysoke nad Jizerou No. 267. He died in 1976 in Plzen.

    Zdenka Sigmundova daughter of Josef Sigmund and Karolina Restránková was born on 31 Oct 1908 in Plzen, Na Lochotine No. 451. She died in 1990 in Plzen.

    Adolf Šváb and Zdenka Sigmundova were married on 17 Sep 1932 in Plzen. They had the following children:

    26. i. **Irena Švábová** was born on 03 Feb 1936 in Plzen. She married Emil Kasl in 1955.
    27. ii. **Zdeněk Šváb** was born on 31 Mar 1940 in Plzen.
    28. iii. **Olga Švábová** was born on 18 Jul 1948 in Plzen. She married Vladimír Pechman in 1968.

18. **Kamil Šváb**-4 (Marie Markéta Marta-3, Jakub-2, Julia-1) was born in 1907 in Vysoke nad Jizerou. He died in 1982 in Praha, Bohemia.

    Augusta (Gusta) Hyblerova daughter of Otto Hybler and (Pavlina) Marie Schönfeldová was born in 1911. She died in 1960.

    Kamil Šváb and Augusta (Gusta) Hyblerova were married in 1936. They had the following children:

    i. **Jan Šváb** was born on 04 Jul 1937 in Praha, CSR. He married Josette Azra on 02 May 1978.

Božena Stroblová was born in 1913. She died in 1981.

Kamil Šváb and Božena Stroblová were married in 1945. They had the following children:

29. i. **Kamil Šváb** was born on 29 Aug 1944 in Prague. He married Dobroslava Rittova in 1968.

Generation 5

19. **Eva Kašpárková**-5 (Ivan-4, Hermina-3, Jakub-2, Julia-1) was born in 1944.

Horatio.

Horatio and Eva Kašpárková married. They had the following children:

i. **David.**

20. **Vladimír Vodička**-5 (Vladimír-4, Kamila-3, Jakub-2, Julia-1) was born on 05 May 1925 in Benešov.

Marie Fiserova.

Vladimír Vodička and Marie Fiserova married. They had the following children:

i. **Marie Vodičková.**

Milada.

Vladimír Vodička and Milada were married before 1954. They had no children.

21. **Helen Edwards (Eisnerova)**-5 (Jiřina-4, Oskar-3, Jakub-2, Julia-1) was born on 29 Apr 1927 in Prague, CSR.

Frank Steiner son of Johann (Hans) Steiner and Růžena Steinbachova was born on 23 Apr 1922 in Prague, Bohemia. He died on 14 Sep 2000 in Scotia, NY.

Frank Steiner and Helen Edwards (Eisnerova) were married on 16 Sep 1948 in New York, NY. They had the following children:

30. i. **Linda Claire Steiner** was born on 01 Mar 1950 in Schenectady, NY. She married Edward Salomon on 05 Jun 1977 in Scotia, NY.

31. ii. **David Henry Steiner** was born on 13 Mar 1952 in Schenectady, NY. He married Carol Ann Mastaliz on 07 Jul 1979 in So. Deerfield, MA.

22. **Eva Edwards (Eisnerová)**-5 (Jiřina-4, Oskar-3, Jakub-2, Julia-1) was born on 21 Jan 1932 in Prague, CSR.

Mila (Miloslav) Rechcigl Jr. son of Miloslav Rechcigl and Marie

Rajtrová was born on 30 Jul 1930 in Mladá Boleslav, CSR.

Mila (Miloslav) Rechcigl Jr. and Eva Edwards (Eisnerová) were married on 29 Aug 1953 in New York, NY. They had the following children:

- 32. i. **John Edward Rechcigl** was born on 27 Feb 1960 in Washington, D.C.. He married Nancy Ann Palko on 30 Jul 1983 in Dover, NJ.
- 33. ii. **Karen Rechcigl** was born on 16 Apr 1962 in Washington, DC. She married Ulysses Kollecas on 25 Aug 1990 in Bethesda, MD.

23. **Janet (Jana) Winn**-5 (Hana-4, Oskar-3, Jakub-2, Julia-1) was born on 08 Jul 1934 in Prague.

    Donald Malcolm was born in 1935. He died in 1975.

    Donald Malcolm and Janet (Jana) Winn were married on 13 Apr 1956 in New York City. They had the following children:

    - 19 i. **Anne Malcolm** was born on 17 Dec 1962 in New York City. She married Richard Tuck on 19 Mar 1993 in New York City.

    Gardner Botsford son of Botsford was born on 07 Jul 1917 in New York, NY. He died on 27 Sep 2004 in New York, NY.

    Gardner Botsford and Janet (Jana) Winn were married on 26 Sep 1975. They had no children.

24. **Marie Winn**-5 (Hana-4, Oskar-3, Jakub-2, Julia-1) was born on 21 Oct 1936 in Prague.

    Allan Miller was born on 05 Dec 1933 in New York City.

    Allan Miller and Marie Winn were married on 28 Apr 1961 in New York City. They had the following children:

    - 35. i. **Michael Winn Miller** was born on 20 Nov 1962. He married Sarah Paul on 30 Dec 1988 in New York City.
    - 36. ii. **Steven David Miller** was born on 14 Apr 1966 in New York City. He married Jennifer Durand on 11 Nov 1995 in San Francisco, CA.

25. **Julie ("Jaska") Švábová**-5 (Vladislav-4, Marie Markéta Marta-3, Jakub-2, Julia-1) was born on 24 Feb 1945 in Tabor.

    Vladimír Sarsa was born on 11 Feb 1943 in Ostrava.

    Vladimír Sarsa and Julie ("Jaska") Švábová were married on 26 Jun 1969 in Ostrava. They had the following children:

    - 37. i. **Olga Sarsova** was born on 26 Dec 1970 in Ostrava. She married

Broniaslav Klementa on 14 Apr 2007 in Na Svatem Kopecku u Olomouce.

    38. ii. **Vladimír Sarsa** was born on 26 Nov 1971 in Ostrava. He married Bronislava Srubkova on 26 Jul 1997 in Ostrava.

26. **Irena Švábová**-5 (Adolf-4, Marie Markéta Marta-3, Jakub-2, Julia-1) was born on 03 Feb 1936 in Plzen.

Emil Kasl was born in 1926.

Emil Kasl and Irena Švábová were married in 1955. They had the following children:

    39. i. **Monika Kaslova** was born on 03 Jun 1958 in Plzen. She married Jiří Chládek on 30 Apr 1978 in Prague, CSR.

    ii. **Tomáš Kasl** was born on 26 Apr 1964 in Plzen.

27. **Zdeněk Šváb**-5 (Adolf-4, Marie Markéta Marta-3, Jakub-2, Julia-1) was born on 31 Mar 1940 in Plzen.

Jaroslava Leimerova was born in 1943.

Zdeněk Šváb and Jaroslava Leimerova married. They had the following children:

    40. i. **Daniel Šváb** was born on 29 Jan 1964 in Plzen. He married Jitka Kopackova in 1992.

Marie Kosorova was born in 1945.

Zdeněk Šváb and Marie Kosorova were married in 1970. They had no children.

28. **Olga Švábová**-5 (Adolf-4, Marie Markéta Marta-3, Jakub-2, Julia-1) was born on 18 Jul 1948 in Plzen.

Vladimír Pechman was born in 1943.

Vladimír Pechman and Olga Švábová were married in 1968. They had the following children:

    41. i. **Radek Pechman** was born on 12 Mar 1969 in Plzen. He married Jitka Slámová in 1992.

    42. ii. **Olga Pechmanová** was born on 12 Mar 1976 in Plzen. She married Tomáš Pech in 1998.

Muchna.

Muchna and Olga Švábová were married after 1976. They had no

children.
29. **Kamil Šváb**-5 (Kamil-4, Marie Markéta Marta-3, Jakub-2, Julia-1) was born on 29 Aug 1944 in Prague.
Dobroslava Rittova was born on 13 Sep 1945.
Kamil Šváb and Dobroslava Rittova were married in 1968. They had the following children:
   i. **Jana Švábová** was born on 17 Jun 1972. She married Franklin Venegas on 16 Jul 1994.

Generation 6

30. **Linda Claire Steiner**-6 (Helen Edwards-5, Jiřina-4, Oskar-3, Jakub-2, Julia-1) was born on 01 Mar 1950 in Schenectady, NY.
Edward Salomon son of Jerome Salomon and Rachel Finchel was born on 12 Feb 1951 in Jersey city, NJ.
Edward Salomon and Linda Claire Steiner were married on 05 Jun 1977 in Scotia, NY. They had the following children:
   i. **Sarah Beth Salomon** was born on 28 Jan 1980 in Chicago, IL.
   ii. **Paul Nathan Salomon** was born on 02 Jan 1983 in Chicago, IL.

31. **David Henry Steiner**-6 (Helen Edwards-5, Jiřina-4, Oskar-3, Jakub-2, Julia-1) was born on 13 Mar 1952 in Schenectady, NY.
Carol Ann Mastaliz daughter of Frank Peter Mastaliz and Helen Carline Macko was born on 26 Oct 1952 (Greenfield, MA).
David Henry Steiner and Carol Ann Mastaliz were married on 07 Jul 1979 in So. Deerfield, MA. They had the following children:
43. i. **Erin Marie Steiner** was born on 01 Aug 1981 in Chicago, IL. She married Michael John Malick on 27 Jul 2013 in Poulsbo, WA.
    ii. **Jonathan Robert Steiner** was born on 30 Dec 1984 in Concord, MA.

32. **John Edward Rechcigl**-6 (Eva Edwards-5, Jiřina-4, Oskar-3, Jakub-2, Julia-1) was born on 27 Feb 1960 in Washington, D.C..
Nancy Ann Palko daughter of Joseph Palko and Mary Rishko was born on 26 Sep 1961 in Morristown, NJ.
John Edward Rechcigl and Nancy Ann Palko were married on 30 Jul 1983 in Dover, NJ. They had the following children:

i. **Gregory John Rechcigl** was born on 19 Dec 1988 in Bradenton, FL.
44. ii. **Kevin Thomas Rechcigl** was born on 09 Oct 1991 in Bradenton, FL. He married Jordan Robbins on 12 May 2018 in Jacksonville, FL.
   iii. **Lindsey Nicole Rechcigl** was born on 03 Nov 1994 in Bradenton, FL.
33. **Karen Rechcigl**-6 (Eva Edwards-5, Jiřina-4, Oskar-3, Jakub-2, Julia-1) was born on 16 Apr 1962 in Washington, DC.
    Ulysses Kollecas son of Christopher Thomas (Kolecas) Collier and Amelia Malatras was born on 20 Mar 1958 in Washington, DC.
    Ulysses Kollecas and Karen Rechcigl were married on 25 Aug 1990 in Bethesda, MD. They had the following children:
       i. **Kristin Kollecas** was born on 04 May 1993 in Albuquerque, NM.
       ii. **Paul Kollecas** was born on 02 Jun 1995 in Albuquerque, NM.
34. **Anne Malcolm**-6 (Janet (Jana)-5, Hana-4, Oskar-3, Jakub-2, Julia-1) was born on 17 Dec 1962 in New York City.
    Richard Tuck was born on 09 Jan 1949 in Newcastleupon-Tyne, England. Richard Tuck and Anne Malcolm were married on 19 Mar 1993 in New York City. They had the following children:
       i. **Sophy Malcolm Tuck** was born on 13 Jul 1993 in Cambridge, England.
35. **Michael Winn Miller**-6 (Marie-5, Hana-4, Oskar-3, Jakub-2, Julia-1) was born on 20 Nov 1962.
    Sarah Paul was born on 29 Dec 1961 in New York City.
    Michael Winn Miller and Sarah Paul were married on 30 Dec 1988 in New York City. They had the following children:
       i. **Isadore 'Izzy' Miller** was born on 20 Nov 1995 in San Francisco, CA.
       ii. **Abigail "Abbey' Nadia Paul Miller** was born on 24 Oct 1996 in New York City.
36. **Steven David Miller**-6 (Marie-5, Hana-4, Oskar-3, Jakub-2, Julia-1) was born on 14 Apr 1966 in New York City.
    Jennifer Durand.

Steven David Miller and Jennifer Durand were married on 11 Nov 1995 in San Francisco, CA. They had the following children:
   i. **Eli Miller** was born on 17 Mar 1999.
   ii. **Clara Miller** was born on 04 Jul 2000 in San Francisco, CA or NYC.
37. **Olga Sarsova**-6 (Julie ("Jaska")-5, Vladislav-4, Marie Markéta Marta-3, Jakub-2, Julia-1) was born on 26 Dec 1970 in Ostrava.
   Broniaslav Klementa son of Josef Klementa and Oldřiška Pavlickova was born on 29 Jun 1966 in Sumperk.
   Broniaslav Klementa and Olga Sarsova were married on 14 Apr 2007 in Na Svatem Kopecku u Olomouce. They had the following children:
   i. **Veronika Klementova** was born on 25 May 2007 in Olomouc.
38. **Vladimír Sarsa**-6 (Julie ("Jaska")-5, Vladislav-4, Marie Markéta Marta-3, Jakub-2, Julia-1) was born on 26 Nov 1971 in Ostrava.
   Bronislava Srubkova was born on 05 Mar 1963 in Pustejov, Bruntal Dist., Czechoslovakia..
   Vladimír Sarsa and Bronislava Srubkova were married on 26 Jul 1997 in Ostrava. They had the following children:
   i. **Milena Sarsova** was born on 03 Jan 1998 in Ostrava, Czechoslovakia.
39. **Monika Kaslova**-6 (Irena-5, Adolf-4, Marie Markéta Marta-3, Jakub-2, Julia-1) was born on 03 Jun 1958 in Plzen.
   Jiří Chládek was born in 1955.
   Jiří Chládek and Monika Kaslova were married on 30 Apr 1978 in Prague, CSR. They had the following children:
   i. **David Chládek** was born on 19 Dec 1978 in Cheb.
   ii. **Ondřej Chládek** was born on 17 Aug 1981 in Cheb.
   iii. **Jan Chládek** was born on 16 Nov 1988 in Cheb.
40. **Daniel Šváb**-6 (Zdeněk-5, Adolf-4, Marie Markéta Marta-3, Jakub-2, Julia-1) was born on 29 Jan 1964 in Plzen.
   Jitka Kopackova.
   Daniel Šváb and Jitka Kopackova were married in 1992. They had the following children:

     i. **Dominika Švábová** was born on 16 Oct 1992 in Plzen.
     ii. **Natalie Švábová** was born on 09 Aug 1998 in Plzen.

41. **Radek Pechman**-6 (Olga-5, Adolf-4, Marie Markéta Marta-3, Jakub-2, Julia-1) was born on 12 Mar 1969 in Plzen.

    Jitka Slámová was born in 1966.

    Radek Pechman and Jitka Slámová were married in 1992. They had the following children:

         i. **Barbora Pechmanová** was born in 1992.

42. **Olga Pechmanová**-6 (Olga-5, Adolf-4, Marie Markéta Marta-3, Jakub-2, Julia-1) was born on 12 Mar 1976 in Plzen.

    Tomáš Pech.

    Tomáš Pech and Olga Pechmanová were married in 1998. They had the following children:

         i. **Karolina Pechová** was born on 22 May 1999 in Plzen.

Generation 7

43. **Erin Marie Steiner**-7 (David Henry-6, Helen Edwards-5, Jiřina-4, Oskar-3, Jakub-2, Julia-1) was born on 01 Aug 1981 in Chicago, IL.

    Michael John Malick was born on 01 Aug 1981 in Chicago, IL.

    Michael John Malick and Erin Marie Steiner were married on 27 Jul 2013 in Poulsbo, WA. They had the following children:

         i. **Henry Francsz Malick** was born on 18 Feb 2018 in Seattle, WA.

44. **Kevin Thomas Rechcigl**-7 (John Edward-6, Eva Edwards-5, Jiřina-4, Oskar-3, Jakub-2, Julia-1) was born on 09 Oct 1991 in Bradenton, FL.

    Jordan Robbins daughter of Douglass Robbins and Ivonne was born on 10 Jan 1992 in Camarillo, CA.

    Kevin Thomas Rechcigl and Jordan Robbins were married on 12 May 2018 in Jacksonville, FL. They had the following children:

         i. **James Douglas Rechcigl** was born on 05 Jan 2021 in Jacksonville, FL.

         ii. **Evelyn Marie Rechcigl** was born 29 May 2023 in Jacksonville, FL.

Meisl Family

Generation 1

1. **Jakub Meisl**-1 was born on 27 Mar 1795 in Žehušice, Kutná Hora District, Bohemia. He died on 08 Jan 1867 in Žehušice, Kutná Hora District, Bohemia.

   Judita Dubova daughter of Dub and Unknown was born in 1804 in Benešov. Jakub Meisl and Judita Dubova married. They had the following children:

   2. i. **Julie Meislova** was born in 1838 in Žehušice, Kutná Hora District, Bohemia. She died on 30 May 1913 in Benešov, Bohemia.
   3. ii. **Anna Meislova** was born on 15 Jul 1830 in Žehušice, Kutná Hora District, Bohemia. She died on 24 Jan 1872 in Turnov, Semily District, Bohemia.
   4. iii. **Gabriela Marie Meisl** was born on 28 Sep 1848 in Žehušice, Kutná Hora District, Bohemia. She died on 08 May 1932 in Prague, Czech..
   iv. **Leopold Meisl**.
   v. **Alexander Meisl** was born on 01 Jun 1825 in Žehušice, Kutná Hora District, Bohemia.
   vi. **Josef Meisl** was born on 13 Sep 1836 in Žehušice, Kutná Hora District, Bohemia.
   vii. **Julie Meisl** was born on 13 May 1838 in Žehušice, Kutná Hora District, Bohemia. She died on 30 May 1913 in Benešov, Bohemia.

Generation 2

2. **Julie Meislova**-2 (Jakub-1) was born in 1838 in Žehušice, Kutná Hora District, Bohemia. She died on 30 May 1913 in Benešov, Bohemia.

   Jakub Taussig son of Markus Stoekler and Julia Taussigová was born in 1827 in Bechovice u Prahy. He died on 25 Feb 1896 in Benešov.

   Jakub Taussig and Julie Meislova married. They had the following children:

   i. **Olga Taussigová** was born on 02 Jul 1862. She died on 04 Mar 1905 in Benešov.

ii. **Julius Taussig** was born on 01 Oct 1862. He died in 1941 in Benešov (probably).

5. iii. **Gabriela Taussigová** was born on 23 Sep 1863. She died on 12 Nov 1927.

iv. **Pavel Taussig** was born in 1864.

v. **Jindřich Taussig** was born in 1867.

vi. **Artur Taussig** was born on 14 Dec 1869.

6. vii. **Hermina Taussigová** was born on 23 Jun 1871. She died in 1927.
7. viii. **Kamila Taussigová** was born on 27 Feb 1873. She died in 1912.
8. ix. **Pavla Taussigová** was born on 18 Jan 1875. She died in 1943.
9. x. **Oskar Taussig** was born on 22 Jun 1876 in Benešov. He died on 08 Nov 1938 in Prague.
10. xi. **Marie Markéta Marta Taussigová** was born on 07 Mar 1879 in Benešov No. 162. She married Adolf Šváb on 15 Oct 1902 in U Matky Bozi pred Tynem, Prague. She died on 22 Jun 1958 in Plzen.

xii. **Jindřich Taussig**.

3. **Anna Meislova**-2 (Jakub-1) was born on 15 Jul 1830 in Žehušice, Kutná Hora District, Bohemia. She died on 24 Jan 1872 in Turnov, Semily District, Bohemia.

Pavel Schönfeld son of Josef Schönfeld and Františka Horzitzky was born on 05 May 1825. He died on 02 Oct 1886 in Turnov, Semily District, Bohemia.

Pavel Schönfeld and Anna Meislova married. They had the following children:

11. i. **František Schönfeld** was born on 10 Aug 1850. He died on 13 Aug 1911 in Turnov, Bohemia ?.
12. ii. **Josef Schönfeld** was born in 1851. He died in 1905.
13. iii. **Julius von Schönfeld** was born in 1853. He died in 1904.
14. iv. **Pavla Schönfeldová** was born in 1855. She died in 1943 in Terezin.
15. v. **Kamila Schönfeldová** was born in 1857. She died on 27 Mar 1920 in Krc.

vi. **Eleanora Schönfeld**.

4. **Gabriela Marie Meisl**-2 (Jakub-1) was born on 28 Sep 1848 in Žehušice, Kutná Hora District, Bohemia. She died on 08 May 1932 in Prague, Czech..

   Emilius Isarel Winternitz was born on 29 Apr 1842 in Opočno, Rychnov nad Kněžnou District, Bohemia. He died on 02 Jan 1917 in Prague, Czech..
   Emilius Isarel Winternitz and Gabriela Marie Meisl married. They had the following children:
   - i. **Anna Marie Winternitz** was born on 25 Oct 1871 in Opočno, Rychnov nad Kněžnou District, Bohemia. She died in 1942 in Treblinka, Poland - Holocaust.
   - ii. **Josefine Josefa Winternitz** was born on 25 Apr 1870 in Opočno, Rychnov nad Kněžnou District, Bohemia. She died on 01 Jul 1921 in Prague, Czech..
   - iii. **Emilie Winternitz** was born on 20 Mar 1877 in Ledce, Mladá Boleslav District, Bohemia. She died on 30 Dec 1934 in Prague, Czech..
   - iv. **Magdalena Winternitz** was born on 23 Nov 1878 in Ledeč, Hradec Králové District, Bohemia,. She died on 09 Sep 1942 in Łódź, Poland - Holocaust.

Generation 3

5. **Gabriela Taussigová**-3 (Julie-2, Jakub-1) was born on 23 Sep 1863. She died on 12 Nov 1927.

   Gustav Weiner son of Moses Weiner and Rosalia Hindl Stricker was born in 1850 in Pisek, Písek District, Bohemia. He died in 1919 in Prague, Czechoslovakia.

   Gustav Weiner and Gabriela Taussigová married. They had the following children:
   - i. **Richard Weiner** was born on 06 Nov 1884 in Pisek, Písek District, Bohemia. He died on 03 Jan 1937 in Prague, Czech..
   - ii. **Kamil Weiner** was born in 1886. He died in 1960.
   - iii. **Marta Weinerova** was born in 1893. She died in 1918.
   17. iv. **Jiří Weiner** was born in 1896.
   18. v. **Zdena Weinerova** was born in 1898. She died in 1975.

6. **Hermina Taussigová**-3 (Julie-2, Jakub-1) was born on 23 Jun 1871. She died in 1927.
   František Kašpárek son of Kašpárek and Unknown.
   František Kašpárek and Hermina Taussigová married. They had the following children:
       i. **Jiří Kašpárek** was born in 1909. He married Zdena Kracmerova in 1939. He died in 1983.
   18. ii. **Ivan Kašpárek** was born in 1910. He died in 1985.
       iii. **Petr Kašpárek** was born in 1912.
7. **Kamila Taussigová**-3 (Julie-2, Jakub-1) was born on 27 Feb 1873. She died in 1912.
   Viktor Vodička son of Vodička and Unknown.
   Viktor Vodička and Kamila Taussigová married. They had the following children:
   19. i. **Vladimír Vodička** was born before 1893. He died on 12 Feb 1954.
       ii. **Marenka Vodičková** was born in 1893. She died on 09 Feb 1898 in Pisek.
8. **Pavla Taussigová**-3 (Julie-2, Jakub-1) was born on 18 Jan 1875. She died in 1943.
   Emil Bloch.
   Emil Bloch and Pavla Taussigová married. They had the following children:
       i. **Karel Bloch**.
   20. ii. **Helena Bloch**.
9. **Oskar Taussig**-3 (Julie-2, Jakub-1) was born on 22 Jun 1876 in Benešov. He died on 08 Nov 1938 in Prague.
   Klára Munková daughter of Rafael Munk and Theresia Steindlerová was born on 21 Dec 1887 in Prague, Bohemia. She died on 18 Jan 1934 in Prague, Bohemia.
   Oskar Taussig and Klára Munková married. They had the following children:
   21. i. **Jiřina Taussigová** was born on 24 Apr 1906 in Prague - Kralovske Vinohrady, Nerudova l. She married Paul J. Edwards (Pavel Eisner)

on 05 Jun 1926 in Prague. She died on 06 Nov 1962 in New York, NY.

22. ii. **Hana Taussigová** was born on 26 Feb 1910 in Prague. She married Joseph (Wiener) Winn in 1933. She died on 14 Mar 1999 in New York, NY.

10. **Marie Markéta Marta Taussigová**-3 (Julie-2, Jakub-1) was born on 07 Mar 1879 in Benešov No. 162. She died on 22 Jun 1958 in Plzen.

Adolf Šváb son of Jan Krtitel Šváb and Barbora Sedláková was born on 18 Apr 1876 in Bystrice No. 138, Benešov Co.. He died on 26 Apr 1954 in Plzen.

Adolf Šváb and Marie Markéta Marta Taussigová were married on 15 Oct 1902 in U Matky Bozi pred Tynem, Prague. They had the following children:

23. i. **Vladislav Šváb** was born on 08 Aug 1903 in Vysoke nad Jizerou. He married Julie Zacharova on 11 Oct 1932 in Prague. He died on 23 Oct 1947 in Tabor, Czechoslovakia.

24. ii. **Adolf Šváb** was born on 15 Apr 1905 in Vysoke nad Jizerou No. 267. He married Zdenka Sigmundova on 17 Sep 1932 in Plzen. He died in 1976 in Plzen.

25. iii. **Kamil Šváb** was born in 1907 in Vysoke nad Jizerou. He married Augusta (Gusta) Hyblerova in 1936. He died in 1982 in Praha, Bohemia.

iv. **Věra Švábová** was born in 1910 in Vysoke nad Jizerou. She married Čeněk Simerka in 1936. She died in 1985 in Plzen.

11. **František Schönfeld**-3 (Anna-2, Jakub-1) was born on 10 Aug 1850. He died on 13 Aug 1911 in Turnov, Bohemia ?.

Augusta Beerová.

František Schönfeld and Augusta Beerová married. They had the following children:

26. i. **Anna Schönfeldová** was born in 1881. She died in 1945 in Osvetim.

27. ii. **(Pavlina) Marie Schönfeldová** was born in 1885. She died in 1932.

12. **Josef Schönfeld**-3 (Anna-2, Jakub-1) was born in 1851. He died in 1905.

Klára Igelova daughter of Elias Igel and Reisel Rosa Selzer.

Josef Schönfeld and Klára Igelova married. They had the following

children:
   i. **Pavla Schönfeldová**.
28. ii. **František Albrecht Schönfeld** was born on 13 Apr 1887 in Semily, Semily District, Bohemia. He died in 1940 in Prague, Bohemia.

13. **Julius von Schönfeld**-3 (Anna-2, Jakub-1) was born in 1853. He died in 1904.

Augusta Picková.

Julius von Schönfeld and Augusta Picková married. They had the following children:
29. i. **Anna Schönfeldová**.
30. ii. **Pavel von Schoenfeld**.
    iii. **Hanus von Schoenfeld**. He died in 1915.
    iv. **Julius von Schoenfeld**. He died in 1914.

14. **Pavla Schönfeldová**-3 (Anna-2, Jakub-1) was born in 1855. She died in 1943 in Terezin.

Rosenfeld.

Rosenfeld and Pavla Schönfeldová married. They had the following children:
31. i. **Pavel (Rosenfeld) Rohan**.
32. ii. **Anna Rosenfeldová**. She died in Osvetim.
33. iii. **Kamila Rosenfeldová** was born in 1980.

15. **Kamila Schönfeldová**-3 (Anna-2, Jakub-1) was born in 1857. She died on 27 Mar 1920 in Krc.

Antal Stasek (Antonín Zemen) son of Antonín Zeman and Anna Šolová was born on 22 Jul 1843 in Stanový, Zlatá Olešnice, Jablonec nad Nisou District, Bohemia. He died on 09 Oct 1931 in Prague, Czech..

Antal Stasek (Antonín Zemen) and Kamila Schönfeldová married. They had the following children:
34. i. **Kamil Zeman (Ivan Olbracht)** was born on 06 Jan 1882 in Semily. He died on 30 Dec 1952 in Praha, CSR.
35. ii. **Vladimír Zeman** was born on 17 Mar 1887. He died on 01 May 1929.

Generation 4

16. **Jiří Weiner**-4 (Gabriela-3, Julie-2, Jakub-1) was born in 1896.
    Kateřina.
    Jiří Weiner and Kateřina married. They had the following children:
    i. **Jadviga Weiner**.
17. **Zdena Weinerova**-4 (Gabriela-3, Julie-2, Jakub-1) was born in 1898. She died in 1975.
    Vladimír Vochoc. He died in 1987.
    Vladimír Vochoc and Zdena Weinerova married. They had the following children:
    i. **Nanynka Vochocova**.
    Antonín Pavel was born in 1887. He died in 1958.
    Antonín Pavel and Zdena Weinerova married. They had no children.
18. **Ivan Kašpárek**-4 (Hermina-3, Julie-2, Jakub-1) was born in 1910. He died in 1985.
    Mila Novotná was born in 1916.
    Ivan Kašpárek and Mila Novotná married. They had the following children:
    36. i. **Eva Kašpárková** was born in 1944.
19. **Vladimír Vodička**-4 (Kamila-3, Julie-2, Jakub-1) was born before 1893. He died on 12 Feb 1954.
    Růžena Krausová.
    Vladimír Vodička and Růžena Krausová married. They had the following children:
    38. i. **Vladimír Vodička** was born on 05 May 1925 in Benešov.
    ii. **daughter Vodička**.
20. **Helena Bloch**-4 (Pavla-3, Julie-2, Jakub-1).
    Salinger.
    Salinger and Helena Bloch married. They had the following children:
    i. **Henry Salinger**.
    Kahn.
    Kahn and Helena Bloch married. They had the following children:
    i. **son Kahn**.

21. **Jiřina Taussigová**-4 (Oskar-3, Julie-2, Jakub-1) was born on 24 Apr 1906 in Prague - Kralovske Vinohrady, Nerudova l. She died on 06 Nov 1962 in New York, NY.

    Paul J. Edwards (Pavel Eisner) son of (Jindřich) Henry Eisner and Hortense Auer was born on 29 Jun 1892 in Prague, Klimentska 1. He died on 27 Jun 1964 in Schenectady, NY.

    Paul J. Edwards (Pavel Eisner) and Jiřina Taussigová were married on 05 Jun 1926 in Prague. They had the following children:
    - 38. i. **Helen Edwards (Eisnerova)** was born on 29 Apr 1927 in Prague, CSR. She married Frank Steiner on 16 Sep 1948 in New York, NY.
    - 39. ii. **Eva Edwards (Eisnerová)** was born on 21 Jan 1932 in Prague, CSR. She married Mila (Miloslav) Rechcigl Jr. on 29 Aug 1953 in New York, NY.

22. **Hana Taussigová**-4 (Oskar-3, Julie-2, Jakub-1) was born on 26 Feb 1910 in Prague. She died on 14 Mar 1999 in New York, NY.

    Joseph (Wiener) Winn son of Maurice Wiener and Alba Růžičková was born on 02 Feb 1901 in Prague. He died on 08 Feb 1983 in New York City. Joseph (Wiener) Winn and Hana Taussigová were married in 1933. They had the following children:
    - 40. i. **Janet (Jana) Winn** was born on 08 Jul 1934 in Prague. She married Donald Malcolm on 13 Apr 1956 in New York City.
    - 41. ii. **Marie Winn** was born on 21 Oct 1936 in Prague. She married Allan Miller on 28 Apr 1961 in New York City.

23. **Vladislav Šváb**-4 (Marie Markéta Marta-3, Julie-2, Jakub-1) was born on 08 Aug 1903 in Vysoke nad Jizerou. He died on 23 Oct 1947 in Tabor, Czechoslovakia.

    Julie Zacharova daughter of Nikolaj Michajlovic Zacharov and Julie Filipovna Obrevko-Zdanov was born on 03 Mar 1901 in Moscow, Russia. She died on 24 Jan 1999 in Tabor, Bbohemia.

    Vladislav Šváb and Julie Zacharova were married on 11 Oct 1932 in Prague. They had the following children:
    - 42. i. **Julie ("Jaska") Švábová** was born on 24 Feb 1945 in Tabor. She married Vladimír Sarsa on 26 Jun 1969 in Ostrava.

24. **Adolf Šváb**-4 (Marie Markéta Marta-3, Julie-2, Jakub-1) was born on 15 Apr 1905 in Vysoke nad Jizerou No. 267. He died in 1976 in Plzen.
Zdenka Sigmundova daughter of Josef Sigmund and Karolina Restránková was born on 31 Oct 1908 in Plzen, Na Lochotine No. 451. She died in 1990 in Plzen.
Adolf Šváb and Zdenka Sigmundova were married on 17 Sep 1932 in Plzen. They had the following children:
    43. i. **Irena Švábová** was born on 03 Feb 1936 in Plzen. She married Emil Kasl in 1955.
    44. ii. **Zdeněk Šváb** was born on 31 Mar 1940 in Plzen.
    45. iii. **Olga Švábová** was born on 18 Jul 1948 in Plzen. She married Vladimír Pechman in 1968.

25. **Kamil Šváb**-4 (Marie Markéta Marta-3, Julie-2, Jakub-1) was born in 1907 in Vysoke nad Jizerou. He died in 1982 in Praha, Bohemia.
Augusta (Gusta) Hyblerova daughter of Otto Hybler and (Pavlina) Marie Schönfeldová was born in 1911. She died in 1960.
Kamil Šváb and Augusta (Gusta) Hyblerova were married in 1936. They had the following children:
    i. **Jan Šváb** was born on 04 Jul 1937 in Praha, CSR. He married Josette Azra on 02 May 1978.
Božena Stroblová was born in 1913. She died in 1981.
Kamil Šváb and Božena Stroblová were married in 1945. They had the following children:
    46. i. **Kamil Šváb** was born on 29 Aug 1944 in Prague. He married Dobroslava Rittova in 1968.

26. **Anna Schönfeldová**-4 (František-3, Anna-2, Jakub-1) was born in 1881. She died in 1945 in Osvetim.
Hugo Iltis was born in 1874. He died in 1927.
Hugo Iltis and Anna Schönfeldová married. They had the following children:
    i. **Augusta Iltisova** was born in 1902. She died in 1983.
    ii. **František Iltis** was born in 1904. He died in 1919.

27. **(Pavlina) Marie Schönfeldová**-4 (František-3, Anna-2, Jakub-1) was

born in 1885. She died in 1932.
Otto Hybler was born about 1880.
Otto Hybler and (Pavlina) Marie Schönfeldová married. They had the following children:
- 47. i. **Otto Hybler** was born in 1909.
- 48. ii. **Eva Hyblerova** was born in 1913.
- 49. iii. **Augusta (Gusta) Hyblerova** was born in 1911. She married Kamil Šváb in 1936. She died in 1960.

28. **František Albrecht Schönfeld**-4 (Josef-3, Anna-2, Jakub-1) was born on 13 Apr 1887 in Semily, Semily District, Bohemia. He died in 1940 in Prague, Bohemia.
Erna Singerova was born on 16 Jul 1897 in Prague, Bohemia. She died in 1944. František Albrecht Schönfeld and Erna Singerova married. They had the following children:
- 50. i. **Pavel (Schönfeld) Tigrid** was born on 27 Oct 1917 in Prague, Bohemia. He died on 31 Aug 2003 in Héricy, Seine-et-Marne, Île-de-France, France.

Olga Kafka was born on 17 Mar 1893 in Pisek, Bohemia. She died in 1942 in Sobibór, Włodawa Dist., Poland - Holocaust.
František Albrecht Schönfeld and Olga Kafka married. They had the following children:
- i. **Gertrude Schönfeld** was born on 13 Mar 1918 in New york, NY.

29. **Anna Schönfeldová**-4 (Julius von-3, Anna-2, Jakub-1).
R. Rosenfeld.
R. Rosenfeld and Anna Schönfeldová married. They had the following children:
- i. **Stella Rosenfeld** was born in 1904.

Willy Fleisher.
Willy Fleisher and Anna Schönfeldová married. They had no children.

30. **Pavel von Schoenfeld**-4 (Julius von-3, Anna-2, Jakub-1).
Weiglova.
Pavel von Schoenfeld and Weiglova married. They had the following children:

i. **Ilse von Schoenfeld.**
31. **Pavel (Rosenfeld) Rohan**-4 (Pavla-3, Anna-2, Jakub-1).
    Roslmeyer.
    Pavel (Rosenfeld) Rohan and Roslmeyer married. They had the following children:
    i. **Marie Rohanová.**
    ii. **Alfred Rohan.**
32. **Anna Rosenfeldová**-4 (Pavla-3, Anna-2, Jakub-1). She died in Osvetim.
    Oscar Pozner. He died in Osvetin.
    Oscar Pozner and Anna Rosenfeldová married. They had the following children:
    51. i. **Erich Pozner** was born in 1978.
    52. ii. **Hans Pozner.**
33. **Kamila Rosenfeldová**-4 (Pavla-3, Anna-2, Jakub-1) was born in 1980.
    Leo Besterman.
    Leo Besterman and Kamila Rosenfeldová married. They had the following children:
    53. i. **Ilse Besterman.**
    ii. **Lea Besterman.**
34. **Kamil Zeman (Ivan Olbracht)**-4 (Kamila-3, Anna-2, Jakub-1) was born on 06 Jan 1882 in Semily. He died on 30 Dec 1952 in Praha, CSR.
    Helena Malirova.
    Kamil Zeman (Ivan Olbracht) and Helena Malirova married. They had the following children:
    i. **Ivanka Olbrachtová** was born on 25 May 1938.
    Slavka.
    Kamil Zeman (Ivan Olbracht) and Slavka married. They had the following children:
    i. **Ivanka Olbrachtová** was born on 25 May 1938.
35. **Vladimír Zeman**-4 (Kamila-3, Anna-2, Jakub-1) was born on 17 Mar 1887. He died on 01 May 1929.
    Marie Wimrova.
    Vladimír Zeman and Marie Wimrova married. They had the following

children:
   i. **Maryška Zemanová** was born in 1915.
55. ii. **Alena Zemanová** was born in 1919.

Generation 5

36. **Eva Kašpárková**-5 (Ivan-4, Hermina-3, Julie-2, Jakub-1) was born in 1944.
    Horatio.
    Horatio and Eva Kašpárková married. They had the following children:
       i. **David**.
37. **Vladimír Vodička**-5 (Vladimír-4, Kamila-3, Julie-2, Jakub-1) was born on 05 May 1925 in Benešov.
    Marie Fiserova.
    Vladimír Vodička and Marie Fiserova married. They had the following children:
       i. **Marie Vodičková**.
    Milada.
    Vladimír Vodička and Milada were married before 1954. They had no children.
38. **Helen Edwards (Eisnerova)**-5 (Jiřina-4, Oskar-3, Julie-2, Jakub-1) was born on 29 Apr 1927 in Prague, CSR.
    Frank Steiner son of Johann (Hans) Steiner and Růžena Steinbachova was born on 23 Apr 1922 in Prague, Bohemia. He died on 14 Sep 2000 in Scotia, NY.
    Frank Steiner and Helen Edwards (Eisnerova) were married on 16 Sep 1948 in New York, NY. They had the following children:
    55. i. **Linda Claire Steiner** was born on 01 Mar 1950 in Schenectady, NY. She married Edward Salomon on 05 Jun 1977 in Scotia, NY.
    56. ii. **David Henry Steiner** was born on 13 Mar 1952 in Schenectady, NY. He married Carol Ann Mastaliz on 07 Jul 1979 in So. Deerfield, MA.
39. **Eva Edwards (Eisnerová)**-5 (Jiřina-4, Oskar-3, Julie-2, Jakub-1) was born on 21 Jan 1932 in Prague, CSR.
    Mila (Miloslav) Rechcigl Jr. son of Miloslav Rechcigl and Marie Rajtrová was born on 30 Jul 1930 in Mladá Boleslav, CSR.

MEISL FAMILY

Mila (Miloslav) Rechcigl Jr. and Eva Edwards (Eisnerová) were married on 29 Aug 1953 in New York, NY. They had the following children:

57. i. **John Edward Rechcigl** was born on 27 Feb 1960 in Washington, D.C.. He married Nancy Ann Palko on 30 Jul 1983 in Dover, NJ.

58. ii. **Karen Rechcigl** was born on 16 Apr 1962 in Washington, DC. She married Ulysses Kollecas on 25 Aug 1990 in Bethesda, MD.

40. **Janet (Jana) Winn**-5 (Hana-4, Oskar-3, Julie-2, Jakub-1) was born on 08 Jul 1934 in Prague.

Donald Malcolm was born in 1935. He died in 1975.

Donald Malcolm and Janet (Jana) Winn were married on 13 Apr 1956 in New York City. They had the following children:

19 i. **Anne Malcolm** was born on 17 Dec 1962 in New York City. She married Richard Tuck on 19 Mar 1993 in New York City.

Gardner Botsford son of Botsford was born on 07 Jul 1917 in New York, NY. He died on 27 Sep 2004 in New York, NY.

Gardner Botsford and Janet (Jana) Winn were married on 26 Sep 1975. They had no children.

41. **Marie Winn**-5 (Hana-4, Oskar-3, Julie-2, Jakub-1) was born on 21 Oct 1936 in Prague.

Allan Miller was born on 05 Dec 1933 in New York City.

Allan Miller and Marie Winn were married on 28 Apr 1961 in New York City. They had the following children:

60. i. **Michael Winn Miller** was born on 20 Nov 1962. He married Sarah Paul on 30 Dec 1988 in New York City.

61. ii. **Steven David Miller** was born on 14 Apr 1966 in New York City. He married Jennifer Durand on 11 Nov 1995 in San Francisco, CA.

41. **Julie ("Jaska") Švábová**-5 (Vladislav-4, Marie Markéta Marta-3, Julie-2, Jakub-1) was born on 24 Feb 1945 in Tabor.

Vladimír Sarsa was born on 11 Feb 1943 in Ostrava.

Vladimír Sarsa and Julie ("Jaska") Švábová were married on 26 Jun 1969 in Ostrava. They had the following children:

i. **Olga Sarsova** was born on 26 Dec 1970 in Ostrava. She married Broniaslav Klementa on Apr 2007 in Na Svatem Kopecku u

Olomouce.

26 ii. **Vladimír Sarsa** was born on 26 Nov 1971 in Ostrava. He married Bronislava Srubkova on 26 Jul 1997 in Ostrava.

43. **Irena Švábová**-5 (Adolf-4, Marie Markéta Marta-3, Julie-2, Jakub-1) was born on 03 Feb 1936 in Plzen.

    Emil Kasl was born in 1926.

    Emil Kasl and Irena Švábová were married in 1955. They had the following children:

    64. i. **Monika Kaslova** was born on 03 Jun 1958 in Plzen. She married Jiří Chládek on 30 Apr 1978 in Prague, CSR.

          ii. **Tomáš Kasl** was born on 26 Apr 1964 in Plzen.

44. **Zdeněk Šváb**-5 (Adolf-4, Marie Markéta Marta-3, Julie-2, Jakub-1) was born on 31 Mar 1940 in Plzen.

    Jaroslava Leimerova was born in 1943.

    Zdeněk Šváb and Jaroslava Leimerova married. They had the following children:

    65. i. **Daniel Šváb** was born on 29 Jan 1964 in Plzen. He married Jitka Kopackova in 1992.

    Marie Kosorova was born in 1945.

    Zdeněk Šváb and Marie Kosorova were married in 1970. They had no children.

45. **Olga Švábová**-5 (Adolf-4, Marie Markéta Marta-3, Julie-2, Jakub-1) was born on 18 Jul 1948 in Plzen.

    Vladimír Pechman was born in 1943.

    Vladimír Pechman and Olga Švábová were married in 1968. They had the following children:

    66. i. **Radek Pechman** was born on 12 Mar 1969 in Plzen. He married Jitka Slámová in 1992.

    67. ii. **Olga Pechmanová** was born on 12 Mar 1976 in Plzen. She married Tomáš Pech in 1998.

    Muchna.

    Muchna and Olga Švábová were married after 1976. They had no children.

46. **Kamil Šváb**-5 (Kamil-4, Marie Markéta Marta-3, Julie-2, Jakub-1) was

born on 29 Aug 1944 in Prague.

Dobroslava Rittova was born on 13 Sep 1945.

Kamil Šváb and Dobroslava Rittova were married in 1968. They had the following children:

>   i. **Jana Švábová** was born on 17 Jun 1972. She married Franklin Venegas on 16 Jul 1994.

47. **Otto Hybler**-5 ((Pavlina) Marie-4, František-3, Anna-2, Jakub-1) was born in 1909.

    Božena.

    Otto Hybler and Božena married. They had the following children:

    68. i. **Alena Hyblerova** was born in 1947.

48. **Eva Hyblerova**-5 ((Pavlina) Marie-4, František-3, Anna-2, Jakub-1) was born in 1913.

    V. Holan.

    W. Holan and Eva Hyblerova married. They had the following children:

    70. i. **Jana Holanova** was born in 1937.

    Bedřich Wiskovsky.

    Bedřich Wiskovsky and Eva Hyblerova married. They had no children.

49. **Augusta (Gusta) Hyblerova**-5 ((Pavlina) Marie-4, František-3, Anna-2, Jakub-1) was born in 1911. She died in 1960.

    Kamil Šváb son of Adolf Šváb and Marie Markéta Marta Taussigová was born in 1907 in Vysoke nad Jizerou. He died in 1982 in Praha, Bohemia. Kamil Šváb and Augusta (Gusta) Hyblerova were married in 1936. They had the following children:

    >   i. **Jan Šváb** was born on 04 Jul 1937 in Praha, CSR. He married Josette Azra on 02 May 1978.

    Karel Storch.

    Karel Storch and Augusta (Gusta) Hyblerova married. They had the following children:

    70. i. **Martin Storch** was born in 1946.

    71. ii. **Anna Storchova** was born in 1947.

50. **Pavel (Schönfeld) Tigrid**-5 (František Albrecht-4, Josef-3, Anna-2, Jakub-1) was born on 27 Oct 1917 in Prague, Bohemia. He died on 31 Aug

2003 in Héricy, Seine-et-Marne, Île-de-France, France.

Ivanka Myskova was born in 1925. She died in 2008.

Pavel (Schönfeld) Tigrid and Ivanka Myskova married. They had the following children:

72. i. **Deborah Tigrid** was born in 1955.
73. ii. **Kateřina Tigridová** was born in 1956.
74. iii. **Gregory Tigrid** was born in 1958.

51. **Erich Pozner**-5 (Anna-4, Pavla-3, Anna-2, Jakub-1) was born in 1978.
    Joyce Smyth.
    Erich Pozner and Joyce Smyth married. They had the following children:
    i. **Rebecca Pozner**.

52. **Hans Pozner**-5 (Anna-4, Pavla-3, Anna-2, Jakub-1).
    Evelin Swallow.
    Hans Pozner and Evelin Swallow married. They had the following children:
    i. **Richard Pozner**.
    ii. **Lora Pozner**.

53. **Ilse Besterman**-5 (Kamila-4, Pavla-3, Anna-2, Jakub-1).
    Pfeifer.
    Pfeifer and Ilse Besterman married. They had the following children:
    i. **Claude Pfeifer**.

54. **Alena Zemanová**-5 (Vladimír-4, Kamila-3, Anna-2, Jakub-1) was born in 1919.
    V. Krotky.
    V. Krotky and Alena Zemanová married. They had the following children:
    i. **Markéta Krotka**.
    ii. **Jan Krotky**.

Generation 6

55. **Linda Claire Steiner**-6 (Helen Edwards-5, Jiřina-4, Oskar-3, Julie-2, Jakub-1) was born on 01 Mar 1950 in Schenectady, NY.
    Edward Salomon son of Jerome Salomon and Rachel Finchel was born

on 12 Feb 1951 in Jersey city, NJ.

Edward Salomon and Linda Claire Steiner were married on 05 Jun 1977 in Scotia, NY. They had the following children:

    i. **Sarah Beth Salomon** was born on 28 Jan 1980 in Chicago, IL.

    ii. **Paul Nathan Salomon** was born on 02 Jan 1983 in Chicago, IL.

56. **David Henry Steiner**-6 (Helen Edwards-5, Jiřina-4, Oskar-3, Julie-2, Jakub-1) was born on 13 Mar 1952 in Schenectady, NY.

Carol Ann Mastaliz daughter of Frank Peter Mastaliz and Helen Carline Macko was born on 26 Oct 1952 (Greenfield, MA).

David Henry Steiner and Carol Ann Mastaliz were married on 07 Jul 1979 in So. Deerfield, MA. They had the following children:

75. i. **Erin Marie Steiner** was born on 01 Aug 1981 in Chicago, IL. She married Michael John Malick on 27 Jul 2013 in Poulsbo, WA.

    ii. **Jonathan Robert Steiner** was born on 30 Dec 1984 in Concord, MA.

57. **John Edward Rechcigl**-6 (Eva Edwards-5, Jiřina-4, Oskar-3, Julie-2, Jakub-1) was born on 27 Feb 1960 in Washington, D.C..

Nancy Ann Palko daughter of Joseph Palko and Mary Rishko was born on 26 Sep 1961 in Morristown, NJ.

John Edward Rechcigl and Nancy Ann Palko were married on 30 Jul 1983 in Dover, NJ. They had the following children:

    i. **Gregory John Rechcigl** was born on 19 Dec 1988 in Bradenton, FL.

77. ii. **Kevin Thomas Rechcigl** was born on 09 Oct 1991 in Bradenton, FL. He married Jordan Robbins on 12 May 2018 in Jacksonville, FL.

    iii. **Lindsey Nicole Rechcigl** was born on 03 Nov 1994 in Bradenton, FL.

58. **Karen Rechcigl**-6 (Eva Edwards-5, Jiřina-4, Oskar-3, Julie-2, Jakub-1) was born on 16 Apr 1962 in Washington, DC.

Ulysses Kollecas son of Christopher Thomas (Kolecas) Collier and Amelia Malatras was born on 20 Mar 1958 in Washington, DC.

Ulysses Kollecas and Karen Rechcigl were married on 25 Aug 1990 in Bethesda, MD. They had the following children:

i. **Kristin Kollecas** was born on 04 May 1993 in Albuquerque, NM.
ii. **Paul Kollecas** was born on 02 Jun 1995 in Albuquerque, NM.

59. **Anne Malcolm**-6 (Janet (Jana)-5, Hana-4, Oskar-3, Julie-2, Jakub-1) was born on 17 Dec 1962 in New York City.
   Richard Tuck was born on 09 Jan 1949 in Newcastleupon-Tyne, England. Richard Tuck and Anne Malcolm were married on 19 Mar 1993 in New York City. They had the following children:
   i. **Sophy Malcolm Tuck** was born on 13 Jul 1993 in Cambridge, England.

60. **Michael Winn Miller**-6 (Marie-5, Hana-4, Oskar-3, Julie-2, Jakub-1) was born on 20 Nov 1962.
   Sarah Paul was born on 29 Dec 1961 in New York City.
   Michael Winn Miller and Sarah Paul were married on 30 Dec 1988 in New York City. They had the following children:
   i. **Isadore 'Izzy' Miller** was born on 20 Nov 1995 in San Francisco, CA.
   ii. **Abigail "Abbey' Nadia Paul Miller** was born on 24 Oct 1996 in New York City.

61. **Steven David Miller**-6 (Marie-5, Hana-4, Oskar-3, Julie-2, Jakub-1) was born on 14 Apr 1966 in New York City.
   Jennifer Durand.
   Steven David Miller and Jennifer Durand were married on 11 Nov 1995 in San Francisco, CA. They had the following children:
   i. **Eli Miller** was born on 17 Mar 1999.
   ii. **Clara Miller** was born on 04 Jul 2000 in San Francisco, CA or NYC.

62. **Olga Sarsova**-6 (Julie ("Jaska")-5, Vladislav-4, Marie Markéta Marta-3, Julie-2, Jakub-1) was born on 26 Dec 1970 in Ostrava.
   Broniaslav Klementa son of Josef Klementa and Oldřiška Pavlickova was born on 29 Jun 1966 in Sumperk.
   Broniaslav Klementa and Olga Sarsova were married on 14 Apr 2007 in Na Svatem Kopecku u Olomouce. They had the following children:
   i. **Veronika Klementova** was born on 25 May 2007 in Olomouc.

63. **Vladimír Sarsa**-6 (Julie ("Jaska")-5, Vladislav-4, Marie Markéta Marta-

3, Julie-2, Jakub-1) was born on 26 Nov 1971 in Ostrava.

Bronislava Srubkova was born on 05 Mar 1963 in Pustejov, Bruntal Dist., Czechoslovakia..

Vladimír Sarsa and Bronislava Srubkova were married on 26 Jul 1997 in Ostrava. They had the following children:

    i. **Milena Sarsova** was born on 03 Jan 1998 in Ostrava, Czechoslovakia.

64. **Monika Kaslova**-6 (Irena-5, Adolf-4, Marie Markéta Marta-3, Julie-2, Jakub-1) was born on 03 Jun 1958 in Plzen.

Jiří Chládek was born in 1955.

Jiří Chládek and Monika Kaslova were married on 30 Apr 1978 in Prague, CSR. They had the following children:

    i. **David Chládek** was born on 19 Dec 1978 in Cheb.

    ii. **Ondřej Chládek** was born on 17 Aug 1981 in Cheb.

    iii. **Jan Chládek** was born on 16 Nov 1988 in Cheb.

65. **Daniel Šváb**-6 (Zdeněk-5, Adolf-4, Marie Markéta Marta-3, Julie-2, Jakub-1) was born on 29 Jan 1964 in Plzen.

Jitka Kopackova.

Daniel Šváb and Jitka Kopackova were married in 1992. They had the following children:

    i. **Dominika Švábová** was born on 16 Oct 1992 in Plzen.

    ii. **Natalie Švábová** was born on 09 Aug 1998 in Plzen.

66. **Radek Pechman**-6 (Olga-5, Adolf-4, Marie Markéta Marta-3, Julie-2, Jakub-1) was born on 12 Mar 1969 in Plzen.

Jitka Slámová was born in 1966.

Radek Pechman and Jitka Slámová were married in 1992. They had the following children:

    i. **Barbora Pechmanová** was born in 1992.

67. **Olga Pechmanová**-6 (Olga-5, Adolf-4, Marie Markéta Marta-3, Julie-2, Jakub-1) was born on 12 Mar 1976 in Plzen.

Tomáš Pech.

Tomáš Pech and Olga Pechmanová were married in 1998. They had the following children:

i. **Karolina Pechová** was born on 22 May 1999 in Plzen.
68. **Alena Hyblerova**-6 (Otto-5, (Pavlina) Marie-4, František-3, Anna-2, Jakub-1) was born in 1947.
Jiří Kos.
Jiří Kos and Alena Hyblerova married. They had the following children:
i. **David Kos.**
69. **Jana Holanova**-6 (Eva-5, (Pavlina) Marie-4, František-3, Anna-2, Jakub-1) was born in 1937.
Jindřich Pokorný was born in 1921.
Jindřich Pokorný and Jana Holanova married. They had the following children:
77. i. **Tereza Pokorná** was born in 1960.
70. **Martin Storch**-6 (Augusta (Gusta)-5, (Pavlina) Marie-4, František-3, Anna-2, Jakub-1) was born in 1946.
Marta Musilová was born in 1948.
Martin Storch and Marta Musilová married. They had the following children:
i. **Jan Storch.**
71. **Anna Storchova**-6 (Augusta (Gusta)-5, (Pavlina) Marie-4, František-3, Anna-2, Jakub-1) was born in 1947.
Kristian Kodet.
Kristian Kodet and Anna Storchova married. They had the following children:
i. **Veronika Kodetova** was born in 1968.
ii. **Johanna Kodetova** was born in 1970.
72. **Deborah Tigrid**-6 (Pavel (Schönfeld)-5, František Albrecht-4, Josef-3, Anna-2, Jakub-1) was born in 1955.
Eric Marguerat.
Eric Marguerat and Deborah Tigrid married. They had the following children:
i. **Natasha Marguerat** was born in 1984.
ii. **Nathan Marguerat** was born in 1987.
iii. **Valentin Marguerat** was born in 1991.

73. **Kateřina Tigridová**-6 (Pavel (Schönfeld)-5, František Albrecht-4, Josef-3, Anna-2, Jakub-1) was born in 1956.

Kateřina Tigridová and unknown spouse married. They had the following children:

    i. **Tommy** was born in 1985.

74. **Gregory Tigrid**-6 (Pavel (Schönfeld)-5, František Albrecht-4, Josef-3, Anna-2, Jakub-1) was born in 1958.

Gregory Tigrid and unknown spouse married. They had the following children:

    i. **Stanislas** was born in 1987.

Generation 7

1 **Erin Marie Steiner**-7 (David Henry-6, Helen Edwards-5, Jiřina-4, Oskar-3, Julie-2, Jakub-1) was born on 01 Aug 1981 in Chicago, IL.

Michael John Malick was born on 01 Aug 1981 in Chicago, IL.

Michael John Malick and Erin Marie Steiner were married on 27 Jul 2013 in Poulsbo, WA. They had the following children:

44. **Henry Francsz Malick** was born on 18 Feb 2018 in Seattle, WA.

2 **Kevin Thomas Rechcigl**-7 (John Edward-6, Eva Edwards-5, Jiřina-4, Oskar-3, Julie-2, Jakub-1) was born on 09 Oct 1991 in Bradenton, FL.

Jordan Robbins daughter of Douglass Robbins and Ivonne was born on 10 Jan 1992 in Camarillo, CA.

Kevin Thomas Rechcigl and Jordan Robbins were married on 12 May 2018 in Jacksonville, FL. They had the following children:

44. **James Douglas Rechcigl** was born on 05 Jan 2021 in Jacksonville, FL.

45. **Evelyn Marie Rechcigl** was born 29 May 2023 in Jacksonville, FL.

3 **Tereza Pokorná**-7 (Jana-6, Eva-5, (Pavlina) Marie-4, František-3, Anna-2, Jakub-1) was born in 1960.

Jura Herz was born in 1936.

Jura Herz and Tereza Pokorná married. They had the following children:

    44. **Anna Elisabeth Herzova**.

Munk Family

Generation 1

1. **Jakub Munk**-1.
   Barbora Arnstein was born in Chotěšov, Bohemia.
   Jakub Munk and Barbora Arnstein married. They had the following children:
   2. i. **Rafael Munk** was born about 1823 in Chotesov, Plzen Region, Bohemia. He died on 22 Oct 1905 in Benešov.
   ii. **Daniel Munk**.
   iii. **Isachiel Munk**.
   iv. **Ariel Munk**.
   3. v. **Gabriel Munk** was born on 05 Apr 1831 in Chotysany. He died on 14 Dec 1896 in Struhařov, Benešov District, Bohemia.
   4. vi. **Abraham Munk** was born in 1822 in Chotesov, Bohemia. He died on 26 Apr 1891 in Dobromerice, Bohemia.

Generation 2

2. **Rafael Munk**-2 (Jakub-1) was born about 1823 in Chotesov, Plzen Region, Bohemia. He died on 22 Oct 1905 in Benešov.
   Theresia Steindlerová daughter of Jakub Steindler and Ludmila Bret was born on 07 Nov 1849. Rafael Munk and Theresia Steindlerová married. They had the following children:
   5. i. **Klára Munková** was born on 21 Dec 1887 in Prague, Bohemia. She died on 18 Jan 1934 in Prague, Bohemia.

3. **Gabriel Munk**-2 (Jakub-1) was born on 05 Apr 1831 in Chotysany. He died on 14 Dec 1896 in Struhařov, Benešov District, Bohemia.
   Anna Frank daughter of Raphael Frank and Anna Kolinska was born on 14 Feb 1835 in Struhařov, Benešov District, Bohemia. She died on 01 Jan 1881 in Struhařov, Benešov District, Bohemia. Gabriel Munk and Anna Frank married. They had the following children:
   i. **Rudolf Munk** was born on 14 Feb 1859 in Struharov.
   ii. **Moriz Munk** was born about 1861. He died on 25 Jun 1885 in Bohemia.

  iii. **Heinrich Munk** was born on 24 Sep 1862. He died on 30 Dec 1929 in Karlovy Vary, Bohemia.

  iv. **Josef Wilhelm Munk** was born on 24 Apr 1865.

  v. **August Munk** was born on 09 Aug 1867 in Struharov. He died in 1942 in Treblinka, Poland - Holocaust.

6. vi. **Emilie Emma Munk** was born on 02 Mar 1869 in Struharov. She died on 18 Aug 1942 in Terezin - Holocaust.

  vii. **Mathilde Munk** was born on 10 Nov 1870. She died on 22 Mar 1871.

  viii. **Beatrice Munk** was born in Dec 1873. She died on 17 Apr 1874 in Struhařov, Benešov District, Bohemia.

7. ix. **Klementine Munk** was born in 1875. She died on 04 May 1900 in Kladno, Bohemia.

  x. **Otilie Munk** was born on 01 May 1875.

  xi. **Wilhelm Munk**.

4. **Abraham Munk**-2 (Jakub-1) was born in 1822 in Chotesov, Bohemia. He died on 26 Apr 1891 in Dobromerice, Bohemia.

Franziska Arnstein daughter of Jonáš Arnstein and Barbara Josepha Kauders was born on 04 Mar 1847 in Pribysice, Neveklov.

Abraham Munk and Franziska Arnstein married. They had the following children:

8. i. **Leopold Munk** was born about 1858. He died in Feb 1923 in Louny, Bohemia.

9. ii. **Karoline Munk** was born on 20 May 1880 in Dobromerice, Bohemia.

10. iii. **Moritz Munk** was born on 27 Sep 1878 in Týnec nad Sázavou, Central Bohemia, Czech Republic.

  iv. **Otto Munk** was born on 17 Nov 1887 in Dobromerice, North Bohemia, Czech Republic.

11. v. **Josef Munk** was born on 10 Oct 1874 in Týnec nad Sázavou, Central Bohemia, Czech Republic. He died on 08 Feb 1939.

12. vi. **Hermine Munk** was born on 25 Apr 1885 in Dobromerice, North Bohemia, Czech Republic. She died on 02 Mar 1923 in Velebudice,

North Bohemia, Czech Republic.
- vii. **Heinrich Munk** was born on 10 Feb 1882 in Dobromerice, North Bohemia, Czech Republic.

13. viii. **Regina Munková** was born on 18 Sep 1877 in Týnec nad Sázavou, Central Bohemia, Czech Republic. She died about 1942 in Lub lin, Poland - Holocaust.

Maria Steindlerová daughter of Jakub Steindler and Ludmila Bret was born in 1838. She died on 29 Apr 1872.

Abraham Munk and Maria Steindlerová married. They had the following children:

- i. **Pauline (Pavla) Munk** was born on 25 Aug 1863 in Tynec.

Generation 3

5. **Klára Munková**-3 (Rafael-2, Jakub-1) was born on 21 Dec 1887 in Prague, Bohemia. She died on 18 Jan 1934 in Prague, Bohemia.

   Oskar Taussig son of Jakub Taussig and Julie Meislova was born on 22 Jun 1876 in Benešov. He died on 08 Nov 1938 in Prague.

   Oskar Taussig and Klára Munková married. They had the following children:

   14. i. **Jiřina Taussigová** was born on 24 Apr 1906 in Prague - Kralovske Vinohrady, Nerudova l. She married Paul J. Edwards (Pavel Eisner) on 05 Jun 1926 in Prague. She died on 06 Nov 1962 in New York, NY.
   15. ii. **Hana Taussigová** was born on 26 Feb 1910 in Prague. She married Joseph (Wiener) Winn in 1933. She died on 14 Mar 1999 in New York, NY.

6. **Emilie Emma Munk**-3 (Gabriel-2, Jakub-1) was born on 02 Mar 1869 in Struharov. She died on 18 Aug 1942 in Terezin - Holocaust.

   Max Lengsfeld was born on 25 Sep 1863 in Neuschloss No. 39. He died on 30 Jul 1930 in Prague, Bohemia.

   Max Lengsfeld and Emilie Emma Munk married. They had the following children:

   - i. **Franz Lengsfeld** was born on 02 Dec 1895 in Prague, Bohemia.
   - ii. **Josef Lengsfeld** was born on 14 Dec 1892 in Prague, Bohemia. He died in 1968.

16. iii. **Anna Lengsfeld** was born on 23 Apr 1894 in Prague, Bohemia. She died on 06 May 1976.

7. **Klementine Munk**-3 (Gabriel-2, Jakub-1) was born in 1875. She died on 04 May 1900 in Kladno, Bohemia.

   Berthold Deutschmann was born on 31 Mar 1852 in Rychnov nad Kněžnou,, Bohemia. He died on 14 Mar 1906 in Kladno, Bohemia.

   Berthold Deutschmann and Klementine Munk married. They had the following children:

   17. i. **Pauline Deutschmann** was born on 30 Mar 1898 in Kladno, Bohemia. She died in May 1942 in Sobibor - Holocaust.

       ii. **Gabriele Deutschmann**.

8. **Leopold Munk**-3 (Abraham-2, Jakub-1) was born about 1858. He died in Feb 1923 in Louny, Bohemia.

   Mathilda Melichar daughter of Melichar and Unknown was born in 1868 in Kolin. She died on 10 Jan 1937.

   Leopold Munk and Mathilda Melichar married. They had the following children:

   18. i. **Hugo Munk** was born on 27 Mar 1894 in Hradek, Moravia. He married Martha about 1930. He died about 1935.

       ii. **Arthur Munk** was born on 18 May 1891. He married Martha after 1945.

   19. iii. **Else Munk** was born on 25 Jan 1890 in Hradek, Bohemia. She died about 1943 in Oswiecim, Poland.

       iv. **Joseph Jacob Bernhard Munk** was born on 17 May 1887. He died in 1887.

       v. **Marie Munk** was born on 24 May 1888 in Hrádek, North Moravia, Czech Republic. She died on 09 May 1942 in Lublin, Poland.

9. **Karoline Munk**-3 (Abraham-2, Jakub-1) was born on 20 May 1880 in Dobromerice, Bohemia.

   Pollak.

   Pollak and Karoline Munk married. They had the following children:

   i. **B. Pollak**.

10. **Moritz Munk**-3 (Abraham-2, Jakub-1) was born on 27 Sep 1878 in Týnec nad Sázavou, Central Bohemia, Czech Republic.

    Ludmila Propper daughter of Ludwig Popper and Cecilie 'Cilli' Kraus was born on 12 Nov 1891 in Panensky Tynec, Bohemia. She died on 12 Dec 1943 in Terezin.

    Moritz Munk and Ludmila Propper married. They had the following children:

        i. **Franziska Helene Munk** was born on 17 Nov 1911 in Most, Bohemia.

11. **Josef Munk**-3 (Abraham-2, Jakub-1) was born on 10 Oct 1874 in Týnec nad Sázavou, Central Bohemia, Czech Republic. He died on 08 Feb 1939.

    Marie Hubscherova was born in 1897. She died in 1943.

    Josef Munk and Marie Hubscherova married. They had the following children:

    20. i. **Josef Munk** was born in 1916. He died in 1987.

12. **Hermine Munk**-3 (Abraham-2, Jakub-1) was born on 25 Apr 1885 in Dobromerice, North Bohemia, Czech Republic. She died on 02 Mar 1923 in Velebudice, North Bohemia, Czech Republic.

    Ludwig Spitz was born on 06 Jun 1878 in Velebudice, North Bohemia, Czech Republic. He died on 20 May 1941 in Dachau, Germany.

    Ludwig Spitz and Hermine Munk married. They had the following children:

        i. **Frederike 'Fritzi' Spitz** was born on 27 Sep 1907 in Most, Bohemia. She died after 17 Mar 1942 in Lublin, Poland - Hholocaust.

    16. ii. **Franziska 'Franzi' Spitz** was born on 09 Jul 1909 in Velebudice, North Bohemia, Czech Republic. She died on 11 Nov 1983 in Prague, Czechoslavakia.

13. **Regina Munková**-3 (Abraham-2, Jakub-1) was born on 18 Sep 1877 in Týnec nad Sázavou, Central Bohemia, Czech Republic. She died about 1942 in Lub lin, Poland - Holocaust.

    Josef Rezek was born on 17 Mar 1867 in Zivohost, Bohemia. He died about 1942 in Poland - Holocaust.

Josef Rezek and Regina Munková married. They had the following children:

    i. **Anna Rezková** was born on 12 Aug 1899 in Lower Austria.

    ii. **Julius Rezek** was born on 26 Jun 1911 in Waldhofen, Lowetr Austria. He died on 22 Oct 1989 in Sydney, Australia.

Generation 4

14. **Jiřina Taussigová**-4 (Klára-3, Rafael-2, Jakub-1) was born on 24 Apr 1906 in Prague - Kralovske Vinohrady, Nerudova l. She died on 06 Nov 1962 in New York, NY.

    Paul J. Edwards (Pavel Eisner) son of (Jindřich) Henry Eisner and Hortense Auer was born on 29 Jun 1892 in Prague, Klimentska 1. He died on 27 Jun 1964 in Schenectady, NY.

    Paul J. Edwards (Pavel Eisner) and Jiřina Taussigová were married on 05 Jun 1926 in Prague. They had the following children:

    22. i. **Helen Edwards (Eisnerova)** was born on 29 Apr 1927 in Prague, CSR. She married Frank Steiner on 16 Sep 1948 in New York, NY.

    23. ii. **Eva Edwards (Eisnerová)** was born on 21 Jan 1932 in Prague, CSR. She married Mila (Miloslav) Rechcigl Jr. on 29 Aug 1953 in New York, NY.

15. **Hana Taussigová**-4 (Klára-3, Rafael-2, Jakub-1) was born on 26 Feb 1910 in Prague. She died on 14 Mar 1999 in New York, NY.

    Joseph (Wiener) Winn son of Maurice Wiener and Alba Růžičková was born on 02 Feb 1901 in Prague. He died on 08 Feb 1983 in New York City. Joseph (Wiener) Winn and Hana Taussigová were married in 1933. They had the following children:

    24. i. **Janet (Jana) Winn** was born on 08 Jul 1934 in Prague. She married Donald Malcolm on 13 Apr 1956 in New York City.

    25. ii. **Marie Winn** was born on 21 Oct 1936 in Prague. She married Allan Miller on 28 Apr 1961 in New York City.

16. **Anna Lengsfeld**-4 (Emilie Emma-3, Gabriel-2, Jakub-1) was born on 23 Apr 1894 in Prague, Bohemia. She died on 06 May 1976.

    Pravomir Novotný was born in 1891. He died on 14 Dec 1966.

    Pravomir Novotný and Anna Lengsfeld married. They had the following

children:
- i. **Pravomir Novotný**.
- ii. **Věra Novotný** was born on 11 Sep 1919. She died on 30 Jun 1958.

17. **Pauline Deutschmann**-4 (Klementine-3, Gabriel-2, Jakub-1) was born on 30 Mar 1898 in Kladno, Bohemia. She died in May 1942 in Sobibor - Holocaust.

    Ernst (Arnošt) Drucker was born on 20 Aug 1896 in Prague, Bohemia. He died in May 1942 in Sobibor - Holocaust.

    Ernst (Arnošt) Drucker and Pauline Deutschmann married. They had the following children:
    - i. **Jan Drucker** was born on 16 Aug 1925. He died in May 1942 in Sobibor - Holocaust.

18. **Hugo Munk**-4 (Leopold-3, Abraham-2, Jakub-1) was born on 27 Mar 1894 in Hradek, Moravia. He died about 1935.

    Martha.

    Hugo Munk and Martha were married about 1930. They had the following children:
    - i. **child Munk**.

    Anna Lustig daughter of Ignaz Lustig and Emilie Siinger was born on 11 Apr 1894 in Korycany, Moravia.

    Hugo Munk and Anna Lustig married. They had no children.

19. **Else Munk**-4 (Leopold-3, Abraham-2, Jakub-1) was born on 25 Jan 1890 in Hradek, Bohemia. She died about 1943 in Oswiecim, Poland.

    Viktor Heller was born on 16 Aug 1882 in Chomutov, Bohemia. He died in 1962. Viktor Heller and Else Munk married. They had the following children:
    - i. **Katharine Heller**.

20. **Josef Munk**-4 (Josef-3, Abraham-2, Jakub-1) was born in 1916. He died in 1987.

    Marie Kvitkova.

    Josef Munk and Marie Kvitkova married. They had the following children:
    - 26. i. **Marie Munková**.

21. **Franziska 'Franzi' Spitz**-4 (Hermine-3, Abraham-2, Jakub-1) was born on 09 Jul 1909 in Velebudice, North Bohemia, Czech Republic. She died on 11 Nov 1983 in Prague, Czechoslavakia.

    Franz Nikl was born on 24 Jan 1907 in Duchcov, North Bohemia, Czech Republic. He died on 13 May 1977 in Prague, Czechoslavakia.

    Franz Nikl and Franziska 'Franzi' Spitz married. They had the following children:

    27. i. **Pavel Nikl** was born on 28 Aug 1946 in Prague, Czechoslavakia.

Generation 5

22. **Helen Edwards (Eisnerova)**-5 (Jiřina-4, Klára-3, Rafael-2, Jakub-1) was born on 29 Apr 1927 in Prague, CSR.

    Frank Steiner son of Johann (Hans) Steiner and Růžena Steinbachova was born on 23 Apr 1922 in Prague, Bohemia. He died on 14 Sep 2000 in Scotia, NY.

    Frank Steiner and Helen Edwards (Eisnerova) were married on 16 Sep 1948 in New York, NY. They had the following children:

    i. **Linda Claire Steiner** was born on 01 Mar 1950 in Schenectady, NY. She married Edward Salomon on 05 Jun 1977 in Scotia, NY.

    ii. **David Henry Steiner** was born on 13 Mar 1952 in Schenectady, NY. He married Carol Ann Mastaliz on 07 Jul 1979 in So. Deerfield, MA.

23. **Eva Edwards (Eisnerová)**-5 (Jiřina-4, Klára-3, Rafael-2, Jakub-1) was born on 21 Jan 1932 in Prague, CSR.

    Mila (Miloslav) Rechcigl Jr. son of Miloslav Rechcigl and Marie Rajtrová was born on 30 Jul 1930 in Mladá Boleslav, CSR.

    Mila (Miloslav) Rechcigl Jr. and Eva Edwards (Eisnerová) were married on 29 Aug 1953 in New York, NY. They had the following children:

    i. **John Edward Rechcigl** was born on 27 Feb 1960 in Washington, D.C.. He married Nancy Ann Palko on 30 Jul 1983 in Dover, NJ.

    ii. **Karen Rechcigl** was born on 16 Apr 1962 in Washington, DC. She married Ulysses Kollecas on 25 Aug 1990 in Bethesda, MD.

24. **Janet (Jana) Winn**-5 (Hana-4, Klára-3, Rafael-2, Jakub-1) was born on 08 Jul 1934 in Prague.

Donald Malcolm was born in 1935. He died in 1975.

Donald Malcolm and Janet (Jana) Winn were married on 13 Apr 1956 in New York City. They had the following children:

    i.   **Anne Malcolm** was born on 17 Dec 1962 in New York City. She married Richard Tuck on 19 Mar 1993 in New York City.

Gardner Botsford son of Botsford was born on 07 Jul 1917 in New York, NY. He died on 27 Sep 2004 in New York, NY.

Gardner Botsford and Janet (Jana) Winn were married on 26 Sep 1975. They had no children.

25. **Marie Winn**-5 (Hana-4, Klára-3, Rafael-2, Jakub-1) was born on 21 Oct 1936 in Prague.

    Allan Miller was born on 05 Dec 1933 in New York City.

    Allan Miller and Marie Winn were married on 28 Apr 1961 in New York City. They had the following children:

        i.   **Michael Winn Miller** was born on 20 Nov 1962. He married Sarah Paul on 30 Dec 1988 in New York City.

        ii.   **Steven David Miller** was born on 14 Apr 1966 in New York City. He married Jennifer Durand on 11 Nov 1995 in San Francisco, CA.

26. **Marie Munková**-5 (Josef-4, Josef-3, Abraham-2, Jakub-1).

    Josef Cihak.

    Josef Cihak and Marie Munková married. They had the following children:

        i.   **Ondřej Cihak**.

27. **Pavel Nikl**-5 (Franziska 'Franzi'-4, Hermine-3, Abraham-2, Jakub-1) was born on 28 Aug 1946 in Prague, Czechoslavakia.

    Unknown.

    Pavel Nikl and Unknown married. They had the following children:

        i.   **Pavla Nikl** was born on 14 Jul 1987 in Prague, Czechoslavakia.

Steindler Family

Generation 1

1. **Jakub Steindler**-1 was born in 1820 in Benešov, Bohemia. He died on 17 Apr 1873 in Benešov, Bohemia.

   Ludmila Bret daughter of Elias Bret and Eva Goldberger was born on 24 Dec 1813 in Golcuv Jenikov, Havlickuv Brod District, Moravia. She died on 13 Dec 1849 in Benešov, Bohemia. Jakub Steindler and Ludmila Bret married. They had the following children:

   2. i. **Maria Steindlerová** was born in 1838. She died on 29 Apr 1872.

       ii. **Francisca Steindlerová** was born on 15 Aug 1840.

       iii. **Anna Steindlerová** was born on 17 Sep 1842.

       iv. **Helena Steindlerová** was born on 26 Apr 1845.

   3. v. **Theresia Steindlerová** was born on 07 Nov 1849.

   Antonie Bret.

   Jakub Steindler and Antonie Bret married. They had the following children:

   4. i. **Moritz Steindler** was born on 15 Dec 1853 in Benešov. He died on 01 Aug 1917 in weinerBenesov, Bohemia.

Generation 2

2. **Maria Steindlerová**-2 (Jakub-1) was born in 1838. She died on 29 Apr 1872.

   Abraham Munk son of Jakub Munk and Barbora Arnstein was born in 1822 in Chotesov, Bohemia. He died on 26 Apr 1891 in Dobromerice, Bohemia.

   Abraham Munk and Maria Steindlerová married. They had the following children:

       i. **Pauline (Pavla) Munk** was born on 25 Aug 1863 in Tynec.

3. **Theresia Steindlerová**-2 (Jakub-1) was born on 07 Nov 1849.

   Rafael Munk son of Jakub Munk and Barbora Arnstein was born about 1823 in Chotesov, Plzen Region, Bohemia. He died on 22 Oct 1905 in Benešov.

   Rafael Munk and Theresia Steindlerová married. They had the following

children:
- 5. i. **Klára Munková** was born on 21 Dec 1887 in Prague, Bohemia. She died on 18 Jan 1934 in Prague, Bohemia.

4. **Moritz Steindler**-2 (Jakub-1) was born on 15 Dec 1853 in Benešov. He died on 01 Aug 1917 in weinerBenesov, Bohemia.

    Fridricha (Bedřiška) Ascher daughter of Bernhard Ascher and Francisca Guttmann was born in 1854 in Pacov. She died on 03 Jul 1886.

    Moritz Steindler and Fridricha (Bedřiška) Ascher married. They had the following children:
    - 6. i. **Marie Steindlerová** was born on 06 Sep 1878 in Benešov. She died on 22 Oct 1942 in Treblinka.
    - 7. ii. **Antonie Steindlerová** was born on 20 Oct 1879 in Benešov. She died on 28 Jul 1942 in Baranovici KZ.
    - 8. iii. **Anna Steindlerová** was born on 29 Jun 1881 in Benešov. She died on 10 Oct 1944 in Auschwitz.
    - 9. iv. **Luisa Steindlerová** was born on 16 Jun 1883 in Benešov. She died on 09 May 1942 in Sobibor Ossowa KZ.
    - 10. v. **Jaroslav Steindler** was born on 25 Mar 1885 in Benešov. He died in 1980 in Praha.

    Klára Abelesova daughter of Josef Abeles and Franziska Schulhof was born on 20 Jun 1864 in Lechovice, Beroun District, Bohemia. She died on 05 Aug 1922 in Benešov, Bohemia.

    Moritz Steindler and Klára Abelesova married. They had the following children:
    - 11. i. **Antonie Steindler** was born on 20 Oct 1879 in Benešov, Bohemia. She died on 28 Jul 1942 in Baranavichy, Brestskaya Voblasts', Belarus - Holocaust.
    - 12. ii. **Bedřiška Steindlerová** was born on 06 Apr 1888 in Benešov, Bohemia. She died on 05 Nov 1959 in Praha, Czechoslovakia.
    - 13. iii. **Ema Steindlerová** was born on 24 Sep 1889 in Benešov. She died on 14 Sep 1966 in Praha.
    - 14. iv. **Josef Steindler** was born on 06 Jun 1891 in Benešov, Bohemia. He died on 01 Jul 1942 in Tabor, Tábor District, Bohemia.

15. v. **Pavel Jiří Steindler** was born on 10 Apr 1893 in Benešov No. 126, Bohemia. He died on 29 Sep 1944 in Auschwitz, Poland - Holocaust.
16. vi. **Božena Steindlerová** was born on 08 Jun 1895 in Benešov. She died on 15 Sep 1971 in Praha.
17. vii. **Karel Steindler** was born on 21 Jan 1897 in Benešov No. 126, Bohemia. He died on 01 Jul 1965 in Sydney, New South Wales, Australia.
18. viii. **Zdenka Steindlerová** was born on 04 Oct 1898 in Benešov. She died on 11 Oct 1944 in Auschwitz KZ.
19. ix. **Ludmila ("Lidka") Steindlerová** was born on 01 Oct 1900 in Benešov. She died in Dec 1925 in Praha.

Generation 3

5. **Klára Munková**-3 (Theresia-2, Jakub-1) was born on 21 Dec 1887 in Prague, Bohemia. She died on 18 Jan 1934 in Prague, Bohemia.
Oskar Taussig son of Jakub Taussig and Julie Meislova was born on 22 Jun 1876 in Benešov. He died on 08 Nov 1938 in Prague.
Oskar Taussig and Klára Munková married. They had the following children:
   20. i. **Jiřina Taussigová** was born on 24 Apr 1906 in Prague - Kralovske Vinohrady, Nerudova l. She married Paul J. Edwards (Pavel Eisner) on 05 Jun 1926 in Prague. She died on 06 Nov 1962 in New York, NY.
   21. ii. **Hana Taussigová** was born on 26 Feb 1910 in Prague. She married Joseph (Wiener) Winn in 1933. She died on 14 Mar 1999 in New York, NY.
6. **Marie Steindlerová**-3 (Moritz-2, Jakub-1) was born on 06 Sep 1878 in Benešov. She died on 22 Oct 1942 in Treblinka.
Bedřich Rosenbaum was born about 1878. He died about 1942.
Bedřich Rosenbaum and Marie Steindlerová married. They had the following children:
   22. i. **Jan (Rosenbaum) Skála** was born about 1899 in Nova Hospoda. He died in 1944 in Terezin.
   23. ii. **Bedřiška Rosenbaumova** was born on 16 Jul 1901. She died on 19 Oct 1944 in Auschwitz KZ.

24. iii. **František Rosenbaum** was born on 05 Sep 1908. He died on 20 Feb 1945 in Dachau KZ.

7. **Antonie Steindlerová**-3 (Moritz-2, Jakub-1) was born on 20 Oct 1879 in Benešov. She died on 28 Jul 1942 in Baranovici KZ.

   Orovan.

   Orovan and Antonie Steindlerová married. They had the following children:

   i. **Bedřiška ("Fritzi") Orovan.**

   Siegfried Gruenwald was born on 26 Nov 1877 in Unin. He died on 28 Jul 1942 in Baranovici KZ.

   Siegfried Gruenwald and Antonie Steindlerová married. They had the following children:

   25. i. **Gertrude Grünwald** was born about 1911. She died about 1992 in Stockholm, Sweden.

   ii. **Marianne Grünwald** was born on 03 Jul 1912 in Gloggnitz, Neunkirchen District, Lower Austria, Austria.

   26. iii. **Anna Grünwald** was born on 03 Jul 1912 in Gloggnitz, Neunkirchen District, Lower Austria, Austria.

8. **Anna Steindlerová**-3 (Moritz-2, Jakub-1) was born on 29 Jun 1881 in Benešov. She died on 10 Oct 1944 in Auschwitz.

   Alois Katz Kalina. He died in 1929 in Praha.

   Alois Katz Kalina and Anna Steindlerová married. They had the following children:

   i. **Josef Katz Kalina** was born on 16 Mar 1909 in Praha. He died on 11 Mar 1942 in Izbica KZ.

   27. ii. **Jiří Katz Kalina** was born in 1910 in Praha. He died in 1984 in Sydney, Australia.

   28. iii. **Milena Katzova Kalinova** was born on 28 Nov 1910. She died in 1943 in Auschwitz KZ.

9. **Luisa Steindlerová**-3 (Moritz-2, Jakub-1) was born on 16 Jun 1883 in Benešov. She died on 09 May 1942 in Sobibor Ossowa KZ.

   Carl Eisner was born on 22 Aug 1868 in Praha. He died on 21 Dec 1920 in Kolin. Carl Eisner and Luisa Steindlerová married. They had the

following children:

29. i. **Bedřiška Eisnerová** was born on 25 May 1905 in Praha. She died on 10 Apr 1997.

10. **Jaroslav Steindler**-3 (Moritz-2, Jakub-1) was born on 25 Mar 1885 in Benešov. He died in 1980 in Praha.

    Marie Andreadisova. She died in Praha.

    Jaroslav Steindler and Marie Andreadisova married. They had the following children:

    30. i. **Stanislav Steindler** was born on 08 Nov 1911. He died in 2000.

    Marusja Voronkova.

    Jaroslav Steindler and Marusja Voronkova married. They had the following children:

    i. **Volodja Steindlerová** was born in 1925. She died in 1947 in England.

11. **Antonie Steindler**-3 (Moritz-2, Jakub-1) was born on 20 Oct 1879 in Benešov, Bohemia. She died on 28 Jul 1942 in Baranavichy, Brestskaya Voblasts', Belarus - Holocaust.

    JUDr Vitezslav Grünwald was born on 26 Nov 1877 in Unín, Moravia. He died on 28 Jul 1942 in Baranavichy, Brestskaya Voblast, Belarus.

    JUDr Vitezslav Grünwald and Antonie Steindler married. They had the following children:

    26. i. **Anna Grünwald** was born on 03 Jul 1912 in Gloggnitz, Neunkirchen District, Lower Austria, Austria.

    25. ii. **Gertrude Grünwald** was born about 1911. She died about 1992 in Stockholm, Sweden.

    iii. **Marianne Grünwald** was born on 03 Jul 1912 in Gloggnitz, Neunkirchen District, Lower Austria, Austria.

    Samuel Caesar Oravan was born on 25 Jun 1873 in Vienna, Austria.

    Samuel Caesar Oravan and Antonie Steindler married. They had the following children:

    i. **Bedřiška 'Fritzi' Oravanov.**

12. **Bedřiška Steindlerová**-3 (Moritz-2, Jakub-1) was born on 06 Apr 1888 in Benešov, Bohemia. She died on 05 Nov 1959 in Praha, Czechoslovakia.

JUDr. **Julius Friedmann** son of Julius Friedmann was born on 25 Jun 1885. He died on 05 Nov 1959 in Praha.

JUDr. Julius Friedmann and Bedřiška Steindlerová married. They had the following children:

    i. **Jiří Friedmann** was born on 17 Sep 1913 in Praha. He died in May 1973 in Praha.

32. ii. **Věra Friedmannova** was born in 1917 in Praha. She died in 1964 in Praha.

33. iii. **Eva Friedmannova** was born on 04 Mar 1922 in Praha.

13. **Ema Steindlerová**-3 (Moritz-2, Jakub-1) was born on 24 Sep 1889 in Benešov. She died on 14 Sep 1966 in Praha.

Josef Hermann was born on 18 Aug 1881 in Dacice, near Pardubice. He died on 27 Oct 1940 in England.

Josef Hermann and Ema Steindlerová married. They had the following children:

33. i. **Adolf Hermann** was born on 01 Jun 1914 in Tabor. He died on 17 Oct 1996 in London.

    ii. **Jiří Hermann** was born on 27 Oct 1917 in Praha. He died in Mar 1922 in Praha.

34. iii. **Hana Hermannova** was born on 25 Jan 1921 in Praha.

14. **Josef Steindler**-3 (Moritz-2, Jakub-1) was born on 06 Jun 1891 in Benešov, Bohemia. He died on 01 Jul 1942 in Tabor, Tábor District, Bohemia.

Anna Vejlupkova was born on 13 Nov 1900. She died on 05 Jul 1963 in Praha. Josef Steindler and Anna Vejlupkova married. They had the following children:

35. i. **Květa Steindlerová** was born on 08 Mar 1922 in Benešov.

36. ii. **Miroslav Steindler** was born on 15 Jul 1923 in Benešov.

37. iii. **Miloš Steindler** was born on 06 Dec 1924 in Benešov. He died on 02 Apr 1996 in Pratteln.

15. **Pavel Jiří Steindler**-3 (Moritz-2, Jakub-1) was born on 10 Apr 1893 in Benešov No. 126, Bohemia. He died on 29 Sep 1944 in Auschwitz, Poland - Holocaust.

Ludmila 'Lidka' Černá was born about 1901. She died in 1984 in Ricany.

Pavel Jiří Steindler and Ludmila 'Lidka' Černá married. They had the following children:

38. i. **Pavel Steindler** was born in 1921. He died on 06 Oct 1983 in New York, NY.

   ii. **Jiří (Steindler) Černý** was born in 1923.

16. **Božena Steindlerová**-3 (Moritz-2, Jakub-1) was born on 08 Jun 1895 in Benešov. She died on 15 Sep 1971 in Praha.

   Josef Friedmann son of Emanuel Friedmann and Františka Gellner was born on 12 Dec 1888 in Vysoký Újezd, Beroun District, Bohemia. He died on 11 Sep 1953 in Prague, Czech..

   Josef Friedmann and Božena Steindlerová married. They had the following children:

   39. i. **Jiřina Friedmannova** was born on 24 Feb 1921 in Pelhrimov. She died on 16 May 1989 in Praha.

   40. ii. **Jaroslava Friedmannova** was born on 27 Feb 1923 in Pelhrimov.

17. **Karel Steindler**-3 (Moritz-2, Jakub-1) was born on 21 Jan 1897 in Benešov No. 126, Bohemia. He died on 01 Jul 1965 in Sydney, New South Wales, Australia.

   Anna Grohmannová was born in 1902. She died in 1990 in Sydney, Australia. Karel Steindler and Anna Grohmannová married. They had the following children:

   41. i. **Karel Steindler** was born on 08 Mar 1927 in Chotěboř. He died in 1989 in Sydney, Australia.

   ii. **Lidka Steindlerová** was born in 1931. She died on 24 Dec 1950 in Sydney, Australia.

18. **Zdenka Steindlerová**-3 (Moritz-2, Jakub-1) was born on 04 Oct 1898 in Benešov. She died on 11 Oct 1944 in Auschwitz KZ.

   MUDr Josef Vohryzek was born on 04 Jun 1897 in Prague, Bohemia. He died on 29 Sep 1944 in Auschwitz, Poland - Holocaust.

   MUDr Josef Vohryzek and Zdenka Steindlerová married. They had the following children:

   42. i. **Ludmila Vohryzkova** was born on 24 May 1932 in Praha.

   43. ii. **Helena Millek Vohryzkova** was born on 27 Oct 1924 in Prahue,

Czech.. She died on 03 Nov 2016 in Zürich, Zürich District, Switzerland.

19. **Ludmila ("Lidka") Steindlerová**-3 (Moritz-2, Jakub-1) was born on 01 Oct 1900 in Benešov. She died in Dec 1925 in Praha.

    Emil Neumann was born on 22 May 1897 in Porici. He died in Mar 1973 in Nathanya, Israel. Emil Neumann and Ludmila ("Lidka") Steindlerová married. They had the following children:

    44. i. **Irena Neumannová** was born on 22 Aug 1925 in Praha. She died on 24 Jan 2007 in DC.

Generation 4

20. **Jiřina Taussigová**-4 (Klára-3, Theresia-2, Jakub-1) was born on 24 Apr 1906 in Prague - Kralovske Vinohrady, Nerudova l. She died on 06 Nov 1962 in New York, NY.

    Paul J. Edwards (Pavel Eisner) son of (Jindřich) Henry Eisner and Hortense Auer was born on 29 Jun 1892 in Prague, Klimentska 1. He died on 27 Jun 1964 in Schenectady, NY.

    Paul J. Edwards (Pavel Eisner) and Jiřina Taussigová were married on 05 Jun 1926 in Prague. They had the following children:

    45. i. **Helen Edwards (Eisnerova)** was born on 29 Apr 1927 in Prague, CSR. She married Frank Steiner on 16 Sep 1948 in New York, NY.
    46. ii. **Eva Edwards (Eisnerová)** was born on 21 Jan 1932 in Prague, CSR. She married Mila (Miloslav) Rechcigl Jr. on 29 Aug 1953 in New York, NY.

21. **Hana Taussigová**-4 (Klára-3, Theresia-2, Jakub-1) was born on 26 Feb 1910 in Prague. She died on 14 Mar 1999 in New York, NY.

    Joseph (Wiener) Winn son of Maurice Wiener and Alba Růžičková was born on 02 Feb 1901 in Prague. He died on 08 Feb 1983 in New York City. Joseph (Wiener) Winn and Hana Taussigová were married in 1933. They had the following children:

    47. i. **Janet (Jana) Winn** was born on 08 Jul 1934 in Prague. She married Donald Malcolm on 13 Apr 1956 in New York City.
    48. ii. **Marie Winn** was born on 21 Oct 1936 in Prague. She married Allan Miller on 28 Apr 1961 in New York City.

22. **Jan (Rosenbaum) Skála**-4 (Marie-3, Moritz-2, Jakub-1) was born about 1899 in Nova Hospoda. He died in 1944 in Terezin.
    Bohumila Pucelikova was born about 1901. She died about 1983.
    Jan (Rosenbaum) Skála and Bohumila Pucelikova married. They had the following children:
    49. i. **Jan Skála** was born about 1931. He died in 1992 in Praha.
    50. ii. **Ivo Skála** was born about 1933.
    51. iii. **Jiří Skála** was born about 1936.
23. **Bedřiška Rosenbaumova**-4 (Marie-3, Moritz-2, Jakub-1) was born on 16 Jul 1901. She died on 19 Oct 1944 in Auschwitz KZ.
    Jiří Schwarz. He died in 1940 in Praha.
    Jiří Schwarz and Bedřiška Rosenbaumova married. They had the following children:
    i. **Helena Schwarzova** was born on 26 Mar 1924. She died between 1944-1945 in concentration camp.
24. **František Rosenbaum**-4 (Marie-3, Moritz-2, Jakub-1) was born on 05 Sep 1908. He died on 20 Feb 1945 in Dachau KZ.
    Anna Benešová was born on 09 Mar 1919. She died on 23 Oct 1944 in Auschwitz KZ. František Rosenbaum and Anna Benešová married. They had the following children:
    i. **Bedrch Rosenbaum** was born on 01 Mar 1940. He died on 23 Oct 1944 in Auschwitz KZ.
25. **Gertrude Grünwald**-4 (Antonie-3, Moritz-2, Jakub-1) was born about 1911. She died about 1992 in Stockholm, Sweden.
    Hans Coudek was born on 04 Oct 1907 in Vienna, Austria. He died on 21 Jun 1993 in Stockholm, Sweden.
    Hans Coudek and Gertrude Grünwald married. They had no children.
    Hans Coudek was born on 04 Oct 1910 in Wien, Austria. He died on 21 Jun 1993 in Stockholm, Sweden.
    Hans Coudek and Gertrude Grünwald married. They had the following children:
    52. i. **Lisa Coudkova** was born in 1946.
26. **Anna Grünwald**-4 (Antonie-3, Moritz-2, Jakub-1) was born on 03 Jul

1912 in Gloggnitz, Neunkirchen District, Lower Austria, Austria.

Rudolf Sponer was born on 08 Sep 1913 in Chrastava, Bohemia. He died on 15 Aug 1994 in Birmingham, West Midlands, UK.

Rudolf Sponer and Anna Grünwald married. They had the following children:

    53. i. **Michael Sponer** was born on 28 Dec 1946 in Birmingham.

27. **Jiří Katz Kalina**-4 (Anna-3, Moritz-2, Jakub-1) was born in 1910 in Praha. He died in 1984 in Sydney, Australia.

Milada Králová. She died in 1990 in Sydney, Australia.

Jiří Katz Kalina and Milada Králová married. They had the following children:

    i. **Jan Kalina** was born in 1941. He died in 1990 in Sydney, Australia.

    ii. **Milan Kalina** was born in 1943.

28. **Milena Katzova Kalinova**-4 (Anna-3, Moritz-2, Jakub-1) was born on 28 Nov 1910. She died in 1943 in Auschwitz KZ.

Vojtěch Berkovic was born on 10 Mar 1904. He died about 1980 in Praha.

Vojtěch Berkovic and Milena Katzova Kalinova married. They had the following children:

    i. **Jiří Berkovic** was born on 20 Feb 1936. He died in 1943 in Auschwitz KZ.

29. **Bedřiška Eisnerová**-4 (Luisa-3, Moritz-2, Jakub-1) was born on 25 May 1905 in Praha. She died on 10 Apr 1997.

Jan Ledvina was born on 13 Jul 1905 in Kralupy. He died in 1972 in Praha.

Jan Ledvina and Bedřiška Eisnerová married. They had the following children:

    i. **Zuzana Ledvinova** was born on 05 Aug 1930 in Praha.

30. **Stanislav Steindler**-4 (Jaroslav-3, Moritz-2, Jakub-1) was born on 08 Nov 1911. He died in 2000.

Unknown.

Stanislav Steindler and Unknown married. They had no children.

Jiřina was born about 1926.

Stanislav Steindler and Jiřina married. They had the following children:

54. i. **Milan Steindler** was born in 1956.

ii. **Michal Steindler** was born in 1968.

31. **Věra Friedmannova**-4 (Bedřiška-3, Moritz-2, Jakub-1) was born in 1917 in Praha. She died in 1964 in Praha.

Georgios Liolios was born about 1904 in Greece. He died about 1975 in Praha. Georgios Liolios and Věra Friedmannova married. They had the following children:

55. i. **Magdalena Lioliosova** was born on 11 Nov 1955 in Praha.

32. **Eva Friedmannova**-4 (Bedřiška-3, Moritz-2, Jakub-1) was born on 04 Mar 1922 in Praha.

Hanus Silvera was born on 22 Jan 1920 in Praha.

Hanus Silvera and Eva Friedmannova married. They had the following children:

i. **Helena Silverová** was born on 21 Aug 1944 in London.

57. ii. **Dana Silverová** was born on 14 Sep 1946 in Praha.

58. iii. **Nada Silverová** was born on 26 Dec 1947 in Praha.

33. **Adolf Hermann**-4 (Ema-3, Moritz-2, Jakub-1) was born on 01 Jun 1914 in Tabor. He died on 17 Oct 1996 in London.

Zdenka Steinová was born on 11 Jun 1914 in Praha.

Adolf Hermann and Zdenka Steinová married. They had the following children:

58. i. **Jana Hermann** was born on 08 Jan 1945 in London.

59. ii. **MichalJosef Hermann** was born on 05 Jun 1949 in Praha.

34. **Hana Hermannova**-4 (Ema-3, Moritz-2, Jakub-1) was born on 25 Jan 1921 in Praha.

Miroslav Pastor was born on 03 Nov 1925.

Miroslav Pastor and Hana Hermannova married. They had the following children:

i. **Josef Pastor** was born on 08 Apr 1955 in Praha.

35. **Květa Steindlerová**-4 (Josef-3, Moritz-2, Jakub-1) was born on 08 Mar 1922 in Benešov.

Jan Kuthan was born on 19 Jun 1905. He died on 28 Feb 1980 in Praha. Jan Kuthan and Květa Steindlerová married. They had the following children:

    60. i. **Květa Kuthanova** was born on 27 Apr 1941.

    61. ii. **Jan Kuthan** was born on 10 Feb 1946 in Hradec Králové.

36. **Miroslav Steindler**-4 (Josef-3, Moritz-2, Jakub-1) was born on 15 Jul 1923 in Benešov.

Eva Petraskova.

Miroslav Steindler and Eva Petraskova married. They had the following children:

    i. **Pavel Steindler** was born on 30 Oct 1957 in Praha.

Alena was born about 1930.

Miroslav Steindler and Alena married. They had the following children:

    i. **Michael Steindler** was born about 1960 in Praha.

37. **Miloš Steindler**-4 (Josef-3, Moritz-2, Jakub-1) was born on 06 Dec 1924 in Benešov. He died on 02 Apr 1996 in Pratteln.

Inka Vyborna was born about 1922 in Plzen.

Miloš Steindler and Inka Vyborna married. They had the following children:

    i. **Iva Steindlerová** was born on 28 Aug 1950 in Plzen.

Růžena Froehlichova was born on 06 Dec 1926 in Uhercice.

Miloš Steindler and Růžena Froehlichova married. They had no children.

38. **Pavel Steindler**-4 (Pavel Jiří-3, Moritz-2, Jakub-1) was born in 1921. He died on 06 Oct 1983 in New York, NY.

Helena Schreiberová was born about 1923.

Pavel Steindler and Helena Schreiberová married. They had the following children:

    62. i. **Pavel Steindler** was born in 1942 in Praha.

Jane.

Pavel Steindler and Jane married. They had the following children:

    i. **Carol Steindler** was born about 1953.

Alena 'Aj'a Vrzanova was born on 16 May 1931. She died on 30 Jul 2015 in New York, NY. Pavel Steindler and Alena 'Aj'a Vrzanova married.

They had no children.
39. **Jiřina Friedmannova**-4 (Božena-3, Moritz-2, Jakub-1) was born on 24 Feb 1921 in Pelhrimov. She died on 16 May 1989 in Praha.
   Jiří Zikula was born on 17 Nov 1921 in Praha. He died on 31 Mar 1994 in Praha. Jiří Zikula and Jiřina Friedmannova married. They had the following children:
   63. i. **Alena Zikulová** was born on 26 Jun 1951 in Praha.
   64. ii. **Eva Zikulová** was born on 18 May 1955 in Praha.
40. **Jaroslava Friedmannova**-4 (Božena-3, Moritz-2, Jakub-1) was born on 27 Feb 1923 in Pelhrimov.
   Miroslav Hruda was born on 25 May 1920 in Trebic.
   Miroslav Hruda and Jaroslava Friedmannova married. They had the following children:
   65. i. **Miroslava Hrudova** was born in Jan 1949 in Kladno.
   66. ii. **Jaroslav Hruda** was born on 15 Jun 1951 in Kladno.
41. **Karel Steindler**-4 (Karel-3, Moritz-2, Jakub-1) was born on 08 Mar 1927 in Chotěboř. He died in 1989 in Sydney, Australia.
   Unknown.
   Karel Steindler and Unknown married. They had no children.
   Elisabeth Sturzenegger.
   Karel Steindler and Elisabeth Sturzenegger married. They had the following children:
      i. **Andrew Karel Steindler** was born in 1986.
      ii. **Lisa Steindler** was born in 1988.
42. **Ludmila Vohryzkova**-4 (Zdenka-3, Moritz-2, Jakub-1) was born on 24 May 1932 in Praha.
   Miroslav Zaruba was born on 20 Jan 1927 in Praha.
   Miroslav Zaruba and Ludmila Vohryzkova married. They had the following children:
   67. i. **Georges Zaruba** was born on 01 Jan 1952 in Montreal.
   68. ii. **Paul Zaruba** was born on 04 Jul 1955 in Montreal, Canada.
43. **Helena Millek Vohryzkova**-4 (Zdenka-3, Moritz-2, Jakub-1) was born on 27 Oct 1924 in Prahue, Czech.. She died on 03 Nov 2016 in Zürich,

Zürich District, Switzerland.

Jiří Grant son of Rudolf Grant (Grünberger) and Jana Fischerová was born on 30 Jun 1920 in Prague, Czech.. He died on 03 Mar 2011 in Berne, Canton of Bern, Switzerland.

Jiří Grant and Helena Millek Vohryzkova married. They had the following children:

    i. **Tomáš Grant** was born on 04 Nov 1950 in Prague, Czech.. He died on 02 Jan 1974 in Chur, Grisons, Switzerland (assassinated).

69. ii. **Peter Grant** was born on 25 Feb 1948 in Prague, Bohemia.

Eduard Milek was born on 17 Mar 1929 in Praha.

Eduard Milek and Helena Millek Vohryzkova married. They had no children.

44. **Irena Neumannová**-4 (Ludmila ("Lidka")-3, Moritz-2, Jakub-1) was born on 22 Aug 1925 in Praha. She died on 24 Jan 2007 in DC.

Henry Weinstein.

Henry Weinstein and Irena Neumannová married. They had no children.

Joseph Lane Kirkland was born on 19 Mar 1922 in South Carolina. He died on 14 Aug 1999 in Washington, DC.

Joseph Lane Kirkland and Irena Neumannová were married in 1973. They had no children.

Norman Lourie was born on 01 Oct 1909 in Johannesburg. He died on 25 Jul 1978 in Israel. Norman Lourie and Irena Neumannová married. They had the following children:

70. i. **Michael Lourie** was born on 14 Aug 1952 in London.

    ii. **Jonathan Lourie** was born on 16 Feb 1962.

Generation 5

45. **Helen Edwards (Eisnerova)**-5 (Jiřina-4, Klára-3, Theresia-2, Jakub-1) was born on 29 Apr 1927 in Prague, CSR.

Frank Steiner son of Johann (Hans) Steiner and Růžena Steinbachova was born on 23 Apr 1922 in Prague, Bohemia. He died on 14 Sep 2000 in Scotia, NY.

Frank Steiner and Helen Edwards (Eisnerova) were married on 16 Sep

1948 in New York, NY. They had the following children:
- 71. i. **Linda Claire Steiner** was born on 01 Mar 1950 in Schenectady, NY. She married Edward Salomon on 05 Jun 1977 in Scotia, NY.
- 72. ii. **David Henry Steiner** was born on 13 Mar 1952 in Schenectady, NY. He married Carol Ann Mastaliz on 07 Jul 1979 in So. Deerfield, MA.

46. **Eva Edwards (Eisnerová)**-5 (Jiřina-4, Klára-3, Theresia-2, Jakub-1) was born on 21 Jan 1932 in Prague, CSR.

    Mila (Miloslav) Rechcigl Jr. son of Miloslav Rechcigl and Marie Rajtrová was born on 30 Jul 1930 in Mladá Boleslav, CSR.

    Mila (Miloslav) Rechcigl Jr. and Eva Edwards (Eisnerová) were married on 29 Aug 1953 in New York, NY. They had the following children:
    - 73. i. **John Edward Rechcigl** was born on 27 Feb 1960 in Washington, D.C.. He married Nancy Ann Palko on 30 Jul 1983 in Dover, NJ.
    - 74. ii. **Karen Rechcigl** was born on 16 Apr 1962 in Washington, DC. She married Ulysses Kollecas on 25 Aug 1990 in Bethesda, MD.

66. **Janet (Jana) Winn**-5 (Hana-4, Klára-3, Theresia-2, Jakub-1) was born on 08 Jul 1934 in Prague.

    Donald Malcolm was born in 1935. He died in 1975.

    Donald Malcolm and Janet (Jana) Winn were married on 13 Apr 1956 in New York City. They had the following children:
    - i. i. **Anne Malcolm** was born on 17 Dec 1962 in New York City. She married Richard Tuck on Mar 1993 in New York City.

    Gardner Botsford son of Botsford was born on 07 Jul 1917 in New York, NY. He died on 27 Sep 2004 in New York, NY.

    Gardner Botsford and Janet (Jana) Winn were married on 26 Sep 1975. They had no children.

48. **Marie Winn**-5 (Hana-4, Klára-3, Theresia-2, Jakub-1) was born on 21 Oct 1936 in Prague.

    Allan Miller was born on 05 Dec 1933 in New York City.

    Allan Miller and Marie Winn were married on 28 Apr 1961 in New York City. They had the following children:
    - 76. i. **Michael Winn Miller** was born on 20 Nov 1962. He married Sarah

Paul on 30 Dec 1988 in New York City.

77. ii. **Steven David Miller** was born on 14 Apr 1966 in New York City. He married Jennifer Durand on 11 Nov 1995 in San Francisco, CA.

49. **Jan Skála**-5 (Jan (Rosenbaum)-4, Marie-3, Moritz-2, Jakub-1) was born about 1931. He died in 1992 in Praha.

Souckova.

Jan Skála and Souckova married. They had the following children:

    i. **Jan Skála.**

79. ii. **daughter Skalová.**

50. **Ivo Skála**-5 (Jan (Rosenbaum)-4, Marie-3, Moritz-2, Jakub-1) was born about 1933.

Ludmila Tesarova was born about 1943.

Ivo Skála and Ludmila Tesarova married. They had the following children:

    i. **Petra Skalová** was born on 17 Dec 1969.

    ii. **Ondřej Skála** was born on 14 Oct 1971.

51. **Jiří Skála**-5 (Jan (Rosenbaum)-4, Marie-3, Moritz-2, Jakub-1) was born about 1936.

Unknown.

Jiří Skála and Unknown married. They had the following children:

    i. **Romana Skalová** was born in 1968.

    ii. **Jiří Skála** was born in 1971.

52. **Lisa Coudkova**-5 (Gertrude-4, Antonie-3, Moritz-2, Jakub-1) was born in 1946.

Unknown.

Unknown and Lisa Coudkova married. They had the following children:

    i. **Tanja Lind** was born on 28 Jun 1972 in Stockholm, Sweden.

    ii. **Katja Lind** was born on 09 Sep 1973 in Stockholm, Sweden.

    iii. **Linus Osterholm** was born in 1982 in Stockholm, Sweden.

    iv. **Rasmus Osterholm** was born in 1985 in Stockholm, Sweden.

53. **Michael Sponer**-5 (Anna-4, Antonie-3, Moritz-2, Jakub-1) was born on 28 Dec 1946 in Birmingham.

Christine Sewell was born on 02 Nov 1949 in Birmigham.

Michael Sponer and Christine Sewell married. They had the following children:
   i. **Nigel Sponer** was born on 02 Oct 1978 in Birmingham.
   ii. **Claire Sponer** was born on 28 Apr 1981 in Birmigham.
54. **Milan Steindler**-5 (Stanislav-4, Jaroslav-3, Moritz-2, Jakub-1) was born in 1956.
   Unknown.
   Milan Steindler and Unknown married. They had the following children:
   i. **child Steindler.**
55. **Magdalena Lioliosova**-5 (Věra-4, Bedřiška-3, Moritz-2, Jakub-1) was born on 11 Nov 1955 in Praha.
   Jaroslav Pořádek.
   Jaroslav Pořádek and Magdalena Lioliosova married. They had the following children:
   i. **Jitka Pořádková** was born about 1978 in Praha.
56. **Dana Silverová**-5 (Eva-4, Bedřiška-3, Moritz-2, Jakub-1) was born on 14 Sep 1946 in Praha.
   Jiří Nedvěd was born on 19 Apr 1938.
   Jiří Nedvěd and Dana Silverová married. They had the following children:
   i. **Jan Nedvěd** was born on 26 Jun 1971 in Zuruch, Switzerland.
   ii. **Daniel Nedvěd** was born on 21 Apr 1974 in Zurich, Switzerland.
57. **Nada Silverová**-5 (Eva-4, Bedřiška-3, Moritz-2, Jakub-1) was born on 26 Dec 1947 in Praha.
   Walter Czurda was born on 05 Apr 1929.
   Walter Czurda and Nada Silverová married. They had the following children:
   i. **Petr Czurda** was born on 09 Jun 1972.
58. **Jana Hermann**-5 (Adolf-4, Ema-3, Moritz-2, Jakub-1) was born on 08 Jan 1945 in London.
   Jiří Malina was born on 07 Oct 1942 in Praha.
   Jiří Malina and Jana Hermann married. They had the following children:
   i. **Marek Malina** was born on 23 Aug 1968 in Gmuend, Ausrtria.

He died on 01 Feb 1988 in London.

ii. **Petra Malinova** was born on 14 Oct 1972 in London.

59. **MichalJosef Hermann**-5 (Adolf-4, Ema-3, Moritz-2, Jakub-1) was born on 05 Jun 1949 in Praha.

    Jeannette Bielinki was born on 04 Dec 1949 in London.

    MichalJosef Hermann and Jeannette Bielinki married. They had the following children:

    i. **Nicolas Hermann** was born on 14 Jun 1976 in London.

    ii. **Sasha Hermann** was born on 15 Oct 1977 in London.

60. **Květa Kuthanova**-5 (Květa-4, Josef-3, Moritz-2, Jakub-1) was born on 27 Apr 1941.

    Jan Kubíček was born on 26 Aug 1938.

    Jan Kubíček and Květa Kuthanova married. They had the following children:

    i. **Dana Kubíčková** was born on 22 Mar 1966 in Praha.

61. **Jan Kuthan**-5 (Květa-4, Josef-3, Moritz-2, Jakub-1) was born on 10 Feb 1946 in Hradec Králové.

    Jitka Kurcova was born on 28 Feb 1952.

    Jan Kuthan and Jitka Kurcova married. They had the following children:

    i. **Jan Kuthan** was born on 12 Jan 1981.

62. **Pavel Steindler**-5 (Pavel-4, Pavel Jiří-3, Moritz-2, Jakub-1) was born in 1942 in Praha.

    Unknown.

    Pavel Steindler and Unknown married. They had the following children:

    i. **child Steindler.**

    ii. **child Steindler.**

    Jana.

    Pavel Steindler and Jana married. They had no children.

    Alena 'Aj'a Vrzanova was born on 16 May 1931. She died on 30 Jul 2015 in New York, NY. Pavel Steindler and Alena 'Aj'a Vrzanova married. They had no children.

63. **Alena Zikulová**-5 (Jiřina-4, Božena-3, Moritz-2, Jakub-1) was born on 26 Jun 1951 in Praha.

Stanislav Svoboda was born on 22 May 1951 in Praha.
Stanislav Svoboda and Alena Zikulová married. They had the following children:
   i.   **Martina Svobodová** was born on 13 Sep 1976 in Praha.
   ii. **Pavel Svoboda** was born on 22 Mar 1978 in Praha.

64. **Eva Zikulová**-5 (Jiřina-4, Božena-3, Moritz-2, Jakub-1) was born on 18 May 1955 in Praha.
   Karel Týra was born on 23 Jun 1952 in Praha.
   Karel Týra and Eva Zikulová married. They had the following children:
      i.   **Jana Týrová** was born on 06 Jul 1979 in Praha.
      ii. **Karel Tyra** was born on 19 Apr 1982 in Praha.

65. **Miroslava Hrudova**-5 (Jaroslava-4, Božena-3, Moritz-2, Jakub-1) was born in Jan 1949 in Kladno.
   Petr Materna was born on 26 Dec 1942 in Praha.
   Petr Materna and Miroslava Hrudova married. They had the following children:
      i.   **Petr Materna** was born on 07 Jul 1976 in Praha.
      ii. **Ondřej Materna** was born on 15 Jun 1980 in Praha.
   Petr.
   Petr and Miroslava Hrudova married. They had the following children:
      i.   **Ondřej** was born about 1979.

66. **Jaroslav Hruda**-5 (Jaroslava-4, Božena-3, Moritz-2, Jakub-1) was born on 15 Jun 1951 in Kladno.
   Jana Linhartova was born on 07 Feb 1955 in Praha.
   Jaroslav Hruda and Jana Linhartova married. They had the following children:
      i.   **Julie Hrudova** was born on 14 Mar 1988 in Praha.

67. **Georges Zaruba**-5 (Ludmila-4, Zdenka-3, Moritz-2, Jakub-1) was born on 01 Jan 1952 in Montreal.
   Danielle Černý was born on 06 Oct 1955 in Sydney, Australia.
   Georges Zaruba and Danielle Černý married. They had the following children:
      i.   **Thomas Zaruba** was born on 22 May 1981 in Paris.

ii. **Denis Zaruba** was born on 29 Mar 1983 in Paris.
iii. **Camille Zarubovaa** was born on 16 Jan 1986 in Paris.
iv. **Antoine Zaruba** was born on 30 Dec 1989 in Paris.
v. **Olivier Zaruba** was born on 05 Jul 1994 in Paris.

68. **Paul Zaruba**-5 (Ludmila-4, Zdenka-3, Moritz-2, Jakub-1) was born on 04 Jul 1955 in Montreal, Canada.
Dominique Roche was born on 25 Oct 1955 in Savigny s. Orge.
Paul Zaruba and Dominique Roche married. They had the following children:
   i. **Juliette Zaruba** was born on 22 Jun 1984 in Bordeaux.
   ii. **Caroline Zaruba** was born on 15 Apr 1987 in Bordeaux.
   iii. **Roman Zaruba** was born on 05 Sep 1990 in Bordeaux.

69. **Peter Grant**-5 (Helena Millek-4, Zdenka-3, Moritz-2, Jakub-1) was born on 25 Feb 1948 in Prague, Bohemia.
Charlotte Oetiker was born on 20 Mar 1953 in Bülach, Zurich, Switzerland. Peter Grant and Charlotte Oetiker married. They had the following children:
   i. **Barbara Grant** was born on 12 May 1982 in Bülach, Zurich, Switzerland.
   ii. **Jan Grant** was born on 14 Jul 1984 in Bülach, Zürich, Switzerland.

70. **Michael Lourie**-5 (Irena-4, Ludmila ("Lidka")-3, Moritz-2, Jakub-1) was born on 14 Aug 1952 in London.
Lea Reznik was born on 09 Apr 1953 in Jerusalem.
Michael Lourie and Lea Reznik married. They had the following children:
   i. **Kineret Lourie** was born on 11 May 1978 in Haifa.
   ii. **Irit Lourie** was born in Oct 1979 in Haifa.
   iii. **Shlomit Lourie** was born on 01 Jun 1982 in Haifa.
   iv. **Nachum Lourie** was born on 03 Feb 1986 in Haifa.

Generation 6

71. **Linda Claire Steiner**-6 (Helen Edwards-5, Jiřina-4, Klára-3, Theresia-2, Jakub-1) was born on 01 Mar 1950 in Schenectady, NY.

STEINDLER FAMILY

Edward Salomon son of Jerome Salomon and Rachel Finchel was born on 12 Feb 1951 in Jersey city, NJ.

Edward Salomon and Linda Claire Steiner were married on 05 Jun 1977 in Scotia, NY. They had the following children:

    i. **Sarah Beth Salomon** was born on 28 Jan 1980 in Chicago, IL.

    ii. **Paul Nathan Salomon** was born on 02 Jan 1983 in Chicago, IL.

72. **David Henry Steiner**-6 (Helen Edwards-5, Jiřina-4, Klára-3, Theresia-2, Jakub-1) was born on 13 Mar 1952 in Schenectady, NY.

Carol Ann Mastaliz daughter of Frank Peter Mastaliz and Helen Carline Macko was born on 26 Oct 1952 (Greenfield, MA).

David Henry Steiner and Carol Ann Mastaliz were married on 07 Jul 1979 in So. Deerfield, MA. They had the following children:

79. i. **Erin Marie Steiner** was born on 01 Aug 1981 in Chicago, IL. She married Michael John Malick on 27 Jul 2013 in Poulsbo, WA.

    ii. **Jonathan Robert Steiner** was born on 30 Dec 1984 in Concord, MA.

73. **John Edward Rechcigl**-6 (Eva Edwards-5, Jiřina-4, Klára-3, Theresia-2, Jakub-1) was born on 27 Feb 1960 in Washington, D.C..

Nancy Ann Palko daughter of Joseph Palko and Mary Rishko was born on 26 Sep 1961 in Morristown, NJ.

John Edward Rechcigl and Nancy Ann Palko were married on 30 Jul 1983 in Dover, NJ. They had the following children:

    i. **Gregory John Rechcigl** was born on 19 Dec 1988 in Bradenton, FL.

80. ii. **Kevin Thomas Rechcigl** was born on 09 Oct 1991 in Bradenton, FL. He married Jordan Robbins on 12 May 2018 in Jacksonville, FL.

    iii. **Lindsey Nicole Rechcigl** was born on 03 Nov 1994 in Bradenton, FL.

74. **Karen Rechcigl**-6 (Eva Edwards-5, Jiřina-4, Klára-3, Theresia-2, Jakub-1) was born on 16 Apr 1962 in Washington, DC.

Ulysses Kollecas son of Christopher Thomas (Kolecas) Collier and Amelia Malatras was born on 20 Mar 1958 in Washington, DC.

Ulysses Kollecas and Karen Rechcigl were married on 25 Aug 1990 in

Bethesda, MD. They had the following children:
  i. **Kristin Kollecas** was born on 04 May 1993 in Albuquerque, NM.
  ii. **Paul Kollecas** was born on 02 Jun 1995 in Albuquerque, NM.

75. **Anne Malcolm**-6 (Janet (Jana)-5, Hana-4, Klára-3, Theresia-2, Jakub-1) was born on 17 Dec 1962 in New York City.
Richard Tuck was born on 09 Jan 1949 in Newcastleupon-Tyne, England. Richard Tuck and Anne Malcolm were married on 19 Mar 1993 in New York City. They had the following children:
  i. **Sophy Malcolm Tuck** was born on 13 Jul 1993 in Cambridge, England.

76. **Michael Winn Miller**-6 (Marie-5, Hana-4, Klára-3, Theresia-2, Jakub-1) was born on 20 Nov 1962.
Sarah Paul was born on 29 Dec 1961 in New York City.
Michael Winn Miller and Sarah Paul were married on 30 Dec 1988 in New York City. They had the following children:
  i. **Isadore 'Izzy' Miller** was born on 20 Nov 1995 in San Francisco, CA.
  ii. **Abigail "Abbey' Nadia Paul Miller** was born on 24 Oct 1996 in New York City.

77. **Steven David Miller**-6 (Marie-5, Hana-4, Klára-3, Theresia-2, Jakub-1) was born on 14 Apr 1966 in New York City.
Jennifer Durand.
Steven David Miller and Jennifer Durand were married on 11 Nov 1995 in San Francisco, CA. They had the following children:
  i. **Eli Miller** was born on 17 Mar 1999.
  ii. **Clara Miller** was born on 04 Jul 2000 in San Francisco, CA or NYC.

78. **daughter Skalová** 6 (Jan 5, Jan (Rosenbaum)-4, Marie-3, Moritz-2, Jakub-1).
Unknown.
Unknown and daughter Skalová married. They had the following children:
  i. **child Unknown.**

Generation 7

79. **Erin Marie Steiner**-7 (David Henry-6, Helen Edwards-5, Jiřina-4, Klára-3, Theresia-2, Jakub-1) was born on 01 Aug 1981 in Chicago, IL.
    Michael John Malick was born on 01 Aug 1981 in Chicago, IL.
    Michael John Malick and Erin Marie Steiner were married on 27 Jul 2013 in Poulsbo, WA. They had the following children:
    i. **Henry Francsz Malick** was born on 18 Feb 2018 in Seattle, WA.

80. **Kevin Thomas Rechcigl**-7 (John Edward-6, Eva Edwards-5, Jiřina-4, Klára-3, Theresia-2, Jakub-1) was born on 09 Oct 1991 in Bradenton, FL.
    Jordan Robbins daughter of Douglass Robbins and Ivonne was born on 10 Jan 1992 in Camarillo, CA.
    Kevin Thomas Rechcigl and Jordan Robbins were married on 12 May 2018 in Jacksonville, FL. They had the following children:
    i. **James Douglas Rechcigl** was born on 05 Jan 2021 in Jacksonville, FL.
    ii. **Evelyn Marie Rechcigl** was born 29 May 2023 in Jacksonville, FL.

Svab Family

Generation 1

1. **Jiří Šváb**-1 was born in Hermanice.
   Veronika Janásková daughter of Jakub Janásek.
   Jiří Šváb and Veronika Janásková married. They had the following children:
   2. i. **Jiří Šváb** was born on 26 Jul 1798 in České Hermanice No. 58.

Generation 2

2. **Jiří Šváb**-2 (Jiří-1) was born on 26 Jul 1798 in České Hermanice No. 58.
   Mariana Doležalová daughter of Unknown and Kristina was born on 22 May 1793 in Hermanice No. 52.
   Jiří Šváb and Mariana Doležalová met. They had the following children:
   3. i. **Jan Šváb** was born on 31 Oct 1819 in České Hermanice No. 55, Litomysl Co.. He married Mariana Nespěchalová on 22 Feb 1841 in České Hermanice.

Generation 3

3. **Jan Šváb**-3 (Jiří-2, Jiří-1) was born on 31 Oct 1819 in České Hermanice No. 55, Litomysl Co..
   Mariana Nespěchalová daughter of Václav Nespěchal and Anna Hubkova was born on 11 Jan 1819 in Norin No. 6, near Chocen, Vysoke Myto Co..
   Jan Šváb and Mariana Nespěchalová were married on 22 Feb 1841 in České Hermanice. They had the following children:
   4. i. **Jan Krtitel Šváb** was born on 28 May 1845 in Bystrice No. 138, Benešov Dist., Bohemia. He married Barbora Sedláková on 08 Jan 1872 in Stahlovi. He died in 1918.

Generation 4

4. **Jan Krtitel Šváb**-4 (Jan-3, Jiří-2, Jiří-1) was born on 28 May 1845 in Bystrice No. 138, Benešov Dist., Bohemia. He died in 1918.
   Barbora Sedláková daughter of Jan Sedlák and Kateřina Sebkova was born on 30 Dec 1848 in Stahlavy No. 54, near Rokycany. She died in 1930.

Jan Krtitel Šváb and Barbora Sedláková were married on 08 Jan 1872 in Stahlovi. They had the following children:

    i. **Jan Šváb**.
6. ii. **Emillie Švábová**.
7. iii. **Marie Švábová** was born on 13 Jul 1873 in Bystrice, Benešov Dist., Bohemia. She died in 1945.
7. iv. **Adolf Šváb** was born on 18 Apr 1876 in Bystrice No. 138, Benešov Co.. He married Marie Markéta Marta Taussigová on 15 Oct 1902 in U Matky Bozi pred Tynem, Prague. He died on 26 Apr 1954 in Plzen.

Generation 5

5. **Emillie Švábová**-5 (Jan Krtitel-4, Jan-3, Jiří-2, Jiří-1).
   A. Pfeffer.
   A. Pfeffer and Emillie Švábová married. They had the following children:
       i. **Antonín Pfeffer** was born on 15 Jan 1904 in Veseli nad Luznici, Tabor Co..
       ii. **Ladislav Pfeffer**.

6. **Marie Švábová**-5 (Jan Krtitel-4, Jan-3, Jiří-2, Jiří-1) was born on 13 Jul 1873 in Bystrice, Benešov Dist., Bohemia. She died in 1945.
   Ladislav Syllaba son of František Syllaba and Anna Vlckova was born on 16 Jun 1868 in Bystrice, Benešov Dist., Bohemia. He died on 30 Dec 1930 in Prague, Czech..
   Ladislav Syllaba and Marie Švábová married. They had the following children:
8. i. **Ludmila Syllabová** was born on 05 Apr 1899. She died in 1996.
       ii. **Jiří Syllaba** was born on 08 Mar 1902 in Praha, CSR. He married Božena Slámová in 1942 in Praha II. He died on 17 May 1997 in Praha,CSR.
9. iii. **Milada Syllabová** was born in 1904.
       iv. **Anna Syllabová** was born in 1896. She died in 1902.

7. **Adolf Šváb**-5 (Jan Krtitel-4, Jan-3, Jiří-2, Jiří-1) was born on 18 Apr 1876 in Bystrice No. 138, Benešov Co.. He died on 26 Apr 1954 in Plzen.
   Marie Markéta Marta Taussigová daughter of Jakub Taussig and Julie Meislova was born on 07 Mar 1879 in Benešov No. 162. She died on 22

Jun 1958 in Plzen.

Adolf Šváb and Marie Markéta Marta Taussigová were married on 15 Oct 1902 in U Matky Bozi pred Tynem, Prague. They had the following children:

10. i. **Vladislav Šváb** was born on 08 Aug 1903 in Vysoke nad Jizerou. He married Julie Zacharova on 11 Oct 1932 in Prague. He died on 23 Oct 1947 in Tabor, Czechoslovakia.
11. ii. **Adolf Šváb** was born on 15 Apr 1905 in Vysoke nad Jizerou No. 267. He married Zdenka Sigmundova on 17 Sep 1932 in Plzen. He died in 1976 in Plzen.
12. iii. **Kamil Šváb** was born in 1907 in Vysoke nad Jizerou. He married Augusta (Gusta) Hyblerova in 1936. He died in 1982 in Praha, Bohemia.
    iv. **Věra Švábová** was born in 1910 in Vysoke nad Jizerou. She married Čeněk Simerka in 1936. She died in 1985 in Plzen.

Generation 6

8. **Ludmila Syllabová**-6 (Marie-5, Jan Krtitel-4, Jan-3, Jiří-2, Jiří-1) was born on 05 Apr 1899. She died in 1996.

Filip.

Filip and Ludmila Syllabová married. They had the following children:
   i. **Eva Filipová**.
   ii. **Hana Filipová**.

9. **Milada Syllabová**-6 (Marie-5, Jan Krtitel-4, Jan-3, Jiří-2, Jiří-1) was born in 1904.

Stretti.

Stretti and Milada Syllabová married. They had the following children:
   i. **Olga Strettiová**.
   ii. **Milada Strettiová**.

10. **Vladislav Šváb**-6 (Adolf-5, Jan Krtitel-4, Jan-3, Jiří-2, Jiří-1) was born on 08 Aug 1903 in Vysoke nad Jizerou. He died on 23 Oct 1947 in Tabor, Czechoslovakia.

Julie Zacharova daughter of Nikolaj Michajlovic Zacharov and Julie Filipovna Obrevko-Zdanov was born on 03 Mar 1901 in Moscow, Russia.

She died on 24 Jan 1999 in Tabor, Bbohemia.

Vladislav Šváb and Julie Zacharova were married on 11 Oct 1932 in Prague. They had the following children:

    13. i. **Julie ("Jaska") Švábová** was born on 24 Feb 1945 in Tabor. She married Vladimír Sarsa on 26 Jun 1969 in Ostrava.

11. **Adolf Šváb**-6 (Adolf-5, Jan Krtitel-4, Jan-3, Jiří-2, Jiří-1) was born on 15 Apr 1905 in Vysoke nad Jizerou No. 267. He died in 1976 in Plzen.

Zdenka Sigmundova daughter of Josef Sigmund and Karolina Restránková was born on 31 Oct 1908 in Plzen, Na Lochotine No. 451. She died in 1990 in Plzen.

Adolf Šváb and Zdenka Sigmundova were married on 17 Sep 1932 in Plzen. They had the following children:

    14. i. **Irena Švábová** was born on 03 Feb 1936 in Plzen. She married Emil Kasl in 1955.

    15. ii. **Zdeněk Šváb** was born on 31 Mar 1940 in Plzen.

    16. iii. **Olga Švábová** was born on 18 Jul 1948 in Plzen. She married Vladimír Pechman in 1968.

12. **Kamil Šváb**-6 (Adolf-5, Jan Krtitel-4, Jan-3, Jiří-2, Jiří-1) was born in 1907 in Vysoke nad Jizerou. He died in 1982 in Praha, Bohemia.

Augusta (Gusta) Hyblerova daughter of Otto Hybler and (Pavlina) Marie Schönfeldová was born in 1911. She died in 1960.

Kamil Šváb and Augusta (Gusta) Hyblerova were married in 1936. They had the following children:

    i. **Jan Šváb** was born on 04 Jul 1937 in Praha, CSR. He married Josette Azra on 02 May 1978.

Božena Stroblová was born in 1913. She died in 1981.

Kamil Šváb and Božena Stroblová were married in 1945. They had the following children:

    17. i. **Kamil Šváb** was born on 29 Aug 1944 in Prague. He married Dobroslava Rittova in 1968.

Generation 7

13. **Julie ("Jaska") Švábová**-7 (Vladislav-6, Adolf-5, Jan Krtitel-4, Jan-3, Jiří-2, Jiří-1) was born on 24 Feb 1945 in Tabor.

Vladimír Sarsa was born on 11 Feb 1943 in Ostrava.

Vladimír Sarsa and Julie ("Jaska") Švábová were married on 26 Jun 1969 in Ostrava. They had the following children:

- 18   i. **Olga Sarsova** was born on 26 Dec 1970 in Ostrava. She married Broniaslav Klementa on 14 Apr 2007 in Na Svatem Kopecku u Olomouce.
- 19   ii. **Vladimír Sarsa** was born on 26 Nov 1971 in Ostrava. He married Bronislava Srubkova on 26 Jul 1997 in Ostrava.

14. **Irena Švábová**-7 (Adolf-6, Adolf-5, Jan Krtitel-4, Jan-3, Jiří-2, Jiří-1) was born on 03 Feb 1936 in Plzen.

    Emil Kasl was born in 1926.

    Emil Kasl and Irena Švábová were married in 1955. They had the following children:

    - 20.   i. **Monika Kaslova** was born on 03 Jun 1958 in Plzen. She married Jiří Chládek on 30 Apr 1978 in Prague, CSR.
    -      ii. **Tomáš Kasl** was born on 26 Apr 1964 in Plzen.

15. **Zdeněk Šváb**-7 (Adolf-6, Adolf-5, Jan Krtitel-4, Jan-3, Jiří-2, Jiří-1) was born on 31 Mar 1940 in Plzen.

    Jaroslava Leimerova was born in 1943.

    Zdeněk Šváb and Jaroslava Leimerova married. They had the following children:

    - 21.   i. **Daniel Šváb** was born on 29 Jan 1964 in Plzen. He married Jitka Kopackova in 1992.

    Marie Kosorova was born in 1945.

    Zdeněk Šváb and Marie Kosorova were married in 1970. They had no children.

16. **Olga Švábová**-7 (Adolf-6, Adolf-5, Jan Krtitel-4, Jan-3, Jiří-2, Jiří-1) was born on 18 Jul 1948 in Plzen.

    Vladimír Pechman was born in 1943.

    Vladimír Pechman and Olga Švábová were married in 1968. They had the following children:

    - 22.   i. **Radek Pechman** was born on 12 Mar 1969 in Plzen. He married Jitka Slámová in 1992.

23. ii. **Olga Pechmanová** was born on 12 Mar 1976 in Plzen. She married Tomáš Pech in 1998.

Muchna.

Muchna and Olga Švábová were married after 1976. They had no children.

17. **Kamil Šváb**-7 (Kamil-6, Adolf-5, Jan Krtitel-4, Jan-3, Jiří-2, Jiří-1) was born on 29 Aug 1944 in Prague.

Dobroslava Rittova was born on 13 Sep 1945.

Kamil Šváb and Dobroslava Rittova were married in 1968. They had the following children:

    i. **Jana Švábová** was born on 17 Jun 1972. She married Franklin Venegas on 16 Jul 1994.

Generation 8

20. **Olga Sarsova**-8 (Julie ("Jaska")-7, Vladislav-6, Adolf-5, Jan Krtitel-4, Jan-3, Jiří-2, Jiří-1) was born on 26 Dec 1970 in Ostrava.

Broniaslav Klementa son of Josef Klementa and Oldřiška Pavlickova was born on 29 Jun 1966 in Sumperk.

Broniaslav Klementa and Olga Sarsova were married on 14 Apr 2007 in Na Svatem Kopecku u Olomouce. They had the following children:

    i. **Veronika Klementova** was born on 25 May 2007 in Olomouc.

19. **Vladimír Sarsa**-8 (Julie ("Jaska")-7, Vladislav-6, Adolf-5, Jan Krtitel-4, Jan-3, Jiří-2, Jiří-1) was born on 26 Nov 1971 in Ostrava.

Bronislava Srubkova was born on 05 Mar 1963 in Pustejov, Bruntal Dist., Czechoslovakia..

Vladimír Sarsa and Bronislava Srubkova were married on 26 Jul 1997 in Ostrava. They had the following children:

    i. **Milena Sarsova** was born on 03 Jan 1998 in Ostrava, Czechoslovakia.

20. **Monika Kaslova**-8 (Irena-7, Adolf-6, Adolf-5, Jan Krtitel-4, Jan-3, Jiří-2, Jiří-1) was born on 03 Jun 1958 in Plzen.

Jiří Chládek was born in 1955.

Jiří Chládek and Monika Kaslova were married on 30 Apr 1978 in Prague, CSR. They had the following children:

    i. **David Chládek** was born on 19 Dec 1978 in Cheb.

    ii. **Ondřej Chládek** was born on 17 Aug 1981 in Cheb.

    iii. **Jan Chládek** was born on 16 Nov 1988 in Cheb.

21. **Daniel Šváb**-8 (Zdeněk-7, Adolf-6, Adolf-5, Jan Krtitel-4, Jan-3, Jiří-2, Jiří-1) was born on 29 Jan 1964 in Plzen.
Jitka Kopackova.
Daniel Šváb and Jitka Kopackova were married in 1992. They had the following children:

    i. **Dominika Švábová** was born on 16 Oct 1992 in Plzen.

    ii. **Natalie Švábová** was born on 09 Aug 1998 in Plzen.

22. **Radek Pechman**-8 (Olga-7, Adolf-6, Adolf-5, Jan Krtitel-4, Jan-3, Jiří-2, Jiří-1) was born on 12 Mar 1969 in Plzen.
Jitka Slámová was born in 1966.
Radek Pechman and Jitka Slámová were married in 1992. They had the following children:

    i. **Barbora Pechmanová** was born in 1992.

23. **Olga Pechmanová**-8 (Olga-7, Adolf-6, Adolf-5, Jan Krtitel-4, Jan-3, Jiří-2, Jiří-1) was born on 12 Mar 1976 in Plzen.
Tomáš Pech.
Tomáš Pech and Olga Pechmanová were married in 1998. They had the following children:

    i. **Karolina Pechová** was born on 22 May 1999 in Plzen.

Weiner Family

Generation 1

1. **Moses Weiner**-1 was born in 1812 in Bechyně, Tábor District, Bohemia. He died in 1893 in Pisek, Písek District, Bohemia.
   Rosalia Hindl Stricker was born in 1817. She died on 18 Apr 1877 in Písek, Písek District, Bohemia. Moses Weiner and Rosalia Hindl Stricker married. They had the following children:
   2. i. **Moritz Weiner**.
   3. ii. **Sophie Weiner**.
   4. iii. **Franziska 'Fann'y Weinerova** was born in 1858 in Bechyne, Tabor Dist., Bohemia. She married Adolf Stránský on 30 Dec 1879 in Bechyne, Tabor Dist., Bohemia. She died before 1934.
   5. iv. **Anna Weinerova**[1] was born in 1850 in Bechyne, Bbohemia. She married Filip Rabl in 1864. She died on 08 Mar 1906 in Pisek, Bohemia.
   6. v. **Gustav Weiner** was born in 1850 in Pisek, Písek District, Bohemia. He died in 1919 in Prague, Czechoslovakia.

Generation 2

2. **Moritz Weiner**-2 (Moses-1). Clara.
   Moritz Weiner and Clara married. They had no children.
   Fanny.
   Moritz Weiner and Fanny married. They had the following children:
   i. **Mica Weinerova**.
3. **Sophie Weiner**-2 (Moses-1).
   Hoffman.
   Hoffman and Sophie Weiner married. They had the following children:
   ii. **Otto Hoffman**.
   8. ii. **Olga Hoffman**.
   9. iii. **Paul Hoffman**.
4. **Franziska 'Fann'y Weinerova**-2 (Moses-1) was born in 1858 in Bechyne, Tabor Dist., Bohemia. She died before 1934.
   Adolf Stránský son of Josef Stránský and Josefine Katz was born on 12

Apr 1850. He died on 01 Oct 1934 in Vienna, Austria.

Adolf Stránský and Franziska 'Fann'y Weinerova were married on 30 Dec 1879 in Bechyne, Tabor Dist., Bohemia. They had the following children:

    i. **Max Stránský** was born on 18 Nov 1880 in Pisek, Bohemia.

9. ii. **Robert Stránský** was born on 05 May 1882 in Pisek, Bohemia. He died on 14 Jun 1942 in Lodz, Poland - Holocaust.

10. iii. **Olga Stránská** was born on 22 Dec 1884 in Pisek, Bohemia. She died in Aug 1971 in New York, NY.

11. iv. **Viktor Stránský** was born on 17 Sep 1893 in Písek, South Bohemia. He died on 04 Sep 1963 in New York, NY.

5. **Anna Weinerova**-2 (Moses-1)[1] was born in 1850 in Bechyne, Bbohemia. She died on 08 Mar 1906 in Pisek, Bohemia.

Filip Rabl son of Moises Rabl and Unknown[1] was born on 01 Apr 1825 in Kardašova Řečice, Pribram Dist., Bohemia. He died about 1903 in Pisek. Filip Rabl and Anna Weinerova were married in 1864. They had the following children:

12. i. **Ludwig Rabl**[1] was born on 01 Nov 1866 in Kardašova Řečice, Pribram Dist., Bohemia[1]. He married Bianca Poláček before 1900. He died on 17 Dec 1925 in Berlin, Germany[1].

    ii. **Josefina Rablova**[1] was born on 28 Dec 1867 in K.R.[1]. She died about 1935 in date is doubtful[1].

    iii. **Maximilian Rabl**[1] was born on 04 Jun 1869 in K.R.[1]. He died on 14 Jan 1915[1].

13. iv. **Berthold Rabl**[1] was born on 25 Mar 1871 in K R. He died on 19 Jun 1932 in Karlovy Vary[1].

    v. **Mathilde Rablova**[1] was born on 29 Aug 1872 in K.R.[1]. She died in 1890[1].

14. vi. **Adele Rablova**[1] was born on 03 Dec 1874 in K.R.[1]. She died on 18 Oct 1950 in Prague[1].

    vii. **Gizela Rablova**[1] was born on 31 Aug 1876[1].

    viii. **Růžena Rabl**[1] was born on 09 Jul 1878[1].

15. ix. **Otto Rabl**[1] was born on 02 Jan 1880[1].

    x. **Josef Rabl**[1] was born on 16 Oct 1881[1].

16. xi. **Richard Rabl**[1] was born on 12 Sep 1883[1].
    xii. **Ernst Rabl**[1] was born in 1884[1]. He died in 1961 in Israel[1].
17. xiii. **Kamila Rablova**[1] was born on 02 Sep 1885[1].
18. xiv. **Rudi Rabl**[1] was born on 23 Mar 1889[1]. He married Elizabeth Chambers after 1940. He died in 1951.
    xv. **Grete Rablova**.

6. **Gustav Weiner**-2 (Moses-1) was born in 1850 in Pisek, Písek District, Bohemia. He died in 1919 in Prague, Czechoslovakia.

   Gabriela Taussigová daughter of Jakub Taussig and Julie Meislova was born on 23 Sep 1863. She died on 12 Nov 1927.

   Gustav Weiner and Gabriela Taussigová married. They had the following children:

   i. **Richard Weiner** was born on 06 Nov 1884 in Pisek, Písek District, Bohemia. He died on 03 Jan 1937 in Prague, Czech..
   ii. **Kamil Weiner** was born in 1886. He died in 1960.
   iii. **Marta Weinerova** was born in 1893. She died in 1918.
20. iv. **Jiří Weiner** was born in 1896.
21. v. **Zdena Weinerova** was born in 1898. She died in 1975.

Generation 3

7. **Olga Hoffman**-3 (Sophie-2, Moses-1).
   Winter.
   Winter and Olga Hoffman married. They had the following children:
   21. i. **Věra Winterova**.

8. **Paul Hoffman**-3 (Sophie-2, Moses-1).
   Unknown.
   Paul Hoffman and Unknown married. They had the following children:
   i. **Helen Hoffmannová**.

9. **Robert Stránský**-3 (Franziska 'Fann'y-2, Moses-1) was born on 05 May 1882 in Pisek, Bohemia. He died on 14 Jun 1942 in Lodz, Poland - Holocaust.

   Arnstein was born on 03 Aug 1890 in Votice, Bohemia. She died on 19 Apr 1944 in Łódź, Poland - Holocaust.

   Robert Stránský and Arnstein married. They had the following children:

i. **Pavell Stránský** was born on 19 Jun 1915 in Vienna, Austria. He died about 1941 in P{oland - Holocaust.
ii. **Hanka Stránská**.

10. **Olga Stránská**-3 (Franziska 'Fann'y-2, Moses-1) was born on 22 Dec 1884 in Pisek, Bohemia. She died in Aug 1971 in New York, NY.

    Dr. Bernhard Elias Schapire was born on 21 Jan 1880 in Ternopil, Ternopil's'ka oblast, Ukraine. He died on 09 Apr 1953.

    Dr. Bernhard Elias Schapire and Olga Stránská married. They had the following children:

    22. i. **Franzi Schapire** was born on 28 Dec 1909 in Vienna, Austria. She died on 03 Oct 2004 in Albany, Albany County, New York.
    23. ii. **Hans Schapire** was born on 26 Aug 1914 in Vienna, Austria. He died on 16 Jan 2013 in Minneapolis, Hennepin County, MN.

11. **Viktor Stránský**-3 (Franziska 'Fann'y-2, Moses-1) was born on 17 Sep 1893 in Písek, South Bohemia. He died on 04 Sep 1963 in New York, NY.

    Ernestine Zerner was born on 28 Feb 1897 in Rosice, Brno Dist., Moravia. She died on 17 Jan 1961 in New York, NY.

    Viktor Stránský and Ernestine Zerner married. They had the following children:

    24. i. **Curt Strand (Stránský)** was born on 13 Nov 1920 in Vienna, Austria.

12. **Ludwig Rabl**-3 (Anna-2, Moses-1)[1] was born on 01 Nov 1866 in Kardašova Řečice, Pribram Dist., Bohemia[1]. He died on 17 Dec 1925 in Berlin, Germany[1].

    Bianca Poláček[1].

    Ludwig Rabl and Bianca Poláček were married before 1900. They had the following children:

    i. **Hans Rabl**[1] was born on 29 Oct 1899 in Karlovy Vary, Bohemia[1]. He died before 1930 in Berlin, Germany.

    Leonie Fraenkel daughter of Gotthilf Fraenkel and Amalie ("Mally") Sandbank[1]. She died in 1945 in Ravensberg.

    Ludwig Rabl and Leonie Fraenkel were married before 1906. They had the following children:

  i. **Ruth Rabl**[1] was born on 09 Nov 1906[1]. She died in 1937[1].

25. ii. **Annemarie Rabl**[1] was born on 04 Jan 1908 in Karlovy Vary, Bohemia[1]. She died on 18 Oct 1971 in Shrewsbury, Shropshire, England, UK[1].

13. **Berthold Rabl**-3 (Anna-2, Moses-1)[1] was born on 25 Mar 1871 in K R. He died on 19 Jun 1932 in Karlovy Vary[1].

Selma Reichl[1] was born on 11 Jul 1879. She died in 1942 in Trostyanetz. Berthold Rabl and Selma Reichl married. They had the following children:

26. i. **Martin Walter Rabl Radcliffe** was born on 02 Dec 1903 in Prague. He died on 04 Jan 1950 in Hastings, England.

27. ii. **Hans Rabl**[1] was born on 01 Apr 1906 in Prague[1]. He died in 1987 in London[1].

  iii. **Ernst Rabl**.

28. iv. **Martin Rabl**[1] was born on 02 Dec 1903 in Prague[1]. He died on 04 Jan 1950 in Hastings[1].

29. v. **Ernest Phillip Rabl**[1] was born on 26 Dec 1913 in Karlovy Vary[1]. He died on 01 Nov 1976 in New York[1].

14. **Adele Rablova**-3 (Anna-2, Moses-1)[1] was born on 03 Dec 1874 in K.R.[1]. She died on 18 Oct 1950 in Prague[1].

Joseph Lebenhart[1] was born in 1874 in Pisek[1]. He died in 1944[1]. Joseph Lebenhart and Adele Rablova married. They had the following children:

30. i. **Hugo Lebenhart**[1].

  ii. **Zdenka Lebenhart**[1] was born in 1901[1]. She died in 1961[1].

31. iii. **Otto Lebenhart (Toman)**[1] was born on 13 Oct 1902 in possibly Pisek[1]. He died on 30 Sep 1966 in Prague[1].

15. **Otto Rabl**-3 (Anna-2, Moses-1)[1] was born on 02 Jan 1880[1].

Berta[1].

Otto Rabl and Berta married. They had the following children:

32. i. **Hans Rabl**[1] was born in Feb 1912[1].

33. ii. **Eugene Rabl**[1] was born in 1914[1].

16. **Richard Rabl**-3 (Anna-2, Moses-1)[1] was born on 12 Sep 1883[1].

Klára[1].
Richard Rabl and Klára married. They had the following children:
  i. **Peter Rabl**[1].
  ii. **Maximilian Rabl**[1] was born on 04 Jun 1869 in K.R.[1]. He died on 14 Jan 1915[1].

17. **Kamila Rablova**-3 (Anna-2, Moses-1)[1] was born on 02 Sep 1885[1].
Carl-Maria Svoboda[1].
Carl-Maria Svoboda and Kamila Rablova married. They had the following children:
  34. i. **Michael Swoboda**[1].

18. **Rudi Rabl**-3 (Anna-2, Moses-1)[1] was born on 23 Mar 1889[1]. He died in 1951.
Elizabeth Chambers[1].
Rudi Rabl and Elizabeth Chambers were married after 1940. They had the following children:
  35. i. **Jula Rabl**[1] was born on 18 Jan 1944 in London, England.
Jula Goldman[1].
Rudi Rabl and Jula Goldman married. They had no children.

19. **Jiří Weiner**-3 (Gustav-2, Moses-1) was born in 1896.
Kateřina.
Jiří Weiner and Kateřina married. They had the following children:
  i. **Jadviga Weiner**.

20. **Zdena Weinerova**-3 (Gustav-2, Moses-1) was born in 1898. She died in 1975.
Vladimír Vochoc. He died in 1987.
Vladimír Vochoc and Zdena Weinerova married. They had the following children:
  i. **Nanynka Vochocova**.
Antonín Pavel was born in 1887. He died in 1958.
Antonín Pavel and Zdena Weinerova married. They had no children.

Generation 4

21. **Věra Winterova**-4 (Olga-3, Sophie-2, Moses-1).
Kupka.

Kupka and Věra Winterova married. They had the following children:
> i. **Ivan Kupka**.
> ii. **Tom Kupka**.

22. **Franzi Schapire**-4 (Olga-3, Franziska 'Fann'y-2, Moses-1) was born on 28 Dec 1909 in Vienna, Austria. She died on 03 Oct 2004 in Albany, Albany County, New York.
Weiss.
Weiss and Franzi Schapire married. They had the following children:
> i. **Esther Weiss**.

Dr. Bernhard Elias Schapire was born on 21 Jan 1880 in Ternopil, Ternopil's'ka oblast, Ukraine. He died on 09 Apr 1953.
Dr. Bernhard Elias Schapire and Franzi Schapire married. They had the following children:
> i. **Irene Schapire**.

23. **Hans Schapire**-4 (Olga-3, Franziska 'Fann'y-2, Moses-1) was born on 26 Aug 1914 in Vienna, Austria. He died on 16 Jan 2013 in Minneapolis, Hennepin County, MN.
Lillian 'Libby' was born about 1924 in Colorado. She died on 25 Nov 2013 in Minneapolis, Hennepin County, MN.
Hans Schapire and Lillian 'Libby' married. They had the following children:
> i. **Julie Schapire**.
> ii. **Irene Schapire** was born after 1944.
> iii. **Esther Schapire** was born in 1952.

24. **Curt Strand (Stránský)**-4 (Viktor-3, Franziska 'Fann'y-2, Moses-1) was born on 13 Nov 1920 in Vienna, Austria.
Fleur Lillian Emanuel was born on 24 Feb 1928 in Bloemfontein, Motheo, Free State, South Africa. She died on 23 Dec 2011 in Snowmass, Pitkin County, CO.
Curt Strand (Stránský) and Fleur Lillian Emanuel married. They had the following children:
> i. **Karen (Strand) Stránský** was born on 16 Feb 1955 in Amityville, Suffolk County, NY. She died on 03 Dec 2006 in

Bennington, Bennington County, VT.

25. **Annemarie Rabl**-4 (Ludwig-3, Anna-2, Moses-1)[1] was born on 04 Jan 1908 in Karlovy Vary, Bohemia[1]. She died on 18 Oct 1971 in Shrewsbury,Shropshire, England, UK[1].

    Hans Lobbenberg[1] was born on 18 May 1896 in Köln, Nordrhein-Westfalen, Germany. He died on 6 Jul 1955 in Shrewsbury, Shropshire, England, UK.

    Hans Lobbenberg and Annemarie Rabl married. They had the following children:

    36. i. **George Lobbenberg** was born on 16 Nov 1922 in Köln-Lindenthal, Nordrhein-Westfalen, Germany. He died on 22 Oct 1970 in Birmingham, West Midlands, England, UK.

    ii. **Peter Lobbenberg** was born on 12 Sep 1939 in Edgware, London, Great Britain, UK.

26. **Martin Walter Rabl Radcliffe**-4 (Berthold-3, Anna-2, Moses-1) was born on 02 Dec 1903 in Prague. He died on 04 Jan 1950 in Hastings, England.

    Mariana Block[1] was born on 24 Oct 1906. She died on 06 Sep 1943 in Auschwitz. Martin Walter Rabl Radcliffe and Mariana Block married. They had the following children:

    i. **Miriam Rabl** was born on 04 Oct 1934 in Prague. She died on 06 Sep 1942 in Auschwitz.

    Mona Bullus[1] was born on 11 Apr 1915 in Bradford[1]. She died on 22 Jan 1972 in Alderney[1].

    Martin Walter Rabl Radcliffe and Mona Bullus were married about 1950. They had the following children:

    37. i. **Nikolas Rabl Radcliffe** was born on 07 Jan 1950.

27. **Hans Rabl**-4 (Berthold-3, Anna-2, Moses-1)[1] was born on 01 Apr 1906 in Prague[1]. He died in 1987 in London[1].

    Moira Wilson[1].

    Hans Rabl and Moira Wilson married. They had the following children:

    38. i. **Preston Rabl**[1] was born on 06 Jan 1949 in London[1].

28. **Martin Rabl**-4 (Berthold-3, Anna-2, Moses-1)[1] was born on 02 Dec

1903 in Prague[1]. He died on 04 Jan 1950 in Hastings[1].

Mariana Block[1] was born on 24 Oct 1906. She died on 06 Sep 1943 in Auschwitz. Martin Rabl and Mariana Block married. They had the following children:

 i. **Miriam Rabl** was born on 04 Oct 1934 in Prague. She died on 06 Sep 1942 in Auschwitz.

Mona Bullus[1] was born on 11 Apr 1915 in Bradford[1]. She died on 22 Jan 1972 in Alderney[1].

Martin Rabl and Mona Bullus married. They had the following children:
37. i. **Nikolas Rabl Radcliffe** was born on 07 Jan 1950.

29. **Ernest Phillip Rabl**-4 (Berthold-3, Anna-2, Moses-1)[1] was born on 26 Dec 1913 in Karlovy Vary[1]. He died on 01 Nov 1976 in New York[1].

Margit Iritzer[1] was born on 07 Mar 1915 in Macov, Czech[1]. She died on 02 Oct 1995 in New York[1]. Ernest Phillip Rabl and Margit Iritzer married. They had the following children:

39. i. **Marion Renee Diana Rabl**[1] was born on 19 Nov 1945 in London[1].

30. **Hugo Lebenhart**-4 (Adele-3, Anna-2, Moses-1)[1].
Viola Jakubovie[1].

Hugo Lebenhart and Viola Jakubovie married. They had the following children:

 i. **Barabara Tomanová**[1] was born on 18 Jan 1950 in Bratislava[1].

31. **Otto Lebenhart (Toman)**-4 (Adele-3, Anna-2, Moses-1)[1] was born on 13 Oct 1902 in possibly Pisek[1]. He died on 30 Sep 1966 in Prague[1].

Christa Heidi Willer daughter of Robert Willer and Mimi Rudinger[1] was born on 12 Apr 1918 in Pisek. She died on 20 Aug 1980 in London. Otto Lebenhart (Toman) and Christa Heidi Willer married. They had the following children:

40. i. **Helena Tomanová**[1] was born on 19 Jun 1947 in Prague[1].

32. **Hans Rabl**-4 (Otto-3, Anna-2, Moses-1)[1] was born in Feb 1912[1].
Ruth Arensberg[1].

Hans Rabl and Ruth Arensberg married. They had the following children:

41. i. **Ronie Rabl**[1] was born on 26 Jan 1944[1].
42. ii. **Irit Rabl**[1] was born on 12 Sep 1953 in Israel[1]. She died on 26 Dec 1997 in Tel Aviv[1].

33. **Eugene Rabl**-4 (Otto-3, Anna-2, Moses-1)[1] was born in 1914[1].
Dagmar[1].
Eugene Rabl and Dagmar married. They had the following children:
43. i. **Monica Rabl**[1].

34. **Michael Swoboda**-4 (Kamila-3, Anna-2, Moses-1)[1].
Christine[1].
Michael Swoboda and Christine married. They had the following children:
44. i. **Andrew Swoboda**[1].
45. ii. **Deborah Swoboda**[1].
Susan[1].
Michael Swoboda and Susan married. They had no children.

35. **Jula Rabl**-4 (Rudi-3, Anna-2, Moses-1)[1] was born on 18 Jan 1944 in London, England.
Roger Westman[1].
Roger Westman and Jula Rabl married. They had the following children:
  i. **Sam Westman**[1].
46. ii. **Sophie Westman**[1].

Generation 5

36. **George Lobbenberg**-5 (Annemarie-4, Ludwig-3, Anna-2, Moses-1) was born on 16 Nov 1922 in Köln-Lindenthal, Nordrhein-Westfalen, Germany. He died on 22 Oct 1970 in Birmingham, West Midlands, England, UK.
Margaret Thomas was born in 1933 in Shrewsbury, Shropshire, England, UK. She died on 20 Apr 2015 in Shrewsbury, Shropshire, England, UK.
George Lobbenberg and Margaret Thomas married. They had the following children:
  i. **Andrew Davidi Lobbenberg**.

37. **Nikolas Rabl Radcliffe**-5 (Martin Walter Rabl-4, Berthold-3, Anna-2, Moses-1) was born on 07 Jan 1950.
Hilary Gibson[1] was born on 03 May 1954 in Bournemouth[1].

Nikolas Rabl Radcliffe and Hilary Gibson married. They had the following children:
   i. **Victoria Emily Rabl Radcliffe**[1] was born on 09 Jul 1981 in Hastings[1].
   ii. **James Martin Antony Rabl Radcliffe**[1] was born on 18 Jun 1983 in Hastings[1].
   iii. **Charlotte Rabl Radcliffe**[1] was born on 04 Nov 1989 in Hastings[1].
38. **Preston Rabl**-5 (Hans-4, Berthold-3, Anna-2, Moses-1)[1] was born on 06 Jan 1949 in London[1].
   Sara Fitzpatrick[1].
   Preston Rabl and Sara Fitzpatrick married. They had the following children:
   i. **Francesca Rabl**[1].
   ii. **Sophia Rabl**[1] was born in 1987 in London[1].
   iii. **Georgina Rabl**[1] was born in 1988 in London[1].
39. **Marion Renee Diana Rabl**-5 (Ernest Phillip-4, Berthold-3, Anna-2, Moses-1)[1] was born on 19 Nov 1945 in London[1].
   Leslie John Edge[1] was born on 29 Jul[1].
   Leslie John Edge and Marion Renee Diana Rabl married. They had the following children:
   i. **Alison Kimberly Diana Edge**[1] was born on 28 Nov 1977 in Montreal[1].
   ii. **Ryan Phillip John Edge**[1] was born on 22 May 1979 in Montreal[1].
41. **Helena Tomanová**-5 (Otto Lebenhart-4, Adele-3, Anna-2, Moses-1)[1] was born on 19 Jun 1947 in Prague[1].
   Robert Bowman[1].
   Robert Bowman and Helena Tomanová married. They had the following children:
   i. **Mark Bowman**[1] was born on 19 Jul 1979 in Gerrands Cross, England[1].
   ii. **Alan Russell Bowman**[1] was born on 05 Aug 1982 in Gerrands

Cross, England[1].

Peter Buffam.
Peter Buffam and Helena Tomanová were married in 1996. They had no children.

Peter Aberley.
Peter Aberley and Helena Tomanová were married in 2000 in Prague, CSR. They had no children.

42. **Ronie Rabl**-5 (Hans-4, Otto-3, Anna-2, Moses-1)[1] was born on 26 Jan 1944[1].
    Edelist[1].
    Edelist and Ronie Rabl married. They had the following children:
    47. i. **Dana Edelist**[1] was born in 1966[1].
    48. ii. **Yael Edelist**[1] was born in 1968[1].

43. **Irit Rabl**-5 (Hans-4, Otto-3, Anna-2, Moses-1)[1] was born on 12 Sep 1953 in Israel[1]. She died on 26 Dec 1997 in Tel Aviv[1].
    Marian Cohn[1].
    Marian Cohn and Irit Rabl married. They had the following children:
    i. **Gaby Cohn**[1] was born on 22 Mar 1978[1].
    ii. **Tal Cohn**[1] was born on 19 Jun 1986[1].

44. **Monica Rabl**-5 (Eugene-4, Otto-3, Anna-2, Moses-1)[1].
    Monica Rabl and unknown spouse married. They had the following children:
    i. **Alon**[1] was born in 1989 in Tel Aviv[1].
    ii. **Ellar**[1] was born in 1989 in Tel Aviv[1].
    iii. **Itamar**[1] was born in 1994[1].

44. **Andrew Swoboda**-5 (Michael-4, Kamila-3, Anna-2, Moses-1)[1].
    ?[1].
    Andrew Swoboda and ? married. They had the following children:
    i. **? Swoboda**[1].

45. **Deborah Swoboda**-5 (Michael-4, Kamila-3, Anna-2, Moses-1)[1].
    ? [1].
    ? and Deborah Swoboda married. They had the following children:
    i. **? ?**[1].

ii. **? ?**[1].
　　　iii. **? ?**[1].
　　　iv. **? ?**[1].
46. **Sophie Westman**-5 (Jula-4, Rudi-3, Anna-2, Moses-1)[1].
    Carlos Lizarraga-Curiel[1].
    Carlos Lizarraga-Curiel and Sophie Westman married. They had the following children:
    　　i. **Benjamine Rabl Lizarraga-Curiel**[1] was born on 13 Jun 1997[1].
    　　ii. **Joshua Lizarraga-Curiel**[1] was born on 31 Mar 2000[1].

Generation 6

47. **Dana Edelist**-6 (Ronie-5, Hans-4, Otto-3, Anna-2, Moses-1)[1] was born in 1966[1].
    Boaz Spector[1].
    Boaz Spector and Dana Edelist married. They had the following children:
    　　i. **Yonatan Spector**[1] was born on 18 Nov 1992[1].
    　　ii. **Yuval Spector** was born about 1996.
    　　iii. **Twin Spector** was born about 2001.
48. **Yael Edelist**-6 (Ronie-5, Hans-4, Otto-3, Anna-2, Moses-1)[1] was born in 1968[1].
    David Levy.
    David Levy and Yael Edelist married. They had the following children:
    　　i. **Ido Levy** was born about 1997.
    　　ii. **Ruth Levy** was born between 1999-2000.

Sources

1 Rabl Family.GED.FTW, Date of Import: Jan 11, 2001.

Kašpárek Family

Generation 1

Jakub Kasparek-1.

Marie Ptackova.

Jakub Kasparek and Marie Ptackova married. They had the following children:

i. **Jan Kašpárek** was born in 1838.

Generation 2

Jan Kašpárek-2 (Jakub-1) was born in 1838.

Marie Servitkova was born in 1849 in Zvold, Zdar nad Sazavou, Vysocina, Moravia. Jan Kašpárek and Marie Servitkova married. They had the following children:

i. **František Jan Kašpárek** was born in 1881 in Zvole, Zdar nad Sazavou, vysocina, Moravia.

Josef Kašpárek was born in 1859 in Zvole, Zdar nad Sazavou, Vysocina, Moravia.

iii. **Frantiska Marta Kašpárkova** was born in 1877 in Zvole, Zdar nad Sazaviou, Vysocina, Moravia.

Generation 3

František Jan Kašpárek-3 (Jan-2, Jakub-1) was born in 1881 in Zvole, Zdar nad Sazavou, vysocina, Moravia.

Hermina Taussigová daughter of Jakub Taussig and Julie Meislova was born on 23 Jun 1871. She died in 1927.

František Jan Kašpárek and Hermina Taussigová married. They had the following children:

JUDr. (George (Jiří) Kašpárek was born on 27 Apr 1909 in Brno, Moravia. He married Zdena Kracmerova in 1939. He died on 20 Feb 1983.

ii. **MUDr. Ivan Kašpárek** was born on 05 Oct 1910 in Brno, Moravia. He died in Jan 1985 in Elgin, IL.

Petr Kašpárek was born on 12 Jun 1912 in Brno, Moravia. He died on 15 Dec 1994 in Laguna Hills, Orange, California, USA.

Frantiska Marta Kašpárkova-3 (Jan-2, Jakub-1) was born in 1877 in Zvole, Zdar nad Sazaviou, Vysocina, Moravia.
Augustin Jindra was born on 27 Sep 1876 in Racice, Vysocina.
Augustin Jindra and Frantiska Marta Kašpárkova married. They had the following children:
>   **Vojtech Jindra**.
>   **Josef Jindra** was born on 09 Feb 1914. He died on 02 May 1987.
>   **Frantisek Jindra**.
>   **Vladimir Jindra**.

Generation 4
MUDr. Ivan Kašpárek-4 (František Jan-3, Jan-2, Jakub-1) was born on 05 Oct 1910 in Brno, Moravia. He died in Jan 1985 in Elgin, IL.
Milada Novotná was born on 07 Feb 1916 in Cesky Brod, Kolin Dist,,Bbohemia. She died on 20 Nov 1989 in Elgin, IL.
MUDr. Ivan Kašpárek and Milada Novotná married. They had the following children:
>   i. **Eva Kašpárková** was born on 13 Feb 1942 in Prague, Czech..

Generation 5
Eva Kašpárková-5 (MUDr. Ivan-4, František Jan-3, Jan-2, Jakub-1) was born on 13 Feb 1942 in Prague, Czech..
Horatio.
Horatio and Eva Kašpárková married. They had the following children:
>   **David**.

Schönfeld Family

Generation 1

Moses Kohn Schönfeld-1 was born in 1711. He died in 1810 in Malá Skála, Jablonec nad Nisou District, bohemia.

Moses Kohn Schönfeld and unknown spouse married. They had the following children:

> i. **Elchanan Josef Schönfeld** was born in 1751. He died on 22 Oct 1813 in Turnov, Semily District, Bohemia.
> **Karl Schönfeld.**

Generation 2

Elchanan Josef Schönfeld-2 (Moses Kohn-1) was born in 1751. He died on 22 Oct 1813 in Turnov, Semily District, Bohemia.

Ester Theresie was born in 1741. She died on 25 Sep 1826 in Turnov, Semily District, Bohemia. Elchanan Josef Schönfeld and Ester Theresie married. They had the following children:

> i. **Josef Schönfeld** was born on 15 Mar 1780. He died in 1860 in Turnov.
> ii. **Blimel Barbara Schönfeld**. She died on 07 Jul 1835.
> iii. **Františka Schönfeld** was born in 1790. She died in 1840.

Generation 3

Josef Schönfeld-3 (Elchanan Josef-2, Moses Kohn-1) was born on 15 Mar 1780. He died in 1860 in Turnov.

Františka Horzitzky was born in 1784 in Golčův Jeníkov, Havlíčkův Brod District, Moravia. She died on 09 Jan 1849 in Turnov, Bohemia.

Josef Schönfeld and Františka Horzitzky married. They had the following children:

> **Barbora Schönfeld** was born in 1808.
> ii. **Johana Jeanette Schönfeld** was born in 1809. She died in 1876.
> **Adolf Abraham Schönfeld** was born in 1810. He died in 1812.
> iv. **Luisa Aloisie Schönfeld** was born in 1812. She died on 13 Jan 1875 in Liberec, Bohemia.
> **Konrad Schönfeld** was born in 1817. He died in 1820.

vi. **Emilie Emma Schönfeld** was born in 1817 in Litomerice, Litoměřice District, Bohemia.

vii. **Anton Schönfeld** was born on 01 Jul 1820. He died on 19 Oct 1869 in Turnov, Bohemia.

Emanuel Schönfeld was born in 1824.

ix. **Pavel Schönfeld** was born on 05 May 1825. He died on 02 Oct 1886 in Turnov, Semily District, Bohemia.

x. **Amalia Agnes Anna Schönfeld** was born on 10 Aug 1815 in Semily, Semily District, Bohemia. She died on 10 Sep 1878.

Blimel Barbara Schönfeld-3 (Elchanan Josef-2, Moses Kohn-1). She died on 07 Jul 1835.

Wolf Weiskopf was born about 1784.

Wolf Weiskopf and Blimel Barbara Schönfeld married. They had the following children:

i. **Konrad Weiskopf** was born about 1816.

ii. **Isak Weiskopf** was born about 1822.

Generation 4

Johana Jeanette Schönfeld-4 (Josef-3, Elchanan Josef-2, Moses Kohn-1) was born in 1809. She died in 1876.

Markus Wertheimer was born in Dolní Kralovice, Benešov District, Bohemia.

Markus Wertheimer and Johana Jeanette Schönfeld married. They had the following children:

Isak Wertheimer.

Alois Wertheimer was born in 1833.

Mariana Wertheimer.

Luisa Aloisie Schönfeld-4 (Josef-3, Elchanan Josef-2, Moses Kohn-1) was born in 1812. She died on 13 Jan 1875 in Liberec, Bohemia.

Josef Winternitz was born in Cerekvice nad Loučnou, Svitavy District, Bohemia. He died on 11 Oct 1896 in Jablonné v Podještědí, Liberec District, Bohemia.

Josef Winternitz and Luisa Aloisie Schönfeld married. They had the following children:

Hermine 'Ojebinka' Winternitz was born on 17 Mar 1841 in Jablonné v Podještědí, Liberec District, Boihemia. She died on 25 Oct 1934 in Semily, Semily District, Bohemia.

ii. **Gustav Winternitz** was born in 1842 in Rumburk, Děčín District, Bohemia. He died on 20 Feb 1919 in Hrádek nad Nisou, Liberec District, Bohemia.

Emilie Emma Schönfeld-4 (Josef-3, Elchanan Josef-2, Moses Kohn-1) was born in 1817 in Litomerice, Litoměřice District, Bohemia.

Selikowsky.

Selikowsky and Emilie Emma Schönfeld married. They had the following children:

Gustav Selikowsky.

Franziska Selikowsky.

Anton Schönfeld-4 (Josef-3, Elchanan Josef-2, Moses Kohn-1) was born on 01 Jul 1820. He died on Oct 1869 in Turnov, Bohemia.

Marie Wilhelmine Raudnitz was born in 1824 in Prague, Bohemia. She died on 01 Feb 1889.

Anton Schönfeld and Marie Wilhelmine Raudnitz married. They had the following children:

Karel Schönfeld. He died in US.

Ida Franziska Schönfeld.

Adolf Schönfeld. He died in Litomerice, Litoměřice District, Bohemia.

iv. **Franz Josef Schönfeld** was born in 1851. He died in 1879 in Kolin, Bohemia.

Heinrich Schönfeld.

Paul Schönfeld.

Amalie Schönfeld was born in 1856. She died in 1941 in Semily, Bohemia.

Sigfried Hynek Schönfeld. He died in Sobotka, Jičín District, Bohemia.

Leopold Schönfeld. He died in Rychnov nad Kněžnou, Bohemia.

Pavel Schönfeld-4 (Josef-3, Elchanan Josef-2, Moses Kohn-1) was born on 05

May 1825. He died on 02 Oct 1886 in Turnov, Semily District, Bohemia.
Anna Meislova daughter of Jakub Meisl and Judita Dubova was born on 15 Jul 1830 in Žehušice, Kutná Hora District, Bohemia. She died on 24 Jan 1872 in Turnov, Semily District, Bohemia. Pavel Schönfeld and Anna Meislova married. They had the following children:

    i. **František Schönfeld** was born on 10 Aug 1850. He died on 13 Aug 1911 in Turnov, Bohemia ?.

    ii. **Josef Schönfeld** was born in 1851. He died in 1905.

    iii. **Julius von Schönfeld** was born in 1853. He died in 1904.

    iv. **Pavla Schönfeldová** was born in 1855. She died in 1943 in Terezin.

    v. **Kamila Schönfeldová** was born in 1857. She died on 27 Mar 1920 in Krc.

    Eleanora Schönfeld.

Amalia Agnes Anna Schönfeld-4 (Josef-3, Elchanan Josef-2, Moses Kohn-1) was born on 10 Aug 1815 in Semily, Semily District, Bohemia. She died on 10 Sep 1878.

Eduard Adolf Malburg (Mautner) was born on 07 Aug 1808 in Smiřice, Hradec Králové District, Bohemia. He died on 02 Sep 1870 in Smiřice, Hradec Králové District, Bohemia.

Eduard Adolf Malburg (Mautner) and Amalia Agnes Anna Schönfeld married. They had the following children:

    Lambertine Malburg (Mautner) was born on 09 Apr 1852 in Smiřice, Hradec Králové District, Bohemia. She died on 08 Dec 1930 in Smiřice, Hradec Králové District, Czechoslovakia.

    Eduard Mautner.

    Pauline Josefine Mautner was born on 07 Apr 1837 in Alt Sankt Johann, Toggenburg, Sankt Gallen, Switzerland. She died on 02 Mar 1909 in Puchbach, Köflach, Voitsberg, Steiermark, Austria.

    iv. **Albrecht Theobald Mautner** was born on 15 Apr 1844 in Smiřice, Hradec Králové District, Bohemia. He died on 17 Aug 1905.

Konrad Weiskopf-4 (Blimel Barbara-3, Elchanan Josef-2, Moses Kohn-1) was born about 1816.

Aspasia Grünfeld.

Konrad Weiskopf and Aspasia Grünfeld married. They had the following children:

> i. **Moritz Weisskopf** was born on 07 Feb 1847 in Bohemia. He died on 09 May 1909 in New York, NY.
>
> ii. **William Whitehead (Weiskopf0** was born on 25 Dec 1856 in East Farmingdale, Suffolk County,. He died on 02 Jun 1932 in New york, NY.

Generation 5

Gustav Winternitz-5 (Luisa Aloisie-4, Josef-3, Elchanan Josef-2, Moses Kohn-1) was born in 1842 in Rumburk, Děčín District, Bohemia. He died on 20 Feb 1919 in Hrádek nad Nisou, Liberec District, Bohemia.

Jenny Schorsch was born on 16 Jun 1844 in Teplicce, Bbohemia.

Gustav Winternitz and Jenny Schorsch married. They had the following children:

> **Adele Winternitz** was born on 28 Nov 1871 in Hrádek nad Nisou, Liberec District, Bohemia.
>
> ii. **Rudolf Salomon Winternitz** was born on 26 Feb 1873. He died in 1944 in Auschwitz, Poiland - Holocaust.
>
> **Dr. Fritz Ernst Winternitz** was born on 05 May 1878 in Hrádek nad Nisou, Liberec District, Bohemia.
>
> **Erwin Winternitz.** He died on 05 Jul 1907 in Varnsdorf, Děčín District, Bohemia.

Franz Josef Schönfeld-5 (Anton-4, Josef-3, Elchanan Josef-2, Moses Kohn-1) was born in 1851. He died in 1879 in Kolin, Bohemia.

Karolina.

Franz Josef Schönfeld and Karolina married. They had the following children:

> **Artur Schönfeld** was born in 1878 in Kolin, Bohemia.

František Schönfeld-5 (Pavel-4, Josef-3, Elchanan Josef-2, Moses Kohn-1) was born on 10 Aug 1850. He died on 13 Aug 1911 in Turnov, Bohemia ?.

Augusta Beerová.

František Schönfeld and Augusta Beerová married. They had the following children:
> i. **Anna Schönfeldová** was born in 1881. She died in 1945 in Osvetim.
>
> ii. **(Pavlina) Marie Schönfeldová** was born in 1885. She died in 1932.

Josef Schönfeld-5 (Pavel-4, Josef-3, Elchanan Josef-2, Moses Kohn-1) was born in 1851. He died in 1905.

Klára Igelova daughter of Elias Igel and Reisel Rosa Selzer.

Josef Schönfeld and Klára Igelova married. They had the following children:
> **Pavla Schönfeldová**.
>
> ii. **František Albrecht Schönfeld** was born on 13 Apr 1887 in Semily, Semily District, Bohemia. He died in 1940 in Prague, Bohemia.

Julius von Schönfeld-5 (Pavel-4, Josef-3, Elchanan Josef-2, Moses Kohn-1) was born in 1853. He died in 1904.

Augusta Picková.

Julius von Schönfeld and Augusta Picková married. They had the following children:
> i. **Anna Schönfeldová**.
>
> ii. **Pavel von Schoenfeld**.
>
> **Hanus von Schoenfeld**. He died in 1915.
>
> **Julius von Schoenfeld**. He died in 1914.

Pavla Schönfeldová-5 (Pavel-4, Josef-3, Elchanan Josef-2, Moses Kohn-1) was born in 1855. She died in 1943 in Terezin.

Rosenfeld.

Rosenfeld and Pavla Schönfeldová married. They had the following children:
> i. **Pavel (Rosenfeld) Rohan**.
>
> ii. **Anna Rosenfeldová**. She died in Osvetim.
>
> iii. **Kamila Rosenfeldová** was born in 1980.

Kamila Schönfeldová-5 (Pavel-4, Josef-3, Elchanan Josef-2, Moses Kohn-1) was born in 1857. She died on 27 Mar 1920 in Krc.

Antal Stasek (Antonín Zemen) son of Antonín Zeman and Anna Šolová was born on 22 Jul 1843 in Stanový, Zlatá Olešnice, Jablonec nad Nisou

District, Bohemia. He died on 09 Oct 1931 in Prague, Czech..

Antal Stasek (Antonín Zemen) and Kamila Schönfeldová married. They had the following children:

> i. **Kamil Zeman (Ivan Olbracht)** was born on 06 Jan 1882 in Semily. He died on 30 Dec 1952 in Praha, CSR.
>
> ii. **Vladimír Zeman** was born on 17 Mar 1887. He died on 01 May 1929.

Albrecht Theobald Mautner-5 (Amalia Agnes Anna-4, Josef-3, Elchanan Josef-2, Moses Kohn-1) was born on 15 Apr 1844 in Smiřice, Hradec Králové District, Bohemia. He died on 17 Aug 1905.

Johanna Jenny Maria Plugmacher was born on 31 Dec 1859.

Albrecht Theobald Mautner and Johanna Jenny Maria Plugmacher married. They had no children.

Stana Radicevics was born on 20 May 1848 in Serbia. She died on 08 Feb 1895.

Albrecht Theobald Mautner and Stana Radicevics married. They had the following children:

> **Marie Elisabeth Malburg** was born on 05 Jul 1875.
>
> **Adolf Eduard Josef Malburg** was born on 13 Jan 1885.

Marie Nitschke was born on 31 Jul 1842 in Wrocław, Wrocław Dist., Poland. She died on 18 Apr 1873.

Albrecht Theobald Mautner and Marie Nitschke married. They had the following children:

> i. **Dr. Oswald Zdenko Maria Malburg** was born on 27 Feb 1871 in Smiřice, Hradec Králové District, Bohemia. He died on 13 Mar 1930 in Smiřice, Hradec Králové District, Bohemia.

Moritz Weisskopf-5 (Konrad-4, Blimel Barbara-3, Elchanan Josef-2, Moses Kohn-1) was born on 07 Feb 1847 in Bohemia. He died on 09 May 1909 in New York, NY.

Karolina Hartmann was born after Feb 1848 in Běšin, Bohemia. She died on 01 Feb 1914 in New york, NY.

Moritz Weisskopf and Karolina Hartmann married. They had the following children:

SCHÖNFELD FAMILY

    Theresia Weisskopf was born on 09 Oct 1876 in New york, NY.
    Julia Johanna Weiskopf was born on 13 Apr 1880.
iii. **Oscar Whitehead (Weiskopf)** was born on 03 Feb 1882 in New york, NY. He died on 23 Mar 1951 in East Farmingdale, Suffolk County, NY.
    Alfred Weiskopf was born on 28 Sep 1886 in New york, NY.
    Ralph Weiskopf.
    Albine Weiskopf was born on 15 Jun 1878 in New york, NY.

William Whitehead (Weiskopf0-5 (Konrad-4, Blimel Barbara-3, Elchanan Josef-2, Moses Kohn-1) was born on 25 Dec 1856 in East Farmingdale, Suffolk County,. He died on 02 Jun 1932 in New york, NY.

Julia Levy was born on 24 Oct 1853. She died on 15 Jan 1920 in New york, NY. William Whitehead (Weiskopf0 and Julia Levy married. They had the following children:

    Leo Weiskopf.
    Lillian Weiskopf.
    Frieda Weiskopf.
    Chester Weiskopf.
    Ralph Weiskopf.
    Milton Weiskopf.

Generation 6

Rudolf Salomon Winternitz-6 (Gustav-5, Luisa Aloisie-4, Josef-3, Elchanan Josef-2, Moses Kohn-1) was born on 26 Feb 1873. He died in 1944 in Auschwitz, Poiland - Holocaust.

Hermine Wodicka daughter of Adolf Wodicka and Marie was born on 19 May 1879 in Kolin, Bohemia. She died in 1944 in Auschwitz, Poland - Holocaust.

Rudolf Salomon Winternitz and Hermine Wodicka married. They had the following children:

    Ella Elsa Winternitz was born on 25 Jan 1904 in Hrádek nad Nisou, Liberec District, Bohemia. She died in 1942 in Łódź, Poland - Holocaust.

Anna Schönfeldová-6 (František-5, Pavel-4, Josef-3, Elchanan Josef-2,

Moses Kohn-1) was born in 1881. She died in 1945 in Osvetim.

Hugo Iltis was born in 1874. He died in 1927.

Hugo Iltis and Anna Schönfeldová married. They had the following children:

> **Augusta Iltisova** was born in 1902. She died in 1983.
>
> **František Iltis** was born in 1904. He died in 1919.

(Pavlina) Marie Schönfeldová-6 (František-5, Pavel-4, Josef-3, Elchanan Josef-2, Moses Kohn-1) was born in 1885. She died in 1932.

Otto Hybler was born about 1880.

Otto Hybler and (Pavlina) Marie Schönfeldová married. They had the following children:

> i. **Otto Hybler** was born in 1909.
>
> ii. **Eva Hyblerova** was born in 1913.
>
> iii. **Augusta (Gusta) Hyblerova** was born in 1911. She married Kamil Šváb in 1936. She died in 1960.

František Albrecht Schönfeld-6 (Josef-5, Pavel-4, Josef-3, Elchanan Josef-2, Moses Kohn-1) was born on 13 Apr 1887 in Semily, Semily District, Bohemia. He died in 1940 in Prague, Bohemia.

Erna Singerova was born on 16 Jul 1897 in Prague, Bohemia. She died in 1944.

František Albrecht Schönfeld and Erna Singerova married. They had the following children:

> i. **Pavel (Schönfeld) Tigrid** was born on 27 Oct 1917 in Prague, Bohemia. He died on 31 Aug 2003 in Héricy, Seine-et-Marne, Île-de-France, France.

Olga Kafka was born on 17 Mar 1893 in Pisek, Bohemia. She died in 1942 in Sobibór, Włodawa Dist., Poland - Holocaust.

František Albrecht Schönfeld and Olga Kafka married. They had the following children:

> **Gertrude Schönfeld** was born on 13 Mar 1918 in New york, NY.

Anna Schönfeldová-6 (Julius von-5, Pavel-4, Josef-3, Elchanan Josef-2, Moses Kohn-1).

R. Rosenfeld.

Rosenfeld and Anna Schönfeldová married. They had the following children:
> **Stella Rosenfeld** was born in 1904.

Willy Fleisher.
Willy Fleisher and Anna Schönfeldová married. They had no children.

Pavel von Schoenfeld-6 (Julius von-5, Pavel-4, Josef-3, Elchanan Josef-2, Moses Kohn-1).

Weiglova.
Pavel von Schoenfeld and Weiglova married. They had the following children:
> **Ilse von Schoenfeld.**

Pavel (Rosenfeld) Rohan-6 (Pavla-5, Pavel-4, Josef-3, Elchanan Josef-2, Moses Kohn-1).

Roslmeyer.
Pavel (Rosenfeld) Rohan and Roslmeyer married. They had the following children:
> **Marie Rohanová.**
> **Alfred Rohan.**

Anna Rosenfeldová-6 (Pavla-5, Pavel-4, Josef-3, Elchanan Josef-2, Moses Kohn-1). She died in Osvetim.

Oscar Pozner. He died in Osvetin.
Oscar Pozner and Anna Rosenfeldová married. They had the following children:
> i. **Erich Pozner** was born in 1978.
> ii. **Hans Pozner.**

Kamila Rosenfeldová-6 (Pavla-5, Pavel-4, Josef-3, Elchanan Josef-2, Moses Kohn-1) was born in 1980.

Leo Besterman.
Leo Besterman and Kamila Rosenfeldová married. They had the following children:
> i. **Ilse Besterman.**
> **Lea Besterman.**

Kamil Zeman (Ivan Olbracht)-6 (Kamila-5, Pavel-4, Josef-3, Elchanan Josef-

2, Moses Kohn-1) was born on 06 Jan 1882 in Semily. He died on 30 Dec 1952 in Praha, CSR.

Helena Malirova.

Kamil Zeman (Ivan Olbracht) and Helena Malirova married. They had the following children:

    i. **Ivanka Olbrachtová** was born on 25 May 1938.

Slavka.

Kamil Zeman (Ivan Olbracht) and Slavka married. They had the following children:

    Ivanka Olbrachtová was born on 25 May 1938.

Vladimír Zeman-6 (Kamila-5, Pavel-4, Josef-3, Elchanan Josef-2, Moses Kohn-1) was born on 17 Mar 1887. He died on 01 May 1929.

Marie Wimrova.

Vladimír Zeman and Marie Wimrova married. They had the following children:

    Maryška Zemanová was born in 1915.

    ii. **Alena Zemanová** was born in 1919.

Dr. Oswald Zdenko Maria Malburg-6 (Albrecht Theobald-5, Amalia Agnes Anna-4, Josef-3, Elchanan Josef-2, Moses Kohn-1) was born on 27 Feb 1871 in Smiřice, Hradec Králové District, Bohemia. He died on 13 Mar 1930 in Smiřice, Hradec Králové District, Bohemia.

Ilona von Puteani was born on 02 Jul 1876 in Szigliget, Hungary. She died in 1980 in Stanz im Mürztal, Mürzzuschlag, Styria, Austria.

Dr. Oswald Zdenko Maria Malburg and Ilona von Puteani married. They had the following children:

    Rudiolf Friedrich Maria Malburg was born on 11 Mar 1910 in miřice, Hradec Králové District, bohemia. He died on 30 Dec 1951 in Stanz im Mürztal, Mürzzuschlag, Styria, Austria.

Oscar Whitehead (Weiskopf)-6 (Moritz-5, Konrad-4, Blimel Barbara-3, Elchanan Josef-2, Moses Kohn-1) was born on 03 Feb 1882 in New york, NY. He died on 23 Mar 1951 in East Farmingdale, Suffolk County, NY.

Mathilda 'Tillie' Jacobs was born in 1888 in New york, NY.

Oscar Whitehead (Weiskopf) and Mathilda 'Tillie' Jacobs married. They had the following children:

> **Ralph Whitehead** was born on 03 Feb 1909 in New york, NY. He died on 22 Aug 1962.
>
> **Marjory Whitehead** was born about 1913 in New York, NY.
>
> **Alfred Whitehead** was born about 1917.

Generation 7

Otto Hybler-7 ((Pavlina) Marie-6, František-5, Pavel-4, Josef-3, Elchanan Josef-2, Moses Kohn-1) was born in 1909.

Božena.

Otto Hybler and Božena married. They had the following children:

> i. **Alena Hyblerova** was born in 1947.

Eva Hyblerova-7 ((Pavlina) Marie-6, František-5, Pavel-4, Josef-3, Elchanan Josef-2, Moses Kohn-1) was born in 1913.

V. Holan.

Holan and Eva Hyblerova married. They had the following children:

> i. **Jana Holanova** was born in 1937.

Bedřich Wiskovsky.

Bedřich Wiskovsky and Eva Hyblerova married. They had no children.

Augusta (Gusta) Hyblerova-7 ((Pavlina) Marie-6, František-5, Pavel-4, Josef-3, Elchanan Josef-2, Moses Kohn-1) was born in 1911. She died in 1960.

Kamil Šváb son of Adolf Šváb and Marie Markéta Marta Taussigová was born in 1907 in Vysoke nad Jizerou. He died in 1982 in Praha, Bohemia. Kamil Šváb and Augusta (Gusta) Hyblerova were married in 1936. They had the following children:

> **Jan Šváb** was born on 04 Jul 1937 in Praha, CSR. He married Josette Azra on 02 May 1978.

Karel Storch.

Karel Storch and Augusta (Gusta) Hyblerova married. They had the following children:

> i. **Martin Storch** was born in 1946.
>
> ii. **Anna Storchova** was born in 1947.

Pavel (Schönfeld) Tigrid-7 (František Albrecht-6, Josef-5, Pavel-4, Josef-3, Elchanan Josef-2, Moses Kohn-1) was born on 27 Oct 1917 in Prague, Bohemia. He died on 31 Aug 2003 in Héricy, Seine-et-Marne, Île-de-France, France.
Ivanka Myskova was born in 1925. She died in 2008.
Pavel (Schönfeld) Tigrid and Ivanka Myskova married. They had the following children:
    i. **Deborah Tigrid** was born in 1955.
    ii. **Kateřina Tigridová** was born in 1956.
    iii. **Gregory Tigrid** was born in 1958.

Erich Pozner-7 (Anna-6, Pavla-5, Pavel-4, Josef-3, Elchanan Josef-2, Moses Kohn-1) was born in 1978.
Joyce Smyth.
Erich Pozner and Joyce Smyth married. They had the following children:
    Rebecca Pozner.

Hans Pozner-7 (Anna-6, Pavla-5, Pavel-4, Josef-3, Elchanan Josef-2, Moses Kohn-1).
Evelin Swallow.
Hans Pozner and Evelin Swallow married. They had the following children:
    Richard Pozner.
    Lora Pozner.

Ilse Besterman-7 (Kamila-6, Pavla-5, Pavel-4, Josef-3, Elchanan Josef-2, Moses Kohn-1).
Pfeifer.
Pfeifer and Ilse Besterman married. They had the following children:
    Claude Pfeifer.

Alena Zemanová-7 (Vladimír-6, Kamila-5, Pavel-4, Josef-3, Elchanan Josef-2, Moses Kohn-1) was born in 1919.
V. Krotky.
Krotky and Alena Zemanová married. They had the following children:
    Markéta Krotka.

Jan Krotky.

Generation 8

Alena Hyblerova-8 (Otto-7, (Pavlina) Marie-6, František-5, Pavel-4, Josef-3, Elchanan Josef-2, Moses Kohn-1) was born in 1947.

Jiří Kos.

Jiří Kos and Alena Hyblerova married. They had the following children:

    David Kos.

Jana Holanova-8 (Eva-7, (Pavlina) Marie-6, František-5, Pavel-4, Josef-3, Elchanan Josef-2, Moses Kohn-1) was born in 1937.

Jindřich Pokorný was born in 1921.

Jindřich Pokorný and Jana Holanova married. They had the following children:

    i. **Tereza Pokorná** was born in 1960.

Martin Storch-8 (Augusta (Gusta)-7, (Pavlina) Marie-6, František-5, Pavel-4, Josef-3, Elchanan Josef-2, Moses Kohn-1) was born in 1946.

Marta Musilová was born in 1948.

Martin Storch and Marta Musilová married. They had the following children:

    Jan Storch.

Anna Storchova-8 (Augusta (Gusta)-7, (Pavlina) Marie-6, František-5, Pavel-4, Josef-3, Elchanan Josef-2, Moses Kohn-1) was born in 1947.

Kristian Kodet.

Kristian Kodet and Anna Storchova married. They had the following children:

    Veronika Kodetova was born in 1968.

    Johanna Kodetova was born in 1970.

Deborah Tigrid-8 (Pavel (Schönfeld)-7, František Albrecht-6, Josef-5, Pavel-4, Josef-3, Elchanan Josef-2, Moses Kohn-1) was born in 1955.

Eric Marguerat.

Eric Marguerat and Deborah Tigrid married. They had the following children:

    Natasha Marguerat was born in 1984.

    Nathan Marguerat was born in 1987.

Valentin Marguerat was born in 1991.

Kateřina Tigridová-8 (Pavel (Schönfeld)-7, František Albrecht-6, Josef-5, Pavel-4, Josef-3, Elchanan Josef-2, Moses Kohn-1) was born in 1956.

Kateřina Tigridová and unknown spouse married. They had the following children:

Tommy was born in 1985.

Gregory Tigrid-8 (Pavel (Schönfeld)-7, František Albrecht-6, Josef-5, Pavel-4, Josef-3, Elchanan Josef-2, Moses Kohn-1) was born in 1958.

Gregory Tigrid and unknown spouse married. They had the following children:

Stanislas was born in 1987.

Generation 9

Tereza Pokorná-9 (Jana-8, Eva-7, (Pavlina) Marie-6, František-5, Pavel-4, Josef-3, Elchanan Josef-2, Moses Kohn-1) was born in 1960.

Jura Herz was born in 1936.

Jura Herz and Tereza Pokorná married. They had the following children:

Anna Elisabeth Herzova.

Rábl Family

Generation 1

Samuel Moises-1[1].

Unknown.

Samuel Moises and Unknown married. They had the following children:

    i. **Abraham Rabl (Samuel)**[1] was born about 1722 in Kardašova Řečice, Jindřichův Hradec District, Bohemia[1]. He died after 1778 in Kardašova Řečice, Jindřichův Hradec District, Bohemia[1].

Generation 2

Abraham Rabl (Samuel)-2 (Samuel-1)[1] was born about 1722 in Kardašova Řečice, Jindřichův Hradec District, Bohemia[1]. He died after 1778 in Kardašova Řečice, Jindřichův Hradec District, Bohemia[1].

Elizabeth was born in 1719. She died in 1814 in Kardašova Řečice, Jindřichův Hradec District, Bohemia.

Abraham Rabl (Samuel) and Elizabeth married. They had the following children:

    i. **Bernard Rabl**[1] was born in K.R.[1]. He died after 1796 in K.R.[1].

    ii. **Samuel Rabl**[1, 2].

    Ewa Rabl was born in 1770.

    Anna Rabl.

    v. **Rachel Rabl** was born in 1752 in Kardašova Řečice, Jindřichův Hradec District, Bohemia. She died on 16 Mar 1824 in Kardašova Řečice, Jindřichův Hradec District, Bohemi.

Generation 3

Bernard Rabl-3 (Abraham Rabl-2, Samuel-1)[1] was born in K.R.[1]. He died after 1796 in K.R.[1].

Ester[1].

Bernard Rabl and Ester married. They had the following children:

    i. **Josef-Marek Rabl**[1]. He died in 1842[1].

    ii. **Wilheim Rabl**[1].

    Benjamine Rabl[1].

Daughters Rabl[1].

v. **Sirach Rabl**[1] was born in 1790 in KR[1].

vi. **Moises Rabl**[1] was born in 1785 in K.R.[1]. He died on 13 Sep 1860 in K.R.[1].

Samuel Rabl-3 (Abraham Rabl-2, Samuel-1)[1, 2].

Samuel Rabl and unknown spouse married. They had the following children:

i. **Abraham Rabl**[1, 2] was born about 1722 in Kardašova Řečice, Jindřichův Hradec District, Bohemi. He died after 1802 in Kardašova Řečice, Jindřichův Hradec District, Bohemi.

Son#3 Rabl[1, 2].

Son#4 Rabl[1, 2].

Daughter#1 Rabl[1, 2].

Daughter#2 Rabl[1, 2].

Daughter#3 Rabl[1, 2].

Daughter#4 Rabl[1, 2].

Daughter#5 Rabl[1, 2].

Daughter#6 Rabl[1, 2].

Daughter#7 Rabl[1, 2].

Son#5 Rabl[1, 2].

Son#6 Rabl[1, 2].

xiii. **Isak Rabl**[1, 2] was born in 1807[1, 2].

Rachel Rabl-3 (Abraham Rabl-2, Samuel-1) was born in 1752 in Kardašova Řečice, Jindřichův Hradec District, Bohemia. She died on 16 Mar 1824 in Kardašova Řečice, Jindřichův Hradec District, Bohemi.

Filip Herrmann was born about 1746. He died on 09 Feb 1824 in Kardašova Řečice, Jindřichův Hradec District, Bohemi.

Filip Herrmann and Rachel Rabl married. They had the following children:

Moses Herrmann was born on 23 Feb 1786 in Kardašova Řečice, Jindřichův Hradec District, Bohemi.

Joseph Herrmann was born on 08 Apr 1788 in Kardašova Řečice, Jindřichův Hradec District, Bohemi. He died in May

1788 in Kardašova Řečice, Jindřichův Hradec District, Bohemi.

iii. **Leopold Herrmann** was born in 1777 in Kardašova Řečice, Jindřichův Hradec District, Bohemia. He died on 07 Dec 1855 in Kardašova Řečice, Jindřichův Hradec District, Bohemia.

Generation 4

Josef-Marek Rabl-4 (Bernard-3, Abraham Rabl-2, Samuel-1)[1]. He died in 1842[1].

Sara Herrman[1].

Josef-Marek Rabl and Sara Herrman married. They had the following children:

i. **Bernard Rabl**[1] was born on 16 Feb 1830[1].

Wilheim Rabl-4 (Bernard-3, Abraham Rabl-2, Samuel-1)[1].

Wilheim Rabl and unknown spouse married. They had the following children:

Marek Rabl[1].

ii. **Jakub Rabl**[1].

Sirach Rabl-4 (Bernard-3, Abraham Rabl-2, Samuel-1)[1] was born in 1790 in KR[1]. Sirach Rabl and unknown spouse married. They had the following children:

i. **Samuel Rabl**[1].

ii. **Salamon Rabl**[1].

Terizie Rabl[1].

Marie Rabl[1].

Untraced Rabl[1].

Moises Rabl-4 (Bernard-3, Abraham Rabl-2, Samuel-1)[1] was born in 1785 in K.R.[1]. He died on 13 Sep 1860 in K.R.[1].

Unknown.

Moises Rabl and Unknown married. They had the following children:

i. **Filip Rabl**[1] was born on 01 Apr 1825 in Kardašova Řečice, Pribram Dist., Bohemia. He married Anna Weinerova in 1864. He died about 1903 in Pisek.

Abraham Rabl-4 (Samuel-3, Abraham Rabl-2, Samuel-1)[1, 2] was born about 1722 in Kardašova Řečice, Jindřichův Hradec District, Bohemi. He died after 1802 in Kardašova Řečice, Jindřichův Hradec District, Bohemi. **Elizabeth Unknown** was born between 1719-1814.

Abraham Rabl and Elizabeth Unknown married. They had the following children:

>**Emanuel Rabl**[1, 2].
>**Jakub Rabl**[1, 2].
>**Rosalie Rabl**[1, 2].
>**Sofie Rabl**[1, 2].
>**Lidmilla Rabl**[1, 2].

Isak Rabl-4 (Samuel-3, Abraham Rabl-2, Samuel-1)[1, 2] was born in 1807[1, 2]. Isak Rabl and unknown spouse married. They had the following children:

>i. **Bernard Rabl**[1, 2] was born in 1841 in K.R.[1, 2]. He died on 08 May 1891 in K.R.[1, 2].

Leopold Herrmann-4 (Rachel-3, Abraham Rabl-2, Samuel-1) was born in 1777 in Kardašova Řečice, Jindřichův Hradec District, Bohemia. He died on 07 Dec 1855 in Kardašova Řečice, Jindřichův Hradec District, Bohemia.

Rosalie Friedmann.

Leopold Herrmann and Rosalie Friedmann married. They had the following children:

>**Jacob Herrmann** was born in 1802 in Kardašova Řečice, Jindřichův Hradec District, Bohemi. He died on 01 Aug 1837.
>ii. **Abraham (Adolf) Herrmann** was born on 17 Jan 1810. He died on 03 Nov 1846.

Generation 5

Bernard Rabl-5 (Josef-Marek-4, Bernard-3, Abraham Rabl-2, Samuel-1)[1] was born on 16 Feb 1830[1].

Kateřina[1].

Bernard Rabl and Kateřina married. They had the following children:

>**Filip Rabl**[1].
>**Alfred Rabl**[1].

Matilda Rabl[1].
Hermina Rabl[1].
Regina Rabl[1].

Jakub Rabl-5 (Wilheim-4, Bernard-3, Abraham Rabl-2, Samuel-1)[1]. Jakub Rabl and unknown spouse married. They had the following children:

Ludvik Rabl[1].
Emil Rabl[1].
Bertha Rabl[1].
iv. Julius Rabl[1].

Samuel Rabl-5 (Sirach-4, Bernard-3, Abraham Rabl-2, Samuel-1)[1]. Samuel Rabl and unknown spouse married. They had the following children:

Max Rabl[1].
Jakub Rabl[1].
Regina Rabl[1].

Salamon Rabl-5 (Sirach-4, Bernard-3, Abraham Rabl-2, Samuel-1)[1].

Kateřina[1].

Salamon Rabl and Kateřina married. They had the following children:

Adolf Rabl[1].
Ludwik Rabl[1].
iii. Julius Rabl[1].

Filip Rabl-5 (Moises-4, Bernard-3, Abraham Rabl-2, Samuel-1)[1] was born on 01 Apr 1825 in Kardašova Řečice, Pribram Dist., Bohemia. He died about 1903 in Pisek.

Anna Weinerova daughter of Moses Weiner and Rosalia Hindl Stricker[1] was born in 1850 in Bechyne, Bbohemia. She died on 08 Mar 1906 in Pisek, Bohemia.

Filip Rabl and Anna Weinerova were married in 1864. They had the following children:

i. **Ludwig Rabl**[1] was born on 01 Nov 1866 in Kardašova Řečice, Pribram Dist., Bohemia[1]. He married Bianca Poláček before 1900. He died on 17 Dec 1925 in Berlin, Germany[1].

Josefina Rablova[1] was born on 28 Dec 1867 in K.R.[1]. She died about 1935 in date is doubtful[1].

Maximilian Rabl[1] was born on 04 Jun 1869 in K.R.[1]. He died on 14 Jan 1915[1].

iv. **Berthold Rabl**[1] was born on 25 Mar 1871 in K R. He died on 19 Jun 1932 in Karlovy Vary[1].

Mathilde Rablova[1] was born on 29 Aug 1872 in K.R.[1]. She died in 1890[1].

vi. **Adele Rablova**[1] was born on 03 Dec 1874 in K.R.[1]. She died on 18 Oct 1950 in Prague[1].

Gizela Rablova[1] was born on 31 Aug 1876[1].

Růžena Rabl[1] was born on 09 Jul 1878[1].

ix. **Otto Rabl**[1] was born on 02 Jan 1880[1].

Josef Rabl[1] was born on 16 Oct 1881[1].

xi. **Richard Rabl**[1] was born on 12 Sep 1883[1].

Ernst Rabl[1] was born in 1884[1]. He died in 1961 in Israel[1].

xiii. **Kamila Rablova**[1] was born on 02 Sep 1885[1].

xiv. **Rudi Rabl**[1] was born on 23 Mar 1889[1]. He married Elizabeth Chambers after 1940. He died in 1951.

Grete Rablova.

Abraham (Adolf) Herrmann-5 (Leopold-4, Rachel-3, Abraham Rabl-2, Samuel-1) was born on 17 Jan 1810. He died on 03 Nov 1846.

Josefina Kohner.

Abraham (Adolf) Herrmann and Josefina Kohner married. They had the following children:

Philipp Herrmann was born in 1843 in Kardašova Řečice, Jindřichův Hradec District, Bohemi.

ii. **Veit Josef Herrmann** was born on 01 Aug 1835 in Kardašova Řečice, Jindřichův Hradec District, Bohemi. He died on 15 Apr 1888 in Uhlirske Janovice, Bohemia.

Generation 6

Julius Rabl-6 (Jakub-5, Wilheim-4, Bernard-3, Abraham Rabl-2, Samuel-1)[1].

Františka Frohlich[1].

Julius Rabl and Františka Frohlich married. They had the following

children:
- i. **Elsa Rabl**[1]. She died in 1960 in USA[1].
- ii. **Ervin Rabl**[1] was born in 1889[1].
- iii. **Otto Rabl**[1] was born on 11 Nov 1909[1].

Ludwig Rabl-6 (Filip-5, Moises-4, Bernard-3, Abraham Rabl-2, Samuel-1)[1] was born on 01 Nov 1866 in Kardašova Řečice, Pribram Dist., Bohemia[1]. He died on 17 Dec 1925 in Berlin, Germany[1].

Bianca Poláček[1].

Ludwig Rabl and Bianca Poláček were married before 1900. They had the following children:

Hans Rabl[1] was born on 29 Oct 1899 in Karlovy Vary, Bohemia[1]. He died before 1930 in Berlin, Germany.

Leonie Fraenkel daughter of Gotthilf Fraenkel and Amalie ("Mally") Sandbank[1]. She died in 1945 in Ravensberg.

Ludwig Rabl and Leonie Fraenkel were married before 1906. They had the following children:

- **Ruth Rabl**[1] was born on 09 Nov 1906[1]. She died in 1937[1].
- ii. **Annemarie Rabl**[1] was born on 04 Jan 1908 in Karlovy Vary, Bohemia[1]. She died on 18 Oct 1971 in Shrewsbury, Shropshire, England, UK[1].

Berthold Rabl-6 (Filip-5, Moises-4, Bernard-3, Abraham Rabl-2, Samuel-1)[1] was born on 25 Mar 1871 in K R. He died on 19 Jun 1932 in Karlovy Vary[1].

Selma Reichl[1] was born on 11 Jul 1879. She died in 1942 in Trostyanetz. Berthold Rabl and Selma Reichl married. They had the following children:

- i. **Martin Walter Rabl Radcliffe** was born on 02 Dec 1903 in Prague. He died on 04 Jan 1950 in Hastings, England.
- ii. **Hans Rabl**[1] was born on 01 Apr 1906 in Prague[1]. He died in 1987 in London[1].

    Ernst Rabl.
- iv. **Martin Rabl**[1] was born on 02 Dec 1903 in Prague[1]. He died on 04 Jan 1950 in Hastings[1].
- v. **Ernest Phillip Rabl**[1] was born on 26 Dec 1913 in Karlovy

Vary[1]. He died on 01 Nov 1976 in New York[1].

Adele Rablova-6 (Filip-5, Moises-4, Bernard-3, Abraham Rabl-2, Samuel-1)[1] was born on 03 Dec 1874 in K.R.[1]. She died on 18 Oct 1950 in Prague[1].

Joseph Lebenhart[1] was born in 1874 in Pisek[1]. He died in 1944[1].

Joseph Lebenhart and Adele Rablova married. They had the following children:

    i. **Hugo Lebenhart**[1].

    Zdenka Lebenhart[1] was born in 1901[1]. She died in 1961[1].

    iii. **Otto Lebenhart (Toman)**[1] was born on 13 Oct 1902 in possibly Pisek[1]. He died on 30 Sep 1966 in Prague[1].

Otto Rabl-6 (Filip-5, Moises-4, Bernard-3, Abraham Rabl-2, Samuel-1)[1] was born on 02 Jan 1880[1].

Berta[1].

Otto Rabl and Berta married. They had the following children:

    i. **Hans Rabl**[1] was born in Feb 1912[1].

    ii. **Eugene Rabl**[1] was born in 1914[1].

Richard Rabl-6 (Filip-5, Moises-4, Bernard-3, Abraham Rabl-2, Samuel-1)[1] was born on 12 Sep 1883[1].

Klára[1].

Richard Rabl and Klára married. They had the following children:

    Peter Rabl[1].

    Maximilian Rabl[1] was born on 04 Jun 1869 in K.R.[1]. He died on 14 Jan 1915[1].

Kamila Rablova-6 (Filip-5, Moises-4, Bernard-3, Abraham Rabl-2, Samuel-1)[1] was born on 02 Sep 1885[1].

Carl-Maria Svoboda[1].

Carl-Maria Svoboda and Kamila Rablova married. They had the following children:

    i. **Michael Swoboda**[1].

Rudi Rabl-6 (Filip-5, Moises-4, Bernard-3, Abraham Rabl-2, Samuel-1)[1] was born on 23 Mar 1889[1]. He died in 1951.

Elizabeth Chambers[1].

Rudi Rabl and Elizabeth Chambers were married after 1940. They had

the following children:
> i. **Jula Rabl**[1] was born on 18 Jan 1944 in London, England.

Jula Goldman[1].

Rudi Rabl and Jula Goldman married. They had no children.

Veit Josef Herrmann-6 (Abraham (Adolf)-5, Leopold-4, Rachel-3, Abraham Rabl-2, Samuel-1) was born on 01 Aug 1835 in Kardašova Řečice, Jindřichův Hradec District, Bohemi. He died on 15 Apr 1888 in Uhlirske Janovice, Bohemia.

Josefina Weleminsky was born on 20 Sep 1835 in Bohouovice.

Veit Josef Herrmann and Josefina Weleminsky married. They had the following children:
> **Emil Herrmann** was born on 09 Jan 1867 in Uhlirske Janovice.
> **Leoo Herrmann** was born on 03 Feb 1879 in Uhlirske Janovice.
> iii. **Anna Herrmann** was born on 25 Sep 1864 in Uhrliske Janovice.
> iv. **Therese Herrmann** was born on 03 Nov 1868 in Uhlirske Janovice.

Generation 7

Elsa Rabl-7 (Julius-6, Jakub-5, Wilheim-4, Bernard-3, Abraham Rabl-2, Samuel-1)[1]. She died in 1960 in USA[1].

Elsa Rabl and unknown spouse married. They had the following children:
> i. **Hanna Rabl**[1].
> ii. **Alena Rabl**[1].

Ervin Rabl-7 (Julius-6, Jakub-5, Wilheim-4, Bernard-3, Abraham Rabl-2, Samuel-1)[1] was born in 1889[1].

Joan[1].

Ervin Rabl and Joan married. They had the following children:
> **Robert Julius Rabl**[1] was born in 1948[1].

Otto Rabl-7 (Julius-6, Jakub-5, Wilheim-4, Bernard-3, Abraham Rabl-2, Samuel-1)[1] was born on 11 Nov 1909[1].

Hedda Lewith[1].

Otto Rabl and Hedda Lewith married. They had the following children:
> **Janette Rabl**[1].

Annemarie Rabl-7 (Ludwig-6, Filip-5, Moises-4, Bernard-3, Abraham Rabl-

2, Samuel-1)[1] was born on 04 Jan 1908 in Karlovy Vary, Bohemia[1]. She died on 18 Oct 1971 in Shrewsbury,Shropshire, England, UK[1].

Hans Lobbenberg[1] was born on 18 May 1896 in Köln, Nordrhein-Westfalen, Germany. He died on Jul 1955 in Shrewsbury, Shropshire, England, UK.

Hans Lobbenberg and Annemarie Rabl married. They had the following children:

>i. **George Lobbenberg** was born on 16 Nov 1922 in Köln-Lindenthal, Nordrhein-Westfalen, Germany. He died on 22 Oct 1970 in Birmingham, West Midlands, England, UK.
>
>>**Peter Lobbenberg** was born on 12 Sep 1939 in Edgware, London, Great Britain, UK.

Martin Walter Rabl Radcliffe-7 (Berthold-6, Filip-5, Moises-4, Bernard-3, Abraham Rabl-2, Samuel-1) was born on 02 Dec 1903 in Prague. He died on 04 Jan 1950 in Hastings, England.

Mariana Block[1] was born on 24 Oct 1906. She died on 06 Sep 1943 in Auschwitz.

Martin Walter Rabl Radcliffe and Mariana Block married. They had the following children:

>i. **Miriam Rabl** was born on 04 Oct 1934 in Prague. She died on 06 Sep 1942 in Auschwitz.
>
>>**Mona Bullus**[1] was born on 11 Apr 1915 in Bradford[1]. She died on 22 Jan 1972 in Alderney[1].

Martin Walter Rabl Radcliffe and Mona Bullus were married about 1950. They had the following children:

>i. **Nikolas Rabl Radcliffe** was born on 07 Jan 1950.

Hans Rabl-7 (Berthold-6, Filip-5, Moises-4, Bernard-3, Abraham Rabl-2, Samuel-1)[1] was born on 01 Apr 1906 in Prague[1]. He died in 1987 in London[1].

Moira Wilson[1].

Hans Rabl and Moira Wilson married. They had the following children:

>i. **Preston Rabl**[1] was born on 06 Jan 1949 in London[1].

Martin Rabl-7 (Berthold-6, Filip-5, Moises-4, Bernard-3, Abraham Rabl-2,

Samuel-1)[1] was born on Dec 1903 in Prague[1]. He died on 04 Jan 1950 in Hastings[1].

Mariana Block[1] was born on 24 Oct 1906. She died on 06 Sep 1943 in Auschwitz.

Martin Rabl and Mariana Block married. They had the following children:

    i. **Miriam Rabl** was born on 04 Oct 1934 in Prague. She died on 06 Sep 1942 in Auschwitz.

        Mona Bullus[1] was born on 11 Apr 1915 in Bradford[1]. She died on 22 Jan 1972 in Alderney[1].

Martin Rabl and Mona Bullus married. They had the following children:

    i. **Nikolas Rabl Radcliffe** was born on 07 Jan 1950.

Ernest Phillip Rabl-7 (Berthold-6, Filip-5, Moises-4, Bernard-3, Abraham Rabl-2, Samuel-1)[1] was born on 26 Dec 1913 in Karlovy Vary[1]. He died on 01 Nov 1976 in New York[1].

Margit Iritzer[1] was born on 07 Mar 1915 in Macov, Czech[1]. She died on 02 Oct 1995 in New York[1]. Ernest Phillip Rabl and Margit Iritzer married. They had the following children:

    i. **Marion Renee Diana Rabl**[1] was born on 19 Nov 1945 in London[1].

Hugo Lebenhart-7 (Adele-6, Filip-5, Moises-4, Bernard-3, Abraham Rabl-2, Samuel-1)[1].

Viola Jakubovie[1].

Hugo Lebenhart and Viola Jakubovie married. They had the following children:

    i. **Barabara Tomanová**[1] was born on 18 Jan 1950 in Bratislava[1].

Otto Lebenhart (Toman)-7 (Adele-6, Filip-5, Moises-4, Bernard-3, Abraham Rabl-2, Samuel-1)[1] was born on 13 Oct 1902 in possibly Pisek[1]. He died on 30 Sep 1966 in Prague[1].

Christa Heidi Willer daughter of Robert Willer and Mimi Rudinger[1] was born on 12 Apr 1918 in Pisek. She died on 20 Aug 1980 in London.

Otto Lebenhart (Toman) and Christa Heidi Willer married. They had the following children:

    i. **Helena Tomanová**[1] was born on 19 Jun 1947 in Prague[1].

Hans Rabl-7 (Otto-6, Filip-5, Moises-4, Bernard-3, Abraham Rabl-2, Samuel-1)[1] was born in Feb 1912[1].
Ruth Arensberg[1].
Hans Rabl and Ruth Arensberg married. They had the following children:
    i. **Ronie Rabl**[1] was born on 26 Jan 1944[1].
    ii. **Irit Rabl**[1] was born on 12 Sep 1953 in Israel[1]. She died on 26 Dec 1997 in Tel Aviv[1].

Eugene Rabl-7 (Otto-6, Filip-5, Moises-4, Bernard-3, Abraham Rabl-2, Samuel-1)[1] was born in 1914[1].
Dagmar[1].
Eugene Rabl and Dagmar married. They had the following children:
    i. **Monica Rabl**[1].

Michael Swoboda-7 (Kamila-6, Filip-5, Moises-4, Bernard-3, Abraham Rabl-2, Samuel-1)[1].
Christine[1].
Michael Swoboda and Christine married. They had the following children:
    i. **Andrew Swoboda**[1].
    ii. **Deborah Swoboda**[1].
Susan[1].
Michael Swoboda and Susan married. They had no children.

Jula Rabl-7 (Rudi-6, Filip-5, Moises-4, Bernard-3, Abraham Rabl-2, Samuel-1)[1] was born on 18 Jan 1944 in London, England.
Roger Westman[1].
Roger Westman and Jula Rabl married. They had the following children:
    i. **Sam Westman**[1].
    ii. **Sophie Westman**[1].

Therese Herrmann-7 (Veit Josef-6, Abraham (Adolf)-5, Leopold-4, Rachel-3, Abraham Rabl-2, Samuel-1) was born on 03 Nov 1868 in Uhlirske Janovice.
Paul Schulhof was born about 1823. He died on 28 Mar 1897 in Nymburk, Bohemia. Paul Schulhof and Therese Herrmann married.

They had the following children:
> i. **Sigmund Schulhof** was born in 1858.

Generation 8

Hanna Rabl-8 (Elsa-7, Julius-6, Jakub-5, Wilheim-4, Bernard-3, Abraham Rabl-2, Samuel-1)[1].

Burri[1].

Burri and Hanna Rabl married. They had the following children:
> **Denise Burri**[1] was born in 1952[1].
>
> **Kitty Burri**[1] was born in 1954[1].

Alena Rabl-8 (Elsa-7, Julius-6, Jakub-5, Wilheim-4, Bernard-3, Abraham Rabl-2, Samuel-1)[1].

De La Flores[1].

De La Flores and Alena Rabl married. They had the following children:
> **Kristina De La Flores**[1].
>
> **Maurica De La Flores**[1].

George Lobbenberg-8 (Annemarie-7, Ludwig-6, Filip-5, Moises-4, Bernard-3, Abraham Rabl-2, Samuel-1) was born on 16 Nov 1922 in Köln-Lindenthal, Nordrhein-Westfalen, Germany. He died on Oct 1970 in Birmingham, West Midlands, England, UK.

Margaret Thomas was born in 1933 in Shrewsbury, Shropshire, England, UK. She died on 20 Apr 2015 in Shrewsbury, Shropshire, England, UK.

George Lobbenberg and Margaret Thomas married. They had the following children:
> **Andrew Davidi Lobbenberg**.

Nikolas Rabl Radcliffe-8 (Martin Walter Rabl-7, Berthold-6, Filip-5, Moises-4, Bernard-3, Abraham Rabl-2, Samuel-1) was born on 07 Jan 1950.

Hilary Gibson[1] was born on 03 May 1954 in Bournemouth[1].

Nikolas Rabl Radcliffe and Hilary Gibson married. They had the following children:
> **Victoria Emily Rabl Radcliffe**[1] was born on 09 Jul 1981 in Hastings[1].
>
> **James Martin Antony Rabl Radcliffe**[1] was born on 18 Jun 1983 in Hastings[1].

>Charlotte Rabl Radcliffe[1] was born on 04 Nov 1989 in Hastings[1].

Preston Rabl-8 (Hans-7, Berthold-6, Filip-5, Moises-4, Bernard-3, Abraham Rabl-2, Samuel-1)[1] was born on 06 Jan 1949 in London[1].

Sara Fitzpatrick[1].

Preston Rabl and Sara Fitzpatrick married. They had the following children:

>**Francesca Rabl**[1].
>
>**Sophia Rabl**[1] was born in 1987 in London[1].
>
>**Georgina Rabl**[1] was born in 1988 in London[1].

Marion Renee Diana Rabl-8 (Ernest Phillip-7, Berthold-6, Filip-5, Moises-4, Bernard-3, Abraham Rabl-2, Samuel-1)[1] was born on 19 Nov 1945 in London[1].

Leslie John Edge[1] was born on 29 Jul[1].

Leslie John Edge and Marion Renee Diana Rabl married. They had the following children:

>**Alison Kimberly Diana Edge**[1] was born on 28 Nov 1977 in Montreal[1].
>
>**Ryan Phillip John Edge**[1] was born on 22 May 1979 in Montreal[1].

Helena Tomanová-8 (Otto Lebenhart-7, Adele-6, Filip-5, Moises-4, Bernard-3, Abraham Rabl-2, Samuel-1)[1] was born on 19 Jun 1947 in Prague[1].

Robert Bowman[1].

Robert Bowman and Helena Tomanová married. They had the following children:

>**Mark Bowman**[1] was born on 19 Jul 1979 in Gerrands Cross, England[1].
>
>**Alan Russell Bowman**[1] was born on 05 Aug 1982 in Gerrands Cross, England[1].

Peter Buffam.

Peter Buffam and Helena Tomanová were married in 1996. They had no children.

Peter Aberley.

Peter Aberley and Helena Tomanová were married in 2000 in Prague, CSR. They had no children.

Ronie Rabl-8 (Hans-7, Otto-6, Filip-5, Moises-4, Bernard-3, Abraham Rabl-2, Samuel-1)[1] was born on 26 Jan 1944[1].

Edelist[1].

Edelist and Ronie Rabl married. They had the following children:

 i. **Dana Edelist**[1] was born in 1966[1].

 ii. **Yael Edelist**[1] was born in 1968[1].

Irit Rabl-8 (Hans-7, Otto-6, Filip-5, Moises-4, Bernard-3, Abraham Rabl-2, Samuel-1)[1] was born on Sep 1953 in Israel[1]. She died on 26 Dec 1997 in Tel Aviv[1].

Marian Cohn[1].

Marian Cohn and Irit Rabl married. They had the following children:

 Gaby Cohn[1] was born on 22 Mar 1978[1].

 Tal Cohn[1] was born on 19 Jun 1986[1].

Monica Rabl-8 (Eugene-7, Otto-6, Filip-5, Moises-4, Bernard-3, Abraham Rabl-2, Samuel-1)[1]. Monica Rabl and unknown spouse married. They had the following children:

 Alon[1] was born in 1989 in Tel Aviv[1].

 Ellar[1] was born in 1989 in Tel Aviv[1].

 Itamar[1] was born in 1994[1].

Andrew Swoboda-8 (Michael-7, Kamila-6, Filip-5, Moises-4, Bernard-3, Abraham Rabl-2, Samuel-1)[1].

?[1].

Andrew Swoboda and ? married. They had the following children:

? Swoboda[1].

Deborah Swoboda-8 (Michael-7, Kamila-6, Filip-5, Moises-4, Bernard-3, Abraham Rabl-2, Samuel-1)[1].

[1].

and Deborah Swoboda married. They had the following children:

 ? ?[1].

 ? ?[1].

 ? ?[1].

? ?[1].

Sophie Westman-8 (Jula-7, Rudi-6, Filip-5, Moises-4, Bernard-3, Abraham Rabl-2, Samuel-1)[1].
Carlos Lizarraga-Curiel[1].
Carlos Lizarraga-Curiel and Sophie Westman married. They had the following children:
> **Benjamine Rabl Lizarraga-Curiel**[1] was born on 13 Jun 1997[1].
> **Joshua Lizarraga-Curiel**[1] was born on 31 Mar 2000[1].

Sigmund Schulhof-8 (Therese-7, Veit Josef-6, Abraham (Adolf)-5, Leopold-4, Rachel-3, Abraham Rabl-2, Samuel-1) was born in 1858.
Gabriele Ella Kapper was born in 1870.
Sigmund Schulhof and Gabriele Ella Kapper married. They had the following children:
> **Erwin Schulhof** was born in 1895 in Prague, Bohemia. He died on 31 May 1914.
> **Rudolf Schulhof** was born on 21 Feb 1891 in Prague, Bohemia.
> **Irma Schulhof** was born in 1906.

Generation 9

Dana Edelist-9 (Ronie-8, Hans-7, Otto-6, Filip-5, Moises-4, Bernard-3, Abraham Rabl-2, Samuel-1)[1] was born in 1966[1].
Boaz Spector[1].
Boaz Spector and Dana Edelist married. They had the following children:
> **Yonatan Spector**[1] was born on 18 Nov 1992[1].
> **Yuval Spector** was born about 1996.
> **Twin Spector** was born about 2001.

Yael Edelist-9 (Ronie-8, Hans-7, Otto-6, Filip-5, Moises-4, Bernard-3, Abraham Rabl-2, Samuel-1)[1] was born in 1968[1].
David Levy.
David Levy and Yael Edelist married. They had the following children:
> **Ido Levy** was born about 1997.
> **Ruth Levy** was born between 1999-2000.

Sources

Rabl Family.GED.FTW, Date of Import: Jan 11, 2001.
Rabl Family.FTW, Date of Import: Jan 11, 2001.

Sedlák Family

Generation 1

Jan Sedlák-1 was born in 1789 in Stahlavy No. 54.

Marie Trefná daughter of Vavrinec Trefný and Marie Hoblova was born in 1789 in Stahlavy. Jan Sedlák and Marie Trefná married. They had the following children:

> i. **Jan Sedlák** was born on 22 Feb 1814 in Nezbavetice. He married Kateřina Sebkova on 21 Nov 1837 in Stahlavy.

Generation 2

Jan Sedlák-2 (Jan-1) was born on 22 Feb 1814 in Nezbavetice.

Kateřina Sebkova daughter of Jan Šebek and Marie Tucaurová was born on 01 Mar 1819 in Stahlavy No. 30.

Jan Sedlák and Kateřina Sebkova were married on 21 Nov 1837 in Stahlavy. They had the following children:

> i. **Barbora Sedláková** was born on 30 Dec 1848 in Stahlavy No. 54, near Rokycany. She married Jan Krtitel Šváb on 08 Jan 1872 in Stahlovi. She died in 1930.
> **Josef Sedlák.**
> **Vojtěch Sedlák.**
> **Jan Sedlák.**

Generation 3

Barbora Sedláková-3 (Jan-2, Jan-1) was born on 30 Dec 1848 in Stahlavy No. 54, near Rokycany. She died in 1930.

Jan Krtitel Šváb son of Jan Šváb and Mariana Nespěchalová was born on 28 May 1845 in Bystrice No. 138, Benešov Dist., Bohemia. He died in 1918. Jan Krtitel Šváb and Barbora Sedláková were married on 08 Jan 1872 in Stahlovi. They had the following children:

> **Jan Šváb.**
> ii. **Emillie Švábová.**
> iii. **Marie Švábová** was born on 13 Jul 1873 in Bystrice, Benešov Dist., Bohemia. She died in 1945.
> iv. **Adolf Šváb** was born on 18 Apr 1876 in Bystrice No. 138, Benešov

Co.. He married Marie Markéta Marta Taussigová on 15 Oct 1902 in U Matky Bozi pred Tynem, Prague. He died on 26 Apr 1954 in Plzen.

Generation 4

Emillie Švábová-4 (Barbora-3, Jan-2, Jan-1).
Pfeffer.
Pfeffer and Emillie Švábová married. They had the following children:
>**Antonín Pfeffer** was born on 15 Jan 1904 in Veseli nad Luznici, Tabor Co..
>**Ladislav Pfeffer**.

Marie Švábová-4 (Barbora-3, Jan-2, Jan-1) was born on 13 Jul 1873 in Bystrice, Benešov Dist., Bohemia. She died in 1945.

Ladislav Syllaba son of František Syllaba and Anna Vlckova was born on 16 Jun 1868 in Bystrice, Benešov Dist., Bohemia. He died on 30 Dec 1930 in Prague, Czech..

Ladislav Syllaba and Marie Švábová married. They had the following children:
>i. **Ludmila Syllabová** was born on 05 Apr 1899. She died in 1996.
>**Jiří Syllaba** was born on 08 Mar 1902 in Praha, CSR. He married Božena Slámová in 1942 in Praha II. He died on 17 May 1997 in Praha, CSR.
>iii. **Milada Syllabová** was born in 1904.
>**Anna Syllabová** was born in 1896. She died in 1902.

Adolf Šváb-4 (Barbora-3, Jan-2, Jan-1) was born on 18 Apr 1876 in Bystrice No. 138, Benešov Co.. He died on 26 Apr 1954 in Plzen.

Marie Markéta Marta Taussigová daughter of Jakub Taussig and Julie Meislova was born on 07 Mar 1879 in Benešov No. 162. She died on 22 Jun 1958 in Plzen.

Adolf Šváb and Marie Markéta Marta Taussigová were married on 15 Oct 1902 in U Matky Bozi pred Tynem, Prague. They had the following children:
>i. **Vladislav Šváb** was born on 08 Aug 1903 in Vysoke nad Jizerou. He married Julie Zacharova on 11 Oct 1932 in Prague. He died

on 23 Oct 1947 in Tabor, Czechoslovakia.

 ii. **Adolf Šváb** was born on 15 Apr 1905 in Vysoke nad Jizerou No. 267. He married Zdenka Sigmundova on 17 Sep 1932 in Plzen. He died in 1976 in Plzen.

 iii. **Kamil Šváb** was born in 1907 in Vysoke nad Jizerou. He married Augusta (Gusta) Hyblerova in 1936. He died in 1982 in Praha, Bohemia.

Věra Švábová was born in 1910 in Vysoke nad Jizerou. She married Čeněk Simerka in 1936. She died in 1985 in Plzen.

Generation 5

7. **Ludmila Syllabová**-5 (Marie-4, Barbora-3, Jan-2, Jan-1) was born on 05 Apr 1899. She died in 1996.

Filip.

Filip and Ludmila Syllabová married. They had the following children:

 Eva Filipová.

 Hana Filipová.

Milada Syllabová-5 (Marie-4, Barbora-3, Jan-2, Jan-1) was born in 1904.

Stretti.

Stretti and Milada Syllabová married. They had the following children:

 Olga Strettiová.

 Milada Strettiová.

Vladislav Šváb-5 (Adolf-4, Barbora-3, Jan-2, Jan-1) was born on 08 Aug 1903 in Vysoke nad Jizerou. He died on 23 Oct 1947 in Tabor, Czechoslovakia.

Julie Zacharova daughter of Nikolaj Michajlovic Zacharov and Julie Filipovna Obrevko-Zdanov was born on 03 Mar 1901 in Moscow, Russia. She died on 24 Jan 1999 in Tabor, Bbohemia.

Vladislav Šváb and Julie Zacharova were married on 11 Oct 1932 in Prague. They had the following children:

 i. **Julie ("Jaska") Švábová** was born on 24 Feb 1945 in Tabor. She married Vladimír Sarsa on 26 Jun 1969 in Ostrava.

Adolf Šváb-5 (Adolf-4, Barbora-3, Jan-2, Jan-1) was born on 15 Apr 1905 in Vysoke nad Jizerou No. 267. He died in 1976 in Plzen.

Zdenka Sigmundova daughter of Josef Sigmund and Karolina

Restránková was born on 31 Oct 1908 in Plzen, Na Lochotine No. 451. She died in 1990 in Plzen.

Adolf Šváb and Zdenka Sigmundova were married on 17 Sep 1932 in Plzen. They had the following children:
- i. **Irena Švábová** was born on 03 Feb 1936 in Plzen. She married Emil Kasl in 1955.
- ii. **Zdeněk Šváb** was born on 31 Mar 1940 in Plzen.
- iii. **Olga Švábová** was born on 18 Jul 1948 in Plzen. She married Vladimír Pechman in 1968.

Kamil Šváb-5 (Adolf-4, Barbora-3, Jan-2, Jan-1) was born in 1907 in Vysoke nad Jizerou. He died in 1982 in Praha, Bohemia.

Augusta (Gusta) Hyblerova daughter of Otto Hybler and (Pavlina) Marie Schönfeldová was born in 1911. She died in 1960.

Kamil Šváb and Augusta (Gusta) Hyblerova were married in 1936. They had the following children:

    Jan Šváb was born on 04 Jul 1937 in Praha, CSR. He married Josette Azra on 02 May 1978.

Božena Stroblová was born in 1913. She died in 1981.

Kamil Šváb and Božena Stroblová were married in 1945. They had the following children:
- 16. i. **Kamil Šváb** was born on 29 Aug 1944 in Prague. He married Dobroslava Rittova in 1968.

Generation 6

Julie ("Jaska") Švábová-6 (Vladislav-5, Adolf-4, Barbora-3, Jan-2, Jan-1) was born on 24 Feb 1945 in Tabor.

Vladimír Sarsa was born on 11 Feb 1943 in Ostrava.

Vladimír Sarsa and Julie ("Jaska") Švábová were married on 26 Jun 1969 in Ostrava. They had the following children:
- i. **Olga Sarsova** was born on 26 Dec 1970 in Ostrava. She married Broniaslav Klementa on Apr 2007 in Na Svatem Kopecku u Olomouce.
- ii. **Vladimír Sarsa** was born on 26 Nov 1971 in Ostrava. He married Bronislava Srubkova on Jul 1997 in Ostrava.

Irena Švábová-6 (Adolf-5, Adolf-4, Barbora-3, Jan-2, Jan-1) was born on 03 Feb 1936 in Plzen.

Emil Kasl was born in 1926.

Emil Kasl and Irena Švábová were married in 1955. They had the following children:

>   i. **Monika Kaslova** was born on 03 Jun 1958 in Plzen. She married Jiří Chládek on 30 Apr 1978 in Prague, CSR.
>
>   **Tomáš Kasl** was born on 26 Apr 1964 in Plzen.

Zdeněk Šváb-6 (Adolf-5, Adolf-4, Barbora-3, Jan-2, Jan-1) was born on 31 Mar 1940 in Plzen.

Jaroslava Leimerova was born in 1943.

Zdeněk Šváb and Jaroslava Leimerova married. They had the following children:

>   i. **Daniel Šváb** was born on 29 Jan 1964 in Plzen. He married Jitka Kopackova in 1992.

Marie Kosorova was born in 1945.

Zdeněk Šváb and Marie Kosorova were married in 1970. They had no children.

Olga Švábová-6 (Adolf-5, Adolf-4, Barbora-3, Jan-2, Jan-1) was born on 18 Jul 1948 in Plzen.

Vladimír Pechman was born in 1943.

Vladimír Pechman and Olga Švábová were married in 1968. They had the following children:

>   i. **Radek Pechman** was born on 12 Mar 1969 in Plzen. He married Jitka Slámová in 1992.
>
>   ii. **Olga Pechmanová** was born on 12 Mar 1976 in Plzen. She married Tomáš Pech in 1998.

Muchna.

Muchna and Olga Švábová were married after 1976. They had no children.

Kamil Šváb-6 (Kamil-5, Adolf-4, Barbora-3, Jan-2, Jan-1) was born on 29 Aug 1944 in Prague.

Dobroslava Rittova was born on 13 Sep 1945.

Kamil Šváb and Dobroslava Rittova were married in 1968. They had the following children:
> **Jana Švábová** was born on 17 Jun 1972. She married Franklin Venegas on 16 Jul 1994.

Generation 7

Olga Sarsova-7 (Julie ("Jaska")-6, Vladislav-5, Adolf-4, Barbora-3, Jan-2, Jan-1) was born on 26 Dec 1970 in Ostrava.

Broniaslav Klementa son of Josef Klementa and Oldřiška Pavlickova was born on 29 Jun 1966 in Sumperk.

Broniaslav Klementa and Olga Sarsova were married on 14 Apr 2007 in Na Svatem Kopecku u Olomouce. They had the following children:
> **Veronika Klementova** was born on 25 May 2007 in Olomouc.

Vladimír Sarsa-7 (Julie ("Jaska")-6, Vladislav-5, Adolf-4, Barbora-3, Jan-2, Jan-1) was born on 26 Nov 1971 in Ostrava.

Bronislava Srubkova was born on 05 Mar 1963 in Pustejov, Bruntal Dist., Czechoslovakia..

Vladimír Sarsa and Bronislava Srubkova were married on 26 Jul 1997 in Ostrava. They had the following children:
> **Milena Sarsova** was born on 03 Jan 1998 in Ostrava, Czechoslovakia.

Monika Kaslova-7 (Irena-6, Adolf-5, Adolf-4, Barbora-3, Jan-2, Jan-1) was born on 03 Jun 1958 in Plzen.

Jiří Chládek was born in 1955.

Jiří Chládek and Monika Kaslova were married on 30 Apr 1978 in Prague, CSR. They had the following children:
> **David Chládek** was born on 19 Dec 1978 in Cheb.
> **Ondřej Chládek** was born on 17 Aug 1981 in Cheb.
> **Jan Chládek** was born on 16 Nov 1988 in Cheb.

Daniel Šváb-7 (Zdeněk-6, Adolf-5, Adolf-4, Barbora-3, Jan-2, Jan-1) was born on 29 Jan 1964 in Plzen.

Jitka Kopackova.

Daniel Šváb and Jitka Kopackova were married in 1992. They had the following children:

> Dominika Švábová was born on 16 Oct 1992 in Plzen.
>
> Natalie Švábová was born on 09 Aug 1998 in Plzen.

Radek Pechman-7 (Olga-6, Adolf-5, Adolf-4, Barbora-3, Jan-2, Jan-1) was born on 12 Mar 1969 in Plzen.

Jitka Slámová was born in 1966.

Radek Pechman and Jitka Slámová were married in 1992. They had the following children:

> **Barbora Pechmanová** was born in 1992.

Olga Pechmanová-7 (Olga-6, Adolf-5, Adolf-4, Barbora-3, Jan-2, Jan-1) was born on 12 Mar 1976 in Plzen.

Tomáš Pech.

Tomáš Pech and Olga Pechmanová were married in 1998. They had the following children:

> **Karolina Pechová** was born on 22 May 1999 in Plzen.

Sebek Family

Generation 1

Václav Šebek-1.

Marie Nosková.

Václav Šebek and Marie Nosková married. They had the following children:

> i. **Jan Šebek** was born on 11 May 1781 in Stahlavy No. 39, okres Rokycany. He married Marie Tucaurová on 08 May 1803.

Generation 2

Jan Šebek-2 (Václav-1) was born on 11 May 1781 in Stahlavy No. 39, okres Rokycany.

Marie Tucaurová daughter of Jakub Tucaur and Marie Přibilová was born on 05 Jan 1788 in Stahlavice No. 18.

Jan Šebek and Marie Tucaurová were married on 08 May 1803. They had the following children:

> i. **Kateřina Sebkova** was born on 01 Mar 1819 in Stahlavy No. 30. She married Jan Sedlák on 21 Nov 1837 in Stahlavy.
>
> **Josef Šebek.**
>
> **Jan Šebek.**
>
> Sebkova.
>
> child Šebek.

Generation 3

Kateřina Sebkova-3 (Jan-2, Václav-1) was born on 01 Mar 1819 in Stahlavy No. 30.

Jan Sedlák son of Jan Sedlák and Marie Trefná was born on 22 Feb 1814 in Nezbavetice.

Jan Sedlák and Kateřina Sebkova were married on 21 Nov 1837 in Stahlavy. They had the following children:

> i. **Barbora Sedláková** was born on 30 Dec 1848 in Stahlavy No. 54, near Rokycany. She married Jan Krtitel Šváb on 08 Jan 1872 in Stahlovi. She died in 1930.
>
> **Josef Sedlák.**

Vojtěch Sedlák.
Jan Sedlák.

Generation 4

Barbora Sedláková-4 (Kateřina-3, Jan-2, Václav-1) was born on 30 Dec 1848 in Stahlavy No. 54, near Rokycany. She died in 1930.

Jan Krtitel Šváb son of Jan Šváb and Mariana Nespěchalová was born on 28 May 1845 in Bystrice No. 138, Benešov Dist., Bohemia. He died in 1918.

Jan Krtitel Šváb and Barbora Sedláková were married on 08 Jan 1872 in Stahlovi. They had the following children:

> **Jan Šváb.**
> ii. **Emillie Švábová.**
> iii. **Marie Švábová** was born on 13 Jul 1873 in Bystrice, Benešov Dist., Bohemia. She died in 1945.
> iv. **Adolf Šváb** was born on 18 Apr 1876 in Bystrice No. 138, Benešov Co.. He married Marie Markéta Marta Taussigová on 15 Oct 1902 in U Matky Bozi pred Tynem, Prague. He died on 26 Apr 1954 in Plzen.

Generation 5

Emillie Švábová-5 (Barbora-4, Kateřina-3, Jan-2, Václav-1).

Pfeffer.

Pfeffer and Emillie Švábová married. They had the following children:

> **Antonín Pfeffer** was born on 15 Jan 1904 in Veseli nad Luznici, Tabor Co..

Ladislav Pfeffer.

Marie Švábová-5 (Barbora-4, Kateřina-3, Jan-2, Václav-1) was born on 13 Jul 1873 in Bystrice, Benešov Dist., Bohemia. She died in 1945.

Ladislav Syllaba son of František Syllaba and Anna Vlckova was born on 16 Jun 1868 in Bystrice, Benešov Dist., Bohemia. He died on 30 Dec 1930 in Prague, Czech..

Ladislav Syllaba and Marie Švábová married. They had the following children:

> i. **Ludmila Syllabová** was born on 05 Apr 1899. She died in 1996.

Jiří Syllaba was born on 08 Mar 1902 in Praha, CSR. He married Božena Slámová in 1942 in Praha II. He died on 17 May 1997 in Praha,CSR.

   iii. **Milada Syllabová** was born in 1904.

   Anna Syllabová was born in 1896. She died in 1902.

Adolf Šváb-5 (Barbora-4, Kateřina-3, Jan-2, Václav-1) was born on 18 Apr 1876 in Bystrice No. 138, Benešov Co.. He died on 26 Apr 1954 in Plzen.

Marie Markéta Marta Taussigová daughter of Jakub Taussig and Julie Meislova was born on 07 Mar 1879 in Benešov No. 162. She died on 22 Jun 1958 in Plzen.

Adolf Šváb and Marie Markéta Marta Taussigová were married on 15 Oct 1902 in U Matky Bozi pred Tynem, Prague. They had the following children:

   i. **Vladislav Šváb** was born on 08 Aug 1903 in Vysoke nad Jizerou. He married Julie Zacharova on 11 Oct 1932 in Prague. He died on 23 Oct 1947 in Tabor, Czechoslovakia.

   ii. **Adolf Šváb** was born on 15 Apr 1905 in Vysoke nad Jizerou No. 267. He married Zdenka Sigmundova on 17 Sep 1932 in Plzen. He died in 1976 in Plzen.

   iii. **Kamil Šváb** was born in 1907 in Vysoke nad Jizerou. He married Augusta (Gusta) Hyblerova in 1936. He died in 1982 in Praha, Bohemia.

   Věra Švábová was born in 1910 in Vysoke nad Jizerou. She married Čeněk Simerka in 1936. She died in 1985 in Plzen.

Generation 6

Ludmila Syllabová-6 (Marie-5, Barbora-4, Kateřina-3, Jan-2, Václav-1) was born on 05 Apr 1899. She died in 1996.

Filip.

Filip and Ludmila Syllabová married. They had the following children:

   Eva Filipová.

   Hana Filipová.

Milada Syllabová-6 (Marie-5, Barbora-4, Kateřina-3, Jan-2, Václav-1) was born in 1904.

Stretti.

Stretti and Milada Syllabová married. They had the following children:

Olga Strettiová.

Milada Strettiová.

Vladislav Šváb-6 (Adolf-5, Barbora-4, Kateřina-3, Jan-2, Václav-1) was born on 08 Aug 1903 in Vysoke nad Jizerou. He died on 23 Oct 1947 in Tabor, Czechoslovakia.

Julie Zacharova daughter of Nikolaj Michajlovic Zacharov and Julie Filipovna Obrevko-Zdanov was born on 03 Mar 1901 in Moscow, Russia. She died on 24 Jan 1999 in Tabor, Bbohemia.

Vladislav Šváb and Julie Zacharova were married on 11 Oct 1932 in Prague. They had the following children:

    i. **Julie ("Jaska") Švábová** was born on 24 Feb 1945 in Tabor. She married Vladimír Sarsa on 26 Jun 1969 in Ostrava.

Adolf Šváb-6 (Adolf-5, Barbora-4, Kateřina-3, Jan-2, Václav-1) was born on 15 Apr 1905 in Vysoke nad Jizerou No. 267. He died in 1976 in Plzen.

Zdenka Sigmundova daughter of Josef Sigmund and Karolina Restránková was born on 31 Oct 1908 in Plzen, Na Lochotine No. 451. She died in 1990 in Plzen.

Adolf Šváb and Zdenka Sigmundova were married on 17 Sep 1932 in Plzen. They had the following children:

    i. **Irena Švábová** was born on 03 Feb 1936 in Plzen. She married Emil Kasl in 1955.

    ii. **Zdeněk Šváb** was born on 31 Mar 1940 in Plzen.

    iii. **Olga Švábová** was born on 18 Jul 1948 in Plzen. She married Vladimír Pechman in 1968.

Kamil Šváb-6 (Adolf-5, Barbora-4, Kateřina-3, Jan-2, Václav-1) was born in 1907 in Vysoke nad Jizerou. He died in 1982 in Praha, Bohemia.

Augusta (Gusta) Hyblerova daughter of Otto Hybler and (Pavlina) Marie Schönfeldová was born in 1911. She died in 1960.

Kamil Šváb and Augusta (Gusta) Hyblerova were married in 1936. They had the following children:

    Jan Šváb was born on 04 Jul 1937 in Praha, CSR. He married

Josette Azra on 02 May 1978.

Božena Stroblová was born in 1913. She died in 1981.

Kamil Šváb and Božena Stroblová were married in 1945. They had the following children:

17. i. **Kamil Šváb** was born on 29 Aug 1944 in Prague. He married Dobroslava Rittova in 1968.

Generation 7

Julie ("Jaska") Švábová-7 (Vladislav-6, Adolf-5, Barbora-4, Kateřina-3, Jan-2, Václav-1) was born on 24 Feb 1945 in Tabor.

Vladimír Sarsa was born on 11 Feb 1943 in Ostrava.

Vladimír Sarsa and Julie ("Jaska") Švábová were married on 26 Jun 1969 in Ostrava. They had the following children:

    i. **Olga Sarsova** was born on 26 Dec 1970 in Ostrava. She married Broniaslav Klementa on Apr 2007 in Na Svatem Kopecku u Olomouce.

    ii. **Vladimír Sarsa** was born on 26 Nov 1971 in Ostrava. He married Bronislava Srubkova on Jul 1997 in Ostrava.

Irena Švábová-7 (Adolf-6, Adolf-5, Barbora-4, Kateřina-3, Jan-2, Václav-1) was born on 03 Feb 1936 in Plzen.

Emil Kasl was born in 1926.

Emil Kasl and Irena Švábová were married in 1955. They had the following children:

    i. **Monika Kaslova** was born on 03 Jun 1958 in Plzen. She married Jiří Chládek on 30 Apr 1978 in Prague, CSR.

Tomáš Kasl was born on 26 Apr 1964 in Plzen.

Zdeněk Šváb-7 (Adolf-6, Adolf-5, Barbora-4, Kateřina-3, Jan-2, Václav-1) was born on 31 Mar 1940 in Plzen.

Jaroslava Leimerova was born in 1943.

Zdeněk Šváb and Jaroslava Leimerova married. They had the following children:

    i. **Daniel Šváb** was born on 29 Jan 1964 in Plzen. He married Jitka Kopackova in 1992.

Marie Kosorova was born in 1945.

Zdeněk Šváb and Marie Kosorova were married in 1970. They had no children.

Olga Švábová-7 (Adolf-6, Adolf-5, Barbora-4, Kateřina-3, Jan-2, Václav-1) was born on 18 Jul 1948 in Plzen.

Vladimír Pechman was born in 1943.

Vladimír Pechman and Olga Švábová were married in 1968. They had the following children:

    i. **Radek Pechman** was born on 12 Mar 1969 in Plzen. He married Jitka Slámová in 1992.

    ii. **Olga Pechmanová** was born on 12 Mar 1976 in Plzen. She married Tomáš Pech in 1998.

Muchna.

Muchna and Olga Švábová were married after 1976. They had no children.

Kamil Šváb-7 (Kamil-6, Adolf-5, Barbora-4, Kateřina-3, Jan-2, Václav-1) was born on 29 Aug 1944 in Prague.

Dobroslava Rittova was born on 13 Sep 1945.

Kamil Šváb and Dobroslava Rittova were married in 1968. They had the following children:

    Jana Švábová was born on 17 Jun 1972. She married Franklin Venegas on 16 Jul 1994.

Generation 8

Olga Sarsova-8 (Julie ("Jaska")-7, Vladislav-6, Adolf-5, Barbora-4, Kateřina-3, Jan-2, Václav-1) was born on 26 Dec 1970 in Ostrava.

Broniaslav Klementa son of Josef Klementa and Oldřiška Pavlickova was born on 29 Jun 1966 in Sumperk.

Broniaslav Klementa and Olga Sarsova were married on 14 Apr 2007 in Na Svatem Kopecku u Olomouce. They had the following children:

    Veronika Klementova was born on 25 May 2007 in Olomouc.

Vladimír Sarsa-8 (Julie ("Jaska")-7, Vladislav-6, Adolf-5, Barbora-4, Kateřina-3, Jan-2, Václav-1) was born on 26 Nov 1971 in Ostrava.

Bronislava Srubkova was born on 05 Mar 1963 in Pustejov, Bruntal Dist., Czechoslovakia..

Vladimír Sarsa and Bronislava Srubkova were married on 26 Jul 1997 in Ostrava. They had the following children:
>   **Milena Sarsova** was born on 03 Jan 1998 in Ostrava, Czechoslovakia.

Monika Kaslova-8 (Irena-7, Adolf-6, Adolf-5, Barbora-4, Kateřina-3, Jan-2, Václav-1) was born on 03 Jun 1958 in Plzen.

Jiří Chládek was born in 1955.

Jiří Chládek and Monika Kaslova were married on 30 Apr 1978 in Prague, CSR. They had the following children:
>   **David Chládek** was born on 19 Dec 1978 in Cheb.
>   **Ondřej Chládek** was born on 17 Aug 1981 in Cheb.
>   **Jan Chládek** was born on 16 Nov 1988 in Cheb.

Daniel Šváb-8 (Zdeněk-7, Adolf-6, Adolf-5, Barbora-4, Kateřina-3, Jan-2, Václav-1) was born on 29 Jan 1964 in Plzen.

Jitka Kopackova.

Daniel Šváb and Jitka Kopackova were married in 1992. They had the following children:
>   **Dominika Švábová** was born on 16 Oct 1992 in Plzen.
>   **Natalie Švábová** was born on 09 Aug 1998 in Plzen.

Radek Pechman-8 (Olga-7, Adolf-6, Adolf-5, Barbora-4, Kateřina-3, Jan-2, Václav-1) was born on 12 Mar 1969 in Plzen.

Jitka Slámová was born in 1966.

Radek Pechman and Jitka Slámová were married in 1992. They had the following children:
>   **Barbora Pechmanová** was born in 1992.

Olga Pechmanová-8 (Olga-7, Adolf-6, Adolf-5, Barbora-4, Kateřina-3, Jan-2, Václav-1) was born on Mar 1976 in Plzen.

Tomáš Pech.

Tomáš Pech and Olga Pechmanová were married in 1998. They had the following children:
>   i. **Karolina Pechová** was born on 22 May 1999 in Plzen.

Vodicka Family

Generation 1

Viktor Vodička-1.

Kamila Taussigová daughter of Jakub Taussig and Julie Meislova was born on 27 Feb 1873. She died in 1912.

Viktor Vodička and Kamila Taussigová married. They had the following children:

    i. **Vladimír Vodička** was born before 1893. He died on 12 Feb 1954.

Marenka Vodičková was born in 1893. She died on 09 Feb 1898 in Pisek.

Viktor Vodička and unknown spouse married. They had the following children:

    i. **Vladimír Vodička** was born before 1893. He died on 12 Feb 1954.

    Marenka Vodičková was born in 1893. She died on 09 Feb 1898 in Pisek.

Generation 2

Vladimír Vodička-2 (Viktor-1) was born before 1893. He died on 12 Feb 1954.

Růžena Krausová.

Vladimír Vodička and Růžena Krausová married. They had the following children:

    i. **Vladimír Vodička** was born on 05 May 1925 in Benešov.

    ii. **daughter Vodička.**

Generation 3

3. **Vladimír Vodička**-3 (Vladimír-2, Viktor-1) was born on 05 May 1925 in Benešov.

Marie Fiserova.

Vladimír Vodička and Marie Fiserova married. They had the following children:

    i. **Marie Vodičková.**

Milada.

Vladimír Vodička and Milada were married before 1954. They had no children.

Ascher Family

Generation 1

1. **Emanuel Ascher**-1 was born in 1776 in Pacov. He died on 22 Feb 1831.

    Johanna Ascher daughter of Pinchas Ascher was born about 1805 in Prague, Bohemia. She died on 04 Jul 1891 in Prague, Bohemia.

    Emanuel Ascher and Johanna Ascher married. They had the following children:

        i. **Bernhard Ascher** was born on 28 Jan 1814 in Pacov. He died on 05 Oct 1899 in Pacov.

        ii. **Hermann Ascher**.

        iii. **Therese Ascher** was born on 31 Aug 1831 in Pacov. She died on 31 May 1898 in Prague, Bohemia.

        iv. **Katharina Ascher** was born in Pacov.

    Maria Glaser was born in Serbia.

    Emanuel Ascher and Maria Glaser married. They had the following children:

    5. i. **Katharina Ascher** was born in Pacov.

Generation 2

Bernhard Ascher-2 (Emanuel-1) was born on 28 Jan 1814 in Pacov. He died on 05 Oct 1899 in Pacov.

Francisca Guttmann was born on 14 Mar 1830 in Pacov. She died on 29 Apr 1902 in Pacov. Bernhard Ascher and Francisca Guttmann married. They had the following children:

    i. **Louise Ascher** was born about 1850 in Prague, Bohemia. She died on 12 Mar 1882 in Prague, Bohemia.

    Johanna Ascher was born in 1853.

    iii. **Fridricha (Bedřiška) Ascher** was born in 1854 in Pacov. She died on 03 Jul 1886.

    iv. **Ignaz Ascher** was born in 1855. He died on 21 Oct 1911 in Pacov.

    v. **Moritz Ascher** was born on 02 Feb 1858 in Pacov. He died on 17 Oct 1937.

    Sigmund Ascher was born in 1868. He died in 1887.

Hermann Ascher-2 (Emanuel-1).

Anna Guttmann daughter of Salomon Guttmann and Therese Rosalia Kafka was born in 1838 in Tabor, bohemia. She died on 21 Feb 1907 in Liberec, bohemia.

Hermann Ascher and Anna Guttmann married. They had the following children:

    i. **Maria Ascher** was born in 1862 in Pacov.

    ii. **Alois Ascher** was born on 10 May 1857 in Pacov, Pelhřimov Distric. He died on 01 Feb 1922 in Vienna, Austria.

    iii. **Joseph Ascher** was born on 24 Dec 1860 in Pacov. He died on 07 May 1942 in Prague, Bohemia.

    iv. **Rudolf Ascher** was born on 02 Mar 1864 in Pacov.

    Sophie Ascher was born in 1866 in Pacov. He died on 18 Feb 1867.

    vi. **Mathilde Ascher** was born on 27 Nov 1858 in Pacov. She died on 23 Jul 1930.

    Sigmund Ascher was born on 12 Dec 1868.

Therese Ascher-2 (Emanuel-1) was born on 31 Aug 1831 in Pacov. She died on 31 May 1898 in Prague, Bohemia.

Ignaz Sommer son of Salomon Sommer and Franziska Ohrenstein was born on 01 Mar 1832 in Budlin. He died on 02 Mar 1909.

Ignaz Sommer and Therese Ascher married. They had the following children:

    Wilhelm Sommer was born on 20 Apr 1864 in Pacov,. He died on 16 Sep 1942 in Terezin holocaust.

    Emilie Sommer. She died on 22 Oct 1942 in Treblinka, Poland - holocaust.

    Wilhelm Sommer was born on 20 Apr 1864 in Pacov,. He died on 16 Sep 1942 in Terezin Holocaust.

    Tobias Sommer was born in 1861 in Vodice, Tábor District, Bohemia. He died on 20 Feb 1896 in Prague, Bohemia.

    Oswald Sommer.

    vi. **Franziska Sommer** was born on 27 Feb 1866 in Vodice,

Bohemia. She died on 20 Oct 1922 in Vienna, Austria.

Emil Sommer was born on 25 May 1862 in Prague, bohemia.

Mathilde Sommer was born on 29 Feb 1868 in Pacov. She died on 25 Apr 1942 in Siegburg, German - Holocaust.

Katharina Ascher-2 (Emanuel-1) was born in Pacov.

Friedmann Meller.

Friedmann Meller and Katharina Ascher married. They had the following children:

    i. **Josefine Meller** was born on 11 Sep 1854 in Pacov, Pelhřimov District. She died on 09 Oct 1915 in Vienna, Austria.

Friedmann Meller was born in 1820 in Pacov.

Friedmann Meller and Katharina Ascher married. They had the following children:

    i. **Emil Meller** was born in 1850. He died on 24 Jun 1924.

    Emilia Meller was born on 01 Feb 1851 in Pacov.

    Carolina Meller was born on 24 Mar 1856 in Pacov.

    iv. **Sigmund Meller** was born on 16 Jan 1858 in Pacov. He died on 13 Oct 1931 in Liberec, bohemia.

    v. **Salomon Meller** was born in 1862. He died on 19 Jun 1900 in Liberec, Bohemia.

    vi. **Josefine Meller** was born on 11 Sep 1854 in Pacov, Pelhřimov District. She died on 09 Oct 1915 in Vienna, Austria.

    Charlotte Meller.

Generation 3

Louise Ascher-3 (Bernhard-2, Emanuel-1) was born about 1850 in Prague, Bohemia. She died on 12 Mar 1882 in Prague, Bohemia.

Adolf Weiss.

Adolf Weiss and Louise Ascher married. They had the following children:

    Emma Weiss.

    Bertha Weiss.

Fridricha (Bedřiška) Ascher-3 (Bernhard-2, Emanuel-1) was born in 1854 in Pacov. She died on 03 Jul 1886.

Moritz Steindler son of Jakub Steindler and Antonie Bret was born on 15 Dec 1853 in Benešov. He died on 01 Aug 1917 in weinerBenesov, Bohemia.

Moritz Steindler and Fridricha (Bedřiška) Ascher married. They had the following children:

    i. **Marie Steindlerová** was born on 06 Sep 1878 in Benešov. She died on 22 Oct 1942 in Treblinka.

    ii. **Antonie Steindlerová** was born on 20 Oct 1879 in Benešov. She died on 28 Jul 1942 in Baranovici KZ.

    iii. **Anna Steindlerová** was born on 29 Jun 1881 in Benešov. She died on 10 Oct 1944 in Auschwitz.

    iv. **Luisa Steindlerová** was born on 16 Jun 1883 in Benešov. She died on 09 May 1942 in Sobibor Ossowa KZ.

    v. **Jaroslav Steindler** was born on 25 Mar 1885 in Benešov. He died in 1980 in Praha.

Ignaz Ascher-3 (Bernhard-2, Emanuel-1) was born in 1855. He died on 21 Oct 1911 in Pacov.

Anna Lustig was born on 27 Jan 1862 in Kopidlno.

Ignaz Ascher and Anna Lustig married. They had the following children:

    i. **Louise Marie Ascher** was born on 30 Mar 1863 in Pacov.

    Hedwig Ascher.

    Ing. Franz Ascher.

Moritz Ascher-3 (Bernhard-2, Emanuel-1) was born on 02 Feb 1858 in Pacov. He died on 17 Oct 1937.

Paula Fluss was born on 12 Jun 1858 in říbor (Freiberg), Nový Jičín District, Moravia. She died on 25 Oct 1954 in Vienna, Austria.

Moritz Ascher and Paula Fluss married. They had the following children:

    i. **Marianne Louise Ascher** was born on 18 Jun 1893 in Vienna, Austria. She died in 1978 in Vienna, Austria.

        Ing. Peter Bernhard Ascher was born on 12 Sep 1904 in Vienna, Austria. He died on 17 Jul 1940 in Sachsenhausen - Holocaust.

Maria Ascher-3 (Hermann-2, Emanuel-1) was born in 1862 in Pacov.
Simon Schwelb was born on 08 Mar 1862 in Tabor, Tábor District, Bohemia. He died on 22 Oct 1942 in Treblinka, Poland - Holocaust.
Simon Schwelb and Maria Ascher married. They had the following children:

> **Margareth Schwelb** was born in 1901 in Varnsdorf, Bohemia.
> **Rudolf Schwelb** was born on 05 Oct 1886 in Tabor, Bohemia.
> **Frederike Schwelb** was born on 02 Sep 1902 in Varnsdorf, Bohemia. She died in 1917.
> iv. **Rose Schwelb** was born on 10 Feb 1896 in Tabor, Bohemia. She died in 1942 in Raasiku.
> **Rudolpf Schwelb** was born on 05 Oct 1886 in Tabor, bohemia.
> vi. **Franziska Schwelb**.
> vii. **Franziska Schwelb**.

Alois Ascher-3 (Hermann-2, Emanuel-1) was born on 10 May 1857 in Pacov, Pelhřimov Distric. He died on 01 Feb 1922 in Vienna, Austria.
Franziska Sommer daughter of Ignaz Sommer and Therese Ascher was born on 27 Feb 1866 in Vodice, Bohemia. She died on 20 Oct 1922 in Vienna, Austria.
Alois Ascher and Franziska Sommer married. They had the following children:

> i. **Leo Emanuel Ascher** was born on 29 Dec 1898 in Slatinice, Olomouc District, Moravia. He died in 1962 in Berkshire, UK.
> **Antonie Ascher** was born on 31 Jul 1838 in Vodice, Tábor District, Bohemia.
> iii. **Herman George Ascher** was born on 11 Aug 1889 in Vodice No. 1., Tábor District, Bohemia. He died on 18 Apr 1943 in Manchester, Greater Manchester, England, UK.

Joseph Ascher-3 (Hermann-2, Emanuel-1) was born on 24 Dec 1860 in Pacov. He died on 07 May 1942 in Prague, Bohemia.
Bertha Klinger was born on 25 May 1875 in Třebovle, 281 63 Kostelec nad Černými Lesy, Kolín District, Bohemia. She died after 14 Oct 1942 in Treblinka, Poland - Holocaust.

Joseph Ascher and Bertha Klinger married. They had the following children:
> **Zdeněk Ascher** was born on 11 Aug 1901.
> **Rudolf Ascher** was born on 30 Sep 1896 in Potštejn, Bohemia.
> **Anna Ascher** was born on 15 Feb 1911 in Prague, Bohemia.
> iv. **Friedrich Ascher** was born on 30 Sep 1896 in Pacov, Pelhřimov District. He died in 1942 in Izbica Ghetto, Poland - Holocaust.

Rudolf Ascher-3 (Hermann-2, Emanuel-1) was born on 02 Mar 1864 in Pacov.

Therese Fischer.

Rudolf Ascher and Therese Fischer married. They had the following children:
> **Viktor Ascher** was born on 02 Nov 1896 in Markvartice, Jablonné v Podještědí, Liberec Dist., Bohemia.
> **Robert Philipp Ascher** was born on 07 Jun 1900 in Jablonné v Podještědí, Liberec District, Bohemia.

Mathilde Ascher-3 (Hermann-2, Emanuel-1) was born on 27 Nov 1858 in Pacov. She died on 23 Jul 1930.

Emil Meller son of Friedmann Meller and Katharina Ascher was born in 1850. He died on 24 Jun 1924.

Emil Meller and Mathilde Ascher married. They had the following children:
> **Heinrich Meller** was born on 13 Jul 1883 in Liberec, Bohemia. He died about 1942 in Holocaust.

Franziska Sommer-3 (Therese-2, Emanuel-1) was born on 27 Feb 1866 in Vodice, Bohemia. She died on 20 Oct 1922 in Vienna, Austria.

Alois Ascher son of Hermann Ascher and Anna Guttmann was born on 10 May 1857 in Pacov, Pelhřimov Distric. He died on 01 Feb 1922 in Vienna, Austria.

Alois Ascher and Franziska Sommer married. They had the following children:
> i. **Leo Emanuel Ascher** was born on 29 Dec 1898 in Slatinice, Olomouc District, Moravia. He died in 1962 in Berkshire, UK.

> > **Antonie Ascher** was born on 31 Jul 1838 in Vodice, Tábor District, Bohemia.
> > iii. **Herman George Ascher** was born on 11 Aug 1889 in Vodice No. 1., Tábor District, Bohemia. He died on 18 Apr 1943 in Manchester, Greater Manchester, England, UK.
>
> **Josefine Meller**-3 (Katharina-2, Emanuel-1) was born on 11 Sep 1854 in Pacov, Pelhřimov District. She died on 09 Oct 1915 in Vienna, Austria.
>
> **Adolf Abraham Hauser** was born on 26 Jun 1853 in Šafov, Znojmo District, Moravia. He died on 15 Apr 1934 in Vienna, Austria.
>
> Adolf Abraham Hauser and Josefine Meller married. They had the following children:
>
> > > **Fredrike Hauser** was born on 21 Apr 1888 in Vienna, Austria. She died in 1942 in Auschwitz, Poland - Holocaust.
> > > **Karoline Hauser** was born on 24 May 1893 in Vienna, Austria. She died on 28 Jun 1969.
> > iii. **Oskar Hauser** was born on 10 Apr 1881 in Vienna, Austria. He died after 26 Feb 1941 in Holocaust.
> > > **Franz Hauser** was born on 20 Oct 1891 in Vienna, Austria. He died on 01 Jul 1942 in Łódź, Poland - Holocaust.
>
> **Emil Meller**-3 (Katharina-2, Emanuel-1) was born in 1850. He died on 24 Jun 1924.
>
> **Mathilde Ascher** daughter of Hermann Ascher and Anna Guttmann was born on 27 Nov 1858 in Pacov. She died on 23 Jul 1930.
>
> Emil Meller and Mathilde Ascher married. They had the following children:
>
> > > **Heinrich Meller** was born on 13 Jul 1883 in Liberec, Bohemia. He died about 1942 in Holocaust.
>
> **Sigmund Meller**-3 (Katharina-2, Emanuel-1) was born on 16 Jan 1858 in Pacov. He died on 13 Oct 1931 in Liberec, bohemia.
>
> **Amalia Pollak.**
>
> Sigmund Meller and Amalia Pollak married. They had the following children:
>
> > i. **Ernst Meller** was born on 11 Oct 1894 in Liberec, Bohemia.

ii. **Frieda Meller** was born on 23 May 1890 in Pilsen, Bohemia. She died in 1942 in Terezin - holocaust.

Katharine Meller was born on 27 Feb 1898 in Liberec, Bohemia. She died about 1942 in Lublin, Poland - Holocaust.

Salomon Meller-3 (Katharina-2, Emanuel-1) was born in 1862. He died on 19 Jun 1900 in Liberec, Bohemia.

Anna Guttmann was born on 30 Oct 1868. She died in 1942 in Teblinka, Poland - Holocaust. Salomon Meller and Anna Guttmann married. They had the following children:

Käthe Meller was born on 03 Dec 1894 in Liberec, bohemia. She died on 21 Jan 1977 in Holon, Center District, Israel.

Gertrud Meller was born on 16 May 1899 in Liberec, Bohemia. She died in 1942 in aly Trascianiec, Minsk, Belarus.

Generation 4

Marie Steindlerová-4 (Fridricha (Bedřiška)-3, Bernhard-2, Emanuel-1) was born on 06 Sep 1878 in Benešov. She died on 22 Oct 1942 in Treblinka.

Bedřich Rosenbaum was born about 1878. He died about 1942.

Bedřich Rosenbaum and Marie Steindlerová married. They had the following children:

i. **Jan (Rosenbaum) Skála** was born about 1899 in Nova Hospoda. He died in 1944 in Terezin.

ii. **Bedřiška Rosenbaumova** was born on 16 Jul 1901. She died on 19 Oct 1944 in Auschwitz KZ.

iii. **František Rosenbaum** was born on 05 Sep 1908. He died on 20 Feb 1945 in Dachau KZ.

Antonie Steindlerová-4 (Fridricha (Bedřiška)-3, Bernhard-2, Emanuel-1) was born on 20 Oct 1879 in Benešov. She died on 28 Jul 1942 in Baranovici KZ.

Orovan.

Orovan and Antonie Steindlerová married. They had the following children:

i. **Bedřiška ("Fritzi") Orovan**.

Siegfried Gruenwald was born on 26 Nov 1877 in Unin. He died on 28 Jul 1942 in Baranovici KZ.

Siegfried Gruenwald and Antonie Steindlerová married. They had the following children:

> i. **Gertrude Grünwald** was born about 1911. She died about 1992 in Stockholm, Sweden.
>
> **Marianne Grünwald** was born on 03 Jul 1912 in Gloggnitz, Neunkirchen District, Lower Austria, Austria.
>
> iii. **Anna Grünwald** was born on 03 Jul 1912 in Gloggnitz, Neunkirchen District, Lower Austria, Austria.

Anna Steindlerová-4 (Fridricha (Bedřiška)-3, Bernhard-2, Emanuel-1) was born on 29 Jun 1881 in Benešov. She died on 10 Oct 1944 in Auschwitz.

Alois Katz Kalina. He died in 1929 in Praha.

Alois Katz Kalina and Anna Steindlerová married. They had the following children:

> **Josef Katz Kalina** was born on 16 Mar 1909 in Praha. He died on 11 Mar 1942 in Izbica KZ.
>
> ii. **Jiří Katz Kalina** was born in 1910 in Praha. He died in 1984 in Sydney, Australia.
>
> iii. **Milena Katzova Kalinova** was born on 28 Nov 1910. She died in 1943 in Auschwitz KZ.

Luisa Steindlerová-4 (Fridricha (Bedřiška)-3, Bernhard-2, Emanuel-1) was born on 16 Jun 1883 in Benešov. She died on 09 May 1942 in Sobibor Ossowa KZ.

Carl Eisner was born on 22 Aug 1868 in Praha. He died on 21 Dec 1920 in Kolin. Carl Eisner and Luisa Steindlerová married. They had the following children:

> i. **Bedřiška Eisnerová** was born on 25 May 1905 in Praha. She died on 10 Apr 1997.

Jaroslav Steindler-4 (Fridricha (Bedřiška)-3, Bernhard-2, Emanuel-1) was born on 25 Mar 1885 in Benešov. He died in 1980 in Praha.

Marie Andreadisova. She died in Praha.

Jaroslav Steindler and Marie Andreadisova married. They had the following children:

> i. **Stanislav Steindler** was born on 08 Nov 1911. He died in 2000.

Marusja Voronkova.

Jaroslav Steindler and Marusja Voronkova married. They had the following children:

> **Volodja Steindlerová** was born in 1925. She died in 1947 in England.

Louise Marie Ascher-4 (Ignaz-3, Bernhard-2, Emanuel-1) was born on 30 Mar 1863 in Pacov.

Karl Guttmann was born on 02 Apr 1875 in Tabor, Bohemia. She died on 16 Oct 1935.

Louise Marie Ascher and Karl Guttmann married. They had the following children:

> **Erich Paul Ascher** was born on 29 Sep 1906 in Vienna, Austria. He died in Jan 1985 in King's Lynn, Norfolk, England, UK.

Marianne Louise Ascher-4 (Moritz-3, Bernhard-2, Emanuel-1) was born on 18 Jun 1893 in Vienna, Austria. She died in 1978 in Vienna, Austria.

Dr. Maximillian Schreyer was born on 25 May 1881 in Drohobycz, Poland. He died on 06 May 1942 in Vienna, Austria.

Dr. Maximillian Schreyer and Marianne Louise Ascher married. They had the following children:

> **Frederike Sussanne Schreyer** was born in 1920. She died in 1937.

Rose Schwelb-4 (Maria-3, Hermann-2, Emanuel-1) was born on 10 Feb 1896 in Tabor, Bohemia. She died in 1942 in Raasiku.

Julius Pimsenstein son of Lazar Pimsenstein and Katharina Steiner was born on 26 Dec 1883 in Kožlany, Bohemia. He died in 1942 in Raasiku, Estonia - Holocaust.

Julius Pimsenstein and Rose Schwelb married. They had the following children:

> **Margarit Pimsenstein** was born on 11 May 1921 in Varnsdorf No. 1600, Bohemia. She died on 01 Nov 2003 in Prague, Bohemia.

Franziska Schwelb-4 (Maria-3, Hermann-2, Emanuel-1).

Robert Reininger was born in 1881.

Robert Reininger and Franziska Schwelb married. They had the following children:

> **Susanna Reininger** was born on 23 May 1911 in Vienna, Austria. She died on 19 Jun 1998 in Tel Aviv, Israel.

Franziska Schwelb-4 (Maria-3, Hermann-2, Emanuel-1).

Robert Reininger was born in 1881.

Robert Reininger and Franziska Schwelb married. They had the following children:

> **Susanna Reininger** was born on 23 May 1911 in Vienna, Austria. She died on 19 Jun 1998 in Tel Aviv, Israel.

Leo Emanuel Ascher-4 (Alois-3, Hermann-2, Emanuel-1) was born on 29 Dec 1898 in Slatinice, Olomouc District, Moravia. He died in 1962 in Berkshire, UK.

Josephine Ascher.

Leo Emanuel Ascher and Josephine Ascher married. They had the following children:

> **Paul Ascher** was born in 1925 in Vienna, Clark, South Dakota, USA. She died in Oct 1998 in Dorset, England, UK.

Herman George Ascher-4 (Alois-3, Hermann-2, Emanuel-1) was born on 11 Aug 1889 in Vodice No. 1., Tábor District, Bohemia. He died on 18 Apr 1943 in Manchester, Greater Manchester, England, UK.

Helen Perason Ross Fleming.

Herman George Ascher and Helen Perason Ross Fleming married. They had the following children:

> i. **George Curie Ascher** was born on 16 Jun 1931 in Glasgow, Scotland, UK. He died on 18 Apr 1891 in Beverley, East Riding of Yorkshire, England, UK.

Friedrich Ascher-4 (Joseph-3, Hermann-2, Emanuel-1) was born on 30 Sep 1896 in Pacov, Pelhřimov District. He died in 1942 in Izbica Ghetto, Poland - Holocaust.

Antonie Cespivová was born in 1900.

Friedrich Ascher and Antonie Cespivová married. They had the following children:

Karel Ascher was born in 1924.

Oskar Hauser-4 (Josefine-3, Katharina-2, Emanuel-1) was born on 10 Apr 1881 in Vienna, Austria. He died after 26 Feb 1941 in Holocaust.

Rosa Seidll was born on 06 Mar 1891 in Alberndorf im Pulkautal, Hollabrunn, Lower Austria, Austria. She died after 26 Feb 1941.

Oskar Hauser and Rosa Seidll married. They had the following children:

> **Marianne Hauser** was born on 30 Nov 1924 (Vienna, Austria). She died after 26 Feb 1941 in Holocaust.

Ernst Meller-4 (Sigmund-3, Katharina-2, Emanuel-1) was born on 11 Oct 1894 in Liberec, Bohemia.

Marie Dittrich was born on 25 Mar 1896 in Liberec, Bohemia.

Ernst Meller and Marie Dittrich married. They had the following children:

> **Hans Georg Meller** was born on 02 Oct 1921 in Liberec, bohemia. He died in May 1981 in New York, NY.
>
> **Fred Fritz Meller** was born on 21 Jun 1929 in Prague, bohemia. He died on 07 Sep 1959.

Frieda Meller-4 (Sigmund-3, Katharina-2, Emanuel-1) was born on 23 May 1890 in Pilsen, Bohemia. She died in 1942 in Terezin - holocaust.

Richard Hartmann was born in 1891 in Pilsen,Bbohemia. He died in Oct 1941 in Terezin - holocaust. Richard Hartmann and Frieda Meller married. They had the following children:

> **Walter Hartmann Hartmann** was born on 09 Apr 1911. He died on 06 Feb 1943 in Lodz, Poland - Holocaust.

Generation 5

Jan (Rosenbaum) Skála-5 (Marie-4, Fridricha (Bedřiška)-3, Bernhard-2, Emanuel-1) was born about 1899 in Nova Hospoda. He died in 1944 in Terezin.

Bohumila Pucelikova was born about 1901. She died about 1983.

Jan (Rosenbaum) Skála and Bohumila Pucelikova married. They had the following children:

> i. **Jan Skála** was born about 1931. He died in 1992 in Praha.
>
> ii. **Ivo Skála** was born about 1933.

iii. **Jiří Skála** was born about 1936.

Bedřiška Rosenbaumova-5 (Marie-4, Fridricha (Bedřiška)-3, Bernhard-2, Emanuel-1) was born on Jul 1901. She died on 19 Oct 1944 in Auschwitz KZ.

Jiří Schwarz. He died in 1940 in Praha.

Jiří Schwarz and Bedřiška Rosenbaumova married. They had the following children:

>**Helena Schwarzova** was born on 26 Mar 1924. She died between 1944-1945 in concentration camp.

František Rosenbaum-5 (Marie-4, Fridricha (Bedřiška)-3, Bernhard-2, Emanuel-1) was born on 05 Sep 1908. He died on 20 Feb 1945 in Dachau KZ.

Anna Benešová was born on 09 Mar 1919. She died on 23 Oct 1944 in Auschwitz KZ. František Rosenbaum and Anna Benešová married. They had the following children:

>**Bedrch Rosenbaum** was born on 01 Mar 1940. He died on 23 Oct 1944 in Auschwitz KZ.

Gertrude Grünwald-5 (Antonie-4, Fridricha (Bedřiška)-3, Bernhard-2, Emanuel-1) was born about 1911. She died about 1992 in Stockholm, Sweden.

Hans Coudek was born on 04 Oct 1907 in Vienna, Austria. He died on 21 Jun 1993 in Stockholm, Sweden.

Hans Coudek and Gertrude Grünwald married. They had no children.

Hans Coudek was born on 04 Oct 1910 in Wien, Austria. He died on 21 Jun 1993 in Stockholm, Sweden.

Hans Coudek and Gertrude Grünwald married. They had the following children:

>i. **Lisa Coudkova** was born in 1946.

Anna Grünwald-5 (Antonie-4, Fridricha (Bedřiška)-3, Bernhard-2, Emanuel-1) was born on 03 Jul 1912 in Gloggnitz, Neunkirchen District, Lower Austria, Austria.

Rudolf Sponer was born on 08 Sep 1913 in Chrastava, Bohemia. He died on 15 Aug 1994 in Birmingham, West Midlands, UK.

Rudolf Sponer and Anna Grünwald married. They had the following children:

    i. **Michael Sponer** was born on 28 Dec 1946 in Birmingham.

Jiří Katz Kalina-5 (Anna-4, Fridricha (Bedřiška)-3, Bernhard-2, Emanuel-1) was born in 1910 in Praha. He died in 1984 in Sydney, Australia.

Milada Králová. She died in 1990 in Sydney, Australia.

Jiří Katz Kalina and Milada Králová married. They had the following children:

    Jan Kalina was born in 1941. He died in 1990 in Sydney, Australia.

    Milan Kalina was born in 1943.

Milena Katzova Kalinova-5 (Anna-4, Fridricha (Bedřiška)-3, Bernhard-2, Emanuel-1) was born on 28 Nov 1910. She died in 1943 in Auschwitz KZ.

Vojtěch Berkovic was born on 10 Mar 1904. He died about 1980 in Praha.

Vojtěch Berkovic and Milena Katzova Kalinova married. They had the following children:

    Jiří Berkovic was born on 20 Feb 1936. He died in 1943 in Auschwitz KZ.

Bedřiška Eisnerová-5 (Luisa-4, Fridricha (Bedřiška)-3, Bernhard-2, Emanuel-1) was born on 25 May 1905 in Praha. She died on 10 Apr 1997.

Jan Ledvina was born on 13 Jul 1905 in Kralupy. He died in 1972 in Praha. Jan Ledvina and Bedřiška Eisnerová married. They had the following children:

    Zuzana Ledvinova was born on 05 Aug 1930 in Praha.

Stanislav Steindler-5 (Jaroslav-4, Fridricha (Bedřiška)-3, Bernhard-2, Emanuel-1) was born on 08 Nov 1911. He died in 2000.

Unknown.

Stanislav Steindler and Unknown married. They had no children.

Jiřina was born about 1926.

Stanislav Steindler and Jiřina married. They had the following children:

    i. **Milan Steindler** was born in 1956.

    Michal Steindler was born in 1968.

George Curie Ascher-5 (Herman George-4, Alois-3, Hermann-2, Emanuel-1) was born on 16 Jun 1931 in Glasgow, Scotland, UK. He died on 18 Apr 1891 in Beverley, East Riding of Yorkshire, England, UK.

Margaret Jane Gibbs was born on 21 Jan 1938 in Grimsby, North East Lincolnshire, England, UK. She died on 08 Aug 2002.

George Curie Ascher and Margaret Jane Gibbs married. They had the following children:

> **Janet Ascher.**
> ii. **Lynne Ascher.**

Generation 6

Jan Skála-6 (Jan (Rosenbaum)-5, Marie-4, Fridricha (Bedřiška)-3, Bernhard-2, Emanuel-1) was born about 1931. He died in 1992 in Praha.

Souckova.

Jan Skála and Souckova married. They had the following children:

> **Jan Skála.**
> ii. **daughter Skalová.**

Ivo Skála-6 (Jan (Rosenbaum)-5, Marie-4, Fridricha (Bedřiška)-3, Bernhard-2, Emanuel-1) was born about 1933.

Ludmila Tesarova was born about 1943.

Ivo Skála and Ludmila Tesarova married. They had the following children:

> **Petra Skalová** was born on 17 Dec 1969.
> **Ondřej Skála** was born on 14 Oct 1971.

Jiří Skála-6 (Jan (Rosenbaum)-5, Marie-4, Fridricha (Bedřiška)-3, Bernhard-2, Emanuel-1) was born about 1936.

Unknown.

Jiří Skála and Unknown married. They had the following children:

> **Romana Skalová** was born in 1968.
> **Jiří Skála** was born in 1971.

Lisa Coudkova-6 (Gertrude-5, Antonie-4, Fridricha (Bedřiška)-3, Bernhard-2, Emanuel-1) was born in 1946.

Unknown.

Unknown and Lisa Coudkova married. They had the following children:

> Tanja Lind was born on 28 Jun 1972 in Stockholm, Sweden.
> Katja Lind was born on 09 Sep 1973 in Stockholm, Sweden.
> Linus Osterholm was born in 1982 in Stockholm, Sweden.
> Rasmus Osterholm was born in 1985 in Stockholm, Sweden.

Michael Sponer-6 (Anna-5, Antonie-4, Fridricha (Bedřiška)-3, Bernhard-2, Emanuel-1) was born on Dec 1946 in Birmingham.

Christine Sewell was born on 02 Nov 1949 in Birmigham.

Michael Sponer and Christine Sewell married. They had the following children:

> **Nigel Sponer** was born on 02 Oct 1978 in Birmingham.
> **Claire Sponer** was born on 28 Apr 1981 in Birmigham.

Milan Steindler-6 (Stanislav-5, Jaroslav-4, Fridricha (Bedřiška)-3, Bernhard-2, Emanuel-1) was born in 1956.

Unknown.

Milan Steindler and Unknown married. They had the following children:

> **child Steindler.**

Lynne Ascher-6 (George Curie-5, Herman George-4, Alois-3, Hermann-2, Emanuel-1).

Alan Havercroft.

Alan Havercroft and Lynne Ascher married. They had the following children:

> i. **Michelle Havercroft.**

Generation 7

daughter Skalová-7 (Jan-6, Jan (Rosenbaum)-5, Marie-4, Fridricha (Bedřiška)-3, Bernhard-2, Emanuel-1).

Unknown.

Unknown and daughter Skalová married. They had the following children:

> **child Unknown.**

Michelle Havercroft-7 (Lynne-6, George Curie-5, Herman George-4, Alois-3, Hermann-2, Emanuel-1).

and Michelle Havercroft married. They had the following children:

> **Harley Currie.**

Stránský Family

Generation 1

Josef Stránský-1.

Josefine Katz.

Josef Stránský and Josefine Katz married. They had the following children:

    i. **Adolf Stránský** was born on 12 Apr 1850. He married Franziska 'Fann'y Weinerova on 30 Dec 1879 in Bechyne, Tabor Dist., Bohemia. He died on 01 Oct 1934 in Vienna, Austria.

    ii. **Salomon Stránský** was born on 17 Oct 1845 in Netřebice, South Bohemia. He died on 14 Mar 1926 in Prague, Czechoslovakia.

Generation 2

Adolf Stránský-2 (Josef-1) was born on 12 Apr 1850. He died on 01 Oct 1934 in Vienna, Austria.

Franziska 'Fann'y Weinerova daughter of Moses Weiner and Rosalia Hindl Stricker was born in 1858 in Bechyne, Tabor Dist., Bohemia. She died before 1934.

Adolf Stránský and Franziska 'Fann'y Weinerova were married on 30 Dec 1879 in Bechyne, Tabor Dist., Bohemia. They had the following children:

    Max Stránský was born on 18 Nov 1880 in Pisek, Bohemia.

    ii. **Robert Stránský** was born on 05 May 1882 in Pisek, Bohemia. He died on 14 Jun 1942 in Lodz, Poland - Holocaust.

    iii. **Olga Stránská** was born on 22 Dec 1884 in Pisek, Bohemia. She died in Aug 1971 in New York, NY.

    iv. **Viktor Stránský** was born on 17 Sep 1893 in Písek, South Bohemia. He died on 04 Sep 1963 in New York, NY.

Eva Bloch was born about 1847 in Ohrazenice. She died on 23 Feb 1874 in Pisek, Bohemia.

Adolf Stránský and Eva Bloch married. They had the following children:

    Malvine Stránský was born on 20 Jul 1876 in Pisek, Písek Distric,, Bohemia. She died before 1945.

Leo **Stránský** was born on 22 Jun 1878 in Pisek, Bohemia. He died about 1942 in Vienna, Austria.

Salomon Stránský-2 (Josef-1) was born on 17 Oct 1845 in Netřebice, South Bohemia. He died on 14 Mar 1926 in Prague, Czechoslovakia.

Lotti Klineberger was born on 16 Nov 1854 in Košolná, Trnavský kraj, Slovakia. She died on 31 Dec 1918 in Prague, Bohemia.

Salomon Stránský and Lotti Klineberger married. They had the following children:

7. i. **Oskar Stránský** was born on 08 Sep 1876 in Prague, Bohemia.

    Melanie Stránský was born on 21 Apr 1878 in Ottakring, Vienna, Austria.

    iii. **Margarete Stránský** was born on 02 Jun 1887 in Prague, Bohemia. She died on 12 Sep 1939 in Berlin, Germany.

Generation 3

Robert Stránský-3 (Adolf-2, Josef-1) was born on 05 May 1882 in Pisek, Bohemia. He died on 14 Jun 1942 in Lodz, Poland - Holocaust.

Arnstein was born on 03 Aug 1890 in Votice, Bohemia. She died on 19 Apr 1944 in Łódź, Poland - Holocaust.

Robert Stránský and Arnstein married. They had the following children:

    Pavell Stránský was born on 19 Jun 1915 in Vienna, Austria. He died about 1941 in P{oland - Holocaust.

    Hanka Stránská.

Olga Stránská-3 (Adolf-2, Josef-1) was born on 22 Dec 1884 in Pisek, Bohemia. She died in Aug 1971 in New York, NY.

Dr. Bernhard Elias Schapire was born on 21 Jan 1880 in Ternopil, Ternopil's'ka oblast, Ukraine. He died on 09 Apr 1953.

Dr. Bernhard Elias Schapire and Olga Stránská married. They had the following children:

    i. **Franzi Schapire** was born on 28 Dec 1909 in Vienna, Austria. She died on 03 Oct 2004 in Albany, Albany County, New York.

    ii. **Hans Schapire** was born on 26 Aug 1914 in Vienna, Austria. He died on 16 Jan 2013 in Minneapolis, Hennepin County, MN.

Viktor Stránský-3 (Adolf-2, Josef-1) was born on 17 Sep 1893 in Písek, South

Bohemia. He died on Sep 1963 in New York, NY.

Ernestine Zerner was born on 28 Feb 1897 in Rosice, Brno Dist., Moravia. She died on 17 Jan 1961 in New York, NY.

Viktor Stránský and Ernestine Zerner married. They had the following children:

    i. **Curt Strand (Stránský)** was born on 13 Nov 1920 in Vienna, Austria.

Oskar Stránský-3 (Salomon-2, Josef-1) was born on 08 Sep 1876 in Prague, Bohemia.

Klára Löwy was born on 05 Apr 1878 in Žihle, Plzeň-North District, Bohemia. She died about 1944 in Auschwitz, Poland - Holocaust.

Oskar Stránský and Klára Löwy married. They had the following children:

    i. **Herta Stránský** was born on 28 Jun 1904.

Margarethe Bette Stránský was born about 1907.

Margarete Stránský-3 (Salomon-2, Josef-1) was born on 02 Jun 1887 in Prague, Bohemia. She died on 12 Sep 1939 in Berlin, Germany.

Richard Aronhold was born on 21 Jan 1878 in Dresden, Saxony, Germany. He died on 09 Apr 1942 in Lodz, Poland - Holocaust.

Richard Aronhold and Margarete Stránský married. They had the following children:

    i. **Doris Aronhold** was born on 12 Mar 1916 in Berlin, Germany. She died on 12 May 1968 in Barranquilla, Atlántico, Colombia.

Generation 4

Franzi Schapire-4 (Olga-3, Adolf-2, Josef-1) was born on 28 Dec 1909 in Vienna, Austria. She died on 03 Oct 2004 in Albany, Albany County, New York.

Weiss.

Weiss and Franzi Schapire married. They had the following children:

    Esther Weiss.

Dr. Bernhard Elias Schapire was born on 21 Jan 1880 in Ternopil, Ternopil's'ka oblast, Ukraine. He died on 09 Apr 1953.

Dr. Bernhard Elias Schapire and Franzi Schapire married. They had the following children:

Irene Schapire.

Hans Schapire-4 (Olga-3, Adolf-2, Josef-1) was born on 26 Aug 1914 in Vienna, Austria. He died on Jan 2013 in Minneapolis, Hennepin County, MN.

Lillian 'Libby' was born about 1924 in Colorado. She died on 25 Nov 2013 in Minneapolis, Hennepin County, MN.

Hans Schapire and Lillian 'Libby' married. They had the following children:

> **Julie Schapire.**
> **Irene Schapire** was born after 1944.
> **Esther Schapire** was born in 1952.

Curt Strand (Stránský)-4 (Viktor-3, Adolf-2, Josef-1) was born on 13 Nov 1920 in Vienna, Austria.

Fleur Lillian Emanuel was born on 24 Feb 1928 in Bloemfontein, Motheo, Free State, South Africa. She died on 23 Dec 2011 in Snowmass, Pitkin County, CO.

Curt Strand (Stránský) and Fleur Lillian Emanuel married. They had the following children:

> **Karen (Strand) Stránský** was born on 16 Feb 1955 in Amityville, Suffolk County, NY. She died on 03 Dec 2006 in Bennington, Bennington County, VT.

Doris Aronhold-4 (Margarete-3, Salomon-2, Josef-1) was born on 12 Mar 1916 in Berlin, Germany. She died on 12 May 1968 in Barranquilla, Atlántico, Colombia.

Gerd Blumenthal was born on 24 Feb 1915 in Greifswald, Mecklenburg-Vorpommern, Germany. He died on 06 Nov 1980 in New York, Queens, NY.

Gerd Blumenthal and Doris Aronhold married. They had the following children:

> **Dennis Blumenthal.**
> **Susana Blumenthal.**

Werner Cohen was born on 25 Nov 1910 in Berlin, Germany. He died on 28 Oct 1955 in Bogota, Cundinamarca, Colombia.

Werner Cohen and Doris Aronhold married. They had no children.

Syllaba Family

Generation 1

František Syllaba-1 was born in 1824. He died in 1894.

Anna Vlckova was born in 1829. She died in 1901.

František Syllaba and Anna Vlckova married. They had the following children:

    Franc Syllaba was born in 1851. He died in 1909.

    ii. **Ladislav Syllaba** was born on 16 Jun 1868 in Bystrice, Benešov Dist., Bohemia. He died on 30 Dec 1930 in Prague, Czech..

    iii. **Karel Syllaba**.

    Emilie Syllabová. She died in 1882.

    v. **Františka Syllabová**.

    Milada Syllaba was born in 1904.

Generation 2

Ladislav Syllaba-2 (František-1) was born on 16 Jun 1868 in Bystrice, Benešov Dist., Bohemia. He died on 30 Dec 1930 in Prague, Czech..

Marie Švábová daughter of Jan Krtitel Šváb and Barbora Sedláková was born on 13 Jul 1873 in Bystrice, Benešov Dist., Bohemia. She died in 1945. Ladislav Syllaba and Marie Švábová married. They had the following children:

    i. **Ludmila Syllabová** was born on 05 Apr 1899. She died in 1996.

    Jiří Syllaba was born on 08 Mar 1902 in Praha, CSR. He married Božena Slámová in 1942 in Praha II. He died on 17 May 1997 in Praha,CSR.

    iii. **Milada Syllabová** was born in 1904.

    Anna Syllabová was born in 1896. She died in 1902.

Karel Syllaba-2 (František-1).

Unknown.

Karel Syllaba and Unknown married. They had the following children:

    Marenka Syllabová.

Františka Syllabová-2 (František-1).

Unknown.

Unknown and Františka Syllabová married. They had no children.
Modroch.
Modroch and Františka Syllabová were married in 1918. They had the following children:
>**Theodor Modroch.**
>ii. **Karel Modroch.**
>**Ladislav Modroch.**

Generation 3

Ludmila Syllabová-3 (Ladislav-2, František-1) was born on 05 Apr 1899. She died in 1996.
Filip.
Filip and Ludmila Syllabová married. They had the following children:
>**Eva Filipová.**
>**Hana Filipová.**

Milada Syllabová-3 (Ladislav-2, František-1) was born in 1904.
Stretti.
Stretti and Milada Syllabová married. They had the following children:
>**Olga Strettiová.**
>**Milada Strettiová.**

Karel Modroch-3 (Františka-2, František-1).
Unknown.
Karel Modroch and Unknown married. They had the following children:
>i. **Dr.Sc Theodor Syllaba** was born on 20 Nov 1925 in Karlovce, Plzen - North Co..

Generation 4

Dr.Sc Theodor Syllaba-4 (Karel-3, Františka-2, František-1) was born on 20 Nov 1925 in Karlovce, Plzen - North Co..
Růžena Blumova was born on 14 Feb 1928 in Chomutov.
Dr.Sc Theodor Syllaba and Růžena Blumova married. They had the following children:
>**Zdenka Syllabová** was born on 02 Nov 1951 in Praha.
>9. ii. **Dagmar Syllabová** was born on 06 Mar 1955 in Praha.

Generation 5

Dagmar Syllabová-5 (Dr.Sc Theodor-4, Karel-3, Františka-2, František-1) was born on 06 Mar 1955 in Praha.

Ivan Nevěřil was born on 23 Dec 1953 in Praha.

Ivan Nevěřil and Dagmar Syllabová married. They had the following children:

    Michal Nevěřil was born on 08 Feb 1978.

    Tereza Nevěřilová was born on 26 Jan 1983.

Winternitz Family

Generation 1

Josef Winternitz-1 was born in Cerekvice nad Loučnou, Svitavy District, Bohemia. He died on 11 Oct 1898 in Jablonné v Podještědí, Liberec District, Boihemia.

Luisa Aloisie Schönfeld daughter of Josef Schönfeld and Františka Horzitzky was born in 1812. She died on 13 Jan 1875 in Liberec, Bohemia.

Josef Winternitz and Luisa Aloisie Schönfeld married. They had the following children:

> **Hermine 'Ojebinka' Winternitz** was born on 17 Mar 1841 in Jablonné v Podještědí, Liberec District, Boihemia. She died on 25 Oct 1934 in Semily, Semily District, Bohemia.
>
> ii. **Gustav Winternitz** was born in 1842 in Rumburk, Děčín District, Bohemia. He died on 20 Feb 1919 in Hrádek nad Nisou, Liberec District, Bohemia.

Generation 2

Gustav Winternitz-2 (Josef-1) was born in 1842 in Rumburk, Děčín District, Bohemia. He died on 20 Feb 1919 in Hrádek nad Nisou, Liberec District, Bohemia.

Jenny Schorsch was born on 16 Jun 1844 in Teplicce, Bbohemia.

Gustav Winternitz and Jenny Schorsch married. They had the following children:

> **Adele Winternitz** was born on 28 Nov 1871 in Hrádek nad Nisou, Liberec District, Bohemia.
>
> ii. **Rudolf Salomon Winternitz** was born on 26 Feb 1873. He died in 1944 in Auschwitz, Poiland - Holocaust.
>
> **Dr. Fritz Ernst Winternitz** was born on 05 May 1878 in Hrádek nad Nisou, Liberec District, Bohemia.
>
> **Erwin Winternitz**. He died on 05 Jul 1907 in Varnsdorf, Děčín District, Bohemia.

Generation 3

Rudolf Salomon Winternitz-3 (Gustav-2, Josef-1) was born on 26 Feb 1873. He died in 1944 in Auschwitz, Poiland - Holocaust.

Hermine Wodicka daughter of Adolf Wodicka and Marie was born on 19 May 1879 in Kolin, Bohemia. She died in 1944 in Auschwitz, Poland - Holocaust.

Rudolf Salomon Winternitz and Hermine Wodicka married. They had the following children:

> **Ella Elsa Winternitz** was born on 25 Jan 1904 in Hrádek nad Nisou, Liberec District, Bohemia. She died in 1942 in Łódź, Poland - Holocaust.

Sommer Family

Generation 1

Adam Sommer-1. He died before 1849.

Maria Mautner.

Adam Sommer and Maria Mautner married. They had the following children:

    i. **Salomon Sommer** was born about 1803. He died after 1857.

    ii. **Rosalia Sommer.**

Generation 2

Salomon Sommer-2 (Adam-1) was born about 1803. He died after 1857.

Franziska Ohrenstein was born on 13 Feb 1803 in Stritez 32, Bohemia. She died on 12 Apr 1857 in Budin No. 8.

Salomon Sommer and Franziska Ohrenstein married. They had the following children:

    i. **Ignaz Sommer** was born on 01 Mar 1832 in Budlin. He died on 02 Mar 1909.

    Abraham Sommer was born on 09 Sep 1828 in Budin No. 7.

    iii. **Rosalia Sommer** was born on 21 Oct 1835 in Budin No. 7.

    Elisabeth Sommer was born on 15 Jul 1842 in Budin no. 16.

    Anna Ohrenstein was born on 08 Aug 1826 in Budin No. 7.

Rosalia Sommer-2 (Adam-1).

and Rosalia Sommer married. They had the following children:

    Karl Sommer was born on 15 Sep 1845.

Generation 3

Ignaz Sommer-3 (Salomon-2, Adam-1) was born on 01 Mar 1832 in Budlin. He died on 02 Mar 1909.

Therese Ascher daughter of Emanuel Ascher and Johanna Ascher was born on 31 Aug 1831 in Pacov. She died on 31 May 1898 in Prague, Bohemia.

Ignaz Sommer and Therese Ascher married. They had the following children:

    Wilhelm Sommer was born on 20 Apr 1864 in Pacov,. He died on 16 Sep 1942 in Terezin - holocaust.

Emilie Sommer. She died on 22 Oct 1942 in Treblinka, Poland - holocaust.

Wilhelm Sommer was born on 20 Apr 1864 in Pacov,. He died on 16 Sep 1942 in Terezin - Holocaust.

Tobias Sommer was born in 1861 in Vodice, Tábor District, Bohemia. He died on 20 Feb 1896 in Prague, Bohemia.

Oswald Sommer.

vi. **Franziska Sommer** was born on 27 Feb 1866 in Vodice, Bohemia. She died on 20 Oct 1922 in Vienna, Austria.

Emil Sommer was born on 25 May 1862 in Prague, bohemia.

Mathilde Sommer was born on 29 Feb 1868 in Pacov. She died on 25 Apr 1942 in Siegburg, German - Holocaust.

Rosalia Sommer-3 (Salomon-2, Adam-1) was born on 21 Oct 1835 in Budin No. 7.

Jacob Wottitzky.

Jacob Wottitzky and Rosalia Sommer married. They had the following children:

Loise Wottitzky was born on 17 Jul 1856.

Anna Wottitzky was born on 11 Jul 1865.

Generation 4

Franziska Sommer-4 (Ignaz-3, Salomon-2, Adam-1) was born on 27 Feb 1866 in Vodice, Bohemia. She died on 20 Oct 1922 in Vienna, Austria.

Alois Ascher son of Hermann Ascher and Anna Guttmann was born on 10 May 1857 in Pacov, Pelhřimov Distric. He died on 01 Feb 1922 in Vienna, Austria.

Alois Ascher and Franziska Sommer married. They had the following children:

i. **Leo Emanuel Ascher** was born on 29 Dec 1898 in Slatinice, Olomouc District, Moravia. He died in 1962 in Berkshire, UK.

Antonie Ascher was born on 31 Jul 1838 in Vodice, Tábor District, Bohemia.

iii. **Herman George Ascher** was born on 11 Aug 1889 in Vodice No.

1., Tábor District, Bohemia. He died on 18 Apr 1943 in Manchester, Greater Manchester, England, UK.

Generation 5

Leo Emanuel Ascher-5 (Franziska-4, Ignaz-3, Salomon-2, Adam-1) was born on 29 Dec 1898 in Slatinice, Olomouc District, Moravia. He died in 1962 in Berkshire, UK.

Josephine Ascher.

Leo Emanuel Ascher and Josephine Ascher married. They had the following children:

> **Paul Ascher** was born in 1925 in Vienna, Clark, South Dakota, USA. She died in Oct 1998 in Dorset, England, UK.

Herman George Ascher-5 (Franziska-4, Ignaz-3, Salomon-2, Adam-1) was born on 11 Aug 1889 in Vodice No. 1., Tábor District, Bohemia. He died on 18 Apr 1943 in Manchester, Greater Manchester, England, UK.

Helen Perason Ross Fleming.

Herman George Ascher and Helen Perason Ross Fleming married. They had the following children:

> i. **George Curie Ascher** was born on 16 Jun 1931 in Glasgow, Scotland, UK. He died on 18 Apr 1891 in Beverley, East Riding of Yorkshire, England, UK.

Generation 6

George Curie Ascher-6 (Herman George-5, Franziska-4, Ignaz-3, Salomon-2, Adam-1) was born on 16 Jun 1931 in Glasgow, Scotland, UK. He died on 18 Apr 1891 in Beverley, East Riding of Yorkshire, England, UK.

Margaret Jane Gibbs was born on 21 Jan 1938 in Grimsby, North East Lincolnshire, England, UK. She died on 08 Aug 2002.

George Curie Ascher and Margaret Jane Gibbs married. They had the following children:

> i. **Janet Ascher**.
> ii. **Lynne Ascher**.

Generation 7

Lynne Ascher-7 (George Curie-6, Herman George-5, Franziska-4, Ignaz-3,

Salomon-2, Adam-1).

Alan Havercroft.

Alan Havercroft and Lynne Ascher married. They had the following children:

   i. **Michelle Havercroft.**

Generation 8

Michelle Havercroft-8 (Lynne-7, George Curie-6, Herman George-5, Franziska-4, Ignaz-3, Salomon-2, Adam-1).

and Michelle Havercroft married. They had the following children:

    Harley Currie

E. Jack Rechcigl's Wife Side

Palko Family

Generation 1

1. **John Palko**-1 was born in Europe.
   Anna Kolesar daughter of Kolesar and Unknown was born in 1879 in Europe. She died in 1949. John Palko and Anna Kolesar married. They had the following children:
   - 2. i. **John Bernard Palko** was born on 07 Feb 1903 in US. He married Anna Kopcho on 07 Jun 1924. He died on 10 Aug 1962 in Alden, PA.
   - 3. ii. **Michael Palko**.
   - 4. iii. **Anna Palko** was born in 1899. She died in 1977.

Generation 2

2. **John Bernard Palko**-2 (John-1) was born on 07 Feb 1903 in US. He died on 10 Aug 1962 in Alden, PA.
   Anna Kopcho daughter of Michael Kopcho and Anna Vanchissen was born on 28 Mar 1906 in Freeland, PA. She died on 22 Dec 1995 in Wilkes-Barre, PA.
   John Bernard Palko and Anna Kopcho were married on 07 Jun 1924. They had the following children:
   - 5. i. **Joseph Palko** was born on 27 Sep 1926 in Nanticoke, PA. He married Mary Rishko on 18 Sep 1954 in Elizabeth, NJ. He died in 2010.
   - 6. ii. **John Palko** was born on 09 Aug 1930 in Alden, PA. He married Ann Marian Sylvia Oakes on 07 Sep 1956. He died on 04 Dec 1995.

3. **Michael Palko**-2 (John-1).
   Unknown.
   Michael Palko and Unknown married. They had the following children:
   - i. **Barbara Palko**.

4. **Anna Palko**-2 (John-1) was born in 1899. She died in 1977.
   Michael Shupek was born in 1896. He died in 1971.
   Michael Shupek and Anna Palko married. They had the following

children:
- i. **Eugenia Shupek.**
- ii. **John Shupek** was born in 1921. He died in 1944.
7. iii. **Anna Shupek** was born in 1922. She died in 1999 in NJ.
8. iv. **Mary Shupek** was born in 1925.

Generation 3

5. **Joseph Palko**-3 (John Bernard-2, John-1) was born on 27 Sep 1926 in Nanticoke, PA. He died in 2010.

   Mary Rishko daughter of Peter Vasilev Rishko and Anna Goidich was born on 27 Nov 1930 in Alden, PA. She died on 03 Dec 1994 in Bradenton, FL.

   Joseph Palko and Mary Rishko were married on 18 Sep 1954 in Elizabeth, NJ. They had the following children:
   - 9. i. **Nancy Ann Palko** was born on 26 Sep 1961 in Morristown, NJ. She married John Edward Rechcigl on 30 Jul 1983 in Dover, NJ.

6. **John Palko**-3 (John Bernard-2, John-1) was born on 09 Aug 1930 in Alden, PA. He died on 04 Dec 1995.

   Ann Marian Sylvia Oakes was born on 07 Jun 1931. She died on 02 Jul 2022.

   John Palko and Ann Marian Sylvia Oakes were married on 07 Sep 1956. They had the following children:
   - 10. i. **Gregory John Palko** was born on 11 Dec 1961 in Irvington, NJ. He married Bonnie Higgins on 21 May 1987.
   - 11. ii. **Sonia Carol Palko** was born on 13 Jun 1963 in Irvington, NJ. She married Robert Salvesen on 22 Sep 1996.
   - 12. iii. **Sylvia Ellen Palko** was born on 04 Oct 1965 in Newark, NJ. She married Ihor Bouts on 02 May 1998.

7. **Anna Shupek**-3 (Anna-2, John-1) was born in 1922. She died in 1999 in NJ.

   Max Freshwater was born in 1920.

   Max Freshwater and Anna Shupek married. They had the following children:
   - i. **Alan Freshwater** was born in 1949.

8. **Mary Shupek**-3 (Anna-2, John-1) was born in 1925.

William Neckorcuk was born in 1926.

William Neckorcuk and Mary Shupek married. They had the following children:

    i. **Gary Neckorcuk** was born in 1952.

    ii. **April Neckorcuk** was born in 1955.

    iii. **Denise Neckorcuk** was born in 1960.

Generation 4

9. **Nancy Ann Palko**-4 (Joseph-3, John Bernard-2, John-1) was born on 26 Sep 1961 in Morristown, NJ.

    John Edward Rechcigl son of Mila (Miloslav) Rechcigl Jr. and Eva Edwards (Eisnerová) was born on 27 Feb 1960 in Washington, D.C..

    John Edward Rechcigl and Nancy Ann Palko were married on 30 Jul 1983 in Dover, NJ. They had the following children:

      i. **Gregory John Rechcigl** was born on 19 Dec 1988 in Bradenton, FL.

   13. ii. **Kevin Thomas Rechcigl** was born on 09 Oct 1991 in Bradenton, FL. He married Jordan Robbins on 12 May 2018 in Jacksonville, FL.

      i. **Lindsey Nicole Rechcigl** was born on 03 Nov 1994 in Bradenton, FL.

10. **Gregory John Palko**-4 (John-3, John Bernard-2, John-1) was born on 11 Dec 1961 in Irvington, NJ.

    Bonnie Higgins was born on 03 Apr 1961.

    Gregory John Palko and Bonnie Higgins were married on 21 May 1987. They had the following children:

      i. **Stephanie Anne Palko** was born on 24 Feb 1996.

    Christine Grier was born on 09 Apr 1968.

    Gregory John Palko and Christine Grier were married on 10 Aug 2015 in Point Pleasant Beach, NJ. They had no children.

11. **Sonia Carol Palko**-4 (John-3, John Bernard-2, John-1) was born on 13 Jun 1963 in Irvington, NJ.

    Robert Salvesen was born on 18 Sep 1957.

    Robert Salvesen and Sonia Carol Palko were married on 22 Sep 1996. They had the following children:

i. **Marlayna Grace Salvesen** was born on 05 Apr 1999 in NJ.

12. **Sylvia Ellen Palko**-4 (John-3, John Bernard-2, John-1) was born on 04 Oct 1965 in Newark, NJ.

    Ihor Bouts was born on 22 Aug 1961 in Mykoliev, Ukraine.

    Ihor Bouts and Sylvia Ellen Palko were married on 02 May 1998 in Woburn, MA. They had the following children:

    i. **John Nicholas Bouts Bouts** was born on 24 May 2002.

    They divorced 20 Sept 2021.

Generation 5

14. **Kevin Thomas Rechcigl**-5 (Nancy Ann-4, Joseph-3, John Bernard-2, John-1) was born on 09 Oct 1991 in Bradenton, FL.

    Jordan Robbins daughter of Douglass Robbins and Ivonne was born on 10 Jan 1992 in Camarillo, CA.

    Kevin Thomas Rechcigl and Jordan Robbins were married on 12 May 2018 in Jacksonville, FL. They had the following children:

    i. **James Douglas Rechcigl** was born on 05 Jan 2021 in Jacksonville, FL.

    ii. **Evelyn Marie Rechcigl** was born 29 May 2023 in Jacksonville, FL.

Kopcho Family

Generation 1

1. **Michael Kopcho**-1 was born on 25 Dec 1875 in Europe. He died in 1945. **Anna Vanchissen** daughter of Vanchissen and Unknown was born in 1879. She died in 1949. Michael Kopcho and Anna Vanchissen married. They had the following children:
   2. i. **Anna Kopcho** was born on 28 Mar 1906 in Freeland, PA. She married John Bernard Palko on 07 Jun 1924. She died on 22 Dec 1995 in Wilkes-Barre, PA.
      ii. **John Kopcho** was born on 28 Jul 1907. He died on 17 Aug 1980.
      iii. **Helen Kopcho**.
   3. iv. **Marie Kopcho** was born on 16 May 1913. She married Russell Swantko on 21 Jan 1934.
   4. v. **Peter Kopcho** was born on 12 Jul 1911.
   5. vi. **Julia Kopcho** was born on 01 Oct 1916. She married Thomas Odgers Lewis on 18 Jun 1936.
   6. vii. **Agnes Kopcho** was born on 29 Sep 1918. She married George Derco on 29 Oct 1945.
      viii. **Joseph Kopcho**.

Generation 2

2. **Anna Kopcho**-2 (Michael-1) was born on 28 Mar 1906 in Freeland, PA. She died on 22 Dec 1995 in Wilkes-Barre, PA.
   John Bernard Palko son of John Palko and Anna Kolesar was born on 07 Feb 1903 in US. He died on 10 Aug 1962 in Alden, PA.
   John Bernard Palko and Anna Kopcho were married on 07 Jun 1924. They had the following children:
   7. i. **Joseph Palko** was born on 27 Sep 1926 in Nanticoke, PA. He married Mary Rishko on 18 Sep 1954 in Elizabeth, NJ. He died in 2010.
   8. ii. **John Palko** was born on 09 Aug 1930 in Alden, PA. He married Ann Marian Sylvia Oakes on 07 Sep 1956. He died on 04 Dec 1995.
3. **Marie Kopcho**-2 (Michael-1) was born on 16 May 1913.
   Russell Swantko was born on 14 Jan 1906. He died on 20 Jun 1983.

KOPCHO FAMILY

Russell Swantko and Marie Kopcho were married on 21 Jan 1934. They had the following children:

9.   i. **Daniel Swantko** was born on 01 Dec 1938. He married Alice on 02 Jun 1962.

10.   ii. **Russell Swantko** was born on 16 Jan 1950.

4. **Peter Kopcho**-2 (Michael-1) was born on 12 Jul 1911.
   Helen Derco was born on 03 Oct 1913.
   Peter Kopcho and Helen Derco married. They had the following children:
   - i. **Michael Kopcho** was born on 12 Jun 1942.
   - ii. **Juliana Kopcho** was born on 07 Aug 1942.

5. **Julia Kopcho**-2 (Michael-1) was born on 01 Oct 1916.
   Thomas Odgers Lewis was born on 19 Jun 1903.
   Thomas Odgers Lewis and Julia Kopcho were married on 18 Jun 1936. They had the following children:
   - i. **Thomas M. Lewis** was born on 31 Jan 1937. He died on 14 Sep 1978.

12.   ii. **Raymond J. Lewis** was born on 05 Oct 1940.
   - iii. **John C. Lewis** was born on 29 Sep 1946. He married Donna Ann Motter on 02 May 1976.

6. **Agnes Kopcho**-2 (Michael-1) was born on 29 Sep 1918.
   George Derco was born on 28 Apr 1920.
   George Derco and Agnes Kopcho were married on 29 Oct 1945. They had the following children:

12.   i. **Agnes Ann Derco** was born on 29 Jul 1946. She married Michael Eltoro on 20 Aug 1966.

13.   ii. **George John Derco** was born on 12 Apr 1958. He married Coleen Krisak on 02 Jun 1988.

Generation 3

7. **Joseph Palko**-3 (Anna-2, Michael-1) was born on 27 Sep 1926 in Nanticoke, PA. He died in 2010.
   Mary Rishko daughter of Peter Vasilev Rishko and Anna Goidich was born on 27 Nov 1930 in Alden, PA. She died on 03 Dec 1994 in Bradenton, FL.

Joseph Palko and Mary Rishko were married on 18 Sep 1954 in Elizabeth, NJ. They had the following children:

    14. i. **Nancy Ann Palko** was born on 26 Sep 1961 in Morristown, NJ. She married John Edward Rechcigl on 30 Jul 1983 in Dover, NJ.

8. **John Palko**-3 (Anna-2, Michael-1) was born on 09 Aug 1930 in Alden, PA. He died on 04 Dec 1995.

    Ann Marian Sylvia Oakes was born on 07 Jun 1931. She died on 02 Jul 2022.

    John Palko and Ann Marian Sylvia Oakes were married on 07 Sep 1956. They had the following children:

      15. i. **Gregory John Palko** was born on 11 Dec 1961 in Irvington, NJ. He married Bonnie Higgins on 21 May 1987.

      16. ii. **Sonia Carol Palko** was born on 13 Jun 1963 in Irvington, NJ. She married Robert Salvesen on 22 Sep 1996.

      17. iii. **Sylvia Ellen Palko** was born on 04 Oct 1965 in Newark, NJ. She married Ihor Bouts on 02 May 1998.

9. **Daniel Swantko**-3 (Marie-2, Michael-1) was born on 01 Dec 1938.

    Alice was born on 24 Jul 1938.

    Daniel Swantko and Alice were married on 02 Jun 1962. They had the following children:

        i. **Daniel Swantko Jr.** was born on 26 May 1963. He married Unknown on 25 Oct 1980.

        ii. **David Swantko** was born on 22 Feb 1966.

        iii. **Lisa Swantko** was born on 21 Jan 1965.

10. **Russell Swantko**-3 (Marie-2, Michael-1) was born on 16 Jan 1950.

    Arlene Novitski was born on 19 May 1953.

    Russell Swantko and Arlene Novitski married. They had the following children:

        i. **Amy Swantko** was born on 26 Oct 1982.

        ii. **Jessie Swantko** was born on 12 Jun 1985.

11. **Raymond J. Lewis**-3 (Julia-2, Michael-1) was born on 05 Oct 1940.

    Carol (Cammie) ann Brysten was born on 25 Aug 1945.

    Raymond J. Lewis and Carol (Cammie) ann Brysten married. They had

the following children:
- 18. i. **2nd Raymond Lewis** was born on 27 Oct 1966.
    - ii. **David Lewis** was born on 05 Sep 1969.
    - iii. **Jeffrey Lewis** was born on 15 Aug 1974.

12. **Agnes Ann Derco**-3 (Agnes-2, Michael-1) was born on 29 Jul 1946.
    Michael Eltoro was born on 07 Sep 1946.
    Michael Eltoro and Agnes Ann Derco were married on 20 Aug 1966. They had the following children:
    - i. **Michael Richard Eltoro** was born on 12 Dec 1967.
    - ii. **Darlene Eltoro** was born on 22 Mar 1970. She married Richard Matthew Homa on 05 Nov 1994.
    - iii. **Brian Christopher Eltoro** was born on 02 Feb 1973.
    - iv. **Melisa Eltoro** was born on 10 Mar 1979.

13. **George John Derco**-3 (Agnes-2, Michael-1) was born on 12 Apr 1958.
    Coleen Krisak was born on 02 Feb 1961.
    George John Derco and Coleen Krisak were married on 02 Jun 1988. They had the following children:
    - i. **Julia Ann Derco** was born on 23 Jan 1995.
    - ii. **James George Derco** was born on 11 Jul 1996.

Generation 4

14. **Nancy Ann Palko**-4 (Joseph-3, Anna-2, Michael-1) was born on 26 Sep 1961 in Morristown, NJ.
    John Edward Rechcigl son of Mila (Miloslav) Rechcigl Jr. and Eva Edwards (Eisnerová) was born on 27 Feb 1960 in Washington, D.C..
    John Edward Rechcigl and Nancy Ann Palko were married on 30 Jul 1983 in Dover, NJ. They had the following children:
    - i. **Gregory John Rechcigl** was born on 19 Dec 1988 in Bradenton, FL.
    - 20. ii. **Kevin Thomas Rechcigl** was born on 09 Oct 1991 in Bradenton, FL. He married Jordan Robbins on 12 May 2018 in Jacksonville, FL.
    - iii. **Lindsey Nicole Rechcigl** was born on 03 Nov 1994 in Bradenton, FL.

15. **Gregory John Palko**-4 (John-3, Anna-2, Michael-1) was born on 11 Dec

1961 in Irvington, NJ.

Bonnie Higgins was born on 03 Apr 1961.

Gregory John Palko and Bonnie Higgins were married on 21 May 1987. They had the following children:

    i. **Stephanie Anne Palko** was born on 24 Feb 1996.

Christine Grier was born on 09 Apr 1968.

Gregory John Palko and Christine Grier were married on 10 Aug 2015 in Point Pleasant Beach, NJ. They had no children.

16. **Sonia Carol Palko**-4 (John-3, Anna-2, Michael-1) was born on 13 Jun 1963 in Irvington, NJ.

    Robert Salvesen was born on 18 Sep 1957.

    Robert Salvesen and Sonia Carol Palko were married on 22 Sep 1996. They had the following children:

        i. **Marlayna Grace Salvesen** was born on 05 Apr 1999 in NJ.

17. **Sylvia Ellen Palko**-4 (John-3, Anna-2, Michael-1) was born on 04 Oct 1965 in Newark, NJ.

    Ihor Bouts was born on 22 Aug.

    Ihor Bouts and Sylvia Ellen Palko were married on 02 May 1998. They had the following children:

        i. **John Nicholas Bouts Bouts** was born on 24 May 2002.

18. **2nd Raymond Lewis**-4 (Raymond J.-3, Julia-2, Michael-1) was born on 27 Oct 1966.

    Jill was born on 26 Dec 1966.

    2nd Raymond Lewis and Jill married. They had the following children:

        i. **3rd Raymond Lewis** was born on 25 Oct.
        ii. **James Lewis** was born on 16 Jan.
        iii. **Scott Lewis** was born on 09 Dec.

Generation 5

19. **Kevin Thomas Rechcigl**-5 (Nancy Ann-4, Joseph-3, Anna-2, Michael-1) was born on 09 Oct 1991 in Bradenton, FL.

    Jordan Robbins daughter of Douglass Robbins and Ivonne was born on 10 Jan 1992 in Camarillo, CA.

    Kevin Thomas Rechcigl and Jordan Robbins were married on 12 May

2018 in Jacksonville, FL. They had the following children:
- i. **James Douglas Rechcigl** was born on 05 Jan 2021 in Jacksonville, FL.
- ii. **Evelyn Marie Rechcigl** was born 29 May 2023 in Jacksonville, FL.

Vanchissen Family

Generation 1

1. **Anna Vanchissen**-1 was born in 1879. She died in 1949.
   Michael Kopcho son of Kopcho and Unknown was born on 25 Dec 1875 in Europe. He died in 1945. Michael Kopcho and Anna Vanchissen married. They had the following children:
   2. i. **Anna Kopcho** was born on 28 Mar 1906 in Freeland, PA. She married John Bernard Palko on 07 Jun 1924. She died on 22 Dec 1995 in Wilkes-Barre, PA.
   ii. **John Kopcho** was born on 28 Jul 1907. He died on 17 Aug 1980.
   iii. **Helen Kopcho**.
   3. iv. **Marie Kopcho** was born on 16 May 1913. She married Russell Swantko on 21 Jan 1934.
   4. v. **Peter Kopcho** was born on 12 Jul 1911.
   5. vi. **Julia Kopcho** was born on 01 Oct 1916. She married Thomas Odgers Lewis on 18 Jun 1936.
   6. vii. **Agnes Kopcho** was born on 29 Sep 1918. She married George Derco on 29 Oct 1945.
   viii. **Joseph Kopcho**.

Generation 2

2. **Anna Kopcho**-2 (Anna-1) was born on 28 Mar 1906 in Freeland, PA. She died on 22 Dec 1995 in Wilkes-Barre, PA.
   John Bernard Palko son of John Palko and Anna Kolesar was born on 07 Feb 1903 in US. He died on 10 Aug 1962 in Alden, PA.
   John Bernard Palko and Anna Kopcho were married on 07 Jun 1924. They had the following children:
   7. i. **Joseph Palko** was born on 27 Sep 1926 in Nanticoke, PA. He married Mary Rishko on 18 Sep 1954 in Elizabeth, NJ. He died in 2010.
   8. ii. **John Palko** was born on 09 Aug 1930 in Alden, PA. He married Ann Marian Sylvia Oakes on 07 Sep 1956. He died on 04 Dec 1995.
3. **Marie Kopcho**-2 (Anna-1) was born on 16 May 1913.

Russell Swantko was born on 14 Jan 1906. He died on 20 Jun 1983.

Russell Swantko and Marie Kopcho were married on 21 Jan 1934. They had the following children:

9.   i. **Daniel Swantko** was born on 01 Dec 1938. He married Alice on 02 Jun 1962.

10. ii. **Russell Swantko** was born on 16 Jan 1950.

4. **Peter Kopcho**-2 (Anna-1) was born on 12 Jul 1911.

   Helen Derco was born on 03 Oct 1913.

   Peter Kopcho and Helen Derco married. They had the following children:

       i. **Michael Kopcho** was born on 12 Jun 1942.

       ii. **Juliana Kopcho** was born on 07 Aug 1942.

52. **Julia Kopcho**-2 (Anna-1) was born on 01 Oct 1916.

    Thomas Odgers Lewis was born on 19 Jun 1903.

    Thomas Odgers Lewis and Julia Kopcho were married on 18 Jun 1936. They had the following children:

        Thomas M. Lewis was born on 31 Jan 1937. He died on 14 Sep 1978.

87. ii. **Raymond J. Lewis** was born on 05 Oct 1940.

        iii. **John C. Lewis** was born on 29 Sep 1946. He married Donna Ann Motter on 02 May 1976.

6. **Agnes Kopcho**-2 (Anna-1) was born on 29 Sep 1918.

   George Derco was born on 28 Apr 1920.

   George Derco and Agnes Kopcho were married on 29 Oct 1945. They had the following children:

   12. i. **Agnes Ann Derco** was born on 29 Jul 1946. She married Michael Eltoro on 20 Aug 1966.

   13. ii. **George John Derco** was born on 12 Apr 1958. He married Coleen Krisak on 02 Jun 1988.

Generation 3

7. **Joseph Palko**-3 (Anna-2, Anna-1) was born on 27 Sep 1926 in Nanticoke, PA. He died in 2010.

   Mary Rishko daughter of Peter Vasilev Rishko and Anna Goidich was born on 27 Nov 1930 in Alden, PA. She died on 03 Dec 1994 in Bradenton, FL.

Joseph Palko and Mary Rishko were married on 18 Sep 1954 in Elizabeth, NJ. They had the following children:

1   i. **Nancy Ann Palko** was born on 26 Sep 1961 in Morristown, NJ. She married John Edward Rechcigl on 30 Jul 1983 in Dover, NJ.

8. **John Palko**-3 (Anna-2, Anna-1) was born on 09 Aug 1930 in Alden, PA. He died on 04 Dec 1995.

   Ann Marian Sylvia Oakes was born on 07 Jun 1931. She died on 02 Jul 2022.

   John Palko and Ann Marian Sylvia Oakes were married on 07 Sep 1956. They had the following children:

   15. i. **Gregory John Palko** was born on 11 Dec 1961 in Irvington, NJ. He married Bonnie Higgins on 21 May 1987.
   16. ii. **Sonia Carol Palko** was born on 13 Jun 1963 in Irvington, NJ. She married Robert Salvesen on 22 Sep 1996.
   17. iii. **Sylvia Ellen Palko** was born on 04 Oct 1965 in Newark, NJ. She married Ihor Bouts on 02 May 1998.

9. **Daniel Swantko**-3 (Marie-2, Anna-1) was born on 01 Dec 1938.

   Alice was born on 24 Jul 1938.

   Daniel Swantko and Alice were married on 02 Jun 1962. They had the following children:

   i. **Daniel Swantko Jr.** was born on 26 May 1963. He married Unknown on 25 Oct 1980.
   ii. **David Swantko** was born on 22 Feb 1966.
   iii. **Lisa Swantko** was born on 21 Jan 1965.

10. **Russell Swantko**-3 (Marie-2, Anna-1) was born on 16 Jan 1950.

    Arlene Novitski was born on 19 May 1953.

    Russell Swantko and Arlene Novitski married. They had the following children:

    i. **Amy Swantko** was born on 26 Oct 1982.
    ii. **Jessie Swantko** was born on 12 Jun 1985.

11. **Raymond J. Lewis**-3 (Julia-2, Anna-1) was born on 05 Oct 1940.

VANCHISSEN FAMILY

Carol (Cammie) ann Brysten was born on 25 Aug 1945.

Raymond J. Lewis and Carol (Cammie) ann Brysten married. They had the following children:

18. i. **2nd Raymond Lewis** was born on 27 Oct 1966.
    ii. **David Lewis** was born on 05 Sep 1969.
    iii. **Jeffrey Lewis** was born on 15 Aug 1974.

12. **Agnes Ann Derco**-3 (Agnes-2, Anna-1) was born on 29 Jul 1946.

Michael Eltoro was born on 07 Sep 1946.

Michael Eltoro and Agnes Ann Derco were married on 20 Aug 1966. They had the following children:

    i. **Michael Richard Eltoro** was born on 12 Dec 1967.
    ii. **Darlene Eltoro** was born on 22 Mar 1970. She married Richard Matthew Homa on 05 Nov 1994.
    iii. **Brian Christopher Eltoro** was born on 02 Feb 1973.
    iv. **Melisa Eltoro** was born on 10 Mar 1979.

13. **George John Derco**-3 (Agnes-2, Anna-1) was born on 12 Apr 1958.

Coleen Krisak was born on 02 Feb 1961.

George John Derco and Coleen Krisak were married on 02 Jun 1988. They had the following children:

    ii. **Julia Ann Derco** was born on 23 Jan 1995.
    iii. **James George Derco** was born on 11 Jul 1996.

Generation 4

14. **Nancy Ann Palko**-4 (Joseph-3, Anna-2, Anna-1) was born on 26 Sep 1961 in Morristown, NJ.

John Edward Rechcigl son of Mila (Miloslav) Rechcigl Jr. and Eva Edwards (Eisnerová) was born on 27 Feb 1960 in Washington, D.C..

John Edward Rechcigl and Nancy Ann Palko were married on 30 Jul 1983 in Dover, NJ. They had the following children:

    i. **Gregory John Rechcigl** was born on 19 Dec 1988 in Bradenton, FL.

20. ii. **Kevin Thomas Rechcigl** was born on 09 Oct 1991 in Bradenton, FL. He married Jordan Robbins on 12 May 2018 in Jacksonville, FL.
    iii. **Lindsey Nicole Rechcigl** was born on 03 Nov 1994 in Bradenton,

FL.

15. **Gregory John Palko**-4 (John-3, Anna-2, Anna-1) was born on 11 Dec 1961 in Irvington, NJ.
    Bonnie Higgins was born on 03 Apr 1961.
    Gregory John Palko and Bonnie Higgins were married on 21 May 1987. They had the following children:
    i. **Stephanie Anne Palko** was born on 24 Feb 1996.
    Christine Grier was born on 09 Apr 1968.
    Gregory John Palko and Christine Grier were married on 10 Aug 2015 in Point Pleasant Beach, NJ. They had no children.

16. **Sonia Carol Palko**-4 (John-3, Anna-2, Anna-1) was born on 13 Jun 1963 in Irvington, NJ.
    Robert Salvesen was born on 18 Sep 1957.
    Robert Salvesen and Sonia Carol Palko were married on 22 Sep 1996. They had the following children:
    i. **Marlayna Grace Salvesen** was born on 05 Apr 1999 in NJ.

17. **Sylvia Ellen Palko**-4 (John-3, Anna-2, Anna-1) was born on 04 Oct 1965 in Newark, NJ.
    Ihor Bouts was born on 22 Aug.
    Ihor Bouts and Sylvia Ellen Palko were married on 02 May 1998. They had the following children:
    i. **John Nicholas Bouts Bouts** was born on 24 May 2002.

18. **2nd Raymond Lewis**-4 (Raymond J.-3, Julia-2, Anna-1) was born on 27 Oct 1966.
    Jill was born on 26 Dec 1966.
    2nd Raymond Lewis and Jill married. They had the following children:
    i. **3rd Raymond Lewis** was born on 25 Oct.
    ii. **James Lewis** was born on 16 Jan.
    iii. **Scott Lewis** was born on 09 Dec.

Generation 5

19. **Kevin Thomas Rechcigl**-5 (Nancy Ann-4, Joseph-3, Anna-2, Anna-1) was born on 09 Oct 1991 in Bradenton, FL.
    Jordan Robbins daughter of Douglass Robbins and Ivonne was born on

10 Jan 1992 in Camarillo, CA.

Kevin Thomas Rechcigl and Jordan Robbins were married on 12 May 2018 in Jacksonville, FL. They had the following children:
    i.   **James Douglas Rechcigl** was born on 05 Jan 2021 in Jacksonville, FL.
    ii. **Evelyn Marie Rechcigl** was born 29 May 2023 in Jacksonville, FL.

Rishko Family

Generation 1

1. **Wasil Rishko**-1 was born on 15 Feb 1861 in Tylawa, Galicia, Poland. He died on 11 Feb 1911 in Alden, PA.

    Mary Kirpan daughter of Nicolaus Kirpan and Theresa Kokula was born on 18 Feb 1865 in Tylawa, Galicia. She died on 16 Aug 1950 in Alden, PA. Wasil Rishko and Mary Kirpan were married about 1886. They had the following children:

    2. i. **Peter Vasilev Rishko** was born on 08 Jun 1890 in Alden Station, PA. He married Anna Goidich in 1914. He died on 08 Feb 1941 in Alden, PA.
    - ii. **John Rishko** was born in 1897 in Alden, PA. He died on 06 Mar 1970 in Alden, PA.
    - iii. **child Rishko**.

Generation 2

2. **Peter Vasilev Rishko**-2 (Wasil-1) was born on 08 Jun 1890 in Alden Station, PA. He died on 08 Feb 1941 in Alden, PA.

    Anna Goidich daughter of Gregory Gojdycz and Martha Barnai was born on 07 Jul 1895 in Jersey City, NJ. She died on 24 Nov 1973 in Linden, NJ.

    Peter Vasilev Rishko and Anna Goidich were married in 1914. They had the following children:

    - i. **Anna Rishko** was born on 07 Jul 1915 in Alden, PA. She died on 24 Oct 1941.
    4. ii. **John Rishko** was born on 22 Jul 1917 in Alden Station, PA. He married Florence Moranski on 22 Jul 1944. He died on 24 Jul 1986 in North Hollywood, Los Angeles, CA.
    5. iii. **George Rishko** was born on 13 May 1919 in Alden, PA. He married Irene Tania Zuk on 20 Feb 1977 in Whippany, NJ.
    - iv. **Helen Rishko** was born on 23 May 1921 in Alden, PA. She died on 26 Dec 2015 in Linden, NJ.

RISHKO FAMILY

  v. **Paul Rishko** was born on 23 Jun 1926 in Alden, PA.

5. vi. **Irene Rishko** was born on 20 Feb 1928 in Alden, PA. She married Daniel E. Lynch on 04 Aug 1951 in Elizabeth, NJ. She died on 20 Feb 2003 in Clark,NJ.

6. vii. **Mary Rishko** was born on 27 Nov 1930 in Alden, PA. She married Joseph Palko on 18 Sep 1954 in Elizabeth, NJ. She died on 03 Dec 1994 in Bradenton, FL.

7. viii. **Mildred Rishko** was born on 27 Apr 1934 in Alden, PA. She married Allistair Duncan Black on 13 Aug 1966 in Syosset, NY.

8. ix. **Peter Rishko** was born on 05 Oct 1936 in Alden, PA. He married Eleanor Giacalone on 09 Oct 1965 in Elizabeth, NJ. He died on 27 Aug 1997 in Clark, NJ.

Generation 3

3. **John Rishko**-3 (Peter Vasilev-2, Wasil-1) was born on 22 Jul 1917 in Alden Station, PA. He died on 24 Jul 1986 in North Hollywood, Los Angeles, CA.

Florence Moranski daughter of Frank Moranski and Mary Genzik was born on 25 Oct 1924 in Dupont, PA.

John Rishko and Florence Moranski were married on 22 Jul 1944. They had the following children:

9. i. **John Richard Rishko** was born on 20 Sep 1954 in Inglewood, NJ. He married Norine Ann Koles on 29 Oct 1977.

10. ii. **Cynthia Marie Rishko** was born on 15 Jul 1956. She married Bruce Lazarus in Oct 1980 in Princeton, NJ.

4. **George Rishko**-3 (Peter Vasilev-2, Wasil-1) was born on 13 May 1919 in Alden, PA.

Irene Tania Zuk was born on 06 Aug 1930.

George Rishko and Irene Tania Zuk were married on 20 Feb 1977 in Whippany, NJ. They had the following children:

11. i. **Lydia Rishko** was born on 27 Aug 1964. She married Roman Klufus on 16 May 1992.

12. ii. **Zina Rishko** was born on 27 Sep 1970.

5. **Irene Rishko**-3 (Peter Vasilev-2, Wasil-1) was born on 20 Feb 1928 in

Alden, PA. She died on 20 Feb 2003 in Clark, NJ.

Daniel E. Lynch was born on 28 Oct 1921. He died on 18 Dec 2009 in Clark, NJ.

Daniel E. Lynch and Irene Rishko were married on 04 Aug 1951 in Elizabeth, NJ. They had the following children:

    i. **Daniel Lynch** was born on 30 Dec 1952.

13. ii. **Maryanne Lynch** was born on 26 Aug 1954.

14. iii. **Michael Lynch** was born on 23 May 1957. He married Pamela Moses on 30 Sep 1989.

15. iv. **Patricia Lynch** was born on 26 Sep 1959. She married John Weilandics on 25 Apr 1987.

6. **Mary Rishko**-3 (Peter Vasilev-2, Wasil-1) was born on 27 Nov 1930 in Alden, PA. She died on 03 Dec 1994 in Bradenton, FL.

    Joseph Palko son of John Bernard Palko and Anna Kopcho was born on 27 Sep 1926 in Nanticoke, PA. He died in 2010.

    Joseph Palko and Mary Rishko were married on 18 Sep 1954 in Elizabeth, NJ. They had the following children:

    16. i. **Nancy Ann Palko** was born on 26 Sep 1961 in Morristown, NJ. She married John Edward Rechcigl on 30 Jul 1983 in Dover, NJ.

7. **Mildred Rishko**-3 (Peter Vasilev-2, Wasil-1) was born on 27 Apr 1934 in Alden, PA.

    Allistair Duncan Black was born on 06 May 1939. He died on 16 Feb 1996 in Hackettstown, NJ.

    Allistair Duncan Black and Mildred Rishko were married on 13 Aug 1966 in Syosset, NY. They had the following children:

        i. **Douglas Alexander Black** was born on 22 Oct 1972. He died on 16 Jul 1998 in Hackettstown, NJ.

8. **Peter Rishko**-3 (Peter Vasilev-2, Wasil-1) was born on 05 Oct 1936 in Alden, PA. He died on 27 Aug 1997 in Clark, NJ.

    Eleanor Giacalone was born on 26 Dec 1938. She died on 10 Jun 1990 in Clark, NJ.

    Peter Rishko and Eleanor Giacalone were married on 09 Oct 1965 in Elizabeth, NJ. They had the following children:

17. i. **Carrie Ann Rishko** was born on 29 Jul 1972 in Clark, NJ. She married Sean Edwin Cusack on 17 Apr 1999 in Princeton, NJ.
18. ii. **Peter Rishko** was born on 27 Dec 1974. He married Jennifer Becmer on 02 Jul 2005.

Generation 4

9. **John Richard Rishko**-4 (John-3, Peter Vasilev-2, Wasil-1) was born on 20 Sep 1954 in Inglewood, NJ.

Norine Ann Koles was born on 04 Sep 1953 in Newark, NJ.

John Richard Rishko and Norine Ann Koles were married on 29 Oct 1977. They had the following children:

19. i. **Kevin John Rishko** was born on 16 Dec 1982 in Tarzana, CA. He married Favianna Francisco on 02 Jun 2007.
    ii. **Shawn Richard Rishko** was born on 27 Dec 1983 in Tarzana, CA. He died on 07 Feb 2006 in Oak Park, CA.
    iii. **Richard Alan Rishko** was born on 27 Mar 1986 in Tarzana, CA.

10. **Cynthia Marie Rishko**-4 (John-3, Peter Vasilev-2, Wasil-1) was born on 15 Jul 1956.

Bruce Lazarus.

Bruce Lazarus and Cynthia Marie Rishko were married in Oct 1980 in Princeton, NJ. They had the following children:

20. i. **Amber Abigail Lazarus** was born on 04 Aug 1984. She married Kevin Hines on 19 Sep 2015 in Lone Tree, CO.
    ii. **Justin Lazarus** was born on 14 Jul 1987.

12. **Lydia Rishko**-4 (George-3, Peter Vasilev-2, Wasil-1) was born on 27 Aug 1964.

Roman Klufus.

Roman Klufus and Lydia Rishko were married on 16 May 1992. They had the following children:

   i. **Andrew Klufus** was born on 18 Jan 1995.
   ii. **Alexandra Klufus** was born on 12 Sep 1996.
   iii. **Larisson Anna Klufus** was born on 29 May 1998.

13. **Zina Rishko**-4 (George-3, Peter Vasilev-2, Wasil-1) was born on 27 Sep 1970.

Mark Zinych.

Mark Zinych and Zina Rishko married. They had the following children:
  i. **Andrea Zinych.**

14. **Maryanne Lynch**-4 (Irene-3, Peter Vasilev-2, Wasil-1) was born on 26 Aug 1954.

    Kenneth Kirchner was born on 09 Jan 1953.

    Kenneth Kirchner and Maryanne Lynch married. They had the following children:
      i. **Andrew Paul Kirchner** was born on 03 May 1982 in Bakersfield, CA.
      ii. **Laura Ann Kirchner** was born on 13 Mar 1985.
      iii. **Jennifer Claire Kirchner** was born on 10 Dec 1987 in Bakersfield, CA.

15. **Michael Lynch**-4 (Irene-3, Peter Vasilev-2, Wasil-1) was born on 23 May 1957.

    Pamela Moses was born on 23 Mar 1960.

    Michael Lynch and Pamela Moses were married on 30 Sep 1989. They had the following children:
      i. **Anna Grace Lynch** was born on 26 Dec 1993.
      ii. **Kelsey Elizabeth Lynch.**

16. **Patricia Lynch**-4 (Irene-3, Peter Vasilev-2, Wasil-1) was born on 26 Sep 1959.

    John Weilandics.

    John Weilandics and Patricia Lynch were married on 25 Apr 1987. They had the following children:
      i. **Allison Elizabeth Weilandics** was born on 15 Jan 1989 in Clark, NJ.
      ii. **Kathryn Anne Weilandics** was born on 25 Oct 1996 in Clark, NJ.

17. **Nancy Ann Palko**-4 (Mary-3, Peter Vasilev-2, Wasil-1) was born on 26 Sep 1961 in Morristown, NJ.

    John Edward Rechcigl son of Mila (Miloslav) Rechcigl Jr. and Eva Edwards (Eisnerová) was born on 27 Feb 1960 in Washington, D.C..

    John Edward Rechcigl and Nancy Ann Palko were married on 30 Jul 1983

in Dover, NJ. They had the following children:
   i. **Gregory John Rechcigl** was born on 19 Dec 1988 in Bradenton, FL.
22. ii. **Kevin Thomas Rechcigl** was born on 09 Oct 1991 in Bradenton, FL. He married Jordan Robbins on 12 May 2018 in Jacksonville, FL.
   iii. **Lindsey Nicole Rechcigl** was born on 03 Nov 1994 in Bradenton, FL.
17. **Carrie Ann Rishko**-4 (Peter-3, Peter Vasilev-2, Wasil-1) was born on 29 Jul 1972 in Clark, NJ.
Sean Edwin Cusack was born on 21 May 1971.
Sean Edwin Cusack and Carrie Ann Rishko were married on 17 Apr 1999 in Princeton, NJ. They had the following children:
   i. **Aiden Cusack** was born on 26 Jun 2005.
   ii. **Connor Cusack** was born on 20 Mar 2007.
18. **Peter Rishko**-4 (Peter-3, Peter Vasilev-2, Wasil-1) was born on 27 Dec 1974.
Jennifer Becmer.
Peter Rishko and Jennifer Becmer were married on 02 Jul 2005. They had the following children:
   i. **Ella Rishko** was born on 26 Jan 2008.
   ii. **Austin Rishko** was born on 12 Dec 2011.
Vlada Solovyaova was born on 02 Oct 1993.
Peter Rishko and Vlada Solovyaova were married on 26 Nov 2018. They had no children.

Generation 5

19. **Kevin John Rishko**-5 (John Richard-4, John-3, Peter Vasilev-2, Wasil-1) was born on 16 Dec 1982 in Tarzana, CA.
Favianna Francisco was born on 26 Aug 1981.
Kevin John Rishko and Favianna Francisco were married on 02 Jun 2007. They had the following children:
   i. **Blakely Kate Rishko** was born on 08 Oct 2012.
   ii. **John Beckham Rishko** was born on 14 Mar 2016.
20. **Amber Abigail Lazarus**-5 (Cynthia Marie-4, John-3, Peter Vasilev-2,

Wasil-1) was born on 04 Aug 1984.

Kevin Hines.

Kevin Hines and Amber Abigail Lazarus were married on 19 Sep 2015 in Lone Tree, CO. They had the following children:

    i.   **Abigail Hines** was born on 21 Oct 2018 in CO.

    ii. **Eillism Hines** was born on 06 Oct 2020 in CO.

21. **Kevin Thomas Rechcigl**-5 (Nancy Ann-4, Mary-3, Peter Vasilev-2, Wasil-1) was born on 09 Oct 1991 in Bradenton, FL.

Jordan Robbins daughter of Douglass Robbins and Ivonne was born on 10 Jan 1992 in Camarillo, CA.

Kevin Thomas Rechcigl and Jordan Robbins were married on 12 May 2018 in Jacksonville, FL. They had the following children:

    i.   **James Douglas Rechcigl** was born on 05 Jan 2021 in Jacksonville, FL.

    ii. **Evelyn Marie Rechcigl** was born 29 May 2023 in Jacksonville, FL.

Goidich Family

Generation 1

Gregory Gojdycz-1 was born in Zdynia, Poland.

Martha Barnai daughter of Stephan Barnai and Yarka was born about 1868 in Zdynia, Poland. She died on 07 Dec 1906.

Gregory Gojdycz and Martha Barnai married. They had the following children:

3.   i. **Mary Goidich** was born on 06 Aug 1892 in Jersey City, NJ. She died on 08 Dec 1963 in Roselle Park, NJ.
4.   ii. **Anna Goidich** was born on 07 Jul 1895 in Jersey City, NJ. She married Peter Vasilev Rishko in 1914. She died on 24 Nov 1973 in Linden, NJ.
    iii. **Andrew Goidich** was born on 08 Dec 1903. He died on 08 Dec 1963 in Lakewood, NJ.

Generation 2

2. **Mary Goidich**-2 (Gregory-1) was born on 06 Aug 1892 in Jersey City, NJ. She died on 08 Dec 1963 in Roselle Park, NJ.

Alex Mulford.

Alex Mulford and Mary Goidich married. They had the following children:

4.   i. **Tom Mulford.**
5.   ii. **Rose Mulford.**
6.   iii. **Magdalene Mulford.**
    iv. **Harry Mulford.**
7.   v. **Mabel Mulford.**
8.   vi. **2nd Alex Mulford.**
    vii. **Anna Mulford.**
    viii. **Josef Mulford.**
    ix. **Beatrice Mulford.**
    x. **Albert Mulford.**
    xi. **Mary Mulford.**

3. **Anna Goidich**-2 (Gregory-1) was born on 07 Jul 1895 in Jersey City, NJ. She died on 24 Nov 1973 in Linden, NJ.

Peter Vasilev Rishko son of Wasil Rishko and Mary Kirpan was born on 08 Jun 1890 in Alden Station, PA. He died on 08 Feb 1941 in Alden, PA. Peter Vasilev Rishko and Anna Goidich were married in 1914. They had the following children:

      i. **Anna Rishko** was born on 07 Jul 1915 in Alden, PA. She died on 24 Oct 1941.

9.   ii. **John Rishko** was born on 22 Jul 1917 in Alden Station, PA. He married Florence Moranski on 22 Jul 1944. He died on 24 Jul 1986 in North Hollywood, Los Angeles, CA.

10.   iii. **George Rishko** was born on 13 May 1919 in Alden, PA. He married Irene Tania Zuk on 20 Feb 1977 in Whippany, NJ.

      iv. **Helen Rishko** was born on 23 May 1921 in Alden, PA. She died on 26 Dec 2015 in Linden, NJ.

      v. **Paul Rishko** was born on 23 Jun 1926 in Alden, PA.

11.   vi. **Irene Rishko** was born on 20 Feb 1928 in Alden, PA. She married Daniel E. Lynch on 04 Aug 1951 in Elizabeth, NJ. She died on 20 Feb 2003 in Clark,NJ.

12.   vii. **Mary Rishko** was born on 27 Nov 1930 in Alden, PA. She married Joseph Palko on 18 Sep 1954 in Elizabeth, NJ. She died on 03 Dec 1994 in Bradenton, FL.

13.   viii. **Mildred Rishko** was born on 27 Apr 1934 in Alden, PA. She married Allistair Duncan Black on 13 Aug 1966 in Syosset, NY.

14.   ix. **Peter Rishko** was born on 05 Oct 1936 in Alden, PA. He married Eleanor Giacalone on 09 Oct 1965 in Elizabeth, NJ. He died on 27 Aug 1997 in Clark, NJ.

Generation 3

4.   **Tom Mulford**-3 (Mary-2, Gregory-1).
Helen.
Tom Mulford and Helen married. They had the following children:
      i. **Tom Mulford.**
      ii. **son Mulford.**

5.   **Rose Mulford**-3 (Mary-2, Gregory-1).
Norman Hyslip.

Norman Hyslip and Rose Mulford married. They had the following children:
- i. **Barbara Hyslip**.

6. **Magdalene Mulford**-3 (Mary-2, Gregory-1).
Massone.
Massone and Magdalene Mulford married. They had the following children:
- i. **Marianne Massone**.

7. **Mabel Mulford**-3 (Mary-2, Gregory-1).
Tom Angelo.
Tom Angelo and Mabel Mulford married. They had the following children:
- i. **Jeffrey Angelo**.

8. **2nd Alex Mulford**-3 (Mary-2, Gregory-1).
2nd Alex Mulford and unknown spouse married. They had the following children:
- i. **dau Mulford**.

9. **John Rishko**-3 (Anna-2, Gregory-1) was born on 22 Jul 1917 in Alden Station, PA. He died on 24 Jul 1986 in North Hollywood, Los Angeles, CA.
Florence Moranski daughter of Frank Moranski and Mary Genzik was born on 25 Oct 1924 in Dupont, PA.
John Rishko and Florence Moranski were married on 22 Jul 1944. They had the following children:
- 15. i. **John Richard Rishko** was born on 20 Sep 1954 in Inglewood, NJ. He married Norine Ann Koles on 29 Oct 1977.
- 16. ii. **Cynthia Marie Rishko** was born on 15 Jul 1956. She married Bruce Lazarus in Oct 1980 in Princeton, NJ.

10. **George Rishko**-3 (Anna-2, Gregory-1) was born on 13 May 1919 in Alden, PA.
Irene Tania Zuk was born on 06 Aug 1930.
George Rishko and Irene Tania Zuk were married on 20 Feb 1977 in Whippany, NJ. They had the following children:
- 17. i. **Lydia Rishko** was born on 27 Aug 1964. She married Roman

Klufus on 16 May 1992.

18. ii. **Zina Rishko** was born on 27 Sep 1970.

11. **Irene Rishko**-3 (Anna-2, Gregory-1) was born on 20 Feb 1928 in Alden, PA. She died on 20 Feb 2003 in Clark,NJ.

Daniel E. Lynch was born on 28 Oct 1921. He died on 18 Dec 2009 in Clark, NJ.

Daniel E. Lynch and Irene Rishko were married on 04 Aug 1951 in Elizabeth, NJ. They had the following children:

   i. **Daniel Lynch** was born on 30 Dec 1952.

19. ii. **Maryanne Lynch** was born on 26 Aug 1954.

20. iii. **Michael Lynch** was born on 23 May 1957. He married Pamela Moses on 30 Sep 1989.

21. iv. **Patricia Lynch** was born on 26 Sep 1959. She married John Weilandics on 25 Apr 1987.

12. **Mary Rishko**-3 (Anna-2, Gregory-1) was born on 27 Nov 1930 in Alden, PA. She died on 03 Dec 1994 in Bradenton, FL.

Joseph Palko son of John Bernard Palko and Anna Kopcho was born on 27 Sep 1926 in Nanticoke, PA. He died in 2010.

Joseph Palko and Mary Rishko were married on 18 Sep 1954 in Elizabeth, NJ. They had the following children:

22. i. **Nancy Ann Palko** was born on 26 Sep 1961 in Morristown, NJ. She married John Edward Rechcigl on 30 Jul 1983 in Dover, NJ.

13. **Mildred Rishko**-3 (Anna-2, Gregory-1) was born on 27 Apr 1934 in Alden, PA.

Allistair Duncan Black was born on 06 May 1939. He died on 16 Feb 1996 in Hackettstown, NJ.

Allistair Duncan Black and Mildred Rishko were married on 13 Aug 1966 in Syosset, NY. They had the following children:

   i. **Douglas Alexander Black** was born on 22 Oct 1972. He died on 16 Jul 1998 in Hackettstown, NJ.

14. **Peter Rishko**-3 (Anna-2, Gregory-1) was born on 05 Oct 1936 in Alden, PA. He died on 27 Aug 1997 in Clark, NJ.

Eleanor Giacalone was born on 26 Dec 1938. She died on 10 Jun 1990 in

Clark, NJ.

Peter Rishko and Eleanor Giacalone were married on 09 Oct 1965 in Elizabeth, NJ. They had the following children:

23. i. **Carrie Ann Rishko** was born on 29 Jul 1972 in Clark, NJ. She married Sean Edwin Cusack on 17 Apr 1999 in Princeton, NJ.
24. ii. **Peter Rishko** was born on 27 Dec 1974. He married Jennifer Becmer on 02 Jul 2005.

Generation 4

15. **John Richard Rishko**-4 (John-3, Anna-2, Gregory-1) was born on 20 Sep 1954 in Inglewood, NJ.

    Norine Ann Koles was born on 04 Sep 1953 in Newark, NJ.

    John Richard Rishko and Norine Ann Koles were married on 29 Oct 1977. They had the following children:
    25. i. **Kevin John Rishko** was born on 16 Dec 1982 in Tarzana, CA. He married Favianna Francisco on 02 Jun 2007.
        ii. **Shawn Richard Rishko** was born on 27 Dec 1983 in Tarzana, CA. He died on 07 Feb 2006 in Oak Park, CA.
        iii. **Richard Alan Rishko** was born on 27 Mar 1986 in Tarzana, CA.

16. **Cynthia Marie Rishko**-4 (John-3, Anna-2, Gregory-1) was born on 15 Jul 1956.

    Bruce Lazarus.

    Bruce Lazarus and Cynthia Marie Rishko were married in Oct 1980 in Princeton, NJ. They had the following children:
    26. i. **Amber Abigail Lazarus** was born on 04 Aug 1984. She married Kevin Hines on 19 Sep 2015 in Lone Tree, CO.
        ii. **Justin Lazarus** was born on 14 Jul 1987.

17. **Lydia Rishko**-4 (George-3, Anna-2, Gregory-1) was born on 27 Aug 1964.

    Roman Klufus.

    Roman Klufus and Lydia Rishko were married on 16 May 1992. They had the following children:
    i. **Andrew Klufus** was born on 18 Jan 1995.
    ii. **Alexandra Klufus** was born on 12 Sep 1996.
    iii. **Larisson Anna Klufus** was born on 29 May 1998.

18. **Zina Rishko**-4 (George-3, Anna-2, Gregory-1) was born on 27 Sep 1970.
    Mark Zinych.
    Mark Zinych and Zina Rishko married. They had the following children:
    i. **Andrea Zinych.**
19. **Maryanne Lynch**-4 (Irene-3, Anna-2, Gregory-1) was born on 26 Aug 1954.
    Kenneth Kirchner was born on 09 Jan 1953.
    Kenneth Kirchner and Maryanne Lynch married. They had the following children:
    i. **Andrew Paul Kirchner** was born on 03 May 1982 in Bakersfield, CA.
    ii. **Laura Ann Kirchner** was born on 13 Mar 1985.
    iii. **Jennifer Claire Kirchner** was born on 10 Dec 1987 in Bakersfield, CA.
20. **Michael Lynch**-4 (Irene-3, Anna-2, Gregory-1) was born on 23 May 1957.
    Pamela Moses was born on 23 Mar 1960.
    Michael Lynch and Pamela Moses were married on 30 Sep 1989. They had the following children:
    i. **Anna Grace Lynch** was born on 26 Dec 1993.
    ii. **Kelsey Elizabeth Lynch.**
21. **Patricia Lynch**-4 (Irene-3, Anna-2, Gregory-1) was born on 26 Sep 1959.
    John Weilandics.
    John Weilandics and Patricia Lynch were married on 25 Apr 1987. They had the following children:
    i. **Allison Elizabeth Weilandics** was born on 15 Jan 1989 in Clark, NJ.
    ii. **Kathryn Anne Weilandics** was born on 25 Oct 1996 in Clark, NJ.
22. **Nancy Ann Palko**-4 (Mary-3, Anna-2, Gregory-1) was born on 26 Sep 1961 in Morristown, NJ.
    John Edward Rechcigl son of Mila (Miloslav) Rechcigl Jr. and Eva Edwards (Eisnerová) was born on 27 Feb 1960 in Washington, D.C..
    John Edward Rechcigl and Nancy Ann Palko were married on 30 Jul 1983 in Dover, NJ. They had the following children:

GOIDICH FAMILY

  i. **Gregory John Rechcigl** was born on 19 Dec 1988 in Bradenton, FL.

28. ii. **Kevin Thomas Rechcigl** was born on 09 Oct 1991 in Bradenton, FL. He married Jordan Robbins on 12 May 2018 in Jacksonville, FL.

  iii. **Lindsey Nicole Rechcigl** was born on 03 Nov 1994 in Bradenton, FL.

23. **Carrie Ann Rishko**-4 (Peter-3, Anna-2, Gregory-1) was born on 29 Jul 1972 in Clark, NJ.
Sean Edwin Cusack was born on 21 May 1971.
Sean Edwin Cusack and Carrie Ann Rishko were married on 17 Apr 1999 in Princeton, NJ. They had the following children:
    i. **Aiden Cusack** was born on 26 Jun 2005.
    ii. **Connor Cusack** was born on 20 Mar 2007.

24. **Peter Rishko**-4 (Peter-3, Anna-2, Gregory-1) was born on 27 Dec 1974.
Jennifer Becmer.
Peter Rishko and Jennifer Becmer were married on 02 Jul 2005. They had the following children:
    i. **Ella Rishko** was born on 26 Jan 2008.
    ii. **Austin Rishko** was born on 12 Dec 2011.
Vlada Solovyaova was born on 02 Oct 1993.
Peter Rishko and Vlada Solovyaova were married on 26 Nov 2018. They had no children.

Generation 5

26. **Kevin John Rishko**-5 (John Richard-4, John-3, Anna-2, Gregory-1) was born on 16 Dec 1982 in Tarzana, CA.
Favianna Francisco was born on 26 Aug 1981.
Kevin John Rishko and Favianna Francisco were married on 02 Jun 2007. They had the following children:
    i. **Blakely Kate Rishko** was born on 08 Oct 2012.
    ii. **John Beckham Rishko** was born on 14 Mar 2016.

27. **Amber Abigail Lazarus**-5 (Cynthia Marie-4, John-3, Anna-2, Gregory-1) was born on 04 Aug 1984.
Kevin Hines.

Kevin Hines and Amber Abigail Lazarus were married on 19 Sep 2015 in Lone Tree, CO. They had the following children:
- i. **Abigail Hines** was born on 21 Oct 2018 in CO.
- ii. **Eillism Hines** was born on 06 Oct 2020 in CO.

28. **Kevin Thomas Rechcigl**-5 (Nancy Ann-4, Mary-3, Anna-2, Gregory-1) was born on 09 Oct 1991 in Bradenton, FL.

    Jordan Robbins daughter of Douglass Robbins and Ivonne was born on 10 Jan 1992 in Camarillo, CA.

    Kevin Thomas Rechcigl and Jordan Robbins were married on 12 May 2018 in Jacksonville, FL. They had the following children:
    - i. **James Douglas Rechcigl** was born on 05 Jan 2021 in Jacksonville, FL.
    - ii. **Evelyn Marie Rechcigl** was born 29 May 2023 in Jacksonville, FL.

F. Karen Rechcigl's Husband Side

Kollecas (Kolecas) Family[10]

The name is of northern Mirditor origin, and surname was derived from Kol Leka. The ancestors could be traced to the ancient Albanian family of Nik Gjinaj.

Generation 1

1. **Spiro Koleka-1.**
   Unknown.
   Spiro Koleka and Unknown married. They had the following children:
   1. i. **Dhimitre Koleka.**

Generation 2

2. **Dhimitre Koleka**-2 (Spiro-1).
   Maria Pilla.
   Dhimitre Koleka and Maria Pilla married. They had the following children:
   3. i. **Costas Kolecas.**
      ii. **Kristo Kolecas.**
   4. iii. **Spiro Koleka.**

Generation 3

3. **Costas Kolecas**-3 (Dhimitre-2, Spiro-1).
   Katera Kaia.
   Costas Kolecas and Katera Kaia married. They had the following children:
   5. i. **Odysseus Kolecas.**
   6. ii. **Dimitri Kolecas.**
4. **Spiro Koleka**-3 (Dhimitre-2, Spiro-1).
   Unknown.

---

[10] The parts of this genealogy may not be entirely accurate because some of the interrelationships could not be verified, particularly with reference to Spiro Koleka.

Spiro Koleka and Unknown married. They had the following children:

    7. i. **Jorgo Kolecas** was born in 1879 in Vuno, Albania. He died in 1940.

Generation 4

5. **Odysseus Kolecas**-4 (Costas-3, Dhimitre-2, Spiro-1).
Sana Ballia.
Odysseus Kolecas and Sana Ballia married. They had the following children:

    8. i. **Anastasios Kolecas** was born in 1888 in Vuno, Albania. He died in 1962.

    ii. **Bsil Kolecas.**

    iii. **Lamoru Kolecas.**

6. **Dimitri Kolecas**-4 (Costas-3, Dhimitre-2, Spiro-1).
Unknown.
Dimitri Kolecas and Unknown married. They had the following children:

    i. **Heralambos Kolecas.**

    ii. **Ilune Kolecas.**

    10. iii. **Antonio Kolecas.**

    iv. **Kome Kolecas.**

    v. **Katere Kolecas.**

7. **Jorgo Koleka**-4 (Spiro-3, Dhimitre-2, Spiro-1) was born in 1879 in Vuno, Albania. He was an Albanian politician, active in the 1920's. He died in 1940.
Unknown.
Jorgo Kolecas and Unknown married. They had the following children:

    10. i. **Pano Koleka.**

    ii. **Thanas Koleka.**

    11. iii. **Spiro Koleka.**

    iv. **Lene Koleka.**

    v. **Aleks Koleka.**

    vi. **Koco Koleka.**

Generation 5

8. **Anastasios Kolecas**-5 (Odysseus-4, Costas-3, Dhimitre-2, Spiro-1) was

born in 1888 in Vuno, Albania. He died in 1962.

Olga Llaguri daughter of Llaguri and Unknown was born in 1900 in Volos, Greece. She died in 1972. Anastasios Kolecas and Olga Llaguri married. They had the following children:

12. i. **Christopher Thomas (Kolecas) Collier** was born on 07 Jan 1922.
    ii. **Odysseus Kolecas** was born in 1924.
13. iii. **Joanna Kolecas** was born on 14 Oct 1928.

9. **Antonio Kolecas**-5 (Dimitri-4, Costas-3, Dhimitre-2, Spiro-1).
   Unknown.
   Antonio Kolecas and Unknown married. They had the following children:
   14. i. **Dhimitraq Kolecas.**
       ii. **Lefteri Kolecas.**

10. **Pano Koleka**-5 (Jorgo-4, Spiro-3, Dhimitre-2, Spiro-1).
    Unknown.
    Pano Koleka and Unknown married. They had the following children:
    i. **Katine Koleka.**
    15. ii. **Minelle Koleka.**

11. **Spiro Koleka**-5 (Jorgo-4, Spiro-3, Dhimitre-2, Spiro-1). (1908-2001). b. in Vuno, nr. Himara. He was an important Albanian statesman, communist politician and military officer during World War II and civil engineer by profession.
    Unknown.
    Spiro Koleka and Unknown married. They had the following children:
    16. i. **Gogo Koleka.**
        ii. **Mile Koleka.**
        iii. **Alegi Koleka.**

Generation 6

12. **Christopher Thomas (Kolecas) Collier**-6 (Anastasios-5, Odysseus-4, Costas-3, Dhimitre-2, Spiro-1) was born on 07 Jan 1922 in Elyria, OH. He died 13 June, 2021 in Germantown, MD.
    Amelia Malatras daughter of Demosthenes Malatras and Malamo Malamosis was born on 03 Apr 1928 in Oak Hill, WV. She died on 22 Jul

2004 in DE.

Christopher Thomas (Kolecas) Collier and Amelia Malatras married. They had the following children:

17. i. **Thomas Kollecas** was born on 25 Jan 1950 in Washington, DC.
    ii. **Melanie Collier** was born on 11 Aug 1952 in Washington, DC.
18. iii. **Ulysses Kollecas** was born on 20 Mar 1958 in Washington, DC. He married Karen Rechcigl on 25 Aug 1990 in Bethesda, MD.
    iv. **Gregory Collier** was born on 02 Nov 1962 in Washington, DC.

He divorced his first wife.

Helen Konstantia Siderapoulos. She was born July 24, 1952 in Serres, Greece and died December 6, 2011.

Christopher Thomas (Kolecas) Collier and Helen Siderapoulos married on 24 August, 1978. They had the following children:

19. **Christina Eliza Collier** was born 29 Oct., 1979 in Washington, DC. She is married to Charles Summers, Jr. They had 3 children:
    i. **Charles Christopher Summers**
    ii. **Blake Alexander Summers**
    iii. **Olivia Katherine Summers**
20. **Joanna Tatiana Collier** was born 1 Oct., 1981 in Washington, DC. She is married to Richard Green. They had 2 children:
    i. **Madelyn Green**
    ii. **Ava Green**

13. **Ulysses Kolecas**-6 (Anastasios-5, Odysseus-4, Costas-3, Dhimitre-2, Spiro-1) was born on 29 Nov 1923 in Elyria, OH. He was a marine hero who lost his life by the effects of the second bombing at Nagasaki. He died 9 Aug 1945. He was awarded The Purple Heart and The Bronze Star.

14. **Joanna Kolecas**-6 (Anastasios-5, Odysseus-4, Costas-3, Dhimitre-2, Spiro-1) was born on 14 Oct 1928 in Elyria, OH.

Pirro Ndrenika was born in 1922 in Vuno, Albania.

Pirro Ndrenika and Joanna Kolecas married. They had the following children:

20. i. **Energjik Ndrenika** was born on 01 Jul 1952 in Himara, Albania.
21. ii. **Elena Ndrenika** was born on 24 Mar 1955 in Vlore, Albania.

iii. **Miranda Ndrenika** was born on 15 Nov 1957 in Durres, Albania.

22. iv. **Irakli Ndrenika** was born on 23 Dec 1967 in Durres, Albania.

15. **Dhimitraq Kolecas**-6 (Antonio-5, Dimitri-4, Costas-3, Dhimitre-2, Spiro-1).

Unknown.

Dhimitraq Kolecas and Unknown married. They had the following children:

23. i. **Andon Kolecas**.
24. ii. **Neli Kolecas**.
    iii. **Thodori Kolecas**.

15. **Minelle Koleka**-6 (Pano-5, Jorgo-4, Spiro-3, Dhimitre-2, Spiro-1).

Unknown.

Minelle Koleka and Unknown married. They had the following children:

   i. **Lintita Koleka**.
   ii. **Rajmondo Koleka**.

16. **Gogo Koleka**-6 (Spiro-5, Jorgo-4, Spiro-3, Dhimitre-2, Spiro-1).

Unknown.

Gogo Koleka and Unknown married. They had the following children:

   i. **Tatjana Koleka**.
   ii. **Spiro Koleka**.

17. **Aneta Koleka**-6 (Spiro-5, Jorgo-4, Spiro-3, Dhimitre-2, Spiro-1). (1938-2010), b. Vuno, Albania was a graduate of medicine.

Kristaq Rama (1932-1998), b. Durres, Albania, was a sculptor.

They married and had 2 children:

   i. **Edi Rama** (1964-), b. Tirana, Albania
   ii. **Olsi Rama** (1969-), b. Tirana, Albania

Generation 7

18. **Thomas Kollecas**-7 (Christopher Thomas (Kolecas)-6, Anastasios-5, Odysseus-4, Costas-3, Dhimitre-2, Spiro-1) was born on 25 Jan 1950.

Diana Plomason.

Thomas Kollecas and Diana Plomason married. They had the following children:

a. **Christopher Kollecas** was born on 22 Jun 1984 in Rockville, MD.
   b. **Lauren Kollecas** was born on 06 May 1987 in Rockville, MD.
19. **Ulysses Kollecas**-7 (Christopher Thomas (Kolecas)-6, Anastasios-5, Odysseus-4, Costas-3, Dhimitre-2, Spiro-1) was born on 20 Mar 1958 in Washington, DC.

Karen Rechcigl daughter of Mila (Miloslav) Rechcigl Jr. and Eva Edwards (Eisnerová) was born on 16 Apr 1962 in Washington, DC.

Ulysses Kollecas and Karen Rechcigl were married on 25 Aug 1990 in Bethesda, MD. They had the following children:
   i. **Kristin Kollecas** was born on 04 May 1993 in Albuquerque, NM.
   ii. **Paul Kollecas** was born on 02 Jun 1995 in Albuquerque, NM.
19. **Christina Eliza Collier**-7 (Christopher Thomas (Kolecas)-6, Anastasios-5, Odysseus-4, Costas-3, Dhimitre-2, Spiro-1) was born 29 Oct., 1979 in Washington, DC.

Charles Summers, Jr., b. 19 July 1914 in Cheverly, MD

Charles Summers and Christina Eliza married on 23, 2002 in Thessalonike Greece. They had the following children:
   i. **Charles Christopher Summers** born 1 Nov., 2002 in Washington, DC.
   ii. **Blake Alexander Summers** born 05 May, 2009 in Silver Spring, MD
   iii. **Olivia Katherine Summers** born 15 Sept 2010 in Rockville, MD
20. **Joanna Tatiana Collier**-7 (Christopher Thomas (Kolecas)-6, Anastasios-5, Odysseus-4, Costas-3, Dhimitre-2, Spiro-1) was born 1 Oct., 1981 in Washington, DC.

Richard Bao Phung Green born on Dec., 1974 in Vietnam.

Joanna and Richard were married on 30 Oct., 2010 in Bethesda, MD. They had the following children:
   i. **Madelyn Lan Green** born on 26 Dec., 2012 in Silver Spring, MD
   ii. **Ava Mai Green** born 25 Oct. 2017, in Silver Spring, MD
21. **Energjik Ndrenika**-7 (Joanna-6, Anastasios-5, Odysseus-4, Costas-3, Dhimitre-2, Spiro-1) was born on 01 Jul 1952 in Himara, Albania.

Vilma Miculi was born on 01 Nov 1958.

Energjik Ndrenika and Vilma Miculi married. They had the following children:
   i.   **Enea Ndrenika** was born on 01 Jun 1984 in Durres.
   ii. **Joanna Ndrenika** was born on 18 Mar 1989 in Durres.
21. **Elena Ndrenika**-7 (Joanna-6, Anastasios-5, Odysseus-4, Costas-3, Dhimitre-2, Spiro-1) was born on 24 Mar 1955 in Vlore, Albania.
   Prokop Kushi was born on 27 May 1944 in Durres.
   Prokop Kushi and Elena Ndrenika married. They had the following children:
   i. **Edmond Kushi** was born on 11 Aug 1979 in Durres.
   ii. **Enita Kushi** was born on 23 Sep 1984 in Tiran.
23 **Irakli Ndrenika**-7 (Joanna-6, Anastasios-5, Odysseus-4, Costas-3, Dhimitre-2, Spiro-1) was born on 23 Dec 1967 in Durres, Albania.
   Migena Shoro.
   Irakli Ndrenika and Migena Shoro married. They had the following children:
   i.   **Joni Ndrenika** was born on 29 Apr 2002.
   ii. **Albi Ndrenika** was born on 18 Mar 2004.
24. **Andon Kolecas**-7 (Dhimitraq-6, Antonio-5, Dimitri-4, Costas-3, Dhimitre-2, Spiro-1).
   Jeti.
   Andon Kolecas and Jeti married. They had the following children:
   i.   **Elona Kolecas**.
   ii. **Anieza Kolecas**.
25. **Neli Kolecas**-7 (Dhimitraq-6, Antonio-5, Dimitri-4, Costas-3, Dhimitre-2, Spiro-1).
   Manol.
   Manol and Neli Kolecas married. They had the following children:
   i.   **Anila Manol**.
   ii. **Ervin Manol**.
26. **Edi Rama**-7 (Dhimitraq-6, Antonio-5, Dimitri-4, Costas-3, Dhimitre-2, Spiro-1). (1964-), b. Tirana, Albania. He is a current Prime Minister of Albania. Previously he was Mayor of Tirana, Albania, (since 2000).

Married first actress **Matilda Makoci** in 1986 and had a son **Gregor** (or **Gregun**) before 1991.They divorced in 1991.

Married second an economist and social civil activist **Linda Basha**. They had a son **Zaho**, b. 2014

27. **Olsi Rama**-7 (Dhimitraq-6, Antonio-5, Dimitri-4, Costas-3, Dhimitre-2, Spiro-1). (1969-), b. Tirana, Albania. He is general director of football club Partizani Tirana.

Malatras Family

Generation 1

1. **Vasiliki Malatras**-1.
   Elizabeth.
   Vasiliki Malatras and Elizabeth married. They had the following children:
   2. i. **Alexander Malatras.**

Generation 2

2. **Alexander Malatras**-2 (Vasiliki-1).
   Lillian Hartopoulos daughter of George Hartopoulos and Yaroula Hartopoulos. Alexander Malatras and Lillian Hartopoulos married. They had the following children:
   i. i. **Demosthenes Malatras** was born on 01 Jan 1890. He married Malamo Malamosis on 26 Oct 1914. He died on 05 Jun 1995.

Generation 3

3. **Demosthenes Malatras**-3 (Alexander-2, Vasiliki-1) was born on 01 Jan 1890. He died on 05 Jun 1995.
   Malamo Malamosis daughter of John Malamosis and Mary.
   Demosthenes Malatras and Malamo Malamosis were married on 26 Oct 1914. They had the following children:
   a. i. **Alexandra Malatras** was born on 10 Sep 1916 in Mamchester, NH. She married Bernard ("Bernie") Thornberg on 28 Mar 1934.
   b. ii. **Louise Malatras** was born on 28 Jun 1919 in Manchester, NH.
   c. iii. **Teddy Malatras** was born on 20 Oct 1923 in Mamchester, NH.
   d. iv. **Amelia Malatras** was born on 03 Apr 1928 in Oak Hill, WV. She died on 22 Jul 2004 in DE.
   e. v. **Lula Malatras** was born on 26 Dec 1929 in Washington, DC.
   f. vi. **John Malatras** was born on 21 Oct 1933 in Washington, DC.

Generation 4

4. **Alexandra Malatras**-4 (Demosthenes-3, Alexander-2, Vasiliki-1) was born on 10 Sep 1916 in Mamchester, NH.

Bernard ("Bernie") Thornberg son of Joseph Thornberg and Alma Masters.

Bernard ("Bernie") Thornberg and Alexandra Malatras were married on 28 Mar 1934. They had the following children:

10. i. **Bernie Thornberg** was born on 06 Jun 1938 in Washington, DC. He married Helen Gianaris on 09 Sep 1967.
11. ii. **Mary Lillian Thornberg** was born on 29 Jan 1943 in Washington, DC.
12. iii. **Denny (Thornberg) Malatras** was born on 03 Nov 1944 in Washington, DC.

5. **Louise Malatras**-4 (Demosthenes-3, Alexander-2, Vasiliki-1) was born on 28 Jun 1919 in Manchester, NH.

    Steve Kokenes son of Constantine Kokenes.

    Steve Kokenes and Louise Malatras married. They had the following children:

    13. i. **Dean Kokenes** was born on 26 Jan 1943 in Washington, DC.
    14. ii. **Alexander Kokenes** was born on 22 Apr 1950 in Washington, DC.
    15. iii. **Christina Kokenes** was born on 16 Jul 1953 in Washington, DC.

6. **Teddy Malatras**-4 (Demosthenes-3, Alexander-2, Vasiliki-1) was born on 20 Oct 1923 in Mamchester, NH.

    Ceil.

    Teddy Malatras and Ceil married. They had the following children:

    16. i. **Steven Malatras.**
        ii. **Dennis Malatras.**
        iii. **Patty Malatras.**

7. **Amelia Malatras**-4 (Demosthenes-3, Alexander-2, Vasiliki-1) was born on 03 Apr 1928 in Oak Hill, WV. She died on 22 Jul 2004 in DE.

    Christopher Thomas (Kolecas) Collier son of Anastasios Kolecas and Olga Llaguri was born on 07 Jan 1922.

    Christopher Thomas (Kolecas) Collier and Amelia Malatras married. They had the following children:

    17. i. **Thomas Kollecas** was born on 25 Jan 1950.
        ii. **Melanie Collier** was born on 11 Aug 1952 in Washington, DC.

MALATRAS FAMILY

  18. iii. **Ulysses Kollecas** was born on 20 Mar 1958 in Washington, DC. He married Karen Rechcigl on 25 Aug 1990 in Bethesda, MD.

   iv. **Gregory Collier** was born on 02 Nov 1962.

2. **Lula Malatras**-4 (Demosthenes-3, Alexander-2, Vasiliki-1) was born on 26 Dec 1929 in Washington, DC.

 Frank Strachan son of Paul Ambrose Strachan and Avery Pearl Bell. Frank Strachan and Lula Malatras married. They had the following children:

   Melanie Strachan was born on 20 Mar 1952.

  5. ii. **Paul Strachan** was born on 28 Mar 1956 in Washington, DC. He married Elizabeth ("Liz") Marie Nance about 16 Jun 1990.

3. **John Malatras**-4 (Demosthenes-3, Alexander-2, Vasiliki-1) was born on 21 Oct 1933 in Washington, DC.

 Lu.

 John Malatras and Lu married. They had the following children:

   Tony Malatras was born about 1950. He died on 07 Apr 1973.

  20. ii. **Mark Malatras** was born about 1960. He died on 30 Dec 1990.

Generation 5

10. **Bernie Thornberg**-5 (Alexandra-4, Demosthenes-3, Alexander-2, Vasiliki-1) was born on 06 Jun 1938 in Washington, DC.

 Helen Gianaris daughter of Peter Gianaris and Mary Koutsouke.

 Bernie Thornberg and Helen Gianaris were married on 09 Sep 1967. They had the following children:

  21. i. **Alexandra Thornberg** was born on 30 Jun 1968. She married Nick Pitas on 11 Dec 1989.

   ii. **Peter John Thornberg** was born on 24 May 1973.

   iii. **Maria Eleni Thornberg** was born on 07 Aug 1983.

11. **Mary Lillian Thornberg**-5 (Alexandra-4, Demosthenes-3, Alexander-2, Vasiliki-1) was born on 29 Jan 1943 in Washington, DC.

 Bel ("Buddy") Faraby Henson.

 Bel ("Buddy") Faraby Henson and Mary Lillian Thornberg married. They had the following children:

i. **Michelle Henson** was born on 17 Feb 1962.

   22. ii. **David Henson** was born on 03 Feb 1964.

3. **Denny (Thornberg) Malatras**-5 (Alexandra-4, Demosthenes-3, Alexander-2, Vasiliki-1) was born on 3 Nov 1944 in Washington, DC.

   Grace.

   Denny (Thornberg) Malatras and Grace married. They had the following children:

   i. **Denny Thornberg** was born on 16 Mar 1966.

   Angie.

   Denny (Thornberg) Malatras and Angie married. They had the following children:

   i. **Rebecca Malatras** was born on 17 Dec 1982.

13. **Dean Kokenes**-5 (Louise-4, Demosthenes-3, Alexander-2, Vasiliki-1) was born on 26 Jan 1943 in Washington, DC.

    Mary Magyar.

    Dean Kokenes and Mary Magyar married. They had the following children:

    i. **Steven Kokenes**.

    ii. **Kristin Kokenes**.

    Jenny Rice.

    Dean Kokenes and Jenny Rice were married in Jul 1987. They had no children.

14. **Alexander Kokenes**-5 (Louise-4, Demosthenes-3, Alexander-2, Vasiliki-1) was born on 22 Apr 1950 in Washington, DC.

    Cathy.

    Alexander Kokenes and Cathy married. They had the following children:

    i. **Matthew Kokenes** was born in Charlotte, NC.

    ii. **Lauren Kokenes** was born in Charlotte, NC.

    Valerie.

    Alexander Kokenes and Valerie married. They had the following children:

    i. **Stephanie Kokenes**.

67. **Christina Kokenes**-5 (Louise-4, Demosthenes-3, Alexander-2, Vasiliki-

1) was born on 16 Jul 1953 in Washington, DC.

John Skiouris son of Kyriakos Skiouris and Lena.

John Skiouris and Christina Kokenes married. They had the following children:

    i   **Lena Skiouris** was born on 22 May 1981 in Athens, Greece.

    ii.   **Kyriakos Skiouris** was born on 04 Jan in Charlotte, NC.

    iii. **Stephanos Skiouris** was born on 05 Sep in Charlotte, NC.

17. **Steven Malatras**-5 (Teddy-4, Demosthenes-3, Alexander-2, Vasiliki-1). **Judy**.

Steven Malatras and Judy married. They had the following children:

    i.   **Cheryl Malatras**.

18. **Thomas Kollecas**-5 (Amelia-4, Demosthenes-3, Alexander-2, Vasiliki-1) was born on 25 Jan 1950.

Diana Plomason.

Thomas Kollecas and Diana Plomason married. They had the following children:

    i.   **Christopher Kollecas** was born on 22 Jun 1984 in Rockville, MD.

    ii. **Lauren Kollecas** was born on 06 May 1987 in Rockville, MD.

19. **Ulysses Kollecas**-5 (Amelia-4, Demosthenes-3, Alexander-2, Vasiliki-1) was born on 20 Mar 1958 in Washington, DC.

Karen Rechcigl daughter of Mila (Miloslav) Rechcigl Jr. and Eva Edwards (Eisnerová) was born on 16 Apr 1962 in Washington, DC.

Ulysses Kollecas and Karen Rechcigl were married on 25 Aug 1990 in Bethesda, MD. They had the following children:

    i.   **Kristin Kollecas** was born on 04 May 1993 in Albuquerque, NM.

    ii. **Paul Kollecas** was born on 02 Jun 1995 in Albuquerque, NM.

19. **Paul Strachan**-5 (Lula-4, Demosthenes-3, Alexander-2, Vasiliki-1) was born on 28 Mar 1956 in Washington, DC.

Elizabeth ("Liz") Marie Nance.

Paul Strachan and Elizabeth ("Liz") Marie Nance were married about 16 Jun 1990. They had the following children:

    i.   **Lydia Strachan** was born on 26 Feb 1991 in Charlotte, NC.

    ii. **Callie Elizabeth Strachan** was born on 26 Apr 1993 in

Charlotte, NC.
20. **Mark Malatras**-5 (John-4, Demosthenes-3, Alexander-2, Vasiliki-1) was born about 1960. He died on 30 Dec 1990.
Christine.
Mark Malatras and Christine married. They had the following children:
    i. **John Demosthenes Malatras** was born in 1990 in Charlotte, NC.

Generation 6

21. **Alexandra Thornberg**-6 (Bernie-5, Alexandra-4, Demosthenes-3, Alexander-2, Vasiliki-1) was born on 30 Jun 1968.
Nick Pitas.
Nick Pitas and Alexandra Thornberg were married on 11 Dec 1989. They had the following children:
    i. **Chrystyna Pitas** was born on 24 Mar 1990 in Washington, DC.
    ii. **Victoria Rose Pitas** was born on 18 Mar 1993 in Washington, DC.
    iii. **Michael Pitas** was born on 06 Nov 1996 in Washington, DC.
22. **David Henson**-6 (Mary Lillian-5, Alexandra-4, Demosthenes-3, Alexander-2, Vasiliki-1) was born on 3 Feb 1964.
Wendy.
David Henson and Wendy married. They had the following children:
    i. **Carlie Henson** was born on 09 Mar 1987.
    ii. **David Henson** was born on 06 Mar 1991.

Llaguri Family

Generation 1

1. **Llaguri-1.**
   Unknown.

   Llaguri and Unknown married. They had the following children:
   1. i. **Olga Llaguri** was born in 1900 in Volos, Greece. She died in 1972.
      ii. **John Llaguri**.
      iii. **child Llaguri**.

Generation 2

2. **Olga Llaguri**-2 (Father-1) was born in 1900 in Volos, Greece. She died in 1972.

   Anastasios Kolecas son of Odysseus Kolecas and Sana Ballia was born in 1888 in Vuno, Albania. He died in 1962.

   Anastasios Kolecas and Olga Llaguri married. They had the following children:
   a. i. **Christopher Thomas (Kolecas) Collier** was born on 07 Jan 1922.
      ii. **Odysseus Kolecas** was born in 1924.
   b. iii. **Joanna Kolecas** was born on 14 Oct 1928.

Generation 3

3. **Christopher Thomas (Kolecas) Collier**-3 (Olga-2, Father-1) was born on 07 Jan 1922.

   Amelia Malatras daughter of Demosthenes Malatras and Malamo Malamosis was born on 03 Apr 1928 in Oak Hill, WV. She died on 22 Jul 2004 in DE.

   Christopher Thomas (Kolecas) Collier and Amelia Malatras married. They had the following children:
   5. i. **Thomas Kollecas** was born on 25 Jan 1950.
      ii. **Melanie Collier** was born on 11 Aug 1952 in Washington, DC.
   6. iii. **Ulysses Kollecas** was born on 20 Mar 1958 in Washington, DC. He married Karen Rechcigl on 25 Aug 1990 in Bethesda, MD.
      iv. **Gregory Collier** was born on 02 Nov 1962.

   Helen Siderapoulos.

Christopher Thomas (Kolecas) Collier and Helen Siderapoulos married. They had the following children:

7. i. **Christina Collier**.

   ii. **Joanna Collier**.

4. **Joanna Kolecas**-3 (Olga-2, Father-1) was born on 14 Oct 1928.
Pirro Ndrenika was born in 1922 in Vuno, Albania.
Pirro Ndrenika and Joanna Kolecas married. They had the following children:

8. i. **Energjik Ndrenika** was born on 01 Jul 1952 in Himara, Albania.

9. ii. **Elena Ndrenika** was born on 24 Mar 1955 in Vlore, Albania.

   iii. **Miranda Ndrenika** was born on 15 Nov 1957 in Durres, Albania.

10. iv. **Irakli Ndrenika** was born on 23 Dec 1967 in Durres, Albania.

Generation 4

5. **Thomas Kollecas**-4 (Christopher Thomas (Kolecas)-3, Olga-2, Father-1) was born on 25 Jan 1950.
Diana Plomason.
Thomas Kollecas and Diana Plomason married. They had the following children:

   i. **Christopher Kollecas** was born on 22 Jun 1984 in Rockville, MD.

   ii. **Lauren Kollecas** was born on 06 May 1987 in Rockville, MD.

6. **Ulysses Kollecas**-4 (Christopher Thomas (Kolecas)-3, Olga-2, Father-1) was born on 20 Mar 1958 in Washington, DC.
Karen Rechcigl daughter of Mila (Miloslav) Rechcigl Jr. and Eva Edwards (Eisnerová) was born on 16 Apr 1962 in Washington, DC.
Ulysses Kollecas and Karen Rechcigl were married on 25 Aug 1990 in Bethesda, MD. They had the following children:

   ii. **Kristin Kollecas** was born on 04 May 1993 in Albuquerque, NM.

   iii. **Paul Kollecas** was born on 02 Jun 1995 in Albuquerque, NM.

7. **Christina Collier**-4 (Christopher Thomas (Kolecas)-3, Olga-2, Father-1).
Charles Summers.
Charles Summers and Christina Collier married. They had the following children:

   i. **Charles Summers**.

8. **Energjik Ndrenika**-4 (Joanna-3, Olga-2, Father-1) was born on 01 Jul 1952 in Himara, Albania.

   Vilma Miculi was born on 01 Nov 1958.

   Energjik Ndrenika and Vilma Miculi married. They had the following children:

   i. **Enea Ndrenika** was born on 01 Jun 1984 in Durres.

   ii. **Joanna Ndrenika** was born on 18 Mar 1989 in Durres.

9. **Elena Ndrenika**-4 (Joanna-3, Olga-2, Father-1) was born on 24 Mar 1955 in Vlore, Albania.

   Prokop Kushi was born on 27 May 1944 in Durres.

   Prokop Kushi and Elena Ndrenika married. They had the following children:

   i. **Edmond Kushi** was born on 11 Aug 1979 in Durres.

   ii. **Enita Kushi** was born on 23 Sep 1984 in Tiran.

10. **Irakli Ndrenika**-4 (Joanna-3, Olga-2, Father-1) was born on 23 Dec 1967 in Durres, Albania.

    Migena Shoro.

    Irakli Ndrenika and Migena Shoro married. They had the following children:

    i. **Joni Ndrenika** was born on 29 Apr 2002.

    ii. **Albi Ndrenika** was born on 18 Mar 2004.

Malamosis Family

Generation 1

1. **John Malamosis**-1.
   Mary.
   John Malamosis and Mary married. They had the following children:
   a. i. **Malamo Malamosis**. She married Demosthenes Malatras on 26 Oct 1914.

Generation 2

2. **Malamo Malamosis**-2 (John-1).
   Demosthenes Malatras son of Alexander Malatras and Lillian Hartopoulos was born on 01 Jan 1890. He died on 05 Jun 1995.
   Demosthenes Malatras and Malamo Malamosis were married on 26 Oct 1914. They had the following children:
   a. i. **Alexandra Malatras** was born on 10 Sep 1916 in Mamchester, NH. She married Bernard ("Bernie") Thornberg on 28 Mar 1934.
   b. ii. **Louise Malatras** was born on 28 Jun 1919 in Manchester, NH.
   c. iii. **Teddy Malatras** was born on 20 Oct 1923 in Mamchester, NH.
   d. iv. **Amelia Malatras** was born on 03 Apr 1928 in Oak Hill, WV. She died on 22 Jul 2004 in DE.
   e. v. **Lula Malatras** was born on 26 Dec 1929 in Washington, DC.
   f. vi. **John Malatras** was born on 21 Oct 1933 in Washington, DC.

Generation 3

3. **Alexandra Malatras**-3 (Malamo-2, John-1) was born on 10 Sep 1916 in Mamchester, NH.
   Bernard ("Bernie") Thornberg son of Joseph Thornberg and Alma Masters.
   Bernard ("Bernie") Thornberg and Alexandra Malatras were married on 28 Mar 1934. They had the following children:
   9. i. **Bernie Thornberg** was born on 06 Jun 1938 in Washington, DC. He married Helen Gianaris on 09 Sep 1967.
   10. ii. **Mary Lillian Thornberg** was born on 29 Jan 1943 in Washington, DC.

    11. iii. **Denny (Thornberg) Malatras** was born on 03 Nov 1944 in Washington, DC.
4. **Louise Malatras**-3 (Malamo-2, John-1) was born on 28 Jun 1919 in Manchester, NH.
   Steve Kokenes son of Constantine Kokenes.
   Steve Kokenes and Louise Malatras married. They had the following children:
   12. i. **Dean Kokenes** was born on 26 Jan 1943 in Washington, DC.
   13. ii. **Alexander Kokenes** was born on 22 Apr 1950 in Washington, DC.
   14. iii. **Christina Kokenes** was born on 16 Jul 1953 in Washington, DC.
5. **Teddy Malatras**-3 (Malamo-2, John-1) was born on 20 Oct 1923 in Mamchester, NH.
   Ceil.
   Teddy Malatras and Ceil married. They had the following children:
   15. i. **Steven Malatras.**
       ii. **Dennis Malatras.**
       iii. **Patty Malatras.**
6. **Amelia Malatras**-3 (Malamo-2, John-1) was born on 03 Apr 1928 in Oak Hill, WV. She died on 22 Jul 2004 in DE.
   Christopher Thomas (Kolecas) Collier son of Anastasios Kolecas and Olga Llaguri was born on 07 Jan 1922.
   Christopher Thomas (Kolecas) Collier and Amelia Malatras married. They had the following children:
   16. i. **Thomas Kollecas** was born on 25 Jan 1950.
       ii. **Melanie Collier** was born on 11 Aug 1952 in Washington, DC.
   17. iii. **Ulysses Kollecas** was born on 20 Mar 1958 in Washington, DC. He married Karen Rechcigl on 25 Aug 1990 in Bethesda, MD.
       iv. **Gregory Collier** was born on 02 Nov 1962.
7. **Lula Malatras**-3 (Malamo-2, John-1) was born on 26 Dec 1929 in Washington, DC.
   Frank Strachan son of Paul Ambrose Strachan and Avery Pearl Bell.
   Frank Strachan and Lula Malatras married. They had the following children:

i. **Melanie Strachan** was born on 20 Mar 1952.

   19. ii. **Paul Strachan** was born on 28 Mar 1956 in Washington, DC. He married Elizabeth ("Liz") Marie Nance about 16 Jun 1990.

8. **John Malatras**-3 (Malamo-2, John-1) was born on 21 Oct 1933 in Washington, DC.

   Lu.

   John Malatras and Lu married. They had the following children:

   i. **Tony Malatras** was born about 1950. He died on 07 Apr 1973.

   19. ii. **Mark Malatras** was born about 1960. He died on 30 Dec 1990.

Generation 4

9. **Bernie Thornberg**-4 (Alexandra-3, Malamo-2, John-1) was born on 06 Jun 1938 in Washington, DC.

   Helen Gianaris daughter of Peter Gianaris and Mary Koutsouke.

   Bernie Thornberg and Helen Gianaris were married on 09 Sep 1967. They had the following children:

   20. i. **Alexandra Thornberg** was born on 30 Jun 1968. She married Nick Pitas on 11 Dec 1989.

   ii. **Peter John Thornberg** was born on 24 May 1973.

   iii. **Maria Eleni Thornberg** was born on 07 Aug 1983.

10. **Mary Lillian Thornberg**-4 (Alexandra-3, Malamo-2, John-1) was born on 29 Jan 1943 in Washington, DC.

    Bel ("Buddy") Faraby Henson.

    Bel ("Buddy") Faraby Henson and Mary Lillian Thornberg married. They had the following children:

    i. **Michelle Henson** was born on 17 Feb 1962.

    21. ii. **David Henson** was born on 03 Feb 1964.

11. **Denny (Thornberg) Malatras**-4 (Alexandra-3, Malamo-2, John-1) was born on 03 Nov 1944 in Washington, DC.

    Grace.

    Denny (Thornberg) Malatras and Grace married. They had the following children:

    i. **Denny Thornberg** was born on 16 Mar 1966.

    Angie.

Denny (Thornberg) Malatras and Angie married. They had the following children:
   i. **Rebecca Malatras** was born on 17 Dec 1982.
12. **Dean Kokenes**-4 (Louise-3, Malamo-2, John-1) was born on 26 Jan 1943 in Washington, DC.
   Mary Magyar.
   Dean Kokenes and Mary Magyar married. They had the following children:
   i. **Steven Kokenes.**
   ii. **Kristin Kokenes. Jenny Rice.**
   Dean Kokenes and Jenny Rice were married in Jul 1987. They had no children.
13. **Alexander Kokenes**-4 (Louise-3, Malamo-2, John-1) was born on 22 Apr 1950 in Washington, DC.
   Cathy.
   Alexander Kokenes and Cathy married. They had the following children:
   i. **Matthew Kokenes** was born in Charlotte, NC.
   ii. **Lauren Kokenes** was born in Charlotte, NC.
   Valerie.
   Alexander Kokenes and Valerie married. They had the following children:
   i. **Stephanie Kokenes.**
14. **Christina Kokenes**-4 (Louise-3, Malamo-2, John-1) was born on 16 Jul 1953 in Washington, DC.
   John Skiouris son of Kyriakos Skiouris and Lena.
   John Skiouris and Christina Kokenes married. They had the following children:
   i. **Lena Skiouris** was born on 22 May 1981 in Athens, Greece.
   ii. **Kyriakos Skiouris** was born on 04 Jan in Charlotte, NC.
   iii. **Stephanos Skiouris** was born on 05 Sep in Charlotte, NC.
15. **Steven Malatras**-4 (Teddy-3, Malamo-2, John-1).
   Judy.
   Steven Malatras and Judy married. They had the following children:
   i. **Cheryl Malatras.**

16. **Thomas Kollecas**-4 (Amelia-3, Malamo-2, John-1) was born on 25 Jan 1950.
    Diana Plomason.
    Thomas Kollecas and Diana Plomason married. They had the following children:
    i. **Christopher Kollecas** was born on 22 Jun 1984 in Rockville, MD.
    ii. **Lauren Kollecas** was born on 06 May 1987 in Rockville, MD.
17. **Ulysses Kollecas**-4 (Amelia-3, Malamo-2, John-1) was born on 20 Mar 1958 in Washington, DC.
    Karen Rechcigl daughter of Mila (Miloslav) Rechcigl Jr. and Eva Edwards (Eisnerová) was born on 16 Apr 1962 in Washington, DC.
    Ulysses Kollecas and Karen Rechcigl were married on 25 Aug 1990 in Bethesda, MD. They had the following children:
    i. **Kristin Kollecas** was born on 04 May 1993 in Albuquerque, NM.
    ii. **Paul Kollecas** was born on 02 Jun 1995 in Albuquerque, NM.
18. **Paul Strachan**-4 (Lula-3, Malamo-2, John-1) was born on 28 Mar 1956 in Washington, DC.
    Elizabeth ("Liz") Marie Nance.
    Paul Strachan and Elizabeth ("Liz") Marie Nance were married about 16 Jun 1990. They had the following children:
    i. **Lydia Strachan** was born on 26 Feb 1991 in Charlotte, NC.
    ii. **Callie Elizabeth Strachan** was born on 26 Apr 1993 in Charlotte, NC.
19. **Mark Malatras**-4 (John-3, Malamo-2, John-1) was born about 1960. He died on 30 Dec 1990.
    Christine.
    Mark Malatras and Christine married. They had the following children:
    i. **John Demosthenes Malatras** was born in 1990 in Charlotte, NC.

Generation 5

20. **Alexandra Thornberg**-5 (Bernie-4, Alexandra-3, Malamo-2, John-1) was born on 30 Jun 1968.
    Nick Pitas.

Nick Pitas and Alexandra Thornberg were married on 11 Dec 1989. They had the following children:
- i. **Chrystyna Pitas** was born on 24 Mar 1990 in Washington, DC.
- ii. **Victoria Rose Pitas** was born on 18 Mar 1993 in Washington, DC.
- iii. **Michael Pitas** was born on 06 Nov 1996 in Washington, DC.

21. **David Henson**-5 (Mary Lillian-4, Alexandra-3, Malamo-2, John-1) was born on 03 Feb 1964.

    Wendy.

    David Henson and Wendy married. They had the following children:
    - i. **Carlie Henson** was born on 09 Mar 1987.
    - ii. **David Henson** was born on 06 Mar 1991.

Hartopoulos Family

Generation 1

1. **George Hartopoulos**-1.
   Yaroula Hartopulos.
   George Hartopoulos and Yaroula Hartopulos married. They had the following children:
   2. i. **Lillian Hartopoulos.**

Generation 2

2. **Lillian Hartopoulos**-2 (George-1).
   Alexander Malatras son of Vasiliki Malatras and Elizabeth.
   Alexander Malatras and Lillian Hartopoulos married. They had the following children:
   3. i. **Demosthenes Malatras** was born on 01 Jan 1890. He married Malamo Malamosis on 26 Oct 1914. He died on 05 Jun 1995.

Generation 3

3. **Demosthenes Malatras**-3 (Lillian-2, George-1) was born on 01 Jan 1890. He died on 05 Jun 1995.
   Malamo Malamosis daughter of John Malamosis and Mary.
   Demosthenes Malatras and Malamo Malamosis were married on 26 Oct 1914. They had the following children:
   4. i. **Alexandra Malatras** was born on 10 Sep 1916 in Mamchester, NH. She married Bernard ("Bernie") Thornberg on 28 Mar 1934.
   5. ii. **Louise Malatras** was born on 28 Jun 1919 in Manchester, NH.
   6. iii. **Teddy Malatras** was born on 20 Oct 1923 in Mamchester, NH.
   7. iv. **Amelia Malatras** was born on 03 Apr 1928 in Oak Hill, WV. She died on 22 Jul 2004 in DE.
   8. v. **Lula Malatras** was born on 26 Dec 1929 in Washington, DC.
   9. vi. **John Malatras** was born on 21 Oct 1933 in Washington, DC.

Generation 4

4. **Alexandra Malatras**-4 (Demosthenes-3, Lillian-2, George-1) was born on 10 Sep 1916 in Mamchester, NH.

Bernard ("Bernie") Thornberg son of Joseph Thornberg and Alma Masters.

Bernard ("Bernie") Thornberg and Alexandra Malatras were married on 28 Mar 1934. They had the following children:

10. i. **Bernie Thornberg** was born on 06 Jun 1938 in Washington, DC. He married Helen Gianaris on 09 Sep 1967.
11. ii. **Mary Lillian Thornberg** was born on 29 Jan 1943 in Washington, DC.
12. iii. **Denny (Thornberg) Malatras** was born on 03 Nov 1944 in Washington, DC.

5. **Louise Malatras**-4 (Demosthenes-3, Lillian-2, George-1) was born on 28 Jun 1919 in Manchester, NH.

Steve Kokenes son of Constantine Kokenes.

Steve Kokenes and Louise Malatras married. They had the following children:

13. i. **Dean Kokenes** was born on 26 Jan 1943 in Washington, DC.
14. ii. **Alexander Kokenes** was born on 22 Apr 1950 in Washington, DC.
15. iii. **Christina Kokenes** was born on 16 Jul 1953 in Washington, DC.

6. **Teddy Malatras**-4 (Demosthenes-3, Lillian-2, George-1) was born on 20 Oct 1923 in Mamchester, NH.

Ceil.

Teddy Malatras and Ceil married. They had the following children:

16. i. **Steven Malatras**.
    ii. **Dennis Malatras**.
    iii. **Patty Malatras**.

7. **Amelia Malatras**-4 (Demosthenes-3, Lillian-2, George-1) was born on 03 Apr 1928 in Oak Hill, WV. She died on 22 Jul 2004 in DE.

Christopher Thomas (Kolecas) Collier son of Anastasios Kolecas and Olga Llaguri was born on 07 Jan 1922.

Christopher Thomas (Kolecas) Collier and Amelia Malatras married. They had the following children:

17. i. **Thomas Kollecas** was born on 25 Jan 1950.
    ii. **Melanie Collier** was born on 11 Aug 1952 in Washington, DC.

18. iii. **Ulysses Kollecas** was born on 20 Mar 1958 in Washington, DC. He married Karen Rechcigl on 25 Aug 1990 in Bethesda, MD.
    iv. **Gregory Collier** was born on 02 Nov 1962.
8. **Lula Malatras**-4 (Demosthenes-3, Lillian-2, George-1) was born on 26 Dec 1929 in Washington, DC.
   Frank Strachan son of Paul Ambrose Strachan and Avery Pearl Bell.
   Frank Strachan and Lula Malatras married. They had the following children:
       i. **Melanie Strachan** was born on 20 Mar 1952.
   19. ii. **Paul Strachan** was born on 28 Mar 1956 in Washington, DC. He married Elizabeth ("Liz") Marie Nance about 16 Jun 1990.
9. **John Malatras**-4 (Demosthenes-3, Lillian-2, George-1) was born on 21 Oct 1933 in Washington, DC.
   Lu.
   John Malatras and Lu married. They had the following children:
       i. **Tony Malatras** was born about 1950. He died on 07 Apr 1973.
   21. ii. **Mark Malatras** was born about 1960. He died on 30 Dec 1990.

Generation 5

10. **Bernie Thornberg**-5 (Alexandra-4, Demosthenes-3, Lillian-2, George-1) was born on 06 Jun 1938 in Washington, DC.
    Helen Gianaris daughter of Peter Gianaris and Mary Koutsouke.
    Bernie Thornberg and Helen Gianaris were married on 09 Sep 1967. They had the following children:
    21. i. **Alexandra Thornberg** was born on 30 Jun 1968. She married Nick Pitas on 11 Dec 1989.
        ii. **Peter John Thornberg** was born on 24 May 1973.
        iii. **Maria Eleni Thornberg** was born on 07 Aug 1983.
11. **Mary Lillian Thornberg**-5 (Alexandra-4, Demosthenes-3, Lillian-2, George-1) was born on 29 Jan 1943 in Washington, DC.
    Bel ("Buddy") Faraby Henson.
    Bel ("Buddy") Faraby Henson and Mary Lillian Thornberg married. They had the following children:
        i. **Michelle Henson** was born on 17 Feb 1962.

22. ii. **David Henson** was born on 03 Feb 1964.

12. **Denny (Thornberg) Malatras**-5 (Alexandra-4, Demosthenes-3, Lillian-2, George-1) was born on 03 Nov 1944 in Washington, DC.

    Grace.

    Denny (Thornberg) Malatras and Grace married. They had the following children:

    i. **Denny Thornberg** was born on 16 Mar 1966.

    Angie.

    Denny (Thornberg) Malatras and Angie married. They had the following children:

    i. **Rebecca Malatras** was born on 17 Dec 1982.

13. **Dean Kokenes**-5 (Louise-4, Demosthenes-3, Lillian-2, George-1) was born on 26 Jan 1943 in Washington, DC.

    Mary Magyar.

    Dean Kokenes and Mary Magyar married. They had the following children:

    i. **Steven Kokenes.**

    ii. **Kristin Kokenes.**

    Jenny Rice.

    Dean Kokenes and Jenny Rice were married in Jul 1987. They had no children.

14. **Alexander Kokenes**-5 (Louise-4, Demosthenes-3, Lillian-2, George-1) was born on 22 Apr 1950 in Washington, DC.

    Cathy.

    Alexander Kokenes and Cathy married. They had the following children:

    i. **Matthew Kokenes** was born in Charlotte, NC.

    ii. **Lauren Kokenes** was born in Charlotte, NC.

    Valerie.

    Alexander Kokenes and Valerie married. They had the following children:

    i. **Stephanie Kokenes.**

15. **Christina Kokenes**-5 (Louise-4, Demosthenes-3, Lillian-2, George-1) was born on 16 Jul 1953 in Washington, DC.

    John Skiouris son of Kyriakos Skiouris and Lena.

John Skiouris and Christina Kokenes married. They had the following children:
> i. **Lena Skiouris** was born on 22 May 1981 in Athens, Greece.
> ii. **Kyriakos Skiouris** was born on 04 Jan in Charlotte, NC.
> iii. **Stephanos Skiouris** was born on 05 Sep in Charlotte, NC.

16. **Steven Malatras**-5 (Teddy-4, Demosthenes-3, Lillian-2, George-1). **Judy.**
Steven Malatras and Judy married. They had the following children:
> i. **Cheryl Malatras.**

17. **Thomas Kollecas**-5 (Amelia-4, Demosthenes-3, Lillian-2, George-1) was born on 25 Jan 1950.
Diana Plomason.
Thomas Kollecas and Diana Plomason married. They had the following children:
> i. **Christopher Kollecas** was born on 22 Jun 1984 in Rockville, MD.
> ii. **Lauren Kollecas** was born on 06 May 1987 in Rockville, MD.

18. **Ulysses Kollecas**-5 (Amelia-4, Demosthenes-3, Lillian-2, George-1) was born on 20 Mar 1958 in Washington, DC.
Karen Rechcigl daughter of Mila (Miloslav) Rechcigl Jr. and Eva Edwards (Eisnerová) was born on 16 Apr 1962 in Washington, DC.
Ulysses Kollecas and Karen Rechcigl were married on 25 Aug 1990 in Bethesda, MD. They had the following children:
> i. **Kristin Kollecas** was born on 04 May 1993 in Albuquerque, NM.
> ii. **Paul Kollecas** was born on 02 Jun 1995 in Albuquerque, NM.

19. **Paul Strachan**-5 (Lula-4, Demosthenes-3, Lillian-2, George-1) was born on 28 Mar 1956 in Washington, DC.
Elizabeth ("Liz") Marie Nance.
Paul Strachan and Elizabeth ("Liz") Marie Nance were married about 16 Jun 1990. They had the following children:
> i. **Lydia Strachan** was born on 26 Feb 1991 in Charlotte, NC.
> ii. **Callie Elizabeth Strachan** was born on 26 Apr 1993 in Charlotte, NC.

20. **Mark Malatras**-5 (John-4, Demosthenes-3, Lillian-2, George-1) was born

about 1960. He died on 30 Dec 1990.

Christine.

Mark Malatras and Christine married. They had the following children:

    i. **John Demosthenes Malatras** was born in 1990 in Charlotte, NC.

Generation 6

21. **Alexandra Thornberg**-6 (Bernie-5, Alexandra-4, Demosthenes-3, Lillian-2, George-1) was born on 30 Jun 1968.

    Nick Pitas.

    Nick Pitas and Alexandra Thornberg were married on 11 Dec 1989. They had the following children:

        i. **Chrystyna Pitas** was born on 24 Mar 1990 in Washington, DC.

        ii. **Victoria Rose Pitas** was born on 18 Mar 1993 in Washington, DC.

        iii. **Michael Pitas** was born on 06 Nov 1996 in Washington, DC.

22. **David Henson**-6 (Mary Lillian-5, Alexandra-4, Demosthenes-3, Lillian-2, George-1) was born on 03 Feb 1964.

    Wendy.

    David Henson and Wendy married. They had the following children:

        i. **Carlie Henson** was born on 09 Mar 1987.

        ii. **David Henson** was born on 06 Mar 1991.

G. Mila Rechcigl's Sister Side

Žďárský Family

Generation 1

1. **Václav Žďárský**-1 was born in Loukov No. 6.
   Unknown.
   Václav Žďárský and Unknown married. They had the following children:
   2. i. **Jan Žďárský** was born in Sobeslavice.

Generation 2

2. **Jan Žďárský**-2 (Václav-1) was born in Sobeslavice.
   Anna Kovářová was born in Zdar No. 12.
   Jan Žďárský and Anna Kovářová married. They had the following children:
   3. i. **Josef Žďárský** was born in Loukov no. 9.
   4. ii. **Kateřina Žďárská** was born in Sobeslavice.

Generation 3

3. **Josef Žďárský**-3 (Jan-2, Václav-1) was born in Loukov no. 9.
   Anna Šimůnková daughter of Josef Šimůnek and Kateřina Srbska was born in Sezemice No. 1. Josef Žďárský and Anna Šimůnková married. They had the following children:
   5. i. **Josef Žďárský** was born on 29 Sep 1849 in Loukov no. 9. He died on 20 Jun 1918.
      ii. **Marie Žďárská** was born on 03 Feb 1854 in Loukov no. 9.
4. **Kateřina Žďárská**-3 (Jan-2, Václav-1) was born in Sobeslavice.
   Matěj Černý was born in Sobeslavice No. 16.
   Matěj Černý and Kateřina Žďárská married. They had the following children:
   6. i. **Alžběta Černá.**

Generation 4

5. **Josef Žďárský**-4 (Josef-3, Jan-2, Václav-1) was born on 29 Sep 1849 in Loukov no. 9. He died on 20 Jun 1918.

   Anna Bičíková daughter of Jan Bičík and Marie Sonska was born on 21 Jan 1855. Josef Žďárský and Anna Bičíková married. They had the following children:

   - 13 i. **Josef Žďárský** was born on 01 Apr 1873 in Loukov no. 9. He married Emilie Holasova on 13 Feb 1900 in Mukarov, Mnichovo Hradiště Co.. He died on 29 Dec 1945.
   - ii. **Marie Žďárská** was born in 1876.
   - iii. **Anna Žďárská** was born in 1882.
   - 8. iv. **Václav Žďárský** was born on 14 Jul 1885 in Jirsko no. 3. He married Anna Pospíšilová on 04 Jun 1912 in Mukarov.
   - v. **Anastazie Žďárská** was born in 1890.
   - 9. vi. **František Žďárský** was born on 10 Jul 1892 in Loukov no. 9. He died on 27 Aug 1919.
   - 10. vii. **Jan Žďárský** was born on 13 Sep 1896 in Loukov no. 9. He died in 1957.

6. **Alžběta Černá**-4 (Kateřina-3, Jan-2, Václav-1).

   František Šifta was born before 1810 in Jivina No. 6.

   František Šifta and Alžběta Černá married. They had the following children:

   - 11. i. **Anna Šiftová** was born on 27 Jun 1834 in Jivina No. 6. She married Antonín Rechziegel on 11 Feb 1851 in Jivina No. 6. She died on 03 Apr 1854 in Slavíkov No. 4.

Generation 5

7. **Josef Žďárský**-5 (Josef-4, Josef-3, Jan-2, Václav-1) was born on 01 Apr 1873 in Loukov no. 9. He died on 29 Dec 1945.

   Emilie Holasova daughter of Josef Holas and Anna Horáková was born on 26 Oct 1877 in Neveklovice.

   Josef Žďárský and Emilie Holasova were married on 13 Feb 1900 in Mukarov, Mnichovo Hradiště Co.. They had the following children:

   - 12. i. **František Václav Žďárský** was born on 22 Aug 1904 in Loukovec.

He died on 01 Jan 1970.

    ii. **Stanislav Žďárský**.

13. iii. **Josef Žďárský** was born on 12 Apr 1901 in Loukovec.

8. **Václav Žďárský**-5 (Josef-4, Josef-3, Jan-2, Václav-1) was born on 14 Jul 1885 in Jirsko no. 3.

Anna Pospíšilová daughter of František Pospíšil and Anna Brzobohatá was born on 11 Jan 1892 in Borovice.

Václav Žďárský and Anna Pospíšilová were married on 04 Jun 1912 in Mukarov. They had the following children:

    i. **Václav Josef Žďárský** was born on 12 Sep 1918 in Jirsko no. 3.

9. **František Žďárský**-5 (Josef-4, Josef-3, Jan-2, Václav-1) was born on 10 Jul 1892 in Loukov no. 9. He died on 27 Aug 1919.

Božena Černá daughter of Josef Černý and Františka Poláková was born on 17 Apr 1896 in Doubrava.

František Žďárský and Božena Černá married. They had the following children:

    i. **Věra Žďárská**.

10. **Jan Žďárský**-5 (Josef-4, Josef-3, Jan-2, Václav-1) was born on 13 Sep 1896 in Loukov no. 9. He died in 1957.

Marie Lamačová daughter of František Lamač and Božena Tomášová was born on 26 Nov 1896 in Prepere.

Jan Žďárský and Marie Lamačová married. They had the following children:

    i. **Eva Žďárská** was born on 25 Dec 1919 in Loukov.

    ii. **Marie Božena Žďárská** was born on 22 Mar 1924 in Loukov. She died on 02 Nov 1931.

    iii. **Vlasta Žďárský** was born in 1930.

15. iv. **Jiří Žďárský** was born on 31 Oct 1937 in Loukov no. 9.

11. **Anna Šiftová**-5 (Alžběta-4, Kateřina-3, Jan-2, Václav-1) was born on 27 Jun 1834 in Jivina No. 6. She died on 03 Apr 1854 in Slavíkov No. 4.

Antonín Rechziegel son of Ing. František Rechziegel and Lidmila Neumanová was born on 22 May 1823 in Slavíkov No. 4, Český Dub Co.. He died on 25 Sep 1888 in Slavíkov No. 4, Cesyu Dub Co..

Antonín Rechziegel and Anna Šiftová were married on 11 Feb 1851 in Jivina No. 6. They had the following children:

15. i. **Anna Rechziegel** was born on 07 Aug 1852 in Slavíkov No. 4. She married Josef Vela on 06 Feb 1872 in Slavíkov No. 4, Vlastibořice parish. She died on 15 Sep 1931 in Sychrov.

   ii. **Josef Rechziegel** was born on 29 Mar 1854 in Slavíkov No. 4. He died on 29 Mar 1854 in Slavíkov No. 4.

Generation 6

12. **František Václav Žďárský**-6 (Josef-5, Josef-4, Josef-3, Jan-2, Václav-1) was born on 22 Aug 1904 in Loukovec. He died on 01 Jan 1970.
    Eliška Foltýnová daughter of Rudolf Foltýn and Marie Řeháková was born on 23 Aug 1905 in Hradeck Králové.
    František Václav Žďárský and Eliška Foltýnová married. They had the following children:

    16. i. **František Žďárský** was born on 21 May 1932 in Turnov. He married Marta Rechcíglová on 03 Oct 1953 in Mladá Boleslav.

    17. ii. **Libor Žďárský** was born on 09 Nov 1936.

13. **Josef Žďárský**-6 (Josef-5, Josef-4, Josef-3, Jan-2, Václav-1) was born on 12 Apr 1901 in Loukovec.
    Marie Šulcová was born in Ujezd.
    Josef Žďárský and Marie Šulcová married. They had the following children:

    i. **Marie Žďárská**.
    ii. **Miluše Žďárská**.

14. **Jiří Žďárský**-6 (Jan-5, Josef-4, Josef-3, Jan-2, Václav-1) was born on 31 Oct 1937 in Loukov no. 9.
    Drahuse Šnajdrová was born in Pencin.
    Jiří Žďárský and Drahuse Šnajdrová married. They had the following children:

    i. **Jiří Žďárský**.
    ii. **Jan Žďárský**.
    iii. **Václav Žďárský**.

15. **Anna Rechziegel**-6 (Anna-5, Alžběta-4, Kateřina-3, Jan-2, Václav-1) was

born on 07 Aug 1852 in Slavíkov No. 4. She died on 15 Sep 1931 in Sychrov.
Josef Vela son of Josef Vela and Rozalie Šídová was born on 17 Mar 1844 in Cervenice No. 8. He died on 02 Dec 1928 in Sychrov.

Josef Vela and Anna Rechziegel were married on 06 Feb 1872 in Slavíkov No. 4, Vlastibořice parish. They had the following children:

    i. **Josef Vela** was born on 19 Apr 1873 in Slavíkov No. 3. He died on 07 Jan 1908 in Třtí.

    ii. **Kateřina Velova** was born on 21 Sep 1874 in Slavíkov No. 3. She died on 15 Nov 1931 in Sychrov. She married Čeněk Adam in Slavíkov.

    iii. **Anna Velova** was born on 12 Apr 1877 in Slavíkov No. 3. She died on 22 Apr 1911 in Hruba Skála (Doubravice).

19. iv. **Alois Jan Vela** was born on 14 May 1888 in Slavíkov No. 3. He married Marie Vysatova on 12 Sep 1916 in Vlastibořice. He died on 07 Oct 1974 in Turnov.

Generation 7

16. **František Žďárský**-7 (František Václav-6, Josef-5, Josef-4, Josef-3, Jan-2, Václav-1) was born on 21 May 1932 in Turnov. He died Feb. 4, 2021 in Liberec, Czech Republic.

Marta Rechcíglová daughter of Miloslav Rechcigl and Marie Rajtrová was born on 23 May 1933 in Mladá Boleslav. She died on 13 Sep 2018 in Mladá Boleslav.

František Žďárský and Marta Rechcíglová were married on 03 Oct 1953 in Mladá Boleslav. They had the following children:

19. i. **Marcela Žďárská** was born on 09 May 1954 in Liberec. She married Miroslav Heralecký on 15 Mar 1975 in Sychrov.

20. ii. **Iveta Žďárská** was born on 29 Aug 1963 in Liberec, Bohemia. She married Vlastimil Berkman on 29 Oct 1983.

17. **Libor Žďárský**-7 (František Václav-6, Josef-5, Josef-4, Josef-3, Jan-2, Václav-1) was born on 09 Nov 1936.
Miuse Ševčíková.

Libor Žďárský and Miuse Ševčíková married. They had the following children:

21. i. **Libor Žďárský** was born in 1960.
    ii. **Monika Žďárská**.
18. **Alois Jan Vela**-7 (Anna-6, Anna-5, Alžběta-4, Kateřina-3, Jan-2, Václav-1) was born on 14 May 1888 in Slavíkov No. 3. He died on 07 Oct 1974 in Turnov.

    Marie Vysatova was born on 14 May 1895 in Praha. She died on 27 Jan 1971 in Turnov.

    Alois Jan Vela and Marie Vysatova were married on 12 Sep 1916 in Vlastibořice. They had the following children:
      i. **Bohumir Vela** was born on 06 Jul 1917 in Sychrov. He married Vlasta Pechanová on 08 May 1956.
    22. ii. **Vladimír Vela** was born on 13 Jul 1922 in Sychrov. He married Alena Vlahova on 22 Jan 1949.

Generation 8

19. **Marcela Žďárská**-8 (František-7, František Václav-6, Josef-5, Josef-4, Josef-3, Jan-2, Václav-1) was born on 09 May 1954 in Liberec.

    Miroslav Heralecký son of Miroslav Heralecký and Marie Bartošová was born on 18 May 1949 in salomonJablonec nad Nisou, Czech.. He died on 20 Feb 2017 in Proseč, Jablonec nad Nisou, Czech..

    Miroslav Heralecký and Marcela Žďárská were married on 15 Mar 1975 in Sychrov. They had the following children:
      i. **Vit Heralecký** was born on 16 Jan 1977 in Jablonec nad Nisou. He married Olga Zrubcová on 13 Jul 1996.
    24. ii. **Zuzana Heralecká** was born on 30 Dec 1978 in Jablonec nad Nisou. She married Jaroslav Egrt on 13 Sep 2002 in Jablonec nad Nisou.
20. **Iveta Žďárská**-8 (František-7, František Václav-6, Josef-5, Josef-4, Josef-3, Jan-2, Václav-1) was born on 29 Aug 1963 in Liberec, Bohemia.

    Vlastimil Berkman was born in 1957.

    Vlastimil Berkman and Iveta Žďárská were married on 29 Oct 1983. They had the following children:
      i. **Tereza Hriníková** was born on 05 Jun 1984 in Jablonec nad Nisou.

    Jaroslav Hrinik son of Jaroslav Hrinik and Milena Preisslerová was born on 17 Apr 1960.

Jaroslav Hrinik and Iveta Žďárská were married on 16 Aug 1991 in Zamek Červená Lhota. They had the following children:

    i. **Eliška Hriníková** was born on 23 Jun 1992 in Jablonec nad Nisou. She married Jan Ottis on 06 Oct 2018 in Jablonec nad Jizerou, East Bohemia, Czech Republic. They had 2 children:

        i. daughter Barbora Ottisová, born 15 July 2021 in Jablonec nad Nisou

        ii. son Václav Ottis, born 11 Feb., 2023. in Jablonec nad Nisou

21. **Libor Žďárský**-8 (Libor-7, František Václav-6, Josef-5, Josef-4, Josef-3, Jan-2, Václav-1) was born in 1960.

Růžena.

Libor Žďárský and Růžena married. They had the following children:

    i. **Jakub Žďárský.**

    ii. **Denisa Žďárská.**

22. **Vladimír Vela**-8 (Alois Jan-7, Anna-6, Anna-5, Alžběta-4, Kateřina-3, Jan-2, Václav-1) was born on 13 Jul 1922 in Sychrov.

Alena Vlahova was born on 03 Apr 1928. She died on 26 May 1982.

Vladimír Vela and Alena Vlahova were married on 22 Jan 1949. They had the following children:

  24. i. **Alena Velova** was born on 05 Jan 1951 in Turnov. She married Ladislav Vodhanel on 12 Jul 1972.

  25. ii. **Vladimír Vela** was born on 17 Dec 1954. He married Raduse Dvořáková on 07 Dec 1979.

Generation 9

23. **Zuzana Heralecká**-9 (Marcela-8, František-7, František Václav-6, Josef-5, Josef-4, Josef-3, Jan-2, Václav-1) was born on 30 Dec 1978 in Jablonec nad Nisou.

Jaroslav Egrt was born on 25 Apr 1974 in Duchcov.

Jaroslav Egrt and Zuzana Heralecká were married on 13 Sep 2002 in Jablonec nad Nisou. They had the following children:

    i. **Kristina Egrtova** was born on 04 Jan 2008 in Liberec.

    ii. **Jaroslav Egrt** was born on 04 Jan 2008 in Liberec.

24. **Alena Velova**-9 (Vladimír-8, Alois Jan-7, Anna-6, Anna-5, Alžběta-4, Kateřina-3, Jan-2, Václav-1) was born on 05 Jan 1951 in Turnov.
Ladislav Vodhanel was born on 29 Dec 1945.
Ladislav Vodhanel and Alena Velova were married on 12 Jul 1972. They had the following children:
    i. **Miroslava Vodhanelova** was born on 22 Dec 1973 in Turnov.

Jindřich Novotný.
Jindřich Novotný and Alena Velova were married on 12 Apr 1976. They had the following children:
    i. **Sarka Novotná** was born on 10 Jun 1977 in Turnov.

25. **Vladimír Vela**-9 (Vladimír-8, Alois Jan-7, Anna-6, Anna-5, Alžběta-4, Kateřina-3, Jan-2, Václav-1) was born on 17 Dec 1954.
Raduse Dvořáková was born on 11 Dec 1959 in Turnov.
Vladimír Vela and Raduse Dvořáková were married on 07 Dec 1979. They had the following children:
    i. **Vladimír Vela** was born on 27 Jul 1980.
    ii. **Jan Vela** was born on 24 Jun 1984.

Foltýn Family

Generation 1

1. **Pavel Foltýn**-1 was born in Stachy No. 203.
   Kateřina Svarcova or Magdalena Wolfova was born in Stachy 55, Stachy No. 73.
   Pavel Foltýn and Kateřina Svarcova or Magdalena Wolfova married. They had the following children:
       i. **František Foltýn.**
   2. ii. **Josef Foltýn** was born on 19 Jun 1847 in Stachy No. 203. He married Alžběta Caisová on 28 Apr 1845.

Generation 2

2. **Josef Foltýn**-2 (Pavel-1) was born on 19 Jun 1847 in Stachy No. 203.
   Alžběta Caisová daughter of Martin Cais and Anna Luhanova.
   Josef Foltýn and Alžběta Caisová were married on 28 Apr 1845. They had the following children:
   3 i. **Rudolf Foltýn** was born on 24 Dec 1875 in Stachy No. 83. He married Marie Řeháková on 18 Jun 1900 in Kukleny, Hradec Králové Co..

Generation 3

3. **Rudolf Foltýn**-3 (Josef-2, Pavel-1) was born on 24 Dec 1875 in Stachy No. 83.
   Marie Řeháková daughter of Václav Řehák and Josefa Smolikova was born on 07 Sep 1878 in Predmerice nad Labem, Hradec Králové Co..
   Rudolf Foltýn and Marie Řeháková were married on 18 Jun 1900 in Kukleny, Hradec Králové Co.. They had the following children:
   4. i. **Eliška Foltýnová** was born on 23 Aug 1905 in Hradeck Králové.
   5. ii. **Rudolf Foltýn.**
   6. iii. **Josef Foltýn.**
   7. iv. **Jaroslava Foltýnová.**
       v. **Vlasta Foltýnová.**

Generation 4

4. **Eliška Foltýnová**-4 (Rudolf-3, Josef-2, Pavel-1) was born on 23 Aug 1905 in Hradeck Králové.

   František Václav Žďárský son of Josef Žďárský and Emilie Holasova was born on 22 Aug 1904 in Loukovec. He died on 01 Jan 1970.

   František Václav Žďárský and Eliška Foltýnová married. They had the following children:

   8. i. **František Žďárský** was born on 21 May 1932 in Turnov. He married Marta Rechcíglová on 03 Oct 1953 in Mladá Boleslav.
   9. ii. **Libor Žďárský** was born on 09 Nov 1936.

5. **Rudolf Foltýn**-4 (Rudolf-3, Josef-2, Pavel-1).

   Rudolf Foltýn and unknown spouse married. They had the following children:

   i. **Nina Foltýnová**.

6. **Josef Foltýn**-4 (Rudolf-3, Josef-2, Pavel-1).

   Josef Foltýn and unknown spouse married. They had the following children:

   i. **Josef Foltýn**.

7. **Jaroslava Foltýnová**-4 (Rudolf-3, Josef-2, Pavel-1).

   Karel Wohlhoefner.

   Karel Wohlhoefner and Jaroslava Foltýnová married. They had the following children:

   i. **Karel Wohlhoefner**.
   ii. **Hana Wohlhoefnerova**.

Generation 5

8. **František Žďárský**-5 (Eliška-4, Rudolf-3, Josef-2, Pavel-1) was born on 21 May 1932 in Turnov.

   Marta Rechcíglová daughter of Miloslav Rechcigl and Marie Rajtrová was born on 23 May 1933 in Mladá Boleslav. She died on 13 Sep 2018 in Mladá Boleslav.

   František Žďárský and Marta Rechcíglová were married on 03 Oct 1953 in Mladá Boleslav. They had the following children:

   10. i. **Marcela Žďárská** was born on 09 May 1954 in Liberec. She

married Miroslav Heralecký on 15 Mar 1975 in Sychrov.

11. ii. **Iveta Žďárská** was born on 29 Aug 1963 in Liberec, Bohemia. She married Vlastimil Berkman on 29 Oct 1983.

9. **Libor Žďárský**-5 (Eliška-4, Rudolf-3, Josef-2, Pavel-1) was born on 09 Nov 1936.

    Miuse Ševčíková.

    Libor Žďárský and Miuse Ševčíková married. They had the following children:

    12. i. **Libor Žďárský** was born in 1960.

    ii. **Monika Žďárská**.

Generation 6

10. **Marcela Žďárská**-6 (František-5, Eliška-4, Rudolf-3, Josef-2, Pavel-1) was born on 09 May 1954 in Liberec.

    Miroslav Heralecký son of Miroslav Heralecký and Marie Bartošová was born on 18 May 1949 in salomonJablonec nad Nisou, Czech.. He died on 20 Feb 2017 in Proseč, Jablonec nad Nisou, Czech..

    Miroslav Heralecký and Marcela Žďárská were married on 15 Mar 1975 in Sychrov. They had the following children:

    i. **Vit Heralecký** was born on 16 Jan 1977 in Jablonec nad Nisou. He married Olga Zrubcová on 13 Jul 1996.

    14. ii. **Zuzana Heralecká** was born on 30 Dec 1978 in Jablonec nad Nisou. She married Jaroslav Egrt on 13 Sep 2002 in Jablonec nad Nisou.

11. **Iveta Žďárská**-6 (František-5, Eliška-4, Rudolf-3, Josef-2, Pavel-1) was born on 29 Aug 1963 in Liberec, Bohemia.

    Vlastimil Berkman was born in 1957.

    Vlastimil Berkman and Iveta Žďárská were married on 29 Oct 1983. They had the following children:

    i. **Tereza Hriníková** was born on 05 Jun 1984 in Jablonec nad Nisou.

    Jaroslav Hrinik son of Jaroslav Hrinik and Milena Preisslerová was born on 17 Apr 1960.

    Jaroslav Hrinik and Iveta Žďárská were married on 16 Aug 1991 in Zamek Červená Lhota. They had the following children:

    i. **Eliška Hriníková** was born on 23 Jun 1992 in Jablonec nad Nisou. She married Jan Ottis on 06 Oct 2018 in Jablonec nad Jizerou, East Bohemia, Czech Republic.

12. **Libor Žďárský**-6 (Libor-5, Eliška-4, Rudolf-3, Josef-2, Pavel-1) was born in 1960.

Růžena.

Libor Žďárský and Růžena married. They had the following children:

    i. **Jakub Žďárský.**

    ii. **Denisa Žďárská.**

Generation 7

13. **Zuzana Heralecká**-7 (Marcela-6, František-5, Eliška-4, Rudolf-3, Josef-2, Pavel-1) was born on 30 Dec 1978 in Jablonec nad Nisou.

Jaroslav Egrt was born on 25 Apr 1974 in Duchcov.

Jaroslav Egrt and Zuzana Heralecká were married on 13 Sep 2002 in Jablonec nad Nisou. They had the following children:

    i. **Kristina Egrtova** was born on 04 Jan 2008 in Liberec.

    ii. **Jaroslav Egrt** was born on 04 Jan 2008 in Liberec.

Heralecký Family

Generation 1

1. **Jan Heralitzky**-1 was born between 1625-1640 in Malomerice. He died in 1682.
   Unknown.
   Jan Heralitzky and Unknown married. They had the following children:
   2. i. **Martin Heraliczky** was born between 1650-1660 in Malomerice, Brno-Obrany. He married Kateřina Chalupová on 27 Jan 1681.

Generation 2

2. **Martin Heraliczky**-2 (Jan-1) was born between 1650-1660 in Malomerice, Brno-Obrany.
   Kateřina Chalupová daughter of Thomas Chalupa and Unknown.
   Martin Heraliczky and Kateřina Chalupová were married on 27 Jan 1681. They had the following children:
   3. i. **Josef Ferdinand Heraleczky** was born on 13 Mar 1681 in Slavice.
   ii. **Pavel Heraleczky** was born on 03 Jan 1685 in Slavice.
   iii. **Thomass Heraleczky** was born on 22 Nov 1687.

Generation 3

3. **Josef Ferdinand Heraleczky**-3 (Martin-2, Jan-1) was born on 13 Mar 1681 in Slavice.
   Unknown.
   Josef Ferdinand Heraleczky and Unknown married. They had the following children:
   4. i. **Jakob Heraleczky** was born between 1700-1716 in Slavice ?. He died between 1756-1786.

Generation 4

4. **Jakob Heraleczky**-4 (Josef Ferdinand-3, Martin-2, Jan-1) was born between 1700-1716 in Slavice ?. He died between 1756-1786.
   Rozina was born in 1697. She died on 24 Aug 1786 in Slavice No. 28.
   Jakob Heraleczky and Rozina married. They had the following children:
   5. i. **Jakob Heraletzky** was born about 1730.

6. ii. **Josef Heraliczky** was born in 1736. He married Mariana Widominska on 03 May 1756 in Slavice. He died on 16 Aug 1786.
7. iii. **Johan Heralezky** was born about 1740.

Generation 5

5. **Jakob Heraletzky**-5 (Jakob-4, Josef Ferdinand-3, Martin-2, Jan-1) was born about 1730.
   Unknown.
   Jakob Heraletzky and Unknown married. They had the following children:
   8. i. **Johann Heraletzky** was born between 1750-1760. He married Kateřina Barteisova on 30 Oct 1780.
6. **Josef Heraliczky**-5 (Jakob-4, Josef Ferdinand-3, Martin-2, Jan-1) was born in 1736. He died on 16 Aug 1786.
   Mariana Widominska was born in 1718 in Mikulovice. She died on 28 Jan 1801 in Slavice No. 28.
   Josef Heraliczky and Mariana Widominska were married on 03 May 1756 in Slavice. They had the following children:
   9. i. **Jan Heralecký** was born in 1758. He married Rozalie Dokulilová on 12 Nov 1786. He died on 23 Feb 1820 in Slavice No. 28.
7. **Johan Heralezky**-5 (Jakob-4, Josef Ferdinand-3, Martin-2, Jan-1) was born about 1740.
   Unknown.
   Johan Heralezky and Unknown married. They had the following children:
   10. i. **Johann Heralezky** was born in 1769 in Slavice. He married Rosina Pelikánová on 17 Jan 1794 in Slavice No. 21.

Generation 6

8. **Johann Heraletzky**-6 (Jakob-5, Jakob-4, Josef Ferdinand-3, Martin-2, Jan-1) was born between 1750-1760.
   Kateřina Barteisova was born in Slavice No. 27.
   Johann Heraletzky and Kateřina Barteisova were married on 30 Oct 1780. They had the following children:
   i. **Anna Heraletzka** was born on 13 Jul 1782 in Slavice No. 27.
   ii. **Maria Heraletzka** was born on 27 Jan 1784 in Slavice No. 27.

She died on 12 Jun 1785 in Slavice No. 27.
- iii. **Anna Heraletzka** was born on 05 Jul 1788.
- iv. **Frantz Heraletzky** was born on 25 Sep 1790.
- v. **Kateřina Heraletzka** was born on 31 Oct 1792.
- 12. vi. **Josef Heralidsky** was born on 16 Mar 1795 in Slavice No. 27. He died on 22 Apr 1881 in Slavice No. 27.
- vii. **Rosalia Heraletzka** was born on 20 Aug 1797.
- viii. **Marie Anna Heraletzka** was born on 06 Apr 1800.
- ix. **Franziska Heraletzka** was born on 02 Mar 1803.

9. **Jan Heralecký**-6 (Josef-5, Jakob-4, Josef Ferdinand-3, Martin-2, Jan-1) was born in 1758. He died on 23 Feb 1820 in Slavice No. 28.

   Rozalie Dokulilová daughter of Jan Dokulil and Veronika Hubačová was born on 17 Aug 1769 in Sokoli. She died on 25 Mar 1821 in Slavice No. 28. Jan Heralecký and Rozalie Dokulilová were married on 12 Nov 1786. They had the following children:
   - 12. i. **Václav Heralecký** was born on 22 Aug 1797 in Slavice No. 28. He married Marie Tomková on 29 May 1821. He died on 29 Jun 1866.
   - ii. **Tomáš Heralecký** was born on 05 Dec 1789. He died on 08 Jul 1790.
   - iii. **Kateřina Heralecká** was born on 13 Nov 1791.
   - iv. **Josefa Heralecká** was born on 16 Nov 1794.
   - v. **Kateřina Heralecká** was born on 14 Nov 1799.
   - 13. vi. **Josef Heralecký** was born on 15 Mar 1802 in Slavice No. 28. He died on 01 Aug 1828 in Slavice No. 6.
   - vii. **Jan Heralecký** was born on 13 Jun 1804.
   - viii. **Mariana Heralecká** was born in 1808.

10. **Johann Heralezky**-6 (Johan-5, Jakob-4, Josef Ferdinand-3, Martin-2, Jan-1) was born in 1769 in Slavice.

    Rosina Pelikánová daughter of Josef Pelikán and Unknown was born in 1771.

    Johann Heralezky and Rosina Pelikánová were married on 17 Jan 1794 in Slavice No. 21. They had the following children:
    - i. **Maria Anna Heralezka** was born on 16 Mar 1794.

HERALECKÝ FAMILY

      ii. **Johan Heralezky** was born on 08 May 1796. He died on 29 Nov 1798.

      iii. **Frantz Heralezky** was born on 16 May 1798.

15. iv. **Mathias Heralicky** was born on 22 Feb 1801 in Slavice No. 21.

      v. **Anna Heralezka** was born on 18 Mar 1803.

Generation 7

11. **Josef Heralidsky**-7 (Johann-6, Jakob-5, Jakob-4, Josef Ferdinand-3, Martin-2, Jan-1) was born on 16 Mar 1795 in Slavice No. 27. He died on 22 Apr 1881 in Slavice No. 27.

    Vertonika Stuchliková daughter of Tomáš Stuchlik was born in 1802 in Petruvky. She died on 24 Jul 1874 in Slaviuce No. 27.

    Josef Heralidsky and Vertonika Stuchliková married. They had the following children:

          i. **Johanna Heraletzka** was born on 18 Jun 1825.

          ii. **Mariana Heraletzka** was born on 19 Dec 1827.

    15. iii. **Josef Beraletzky** was born on 24 Sep 1830 in Slavice No. 27. He married Františka Klepackova on 27 Nov 1849. He died on 28 Jul 1861.

12. **Václav Heralecký**-7 (Jan-6, Josef-5, Jakob-4, Josef Ferdinand-3, Martin-2, Jan-1) was born on 22 Aug 1797 in Slavice No. 28. He died on 29 Jun 1866.

    Marie Tomková daughter of Marej Tomek and Františka Krschka was born on 09 Jan 1797 in Slavice No. 24.

    Václav Heralecký and Marie Tomková were married on 29 May 1821. They had the following children:

          i. **Františka Heralecká** was born on 23 Aug 1824.

          ii. **Mariana Heralecká** was born on 04 Dec 1826.

    17. iii. **Jan Heralecký** was born on 27 Dec 1828 in Slavice No. 28. He married Anežka Svobodová on 10 Sep 1855 in Bohusice No. 6. He died in Bohusice.

          iv. **Kateřina Heralecká** was born on 18 Aug 1831.

    17. v. **František Heralecký** was born on 19 Oct 1832 in Slavice No. 28. He died in 1906 in Slavice No. 28.

          vi. **Pavlina Heralecká** was born on 27 Jul 1835.

13. **Josef Heralecký**-7 (Jan-6, Josef-5, Jakob-4, Josef Ferdinand-3, Martin-2,

Jan-1) was born on 15 Mar 1802 in Slavice No. 28. He died on 01 Aug 1828 in Slavice No. 6.

Kateřina Wrchotova daughter of Matous Wrchota and Unknown was born in Mikulovice. Josef Heralecký and Kateřina Wrchotova married. They had the following children:
   i. **Jakob Heralecký** was born on 17 Jul 1826. He died on 17 Nov 1846 in Slavice No. 6.
   ii. **Kateřina Heralecká** was born on 29 Sep 1828 in Slavice No 15?. She died on 22 Feb 1829.

23 **Mathias Heralicky**-7 (Johann-6, Johan-5, Jakob-4, Josef Ferdinand-3, Martin-2, Jan-1) was born on 22 Feb 1801 in Slavice No. 21.

Alžběta Charvatova daughter of Johann Charvat and Unknown. Mathias Heralicky and Alžběta Charvatova married. They had the following children:
   i. **child Heralicky**.
   ii. **Anton Heralicky** was born on 12 May 1831.
   iii. **Maria Heralicka** was born on 12 May 1837.

Generation 8

15. **Josef Beraletzky**-8 (Josef-7, Johann-6, Jakob-5, Jakob-4, Josef Ferdinand-3, Martin-2, Jan-1) was born on 24 Sep 1830 in Slavice No. 27. He died on 28 Jul 1861.

   Františka Klepackova was born on 29 Nov 1829 in Domamil.

   Josef Beraletzky and Františka Klepackova were married on 27 Nov 1849. They had the following children:
   i. **Marie Beraletzká** was born on 19 Feb 1851.
   ii. **Jan Beraletzky** was born on 04 May 1853.
   iii. **František Beraletzky** was born on 09 Jul 1855.
   iv. **Josef Beraletzky** was born on 04 Dec 1857.

16. **Jan Heralecký**-8 (Václav-7, Jan-6, Josef-5, Jakob-4, Josef Ferdinand-3, Martin-2, Jan-1) was born on 27 Dec 1828 in Slavice No. 28. He died in Bohusice.

   Anežka Svobodová daughter of Matěj Svoboda and Mariana Schabatková was born in 1833 in Bohusice No. 6.

Jan Heralecký and Anežka Svobodová were married on 10 Sep 1855 in Bohusice No. 6. They had the following children:

    i. **Jan Heralecký** was born on 26 Oct 1856.

    ii. **Antonie Heralecká** was born on 29 May 1858. She married František Hevr on 08 Feb 1881.

18. iii. **Jan Heralecký** was born on 27 Dec 1859. He married Kateřina Trojanová on 11 Nov 1887. He died on 03 May 1927.

    iv. **František Heralecký** was born on 10 Mar 1861.

    v. **Josefa Heralecký** was born on 18 Mar 1863.

19. vi. **Antonín Heralecký** was born on 20 Apr 1865 in Bohusice No. 16. He died in Jan 1944.

    vii. **Terezie Heralecká** was born on 10 Apr 1867.

    viii. **František Heralecký** was born on 31 Mar 1870.

20. ix. **Eduard Heralecký** was born on 30 Mar 1873. He died in 1938.

17. **František Heralecký**-8 (Václav-7, Jan-6, Josef-5, Jakob-4, Josef Ferdinand-3, Martin-2, Jan-1) was born on 19 Oct 1832 in Slavice No. 28. He died in 1906 in Slavice No. 28.

Antonie Klepackova was born in 1841 in Domamil. She died in 1919.

František Heralecký and Antonie Klepackova married. They had the following children:

21. i. **Jan Heralecký** was born on 24 Dec 1860 in Slavice No. 28. He married Antonie Pokorná on 23 Nov 1886. He died on 26 Nov 1956.

    ii. **Antonie Heralecká** was born on 26 Dec 1862.

    iii. **Františka Heralecká** was born on 25 Dec 1864.

    iv. **Anežka Heralecká** was born on 19 Jan 1866 in Slavice No. 28.

    v. **Marie Heralecká** was born on 22 Jan 1868 in Slavice No. 28. She married Josef Chromý on 23 Feb 1892.

    vi. **Františka Heralecká** was born on 04 Apr 1870 in Slavice No. 28.

22. vii. **Antonín Heralecký** was born on 25 Apr 1872 in Slavice No. 28. He married Petronela Klobouckova before 1910. He died in 1952 in Kolovraty (Litohor).

23. viii. **František Heralecký** was born on 01 Dec 1874 in Slavice No. 28. He died in 1943.

24. ix. **Josef Heralecký** was born on 01 Aug 1877 in Slavice No. 28. He married Emilie Nechodomova on 17 Jul 1919 in Trebic. He died on 29 Apr 1929 in Slavice.

    x. **Anastazie Heralecká** was born on 24 Aug 1879.

    xi. **Terezie Heralecká** was born on 24 Aug 1879.

25. xii. **Augustin Heralecký** was born on 03 Dec 1883 in Slavice. He died in Aug 1957 in Okrisky.

Generation 9

18. **Jan Heralecký**-9 (Jan-8, Václav-7, Jan-6, Josef-5, Jakob-4, Josef Ferdinand-3, Martin-2, Jan-1) was born on 27 Dec 1859. He died on 03 May 1927.

Kateřina Trojanová was born on 12 Oct 1865 in Blatnice. She died on 30 Jan 1927.

Jan Heralecký and Kateřina Trojanová were married on 11 Nov 1887. They had the following children:

26. i. **Karla Heralecká** was born on 19 Oct 1889.

    ii. **Antonie Heralecká** was born on 15 Jul 1893.

27. iii. **František Heralecký** was born on 26 Jan 1895 in Bohusice No. 16. He married Marie Stumpolova on 13 Jul 1927. He died in 1984.

    iv. **Karel Heralecký** was born on 08 Nov 1896. He died in 1915.

28. v. **Josef Heralecký** was born on 13 Feb 1898. He married Marie Tučková on 19 Jan 1932 in Hrusovany nad Jevickou.

    vi. **Anna Heralecká** was born on 02 Aug 1902.

    vii. **Jan Heralecký** was born in 1891.

19. **Antonín Heralecký**-9 (Jan-8, Václav-7, Jan-6, Josef-5, Jakob-4, Josef Ferdinand-3, Martin-2, Jan-1) was born on 20 Apr 1865 in Bohusice No. 16. He died in Jan 1944.

Marie Němcová was born on 03 Dec 1868 in Bocov. She died in 1937. Antonín Heralecký and Marie Němcová married. They had the following children:

29. i. **Marie Heralecká** was born in 1893. She died in 1968.

    ii. **Františka Heralecká** was born in 1895. She died in 1937.

    iii. **Růžena Heralecká** was born in 1897. She died in 1921.

30. iv. **Antonín Heralecký** was born on 05 May 1899 in Bohusice No.

16. He died on 15 Jul 1966.
31. v. **Jan Heralecký** was born in 1901. He died in 1972.

20. **Eduard Heralecký**-9 (Jan-8, Václav-7, Jan-6, Josef-5, Jakob-4, Josef Ferdinand-3, Martin-2, Jan-1) was born on 30 Mar 1873. He died in 1938.
Kateřina Husova was born on 10 Apr 1867 in Bohusice No. 6.
Eduard Heralecký and Kateřina Husova married. They had the following children:
32. i. **Eduard Heralecký** was born in 1902. He died in 1992.
33. ii. **Matylda Heralecká** was born in 1909.

21. **Jan Heralecký**-9 (František-8, Václav-7, Jan-6, Josef-5, Jakob-4, Josef Ferdinand-3, Martin-2, Jan-1) was born on 24 Dec 1860 in Slavice No. 28. He died on 26 Nov 1956.
Antonie Pokorná daughter of Matěj Pokorný and Kateřina Krelikova was born on 15 Sep 1857 in Slavice No. 36. She died on 19 Apr 1936.
Jan Heralecký and Antonie Pokorná were married on 23 Nov 1886. They had the following children:
   i. **Milada Heralecká**.
   ii. **Božena Heralecká**.
   iii. **Marie Heralecká**.
35. iv. **Antonín Heralecký** was born on 26 Apr 1893 in Slavice No. 36. He died on 20 Dec 1971.
36. v. **Jaroslav Heralecký** was born in 1887. He married Marie Tvarůžková about 1924.

22. **Antonín Heralecký**-9 (František-8, Václav-7, Jan-6, Josef-5, Jakob-4, Josef Ferdinand-3, Martin-2, Jan-1) was born on 25 Apr 1872 in Slavice No. 28. He died in 1952 in Kolovraty (Litohor).
Petronela Kloubouckova.
Antonín Heralecký and Petronela Kloubouckova were married before 1910. They had the following children:
   i. **Marie Heralecká** was born in 1910. She died in 1995.
   ii. **Františka Heralecká** was born in 1913. She died in 1991.
Kateřina Musilová.
Antonín Heralecký and Kateřina Musilová were married before 1916.

They had the following children:
- i. **Antonín Heralecký** was born in 1916.
- 36. ii. **Jan Heralecký** was born in 1921.
- iii. **Anežka Heralecká** was born in 1922.

23. **František Heralecký**-9 (František-8, Václav-7, Jan-6, Josef-5, Jakob-4, Josef Ferdinand-3, Martin-2, Jan-1) was born on 01 Dec 1874 in Slavice No. 28. He died in 1943.

    Marie Vitkova was born on 13 Aug 1885 in Petruvky. She died on 03 Oct 1959. František Heralecký and Marie Vitkova married. They had the following children:
    - 37. i. **Františka Heralecká** was born on 06 Jun 1908 in Slavice No. 28. She died on 01 Apr 1988 in Slavice No. 23.
    - 38. ii. **Alois Heralecký** was born on 16 Sep 1909 in Slavice No. 28. He died on 17 Jul 1994 in Slavice No. 23.
    - 39. iii. **František Heralecký** was born on 06 Oct 1912 in Slavice No. 23.
    - 40. iv. **Karel Heralecký** was born on 30 Oct 1917. He married Jaroslava Zahradnickova on 05 Jan 1946. He died on 01 Jul 1988.

24. **Josef Heralecký**-9 (František-8, Václav-7, Jan-6, Josef-5, Jakob-4, Josef Ferdinand-3, Martin-2, Jan-1) was born on 01 Aug 1877 in Slavice No. 28. He died on 29 Apr 1929 in Slavice.

    Emilie Nechodomova was born on 29 Jan 1888 in Slavice No. 23. She died on 03 Jul 1967.

    Josef Heralecký and Emilie Nechodomova were married on 17 Jul 1919 in Trebic. They had the following children:
    - 41. i. **Marie Heralecká** was born on 18 Mar 1920 in Trebic. She married Josef Kolar on 08 Aug 1945.
    - 42. ii. **Kvetoslava Heralecká** was born on 09 Apr 1921.
    - 43. iii. **Josef Heralecký** was born on 02 Feb 1922. He died on 26 Feb 2001 in Hartvikovice.
    - 44. iv. **Emilie Heralecká** was born on 22 Nov 1925 in Hartvikovice No. 36. She married Josef Lekl on 13 Feb 1968 in Prostejov.

25. **Augustin Heralecký**-9 (František-8, Václav-7, Jan-6, Josef-5, Jakob-4, Josef Ferdinand-3, Martin-2, Jan-1) was born on 03 Dec 1883 in Slavice.

He died in Aug 1957 in Okrisky.

Anna Řehořová daughter of Jakub Řehoř and Anna Studihrachová was born on 19 Jul 1886 in Lucnici Co. (Dolni Bukovsko No. 55, Veseli n). She died on 16 Dec 1968 in Okrisky.

Augustin Heralecký and Anna Řehořová married. They had the following children:

    i. **Augustin Heralecký**.

45. ii. **Miroslav Heralecký** was born on 05 Sep 1915 in České Budejovice, České Budejovice Co.. He married Marie Bartošová on 11 Nov 1941 in Prague-Zizkov. He died on 10 Jun 1993 in Proseč, Jablonec nad Nisou.

46. iii. **Vladimír Heralecký** was born on 18 Dec 1918 in Jemnice. He died on 19 Dec 1991 in Okrisky.

Generation 10

26. **Karla Heralecká**-10 (Jan-9, Jan-8, Václav-7, Jan-6, Josef-5, Jakob-4, Josef Ferdinand-3, Martin-2, Jan-1) was born on 19 Oct 1889.

Karel Holčapek.

Karel Holčapek and Karla Heralecká married. They had the following children:

    i. **Karla Holcapkova** was born on 12 Oct 1917.

27. **František Heralecký**-10 (Jan-9, Jan-8, Václav-7, Jan-6, Josef-5, Jakob-4, Josef Ferdinand-3, Martin-2, Jan-1) was born on 26 Jan 1895 in Bohusice No. 16. He died in 1984.

Marie Stumpolova was born in Bohusice No. 32.

František Heralecký and Marie Stumpolova were married on 13 Jul 1927. They had the following children:

47. i. **Marie Heralecká** was born on 04 Aug 1928.

48. ii. **František Heralecký** was born on 26 Jan 1930.

28. **Josef Heralecký**-10 (Jan-9, Jan-8, Václav-7, Jan-6, Josef-5, Jakob-4, Josef Ferdinand-3, Martin-2, Jan-1) was born on 13 Feb 1898.

Marie Tučková.

Josef Heralecký and Marie Tučková were married on 19 Jan 1932 in Hrusovany nad Jevickou. They had the following children:

    i. **Marie Heralecká** was born in 1935.

ii. **Josef Heralecký**.
29. **Marie Heralecká**-10 (Antonín-9, Jan-8, Václav-7, Jan-6, Josef-5, Jakob-4, Josef Ferdinand-3, Martin-2, Jan-1) was born in 1893. She died in 1968.
Josef Forman was born in 1888 in Vicenice. He died in 1938.
Josef Forman and Marie Heralecká married. They had the following children:
49. i. **Josef Forman** was born in 1923.
50. ii. **Marie Formanová** was born in 1925.
    iii. **Jiří Forman** was born in 1927.
    iv. **Františka Formanová** was born in 1929.
30. **Antonín Heralecký**-10 (Antonín-9, Jan-8, Václav-7, Jan-6, Josef-5, Jakob-4, Josef Ferdinand-3, Martin-2, Jan-1) was born on 05 May 1899 in Bohusice No. 16. He died on 15 Jul 1966.
Terezie Prinosilova was born on 10 Oct 1907. She died on 29 Mar 1981. Antonín Heralecký and Terezie Prinosilova married. They had the following children:
    i. **Terezie Heralecká** was born in 1930. She died in 1931.
52. ii. **Marie Heralecká** was born in 1931.
53. iii. **Antonie Heralecká** was born in 1933.
54. iv. **Antonín Heralecký** was born on 24 May 1934 in Bohusice No. 16.
    v. **Jan Heralecký** was born in 1937. He died in 1938.
31. **Jan Heralecký**-10 (Antonín-9, Jan-8, Václav-7, Jan-6, Josef-5, Jakob-4, Josef Ferdinand-3, Martin-2, Jan-1) was born in 1901. He died in 1972.
Amalie Kolarova was born in 1911 in Sukov. She died in 1999.
Jan Heralecký and Amalie Kolarova married. They had the following children:
54. i. **Jana Heralecká** was born in 1939.
55. ii. **Zdena Heralecká** was born in 1940.
32. **Eduard Heralecký**-10 (Eduard-9, Jan-8, Václav-7, Jan-6, Josef-5, Jakob-4, Josef Ferdinand-3, Martin-2, Jan-1) was born in 1902. He died in 1992.
Marie Splichalova was born in 1909.
Eduard Heralecký and Marie Splichalova married. They had the following children:

56. i. **Eduard Heralecký** was born in 1934.
57. ii. **Mario Heralecký** was born in 1937.
58. iii. **Oldrřch Heralecký** was born in 1950.
    iv. **Ludmila Heralecká** was born in 1951.
33. **Matylda Heralecká**-10 (Eduard-9, Jan-8, Václav-7, Jan-6, Josef-5, Jakob-4, Josef Ferdinand-3, Martin-2, Jan-1) was born in 1909.
    Josef Vondráček was born in 1903. He died in 1987.
    Josef Vondráček and Matylda Heralecká married. They had the following children:
    i. **Marie Vondrackova** was born in 1932.
    ii. **Josef Vondráček** was born in 1933.
59. iii. **Anna Vondrackova** was born in 1935.
    iv. **František Vondráček** was born in 1944.
34. **Antonín Heralecký**-10 (Jan-9, František-8, Václav-7, Jan-6, Josef-5, Jakob-4, Josef Ferdinand-3, Martin-2, Jan-1) was born on 26 Apr 1893 in Slavice No. 36. He died on 20 Dec 1971.
    Anastazie was born on 21 Dec 1898. She died on 16 Mar 1962.
    Antonín Heralecký and Anastazie married. They had the following children:
    60. i. **Antonín Heralecký** was born on 11 May 1928. He died on 01 Oct 1983.
    61. ii. **Jan Heralecký** was born on 18 Jul 1930 in Telc. He married Marie Svatonová on 28 May 1955. He died on 15 Jun 1997.
        iii. **Vladimír Heralecký** was born on 18 Jul 1930. He died on 03 Jan 1933.
    63. iv. **Jaromír Heralecký** was born on 29 Nov 1933. He married Zdena Vetcha on 18 Jun 1960.
35. **Jaroslav Heralecký**-10 (Jan-9, František-8, Václav-7, Jan-6, Josef-5, Jakob-4, Josef Ferdinand-3, Martin-2, Jan-1) was born in 1887.
    Marie Tvarůžková.
    Jaroslav Heralecký and Marie Tvarůžková were married about 1924. They had the following children:
    63. i. **Jaroslav Heralecký** was born on 14 Oct 1924 in Kozlov. He

married Věra Hrazdirová on 22 Dec 1945.

36. **Jan Heralecký**-10 (Antonín-9, František-8, Václav-7, Jan-6, Josef-5, Jakob-4, Josef Ferdinand-3, Martin-2, Jan-1) was born in 1921.

    Květoslava Muková was born in 1928.

    Jan Heralecký and Květoslava Muková married. They had the following children:

    64. i. **Jana Heralecká**.
    65. ii. **Marie Heralecká**.

37. **Františka Heralecká**-10 (František-9, František-8, Václav-7, Jan-6, Josef-5, Jakob-4, Josef Ferdinand-3, Martin-2, Jan-1) was born on 06 Jun 1908 in Slavice No. 28. She died on 01 Apr 1988 in Slavice No. 23.

    Adolf Pokorný was born on 28 May 1905 in Slavice. He died on 16 Jun 1985 in Slavice. Adolf Pokorný and Františka Heralecká married. They had the following children:

    66. i. **Miloš Pokorný** was born on 22 Oct 1944.
    67. ii. **Marie Pokorná** was born on 05 Dec 1933 in Slavice.
    68. iii. **Jiřina Pokorná** was born on 18 Jan 1936. She married Jaroslav Kopecny on 26 Oct 1957.

38. **Alois Heralecký**-10 (František-9, František-8, Václav-7, Jan-6, Josef-5, Jakob-4, Josef Ferdinand-3, Martin-2, Jan-1) was born on 16 Sep 1909 in Slavice No. 28. He died on 17 Jul 1994 in Slavice No. 23.

    Blažena Sobotková was born on 13 Apr 1913. She died on 24 Feb 1962. Alois Heralecký and Blažena Sobotková married. They had the following children:

    69. i. **Alois Heralecký** was born on 15 May 1940. He married Irena Eschenauerová on 21 Jul 1962.
    70. ii. **Vladimír Heralecký** was born on 18 Nov 1941 in Slavice No. 28.
    71. iii. **Dana Heralecká** was born on 02 Apr 1946. She married Josef Vanicek on 24 Oct 1964.
    72. iv. **Blanka Heralecká** was born on 14 Aug 1951. She married Josef Pecka on 14 Jul 1971.

39. **František Heralecký**-10 (František-9, František-8, Václav-7, Jan-6, Josef-5, Jakob-4, Josef Ferdinand-3, Martin-2, Jan-1) was born on 06 Oct

1912 in Slavice No. 23.

Věra Mikeskova was born on 16 Sep 1920 in Trebic.

František Heralecký and Věra Mikeskova married. They had the following children:

73.   i. **Věra Heralecká** was born on 05 Apr 1943.
74.   ii. **Borivoj Heralecký** was born on 02 May 1946 in Trebic. He married Jana Ulmanova on 07 Dec 1968.
75.   iii. **Sylvie Heralecká** was born on 09 Nov 1950. She married Jan Brátka on 12 Sep 1975.

40. **Karel Heralecký**-10 (František-9, František-8, Václav-7, Jan-6, Josef-5, Jakob-4, Josef Ferdinand-3, Martin-2, Jan-1) was born on 30 Oct 1917. He died on 01 Jul 1988.

Jaroslava Zahradnickova was born on 26 Mar 1928 in Mastnik No. 20.

Karel Heralecký and Jaroslava Zahradnickova were married on 05 Jan 1946. They had the following children:

76.   i. **Jaroslava Heralecká** was born on 08 Jun 1946. She married Petr Vojtek on 08 Aug 1966.
77.   ii. **Helena Heralecká** was born on 17 Aug 1950. She married Milan Nestrojil on 28 Aug 1971.
78.   iii. **Jitka Heralecká** was born on 14 Feb 1952. She married Vlado Lavický on 29 Jul 1973.

41. **Marie Heralecká**-10 (Josef-9, František-8, Václav-7, Jan-6, Josef-5, Jakob-4, Josef Ferdinand-3, Martin-2, Jan-1) was born on 18 Mar 1920 in Trebic.

Josef Kolar was born on 29 May 1920 in Namesti nad Oslavou.

Josef Kolar and Marie Heralecká were married on 08 Aug 1945. They had the following children:

79.   i. **Josef Kolar** was born on 09 Apr 1949 in Trebic. He married Eva Jandová on 14 Sep 1985.
    ii. **child Kolar**.

42. **Kvetoslava Heralecká**-10 (Josef-9, František-8, Václav-7, Jan-6, Josef-5, Jakob-4, Josef Ferdinand-3, Martin-2, Jan-1) was born on 09 Apr 1921.

Lubomir Zak.

Lubomir Zak and Kvetoslava Heralecká married. They had the following children:

80. i. **Květoslav Zak.**

81. ii. **Lubomira Zakova.**

43. **Josef Heralecký**-10 (Josef-9, František-8, Václav-7, Jan-6, Josef-5, Jakob-4, Josef Ferdinand-3, Martin-2, Jan-1) was born on 02 Feb 1922. He died on 26 Feb 2001 in Hartvikovice.

    Anežka Outulna was born on 28 Nov 1927.

    Josef Heralecký and Anežka Outulna married. They had the following children:

    82. i. **Emilie Heralecká** was born on 03 Jul 1955 in Ocmanice. She married Miroslav Smutny in Ocmanice.

    83. ii. **Josef Heralecký** was born on 01 Feb 1958 in Hartvikovice.

44. **Emilie Heralecká**-10 (Josef-9, František-8, Václav-7, Jan-6, Josef-5, Jakob-4, Josef Ferdinand-3, Martin-2, Jan-1) was born on 22 Nov 1925 in Hartvikovice No. 36.

    Josef Lekl son of Josef Lekl and Anna Angettrova was born on 07 Dec 1924 in Olomouc - Hodolany.

    Josef Lekl and Emilie Heralecká were married on 13 Feb 1968 in Prostejov. They had the following children:

    84. i. **Libor Lekl** was born on 13 May 1968. He married Slavomira Popelková on 25 Jan 1992 in Strazisko.

45. **Miroslav Heralecký**-10 (Augustin-9, František-8, Václav-7, Jan-6, Josef-5, Jakob-4, Josef Ferdinand-3, Martin-2, Jan-1) was born on 05 Sep 1915 in České Budejovice, České Budejovice Co.. He died on 10 Jun 1993 in Proseč, Jablonec nad Nisou.

    Marie Bartošová daughter of František Bartos and Anna Bondy was born on 20 Feb 1925 in Kejzlice. She died on 22 Jul 2002 in Jablonec.

    Miroslav Heralecký and Marie Bartošová were married on 11 Nov 1941 in Prague-Zizkov. They had the following children:

    85. i. **Daniela Heralecká** was born on 24 May 1945 in Praha. She married Miroslav Hejatko in Liberec.

    86. ii. **Miroslav Heralecký** was born on 18 May 1949 in salomonJablonec

nad Nisou, Czech.. He married Marcela Žďárská on 15 Mar 1975 in Sychrov. He died on 20 Feb 2017 in Proseč, Jablonec nad Nisou, Czech..

46. **Vladimír Heralecký**-10 (Augustin-9, František-8, Václav-7, Jan-6, Josef-5, Jakob-4, Josef Ferdinand-3, Martin-2, Jan-1) was born on 18 Dec 1918 in Jemnice. He died on 19 Dec 1991 in Okrisky.

    Jarmila Kruzikova was born on 19 Nov 1921.

    Vladimír Heralecký and Jarmila Kruzikova married. They had the following children:

    87. i. **Vladimír Heralecký** was born on 25 Jun 1946.
    88. ii. **Miroslav Heralecký** was born on 09 Dec 1949. He married Lenka Indrova on 24 Nov 1979 in Trebic.
    89. iii. **Jarmila Heralecká** was born on 27 Dec 1954. She married Jan Fudor on 06 Aug 1977.

Generation 11

47. **Marie Heralecká**-11 (František-10, Jan-9, Jan-8, Václav-7, Jan-6, Josef-5, Jakob-4, Josef Ferdinand-3, Martin-2, Jan-1) was born on 04 Aug 1928.

    František Jonáš.

    František Jonáš and Marie Heralecká married. They had the following children:

    i. **František Jonáš**.

48. **František Heralecký**-11 (František-10, Jan-9, Jan-8, Václav-7, Jan-6, Josef-5, Jakob-4, Josef Ferdinand-3, Martin-2, Jan-1) was born on 26 Jan 1930.

    Ludmila Papoušková was born in 1937 in Bohusice No. 322.

    František Heralecký and Ludmila Papoušková married. They had the following children:

    i. **Marie Heralecká** was born in 1955.
    ii. **František Heralecký** was born in 1958.
    iii. **Miloš Heralecký**.
    iv. **Blanka Heralecká**.
    v. **Cestmir Heralecký**.

49. **Josef Forman**-11 (Marie-10, Antonín-9, Jan-8, Václav-7, Jan-6, Josef-5,

Jakob-4, Josef Ferdinand-3, Martin-2, Jan-1) was born in 1923.
Slavka Jonasova.
Josef Forman and Slavka Jonasova married. They had the following children:
  i. **Josef Forman** was born in 1949. He died in 1995.
91. ii. **Jiří Forman** was born in 1957.
  iii. **Stanislava Formanová.**
  iv. **Bohuslav Forman.**

50. **Marie Formanová**-11 (Marie-10, Antonín-9, Jan-8, Václav-7, Jan-6, Josef-5, Jakob-4, Josef Ferdinand-3, Martin-2, Jan-1) was born in 1925.
Antonín Michal was born in 1919.
Antonín Michal and Marie Formanová married. They had the following children:
  i. **Marie Michalova.**
  ii. **Antonín Michal.**
  iii. **Jana Michalova.**

51. **Marie Heralecká**-11 (Antonín-10, Antonín-9, Jan-8, Václav-7, Jan-6, Josef-5, Jakob-4, Josef Ferdinand-3, Martin-2, Jan-1) was born in 1931.
Leoplod Malena was born in 1930.
Leoplod Malena and Marie Heralecká married. They had the following children:
91. i. **Marie Malenova** was born in 1955.
92. ii. **Antonín Malena.**
93. iii. **Zdena Malenova** was born in 1957.
94. iv. **Jiří Malena** was born in 1962.

52. **Antonie Heralecká**-11 (Antonín-10, Antonín-9, Jan-8, Václav-7, Jan-6, Josef-5, Jakob-4, Josef Ferdinand-3, Martin-2, Jan-1) was born in 1933.
Bohuslav Bulíček was born in 1928. He died in 1998.
Bohuslav Bulíček and Antonie Heralecká married. They had the following children:
95. i. **Bohuslav Bulíček** was born in 1962.
96. ii. **Miroslav Bulíček** was born in 1964.

53. **Antonín Heralecký**-11 (Antonín-10, Antonín-9, Jan-8, Václav-7, Jan-6,

Josef-5, Jakob-4, Josef Ferdinand-3, Martin-2, Jan-1) was born on 24 May 1934 in Bohusice No. 16.

Marie Dvořáková was born on 25 Mar 1938.

Antonín Heralecký and Marie Dvořáková married. They had the following children:

97. i. **Antonín Heralecký** was born on 13 Sep 1957.

98. ii. **Libuše Heralecká** was born on 10 Jun 1959.

iii. **Petra Heralecká** was born on 31 May 1976.

54. **Jana Heralecká**-11 (Jan-10, Antonín-9, Jan-8, Václav-7, Jan-6, Josef-5, Jakob-4, Josef Ferdinand-3, Martin-2, Jan-1) was born in 1939.

Václav Holik was born in Ctidruzice.

Václav Holik and Jana Heralecká married. They had the following children:

i. **Jiří Holik**.

ii. **Pavel Holik**.

55. **Zdena Heralecká**-11 (Jan-10, Antonín-9, Jan-8, Václav-7, Jan-6, Josef-5, Jakob-4, Josef Ferdinand-3, Martin-2, Jan-1) was born in 1940.

Ladislav Vejtasa was born in Lukov (now Pelhrimov).

Ladislav Vejtasa and Zdena Heralecká married. They had the following children:

i. **Roman Vejtasa**.

ii. **Milan Vejtasa**.

56. **Eduard Heralecký**-11 (Eduard-10, Eduard-9, Jan-8, Václav-7, Jan-6, Josef-5, Jakob-4, Josef Ferdinand-3, Martin-2, Jan-1) was born in 1934.

Jaroslava Brhelová was born in 1934.

Eduard Heralecký and Jaroslava Brhelová married. They had the following children:

99. i. **Jaroslava Heralecká**.

100. ii. **Hana Heralecká**.

57. **Mario Heralecký**-11 (Eduard-10, Eduard-9, Jan-8, Václav-7, Jan-6, Josef-5, Jakob-4, Josef Ferdinand-3, Martin-2, Jan-1) was born in 1937.

Krystina Rybova was born in 1938.

Mario Heralecký and Krystina Rybova married. They had the following

children:

101. i. **Petra Heralecká**.

58. **Oldrřch Heralecký**-11 (Eduard-10, Eduard-9, Jan-8, Václav-7, Jan-6, Josef-5, Jakob-4, Josef Ferdinand-3, Martin-2, Jan-1) was born in 1950.
    Stanislava Wildova.
    Oldrřch Heralecký and Stanislava Wildova married. They had the following children:
    - i. **Pavel Heralecký**.
    - ii. **Tomáš Heralecký**.
    - iii. **Vit Heralecký**.
    - iv. **Petr Heralecký**.

    Marie.
    Oldrřch Heralecký and Marie married. They had no children.

59. **Anna Vondrackova**-11 (Matylda-10, Eduard-9, Jan-8, Václav-7, Jan-6, Josef-5, Jakob-4, Josef Ferdinand-3, Martin-2, Jan-1) was born in 1935.
    Jackovic was born in 1944.
    Jackovic and Anna Vondrackova married. They had the following children:
    - i. **Eliška Jackovicová**.
    - ii. **Borek Jackovic**.
    - iii. **Terezie Jackovicová**.

60. **Antonín Heralecký**-11 (Antonín-10, Jan-9, František-8, Václav-7, Jan-6, Josef-5, Jakob-4, Josef Ferdinand-3, Martin-2, Jan-1) was born on 11 May 1928. He died on 01 Oct 1983.
    Dana Mejzlikova was born on 19 Nov 1934.
    Antonín Heralecký and Dana Mejzlikova married. They had the following children:

    102. i. **Pavel Heralecký** was born on 26 Dec 1954 in Trebic. He married Jana Pechová on 19 Sep 1975 in Luka nad Jihlavou.
    103. ii. **Antonín Heralecký** was born on 19 Sep 1956 in Jihlava. He married Libuše Oksinova on 28 Aug 1981 in Jihlava.

61. **Jan Heralecký**-11 (Antonín-10, Jan-9, František-8, Václav-7, Jan-6, Josef-5, Jakob-4, Josef Ferdinand-3, Martin-2, Jan-1) was born on 18 Jul 1930 in

Telc. He died on 15 Jun 1997.

Marie Svatonová was born on 26 Aug 1935.

Jan Heralecký and Marie Svatonová were married on 28 May 1955. They had the following children:

    104. i. **Jan Heralecký** was born on 24 Jun 1957 in Trebic. He married Jiřina Blahutková on 30 Dec 1982 in Telc.

62. **Jaromír Heralecký**-11 (Antonín-10, Jan-9, František-8, Václav-7, Jan-6, Josef-5, Jakob-4, Josef Ferdinand-3, Martin-2, Jan-1) was born on 29 Nov 1933.

Zdena Vetcha was born on 28 Feb 1940.

Jaromír Heralecký and Zdena Vetcha were married on 18 Jun 1960. They had the following children:

    105. i. **Jaromír Heralecký** was born on 02 Aug 1961. He married Denisa Minarcikova on 25 Jun 1983.

    106. ii. **Lenka Heralecká** was born on 11 Feb 1964. She married Jiří Jurka on 16 Nov 1986.

63. **Jaroslav Heralecký**-11 (Jaroslav-10, Jan-9, František-8, Václav-7, Jan-6, Josef-5, Jakob-4, Josef Ferdinand-3, Martin-2, Jan-1) was born on 14 Oct 1924 in Kozlov.

Věra Hrazdirová was born on 08 Oct 1923 in Brno.

Jaroslav Heralecký and Věra Hrazdirová were married on 22 Dec 1945. They had the following children:

    107. i. **Jaroslav Heralecký** was born on 24 May 1946. He married Milada Ticha on 01 Jun 1968.

    108. ii. **Marie Heralecká** was born on 14 Oct 1949. She married Zdeněk Svoboda on 17 Feb 1968.

    109. iii. **Ladislav Heralecký** was born on 27 May 1954 in Trebic. He married Vlasta Flodrova on 21 Apr 1976.

64. **Jana Heralecká**-11 (Jan-10, Antonín-9, František-8, Václav-7, Jan-6, Josef-5, Jakob-4, Josef Ferdinand-3, Martin-2, Jan-1).

Josef Mafek.

Josef Mafek and Jana Heralecká married. They had the following children:

i. Josef Mafek.
   ii. Jan Mafek.
   iii. Pavel Mafek.
65. **Marie Heralecká**-11 (Jan-10, Antonín-9, František-8, Václav-7, Jan-6, Josef-5, Jakob-4, Josef Ferdinand-3, Martin-2, Jan-1).
   Brinek.
   Brinek and Marie Heralecká married. They had the following children:
   i. **Marie Brinkova.**
   ii. **Oldrřch Brinek.**
   iii. **Kamil Brinek.**
66. **Miloš Pokorný**-11 (Františka-10, František-9, František-8, Václav-7, Jan-6, Josef-5, Jakob-4, Josef Ferdinand-3, Martin-2, Jan-1) was born on 22 Oct 1944.
   Blažena Holeckova.
   Miloš Pokorný and Blažena Holeckova married. They had the following children:
   i. **Iva Pokorná.**
   ii. **Lenka Pokorná.**
   iii. **Luděk Pokorný.**
67. **Marie Pokorná**-11 (Františka-10, František-9, František-8, Václav-7, Jan-6, Josef-5, Jakob-4, Josef Ferdinand-3, Martin-2, Jan-1) was born on 05 Dec 1933 in Slavice.
   Albin Maly was born about 1926. He died about 1964.
   Albin Maly and Marie Pokorná married. They had the following children:
   110. i. **Pavel Maly** was born on 20 Oct 1960.
68. **Jiřina Pokorná**-11 (Františka-10, František-9, František-8, Václav-7, Jan-6, Josef-5, Jakob-4, Josef Ferdinand-3, Martin-2, Jan-1) was born on 18 Jan 1936.
   Jaroslav Kopecny was born on 16 Oct 1935.
   Jaroslav Kopecny and Jiřina Pokorná were married on 26 Oct 1957. They had the following children:
   111. i. **Alena Kopecna.**

ii. **Jiřina Kopecna** was born on 07 Aug 1958.
69. **Alois Heralecký**-11 (Alois-10, František-9, František-8, Václav-7, Jan-6, Josef-5, Jakob-4, Josef Ferdinand-3, Martin-2, Jan-1) was born on 15 May 1940.

    Irena Eschenauerová was born on 22 Sep 1941 in Budickovice.

    Alois Heralecký and Irena Eschenauerová were married on 21 Jul 1962. They had the following children:

    112. i. **Jana Heralecká** was born on 17 Feb 1963.

70. **Vladimír Heralecký**-11 (Alois-10, František-9, František-8, Václav-7, Jan-6, Josef-5, Jakob-4, Josef Ferdinand-3, Martin-2, Jan-1) was born on 18 Nov 1941 in Slavice No. 28.

    Marie Tomková was born on 23 Jan 1947.

    Vladimír Heralecký and Marie Tomková married. They had the following children:

    113. i. **Leos Heralecký** was born on 21 Mar 1972. He married Radka Jicinska on 19 Dec 1992.
    114. ii. **Vladimír Heralecký** was born on 02 Oct 1968.

71. **Dana Heralecká**-11 (Alois-10, František-9, František-8, Václav-7, Jan-6, Josef-5, Jakob-4, Josef Ferdinand-3, Martin-2, Jan-1) was born on 02 Apr 1946.

    Josef Vanicek was born on 17 Dec 1941.

    Josef Vanicek and Dana Heralecká were married on 24 Oct 1964. They had the following children:

    115. i. **Dana Vanickova** was born on 10 Jun 1965. She married Pavel Pekař on 15 Jul 1989.
    116. ii. **Romana Vanickova** was born on 19 Aug 1966. She married Jaroslav Popovský on 19 Jul 1986.
    117. iii. **Iva Vanickova** was born on 05 Apr 1973. She married Jan Vrbka on 11 Jul 1992.

72. **Blanka Heralecká**-11 (Alois-10, František-9, František-8, Václav-7, Jan-6, Josef-5, Jakob-4, Josef Ferdinand-3, Martin-2, Jan-1) was born on 14 Aug 1951.

    Josef Pecka was born on 13 Feb 1948.

Josef Pecka and Blanka Heralecká were married on 14 Jul 1971. They had the following children:

    118. i. **Tomáš Pecka** was born on 05 Jun 1972.

    119. ii. **Aleš Pecka** was born on 04 Mar 1975. He married Andrea Nováková on 15 Apr 1994.

73. **Věra Heralecká**-11 (František-10, František-9, František-8, Václav-7, Jan-6, Josef-5, Jakob-4, Josef Ferdinand-3, Martin-2, Jan-1) was born on 05 Apr 1943.

Milan Jurcik was born on 06 Nov 1940.

Milan Jurcik and Věra Heralecká married. They had the following children:

    120. i. **Kateřina Jurcikova** was born on 24 Feb 1965.

    ii. **Marek Jurcikova** was born on 22 Apr 1971.

74. **Borivoj Heralecký**-11 (František-10, František-9, František-8, Václav-7, Jan-6, Josef-5, Jakob-4, Josef Ferdinand-3, Martin-2, Jan-1) was born on 02 May 1946 in Trebic.

Jana Ulmanova was born on 21 Jun 1949.

Borivoj Heralecký and Jana Ulmanova were married on 07 Dec 1968. They had the following children:

    121. i. **Kamila Heralecká** was born on 04 May 1969. She married Wilerth on 22 Apr 1989.

    122. ii. **Jana Heralecká** was born on 27 Dec 1973. She married Simansky on 25 Jan 1997.

75. **Sylvie Heralecká**-11 (František-10, František-9, František-8, Václav-7, Jan-6, Josef-5, Jakob-4, Josef Ferdinand-3, Martin-2, Jan-1) was born on 09 Nov 1950.

Jan Brátka was born on 18 Jul 1950.

Jan Brátka and Sylvie Heralecká were married on 12 Sep 1975. They had the following children:

    i. **Karolina Brátková** was born on 26 Mar 1976.

    ii. **Sylvie Brátkova** was born on 15 Feb 1978.

    iii. **Jana Brátková** was born on 03 Nov 1982.

76. **Jaroslava Heralecká**-11 (Karel-10, František-9, František-8, Václav-7,

Jan-6, Josef-5, Jakob-4, Josef Ferdinand-3, Martin-2, Jan-1) was born on 08 Jun 1946.

Petr Vojtek was born on 09 Jun 1942 in Trebic.

Petr Vojtek and Jaroslava Heralecká were married on 08 Aug 1966. They had the following children:

    123. i. **Michael Vojtek** was born on 11 Sep 1969. He married Kateřina Mala on 25 Jul 1992.

ii. **Martin Vojtek** was born on 03 Feb 1972.

77. **Helena Heralecká**-11 (Karel-10, František-9, František-8, Václav-7, Jan-6, Josef-5, Jakob-4, Josef Ferdinand-3, Martin-2, Jan-1) was born on 17 Aug 1950.

Milan Nestrojil was born on 16 Nov 1947.

Milan Nestrojil and Helena Heralecká were married on 28 Aug 1971. They had the following children:

    124. i. **Tomáš Nestrojil** was born on 28 Aug 1973.

    ii. **Simona Nestrojilova** was born on 31 Dec 1981.

78. **Jitka Heralecká**-11 (Karel-10, František-9, František-8, Václav-7, Jan-6, Josef-5, Jakob-4, Josef Ferdinand-3, Martin-2, Jan-1) was born on 14 Feb 1952.

Vlado Lavický was born on 29 Jun 1947.

Vlado Lavický and Jitka Heralecká were married on 29 Jul 1973. They had the following children:

    i. **Petr Lavický** was born on 02 Nov 1977.

    ii. **Eva Lavicka** was born on 31 Jan 1982.

    iii. **Helena Lavicka** was born on 31 Jan 1982.

    iv. **Jan Lavický** was born on 31 Jan 1982.

79. **Josef Kolar**-11 (Marie-10, Josef-9, František-8, Václav-7, Jan-6, Josef-5, Jakob-4, Josef Ferdinand-3, Martin-2, Jan-1) was born on 09 Apr 1949 in Trebic.

Eva Jandová was born on 15 Jan 1955.

Josef Kolar and Eva Jandová were married on 14 Sep 1985. They had the following children:

    i. **Josef Kolar** was born on 07 Oct 1986.

ii. **Eva Kolarova** was born on 16 May 1988.
80. **Květoslav Zak**-11 (Kvetoslava-10, Josef-9, František-8, Václav-7, Jan-6, Josef-5, Jakob-4, Josef Ferdinand-3, Martin-2, Jan-1).
Unknown.
Květoslav Zak and Unknown married. They had the following children:
i. **Vlastimil Zak.**
ii. **Alexandra Zakova.**
iii. **Tana Zakova.**
81. **Lubomira Zakova**-11 (Kvetoslava-10, Josef-9, František-8, Václav-7, Jan-6, Josef-5, Jakob-4, Josef Ferdinand-3, Martin-2, Jan-1).
Holub.
Holub and Lubomira Zakova married. They had the following children:
i. **Kvetoslava Holubová.**
ii. **Lubomira Holubová.**
iii. **Zdeněk Holub.**
iv. **Zbyněk Holub.**
82. **Emilie Heralecká**-11 (Josef-10, Josef-9, František-8, Václav-7, Jan-6, Josef-5, Jakob-4, Josef Ferdinand-3, Martin-2, Jan-1) was born on 03 Jul 1955 in Ocmanice.
Miroslav Smutny.
Miroslav Smutny and Emilie Heralecká were married in Ocmanice. They had the following children:
i. **Simona Smutna.**
ii. **Kateřina Smutna.**
83. **Josef Heralecký**-11 (Josef-10, Josef-9, František-8, Václav-7, Jan-6, Josef-5, Jakob-4, Josef Ferdinand-3, Martin-2, Jan-1) was born on 01 Feb 1958 in Hartvikovice.
Jana Kopuleta was born on 25 Apr 1961.
Josef Heralecký and Jana Kopuleta married. They had the following children:
i. **Tomáš Heralecký** was born on 23 Oct 1979.
ii. **Pavla Heralecká** was born on 19 Dec 1980.
84. **Libor Lekl**-11 (Emilie-10, Josef-9, František-8, Václav-7, Jan-6, Josef-5,

Jakob-4, Josef Ferdinand-3, Martin-2, Jan-1) was born on 13 May 1968.
Slavomira Popelková was born on 18 Jun 1970 in Strazisko No. 92.
Libor Lekl and Slavomira Popelková were married on 25 Jan 1992 in Strazisko. They had the following children:

    i. **Tomáš Lekl** was born on 22 May 1992.

85. **Daniela Heralecká**-11 (Miroslav-10, Augustin-9, František-8, Václav-7, Jan-6, Josef-5, Jakob-4, Josef Ferdinand-3, Martin-2, Jan-1) was born on 24 May 1945 in Praha.
Miroslav Hejatko was born on 01 May 1940 in Brno.
Miroslav Hejatko and Daniela Heralecká were married in Liberec. They had the following children:

    i. **Daniela Hejatkova** was born on 21 Feb 1968 in Jablonec nad Nisou.

  126. ii. **Magdalena Hejatkova** was born on 08 Feb 1975 in Jablonec nad Nisou. She married Pavel Fiser on 19 Dec 1998 in Liberec.

86. **Miroslav Heralecký**-11 (Miroslav-10, Augustin-9, František-8, Václav-7, Jan-6, Josef-5, Jakob-4, Josef Ferdinand-3, Martin-2, Jan-1) was born on 18 May 1949 in salomonJablonec nad Nisou, Czech.. He died on 20 Feb 2017 in Proseč, Jablonec nad Nisou, Czech..
Marcela Žďárská daughter of František Žďárský and Marta Rechcíglová was born on 09 May 1954 in Liberec.
Miroslav Heralecký and Marcela Žďárská were married on 15 Mar 1975 in Sychrov. They had the following children:

    i. **Vit Heralecký** was born on 16 Jan 1977 in Jablonec nad Nisou. He married Olga Zrubcová on 13 Jul 1996.

  126. ii. **Zuzana Heralecká** was born on 30 Dec 1978 in Jablonec nad Nisou. She married Jaroslav Egrt on 13 Sep 2002 in Jablonec nad Nisou.

87. **Vladimír Heralecký**-11 (Vladimír-10, Augustin-9, František-8, Václav-7, Jan-6, Josef-5, Jakob-4, Josef Ferdinand-3, Martin-2, Jan-1) was born on 25 Jun 1946.
Marcela Černínová.
Vladimír Heralecký and Marcela Černínová married. They had the

following children:
  i. **Lenka Heralecká**.
  ii. **Martin Heralecký**.

88. **Miroslav Heralecký**-11 (Vladimír-10, Augustin-9, František-8, Václav-7, Jan-6, Josef-5, Jakob-4, Josef Ferdinand-3, Martin-2, Jan-1) was born on 09 Dec 1949.
    Lenka Indrova was born on 21 Jun 1959.
    Miroslav Heralecký and Lenka Indrova were married on 24 Nov 1979 in Trebic. They had the following children:
      i. **Čeněk Heralecký** was born on 11 Dec 1981.
      ii. **Aleš Heralecký** was born on 03 Dec 1984.

89. **Jarmila Heralecká**-11 (Vladimír-10, Augustin-9, František-8, Václav-7, Jan-6, Josef-5, Jakob-4, Josef Ferdinand-3, Martin-2, Jan-1) was born on 27 Dec 1954.
    Jan Fudor was born on 20 May 1956.
    Jan Fudor and Jarmila Heralecká were married on 06 Aug 1977. They had the following children:
      i. **Jiří Fudor** was born on 26 May 1978.
      ii. **Jana Fudorova** was born on 02 Jul 1983.

Generation 12

90. **Jiří Forman**-12 (Josef-11, Marie-10, Antonín-9, Jan-8, Václav-7, Jan-6, Josef-5, Jakob-4, Josef Ferdinand-3, Martin-2, Jan-1) was born in 1957.
    Libuše Havelková.
    Jiří Forman and Libuše Havelková married. They had the following children:
      i. **child Forman**.

91. **Marie Malenova**-12 (Marie-11, Antonín-10, Antonín-9, Jan-8, Václav-7, Jan-6, Josef-5, Jakob-4, Josef Ferdinand-3, Martin-2, Jan-1) was born in 1955.
    Josef Palko.
    Josef Palko and Marie Malenova married. They had the following children:
      i. **Hanka Palkova**.

ii. **Tomáš Palko.**
92. **Antonín Malena**-12 (Marie-11, Antonín-10, Antonín-9, Jan-8, Václav-7, Jan-6, Josef-5, Jakob-4, Josef Ferdinand-3, Martin-2, Jan-1).
Marie Lorencova.
Antonín Malena and Marie Lorencova married. They had the following children:
   i. **Barbora Malenova** was born in 1983.
   ii. **Štěpán Malena** was born in 1985.
93. **Zdena Malenova**-12 (Marie-11, Antonín-10, Antonín-9, Jan-8, Václav-7, Jan-6, Josef-5, Jakob-4, Josef Ferdinand-3, Martin-2, Jan-1) was born in 1957.
Jiří Šimeček.
Jiří Šimeček and Zdena Malenova married. They had the following children:
   i. **Vit Šimeček** was born in 1972.
94. **Jiří Malena**-12 (Marie-11, Antonín-10, Antonín-9, Jan-8, Václav-7, Jan-6, Josef-5, Jakob-4, Josef Ferdinand-3, Martin-2, Jan-1) was born in 1962.
Vladka Nikrmajerova.
Jiří Malena and Vladka Nikrmajerova married. They had the following children:
   i. **Markéta Malenova** was born in 1978.
   ii. **Vendula Malenova** was born in 1982.
   iii. **Gabina Malenova** was born in 1987.
   iv. **Nikola Malena** was born in 1989.
95. **Bohuslav Bulíček**-12 (Antonie-11, Antonín-10, Antonín-9, Jan-8, Václav-7, Jan-6, Josef-5, Jakob-4, Josef Ferdinand-3, Martin-2, Jan-1) was born in 1962.
Iveta Navrátilová.
Bohuslav Bulíček and Iveta Navrátilová married. They had the following children:
   i. **Anna Buličková.**
   ii. **Jakub Bulíček.**
96. **Miroslav Bulíček**-12 (Antonie-11, Antonín-10, Antonín-9, Jan-8,

Václav-7, Jan-6, Josef-5, Jakob-4, Josef Ferdinand-3, Martin-2, Jan-1) was born in 1964.

Jarka Svitakova.

Miroslav Bulíček and Jarka Svitakova married. They had the following children:

    i.   **Tomáš Bulíček.**

    ii. **Katka Buličková.**

97. **Antonín Heralecký**-12 (Antonín-11, Antonín-10, Antonín-9, Jan-8, Václav-7, Jan-6, Josef-5, Jakob-4, Josef Ferdinand-3, Martin-2, Jan-1) was born on 13 Sep 1957.

Marie Urbankova was born on 25 Dec 1958.

Antonín Heralecký and Marie Urbankova married. They had the following children:

    i.   **Tomáš Heralecký** was born on 22 Jun 1978.

    ii. **Andrea Heralecká** was born on 31 Jan 1981.

    iii. **Lukáš Heralecký** was born on 10 Jul 1989.

98. **Libuše Heralecká**-12 (Antonín-11, Antonín-10, Antonín-9, Jan-8, Václav-7, Jan-6, Josef-5, Jakob-4, Josef Ferdinand-3, Martin-2, Jan-1) was born on 10 Jun 1959.

Jaroslav Fodor was born in 1957.

Jaroslav Fodor and Libuše Heralecká married. They had the following children:

    i.   **Michal Fodor** was born in 1982.

    ii. **Jana Fodorová** was born in 1985.

99. **Jaroslava Heralecká**-12 (Eduard-11, Eduard-10, Eduard-9, Jan-8, Václav-7, Jan-6, Josef-5, Jakob-4, Josef Ferdinand-3, Martin-2, Jan-1).

Ladislav Prais.

Ladislav Prais and Jaroslava Heralecká married. They had the following children:

    i.   **Edita Praisová.**

    ii. **Tomáš Prais.**

    iii. **Daniel Prais.**

100. **Hana Heralecká**-12 (Eduard-11, Eduard-10, Eduard-9, Jan-8, Václav-7,

Jan-6, Josef-5, Jakob-4, Josef Ferdinand-3, Martin-2, Jan-1).

Jiří Lestucek.

Jiří Lestucek and Hana Heralecká married. They had the following children:

    i. **Jan Lestucek.**

    ii. **Hana Lestuckova.**

101. **Petra Heralecká**-12 (Mario-11, Eduard-10, Eduard-9, Jan-8, Václav-7, Jan-6, Josef-5, Jakob-4, Josef Ferdinand-3, Martin-2, Jan-1).

    Petr Zidek.

    Petr Zidek and Petra Heralecká married. They had the following children:

        i. **Dalibor Zidek.**

    Jaroslav Sladkovsky.

    Jaroslav Sladkovsky and Petra Heralecká married. They had no children.

102. **Pavel Heralecký**-12 (Antonín-11, Antonín-10, Jan-9, František-8, Václav-7, Jan-6, Josef-5, Jakob-4, Josef Ferdinand-3, Martin-2, Jan-1) was born on 26 Dec 1954 in Trebic.

    Jana Pechová was born on 26 Jun 1956 in Jihlava.

    Pavel Heralecký and Jana Pechová were married on 19 Sep 1975 in Luka nad Jihlavou. They had the following children:

        i. **Kamil Heralecký** was born on 19 Mar 1976.

        ii. **Pavel Heralecký** was born on 15 Jan 1984.

103. **Antonín Heralecký**-12 (Antonín-11, Antonín-10, Jan-9, František-8, Václav-7, Jan-6, Josef-5, Jakob-4, Josef Ferdinand-3, Martin-2, Jan-1) was born on 19 Sep 1956 in Jihlava.

    Libuše Oksinova was born on 04 Apr 1961.

    Antonín Heralecký and Libuše Oksinova were married on 28 Aug 1981 in Jihlava. They had the following children:

        iii. **Antonín Heralecký** was born on 15 Feb 1983.

        iv. **Jan Heralecký** was born on 12 Jan 1985.

104. **Jan Heralecký**-12 (Jan-11, Antonín-10, Jan-9, František-8, Václav-7, Jan-6, Josef-5, Jakob-4, Josef Ferdinand-3, Martin-2, Jan-1) was born on 24 Jun 1957 in Trebic.

Jiřina Blahutková was born on 10 Jun 1957.
Jan Heralecký and Jiřina Blahutková were married on 30 Dec 1982 in Telc. They had the following children:
- v. **Petr Heralecký** was born on 21 Oct 1983.
- vi. **Jan Heralecký** was born on 04 Oct 1985.
- vii. **Marie Heralecká** was born on 10 May 1989.
- viii. **Vojtěch Heralecký** was born on 19 Feb 1993.
- ix. **Terezie Heralecký** was born on 10 Feb 1995.

105. **Jaromír Heralecký**-12 (Jaromír-11, Antonín-10, Jan-9, František-8, Václav-7, Jan-6, Josef-5, Jakob-4, Josef Ferdinand-3, Martin-2, Jan-1) was born on 02 Aug 1961.
Denisa Minarcikova was born on 16 Jun 1987 in Znojmo.
Jaromír Heralecký and Denisa Minarcikova were married on 25 Jun 1983. They had the following children:
- i. **Jaromír Heralecký** was born on 26 Sep 1984.
- ii. **Denisa Heralecká** was born on 16 Jun 1987.

106. **Lenka Heralecká**-12 (Jaromír-11, Antonín-10, Jan-9, František-8, Václav-7, Jan-6, Josef-5, Jakob-4, Josef Ferdinand-3, Martin-2, Jan-1) was born on 11 Feb 1964.
Jiří Jurka.
Jiří Jurka and Lenka Heralecká were married on 16 Nov 1986. They had the following children:
- i. **Jiří Jurka**.
- ii. **Vit Jurka**.

107. **Jaroslav Heralecký**-12 (Jaroslav-11, Jaroslav-10, Jan-9, František-8, Václav-7, Jan-6, Josef-5, Jakob-4, Josef Ferdinand-3, Martin-2, Jan-1) was born on 24 May 1946.
Milada Ticha was born on 12 Jan 1947 in Moravske Budejovice.
Jaroslav Heralecký and Milada Ticha were married on 01 Jun 1968. They had the following children:
- iii. **Lenka Heralecká** was born on 03 May 1969. She married Pavel Venuta on 17 Dec 1994.
- iv. **Jaroslav Heralecký** was born on 15 Apr 1974.

v. **Petra Heralecká** was born on 10 Jul 1975.

108. **Marie Heralecká**-12 (Jaroslav-11, Jaroslav-10, Jan-9, František-8, Václav-7, Jan-6, Josef-5, Jakob-4, Josef Ferdinand-3, Martin-2, Jan-1) was born on 14 Oct 1949.

    Zdeněk Svoboda was born on 04 Aug 1945. He died on 27 Sep 1999.

    Zdeněk Svoboda and Marie Heralecká were married on 17 Feb 1968. They had the following children:

    vi. **Tomáš Svoboda** was born on 27 May 1968. He married Barbara Capova on 31 Jan 1991.

109. **Ladislav Heralecký**-12 (Jaroslav-11, Jaroslav-10, Jan-9, František-8, Václav-7, Jan-6, Josef-5, Jakob-4, Josef Ferdinand-3, Martin-2, Jan-1) was born on 27 May 1954 in Trebic.

    Vlasta Flodrova was born on 14 Dec 1951 in Brno.

    Ladislav Heralecký and Vlasta Flodrova were married on 21 Apr 1976. They had the following children:

    vii. **Petr Heralecký** was born on 21 Aug 1976.

    viii. **Jan Heralecký** was born on 24 Jul 1980.

    iii. **Věra Heralecká** was born on 15 Apr 1984. She died on 11 Jul 1992.

110. **Pavel Maly**-12 (Marie-11, Františka-10, František-9, František-8, Václav-7, Jan-6, Josef-5, Jakob-4, Josef Ferdinand-3, Martin-2, Jan-1) was born on 20 Oct 1960.

    Dagmar Novosadová.

    Pavel Maly and Dagmar Novosadová married. They had the following children:

    i. **Iva Mala** was born in 1985.

    ii. **Radka Mala** was born in 1988.

111. **Alena Kopecna**-12 (Jiřina-11, Františka-10, František-9, František-8, Václav-7, Jan-6, Josef-5, Jakob-4, Josef Ferdinand-3, Martin-2, Jan-1).

    Pazderník.

    Pazderník and Alena Kopecna married. They had the following children:

    iii. **Michal Pazderník** was born on 18 Nov 1982.

    iv. **Iveta Pazderníková** was born on 20 Aug 1985.

v. **Vendula Pazderníková** was born on 07 Oct 1991.

Dusan Sobotka.

Dusan Sobotka and Alena Kopecna married. They had the following children:

i. **Vendula Sobotkova** was born on 07 Oct 1991.

112. **Jana Heralecká**-12 (Alois-11, Alois-10, František-9, František-8, Václav-7, Jan-6, Josef-5, Jakob-4, Josef Ferdinand-3, Martin-2, Jan-1) was born on 17 Feb 1963.

Luboš Kamenik.

Luboš Kamenik and Jana Heralecká married. They had the following children:

i. **Robert Kamenik** was born on 30 Aug 1982.
ii. **Petr Kamenik** was born on 20 Aug 1986.

113. **Leos Heralecký**-12 (Vladimír-11, Alois-10, František-9, František-8, Václav-7, Jan-6, Josef-5, Jakob-4, Josef Ferdinand-3, Martin-2, Jan-1) was born on 21 Mar 1972.

Radka Jicinska was born on 07 Mar 1973.

Leos Heralecký and Radka Jicinska were married on 19 Dec 1992. They had the following children:

iii. **Lukáš Heralecký** was born on 24 Jun 1993.
ii. **Tomáš Heralecký** was born on 03 Apr 2000.

114. **Vladimír Heralecký**-12 (Vladimír-11, Alois-10, František-9, František-8, Václav-7, Jan-6, Josef-5, Jakob-4, Josef Ferdinand-3, Martin-2, Jan-1) was born on 02 Oct 1968.

Unknown.

Vladimír Heralecký and Unknown married. They had the following children:

i. **Vladimír Heralecký.**

115. **Dana Vanickova**-12 (Dana-11, Alois-10, František-9, František-8, Václav-7, Jan-6, Josef-5, Jakob-4, Josef Ferdinand-3, Martin-2, Jan-1) was born on 10 Jun 1965.

Pavel Pekař was born on 23 Oct 1965.

Pavel Pekař and Dana Vanickova were married on 15 Jul 1989. They had

the following children:
- ii. **Lenka Pekařová** was born on 25 Dec 1989.
- iii. **Tomáš Pekař** was born on 26 Mar 1991.

116. **Romana Vanickova**-12 (Dana-11, Alois-10, František-9, František-8, Václav-7, Jan-6, Josef-5, Jakob-4, Josef Ferdinand-3, Martin-2, Jan-1) was born on 19 Aug 1966.

    Jaroslav Popovský was born on 24 Sep 1964.

    Jaroslav Popovský and Romana Vanickova were married on 19 Jul 1986. They had the following children:
    - i. **Michaela Popovská** was born on 20 Jan 1987.
    - ii. **Radek Popovský** was born on 01 Apr 1989.

117. **Iva Vanickova**-12 (Dana-11, Alois-10, František-9, František-8, Václav-7, Jan-6, Josef-5, Jakob-4, Josef Ferdinand-3, Martin-2, Jan-1) was born on 05 Apr 1973.

    Jan Vrbka was born on 14 Nov 1969.

    Jan Vrbka and Iva Vanickova were married on 11 Jul 1992. They had the following children:
    - i. **Jan Vrbka** was born on 27 Dec 1992.

118. **Tomáš Pecka**-12 (Blanka-11, Alois-10, František-9, František-8, Václav-7, Jan-6, Josef-5, Jakob-4, Josef Ferdinand-3, Martin-2, Jan-1) was born on 05 Jun 1972.

    Mirka Dobesova was born on 02 May 1975 in Vycapy.

    Tomáš Pecka and Mirka Dobesova married. They had the following children:
    - i. **Tomáš Pecka** was born on 06 Feb 1992.
    - ii. **Jan Pecka** was born on 06 Feb 1997.

119. **Aleš Pecka**-12 (Blanka-11, Alois-10, František-9, František-8, Václav-7, Jan-6, Josef-5, Jakob-4, Josef Ferdinand-3, Martin-2, Jan-1) was born on 04 Mar 1975.

    Andrea Nováková was born on 10 Oct 1974.

    Aleš Pecka and Andrea Nováková were married on 15 Apr 1994. They had the following children:
    - i. **Nikola Pecková** was born on 16 Sep 1994.

120. **Kateřina Jurcikova**-12 (Věra-11, František-10, František-9, František-8, Václav-7, Jan-6, Josef-5, Jakob-4, Josef Ferdinand-3, Martin-2, Jan-1) was born on 24 Feb 1965.
    Ivo Poukar was born on 24 Dec 1960.
    Ivo Poukar and Kateřina Jurcikova married. They had the following children:
    i. **Kateřina Poukarová** was born on 10 Apr 1990.
    ii. **Anna Poukarová** was born on 09 Sep 1996.
121. **Kamila Heralecká**-12 (Borivoj-11, František-10, František-9, František-8, Václav-7, Jan-6, Josef-5, Jakob-4, Josef Ferdinand-3, Martin-2, Jan-1) was born on 04 May 1969.
    Wilerth.
    Wilerth and Kamila Heralecká were married on 22 Apr 1989. They had the following children:
    i. **Jan Wilerth** was born on 17 Nov 1989.
    ii. **Karolina Wilerth** was born on 15 Nov 1990.
122. **Jana Heralecká**-12 (Borivoj-11, František-10, František-9, František-8, Václav-7, Jan-6, Josef-5, Jakob-4, Josef Ferdinand-3, Martin-2, Jan-1) was born on 27 Dec 1973.
    Simansky.
    Simansky and Jana Heralecká were married on 25 Jan 1997. They had the following children:
    i. **Jonáš Simansky** was born on 02 May 1997.
123. **Michael Vojtek**-12 (Jaroslava-11, Karel-10, František-9, František-8, Václav-7, Jan-6, Josef-5, Jakob-4, Josef Ferdinand-3, Martin-2, Jan-1) was born on 11 Sep 1969.
    Kateřina Mala was born on 22 Apr 1973.
    Michael Vojtek and Kateřina Mala were married on 25 Jul 1992. They had the following children:
    i. **Michaela Vojtkova** was born on 26 Jan 1993.
124. **Tomáš Nestrojil**-12 (Helena-11, Karel-10, František-9, František-8, Václav-7, Jan-6, Josef-5, Jakob-4, Josef Ferdinand-3, Martin-2, Jan-1) was born on 28 Aug 1973.

Radka Vejmelkova was born on 28 Dec 1972.

Tomáš Nestrojil and Radka Vejmelkova met. They had the following children:

    i.   **Anna Nestrojil** was born on 14 Mar 2000.

125. **Magdalena Hejatkova**-12 (Daniela-11, Miroslav-10, Augustin-9, František-8, Václav-7, Jan-6, Josef-5, Jakob-4, Josef Ferdinand-3, Martin-2, Jan-1) was born on 08 Feb 1975 in Jablonec nad Nisou.

Pavel Fiser was born on 06 Nov 1968 in Praha.

Pavel Fiser and Magdalena Hejatkova were married on 19 Dec 1998 in Liberec. They had the following children:

    i.   **Pavel Fiser** was born on 02 May 1999 in Jablonec nad Nisou.

126. **Zuzana Heralecká**-12 (Miroslav-11, Miroslav-10, Augustin-9, František-8, Václav-7, Jan-6, Josef-5, Jakob-4, Josef Ferdinand-3, Martin-2, Jan-1) was born on 30 Dec 1978 in Jablonec nad Nisou.

Jaroslav Egrt was born on 25 Apr 1974 in Duchcov.

Jaroslav Egrt and Zuzana Heralecká were married on 13 Sep 2002 in Jablonec nad Nisou. They had the following children:

    i.   **Kristina Egrtova** was born on 04 Jan 2008 in Liberec.

    ii.   **Jaroslav Egrt** was born on 04 Jan 2008 in Liberec.

H. Mila Rechcigl's Mother's Sister Side

Koubik Family

Generation 1

1. **Koubik**-1.
   Koubik and unknown spouse married. They had the following children:
   2. i. **Miroslav Koubik** was born in 1908 in Terezin. He married Marta Rajtrová on 26 Jul 1938 in Praha. He died in 1968 in Havlickuv Brod.
      ii. **Jiří Koubik.**

Generation 2

2. **Miroslav Koubik**-2 (Father-1) was born in 1908 in Terezin. He died in 1968 in Havlickuv Brod.
   Marta Rajtrová daughter of Čeněk Rajtr and Marie Dandová was born on 10 Jan 1909 in Dolanky u Bakova. She died on 29 Nov 1982 in Mladá Boleslav.
   Miroslav Koubik and Marta Rajtrová were married on 26 Jul 1938 in Praha. They had the following children:
   3. i. **Jiří Koubik** was born on 29 Jan 1940 in Prague. He married Jiřina Muellerová on 31 Jan 1962 in Praha. He died on 26 Jun 1998 in Brandys nad Labem.

Generation 3

3. **Jiří Koubik**-3 (Miroslav-2, Father-1) was born on 29 Jan 1940 in Prague. He died on 26 Jun 1998 in Brandys nad Labem.
   Jiřina Muellerová was born on 27 Feb 1943 in Buda.
   Jiří Koubik and Jiřina Muellerová were married on 31 Jan 1962 in Praha. They had the following children:
   4. i. **Marta Koubikova** was born on 04 Jul 1962 in Mladá Boleslav. She married Vladimír Stibor on 17 Apr 1981.
   5. ii. **2nd Jiří Koubik** was born on 13 May 1965 in Praha. He married Andrea Dunebierová on 4 Apr 1987 in Brandys nad Labem.

Generation 4

4. **Marta Koubikova**-4 (Jiří-3, Miroslav-2, Father-1) was born on 04 Jul 1962 in Mladá Boleslav.
   Vladimír Stibor was born on 04 Jun 1959 in Praha.
   Vladimír Stibor and Marta Koubikova were married on 17 Apr 1981. They had the following children:
   - 6. i. **Lucie Stiborová** was born on 29 Aug 1982 in Mladá Boleslav.
     - ii. **Tadeáš Stibor** was born on 25 Jul 1988 in Mladá Boleslav.

5. **2nd Jiří Koubik**-4 (Jiří-3, Miroslav-2, Father-1) was born on 13 May 1965 in Praha.
   Andrea Dunebierová was born on 25 Nov 1964 in Praha.
   2nd Jiří Koubik and Andrea Dunebierová were married on 04 Apr 1987 in Brandys nad Labem. They had the following children:
   - 7. i. **Roman Koubik** was born on 07 Aug 1987 in Brandys nad Labem.
     - ii. **Vojtěch Koubik** was born on 24 Mar 1989 in Brandys nad Labem.

Generation 5

6. **Lucie Stiborová**-5 (Marta-4, Jiří-3, Miroslav-2, Father-1) was born on 29 Aug 1982 in Mladá Boleslav.
   Novotný.
   Novotný and Lucie Stiborová married. They had the following children:
   - i. **Tobias Novotný**.

7. **Roman Koubik**-5 (2nd Jiří-4, Jiří-3, Miroslav-2, Father-1) was born on 07 Aug 1987 in Brandys nad Labem.
   Martina.
   Roman Koubik and Martina married. They had the following children:
   - i. **Roman Koubik**.

I. Eva Edwards's Sister Side

Steiner Family

Generation 1

1. **Adolf Steiner**-1 was born in 1849 in Prostejov, Moravia. He died in 1904. **Rosa Neumannová** was born in 1851 in Podivin, Moravia. She died in 1935. Adolf Steiner and Rosa Neumannová married. They had the following children:

   2. i. **Alfred Steiner** was born in 1876 in Zidlochovice, nr Brno. He died in 1942.
   3. ii. **Johann (Hans) Steiner** was born on 06 Jun 1877 in Zidlochovice, near Brno. He died in 1957.
   iii. **Gisela Steiner** was born in 1880 in Zidlochovice. She died in 1900.
   4. iv. **Anna Steiner** was born in 1882 in Zidlochovice, nr Brno. She died in 1952.
   5. v. **Olga Steiner** was born in 1883 in Zidlochovice, nr Brno. She died in 1952.

Generation 2

2. **Alfred Steiner**-2 (Adolf-1) was born in 1876 in Zidlochovice, nr Brno. He died in 1942.
   Olly Rosenfeld.
   Alfred Steiner and Olly Rosenfeld married. They had the following children:
   i. **Julius Steiner** was born on 06 Jun 1908.
   ii. **Otto Steiner** was born on 06 Jun 1908.

3. **Johann (Hans) Steiner**-2 (Adolf-1) was born on 06 Jun 1877 in Zidlochovice, near Brno. He died in 1957.
   Růžena Steinbachova daughter of Adolf Steinbach and Marie Hartmann was born on 26 Apr 1892 in Strebsko, nr Pribram, Bohemia. She died on 06 Apr 1980 in New York, NY.
   Johann (Hans) Steiner and Růžena Steinbachova married. They had the following children:

6. i. **Frank Steiner** was born on 23 Apr 1922 in Prague, Bohemia. He married Helen Edwards (Eisnerova) on 16 Sep 1948 in New York, NY. He died on 14 Sep 2000 in Scotia, NY.

4. **Anna Steiner**-2 (Adolf-1) was born in 1882 in Zidlochovice, nr Brno. She died in 1952.
Gustav Teltscher.
Gustav Teltscher and Anna Steiner married. They had the following children:

   i. **Otto Teltscher** was born in 1906. He married Frances Loewy in 1958. He died on 23 Aug 1971.
7. ii. **Carl Teltscher** was born in 1908. He died in 1980.

5. **Olga Steiner**-2 (Adolf-1) was born in 1883 in Zidlochovice, nr Brno. She died in 1952.
Emil Mandel.
Emil Mandel and Olga Steiner married. They had the following children:

   i. **Alice Mandel** was born on 02 Apr 1909. She married Lothar Beran in 1935. She died on 22 Apr 1993.
8. ii. **Ernest Mandel** was born on 05 Mar 1911. He died on 19 May 1987.

Generation 3

6. **Frank Steiner**-3 (Johann (Hans)-2, Adolf-1) was born on 23 Apr 1922 in Prague, Bohemia. He died on 14 Sep 2000 in Scotia, NY.
Helen Edwards (Eisnerova) daughter of Paul J. Edwards (Pavel Eisner) and Jiřina Taussigová was born on 29 Apr 1927 in Prague, CSR.
Frank Steiner and Helen Edwards (Eisnerova) were married on 16 Sep 1948 in New York, NY. They had the following children:

9. i. **Linda Claire Steiner** was born on 01 Mar 1950 in Schenectady, NY. She married Edward Salomon on 05 Jun 1977 in Scotia, NY.
10. ii. **David Henry Steiner** was born on 13 Mar 1952 in Schenectady, NY. He married Carol Ann Mastaliz on 07 Jul 1979 in So. Deerfield, MA.

7. **Carl Teltscher**-3 (Anna-2, Adolf-1) was born in 1908. He died in 1980.
Unknown.
Carl Teltscher and Unknown married. They had the following children:

      i. **Gary Teltscher**.

      ii. **Lawrence Teltscher**.

8. **Ernest Mandel**-3 (Olga-2, Adolf-1) was born on 05 Mar 1911. He died on 19 May 1987.

   Lore Jacoby.

   Ernest Mandel and Lore Jacoby married. They had the following children:

      i. **Curtis Mandel** was born on 18 Oct 1956.

Generation 4

9. **Linda Claire Steiner**-4 (Frank-3, Johann (Hans)-2, Adolf-1) was born on 01 Mar 1950 in Schenectady, NY.

   Edward Salomon son of Jerome Salomon and Rachel Finchel was born on 12 Feb 1951 in Jersey city, NJ.

   Edward Salomon and Linda Claire Steiner were married on 05 Jun 1977 in Scotia, NY. They had the following children:

      i. **Sarah Beth Salomon** was born on 28 Jan 1980 in Chicago, IL.

      ii. **Paul Nathan Salomon** was born on 02 Jan 1983 in Chicago, IL.

10. **David Henry Steiner**-4 (Frank-3, Johann (Hans)-2, Adolf-1) was born on 13 Mar 1952 in Schenectady, NY.

    Carol Ann Mastaliz daughter of Frank Peter Mastaliz and Helen Carline Macko was born on 26 Oct 1952 (Greenfield, MA).

    David Henry Steiner and Carol Ann Mastaliz were married on 07 Jul 1979 in So. Deerfield, MA. They had the following children:

11. i. **Erin Marie Steiner** was born on 01 Aug 1981 in Chicago, IL. She married Michael John Malick on 27 Jul 2013 in Poulsbo, WA.

      ii. **Jonathan Robert Steiner** was born on 30 Dec 1984 in Concord, MA.

Generation 5

11. **Erin Marie Steiner**-5 (David Henry-4, Frank-3, Johann (Hans)-2, Adolf-1) was born on 01 Aug 1981 in Chicago, IL.

    Michael John Malick was born on 01 Aug 1981 in Chicago, IL.

    Michael John Malick and Erin Marie Steiner were married on 27 Jul 2013 in Poulsbo, WA. They had the following children:

      i. **Henry Francsz Malick** was born on 18 Feb 2018 in Seattle, WA.

Steinbach Family

Generation 1

1. **Simon Steinbach**-1 was born in 1805 in Vysoka, Bohemia. He died in 1884.

    Rosalie Weiskopf daughter of Abraham Weisskopf and Eva Ohrenstein was born in 1814. She died in 1901.

    Simon Steinbach and Rosalie Weiskopf married. They had the following children:

    2. i. **Lewis Weisskopf Steinbach M.D.** was born on 04 Jun 1851 in Vysoka, bohemia. He died on 10 Feb 1913 in Philadelphia, PA.
    3. ii. **Adolf Steinbach** was born on 23 Dec 1855 in Vysoka, Bohemia. He married Marie Hartmann in 1889. He died on 15 Aug 1931.
    4. iii. **Therese Steinbach** was born after 1856.
        iv. **Lotte Steinbach** was born after 1857.
        v. **Katie Steinbach** was born after 1858.
        vi. **Child Steinbach**.

Generation 2

2. **Lewis Weisskopf Steinbach M.D.**-2 (Simon-1) was born on 04 Jun 1851 in Vysoka, bohemia. He died on 10 Feb 1913 in Philadelphia, PA.

    Johanna Rosenbaum was born on 15 Jun 1863 in Philadelphia, PA. She died on 01 Mar 1934 in Philadelphia, PA.

    Lewis Weisskopf Steinbach M.D. and Johanna Rosenbaum married. They had the following children:

    5. i. **Edna Steinbach** was born in 1891. She died in 1981.
    6. ii. **Florence Steinbach** was born in 1891. She died in 1981.
    7. iii. **Madeline Florence Steinbach** was born on 27 May 1891 in Philadelphia, PA. She died on 26 Oct 1981 in Wyncote, PA.
    8. iv. **Blanche Steinbach**.
    9. v. **Simon Steinbach**. He died in 1945.
    10. vi. **Ruth Steinbach**.

3. **Adolf Steinbach**-2 (Simon-1) was born on 23 Dec 1855 in Vysoka, Bohemia. He died on 15 Aug 1931.

Marie Hartmann daughter of Jakub Hartmann and Klára Seligmann was born on 06 Nov 1863. She died in 1927.

Adolf Steinbach and Marie Hartmann were married in 1889. They had the following children:

11. i. **Paula Steinbachova** was born in 1887. She died in 1944.
    ii. **Ella Steinbachova** was born in 1890. She died in 1942.
12. iii. **Růžena Steinbachova** was born on 26 Apr 1892 in Strebsko, nr Pribram, Bohemia. She died on 06 Apr 1980 in New York, NY.
    iv. **Karel Steinbach** was born on 07 Jun 1894 in Strebsko, nr Pribram, Bohemia. He died on 31 Dec 1990 in New York, NY.

Unknown. She died in 1889.

Adolf Steinbach and Unknown married. They had the following children:

11. i. **Paula Steinbachova** was born in 1887. She died in 1944.

4. **Therese Steinbach**-2 (Simon-1) was born after 1856.

Joseph Pollak.

Joseph Pollak and Therese Steinbach married. They had the following children:

13. i. **Berthold Steinbach Pollak** was born in 1873. He died in 1960.

Generation 3

5. **Edna Steinbach**-3 (Lewis Weisskopf-2, Simon-1) was born in 1891. She died in 1981.

Marshall Coyne.

Marshall Coyne and Edna Steinbach married. They had the following children:

14. i. **Jeannie Coyne** was born in 1912.

6. **Florence Steinbach**-3 (Lewis Weisskopf-2, Simon-1) was born in 1891. She died in 1981.

Frank E. Hahn was born in 1879.

Frank E. Hahn and Florence Steinbach married. They had the following children:

16. i. **Frank E. Hahn Jr.** was born in 1912.

7. **Madeline Florence Steinbach**-3 (Lewis Weisskopf-2, Simon-1) was

born on 27 May 1891 in Philadelphia, PA. She died on 26 Oct 1981 in Wyncote, PA.

Frank Eugene Hahn son of Henry Hahn and Clara Heiman was born on 22 Jan 1879 in Philadelphia, PA. He died on 05 Feb 1962 in Philadelphia, PA.

Frank Eugene Hahn and Madeline Florence Steinbach married. They had the following children:

    i. **Frank Eugene Hahn Jr.** was born on 19 Jan 1912 in Phiadelphia, PA. He died on 18 Feb 2008 in Philadelphia, PA.

8. **Blanche Steinbach**-3 (Lewis Weisskopf-2, Simon-1).
Leonard Adler Goldheim.
Leonard Adler Goldheim and Blanche Steinbach married. They had the following children:
16. i. **Samuel Lewis Goldheim.**

9. **Simon Steinbach**-3 (Lewis Weisskopf-2, Simon-1). He died in 1945.
Lydia Pollitz. She died in 1924.
Simon Steinbach and Lydia Pollitz married. They had the following children:
17. i. **Edna Steinbach.** She died in 1964.
Violet.
Simon Steinbach and Violet married. They had no children.

10. **Ruth Steinbach**-3 (Lewis Weisskopf-2, Simon-1).
Lester Steppacher.
Lester Steppacher and Ruth Steinbach married. They had the following children:
    i. **Lester G. Steppacher Jr.** was born in 1919.
19. ii. **Ruth Steppacher** was born in 1921. She died in 1994.
20. iii. **Mildred Steppacher** was born in 1923.

11. **Paula Steinbachova**-3 (Adolf-2, Simon-1) was born in 1887. She died in 1944.
Theo Wentz.
Theo Wentz and Paula Steinbachova married. They had the following children:

i. **Margret (Grete) Wentz** was born in 1918.
12. **Růžena Steinbachova**-3 (Adolf-2, Simon-1) was born on 26 Apr 1892 in Strebsko, nr Pribram, Bohemia. She died on 06 Apr 1980 in New York, NY.
Johann (Hans) Steiner son of Adolf Steiner and Rosa Neumannová was born on 06 Jun 1877 in Zidlochovice, near Brno. He died in 1957.
Johann (Hans) Steiner and Růžena Steinbachova married. They had the following children:
   20. i. **Frank Steiner** was born on 23 Apr 1922 in Prague, Bohemia. He married Helen Edwards (Eisnerova) on 16 Sep 1948 in New York, NY. He died on 14 Sep 2000 in Scotia, NY.
13. **Berthold Steinbach Pollak**-3 (Therese-2, Simon-1) was born in 1873. He died in 1960.
Henriette Cohen was born in 1896.
Berthold Steinbach Pollak and Henriette Cohen married. They had the following children:
   21. i. **Rose Pollak**.
   22. ii. **Luise Pollak**.
Louise Gruber.
Berthold Steinbach Pollak and Louise Gruber married. They had the following children:
   i. **Louise Theresa Pollak**.

Generation 4

14. **Jeannie Coyne**-4 (Edna-3, Lewis Weisskopf-2, Simon-1) was born in 1912.
Kjell Mossige was born in Norway.
Kjell Mossige and Jeannie Coyne married. They had the following children:
   i. **Liv Mossige**.
   ii. **Annette Mossige**.
   iii. **Ellen Mossige**.
   24. iv. **Edna Mossige**.
15. **Frank E. Hahn Jr.**-4 (Florence-3, Lewis Weisskopf-2, Simon-1) was born in 1912.
Margaret Berg was born in 1916.

Frank E. Hahn Jr. and Margaret Berg married. They had the following children:

1   i. **3rd Frank E Hahn** was born in 1938.

2   ii. **Judith Ann Hahn** was born in 1942.

16. **Samuel Lewis Goldheim**-4 (Blanche-3, Lewis Weisskopf-2, Simon-1).

    Ruth Ulman.

    Samuel Lewis Goldheim and Ruth Ulman married. They had the following children:

    i.   **Leonard Goldheim.**

    ii.   **David Goldheim.**

17. **Edna Steinbach**-4 (Simon-3, Lewis Weisskopf-2, Simon-1). She died in 1964.

    Charles Gold.

    Charles Gold and Edna Steinbach married. They had the following children:

    26. i. **Lydia Gold.**

         ii. **Joanne Gold** was born in 1955.

18. **Ruth Steppacher**-4 (Ruth-3, Lewis Weisskopf-2, Simon-1) was born in 1921. She died in 1994.

    Lewis M. Affelder was born in 1914. He died in 1995.

    Lewis M. Affelder and Ruth Steppacher married. They had the following children:

    27. i. **Margaret Affelder.**

    28. ii. **Jenne Affelder.**

19. **Mildred Steppacher**-4 (Ruth-3, Lewis Weisskopf-2, Simon-1) was born in 1923.

    Willard Bonwit was born in 1922. He died in 1981.

    Willard Bonwit and Mildred Steppacher married. They had the following children:

    i.   **David M. Bonwit.**

    ii.   **Susan Bonwit.**

    iii. **Willard Bonwit Jr..**

    iv. **Nancy Bonwit** was born in 1953.

v. **Andrew Bonwit** was born in 1958.

20. **Frank Steiner**-4 (Růžena-3, Adolf-2, Simon-1) was born on 23 Apr 1922 in Prague, Bohemia. He died on 14 Sep 2000 in Scotia, NY.

    Helen Edwards (Eisnerova) daughter of Paul J. Edwards (Pavel Eisner) and Jiřina Taussigová was born on 29 Apr 1927 in Prague, CSR.

    Frank Steiner and Helen Edwards (Eisnerova) were married on 16 Sep 1948 in New York, NY. They had the following children:

    29. i. **Linda Claire Steiner** was born on 01 Mar 1950 in Schenectady, NY. She married Edward Salomon on 05 Jun 1977 in Scotia, NY.
    30. ii. **David Henry Steiner** was born on 13 Mar 1952 in Schenectady, NY. He married Carol Ann Mastaliz on 07 Jul 1979 in So. Deerfield, MA.

21. **Rose Pollak**-4 (Berthold Steinbach-3, Therese-2, Simon-1).
    Philip Birnbaum.
    Philip Birnbaum and Rose Pollak married. They had the following children:

    i. **Philip Birnbaum.**

22. **Luise Pollak**-4 (Berthold Steinbach-3, Therese-2, Simon-1).
    A. Kruger.
    A. Kruger and Luise Pollak married. They had the following children:

    i. **Alfred Kruger Jr..**
    32. ii. **Virginia Kruger.**

Generation 5

23. **Edna Mossige**-5 (Jeannie-4, Edna-3, Lewis Weisskopf-2, Simon-1).
    John Herman.
    John Herman and Edna Mossige married. They had the following children:

    i. **Ellen Herman.**

24. **3rd Frank E Hahn**-5 (Frank E.-4, Florence-3, Lewis Weisskopf-2, Simon-1) was born in 1938.

    Helen Zimmermann was born in 1937.

    3rd Frank E Hahn and Helen Zimmermann married. They had the following children:

    32. i. **Jeffrey Alan Hahn** was born in 1960.

25. **Judith Ann Hahn**-5 (Frank E.-4, Florence-3, Lewis Weisskopf-2, Simon-1) was born in 1942.
    Mitchell Alvin Kramer was born in 1933.
    Mitchell Alvin Kramer and Judith Ann Hahn married. They had the following children:
    33. i. **Barbara Helene Kramer** was born in 1963.
26. **Lydia Gold**-5 (Edna-4, Simon-3, Lewis Weisskopf-2, Simon-1).
    John Savelle.
    John Savelle and Lydia Gold married. They had the following children:
    i. **Eli Savelle** was born in 1994.
27. **Margaret Affelder**-5 (Ruth-4, Ruth-3, Lewis Weisskopf-2, Simon-1).
    Barry Cain.
    Barry Cain and Margaret Affelder married. They had the following children:
    i. **Andrea Cain**.
28. **Jenne Affelder**-5 (Ruth-4, Ruth-3, Lewis Weisskopf-2, Simon-1).
    Jeff Weissglass.
    Jeff Weissglass and Jenne Affelder married. They had the following children:
    i. **Daniel Weissglass**.
    ii. **Charles Weissglass**.
29. **Linda Claire Steiner**-5 (Frank-4, Růžena-3, Adolf-2, Simon-1) was born on 01 Mar 1950 in Schenectady, NY.
    Edward Salomon son of Jerome Salomon and Rachel Finchel was born on 12 Feb 1951 in Jersey city, NJ.
    Edward Salomon and Linda Claire Steiner were married on 05 Jun 1977 in Scotia, NY. They had the following children:
    i. **Sarah Beth Salomon** was born on 28 Jan 1980 in Chicago, IL.
    ii. **Paul Nathan Salomon** was born on 02 Jan 1983 in Chicago, IL.
30. **David Henry Steiner**-5 (Frank-4, Růžena-3, Adolf-2, Simon-1) was born on 13 Mar 1952 in Schenectady, NY.
    Carol Ann Mastaliz daughter of Frank Peter Mastaliz and Helen Carline Macko was born on 26 Oct 1952 (Greenfield, MA).

David Henry Steiner and Carol Ann Mastaliz were married on 07 Jul 1979 in So. Deerfield, MA. They had the following children:

34. i. **Erin Marie Steiner** was born on 01 Aug 1981 in Chicago, IL. She married Michael John Malick on 27 Jul 2013 in Poulsbo, WA.

ii. **Jonathan Robert Steiner** was born on 30 Dec 1984 in Concord, MA.

31. **Virginia Kruger**-5 (Luise-4, Berthold Steinbach-3, Therese-2, Simon-1). **Becker**.

Becker and Virginia Kruger married. They had the following children:

i. **3 children Becker**.

Generation 6

32. **Jeffrey Alan Hahn**-6 (3rd Frank E-5, Frank E.-4, Florence-3, Lewis Weisskopf-2, Simon-1) was born in 1960.

Shery Levy was born in 1961.

Jeffrey Alan Hahn and Shery Levy married. They had the following children:

i. **Allison Hahn** was born in 1988.

ii. **Lawrence Hahn** was born in 1985.

33. **Barbara Helene Kramer**-6 (Judith Ann-5, Frank E.-4, Florence-3, Lewis Weisskopf-2, Simon-1) was born in 1963.

David Rosenfeld was born in 1964.

David Rosenfeld and Barbara Helene Kramer married. They had the following children:

i. **Anna Kramer Rosenfeld** was born in 1995.

34. **Erin Marie Steiner**-6 (David Henry-5, Frank-4, Růžena-3, Adolf-2, Simon-1) was born on 01 Aug 1981 in Chicago, IL.

Michael John Malick was born on 01 Aug 1981 in Chicago, IL.

Michael John Malick and Erin Marie Steiner were married on 27 Jul 2013 in Poulsbo, WA. They had the following children:

i. **Henry Francsz Malick** was born on 18 Feb 2018 in Seattle, WA.

Salomon Family

Generation 1

Nathan Solomon-1 was born in 1890 in Kalicz, Poland. He died on 11 Jan 1964 in New York, NY.

Ida Liebner was born in 1898 in New York. She died in 1983 in New York, NY.

Nathan Solomon and Ida Liebner married. They had the following children:

    i. **Hannah Solomon** was born in 1915. She died about 1965.

    ii. **Jerome Salomon** was born on 15 Sep 1919 in Philadelphia, PA. He married Rachel Finchel in 1944 in New Jersey. He died on 04 Jun 1979 in New Jersey.

    iii. **Selma Solomon** was born about 05 Jun 1922. She married Morris Weintraub on 14 Dec 1942.

Generation 2

Hannah Solomon-2 (Nathan-1) was born in 1915. She died about 1965.

Irving Sherman.

Irving Sherman and Hannah Solomon married. They had the following children:

    i. **Carol Sherman** was born in 1943.

    ii. **Albert Sherman** was born in 1945.

Jerome Salomon-2 (Nathan-1) was born on 15 Sep 1919 in Philadelphia, PA. He died on 04 Jun 1979 in New Jersey.

Rachel Finchel daughter of Leon (Finkel) Finchel and Sarah Finkel was born on 07 Feb 1925 in New York, NY.

Jerome Salomon and Rachel Finchel were married in 1944 in New Jersey. They had the following children:

    i. **Arthur Salomon** was born on 11 Dec 1945 in San Francisco, CA.

    ii. **Edward Salomon** was born on 12 Feb 1951 in Jersey city, NJ. He married Linda Claire Steiner on 05 Jun 1977 in Scotia, NY.

Selma Solomon-2 (Nathan-1) was born about 05 Jun 1922.

Morris Weintraub.

Morris Weintraub and Selma Solomon were married on 14 Dec 1942. They had the following children:
- i. **Allen Weintraub** was born in 1943.
- ii. **Connee Weintraub** was born in 1945.
- iii. **Floyd Weintraub** was born in 1949.
- 12. iv. **Amy Weintraub** was born in 1956.

Generation 3

Carol Sherman-3 (Hannah-2, Nathan-1) was born in 1943.
Leonard Goldsnith.
Leonard Goldsnith and Carol Sherman married. They had the following children:
- i. **Heidi Goldsnith** was born in 1968.
    Randi Goldsnith-adopted.

Albert Sherman-3 (Hannah-2, Nathan-1) was born in 1945.
Unknown.
Albert Sherman and Unknown married. They had the following children:
Daughter Sherman.
Kate Loitz.
Albert Sherman and Kate Loitz married. They had no children.

Arthur Salomon-3 (Jerome-2, Nathan-1) was born on 11 Dec 1945 in San Francisco, CA.
Judith Schlosberg was born on 15 Jan 1948 in New Jersey.
Arthur Salomon and Judith Schlosberg married. They had the following children:
Jennie Rebecca Salomon was born in 1981 in MD.

Edward Salomon-3 (Jerome-2, Nathan-1) was born on 12 Feb 1951 in Jersey city, NJ.
Linda Claire Steiner daughter of Frank Steiner and Helen Edwards (Eisnerova) was born on 01 Mar 1950 in Schenectady, NY.
Edward Salomon and Linda Claire Steiner were married on 05 Jun 1977 in Scotia, NY. They had the following children:
Sarah Beth Salomon was born on 28 Jan 1980 in Chicago, IL.
Paul Nathan Salomon was born on 02 Jan 1983 in Chicago, IL.

Allen Weintraub-3 (Selma-2, Nathan-1) was born in 1943.

Unknown.

Allen Weintraub and Unknown married. They had the following children:

 Jennifer Weintraub.

 Rebeca Weintraub.

 Alexandra Weintraub.

Connee Weintraub-3 (Selma-2, Nathan-1) was born in 1945.

Unknown.

Unknown and Connee Weintraub married. They had the following children:

 Scott Unknown.

 Neal Unknown.

 Heather Unknown.

Floyd Weintraub-3 (Selma-2, Nathan-1) was born in 1949.

Unknown.

Floyd Weintraub and Unknown married. They had the following children:

 Abigail Weintraub.

Amy Weintraub-3 (Selma-2, Nathan-1) was born in 1956.

Unknown.

Unknown and Amy Weintraub married. They had the following children:

 Annie Unknown.

 Son Unknown.

Generation 4

Heidi Goldsnith-4 (Carol-3, Hannah-2, Nathan-1) was born in 1968.

Steve Moore.

Steve Moore and Heidi Goldsnith married. They had the following children:

 Daughter Moore.

J. Eva Edwards' Mother's Sister Side

Winn (Wiener) Family

Generation 1

1. **Maurice Wiener**-1.
   Alba Růžičková daughter of David Růžička and Johanna Reskova.
   Maurice Wiener and Alba Růžičková married. They had the following children:
   - 2. i. **Joseph (Wiener) Winn** was born on 02 Feb 1901 in Prague. He married Hana Taussigová in 1933. He died on 08 Feb 1983 in New York City.
   - 3. ii. **Marie Wienerova** was born in 1899. She married Josef Krajbich about 1918. She died in 1986.

Generation 2

4. **Joseph (Wiener) Winn**-2 (Maurice-1) was born on 02 Feb 1901 in Prague. He died on 08 Feb 1983 in New York City.
   Hana Taussigová daughter of Oskar Taussig and Klára Munková was born on 26 Feb 1910 in Prague. She died on 14 Mar 1999 in New York, NY.
   Joseph (Wiener) Winn and Hana Taussigová were married in 1933. They had the following children:
   - 4. i. **Janet (Jana) Winn** was born on 08 Jul 1934 in Prague. She married Donald Malcolm on 13 Apr 1956 in New York City.
   - 5. ii. **Marie Winn** was born on 21 Oct 1936 in Prague. She married Allan Miller on 28 Apr 1961 in New York City.

5. **Marie Wienerova**-2 (Maurice-1) was born in 1899. She died in 1986.
   Josef Krajbich son of Krajbich and Unknown was born in 1899. He died in 1977.
   Josef Krajbich and Marie Wienerova were married about 1918. They had the following children:
   - 19. i. **Ivan Krajbich** was born in 1920. He died in 1985.
   - 20. ii. **George Krajbich** was born in 1922. He died in 1988.

iii. **Marie Krajbichova** was born in 1924. She died in 1924.

Generation 3

4. **Janet (Jana) Winn**-3 (Joseph (Wiener)-2, Maurice-1) was born on 08 Jul 1934 in Prague. She died July 14, 2023 in Manhattan, NY.
   Donald Malcolm was born in 1935. He died in 1975.
   Donald Malcolm and Janet (Jana) Winn were married on 13 Apr 1956 in New York City. They had the following children:
   - 8. i. **Anne Malcolm** was born on 17 Dec 1962 in New York City. She married Richard Tuck on 19 Mar 1993 in New York City.

   Gardner Botsford son of Botsford was born on 07 Jul 1917 in New York, NY. He died on 27 Sep 2004 in New York, NY.
   Gardner Botsford and Janet (Jana) Winn were married on 26 Sep 1975. They had no children.

5. **Marie Winn**-3 (Joseph (Wiener)-2, Maurice-1) was born on 21 Oct 1936 in Prague.
   Allan Miller was born on 05 Dec 1933 in New York City.
   Allan Miller and Marie Winn were married on 28 Apr 1961 in New York City. They had the following children:
   - 9. i. **Michael Winn Miller** was born on 20 Nov 1962. He married Sarah Paul on 30 Dec 1988 in New York City.
   - 10. ii. **Steven David Miller** was born on 14 Apr 1966 in New York City. He married Jennifer Durand on 11 Nov 1995 in San Francisco, CA.

6. **Ivan Krajbich**-3 (Marie-2, Maurice-1) was born in 1920. He died in 1985.
   Dagmar Králová was born in 1926.
   Ivan Krajbich and Dagmar Králová married. They had the following children:
   - 11. i. **2nd Ivan Krajbich** was born in 1947.
   - 12. ii. **Hana Krajbich** was born in 1948.
   - iii. **Tomáš Krajbich** was born in 1953.

7. **George Krajbich**-3 (Marie-2, Maurice-1) was born in 1922. He died in 1988.
   Ingeborg Wenzel was born in 1924. She died about 1978.
   George Krajbich and Ingeborg Wenzel married. They had no children.

Zdenka Zlobická was born in 1947.

George Krajbich and Zdenka Zlobická married. They had the following children:
    i.   **Elizabeth Krajbich** was born in 1983.

Generation 4

8. **Anne Malcolm**-4 (Janet (Jana)-3, Joseph (Wiener)-2, Maurice-1) was born on 17 Dec 1962 in New York City.
    Richard Tuck was born on 09 Jan 1949 in Newcastleupon-Tyne, England.
    Richard Tuck and Anne Malcolm were married on 19 Mar 1993 in New York City. They had the following children:
    i.   **Sophy Malcolm Tuck** was born on 13 Jul 1993 in Cambridge, England.

9. **Michael Winn Miller**-4 (Marie-3, Joseph (Wiener)-2, Maurice-1) was born on 20 Nov 1962.
    Sarah Paul was born on 29 Dec 1961 in New York City.
    Michael Winn Miller and Sarah Paul were married on 30 Dec 1988 in New York City. They had the following children:
    i.   **Isadore 'Izzy' Miller** was born on 20 Nov 1995 in San Francisco, CA.
    ii. **Abigail "Abbey' Nadia Paul Miller** was born on 24 Oct 1996 in New York City.

10. **Steven David Miller**-4 (Marie-3, Joseph (Wiener)-2, Maurice-1) was born on 14 Apr 1966 in New York City.
    Jennifer Durand.
    Steven David Miller and Jennifer Durand were married on 11 Nov 1995 in San Francisco, CA. They had the following children:
    i.   **Eli Miller** was born on 17 Mar 1999.
    ii. **Clara Miller** was born on 04 Jul 2000 in San Francisco, CA or NYC.

11. **2nd Ivan Krajbich**-4 (Ivan-3, Marie-2, Maurice-1) was born in 1947.
    Suzanne G. William was born in 1953.
    2nd Ivan Krajbich and Suzanne G. William married. They had the

following children:
- i. **3rd Ivan Krajbich** was born in 1983.
- ii. **Alan Krajbich** was born in 1987.
- iii. **Victoria Lee Krajbich** was born in 1990.

12. **Hana Krajbich**-4 (Ivan-3, Marie-2, Maurice-1) was born in 1948.
    Karl Otta was born in 1948.
    Karl Otta and Hana Krajbich married. They had the following children:
    - i. **Hana Otta** was born in 1977.
    - ii. **Dagmar Otta** was born in 1980.
    - iii. **Karel Otta** was born in 1985.

Růžička Family

Generation 1

1. **Jakob Růžička**-1. **Anna.**
   Jakob Růžička and Anna married. They had the following children:
   2. i. **David Růžička** was born in 1816. He died in 1890.
   3. ii. **Theresia Růžičkova.**

Generation 2

2. **David Růžička**-2 (Jakob-1) was born in 1816. He died in 1890.
   Johanna Reskova was born in 1835. She died in 1921.
   David Růžička and Johanna Reskova married. They had the following children:
   4. i. **Herman Jan Krt. Růžička** was born on 09 Nov 1887 in Drasetice, Dobris Co.. He married Aloise Ludmila Faulová on 03 Aug 1922 in Prague, CSR.
   5. ii. **Rosa Růžičková.**
   6. iii. **Marie Růžičková** was born on 06 Jan 1852 in Borotice, Příbram District, bohemia.
   7. iv. **Mathilda Růžičková.**
       v. **Adolf Růžička.**
       vi. **Jacob Růžička.**
   8. vii. **Bedřich Růžička.**
       viii. **Emanuel Růžička.**
       ix. **Julia Růžičková.**
       x. **Samuel Růžička.**
   9. xi. **Berta Růžičková.**
   10. xii. **Jindřich Růžička.**
   11. xiii. **Alba Růžičková.**
       xiv. **Josef Růžička.**
   12. xv. **Theresa 'Rosa' Růžička** was born on 09 Apr 1857 in Borotice, Příbram District, Bohemia. She died in 1935 in Chicago, IL.

9. **Theresia Růžičkova**-2 (Jakob-1).
   Moses Klein.

Moses Klein and Theresia Růžičkova married. They had the following children:
- i. **Joseph Klein** was born on 04 Nov 1853 in Borotice, Příbram District, Bohemia.
- ii. **Emanuel Klein** was born on 18 Mar 1850 in Borotice, Příbram District, Bohemia.
- iii. **Mauritz Klein** was born on 11 Aug 1856 in Borotice, Příbram District, Bohemia. He died on 14 Mar 1857 in Borotice, Příbram District, Bohemia.
- iv. **Leopold Klein** was born on 01 Jun 1851 in Borotice, Příbram District, bohemia.
- v. **Bernard Klein** was born on 24 Jun 1859 in Borotice, Příbram District, bohemia.

Generation 3

4. **Herman Jan Krt. Růžička**-3 (David-2, Jakob-1) was born on 09 Nov 1887 in Drasetice, Dobris Co..

    Aloise Ludmila Faulová daughter of Bedřich Faul and Eliška Weilova was born on 07 Jun 1896 in Golcuv Jenikov No, 195, Caslav Co..

    Herman Jan Krt. Růžička and Aloise Ludmila Faulová were married on 03 Aug 1922 in Prague, CSR. They had the following children:

    - 13. i. **Anthony Růžička Rushford**.

5. **Rosa Růžičková**-3 (David-2, Jakob-1).

    Ludwig Ginsburg.

    Ludwig Ginsburg and Rosa Růžičková married. They had the following children:
    - i. **Joseph Ginsburg**.
    - 14. ii. **Malva Ginsburgova**.
    - 15. iii. **Elsa Ginsburgova**.
    - 16. iv. **Anna Ginsburg**.
    - v. **Fred Burg Ginsburg**.
    - vi. **Zdeněk Ginsburg**.
    - vii. **Arthur Ginsburg**.
    - 17. viii. **Roderick Ginsburg**.

18. ix. **Wilma Ginsburg**.

6. **Marie Růžičková**-3 (David-2, Jakob-1) was born on 06 Jan 1852 in Borotice, Příbram District, bohemia.
   Josef Roubíček.
   Josef Roubíček and Marie Růžičková married. They had the following children:
   19. i. **Blanche Roubíček**.

7. **Mathilda Růžičková**-3 (David-2, Jakob-1).
   Julius Roubíček.
   Julius Roubíček and Mathilda Růžičková married. They had the following children:
       i. **Karla Roubíčková** was born on 04 Aug 1890 in Nový Knín, Příbram District, Bohemia. She died in Oct 1944 in Auschwitz, Poland - Holocaust.
   20. ii. **Ludmila 'Lida' Roubíčková** was born on 01 Nov 1899. She died on 17 Sep 1980.
   21. iii. **Marie Roubíček**.
       iv. **Beda Roubíček**.
   22. v. **Alba Roubíček**.
       vi. **Hermira Roubíčková**.
       vii. **Ludvik Roubíček**.
       viii. **Kamila Roubíček**.
       ix. **Zdenka Roubíčková**.

8. **Bedřich Růžička**-3 (David-2, Jakob-1).
   Maryla.
   Bedřich Růžička and Maryla married. They had the following children:
   23. i. **Jaroslav Růžička** was born on 03 Oct 1893. He died on 13 May 1943 in Terezin - Holocaust.
       ii. **Kristina Růžičková**.

9. **Berta Růžičková**-3 (David-2, Jakob-1).
   Samuel Rubin.
   Samuel Rubin and Berta Růžičková married. They had the following children:

- i. **Jiřina Rubinová.**
- ii. **Ernest Rubin.**
- iii. **Emma Rubinova.**
- iv. **Mila Rubin.**
24. v. **Arthur Rubin.**
25. vi. **Joseph Rubin.**
26. vii. **Olga Rubinová** was born on 14 Oct 1904 in Czechoslovakia. She married Karel Vrzal in 1924. She died on 11 Dec 1979 in New York, NY.

10. **Jindřich Růžička**-3 (David-2, Jakob-1).
    Pavla Sternschussova.
    Jindřich Růžička and Pavla Sternschussova married. They had the following children:
    27. i. **Jiřina Růžičková.** She died in Auschwitz.
    28. ii. **Karel Růžička.** He died in Mar 1946 in ne Sadska, CSR, while trying to escape death march.
    29. iii. **Zdena Růžičková.**
    30. iv. **Vlasta Růžičková.**
    23. v. **Jaroslav Růžička** was born on 03 Oct 1893. He died on 13 May 1943 in Terezin - Holocaust.

11. **Alba Růžičková**-3 (David-2, Jakob-1).
    Maurice Winer.
    Maurice Winer and Alba Růžičková married. They had no children.
    Maurice Wiener.
    Maurice Wiener and Alba Růžičková married. They had the following children:
    31. i. **Joseph (Wiener) Winn** was born on 02 Feb 1901 in Prague. He married Hana Taussigová in 1933. He died on 08 Feb 1983 in New York City.
    32. ii. **Marie Wienerova** was born in 1899. She married Josef Krajbich about 1918. She died in 1986.

12. **Theresa 'Rosa' Růžička**-3 (David-2, Jakob-1) was born on 09 Apr 1857 in Borotice, Příbram District, Bohemia. She died in 1935 in Chicago, IL.

Ludwig Ginsburg was born on 30 Mar 1858 in Zavadilka, Jizbice, Nymburk, Bohemia. He died on 07 Nov 1919 in Chicago, IL.

Ludwig Ginsburg and Theresa 'Rosa' Růžička married. They had the following children:

33. i. **Malvina Ginsburg.**

Generation 4

13. **Anthony Růžička Rushford**-4 (Herman Jan Krt.-3, David-2, Jakob-1).
    Allison.
    Anthony Růžička Rushford and Allison married. They had the following children:
    - i. **Sally Rushford.**
    - ii. **Robert Rushford.**
    - iii. **Andy Rushford.**
    - iv. **John Rushford.**

14. **Malva Ginsburgova**-4 (Rosa-3, David-2, Jakob-1).
    Calatka.
    Calatka and Malva Ginsburgova married. They had the following children:
    - i. **Irma Calatka.**
    - ii. **William Calatka.**

    Pollak.
    Pollak and Malva Ginsburgova married. They had no children.

15. **Elsa Ginsburgova**-4 (Rosa-3, David-2, Jakob-1).
    Reinish.
    Reinish and Elsa Ginsburgova married. They had the following children:
    - i. **Carl Reinish.**
    - ii. **Herbert Reinish.**

16. **Anna Ginsburg**-4 (Rosa-3, David-2, Jakob-1).
    Schawzkopf.
    Schawzkopf and Anna Ginsburg married. They had the following children:
    - i. **Roy Schawzkopf.**
    - ii. **Hannah Schawzkopf.**

17. **Roderick Ginsburg**-4 (Rosa-3, David-2, Jakob-1).
    Unknown.
    Roderick Ginsburg and Unknown married. They had the following children:
    i. **Allen Ginsburg.**
18. **Wilma Ginsburg**-4 (Rosa-3, David-2, Jakob-1).
    Mautner.
    Mautner and Wilma Ginsburg married. They had the following children:
    i. **Robert Mautner.**
    ii. **Rose Mautner.**
    Loewy.
    Loewy and Wilma Ginsburg married. They had no children.
19. **Blanche Roubíček**-4 (Marie-3, David-2, Jakob-1).
    Thielmann.
    Thielmann and Blanche Roubíček married. They had the following children:
    i. **Margit Thielmann.**
18. **Ludmila 'Lida' Roubíčková**-4 (Mathilda-3, David-2, Jakob-1) was born on 01 Nov 1899. She died on 17 Sep 1980.
    Ondřej Sekora son of Ondřej Sekora and Ludmila Roubíčková was born on 25 Sep 1899 in Kralovo Pole, Brno District, Moravia. He died on 04 Jul 1967 in OndřejPrague, Czech..
    Ondřej Sekora and Ludmila 'Lida' Roubíčková married. They had the following children:
    i. **Dagmar Sekorová.**
    ii. **Ondřej Sekora** was born in 1931. He died in 2004.
21. **Marie Roubíček**-4 (Mathilda-3, David-2, Jakob-1).
    Nedoma.
    Nedoma and Marie Roubíček married. They had the following children:
    i. **Jarca Nedoma.**
22. **Alba Roubíček**-4 (Mathilda-3, David-2, Jakob-1).
    Spitzer.
    Spitzer and Alba Roubíček married. They had the following children:

i. Eva Spitzer.
23. **Jaroslav Růžička**-4 (Bedřich-3, David-2, Jakob-1) was born on 03 Oct 1893. He died on 13 May 1943 in Terezin - Holocaust.
Leopoldina 'Poldi' Lederer was born on 07 Mar 1896.
Jaroslav Růžička and Leopoldina 'Poldi' Lederer married. They had the following children:
  i. **Zuzana Růžičková** was born on 14 Jan 1927 in Plzen, Bohemia. She died on 27 Sep 2017 in Prague, Czech..
24. **Arthur Rubin**-4 (Berta-3, David-2, Jakob-1).
Truda Kapelusova.
Arthur Rubin and Truda Kapelusova married. They had the following children:
  i. **Ivo Rubin**.
25. **Joseph Rubin**-4 (Berta-3, David-2, Jakob-1).
Jindriska.
Joseph Rubin and Jindriska married. They had the following children:
  i. **Eva Rubinova**.
  ii. **Edith Rubinova**.
26. **Olga Rubinová**-4 (Berta-3, David-2, Jakob-1) was born on 14 Oct 1904 in Czechoslovakia. She died on 11 Dec 1979 in New York, NY.
Karel Vrzal was born about 04 Aug 1901.
Karel Vrzal and Olga Rubinová were married in 1924. They had the following children:
  i. **Eva Olga Vrzalova** was born on 26 Jun 1925 in Chicago, IL. She died on 04 Oct 1987 in Houston, TX.
  34. ii. **Věra C. Vrzalova** was born on 09 Mar 1933 in Chicago, IL.
Eric Tausig.
Eric Tausig and Olga Rubinová were married about 1946. They had the following children:
  35. i. **Paul Eric Tausig** was born on 30 Jun 1947 in New York, NY.
27. **Jiřina Růžičková**-4 (Jindřich-3, David-2, Jakob-1). She died in Auschwitz.
Jiří Reich. He died in Plzen.
Jiří Reich and Jiřina Růžičková married. They had the following children:

36. i. **Sona Reichová**.
28. **Karel Růžička**-4 (Jindřich-3, David-2, Jakob-1). He died in Mar 1946 in ne Sadska, CSR, while trying to escape death march.
    Kamila Hermannova.
    Karel Růžička and Kamila Hermannova married. They had the following children:
    i. **Dagmar Růžička**.
29. **Zdena Růžičková**-4 (Jindřich-3, David-2, Jakob-1).
    Senk was born in Prague.
    Senk and Zdena Růžičková married. They had the following children:
    i. **Zdeněk Senk**.
    37. ii. **Eva Senková**.
30. **Vlasta Růžičková**-4 (Jindřich-3, David-2, Jakob-1).
    Karas Arnošt Katz.
    Karas Arnošt Katz and Vlasta Růžičková married. They had the following children:
    i. **Jiří Katz**.
    ii. **Věra Katz**.
31. **Joseph (Wiener) Winn**-4 (Alba-3, David-2, Jakob-1) was born on 02 Feb 1901 in Prague. He died on 08 Feb 1983 in New York City.
    Hana Taussigová daughter of Oskar Taussig and Klára Munková was born on 26 Feb 1910 in Prague. She died on 14 Mar 1999 in New York, NY. Joseph (Wiener) Winn and Hana Taussigová were married in 1933. They had the following children:
    38. i. **Janet (Jana) Winn** was born on 08 Jul 1934 in Prague. She married Donald Malcolm on 13 Apr 1956 in New York City.
    39. ii. **Marie Winn** was born on 21 Oct 1936 in Prague. She married Allan Miller on 28 Apr 1961 in New York City.
32. **Marie Wienerova**-4 (Alba-3, David-2, Jakob-1) was born in 1899. She died in 1986.
    Josef Krajbich son of Krajbich and Unknown was born in 1899. He died in 1977.
    Josef Krajbich and Marie Wienerova were married about 1918. They had

the following children:

40. i. **Ivan Krajbich** was born in 1920. He died in 1985.
41. ii. **George Krajbich** was born in 1922. He died in 1988.
    iii. **Marie Krajbichova** was born in 1924. She died in 1924.

33. **Malvina Ginsburg**-4 (Theresa 'Rosa'-3, David-2, Jakob-1).
    Joe Pollak.
    Joe Pollak and Malvina Ginsburg married. They had no children.
    Eduard Oplatka son of Josef Oplatka and Franziska 'Fanny' Geber was born on 21 Oct 1881 in Odolena Voda, Prague-East District, Bohemia. He died on 31 Dec 1945 in Chicago, IL. Eduard Oplatka and Malvina Ginsburg married. They had the following children:
    i. **William E. Oplatka** was born on 01 Mar 1910. He died on 13 Feb 2000 in Riverside, Cook Co., IL.
42. ii. **Irma Florence Oplatka** was born on 26 Apr 1914.

Generation 5

34. **Věra C. Vrzalova**-5 (Olga-4, Berta-3, David-2, Jakob-1) was born on 09 Mar 1933 in Chicago, IL.
    Theodore Karger son of Daniel Karger and Grace was born on 11 Feb 1928 in Brooklyn, NY. He died on 11 Jun 1988.
    Theodore Karger and Věra C. Vrzalova married. They had the following children:
    i. **Douglas Karger** was born on 10 Jan 1958 in Queens, NY.
    ii. **Daniel Karger** was born on 03 Aug 1959 in Queens, NY.
    iii. **David Karger** was born on 16 Jan 1963 in Greenwich, CT.

35. **Paul Eric Tausig**-5 (Olga-4, Berta-3, David-2, Jakob-1) was born on 30 Jun 1947 in New York, NY.
    Lorraine Brod.
    Paul Eric Tausig and Lorraine Brod married. They had the following children:
    i. **David James Tausig** was born about May 1982.
    ii. **Caroline Tausig** was born about Aug 1989.

36. **Sona Reichová**-5 (Jiřina-4, Jindřich-3, David-2, Jakob-1).
    Jiří Bloch.

Jiří Bloch and Sona Reichová married. They had the following children:
  i. **Dahlia Bloch**.
  ii. **David Bloch**.

37. **Eva Senková**-5 (Zdena-4, Jindřich-3, David-2, Jakob-1).
    František Paul was born on 28 Apr 1898 in Pardubice. He died on 06 Nov 1976 in Praha, CSR. František Paul and Eva Senková married. They had the following children:
    43. i. **Jana Paulová** was born on 19 Feb 1955 in Praha, CSR. She married Milan Svoboda in 1977.
        ii. **Eva Paulová**.
        iii. **Zdena Paulová**.
        iv. **Franta Paul**. He died in 1979.

38. **Janet (Jana) Winn**-5 (Joseph (Wiener)-4, Alba-3, David-2, Jakob-1) was born on 08 Jul 1934 in Prague.
    Donald Malcolm was born in 1935. He died in 1975.
    Donald Malcolm and Janet (Jana) Winn were married on 13 Apr 1956 in New York City. They had the following children:
    44. i. **Anne Malcolm** was born on 17 Dec 1962 in New York City. She married Richard Tuck on 19 Mar 1993 in New York City.
    Gardner Botsford son of Botsford was born on 07 Jul 1917 in New York, NY. He died on 27 Sep 2004 in New York, NY.
    Gardner Botsford and Janet (Jana) Winn were married on 26 Sep 1975. They had no children.

39. **Marie Winn**-5 (Joseph (Wiener)-4, Alba-3, David-2, Jakob-1) was born on 21 Oct 1936 in Prague.
    Allan Miller was born on 05 Dec 1933 in New York City.
    Allan Miller and Marie Winn were married on 28 Apr 1961 in New York City. They had the following children:
    45. i. **Michael Winn Miller** was born on 20 Nov 1962. He married Sarah Paul on 30 Dec 1988 in New York City.
    46. ii. **Steven David Miller** was born on 14 Apr 1966 in New York City. He married Jennifer Durand on 11 Nov 1995 in San Francisco, CA.

40. **Ivan Krajbich**-5 (Marie-4, Alba-3, David-2, Jakob-1) was born in 1920. He

died in 1985.

Dagmar Králová was born in 1926.

Ivan Krajbich and Dagmar Králová married. They had the following children:

47. i. **2nd Ivan Krajbich** was born in 1947.
48. ii. **Hana Krajbich** was born in 1948.
    iii. **Tomáš Krajbich** was born in 1953.

41. **George Krajbich**-5 (Marie-4, Alba-3, David-2, Jakob-1) was born in 1922. He died in 1988.

Ingeborg Wenzel was born in 1924. She died about 1978.

George Krajbich and Ingeborg Wenzel married. They had no children.

Zdenka Zlobická was born in 1947.

George Krajbich and Zdenka Zlobická married. They had the following children:

    i. **Elizabeth Krajbich** was born in 1983.

42. **Irma Florence Oplatka**-5 (Malvina-4, Theresa 'Rosa'-3, David-2, Jakob-1) was born on 26 Apr 1914.

Raymond Schwarzkopf was born on 07 Apr 1911 in Chicago, IL. He died on 05 Jan 1996 in Miami, FL.

Raymond Schwarzkopf and Irma Florence Oplatka married. They had the following children:

    i. **Tommy Schwarzkopf**.

Generation 6

43. **Jana Paulová**-6 (Eva-5, Zdena-4, Jindřich-3, David-2, Jakob-1) was born on 19 Feb 1955 in Praha, CSR.

Milan Svoboda was born on 10 Dec 1951 in Praha, CSR.

Milan Svoboda and Jana Paulová were married in 1977. They had the following children:

    i. **child Svoboda**.

44. **Anne Malcolm**-6 (Janet (Jana)-5, Joseph (Wiener)-4, Alba-3, David-2, Jakob-1) was born on 17 Dec 1962 in New York City.

Richard Tuck was born on 09 Jan 1949 in Newcastleupon-Tyne, England.

Richard Tuck and Anne Malcolm were married on 19 Mar 1993 in New

York City. They had the following children:
i. **Sophy Malcolm Tuck** was born on 13 Jul 1993 in Cambridge, England.

45. **Michael Winn Miller**-6 (Marie-5, Joseph (Wiener)-4, Alba-3, David-2, Jakob-1) was born on 20 Nov 1962.
Sarah Paul was born on 29 Dec 1961 in New York City.
Michael Winn Miller and Sarah Paul were married on 30 Dec 1988 in New York City. They had the following children:
i. **Isadore 'Izzy' Miller** was born on 20 Nov 1995 in San Francisco, CA.
ii. **Abigail 'Abbey' Nadia Paul Miller** was born on 24 Oct 1996 in New York City.

46. **Steven David Miller**-6 (Marie-5, Joseph (Wiener)-4, Alba-3, David-2, Jakob-1) was born on 14 Apr 1966 in New York City.
Jennifer Durand.
Steven David Miller and Jennifer Durand were married on 11 Nov 1995 in San Francisco, CA. They had the following children:
i. **Eli Miller** was born on 17 Mar 1999.
ii. **Clara Miller** was born on 04 Jul 2000 in San Francisco, CA or NYC.

47. **2nd Ivan Krajbich**-6 (Ivan-5, Marie-4, Alba-3, David-2, Jakob-1) was born in 1947.
Suzanne . G. William was born in 1953.
2nd Ivan Krajbich and Suzanne . G. William married. They had the following children:
i. **3rd Ivan Krajbich** was born in 1983.
ii. **Alan Krajbich** was born in 1987.
iii. **Victoria Lee Krajbich** was born in 1990.

51. **Hana Krajbich**-6 (Ivan-5, Marie-4, Alba-3, David-2, Jakob-1) was born in 1948.
Karl Otta was born in 1948.
Karl Otta and Hana Krajbich married. They had the following children:
i. **Hana Otta** was born in 1977.

ii. **Dagmar Otta** was born in 1980.
iii. **Karel Otta** was born in 1985.

Krajbich Family

Generation 1

1. **Josef Krajbich**-1 was born in 1899. He died in 1977.
   Marie Wienerova daughter of Maurice Wiener and Alba Růžičková was born in 1899. She died in 1986.
   Josef Krajbich and Marie Wienerova were married about 1918. They had the following children:
   - 2. i. **Ivan Krajbich** was born in 1920. He died in 1985.
   - 3. ii. **George Krajbich** was born in 1922. He died in 1988.
   - iii. **Marie Krajbichova** was born in 1924. She died in 1924.

Generation 2

2. **Ivan Krajbich**-2 (Josef-1) was born in 1920. He died in 1985.
   Dagmar Králová was born in 1926.
   Ivan Krajbich and Dagmar Králová married. They had the following children:
   - 4. i. **2nd Ivan Krajbich** was born in 1947.
   - 5. ii. **Hana Krajbich** was born in 1948.
   - iii. **Tomáš Krajbich** was born in 1953.

3. **George Krajbich**-2 (Josef-1) was born in 1922. He died in 1988.
   Ingeborg Wenzel was born in 1924. She died about 1978.
   George Krajbich and Ingeborg Wenzel married. They had no children.
   Zdenka Zlobická was born in 1947.
   George Krajbich and Zdenka Zlobická married. They had the following children:
   - i. **Elizabeth Krajbich** was born in 1983.

Generation 3

4. **2nd Ivan Krajbich**-3 (Ivan-2, Josef-1) was born in 1947.
   Suzanne . G. William was born in 1953.
   2nd Ivan Krajbich and Suzanne . G. William married. They had the following children:
   - i. **3rd Ivan Krajbich** was born in 1983.
   - ii. **Alan Krajbich** was born in 1987.

    iii. **Victoria Lee Krajbich** was born in 1990.
5. **Hana Krajbich**-3 (Ivan-2, Josef-1) was born in 1948.
Karl Otta was born in 1948.
Karl Otta and Hana Krajbich married. They had the following children:
    i. **Hana Otta** was born in 1977.
    ii. **Dagmar Otta** was born in 1980.
    iii. **Karel Otta** was born in 1985.

Ginsburg (Günsburg) Family

Generation 1

Anna Günsburg-1.

Unknown.

Unknown and Anna Günsburg married. They had the following children:
  i. **Ignaz Günsburg** was born about 1828 in Zavodilka, Jizbice, Nymburk Dist., Bohemia.
  ii. **Albert Vojtěch Günsburg** was born in 1833 in Zavadilka, Jizbice, Nymburk Dist., Bohemia. He died on 11 Nov 1901 in Písková Lhota, Mladá Boleslav Dist., Bohemia.
  iii. **Philipp Günsburg** was born about 1833 in Zavadilka, Jizbice, Nymburk Dist., Bohemia.

Generation 2

Ignaz Günsburg-2 (Anna-1) was born about 1828 in Zavodilka, Jizbice, Nymburk Dist., Bohemia.

Anna Sommer was born about 1830 in Polsberg, Poděbrady, Nymburk Dist., Bohemia.

Ignaz Günsburg and Anna Sommer married. They had the following children:
  i. **Alois Günsburg** was born on 11 Jul 1856 in Zavadilka, Jizbice, Nymburk Dist., Bohemia.
  ii. **Ludwig Ginsburg** was born on 30 Mar 1858 in Zavadilka, Jizbice, Nymburk, Bohemia. He died on 07 Nov 1919 in Chicago, Cook County, Illinois.

Albert Vojtěch Günsburg-2 (Anna-1) was born in 1833 in Zavadilka, Jizbice, Nymburk Dist., Bohemia. He died on 11 Nov 1901 in Písková Lhota, Mladá Boleslav Dist., Bohemia.

Rosalia Seidl was born in 1824 in Podlužany, Rožďalovice, Nymburk Dist., Bohemia. She died on 27 Oct 1913 in Písková Lhota 40, Mladá Boleslav Dist., Bohemia.

Albert Vojtěch Günsburg and Rosalia Seidl married. They had the following children:

i. **Eduard Günsburg** was born on 01 Nov 1858 in Zábrdovice, Křinec, Nymburk Dist., Bohemia. He died on 10 Jan 1898 in Prague, Bohemia.

ii. **Alois Günsburg** was born on 28 Nov 1861 in "Neuhof", near, Nymburk, Nymburk District, Bohemia. He died on 28 May 1918 in Písková Lhota č. 40.

Anna Günsburg was born on 22 Aug 1863 in Neuhof" near, Nymburk, Nymburk District, Bohemia.

Karl Günsburg was born on 26 Dec 1865 in Křinec, Nymburk District, Bohemia.

Philipp Günsburg-2 (Anna-1) was born about 1833 in Zavadilka, Jizbice, Nymburk Dist., Bohemia.

Anny Steiner was born about 1836 in Písková Lhota, Nymburk District, Bohemia.

Philipp Günsburg and Anny Steiner married. They had the following children:

Emilie Günsburg was born on 15 Apr 1864 in Cilec, Nymburk District, Bohemia.

Generation 3

Alois Günsburg-3 (Ignaz-2, Anna-1) was born on 11 Jul 1856 in Zavadilka, Jizbice, Nymburk Dist., Bohemia.

Theresia Koretz was born about 1858. She died on 08 Dec 1935 in Prague, Czech.. Alois Günsburg and Theresia Koretz married. They had the following children:

Emil Günsburg was born on 23 Apr 1886 in Patek, Nymburk Dist., Bohemia.

ii. **Ernest Günsburg** was born on 07 Jun 1887 in Patek. Nymburk Dist., Bohemia. He died after 09 May 1942 in Sobibór, Włodawa Dist., Poland - Holocaust.

Gottlieb Günsburg was born on 15 Oct 1888 in Patek, Nymburk Dist., Bohemia. He died after 20 Jan 1943 in Auschwitz, Oswiecim, Poland.

Leopold Günsburg was born about 1895. He died about 16 May

1936.

Ludwig Ginsburg-3 (Ignaz-2, Anna-1) was born on 30 Mar 1858 in Zavadilka, Jizbice, Nymburk, Bohemia. He died on 07 Nov 1919 in Chicago, Cook County, Illinois.

Therese Rose Růžičková daughter of David Růžička and Johanna Reskova was born on 09 Apr 1857 in Borotice, Pribram Dist., Bohemia. She died in 1935 in Chicago, Cook Co., IL.

Ludwig Ginsburg and Therese Rose Růžičková married. They had the following children:

> **Joseph Ginsburg** was born on 07 Oct 1882 in Podebrady, Nymburk Dist., Bohemia.
>
> **Otto Ginsburg** was born on 07 Nov 1883 in Poděbrady, Nymburk District, Bohemia. He died on 21 Oct 1884 in Podebrady, Nymburk Dist., Bohemia.
>
> iii. **Malvina Ginsburgova** was born in 1885 in Podebrady, Nymburk Dist., Bohemia. She died in 1974.
>
> **Arthur Ginsburg** was born on 13 Aug 1886 in Podebrady, Nymburk Dist., Bohemia.
>
> **Rudolf Ginsburg** was born on 10 Apr 1888 in Poděbrady, Nymburk District, Bohemia. He died on 08 Jul 1888 in Poděbrady, Nymburk District, Bohemia.
>
> vi. **Elsie Ginsburgova** was born in 1889 in Podebrady, Nymburk Dist., Bohemia. She died in 1952.
>
> vii. **Zdenek Ginsburg** was born on 24 Sep 1890 in Czech.. He died on 09 Mar 1971 in Chicago, IL.
>
> viii. **Vilma Ginsburg** was born on 11 Nov 1892 in Podebrady, Nymburk Dist., Bohemia. She died on 30 Dec 1990 in Los Angeles, Los Angeles County, CA.
>
> ix. **Anna Ginsburg** was born in 1894 in Podebrady, Nymburk Dist., Bohemia. She died in 1975 in Seal Beach, Orange Co., CA.
>
> x. **Friedrich Burg** was born on 09 Jan 1896 in Podebrady, Nymburk Dist., Bohemia. He died on 23 Aug 1995.
>
> xi. **Roderick Oldrich Ginter** was born on 27 May 1899 in Bohemia.

He died on 19 May 1987 in Harvey, Cook County, Illinois.

Eduard Günsburg-3 (Albert Vojtěch-2, Anna-1) was born on 01 Nov 1858 in Zábrdovice, Křinec, Nymburk Dist., Bohemia. He died on 10 Jan 1898 in Prague, Bohemia.

Ewa Neumann was born about 1851 in Luštěnice, Mladá Boleslav District, Bohemia. Eduard Günsburg and Ewa Neumann married. They had the following children:

    i. **Leopold Günsburg** was born on 28 Apr 1884 in Mlada Boleslav, Mladá Boleslav District, Bohemia. He died on 05 Aug 1944 in Prague, Bohemia.

    ii. **Josef Günsburg** was born on 25 Aug 1886 in Zavadilka, Jizbice, Nymburk Dist., Bohemia. He died in 1943 in Auschwitz II-Birkenau, Gmina Oświęcim, Poland (Holocaust).

Alois Günsburg-3 (Albert Vojtěch-2, Anna-1) was born on 28 Nov 1861 in "Neuhof", near, Nymburk, Nymburk District, Bohemia. He died on 28 May 1918 in Písková Lhota č. 40.

Florence (Flora) Fischer was born on 30 Jan 1862 in Písková Lhota, Mladá Boleslav Dist., Bohemia. Alois Günsburg and Florence (Flora) Fischer married. They had the following children:

    Rose Günsburg was born on 01 Jul 1894 in Zámostí, Písková Lhota, Mladá Boleslav Dist., Bohemia. She died about 1943 in ransport B, no. 697 (21. 10. 1941, Prague -> Łódź) (concentration camp).

Generation 4

Ernest Günsburg-4 (Alois-3, Ignaz-2, Anna-1) was born on 07 Jun 1887 in Patek. Nymburk Dist., Bohemia. He died after 09 May 1942 in Sobibór, Włodawa Dist., Poland - Holocaust.

Marie Morawetz was born on 19 Nov 1893 in Kamberk, Benešov District, Bohemia. She died after 09 May 1942 in Sobibór, Włodawa Dist., Poland - Holocaust.

Ernest Günsburg and Marie Morawetz married. They had the following children:

    Alena Günsburg was born on 25 Sep 1920. She died after 09

May 1942 in obibór, Włodawa Dist., Voivodeship, Poland (Holocaust).

Ludvik Günsburg was born on 01 Jan 1925. He died after 09 May 1942 in Sobibór, Włodawa Dist., Poland - Holocaust.

Malvina Ginsburgova-4 (Ludwig-3, Ignaz-2, Anna-1) was born in 1885 in Podebrady, Nymburk Dist., Bohemia. She died in 1974.

Edward Oplatka was born in 1881 in Odolena Voda, Prague-East District, Bohemia. He died in 1945. Edward Oplatka and Malvina Ginsburgova married. They had the following children:

> **Irma Oplatka.**
>
> **William Oplatka.**

Joe Pollak was born in 1883 in Zaluzi, Bohemia. He died in 1962.

Joe Pollak and Malvina Ginsburgova married. They had no children.

Elsie Ginsburgova-4 (Ludwig-3, Ignaz-2, Anna-1) was born in 1889 in Podebrady, Nymburk Dist., Bohemia. She died in 1952.

Reinish.

Reinish and Elsie Ginsburgova married. They had the following children:

> **Carl Reinish.**
>
> **Herbert Reinish.**

Zdenek Ginsburg-4 (Ludwig-3, Ignaz-2, Anna-1) was born on 24 Sep 1890 in Czech.. He died on 09 Mar 1971 in Chicago, IL.

Irma Mautner was born on 27 Mar 1891 in Pisek, Písek Distric,, Bohemia. She died on 01 May 1971 in Chicago, IL.

Zdenek Ginsburg and Irma Mautner married. They had the following children:

> i. **Lucille Rose Ginsburg.**
>> **Georgiana Vera Ginsburg** was born on 16 Dec 1920 in Chicago, Cook County, Illinois. She died on 17 Dec 2013 in Shalom Memorial Park, Arlington Heights, Cook County, Illinois, U.

Vilma Ginsburg-4 (Ludwig-3, Ignaz-2, Anna-1) was born on 11 Nov 1892 in Podebrady, Nymburk Dist., Bohemia. She died on 30 Dec 1990 in Los Angeles, Los Angeles County, CA.

Max Mautner was born on 05 May 1891 in Mladá Vožice, Tábor Dist., Bohemia. He died on 24 Nov 1925 in Chicago, IL.

Max Mautner and Vilma Ginsburg married. They had the following children:

>**Robert Mautner** was born on 16 Jun 1924 in Chicago, Cook County, Illinois. He died on 28 Dec 2001 in Marin County, California.
>
>**Rose Mautner.**
>
>**daughter Mautner.**

Charles F. Lowy (Löwy) was born on 17 Jun 1874 in Vojslavice, Pelhrimov Dist., Vysocina, Moravia.

Charles F. Lowy (Löwy) and Vilma Ginsburg married. They had the following children:

>**Lucille A. Löwy** was born about 1906 in Chicago, Cook Co., IL.

Anna Ginsburg-4 (Ludwig-3, Ignaz-2, Anna-1) was born in 1894 in Podebrady, Nymburk Dist., Bohemia. She died in 1975 in Seal Beach, Orange Co., CA.

Emil Schawzkopf was born about 1892 in Czech.. He died in 1976.

Emil Schawzkopf and Anna Ginsburg married. They had the following children:

>**Roy Schawzkopf.**
>
>**Hannah Schawzkopf.**

Friedrich Burg-4 (Ludwig-3, Ignaz-2, Anna-1) was born on 09 Jan 1896 in Podebrady, Nymburk Dist., Bohemia. He died on 23 Aug 1995.

Erna Vodicka was born on 27 Oct 1896 in Petrovice, Pribram Dist.,Bohemia. She died on 22 Mar 1985 in Los Angeles, CA.

Friedrich Burg and Erna Vodicka married. They had the following children:

>i. **Blamche Dorothy Burg.**
>
>**son Burg.**

Roderick Oldrich Ginter-4 (Ludwig-3, Ignaz-2, Anna-1) was born on 27 May 1899 in Bohemia. He died on 19 May 1987 in Harvey, Cook County, Illinois.

Francis Sylvia Taussig was born on 01 Jan 1901 in Czech.. She died on

17 Apr 1996 in Orange, Orange Co., CA.

Roderick Oldrich Ginter and Francis Sylvia Taussig married. They had the following children:

    Allan Victor Ginter was born on 26 Jun 1923 in Chicago, Cook County, Illinois.

    Edward Max Ginter was born on 18 Jul 1926 in Chicago, Cook County, Illinois.

Helga Mandl.

Roderick Oldrich Ginter and Helga Mandl married. They had no children.

Leopold Günsburg-4 (Eduard-3, Albert Vojtěch-2, Anna-1) was born on 28 Apr 1884 in Mlada Boleslav, Mladá Boleslav District, Bohemia. He died on 05 Aug 1944 in Prague, Bohemia.

Unknown.

Leopold Günsburg and Unknown married. They had the following children:

    Otomar Günsburg.

Josef Günsburg-4 (Eduard-3, Albert Vojtěch-2, Anna-1) was born on 25 Aug 1886 in Zavadilka, Jizbice, Nymburk Dist., Bohemia. He died in 1943 in Auschwitz II-Birkenau, Gmina Oświęcim, Poland (Holocaust).

Hermine Weiss was born on 25 Feb 1887. She died in 1943 in Auschwitz II-Birkenau, Gmina Oświęcim, Poland (Holocaust).

Josef Günsburg and Hermine Weiss married. They had the following children:

    Jiřinka Ginsburgová was born on 05 Mar 1915 in Veselice, Mladá Boleslav District, Bohemia. She died in 1943 in Auschwitz II-Birkenau, Gmina Oświęcim, Poland (Holocaust).

Generation 5

Lucille Rose Ginsburg-5 (Zdenek-4, Ludwig-3, Ignaz-2, Anna-1).

Robert 'Bob' Jevert Eckels was born on 18 Oct 1922 in Bayfield, Bayfield County, WI. Robert 'Bob' Jevert Eckels and Lucille Rose Ginsburg married. They had the following children:

son Eckels.
son Eckels.
son Eckels.

Blamche Dorothy Burg-5 (Friedrich-4, Ludwig-3, Ignaz-2, Anna-1).

Norman Leslie Ginsburg was born on 23 Dec 1922 in Illinois. He died on 28 Dec 2008 in Laguna Woods, CA.

Norman Leslie Ginsburg and Blamche Dorothy Burg married. They had the following children:

i. **Judith Ellen Ginsburg**.

Generation 6

Judith Ellen Ginsburg-6 (Blamche Dorothy-5, Friedrich-4, Ludwig-3, Ignaz-2, Anna-1).

Weiner.

Weiner and Judith Ellen Ginsburg married. They had the following children:

Erica Allison Weiner.
son Weiner.
son Weiner.

V.

ANCESTOR CHARTS of KEY FAMILIES

Ancestors of Miloslav Rechcigl, Sr.

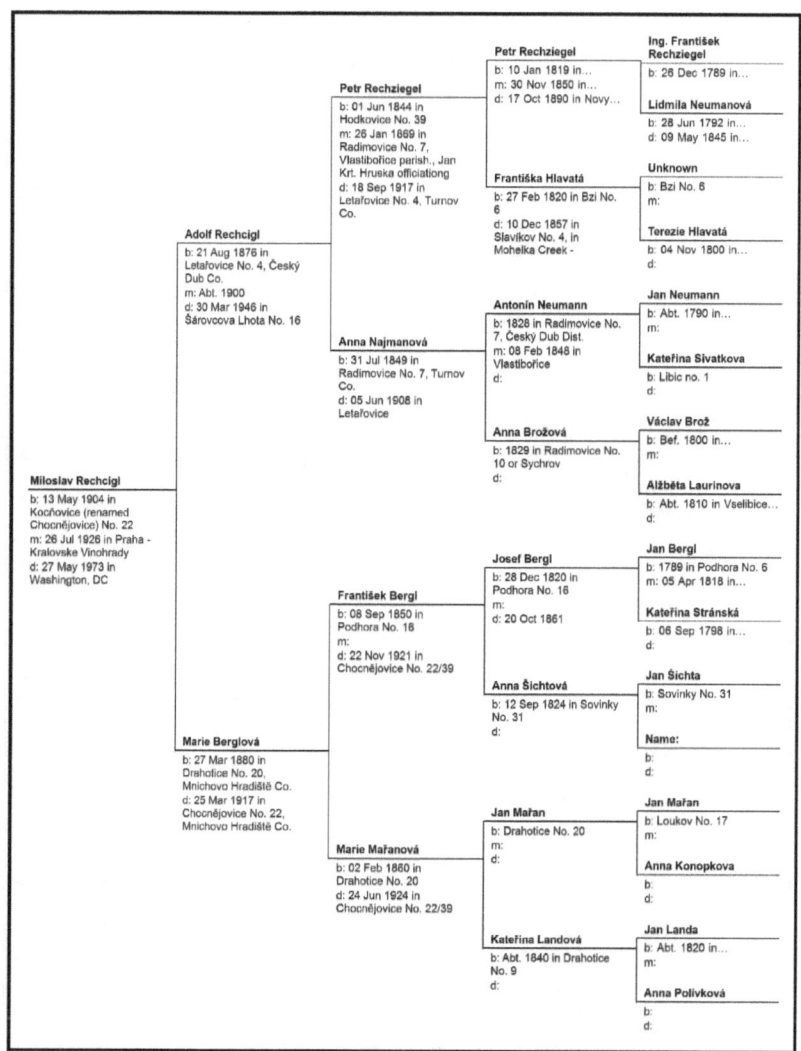

B. Ancestors of Marie Rajtrova

Marie Rajtrová
b: 05 Jul 1905 in Dolanky No. 7, Mnichovo Hradiště Co.
m: 26 Jul 1926 in Praha - Kralovske Vinohrady
d: 13 Apr 1982 in Mladá Boleslav

- **Čeněk Rajtr**
  b: 01 Jul 1874 in nky No. 7, Mnichovo Hradiště Dist.,
  m: 02 Jul 1904 in Mnichovo Hradiště
  d: 27 Oct 1956 in Dolánky No. 7, Mnichovo Hradiště Dist.,
  - **Jan Václav Rajtr**
    b: 12 May 1847 in Zvířetice No. 11, Mnichovo Hradiště Co.
    m: 09 Jun 1868
    d: 19 Sep 1903 in Dolanky No. 7
    - **Václav Rajtr**
      b: 15 Sep 1783 in Zvířetice No. 11
      m:
      - **Václav Rajtr**
        b: 15 Sep 1783 in
        m: 28 Jan 1806 in...
      - **Dorota Strojsová**
        b: 24 Jan 1780 in...
        d:
    - **Barbora Koštejn**
      b: 25 Dec 1815 in Zviretica
      d: 28 May 1887 in Chudoplesy No. 9
      - **Jan Koštejn**
        b:
        m:
      - **Terezie Pazderníková**
        b: Bitouchov No. 8....
        d:
  - **Anna Najmanová**
    b: 26 Dec 1841 in Dolanky No. 7, Mnichovo Hradiště Co.
    d: 05 Aug 1900 in Dolanky, Mnichovo Hradiště Co.
    - **Josef Najman**
      b: Dolanky No. 7, Mnichovo Hradiště Co.
      m:
      d:
      - **Vojtěch Najman**
        b: Kopernik No. 2,...
        m:
      - **Anna Gintrova**
        b: Kopernik No. 4,...
        d:
    - **Alžběta Bartonova**
      b: Dneboh No. 9, Mnichovo Hradiště Co.
      d:
      - **Václav Barton**
        b: Dneboh No. 9,...
        m:
      - **Anna Nohýnková**
        b: Sychrov No. 2,...
        d:

- **Marie Dandová**
  b: 31 Jan 1882 in Hoškovice, No. 14, Mnichovo Hradiště Dist,
  d: 05 Jan 1967 in Dolanky No. 7, Mnichovo Hradiště Co.
  - **František Antonín Danda**
    b: 10 Jun 1857 in Hoškovice, No. 2, Mnichovo Hradiště Dist, Bohemia
    m: 04 Feb 1881 in Manikovice No. 21
    d: 07 Jun 1900 in Hoškovice, No. 14, Mnichovo Hradiště Dist, Bohemia
    - **František Danda**
      b: 01 Aug 1817 in Hoškovice, Mnichovo Hradiště Dist, Bohemia
      m:
      d: 04 Mar 1904 in Podolí No. 8
      - **Josef Danda**
        b: 11 Jun 1783 in
        m: 30 Jun 1805 in...
      - **Barbora Burlánková**
        b: 24 Mar 1776 in...
        d:
    - **Kateřina Nováková**
      b: 03 Jun 1826 in Daješice no. 5
      d: 29 May 1912 in Podolí No. 8
      - **Jan Novák**
        b:
        m: 14 Feb 1843 in...
      - **Dorota Reslerová**
        b:
        d:
  - **Josefa Cimrová**
    b: 01 Jan 1859 in Manikovice No. 11, Mnichovo Hradiště Dist.
    d: 27 Aug 1923 in Hoškovice No. 14, Mnichovo Hradiště Dist.
    - **František Cimr**
      b: 31 Mar 1823 in Manikovice No. 11, Mnichovo Hradiště Co.
      m:
      d: 22 Mar 1884
      - **Josef Cimr**
        b: Manikovice No. 11
        m:
      - **Kodrova ? Anna Kochova**
        b: Bitouchov
    - **Anna Ferklová**
      b: Rostkov No. 3, Mnichovo Hradiště Co.
      d:
      - **Josef Ferkl**
        b: Rostkov No. 3
        m:
      - **Alžběta Filipová**
        b: Abt. 1800 in Sovenice
        d: 11 Aug 1870

C. Ancestors of Paul Edwards (Eisner)

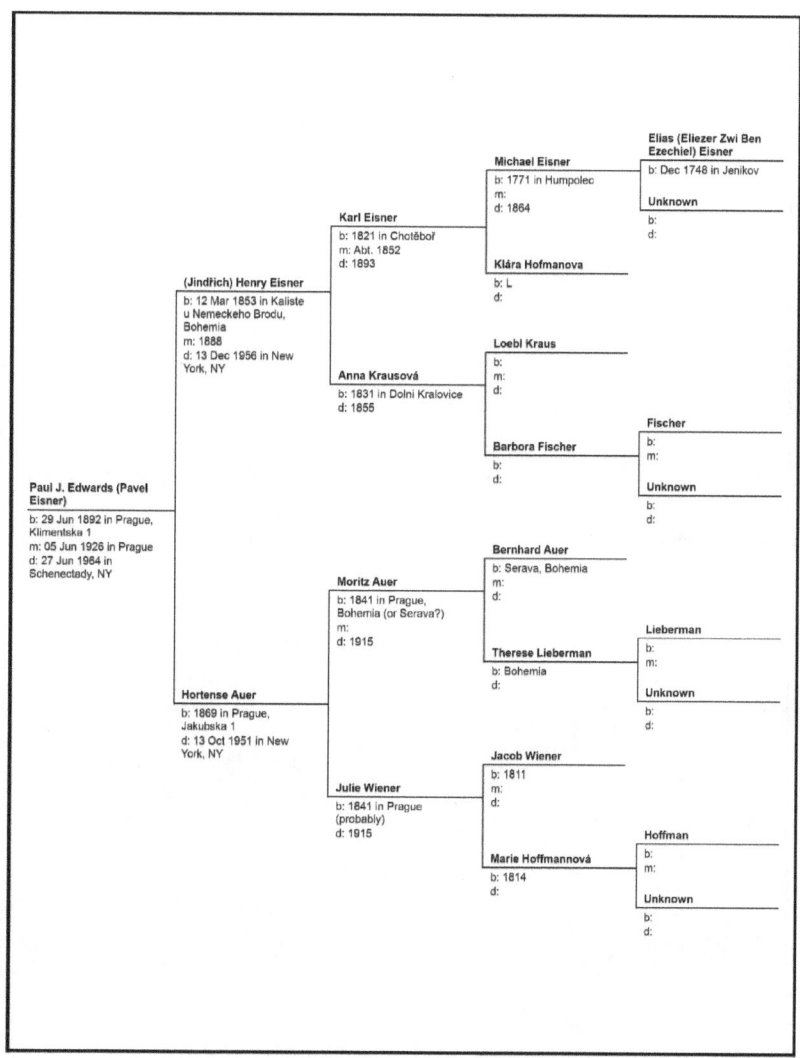

D. Ancestors of Jirina Taussigova

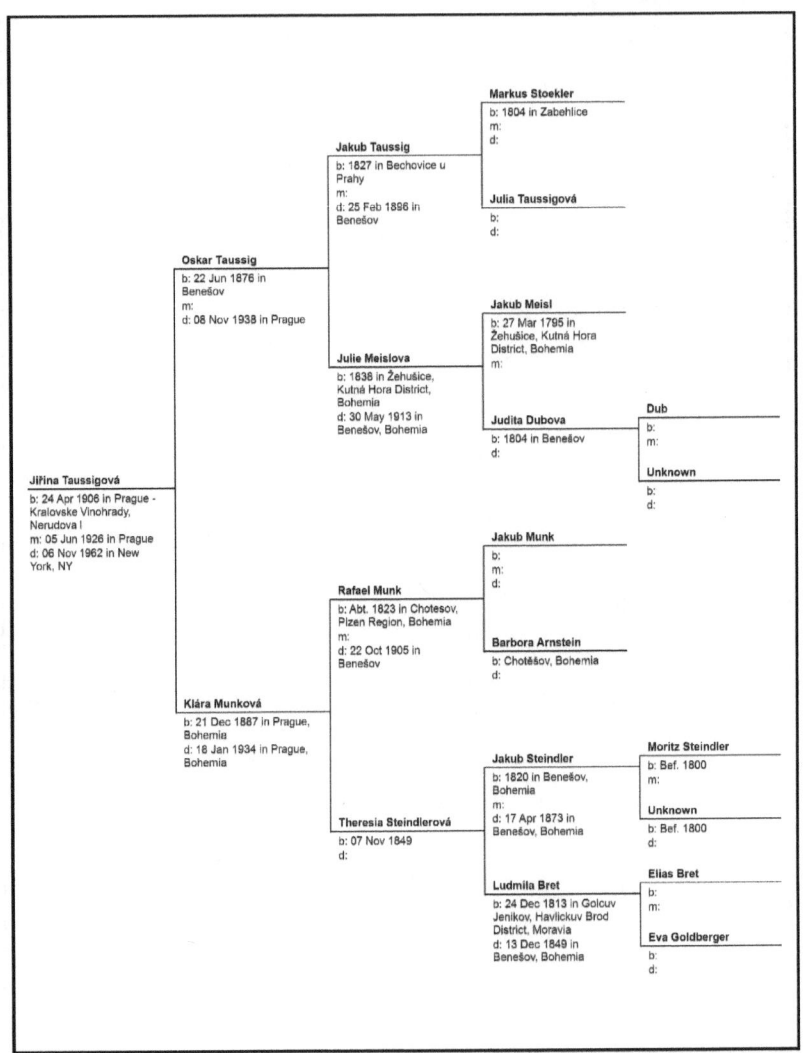

VI.

SELECTED BIOGRAPHIES

A. The Rechcigl Family

Rechcigl family had its origins in the Northeastern Bohemia, in the Moheka River Valley, neighboring on the most beautiful region of Bohemia, appropriately called 'Český Ráj,' meaning 'Czech Paradise.' The earliest known ancestor of the family, František, lived in Slavíkov, from which the family spread southward along the Mohelka Valley and settled in the following villages: Třtí, Žďárek, Hodkovicve, Letařovice and Chocnějovice. Some families members moved even further inland, i.e.., Malá Bělá and Šárovcova Lhota. All the Rechcígls in the Mohelka Valley were, by tradition, flour millers. The mill was usually inherited by the oldest son. However, among Rechcígls, it was traditional for the father to purchase mills for his other sons as well. Miller's trade in those days belonged to among the best professions and it is no wonder that they Rechcigls stuck with it. A miller, who was normally called by everyone 'Pan Otec' (Mr. Father), was usually considered the most important person in the entire community, partly because of his economic status and partly because of his knowledge and wisdom. To become a miller, one had to be not only a good agriculturist, but also had to master of the rather complex milling technology, in addition to being a good businessman.

The first member of the family to emigrate to America was Miloslav Rechcigl (1904-1973), and his son, of the same name, who added the suffix 'Jr.' not to confuse the names.

Their descendants and close relatives are listed in alphabetical order below.

Kristin Kollecas (1993-), b. Albuquerque, NM, daughter Karen Rechcigl (1962-) of Czech immigrant parents, and Ulysses Kollecas, has chosen pharmacy for her career. At age 13, she and her family moved to Naples, Florida where she attended Gulf Coast High School and graduated in the top 5% in her class while receiving multiple Varsity letters in soccer, golf, and tennis. Kristin subsequently graduated summa cum laude from Florida State University with a Bachelor's Degree in Nutrition & Food Science (B.S., 2014) and summa cum laude from University of Florida with a Doctor of Pharmacy Degree (Pharm.D., 2018). She completed a two-year Medical Managed Care Postdoctoral Fellowship at Sanofi Genzyme and MCPHS University, where she supported various disease states including Multiple Sclerosis, Immunology, Oncology, and Rare Blood Disorders. After completion of her Postdoctoral Fellowship, she accepted a position within the same company as a Medical Managed Care Liaison and subsequently was promoted to Associate Director of Medical Value & Outcomes covering Regional Payer Accounts in the Northeast region of the US.

Paul Kollecas (1995-), b. Albuquerque, NM, son of Karen Rechcigl (1962-) of Czech immigrant parents, and Ulysses Kollecas, is a telecommunications finance & product professional. At age 11, he and his family moved to Naples, Florida where he attended Gulf Coast High School and graduated in the top 5%. During his time in Florida, Paul served as an official for competitive soccer games, founded the Political Awareness Club, worked for a small business in a business operations capacity, and participated in Congressional and Presidential campaigns. Paul subsequently graduated summa cum laude from Florida State University with a Bachelor's Degree in Economics (B.S., 2016), where he served as an Orientation Leader (2015) and worked in Real Estate and Public Advocacy organizations. Since graduation, Paul has been with Comcast Business (s. 2017) at its headquarters in Philadelphia supporting both Finance and Product. In Finance, Paul served on the HQ Financial Planning &

Analysis team where he supported the Administrative, Access Solutions, Sales, and Marketing organizations as a financial liaison as well as supporting HQ strategic analysis and long-term planning for the company. As of 2020, Paul is a Product Manager for the Voice Portfolio supporting cross-portfolio initiatives, compliance, and the communications transformation initiative.

Gregory 'Greg' J. Rechcigl (1988-), b. Bradenton, FL, son of Jack Rechcigl (1960-) and Nancy Palko (1961-), and grandson of Czech immigrant grandparents, is a health science administrator. He studied health services administration at University of Central Florida (B.S., 2011; M.S., 2013), followed with an internship at Manatee Memorial Hospital, working directly with a Hospital Vice President. Subsequently, he worked, as a surgical service assistant, for VA Medical Center in Orlando, FL for two years. During that time he had the opportunity to work in several departments including Human Resources, Mental Health and Surgery Services, which enabled him to gain valuable experience in the operations and management of different departments within the VA health system and broadened his knowledge in health administrative services. He then served as a Client Services Manager with Bayada Home Health Care, managing the office, as well as the field staff of 70 employee and coordinating services for clients. Currently, he holds the position of the Health Administrator at the Wellpath - East Arkansas Regional Unit, Arkansas Dept of Corrections, at Brickeys, AR, to which he was promoted, after first being engaged as an Assistant Health Services Administrator for about a year and a half. This is a prestigious, and greatly demanding position, with the responsibility for running a large hospital. In his next years, he improved operational efficiencies and teamed up with local resources to improve care and provide a better work environment. This has led to decreased expenditures and an increase in morale and retention of the hospital staff. In 2021, he moved to Nashville, TN, where he was offered a position at Vanderbilt University Medical Center. He started in August 2021 as the Assistant Director of Anesthesiology. This is a new and fun role that allows him to use his creative thought process and problem-solving skills to come up with new projects to benefit the Department. His first assignment was developing a new VUMC Policy and Procedure structuring the communication and representation of Non-Physician Providers. This was a robust and very controversial topic that required vast research and collaboration. Next, to help staffing and market our locations that we needing more support, he implanted quarterly lunch and learn events to get current staff more engaged in other locations. With two events complete and plans for future events, these lunch and learns were a success. These events led an increase in credentialing at offsite locations that were having staffing troubles. He is also working on many other projects to help with the current space issues and is working diligently to turn offices into hotel spaces to provide more use. An innate naturalist, loving fishing and hunting and the outdoors, he attained the rank of 'Eagle Scout, at very young age. His natural outgoing and extroverted personality enriches his behavior and ensures successful career.

John 'Jack' E. Rechcigl (1960-), b. Washington, DC, son of Czech immigrant parents, Míla Rechcigl (1930-) and Eva Edwards (1932-), graduated from the Univ. of Delaware, majoring in plant science (B.S., 1982) and studied soil science at Virginia Polytechnic Inst. and State Univ., Blacksburg (M.S., 1983; Ph.D., 1986). He joined the faculty of the Univ. of Florida in 1986, as asst. professor of soil science and water quality, in 1991 was promoted to associate professor and in 1996 attained full professorship. In 1999 he was named Univ. of Florida Research Foundation Professor. He also holds the Honorary Professorship at the Czech Univ. of Agriculture in Prague. He was initially based at the Range Cattle Research and Education Center at Ona, FL (1986-2000), prior to his appointment as Director of Gulf Coast Research and Education Center in Bradenton (2000-01) and then at a brand new, state-of-the-art Center in Balm (s. 2001). In 2020, he was given an additional responsibility by being also named Director of Fort Lauderdale Research and Education Center. Dr. Rechcigl is recognized nationally and internationally for his research on the beneficial uses of organic wastes and industrial by-products as fertilizers for agricultural crops. He has been a frequent speaker at national and international workshops and conferences and has consulted in various countries including Brazil, Nicaragua, Venezuela, Australia, Taiwan, Philippines, South Africa and the Czech Republic and Slovakia. He has authored over 300 publications, including contributions to books, monographs, and articles in periodicals in the fields of soil fertility, environmental quality, and water pollution. He served as associate editor of the *Soil and Crop Science Society Proceedings*, prior to assuming the responsibility as editor-in-chief of the *Agriculture and Environmental Book Series*. Among other, he edited monographs: *Soil Amendments and Environmental Quality* (1995), *Soil Amendments: Impacts on Biotic Systems* (1995), *Environmentally Safe Approaches to Crop Disease Control* (1997), *Agricultural Uses of By-Products and Wastes in Agriculture* (1997), *Biological and Biotechnological Control of Insect Pests* (1998) and *Insect Pest Management: Techniques for Environmental Protection* (2000).

Karen Rechcigl (1962-), b. Washington, DC, the daughter of Czech immigrant parents, Mila Rechcigl (l 1930-) and Eva Edwards (1932-), received her education at Univ. of Maryland, where she majored in horticulture and pest management. She worked as an ornamental integrated pest management specialist for several years before she decided to pursue the business management line. Because of her winning personality and organizational ability, she developed extraordinary skills as a salesperson and an account representative. Whatever position she has ever held, she always outshined her co-workers. Although management positions have been offered to her, she declined them all, not wanting to become a paper pusher, preferring to work with people. Among other, she became business account executive at Metro Mobile Co., Albuquerque, NM, Bell Atlantic Co., Cellular One and ALLTELL. She then was associated with Comcast. Corp, and was based in Naples, Florida. She had repeatedly earned a membership in the President's Cabinet for her outstanding performance. She was named the Top Representative of the entire Region and the Top Representative of the Company. Currently she is an account executive for DS Services Crystal Springs. In her new job, she made a fantastic sale to an entire community which took several months to execute, even with assistance of other employees. Consequently, she was given a title of Territory Account Executive. She was married to Ulysses C. Kollecas (1958-) from whom she is now divorced. They had a daughter, Kristin and a son, Paul.

Kevin Thomas Rechcigl (1991-), b. Bradenton, FL, son of Jack Rechcigl (1960-) and Nancy Palko (1961-), and grandson of Czech immigrant grandparents, is an Internal Medicine Physician at Baptist Medical Center in Jacksonville, FL. He is a graduate of University of Florida, where he majored in microbiology and cell science (B.S., cum laude, 2014). He then pursued his doctorate degree in medicine at Nova Southeastern University College of Osteopathic Medicine (NSU-COM), Ft. Lauderdale, FL (D.O., 2018). He then went on to complete his internal medicine residency at University of Florida College of Medicine. As an undergraduate, he was engaged as a research assistant in the Department of Microbiology and Cell Science. Subsequently, he served as Graduate Research Assistant at NSU. He was an active participant in the Student Government

Association and Sigma Sigma Phi National Osteopathic Medicine Honors Fraternity. During his studies he was also a recipient of a number of recognitions, including Dean's List and elected to membership in Delta Epsilon Iota Academic Honor Society, and Sigma Sigma Phi Honors Fraternity. Kevin currently resides in Jacksonville FL with his wife Jordan and son, James Rechcigl.

Lindsey Rechcigl (1994-), b. Bradenton, FL, daughter of Jack Rechcigl (1960-) and Nancy Palko (1961-), and granddaughter of Czech immigrant grandparents, graduated from University of Florida, majoring in nutritional sciences (B.S., 2017) and minoring in leadership. She continued her studies in the same University, receiving Master's degree in public health in 2018. She graduated with summa cum laude with the 4.0 point score, the highest score possible. She graduated from Nova Southeastern University Physician Assistant program in Ft. Lauderdale, FL, with her Master of Medical Science (M.M.S., 2021). Lindsey currently works as a certified physician assistant at a family medicine practice, AllCare Medical Centers, in Bradenton, FL.

Her previous work experience includes, serving as medical assistant at Scola Podiatry (January 2017-May 2018) and medical assistant at Arsenault Dermatology (June 2018-May 2019). She is CPR Certified and was elected to membership in Phi Kappa Phi Honor Society, the Order Omega and the National Society of Collegiate Scholars.

Miloslav Rechcigl, Sr. (1904-1973), b. Chocnějovice, a municipality in the Mladá Boleslav District, Bohemia, son of Adolf Rechcigl (1876-1946) and Marie Berglová (1880-1917), was trained as a miller. However, he devoted most of his career to politics and as a business executive. Rechcigl was an active member of the Agrarian Party in Czechoslovakia before the World War II. In 1935 he was elected to the Czechoslovak Parliament as its youngest member. In this capacity, he devoted his energies to economic problems, and served on several committees, relating to agriculture, industry and commerce, and international relations. He was a reporter for trade agreements for a number of countries, and for agricultural trade issues, in general. The occupation of the country by the Nazis interrupted Rechcigl's political career. In spite of his active involvement in the underground resistance movement against the Nazis, as a non-communist political figure he became a target of persecution after the Communist takeover in 1948. After two failed attempts by the Secret Police to arrest him while he was hospitalized with a serious illness, he illegally crossed the border to Germany in May 1948. After some time in a Displaced persons camp in Germany, he went to Paris, where he became a member of the Executive Committee of the Council of Free Czechoslovakia. In February 1950, he arrived in the United States, where, after several years of manual work in New York City, he joined Radio Free Europe as chief editor of the Czechoslovak agricultural program. In 1956 he was transferred from New York to Munich, Germany. In 1970, he returned to the United States, where he died as a US naturalized citizen in Washington, D.C. on May 27, 1973. Before entering the political scene, he operated a family flour mill in his native village, which he managed for his father from the age of 22, upon graduating from the Prague commercial academy. Two years later he assumed ownership of the mill and independently managed it, together with the adjacent farm. Since 1928, he worked in various professional organizations of millers, including the Millers' Association, Trade Millers' Alliance of Czechoslovakia, Czech Territorial Union of Millers and the Central Union of Millers in Czechoslovakia of which he became executive secretary. He also founded the Millers' Cooperative and became its vice president. In 1938, through his initiative, the supreme organization of Czechoslovak millers was established under the name Central Office of Czechoslovak Millers and he became its president. Furthermore, he also worked in professional agricultural organizations and became a member of all such organizations in his district. He was a council member of the Czech Agricultural Board in Prague, chairman of its economic section, a member of the cultivator committee, and a member of the Central Office of Agricultural Board in Czechoslovakia. He became a member of the Czechoslovak Agricultural Academy and officer of agricultural economists. In addition, he held membership in the auditing committee for the County Farmers' Savings Bank in Mnichovo Hradiště. Rechcigl was vice-chairman of the water agricultural organization in his district and an officer of the Water Agricultural Union of Czechoslovakia, chairman of the Economic Council in Mladá Boleslav, executive secretary of the Economic Institute of North Bohemia, and vice president of the Union of Economic Councils, as well as chairman of the Committee for Regulating the River Jizera and its Tributaries. Rechcigl's extensive archival material has been deposited in the University of Minnesota's Immigration History Research Center (IHRC). He was married to Marie Rajtrová (1905-1982). They had 2 children, son Miloslav (1930-) and a daughter Marta (1933- 2018).

Miloslav 'Míla' Rechcigl, Jr. (1930-), b. Mladá Boleslav, Czech., son of Miloslav Rechcigl (1904-1973) and Marie Rajtrová (1905-1982,) was born in Czechoslovakia to a son of the youngest member of the Czechoslovak Parliament. He spent the War years under Nazi occupation and after the Communist's coup d'état escaped to the West and in 1950 immigrated to the US. After receiving a scholarship, he went to Cornell University where he studied from 1951-58, receiving his B.S., M.N.S., and Ph.D. degrees there, specializing in biochemistry, nutrition, physiology, and food science. He then spent two years conducting research at the

National Institutes of Health as a postdoctoral research fellow. Subsequently he was appointed to the staff of the Laboratory of Biochemistry at the National Cancer Institute (NCI). For some 10 years, while he was at NCI, he conducted extensive research relating to cancer biochemistry and enzyme turnover in vivo. During 1968-69, he was selected for one year of training in a special USPHS executive program in research management, grants administration, and science policy. This led to his appointment as Special Assistant for Nutrition and Health in the Health Services and Mental Health Administration. In 1970, he joined the Agency for International Development (AID), US Department of State, as Nutrition Advisor and soon after was promoted to the position of Chief of Research and Institutional Grants Division. Later he became a Director with the responsibility for reviewing, administering and managing AID research. He is the author or editor of over 30 books and handbooks in the field of biochemistry, physiology, nutrition, food science and technology, agriculture, and international development, in addition to a large number of peer-reviewed original scientific articles and book chapters. Apart from his purely scientific endeavors, as a researcher and science administrator, Dr. Rechcigl devoted over 50 years of his life to the Czechoslovak Society of Arts and Sciences (SVU). In 1960-62 he served as Executive Secretary of the SVU Washington DC Chapter. He was responsible for the first two Society's World Congresses, both of which were a great success, and which put the Society on the world map. For a number of years, he then directed the publication program of the Society.

He also edited the Congress lectures and arranged for their publication, under the title *The Czechoslovak Contribution to World Culture* (1964, 682 p.) and *Czechoslovakia Past and Present* (1968, 2 volumes, 1900 p.). The publications received acclaim in the

American academic circles and greatly contributed to the growing prestige of the Society worldwide.

Dr. Rechcigl was also involved, one way or another, with most of the subsequent SVU World Congresses, including the SVU Congresses in Prague, Brno, Bratislava, Washington, Plzeň, Olomouc and České Budějovice. Prior to his last term as the SVU President (2004-06), he held similar posts during 1974-76, 1976-78, and again in 1994-96, 1996-98, 1998-2000, 2000-02, 2002-04. Together with his devoted wife Eva, he published eight editions of the *SVU Biographical Directory*, the last of which was printed in Prague in 2003. He was instrumental in launching a new English periodical *Kosmas - Czechoslovak and Central European Journal*. It was his idea to establish the SVU Research Institute and to create the SVU Commission for Cooperation with Czechoslovakia, and its Successor States, which played an important role in the first years after the Velvet Revolution of 1989. Under the sponsorship of the Research Institute, he and his colleagues conducted a series of seminars about research management and the art of 'grantsmanship' for scientists and scholars, as well as for the administrators, and science policy makers, at Czech and Slovak universities, the Academies of Sciences and the Government. He was also instrumental in establishing the National Heritage Commission with the aim of preserving Czech and Slovak cultural heritage in America. Under its aegis, he has undertaken a comprehensive survey of Czech-related historic sites and archival materials in the US. Based on this survey, he has prepared a detailed listing, *Czech-American Historic Sites, Monuments, and Memorials,* which was published through the courtesy of Palacký University in Olomouc (2004). The second part of the survey, bearing the title *Czechoslovak American Archivalia,* was also published by Palacký University (2004). In this connection, he also organized several important conferences, one in Texas in 1997, the second in

Minnesota (1999), the third in Nebraska (2001), and the fourth in Iowa (2003). Through his initiative, a special Working Conference on 'Czech & Slovak American Materials and their Preservation' was also held at the Czech and Slovak Embassies in Washington, DC in November 2003. It was an exceptionally successful conference which led to the establishment of the new Czech & Slovak American Archival Consortium (CSAAC). Later, he also organized, jointly with the ACSCC of North Miami, a conference on 'Czech and Slovak Heritage on Both Sides of the Atlantic', 17-20 March 2005. The conference was co-sponsored by the US Commission for the Preservation of America's Heritage Abroad, under the aegis of both Presidents of the Czech and Slovak Republics. For a number of years, Mila also held the position of SVU Archivist. In this capacity, he had organized the Society's fairly complete archival collection, which he then had deposited in several prestigious depositories, i.e., University of Minnesota's Immigration History Research Center (IHRC), University of Nebraska, Palacký University in Olomouc, Czech Republic, and most recently, at the National Archives in Prague.

Among historians, Dr. Rechcigl is well known for his studies on history, genealogy, and bibliography of American Czechs and Slovaks. A number of his publications deal with the early immigrants from the Czechlands and Slovakia, including the migration of Moravian Brethren to America. In the last few years he has been working on the cultural contributions of American Czechs and Slovaks. A selection of his biographical portraits of prominent Czech-Americans from the 17th century to date had been published in Prague, under the title *Postavy naší Ameriky* (Personalities of our America) (2000; 350 p.) On the occasion of his 75th birthday, SVU published a collection of his essays, under the title Czechs and Slovaks in America (2005; 316 p.). Three years later, he published a voluminous monograph, *On Behalf of their Homeland: Fifty Years of SVU*, an eyewitness account of the history of the Czechoslovak Society of Arts and Sciences (2008; 671 p, 28 p. ill.). And finally, on the occasion of his 80th birthday, the SVU published his personal memoirs, *Czechmate, From Bohemian Paradise to America Haven* (2011). In the same year, Rechcigl published his unique *Czech American Bibliography. A Comprehensive Listing with Focus on the US and with Appendices on Czechs in Canada and Latin America* (2011). In 2013, he published *Czech American Timeline. Chronology of Milestones in the History of Czechs in America* and, in 2015, *Czech It Out. Czech American Biography Sourcebook.* The latter, which has been patterned after the Almanac of Famous People (2011), provides a wealth of information on a variety of sources relating to biographical information about notable Czech Americans, including individual biographies, major national and local biographical compendia, ethnic sources and subject compendia, and finally family histories and genealogies.

In 2016, he wrote a 3-volume monumental comprehensive *Encyclopedia of Bohemian and Czech American Biography,* covering a universe, starting soon after the discovery of the New World, through the escapades and significant contributions of Bohemian Jesuits and Moravian Brethren in the 17th and 18th centuries, and the mass migration of the Czechs after the Revolutionary Year of 1848, up to the early years of the 20th century, and the influx of refugees from Nazism and Communism. As the Czech Ambassador to the US, H.E. Petr Gandalovič noted in his Foreword to this book, Mila Rechcigl has written a monumental work, representing a culmination of his life achievement as a historian of Czech America. He compares him to the famed Thomas Čapek, who wrote his classical books about Czech immigrants in America, almost a century ago, whom he may have surpassed.

One of his latest endeavors has been a history of Czech Americans, under the title *Beyond the Sea of Beer or Czech America as Few People Know It*, published in Bloomington, IN, by AuthorHouse in 2017. It is a comprehensive history of emigrants from the Historic Lands of the Bohemian Crown and its successor States, including Czechoslovakia and the Czech Republic, based on the painstaking lifetime research of the author. The reader will find lots of new information in this book that is not available elsewhere. The title of the book comes from a popular song of the famous Czech artistic duo, Voskovec and Werich, who described America in those words when they lived here, reflecting on their love for this country. It covers the period starting soon after the discovery of the New World to date. The emphasis is on the US, although Canada and Latin America are also covered. It covers the arrival and the settlement of the immigrants in various states and regions of America, their harsh beginnings, the establishment of their communities, and their organization. A separate section is devoted to the contributions of notable individuals in different areas of human endeavor, including Bohemians, Moravians, Bohemian Jews, and the Slovaks. Nothing like this has ever been published since the time Thomas Čapek wrote his classic *The Čechs (Bohemians) in America* some one hundred years ago.

In 2018, he authored *Czechs Won't Get lost in the World, Let Alone in America*, featuring a panorama of selected personalities, whose roots had origin in the Czech Lands and who, in the US, reached extraordinary success and who, with their activities, substantially influenced the growth and development of their new homeland. It is a saga of plain, as well as powerful, people whose influence and importance of often exceeded the borders of the US. A great portion of included individuals may be unknown to readers since it concerns persons whose Czech origin was usually not known.

The book was published in Bloomington, IN by AuthorHouse.

This was followed by another first, *American Jews with Czechoslovak Roots*, also published by AuthorHouse, a pioneering, comprehensive bibliography, bio-bibliography and historiography of writings relating to American Jews with ancestry in the former Czechoslovakia and its Successor States, the Czech and the Slovak Republics, which has never before been attempted. As the reader will find out, the listed individuals have been involved, practically, in every field of human endeavor, in numbers that surprise.

His two last books bear the titles *Notable Americans with Slovak Roots* (2019) and *Notabl American Women with Czechoslovak Roots* (2019). The purpose of these two monographs has been to correct some of the shortcomings that have existed in literature. No comprehensive study about the American Slovaks nor about the American Women of Czechoslovak ancestry has ever been attempted before. As these books demonstrate, the lack of existing information has, not at all, been a reflection of the paucity of work done by these individuals. Their contributions have been distinctive and truly remarkable.

And to crown it all, an extraordinary new book hit the press. In contrast to American ethnic literature that usually relates to immigrants, the new monograph's focus is on Americans who married them, specifically to American men whose spouses were women with Czech or Bohemian roots. Czech women, apart from being beautiful and charming, are known for their extraordinary distinctive character, i.e., independent spirit and nonconforming behavior. And, Lest we Forget, their cuisine art has no equal. It is for these reasons, why the Americans like to marry them. The book, to which Czech Ambassador Kmoníček wrote a complimentary Foreword, is appropriately titled: *Celebrities and Less Famed Americans*

Married to Women of Bohemian and Czech Ancestry and their Progeny.

However, that was not the end of it. *American Learned Men and Women with Czechoslovak Roots; American Men and Women in Medicine, Applied Sciences and Engineering; Notable Americans of Czechoslovak Ancestry in Arts and Letters and in Education; and Notable Czech and Slovak Americans from Explorers and Pioneer Colonists through Activists to Public Figures Diplomats, Professionals, Entrepreneurs and Sports Competitors,* followed soon after. (2020-2021).

In 1970, the International College of Applied Nutrition presented him an Honor Scroll in recognition of his contributions to their scientific program and progress. In 1978, SVU recognized his contributions to natural sciences, by bestowing on him, its highest award, the Honorary Membership in the Society. In 1991, on the occasion of its 100th anniversary, the Czechoslovak Academy of Sciences awarded him the Hlávka Memorial Medal. Subsequently, he was also given the Bolzano and the Comenius Medals. In 1998 he received a newly established prize "Gratias agit" from the Czech Minister of Foreign Affairs, in addition to receiving a special award from the Ambassador of Czech Republic in the US, Alexander Vondra, for his tireless contribution to the Celebration of the 80th Anniversary of the founding of the Independent Czechoslovak State. In 1999, he received from the hands of President Václav Havel a Memorial Presidential Medal. More recently, he was given an honorary title 'Admiral of the Nebraska Navy' by the Governor of Nebraska and the key to the Capital of Nebraska by the Mayor of Lincoln and the SVU Prague Chapter awarded him '2002 Praha SVU Award'. In 2002, on the occasion of SVU World Congress in Plzeň, Prof. Ing. Zdeněk Vostracký, DrSc., Rector of the University of Wert Bohemia, presented him a special commendation for the "development of academic, cultural and social relations between the Czech Republic and the expatriate communities." In 2005, Minister of Foreign Affairs of the Czech Republic honored him by awarding him Jan Masaryk Medal for his contributions in preserving and fostering relations between the Czech Republic and the United States. In February 2010, President of the Senate of the Parliament of the Czech Republic presented him a Silver Medal of the Senate for his efforts on behalf of Czechs abroad and for fostering of good name and the traditions of the Czech Republic. In 2012 he was awarded by the Minister of Interior of the Czech Republic Jan Kubice a medal for his lifetime contributions to the Czech archival science. In 2020, he was recipient of the Czech Ministry of Foreign Affairs' Medal of Merit in Diplomacy a Medal of Merit Diplomacy, for his lifetime contribution to the advancement of Czech-American Relations.

Since 1953, he has been married to his devoted wife Eva, who has been a strong supporter to her husband in all his endeavors. They are parents of two highly successful children, Jack E. Rechcigl (1960-) and Karen Rechcigl Kollecas (1962-).

Nancy Rechcigl (1961-), b. Morristown, NJ, the daughter of Joseph Palko (1926-2010.) and Mary Rishko (1930-1994), of Slovak and Ruthenian ancestry, respectively, is married to Jack Rechcigl. She studied plant sciences at Univ. of Delaware (B.S., 1983) and plant pathology and plant virology at Virginia Polytechnic Inst. and State Univ. (M.S., 1986). She began her career as a plant pathologist for the Ball Pan American Plant Company in Parrish, FL. In 1989, she took a position as a County horticultural agent working jointly for the University of Florida and Manatee County Extension Service. In 1995, she accepted a position with Yoder Brothers, Inc. for 10 years, as a crop health manager for their production facilities, specializing in plant disease and entomological problems of floricultural crops (1995-2005). She joined Syngenta Professional Products in September 2005 as a field technical manager for Ornamentals. In this role, she provides technical assistance and training to Syngenta sales representatives and to customers on Syngenta professional products and issues related to ornamental crop production. (She serves as a champion for Syngenta T&O active ingredients, generating awareness and developing new uses for Syngenta professional products.) She is the co-editor of *Environmentally Safe approaches to Crop Disease Control* (1997), *Biological and Biotechnological Control of Insect Pests* (1998) *and Insect Pest Management. Techniques for Environmental Protection* (2000).

B. Edwards (Eisner) Family

The earliest known ancestor of the Eisner family, which was the family's original surname, was Reb Jehuda ben Salamon. His son Elias was born in December 1748. At his circumcision on January 8, 1749, he was given the name Elizer Zwi ben Ezechel. On May 17, 1785, he took the name Eisner because he worked with iron, having n been probably a blacksmith. The German word for iron is Eisen - thus the name.

Elias Eisner was born in the town on Jeníkov and worked in Prague. His son Michael was born in Humpolec, while the son of the latter, Karl Eisner, was born in Chotěboř.

The earliest member of this family who emigrated to America was Henry (Jindřich) Eisner, the son of the above Karl Eisner. He was actually brought to the US, together with his wife, by his son Pavel Eisner. In fact, the latter is credited for bringing the Eisner family and close relative, including the family of his sister-in-law, to the US, thus saving them from the Holocaust. Most of them changed their name Edwards in the US..

His descendants and other close relatives in America are listed below in alphabetical order.

Charles Edwards (orig. Karel Eisner) (1894-1986), b. Prague, Bohemia, son of Henry (Jindřich) Eisner (1853-1956) and Hortense Auerová (1869-1951). He was a jeweler. He as married to Marta Hanáková (1905-1985) of Liberec, Bohemia. They had 2 daughters: Joan (Hana) Edwards (Eisnerova); and Doris Věra Edwards (Eisnerová).

Dorothy 'Doris' Edwards (orig. Eisnerová) (1932-), b. Prague,

Czech., daughter of Charles (Karel) Eisner (1894-1986) and Marta Hanáková (1905-1985). She was married to Jack Gordon (1929-2020) of Brooklyn, NY. He was the son of the Oscar-winning composer-lyricist Mack Gordon. He was a former president of MGM International Distribution. Following his service in the U.S. Army during the Korean War, Gordon was employed by MGM as an interim employee in the studio's 16mm department. Gordon entered MGM's distribution department in the mid-1950s. In 1972, he was appointed vice president of MGM International. He was promoted to executive vice president in 1979. Following MGM's merger with United Artists in 1981, Gordon became senior vice president of international distribution. Two years later, he was named president of MGM/UA International. He continued to operate in the role for 14 years until his retirement in 1997. The had 2 sons and 1 daughter: Wayne Peter Gordon (1957-), Mellissa Rose Gordon (1960-) and Dean Mark Gordon (1963-).

Eva Edwards (orig. Eisnerová) (1932-), b. Prague, Czech., daughter of Pavel Edwards (1892-1964) and Jiřina Taussigová (1906-1962), studied at Packer Collegiate Inst., Brooklyn, NY and continued her studies at Hofstra Coll. (later Univ.), Long Island, NY, majoring in sociology (B.A., 1953). She was first employed as a physics librarian at Cornell Univ. (1953). After moving to Washington, DC area, she got a job as a research library assistant at Washington Public Library (1958-59). In 1970 she began teaching at a nursery school, which she did for a number of years. She was of great assistance to her husband Mila Rechcigl in his leadership positions in the Czechoslovak Society of Arts and Sciences (SVU). She authored or co-authored eight editions of the *SVU Biographical Directory* (1966, 1968, 1972, 1978, 1983, 1988, 1992 and 2003) which became important reference works. She is married to Miloslav 'Mila' Rechcigl, Jr. (1930-) and they have a son, Jack Rechcigl (1960-) and Karen Rechcigl (1932-).

Helen Edwards (originally Eisnerová) (1927-), b. Prague, Czech., daughter of Pavel Edwards (1892-1964) and Jiřina Taussigová (1906-1962), immigrated to the United States in 1939. She attended Brooklyn Friends School, graduated from Vassar College with a degree in psychology (B.A., 1948), and received a postgraduate degree in developmental reading at SUNY, Albany (M.S., 1971). She taught elementary school in Idaho Falls, Idaho (1965-67), and Scotia, NY(1967-86). After retirement in 1986 she tutored for Literacy Volunteers of America, and volunteered in the Schenectady County Public Library, Civic Playhouse, Proctor's Theatre, and Unitarian Society. She was married to Frank C. Steiner (1922-2000) and they had 1 daughter, Linda Steiner (1950-), 1 son, David Steiner (1952).

Henry Edwards (orig. Jindřich Eisner) (1853-1956), b. Kaliště, Bohemia, son of Karl Eisner (1821-1893) and Anna Krausová (1831-1855) He was a jeweler. He was married to Hortense Auerová (1869-1951) of Prague, Bohemia. They had 3 sons. The all immigrated to the US. Their noble descendants are listed alphabetically below.

Joan Edwards (orig. Hana Eisnerová) (1930-2021), b. Prague, Czech., daughter of Charles (Karel) Eisner (1894-1986) and Marta Hanáková (1905-1985), was trained as a nurse. She attended Keuka College (BSs., 1952), where she received concurrently R.N. license. She was married to Bernard Hulkower (1928-2017) of Brooklyn, NY. He was a lawyer. He was graduate of Brooklyn College (A.B.,1950) and the University of Michigan Law School (1953). He was admitted to practice in New York in 1972, after being discharged from the Army. They had 2 sons: Seth Hulkower (1958-) and Daniel Hulkower (1961-).

Paul J. Edwards (orig. Pavel Eisner) (1892-1964), b. Prague, Bohemia, son of Jindřich Eisner (1853-1956) and Hortense Auerová (1869-1951), studied law at Charles Univ. and at St. John's

University. After receiving his American law degree, he opened his own law firm in NYC where he specialized in international law. His clientele included many Czech refugees whom he frequently did not charge, found them jobs and housing and made their lives easier. Until the communist takeover of Czechoslovakia in 1948, he was an advisor to the Czechoslovak Embassy and General Consulate in the US. He translated Alois Rašín's book *Czechoslovak National Economy* from the Czech original into German. He was married to Jiřina Taussigová. They had 2 daughters: Helen Edwards and Eva Edwards.

Andrea Savilla Eisner (1959-), b. Sewell, Chile, SA, daughter of Thomas Michael Eisner (1931-1992) and Savilla Gamble (1937-), is married to Todd Allen Barnett. They have 2 children: Benjamin Michael Barnett (1997-) and another child.

Andrew Calvin Eisner (1974-), b. New York, NY, son of Stephen A. Eisner (1932-) and Arlene Zohn (1940-), married to Stacy Lynn Hirschberg (1971-).

Douglas Randall Eisner (1978-), b. New York, NY, son of Stephen A Eisner (1932-) and Arlene Zohn (1940-).

Philip Robert Eisner (1965-), b. R. Worth, TX, son of Thomas Michael Eisner (1931-1992) and Savilla Gamble (1937-)

Robert Eisner (1898-1984), b. Prague, Bohemia, son of Jindřich Eisner (1853-1956) and Hortense Auerová (1869-1951) was in clothing business. He was married to Mitzi Kratzigová (1900-1991). They had 2 sons: Thomas Michael Eisner (1931-1992) and Stephen Alexander Eisner (1932-)

Stephen Alexander Eisner (1932-), b. Prague, Czech., son of Robert Eisner (1898-1984) and Mitzi Kratzigová (1900-1991). He was married to Arlene Zohn (1940-). They had 2 sons: Andrew Calvin Eisner (1974-) and Douglas Randall Eisner (1958).

Stephen Mark Eisner (1958-), b. Chuquisaca, Chile, SA, son of Thomas Michael Eisner (1931-1992) and Savilla Gamble (1937-). He married in 1986 Suzanne Johnson. They hav2 children: Kathryn Biss Eisner (1988-) and Patrick Thomas Eisner (1994-).

Thomas Michael Eisner (1931-1992), b. Prague, Czech, son of Robert Eisner (1898-1984) and Mitzi Kratzigová (1900-1991). He was married to Savilla Gamble (1937-). The had 2 sons and 1 daughter: Stephen Mark Eisner (1958-), Andrea Savilla Eisner (1959-) and Philip Robert Eisner (1965-). He married as his second wife, Kim Davey (1949-).

Dean Mark Gordon (1963-), b. Long Island, NY, son of Doris Edwards (1932-) and Jack Gordon (1929-2020) is married to Angela Muller (1964-) of Los Angeles, CA. They have 3 children: Sam Walter Gordon (1994-), Joseph Charles Gordon (1996) and Greta Kelly Gordon ((1998-).

Melissa Rose Gordon (1960-), b. Queens, NY, daughter of Doris Edwards (1932-) and Jack Gordon (1929-2020). She is married to Jeffery Gordon (1953-) of Los Angeles, CA. They nave 3 children: Brandon Andrew Clark (1989-), Madison Ross Clark (1994) and Katin Elizabeth Clark (1999).

Wayne Peter Gordon (1957-), b. Queens, NY, son of Doris Edwards (1932-) and Jack Gordon (1929-2020) is married to Clare Lin Ward (1964-) of NYC. They have 2 children: Dominick Lin Gordon (1993-) and Anthony John Gordon (1995-).

Anna Maria Hulkower (1990-), daughter of Daniel Hulkower (1961-) and Lynda Greenberg (1954-) attended many different schools, ultimately graduating from the State University of New York at Purchase, with a degree in Media, Society, and the Arts. She currently lives with a boyfriend Walker, a psychotherapist, in Oklahoma City, where she is employed as a senior editor of a production house. Todate she has worked on several award-winning documentaries.

Daniel Aaron Hulkower (1961-), b. Queens NY, the son of Joan Edwards (1930-2021) of Prague, Czech., and the lawyer Bernard Hulkower (1928-2017), studied marketing with minor in psychology at Lehigh University (B.S., 1984). He was a national sales manager at Herculite Products, Inc. (1986-96); director, New Business Development (1998-2001); vice president, Client and Sales Development NEW (2001-2010); vice president, general manager, Client Services, NEW Asurion (2010-14); sales independent consultant (2014); senior vice president, business development, After, Inc. (s. 2015). In 1989, he was married to Lynda Greenberg (1954-), from whom he later divorced. They had 2 children: Anna Marta Hulkower (1990-) and Isabel Sophia Hulkower (1994-). In 2018, he married Miriam G. Fischer.

Isabel Hulkower (1994-), daughter of Daniel Hulkower (1961-) and Lynda Greenberg (1954-) is a graduate of Oberlin College (B.A., 2016), where she specialized in Law and Society. She then worked on a farm in Reston, VA, which is owned by her childhood Hebrew School teacher. Concurrently she attends school nearby to become a acupuncturist.

Sasha Hulkower (1997-), daughter of Joan Edwards (1930-2021) and Seth Hulkower (1958-), is a graduate of Tufts University (B.A., 2019), where she specialized in American studies. She had internship with Huerto Roma Verde, Mexico City, where she assisted with gardening, harvesting and composting projects at

Mexico City's largest Urban Farm & garden. Presently, she is a project manager with Powerful Pathways, NYC.

Seth Hulkower (1958-), b. Queens, NY, the son of Joan Edwards (1930-2021) of Prague, Czech. and the lawyer Bernard Hulkower (1928-2017), studied mechanical engineering at Tufts University (B.S.M.E., 1981) and technology and policy at MIT (M.S., 1986). He was senior associate with Putnam Hayes & Bartlett (1990-92); vice president of Merrill International, Ltd. (1994-96); chief operating officer at Long Island Power Authority (1996-2007); senior vice president of IFF International (2012-14); and recently president of the Strategic Energy Advisory Services, LLC (s. 2008). Strategic Energy brings an entrepreneurial focus to business challenges related to the energy industry. He is married to Lissa Perlman (1956-). They have 2 children: Talia Minna Hulkower (1994-) and Sasha Regina Hulkower (1996-).

Talia Mina Hulkower (1994-), daughter of Joan Edwards (1930-2021) and Seth Hulkower (1958-), is a graduate of Tufts University (B.A., 2016), where she majored in international relations. She spent a full year of her undergraduate education at the University of Buenos Aires, where she became fluent in Spanish. She then studied business administration at Yale School of Management (M.B.A., 2022). She has traveled extensively. She currently resides in Washington, DC,, where she is employed as a program officer at a company working on government-funded international aid and development projects.

Sarah Salomon (1980-), b. Chicago, IL, daughter of Linda C. Steiner (1950-) and Edward Salomon (1951-), grew up in New Jersey. She earned her BA in Anthropology at Northwestern University (magna cum laude), after which she spent a year as a Dunn Fellow working in the Washington, DC Office of the Governor of Illinois. She earned her MBA (also magna cum laude) at UCLA's Anderson School of Management. She then spent one year at the IE Business School in Madrid. An active volunteer with a number of charities, she was named Virginia's volunteer of the month for her work with the Carpenter's Shelter, which helps homeless to achieve sustainable independence. She also worked for Youth Venture, a social entrepreneurial project to activate youth as changemakers. Sarah Salomon is now a Principal in the merger and acquisition management consulting group at Mercer, based in Chicago, Illinois.

David H. Steiner (1952-), b. Schenectady, NY, son of Frank Steiner (1922-2000) and Helen Edwards (orig. Eisner) (1927-), studied mechanical engineering at WPI (B.S., 1974). Although he is a Mechanical Engineer by training, he has spent his career building plants in the chemical industry. As Chief Project Engineer with WR Grace for thirty years he was involved in chemical plant design, process improvement and troubleshooting in 27 locations worldwide. Moving to Baton Rouge, he was on the construction team to build a $200 million polyacrylamide plant on a Greenfield site that was covered in sugar cane when first started. Recently, he was coaxed out of retirement living near his y grandson to work for a start-up company recycling/upcycling lithium batteries as program manager of Ascend Elements located in Westford, MA. He is married to Carol Mastaliz (1953-) of Greenfield, MA. They have a daughter, Erin Steiner (1981-) and a son Jonathan Steiner (1984-).

Erin Steiner (1981-), b. Chicago, IL, daughter of David H. Steiner (1952-) and Carol Mastaliz (1952-), received a B.A. in zoology from Connecticut College in 2003. Before returning to school, she worked as a North Pacific Groundfish Observer and spent two years in Bolivia as a Peace Corps Volunteer. She received an M.S. in fisheries from the University of Alaska in 2009. Erin joined the Northwest Fisheries Science Center in 2011 after spending two years working at the NOAA Fisheries Office of Science and Technology as a Knauss Sea Grant Fellow and as a full-time employee in Washington, DC. She is married to Michael L. Malick (1981-) Hershey, PA. He is a fish biologist, having studied at Mansfield University (B.S., 2006), UAF (M.S., 2008), with Doctorate in natural resource management from Simon Fraser University (Ph.D., 2017).

Linda Steiner (1950-), b. Schenectady, NY, daughter of Helen Edwards (orig. Eisner) (1948-), and Frank Steiner (1922-2000), attended Smith College and earned her Ph.D. (1979) at the University of Illinois, Urbana-Champaign. While in graduate school she taught undergraduate courses and was also the director of a rape counseling and advocacy center in Champaign County, Illinois. Her first full-time faculty positions were at Governors State University, in Illinois. (1978-91) and Rutgers University (1991-2006), where she chaired the department of Journalism and Media Studies. She is now a Professor at the Merrill College of Journalism, Univ. of Maryland (s. 2006), and director of UMD's ADVANCE Program for Inclusive Excellence. Her research areas include media history, alternative and new media, and, most centrally, women in the media, and feminist ethics. Steiner is a co-author of *And Baby Makes Two: Motherhood without Marriage* (1984) and *Women and Journalism* (2004). She has co-edited seven books, most recently *Newswork and Precarity* (2021), *Front Pages, Front Lines: Media and the Fight for Women's Suffrage* (2020), which was named a *Choice* Outstanding Academic Title for 2021, and *Journalism, Gender and Power* (2019). Steiner is a Fellow of the International Communication Association. She was president of the Association for Education in Journalism and Mass Communication, which also named her Outstanding Woman of the Year in Journalism and Mass Communication Education and gave her its Distinguished Service to Research Award. She and her husband Edward Salomon (1951-), a lawyer, have a daughter, Sarah Salomon (1980-) and a son, Paul Salomon (1983-).

VII. Selected Gazetteer

Albrechtice
Albrechtsdorf see Albrechtice
Alsovice
Altendorf see Stara Ves
Antoninov
Antoniwald see Antoninov
Bakov nad Jizerou
Bechovice
Bedrichov
Beneschau see Benesov
Benesov
Bergmannsdorf see Havirna
Bezdecin
Boehmisch Aicha see Cesky Dub
Boehmisch Truebau see Ceska Trebova
Boesching see Bezdecin
Bohdalovice
Bohdalowitz see Bohldalovice
Bohumilec - Hlavaty, Mares
Borovice - Kosek
Brandys nad Labem - Koubik
Bratrikov
Bratschikow see Bratrikov
Brno - Mateju,
Bruenn see Brno
Buda
Burinsko - Kosek, Sedlacek

Buschdoerfel see Hajek
Bystrice
Bytouchov - Strojsa
Bzi
Caslav - Pellant
Cervenice - Vela
Cerveny Kostelec
Ceska Ttebova - Vesely
Ceske Hermanice
Cesky Dub - Hauzr, Mares, Rechcigl, Rechcigel
Chlistov
Chocnejovice - Bad alec, Bergl. Ferkl, Rechcigl
Chotebor
Chvalcovice - Bartos, Cizkovice, Rechcigel
Dalesice - Novak
Daleschitz see Dalesice
Dehtary
Desna
Dessendorf see Desna
Deutsch Brod see Havlickuv Brod
Dneboh - Hrusa
Dobra Studnice
Dobra Voda - Stepanek
Doenis see Donin

Dolanky - Bartos, Najman, Rajtr
Dolni Kralovice
Dolni Maxov
Dolni Rokytnice
Donin
Doubi - Ruta
Doubravice
Drahotice - Bartos, Flanderka,
　　Hozakova, Landa, Maran
Drschke *see* Drzkov
Drschkow *see* Drzkov
Drzkov
Dynekyry - Safranek
Eisenbrod *see* Zelezny Brod
Felhauser *see* Polni Domky
Friedrichswald *see* Bedrichov
Friedland *see* Frydlant
Frydlant
Friedstein *see* Frydstejn
Frydstejn
Gablonz an der Neisse *see*
　　Jablonec nad Nisou
Gerstorf
Gistei *see* Jistebsko
Goersdorf *see* Gerstorf
Grafendorf *see* Hrabetice
Granzendorf *see* Hranicna
Grottau *see* Hradek nad Nisou
Gruenwald an der Neisse *see*
　　Mseno nad Nisou
Gutbrunn *see* Dobra Studnice
Hajek
Halschowitz *see* Alsovice

Haratice
Haratitz *see* Haratice
Havirna
Havirov
Havlickuv Brod
Hennersdorf *see* Jindrichov
Hochstadt an Iser *see* Vysoke
　　nad Jizerou
Hodkovice nad Mohelkou -
　　Najman, Rechziegel
Honsberg *see* Janov nad Nisou
Horice - Rechcigl
Horni Litvinov - Reckziegel
Horni Mohelnice - Dvorak,
　　Jihlavec
Horschitz *see* Horice
Hoskovice - Bukvicka,
　　Burianek, Danda, Novak,
　　Stejskal
Hrabetice
Hradcany - Kolomaznik
Hradec - Lochman
Hradec Kralove - Brozek,
　　Husak, Mejzlik, Pellant
Hradek nad Nisou
Hranicna
Hruby Rohozec
Hubalov
Humpolec
Humpoletz *see* Humpolec
Huntirov
Hut - Reckziegel, Hubner
　　Novotny

Jablonec nad Nisou - Heralecky, Hrinik, Rajtr, Reckziegel, Tresnak
Janov nad Nisou - Reckziegel
Janovice
Jenikov
Jenisovice
Jenschowitz *see* Jenisovice
Jermanice
Jestrabi
Jicin - Husak, Sif, Teesnak, Vich, Zajicek
Jilau see Jilove u Drzkova.
Jilove - Ullrich
Jilove u Drzkova
Jilowei *see* Jilove
Jindrichov - Reckziegel
Jirkau *see* Jirkov
Jistebsko - Reckziegel, Hoffmann
Jistei *see* Jistebsko
Jitschin *see* Jicin
Jivina - Broz, Cinka
Johannesberg *see* Janov nad Nisou
Josefodol *see* Josefuv Dul
Josefsthal *see* Josefuv Dul
Josefuv Dul - Reckziegel
Jungbunzlau see Mlada Boleslav
Kacanovy - Francu, Karasek, Lamac, Studnicka
Kahler Berg see Lysa Hora

Kalek - Reckziegel
Kaliste
Kallich - *see* Kalek
Kamenice
Kamnitz *see* Kamenice
Karlsberg *see* Karlov
Karlov
Karlovy Vary - Mueller, Stuchl
Karlsbad *see* Karlovy Vary
Klamorna - Jira
Klein Rohosetz see *Maly* Rohozec
Klainskal, Klein Skal - *see* Mala Skala
Klicnov
Klitschnei *see* Klicnov
Knezmosr - Brzobohaty, Rajtr, Verner
Kocnovice *see* Chocnejovice
Kocourov
Kohleruv kopec Koehlerberg
Kohoutovice
Kokonin
Kolin
Komarov u Horovic -Krikava, Nemec, Rechcigl
Kopain *see* Kopanina
Kopanina
Korenov
Koryta - Adam, Burianek, Kotatko,Vencl
Kukan *see* Kokonin
Kridlovaciny - Louda

Kunnersdorf *see* Kunratice
Kunratice
Labau *see* Hut
Lautschney *see* Loucna
Letarovice - Mizera, Pycha, Rechcigl
Liberec - Bic, Bobek, Egrt, Pabista, Zdarsky
Libic
Liebenau *see* Hodkovice
Lisny u Snehova
Litomerice - Gabriel, Rechziegel, Svoboda
Loucna nad Nisou - Reckziegel
Loukov - Maran, Picek
Loukovec - Michalek
Loukovicky
Louschnitz *see* Louznice
Louznice
Lucany nad Nisou
Luxdorf *see* Lukasov
Maffersdorf *see* Vratislavice
Mala Bela
Mala Libic
Mala Skala - Reckziegel
Malcice
Maly Rohozec - Reckziegel
Manikovice - Cimr, Sverma
Marschowits *see* Marsovice
Marsovice
Maxdorf *see* Maxov
Maxov - Reckziegel
Melnik nad Labem

Mlada Boleslav - Bukvicka, Kostejn, Lauryn, Pecina, Rechcigl, Sedlacek, Stibor, Zdarsky
Mlcechvosty
Mnichovo Hradiste - Danda, Hyka
Mohelnice nad Jizerou
Mokriny - Reckziegel
Mokrzin *see* Mokriny
Morchenstern *see* Smrzovka
Mseno nad Nisou
Muenchengraatz *see* Mnichovo Hradiste
Mukarov - Jihlavec
Mukarschow *see* Mukarov
Mukarow *see* Mukarov
Munkovice
Muzsky - Brzobohaty, Rajtr
Nabsel *see* Bzi
Nabzi *see* Bzi
Nacetin - Reckziegel
Natzschung *see* Nacetin
Nemecky Brod *see* Havlickuv Brod
Nesvacily
Neudorf a. N. *see* Nova Ves nad Nisou
Neveklovice - Bergl, Kesner
Nova Paka
Nova Ves nad Nisou
Nova Ves u Bakova - Balak, Studnicny

SELECTED GAZETTEER

Novy Bydzov - Rechcigl
Novy Jicin
Oberleutensdorf *see* Horni
    Litvinov
Odolenovice - Reckziegel
Oujezd - Havlik
Pacerice - Reckziegel
Pardubice - Kvapil, Rechziegel
Patzerschitz - see Pacerice
Pelikovice
Pelkowitz *see* Pelikovice
Pencin
Petrusovice
Pilsen *see* Plzen
Pintschei *see* Pencin
Plavy
Plaw *see* Plavy
Plzen
Podhora - Bergl
Podoli - Hrusa, Sverma
Podrby
Polaun *see* Polubny
Polubny
Prag *see* Praha
Praha - Illek, Koubik, Mateju,
    Pellant, Rechcigel, Sip
Prepere u Turnova - Rajtr
Pribyslavice - Krausner
Prichovice - Reckziegel
Proschwitz *see* Prosec nad
    Nisou
Prosec - Stejskal, Srytr, Stejskal
Prosec nad Nisou - Heralecky

Prisovice - Janecek, Prihoda
Prostejov
Przichowitz *see* Prisovice
Ptyrov - Lauryn, Prskavec,
    Sverma
Radcice
Radimovice - Broz, Najman
Radl *see* Radlo
Radlo
Radonovice
Radonowitz *see* Radonovice
Radostin - Rechziegel, Rechcigl,
    Roubicek
Radschitz see Radcice
Radvanice
Rakovnik - Kamenik, Rajtr
Rauschengrund *see* Horni
    Litvinov
Reichenau *see* Rychnov
Reichenberg *see* Liberec
Reiditz *see* Rejdice
Reinowitz *see* Rynovice
Ridwaltitz see Rydvaltice
Rochlice
Rochlitz see Rochlice
Rohosetz *see* Rohozec
Rohozec
Roven - Holaj
Rostkov - Ferkl
Rudolfov
Rudolfstahl *see* Rudolfov
Ruzodol
Rydvaltice

Rynovice
Sadska
Sarovcova Lhota - Rechcigl
Sassadel *see* Zasada
Schenkenhahn *see* Tesarov
Scherau *see* Vserava
Scheringen *see* Zdarek
Schumburg *see* Sumburk
Schumburg-Gistei see Krasna
Sedlejovice
Sedlistky - Maruska
Seidenschwanz *see*
    Vrchoslavice
Semily
Sestronovice - Reckziegel
Sestronowitz *see* Sestronovice
Sezemice - Fanta, Burianek,
    Retr
Skal
Skuchrow *see* Skuhrov
Slavikov - Beran, Rechziegel,
    Vela
Smrzov - Hauzr
Smrzovka - Reckziegel
Snehov
Sniehow *see* Snehov
Sobeslavice - Pelant
Sobotice
Sovenice - Filip
Sovinky - Sichta
Stahlavy
Stanovy
Stanow *see* Stanovy

Stara Ves
Stare Smrkovce
Stefansruh see Prichovice
Steiniger Bach *see* Kamenice
Stirbon see Jestrabi
Stranov - Tomes
Straziste - Rajtr
Strebsko
Svatonovice - Reckziegel
Svetla pod Jestedem
Svijansky Ujezd
Svijany
Swatanowitz see Svatonovice
Sychrov - Vela
Tabor
Tanvald
Tanwald *see* Tanvald
Tesarov
Travnicek - Jisl
Trti - Fanta, Janecek, Kostka,
    Rechziegel
Tschichkowitz *see* Ciskovice
Turnau *see* Turnoc
Turnov - Bicek, Hunat, Kesner,
    Rechziegel, Vela, Zdarsky
Unter-Kralowitz see Dolni
    Kralovice
Unter-Maxdorf *see* Dolni Maxov
Vesec - Sip
Veseli nad Lisou
Vlastiborice - Boelman, Najman
Vlcetin
Voderady

SELECTED GAZETTEER

Vorklebice
Vranany
Vratislavice nad Nisou
Vresne
Vrkoslavice
Vselibice
Vysoke nad Jizerou
Wetterstein *see* Trti
Wirkoslawitz *see* Vrkoslavice
Wlastiborsch *see* Vlastiborice

Wodalenovic *see* Odolonovice
Wuzelsdorf *see* Korenov
Zabehlice
Zahusice
Zasada
Zaskali
Zdarek - Rechcigl, Reckziegel
Zelezny Brod
Zidlichovice
Zviretice - Kostejn, Rajtr

BIBLIOGRAPHY

Rechcigl Family

"Rechcigl Family from Bohemia." By Miloslav Rechcigl, Jr. In: Rootsweb. See - https://wc.rootsweb.com/trees/211065/I0006/miloslav-rechcigl/individual

"Petr Rechziegel," in: GENi. See - https://www.geni.com/people/Petr-Rechziegel/6000000020571187956?through=6000000020560090914

Rodokmen rodu Rechcigel. Zpracoval Vladko Rechcigel. N.p: The Author, N.d.

"Mila Rechcigl." In: Wikipedia. See - https://en.wikipedia.org/wiki/Mila_Rechcigl

"Miloslav Rechcigl, Sr." in: Wikipedia. See - https://en.wikipedia.org/wiki/Miloslav_Rechcigl_Sr.

"Miloslav Rechcigl, Sr.. Papers," in: The Immigration History Research Center, University of Minnesota, 311 Andersen Library, Minneapolis, MN.

"Mila Rechcigl," in: LinkedIn. See - https://www.linkedin.com/in/mila-rechcigl-2492ba36/

"Jack Rechcigl," in: LinkedIn. See - https://www.linkedin.com/in/jack-rechcigl-98ba691a/

"Miloslav Rechcigl, Jr. Papers," in: The Immigration History Research Center, University of Minnesota, 311 Andersen Library, Minneapolis, MN.

On Behalf of Their Homeland: Fifty Years of SVU .An Eyewitness Account of the History of the Czechoslovak Society of Arts and Sciences (SVU). By One of the Founders and SVU President for Many Years Dr. Miloslav Rechcigl, Jr.

Boulder, CO: East European Monographs, 2008.

Czechmate. From Bohemian Paradise to American Haven. A Personal Memoir. By Miloslav Rechcigl, Jr. Bloomington, IN, 2011. 771p.

Pro vlast. Padesat let Společnosti pro vědy a uměn (SVU). Milolav Rechcigl, ml.. Praha: Academia, 2012.

Over the Hill. Says Who? Sequel to *Czechmate*. By Miloslav Rechcigl, Jr. (in press).

Bergl Family

"Descendants of Josef Bergl and Anna Sichtova," in: Rechcigl Family from Bohemia. By Miloslav Rechcigl, Jr. Rootsweb . See - https://wc.rootsweb.com/trees/211065/I0260/josef-bergl/individual

"Descendants of Frantisek Bergl and Marie Maranova," in: GENi. See - https://www.geni.com/people/Marie-Maranova/6000000020560152812?through=6000000020559910308

Rajtr Family

"Descendants of Vaclav Rajtr and Dorota Strojsova," in: Rechcigl Family from Bohemia. By Miloslav Rechcigl, Jr. Rootsweb. See - https://wc.rootsweb.com/trees/211065/I0281/vaclav-rajtr/individual.

"Descendants of Vaclav Rajtr and Dorota Strojsova," in: GENi. See - https://www.geni.com/people/Vaclav-Rajtr/6000000020571122498?through=6000000020571133521

Danda Family

"Descendants of Josef Danda and Barbora Buriankova," in: Rechcigl Family from Bohemia. By Miloslav Rechcigl, Jr. Rootsweb. See - https://wc.rootsweb.com/trees/211065/I1907/josef-danda/individual

"Descendants of Frantisek Danda and Josefa Cimrova," in: GENi. See - https://www.geni.com/people/Frantisek-Danda/6000000020560112951?through=6000000020560058150

Edwards (Eisner) Family

"Descendants of Ezechiel and Reb Jehuda ben Salomon," in: Rechcigl Family from Bohemia. By Miloslav Rechcigl, Jr. Rootsweb. See - https://wc.rootsweb.com/trees/211065/I0893/-ezechiel/individual.

"(Eliezer Zwi Ben Ezechiel) Elias Eisner Eisner," in: GENi. See - https://www.geni.com/people/Eliezer-Zwi-Ben-Ezechiel-Elias-Eisner-Eisner/6000000020557083630?through=6000000020558429215

Reminiscences of a Native of Prague. By Paul J. Edwards (Dr. Pavel Eisner). Rockville, MD: The Author, 1993. 127p.

Joan Hulkower. Caring, Nurturing, Lovng. By Alan D. Bergman. Port Washington, NY: The Author, 2020.

Building a Life. My Adventures from World War II. Prague to the American Dream. A Life Story Memoir, 2022. By Stephen Eisner. 388p.

Auer Family

"Descendants of Bernhard Auer andTherese Lieberamn," in: Rechcigl Family from Bohemia. By Miloslav Rechcigl, Jr. Rootsweb. See - https://wc.rootsweb.com/trees/211065/I0317/bernhard-auer/individual.

"Descendants of Matias Auer and Anna Auer." In: GENi. See - https://www.geni.com/people/Mathias-Auer/6000000131300575983?through=6000000131300883895

Taussig Family

"Descendants of Julia Taussigova and Makus Stoekler," in: Rechcigl

Family from Bohemia. By Miloslav Rechcigl, Jr. Rootsweb. See - https://wc.rootsweb.com/trees/211065/I0090/julia-taussigova/individual.

"Descendants of Julia Taussigova and Markus Stoekler," in: GENi. See - https://www.geni.com/people/Markus-Stoekler/6000000020558273250?through=6000000020558345101

"Descendants of Jakub Kasparek and Marie Ptackova," in: GENi. See - https://www.geni.com/people/Jakub-Kašpárek/6000000009168737485?through=6000000009168465610.

"Desecendants of Adolf Jan Svab and Marie Marketa Taussigova (1879-1956)," in: GENi. See - https://www.geni.com/people/Marie-Taussigova/6000000020560260821?through=6000000020560106282

Munk Family

"Desecendants of Abraham Munk and Unknown.," in: Rechcigl Family from Bohemia. By Miloslav Rechcigl, Jr. Rootsweb. See - https://wc.rootsweb.com/trees/211065/I2890/abraham-munk/individual.

"Descendants of Jakob Munk and Barbara Arnstein," in: GENi. See - https://www.geni.com/people/Barbara-Munk/6000000019433446089?through=6000000020560236237

"Descendants of Moritz Steindler," in: GENi. See - https://www.geni.com/people/Moritz-Steindler/6000000018915729599?through=6000000019299659606.

Steiner Family

"Descendantsof Adolf Steiner and Rosa Neumann," in: Rechcigl Family from Bohemia. By Miloslav Rechcigl, Jr. Rootsweb. See - https://wc.rootsweb.com/trees/211065/I1037/adolf-steiner/individual.

"Descendants of Adolf Steiner and Rosa Neumann," in: GENi. See - https://www.geni.com/people/Adolf-Steiner/6000000020572987027?through=6000000020572974055

Raw Carrots for Breakfast. By Helen Steiner, Schenectady, NY: The Author, 1998. 145p.

Tales of Two Continents. By Frank Steiner. Schenectady, NY: The Author, 1999.. 85p.

Steinbach Family

"Descendants of Simon Steinbach and Rosalie Weiskopf," in: Rechcigl Family from Bohemia. By Miloslav Rechcigl, Jr. Rootsweb.See - https://wc.rootsweb.com/trees/211065/I0938/simon-steinbach/individual.

"Descendants of Lazar Steinbach and Karolina Polak," in: GENi. See - https://www.geni.com/people/Lazar-Steinbach/6000000033163657256?through=6000000006578543384.

Svědek téměř stoletý. By Dr. Karel Steinbach. Zpracoval Viktor Fischl. Praha: Státni pedagogické nakladatelství, 1990. 128p.

Winn (Wiener) Family

"Descendants of Abraham (ben) Lazar / Wiener and Rosina Wiener (bat) Jakob," in: GENi. See - https://www.geni.com/people/Abraham-ben-Lazar-Wiener/6000000070065138821?through=6000000070073313822

"Descendants of Jakob Ruzicka and Anna Ruziczka," in: GENi. See - https://www.geni.com/people/Jakob-Růžička/6000000033090151099?through=6000000033090413841

"Descendants of josef Krajbich and Marie (Marenka) Wienerova," in:

BIBLIOGRAPHY

GENi. See - https://www.geni.com/people/Marie-Mařenka-Wienerova/6000000069869719911?through=6000000020572674478

Alcantara. Z dila MUDr. J. A.Winna. Praha: Pražská imaginace a Lege artis,1992.

"Winn Family Collection," in: Center for Jewish History, Leo Back Instititute, NYC. Identifier: AR 25493. Referenced in: https://archives.cjh.org/repositories/5/resources/10514

"Pavel and Winn Family Collection," in: Center for Jewish History, Leo Baeck Institute, NYC. Identifier: !R 25076. Referenced in: https://archives.cjh.org/repositories/5/resources/14211

"Winn Literary Works of Joseph A. Winn - Alcantara (Josef Wiener," in Center for Jewish History., Leo Baeck Institute, NYC. Identifier: Referenced in: https://archives.cjh.org/repositories/5/archival_objects/944689

GALLERY

Figure 1. Rechcígl Mill in Chocnějovice

Figure 2. View of the village Chocnějovice

Figure 3. Rechcígl family gravesite at Chocnějovice cemetery

Figure 4. Wedding picture of Mila's paternal grandparents: Adolf Rechcígl and Marie Berglová, around 1900

Figure 5. Wedding picture of Míla's maternal grandparents: Čeněk Rajtr and Marie Dandová, July 2, 1904

Figure 6. Míla's paternal grandmother Marie (Berglová) Rechcíglová with her children: Miloslav (Mila's father) and Aninka in 1915

Figure 7. Wedding picture of Míla's parents, Miloslav Rechcígl and Marie Rajtrová, July 26, 1926

Figure 8. Míla's mother in her younger days

Figure 9. Míla with his sister Marta in 1935

Figure 10. Míla, his sister, Vláďa Filip, František Slaba, Marie Slabová and their daughter Eva

Figure 11. Míla graduating picture from Gymnasium, 1949

Figure 12. Míla's father talking to his Homeland on Radio Free Europe, New York, 1952

Figure 13. Míla's father in Munich, Germany, in the mid50s

Figure 14. Eva Edwards, Míla's future wife, around 1950

Figure 15. Wedding picture of Míla Rechcígl and Eva Edwards, New York City, August 29, 1953

Figure 16. Eva's parents: Pavel E. and Jiřina Edwards, 1953

Figure 17. Míla's and Eva's children, Jack and Karen, around 1963

Figure 18. Wedding picture of Míla's sister Marta Rechcíglová and Franta Žďárský, October 3, 1953

Figure 19. Míla's sister and husband Franta Žďárský with their daughters Marcela and Iveta in 1966

Figure 20. Míla during science administrative training, NIH, Bethesda, MD, 1969

Figure 21. Jack Rechcígl graduating from High School, 1978

Figure 22. Karen Rechcigl graduating from High School, 1980

Figure 23. Wedding picture of Jack Rechcigl and Nancy Palko, July 30, 1983

Figure 24. Wedding picture of Karen Rechcigl and Ulysses Kollecas, August 25, 1990

Figure 25. Míla and Eva with their daughter Karen at her wedding, 1990

Figure 26. Mila's niece Marcela with her husband Mirek Heralecký and their children Zuzanka and Vítek, in 1993

GALLERY

Figure 27. Míla's niece Iveta and her husband Jarda Hriník, Mila's sister and her husband Franta Žďárský and Iveta's children Terézka and Eliška, in 1993

Figure 28. The US Rechcígl clan, 1997

Figure 29. Míla, the way he looked around 2000.

Figure 30. The Rechcígl clan at Seabrook, SC, celebrating Míla's and Eva's Golden wedding anniversary (2003)

GALLERY

Figure 31. Míla upon retirement from SVU - SVU Congress, České Budějovice, 2006

Figure 32. Jack and Nancy with children Greg, Kevin and Lindsey, 2008

Figure 33. Rechcígls' gathering in Bradenton, June 2010

Figure 34. Karen with her children Kristin and Paul, 2010

GALLERY

Figure 35. Kevin Rechcigl's and Jordan Robbins' wedding (2018)

Figure 36. The latest addition to Mila and Eva Rechcigl's family: the great grandson James Douglas Rechcigl and a great granddaughter Evelyn Marie Rechcigl, with their parents Kevin and Jordan Rechcigl.

Figure 37. Paul Edwards' parents, Jindřich and Hortense Eisner, on April 22, 1941, in Cuba, a stop on their voyage to the United States

Figure 38. Helen Edwards and Eva Edwards with their paternal grandparents, Jindřich and Hortense Edwards (Eisner)

Figure 39. Mila receiving Medal in Diplomacy from the Czech Ministry of Affairs; on picture with the Czech Ambassador Hynek Kmoníček, who presented him the Medal at the festive dinner at the Czech Embassy in the presence of the entire Mila's family (2021)

Figure 40. Mila Rechcigl's clan, with the Amb. Kmoníček and his wife, in front of the Czech Embassy, on the occasion of Mila's receiving the Medal of Diplomacy

Figure 41. Engagement of Mila's and Eva's granddaughter Kristin Marie Kollecas and Michael Andrew Wells at Grand Teton Park, July 7, 2022

Figure 42. Engagement of Mila's and Eva's grandson Gregory 'Greg' J. Rechcigl and Mary "Kristen" Lee at Narrows of Harpeth River State Park, TN, June 10, 2023

Figure 43. Jack Rechcigl's Clan on Vacation in Panama (August 2023).

www.ingramcontent.com/pod-product-compliance
Lightning Source LLC
LaVergne TN
LVHW040129080526
838202LV00042B/2848